NON CIRCULA

Federal Income Taxation of Corporations and Shareholders

FIFTH EDITION

BORIS I. BITTKER

Sterling Professor of Law Emeritus, Yale University

JAMES S. EUSTICE

Professor of Law, New York University

WARREN, GORHAM & LAMONT
Boston • New York

This publication is designed to provide accurate and authoritative information in regard to the subject matter covered. In publishing this book, neither the authors nor the publisher is engaged in rendering legal, accounting, or other professional service. If legal advice or other expert assistance is required, the services of a competent professional should be sought.

Preface

SINCE 1979, when the fourth edition of this work was published, the world of Subchapter C has been convulsed by an increasingly revolutionary series of legislative changes, beginning with the Tax Equity and Fiscal Responsibility Act of 1982 and the Tax Reform Act of 1984 and culminating in the Tax Reform Act of 1986. Because scarcely a corner of this treatise escaped this legislative assault, the supplement grew to the size of an independent volume. This made a revision of the fourth edition imperative. Our work commenced in 1985, but the 1986 legislation engulfed us in midstream, requiring the most complete revision of this work since our collaboration began, more than 20 years ago, with the second edition. Our retention of the original chapter titles and sequence belies the degree of change in the text; every chapter has been revised, and the changes in Chapters 4, 5, 7, 9, 11, 16, and 17 are particularly sweeping.

Holding the present edition to a single volume has required great restraint, and the reader is advised to retain the fourth edition for a more expansive historical treatment of pre-1986 law, especially in the areas of distributions in kind, stock redemptions, liquidations, collapsible corporations, and loss carry-overs.

The attention of readers is called to the volume of forms, published as a companion piece to this treatise under the title *Federal Income Taxation of Corporations and Shareholders: Forms*. The forms volume presents interrelated sets of documents illustrating many corporate-shareholder transactions, keyed and cross-referenced to the corresponding discussion in this work of the applicable legal principles.

We are most grateful to generations of students, readers, and colleagues for their many helpful comments over the years, and especially to the following for their contributions to this edition: Andrew N. Berg, Karen Brown, John M. Hughes, Thomas G. Hungar, Marci Kelly, Michael Lang, John P. McDonnell, Frederic Nicolson, Daniel Schneider, Gordon W. Stewart, and Stephen H. Willard.

Like its predecessors, this edition of our treatise is dedicated to Gerald L. Wallace. More than 40 years ago, in one of his rare excursions into print, Gerry expressed doubt about the *General Utilities* doctrine, whose belated demise is reflected in almost every chapter of this revision. It is particularly timely, therefore, that we reaffirm our admiration for Gerry's unrivaled contribution to legal education in the field of taxation.

BORIS I. BITTKER
JAMES S. EUSTICE

New Haven, Conn.
New York, N.Y.
August, 1987

Summary of Contents

Table of Contents

CHAPTER 3

Organization of a Corporation: Section 351 and Related Problems

CHAPTER 4

Debt vs. Equity in the Corporation's Capital Structure

CHAPTER 5

The Corporation Income Tax

CHAPTER 6

Corporate Elections Under Subchapter S

CHAPTER 7

Dividends and Other Nonliquidating Distributions

CHAPTER 8

Penalty Taxes on Undistributed Corporate Income

CHAPTER 9

Stock Redemptions and Partial Liquidations

CHAPTER 10

Preferred Stock Bailouts

CHAPTER 11

Complete Liquidations

Part A.   The General Rule: Complete Liquidations Treated
          as Sales of the Liquidating Corporation's Stock

CHAPTER 12

Collapsible Corporations

CHAPTER 13

Corporate Divisions

CHAPTER 14

Corporate Reorganizations

Part A.   General Considerations

CHAPTER 15

Affiliated Corporations

CHAPTER 16

Corporate Tax Attributes: Survival and Transfer

CHAPTER 17

Foreign Corporations and Foreign-Source Income

CHAPTER 1

Introductory

¶ 1.01   THE CORPORATE INCOME TAX

The federal government has taxed the income of corporations continuously since the Payne-Aldrich Tariff Act of 1909, which antedated the adoption of the sixteenth amendment by four years.[1] Corporate income was taxed even earlier, by the income tax of 1894, but the Supreme Court held in *Pollock v. Farmers' Loan & Trust Co.* that a federal tax on income from real estate and personal property was a direct tax that had to be apportioned among the states in proportion to population under U.S. Const. art. I, §9, cl. 2 and that the rest of the taxing scheme (including the tax on corporations)

---

[1] The principal constitutional provisions regarding taxation are:

Article I, Section 8, Clause 1: "The Congress shall have Power to lay and collect Taxes, Duties, Imposts and Excises, to pay the Debts and provide for the common Defence and general Welfare of the United States; but all Duties, Imposts and Excises shall be uniform throughout the United States."

Article I, Section 9, Clause 4: "No Capitation, or other direct, Tax shall be laid, unless in Proportion to the Census or Enumeration herein before directed to be taken."

Amendment XVI: "The Congress shall have power to lay and collect taxes on incomes, from whatever source derived, without apportionment among the several States, and without regard to any census or enumeration."

See also U.S. Const., art. I , §2, cl. 3, and art. I, §7, cl. 1.

1 - 1

was so inextricably bound up with these unconstitutional portions that the entire statute must fall.[2] Profiting by this experience, the 1909 Act was levied "with respect to the carrying on or doing business" by corporations (as well as joint stock companies, associations, and insurance companies); this change in approach led the Supreme Court, in *Flint v. Stone Tracy Co.*, to find that what Congress had imposed was not a direct tax but an excise or indirect tax upon "the exercise of the privilege of doing business in a corporate capacity":

> [T]he tax is imposed not upon the franchises of the corporation, irrespective of their use in business, nor upon the property of the corporation, but upon the doing of corporate or insurance business, and with respect to the carrying on thereof, in a sum equivalent to 1 per centum upon the entire net income over and above $5,000 received from all sources during the year; that is, when imposed in this manner it is a tax upon the doing of business, with the advantages which inhere in the peculiarities of corporate or joint stock organizations of the character described.[3]

Since the tax was not a direct tax, the Constitution did not require it to be apportioned according to population. The Court then went on to hold that corporate activities were subject to federal taxation even though carried on under a state charter; that the tax was uniform "throughout the United States" as required by the constitution even though individual proprietors and partnerships were not taxed; that the tax was not a direct tax merely because it reached income from municipal bonds and other nontaxable securities; and that various other constitutional objections were equally invalid.

By virtue of *Flint v. Stone Tracy Co.*, the corporate income tax was well entrenched in the federal fiscal system by 1913, when the Sixteenth Amendment, empowering Congress "to lay and collect taxes on incomes, from whatever source derived, without apportionment among the several states, and without regard to any census or enumeration," was adopted. Because *Flint v. Stone Tracy Co.* validated the 1909 measure as a tax on "the exercise of the privilege of doing business in a corporate capacity," it did not explicitly destroy the protection afforded by *Pollock v. Farmers' Loan & Trust Co.* to passive income received from real estate or personal property by a corporation that engaged in no other activities.[4] By empowering Congress to reach

---

[2] Pollock v. Farmers' Loan & Trust Co., 158 US 601 (1895).

[3] Flint v. Stone Tracy Co., 220 US 107, 145–146 (1911).

[4] In Flint v. Stone Tracy Co., supra note 3, however, the Court held (at 165) that income from investments in municipal bonds and other nontaxable securities and in real estate and personal property not used in the business could be taxed. The Court did not have occasion to decide whether income from passive investments could be taxed if the corporation was not engaged in doing business within the meaning of the taxing statute, Compare Zonne v. Minneapolis Syndicate, 220 US 187 (1911), with McCoach v. Minehill & S.H. Ry., 228 US 395 (1913).

such income without apportionment, the Sixteenth Amendment may have enlarged the federal power to tax corporate income. With this possible exception, however, the federal corporate income tax, unlike the federal income tax on individuals, seems to owe nothing to the sixteenth amendment.

The 1909 Act imposed a tax of one percent of net income with an exemption of $5,000 per corporation. In contrast, the Tax Reform Act of 1986 imposes rates of 15 percent on the first $50,000 of taxable income, 25 percent on the next $25,000, and 34 percent on amounts above $75,000 (replacing a five-bracket schedule ranging from 16 percent on the first $25,000 of taxable income to 46 percent of amounts above $100,000.)[5]

The term "corporation" is defined by §7701(a)(3) of the Code to include associations and joint stock companies. Thus, the tax is imposed on some enterprises that do not constitute corporations under state law.[6]

With some exceptions,[7] the taxable income of a corporation is computed in essentially the same fashion as an individual's taxable income. Thus, the corporation's annual accounting period (calendar year or fiscal year) is employed; the corporation's regular accounting method (cash receipts and disbursements, accrual, completed contract, and so forth) is controlling unless it does not clearly reflect income; the corporation must include in gross income, and may deduct, most of the items that are taxable to or deductible by individuals; and the Service may reallocate income and deductions among two or more businesses under common control in order to reflect income accurately, whether these businesses are incorporated or not. Similarly, the grand principles or doctrines of income taxation (e.g., no assignment of earned income, substance over form, business purpose, and step transactions) are applicable to corporations as well as to individuals.[8] Finally, most of the administrative provisions of the Code governing the filing of returns and payment of tax, assessments, collection, interest on deficiencies and overpayments, penalties, procedure in the Service, and litigation are equally applicable to both corporations and individuals.

As will be seen in Chapter 5, where the major deviations between the corporate income tax and the individual income tax are discussed, the most vexing tax problems in the use of the corporation as a method of carrying on business do not arise in determining the corporation's income tax liability. The principal difficulties arise, rather, because (1) distributed corporate

---

[5] The lower rates applicable to the first few tax brackets phase out at $335,000; these lower rate brackets also create an incentive to multiply the number of corporate entities, but this income-splitting tactic, formerly quite popular, is seriously restricted by current law. See infra ¶ 15.02.

[6] For analysis of §7701(a)(3), see infra ch. 2, especially ¶¶ 2.01–2.07.

[7] See infra ¶ 5.02.

[8] See infra ¶ 1.05.

income is taxed to the shareholder, while undistributed income is not; (2) an exchange of stock or securities by the investor may or may not be an appropriate occasion for recognizing gain or loss; and (3) transactions between a corporation and its shareholders are often not conducted at arm's length. Chapters 3 through 16 of this treatise address in detail the ramifications of these problems, but a few words of introduction may be in order.

¶ 1.02　UNDISTRIBUTED CORPORATE INCOME

Under the Code, corporate income is taxed to a corporation as received or accrued, but shareholders are taxed only when, as, and if the corporate earnings are distributed to them.[9] Thus, it may be advantageous for entrepreneurs to operate in corporate form rather than as sole proprietors or partners of an unincorporated enterprise, since the corporation's tax on a given amount of business profits may be less than the individual income tax would be.

From the end of World War II until enactment of the Tax Reform Act of 1986, this advantage was very pronounced, because the top corporate rate was ordinarily at least 20 percentage points below the top individual rate; entrepreneurs could thus save at least $200,000 in taxes by shifting $1 million of business profits from an individual tax return to a corporate return. While the 1986 Act precludes savings of this magnitude because it virtually eliminated the disparity between the top rates, it nonetheless preserves a modest opportunity to reduce taxes by shifting $50,000 of business profits from the top individual bracket (28 percent) to the bottom corporate bracket (15 percent).[10] The resulting tax savings, however, cannot be multiplied by creating a number of satellite corporations because, as explained in more

---

[9] The government argued in Eisner v. Macomber, 252 US 189 (1920), that a shareholder could be taxed under the Sixteenth Amendment on his "share in the accumulated profits of the corporation even before division by the declaration of a dividend of any kind." The argument was rejected, "since the Amendment applies to income only, and what is called the stockholder's share in the accumulated profits of the company is capital, not income." Id. at 219. Whether the Supreme Court would adhere to this view today is problematical, but Congress has not attempted to compel shareholders to report undistributed corporate income, except in the limited instances of foreign personal holding companies and controlled foreign corporations (infra ¶¶ 17.23 and 17.32). Optional inclusion of undistributed income, as under Subchapter S (infra ch. 6) or the consent dividend procedure (infra ¶ 8.24) is, of course, another matter altogether.

[10] The rate changes made by the 1986 Act are subject to transitional adjustments for 1987 and are scheduled to take full effect in 1988. See Eustice, Kuntz, Lewis & Deering, The Tax Reform Act of 1986: Analysis and Commentary ¶ 2.02 (Warren, Gorham & Lamont, Inc., 1987).

detail in Chapter 15, corporations under common control are required to divide among themselves a single set of particular tax benefits, including the lower tax brackets.[11]

Moreover, the Service is armed with a variety of statutory weapons for attacking attempts to exploit the normal insulation of undistributed corporate income from the individual tax rates applicable to the corporation's shareholders. First, §482 empowers the Service to reallocate gross income, deductions, credits, and other tax allowances between two or more businesses or organizations under common control if necessary to clearly reflect their respective incomes.[12] Second, an accumulated earnings tax is imposed by §531 on the undistributed income of a corporation formed or availed of for the purpose of avoiding the income tax by accumulating instead of distributing its earnings.[13] Ordinarily, this tax is applicable only if the corporation has accumulated its earnings beyond the reasonable needs of its business. Third, the personal holding company tax is imposed by §541 on the undistributed income of a "personal holding company," which, roughly speaking, embraces corporations whose principal function is the collection of dividends, interest, and other passive income, as well as so-called incorporated talents and incorporated country estates and yachts.[14] Because, however, relatively few corporations run afoul of §482 and even fewer are subjected to either the accumulated earnings tax of §531 or the personal holding company tax of §541, use of the corporation as a temporary or permanent refuge from individual income tax rates has been one of the principal landmarks of our tax landscape.

As a practical matter, earnings can be accumulated in the corporation only if the shareholders have no immediate need for the funds for living or other personal expenses. For shareholders in this happy position, a corporation can be attractive because business or investment income may be accumulated year after year, with the stock eventually passed on at the shareholders' death. The heirs can then liquidate the corporation or sell the stock; since the stock obtains a stepped-up basis under §1014 equal to its fair market value on the date of the testator's death, the heirs can receive the corporate assets or their equivalent in sales proceeds at no tax cost. In this event, the corporate earnings are not subjected to the individual income tax either during the original shareholder's life or thereafter.

If, on the other hand, the financial needs of the shareholders make it difficult or impossible for them to allow the business profits to accumulate

---

[11] See §1561, discussed infra ¶ 15.02.

[12] For §482, see generally infra ¶ 15.03. See also §269A, a similar provision applicable to certain personal service corporations, discussed infra ¶ 2.07.

[13] See infra ¶ 8.01.

[14] See infra ¶ 8.02.

in the corporate treasury, they have to be content with halfway measures. One possibility, probably typical of most successful closely held corporations, is to draw down in salary and dividends enough of the earnings to meet living expenses, allowing only the balance to accumulate. More sophisticated devices often used by shareholders in the past to realize on corporate earnings without paying tax at the individual income tax rate are redemptions of stock, partial liquidations, and complete liquidations, all of which are on occasion treated as sales of stock, with the profit being taxed as long-term capital gains rather than as ordinary income.[15] The 1986 Act's elimination of the rate differential between ordinary income and long-term capital gains, however, undermined this gambit, except for shareholders who happen to have offsetting capital losses; it remains to be seen whether the rate differential will be reinstated by Congress.[16]

¶ 1.03　DISTRIBUTED CORPORATE INCOME

Although accumulated corporate income is not subjected to the individual income tax rates, the other face of the coin is that corporate income distributed as dividends to shareholders is taxable as personal income. This characteristic of the federal tax system—the so-called double taxation of distributed corporate income—can be illustrated by assuming a single rate of 30 percent applicable to both personal and corporate income, applied first at the corporate level to business income of $500,000, and then to the corporation's after-tax income of $350,000 ($500,000 less corporate income tax of $150,000) when distributed in the form of dividends to the shareholder. The result is an after-tax residual of $245,000 ($350,000 less individual tax of $105,000) for the shareholder, as compared with an after-tax amount of $350,000 if the same business had been conducted in the form of a sole proprietorship rather than through a corporation.

This is not the place for an extended discussion of the equity and economic consequences of imposing independent taxes on the corporation and its shareholders, but surely the real issue is not whether in legal form there are two separate taxes. For many closely held enterprises, which can choose between the corporation and either the proprietorship or the partnership as a method of doing business, the Code offers an election; some find it

---

[15] For the tax effects of these transactions, see infra ¶¶ 9.04–9.12 (redemptions and partial liquidations) and ¶ 11.03 (complete liquidations).

[16] The Conference Report on the 1986 Act states that "[t]he statutory structure for capital gains is retained in the Code to facilitate reinstatement of a capital gains rate differential if there is a future tax rate increase." H.R. Rep. No. 841, 99th Cong., 2d Sess. II–106 (1986).

cheaper rather than more expensive to follow the double tax route. For those that must use the corporation for business reasons, the real issue is not the validity of the label "double taxation" but whether the corporation is taxed more heavily than competing proprietorships and partnerships without compensating tax or other advantages. For publicly held enterprises, the real issue is whether corporate earnings are overtaxed (or undertaxed) in relation to other types of income and the demands of national fiscal policy, problems that in turn pose the unsolved question of whether the burden of the corporation's income tax falls on the shareholder or is shifted to other factors of production and/or to consumers of the corporation's output.[17]

Moreover, for some closely held enterprises, double taxation is avoided by an election under Subchapter S, which subjects the corporation's earnings, whether distributed or not, to taxation only at the shareholder level;[18] thus, the owners of the enterprise obtain the non-tax advantages of operating in corporate form (such as limited liability) without subjecting the business profits to corporate taxation. Another common method of mitigating the potential burden of double taxation is the payment of salaries to shareholder-employees of family corporations. Since these amounts can be deducted by the corporation as business expenses under §162, this portion of the business profits is taxed only at the shareholder-employee level. For many closely held businesses, salaries to shareholder-employees afford a method of withdrawing business profits in large part or even in their entirety, with the result that in these instances the federal income tax liability is about the same as if the enterprise had been conducted as a proprietorship or partnership.

Such an arrangement is feasible only to the extent that the compensation paid to the shareholder-employee can be justified as "a reasonable allowance . . . for personal services actually rendered" so as to be deductible under §162; if the compensation is excessive, it will be disallowed as a corporate deduction pro tanto.[19] Although the possibility of disallowance is always present, especially if earnings fluctuate widely and shareholder salaries are adjusted from year to year to exhaust the earnings, many closely held corporations are able to pay out their entire business earnings, give or take a few dollars, year after year. Other methods by which shareholders

---

[17] See Pechman, Who Paid the Taxes, 1966–1985? (Brookings, 1985), 29, 31–33, and studies there cited. For the so-called double taxation of corporate income and the related issue of integrating the corporate and individual income taxes, see generally McLure, Must Corporate Income Be Taxed Twice? (Brookings, 1979); Pechman, Federal Tax Policy (Brookings, 4th ed., 1983) 129–182; Warren, The Relation and Integration of Individual and Corporate Income Taxes, 94 Harv. L. Rev. 719 (1981) (analysis of integration proposals and ALI Draft Report on Subchapter C); infra ¶ 1.08.

[18] See infra ¶ 6.06.

[19] See infra ¶ 7.05, text at notes 80–84.

may withdraw funds from the corporation in a form that will give rise to a deduction at the corporate level are (1) interest on loans to the corporation, (2) rent on property leased by the shareholders to the corporation, and (3) royalties on patents owned by the shareholders and used by the corporation under licenses. As with salaries, however, these payments must be justified as bona fide arrangements rather than disguised dividends.[20]

Entrepreneurs can also avoid a second round of taxation by eschewing distributions of the corporate earnings until the stock can be exchanged for the stock of a publicly held corporation in a tax-free exchange[21] or by holding the stock of the original corporation until death, when it passes by will to their beneficiaries with a new basis equal to its fair market value at that time.

Finally, it is worth recording that before enactment of the Tax Reform Act of 1986, the double taxation of corporation income did not necessarily create an economic burden, since the shareholders could convert the corporation's undistributed earnings into cash by selling their stock and reporting the profits as long-term capital gains, the tax rate on such gains being dramatically lower than the rate on ordinary income. For example, if individuals were taxed on ordinary income and long-term capital gains at 70 and 25 percent respectively and the corporate rate was 48 percent, business profits of $100,000 would result in after-tax income of $52,000 ($100,000 less tax of $48,000) for the corporation; if the shareholders realized this amount by selling their stock, the tax on their long-term capital gains was $13,000 (25 percent of $52,000), leaving them with $39,000 ($52,000 less $13,000) net after taxes as compared with $30,000 ($100,000 less $70,000) if the business profits had been realized by a sole proprietorship. In practice, of course, such sales were not annual events; instead, the shareholders allowed the business profits to accumulate for years or even decades so that a sale of the stock would reflect a long-term accumulation, including the corporation's profits from reinvesting the retained earnings. This regime, under which double taxation could often be preferable to a single tax, ended when the 1986 Act eliminated the rate differential between ordinary income and long-term capital gains and imposed a higher top tax rate on corporations than on individuals.

¶ 1.04　EXCHANGES OF CORPORATE STOCK AND SECURITIES

Another persistent problem in the taxation of corporations and their investors is the treatment of exchanges of corporate stock and securities. If

---

[20] See infra ¶ 7.05, text at notes 97–98 and 108.

[21] For mergers and other tax-free reorganizations, see infra ¶¶ 14.10–14.20.

stock or securities are sold, the seller is of course taxed on the profit (or may deduct his loss), and ordinarily the gain or loss is capital gain or loss. If he exchanges stock or securities for other property (e.g., real estate, racehorses, or groceries), his gain or loss is recognized in a similar fashion, since under the Code an exchange or barter of property is ordinarily taxed in the same manner as a sale.

There are, however, a variety of transactions in which the taxpayer's gain or loss goes unrecognized under the Code, either because it is regarded as inchoate or unrealized or because nonrecognition is thought to be good economic policy; and many of these nonrecognition transactions involve corporate stock or securities. When gain or loss goes unrecognized on an exchange, the taxpayer's original basis ordinarily carries over and attaches to the property received by him, so that the nonrecognition provisions are sometimes called "postponement provisions" on the theory that the unrecognized gain or loss will be taken into account when the new property is sold. Even if this occurs, no allowance is made for the delay in recognizing the gain or loss, and the tax rates or the taxpayer's other income, or both, may be different in the year of sale.

An example is the transfer by an individual proprietor of his business assets to a newly formed corporation in exchange for all of its stock: Even if the assets have appreciated or depreciated in value, so that the stock received for the assets is worth more or less than the basis of the assets exchanged, the transferor's gain or loss goes unrecognized under §351.[22] On these facts, it can plausibly be argued that the transferor's gain or loss is too problematical to warrant recognition for tax purposes.

A more controversial example is the exchange of stock of one corporation for the stock of a second corporation into which the first is to be merged; the stock received may be worth 10 times (or one tenth) the basis of the old stock, but the shareholder's gain or loss ordinarily goes unrecognized under §354.[23] If the two corporations were already under common control, the merger might be regarded as no more than a change of form, not justifying the recognition of gain or loss. Even here, however, it might be argued that unrealized appreciation or depreciation on property should be taken into account as soon as the owner makes a change in the manner of holding it that will have significant legal consequences either for taxation or for other matters. Moreover, what if the first corporation is a one-man enterprise, owning an office building, and it is merged into a widely held steel-manufacturing firm? Should the shareholder's gain or loss go unrecognized when his economic status is so drastically altered? As will be seen throughout this treatise, a recurring problem in the taxation of the corporation and

---

[22] See infra ¶ 3.01.

[23] See infra ¶ 14.01.

its shareholders is the determination of when an exchange of stock or securities is a taxable occasion, so that the investor's gain or loss is to be recognized, and when it comes within one of the numerous nonrecognition provisions of the Code.

The recognition-nonrecognition dichotomy does not exhaust the possibilities in this area, however, since an exchange may resemble a dividend rather than a sale. For example, if two corporations owned by the same person are merged and the surviving corporation issues bonds in exchange for the stock of the absorbed corporation, the result may be substantially the same as if one of the corporations had distributed bonds—or even cash—to its shareholder without any merger. If so, it would be appropriate to treat the bonds as a dividend to the extent of their fair market value, a result that would be very different from treating the transaction as either a sale or a nonrecognition transaction. Another example of the possibility that an exchange may be treated for tax purposes as a dividend is the redemption of stock by a one-person corporation from its sole shareholder: Since he remains in complete control of the corporation despite the redemption of part of his stock and since the redemption is the functional equivalent of a dividend in virtually all respects, it is so treated for tax purposes.[24]

¶ 1.05   THE CORPORATION AS AN ENTITY

For centuries, legal philosophers have disagreed about the nature of the corporation, and the courts concurrently have had to decide in concrete cases whether corporations should be treated as entities wholly independent of their shareholders or as groups with a legal status dependent upon the identity and behavior of the shareholders. Judicial decisions have cleaved to no single doctrine, to the disappointment of the philosophers and the despair of text writers, and the diversity of legal approaches found in other branches of the law is well mirrored by the tax law.[25]

In general, of course, the Code treats each corporation as an independent tax-paying entity, unaffected by the personal characteristics of its shareholders or changes in their composition as a result of transfers of stock from old shareholders to new ones. A domestic corporation must ordinarily pay the corporate income tax even though its stock is owned entirely by one person, by a tax-exempt organization, or by nonresident aliens beyond U.S.

---

[24] See infra ¶ 9.06.

[25] For example, in Hair Indus. Ltd. v. US, 340 F2d 510 (2d Cir. 1965), it was held that a one-person corporation could not refuse to produce its records in response to a Service subpoena on the ground that they might incriminate its sole shareholder. See generally Bellis v. US, 417 US 85 (1974).

jurisdiction. Similarly, a corporation's taxable year is not terminated by the fact that some or even all of its stock changes hands; nor does such a shift in ownership ordinarily alter the corporation's basis for its assets, earnings and profits account, method of accounting, or other tax attributes. Moreover, transactions between a corporation and its shareholders ordinarily have the same tax consequences as similar transactions with outsiders.

There are, however, many statutory exceptions to the general principle of treating the corporation as wholly independent of its shareholders.[26] Among these exceptions are:

(1) Section 267, forbidding or deferring the deduction of certain losses, expenses, and interest incurred in transactions between a corporation and certain of its shareholders;[27]

(2) Section 269, disallowing certain tax benefits if control of a corporation is acquired for the principal purpose of tax avoidance;[28]

(3) Section 401(a)(4), providing that a stock bonus, pension, or profit-sharing plan qualifies for certain tax benefits only if it does not discriminate inter alia in favor of shareholders;

(4) Section 531, imposing an additional tax on a corporation that is formed or availed of for the purpose of avoiding the income tax on shareholders by accumulating instead of distributing its earnings;[29]

(5) Section 541, imposing an additional tax on personal holding companies, which are defined in part by reference to the number of shareholders;[30]

(6) Section 382, limiting or disallowing the net operating loss carryover in cases where stock ownership shifts in specified ways;[31]

(7) Section 341(e)(5)(A), which for certain purposes treats the corporation's assets as noncapital assets if they would have this character in the hands of a shareholder;[32] and

(8) Sections 267(c)(1), 318(a)(2)(C), and 544(a)(1), which for certain purposes treat stock owned by a corporation as if it were owned

---

[26] Sometimes, but not always, a transaction between a corporation and an affiliate (another corporation or organization under common control) is as vulnerable as if it had occurred between the corporation and its shareholders. See infra ¶ 15.03.

[27] See infra ¶ 5.04.

[28] See infra ¶ 16.21.

[29] See infra ¶ 8.01.

[30] See infra ¶ 8.20.

[31] See infra ¶¶ 16.23–16.25.

[32] See infra ¶ 12.06.

by the corporation's shareholders (and vice versa under §318(a)(3)(C)).

The foregoing is by no means an exhaustive catalogue of the statutory provisions that take account of stock ownership in prescribing the tax results of transactions by the corporation or its shareholders, or both. Even so, these provisions can appropriately be described as exceptions to the statutory principle that the corporation is for tax purposes an independent entity.

It is equally accurate to say that the courts ordinarily take the corporation at face value and do not merge it with its shareholders. There are exceptions in the judicial arena to this generalization, just as in the Code, but the judicial exceptions are less susceptible to classification or even description. A restatement by Judge Learned Hand of the principles emerging from the leading cases demonstrates the high level of abstraction that inevitably attends any generalization in this area:

[The tax] result depends upon whether, in the situation just disclosed, we should recognize transactions of sale or exchange between a corporation and its sole shareholder; and our decision turns upon three decisions of the Supreme Court: Burnet v. Commonwealth Improvement Company . . . ; Higgins v. Smith . . . , and Moline Properties, Inc. v. Commissioner. . . . In the first of these the question was whether it was proper to tax a corporation for profits upon transactions between itself and a decedent's estate which owned all its shares. The court merely declared that, since a corporation was for most purposes recognized as a separate jural person, and since the situation was not one of the exceptions where the "corporate form" should be "disregarded," it should be taxed upon its gains, regardless of the fact that no living person had gained or lost a cent. When Higgins v. Smith . . . was before us . . . we assumed that this rule held good in a case where the Commissioner had refused to allow a deduction to the sole shareholder of losses sustained in transactions between him and his corporation. In this we were in error, however, for the Supreme Court held that, although the Treasury might insist upon the separate personality of the corporation when it chose, it might also disregard it, when it chose. It explained Burnet v. Commonwealth Improvement Co. . . . by saying that "a taxpayer is free to adopt such organization of his affairs as he may choose and having elected to do some business as a corporation, he must accept the tax disadvantages. On the other hand, the Government may not be required to acquiesce in the taxpayer's election of that form for doing business which is most advantageous to him. The Government may look at actualities and upon determination that the form employed of doing business or carrying out the tax event is unreal or a sham may sustain or disregard the effect of the fiction as best serves the purpose of the tax statute. . . . It is command of income and its benefits which marks the real owner of property."

This language we later interpreted as meaning that "the Treasury may take a taxpayer at his word, so to say; when that serves its purpose, it may treat the corporation as a separate person from himself; but that is a rule which works only in the Treasury's own favor; it cannot be used to deplete the revenue." United States v. Morris & Essex R. Co. . . . Again we were wrong; we neglected to observe that the corporate "form" must be "unreal or a sham," before the Treasury may disregard it; we had taken too literally the concluding language that it was the "command of income and its benefits which marks the real owner of property."

This error was made plain in the third decision of the Supreme Court—Moline Properties, Inc. v. Commissioner. . . . In that case the question was whether the corporation might insist upon the Treasury's including capital gains within the gross income of its sole shareholder, and the court decided that it might not. That was the same situation as existed in Burnet v. Commonwealth Improvement Co., *supra*. The gloss then put upon Higgins v. Smith, *supra*, was deliberate and is authoritative: it was that, whatever the purpose of organizing the corporation, "so long as that purpose is the equivalent of business activity or is followed by the carrying on of business by the corporation, the corporation remains a separate taxable entity." . . . That, as we understand it, is the same interpretation which was placed upon corporate reorganizations in Gregory v. Helvering . . . and which has sometimes been understood to contradict the doctrine that the motive to avoid taxation is never, as such, relevant. In fact it does not trench upon that doctrine; it merely declares that to be a separate jural person for purposes of taxation, a corporation must engage in some industrial, commercial, or other activity besides avoiding taxation: in other words, that the term "corporation" will be interpreted to mean a corporation which does some "business" in the ordinary meaning; and that escaping taxation is not "business" in the ordinary meaning.[33]

---

[33] National Inv. Corp. v. Hoey, 144 F2d 466, 467–468 (2d Cir. 1944). For further discussion, see infra ¶ 2.10 (dummy corporations) and ch. 16; Cleary, The Corporate Entity in Tax Cases, 1 Tax L. Rev. 3 (1945); Rice, Judicial Techniques in Combatting Tax Avoidance, 51 Mich. L. Rev. 1021 (1953); Paul, Restatement of the Law of Tax Avoidance, Studies in Federal Taxation 9-157 (1937); Cohen, Taxing the State of Mind, 12 Tax Executive 200 (1960); Hobbet, The Corporate Entity: When Will It Be Recognized for Federal Tax Purposes? 30 J. Tax'n 74 (1969); Barr, A Threat to the Lifeless Corporate Skeleton: Disregarding the Corporate Entity, 51 Taxes 555 (1973).

For special problems in the recognition of corporations whose income is solely or largely derived from the personal services of controlling shareholders, see infra ¶ 2.07.

For the recognition of a corporation as a separate entity while treating it as its controlling shareholder's alter ego for the purpose of imposing shareholder liability for the corporation's taxes, see Wolfe v. US, 798 F2d 1241 (9th Cir. 1986).

One of the difficulties with generalizations about disregard of the corporate entity—Judge Hand's included—is that issues are never presented to the courts, and are almost never decided, on the theory that the corporation is to be disregarded for all tax purposes. It is entirely possible, indeed it is likely, that the identity of interest between the corporation and its shareholders will triumph for some purposes and not for others. Thus, *Higgins v. Smith*, cited by Judge Hand, held that a shareholder could not deduct a loss incurred on a sale of depreciated property to his wholly owned corporation,[34] but it is far from clear that the government would be entitled to tax income received by the corporation from other property, or even from the property thus transferred, to the shareholder. Similarly, even though a corporation engages in industrial or commercial activity, particular transactions with shareholders may be disregarded or recast for tax purposes, while other transactions by the same corporation with outsiders or even with its shareholders are fully honored.[35]

The value of generalizations about corporate entity and taxation is impaired still further by the fact that the broad judicial principles of income taxation are as applicable to corporations and their shareholders as to other taxpayers, so that "disregard of the corporate entity" may be merely a label for a tax result that would be reached as to individuals, estates, trusts, or partnerships by the application of other fundamental principles of income taxation.[36] Conversely, these principles may be employed by the courts in reaching a result that could, alternatively, be regarded as a partial or total

---

[34] Higgins v. Smith, 308 US 473 (1940). The taxable year in this case antedated the enactment of §267(a)(1), explicitly disallowing deductions for such losses (infra ¶ 5.04).

[35] For illustrations of judicial approaches to the corporate entity problem, see Noonan v. CIR, 52 TC 907 (1969), aff'd per curiam, 451 F2d 992 (9th Cir. 1971) (corporate limited partners, formed by general partners to avoid taxes, disregarded as shams); Jerome I. Roubik, 53 TC 365 (1969) (service corporation held valid entity, but all its income taxed to shareholders as true earners of the income); Baltimore Aircoil Co. v. US, 333 F. Supp. 705 (D. Md. 1971) (dominated subsidiary disregarded, and parent's expenses on behalf of subsidiary allowed as deductions incurred for benefit of de facto division); Perry R. Bass, 50 TC 595 (1968) (controlled foreign corporation held viable corporate entity, even though organized to reduce taxes on oil income under U.S.-Swiss treaty); Hospital Corp. of Am., 81 TC 520 (1983) (same); Ross Glove Co. v. CIR, 60 TC 569 (1973) (foreign tax haven corporation engaged in bona fide viable business and corporate entity respected); Owens v. CIR, 568 F2d 1233 (6th Cir. 1977) (purported sale of stock treated as indirect distribution of assets to shareholders where corporation no longer served any business purpose); see also ¶ 2.07 (tax status of personal service corporations), ¶ 2.10 (tax status of dummy and nominee corporations), and infra ¶ 15.03 (reallocations of income between affiliated corporations).

[36] See generally Bittker, Federal Taxation of Income, Estates and Gifts, ¶ 4.3 (Warren, Gorham & Lamont, Inc., 1981).

disregard of the corporate entity. Applications of these principles will be frequently encountered in later chapters of this book, and only a brief mention of them will be made at this point:

1. No assignment of earned income. In the famous case of *Lucas v. Earl*, the Court held that a husband was taxable on his entire earnings despite an agreement made with his wife (before the Sixteenth Amendment was adopted) that each would have a one-half interest in the other's earnings.[37] The court said that "the statute could tax salaries to those who earned them and provide that the tax could not be escaped by anticipatory arrangements and contracts however skilfully devised to prevent the salary when paid from vesting even for a second in the man who earned it" and that "no distinction can be taken according to the motives leading to the arrangement by which the fruits are attributed to a different tree from that on which they grew."[38] In *Helvering v. Horst*, the same theory was applied to an assignment of investment income.[39] These assignment of income principles apply with equal force to corporate transactions.[40]

2. Substance over form. One of the persistent problems of income taxation, as of other branches of the law, is the extent to which legal consequences should turn on the substance of a transaction rather than on its form. It is easy to say that substance should control, but in practice form usually has some substantive consequences, so that if two transactions differ in form, they are probably not identical as to substance. Even so, they may be sufficiently similar to warrant identical tax treatment. Thus, a loan by a shareholder to his corporation may be treated as an equity investment,[41] a salary paid by the corporation to the shareholder may be treated as a dividend,[42] and a sale of property by the shareholder may be treated as if made by the corporation[43] or ignored as a sham, as in *National Lead Co. v. CIR*.[44]

---

[37] Lucas v. Earl, 281 US 111 (1930).

[38] Id. at 114–115.

[39] Helvering v. Horst, 311 US 112 (1940).

[40] See generally infra ¶ 2.07; Lyon & Eustice, Assignment of Income: Fruit and Tree as Irrigated by the P.G. Lake Case, 17 Tax L. Rev. 293, 396 (1962); Eustice, Contract Rights, Capital Gain, and Assignment of Income—The Ferrer Case, 20 Tax L. Rev. 1, 51 (1964).

[41] See ¶ 4.04.

[42] See ¶ 7.05.

[43] See ¶ 11.07.

[44] National Lead Co. v. CIR, 336 F2d 134 (2d Cir. 1964) (also held a continuing transactional nullity). For discussions of this vague but pervasive doctrine, see

3. Business purpose. It is often said that a transaction is not given effect for tax purposes unless it serves some purpose other than tax avoidance. The leading case in this area is *Gregory v. Helvering*,[45] involving a corporate reorganization, and the theory has had its fullest flowering in this area of tax law; but it is by no means confined in its application to corporate reorganizations or even to the corporation-shareholder relationship.[46]

4. Step transactions. A business transaction, like the rest of life, has no clearly defined beginning or end, but it is necessary in practice to cut it, usually chronologically, into segments for tax purposes. If the segment is too thin, however, the tax results may be unfair to the taxpayer or to the government, or to both. In viewing a dynamic whole, the courts often say that an integrated transaction must not be broken into independent steps or, conversely, that the separate steps must be taken together in attaching tax consequences. The so-called step-transaction doctrine is often encountered in the taxation of corporations and shareholders, but its scope is much broader.[47]

In enunciating or applying these principles or doctrines, the courts often omit any reference to specific statutory provisions as if they were laying down a kind of common law of income taxation. Sometimes, however, the following statutory provisions are cited as if they either supported these broad principles or were alternative routes to the same result:

1. Section 61(a), defining "gross income." In *Helvering v. Clifford*, the Supreme Court held that a grantor of a short-term trust of which his wife was the beneficiary was taxable on the trust income under §22(a) of the 1939 Code (§61(a) of current law) on the ground that the trust effected only "a temporary reallocation of income within an intimate family group" and did not deprive the grantor "of the substance of full enjoyment of all the rights which previously he had in the property."[48] The language of the opinion, although anchored to §61(a), echoes the "no assignment of earned income"

Chirelstein, Learned Hand's Contribution to the Law of Tax Avoidance, 77 Yale L.J. 440 (1968); Lyon & Eustice, Federal Income Taxation, 36 NYU L. Rev. 642 (1961); Isenberg, Musings on Form and Substance in Taxation, 49 U. Chi. L. Rev. 859 (1982).

[45] Gregory v. Helvering, 293 US 465 (1935), discussed infra ¶ 13.02.

[46] For detailed analysis, see infra ¶ 14.51.

[47] For applications, see infra ¶¶ 3.09, 14.51, 14.52, 14.54; for general discussion, see Bittker, supra note 36, at ¶ 4.3.5.

[48] Helvering v. Clifford, 309 US 331 (1940).

cases, the "substance over form" cases, and, although less explicitly, the "business purpose" cases.[49]

2. Section 446(b), requiring an accounting method that clearly reflects income. Although the taxpayer's method of accounting is normally controlling in computing taxable income, the government may prescribe another method under §446(b) if the taxpayer has no method or if his method "does not clearly reflect income."[50]

3. Section 482, permitting the government to reallocate gross income, deductions, and so forth among two or more organizations under common control. When a business enters into transactions with another business controlled by the same interests, appearances are often deceiving. Under §482, the Service has the power to distribute, apportion, or allocate gross income, deductions, credits, or allowances between or among two or more organizations, trades, or businesses that are "owned or controlled directly or indirectly by the same interests," if it determines that such action is necessary to prevent evasion of taxes or to clearly reflect the income of any of the organizations, trades, or businesses. The statute is expressly made applicable whether the enterprises or entities are incorporated or not. The provision has been applied "to circumstances involving an improper manipulation of financial accounts, an improper juggling of the accounts between the related organizations, an improper 'milking' of one business for the benefit of the other, or some similar abuse of proper financial accounting, all made possible by the control of the two businesses by the same interests."[51]

4. Sections 269, 382–383, 1551, and 1561. These are specialized provisions applicable to particular problems that are examined in detail later in this work.[52]

---

[49] For an application in the field of corporate taxation, see Johnson v. CIR, 78 TC 882 (1982). Compare Hospital Corp. of Am., supra note 35. For assignments of income between affiliated corporations, see infra ¶¶ 15.03 and 15.04; supra note 40.

[50] For an example of the use of §446(b) in the corporate area, see infra ¶ 11.07 text at note 68.

[51] Simon J. Murphy Co. v. CIR, 231 F2d 639 (6th Cir. 1956); Stanley W. Haag, 88 TC 32 (1987); see also infra ¶¶ 2.07 and 15.03.

[52] For discussion of these provisions, see infra ¶ 16.21 (§269, permitting the Service to disallow deductions, credits, and tax allowances if tax avoidance is the principal purpose for acquiring control of a corporation); ¶ 2.07 (§269A, a specialized version of §482 applicable to certain personal service corporations); ¶ 16.23 (§§382–383, limiting or disallowing the use of net operating losses and certain other tax allowances following specified changes in stock ownership or control); ¶ 15.02

The foregoing judicial principles and statutory provisions, which often overlap in practice, are a useful deterrent to tax avoidance schemes of varying scope and ingenuity. Forcing transactions heavily freighted with tax motives to withstand judicial analysis in the context of these principles, vague and uncertain in application though they may be, is more salutary than uncompromising literalism in applying the statutory system for taxing corporations and shareholders.

¶ 1.06 SPECIAL CLASSES OF CORPORATIONS

Because of their specialized character, the following classes of corporations are outside the scope of this work:

1. Regulated investment companies. Certain investment companies (primarily those registered under the Investment Company Act of 1940), including mutual funds, may elect to be taxed under Subchapter M (§§851–855 and 860), under which, in general, the corporation is taxed only on undistributed income, while the shareholders report the distributed income as ordinary income or capital gain, as the case may be. An elaborate network of conditions must be satisfied to qualify for the election, of which the salient features are that 90 percent of gross income must be derived from dividends, interest, and gains on the sale of stock or securities, and that the corporation's investments must be diversified as prescribed by §851(b)(4).

2. Real estate investment trusts. Sections 856–860 provide that certain real estate investment trusts be treated as corporations if requisite percentages of their income are distributed to their beneficiaries. Under a conduit principle similar to that applicable to mutual funds, the distributed income of a qualifying REIT is taxed to the distributees but not to the trust itself.[53]

3. Real estate mortgage investment conduits. Under §§860A–860G, enacted in 1986, certain organizations formed to hold a fixed pool of real

---

(§§1551 and 1561, disallowing or allocating certain tax benefits among two or more corporations under common control).

[53] See Allen & Fisher, Real Estate Investment Trusts, Tax Mgt. (BNA) No. 107-5th (1986); Halpern, Real Estate Investment Trusts and the Tax Reform Act of 1976, 31 Tax Lawyer 329 (1978); Eustice, Kuntz, Lewis & Deering, supra note 10, at ¶ 2.06[3].

estate mortgages and issuing multiple classes of interests therein are in general not treated as taxable entities (whether created as corporations, trusts or partnerships), but as conduits whose income is taxed only at the investor level.[54]

4. Small business investment companies. The Small Business Investment Act of 1958 provided for the creation of corporations to make capital available to small businesses by the purchase of convertible debentures. Under §1243, a loss incurred by a small business investment company on such debentures is treated as an ordinary, rather than a capital, loss.[55] As for the shareholders of a small business investment company, under §1242 worthless stock gives rise to an ordinary rather than a capital loss, and if the loss is not fully used in the year it is incurred, the excess may be carried over under §172 (net operating loss deduction) as if incurred in the shareholder's trade or business.[56]

These provisions apply only to corporations operating under the Small Business Investment Act of 1958, and should not be confused with the more widely applicable provisions of §1244 or Subchapter S, both of which apply to "small business corporations" but use the term in different senses.[57]

5. Banks and trust companies. Subchapter H (§§581–597) provides special rules for certain banks, trust companies, and common trust funds maintained by banks.[58]

6. Insurance companies. Subchapter L contains intricate and specialized provisions for the taxation of life insurance companies (§§801–818), mutual insurance companies (except life and a few other companies) (§§821–826), and other insurance companies (primarily casualty companies) (§§831–832).[59]

---

[54] See generally H.R. Rep. No. 841, 99th Cong., 2d Sess. II-225 (1986); Eustice, Kuntz, Lewis & Deering, supra note 10, at ¶ 2.06[2].

[55] See also §243(a)(2), providing that the dividends-received deduction (infra ¶ 5.06) for such a company is 100 percent rather than the usual 80 percent of dividends received.

[56] See Comment, The Small Business Investment Act of 1958, 47 Calif. L. Rev. 144 (1959).

[57] For §1244 and Subchapter S, see infra ¶ 4.24 and ch. 6 respectively.

[58] See Clark, The Federal Income Taxation of Financial Intermediaries, 84 Yale L.J. 1603 (1975).

[59] See generally Antes, Taxation of Insurance Companies (Matthew Bender, 2d ed., 1986).

7. Cooperatives. Cooperative organizations are, in general, allowed to exclude from income any patronage refunds or dividends allocated to members; and some organizations (so-called exempt cooperatives) are, in addition, generally exempted from the corporate tax by §521.[60]

8. Tax exempt corporations. Section 501(c) grants tax exemption to a number of corporations, primarily nonprofit institutions (e.g., charitable, educational, and religious organizations; federal instrumentalities; civic leagues; labor unions; social clubs; credit unions; cemetery companies) and mutual or cooperative organizations that provide economic benefits for their members only (fraternal benefit societies; voluntary employees' associations providing life, sickness, or similar benefits; local teachers' retirement funds; local benevolent life insurance associations; and mutual irrigation or telephone companies). In some instances, the organization must be a corporation to enjoy the tax exemption; in other cases, any legal form (e.g., corporation, trust, association) qualifies if the organization serves the purposes set out in §501(c).

A corporation operated for the primary purpose of carrying on a trade or business for profit (a "feeder corporation") does not qualify for tax exemption, however, even though its profits are payable to an exempt organization (§502). Moreover, *all* tax exempt organizations are taxed on their unrelated business taxable income by §511 and lose their exemption completely if they abuse their status by engaging in a prohibited transaction (§503), and they are subject to a network of other restrictions.[61]

¶ 1.07 THE CORPORATION VS. THE PARTNERSHIP

Although explication of the tax treatment of partnerships is beyond the scope of this work,[62] a brief comparison of the salient differences for tax purposes between the corporation and the partnership may be helpful.

---

[60] See generally Clark & Erickson, Taxation of Cooperatives, Tax Mgmt. (BNA) 229-2d (1984); Bittker, supra note 36, at ch. 104.

[61] See generally Hopkins, The Law of Tax-Exempt Organizations (Ronald Press, 3d ed., 1979); Weithorn, Tax Techniques for Foundations and Other Exempt Organizations (Matthew Bender, 1980); Treusch & Sugarman, Tax-Exempt Charitable Organizations (ALI-ABA 1979); Bittker, supra note 36 at chs. 100–103; Bittker & Rahdert, The Exemption of Nonprofit Organizations From Federal Income Taxation, 85 Yale L.J. 299 (1976).

[62] See generally Solomon & Lurie, Choice of Entity, 456 Tax Mgt. (BNA) (1986); McKee, Nelson & Whitmire, Federal Taxation of Partnerships and Partners (Warren, Gorham & Lamont, Inc., 1977); Willis, Pennell, & Postlewaite, Tax Partnership Taxation (Shepard's/McGraw-Hill, 3d ed., 1981).

1. Organization. A partner does not recognize gain or loss on contributing property to a partnership (§721); the basis of the property carries over to the partnership (§723), and it also governs the partner's basis for his interest in the partnership (§722). Substantially identical rules are ordinarily applicable to contributions of property by a shareholder to a corporation, but in unusual circumstances the transfer of property produces gain or loss for the shareholder.[63]

2. Taxability of income. The corporation is taxed on its income (computed after allowance for bona fide salaries, rent, or other business expenses if any, paid to shareholders); any amounts distributed to the shareholders as dividends are ordinarily taxed to them as ordinary income. Undistributed income is not subject to the individual income tax, but it may become subject to the accumulated earnings tax or the personal holding company tax[64] in the hands of the corporation.

Partnerships are not taxed as such (§701), but partners are taxed on their pro rata shares of the firm's income, whether it is distributed to them or not. Under the prevailing conduit theory, the character of such items as ordinary income, capital gains and losses, charitable contributions, tax-exempt interest, and so forth carries over to the partner (§702).

3. Deductibility of losses. Corporate losses can be deducted by the corporation itself, subject to certain carry-back and carry-forward rules applicable to net operating losses (§172) and capital losses (§1212). Shareholders may not avail themselves of unused corporate losses, except that they may deduct losses on worthless stock, ordinarily as a capital loss unless the stock is Section 1244 stock.[65]

Partnership losses are deducted directly by the partners to the extent of the partners' adjusted bases for their interests in the partnership (§704(d)). For this reason, it is not uncommon to organize a hazardous enterprise as a partnership, thus allowing the investors to offset the partnership's losses against their other income and to convert to a corporation if and when success is achieved. Section 183, disallowing certain deductions if an activity is not engaged in for profit, is applicable to partners but not to corporations except for those electing to be taxed as partnerships under Subchapter S.[66]

---

[63] See infra ¶ 3.01.

[64] See infra ¶¶ 8.01–8.09 (accumulated earnings tax) and ¶¶ 8.20–8.24 (personal holding company tax).

[65] See ¶ 4.24.

[66] For §183, see infra ¶ 5.04; see also Regs. §1.702-1(a)(8)(ii) (partners subject to §183). For corporations electing under Subchapter S to be taxed, in the main, as partnerships, see ch. 6.

4. Fiscal year. A corporation may select its own taxable year, whereas a partnership must use the taxable year of its principal partners unless a business purpose for another taxable year is established.[67]

5. Shareholders and partners as employees. Because shareholders can become employees of their own corporation, they can be included in pension, profit-sharing, stock option, deferred compensation, wage continuation, group life insurance, and employee death benefit plans, subject to a variety of nondiscrimination provisions designed to prevent excessive deductions and exclusions under plans favoring highly compensated and shareholder employees. Partners can participate in qualified pension and profit-sharing plans (subject to certain restrictions that do not apply to shareholder-employees); but since partners are not employees of their partnerships (not even if they receive amounts designated as a salary for services), they do not ordinarily qualify for tax favored employee fringe benefits.[68]

6. Income splitting. Income splitting within a family through the use of a partnership is affected by §704(e), requiring the donor of an interest in a partnership to receive a reasonable allowance for his personal services before the donee's distributive share of the firm's income is computed. If shares of a corporation are given to children or other donees, however, the donor may contribute services to the corporation without receiving compensation, even though this may increase the value of the donee's stock or the amount of dividends paid to him.

7. Sales. On selling stock, shareholders realize capital gains or losses unless they are dealers in securities or the corporation is collapsible.[69] The sale of partnership interests similarly produces capital gains or losses, except for amounts received for unrealized receivables and substantially appreciated inventory items.[70]

8. Liquidation. Shareholders ordinarily realize capital gains or losses on the complete liquidation of a corporation, except for collapsible corpora-

---

[67] For partnership taxable years, see §706. For a restriction on the freedom of corporations to select a taxable year, see §441(i) (certain personal service corporations required to use calendar year, unless allowed to select a fiscal year by the IRS).

[68] See generally McKee, Nelson & Whitmire, supra note 62, at ¶ 2.03.

[69] For collapsible corporations, see generally infra ¶¶ 12.01–12.07.

[70] See §§741 and 751.

tions and the liquidation of subsidiaries.[71] Partial liquidations and some stock redemptions also produce capital gains or losses; other stock redemptions are taxed as dividends.[72] The liquidation of a partner's interest also ordinarily produces capital gains or losses, subject to special rules in the case of retiring and deceased partners.[73]

On the other hand, a corporation's liquidating distribution of appreciated or depreciated property ordinarily generates gains or losses;[74] but these transactions are not taxable events in the case of partnerships.

¶ 1.08 INTEGRATION OF CORPORATE AND INDIVIDUAL TAXES

Concerns have been voiced by Treasury officials and members of Congress that our present statutory system of double taxation for corporate earnings is inhibiting capital formation and contributing significantly to the technical complexity of the law. To remedy these defects, various proposals for integrating the corporate and individual income taxes have been suggested, the principal alternative forms of which are the following:

(1) Full integration, or eliminating the corporate income tax completely and taxing all corporate earnings directly to the shareholders at the regular personal tax rates (for a partial prototype of this approach, the Subchapter S provisions would presumably be the model);[75]

(2) Partial integration, or allowing a deduction to the corporation for dividends paid to its shareholders (thus largely obviating one of the primary distinctions between debt and equity);[76] and

---

[71] For collapsible corporations and liquidations of subsidiaries, see infra ch. 12 and ¶ 11.40 respectively.

[72] For stock redemptions, see infra ¶ 9.02.

[73] See §§731 and 736; for receivables and substantially appreciated inventory, see §§741 and 751.

[74] See infra ¶ 11.06.

[75] See also the current popularity of so-called master limited partnerships, infra ¶ 2.04, text at note 53. For other self-help techniques, see infra ch. 4 and ¶ 7.05; see also ¶ 2.07.

[76] See infra ¶ 4.02.

The Treasury Report on Tax Simplification and Reform, released November 27, 1984, adopted this approach (it would allow a corporate-level deduction for one-half of dividends paid from previously taxed earnings). See Sheppard, Corporate Integration, The Proper Way to Eliminate the Corporate Tax, 27 Tax Notes 637 (1985).

In its May 29, 1985 submission to Congress, a revised version of the Treasury's modified corporate integration proposal, the deduction for dividends was scaled

(3) Allowing a credit to the shareholders for some part of the corporate tax (which credit would most likely be keyed to dividend distributions, on a grossed-up method).[77]

Which of these proposals, if any, will be reproposed by the Treasury, and in what form they will finally, if ever, emerge from Congress, are questions presently beyond reasonable predictability. Experience indicates, however, that a meaningful integration system is not likely to be forthcoming for some time.[78] Some have suggested that the trend to convert to master limited partnerships[79] is a form of do-it-yourself integration, or at least an acceptable pressure valve to enable Congress to resist adoption of a formal integration regime.

---

back to 10 percent. See Buchanan, The Dividend Paid Deduction Proposal: Separating Myth From Reality, 28 Tax Notes 97, July 1, 1985 (criticizing both the Treasury I and II proposals).

The House Tax Reform Bill of 1985 (H.R. 3838) approved a watered-down version of the Treasury proposal that provided for a 10 percent dividend-paid deduction to be phased in over 10 years commencing in 1988. (These provisions were in §311(a) of the House Bill, which would have added §§231–234 to the Code.) Such dividends would be deductible only to the extent they were paid from a qualified dividend account (consisting generally of taxable earnings), and then only if they constituted ordinary §301 dividends to the recipient. The dividends-paid deduction proposal also was tied into a scale-back of the §243 dividends-received deduction for corporate shareholders, infra ¶ 5.06, which amount was phased down to 70 percent over the 10-year period from 1988 through 1997.

The House Bill proposal for a corporate-level dividends-paid deduction, modest though it may have been, was not included in either the Senate Tax Reform Bill or the final Conference Bill. For analysis, see Simon, Comments on the Dividends Paid Deduction of H.R. 3838, 31 Tax Notes 609 (May 15, 1986).

[77] For a similar system, see the discussion of the deemed paid foreign tax credit, infra ¶ 17.11.

[78] For discussions of this subject, see Leonard, A Pragmatic View of Corporate Integration, 35 Tax Notes 889 (June 1, 1987); McLure, Integration of the Personal and Corporate Income Taxes: The Missing Element in Recent Tax Reform Proposals, 88 Harv. L. Rev. 532 (1975); McLure, Integration of the Income Taxes: Why and How, 2 J. Corp. Tax'n 429 (1976); N.Y. State Bar Association, Tax Section, Report on the Integration of Corporate and Individual Income Taxes, 31 Tax L. Rev. 37 (1977); Gourevitch, Corporate Tax Integration: The European Experience, 31 Tax L. Rev. 65 (1977); Clark, The Morphogenesis of Subchapter C: An Essay in Statutory Evolution and Reform, 87 Yale L.J. 90 (1977); Treasury Department, Blueprints for Basic Tax Reform 68–75 (1977); Joint Comm. on Taxation, Tax Policy and Capital Formation (Comm. Print 1977); Break & Pechman, Federal Tax Reform: The Impossible Dream? 90–104 (Brookings, 1975); Feldstein & Frisch, Corporate Tax Integration: The Estimated Effects on Capital Accumulation and Tax Distribution of Two Integration Proposals, 30 Nat'l Tax J. 37 (1977); Warren, supra note 17; Pechman, supra note 17; and supra notes 75 and 76.

[79] See infra ¶ 2.04. See generally Canellus, Corporate Integration: By Design or By Default, 35 Tax Notes 999 (1987).

CHAPTER 2

Definition of a Corporation

¶ 2.01   INTRODUCTORY

Section 11(a) of the Code imposes a tax on the taxable income of "every corporation" but does not define the term "corporation." The Code's definitional section, however, provides in §7701(a)(3) that "the term 'corporation' includes associations, joint stock companies, and insurance companies." Although this "definition" leaves much to be desired in the way of precision, the issue of whether a business organization constitutes a "corporation" for federal tax purposes is not often encountered in practice. When the issue does arise, the definitional problem typically is whether the enterprise is an "association" (to be treated as a corporation) or some other form of tax entity (e.g., partnership, trust, or proprietorship).

1. Role of federal and local law. In reaching out to impose corporate tax status on some entities that are not classified as corporations by state law, a practice going as far back as the income tax of 1894,[1] Congress presumably had in mind the fact that a business entity may resemble a corporation in form and function without having a state charter. In *Flint v. Stone Tracy Co.,* for example, the Supreme Court sustained imposition of the corporate income tax on joint stock companies on the ground that they share many of the benefits of corporate organization, referring to the advantages that arise from corporate or quasi-corporate organization; and in *Burk-Waggoner Oil Association v. Hopkins*, the Court observed that "nothing in the Constitution precludes Congress from taxing as a corporation an association which, although unincorporated, transacts its business as if it were incorporated."[2] Conversely, the fact that a state has conferred the label of "corporation" on a business organization should not per se control its status for federal tax purposes, since this issue is inherently a question of federal, rather than state, law.[3]

On the other hand, as the regulations recognize, local law must of necessity govern the legal relationships of an organization's associates (1) among themselves, (2) to third persons (e.g., customers, suppliers, creditors, and employees), and (3) to the property of the venture, even though these factors in turn are taken into account in determining the organization's federal tax status.[4]

Thus, classifying an entity as a corporation is essentially a dual process: Federal law governs the corporate characteristics that must be present in order to find a "tax law" corporation, but state law determines whether the organization possesses these legal earmarks.

2. Classification issues and stakes. The question of corporate classification most often arises in the context of whether the profits of a particular organization are subject to the corporate tax of §11(a) (and, as a corollary thereto, whether distribution of those profits to its beneficial owners will be subject to a second round of taxation, as dividends, under the rules of §§301

---

[1] 28 Stat. 509, at 556.

[2] Flint v. Stone Tracy Co., 220 US 107, 146, 151 (1911); Burk-Waggoner Oil Ass'n v. Hopkins, 269 US 110, 114 (1925).

[3] Despite O'Neill v. US, 410 F2d 888 (6th Cir. 1969), where the court invalidated the 1965 professional corporations regulations (infra ¶ 2.06) to the extent that they failed to follow the state law label of "corporation," it is doubtful that a local law corporate label alone would or should control the federal tax classification issue. See Worthy, IRS Chief Counsel Outlines What Lies Ahead for Professional Corporations, 32 J. Tax'n 88 (1970).

[4] See Regs. §301.7701-1(c). For a similar approach in classifying foreign organizations, see Rev. Rul. 73-254, 1973-1 CB 613 (foreign law determines relevant legal relationships, but federal tax law determines whether these relationships denote corporate or unincorporated status); see also infra text at notes 40–42.

and 316 (see Chapter 7)). But once corporate status is found, *all* the consequences of operating in corporate form will flow from this determination; that is, the panoply of tax rules relating to the treatment of corporations and shareholders will govern the organization, operation, liquidation, and reorganization of the enterprise and the taxability of distributions to its associates. On the other hand, if noncorporate status exists, the tax consequences will be controlled by other applicable Code provisions (e.g., Subchapter J for trusts and beneficiaries or Subchapter K for partners and partnerships).

Taxpayers may seek to avoid corporate status for reasons other than the double taxation consequences noted previously. Thus, conduit treatment may be desired in order to pass through operating losses of the venture current to its owner or to preserve the special tax character of certain items of income or deduction (e.g., tax-exempt interest, long-term capital gain, percentage depletion, and depreciation). To be sure, some corporations can obtain the benefits of conduit treatment in one form or another (e.g., S corporations (see Chapter 6), mutual funds, and real estate investment trusts and certain other special classes of corporations (see Chapter 1)), but the partnership or trust device often provides a simpler method of attaining this goal. Consequently, real estate, theatrical, and natural resource ventures are often organized in partnership form to gain conduit benefits for their investors. At the other end of the scale are investors who seek to obtain rather than avoid corporate status so that they can become "employees" of the enterprise and thus obtain the deferred compensation benefits of qualified pension and profit-sharing plans and such employee fringe benefits as the excludable employee death benefits, nontaxable meals and lodging furnished for the convenience of the employer, and stock option plans.[5] In addition, income-splitting goals are sometimes easier to accomplish through use of a corporation to shelter business income from the rates applicable to individuals.

3. General observations. In the absence of a statutory definition of "corporation," the task of definition has fallen by default to the courts and the Service. The judicial approach to this problem has generally been flexible, focusing on "all the facts and circumstances" to determine whether the form and function of the organization in question cause it to more nearly resemble a corporation or whether its characteristics instead warrant classifi-

---

[5] Disparities in the extent to which these and other tax allowances are available to incorporated as compared with unincorporated enterprises have been greatly reduced since the 1980s, but not all gaps have been closed. See generally Rands, Closely Held Businesses: Tax Advantages and Disadvantages of the Different Forms of Business Organizations, 91 Comm. L.J. 61 (1986); Harris, Parity in Employee Benefit Plans and Fringe Benefits for the Self-Employed After TEFRA and TRA '84, 62 Taxes 529 (1984).

cation as a partnership, trust, or some other type of noncorporate enterprise. This approach is not an exact science, and, because of the heavily factual nature of the classification issue, a determination of status by a trier of fact is not readily reversed on appeal. In contrast, the approach of the regulations to the corporate classification problem is mechanical; a majority of corporate characteristics is required to tip the scales. As interpretative regulations (as opposed to legislative regulations issued under authority delegated by Congress to the Treasury Department), however, they have not elicited special deference by the courts.

The corporate classification area has long been marked by fluidity, confusion, and controversy. Although the Service often attempts to force corporate status on reluctant taxpayers who claim that they are partners or joint venturers, the shoe is sometimes on the other foot, and the Service usually refuses to issue advance rulings on the tax status of particular organizations. Decisions to embrace the corporate form of organization should be carefully considered, since a corporation, like a lobster pot, is easy to enter, difficult to live in, and painful to get out of.

4. Unscrambling the eggs on a change of classification. Although there is an abundance of litigation on the proper classification of various business organizations, there is surprisingly little authority regarding the problems that arise when an organization is authoritatively classified as a partnership or trust after reporting on the corporate basis for a period of years or vice versa. If the statute of limitations on the earlier years has not run, the eggs can be unscrambled by filing amended returns, under which the tax liability of all parties can be recomputed as a prelude to the appropriate additional payments and refunds. If, however, any earlier years are closed by the statute of limitations and this circumstance is not mitigated under §§1311–1314 by the assertion of inconsistent positions by either the government or the taxpayers, the errors of the past will go uncorrected. In such a case, however, the courts may apply an estoppel doctrine to prevent a current benefit from being built on an uncorrectible error.[6]

In the few instances in which the question has been raised, it has been held that a change to the correct method of reporting by an organization that has erroneously reported as a corporation does not constitute its "liquidation."[7] In Rev. Rul. 70-101, the Service ruled that a professional service organization that had been reporting its income as a partnership in accor-

---

[6] See Alderson v. Healy, 15 AFTR2d 536 (D. Mont. 1965); Demmon v. US, 321 F2d 203 (7th Cir. 1963).

[7] Rev. Rul. 63-107, 1963-1 CB 71 (change in status due to change in regulations); Rev. Proc. 65-27, 1965-2 CB 1017; infra note 59 (professional service organizations).

dance with existing regulations but that the Service now agreed was entitled to be treated as a corporation, would not be required to report income as a corporation for years ending before the date of the ruling.[8]

¶ 2.02   "ASSOCIATIONS" IN GENERAL

1. Corporate classification criteria: case law background. The leading case in this area is *Morrissey v. CIR*, holding that the corporate income tax was properly imposed on a trust created to develop certain real estate. In reaching its decision, the Supreme Court noted that "it is impossible in the nature of things to translate the statutory concept of 'association' into a particularity of detail that would fix the status of every sort of enterprise or organization which ingenuity may create," and that "the inclusion of associations with corporations [in the statutory definition] implies resemblance; but it is resemblance and not identity."[9] The classification approach employed by the Court in *Morrissey* was a balancing process in which the characteristics of the organization under examination were compared with the characteristics of "typical" or "ordinary" corporations. This approach, involving as it does the exercise of judgment on facts that are almost never duplicated, has been characterized by fluidity and confusion, especially in the penumbral zone of hybrid entities possessing some, but not all, of the basic corporate indicia.

The principal structural or formal characteristics of a corporation noted by the Court in *Morrissey* were: (1) associates; (2) an objective to carry on a trade or business and divide the profits; (3) continuity of the life of the enterprise, notwithstanding the death, disability, or withdrawal of its members; (4) the opportunity for centralized management by representatives of the owners; (5) the privilege of limited liability for the owners; (6) free transferability of beneficial interests in the organization; and (7) holding title to property as an entity. The *Morrissey* opinion did not say which, if any, of these criteria were controlling, other than to note that associates and a business objective were essential for corporate status. Furthermore, there was no indication that a mechanical balancing of these various factors was required, nor did the Court imply that the relevant corporate indicia had to be identical to the comparable characteristics of a pure corporation, the requirement being resemblance to a corporation, not identity. Finally, while some of the *Morrissey* corporate factors are common to trusts and partnerships as well as

---

[8] Rev. Rul. 70-101, 1970-1 CB 278.

[9] Morrissey v. CIR, 296 US 344, 356 (1935). See generally Rands, Organizations Classified as Corporations for Federal Tax Purposes, 59 St. John's L. Rev. 657 (1985).

to corporations, the Court gave no consideration as to how such overlapping characteristics were to be treated.

2. The association regulations. The first six of the seven corporate characteristics listed by the Court in *Morrissey* were codified by Regs. §301.7701-2 (promulgated in 1960) as the "major characteristics ordinarily found in a pure corporation which, taken together, distinguish it from other organizations." Unlike *Morrissey*, however, the regulations establish an arithmetic criterion: An unincorporated organization is not classified as a corporation unless it has more corporate characteristics than noncorporate characteristics.[10] In making this comparison, characteristics that are common to both corporate and noncorporate organizations are disregarded. For example, in determining whether a partnership has more corporate than noncorporate characteristics, the facts that it has associates and that its objective is to carry on business for profit and to divide the gains therefrom are not taken into account, since these factors are common to corporations and partnerships.[11]

Of the six characteristics listed in the regulations, two, associates and an objective to carry on business for joint profit, are essentially negative criteria; absent associates or a joint profit objective, an arrangement among co-owners for the development of property for their separate profit is not classified as a corporation.[12] (In applying this filter, however, the case law allows a single-owner organization to satisfy the associates requirement, despite its plural form, by analogy to sole-shareholder corporations.[13]) The other four

---

[10] Regs. §301.7701-2(a)(3); see Phillip G. Larson, 66 TC 159, 185 (1976) (acq.) (superseding an earlier opinion, 65 TC No. 10 (Oct. 21, 1975)), noting that the regulations accord equal weight to each of these factors and observing that, were it not for this official "thumb on the scales," the court would have weighted each factor "according to the degree of corporate similarity it provides." For an extended dissent describing the regulations as "patently erroneous," see id. at 202.

For early comments on the 1960 rules, see Fox, The Maximum Scope of the Association Concept, 25 Tax L. Rev. 311 (1970); Lyons, Comments on the New Regulations on Associations, 16 Tax L. Rev. 441 (1961); Zarky, Unincorporated Organizations Taxable as Corporations, 1961 S. Cal. Tax. Inst. 277.

[11] Regs. §301.7701-2(a)(3); see also Regs. §301.7701-2(a)(2) (organization cannot be classified as corporation if it lacks objective to carry on business for profit).

[12] Regs. §301.7701-2(a)(2).

[13] See John B. Hynes, Jr., 74 TC 1266, 1279–1281 (1980) ("when there is a single owner, the regulations are not intended to require multiple associates or a sharing of profits among them"); see also Lombard Trustees, Ltd. v. CIR, 136 F2d 22 (9th Cir. 1943). A one-owner organization, however, may encounter difficulties in establishing that it possesses such corporate characteristics as continuity of life and centralized management; see A.A. Lewis & Co. v. CIR, 301 US 385 (1937); Knoxville Truck Sales & Serv., Inc., 10 TC 616 (1948) (acq.); Coast Carton Co., 10 TC 894 (1948)

major characteristics are examined in some detail in the regulations, with illustrative examples.[14] While in theory still other corporate characteristics may be taken into account in applying the more-corporate-than-noncorporate-characteristics test, in practice unincorporated organizations are rarely classified as corporations unless they have three or more of the following major corporate characteristics:

(1) *Continuity of life.* This factor is present if the death, disability, or withdrawal of any member of the organization will not cause the organization's dissolution. It is not created, however, by a conventional agreement among partners to refrain from causing dissolution, if (as is usually, if not always, true) a demand for a dissolution, although in violation of the agreement, would be effective under local law.[15]

(2) *Centralized management in representative capacity.* To satisfy this factor, the exclusive and continuing power to make necessary management decisions must be concentrated in a managerial group (composed of less than all the members) that has the authority to act on behalf of the organization independently of its members. What is crucial is the focus of authority in the hands of a particular group, in contrast to the mutual agency relationship of a partnership, in which each member can bind the organization by his acts; the corporate form "abhors anarchy of authority."[16]

(3) *Limited liability.* The owners of a corporation typically are liable for its debts (whether created by contract or tort) only to the extent of the corporate property. If creditors of the organization may seek satisfaction of their unpaid claims by proceeding against the individual members, this corporate characteristic is not present. Moreover, limited liability is not created for this purpose by an agreement shifting responsibility for the organization's liabilities from

---

(nonacq.); see also Rev. Rul. 77-214, 1977-1 CB 408, enunciating a "single economic interest" theory, discussed infra text at notes 40–42.

[14] Regs. §§301.7701-2(b)–301.7701-2(g). For other factors, see infra text at notes 20–22.

[15] Zuckman v. US, 524 F2d 729, 736 (Ct. Cl. 1975); see also Glensder Textile Co., 46 BTA 176 (1942) (acq.) (contingent continuity arising from provision in limited partnership's charter authorizing surviving general partners to continue business on death, retirement, or incapacity of another general partner, held not analogous to continuity of life enjoyed by corporations); Estate of Smith v. CIR, 313 F2d 724 (8th Cir. 1963) (continuity lacking if individual participants can withdraw their investments at will).

[16] The general partners of a limited partnership ordinarily constitute central management, but this factor may be negated if they can be removed by the limited partners; Regs. §301.7701-2(c)(4), discussed infra text at note 45.

members of the group to other persons if under local law the indemnified persons remain liable to the organization's creditors.[17]

(4) *Free transferability of interests.* This factor is present if a member is free to assign all the attributes of his beneficial interest in the organization without the consent of other members. Thus, a member must be free to transfer not only his interest in the profits of the venture but also his rights to share in its control and assets, and such a transfer must not work a dissolution of the organization under local law. If an organization's members can transfer their interests to outsiders only after offering them to the other insiders at fair market value, the regulations state that "this modified corporate characteristic will be accorded less significance" than an unqualified right to transfer the interest.[18] However, this reduction in value is of limited importance, since if any two other corporate characteristics are present, modified transferability tips the scales in favor of corporate classification just as conclusively as would full transferability; on the other hand, even full transferability is insufficient if the organization has only one other corporate characteristic.[19]

The regulations state that "other factors may be found in some cases which may be significant in classifying an organization as an association, a partnership, or a trust,"[20] but the regulations neither identify these other factors nor suggest how they are to be weighed. Moreover, a number of plausible candidates for "other-factor" status were deprived of any independent force in classifying limited partnerships by an important 1979 Service ruling that they be treated as significant only in determining the presence of the four corpo-

---

[17] For background regarding the reference in the regulations to agreements that are ineffective under local law, see infra note 46.

For an abortive attempt by the Service to promote limited liability into a super factor that, if present, would require an organization to be classified as a corporation regardless of its other characteristics, see Burke, Jr., & Sessions, The Wyoming Limited Liability Company: An Alternative to Sub S and Limited Partnerships? 54 J. Tax'n 232 (1981); Rosen, Effect of Proposed Amendments to Section 7701 Regulations on Leveraged Leases, 9 J. Corp. Tax'n 53 (1982). The proposed regulations discussed in these articles were withdrawn in 1982 by IRS News Release IR-82-145, 1983 P-H Memo. TC ¶ 54,703. But see Rev. Proc. 87-3, §5.35, 1987-1 IRB 27 (pending resolution of issue by published ruling, revenue procedure, or regulations, rulings will not be issued on the classification of limited liability companies).

[18] Regs. §301.7701-2(e)(2).

[19] For the use of other factors in combination with modified transferability, see infra text at notes 20–22.

[20] Regs. §301.7701-2(a)(1). But see the final sentence of Regs. §301.7701-2(a)(2), which seems to place *sole* reliance on the four factors listed in the regulations.

rate characteristics listed previously.[21] Among these secondary corporate characteristics are (1) the division of limited partnership interests into units that are marketed in the same way as corporate securities; (2) a managing partner's discretionary right to retain or distribute profits; and (3) the denial to limited partners of the right to vote on the election and removal of general partners and on the sale of partnership assets. This "second-class status" of course binds only the Service; it does not prevent *taxpayers* from seeking to persuade courts that the factors listed in the ruling should be given greater weight than the ruling allows if the taxpayer is seeking to obtain, rather than to avoid, corporate classification in a particular case.[22]

Because the four-factor analysis of the regulations is applied with some variations in emphasis to trusts, limited partnerships, tax shelter partnerships, professional service corporations, and joint ventures, these categories of organizations are examined in more detail in the paragraphs that follow.

¶ 2.03   TRUSTS AS "ASSOCIATIONS"

At first blush, virtually all trusts would seem to qualify for corporate classification, since they possess all four of the major corporate characteristics: (1) Management is centralized in the trustee; (2) neither the trustee nor the beneficiaries are personally liable for the trust's debts; (3) the trust ordinarily continues to exist despite the death, bankruptcy, or incapacity of the trustee or the beneficiaries; and (4) the beneficiaries are usually free to transfer their interests. The regulations, however, intervene by stating that since these characteristics are generally common to both trusts and corporations, they are not material in distinguishing between them; thus, the classification of trusts "depends on whether there are associates and an objective to carry on business and divide the gains therefrom."[23]

---

[21] Rev. Rul. 79-106, 1979-1 CB 448; see also Phillip G. Larson, supra note 10, at 184.

[22] But see supra note 19.

[23] Regs. §301.7701-2(a)(2). See generally Doolin, Determining the Taxable Status of Trusts That Run Businesses, 70 Cornell L. Rev. 1143 (1985); Stephens & Freeland, The Federal Tax Meaning of Estates and Trusts, 18 Tax L. Rev. 251 (1963).

For the status of a business trust that had only one beneficiary, who was also the grantor and one of three trustees, see John B. Hynes, Jr., supra note 13, at 1279 et seq. (1980) (despite one-person ownership, trust had associates and an objective to carry on business for joint profit); note, however, that the court went on to examine the trust's *other* corporate characteristics, although this seemed unnecessary under the regulations.

For the effect of a trustee's unexercised powers to shift from passive investments into the conduct of an active business, see Elm Street Realty Trust, 76 TC 803 (1981) (acq.) (trust created as estate planning vehicle to hold rental property had business

In applying these two criteria, the regulations distinguish between ordinary trusts and business trusts. An "ordinary trust" is an arrangement created by will or inter vivos declaration under rules applied by chancery or probate courts to protect and conserve property for beneficiaries who usually "do no more than accept the benefits" of the arrangement rather than participate in planning or creating it.[24] Such an arrangement is ordinarily treated as a trust (rather than as an association and therefore a corporation) if its purpose "is to vest in trustees responsibility for the protection and conservation of property for beneficiaries who cannot share in the discharge of this responsibility and, therefore, are not associates in a joint enterprise for the conduct of business for profit."[25]

These ordinary trusts are distinguished by the regulations from business trusts, which "generally are created by the beneficiaries simply as a device to carry on a profit-making business which normally would have been carried on through business organizations that are classified as corporations *or partnerships* under the Internal Revenue Code."[26] In referring to partnerships, the regulations do not seem to be concerned with efforts to eliminate such conventional trust characteristics as continuity of existence or limited liability, but rather to suggest that persons associating with each other to conduct a business usually choose to do so either in corporate or partnership form.[27]

As formulated by the regulations, the criteria for distinguishing between ordinary and business trusts can usually be applied with ease, but there are troublesome exceptions.[28] Furthermore, the regulations themselves

---

objective because of trustees' broad powers; but beneficiaries were not associates because they did not affirmatively plan or enter into joint enterprise and could not exercise "unfettered, significant influence" on trustee; extensive discussion), and cases there cited at 811–813; Harry M. Bedell, Jr., 86 TC 1207 (1986) (accord).

[24] Regs. §301.7701-4(a).

[25] Id.

[26] Regs. §301.7701-4(b) (emphasis supplied); see also Howard v. US, 1984-1 USTC ¶ 9494 (Cl. Ct. 1984) (subsequent purchasers of beneficial interests in business trust are associates; term is not limited to organizers of enterprise).

[27] If the facts warrant, however, a trust engaged in business activities may be treated as a partnership rather than as either an ordinary trust or an association. See Clyde W. Grove, 54 TC 799 (1970). Compare Outlaw v. US, 494 F2d 1376 (Ct. Cl.), cert. denied, 419 US 844 (1974) (self-styled trust more nearly resembled association than ordinary trust or partnership).

[28] See, e.g., Howard v. US, supra note 26 (trust to exploit mineral deposits on lands owned by railroad that was created for benefit of latter's shareholders; held taxable as business trust); Helvering v. Coleman-Gilbert Assocs., 296 US 369 (1935) (trusts for operation and management of rental real estate were associations); Helvering v. Combs, 296 US 365 (1935) (trust to finance and drill an oil well; same result); Mid-Ridge Inv. Co. v. US, 324 F2d 945 (7th Cir. 1963) (rental real estate management trust held taxable as a corporation); Rev. Rul. 72-75, 1972-1 CB 401

contain two warnings against treating formalities as conclusive.[29] First, the fact that the corpus of a trust is not supplied by the beneficiaries does not conclusively establish that the arrangement is an ordinary trust. Thus, if parents transfer the assets of a family business to themselves as trustees for their children, the trust risks being classified as an association (taxable as a corporation), even though the children did not supply the capital or take the initiative in associating themselves with each other to conduct the business. If, however, the transferred assets consist of rental property, the trust will probably not be classified as an association, even if the trustee is empowered to expand or shift from passive investments into an active business, unless the children can be characterized as associates because they have the power, as beneficiaries, to push the trustee in that direction.[30] Second, persons engaged in business cannot escape association status by conveying the assets to a trustee for their own benefit as purported beneficiaries of a trust.

The regulations go on to deal with investment trusts, stating that so-called management trusts are associations and that fixed investment trusts are also associations if the investment of the certificate holders can be varied, but not otherwise.[31] In several rulings, the Service has applied the no-

---

(California business trust engaged in practice of medicine held taxable as association because of centralized management, continuity of existence, and shares freely transferable to California-licensed physicians); Rev. Rul. 72-120, 1972-1 CB 402 (same for Ohio trust, subject to continuing effectiveness of trust instrument under local law); Rev. Rul. 72-122, 1972-1 CB 405 (same for Colorado trust). But see Rohman v. US, 275 F2d 120 (9th Cir. 1960) (passive holding of rental real estate did not, on facts, make trust an association).

[29] Regs. §301.7701-4(b).

[30] See Elm Street Realty Trust, supra note 23. For a testamentary trust that escaped classification as an association despite its conduct of a business because the beneficiaries (whose interests were not transferable) were not associates, see Harry M. Bedell, Jr., 86 TC 1207 (1986) (suggesting that decision, based on its own record, is a precedent of limited value). For royalty trusts created by corporate distributions to shareholders, see Gelinas, Mineral Royalty Trust Transactions: The Use of the Grantor Trust to Avoid Corporate Income Tax, 37 Tax L. Rev. 225 (1982).

[31] Regs. §301.7701-4(c), citing CIR v. North Am. Bond Trust, 122 F2d 545 (2d Cir. 1941), cert. denied, 314 US 701 (1942) (in this decision, the court contrasted the facts before it with those of a companion case, CIR v. Chase Nat'l Bank, 122 F2d 540 (2d Cir. 1941), where the trustee had virtually no power to alter the nature of a certificate holder's investment); see also Rev. Rul. 75-192, 1975-1 CB 384 ("power to vary investments" within meaning of regulations means "some kind of managerial power [in trustee or other person] over the trusteed funds that enables him to take advantage of variations in the market to improve the investment of all the beneficiaries"; issue is existence of power, not whether it has been exercised); Cleveland Trust Co. v. CIR, 115 F2d 481 (6th Cir. 1940), cert. denied, 312 US 704 (1941) (trust created to hold title to real property subject to a long-term lease was not an association, even though beneficial interests were sold to the public, because the trustee was required to pay over the rents periodically to the beneficiaries and, in the event of a sale, was to distribute the

variation principle to mortgage pools organized as trusts with transferable certificates of beneficial interest, the trustees of which must distribute the interest and principal as collected rather than reinvest these amounts.[32] Under regulations promulgated in 1986, however, an arrangement with more than one class of investors cannot qualify as a fixed investment trust, even if the trustees cannot alter the nature of the original investments or reinvest their proceeds, because "an arrangement with multiple classes of ownership enables investors to fulfill varying profit-making objectives through the division of rights, and the sharing of risks, in certain assets."[33]

So-called liquidating trusts, organized to liquidate and distribute the assets transferred to them, are treated as trusts by the regulations rather than as associations if their activities are reasonably necessary to and consistent with the accomplishment of this winding-up objective;[34] if, however, the liquidation is unreasonably prolonged or the limited purpose is obscured by the conduct of business activities, the organization will lose its trust status. Examples of liquidating trusts include trusts created to liquidate a single parcel of real estate or to effect an expeditious disposal of the assets of an estate or a dissolved corporation.[35] The regulations also treat bondholders'

---

proceeds rather than reinvest them). Compare Main-Hammond Land Trust v. CIR, 200 F2d 308 (6th Cir. 1952) (trust held an association on similar facts); Royalty Participation Trust, 20 TC 466 (1953) (acq.); Rev. Rul. 61-175, 1961-2 CB 128 (investment trust taxable as an ordinary trust); Rev. Rul. 64-220, 1964-2 CB 335 (passive land trust taxable as partnership rather than as association or trust).

[32] See Rev. Rul. 84-10, 1984-1 CB 155 (Federal National Mortgage Association-backed residential mortgage pool taxable as trust), and rulings there cited.

[33] Regs. §301.7701-4(c). The regulations do allow trust status, however, if multiple-class interests are merely incidental to the main custodial purpose of the arrangement; see Regs. §301.7701-4(c)(2), Examples (2) and (4). See generally Taylor, Debt/Equity and Other Tax Distinctions: How Far Can We Go? 62 Taxes 848, 850–852 (1984); Walter & Strassen, The Americus Trust "Prime" and "Score" Units, 65 Taxes 222 (1987).

[34] Regs. §301.7701-4(d); Rev. Rul. 80-150, 1980-1 CB 316. For the conditions that must be met to obtain advance rulings on the status of liquidating trusts, see Rev. Proc. 82-58, 1982-2 CB 847; see also infra ¶ 11.64 regarding the use of liquidating trusts in conjunction with corporate liquidations.

[35] Compare Helvering v. Washburn, 99 F2d 478 (8th Cir. 1938) (trust to liquidate large tract of grazing land held not taxable as corporation; management activity during liquidation process was minimal, and dominant purpose was to effect sale); Mullendore Trust Co. v. US, 271 F2d 748 (10th Cir. 1959) (upon termination of trust taxable as association, trustees carried on business during winding up to increase yield from assets; held an association, despite paramount objective to liquidate); see also US v. Homecrest Tract, 160 F2d 150 (9th Cir. 1947) (liquidation process held trade or business; trust taxed as corporation); Abraham v. US, 406 F2d 1259 (6th Cir. 1969) (liquidating trust taxed as corporation because it had *power* to conduct business and otherwise resembled a corporation, even though no business was in fact conducted); Rev. Rul. 63-228, 1963-2 CB 229 (creditors' liquidating trust not an

protective committees and voting trusts formed to protect the interests of security holders during insolvency proceedings as liquidating trusts, so long as they are not used to "further the control or profitable operation of a going business on a permanent basis."[36]

¶ 2.04 PARTNERSHIPS AS "ASSOCIATIONS"

As noted previously, the regulations provide that an unincorporated organization, such as a partnership, is an association taxable as a corporation if it has more corporate than noncorporate characteristics, but that, in applying this principle to partnerships, two factors—associates and an objective to carry on business and divide the gains therefrom—are disregarded because they are generally common to both corporations and partnerships.[37]

So far as the other characteristics of corporations are concerned, general partnerships subject to the Uniform Partnership Act are characterized by diffused rather than centralized management because of the mutual agency existing among the partners; they lack continuity of life, because the death, bankruptcy, or withdrawal of any partner causes a dissolution of the organization; the partners are subject to unlimited rather than limited liability to creditors of the organization, and partnership interests cannot be transferred without the consent of the other partners. Even if these conventional attributes of general partnerships are restricted by the partnership agreement, such internal arrangements do not bind outsiders without notice, and breaches of the agreement (e.g., refusals to abide by the managerial decisions of a designated general partner or to consent to any request by a partner wishing to transfer his or her interest) are ordinarily legally effective, even though they may subject the repudiating partner to liability for damages.[38] As a result, general partnerships ordinarily lack all four of the major corporate characteristics; in the absence of an unexpected combination of bizarre features of local law, it is

---

association); Rev. Rul. 75-379, 1975-2 CB 505 (same for liquidating trust holding long-term, unmarketable note).

For an analogous distinction in determining for capital gain purposes whether assets are held for sale to customers in the ordinary course of the taxpayer's business (ordinary income) or are merely liquidated in an orderly fashion (capital gain), see Bittker, Federal Taxation of Income, Estates and Gifts (Warren, Gorham & Lamont, Inc., 1981), Vol. 2, ¶ 51.2.4.

[36] Regs. §1.301.7701-4(d).

[37] Regs. §§1.301.7701-2(a)(2) and 1.301.7701-2(a)(3); supra ¶ 2.02. See generally McKee, Nelson & Whitmire, Federal Taxation of Partnerships and Partners (Warren, Gorham & Lamont, Inc., 1977), ¶ 3.06.

[38] See Zuckman v. US, supra note 15, at 734–737 (extended analysis of provision of limited partnership agreement purporting to create continuity of life).

difficult to envision a general partnership with enough corporate characteristics to constitute an association under the regulations.[39]

Attention must be directed, however, to the cloudy status of a partnership all of whose partners are subsidiaries of a common parent. In 1977, the Service floated a so-called single economic interest theory, concerned specifically with the status of an organization created under German law.[40] The theory disregarded the ostensible independence of the partners in this situation, at least where the purported partnership organization is a foreign entity, because the partners are controlled by a single master. Even if the entity is not ordinarily characterized by centralized management or freely transferable shares, it is arguable that these corporate characteristics are present when all of the partners are subject to the managerial and transfer decisions of the common parent. It is similarly arguable that the entity has the corporate characteristic of perpetual existence, since no partner can force a dissolution (e.g., by withdrawal or on the bankruptcy of another partner) if the common parent wants the entity to continue. The validity of the single economic interest theory was sidestepped by the Court of Appeals for the Ninth Circuit in what initially seemed to be a test case, and hence it remains to be determined.[41] Moreover, although the rationale of the Service ruling could be extended to domestic organizations, it did not overrule or even cite an earlier ruling holding that a domestic partnership would be recognized as such, even though its partners were all subsidiaries of a single domestic parent.[42]

Limited partnerships, whether subject to the original Uniform Limited Partnership Act or to the revised version of this Act, come somewhat closer than general partnerships to association status, but not close enough to cross the line, except in extreme cases. A limited partnership's managerial authority is ordinarily vested in the general partner, but it has been held that this does not ordinarily constitute centralized management as that term is used

---

[39] For the status of so-called partnership associations authorized by the laws of Ohio and a few other states, see Regs. §301.7701-3(c) (usual corporate resemblance principles apply); Giant Auto Parts, Ltd., 13 TC 307 (1949) (Ohio partnership association classified as association, but decision reserved on whether all such Ohio organizations would be so classified); see also supra note 17 regarding limited liability companies.

[40] Rev. Rul. 77-214, 1977-1 CB 408; see generally N.Y. State Bar Association, Tax Section, Report on Foreign Entity Characterization for Federal Income Tax Purposes, 35 Tax L. Rev. 167 (1980).

[41] MCA, Inc. v. US, 685 F2d 1099 (9th Cir. 1982) (unincorporated foreign organization owned by a controlled foreign corporation and an employees' trust; unlike the facts hypothesized in Rev. Rul. 77-214, 1977-1 CB 408, the two owners, although related, had separate economic interests; court would not presume that trustees would act in breach of fiduciary duties to trust beneficiaries).

[42] Rev. Rul. 75-19, 1975-1 CB 382; see also Regs. §301.7701-2(b)(3) (last sentence).

in the regulations, because the general partner acts as a proprietor on his own account rather than as a representative of the limited partners.[43] If, however, the limited partners own substantially all of the interests in the partnership, the regulations treat the general partner's managerial authority as similar to the power of the board of directors of a corporation.[44] Moreover, the regulations provide that if the limited partners can remove a general partner, all facts and circumstances must be taken into account in determining whether the partnership possesses centralized management;[45] the premise of this statement is evidently that the power of removal is analogous in some circumstances to the power of shareholders to remove corporate directors and may indicate that the general partner, while in power, acts as the partners' centralized representative in managing the enterprise.

The regulations also acknowledge that a limited partnership has the corporate characteristic of limited liability if the general partner has no substantial assets (other than his interest in the partnership) that can be reached by partnership creditors and is merely a dummy acting as the agent of the limited partners.[46]

On the other hand, the regulations state flatly that limited partnerships subject to the Uniform Limited Partnership Act (or to its later revised version) lack continuity of life,[47] and it seems very unlikely that a general partner's interest in such a partnership can be freely transferred. Given the absence of these two corporate characteristics, investors organizing a limited partnership who *want* to qualify as an association must work hard to achieve this result

---

[43] Phillip G. Larson, supra note 10, at 176–179; see also Glensder Textile Co., supra note 15 (if limited partners cannot remove general partners, relationship between limited and general partners is not analogous to shareholder-director relationship).

[44] Regs. §301.7701-2(c)(4); see also Zuckman v. US, supra note 15, at 738 (general partner's interest not attributed to limited partner in determining whether limited partners own substantially all interests in partnership).

[45] Regs. §301.7701-2(c)(4).

[46] Regs. §301.7701-2(d)(2). But see Zuckman v. US, supra note 15 (noting that if a corporate general partner *is* a dummy, then the limited partners, as its principals, are themselves subject to unlimited liability for its actions.).

The final sentence of Regs. §301.7701-2(d)(2) (stating that limited liability exists if the partnership agreement provides that general partners are not liable for partnership debts unless that provision is ineffective under local law) was based on an ambiguity in the Revised Uniform Limited Partnership Act as originally promulgated; §403(b) of this Act now makes it clear that the unlimited liability of general partners cannot be nullified by the partnership agreement. See TD 7889, 1983-1 CB 362.

[47] Regs. §§1.301.7701-2(b)(3) and 1.301.7701-2(a)(5); see also Rev. Rul. 74-320, 1974-2 CB 404 (re effect of certain amendments to California statute that eliminate continuity of life; for state laws corresponding to the Uniform Limited Partnership Act, see Rev. Rul. 86-30, 1986-1 CB 370 and earlier rulings there cited.

and may fail despite their best efforts; conversely, a limited partnership that qualifies *involuntarily* as an association is surely a rare and ignorant bird.

During the 1970s, when tax shelters appeared to sprout like crabgrass on suburban lawns, the Service came to rue the strong anti-association bias of the regulations; it struggled to impose association status on limited partnerships, the legal form used by most tax shelters, in order to prevent their deductions and losses from being passed through to the limited partners-investors. In 1972, the Service focused on those limited partnerships whose only general partner was a corporation, announcing that it would not rule such an entity a partnership for federal tax purposes if (1) the limited partners owned (directly, indirectly, or by attribution) more than 20 percent of the stock of the corporate general partner or any of its affiliates; (2) the corporate partner's net worth was less than certain specified amounts related to the number of limited partnerships involved and their total capital contributions; or (3) the purchase of a limited partnership interest entails the purchase, whether mandatory or discretionary, of a security of the corporate partner or its affiliates.[48] This no-ruling policy was extended in 1974 to all limited partnerships if (1) the general partners as a group have less than a one percent interest in each material item of partnership income, gain, loss, deduction, or credit throughout the partnership's existence; (2) the deductions to be claimed by the partners as their distributive share of losses during the first two years of partnership operations exceed the equity capital invested in the partnership; or (3) any creditor making a nonrecourse loan thereby obtains an interest in the partnership's profits, capital, or property, except as a secured creditor.[49]

Both of these administrative procedures were promulgated as guidelines to the issuance of advance rulings and were not intended as substantive rules for the determination of partnership status or criteria to be used in auditing tax returns. In practice, many, if not most, tax shelters were marketed on the basis of opinions of counsel, and no ruling was requested; but it is likely that some promoters chose to conform to the guidelines even where they did not intend to apply for a ruling in order to have a second string for their bows in case arguments based on the general tax rules governing association status failed to carry the day.

Although the 1972 and 1974 guidelines remain in force,[50] they have not picked up any support in the litigated cases involving tax shelters. Moreover,

---

[48] Rev. Proc. 72-13, 1972-1 CB 735. For extended analysis, see Huntington, Partnerships—Statutory Outline and Definition, 161 Tax Mgmt. (BNA) 3d, at A-29 et seq. (1986).

[49] Rev. Proc. 74-17, 1974-1 CB 438; see also Rev. Proc. 75-16, 1975-1 CB 676 (checklist of information to be submitted for partnership status rulings); Huntington, supra note 48.

[50] See Rev. Proc. 87-1, §8.05, 1987-1 IRB 7; see also Rev. Proc. 87-3, §3.43, 1987-1 IRB 27.

the Service has lost two important cases involving the classification of limited partnerships with sole corporate general partners;[51] and, although the Service has subsequently had a string of victories in disallowing deductions claimed by tax shelter limited partners, these cases have involved not association status, but such abusive features as grossly exaggerated valuations or nonrecourse financing based on dreams. Finally, a set of proposed regulations that would have replaced the anti-association predisposition of the existing regulations with exactly the opposite (i.e., a strong presumption that limited partnerships are associations) was withdrawn by the Service just two days after it was promulgated.[52]

In determining whether a purported partnership will be classified as such or instead be treated as an association, neither the regulations nor the cases have traditionally looked to the number of partners or the extent to which partnership interests are actually transferred; but the burgeoning in recent years of so-called master limited partnerships with hundreds or thousands of limited partners, holding publicly traded interests, has stimulated concern in the Treasury and Congress about the status of these organizations. MLPs were originally developed as investment vehicles to combine the interests of limited partners in existing closely held oil and gas tax shelters, thus substituting publicly traded interests for the partners' previously unmarketable rights; but the device was also used by public corporations to distribute mineral royalties to their shareholders, thereby liberating this segment of their business income from corporate taxes.[53] These pioneering ventures involved income-producing assets that required little management and

---

[51] See Phillip G. Larson, supra note 10, and Zuckman v. US, supra note 15; see also Rev. Rul. 79-106, 1979-1 CB 448 (acquiescence in *Larson*).

[52] See FR Doc. 77-843, 42 Fed. Reg. 1489 (Jan. 7, 1977), withdrawing FR Doc. 76-38491, 42 Fed. Reg. 1038 (Jan. 5, 1977). See generally Fisher, Classification Under Section 7701–The Past, Present, and Prospects for the Future, 30 Tax Lawyer 627 (1977).

[53] See Limberg, Master Limited Partnerships Offer Significant Benefits, 65 J. Tax'n 84 (1986), and articles there cited; Transcript, Publicly Traded Limited Partnerships: An Emerging Financial Alternative to the Public Corporation, 39 Bus. Law. 709 (1984). For policy issues, see Sheppard, Rethinking Limited Partnership Taxation, 30 Tax Notes 877 (1986); Hobbet, Limited Partnerships: Associations or Partnerships? 22 San Diego L. Rev. 105 (1985); see also 31 Tax Notes 1063 (1986) (Treasury favors taxing publicly traded limited partnerships as corporations); Freeman, . . . Strategies for the Methodical Disincorporation of America After the Tax Reform Act of 1986, 64 Taxes 962 (1986); Friedrich, The Unincorporation of America? 14 J. Corp. Tax'n 3 (1987).

See generally Joint Comm. on Taxation pamphlet, Federal Income Tax Treatment of Pass-Through Entities (June 9, 1986), prepared for hearings by the House Ways and Means Committee on June 9–10, 1986, printed in DTR (BNA) No. 111, at J-1 (June 10, 1986); Sheppard, Sleeping Dogs, Publicly Traded Limited Partnerships Come of Age, 34 Tax Notes 1254 (1987); Sheppard, 35 Tax Notes 86 (1987).

would not be replaced when exhausted; however, the appeal of partnership interests that can be traded but are exempt from the corporate income tax has spread from these passive pools of income-producing assets to actively managed businesses.

¶ 2.05 SYNDICATES, JOINT VENTURES, ETC., AS "ASSOCIATIONS"

A syndicate, pool, joint venture, or other unincorporated group that carries on a business, financial operation, or venture is taxable as a partnership under the regulations unless it constitutes a trust, an estate, or an association.[54] To be taxable as an association, however, the organization must possess not only the characteristics of "associates" and "a business objective," but also a majority of the other four major corporate criteria (continuity, centralized management, limited liability, and transferability). As a consequence of these requirements, syndicates and joint ventures are rarely treated as associations.[55]

In the oil and gas industry, dispersion of ownership and investment has led to the frequent use of joint arrangements for exploiting mineral resources. Because the form and effect of these agreements are dictated by the special characteristics of this industry, discussion of them is beyond the scope of this work.[56] One aspect of this problem, however, is worthy of special note: The regulations state that "since associates and an objective to carry on business for joint profit are essential characteristics of all organiza-

---

[54] Regs. §301.7701-3(a); see §761(a) for a statutory endorsement of this definition. The second sentence of §761(a) authorizes the Treasury to exclude certain organizations from the ambit of the partnership provisions, a power that has been exercised by Regs. §1.761-2(a)(2). These regulations, in addition to their principal purpose of limiting the election afforded by §761(a), point the way toward avoidance of association status; that is, if an unincorporated group is organized and conducted so as to qualify for the §761(a) election, it will, by the same token, not be taxable as a corporation.

[55] See, e.g., Junior Miss Co., 14 TC 1 (1950) (acq.); Bloomfield Ranch v. CIR, 167 F2d 586 (9th Cir.), cert. denied, 335 US 820 (1948); Rev. Rul. 68-344, 1968-1 CB 569 (joint venture of four corporations to own electricity generating plants as tenants in common, each with right to take its share of power for distribution to its own customers, constituted partnership rather than association).

See generally Rabinowitz, Realty Syndication: An Income Tax Primer for Investor and Promoter, 29 J. Tax'n 92 (1968).

[56] See generally Casey, The Strange Case of the Tax Partnership, 40 NYU Inst. on Fed. Tax'n ch. 11 (1982), and articles there cited; see also Bruen, Federal Income Tax Aspects of Oil and Gas Ventures—A Summary for the Investor, 14 Tax L. Rev. 353, 362–373 (1959); Sneed, More About Associations in the Oil and Gas Industry, 33 Tex. L. Rev. 168 (1954).

tions engaged in business for profit . . . the absence of either of these essential characteristics will cause an arrangement among co-owners of property for the development of such property for the *separate* profit of each not to be classified as an association."[57] The last portion of this sentence appears to incorporate the Service's long-standing position in IT 3930 that certain joint operating agreements for the development of mineral properties did not constitute associations because such arrangements were operations for the separate, rather than joint, profit of their members.[58]

¶ 2.06 PROFESSIONAL CORPORATIONS AND PROFESSIONAL ASSOCIATIONS

Since 1970, the letterheads of many lawyers, doctors, architects, accountants, and other licensed purveyors of professional services have been sprinkled with the initials "P.C." and "P.A.," for "professional corporation" and "professional association." These abbreviations announce that these providers of services, who are not allowed to incorporate under the state's general business corporation law, have organized a corporation under a special law restricted to licensed practitioners.

The urge to incorporate personal service enterprises generally reflects the desire to take advantage of a Code provision that grants a more generous deduction or other tax allowance for corporate employee benefit plans than for similar plans created by self-employed individuals. This urge went unrequited for many years because state-licensed professionals were not usually allowed to practice in corporate form. In the late 1950s, however, states started to authorize the creation of professional corporations; and the resulting gold rush rapidly gained momentum after 1970, when the Service, having lost a string of cases seeking to establish that these newfangled organizations more nearly resembled partnerships than traditional corporations, gave up and announced that it would classify them as associations.[59]

---

[57] Regs. §301.7701-2(a)(2) (emphasis added).

[58] IT 3930, 1948-2 CB 126. However, the failure of co-owners to retain the power to deal separately with their own property interests and the production therefrom could result in a finding of association status. See, e.g., US v. Stierwalt, 287 F2d 855 (10th Cir. 1961); John Provence No. 1 Well v. CIR, 321 F2d 840 (3d Cir. 1963). For elaborations and interpretations of IT 3930, see IT 3948, 1949-1 CB 161; Rev. Rul. 58-166, 1958-1 CB 324; Bush No. 1, c/o Stone Street Lands Co., 48 TC 218 (1967) (acq.) (oil investment partnership not taxable as an association).

[59] See Rev. Rul. 70-101, 1970-1 CB 278 (list of qualifying state statutes), as amplified and modified by later revenue rulings listed in Rev. Rul. 77-31, 1977-1 CB 409; see also Rev. Rul. 71-434, 1971-2 CB 430 (Ohio professional service organization taxable as association, since it had requisite corporate characteristics, even

The 1970 ruling states that a professional service organization "must be both organized and operated as a corporation" to qualify as such,[60] and even then, the ruling concedes only that the entity is to be classified as an association (and therefore as a corporation), pointedly reserving the right of the Service to assert "any issues against such organization other than that of classification." These issues, which in any given case may be more important than the group's classification, include (1) the allocation of some or all of the earnings to the shareholder-employee;[61] (2) assertion of the personal holding company tax if the corporation is closely held and a person owning 25 percent or more of the stock is designated "by name or by description" in the corporation's service contracts as the one required to perform the agreed services;[62] (3) disallowance of corporate compensation deductions under §162 as excessive and unreasonable, with the disallowed component being taxed to the shareholder-employees as a constructive dividend;[63] and (4)

---

though not organized under local business corporation or professional corporation statute); Rev. Rul. 71-277, 1971-1 CB 422 (Pennsylvania professional association also taxable as a corporate-association, since it possessed requisite corporate characteristics); Rev. Rul. 71-574, 1971-2 CB 432 (same).

For detailed analysis of the current tax status of professional service organizations, see Warren and Dunkle, Professional Corporations—Organization and Operation, Tax Mgmt. (BNA) No. 334, at A-37 (1980); see also Braverman, Partnerships of Professional Corporations, 32 Tulane Tax Inst. J. (1982) (detailed outline).

For the cases lost by the Service on the classification issue, see Rev. Rul. 70-101, supra; see also US v. Empey, 406 F2d 157 (10th Cir. 1969); Kurzner v. US, 413 F2d 97 (5th Cir. 1969). For a review of this pre-1970 history by two grizzled veterans of the old battles, see Bittker, Professional Service Organizations: A Critique of the Literature, 23 Tax L. Rev. 429 (1968); Eaton, 17 Business Organizations (Professional Corporations and Associations) ch. 5 (Matthew Bender, 1970–1985); see also ¶ 2.06 of the Fourth Edition of this treatise.

[60] Although it involved pre-1970 years, Jerome J. Roubik, 53 TC 365 (1969), is a veritable how-not-to-do-it guide to the requirement of Rev. Rul. 70-101, 1970-1 CB 278, that the personal service organization must be operated (not merely organized) as a corporation.

[61] See generally infra ¶ 2.07.

[62] See infra ¶ 8.22.

[63] For the reasonableness of compensation paid by professional corporations to their dominant shareholder-employees, see, e.g., Anthony La Mastro, 72 TC 377 (1979); Bianchi v. CIR, 66 TC 324 (1976), aff'd per curiam, 553 F2d 93 (2d Cir. 1977); Eduardo Catalano, ¶ 79,183 P-H Memo. TC (1979); see also Isaacson, Rosenbaum, Spiegleman & Friedman, P.C. v. US, 1979-2 USTC ¶ 9463 (Ct. Cl. 1979) (reasonable compensation issue a question of federal tax law, not state law); Rosenbaum, The Court of Claims' Handling of a Legal PC's Reasonable Compensation: Problems Remain, 55 J. Tax'n 138 (1981).

For the treatment of excessive compensation as a constructive dividend, see generally infra ¶ 7.05, para. 1.

exposure to the unreasonable accumulations tax of §531 if the corporation needs little capital to operate.[64]

Not content with these Service warnings that professional corporations would not necessarily achieve their objectives without challenge, Congress has by statute progressively narrowed the gap between the tax allowances available to corporations and those granted to self-employed persons,[65] and the Tax Reform Act of 1986 promises that, commencing in 1988 and for the first time in more than 50 years, the top tax rate for corporations will be higher than the top rate for individuals.[66] When the rapidly vanishing advantages of professional corporations are weighed in the cold light of day against the tax problems incorporation can generate, corporate status may lose its glamour, and the enormous expenditure of legal time and talent in the professional corporation struggle may bring to mind Southey's comment on the Battle of Blenheim, "But 'twas a famous victory."

¶ 2.07 PERSONAL SERVICE CORPORATIONS

In a series of cases in the 1970s and early 1980s, the Service attempted to tax most or all of the income of some personal service corporations to their sole or principal shareholders if these individuals performed the services that generated the corporation's earnings.[67] The impetus for this campaign was that the top individual tax rate was 20 percentage points or more higher during the taxable years in dispute than the top corporate rate. The Tax Reform Act of 1986, however, not only drastically narrowed the gap between the highest individual and corporate tax rates, but reversed the stakes, since the top

---

[64] See infra ¶ 8.03.

[65] See generally Thompson & New, What Structure Is Best for Your Law Firm? 72 A.B.A. J. 53 (1986), which lists the tax advantages favoring professional corporations immediately before enactment of the Tax Reform Act of 1986. Section 89, enacted in 1986, increases the economic cost of some employee benefit plans if highly compensated employees are favored over the rank and file; §441(i), also enacted in 1986, limits the right of personal service corporations (infra ¶ 2.07) to adopt a taxable year other than the calendar year.

[66] The top 1987 corporate rate (40 percent) also exceeds the top individual rate, but only slightly. Even under the rates scheduled to take effect in 1988, however, a tax savings will result if income can be shifted from the top personal bracket to the bottom two corporate brackets.

[67] See generally Manning, The Service Corporation—Who Is Taxable on Its Income: Reconciling Assignment of Income Principles, Section 482, and Section 351, 37 U. Miami L. Rev. 653 (1983); Wood, The Keller, Foglesong, and Pacella Cases: 482 Allocations, Assignments of Income, and New §269A, 10 J. Corp. Tax'n 65 (1983); Bailey, Section 482 and the Aftermath of Foglesong: The Beginning or the End for the Personal Service Corporation, 15 Ind. L. Rev. 639 (1982).

individual rate is to become 28 percent in 1988, as compared with a top rate of 34 percent for corporations. Although these rate changes obviously reduce the incentive to shift personal service income to controlled corporations, some situations remain in which this practice can pay off (e.g., if the corporation has offsetting losses, or if income can be moved from the individual's top bracket to the corporation's bottom two brackets); taxpayer efforts to exploit these residual tax-saving opportunities will no doubt elicit continuing vigorous counterattacks by the Service. Thus, the pre-1987 litigated cases discussed in the following text are far from moribund, although they will almost certainly be invoked less frequently than in the past.

Some of these cases involved services performed by physicians or other state-licensed individuals who practiced through specially incorporated professional corporations or associations,[68] and, in some, the corporation's only customer was a related enterprise owned by the corporation's shareholder-employees; but also included were cases involving a wide range of business activities whose single common thread was the fact that most, if not all, of the income was attributable to the controlling shareholder's personal skill and effort.

An occasional incorporated talent case falls afoul of the specialized personal holding company provisions. For example, a film star may contract to work for a wholly owned corporation for a modest salary, and the corporation may then enter into a loan-out agreement under which the shareholder-employee's services are made available to a producer at their (much higher) market value. Such an arrangement can trigger a penalty tax of 28 percent of the corporation's undistributed income; but this extreme remedy is reserved for extreme situations, and, as explained later in this treatise, it is not difficult for well-advised taxpayers to plan their way around the intricate but mechanical personal holding company rules.[69] As a result, Service attacks on the shifting of personal service income from shareholder-employees to their controlled corporations are ordinarily based on more amorphous, and hence less predictable, grounds, of which the following are the most important:

1. Disregard of the corporate entity. The most drastic approach to incorporated talents is to disregard the corporate entity as a sham on the theory that its only purpose is tax avoidance, and to tax the income directly to the shareholder-employee. In an early case involving film and stage actor Charles Laughton, the Court of Appeals for the Ninth Circuit held that "the question is whether Laughton's hiring of himself to [a wholly owned corporation] for a salary substantially less than the compensation for which the corporation supplied his services as its employee to various motion picture

---

[68] For the recognition of these entities as true corporations, see supra ¶ 2.06.

[69] See infra ¶ 8.20.

producers, constituted, in effect a single transaction by Laughton in which he received indirectly the larger sum paid by the producers."[70] In promulgating this single transaction theory, the court reversed the Board of Tax Appeals, which had held that the corporate entity was entitled to be honored because it was formed for and served a business purpose; and the case was remanded for further findings.

In later cases, however, the courts have held, in accordance with *Moline Properties v. CIR*, that the corporation constitutes an entity for tax purposes if it was organized for a business purpose or if, regardless of the motive for its creation, it engaged in substantial business activity.[71] In practice, the latter criterion seems to require little if anything more than the observance of bookkeeping formalities and similar nonburdensome practices in executing contracts, maintaining a separate bank account, holding property in the corporate name, and representing the corporation to third parties as an independent organization.[72] If these niceties are not maintained, however, it is anyone's guess whether the deficiencies will be fatal to the taxpayer's claim or will be excused as minor departures from a pattern of compliance.[73]

---

[70] CIR v. Laughton, 113 F2d 103 (9th Cir. 1940). The case was remanded to the Board of Tax Appeals for findings of ultimate fact on the issue as stated; the proceedings on remand are not reported. But see Fox v. CIR, 37 BTA 271 (1938) (Fontaine Fox, syndicated newspaper cartoonist, not taxed on amounts received by Reynard, his controlled corporation; court did not look through Reynard to find Fox hiding behind it).

[71] Moline Properties v. CIR, 319 US 436 (1943); see, e.g., Jones v. CIR, 64 TC 1066, 1076 (1975) (court reporter's wholly owned corporation, organized to shift income from high personal to low corporate tax brackets, was viable tax entity because it engaged in substantial business activity, even though it was not organized for a legitimate business purpose; but the Service's allocation of part of corporate income to shareholder-employee under §§61(a) and 482 upheld); Bell v. CIR, ¶ 82,660 P-H Memo. TC (1982) (comparing factors indicating business activity by personal service corporation owned by families of three physicians with adverse factors; favorable factors held controlling); Horn v. CIR, ¶ 82,741 P-H Memo. TC (1982) (business purpose lacking, since accumulating income for children of shareholder-employees was personal objective, obtaining tax advantages is not business activity, and limiting personal liability was afterthought, rather than purpose for incorporation; as to alleged conduct of business activity after incorporation, favorable factors outweighed by unfavorable ones); see also supra ¶ 1.05.

[72] See, e.g., Achiro v. CIR, 77 TC 881, 901 (1981) (landfill management company hired and contracted with employees, supplied services to customers, kept its own books, paid taxes, filed tax returns, created pension plan, and so forth; held corporate entity entitled to recognition); compare Noonan v. CIR, 451 F2d 992 (9th Cir. 1971) (Tax Court upheld in disregarding corporations that "paid no dividends, had no employees, maintained no telephones, telephone listings, or separate business addresses, and engaged in no substantive business activities").

[73] See Horn v. CIR, supra note 71 (taxpayers ignored corporation's separate identity "in too many respects for us to honor it"); Roubik v. CIR, supra note 60 (book-

Moreover, the Tax Court has held that a showing of substantial business activity in the post-incorporation period was sufficient, even if the corporation was organized to obtain tax advantages for the shareholder-employee (e.g., through a medical reimbursement plan) that are not available to sole proprietors:

> The Code provisions relating to qualified retirement and medical plans are a deliberate congressional bestowal of benefits upon employers and employees; efforts to obtain the advantages of these benefits, by way of conducting business in the corporate form, are not to be deemed to render the taxpayer culpable of illegal tax avoidance or evasion.[74]

Although the court did not say so, disparities between the individual and corporate income tax rates also reflect a deliberate congressional bestowal of benefits on whichever business form qualifies for the more favorable rate. It is not clear, however, that shifting income to a corporation solely to take advantage of a lower tax rate would be received with the same tolerance as using a corporation to qualify for a tax-favored employee benefit or other substantive allowance.

2. Assignment of income doctrine. Although the assignment of income doctrine is encountered throughout the corporate tax area,[75] shareholder-employees of personal service corporations have traditionally ranked high on the Service's list of suspicious characters. When the Service asserts that the creation or operation of a corporation amounts to an anticipatory assignment of *all* of the controlling shareholder's personal service income, however, the result is substantially the same as if the corporate entity were disregarded, at least for the taxable year or years in question; and the courts have been reluctant to sanction this outcome. Thus, in *Keller v. CIR*, decided in 1981, the Tax Court observed that the "[t]he [legislative] policy favoring the recognition of corporations as entities independent of their shareholders

---

keeping entries and bank accounts insufficient where corporation owned no property, had no contracts except with shareholder-employees, and did not enter into its own arrangements with customers to whom its shareholder-employee rendered services). Compare Keller v. CIR, 77 TC 1014, 1031–1032 (1981), aff'd, 723 F2d 58 (10th Cir. 1983) (deficiencies outweighed by corporate business activity); Fatland v. CIR, ¶ 84,489 P-H Memo. TC (1984) (favorable factors outweighed unfavorable ones).

[74] Keller v. CIR, supra note 73, 77 TC at 1029–1030; see also Achiro v. CIR, 77 TC 881, 895–896, and 901, n.25 (1981) (corporation entitled to recognition if organizational and operational requirements are met "regardless of the fact that it was formed to take advantage of the richer corporate retirement plans"; no need to decide whether formation to obtain such tax benefits "is the equivalent of a business activity").

[75] See generally supra ¶ 1.05.

requires that we not ignore the corporate form so long as the corporation actually conducts business."[76] In the same vein, but more graphically, the Court of Appeals for the Seventh Circuit decried a Service effort "to dismantle" a personal service corporation on assignment of income grounds, saying that "there is no need to crack walnuts with a sledgehammer," since the Service could instead invoke its §482 power to reallocate gross income and other tax allowances among two businesses under common control.[77] In a later installment of the same case, however, the court held that the Service could not crack the walnuts even with §482.[78]

The ultimate question in assignment of income cases—who earned the income[79]—is the same whether the court must choose between a personal service corporation and its controlling shareholder-employee or, as in such landmark cases as *Lucas v. Earl*, between the person performing the services and a member of his or her family.[80] In cases such as *Lucas v. Earl*, however, the alleged assignee of the income is ordinarily a passive donee who cannot claim to have made any contribution to the income-generating process. In contrast, personal service corporations, with invested capital, employees, names known to the trade, and good will, are often instruments by which business activities are conducted; thus, it is not excessively anthropomorphic to say that a corporation built a bridge or repaired a TV set, even if the achievement required the labor and skill of the corporation's principal shareholder. Since corporations—whether large or small, and whether owned by thousands of shareholders or by a single shareholder-employee—can operate only through individual employees, the true earner of the corporate income cannot be determined "by merely pointing to the one actually turning the spade."[81] The decisional process, according to the Tax Court, is more complex:

---

[76] Keller v. CIR, supra note 73, 77 TC at 1031.

[77] Foglesong v. CIR, 621 F2d 865, 872 (7th Cir. 1980) (remanding for consideration of the Service's claim under §482); for the opinion on remand, see 77 TC 1102 (1981) (upholding allocation of 98 percent of corporate income to controlling shareholder, who was sole income-generating employee), rev'd, 691 F2d 848 (7th Cir. 1982) (§482 applies only if there are two or more businesses under common control; shareholder-employee worked exclusively for corporation, and hence was not engaged in a separate business). If the court had decided that §482 was inapplicable *before* reaching the assignment of income issue, query whether the latter theory would have been dismissed so summarily. Compare Haag v. CIR, 88 TC No. 32 (1987).

[78] See infra text at notes 86–96.

[79] For this formulation, see Johnson v. CIR, 78 TC 882, 890–891 (1982), and cases there cited.

[80] Lucas v. Earl, 281 US 111 (1930).

[81] Johnson v. CIR, supra note 79, at 890.

While the generally accepted test for resolving the "who is taxed" tension is who actually earns the income, that test may easily become sheer sophistry when the "who" choices are a corporation or its employee. Whether a one-person professional service corporation or a multi-faceted corporation is presented, there are many cases in which, in a practical sense, the key employee is responsible for the influx of moneys. Nor may a workable test be couched in terms of for whose services the payor of the income intends to pay. In numerous instances, a corporation is hired solely in order to obtain the services of a specific corporate employee.

Given the inherent impossibility of logical application of a per se actual earner test, a more refined inquiry has arisen in the form of who controls the earning of the income. . . . An examination of the case law from *Lucas v. Earl* hence reveals two necessary elements before the corporation, rather than its service-performed employee, may be considered the controller of the income. First, the service-performer employee must be just that—an employee of the corporation whom the corporation has the right to direct or control in some meaningful sense . . . Second, there must exist between the corporation and the person or entity using the services a contract or similar indicium recognizing the corporation's controlling position.[82]

Although the contours of this bifurcated control over the income test remain to be developed by the courts, a contract between a personal service corporation and its shareholder-employee should ordinarily be effective unless it (1) fails to supersede a prior contract between the shareholder-employee and the customers to whom the services are rendered, (2) is disregarded in practice, or (3) is ineffective under local law because the corporation cannot legally practice in the area.[83] In the end, therefore, the control test may produce patent artificiality;[84] but if so, this is the inevitable result of "tax laws that permit the conceptually difficult arrangement where an individual performs services thereby earning the income that is received and the next day performs the same services and the compensation, when paid to a corporation wholly owned by that individual, is said to have been earned by the corporation."[85] Another way of putting the point is to say that the assignment of income doctrine is caught in a

---

[82] Id. at 891 (citations omitted).

[83] See, e.g., Roubik v. CIR, supra note 60 (contracts were between shareholder-employee and customers); Jones v. CIR, supra note 71 (court reporter's license ran to individual, not to his controlled corporation).

[84] American Sav. Bank v. CIR, 56 TC 828, 839 (1971) (extensive analysis of facts; earning of certain income held controlled by corporation, balance by shareholder-employees).

[85] Id.

vicious circle if the laborer wielding the spade owns his corporate employer and the employer is treated as a separate taxable entity because it owns the spade.

Even if the enterprise fails to pass the amorphous control test, the assignment of income doctrine does not necessarily justify an allocation of all of the corporate income to the controlling shareholder-employee. It should not, for example, encompass corporate income that is not attributable to the controlling individual's personal efforts, such as amounts properly attributable to the corporation's invested capital.

3. Reallocation under §482. Even if a personal service corporation's status as a separate taxable entity is honored and the assignment of income doctrine is inapplicable, the Service may be able to reallocate part of the corporation's income to its controlling shareholder-employee under §482. This provision, which is examined in more detail later in this treatise,[86] permits gross income (as well as deductions, credits, and other tax allowances) to be reallocated between or among two or more related organizations, trades, or businesses if this "is necessary in order to prevent evasion of taxes or clearly to reflect the income of any of such organizations, trades, or businesses."

In applying §482, the Service and the courts must determine whether the arrangement between the personal service corporation and its controlling shareholder-employee is comparable to an arm's-length transaction between two independent parties,[87] a standard that is satisfied if the shareholder-employee's compensation reasonably reflects the value of his services. In making this judgment, any fringe benefits provided by the corporation must be taken into account; and the Tax Court has suggested that tax-free corporate benefits may be worth more than an equal amount of taxable cash.[88] If the shareholder-employee is inadequately compensated, the Service can impute an additional amount as required to achieve an arm's-length result, as is done for family partnerships under §704(e)(2) and for S corporations under §1366(a).[89]

This exposition of §482's relationship to personal service corporations assumes that the controlling shareholder-employee is engaged in an independent business, separate from the corporation's business, since §482 permits

---

[86] See infra ¶ 15.03; Bittker, supra note 35, at ¶ 79.

[87] Regs. §§1.482-1(b)(1) and 1.482-2(b)(3). See also Haag v. CIR, supra note 77, and Achiro v. CIR, supra note 72, at 896–900 and cases there cited; infra ¶ 15.03.

[88] Keller v. CIR, supra note 73, 77 TC 1028.

[89] For §704(e)(2), see McKee, Nelson & Whitmire, Federal Taxation of Partnerships and Partners (Warren, Gorham & Lamont, Inc., 1977), ¶ 14.05; for §1366(a), see infra ¶ 6.06. See generally Haag v. CIR, supra note 77 (§482).

income to be reallocated only "[i]n the case of two or more organizations, trades or businesses." The two-business requirement is readily satisfied if the shareholder-employee renders services not only to the controlled corporation, but also to unrelated third parties in his or her personal capacity.[90] In an important but debatable decision, however, the Court of Appeals for the Seventh Circuit held that a shareholder-employee who works exclusively for his controlled corporation is not engaged in a separate business and hence cannot be the target of a reallocation under §482.[91] In espousing this view, the court was divided. The dissent is more consistent with the widespread recognition in analogous contexts that shareholder-employees are engaged in the business of acting as corporate employees or executives and that this business is separate from, and must not be amalgamated with, the corporation's own business.[92] Moreover, it is virtually self-evident that the earnings of shareholder-employees and their controlled corporations are distorted in an economic sense unless the former are adequately compensated for the services rendered by them to the latter.

It must be acknowledged, however, that the reallocation of corporate income to controlling shareholder-employees under §482 is tantamount to requiring them to receive, or at least to report, reasonable compensation for their services, and that if such imputations (as distinguished from the time-honored practice of disallowing *deductions* for *excessive* compensation[93]) became common, they would constitute a striking innovation in the context of closely held corporations. Moreover, once it gained momentum, the use of §482 for this purpose might not be confined to incorporated talents, but could gradually encompass the shareholder-employees of controlled mercantile and manufacturing corporations, to which a portion of the corporation's income might be imputed to reflect the value to their employers of their organizational, marketing, and technical inventive skills.

---

[90] See, e.g., Borge v. CIR, 405 F2d 673 (10th Cir. 1968) (entertainer shifted part of his income to wholly owned corporation; reallocation upheld under §482).

[91] Foglesong v. CIR, supra note 77; contra Haag v. CIR, supra note 77.

[92] See, e.g., Gould v. CIR, 64 TC 132 (1975) (amount paid by employee-shareholder deductible under §162(a) because made to protect his job); Noland v. CIR, 269 F2d 108 (4th Cir.), cert. denied, 361 US 885 (1959) (corporate executive can deduct expenses essential to continuance of his employment; but on facts, particular expense was allocable to corporation rather than to employee); US v. Generes, 405 US 93 (1972) (recognizing that losses on loans extended by shareholder-employee to controlled corporation are incurred in his trade or business if dominant motive for loans is protection of job; but holding that this was not established by facts). See generally Bittker, supra note 35, ¶¶ 20.1.2, 20.1.4, and 33.6.

[93] See infra ¶ 7.05, para. 1.

Almost 40 years ago, it was asserted that the imputation of reasonable salaries to the undercompensated shareholder-employees of family corporations "would probably require a specific statute,"[94] but the recent case law, as just outlined, suggests that an adequate statutory foundation has existed undetected since 1921, when the precursor of §482 was enacted.[95] Thus, we live and learn; as Justice Frankfurter once observed, "Wisdom too often never comes, and so one ought not to reject it merely because it comes late."[96] On the other hand, given the scheduled elimination of the pre-1987 disparity between the top personal and corporate tax rates, it seems unlikely for the forseeable future that the Service will launch a systematic campaign to impute reasonable salaries to controlling shareholders of personal service corporations, especially if the imputed amounts are deductible by the corporate payor deductible at 34 percent and taxable to the recipient at only 28 percent. Thus, the belatedly acquired wisdom may in fact be too late here.

4. Denial or allocation of tax benefits under §269. If control of a corporation is "acquired" (a statutory term that includes the *creation* of a controlled corporation) by a person or group of persons for the principal purpose of avoiding federal income tax by securing a tax benefit that the acquiring person or persons would not otherwise enjoy, §269 empowers the Service to disallow the sought-after deduction, credit, or other tax allowance. This broad grant of supervisory power to the Service is as applicable to personal service corporations as to any other type; but in practice, §269's bark is worse than its bite. This is because, as explained later in this treatise, taxpayers can usually rebut the Service's claim that the principal purpose for acquiring a corporation is tax avoidance by showing that it serves a business purpose, such as protecting the shareholders against personal liability for its projected activities.[97]

5. Restrictions on personal service corporations serving a single customer. Section 269A, enacted in 1982, amalgamates the "principal purpose" feature of §269 with the broad authority to reallocate income, deductions,

---

[94] Johnson, Taxing Dividends of Family Corporations—A Dissent, 2 Tax L. Rev. 566, 568 (1947), responding to Alexandre, The Corporate Counter-part of the Family Partnership, id. 493.

For the determination of reasonable compensation in applying §482 to professional corporations, see supra note 63.

[95] See infra ¶ 15.03.

[96] Henslee v. Union Planters Bank, 335 US 595–600 (1949).

[97] See generally infra ¶ 16.21. See also Achiro, supra note 72, and Keller, supra note 73.

and other allowances granted to the Service by §482; but the resulting remedy applies only to a narrowly defined class of personal service corporations. Section 269A authorizes the reallocation of a corporation's income, deductions, and other tax allowances, if (1) its principal activity is the performance of personal services; (2) the services are substantially performed by employee-owners; (3) substantially all of its services are performed for or on behalf of a single other corporation, partnership, or entity (all related persons being treated as a single entity); and (4) the principal purpose for forming or using the corporation is the avoidance of federal income tax by reducing the income of any employee-owner or securing for any such person the benefit of a tax allowance that would not otherwise be available.[98] The term "employee-owner" is defined by §269A(b)(2) to mean an employee owning at any time during the relevant taxable year more than 10 percent of the corporation's outstanding stock, after taking into account constructive ownership under a broadened version of §318(a)(2)(C).[99]

In addition to adopting the principal purpose requirement that has been a practical barrier to reallocations under §269, §269A applies only to a limited class of personal service corporations (i.e., those with a single customer, such as a corporation organized by an anesthetist or pathologist to supply his or her services to a hospital).[100] It does not, therefore, affect corporations serving a variety of customers, as do many so-called loan-out corporations organized by performers and directors in the entertainment industry.[101] Moreover, the dramatic narrowing in recent years of the traditional disparities between the top individual and corporate tax rates and between the amounts that could be contributed to individual and corporate retirement plans has substantially reduced the appeal of personal service corporations. It may turn out, therefore, that Congress erected §269A as a fence around the chicken coop just before removing the chickens.

---

[98] For a partial list of tax benefits subject to §269A, see Prop. Regs. §1.269A-1(b)(6).

[99] For §318(a)(2)(C), see infra ¶ 9.03.

[100] See, e.g., Keller v. CIR, supra note 73, involving a corporation organized by a pathologist to take his place in a partnership of pathologists; H.R. Conf. Rep. No. 760, 97th Cong., 2d Sess. 634 (1982), 1982-2 CB 600, 680 (§269A intended to "overturn the results reached in cases like *Keller v. Commissioner* . . ., where the corporation served no meaningful business purpose other than to secure tax benefits which would not otherwise be available"). For another legislative remedy involving personal service organizations, see §414(m) (aggregating employees of all members of an "affiliated service group" in applying qualified pension plan rules, etc.).

[101] See generally Halperin, Use of Loan-Out Corporations Has Been Limited, But Advantages Remain, 65 J. Tax'n 74 (1986).

¶ 2.08 DEFECTIVELY ORGANIZED CORPORATIONS

Organizations that purport to be corporations but have failed to attain de jure status under local law have been held taxable as corporations, either on the theory that the term "corporation" includes organizations that are de facto corporations under state law, or on the theory that a defectively organized corporation is an association.[102] If a de facto corporation attains de jure status during a taxable year, it is probably to be treated as a single taxpayer for the entire period.[103] Use of the association theory in cases where the enterprise does not even attain de facto status under state law, however, is open to question in that an enterprise that would be treated as an ordinary partnership under state law cannot attain association status for want of the corporate characteristics of continuity of existence, transferability of interests, limited liability, and centralized management.[104]

¶ 2.09 CORPORATIONS IN THE PROCESS OF WINDING UP

Similar problems of ascertaining corporate identity can occur at the close of an organization's legal life. At what point does the enterprise cease to exist as a corporation and assume another character (e.g., partnership, trust, proprietorship) for federal income tax purposes? On several occasions, an organization that was continued in the guise of a corporation after expiration of its corporate charter was held taxable as an association.[105] Simi-

---

[102] For difficulties in applying the de facto theory, see Ballantine, Corporations, 68–100 (Callaghan & Co., rev. ed. 1946); see also R.L. Brown Coal & Coke Co., 14 BTA 609 (1928) (acq.); Soeder v. US, 142 F2d 236 (6th Cir.), cert. denied, 323 US 720 (1944); Skarda v. CIR, 250 F2d 429 (10th Cir. 1957) (enterprise held to be a corporation whose losses were not deductible by stockholders, although there were no meetings of stockholders, no bylaws were adopted, officers were not formally elected, and so forth).

[103] See Camp Wolters Land Co. v. CIR, 160 F2d 84 (5th Cir. 1947), which also deals with transactions by promoters preceding the attainment of de facto status.

[104] See J.W. Frentz, 44 TC 485 (1965), aff'd per curiam, 375 F2d 662 (6th Cir. 1967) (organization held not in existence as corporation, either de jure or de facto, when it attempted to elect under Subchapter S); Enola C. Hartley, ¶ 67,038 P-H Memo. TC (1967) (no de facto corporation prior to attempt to form corporation under state law).

[105] Coast Carton Co. v. CIR, 149 F2d 739 (9th Cir. 1945); Crocker v. CIR, 84 F2d 64 (7th Cir. 1936). But see Garris Inv. Corp., ¶ 82,038 P-H Memo. TC (1982) (corporation with cancelled charter held not a taxable entity even though it continued as nominal owner of legal title).

larly, a corporation in the process of winding up its affairs prior to liquidation and dissolution continues to be taxable as a corporation until its corporate existence terminates. [106]

In order to assure an orderly liquidation, corporations sometimes convey their assets to trustees (often one or more of the directors), either pursuant to state statutory procedures or otherwise. The regulations state that "gain or loss is recognized to a corporation on all sales by it, whether directly or indirectly (as through trustees or receivers)," and that "a corporation does not go out of existence if it is turned over to trustees who continue to operate it." [107] Thus, if the trustees are acting in a representative capacity on behalf of the corporation, their actions will be attributed to the corporation, which will be taxed on the income (or will obtain the benefit of deductions) produced thereby. [108] A trust whose sole purpose is to dispose of the remaining corporate property in an orderly fashion on behalf of the liquidating corporation and its shareholders, however, must be distinguished from a trust that does not dispose of the assets expeditiously or engages in a new and unrelated venture; in the latter case, the organization may be taxed as an association in its own right. [109]

A liquidating or dissolving corporation may distribute its assets in kind to its shareholders, and they may select a trustee, agent, or other representative to hold, manage, or dispose of the assets on their behalf. Such a repre-

---

[106] See National Metropolitan Bank v. US, 345 F2d 823 (Ct. Cl. 1965) (bank in liquidation held to continue in existence for tax return purposes); Anbaco-Emig Corp., 49 TC 100 (1967) (acq.) (no de facto dissolution despite sale of operating assets and two-year period of inactivity before starting new business). Compare Sigurd N. Hersloff, 46 TC 545 (1966) (acq.) (dissolved corporations were fully liquidated; trustees acted thereafter on behalf of shareholders rather than corporations); Rev. Rul. 61-191, 1961-2 CB 251 (de facto dissolution can occur without de jure dissolution under state law, in which event post-dissolution net operating loss cannot be carried back to earlier year). See also Regs. §1.6012-2(a)(2) (re corporate existence); infra ¶¶ 11.02 and 11.05–11.08.

[107] Regs. §1.336-1. For the effect of this procedure on the corporation's taxable year, see §§443(a)(2) and 443(b)(2)(ii); see also Regs. §1.6012-3(b)(4) as to filing of returns.

[108] Regs. §1.6012-2(a)(2). See Hersloff v. US, 310 F2d 947 (Ct. Cl. 1962), cert. denied, 373 US 923 (1963), for extensive discussion. The importance of this principle was reduced by the 1954-87 version of §337, which provided that a liquidating corporation would not recognize gain or loss on certain sales of property during the twelve-month period following its adoption of a plan of complete liquidation. (See discussion infra ¶ 11.06.) With the repeal of §337 (and §336) by the Tax Reform Act of 1986 (infra ¶ 11.06), corporations are taxable on their liquidating sales and distributions, regardless of who effects them (infra ¶¶ 11.60 and 11.61).

[109] See generally Charles Goodman, ¶ 46,300 P-H Memo. TC (1946) (year 1938— Issue G); J.W. Wells Lumber Co. Trust A, 44 BTA 551 (1941).

sentative is not a continuation of the corporation, and the status of the enterprise must be determined on its own characteristics,[110] but the line between a corporate-chosen trustee in dissolution and a shareholder representative is, in practice, not easily drawn.

¶ 2.10 DISREGARD OF THE CORPORATE ENTITY: NOMINEE AND DUMMY CORPORATIONS

As noted earlier, the mere existence of a corporation will not, of itself, require its recognition as an independent taxable entity.[111] The courts have always felt free, where the facts warrant, to determine that an entity was not what it was purported to be or that a transaction was consummated by a taxpayer other than the formal principal, and to invoke in support of their conclusions such vague doctrines as business purpose, form versus substance, sham arrangement, economic reality, and step transactions. Many of the decisions in this area have involved artificial arrangements heavily charged with tax avoidance motives; in such instances, it is not surprising that the courts are willing to recast the form of a challenged transaction to prevent violation of the spirit, if not the letter, of the taxing statute.

One aspect of this problem, however, warrants special note. A corporation, like an individual, may act as an agent or nominee for another person without becoming taxable on income collected by it on behalf of its principal. Thus, if a corporation is a mere dummy or alter ego for its shareholders, serving no other function and engaging in no significant business activity, its separate taxable identity may be disregarded. Requests to ignore a corporate entity, or to treat it as a mere nominee of the shareholders, have come most often at the behest of the Service,[112] but taxpayers have also sometimes argued successfully that a corporation should either be disregarded or treated as an agent for tax purposes, so that its income and deductions could be attributed directly to its shareholders. For example, in *Paymer v. CIR*, it was held that a corporation serving as a passive dummy to take and hold title to real property, as a blind to deter the creditors of one of its sharehold-

---

[110] See Regs. §301.7701-4(d) as to the possible corporate status of certain liquidating trusts; see also supra ¶ 2.03. For guidelines for rulings on the status of liquidating trusts, see Rev. Proc. 82-58, 1982-2 CB 847; Westin, Shareholders' Liquidating Trusts After Revenue Procedure 80-54, 9 J. Corp. Tax'n 63 (1982).

[111] See supra ¶¶ 1.05 and 2.07.

[112] See, e.g., Factor v. CIR, 281 F2d 100 (9th Cir. 1960), cert. denied, 364 US 933 (1961) (shareholder taxed on income of his corporation under agency theory; fraud penalty also upheld); Johansson v. US, 336 F2d 809 (5th Cir. 1964) (corporate income taxed directly to shareholder who earned it).

ers, was not taxable on the income from the property.[113] If the entity has not been completely inert, however, the taxpayer is likely to meet both administrative and judicial resistance when he seeks to disregard the separate existence of his own creature. Thus, it was held in *CIR v. State-Adams Corp.* that a corporation engaging in any business activity, such as mortgaging property, executing leases, collecting rentals, making improvements, maintaining a bank account, or negotiating sales, could not be regarded as a mere agent or nominee of its shareholders.[114]

As an original proposition, the theory that business activity is inconsistent with the status of agent or nominee seems dubious. Agents are often employed to execute leases, collect rents, negotiate sales, and otherwise manage property. The theory finds some support, however, in *Moline Properties, Inc. v. CIR*, where the Supreme Court observed:

> Whether the purpose [of incorporating] be to gain an advantage under the law of the state of incorporation or to avoid or to comply with the demands of creditors or to serve the creator's personal or undisclosed convenience, so long as that purpose is the equivalent of business activity or is followed by the carrying on of business by the corporation, the corporation remains a separate taxable entity.[115]

A few years later, the Supreme Court held in *National Carbide Co. v. CIR* that three subsidiary corporations were taxable on income earned in certain business operations, although they were obligated by contract to pay over to their common parent all profits in excess of 6 percent of their capital stock (which was nominal in amount).[116] A portion of the *National Carbide Co.*

---

[113] Paymer v. CIR, 150 F2d 334 (2d Cir. 1945); see also Jackson v. CIR, 233 F2d 289 (2d Cir. 1956); Baltimore Aircoil Co. v. US, 333 F. Supp. 705 (D. Md. 1971) (subsidiary held a mere branch of parent, which could deduct expenses incurred on its behalf); Rev. Rul. 75-31, 1975-1 CB 10 (corporation merely a nominee or agent for New York limited partnership); Rev. Rul. 76-26, 1976-1 CB 10 (principle of Rev. Rul. 75-31 extended to nonrecourse financing; agency title holding by corporate general partner for benefit of limited partnership approved on facts).

[114] CIR v. State-Adams Corp., 283 F2d 395 (2d Cir. 1960), cert. denied, 365 US 844 (1961); see also Ogiony v. CIR, 617 F2d 14 (2d Cir.), cert. denied, 449 US 900 (1980); Given v. CIR, 238 F2d 579 (8th Cir. 1956); Lloyd F. Noonan, 52 TC 907 (1969), aff'd per curiam, 451 F2d 992 (9th Cir. 1971) (corporate limited partners disregarded as shams); Taylor v. CIR, 445 F2d 455 (1st Cir. 1971) (corporate entity not a mere straw; too much business activity). Compare Humana, Inc. & Subsidiaries, 88 TC 197 (1987) (captive insurance subsidiary respected as separate entity, but parent's deductions for premiums paid to subsidiary denied on ground that affiliation negated true insurance as distinguished from self-insurance reserve); accord Clougherty Packing Co. v. CIR, 811 F2d 1297 (9th Cir. 1987).

[115] Moline Properties, Inc. v. CIR, supra note 71, at 438–439.

[116] National Carbide Corp. v. CIR, 336 US 422 (1949).

opinion is often described as announcing that six factors must be weighed in determining whether a principal-agency relationship exists:

> What we have said does not foreclose a true corporate agent or trustee from handling the property and income of its owner-principal without being taxable therefor. Whether the corporation [1] operates in the name and for the account of the principal, [2] binds the principal by its action, [3] transmits money received to the principal, and [4] whether receipt of income is attributable to the services of employees of the principal and to assets belonging to the principal are some of the relevant considerations in determining whether a true agency exists. [5] If the corporation is a true agent, its relations with its principal must not be dependent upon the fact that it is owned by the principal, if such is the case. [6] Its business purpose must be the carrying on of the normal duties of an agent. [117]

Although these Supreme Court decisions are frequently quoted in support of the theory that business activity is inconsistent with an agency relationship between the corporation and its shareholders, they do not fully support this theory. A better explanation of these cases is that the corporation must establish that it is an agent for its shareholders (with respect to the transactions in question) by evidence other than the control that shareholders automatically possess over their corporations. [118] If the corporation

---

[117] Id. at 437; bracketed numerals supplied by Roccaforte v. CIR, 708 F2d 986, 989 (5th Cir.), reh'g denied, 715 F2d 577 (5th Cir. 1983), which contrasts the first four factors (merely relevant considerations) with the fifth and sixth (mandatory and absolute), and rejects the principal-agency taxpayer's claim; for a persuasive contrary view with extended anlysis, see Florenz R. Ourisman, 82 TC 171, 185 (1984), vacated, 760 F2d 541 (4th Cir. 1985) (divided court) (fifth factor not mandatory; agency established); see also Bollinger v. CIR, 807 F2d 65 (6th Cir. 1986), cert. granted June 8, 1987 (same as Tax Court view). For other cases employing the six-factor analysis, see Vaughn v. US, 740 F2d 941 (Fed. Cir. 1984) (agency not established); Jones v. CIR, 640 F2d 745 (5th Cir.), reh'g denied, 647 F2d 1121 (5th Cir.), cert. denied, 454 US 965 (1981) (same); George v. CIR, 803 F2d 144 (5th Cir. 1986) (same), and cases there cited.

See generally Miller, The Nominee Conundrum: The Live Dummy Is Dead, But the Dead Dummy Should Live, 34 Tax L. Rev. 213 (1979); Green, Recent Developments in the Federal Tax Law Treatment of Nominee Corporations, 13 Fla. St. U. L. Rev. 361 (1985); Baker & Rothman, Nominee and Agency Corporations: Grasping for Straws, 33 NYU Inst. on Fed. Tax'n 1255 (1975); Bertane, Tax Problems of the Straw Corporations, 20 Vill. L. Rev. 735 (1975); Baker & Rothman, Straw Corporations: New Cases Shed Light on Tax Recognition Criteria, 45 J. Tax'n 84 (1976).

[118] See Harrison Property Management Co. v. US, 475 F2d 623 (Ct. Cl. 1973), cert. denied, 414 US 1130, reh'g denied, 415 US 952 (1974) (held, in effect, that shareholders cannot use their own corporation as agent or nominee; purported agency agreement disregarded because relation of corporation to its shareholders wholly dependent on corporate-shareholder status rather than principal-agent sta-

merely holds title to property and the management functions are carried on by the shareholders, it is comparatively easy to infer that the corporation is acting only as an agent or nominee. But if the corporation not only holds title but also manages the property or business operations, there is less reason to draw this inference; if the shareholders disclaim responsibility for the corporation's activities, they are ipso facto rejecting the status of principals. It is significant that the relationship between the corporation and its shareholders has been ambiguous in most of the litigated cases; there seem to be few, if any, decided cases in which the corporation was avowedly an agent of the shareholders for such purposes as binding them on contracts, pledging their credit, accepting service of process, and so forth.[119] It is of course possible that the shareholders are bound by the actions of the corporation even in the absence of an explicit agreement to this effect, and, if this can be established in a particular case, the corporation might be regarded as an agent for tax purposes also. But the taxpayer can hardly expect to receive the benefit of the doubt if the relationship has been deliberately left ambiguous, to be clarified only if some tax advantage looms on the horizon.

Because of the ineluctably factual nature of the nominee-agency issue, the decided cases are scattered along a spectrum, so that generalizations and, a fortiori, predictions, are perilous. Taxpayers who want to strengthen their cases are well advised to use unrelated (and compensated) third-party entities for nominee functions when feasible. If this is not convenient or possible and beneficial ownership of the property is divided between two or more families or unrelated persons, some protection may be achieved by vesting one of the individuals or groups with control over the purported nominee.[120]

tus); Dave Stillman, 60 TC 897 (1973) (corporation not agent of shareholders because no agency agreement existed and corporation not compensated for its services). For more on this problem, see Interstate Transit Lines v. CIR, 319 US 590, reh'g denied, 320 US 809 (1943) (parent denied deduction under §162(a) for payment to defray subsidiary's operating deficit for taxable year, although by contract, parent was to receive subsidiary's profits and reimburse it for losses); Fishing Tackle Prods. Co., 27 TC 638 (1957) (acq.) (deduction allowed in similar circumstances).

[119] But see Bollinger v. CIR, supra note 117 (where corporation acted like normal agent and was finally treated as such). Certiorari has been granted to resolve this conflict.

[120] See Moncrief v. US, 730 F2d 276 (5th Cir. 1984), where the court distinguished its earlier decision in Roccaforte v. CIR, supra note 117, and held that an agency relationship had been established because, among other things, the agent was owned by an individual who owned only 25 percent of the principal; see also Raphan v. US, 759 F2d 879 (Fed. Cir.), cert. denied, 106 S. Ct. 129 (1985) (corporate agent owned by 50 percent partner of principal; agency claim upheld); Frink v. CIR, 798 F2d 106 (4th Cir. 1986) (partnership denied right to deduct losses incurred by corporation where common control existed, despite disparity in ownership); George v. CIR, supra note 117 (same result when other members of partnership appealed to different circuit court).

Such disproportionate control reduces, although it does not eliminate, the possibility that "a common principal is merely choosing [for tax purposes] which of two controlled entities it will employ to deal with the property."[121]

¶ 2.11 SUCCESSOR CORPORATIONS

As stated earlier, a corporation's tax attributes are not ordinarily affected by changes in the ownership of its stock or the character of its business activities.[122] The same can be said of such changes in its financial structure as a recapitalization. If the corporation participates in a merger or consolidation or if its assets are acquired by another corporation, however, myriad questions arise: Does the taxable year end? Does the basis of property carry over to the resulting corporation? Does it inherit its predecessor's earnings and profits and net operating loss and capital loss carryovers? Must or may new elections be made as to accounting methods, inventory valuation, depreciation, and installment sales? Section 381, discussed later in this treatise, prescribes a comprehensive set of rules for the preservation of tax attributes, "based upon economic realities rather than upon such artificialities as the legal form of the reorganization."[123]

The carry-over of tax attributes from one corporation to another can lead to the acquisition of corporations primarily because of these attributes. Although on occasion any of the items that are preserved for the acquiring corporation may be a valuable prize, the most commonly sought attribute is a net operating loss carry-over; and advertisements for defunct corporations with such carry-overs sometimes appear in the pages of the financial press. However, the Service is armed with various statutory weapons for attacking such transactions, especially §269 (applicable to any tax attributes that may underlie an acquisition) and §382 (applicable to the net operating loss carry-over and, by virtue of §383, to certain other tax allowances).[124]

---

[121] See Raphan v. US, supra note 120, at 883; see also Bollinger v. CIR, supra note 117 (corporate agency respected regardless of control); the Supreme Court will be revisiting this issue in view of the grant of certiorari in *Bollinger*.

[122] Supra ¶ 1.05.

[123] S. Rep. No. 1622, 83d Cong., 2d Sess. 52 (1954); see infra ¶ 16.10.

[124] See infra ¶ 16.20.

CHAPTER 3

Organization of a Corporation: Section 351 and Related Problems

¶ 3.01   INTRODUCTORY

In general, a corporation does not recognize either gain or loss on issuing its stock.[1] As to the shareholder, the acquisition of stock for cash similarly entails no immediate tax consequences:[2] He has made an investment, the gain or loss on which will be reckoned only when he sells or otherwise disposes of his stock or when, to his chagrin, it becomes worthless.

If the purchaser acquires the stock in exchange for appreciated or depreciated property rather than for money, however, it may be necessary to recognize gain or loss on the transaction. The transfer of the property to the corporation in exchange for the stock is a "sale or other disposition" of the property within the meaning of §1001(a), upon which the transferor realizes gain or loss equal to the difference between the adjusted basis of the property given up and the value of the stock received in exchange. By virtue of §1001(c), the entire amount of this gain or loss is to be recognized by the transferor of the property unless the transaction falls within one of the nonrecognition provisions of the Code.[3]

Since property is frequently transferred for corporate stock or securities, especially on the organization of a new corporation, the following nonrecognition provisions relating to such transactions are of great importance:

(1) Section 351, providing that no gain or loss shall be recognized if property is transferred to a corporation solely in exchange for its stock or securities, and if the transferor or transferors control the corporation immediately after the exchange; and

(2) Section 361(a), providing that no gain or loss shall be recognized if a corporation that is a party to a reorganization transfers property to another corporation a party to the reorganization.

This chapter deals primarily with transfers under §351.[4] This section of the Code is of particular importance when individual proprietorships and partnerships are incorporated. It also embraces the transfer of property to a

---

[1] Infra ¶ 3.12.

[2] This is based on the assumption that the shareholder pays the fair market value for the shares; a bargain purchase might constitute compensation for services or other taxable income. See Rev. Rul. 68-43, 1968-1 CB 146; Oliver R. Aspergren, Jr., 51 TC 945 (1969) (nonacq.) (bargain purchase of stock not compensatory transaction to buyer); cf. Lowndes v. US, 384 F2d 635 (4th Cir. 1967) (bargain purchase taxable event).

[3] See Jefferson Livingston, 18 BTA 1184 (1930) (acq.) (taxable event under pre-§351 law).

[4] See generally Rev. Proc. 83-59, 1983-2 CB 575 (checklist of information required in requests for rulings under §351).

previously organized corporation by its controlling shareholders. Section 361(a) is discussed in Chapter 14. It may be noted at this point, however, that a transfer may qualify under both §351(a) and §361(a) (e.g., when a corporation creates a subsidiary by transferring part of its property for all the stock of the subsidiary and then distributes the subsidiary's stock as described in §368(a)(1)(D)).[5]

Whether a transaction qualifies under §351 is a question that may arise either at the time the transaction occurs or at some later date. When the transaction occurs, the applicability of §351 is critical because it determines whether the transferor recognizes gain or loss on the transfer. But the applicability of §351 may be put in issue later on, when the transferor sells the stock received for the transferred property, since the basis for the stock depends upon whether the transaction in which the property was acquired met the conditions of §351. If it did, the basis of the stock is the same as the basis of the property that was given up.[6] If, on the other hand, the exchange was not within §351, the basis of the stock is its cost,[7] ordinarily the fair market value of the property given up. The corporation's basis for the property transferred to it similarly depends, under §362, upon whether the transfer met the requirements of §351. As a result, controversy over the application of §351 to a given transaction may arise decades after the transaction occurred.[8]

The basic premise of §351 is that a transfer of appreciated or depreciated property to a corporation controlled by the transferor works a change of form only, which should not be an occasion for reckoning up the transferor's gain or loss on the transferred property. In *Portland Oil Co. v. CIR*, for example, the Court of Appeals for the First Circuit said:

> It is the purpose of [§351] to save the taxpayer from an immediate recognition of a gain, or to intermit the claim of a loss, in certain transactions where gain or loss may have accrued in a constitutional sense, but where in a popular and economic sense there has been a mere change in the form of ownership and the taxpayer has not really "cashed in" on the theoretical gain, or closed out a losing venture.[9]

---

[5] See generally infra ¶ 3.19.

[6] Section 358.

[7] Section 1012.

[8] See, e.g., Manhattan Bldg. Co., 27 TC 1032 (1957) (acq.) (corporation's basis for property sold in 1945 depended on whether acquisition in 1922 qualified under §351's predecessor).

[9] Portland Oil Co. v. CIR, 109 F2d 479, 488 (1st Cir.), cert. denied, 310 US 650 (1940); see also S. Rep. No. 275, 67th Cong., 1st Sess., reprinted in 1939-1 CB (Part 2) 181, 188–189, recommending enactment of §351 as part of the Revenue Act of 1921 (nonrecognition provisions will "not only permit business to go forward with the readjustments required by existing conditions but also will considerably increase

The premise upon which §351 rests is in general sound, even though for most purposes the controlled corporation is treated as an entity separate from its shareholders. In point of fact, however, the language of §351 goes beyond its purpose and embraces some transfers that arguably ought to be treated as sales, because the taxpayer has cashed in on the gain, either in whole or in part.

Thus, §351 is not restricted to transfers by a single individual to his or her one-person corporation; it also embraces transfers by two or more persons to a corporation that they control collectively. If A owns a patent with a cost of $1,000 and a fair market value of $10,000 and B owns land with a cost of $20,000 and a value of $10,000 and they transfer their property to a new corporation in exchange for the stock (each taking half), one might argue that the transfer is not merely a matter of form and that their economic positions have changed sufficiently so that A's gain ($9,000) and B's loss ($10,000) should be recognized. But it has long been established that §351 embraces transfers of property by two or more persons who were not previously associated, on the ground that "instead of the transaction having the effect of terminating or extinguishing the beneficial interests of the transferors in the transferred property, after the consummation of the transaction the transferors continue to be beneficially interested in the transferred property and have dominion over it by virtue of their control of the new corporate owner of it."[10]

While in many cases the transferors of property to a controlled corporation "continue to be beneficially interested in the transferred property," there are occasions when their interest is so attenuated that the transaction can hardly be regarded as a matter of form alone. For example, if the owner of a corner grocery store transfers his assets to a newly organized corporation for 0.01 percent of the stock, and a national grocery chain simultaneously transfers its assets in exchange for the other 99.99 percent of the stock, the national company continues to be "beneficially interested in the transferred property." This is hardly true, however, of the individual transferor who intends to forget Mrs. Klotz's complaints about the pork chops and instead to devote more time to reading the *Wall Street Journal*. Similarly, if two partners in a going enterprise transfer their business assets to a newly organized corporation, one taking back all of its stock while the other receives nothing but bonds, it may be unrealistic to describe the latter's new economic status as the continuation of a beneficial interest in the underlying assets. As will be seen later in this chapter, the courts may respond to dra-

---

the revenue by preventing taxpayers from taking colorable losses in wash sales and other fictitious exchanges").

[10] American Compress & Warehouse Co. v. Bender, 70 F2d 655, 667 (5th Cir. 1934).

matic situations of this type by refusing to apply §351 to transactions that satisfy the letter of the law but seem to contravene its spirit, and Congress has intervened in at least one area to curb a perceived abuse.[11] Fortunately for the tax adviser, however, marginal cases of this type are relatively rare, and most transactions seeking to qualify for nonrecognition under §351 are relatively straightforward.

As for the details of §351, these are its major requirements:

(1) One or more persons must transfer property to a corporation;

(2) The transfer must be solely in exchange for stock or securities in such corporation; and

(3) The transferor or transferors must be in control of the corporation immediately after the exchange. The term "control" is defined by §368(c).

If these requirements are met, (1) the transferor or transferors recognize neither gain nor loss on the exchange; (2) under §362, the transferee corporation takes over the transferor's basis for the property received by it; and (3) under §358, the transferor's basis for the stock or securities received by him is the same as his basis for the property transferred.

¶ 3.02   TRANSFER OF PROPERTY

Section 351 provides that gain or loss shall not be recognized if property is exchanged solely for stock or securities of a controlled corporation. Except for the three specific exclusions of §351(d) (relating to services, certain debt, and accrued interest), the term "property" is not defined by statute,[12] but the absence of a definition has not ordinarily been troublesome. Although the term as used in other provisions of the Code does not always embrace money, it does include money under §351.[13] There is a compelling reason for so construing the term property under §351. A newly organized corporation almost always needs cash for working capital, and if §351 did not permit the tax-free transfer of money to such a corporation, it would either lose much of its usefulness or invite evasion in the form of a transfer of cash in an allegedly independent transaction after the other assets had been transferred under §351. Moreover, the transferor corporation's own

---

[11] See infra ¶ 3.04, text at note 45 (status of transferors receiving securities but no stock); ¶ 3.15 (transfers of stock and securities to investment companies).

[12] The definition of property in §317(a) is applicable only to Part I of Subchapter C, which does not include §351.

[13] Rev. Rul. 69-357 1969-1 CB 101; George M. Holstein, 23 TC 923 (1955).

stock would seem to constitute property for purposes of §351 (e.g., where a parent exchanges its newly issued, or treasury, stock for stock of a controlled subsidiary), although there are no cases squarely to this effect.[14]

1. Services and assets created by services. Section 351(d)(1), the first of the exclusions mentioned previously, provides that stock or securities issued for services is not considered as issued for property. The function of this restriction is to require that the value of stock or securities received as compensation for services be reported by the recipient as current ordinary income, rather than as capital gain when and if the stock or securities are sold.

An exchange is not automatically cast out of §351, however, merely because the corporation issues stock or securities for services. The effect of §351(d)(1), rather, is that a person receiving stock or securities in exchange for services cannot be counted in determining whether the transferors of property are in control of the transferee corporation immediately after the exchange. But if the persons who transfer property *are* in control, their exchange of property for stock or securities qualifies under §351, even though at the same time stock or securities are issued for services to one or more other persons. Moreover, if a person who transfers property in exchange for stock or securities *also* receives stock or securities in exchange for services, that stock (whether received for property or services) is counted in determining whether the transferors of property have control of the corporation, unless the property transferred is of nominal value, so that it serves merely to camouflage the true nature of the transaction.[15] Finally, the disqualification of services by §351 probably does not apply to stock or securities issued for property that was, in turn, earned through the performance of services.[16]

----

[14] See Rev. Rul. 74-503, 1974-2 CB 117 (corporation's transfer of treasury stock to controlled subsidiary a tax-free transfer of property under §351; treasury stock has zero basis, regardless of cost; see infra notes 110 and 124). See also infra ¶¶ 7.21, 14.53; §317(a) (definition of property); Banoff, How IRS' New Zero-Basis Approach Will Affect Corporate Tax Planning, 42 J. Tax'n 96 (1975).

[15] See Regs. §1.351-1(a)(1)(ii); William S. James, 53 TC 63 (1969) (value of stock received for services taxable to recipient; concurrent transfer of property by another person also taxable because he received less than requisite 80 percent control); Rev. Rul. 79-194, 1979-1 CB 145 (disregarding nominal property transfers); Estate of Kamborian v. CIR, 468 F2d 219 (1st Cir. 1972) (accommodation exchange disregarded for 80 percent control test; transferors must have substantial economic nexus with each other); Rev. Proc. 77-37, §3.07, 1977-2 CB 568 (for ruling purposes, property not of excessively small value if it equals at least 10 percent of value of stock or securities already owned by transferor or to be received for services by transferor).

[16] See Roberts Co. v. CIR, 5 TC 1 (1945) (acq.) (interest in property arising under attorney's contingent fee agreement is property); Fahs v. Florida Mach. & Foundry Co., 168 F2d 957 (5th Cir. 1948) (claim that recipient of stock had earned

To illustrate: If *A* and *B* transfer property to a newly organized corporation for 78 percent of its stock, and *C*, as part of the same transaction, receives 22 percent of the stock for services rendered to the corporation, the transfer does not qualify under §351 because the transferors of property (*A* and *B*) have less than 80 percent of the stock and hence do not have "control," as that term is defined by §368(c) for purposes of §351. If, however, *A* and *B* received 80 percent or more of the stock, and *C* received 20 percent or less, the exchange would qualify. Moreover, if *A* and *B* received 78 percent of the stock for property and *C* received 22 percent for a combination of services and property, the transfer would qualify (although, as to *C*, the stock received for services would produce taxable income) unless *C*'s transfer of property was nominal in amount or merely a sham designed to support a claim by *A* and *B* for nonrecognition of gain or loss.

Disqualification in §351(d)(1) of stock or securities issued for services seems to assume that the services were rendered *to the corporation.* The transaction takes on another complexion if the services were performed for someone else, such as one of the transferors of property. An example is the individual proprietor who incorporates his business, taking part of the stock himself and directing that the rest be issued to an employee as compensation for services performed in years past. Such a transaction is to be treated as though all the stock had been issued first to the proprietor in exchange for the assets of the business, with part of it being used by him to pay his debts. The incorporation would qualify under §351 if the proprietor retained at least 80 percent of the stock;[17] even if he retained less than 80 percent, it might qualify if the loss of control (as defined by §368(c)) was not an integral part of the transaction.[18]

If the proprietor in such a case is regarded as paying his debt to the employee with stock (as suggested by Regs. §1.351-1(b)(2), Example (1)), he will recognize gain or loss on the difference between the amount of the debt and the adjusted basis of the stock. In the alternative, the transaction might be regarded as a transfer of property by the proprietor in exchange for stock and an assumption of his indebtedness by the corporation, followed by a payment of the debt by the corporation.[19]

---

equitable interest in transferred property rejected on the facts, with possible implication that, on stronger facts, alleged equitable owner would be a transferor of property).

[17] Regs. §§1.351-1(b)(1), 1.351-1(b)(2).

[18] See G. & W.H. Corson, Inc., ¶ 53,242 P-H Memo. TC (1953); infra ¶ 3.09.

[19] On the tax consequences of such an assumption of the transferor's debt, see infra ¶ 3.06.

In practice, of course, it may be difficult to determine whether stock is issued for services performed in the past for one of the transferors, as an incentive (or reward) for the future performance of services for the transferee corporation, or both.[20] *US v. Frazell* is a graphic example of this difficulty.[21] Here, the taxpayer earned a contingent 13 percent interest in the assets of an oil partnership by performing geological services. Shortly before this interest was to vest in the taxpayer, the partnership was terminated, and its assets were transferred to a newly created corporation, with the taxpayer receiving 13 percent of the corporation's stock in exchange for his partnership interest. The court held that the value of the stock was taxable compensation for his prior services to the partnership, although Regs. §1.351-1(a)(1)(i) refers only to services "rendered or to be rendered to or for the benefit of the issuing corporation." Evidently, the court did not regard a cash-basis taxpayer's claim for compensation rendered to a third person (i.e., the partnership) as "property" under §351, although it also suggested an alternative theory for its result, i.e., that the taxpayer's compensation claim vested and became taxable to him prior to the incorporation transfer. Under this theory, the claim would qualify as property in determining whether the exchange was tax-free under §351.[22]

The problem before the court in the *Frazell* case—whether income must be recognized on the incorporation of a going business when previously untaxed rights or claims created by personal services are transferred for stock—is reminiscent of cases in the capital gain area involving such items as industrial know-how, trade names, professional goodwill, trade secrets, employment contracts, and so forth. Profit on the sale of such assets has sometimes been denied capital gain status, partly on the ground that the transferred item did not constitute "property" within the meaning of §1221. Since §351 was intended to permit the tax-free incorporation of going businesses, there is less reason to interpret "property" as used in §351 to exclude such commonly encountered items.[23] The lack of an extensive body of law in

---

[20] See Herwitz, Allocation of Stock Between Services and Capital in the Organization of a Close Corporation, 75 Harv. L. Rev. 1098 (1962).

[21] US v. Frazell, 335 F2d 487 (5th Cir.), reh'g denied, 339 F2d 885 (5th Cir. 1964), cert. denied, 380 US 961 (1965); for opinion on remand, see 269 F. Supp. 885 (W.D. La. 1967).

[22] See also Garrett v. Campbell, 360 F2d 382 (5th Cir. 1966); Elihu B. Washburne, ¶ 68,122 P-H Memo. TC (1968); Deshotels v. US, 450 F2d 961 (5th Cir. 1971), cert. denied, 406 US 920 (1972).

[23] See US v. Stafford, 727 F2d 1043 (11th Cir. 1984) (real estate developer's transfer of unenforceable letter of intent and loan commitment qualified as transfer of property under §351); Rev. Rul. 79-288, 1979-2 CB 139 (corporate name and goodwill associated with it constitute property if subject to legal protection under local law); Hospital Corp. of Am., 81 TC 520 (1983) (diversion of corporate opportu-

this area implies that the administrative practice of the Service has been in accord with this suggestion. At the same time, however, it must be recognized that in appropriate cases, the Service could rightly treat an alleged transfer of property as a device, in whole or in part, to compensate the transferor for past services or to convert an income item whose sale would produce ordinary income into a block of stock that can qualify as a capital asset on sale.

2. Open-account debt. If stock or securities are issued for the transferee corporation's debt and the debt is not evidenced by a security, that debt is not treated as property, by virtue of §351(d)(2). This exclusion, enacted as part of the Bankruptcy Tax Act of 1980, was evidently intended to permit open-account creditors to claim an immediate bad-debt deduction even though they receive stock or securities of the debtor in a bankruptcy proceeding; [24] but it is not confined to insolvency situations or losses. Thus, the purchaser of an open-account debt at a discount could realize and recognize gain if the debt were later exchanged for stock of the debtor corporation with a value exceeding the transferor's adjusted basis for the debt.

3. Accrued interest. Under §351(d)(3), stock or securities issued to discharge interest on the transferee corporation's debt are not treated as property and thus do not qualify for nonrecognition if the interest accrued on or after the beginning of the transferor's holding period for the debt. Like

---

nity to negotiate and perform contract with foreign client not a transfer of property under §§351 and 367); E.I. duPont de Nemours & Co. v. US, 471 F2d 1211 (Ct. Cl. 1973) (grant of nonexclusive license a transfer of property under §351, because rights granted were perpetual and irrevocable); Rev. Rul. 64-56, 1964-1 CB 133 (transfer of industrial know-how qualifies for nonrecognition under §351 under certain conditions); Rev. Rul. 71-564, 1971-2 CB 179 (trade secrets); CIR v. P.G. Lake, Inc., 356 US 260, reh'g denied, 356 US 964 (1958) (transfer of potential income item did not qualify for nonrecognition of gain under §1031); Rev. Rul. 70-45, 1970-1 CB 17 (goodwill of one-person personal service business can be capital asset); Rev. Rul. 65-261, 1965-2 CB 281 (celebrity's name, publicity, and so forth, not a capital asset); Rev. Proc. 69-19, 1969-2 CB 301 (conditions for issuing favorable §367 rulings on the property status of know-how and/or other technical information); Rev. Proc. 74-36, 1974-2 CB 49 (same for domestic transfers); infra ¶ 3.17. See generally Lyon & Eustice, Assignment of Income: Fruit and Tree as Irrigated by the *P.G. Lake* Case, 17 Tax L. Rev. 293, 424 (1962); Eustice, Contract Rights, Capital Gain, and Assignment of Income—The *Ferrer* Case, 20 Tax L. Rev. 1 (1964).

[24] For prior law to the contrary, see Rev. Rul. 77-81, 1977-1 CB 97. For a broader exemption from the nonrecognition principle of §351, limited to Title 11 and similar judicially supervised insolvency arrangements, see §351(e)(2), which applies whether the transferred debt is evidenced by a security or not. See also §1276(d)(1)(C), added by the Tax Reform Act of 1986 (transferor of market discount bond taxable on accrued gain despite §351); for market discount generally, see infra ¶ 4.44.

§351(d)(2), summarized previously, this provision, while enacted as part of the Bankruptcy Tax Act of 1980, is not confined to insolvency situations. As discussed later in this chapter, the courts have reached similar results in certain situations involving the midstream transfer of so-called income items in exchange for stock or securities of a controlled corporation.[25]

¶ 3.03   EXCHANGE FOR STOCK OR SECURITIES: PROBLEMS OF CLASSIFICATION

1. "Exchange" requirement. By referring to transfers of property in "exchange" for stock or securities, §351 apparently incorporates the similar requirement of §1222 that property must be transferred in a sale or exchange to qualify for capital gain treatment. Sale or exchange problems under §351 have arisen most often in the case of assignments of intangibles (e.g., patents or technical information) to a controlled corportation where the transferor retains substantial economic interests in the transferred property; the failure to assign all substantial rights in the property may cause the transaction to be treated as a license rather than an exchange. In order to avoid this treatment, the transferee must acquire the exclusive rights to the use, exploitation, and disposition of the property within a designated area for the foreseeable economic life of the property.[26]

If the transaction extinguishes the transferor's property rights, it may fail to constitute an exchange, so that gain on the stock or securities received would be taxable currently as ordinary income. This situation could arise where the shareholder-transferor converts a debt owed to him by the transferee into stock (i.e., collects the claim by taking additional stock); unless §1271(a)(1) provides the necessary exchange treatment, §351 would not apply to this transaction.[27]

---

[25] See infra ¶ 3.17.

[26] For decisions regarding whether a transaction constituted a sale, a §351 exchange, a license, or a dividend, see A.E. Hickman, 29 TC 864 (1958) (acq.) (sale of patent on royalty pay-out basis held capital gain transaction, not dividend); Rev. Rul. 64-56, 1964-1 CB 133 (not a §351 exchange where transferor retained substantial rights in transferred property); Rev. Rul. 71-564, 1971-2 CB 179 (transfer of know-how an exchange under §351 if term lasts until trade secret becomes public knowledge and is no longer protectable under local law in country of use); E.I. duPont De Nemours & Co. v. US, supra note 23.

[27] See Jack Ammann Photogrammetric Eng'rs, Inc. v. CIR, 341 F2d 466 (5th Cir. 1965); see also Rev. Rul. 57-296, 1957-2 CB 234 (parent's transfer of wholly owned subsidiary's notes for over 80 percent of subsidiary's stock held a §351 transaction); Rev. Rul. 77-81, 1977-1 CB 97 (exchanges of creditor claims for 85 percent of debtor's stock held §351 transaction); Rev. Rul. 73-423, 1973-2 CB 161 (transfer of §453 obligation in §351 exchange held an accelerating disposition under

2. Stock or securities. Section 351(a) permits the tax-free transfer of property to a controlled corporation only if the transfer is "solely in exchange for stock or securities" in such corporation. While there have been numerous decisions construing the term "stock or securities" as used in §351, it also has been held that the term has the same meaning here as in §§354(a)(1) and 361(a), providing for the nonrecognition of gain or loss on an exchange in the course of a corporate reorganization.[28]

As used in the reorganization sections, the term "stock or securities" does not include short-term notes. The reason for this restrictive construction of the term is that the underlying purpose of the reorganization sections is to permit the tax-free transfer of property only if the transfer is not analogous to a sale.[29] Where short-term notes are received for the property, courts construing the reorganization sections have held that the transaction is so akin to a sale that any gain realized by the transferor should be recognized to the extent of the value of the short-term notes.

In the leading case on this question, *Pinellas Ice & Cold Storage Co. v. CIR,* the Supreme Court rested its decision partly on the theory that the transaction (a transfer of property for cash and short-term notes) fell entirely outside the intended ambit of the reorganization sections: "[T]o be within the exemption the seller must acquire an interest in the affairs of the purchasing company more definite than that incident to ownership of its short-term purchase-money notes."[30] Although this was not only an appropriate but also a sufficient ground for its determination, the Court also said that the notes "were not securities within the intendment of the act."[31] This part of the *Pinellas* opinion has been cogently criticized,[32] but it is now so well imbedded in the law that the later decisions in this area have been preoccupied with the tantalizing question, how long is too long? And even when the classification of notes as "securities" is said to depend upon an "overall evaluation of the nature of the debt," the length of time to maturity usually

---

§453B(a)(1)). But see §§368(a)(1)(E) and 354(a), infra ¶ 14.17. See also §351(d)(2), supra text at note 24.

[28] See Lloyd-Smith v. CIR, 116 F2d 642, 644 (2d Cir.), cert. denied, 313 US 588 (1941). For use of the phrase "stock or securities" in the reorganization area, see infra ¶¶ 14.11 and 14.31. However, proposed reform legislation, the Senate Finance Committee Staff report, The Subchapter C Revision Act of 1985, S. Print 47, 99th Cong., 1st Sess. (1985), would treat as boot the excess, if any, of the issue price of securities received over the adjusted basis of securities surrendered in the exchange. See proposed §351(b); see also infra ¶ 3.05.

[29] Regs. §1.368-1(b).

[30] Pinellas Ice & Cold Storage Co. v. CIR, 287 US 462, 470 (1933).

[31] Id. at 468–469.

[32] Griswold, "Securities" and "Continuity of Interest," 58 Harv. L. Rev. 705 (1945).

is regarded as the most important single earmark. Notes with a five-year term or less rarely seem able to qualify as securities, while a term of 10 years or more ordinarily is sufficient to bring them within the statute.[33] It should also be noted that a debt instrument may be found to be a substitute for stock if the corporation is undercapitalized or if the parties do not intend to treat the obligation as a true debt.[34]

The leading case on the securities status of debt obligations issued in a §351 exchange is *Camp Wolters Enterprises, Inc. v. CIR,* where the Tax Court phrased the test as follows:

> The test as to whether notes are securities is not a mechanical determination of the time period of the note. Though time is an important factor, the controlling consideration is an overall evaluation of the nature of the debt, degree of participation and continuing interest compared with similarity of the note to a cash payment, the purpose of the advances, etc. It is not necessary for the debt obligation to be the equivalent of stock since [§351] specifically includes both "stock" and "securities."[35]

Thus, "securities" are investment interests that give the creditor-holder a participation in the affairs of the debtor corporation somewhere to the east

---

[33] See, e.g., Bradshaw v. US, 683 F2d 365 (Ct. Cl. 1982) (promissory notes payable in installments over 2½–6½ years did not constitute securities); Regs. §1.371-1(a)(5) (short-term purchase-money notes not securities); Prentis v. US, 273 F. Supp. 460 (S.D.N.Y. 1967) (6-month notes held securities in substance, since they were issued in plan for later issue of preferred stock); US v. Hertwig, 398 F2d 452 (5th Cir. 1968) (12½-year installment notes held securities); Turner v. CIR, 303 F2d 94 (4th Cir.), cert. denied, 371 US 922 (1962), reh'g denied, 371 US 965 (1963) (demand note not a security); D'Angelo Assocs., Inc., 70 TC 121 (1978) (contra); US v. Mills, 399 F2d 944 (5th Cir. 1968) (one-year note a security); Campbell v. Carter Found. Prod. Co., 322 F2d 827 (5th Cir. 1963); Baker Commodities, Inc., 48 TC 374 (1967), aff'd (other issues), 415 F2d 519 (9th Cir. 1969), cert. denied, 397 US 988 (1970); George A. Nye, 50 TC 203 (1968) (acq.); Wham Constr. Co. v. US, 600 F2d 1052 (4th Cir. 1979) (retained intracompany accounts receivable did not constitute boot received on incorporation of two-business corporation; no change of substance). But see Rev. Rul. 80-228, 1980-2 CB 115 (contra; *Wham* will not be followed). See also infra ¶ 3.14 (sale vs. §351 exchange); infra ch. 4 (corporate capital structure).

See generally Goldstein, Corporate Indebtedness to Shareholders: "Thin Capitalization" and Related Problems, 16 Tax L. Rev. 1 (1960); Note, Section 351 Transfers to Controlled Corporations: The Forgotten Term—"Securities," 114 U. Pa. L. Rev. 314 (1965).

The Service does not ordinarily rule on the debt or security status of obligations issued in a §351 exchange (Rev. Proc. 87-3, §4.19, 1987-1 IRB 27).

[34] See infra ¶ 4.02.

[35] Camp Wolters Enters., Inc. v. CIR, 22 TC 737, 750–751 (1954) (acq.), aff'd, 230 F2d 555 (5th Cir.), cert. denied, 352 US 826 (1956); see also George A. Lagerquist, ¶ 87,185 P-H Memo. TC (1987) (notes securities because of risk).

of equity and to the west of cash or its equivalent. Another approach, which at times may be as practical, is to define a security as "a piece of paper evidencing a corporate debt with mermaids and a steam locomotive engraved at the top."

The fact that short-term notes may not constitute stock or securities as those terms are used in §351 does not automatically exclude a transaction from the benefits of §351. If the transfer otherwise qualifies under §351 (e.g., if the transferors exchange property for a combination of stock and short-term notes), the notes come within the ambit of §351(b)(1). Under this provision, if the transferor of property receives not only "stock or securities," which can be received tax-free under §351(a) (nonrecognition property), but also "other property or money" (boot), the gain on the exchange (if any) is recognized, but in an amount not in excess of the money plus the fair market value of the other boot.

> *To illustrate:* Assume that *A* transfers property with an adjusted basis of $10,000 and a fair market value of $50,000 to a corporation for all its stock (worth $45,000) plus $5,000 of short-term notes (having a fair market value equal to their face amount). *A*'s gain is $40,000 (fair market value of stock and notes received less adjusted basis of property given by him), but it is recognized only to the extent of $5,000, the fair market value of the notes.[36]

Most of the turmoil over the meaning of stock or securities has concerned debt instruments, and it has generally been assumed that the term "stock" is virtually self-defining. The regulations, however, state that stock rights and stock warrants do not come within the term stock or securities.[37] The inspiration for this statement may be *Helvering v. Southwest Consolidated Corp.*, holding that warrants are not voting stock within the meaning of §368(a)(1)(B), relating to corporate reorganizations.[38] Perhaps potential equity interests such as stock rights and warrants should not be taken into account in determining whether the transferors of property are in control of the corporation immediately after the exchange[39], but if they do have control, there seems to be no good reason for disqualifying a transfer of property for stock rights or warrants or for treating

---

[36] For more on the tax treatment of boot, see infra ¶ 3.05. However, proposed legislation for the reform of Subchapter C (supra note 28) would treat all securities as boot per se.

[37] Regs. §1.351-1(a)(1), last sentence.

[38] Helvering v. Southwest Consol. Corp., 315 US 194, reh'g denied, 315 US 829, 316 US 710 (1942).

[39] See infra ¶ 3.09.

them as boot. A Tax Court case accepts this view with respect to contingent rights to acquire additional stock, a position that seems equally applicable to rights and warrants.[40]

¶ 3.04 "STOCK OR SECURITIES": THE CONTINUITY-OF-INTEREST DOCTRINE

In the *Pinellas* case, the Supreme Court said not only that short-term notes are not securities, but also that they do not give the transferor "an interest in the affairs" of the transferee corporation that will qualify under the reorganization provisions.[41] This judicial requirement of a continuity of interest was developed more fully in later cases. In *LeTulle v. Scofield*, for example, it was employed to disqualify a reorganization in which the transferor of property received bonds plus cash, but no stock, from the transferee corporation.[42] The continuity-of-interest doctrine, which is set out in Regs. §1.368-1(b), does not derive from any specific language in the reorganization sections. It is instead a doctrine of judicial origin based on what is conceived to be the unstated but fundamental statutory purpose of providing for nonrecognition of gain or loss only if the reorganization exchange is distinguishable from a sale.[43] It should be noted that there is a drastic difference between (1) holding that an exchange fails to qualify under §351 because the transferor does not retain a continuing proprietary interest, and (2) holding that some of the instruments received by the transferor do not constitute stock or securities. In the former case, the entire gain or loss is recognized; in the latter situation, if the transferor also receives stock evidencing a substantial continuity of interest, gain is recognized only to the extent of the unqualified instruments (or boot).

In a 1973 ruling, the Service held that the continuity-of-interest principle was satisfied and that §351 applied when four individuals, who owned all of the stock of a corporation, transferred property to it solely for securities.[44]

---

[40] See James C. Hamrick, 43 TC 21 (1964) (acq.), remanded by agreement, 17 AFTR2d 357 (4th Cir. 1965); Carlberg v. US, 281 F2d 507 (8th Cir. 1960) (certificates of contingent interest in reserved shares held stock). But see Gordon v. CIR, 424 F2d 378 (2d Cir.), cert. denied, 400 US 848 (1970) (rights to buy corporate property not stock). See also infra ¶¶ 14.31 and 14.56.

[41] See Pinellas Ice & Cold Storage Co. v. CIR, supra note 30.

[42] Le Tulle v. Scofield, 308 US 415, reh'g denied, 309 US 694 (1940).

[43] For discussion, see infra ¶ 14.11. But cf. Helvering v. Cement Investors, Inc. 316 US 527 (1942) (failure to qualify as a reorganization did not preclude application of §351).

[44] Rev. Rul. 73-473, 1973-2 CB 115, citing Parkland Place Co. v. US, 354 F2d 916 (5th Cir. 1966).

However, in a contrasting ruling issued at the same time involving four other individuals who transferred property to a newly created corporation that issued all of its stock to three of them and securities to the fourth, the Service ruled that the transfers for stock qualified under §351 but that the securities received by the fourth transferor did not provide him with a continuing proprietary interest; consequently, any gain or loss realized by him on the exchange was recognized.[45] Application of the continuity-of-interest principle on a transferor-by-transferor basis is also illustrated by a 1984 ruling involving a complex acquisition of all of the stock of a target company. Its public shareholders received cash for their shares (86 percent of the total), but an insider who was unwilling to enter into a taxable transaction received stock for his 14 percent interest. The individual's transfer was held by the Service to qualify under §351 in view of his continuing interest in the acquiring corporation even though it was part of a larger acquisitive transaction in which sales for cash were predominant.[46]

¶ 3.05   SOLELY IN EXCHANGE: THE RECEIPT OF "BOOT"

Section 351 provides that no gain or loss shall be recognized if property is transferred to a controlled corporation solely in exchange for stock or securities in such corporation. It has already been pointed out that if the transferor or transferors receive from the controlled corporation not only stock or securities but also short-term notes, they are required by §351(b) to recognize their gain (if any) to the extent of the fair market value of the notes. The rule of §351(b) comes into play whenever the exchange would qualify under §351(a) except for the fact that the transferor or transferors have received not only stock or securities (nonrecognition property) but also money or other property (boot). At the same time, §351(b) requires the recognition of gain only if gain has been realized under §1001.

To illustrate: If taxpayer *A* transfers property with an adjusted basis of $10,000 and a fair market value of $50,000 to a controlled corporation

---

[45] Rev. Rul. 73-472, 1973-2 CB 114. Note that the ruling excluded the fourth transferor from the control group, thereby enabling the other three transferors who received all the stock to qualify for §351 recognition. See also Rev. Rul. 79-70, 1979-1 CB 144 (stock sold by transferor of property under prearranged plan not counted in satisfying control requirement of §351, even though purchaser simultaneously purchased securities for cash from transferee corporation).

[46] Rev. Rul. 84-71, 1984-1 CB 106 (revoking two 1980 rulings—Rev. Rul. 80-284, 1980-2 CB 117 and Rev. Rul. 80-285, 1980-2 CB 119—that enunciated the larger acquisitive transaction theory). But proposed legislation for the reform of Subchapter C, supra note 28, would overrule Rev. Rul. 84-71 and preempt §351 if the transfer were part of an acquisitive transaction.

in exchange for stock worth $30,000, cash of $10,000, and other property with a fair market value of $10,000, the gain under §1001 is $40,000, but only $20,000 of it is recognized under §351(b).[47] The computation is as follows:

(1) Amount realized:
    (a) Stock $30,000
    (b) Cash (boot)   10,000
    (c) Other property (boot)   10,000
    (d) Total $50,000
(2) Less: adjusted basis of property transferred   10,000
(3) Gain realized $40,000
(4) Gain recognized ((1)(b) plus (1)(c), or (3), whichever is less) $20,000

If the adjusted basis of the property (line (2) above) were $45,000 instead of $10,000, the gain realized would be only $5,000, and only this amount would be recognized under §351(b). If the adjusted basis of property were more than $50,000, there would be a realized loss under §1001, but, by virtue of §351(b)(2), it could not be recognized even though boot was received.[48]

---

[47] For problems in valuing boot, see infra ¶ 11.03. For a case allowing cost recovery reporting upon the collection of speculative boot, see Magnus v. CIR, 259 F2d 893 (3d Cir. 1958). For proposed legislation for the reform of Subchapter C, see supra note 28.

For the possibility of reporting boot gain on the installment method under §453(f)(6) if it is attributable to the transferee corporation's debt instruments, see Prop. Regs. §1.453-1(f)(3)(ii); Cain, Taxation of Boot Notes in a 351/453 Transaction 27 S. Tex. L.J. 61 (1985); New York State Bar Ass'n Tax Section, A Report on Proposed Regulations Under Section 453(f)(6)—Installment Obligations Received in Certain Nonrecognition Exchanges, 24 Tax Notes 297 (1984); Dentino & Walker, Impact of the Installment Sales Revision Act of 1980 on Evidences of Indebtedness in a Section 351 Transaction, 9 J. Corp. Tax'n 330 (1983); Bogdanski, Closely Held Corporations, 11 J. Corp. Tax'n 268 (1984). For basis results, see infra notes 110, 117, and 119. See also §453(g) if property is depreciable.

[48] Another barrier to recognition of the loss is §267(a)(1), which disallows losses on sales or exchanges between related taxpayers, whose ownership of stock is determined by complex attribution rules that take into account stock owned by members of the taxpayer's family (as defined), and other like considerations. Sections 267(a)(1) and 351(b)(2) overlap in many cases (e.g., where the transferor has 80 percent control), although §267 may have the broader coverage (as where only 51 percent control is present); but see §267(b)(3), enacted in 1984, which extended §267(f) (a loss *deferral* rule) to related corporate groups, infra ¶ 5.04; Rev. Rul. 72-151, 1972-1 CB 225 (possibility of overlap between §§1031 and 267).

When gain must be recognized because boot has been received in a §351 exchange, the character of the asset transferred usually determines whether the gain is ordinary income or capital gain and, in the latter case, whether it is long- or short-term gain. If, however, the property transferred by the taxpayer qualifies for depreciation, amortization, or certain other accelerated deductions, the capital gain component of the taxpayer's recognized profit may be converted, in whole or in part, into ordinary income by any of a number of recapture and similar remedial provisions; if it is investment credit property, the transfer may trigger the recapture of part or all of the previously allowed credit. The most important of these provisions are:

(1) Section 1239, providing that gain recognized on the transfer of depreciable property to a corporation cannot be treated as capital gain if more than 50 percent of the transferee corporation's stock is owned directly, indirectly, or constructively by the transferor;[49]

(2) Section 1245, providing for the recapture of post-1961 depreciation as ordinary income if gain is recognized on a §351 transfer of certain types of property (other than real property);

(3) Section 1250, providing for the recapture of post-1963 depreciation on similar transfers of real property, but in more limited circumstances; and

(4) Section 47(a), providing for recapture of the investment credit allowed by §38 on a premature disposition of the property or if it ceases to be §38 property. This provision, unlike those mentioned above, applies whether gain is recognized on the transfer of the property or not; but a §351 transfer of a going business ordinarily comes within §47(b)'s exemption of "a mere change in the form of

---

If both §351 and §267 apply, the former presumably takes precedence, although no authority exists in the case of overlaps here.

[49] The Tax Reform Act of 1986 conformed the §1239 control line to §267. See also Robishaw v. US, 616 F2d 507 (Ct. Cl. 1980) (time for measuring §1239 control is before the sale in question rather than after); Rev. Rul. 75-514, 1975-2 CB 116 (§1239 applies if transferor was in control at initiation of transaction, even though it results in drop in ownership below 50 percent benchmark); Regs. §1.1239-1(c)(3) (in case of person-to-entity transfer, test after the transaction; but in case of entity-to-person transfer, test before *or* after transaction); see also §453(g) (no §453 if depreciable and §267 related buyer).

For the possibility of taking the value of control into account in determining whether the ownership of less than, or exactly, 80 percent of the outstanding shares gave the taxpayer more than 80 percent *by value* (the statutory requirement under §1239 before its amendment in 1986) see US v. Parker, 376 F2d 402 (5th Cir. 1967) (blockage and effect of buy-sell agreement relevant); Harry Trotz, ¶ 67,139 P-H Memo. TC (1967) (contra); Dahlgren v. US, 553 F2d 434 (5th Cir.), reh'g denied, 557 F2d 456 (1977) (control premium made 79.75 percent of shares by number worth more than 80 percent by value).

conducting the trade or business so long as the property is retained in such trade or business as section 38 property and the taxpayer retains a substantial interest in such trade or business." [50]

Because §351 exchanges seldom involve the receipt of boot by the transferors, the Service and the courts have not had to face up to a number of questions in the computation, recognition, and characterization of gain that are not explicitly answered by the statutory provision. These questions grow out of the fact that the property transferred may consist not of a single asset (as assumed in the previous example) but of several assets, each with its own adjusted basis, fair market value, status as capital or ordinary, and holding period. Thus, if the property transferred in the previous example consisted of two assets, with an adjusted basis of $25,000 each but a fair market value of $5,000 for one and $45,000 for the other, there would be no realized gain if their adjusted bases were combined on line (2); but if each asset were taken separately, there would be a realized gain of $20,000 on the first and a realized loss of $20,000 on the second. The realized loss would not be recognized by virtue of §351(b)(2); the amount of the realized gain to be recognized under §351(b)(1) would depend on the method used to allocate the stock, cash, and other property received between the two assets given up by the transferor. If the consideration received were allocated to the assets according to their relative fair market values, the appreciated asset would account for nine tenths of the stock, cash, and other property, with the result that the $20,000 of realized gain on this asset would be recognized to the extent of its share of the boot ($18,000). [51]

Instead of using relative fair market values in allocating the consideration received, it might be allocated according to the adjusted basis of the assets transferred or relative to the appreciation involved. A relative basis allocation has little to commend it; in the foregoing example, it would assume that property with a fair market value of $5,000 accounted for

---

[50] See S. Rep. No. 1881, 87th Cong., 2d Sess. (1962), reprinted in 1962-3 CB 707, 856, citing the incorporation of a going business under §351 as an example of this exception; Loewen v. CIR, 76 TC 90 (1981) (on incorporation, §38 property and other assets of farming and cattle-feeding business were transferred, but real estate was retained by individual transferors and leased to transferee corporation; held recapture of investment credits not required); Rev. Rul. 83-65, 1983-1 CB 10 (accord with *Loewen*; what is required is that retained and transferred property be used collectively after the transfer); James Soares, 50 TC 909 (1968) (incorporation of partnership held taxable disposition under §47(a) as to partner who acquired only 7.2 percent in corporation).

[51] See Rev. Rul. 68-55, 1968-1 CB 140 (realized gain or loss computed asset by asset; boot allocated in proportion to relative asset values); Rev. Rul. 67-192, 1967-2 CB 140; Regs. §1.1245-4(c) (allocation of boot in proportion to asset values); Rabinovitz, Allocating Boot in Section 351 Exchanges, 24 Tax L. Rev. 337 (1969); see also Rev. Rul. 85-164, 1985-2 CB 117, infra ¶ 3.10.

$25,000 of the consideration received. A better case can be made for allocating boot exclusively to appreciated property up to the amount of the realized gain thereon on the ground that it is responsible for the recognition of gain;[52] if this approach were employed in the example just given, there would be $20,000 of recognized gain on the appreciated property. The example can be complicated further by assuming that some assets are capital assets and some ordinary, that the holding periods of the capital assets vary, that some of the assets are subject to the depreciation recapture rules of §1245 or §1250, and so forth.

In other areas involving similar problems, an asset-by-asset approach has carried the day as against an aggregate approach;[53] this seems to imply that each category of consideration received should be allocated separately to the transferred assets by reference to their relative market values. On balance, this seems to involve fewer complexities and anomalies than any other method of allocating the gain to be recognized.

If the exchange agreement explicitly adopts its own method of allocating the consideration to be paid for the transferred property (e.g., assigning stock and securities exclusively to the appreciated property, and boot exclusively to assets on which there is no realized gain), is the agreed allocation controlling? In view of the non-arm's-length character of the average §351 transaction, this does not seem to be a very promising route; but if the allocation serves a business purpose and is free of self-dealing because there are several independent transferors, perhaps it will pass muster. Another possibility in this area is a tax-free §351 exchange of the appreciated property and a separate sale or exchange of the depreciated property for the boot. If prearranged, however, the two transfers may be amalgamated for tax purposes in the name of the step-transaction doctrine.[54]

¶ 3.06 ASSUMPTION OF LIABILITIES

On many §351 exchanges, particularly when a going business is incorporated, the transferee corporation assumes liabilities of the transferor or takes property subject to liabilities. What is the effect of its doing so? In the

---

[52] This approach was followed by the Tax Court in Jack L. Easson, 33 TC 963 (1960), rev'd on other grounds, 294 F2d 653 (9th Cir. 1961).

[53] See Williams v. McGowan, 152 F2d 570 (2d Cir. 1945); Estate of Johnson v. CIR, 42 TC 441 (1964), aff'd per curiam, 355 F2d 931 (6th Cir. 1965); US Holding Co., 44 TC 323 (1965); Curtis v. US, 336 F2d 714 (6th Cir. 1964); Regs. §1.357-2. But see Sayer v. US, 163 F. Supp. 495 (S.D. W. Va. 1958) (Service's attempt to apportion boot on basis of relative values rejected in context of §1031 exchange). See also §1060 (added by the Tax Reform Act of 1986).

[54] See infra ¶ 3.14.

income tax's early years, it was assumed that such a transaction would not require the recognition of gain under §351 or under the analogous reorganization sections. In *US v. Hendler,* however, the Supreme Court held that the assumption and payment by a transferee corporation of a liability of the transferor would constitute boot to the transferor, at least in some circumstances, under the reorganization provisions.[55]

Immediately after winning this decision, the Treasury Department recognized that a host of earlier incorporations and reorganizations, thought to be tax-free when consummated, might in fact have been partially taxable because of the assumption of liabilities. Unless estoppel or a similar doctrine was applicable,[56] the transferee corporation would be entitled to step up its basis for the assets received by it to reflect the gain that should have been recognized on the exchange[57]; and such a stepped-up basis would impair the revenue by increasing the corporation's depreciation deductions for any depreciable assets received on the exchange and by reducing its gain or increasing its loss on any subsequent disposition of the assets. Similarly, the transferors could step up the basis of the stock or securities received by them on the exchange. It was also perceived that if gain were to be recognized upon a reorganization or incorporation whenever the transferee assumed a liability of the transferor or took property subject to a liability, the usefulness of §351 and similar nonrecognition provisions would be seriously impaired.

The upshot was that the Treasury Department promptly urged Congress to enact legislation that would relinquish the victory it had just won in the *Hendler* case by providing that an assumption of liability by the transferee corporation (or its receipt of property subject to a liability) in an otherwise nontaxable exchange would not constitute boot to the transferor.[58] Congress responded in 1939 with the statutory principles that are now, with minor changes, embodied in the general rule of §357(a) and the exception of §357(b). Another exception to the general rule, §357(c), was added in 1954.[59]

1. General rule. By virtue of the general rule of §357(a), the transferee corporation's assumption of liability or its acquisition of property subject to a

---

[55] US v. Hendler, 303 US 564, reh'g denied, 304 US 588 (1938).

[56] See infra notes 112 and 117.

[57] See infra ¶ 3.11.

[58] The *Hendler* victory was rendered pyrrhic in 1939, when the tax upheld by that case was refunded to the taxpayer by Congress, Pub. L. No. 76-379, §910, 53 Stat. 1402 (1939).

[59] See generally Layva, Corporations—Assumptions of Liabilities, Tax Mgmt. Portfolio (BNA) No. 233-3d (1985); Burke, Jr. & Chisholm, Section 357: A Hidden Trap in Tax-Free Incorporations, 25 Tax L. Rev. 211 (1970); Surrey, Assumption of Indebtedness in Tax-Free Exchanges, 50 Yale L.J. 1 (1940).

liability is not treated as money or other property; nor does it prevent the exchange from qualifying under §351. Thus, the incorporation of property or a going business ordinarily qualifies as a tax-free transaction under §351, even though the corporation assumes or acquires property subject to liabilities.

> *To illustrate: A* transfers property with a basis of $40,000 and a value of $100,000 (but subject to a mortgage of $30,000) to controlled corporation *X* in exchange for stock worth $70,000 and *X*'s assumption of the mortgage. *A*'s realized gain is $60,000 (value of the *X* stock plus assumption of *A*'s debt, less *A*'s basis for the property), but his recognized gain is zero, since §357(a) provides that the assumed liability is not to be counted as boot under §351(b). *A*'s basis for his stock will be $10,000 under §358 (property basis of $40,000 less the assumed liability of $30,000), and *X*'s basis for the property will be $40,000 under §362(a)(1).[60]

While the application of §357 is ordinarily straightforward, there are several problems of interpretation. Thus, if the transferor's liability is *discharged* on the transfer (by payment, or by a novation between the creditor and the corporate transferee), would this event fall outside §357(a) on the ground that the transferee neither assumed the debt nor took property subject to it? Would it generate taxable boot or cancellation of indebtedness income to the transferor? Since the *Hendler* case itself involved a prompt (and no doubt prearranged) payment of the assumed liabilities by the transferee corporation, §357(a) ought to be construed to cover this situation as well as a discharge of the liability that is simultaneous with the exchange. Moreover, if the transferor's liability is not discharged by payment or novation at the time of the exchange, and the transferor remains liable (ordinarily in the capacity of a surety), a later payment of the debt by the transferee[61] ought not to be treated as taxable income to the transferor. Otherwise, the utility of §357 would be undermined, and many incorporation transfers would become partially taxable, thus frustrating the purpose that prompted Congress to overrule the *Hendler* decision by enacting §357. The statutory language leaves something to be desired in the way of clarity, but the courts have been chary about reopening an area that Congress attempted to put to rest.[62]

---

[60] The basis provisions are discussed infra ¶¶ 3.10 (transferor's basis) and 3.11 (transferee corporation basis).

[61] For situations in which the transferee corporation may be able to deduct payments of such liabilities, see infra ¶ 3.11, note 118.

[62] See Jewell v. US, 330 F2d 761 (9th Cir. 1964); Easson v. CIR, supra note 52; Arthur L. Kniffen, 39 TC 553 (1962). In effect, these cases regard the tax-avoidance and business-purpose restrictions of §357(b) as the appropriate safeguards against improprieties under §357(a). See also Rev. Rul. 80-240, 1980-2 CB 116 (transitory borrowing by agent and subsequent novation not true assumption transaction); Rev.

2. Exception for tax-avoidance transactions. Although the principle of §357(a) makes good sense as a general rule, it might tempt the transferor of property under §351 to borrow against the property just before the exchange, with the intention of keeping the borrowed funds and causing the corporation either to assume the liability or to take the property subject to it. For the transferor, this chain of events could be the equivalent of receiving cash boot from the corporation in exchange for unencumbered property; but if the general rule of §357(a) were applicable, the corporation's assumption of the liability or acquisition of the property subject to it would not be treated as boot. To frustrate liability bail-out transactions of this type, §357(b) carves out an exception to the general rule of §357(a): The assumption or acquisition is to be treated as money received by the transferor (i.e., as boot under §351(b)) if "taking into consideration the nature of the liability and the circumstances in the light of which the arrangement for the assumption or acquisition was made, it appears that the principal purpose of the taxpayer . . . was a purpose to avoid Federal income tax on the exchange, or . . . if not such purpose, was not a bona fide business purpose."[63] Although the statute itself speaks only of a bona fide business purpose, the regulations provide that the income tax returns of the transferor and the corporation for the year of the exchange must state "the *corporate* business reason" for the assumption of any liability (emphasis added).[64] Moreover, §357(b)(1) provides that if an improper purpose exists with respect to *any* liability, the total amount of *all* liabilities involved in the exchange is considered money received by the taxpayer; and Regs. §1.357-(c) emphasize the point that a single bad apple spoils the entire barrel.

The tax-avoidance approach of §357(b) would probably apply not only to the hypothetical case of a liability created just before the §351 exchange in order to wring some cash out of the transaction but also to the assumption by a transferee corporation of personal obligations (grocery bills, rent, alimony, and so forth) that are not ordinarily taken over in a §351 exchange unless there was a bona fide business purpose for such unusual action. On the other hand, the general rule of §357(a) rather than the exception of

---

Rul. 74-477, 1974-2 CB 116 (transferee assumed and paid expenses incurred by transferor for appraisal fees, legal fees, and shipping and packaging costs associated with transfer of property for stock; held, transferee can assume liabilities arising out of transfer of property under §351 without boot consequences to transferor; conversely, transferor payments constitute capital contributions).

[63] For the burden of proof in this area, see the cryptic language of §357(b)(2), providing that *if* the burden of proof falls on the taxpayer, then the burden must be sustained by the clear preponderance of evidence.

[64] Regs. §§1.351-3(a)(6), 1.351-3(b)(7); see also Rev. Proc. 83-59, 1983-2 CB 575. See generally Greiner, Behling & Moffett, Assumption of Liabilities and the Improper Purpose—A Reexamination of Section 357(b), 32 Tax Lawyer 111 (1978).

§357(b) should ordinarily be applicable to mortgages placed on business assets in the ordinary course of business, trade obligations, bank loans, customers' deposits, and the like; and this should be true even though at the time of the §351 exchange the transferor is able to pay such obligations himself but chooses instead to have the transferee corporation assume, or take property subject to, them.[65] Moreover, borrowing on the eve of a transfer under §351 is not necessarily fatal, since the taxpayer may be able to establish valid business reasons for the action.[66]

   3. **Exception for liabilities in excess of basis.** Under §357(c), if the liabilities encumbering the transferred property or assumed by the transferee corporation exceed the aggregate adjusted basis of the properties transferred, the excess is to be considered as a gain on the sale or exchange of such property.[67]

   To illustrate: A exchanges property with an adjusted basis of $10,000 and a fair market value of $70,000 subject to a mortgage liability of $30,000 for stock of a controlled corporation worth $40,000 and the transferee's assumption of the mortgage. *A*'s realized gain under §1001

---

[65] For cases holding §357(b) applicable to an assumption of liabilities, see Thompson v. Campbell, 353 F2d 787 (5th Cir. 1965); Campbell v. Wheeler, 342 F2d 837 (5th Cir. 1965); Bryan v. CIR, 281 F2d 238 (4th Cir. 1960), cert. denied, 364 US 931 (1961). Section 357(b) was held not applicable in W.H.B. Simpson, 43 TC 900 (1965) (acq.) (desire to avoid future taxes under §§531 and 541 not fatal); Easson v. CIR, supra note 52; Jewell v. US, supra note 62; Estate of Stoll, 38 TC 223 (1962) (acq. and nonacq.) (1939 Code; estate planning); see also Wolf, Jr. v. CIR, 357 F2d 483 (9th Cir. 1966) (transfer of stock subject to binding redemption contract not qualified for §351 treatment).

[66] See ISC Indus., Inc., ¶ 71,283 P-H Memo. TC (1971); Rev. Rul. 79-258, 1979-2 CB 143 (§357(b) not applicable where parent incurred new debt, used proceeds to pay off old debt that creditor would not allow to be assumed, and subsidiary then assumed new debt).
   Proposed legislation (the Subchapter C Revision Act of 1985, supra note 28) would replace the tax-avoidance motive test of §357(b) with a new objective test, i.e., whether the debt is purchase-money debt or otherwise has a sufficient business nexus to the transferee's use of the property.

[67] See generally Diedrich v. CIR, 457 US 191 (1982) (donor taxable on transfer of property with obligation to pay donor's gift-tax liability to extent that liability exceeded adjusted basis of donated property); see also Cooper, Negative Basis, 75 Harv. L. Rev. 1352 (1962).
   The relationship of §§357(b) and 357(c) to contributions of mortgaged property to the corporation's capital (infra ¶ 3.13) remains to be worked out; see Rev. Rul. 64-155, 1964-1 CB 138 (capital contribution treated as §351 transaction); contra, Abegg v. CIR, 429 F2d 1209 (2d Cir. 1970), cert. denied, 400 US 1008 (1971); but contra to *Abegg* is Sol Lessinger, 85 TC 824 (1985).

is $60,000 (the value of the stock received plus the liability assumed, less the property's basis); under §357(c), he must recognize gain in the amount of $20,000. Since A has so far received a return of $30,000 (the amount of the mortgage liability assumed by the transferee) on an investment of $10,000, his taxable gain of $20,000 under §357(c) corresponds to his economic gain. The balance of A's realized gain ($40,000) will be recognized if the stock is sold for its market value ($40,000), since the basis of the stock will have been reduced to zero under §358(d)[68] to take account of the liability assumed by the corporate transferee.

Although the example just used to illustrate §357(c) involves a realized gain to the transferor on the §351 exchange, A is taxed on the excess of liabilities-over-basis regardless of the amount of gain realized and even if none is realized. Thus, his gain on the transaction would be $20,000 even if the value of the transferred property was only $25,000 (i.e., $5,000 less than the mortgage). He might argue against this result on the ground that there is a substantial likelihood of default by the corporation, but the mandate of §357(c) is clear.[69]

In 1978, Congress enacted §357(c)(3) to shield deductible liabilities of a cash basis transferor from the reach of §357(c). Under prior law, §357(c) could be an unexpected pitfall for cash-basis taxpayers who transferred zero-basis receivables for stock and an assumption of the transferor's

---

[68] See infra ¶ 3.10.

[69] See George W. Wiebusch, 59 TC 777 (1973), aff'd per curiam, 487 F2d 515 (8th Cir. 1973); Rev. Rul. 68-629, 1968-2 CB 154 (gain recognized under §357(c) even though transferor gave note to corporate transferee for excess of assumed liabilities over asset bases; transferor had zero basis in his own note); Velma Alderman, 55 TC 662 (1971) (same); George F. Smith, 84 TC 889 (1985) (same); David Rosen, 62 TC 11 (1974), aff'd without opinion, 515 F2d 507 (3d Cir. 1975) (§357(c) applies even though transferor remains personally liable on debts assumed by corporate transferee, which was virtually insolvent). But see Jackson v. CIR, 708 F2d 1402 (9th Cir. 1983) (no application of §357(c) where transferor remained personally liable on debt and corporation did not assume debt on transferred property). See Bogdanski, Closely Held Corporations, 10 J. Corp. Tax'n 357 (1984); Bernstein, Avoiding Zero Basis Problems in Capital Contributions of Debt Obligations, 50 J. Tax'n 302 (1979); Tiller, Contributing Partnership Interests to a Corporation: "Liabilities" After Smith, 2 J. Partnership Tax'n 316 (1986).

In the case of nonrecourse indebtedness, §7701(g), enacted in 1984, requires the encumbered property to be treated as having a fair market value of not less than the debt. See generally CIR v. Tufts, 461 US 300, reh'g denied, 463 US 1215, on remand, 712 F2d 199 (1983); Joint Comm. on Taxation, General Explanation of Revenue Provisions of the Tax Reform Act of 1984, 98th Cong., 1st Sess. 239 (Staff Report 1984) (§7701(g) "limited in application to those Code provisions which *expressly* refer to the fair market value of property" (emphasis added)).

accounts payable, since §357(c), if applied literally, produced taxable ordinary income to the extent that the liabilities exceeded the zero basis of the receivables. In several litigated cases, however, the courts rescued taxpayers from the rigorous application of §357(c) by holding that (1) §357(c) did not apply to assumptions of "deductible" liabilities of the transferor, or (2) the transferor, while realizing §357(c) income, was entitled to an offsetting deduction to the extent that the transferee corporation paid the liabilities in the year of the transfer.[70]

Section 357(c)(3), as added in 1978, codifies the first of these two escape hatches into law, but it does not affect the status of these liabilities under §357(b). A correlative amendment to §358(d) eliminates these deductible liabilities in calculating the basis of the stock received by the transferor.[71]

4. Character of §357(c) gain. Gain recognized by virtue of §357(c) must be reported as ordinary income, long-term capital gain, or short-term capital gain according to the nature and the holding period of the transferred property. The language of §357(c) does not attempt to characterize the *nature* of this gain, it is merely an exception to nonrecognition treatment under §351.[72] Similarly, if more than one type of property is transferred, the recognized gain apparently must be allocated among the various classes of assets in proportion to their relative fair market values.[73]

5. Computation of amount of §357(c) gain. In determining whether §357(c) is applicable, the aggregate amount of the liabilities is compared with the aggregate adjusted basis of the assets transferred. To return to the

---

[70] For the principal pre-1978 cases and the position taken by the Service with respect to them, see Rev. Rul. 80-199, 1980-2 CB 122. See generally Kahn & Oesterle, A Definition of "Liabilities" in Internal Revenue Code Sections 357 and 358(d), 73 Mich. L. Rev. 461 (1975), and other articles cited therein.

See also William P. Orr, 78 TC 1059 (1982) (refundable customer deposits did not constitute deductible liabilities under pre-1978 law), which seems equally applicable in construing §357(c)(3)(A)(i), as enacted in 1978.

[71] See infra ¶ 3.10, note 114. See generally Truskowski, Section 358(d) and the Cash Basis Taxpayer, 56 Taxes 555 (1978); Banoff, Incorporation of Partnerships With Negative Capital Accounts: Can Gain Be Avoided? 60 Taxes 411 (1982).

[72] It may be argued that the character of the asset is the controlling factor in determining the nature of the recognized §357(c) gain, precluding resort to the hotchpot rules of §1231; but it seems relatively clear that Congress merely dealt with the recognition of gain under §357(c), leaving the classification of that gain to other general definitional rules in the Code. The Service assumed this result in Rev. Rul. 60-302, 1960-2 CB 223 (holding that §1239 applied to gain recognized under §357(c)), and this conclusion would likewise embrace such provisions as §§1245 and 1250.

[73] See discussion supra ¶ 3.05; Regs. §1.357-2(b).

previous example, if A had transferred not only property with a basis of $10,000 subject to a mortgage of $30,000 but also unencumbered property with a basis of $10,000, the gain to be reported would be only $10,000 (liability of $30,000, less aggregate basis of $20,000).[74] Although it may at first seem strange that A can reduce his gain by transferring other property along with the mortgaged property, the theory underlying §357(c)'s use of the total basis of all property transferred as the measure of A's gain may be that the properties transferred constitute a single investment of $20,000 from which A's total return so far amounts to $30,000.

If there are two or more transferors, it would seem appropriate to apply §357(c) on a person-by-person basis rather than to aggregate all property transferred by all transferors, but neither §357(c) itself nor the regulations are explicit on this point. To be sure, the language of §357(c) ("the total of the adjusted basis of the property transferred pursuant to such exchange") may imply that the total basis of all properties transferred *by all transferors* is to be employed in determining the gain, but an absurd result would be produced thereby. Thus, if A transferred properties with a total basis of $20,000 but subject to a mortgage of $30,000 and B simultaneously transferred unencumbered property with a basis of $7,000, the gain to be recognized under §357(c), if computed by aggregating A and B, would be $3,000 (mortgage of $30,000 less total basis of $27,000). This result is curious, since A has enjoyed an economic gain of $10,000; it would be even more curious if the $3,000 gain thus computed were allocated between A and B, since the value of the property transferred by B, and hence the value of the stock or securities received by him, may be less than the adjusted basis of the property transferred by him. An aggregate approach to §357(c) would also produce difficulties in the calculation of the transferors' basis for the stock and securities received by them. Since the language of §357(c) does not unmistakably require A and B to be lumped together, it should be applied person by person so that on the foregoing facts A would recognize $10,000 of gain regardless of the basis of property transferred by other persons.[75]

6. Overlap between §§357(b) and 357(c). It is possible for a transfer of property to be subject to both §357(b), because of the transferor's improper purpose, and to §357(c), because the liabilities exceed the basis of the transferred property. In this event, §357(b) takes precedence, with the result that the entire amount of liabilities, not just the excess of the liabilities over the property's adjusted basis, is boot.[76]

---

[74] Regs. §1.357-2(a).

[75] See Rev. Rul. 66-142, 1966-2 CB 66, which so holds.

[76] An interesting problem in the relationship between §§357(b) and 357(c) is to be found in W.H.B. Simpson, supra note 65, holding that the taxpayer's effort to

7. Effect of default by transferee corporation. Both §§357(b) and 357(c) compute the transferor's gain on the assumption that the indebtedness giving rise to the gain will be paid by the transferee corporation. If the transferor is called upon to pay the debt as a result of the transferee's default, the outlay should be either added to the basis of the transferor's stock or securities received on the exchange or deducted as a loss.

8. Overlap between §§351 and 304. In an acquisition by one corporation of another, the acquiring corporation often borrows to purchase the stock of the target corporation and then shifts liability for the debt to another corporation in a §351 transaction (e.g., by transferring the target company's stock, subject to the debt, to a new holding company). If assuming or taking subject to the acquiring party's purchase-money debt is viewed as a distribution of "property" within the meaning of §304, which relates to redemptions and similar transactions between brother-sister and parent-subsidiary corporations, the acquiring party may get a nasty shock: The amount of the debt may have to be treated as a dividend. In general, however, such an outcome is negated by §304(b)(3)(B), which determines which provision takes precedence when §§304 and 351 overlap.[77]

¶ 3.07　CONTROL: THE 80 PERCENT RULE

Section 351 applies only if the transferors of property are "in control" of the corporation, as defined in §368(c), immediately after the exchange.[78] Their control need not be acquired through the exchange itself, however; §351 embraces a transfer of property to a corporation already controlled by the transferor as well as transfers to newly organized corporations.[79]

---

avoid the effect of §357(c) by keeping the liabilities assumed to an amount just below the basis of the transferred assets did not constitute tax avoidance under §357(b); see also Rev. Rul. 78-330, 1978-2 CB 147 (parent shareholder's cancellation of subsidiary's debt prior to merger into sister subsidiary in order to avoid §357(c) gain did not violate §357(b), citing *Simpson*).

[77] See infra ¶ 9.12.

[78] For cases and rulings holding that persons transferring nominal amounts of property cannot be counted in determining whether the persons transferring property have the requisite control, see supra note 15. Moreover, the control group is limited to persons transferring property to the corporation whose control is relevant; see Rev. Rul. 84-44, 1984-1 CB 105 (person transferring property to subsidiary of controlled corporation not counted). For problems in determining whether persons acquiring stock or securities for cash constitute part of the control group, see supra note 45.

[79] See, e.g., Rev. Rul. 73-473, 1973-2 CB 115.

The term "control" is defined by §368(c) to mean the ownership of (1) at least 80 percent of the total combined voting power of all classes of stock entitled to vote, and (2) at least 80 percent of the total number of shares of all other classes of stock of the corporation.[80] In many cases, §368(c) presents no problems of interpretation, either because the corporation issues only one class of stock or because the transferors receive all stock of all classes. This is fortunate, because there are almost no guides to the meaning of "total combined voting power" or of "stock entitled to vote."[81] The term "stock entitled to vote" presumably does not include stock having merely the power under local law to vote on such extraordinary events as charter amendments, mergers, sales of assets, and so forth, since in most states all classes of stock have voting power of this character; if such stock were regarded as stock entitled to vote, the statutory category of other classes of stock would be a vacuum. As to stock with contingent voting rights, such as preferred stock that may vote for directors if dividends are passed for a stated period, Regs. §1.302-3(a)(3) states that such stock is generally not voting stock until the specified event occurs, but it may be that "stock entitled to vote," the term employed in §368(c), is not identical with "voting stock" as that term is used in §302 and elsewhere.[82]

Once the stock entitled to vote has been identified and segregated, it is necessary to determine whether the transferors of property own 80 percent or more of the total combined voting power. Presumably, this requires a realistic weighting of the stock's right to vote, so that ownership of less than 80 percent of the total market value or the total number of shares may qualify, but difficulties may arise if the shares are not fungible as regards their power to vote. It is usually assumed that the computation of total combined voting power is not to take account of shareholders' voting agreements or

---

[80] For this purpose, ownership must be direct, not by attribution; see Brams v. CIR, 734 F2d 290 (6th Cir. 1984); Rev. Rul. 56-613, 1956-2 CB 212; Rev. Rul. 78-130, 1978-1 CB 114.

[81] This phrase is also to be found in §302(b)(2)(B), infra ¶ 9.04. See also §1504(a), relating to consolidated returns and employing the terms "voting power" and "nonvoting stock" (infra ¶ 15.21) (must have 80 percent of vote and value here). The Tax Reform Act of 1986 conformed the control definition of various other sections (e.g., §§332 and 338) to the consolidated return eligibility provisions in §1504(a) (infra ¶ 15.21), although still with no attribution rules. The proposed Subchapter C Revision Act of 1985 (supra note 28) would do the same for §351.

[82] See Rev. Rul. 66-339, 1966-2 CB 274 (voting agreements, warrants, options, rights, and convertible debentures held not voting securities). Whether disproportionate voting rights will destroy voting-stock status is unclear; for example, if stock has an 80 percent interest in earnings and assets, but only a 10 percent vote, it may not qualify as true voting stock under §368(c). For other consequences of voting-stock classification, see infra ¶¶ 14.13 and 14.14 (Type B and Type C reorganizations).

similar arrangements even though they may alter the balance of power; but the question is not foreclosed by case law or rulings.[83]

If there are other classes of stock, the transferors to qualify under §351 must own at least 80 percent of the total number of such shares. There is no good reason why the statute should require control of such stock to be ascertained by total number (a test that has no relevance to the policy underlying §351) rather than by market value, except perhaps to avoid the necessity of an appraisal. Although §368(c) appears to lump all nonvoting shares together regardless of class or privileges, the Service ruled that "80 percent of the total number of shares of all other classes of stock," as used in §368(c), means 80 percent of the total number of shares of *each class* of stock.[84]

¶ 3.08   TWO OR MORE TRANSFERORS

As the language of §351 explicitly recognizes, there is sometimes more than one transferor of property. In such cases, the transaction qualifies as tax-free under §351 if the transferors *as a group* are in control of the corporation immediately after the exchange.[85]

When there are two or more transferors, each one ordinarily, as a result of arm's-length bargaining, receives stock or securities with a fair market value equal to that of the assets he transfers; but on occasion there may be discrepancies between the value of the assets given up and the value of the stock or securities received. Do such variations in value affect the tax consequences of the transaction?

Before 1954, the statute provided for nonrecognition of gain or loss in the case of an exchange by two or more persons "only if the amount of the stock and securities received by each is substantially in proportion to his interest in the property prior to the exchange." The policy underlying this requirement, which if violated led to the full recognition of gain or loss by all parties to the exchange, was obscure, and there were also uncertainties in its

---

[83] See Federal Grain Corp., 18 BTA 242 (1929) (control means ownership of the voting stock, not actual exercise of the voting rights). Rev. Rul. 63-226, 1963-2 CB 341, held that shareholder restrictive voting agreements created more than one class of stock, disqualifying a Subchapter S election, but was revoked by Rev. Rul. 73-611, 1973-2 CB 312; see infra ¶ 6.02.

[84] See Rev. Rul. 59-259, 1959-2 CB 115. Compare §1504 (infra ¶ 15.21), where parent must own 80 percent of vote and value of the subsidiary's stock in order to consolidate.

[85] See Burr Oaks Corp., 43 TC 635, 651 (1965), aff'd, 365 F2d 24 (7th Cir. 1966), cert. denied, 385 US 1007 (1967).

application.[86] It was eliminated in 1954; the Senate Report on the 1954 Code states that §351 is to be applied "irrespective of any disproportion of the amount of stock or securities received by [a transferor] as a result of the transfer."[87] The report goes on, however, to say that if the disproportion in value "results in an event taxable under other provisions of this code, your committee intends that such distribution will be taxed in accordance with its true nature."

This theme is embodied in the regulations, which provide that "in appropriate cases the transaction may be treated as if the stock and securities had first been received in proportion [to the value of the property transferred] and then some of such stock and securities had been used to make gifts [subject to gift tax under §2501], to pay compensation [taxable as income under §61(a)(1)], or to satisfy obligations of the transferor of any kind."[88] If a transaction is so realigned, in addition to the tax consequences suggested by the extract from the regulations, the transferor may have to recognize gain or loss on his constructive disposition of the stock or securities and may in some situations be entitled to a business expense deduction under §162(a).[89] A realignment of stock may also affect the computation of control, since the transferors of property may be treated as constructively owning, immediately after the exchange, more shares than are issued to them, at least if their use of shares to make gifts, pay compensation, and so forth, is not an integral step in the entire transaction.[90]

¶ 3.09   CONTROL IMMEDIATELY AFTER THE EXCHANGE

The statute requires the transferors of property to be in control of the corporation "immediately after the exchange." The regulations say of this

---

[86] See generally Hoffman, The Substantial Proportionment Requirement of [1939 Code] Section 112(b)(5), 5 Tax L. Rev. 235 (1950).

[87] S. Rep. No. 1622, 83d Cong., 2d Sess. 264 (1954).

[88] Regs. §1.351-1(b)(1); see also the cross references in §§351(f)(3) and 351(f)(4).

[89] See Rev. Rul. 73-233, 1973-1 CB 179 (threshhold capital contribution of stock by majority shareholder to induce minority shareholders to vote for merger realigned as pro rata reorganization exchange, followed by taxable disposition by majority shareholder and receipt of income by minority shareholders for their vote); Rev. Rul. 76-454, 1976-2 CB 102 (A owned all of X; A organized Y with $50 cash and got all Y common stock, while X bought all Y preferred stock for $250; on liquidation, assets of Y were split equally between common and preferred; held valid §351 exchange despite disproportion in favor of common, but transaction realigned, and X deemed to have received its allocable portion of Y common and to have distributed it to A as a dividend).

[90] See infra ¶ 3.09 on the phrase "immediately after the exchange."

requirement: "The phrase 'immediately after the exchange' does not necessarily require simultaneous exchanges by two or more persons, but comprehends a situation where the rights of the parties have been previously defined and the execution of the agreement proceeds with an expedition consistent with orderly procedure."[91] Under this interpretation, the stockholdings of two or more transferors can be aggregated in determining whether they control the corporation immediately after the exchange if their transfers are part of a single transaction. Thus, if *A* owns all the stock of a corporation, consisting of 100 shares, and if the corporation is to be expanded by issuing 200 shares to *B* for property, and 200 more shares to *C* for other property, *B* and *C* will be in control of the corporation immediately after the exchange (by virtue of owning 400 out of 500 shares, or 80 percent), even though *B*'s exchange is not simultaneous with *C*'s.

There has been litigation in abundance over the requirement that the transferors control the transferee corporation immediately after the exchange, the principal problem being whether the statute is satisfied if the transferors own 80 percent or more of the stock for a moment but thereafter dispose of some shares so that they are left with less than the 80 percent required by §§351 and 368(c). Such a loss of control may occur if the transferors dispose of part of their stock to donees or purchasers, if the corporation issues additional stock to investors or employees, or in some other manner.[92]

Although some early decisions held or suggested that momentary control was sufficient,[93] the statutory requirement is not satisfied under current law if the transferors of property agree beforehand to transfer enough of their stock to lose control or if such a transfer is an integral part of the plan of incorporation. An illustration of this attitude is *Manhattan Building Co.*, which concerned the transfer of certain assets by one Miniger to Electric Auto-Lite Co. in exchange for 250,000 shares of common stock and $3 million in bonds. Miniger had purchased the assets in question with borrowed funds under an agreement requiring him to transfer the assets to Auto-Lite in exchange for the stock and bonds, to deliver the bonds and 75,000 shares of stock to the lender (a firm of investment bankers), and to turn back 49,000 shares to Auto-Lite as a contribution to capital. The question before the court was whether the predecessor of §351 was applicable to this transaction, under which Miniger fleetingly owned 100 percent of the stock, but less than the requisite 80 percent when the plan was fully consummated.

---

[91] Regs. §1.351-1(a)(1).

[92] When a corporation is a transferor of property, it may distribute its share of the control stock to its own shareholders or transfer it to a subsidiary or affiliate; for the effect of such transactions, see §351(c), discussed infra text at notes 102–104.

[93] See, e.g., Portland Oil Co. v. CIR, supra note 9.

This depends upon whether the transfer of assets to Auto-Lite in exchange for its stock and bonds and the transfer of stock and bonds to the underwriters were mutually interdependent transactions. The test is, were the steps taken so interdependent that the legal relations created by one transaction would have been fruitless without a completion of the series.... In the present case when the transfer of assets to Auto-Lite occurred on July 17, 1922, Miniger was under a binding contract to deliver the bonds and 75,000 shares of stock to the underwriters and to return 49,000 shares to the corporation.... Miniger could not have completed the purchase of the assets without the cash supplied by the underwriters and could not have had the cash except in exchange for the bonds and stock and could not have secured the bonds and stock except for the assets. After the exchanges Miniger had ... less than 80 percent, of the voting stock. At no time did he have the right to hold more.... The 1922 transaction was taxable as the petitioner contends.[94]

In reaching this conclusion, the court cited and distinguished *American Bantam Car Co. v. CIR*, which also involved a loss of control as a result of an underwriting agreement but which was held to qualify for nonrecognition under the predecessor of §351.[95] In this case, the owners of a manufacturing business transferred its assets with $500 in cash to a new corporation in exchange for all of the common stock under a plan calling for a sale of preferred stock by the corporation to the public through underwriters who were to receive, in addition to their underwriting discounts and commissions, certain amounts of the common stock (from the transferor shareholders) when

---

[94] Manhattan Bldg. Co., 27 TC 1032, supra note 8, at 1042. For rulings and other cases of like import, see Hazeltine Corp. v. CIR, 89 F2d 513 (3d Cir. 1937); Intermountain Lumber Co., 65 TC 1025 (1976) (binding obligation by incorporator to sell 50 percent of stock broke control); Rev. Rul. 70-140, 1970-1 CB 73 (incorporation followed by planned disposition of stock broke control); Rev. Rul. 70-225, 1970-1 CB 80 (spin-off of new subsidiary, followed by planned disposition of distributed stock, a taxable transaction); Rev. Rul. 70-522, 1970-2 CB 81 (reciprocal agreement to exchange 49 percent of stock of newly organized subsidiaries broke control for both transferors); supra ¶ 3.04 and infra ¶¶ 3.19, 14.51 and 14.52. Compare Penn-Dixie Steel Corp., 69 TC 837 (1978) (cross-options). But see generally Keller, The Tax Effects of a Shareholder's Post-Incorporation Sale of Stock: A Reappraisal, 2 Tax L.J. 89 (1985) (arguing against this view).

Transfers by one member of the control group to another do not destroy the requisite control; see Rev. Rul. 79-194, 1979-1 CB 145 (Situation 1); in the ruling's Situation 2, however, control was lost because 51 percent of the stock was sold to investors who had transferred merely nominal amounts of property to the corporation and who could not, therefore, be treated as transferors of property in determining control (see supra note 15).

[95] American Bantam Car Co., 11 TC 397 (1948), aff'd per curiam, 177 F2d 513 (3d Cir. 1949), cert. denied, 339 US 920 (1950).

and if they succeeded in selling the preferred stock to the public. The transfer of the assets to the new corporation for 300,000 shares of common stock occurred on June 3, 1936; five days later, the new corporation executed a contract with the underwriters for the sale of the preferred stock, and the shareholders agreed that the underwriters would receive 100,000 shares of their common stock in specified installments as and if the preferred stock was sold; in October 1937, the underwriters received 87,900 shares of the common stock for their services. Although the transferors thus held less than 80 percent of the common stock after October 1937, when the 87,900 shares were transferred to the underwriters, the Tax Court held that the requisite control in the transferors existed in June 1936—immediately after the exchange—and that the loss of control in October 1937 was not an integral part of the transaction:

> The understanding with the underwriters for disposing of the preferred stock, however important, was not a *sine qua non* in the general plan, without which no other step would have been taken. While the incorporation and exchange of assets would have been purposeless one without the other, yet both would have been carried out even though the contemplated method of marketing the preferred stock might fail. The very fact that in the contracts of June 8, 1936, the associates retained the right to cancel the marketing order and, consequently the underwriters' means to own common stock issued to the associates, refutes the proposition that the legal relations resulting from the steps of organizing the corporation and transferring assets to it would have been fruitless without the sale of the preferred stock in the manner contemplated.[96]

In a later case, the Tax Court summarized this freedom-of-action approach as follows:

> A determination of "ownership," as that term is used in section 368(c) and for purposes of control under section 351, depends upon the obligations and freedom of action of the transferee with respect to the stock when he acquired it from the corporation. Such traditional ownership attributes as legal title, voting rights, and possession of stock certificates are not conclusive. If the transferee, as part of the transaction by which the shares were acquired, has irrevocably foregone or relinquished at that time the legal right to determine whether to keep the shares, ownership in such shares is lacking for purposes of section 351. By contrast, if there are no restrictions upon freedom of action at the time he acquired the shares, it is immaterial how soon thereafter the transferee elects to dispose of his stock or whether such disposition is in

---

[96] Id. at 406–407.

accord with a preconceived plan not amounting to a binding obligation.[97]

As generalizations go, this seems quite satisfactory, with an added caveat for
situations where the loss of control, although not pursuant to a binding obligation, is both part of a preconceived plan and also a sine qua non thereof.
One can then say, in the words of the *Manhattan Building Co.* case, that "the
steps taken [were] so interdependent that the legal relations created by one
transaction would have been fruitless without a completion of the series."[98]
Moreover, in applying the binding obligation principle, a distinction should
be drawn between sales of their stock *by members of the control group* that can
result in a loss of control (because the buyers transfer nothing to the corporation and hence do not become part of the control group) and sales of stock *by
the corporation itself*, since purchasers from the corporation can become part
of the control group by virtue of their transfers of cash to the corporation.[99]
    Although the courts have not distinguished between commercial and
noncommercial transactions when deciding whether a loss of control after
the exchange is fatal, much can be said for treating these situations differently. If the transferors of property receive all of the stock of the transferee
corporation and then reduce their ownership below the requisite 80 percent
by giving some of the stock to their spouses or children, the courts have
usually found it possible to apply §351. For example, *Wilgard Realty Co. v.
CIR* concerned a transfer of property for all the stock of a newly organized
corporation. On the same day that the transferor received the stock, he gave
more than 20 percent of it to members of his family. The court held that the
transfer of the property to the corporation was a tax-free exchange under
§351, not on the narrow ground that the transferor owned the shares of the
corporation for an instant, but on a broader ground:

> In the absence of any restriction upon [the transferor's] freedom of
> action after he acquired the stock, he had "immediately after the
> exchange" as much control of the [corporation] as if he had not before
> made up his mind to give away most of his stock and with it conse-
> quently his control. And that is equally true whether the transaction is

---

[97] Intermountain Lumber Co., supra note 94, at 1031–1032 (numerous citations
omitted).

[98] Supra text at note 94.

[99] See Rev. Rul. 78-294, 1978-2 CB 141. But see Rev. Rul. 79-70, 1979-1 CB 144
(where *X* transferred property for *N*'s stock and sold 40 percent of the stock to *Y*,
which paid cash to *N* for *N*'s securities, *Y* is not part of control group; it owned no *N*
stock before the transaction and acquired none from *N* in the transaction). For
detailed analysis, see Tillinghast & Paully, The Effect of the Collateral Issuance of
Stock or Securities on the "Control" Requirement of Section 351, 37 Tax L. Rev. 251
(1982); Keller, supra note 94.

viewed as a whole or as a series of separate steps. . . . Where the recipient of the stock on the exchange has not only the legal title to it "immediately after the exchange" but also the legal right then to determine whether or not to keep it with the control that flows from such ownership, the requirements of the statute are fully satisfied.[100]

The same principle has been applied to a case in which the stock was issued directly to the donees on the sensible ground that what matters is "the power of the transferor [of property] to designate who will receive the stock rather than the precise moment that the power was exercised."[101]

Finally, note should be taken of §351(c), providing that if a corporate transferor receives stock in §351 exchange, the fact that it distributes part or all of the stock to its own shareholders is not taken into account. Thus, despite a transferor's fleeting ownership of the shares, they are counted in determining whether the distributing corporation is in control of the transferee corporation immediately after the property-for-stock exchange.[102]

Instead of distributing stock upstream as explicitly permitted by §351(c), a corporate transferor of property may wish to transfer stock received in an §351 transaction downstream to a subsidiary. There is no counterpart of §351(c) exonerating such transfers, nor is there a statutory sanction for attributing the subsidiary-held stock back to the parent in determining whether the transferors of property own 80 percent of the stock immediately after the exchange.[103] If, however, the transfer of the stock is not an integral part of the plan, the freedom-of-action principle discussed previously would seem to apply[104] so that the control requirement would be satisfied despite the prompt transfer of part or all of the stock.

----

[100] Wilgard Realty Co. v. CIR, 127 F2d 514, 516 (2d Cir.), cert. denied, 317 US 655 (1942).

[101] D'Angelo Assocs. v. CIR, supra note 33, at 133; see also Stanton v. US, 512 F2d 13 (3d Cir. 1975). These cases leave little room for the contrary holding of Fahs v. Florida Mach. & Foundry Co., supra note 16, unless it is construed to involve an absence of control pursuant to a long-standing contractual obligation contemplating that the transferor of property would receive only one-half of the stock.

[102] See Rev. Rul. 68-298, 1968-1 CB 139 (corporation transferred property to newly formed subsidiary in exchange for all of its stock and distributed 25 percent thereof in redemption of one of its shareholder's stock; held §351(c) applied even though distributee's stock-ownership interest in distributing corporation was terminated by distribution); Rev. Rul. 62-138, 1962-2 CB 95 (§351(c) applied in context of corporate division under §355).

Proposed legislation (the Subchapter C Revision Act of 1985, supra note 28) would expand the anti-decontrol concept of §351(c) to include dispositions of recently incorporated active business subsidiaries by corporate transferors.

[103] See supra note 80.

[104] Supra text at note 97. See also Regs. §1.368-2(j)(4), infra ¶ 14.15.

The control requirement looks to the ownership of the transferee corporation's stock immediately after the exchange; it says nothing about ownership of the transferred property. In a 1977 ruling, the Service passed on the status of a transfer by corporation *P* of property to its wholly owned *S-1* in exchange for additional *S-1* stock. This transfer was followed by a transfer by *S-1* of the same property to *its* wholly owned subsidiary, *S-2*, in exchange for additional *S-2* stock. The Service ruled that the transfers, although admittedly parts of a single plan, constituted two separate transactions, each of which satisfied the requirements of §351; it did not succumb to the temptation to rule that in effect *P* transferred the property to *S-2* in exchange for *S-1* stock and that *P* was not in control of *S-2* immediately after the hypothetical exchange.[105] A 1983 ruling amplified the 1977 ruling to cover a plan in which the transferor's wholly owned subsidiary transferred the assets to an affiliated partnership rather than to a second-tier subsidiary.[106]

Do the transferors have control immediately after the exchange if another person has an option to acquire enough shares, either from the corporation or from the transferors themselves, to terminate their control? In the *American Bantam Car Co.* case, the Tax Court relied in part on the fact that the transferors would lose control only if the underwriters sold enough preferred stock to the public to earn the promised common stock.[107] This approach, which looks to the likelihood that the option will be exercised, has much to commend it. The option can be properly disregarded if there is a genuine possibility that it will not be taken up; but if its exercise is a foregone conclusion (e.g., if only a nominal consideration is payable for valuable stock), it may take the transaction outside of §351 unless the optionholder can himself be regarded as a transferor of property to be aggregated with the other transferors in computing control or unless the transfer of property and the option are not integral steps in a single transaction.

¶ 3.10   THE TRANSFEROR'S BASIS

When gain or loss goes unrecognized at the time of an exchange, the transferor's basis for the property given up is ordinarily preserved and applied to the property received. Section 358 applies this principle to an

---

[105] Rev. Rul. 77-449, 1977-2 CB 110; see also Rev. Rul. 83-34, 1983-1 CB 79 (same result where subsidiaries were 80 percent instead of wholly owned). See generally Fisher, Does Rev. Rul. 77-449 Signal a Change in IRS Application of the Step-Transaction Doctrine? 51 J. Tax'n 76 (1979).

[106] Rev. Rul. 83-156, 1983-2 CB 66.

[107] Supra note 95. See also Rev. Rul. 82-150, 1982-2 CB 110 (call option may be the equivalent of present ownership).

exchange under §351. In the simplest situation—i.e., an exchange under §351 of property solely for stock or securities (nonrecognition property)— §358(a)(1) provides that the basis of the stock or securities received is the same as the basis of the property transferred. If several classes of stock and securities are received, §358(b)(1) requires an allocation of the basis of the property transferred among the various classes of stock and securities received on the exchange, and Regs. §1.358-2(b) provides that the allocation be in proportion to the market values of the stock and securities received. Thus, if the basis of the transferred property was $50,000 and the transferor received in exchange common stock worth $60,000 and bonds worth $40,000, the basis of the stock would be $30,000 (60,000/100,000 × 50,000) and the basis of the bonds would be $20,000 (40,000/100,000 × 50,000). Assuming no later fluctuations in value, the transferor would realize $30,000 of gain on selling the stock and $20,000 of gain on selling the bonds. This total gain of $50,000, it will be noted, would be equal to the gain that went unrecognized on the exchange itself because of §351(a)—i.e., the difference between the basis of the property transferred and the value of the stock and bonds received in exchange.

The gain of $50,000 would ordinarily qualify as capital gain, regardless of the nature of the property. If, however, the bonds did not bear interest at the rates specified by §§483 and 1274, interest may have to be imputed under those provisions; even if the stated interest rate were adequate, the bonds may be subject to the market discount rules of §1276 because their market value ($40,000) exceeds their adjusted basis ($20,000).[108]

If the transferred property's basis in the above example had been $150,000, the stock basis would be $90,000 and the basis of the bonds would be $60,000, reflecting a potential loss of $30,000 in the stock and $20,000 in the bonds that equals the loss unrecognized because of §351. Proposed reform legislation, however, would step down the transferor's outside basis to $100,000 (the value of the transferred property) in the case of incorpora-

---

[108] The imputed interest rules of §483 apply to "any contract for the sale or exchange of any property," including nonrecognition transactions, while §1274 applies even more broadly to all debt instruments issued for property and virtually subsumes §483 after 1984. See Eustice, The Tax Reform Act of 1984; A Selective Analysis, (Warren, Gorham & Lamont, Inc., 1984) ¶ 2.02[2]; ¶ 4.42; Branda, Jr., Imputed Interest and Fictitious Sales Prices: The Unexpected Effects of Section 483, 21 J. Tax'n 194 (1964). For the application of the market discount rules of §1276, see Joint Committee on Taxation, General Explanation of the Tax Reform Act of 1984, supra note 69, which states that market discount is created by §351 exchanges "under a literal interpretation of the statute," but that Congress did not intend this result; §1278(a)(1)(C)(i), enacted in 1986, providing that the term "market discount bond" does not include bonds acquired by the taxpayer at their original issue. Under §1276(d)(1)(C), however, *accrued* market discount on bonds transferred in a §351 exchange is taxable at that time; supra note 24.

tion transfers of property with a built-in loss; thus the basis of the stock and bonds in the above example would be $60,000 and $40,000 respectively if this reform proposal were enacted. [109]

Section 358 is also applicable if the transferor received boot on the exchange. In such a case, §351(b)(1) would have required him to recognize his gain on the exchange (if any were realized, i.e., if the value of what he received exceeded the adjusted basis of the property he gave up) to the extent of the value of the boot. Section 358(a)(2) provides that the boot (except money) be given a basis equal to its fair market value. And §358(a)(1) provides that the basis of the nonrecognition property (i.e., the stock or securities received on the exchange) is the same as the basis of the property given up, minus the money and the fair market value of the boot received, plus the gain recognized on the exchange. [110]

To illustrate: Assume that the transferor of property that had an adjusted basis of $4,000 received on the exchange stock and bonds worth $8,000, cash in the amount of $1,500, and other property worth $500. His realized gain of $6,000 (value received of $10,000, less adjusted basis of $4,000) would be recognized under §351(b) to the extent of the boot, or $2,000. The basis of the other property received, under §358(a)(2), would be its fair market value, $500. The basis of the stock and bonds (the nonrecognition property) would be $4,000 (adjusted basis of property given up, $4,000, less cash of $1,500, and other property of $500, plus gain recognized of $2,000), to be allocated between the stock and bonds in proportion to their respective values. [111] The computation is as follows:

---

[109] See Subchapter C Revision Act of 1985, supra note 28.

[110] For the effect on basis of installment sale treatment under §453, see Prop. Regs. §1.453-1(f)(3)(ii) (transferor gets immediate basis credit). But see infra notes 117 and 119 for the transferee's basis (step-up tracks transferor's reporting of gain).

Rev. Rul. 70-271, 1970-1 CB 166 holds that additional payments by the transferor (e.g., liability assumptions by the transferor) result in an upward basis adjustment; see also Rev. Rul. 74-503, 1974-2 CB 117 (where transferor's own stock is transferred, basis is determined under §362(a), not §358, and basis in its own stock is always zero).

Section 358(a)(1)(B)(i), providing for a further upward adjustment if any part of the property received on the exchange was treated as a dividend, is primarily concerned with certain transactions under §306 (infra ch. 10), according to the Senate Report on the 1954 Code. See S. Rep. No. 1622, supra note 87, at 271. In unusual circumstances, however, the provision might be applicable to an exchange under §351. See infra ¶ 3.16.

[111] The same result for the nonrecognition property can be reached by starting with its fair market value ($8,000) and reducing this by the realized but unrecognized gain ($4,000) (or, in case of a loss, increasing it by the unrecognized loss).

(1) Amount realized:
    (a)   Stock and bonds $ 8,000
    (b)   Cash   1,500
    (c)   Other property   500
(2) Total $10,000
(3) Less: Adjusted basis of transferred property   4,000
(4) Gain realized $ 6,000
(5) Gain recognized (((1)(b) plus (1)(c), or (4),
          whichever is less) $2,000
(6) Basis of property received:
    (a)   Cash   NA
    (b)   Other property (fair market value) $ 500
    (c)   Stock and bonds (line (3), less (1)(b) and
              (1)(c), plus (5)) $4,000

If the stock and bonds were then sold for their market value ($8,000), the owner would recognize $4,000 of gain, which, added to the $2,000 of gain recognized at the time of the §351 exchange, would equal his full economic gain of $6,000 (total value of $10,000 received on the exchange, less adjusted basis of original property of $4,000).

The reader will have noted that the basis of the property received on the exchange reflects, under §358(a)(1)(B)(ii), the "amount of gain to the taxpayer which *was recognized*" on the §351 exchange. What if the transferor treats an exchange as nontaxable but later claims a stepped-up basis for the stock and securities received by him on the ground that gain *should have been recognized*? There is authority by analogy for allowing him to use the stepped-up basis, at least where the failure to recognize gain on the exchange was not fraudulent or otherwise blameworthy.[112]

Proposed legislation (the Subchapter C Revision Act of 1985, supra note 28) would treat debt securities as boot per se and would also step down outside basis where potential loss property was incorporated.

[112] See Margaret S. Bullock, ¶ 44,406 P-H Memo. TC (1944); Bennet v. Helvering, 137 F2d 537 (2d Cir. 1943); see also Fahs v. Florida Mach. & Foundry Co., supra note 16, holding that the transferee corporation, whose basis for the transferred assets is also dependent upon whether the exchange was a taxable transaction, is not estopped by the errors of the transferor. However, if the transferor insists upon a stepped-up basis, the government may assess an additional tax against him for the year of the exchange, notwithstanding the running of the statute of limitations. See §1312(7); Regs. §1.1312-7(c), Example (1)(ii) (which assumes that the transferor is not estopped to claim a stepped-up basis); Burford, Basis of Property After Erroneous Treatment of a Prior Transaction, 12 Tax L. Rev. 365, 370 (1957).

If the transferee corporation assumed a liability of the transferor or took property subject to a liability, §358(d) provides that the amount of the liability should be treated as money received by the transferor upon the exchange. This requirement, which is applicable whether the liability gave rise to income at the time of the exchange under §357(b) or §357(c), or came within the general rule of §357(a),[113] has the effect of reducing the basis that would otherwise be allocated under §358(a)(1) to the nonrecognition property by the amount of the liability.

> *To illustrate:* If *A* transfers property with a cost basis of $50,000 to a corporation for all of its stock plus the assumption of a $30,000 mortgage, *A*'s basis for the stock will be $20,000. If *A* then sells the stock for $25,000, he will realize $5,000 of gain. Provided the mortgage is discharged in due course, this tax treatment accords with economic reality: *A*'s net investment was $20,000 (the cost of the land less the amount of the mortgage) and he ultimately realized $25,000.
>
> If the transferee corporation fails to pay the debt at maturity and *A* is called upon to pay it, however, *A* would presumably be entitled to increase the basis of his stock (if he still owns it) by the amount of his outlay or to take a deduction under §165 or §166. There is a possibility that if the stock had been sold by *A* before he was called upon to pay the debt, his loss on payment would be treated as a capital loss because the sale of the stock was a capital gain transaction.[114]

On selling stock or securities received tax-free under §351(a), the transferor determines his holding period under §1223(1) by including the period during which he held the transferred property (tacking), provided the transferred property was either a capital asset or a §1231(b) asset. If the transferred property consisted of a mixture of capital assets, §1231(b) assets, and noncapital assets, as in the ordinary case of incorporating a going business, it may be

---

For the converse situation, see Gooding v. US, 326 F2d 988 (Ct. Cl.), cert. denied, 379 US 834 (1964) (following a court determination that an exchange, which the taxpayer-transferor had treated as partially taxable, was wholly tax-free as to the corporate transferee, the transferor sought a refund under §§1311–1314; held §1312(7) applied, although it would seem that a §1311 adjustment should have awaited the outcome of a dispute on a sale by the taxpayer of his stock). See §1312(7)(B); Regs. §1.1312-7(c), Example (5); Turner Constr. Co., 364 F2d 525 (2d Cir. 1966); for opinion on remand, see Prentis v. US, supra note 33; infra note 117.

[113] See supra ¶ 3.06.

[114] See Rees Blow Pipe Mfg. Co., 41 TC 598 (1964), aff'd per curiam, 342 F2d 990 (9th Cir. 1965) (comparable result under §1031); Thatcher v. CIR, 533 F2d 1114 (9th Cir. 1976) (transferor's stock basis zero because of offsetting deduction against §357(c) liability assumption gain); see also §358(d)(2) excluding liabilities exempted by §357(c)(3) from the operation of §358(d); supra note 71; infra note 118.

necessary to make an allocation under §1223(1), with the result either that some of the shares or securities received will have a holding period dating from the §351 exchange while others will have longer holding periods, or that each share or security will be divided for holding period purposes.

Tacking is provided for by §1223(1) if the property whose holding period is to be determined has, for determining gain or loss on a sale or exchange, "the same basis in whole or in part . . . as the property exchanged." This requirement is readily satisfied if the §351 exchange is wholly tax-free. If boot is received, the stock's basis is determined *by reference* to the basis of the property given up, and this may constitute a use of that basis in part; but if the transferor's gain is wholly recognized on the exchange, this interpretation of the term "in part" is more doubtful.[115]

While the stock or securities derive their basis and holding periods from the transferred properties, capital asset status (or the lack of it) for the stock or securities is *not* a characteristic that is inherited from the property exchanged therefor.

Can the transferor deliberately transfer some assets for stock and others for securities in order to control the basis or holding period of the stock and securities received? It is doubtful that such an earmarking of the transferred property would succeed if both transfers were interdependent steps in a single transaction. Section 358 and the regulations promulgated under it seem to contemplate that the aggregate basis of the property transferred will be assigned to the properties received, leaving little room for any planning of basis by the foresighted taxpayer, and §1223(1) is no more helpful, since its applicability depends upon §358.[116]

¶ 3.11   THE TRANSFEREE CORPORATION'S BASIS

Section 362(a) provides that the basis to the transferee corporation of the property received on the exchange will be the transferor's basis for the

---

[115] But see Citizens Nat'l Bank of Waco v. US, 417 F2d 675 (5th Cir. 1969).

In permitting tacking only if the property given up was a capital or §1231 asset, §1223(1) seems to embrace §1231 assets even if subject to ordinary income treatment by virtue of the depreciation recapture rules of §1245 or §1250. Such an asset can be said to be described in §1231, as required by §1223(1).

As to whether the basis of various assets is traced into the individual shares of stock or securities received by the transferor or instead merges into an average or fungible basis for the acquired nonrecognition property, see infra ¶ 14.34, para. 3, and infra note 116.

[116] See Nassau Lens Co. v. CIR, 35 TC 268 (1960), remanded, 308 F2d 39 (2d Cir. 1962), suggesting this conclusion; supra ¶ 3.05, last paragraph. But compare Leonard Osrow, 49 TC 333 (1968) (acq.); Rev. Rul. 85-164, 1985-2 CB 117 (basis and holding periods must be allocated pro rata, not by designation to specific exchanges).

property, increased in the amount of gain recognized to the transferor. What if the transferor erroneously recognized (or erroneously failed to recognize) gain on the prior exchange? Does §362 mean *actual* recognition, or should this language be read as meaning recognizable? The latter construction has won judicial support, whether the transferor's error was in recognizing or in failing to recognize gain.[117] The assumption of liabilities by the transferee does not enter into the computation of its basis for the transferred property unless gain is recognized to the transferor under §357; if the assumed liabilities are part of its acquisition cost for the assets, it cannot deduct the amounts paid to discharge these liabilities or add them to its inherited tax basis.[118] The transferor's basis may also be subject to special adjustment rules, such as the "lower of cost or value" rule in the case of personal-use property that is converted to income-producing or business functions.[119]

The discharge or satisfaction of debt securities that were issued by the transferee in a tax-free exchange for property under §351(a) should not result in a stepped-up basis for the acquired properties. No gain is recog-

---

[117] Truck Terminals, Inc., v. CIR, 314 F2d 449 (9th Cir. 1963) (erroneous recognition of gain); Fahs v. Florida Mach. & Foundry Co., discussed supra note 112 (erroneous recognition); see also Regs. §1.1312-7(c), Example (1)(i), assuming that the transferee corporation is not estopped to claim a stepped-up basis and that this will not open up the statute of limitations as to the transferor; Las Cruces Oil Co., 62 TC 764 (1974) (acq.) (corporate transferee not bound by basis errors of transferor); see also Prop. Regs. §1.453-1(f)(3)(ii) (transferee's basis step-up delayed if transferor reports gain under §453).

[118] Section 362(a)(1) makes no allowance for the liabilities except to the extent that gain was recognized as a result of §357(b) or §357(c); see also H.R. Rep. No. 855, 76th Cong., 1st Sess. 20 (1939) (no changes in inherited tax basis where transferee subsequently discharges the liabilities). For cases denying a deduction for the amount paid on the ground that it is part of the transferee's cost of acquiring the property, see Holdcroft Transp. Co. v. CIR, 153 F2d 323 (8th Cir. 1946); Rodney, Inc. v. CIR, 145 F2d 692 (2d Cir. 1944); M. Buten & Sons, ¶ 72,044 P-H Memo. TC (1972) (no deduction for assumed liabilities); Mark O. Leavitt, ¶ 72,113 P-H Memo. TC (1972) (same).

For the transferee corporation's right to deduct payments to discharge assumed liabilities (e.g., for continuing business expenses) that would have generated deductions on payment by the transferor, see Rev. Rul. 80-198, 1980-2 CB 113 (trade accounts payable); Rev. Rul. 83-155, 1983-2 CB 38 (payments owing by transferor partnership to retired partner or spouse of deceased partner; held deductible by transferee corporation); see also §358(d)(2) (no adjustment to basis for liabilities described by §357(c)(3) relating to deductible and other excluded liabilities); supra notes 71 and 114.

[119] See Regs. §1.167(g)-1; see also Au v. CIR, 330 F2d 1008 (9th Cir. 1964), cert. denied, 379 US 960 (1965) (personal car transferred to partnership); Rev. Rul. 69-117, 1969-1 CB 103 (accrual-basis transferee corporation required to take zero basis for transferred inventory items that previously had been expensed by cash-basis transferor); Prop. Regs. §1.453-1(f)(3)(ii) (if transferor reports boot gain under §453, transferee's basis step-up is delayed; supra notes 47, 110, and 117.)

nized to the transferor under §351(b) on the transfer in exchange for these securities (as required by §362(a) in order to obtain an increase in basis). Even though the transferor realizes gain when the securities are paid off, this is treated as an unrelated event.[120]

Neither the Code nor the regulations state how the carried-over basis is to be allocated by the transferee corporation among the various assets received. For example, if the controlled corporation issues stock in exchange for an asset with an adjusted basis to the transferor of $10,000 and a value of $10,000 and another asset with an adjusted basis of $20,000 and a value of $50,000, is the aggregate basis of $30,000 to be divided between the two assets in proportion to their market values, or should the old basis of each asset be preserved intact? In *P.A. Birren & Son v. CIR*, it was held under the predecessor of §362(a) that the transferee corporation steps into the shoes of the transferor, preserving intact the old basis for each asset received on the exchange.[121]

This rule, which has the virtue of avoiding an appraisal of the assets at the time of the exchange, will ordinarily be helpful to the taxpayer when a going concern is incorporated. If the transferor's aggregate basis for all the assets of the business had to be allocated by the transferee corporation in proportion to the market values of the various assets, a portion of the total basis, perhaps a substantial portion, would usually have to be allocated to goodwill. This would often be disadvantageous to the transferee corporation, because it would reduce the basis of inventory and similar property (which presumably will be sold within a reasonable period) and of machinery, equipment, and plant (on which depreciation is allowed) while increasing the basis of goodwill, which would ordinarily not be sold or depreciated. Under the *Birren* case, however, there is no such reallocation of basis.

If the §351 exchange was partly taxable because boot was received, §362(a) provides that the basis to be assigned to the transferred assets is to be increased by the amount of gain recognized. But neither the Code nor the regulations state how this increase should be allocated among the various assets. One method would be for the corporation to take over the transferor's basis for each asset increased by the same percentage that the gain recognized bears to the aggregate old basis. Thus, if the total old basis was $25,000 and the gain recognized was $5,000, the basis of each transferred asset would be increased by 20 percent. This method has the advantage of simplicity, since it

---

[120] See Schweitzer & Conrad, Inc., 41 BTA 533 (1940); Levin, The Case for a Stepped-Up Basis to the Transferee in Certain Reorganizations, 17 Tax L. Rev. 511 (1962).

[121] P.A. Birren & Son v. CIR, 116 F2d 718 (7th Cir. 1940); see also Gunn v. CIR, 25 TC 424, 438 (1955), aff'd per curiam, 244 F2d 408 (10th Cir.), cert. denied, 355 US 830 (1957). But cf. §1060 (enacted in 1986), infra ¶ 11.11, and General Explanation of the Tax Reform Act of 1986, at 359 (1987).

requires no appraisal of the transferred assets, but it is open to the objection that an asset's increase in basis may bear no relationship to its contribution to the recognition of gain. In the alternative, the gain could be allocated among the assets in proportion to their market values at the time of the exchange or in proportion to their actual increase in value above basis. Both alternatives would require an appraisal, but the latter one would have the merit of assigning the increase in basis to the assets responsible for it.[122]

If the corporation disposes of any of the assets transferred to it under §351 in a transaction that produces capital gain or loss, the transferor's holding period can be tacked under §1223(2). It may be, moreover, that the transferor's holding period can be tacked under §1223(2), even though the property became a capital asset only when it was acquired by the transferee corporation.[123]

¶ 3.12   CORPORATE GAIN OR LOSS ON ISSUE OR SALE OF STOCK

Section 1032 provides for the nonrecognition of gain or loss by a corporation receiving "money or other property in exchange for [its own] stock (including treasury stock)."[124] The reference to treasury stock, although enclosed in parentheses, is actually the crux of §1032, since the provision was enacted to reject the result reached by some cases under pre-1954 law that required gain to be recognized if a corporation "dealt in its own shares as it might in the shares of another corporation"—for example, by using

---

[122] See generally supra ¶ 3.05.

[123] See CIR v. Gracey, 159 F2d 324 (5th Cir. 1947); §1223(2) was not amended in 1954, as was §1223(1), to nullify the *Gracey* rule. For further discussion of tacking, see supra note 115.

[124] Since 1984, §1032(b) applies the same nonrecognition rule to gains and losses realized by a corporation on a lapse or an acquisition of an option to buy or sell its own stock, including treasury shares. See generally Pesiri, Untangling the Warrant Web, 23 Tax Notes 525 (1984).

For a solvent corporation's obligation to report income from the cancellation of its debt for less than its face amount on issuing stock in exchange for debt securities in a so-called debt-equity swap, see §108(e)(10)(A), infra ¶ 4.25, text at notes 165 and 167. For the effect on loss carry-over limitations of gain realized from the discharge of debt for less than its face amount, see §382(1)(5)(C), infra ¶ 16.25.

Section 1032 applies only to a corporation's transactions in *its own* stock or securities; for the use of stock or securities of other corporations, including parent and subsidiary corporations, see Rev. Rul. 70-305, 1970-1 CB 169, modified by Rev. Rul. 74-503, 1974-2 CB 117 (subsidiary's open-market purchases of parent's stock and resale to outsiders not protected by §1032 because not stock of the selling corporation; but treasury stock always has a zero basis).

appreciated treasury shares with a basis of $25,000 (the amount paid when they were repurchased from the original owner) to pay for property with a fair market value of $100,000.[125] By contrast, pre-1954 law did not recognize gain or loss if authorized but previously unissued stock (regardless of its par, stated, or fair market value) was used to acquire property, because such a transaction did not involve "dealing in its own shares as it might in the shares of another corporation." Because this tax distinction did not reflect any business or financial differences between treasury and previously unissued stock, it was repudiated by the enactment of §1032.

Although §1032 itself refers only to transactions involving the issue of stock for money or other property, the regulations apply the same nonrecognition principle to the use of stock to pay for services,[126] a sensible extension, since otherwise this anomalous distinction between treasury shares and previously unissued shares would be perpetuated in stock-for-services exchanges.

The regulations also clarify a statutory ambiguity in determining the corporation's basis for property acquired in exchange for stock. Although §1032(b) refers to §362 as though it were the only provision governing the corporation's basis, the regulations state that §362 is applicable if the exchange qualifies under §351 or under the reorganization provisions,[127] but that the basis of property acquired by the corporation in *taxable* exchanges is governed by §1012 (basis of property is "cost"). Thus, if stock is issued to acquire property from an outsider, the basis of the property to the corporation will be its cost, which is ordinarily, although not always, the fair market value of the stock given up.[128]

---

[125] Regs. §118, §39.22(a)-15(b); the cases are reviewed in Penn-Texas Corp. v. US, 308 F2d 575 (Ct. Cl. 1962); see also Hercules Powder Co. v. US, 337 F2d 643 (Ct. Cl. 1964).

For explicit rejection of the pre-1954 dealing-in-its-own-shares doctrine, see Regs. §1.1032-1(a).

[126] Regs. §1.1032-1(a); see CIR v. Fender Sales, Inc., 338 F2d 924 (9th Cir. 1964), cert. denied, 382 US 813 (1965) (no corporate income under §1032 on issue of shares in payment of corporate debts to shareholders); National Can Corp. v. US, 687 F2d 1107 (7th Cir. 1982) (§1032 precludes recognition of gain on issue of stock to satisfy conversion feature of subsidiary's bonds). Compare ITT & Affiliated Cos. v. CIR, 77 TC 60, 80, n.23 (1981), aff'd per curiam (other issues), 704 F2d 252 (2d Cir. 1983) (parent gets basis in bonds of subsidiary equal to value of stock issued on conversion of bonds). See generally Eustice, Cancellation of Indebtedness and the Federal Income Tax: A Problem of Creeping Confusion, 14 Tax L. Rev. 225, 238 (1959).

For the tax effects of issuing stock and securities in a bankruptcy proceeding, see infra ¶ 14.20.

[127] For §351, see supra ¶ 3.11; for reorganization provisions, see infra ch. 14.

[128] For determination of basis in the context of taxable exchanges, see Philadelphia Park Amusement Co. v. US, 126 F. Supp. 184 (Ct. Cl. 1954); Moore-McCor-

The term "stock" is not defined in §1032 or elsewhere in the Code, and on several occasions the courts have had to say whether a corporation was entitled to the benefit of §1032 on receiving payment for rights embodied in a document of ambiguous character. Thus, *Community T.V. Association v. US* held that amounts received for so-called Class B stock, which had to be purchased as a condition to the receipt of television services to be furnished by the issuing corporation, did not qualify for exemption under §1032 and thus constituted taxable income to the corporation under §61.[129] The stock was redeemable at par and did not entitle the owner to vote, participate in the profits of the company, or share in its assets on liquidation until the Class A stock had been paid in full. A similar result was reached with respect to fees paid for membership certificates in a cooperative organization, even though the holders were entitled to vote and to share in assets on liquidation, because the substance of the transaction was a payment for the privilege of buying goods at a savings rather than an equity investment in the taxpayer.[130]

The relationship between the nonrecognition of gain or loss on §1032 transactions and certain other statutory provisions is obscure. A 1962 ruling carries forward the pre-1954 rule that the fair market value of stock issued as compensation for services rendered may be deducted as a business expense if a payment of cash would have given rise to such a deduction, and presumably the same rule would apply to stock issued for property if a cash payment would have been deductible.[131] The ruling seems proper; a deduction does not conflict with §1032's purpose of recognizing neither gain nor loss on the receipt of money or property in exchange for stock. The same can be said of an allowance under §248 (amortization of organizational expenses), or a deduction, when appropriate, for the value of stock issued in payment for the corporation's organizational expenses.[132] If a corporation is to be paid in

mack Lines, Inc., 44 TC 745 (1965) (acq.); Seas Shipping Co. v. CIR, 371 F2d 528 (2d Cir.), cert. denied, 387 US 943 (1967); Amerada-Hess Corp. v. CIR, 517 F2d 75 (3d Cir.), cert. denied, 423 US 1037 (1975); ITT & Affiliated Cos., supra note 126.

[129] Community T.V. Ass'n v. US, 203 F. Supp. 270 (D. Mont. 1962).

[130] See Affiliated Gov't Employees' Distrib. Co. v. CIR, 322 F2d 872 (9th Cir. 1963), cert. denied, 376 US 950 (1964); see also Rev. Rul. 61-18, 1961-1 CB 5 (excess of amount received over value of stock issued taxed as income to issuing corporation); University Country Club, Inc., 64 TC 460 (1975) (acq.) (corporation's Class B stock held not a proprietary interest but represented privilege to use club's facilities; thus, receipts from sale taxable as ordinary income).

[131] See Rev. Rul. 62-217, 1962-2 CB 59, modified by Rev. Rul. 74-503, 1974-2 CB 117; for pre-1954 law, see International Freighting Corp. v. CIR, 135 F2d 310 (2d Cir. 1943); Montana Power Co. v. US, 171 F. Supp. 943 (Ct. Cl. 1959); see also Rev. Rul. 75-348; 1975-2 CB 75.

[132] See Hollywood Baseball Ass'n, 42 TC 234 (third issue), aff'd on other issues, 352 F2d 350 (1964), vacated, 383 US 24 (1966); Duncan Indus. Inc., 73 TC 266 (1979). For §248, see infra ¶ 5.06.

installments for stock over a period of time, the regulations under §483 indicate that interest will be imputed on the deferred payments if the contract does not stipulate an adequate rate of return.[133] Although §483 was enacted to prevent interest income from being received under the guise of capital gain, its language is sweeping, and the regulation simply makes explicit the interest element that is implicit in the arrangement in any event.[134]

¶ 3.13   CONTRIBUTIONS TO CAPITAL

1. General; Corporate nonrecognition of income. Section 118, providing that gross income shall not include contributions to the corporation's capital, was enacted in 1954 as a restatement of "existing law as developed through administration and court decisions."[135] In the case of pro rata contributions by shareholders, the exclusion from gross income might be regarded as a corollary to §1032, under which the issue of stock does not produce corporate gain or loss, as discussed in the previous section. The purpose of §118 was not to confirm existing law with respect to contributions made by shareholders, however, but to give congressional blessing to pre-1954 cases holding that certain contributions by nonshareholders were not taxable as income:

> It [§118] deals with cases where a contribution is made to a corporation by a governmental unit, chamber of commerce, or other association of individuals having no proprietary interest in the corporation. In many such cases, because the contributor expects to derive indirect benefits, the contribution cannot be called a gift; yet the anticipated future benefits may also be so intangible as to not warrant treating the contribution as a payment for future services.[136]

---

[133] See Regs. §1.483-1(b)(6), Example (6); ¶ 14.56. For the virtual absorption of §483 by §1274 (added in 1984), see Eustice, supra note 108; infra ¶ 4.42.

[134] The uncertain relationship between §1032 and §453 (installment obligations) was explored in a case involving an unusual set of facts, Jack Ammann Photogrammetric Eng'rs, Inc. v. CIR, supra note 27 (corporation issued stock in exchange for its installment obligations, previously issued in payment for certain assets; held acquisition and cancellation of corporation's obligations not a disposition by it under §453; court indicated that transferor was the one that should have been taxed, infra ¶ 3.17); see also Rev. Rul. 73-423, supra note 27 (corporate debtor protected by §1032 where shareholder-creditor transfers §453 installment obligation in §351 exchange; theory of *Ammann* followed).

[135] S. Rep. No. 1622, supra note 87, at 190.

[136] Id. at 18–19. See generally Landis, Contributions to Capital of Corporations, 24 Tax L. Rev. 241 (1969); Reiling, Warrants in Bond-Warrant Units: A Survey and Assessment, 70 Mich. L. Rev. 1411 (1972) (general analysis of legal, economic, finan-

It will be noted that §118 applies only if the transaction is a contribution to the capital of the taxpayer and does not define the term "contribution to capital" except by providing in §118(b) that the term does not include contributions in aid of construction or other contributions by customers or potential customers.[137] The regulations distinguish between (1) contributions "by a governmental unit or civic group to induce the corporation to locate its business in a particular community or to expand its operating facilities" that are subject to §118, and (2) payments for goods or services rendered and subsidies paid to induce the corporation to limit its production, to which §118 is inapplicable.[138] Contributions made by customers to a regulated public utility to aid in construction were treated specially by §118(b), which was added in 1976 and which exempted such payments from tax, but denied such additional tax benefits as deductions, investment credits, and increases in basis[139]; but the exemption was repealed by the Tax Reform Act of 1986, and §118(b) now specifically requires such amounts to be included in income.

The indicia that have been thought relevant in determining whether an amount received by a corporation (either from a shareholder or from an

---

cial, and tax aspects of warrants); Pearson, *U.S. v. CB&Q R.R.*: A New Test for Non-Shareholder Contributions to Capital, 27 Tax Lawyer 503 (1974); Note, Contributions to the Capital of a Corporation: A Reexamination, 44 U. Cin. L. Rev. 549 (1975).

[137] Regs. §1.118-1. In US v. Chicago, B. & Q. R.R., 412 US 401 (1973), involving nonshareholder contributions to capital before the 1954 amendments to §362(c), the Court listed the following characteristics of a nonshareholder capital contribution: It must become a permanent part of the transferee's working capital structure; it must not be compensatory in character; it must be bargained for; the asset transferred must foreseeably result in benefits to the transferee commensurate with its value; and the asset must ordinarily be employed in, or contribute to, the production of additional income, and its value must be assured in that respect.

From 1976 to 1986, contributions by customers to regulated public utilities in aid of construction were exempt from taxation, but the utilities were not allowed depreciation and other tax allowances with respect to the resulting expenditures.

[138] See State Farm Road Corp., 65 TC 217 (1975) (judicial and legislative history of §118; corporation in business of constructing and operating sewage disposal systems financed construction by imposing nonrefundable tie-in charges on prospective customers; held taxable income rather than capital contributions); Rev. Rul. 75-300, 1975-2 CB 23 (unclaimed customer refunds, not capital contributions); Rev. Rul. 68-558, 1968-2 CB 415; Concord Village, Inc., 65 TC 142 (1975) (unexpended funds collected by housing co-op from member occupants that were earmarked and accumulated in painting and operating reserves were taxable income; amounts accumulated in replacement reserve for capital expenditures were excludable capital contributions); Rev. Rul. 75-371, 1975-2 CB 52 (same).

[139] For treatment prior to the 1976 amendment, see Larson, Jr. & Jove, Customer Contributions to Utilities Continue to Create Income Problems, 45 J. Tax'n 194 (1976).

outsider) is a tax-free contribution to its capital under §118 include the corporation's need for additional capital; the expectation of ultimate return through an increase in the contributor's equity in the corporation; the intent or purpose of the contribution (i.e., whether the payment is for the benefit of the corporation's capital position, or constitutes consideration for corporate goods or services rendered or to be rendered for the benefit of the payer); whether the contribution is voluntary and pro rata among the shareholders; and the form of the contribution (e.g., a lump-sum payment of money or property, as opposed to annual periodic payments in the nature of dues or fees). [140]

Many of the contribution-to-capital cases have arisen in the context of a forgiveness of corporate indebtedness by shareholder-creditors. The regulations state that a shareholder who gratuitously forgives a debt owed to him by his corporation has made a contribution to capital to the extent of the principal of the debt; [141] but this provision does not take account of §108(e)(6), enacted in 1980. Under this provision, §118 is made inapplicable to contributions to capital by shareholder-creditors, and the corporation is instead treated as having satisfied the debt with cash in an amount equal to the adjusted basis of the debt in the hands of the shareholder.

By virtue of this as-if treatment, the tax results to the corporation are governed by §108, relating to cancellation of indebtedness income. If the shareholder's adjusted basis for the debt is equal to the face amount of the debt (e.g., if the shareholder lent the face amount in cash to the corporation), the corporation realizes no income when the shareholder's claim is contributed to its capital, because the hypothetical payment by the corporation does not exceed the claim's adjusted basis in the hands of the shareholder. On the other hand, if (1) the debt reflects an amount owed to the share-

---

[140] See United Grocers, Ltd. v. US, 308 F2d 634 (9th Cir. 1962); Edwards v. Cuba R.R. Co., 268 US 628 (1925); Detroit Edison Co. v. CIR, 319 US 98 (1943); Brown Shoe Co. v. CIR, 339 US 583 (1950); Teleservice Co. v. CIR, 254 F2d 105 (3d Cir.), cert. denied, 357 US 919 (1958); Maryland Jockey Club v. US, 189 F. Supp. 70 (D. Md. 1960), aff'd per curiam, 292 F2d 469 (4th Cir. 1961); Federated Dep't Stores, Inc. v. CIR, 426 F2d 417 (6th Cir. 1970) (§118 applied to nonshareholder capital contributions by real estate developer); followed in May Dep't Stores Co., ¶ 74,253 P-H Memo. TC (1974), aff'd per curiam, 519 F2d 1154 (8th Cir. 1975) (gift of land by shopping center developer to induce corporation to locate in project held tax-free §118 capital contribution). But see John B. White, Inc., 55 TC 729 (1971), aff'd per curiam, 458 F2d 898 (3d Cir.), cert. denied, 409 US 876 (1972) (payment by auto company to its distributor to induce a change of location taxable).

See generally Sneed, The Criteria of Federal Income Tax Policy, 17 Stan. L. Rev. 567, 604–613 (1965).

[141] See Regs. §1.61-12(a). Sometimes the taxpayer relies in the alternative on the assertion that there was no indebtedness to cancel because the advance in question was in fact an equity investment; see J.A. Maurer, Inc., 30 TC 1273 (1958) (acq.).

holder for services performed for the corporation, and (2) the corporation, reporting on an accrual basis, deducted the debt with tax benefit, but the shareholder, being a cash basis taxpayer, did not take the debt into income, the debt has a zero basis in the shareholder's hands; and if the shareholder contributes the debt to the corporation's capital, the corporation realizes cancellation of indebtedness income equal to the face amount owing.[142] Insolvent debtors, however, do not have to report this amount currently if they elect under §108(b)(5) to reduce the basis of their depreciable assets by the amount of income realized under §108(a).

The capital contribution concept is often invoked in cases involving alleged purchases of property by a corporation from its shareholders if the arrangement shows an intention to commit the property to the risks of the business or if the corporation is thinly capitalized. Here it is ordinarily the government rather than the taxpayer that seeks to characterize the transaction as a contribution to capital.[143]

2. Corporate basis. Section 362(a)(2) provides that the corporation's basis for property acquired as paid-in surplus or as a contribution to capital should be the same as the transferor's basis. This rule is comparable to §362(a)(1), under which property received by the corporation in exchange

---

[142] The example in the text assumes that the corporation was not forbidden to accrue the salary expense by §267(a)(2) (summarized in ¶ 5.04, text at note 27), which defers to certain deductions attributable to unpaid amounts owed by an accrual method taxpayer to a related cash-method taxpayer. If, however, §267(a)(2) did apply (because the shareholder-employee owned directly, indirectly, or constructively more than 50 percent of the corporation's stock), the corporation would not currently have been allowed to deduct the accrued salary; its hypothetical payment of zero to discharge the debt would not generate any cancellation of indebtedness income because the corporation derived no prior tax benefit when it accrued the amount owed.

Section 108(e)(6) was enacted to alter the result in Putoma Corp. v. CIR, 601 F2d 734 (5th Cir. 1979) (divided court), which held that the tax-benefit doctrine, relied on by the government in arguing that a corporation realized income when a cash-basis shareholder-creditor cancelled accrued interest deducted by the corporation, was superseded by §118. The court also ruled that the cancellation was a nontaxable gift. Section 108(e)(6) does not explicitly address the latter ground for the *Putoma Corp.* result, but the Senate Finance Committee's report on §108(e)(6) states that "it is intended that there will not be any gift exception in a commercial context (such as a shareholder-corporation relationship) to the general rule that income is realized on discharge of indebtedness." S. Rep. No. 1035, 96th Cong., reprinted in 1980-2 CB 620, 629, n.22.

For corporate income where debt is eliminated in an exchange of stock for debt securities in a so-called debt-equity swap, see infra ¶ 4.25, text at note 167.

[143] See infra ¶ 3.14 (sale vs. §351 exchange); infra ch. 4 ("loan" vs. capital contribution).

for stock in a transaction under §351 retains the transferor's basis. Taken in conjunction, §§362(a)(1) and 362(a)(2) provide for the preservation of basis whether or not the shareholder gets stock in exchange, thus recognizing the fact that the receipt of stock is a matter of indifference if the shareholders' contributions are pro rata.

Since *an outsider's* contribution to a corporation's capital increases the corporation's net worth at no tax cost under §118, however, §362(c)(1) provides that property that is "not contributed by a shareholder as such" will have a zero basis in the hands of the transferee corporation, while §362(c)(2) provides that if the contribution consists of money, the corporation must reduce the basis of any property acquired within the following 12-month period with the contributed money, and if enough property is not so acquired, the basis of other property held by the corporation must be reduced pro tanto.[144] Like §118, §362(c) is applicable only if the property or money constitutes a contribution to capital; if it is received as payment for goods or services, no adjustment to basis is required. Section 362(c) is evidently also inapplicable to property or money received by a corporation as a gift; if so, the corporation would carry over the donor's basis under §1015.[145]

---

[144] Section 362(c). The phrase "not contributed by a shareholder as such" presumably includes a civic booster who happens to be a shareholder of the corporation if his contribution is out of proportion to his proprietary interest in the corporation. But what of a contribution by a major shareholder to a poverty-stricken corporation if the other shareholders do not contribute proportionately? If the contributor's main interest is salvaging the value of his stock, the contribution should be regarded as made by a "shareholder as such," subject to §362(a)(2) rather than to §362(c). See Henry J. Wolfers, 69 TC 975 (1978) (§362(c) preempts case law regarding nonshareholder capital contributions).

For the method of reducing basis under §362(c), see Regs. §1.362-2; Federated Dep't Stores, Inc., supra note 140. The proper basis adjustment on a cancellation of indebtedness is left unclear, but arguably it should be treated as money; see Greer v. CIR, 230 F2d 490 (5th Cir. 1956) (pre-1954 taxable year); see also Denver & Rio Grande W.R.R. Co. v. US, 505 F2d 1266 (Ct. Cl. 1974) (contingently refundable advances used by railroad to finance construction of spur line to service lender's products, repayable over 10 years under a contingency formula, depending on lender's use of spur; held includable in basis as advances were repaid).

[145] As to amounts received as payment for goods or services, see supra note 140. As to gifts, see S. Rep. No. 1622, supra note 87, at 272; H.R. Rep. No. 1337, 83d Cong., 2d Sess., at A128 (1954); Bothin Real Estate Co. v. CIR, 90 F2d 91 (9th Cir. 1937); Veterans Found. v. CIR, 317 F2d 456 (10th Cir. 1963) (used clothing and other items donated to taxpayer for sale in thrift stores were contributions to capital with zero basis under §362(c) rather than gifts with carryover basis under §1015); see also Estate of Hitchon, 45 TC 96 (1965) (acq.) (gift by one shareholder to corporation, if intended to benefit other shareholders, entitles them to increase the basis of their shares); Rev. Rul. 74-329, 1974-2 CB 269 (bequest to corporation entitles shareholders to increase stock basis if bequest intended to benefit shareholders; no distinction between a bequest of property and a bequest of corporation's own shares).

3. Treatment of contributor. If the person making the contribution is a shareholder, the contribution is ordinarily reflected in an increased basis for his stock.[146] If the contribution is made in property other than money, however, it is not clear whether the basis of the stock is to be increased by the basis or the fair market value of the property. If the contribution is voluntary, it does not produce gain or loss to the shareholder; in this event, the shareholder should probably be regarded as contributing the basis of the property rather than its fair market value. If the property is transferred to the corporation in payment of an assessment, however, the shareholder realizes gain or loss on discharging his indebtedness with property; and the basis of his stock should be increased by the fair market value of the property.[147]

Nonshareholder contributions to a corporation's capital might be deductible business expenses (e.g., if the contributor expects to derive busi-

---

[146] See Reg. §1.118-1, stating that voluntary pro rata payments by shareholders are "in the nature of assessments upon, and represent an additional price paid for" the stock; see also Tilford v. CIR, 705 F2d 828 (6th Cir.), cert. denied, 464 US 992 (1983) (divided court) (upholding §83 regulations providing that sale by shareholder of stock to employee of corporation for services to the corporation constitutes contribution to capital; shareholder not entitled to deduct loss on sale); Leroy Frantz, 83 TC 162 (1984), aff'd, 784 F2d 119 (2d Cir. 1986) (accord); Comment, Frantz v. Commissioner: Non-Pro Rata Surrender of Stock to the Issuing Corporation, 38 Tax Lawyer 739 (1985).

[147] See Edward Mallinckrodt, Jr., 38 BTA 960, 969 (1983) (nonacq.) (increase by basis of contributed property); Greer v. CIR, supra note 144 (increase by fair market value). The latter decision is of doubtful validity; it is difficult to see why a shareholder should obtain an increased basis for his investment in a controlled corporation by making a capital contribution of property without taking back additional stock, while the receipt of stock or securities on a §351 transfer would require a substitution of basis under §358, supra ¶ 3.10; see also Rev. Rul. 64-155, 1964-1 CB 138, and Sol Lessinger, 85 TC 824 (1985) (treat as constructive §351 exchange when made by sole shareholder); Regs. §1.304-2(a) (increase by basis of contributed property); Rev. Rul. 70-291, 1970-1 CB 168 (pro rata surrender of stock held nontaxable capital contribution; shareholders increase basis of remaining shares by basis of contributed shares; see also S. Rep. No. 552, 91st Cong., 1st Sess. 123–124 (1969) (under §83, shareholders' payments of restricted property on behalf of their corporation constitute contributions to its capital, with an increase in their stock basis and a taxable gain or loss to the employer corporation unless §1032 applies); Regs. §1.83-6(d) (parent's transfer of its stock is a capital contribution to subsidiary of basis; subsidiary apparently recognizes gain on transfer). But see Rev. Rul. 80-76, 1980-1 CB 15 (subsidiary gets deduction under §83(h) but does not recognize gain); Tilford v. CIR, supra note 146. See generally Nolan, Deferred Compensation and Employee Options Under the New Section 83 Regulations, 57 Taxes 790, 793–795 (1979).

Finally, if the contribution is made by a 100 percent shareholder, there is authority for treating the transaction as a constructive §351 exchange despite the failure to issue additional stock; see Rev. Rul. 64-155, and Sol Lessinger, supra note 147.

ness benefits from the relocation of industry in his area);[148] and occasionally a shareholder's contribution, especially if not pro rata, can qualify for deduction.[149]

¶ 3.14 TRANSFER UNDER §351 VS. SALE

It is sometimes necessary to determine whether the transfer of property to a controlled corporation qualifies as a transfer under §351 or constitutes, instead, an ordinary sale of the property. If §351 governs, the transfer is either wholly tax-free or taxable to the extent of any boot received, but no loss is recognized. On the other hand, if the transfer is a sale, the transferor recognizes gain (or loss, unless §267 applies)[150] under §1001. For this reason, owners of property that has declined in value sometimes wish to sell it to a corporation controlled by them and deduct their loss without losing control of the property. The transferee corporation's basis for the transferred assets is also affected by whether the transfer falls under §351 or is a sale. If §351 is applicable, the corporation must carry over the transferor's basis, while if the transaction is a sale, the corporation's basis is its costs.

Relying on these principles, owners of appreciated land that is ripe for subdivisions or other building projects sometimes endeavor to sell the land to a controlled corporation so that (1) the appreciation is taxed to them as capital gain (possibly over a period of years, if a §453(b) installment sale is made; and (2) the corporation starts with a higher basis for the land and hence realizes correspondingly less ordinary income from its sale. If success-

---

[148] See IT 3706, 1945 CB 87 (contributions to civic development fund); but see Rev. Rul. 69-43, 1969-1 CB 310 (IT 3706 ruled obsolete).

[149] Julius C. Miller, 45 BTA 292 (1941) (nonacq.) (shareholder allowed to deduct difference between basis of stock surrendered to improve corporation's capital status and proportionate benefit to his remaining stock); Charles H. Duell, ¶ 60,248 P-H Memo. TC (1960) (accord). But see Schleppy v. CIR, 601 F2d 196 (5th Cir. 1979) (non-pro rata contribution of stock to improve financial condition constituted non-taxable, nondeductible addition to basis of remaining stock held by contributing shareholder); Tilford v. CIR, supra note 146; Frantz v. CIR, supra note 146. But contra to *Frantz* and *Schleppy* is Fink v. CIR, 789 F2d 427 (6th Cir. 1986), cert. granted (1986) (shareholder allowed ordinary loss on contribution back of stock to improve financial condition). See generally Bolding, Non-Pro Rata Stock Surrenders: Capital Contribution, Capital Loss or Ordinary Loss, 32 Tax Lawyer 275 (1979); Johnson, Deduction of Nonprorata Shareholder Contributions Is a Violation of the Principles of Taxation, 32 Tax Notes 267 (1986); Dickens, Is the *Fink* Decision Really What It Appears to Be? 14 J. Corp. Tax'n 55 (1987).

[150] In addition to §267, see Higgins v. Smith, 308 US 473 (1940) (disallowing a claimed loss on a sale by a shareholder to his one-man corporation), which creates the possibility that some losses not automatically disallowed by §267 will nevertheless be held nondeductible after a judicial appraisal of all the facts.

ful, this plan permits the business profits ultimately realized by selling the land to outsiders to be divided between the individual (reporting capital gain) and the corporation (reporting ordinary income), whereas a transfer of the land to the corporation under §351 would result in the corporation's realizing the entire profit as ordinary income.[151]

A sale may also be preferred over a §351 exchange as a means of stepping up the basis of depreciable property: If business equipment or real property with high current market value has a low adjusted basis, the owner may sell it to a controlled corporation in order to give the corporation a stepped-up basis for depreciation at the cost to him of a capital gain under §1231.[152] In cases of this sort, where the owner of property is seeking to give his corporation a stepped-up basis for assets at the cost of a capital gain to himself, an alternative to a sale is a transfer of the property under §351 in exchange for stock plus cash, short-term notes, or other taxable boot. The §351 route is not always a feasible alternative, however, since the use of short-term notes or other boot may have business disadvantages.[153]

Recognizing that the courts may convert what the parties have called a sale into a tax-free §351 exchange in which the transferee corporation must take over the transferor's basis for the property, we turn now to the factual patterns in which the issue usually presents itself.

If property is to be transferred to a controlled corporation solely for stock or securities, it is difficult to see how the parties can avoid §351(a). Section 351 is applicable "if property is transferred to a corporation . . . solely in exchange for stock or securities," and the impact of this language

---

[151] For a successful example of this technique, see Bradshaw v. US, supra note 33 (sale of undeveloped land to newly organized corporation for installment notes maturing over 2½ to 6½ years held true sale, producing capital gain for transferors). For the possibility that the securities will create imputed interest under §§483 and 1274 or market discount under §1276, see supra note 108.

Proposed reform legislation (supra note 28) would subject installment sales by 20 percent shareholders to §351 treatment, delaying the transferee's basis step-up until gain is reported by the seller-transferor, supra notes 117 and 119.

See also §453(g)(1)(B) as amended by the Tax Reform Act of 1986, for a similar rule involving contingent price sales of depreciable property between related (more than 50 percent) parties.

[152] See supra ¶ 3.05 for the possible application of §§1239, 1245, and 1250 to sales or other taxable transfers of depreciable property. See also Ellis, Tax Problems in Sales to Controlled Corporations, 21 Vand. L. Rev. 196 (1968); Harley, Dealings Between Closely Held Corporations and Their Stockholders, 25 Tax L. Rev. 403 (1970); proposed reform legislation as to installment sales by 20 percent shareholders, supra note 151.

[153] The Service ordinarily refuses to rule whether obligations issued in a §351 exchange constitute stock, securities, or boot; Rev. Proc. 87-3, §4.19, 1987-1 IRB 27. For the effect of proposed legislation on the treatment of securities received in a §351 exchange, see supra note 28.

can hardly be avoided by affixing the label sale to the transfer. In more naive days, it was sometimes thought that the organizers of a corporation, wishing to deduct a loss on depreciated property, could purchase the corporation's stock for cash and then successfully sell the property to it for the cash just paid in, but the quietus was put on such transactions as early as 1932, in *Labrot v. Burnet,*[154] and the device is not likely to be revived. Protection against §351 in these circumstances, moreover, would be indefensible because it would convert §351 into an optional provision, in contravention of the congressional purpose.

Even if the transaction is cast in the form of a sale of property for stock or securities plus cash or other property, its tax consequences should be governed by §§351(a) and 351(b), so that the transferor should recognize gain (but not loss) to the extent of the boot. The language of §351 is broad enough to embrace the transaction, and a contrary construction would endow the transferor with an option that was not intended by Congress. (As suggested above, however, if the transferor's purpose is to give the property a stepped-up basis in the hands of the corporation rather than to enjoy a deductible loss, a transfer under §351 for stock or securities and boot may be a satisfactory alternative to a sale.) Nor should the tax consequences of such a transfer be altered by dividing it into a sale of some of the property for cash and a transfer of the balance for stock or securities if the two steps are integral parts of a single transaction.[155]

On the other hand, if the property is transferred to a controlled corporation solely for cash or property, the transfer cannot qualify under either §351(a) (which requires that the sole consideration be stock or securities) or §351(b) (which permits the receipt of boot, but only if the transferor has *also received stock or securities*).[156] Conversely, if the transferor does not have 80

---

[154] Labrot v. Burnet, 57 F2d 413 (D.C. Cir. 1932); see also Six Seam Co. v. US, 524 F2d 347 (6th Cir. 1975) (transfer of cash to wholly owned subsidiary for additional stock, immediately after which subsidiary purchased operating assets from parent; held §351 exchange with carry-over basis; not a sale).

[155] See Houck v. Hinds, 215 F2d 673 (10th Cir. 1954); Baker Commodities, Inc., supra note 33 (incorporation followed by sale of assets for long-term installment notes held §351 exchange for stock and securities); George A. Nye, supra note 33 (same); but see Sylvan Makover, ¶ 67,053 P-H Memo. TC (1967) (transfer of assets after initial §351 exchange recognized as separate step, independent of incorporation transaction); Stevens Pass, Inc., 48 TC 532 (1967) (separate purchase); Robert W. Adams, 58 TC 41 (1972) (incorporation followed by sale for short-term note held a single §351 transaction, but note was boot rather than security, so gain recognized under §351(b)); see also D'Angelo Assocs., supra note 33 (wholly tax-free §351 transaction, not sale).

[156] See Bradshaw v. US, supra note 33. The transfer may be treated as a bona fide sale to the extent of the transferred property's fair market value, but a dividend or other distribution to the extent of any excess to be paid above that amount. See

percent control of the transferee corporation (alone or with other transferors) immediately after the exchange, the transfer falls outside §351 and gain
or loss is recognized under §1001.

Section 351 may be equally inapplicable if the corporation issues no
stock or securities but agrees to pay for the property at a specified time in
the future or in installments. Although it finds support in the language of
§351, this conclusion allows form to control, since there may be no economic
difference to the parties between a controlled corporation's promise to pay
and its bonds or debentures. Moreover, it has been held that an installment
sales contract (under which the property was sold to a controlled corporation, the sales price to be paid in ten equal annual installments) was not a
"security" as that term is used in §351.[157] The court distinguished between
an instrument evidencing "a continuing interest in the affairs of the corporation" and one intended "to effect a termination of such a continuing interest," a distinction that is not easy to apply.[158]

The preceding discussion focused on whether or not §351 is applicable
to particular transactions. It would be perilous, however, to assume that a
transaction falling outside §351 is *necessarily* a sale merely because it bears
that label. For example, if property is transferred to a controlled corporation
solely for cash, §351 is inapplicable for the reasons stated above; but the
taxpayer may still have to establish that the transfer is a sale rather than a
contribution of the property to capital coupled with a distribution of cash.
Moreover, the taxpayer must be prepared to establish that appearances correspond with reality. The Service has more than once argued, sometimes
with success, that a corporation's promise to pay for property should be
disregarded either because the corporation's capitalization was too thin or

---

Arthur M. Rosenthal, ¶ 65,254 P-H Memo. TC (1965); Crabtree v. CIR, 22 TC 61
(1954), aff'd per curiam, 221 F2d 807 (2d Cir. 1955); infra ¶ 3.16; see also Rev. Rul.
64-155 and Sol Lessinger, supra note 147, finding a constructive §351 exchange
where the transferor is a 100 percent shareholder, despite the failure to issue additional stock (a meaningless event in this case).

[157] Warren H. Brown, 27 TC 27 (1956) (acq.); see also Bradshaw v. US, supra
note 33. But see proposed reform legislation, supra note 151, that would subject such
a sale to §351 (and delay a basis step-up for the acquired property).

[158] See generally supra ¶ 3.03. For decisions finding alleged sales for installment
obligations to be §351 exchanges for "securities," see *Baker Commodities* and *Nye*,
supra note 33, and authorities cited therein; see also Burr Oaks Corp. v. CIR, supra
note 85; Foresun, Inc. v. CIR, 348 F2d 1006 (6th Cir. 1965); Marsan Realty Corp.,
¶ 63,297 P-H Memo. TC (1963); Stanley, Inc. v. Schuster, 421 F2d 1360 (6th Cir.
1970); see also Dennis v. CIR, 473 F2d 274 (5th Cir. 1973).

However, "sale" treatment was upheld in Murphy Logging Corp. v. US, 378
F2d 222 (9th Cir. 1967); Piedmont Corp. v. CIR, 388 F2d 886 (4th Cir. 1968); Gyro
Eng'g Corp. v. US, 417 F2d 437 (9th Cir. 1969); Charles E. Curry, 43 TC 667 (1965)
(acq. and nonacq.); Bradshaw v. US, supra note 33.

for some other reason, and that a self-styled sale should be treated either as a §351 transfer or as a contribution to capital.[159]

It should also be noted that the shoe may be on the other foot: The taxpayer may seek to apply §351 to a transaction (usually a transfer of appreciated property) that, for practical purposes, is tantamount to a sale. If at the outset the parties characterized the transaction as a sale, the courts are not likely to welcome a belated claim that it was "really" a §351 exchange, even if the technical elements of estoppel are not present.[160]

More foresighted taxpayers may attempt to cloak a transaction from its inception in the form of a §351 exchange, but two important Service rulings indicate that such efforts may be frustrated. Both cases involved the transfer of appreciated property by an individual, A, for what was, in the end, a minority stock interest in the acquiring corporation. In the first gambit, A transferred the property to newly organized X Company for its stock; Y Company simultaneously transferred its assets to X for stock of X and then liquidated. Literally, §351 applied to the transfers by A and Y, but the Service ruled that X was organized merely for the purpose of enabling A to transfer his property on a tax-free basis and hence was a mere continuation of Y. Since A did not control Y (or its alter ego, X), as required by §351 for a tax-free transfer by A to Y for the latter's stock, A's transfer was a taxable event.[161] The second ruling rejected an elaborate variation on the preceding plan, under which A similarly transferred the property to newly organized X, and Y then acquired all of the X stock from A solely for its own stock in a putative Type B reorganization exchange. Taken at face value, the transaction consisted of two nontaxable exchanges, viz., the incorporation transfer by A to X that is protected in a literal sense by §351, and the subsequent stock-for-stock exchange by A with Y that likewise falls under a literal reading of §§368(a)(1)(B) and 354(a). Upon closer scrutiny, however, the transaction could just as easily be viewed as a taxable exchange of A's property for Y stock (A not being in "control" of Y), followed by Y's transfer of the property to a newly created subsidiary, X; and the Service ruled that it was a taxable sale when viewed in this light.[162]

---

[159] See supra ¶ 3.13, infra ¶ 4.04.

[160] See Harry F. Shannon, 29 TC 702 (1958).

[161] Rev. Rul. 68-349, 1968-2 CB 143; see also Rev. Rul. 75-292, 1975-2 CB 333 (exchange of real estate for other real estate, followed by §351 transfer of acquired property to controlled corporation in prearranged transaction, held taxable). Compare Magneson v. CIR, 753 F2d 1490 (9th Cir. 1985) (second-step transfer to partnership distinguished).

[162] Rev. Rul. 70-140, 1970-1 CB 73; see also Rev. Rul. 80-221, 1980-2 CB 107 (use of temporary §351 transfer as vehicle to effect corporate-level asset sale).

In E.G. Rodman, 57 TC 113 (1971), involving an incorporation transfer of property followed by a previously planned exchange of stock of the transferee for stock of

¶ 3.15   TRANSFERS TO INVESTMENT COMPANIES

As previously noted, if two or more unrelated persons transfer separately owned property to a controlled corporation in exchange for its stock or securities, §351 permits them to achieve a degree of diversification without recognizing gain; [163] and if the diversification is sufficiently dramatic, the transaction may be tantamount to a sale. Exploiting this feature of §351, so-called swap funds were devised in the early 1960s to permit unrelated investors holding highly appreciated securities to unlock their positions without being taxed, by exchanging their securities for the shares of a newly organized mutual fund to be managed by the promoter of the plan. In a series of private rulings, the Service initially held that §351 applied to these exchanges, but it later had second thoughts; and in 1966, Congress, recognizing that these transactions were more like sales than conventional §351 transactions, enacted the statutory predecessor of §351(e)(1), which makes the nonrecognition principle of §351 inapplicable to transfers of property "to an investment company." [164]

Badly needed flesh is added to this statutory skeleton by the regulations, which provide that the prohibited transfers are those that (1) result, directly or indirectly, in diversification of the transferors' interests, and (2) are made to a regulated investment company, a real estate investment trust, or a corporation more than 80 percent of whose assets (excluding cash and nonconvertible debt securities) are held for investment and consist of readily marketable stock or securities or of interests in regulated investment companies or real estate investment trusts. [165] Expanding on these criteria, the regulations state that (1) diversification occurs if two or more persons transfer nonidentical assets to the corporation unless these assets are an insignificant portion of the total value of the transferred properties; (2) securities are held for investment unless they are dealer property, or are used in a banking, insurance, brokerage, or similar business; and (3) securities are readily marketable if (but only if) they are part of a class that is traded on a securities

---

an acquiring corporation, the taxpayer stipulated application of Rev. Rul. 70-140. See also Earl Vest, 57 TC 128 (1971), modified on other grounds, 481 F2d 238 (5th Cir.), reh'g denied, 481 F2d 404, cert. denied, 414 US 1092 (1973) (incorporation transfer and subsequent stock-for-stock exchange upheld as separate tax-free transactions; Maurice Weikel, ¶ 86,058 P-H Memo. TC (same).

For more on the overlap between §351 and the reorganization provisions, see infra ¶ 3.19 and footnotes thereto. See generally Wood, Business Purpose and Step-Transaction Doctrines, 13 J. Corp. Tax'n 377 (1987).

[163] See supra ¶ 3.01.

[164] See generally Chirelstein, Tax Pooling and Tax Postponement—The Capital Exchange Funds, 75 Yale L.J. 183 (1965).

[165] Regs. §1.351-1(c)(1).

exchange or traded or quoted regularly in the over-the-counter market.[166] Note that if a diversifying transfer to an investment company occurs, *losses* will be recognized as well as gains.

These regulations impose restrictions on §351(c)(1) that are not required by the unqualified statutory references to transfers of property to an investment company. On the other hand, a caveat against pushing too close to the outer limits of the regulations is provided by the Service's list of areas under extensive study, in which rulings will not be issued until unsettled questions are resolved, such as

> [w]hether section 351 applies to the transfer of widely held developed or underdeveloped real property or interests therein; widely held oil and gas properties or interests therein; or any similarly held properties or interests to a corporation in exchange for shares of stock of such corporation when (i) the transfer is the result of solicitation by promoters, brokers, or investment houses, or (ii) the transferee corporation's stock is issued in a form designed to render it readily tradable.[167]

¶ 3.16 TRANSFER UNDER §351 VS. DIVIDEND

The regulations under §351 suggest the possibility that a distribution by a corporation of its stock or securities "in connection with an exchange subject to section 351(a)" may have "the effect of the distribution of a taxable dividend."[168] Although this part of the regulations does not identify the circumstances under which such a distribution might occur, there are at least these possibilities:

(1) A transfer of property to a controlled corporation in exchange for stock and securities having a value greater than the property transferred. The excess value might be treated as a distribution under §301.[169]

(2) A transfer of property to a controlled corporation in exchange for securities if the transfer was merely a device, lacking in business

---

[166] Id. Option rights (warrants, convertible debentures, and so forth) in marketable securities are themselves treated as marketable. See Rev. Rul. 87-9, 1987-5 IRB 4 (traded stock of one corporation and cash, 11 percent, had diversifying effect).

[167] Rev. Proc. 87-3, §5.16 1987-1 IRB 27; see Winston, The IRS' No-Ruling Policy on Exchange Offers, 61 Taxes 375 (1983).

For the status of transfers to partnership swap funds, see McKee, Nelson & Whitmire, Federal Taxation of Partnerships and Partners (Warren, Gorham & Lamont, Inc., 1977), ¶ 4.09.

[168] See Regs. §1.351-2(d).

[169] See Regs. §1.301-1(j).

purpose, for extracting the securities from the corporation. The government might assert that a transfer in these circumstances was really a contribution to capital coupled with a distribution of securities taxable under §301.

(3) A reincorporation.[170]

(4) A transfer of stock of an affiliated corporation in a transaction covered by §304.[171]

In warning of the possibility that a dividend may occur in conjunction with a §351 exchange, Regs. §1.351-2(d) speaks only of a distribution of stock or securities. But it is equally possible that a distribution of money or other property would, in the circumstances described above, be taxed as a dividend under §301 rather than as boot under §351(b),[172] even though it is coupled with the receipt of stock or securities.

¶ 3.17　MIDSTREAM TRANSFERS OF POTENTIAL INCOME

By providing for the nonrecognition of gain or loss on the transfer of property to a controlled corporation and for a carryover of the transferor's basis, §§351 and 362 contemplate as a general principle that the unrecognized gain or loss will be taken into account by the transferee corporation when it disposes of the property received. When a going business is incorporated, however, the transferred assets do not ordinarily consist solely of investment property, but include inventory, accounts receivable, property under contract or earmarked for customers, materials and supplies whose cost was deducted by the transferor on acquisition, work in process, installment obligations, contract rights, and other items that would have generated taxable income to the transferor in the ordinary course of business, possibly within a few days or weeks. Attention has already been called to the possibility that some claims and other items of this character, especially if created by the transferor's personal services, may not constitute "property" within the meaning of §351(a), in which event the transferor's receipt of stock or

---

[170] See infra ¶ 3.20.

[171] In general, §304 takes precedence when it overlaps with §351; see generally infra ¶ 9.12.

[172] For recognition of this possibility, see Arthur M. Rosenthal, supra note 156; Dunn v. US, 259 F. Supp. 828 (W.D. Okla. 1966), aff'd, 400 F2d 679 (1968); Wolf v. CIR, supra note 65; Rev. Rul. 78-422, 1978-2 CB 129; Rev. Rul. 80-239, 1980-2 CB 103. See generally Blanchard, The Service's Recent Attack: Taxation of Section 351 Exchanges Between Shareholders and Newly Organized Holding Companies, 35 Tax Lawyer 163 (1981) (analyzing Rev. Rul. 80-239).

securities of the controlled corporation in exchange for the item in question will result in taxable income under §61(a) or §1001.[173] Even if the property requirement of §351 is fully satisfied, however, the taxpayer must contend with the possibility that the statutory provision for nonrecognition of gain is subordinate in certain cases to such basic doctrines as the assignment-of-income and tax-benefit principles or to the Service's statutory authority under §§446(b) and 482 to require a different accounting method or an allocation of income and deductions in order to "clearly reflect income." When applicable, these rules require the transferors to take certain items into account in their own return rather than shifting that burden to the transferee corporation. Although these principles should not be permitted to frustrate the congressional desire to facilitate the incorporation of going businesses by enacting §351's rule of nonrecognition of gain and loss, it is equally unreasonable to assume that §351 transcends all other statutory and judicial principles of tax liability.[174] Because no standards susceptible of extrapolation to other instances have as yet emerged in this area, the best that can be done at this point is to mention some of the trouble spots and summarize the results that have been reached.[175]

1. **Assignment of income.** Despite §351, and in reliance on such cases as *Lucas v. Earl* and *Helvering v. Horst*, a taxpayer transferring a claim for personal services has been taxed when (1) the transferee corporation collected the amount due; (2) a newly formed corporation's sale of growing crops has been treated as a sale by the transferor, who held them until shortly before harvesting; and (3) a shareholder who canceled his claim for unpaid salary against a controlled corporation in exchange for its stock was held to have disposed of the claim for value.[176]

---

[173] Supra ¶ 3.02.

[174] A similar problem of allocating items between transferor and transferee can arise on the liquidation of a corporation, especially if a going business is transferred to the shareholders; and many of the cases in this area have implications for §351 exchanges. See infra ¶ 11.07.

[175] See generally Manning, The Service Corporation—Who Is Taxable On Its Income: Reconciling Assignment of Income Principles, Section 482, and Section 351, 37 U. Miami L. Rev. 657 (1984); Goldstein, Tax-Free Incorporation: Are Courts Today Taking Too Restrictive View of Section 351, 39 J. Tax'n 165 (1973); Lyon & Eustice, supra note 23; Eustice, supra note 23; Baldwin, Section 351 of the Internal Revenue Code and Mid-Stream Incorporations, 38 U. Cin. L. Rev. 96 (1969).

[176] Lucas v. Earl, 281 US 111 (1980); Helvering v. Horst, 311 US 112 (1940); See Brown v. CIR, 115 F2d 337 (2d Cir. 1940) (claim for legal fees); Clinton Davidson, 43 BTA 576 (1941) (acq.) (insurance commissions); Adolph Weinberg, 44 TC 233 (1965), aff'd per curiam sub nom. CIR v. Sugar Daddy, Inc., 386 F2d 836 (9th Cir. 1967) (growing crops), cert. denied, 392 US 929 (1968); CIR v. Fender Sales,

On the other hand, an important 1980 ruling[177] recognizes that the function of §351 would be frustrated if cash basis transferors were routinely taxed on the accounts receivable of a going business when the enterprise is incorporated, and the Service accordingly ruled that the assignment-of-income doctrine is not applicable if there is no tax-avoidance purpose for the transaction. Thus, assuming a business purpose, the accounts receivable generate income when collected by the transferee corporation, just as the accounts payable generate deductions when paid.[178]

2. Reallocations under §482. Section 482, as explained in more detail in Chapter 15, authorizes the Service to allocate income, deductions, and other tax items between two or more businesses under common control if necessary to clearly reflect their respective incomes. For example, if a corporation engages in transactions with a business conducted by its shareholders in proprietorship or partnership form, the Service can invoke §482 to insure that the intrafamily prices conform to an arm's-length standard. But §482 is not limited to these post-incorporation transactions; it can also be applied *at the time of incorporation* (e.g., to nullify a tax-motivated selection of which accounts receivable or accounts payable are to be transferred to a newly organized corporation or a transfer of appreciated property at a time dictated by tax rather than business considerations.[179] There is also authority for the application of §482 at the time of incorporation, even though the transferors do not engage in business transactions with the corporation *thereafter*, and the corporation, being newly created, had no *earlier* transactions with the transferors—that is, §482's requirement of two or more related businesses is satisfied by the fact that the related parties conducted two businesses in the same taxable year, even though the first terminated when the second began.[180]

Inc., supra note 126 (stock-for-salary claim). But see H.B. Zachry Co., 49 TC 73 (1967) (exchange of a carved-out oil payment); Arthur L. Kniffen, supra note 62 (accrued interest on assigned notes not taxable to transferor in §351 exchange).

[177] Rev. Rul. 80-198, 1980-2 CB 113, citing Hempt Bros. v. CIR, 490 F2d 1172, cert. denied, 419 US 826 (1974), and distinguishing Brown v. CIR, supra note 176.

[178] For the transferee corporation's right to deduct accounts payable if the transferor could have deducted them, see supra note 118.

[179] See Foster v. CIR, 756 F2d 1430 (9th Cir. 1985) (tax-motivated transfers of appreciated land in course of real estate development); Rev. Rul. 80-198, 1980-2 CB 113 (§482 applicable "when the timing of the incorporation improperly separates income from related expenses"); Peck v. CIR, 752 F2d 469 (9th Cir. 1985).

See generally Adess, The Role of Section 482 in Nonrecognition Transactions—The Outer Edges of Its Application, 57 Taxes 946 (1979); and Martin, Section 482 and the Nonrecognition Provisions: Resolving the Conflict, 77 Nw. U.L. Rev. 670 (1982); infra ¶ 15.03.

[180] Central Cuba Sugar Co. v. CIR, 198 F2d 214 (2d Cir.), cert. denied, 344 US 874 (1952) (taxpayer transferred all assets to a newly organized corporation in

3. Proper accounting method under §446(b). Section 446(b), permitting the Service to compute income under a proper accounting method if the one employed by the taxpayer does not clearly reflect its income, can be invoked in the context of §351.[181] In *Palmer v. CIR*, for example, a taxpayer who had been reporting income from a construction business using the completed-contract method of accounting transferred the business to a controlled corporation shortly before the major payment fell due for work that was largely completed before the transfer.[182] The court upheld an adjustment based on the percentage-of-completion accounting method and reflecting the taxpayer's ratable share of the net income earned before incorporation, thereby allocating a substantial portion of the corporate income back to him.

4. Tax-benefit rule and related problems. In *Nash v. US*, the Supreme Court rejected an attempt by the Service to tax the transferor of a going business on its bad debt reserve when the business assets were transferred to a newly created corporation.[183] Although the transferor's additions to the reserve in the preincorporation years had generated tax benefits and he no longer needed the reserve, the Court held that the transfer of the accounts receivable for stock of the transferee did not constitute a "recovery" of the reserve within the meaning of the tax-benefit doctrine.[184]

To insure that any unnecessary portion of the bad debt reserve will ultimately be taken into income, however, it seems appropriate to require the transferee corporation to reduce the face amount of the accounts receivable transferred to it by the amount of the previously deducted reserve in computing its basis for the receivables.[185] Thus, if the full face amount is col-

---

exchange for the latter's stock, which taxpayer distributed to its own shareholders, in exchange for their shares); see also Regs. §1.482-1(d)(5) (§482 applies in context of §351 exchange). Compare Eli Lilly & Co., 84 TC 996 (1985); G.D. Searle & Co., 88 TC 252 (1987).

[181] See infra ¶¶ 15.03–15.04.

[182] Palmer v. CIR, 267 F2d 434 (9th Cir.), cert. denied, 361 US 821 (1959).

[183] Nash v. US, 398 US 1 (1970).

[184] For a subsequent Supreme Court opinion holding that a technical "recovery" is not a prerequisite to application of the tax-benefit doctrine, see Hillsboro Nat'l Bank v. CIR, 460 US 370 (1983). See generally Bittker, Federal Taxation of Income, Estates and Gifts (Warren, Gorham and Lamont, Inc., 1981), ¶ 5.7.

[185] Rev. Rul. 78-280, 1978-2 CB 139 (effect on basis and tax results to transferee of later collections and losses). See generally O'Hare, Statutory Nonrecognition of Income and the Overriding Principle of the Tax Benefit Rule in the Taxation of Corporations and Shareholders, 27 Tax L. Rev. 215 (1972); Raskind, The Tax Treatment of the Reserve for Bad Debts on Incorporation: The Supreme Court Resolution in *Nash*, 31 Ohio St. L.J. 411 (1970).

lected, the transferee corporation would realize income equal to the amount deducted by the transferor before the §351 exchange.

The transferor's substituted basis for the transferee's stock under §358 apparently is determined by reference to the net value of the receivables (i.e., face, less the amount of the untaxed reserve). Hence, even if the receivables turn out to be worth more than this amount (e.g., are collected at face by the transferee), later sales of stock by the transferor give rise to capital gain rather than ordinary income, even if the gain is due in whole or in part to the previously deducted reserve.

In reaching its conclusion in the *Nash* case, the Court stated that the stock received by the transferors was "equal in value to the net worth of the accounts transferred, that is the face value less the amount of the reserve for bad debts." [186] This factual premise suggests that a different result might have been reached if the stock issued had been worth more than this net amount; while the case does not necessarily invite an inquiry into this issue in other bad debt reserve cases, the Court may have left room for the tax-benefit doctrine in other situations (i.e., if the transferors had deducted the cost of materials and supplies having a short useful life, and if some or all of the deducted items were still on hand at the time of the transfer and were reflected in the value of the stock received by the transferor). [187]

5. Business purpose, step transactions, and other principles. The transfer to a second corporation controlled by the transferors of stock on which a large dividend was about to be paid without any business purpose, but in the hope of qualifying the dividend for the dividends-received deduction of §243, was held to be ineffective in Rev. Rul. 60-331, with the result that the dividend was taxable to the individual transferors. [188] In the same vein, a transfer of property to a corporation with no purpose other than to prepare for a sale or exchange of the stock in the hope of reporting capital gain

---

[186] Supra note 183, at 4. Since other assets were also transferred, the value of the stock was not limited to the value of the receivables; the Court presumably meant that the fair market value of the accounts was their face amount less the reserve and that the value of the stock reflected this net amount.

[187] For the deduction of short-lived items, see Regs. §1.162-6. In at least one area (the recapture of depreciation deductions that prove in retrospect to have been excessive), however, the existence of statutory solutions (§§1245 and 1250) that explicitly limit their applicability in §351 exchanges appears to preempt the possibility of a recapture on tax-benefit principles. See Rev. Rul. 71-569, 1971-2 CB 314; see also §1276(d)(1).

[188] Rev. Rul. 60-331, 1960-2 CB 189; but see George Cukor, ¶ 68,107 P-H Memo. TC (1968) (contra as to §351 exchange of stock dividend on). But cf. Silco v. US, 779 F2d 282 (5th Cir. 1986).

For the dividends-received deduction of §243, see infra ¶ 5.05.

thereon may be disregarded, in which event the transaction will be treated as a direct sale of the property itself.[189]

Aside from these doctrines of vague ambit that are sometimes overlapping routes to the same end, a number of statutory provisions require the transferor of certain types of property to report income on a disposition or other transfer. These provisions sometimes explicitly provide whether a §351 exchange is to be so treated (as in §§1245 and 1250, exempting §351 transfers if wholly tax-free); but sometimes this matter is left to administrative and judicial construction. An example is §453 (relating to installment obligations) under which the regulations and cases hold that a §351 transaction does not constitute a taxable disposition of such assets.[190]

Finally, it should be emphasized that the corporate transferee, despite the continuity-of-ownership and business-enterprise characteristics of the §351 transaction, nevertheless constitutes a separate taxable entity from its transferors, with its own method of accounting, taxable period, and other election privileges. Hence it cannot be viewed as merely the formal extension or alter ego of its incorporators absent a showing of facts that would cause disregard of its corporate entity.[191]

¶ 3.18 COLLATERAL PROBLEMS OF INCORPORATING A GOING BUSINESS

Switching from a sole proprietorship or partnership to the corporate form of doing business can raise numerous collateral problems in addition to those relating to qualification and effect of the §351 exchange itself. Some

---

[189] See West Coast Mktg. Corp., 46 TC 32 (1966); Rev. Rul. 70-140, supra note 94; Maurice Weikel, supra note 162 (contra). Compare James Hallowell, 56 TC 600 (1971) (property contributed to corporation and resold pursuant to single plan resulted in taxable gain to transferor). But see Eleanor H. Smalley, ¶ 73,085 P-H Memo. TC (1973) (contribution of stock to corporation, followed by corporate sale of property, held not to be a sham transaction; gain taxable to corporation rather than shareholder). See also Stewart v. CIR, 714 F2d 977 (9th Cir. 1983) (shareholder taxable on corporate resale of contributed property). But compare Stewart v. US, 739 F2d 411 (9th Cir. 1984).

[190] See Regs. §1.453-9(c)(2); for current law, see §453 A; for the special case of status of debts owed to the transferor by the transferee corporation, see Jack Ammann Photogrammetric Eng'rs, Inc. v. CIR, supra note 27; Rev. Rul. 73-423, 1973-2 CB 161; §351(d)(2), supra text at note 24.

[191] See Ezo Prods. Co., 37 TC 385 (1961) (transferee corporation not same taxpayer as transferor in applying §481, relating to adjustments required on change of accounting method); Regs. §1.167(c)-1(a)(6) (similar theory in determining original use of depreciable transferred property); Dearborn Gage Co., 48 TC 190 (1967) (relation of §481 adjustments for inventory valuation where property acquired in §351 exchange); Rev. Rul. 85-134, 1985-2 CB 160. See also ¶ 1.05, infra ¶ 3.18.

of these problems have been noted in preceding sections of this chapter;[192] others are discussed in other chapters of this work, but deserve brief mention at this point.

1. The transferors. When incorporating a going business that has been conducted as a sole proprietorship or partnership, the transferors may want to hold back some of the assets from the §351 exchange, preferring instead to lease or license these properties to the corporation in a separate transaction. Related party dealings of this sort have their own tax hurdles to surmount,[193] but disqualification of the §351 exchange does not appear to be one of their consequences. Indeed, shareholder leasing of retained assets to a controlled corporation is a standard technique for subsequently extracting money on a tax-deductible basis from the corporation. If the terms are fair, the transaction is respected; but if overreaching is present, §482 and constructive dividend exposure results.[194]

When a partnership desires to incorporate, the form of the transaction is often a matter of indifference to the parties; thus, the partnership can transfer its properties to the new corporation in exchange for its stock, then it can either continue in existence, holding the stock as partnership property, or liquidate, distributing the stock to the partners in complete liquidation.[195] Alternatively, the partnership can liquidate first, distributing its assets in kind to the partners; they can then transfer the assets to the corporation in exchange for its stock. A third route is a transfer by the partners of their partnership interests to the corporation for stock, followed by a liquidation of the partnership and a distribution of its assets to the corporation. These routes ordinarily have the same practical consequences, but the Service ruled in 1984 that they have different federal tax results for both the transferors (e.g., under §1244, relating to losses on certain small business corporations) and the transferee corporation (e.g., its basis and the holding period for the transferred assets).[196] The ruling, however, rests on a detailed examination of the special tax rules prescribed for partnerships by Subchapter K, and it is hence beyond the scope of this work.[197]

---

[192] E.g., supra ¶¶ 3.05, 3.06, 3.14, 3.16, and 3.17.

[193] See infra ¶¶ 7.05, 15.03, and 15.04.

[194] See supra text at notes 178–180; see also infra ¶¶ 7.05, 15.03.

[195] If the stock is distributed directly to the partners, bypassing the partnership, see Miller Bros. Elec., 49 TC 446 (1968) (§351 applies; stock constructively received by partnership).

[196] Rev. Rul. 84-111, 1984-2 CB 88, revoking Rev. Rul. 70-239, 1970-1 CB 74.

[197] See Barrie & Jones, Incorporating an Ongoing Partnership: Selecting The Appropriate Method, 3 J. Partnership Tax'n 335 (1987); Bogdanski, Closely Held Corporations, 11 J. Corp. Tax'n 367 (1985); McKee, Nelson & Whitmire, Federal

2. The transferee corporation. The transferee corporation, if newly organized, becomes "a taxpayer" with all burdens and benefits that status entails. Thus, with the filing of its first required return, it has the right to choose its taxable period (calendar or fiscal year), its method of accounting (cash, accrual, or hybrid), its inventory, bad-debt write-off, and depreciation or amortization methods, use of installment reporting, and other similar timing options.[198] Since §381 does not apply to the usual §351 transaction, the transferee corporation is neither required nor permitted to take over the tax attributes of its transferors, other than the basis and holding period of properties transferred to it upon incorporation.[199] Other options that may be available to the newly organized corporation include the Subchapter S election not to be subject to corporate taxes on its income and to pass through operating losses to its shareholders (see Chapter 6), and, if it is a subsidiary, the possibility of filing consolidated returns with its parent.[200]

¶ 3.19 RELATION OF §351 TO REORGANIZATION PROVISIONS

As noted previously, a §351 transaction may occur as part of, or as an alternative to, a tax-free reorganization.[201] Thus, incorporation of a new subsidiary, which constitutes a §351 exchange, may also qualify as a Type D reorganization[202] if the new subsidiary's stock is distributed in a transaction that qualifies under §354 or §355. The fact that §351—as well as §354 or §361—applies to the incorporation transfer ordinarily is a matter of indifference to the parties, since nonrecognition treatment is accorded to the trans-

---

Taxation of Partnerships and Partners (Warren, Gorham & Lamont, Inc., 1977), ¶ 17.03; Banoff, supra note 71.

[198] See supra notes 190–191; Regs. §§1.441-1(b)(3), 1.446-1(e)(1), and 1.6012-2(a)(2). But see §441(i) and 448, added by the Tax Reform Act of 1986, limiting corporate taxpayers' use of the cash method and requiring "personal service corporations" (supra ¶ 2.07) to adopt a calendar year for tax-reporting purposes. See infra ¶ 5.07.

[199] See infra ¶¶ 16.11 and 16.14. If the §351 transaction also constitutes a tax-free reorganization as mentioned in §381(a), however, carry-over treatment seems to apply. See infra ¶ 3.19 for discussion of these overlap possibilities. For the transferee corporation's basis and holding period for the transferred assets, see supra ¶ 3.11.

[200] Infra ¶ 15.20. For the recognition of separate corporate entity status, see supra ¶ 1.05 and ch. 2; for limitations on the tax benefits of multiple corporations, see infra ¶ 15.01; for restrictions on the use or enjoyment of certain corporate tax attributes, see infra ¶ 16.20.

[201] Supra ¶¶ 3.01, 3.14, and 3.17.

[202] Infra ¶ 14.16.

feror in either event. Collateral effects may attach to a reorganization that do not apply in the case of simple §351 transactions, however, such as the carryover of tax attributes under §381, boot dividend possibilities under §356(a)(2), and different ruling criteria under §367.[203]

In general, it would seem that the reorganization rules ought to prevail over those of §351 where the two overlap, in view of the more comprehensive statutory patterns and principles applicable to the former. Surprisingly, however, there is little specific authority on this question, and the most that can be said is that much is still an open question in this area.

The overlap possibilities between §351 and the reorganization provision could occur in the following situations:

(1) A corporation's transfer of all of its properties to a new corporation in exchange for all of the new corporation's stock and its subsequent distribution of the stock in complete liquidation (i.e., the entity's reincorporation in a different corporate shell) qualifies under §351, but it also constitutes a Type D reorganization (and could be considered a Type F reorganization,[204] or a Type A reorganization if effected pursuant to state merger law[205]). Clearly, §381, which applies to reorganizations but does not refer to §351 exchanges, should apply to this transaction. Whether §357(c) gain (liability in excess of basis) would result here, however, is a more difficult question; §357(c)(1) applies to §351 exchanges and to those §361 exchanges that constitute Type D reorganiations, but not, presumably, to Type A or Type F reorganizations. It could be argued that since §351 applies here, §357(c) should come into play, since the §351 transaction is not ousted from jurisdiction by the concurrent application of §361. On the other hand, a mere reincorporation (Type F) reorganization seems an inappropriate time to impose a tax under §357(c), and it appears that §357(c) would be held inapplicable.[206]

(2) The transfer of stock of a controlled corporation for stock of another controlled corporation qualifies as a Type B reorganization[207] as well as a §351 exchange, so that the transferor would obtain nonrecognition under both §§354 and 351. Rev. Rul. 70-433 held that §351 applies to this situation and that the transferor did not need a §367 ruling because the transferee was a domestic cor-

---

[203] For §381, see infra ch. 16. For ¶ 356(a)(2), see infra ¶ 14.34. For §367, see infra ch. 17, pt. E.

[204] Infra ¶ 14.18.

[205] Infra ¶ 14.12.

[206] Rev. Rul. 79-289, 1979-2 CB 145, so holds; see also Rev. Rul. 68-349, 1968-2 CB 143.

[207] Infra ¶ 14.13.

poration, even though §354 (which ordinarily requires a §367 ruling) also applied.[208]

(3) A corporation that transfers substantially all its assets to a controlled corporation, but does not liquidate, apparently has effected a technical Type C reorganization,[209] in addition to a §351 exchange. Does §357(c), which covers §351 exchanges but not Type C reorganizations, apply? It would seem that §351 alone should support application of §357(c) here, in view of the predominantly §351 character of this transaction (unlike the other situations considered herein, where the role of §351 is incidental to the transaction).[210]

(4) A §351 transaction may constitute an integral step in a tax-free reorganization, but the various steps in the plan, including the §351 segment, may be rearranged by the Service to reflect the economic substance of the transaction. Thus, liquidation of a corporation followed by a reincorporation of its operating assets in a new controlled corporation may be recast as a corporate level reorganization under §368(a)(1)(D).[211] Also, Rev. Rul. 68-349 holds that an accommodation corporate transferee may be disregarded (by treating the transferor as if it had merely reincorporated in a new corporate shell) in order to tax the other transferors of property. Finally, Rev. Rul. 70-140 warns that a preliminary §351 incorporation transaction in preparation for a planned Type B reorganization exchange (stock for stock) may be recast as a taxable exchange of assets for stock. On the other hand, Rev. Rul. 68-357 recognizes the possibility that §351 can coexist in tandem with a Type C reorganization without destroying the tax-free character of either transaction.[212]

---

[208] Rev. Rul. 70-433, 1970-2 CB 82; see also Rev. Rul. 74-502, 1974-2 CB 116 (transfer of stock of existing public corporation to new corporation for latter's common and nonvoting preferred stock, so former shareholders of old corporation had control of new corporation; held exchange qualified under §351). For the application of §306, requiring gain on dispositions of §306 stock to be reported as ordinary income, see Rev. Rul. 79-274, 1979-2 CB 131 (overlap of Type B reorganization and §351; voting preferred received pro rata by transferors held §306 stock if transferee has earnings and profits in its first taxable year); for current law, see §306(c)(3) (added in 1982). See generally (for prior law) Corry, Preferred Stock Issued in Tax-Free Exchanges: Does Section 306 Apply? 35 Tax L. Rev. 113 (1979).

[209] Infra ¶ 14.14.

[210] Rev. Rul. 76-188, 1976-1 CB 99 (§357(c) applies to §351 transfer that also qualified as Type C reorganization where parent transferred substantially all its assets subject to liabilities in excess of basis to new subsidiary and stayed alive as holding company). But see §368(a)(2)(G), added in 1984 (transferor must now liquidate in a Type C reorganization unless waived by the Service).

[211] Infra ¶ 3.20.

[212] Rev. Rul. 68-357, 1968-2 CB 144; Rev. Rul. 68-349, 1968-2 CB 143; Rev. Rul. 70-140, 1970-1 CB 73; see also Rev. Rul. 76-123, 1976-1 CB 94 for another combina-

(5) Inspired by some of the broader implications of Rev. Rul. 76-123,[213] use of §351 as an alternative acquisition method to the tax-free reorganization provisions of §368 has been suggested in view of the more relaxed limitations of the former. For example, creating a preliminary holding company owned jointly by the acquiring corporation and those shareholders of the target company who want nonrecognition treatment can allow the remaining shareholders of the target to be bought out for cash, debt securities, or nonvoting stock (or a combination thereof), presumably without rendering the initial incorporation transaction taxable under §351. (In an extreme case, the acquiring corporation could even obtain a cost basis for the acquired corporation's stock or assets if proper planning were adopted.) As noted earlier in this chapter, the Service revoked its initially hostile position and held in 1984 that §351 applies to this sort of transaction, even though it is part of a larger acquisitive transaction; but proposed reform legislation would reverse this priority and subordinate §351 to the general acquisition regime. If enacted, this proposal would revert to the original view of two rulings issued in 1980.[214]

¶ 3.20 REINCORPORATIONS

If a corporation pays a dividend by issuing its bonds or debentures to its shareholders, the distribution, for reasons discussed in Chapter 7, will be taxed about the same as a distribution of property. But if the corporation is liquidated and the stockholders, by prearrangement, then transfer the assets to a newly organized corporation in exchange for stock and bonds or debentures, can they treat the transaction for tax purposes as (1) a liquidation of the old corporation (which is an occasion for recognizing capital gain or loss,

---

tion of a §351 exchange with a Type C reorganization; Rev. Rul. 78-130, 1978-1 CB 114 (illustration of §351, Type D reorganization and Type C reorganization overlap). Rev. Rul. 68-357 and Rev. Rul. 76-123 were distinguished in Rev. Rul. 84-44, 1984-1 CB 105 (stock not aggregated where one corporation merged into subsidiary for stock of parent and another corporation transferred assets to the parent for less than control; since second transferor was the only transferor of property to corporation issuing stock, §351 control was not obtained).

[213] Supra note 212.

[214] Rev. Rul. 84-71, 1984-1 CB 106, revoking Rev. Rul. 80-284, 1980-2 CB 117, and Rev. Rul. 80-285, 1980-2 CB 119. See Friedrich, Recent Developments, 11 J. Corp. Tax'n 290 (1984). For a defense of the revoked 1980 rulings, see Samuels, The Limited Role of Section 351 in Corporate Acquisitions, 60 Taxes 955 (1982). The reform proposals are contained in the Supchapter C Revision Act of 1985, supra note 28.

but may even be tax-free[215]), and (2) a tax-free exchange of property for the stock and securities of the new corporation, under §351? If so, they will have accomplished their purpose without realizing the ordinary income that is usually produced by a distribution of securities by a going corporation. It is possible, of course, that the courts would disregard the liquidation of the old corporation and the creation of the new as a sham, giving effect only to the distribution of securities and taxing it as a dividend. Another approach would be to give effect to the liquidation, but to treat the reincorporation as consisting of (1) an exchange of assets for stock, tax-free under §351, and (2) a separable distribution of securities, taxable as a dividend.[216] Reincorporations flourished for years as tax-avoidance devices of significant potentialities, at least in the discussion of tax advisers, and the problem just mentioned is only a small segment of this area, which will be discussed at greater length in conjunction with corporate liquidations and reorganizations.[217]

¶ 3.21   TRANSFERS UNDER §351 TO FOREIGN CORPORATIONS

Transfers of property to a foreign corporation present special problems in addition to those previously discussed. Section 367 provides that, in determining the extent to which gain shall be recognized in a §351 exchange, a foreign corporation is not considered a corporation unless certain prescribed statutory requirements in §367(a) are satisfied. Despite the curious language of §367 ("a foreign corporation shall not be considered as a corporation"), its effect is to require partial or complete recognition of the gain realized by the transferor on the exchange; the transferee does not lose its corporate status in determining such matters as its basis for transferred property, earnings and profits, and existence as a separate taxable entity.[218]

---

[215] See infra ¶ 11.01.

[216] See Regs. §1.301-1(1).

[217] Infra ¶¶ 11.05 and 14.54.

[218] For detailed analysis, see infra ch. 17, pt. E.

CHAPTER 4

Debt vs. Equity in the Corporation's Capital Structure

PART D. CONVERTIBLE AND OTHER EQUITY-FLAVORED
SECURITIES

PART A.   DEBT VS. EQUITY: PROBLEMS OF CLASSIFICATION

¶ 4.01 INTRODUCTORY

The organizers of a corporation normally have freedom, within the limits imposed by state law and business needs, to create a capital structure either of equity alone (including different classes of stock, such as common and preferred), or of combined equity and debt. In deciding whether to use debt as well as equity to evidence contributions to the corporation, they are ordinarily aware that creditors whose claims are not satisfied when due can force the corporation into bankruptcy, while discontented shareholders can only vote or agitate to oust the board of directors. This difference between debt and equity, however, may not be troublesome if it is contemplated that the debt will be held in proportion to stock and that the relationship among the organizers of a corporation will continue to be harmonious, since in times of financial trouble they are likely to behave the same whether they are shareholder-creditors of the corporation or are merely shareholders. Thus, for the organizers of a closely held corporation, the choice between an all-stock capital structure and a combination of debt and equity may, in the end, rest primarily on tax considerations.

If, however, the corporation must look to outsiders for financing, whether at its inception or later in its history, the shareholder cannot expect defaults to be tolerated; tax considerations are less likely to be decisive in choosing between debt and equity than the legal rights conferred on the outsiders by the type of financing employed. Even so, the tax consequences of the debt-equity option are ordinarily taken into account, and they are sometimes weighty enough to tip the scales.

The choice between debt and equity can affect the tax status of the corporation and its investors in many different ways,[1] the two most commonly encountered of which are the following:

---

[1] For an extensive compilation of the divergent tax effects of debt and equity, see Plumb, The Federal Income Tax Significance of Corporate Debt: A Critical

1. Current distributions. Section 163(a) allows "all interest paid or accrued within the taxable year on indebtedness" to be deducted by the payor corporation; no comparable deduction is allowed for distributions to the corporation's shareholders.[2] Since these payments are ordinarily taxed to noncorporate recipients in the same way whether they constitute interest on debt or distributions on stock, §163(a) usually encourages the corporation to meet its financing needs by borrowing rather than by issuing stock.[3] This generalization must be qualified for entities in certain special circumstances, such as (1) corporations that are incurring losses and cannot use the interest deduction either currently or in the foreseeable future; (2) corporations without earnings and profits, whose distributions to shareholders are ordinarily nontaxable returns of capital up to the adjusted basis of their shares;[4] and (3) corporations whose stock is held by other corporations, since intracorporate dividends qualify for an 80 percent or 100 percent deduction under §243(a)[5] while interest is fully

---

Analysis and a Proposal, 26 Tax L. Rev. 369 (1971). For policy issues raised by the deductibility of interest, see Andrews, Tax Neutrality Between Equity Capital and Debt, 30 Wayne L. Rev. 1057 (1984), articles cited therein, and comments by McLure & Kahn, id. at 1073 and 1081; Sheppard, Should Junk Bond Interest Deductions Be Allowed? 34 Tax Notes 1142 (1987).

[2] This fundamental distinction is subject to minor exceptions; e.g., §279, discussed infra ¶ 4.26, disallows interest on debt incurred in certain debt-financed corporate acquisitions, and §247 allows dividends paid on certain preferred stock of public utilities to be deducted. For the timing of the issuer's deduction and the lender's inclusion in income when interest takes the form of original issue discount, see infra ¶ 4.40.

[3] An additional push in the direction of debt was supplied before 1969, when original issue discount gave rise to current deductions by the issuer but was not taxable to cash-basis holders of the debt until payment at maturity; as explained infra ¶ 4.40, the lender is now taxed currently on original issue discount under an economic accrual regime.

[4] For non-dividend distributions, see §301(c), discussed infra ¶ 7.02.

[5] For discussion of §243, see infra ¶ 5.05, which also discusses §246A, reducing the 80 percent deduction for dividends from debt-financed portfolio stock (as defined). See also Ragland Inv. Co. v. CIR, 52 TC 867 (1969), aff'd per curiam, 435 F2d 118 (6th Cir. 1970) (transaction deliberately structured to create preferred stock in order to qualify for §243 dividends-received deduction; held successful).

That the mitigating effect of the 80 percent deduction for dividends received by corporations is incomplete can be illustrated by comparing it with the tax effects of a payment of deductible interest. If the creditor and debtor are subject to the same marginal tax rate, the payment of interest is a transaction on which no net tax is levied, since the creditor's tax on receiving the interest is exactly offset by the tax savings realized by the debtor from the deduction. By contrast, if dividends are paid and if the shareholder's marginal rate is 34 percent, a net tax of 6.8 percent is levied (34 percent of 20 percent). Thus, a shareholder realizes no difference between preferred stock paying 8 percent and a debt instrument paying 11.3 percent, since the after-tax rate return (taking into account the 80 percent deduction for dividends) is

taxable (assuming the creditor is a tax-paying entity). By and large, however, these countervailing possibilities do not seriously offset the pro-debt bias of the interest deduction.

2. Recovery of investment. From the issuing corporation's perspective, the repayment of debt at maturity is not a taxable event, and the same is true of a redemption of stock, assuming in either case that appreciated property is not used to effect the transaction and, in the case of debt, that there is no unamortized original issue discount or premium.[6]

From the investor's point of view, however, the comparison between debt and equity is more complicated. Ordinarily, shareholders of publicly held corporations whose stock is redeemed apply the proceeds against the adjusted basis of the stock and realize capital gain or loss to the extent of any excess or shortfall.[7] Creditors are similarly entitled to receive repayment of their loans tax-free; but if the payment at maturity exceeds the adjusted basis of the debt being discharged, the gain is taxed as ordinary income rather than as capital gain to the extent of any accrued market discount.[8]

The tax treatment of debt and equity diverges much more dramatically in the case of closely held corporations, whose shareholders may be required to report the entire amount received on the redemption of their stock as ordinary income (with no offset for the adjusted basis of the stock), unless the redemption completely terminates the shareholder's interest in the corporation or is substantially disproportionate relative to the other sharehold-

---

the same: 7.46 percent. A creditor, on the other hand, realizes no difference between preferred stock paying an 8 percent nondeductible dividend and a debt instrument paying deductible interest of 12.12 percent, since the after-tax cost of either is 8 percent. Accordingly, if the parties switch from preferred stock to debt and agree on any rate between 11.3 percent and 12.12 percent, both are better off, other matters being equal. If the creditor is not a tax-paying entity (e.g., it has current losses or is exempt under §§401 or 501), however, the pro-debt bias is significant.

[6] For distributions of appreciated or depreciated property in redemption of stock, see §311, discussed infra ¶ 7.21; for the recognition of gain or loss when appreciated or depreciated property is used to discharge debt, see, e.g., Schultz v. CIR, 59 TC 559, 565 (1973) (transfer of property to discharge debt is taxable as though creditor bought property and debtor used hypothetical payment to discharge debt). For OID and premium, see infra ¶¶ 4.40 and 4.60.

[7] The capital gain/loss result was more important before the Tax Reform Act of 1986 repealed the rate differential for long-term capital gains, but it remains significant in some circumstances (e.g., if the shareholder has offsetting capital losses). Redemptions by public corporations are not exempted per se from the rules of §302, discussed in ¶ 9.02, but their redemptions are likely to meet the criterion of §302(b)(1) ("not essentially equivalent to a dividend"), discussed infra ¶ 9.06.

[8] See §1276, discussed infra ¶ 4.44; for similar treatment of OID on certain obligations issued before May 28, 1969, see §§1271(c)(1) and 1271(c)(2).

ers.[9] By contrast, the creditors of closely held corporations, even if they also own stock in the enterprise, are taxed in the same manner as creditors of publicly held corporations—that is, they can recover the adjusted basis of the claim tax-free, and are taxed only to the extent of any excess received.

This opportunity for investors in closely held corporations to withdraw their debt investments painlessly rivals the interest deduction in encouraging them to split their investment between debt and equity rather than to use an all-stock capital structure. For reasons examined in subsequent chapters of this treatise, however, corporations that do not issue debt at the outset ordinarily find that the void cannot be filled at a later date (e.g., by recapitalizing the corporation) without adverse tax consequences to the shareholders.[10]

The capital asset status of debt, as compared with equity, is discussed later in this chapter, as is the divergent treatment of debt and equity when the investment becomes worthless.[11] Various other tax differences between these two investment vehicles are examined elsewhere in this work, a sampling of which, set out only to illustrate the pervasive distinction between debt and equity, is as follows: (1) A corporation cannot make a Subchapter S election or retain that status if it has more than one class of stock outstanding, but there is no limit on the number of classes of debt instruments it can issue;[12] (2) stock qualifies more readily than debt for tax-free distributions in corporate reorganizations;[13] and (3) while dividends and interest are sometimes aggregated in determining whether a corporation is subject to the punitive personal holding company tax, in other circumstances dividends are more damaging than interest (or vice versa).[14]

In addition to these differences between debt and equity, the Code sometimes draws distinctions *within* each of these broad categories. Thus, as noted elsewhere in this treatise, it may sometimes be necessary to distinguish between common and preferred stock, voting and nonvoting stock, or securities and other debt instruments.[15]

---

[9] See generally infra ¶ 9.04 (substantially disproportionate redemptions) and ¶ 9.05 (terminations of shareholder's entire interest). For the transfer of the basis of the redeemed shares to other shares, see infra ¶ 9.32.

[10] See Bazley v. CIR, 331 US 737 (1947), discussed infra ¶ 14.17. This prejudice against an all-stock capital structure does not apply to corporations electing under Subchapter S; see infra ch. 6.

[11] See infra ¶ 4.20 (capital asset status) and ¶ 4.22 (deductions for worthlessness).

[12] Infra ¶ 6.02.

[13] Infra ¶ 14.34.

[14] Infra ¶ 8.21; see also Plumb, supra note 1.

[15] See, e.g., supra ¶¶ 3.03 (securities vs. other evidences of indebtedness), infra 7.43 (preferred stock), 10.03 (common stock), and 14.13 ("voting stock"); see also the

Two further points affecting the capital structure of corporations at the planning stage should be noted here:

1. Registration of obligations. Section 163(f) disallows deductions for interest on so-called registration-required obligations unless they are in registered form (i.e., including book entries qualifying under the regulations). This provision was enacted in 1982 to discourage the use of bearer instruments as a means of avoiding income, estate, and gift taxes and of facilitating illegal activities. Registration is not required, however, for obligations that (1) mature in one year or less, (2) are not of a type offered to the public, or (3) meet conditions designed to ensure that they will be marketed only to non-U.S. persons and that the interest will be payable outside the United States and its possessions.[16]

2. Leases and licenses as alternatives to debt or equity. The organizers of a corporation sometimes can choose between (1) transferring property to the corporation in exchange for debt or stock and (2) retaining the property but making it available to the corporation by lease or license, particularly when incorporating a going business that has been operated as a sole proprietorship or partnership. If, for example, buildings, machinery, or patents are rented or licensed from the corporation's shareholders for amounts that can be justified by reference to the assets' fair market value, the corporation can deduct the payment as a business expense under §162(a), much as it could deduct interest payments if it had acquired the property outright in exchange for bonds or other obligations; growth in the value of the property inures to the benefit of the shareholders in their personal capacities after the lease or license expires.

¶ 4.02   DEBT OR EQUITY? CLASSIFICATION PROBLEMS

In attaching different tax consequences to debt as compared with equity, the Code necessarily presupposes that these alternative ways of investing in a corporation can be distinguished from one another; but the Code itself does not fix the boundary line. A 1969 attempt by Congress to pass the definitional buck to the Treasury proved to be a fiasco.[17] The crux

---

extensive examination of "The Not-to-Be-Forgotten Term 'Securities' " in Plumb, supra note 1, at 555–574.

[16] See generally Kessler, The Corporate Debt Registration Requirements: Hidden Trap for Close Corporations, 64 Taxes 398 (1986).

[17] Section 385, discussed infra text at notes 33–35.

of the classification problem is that debt and equity are labels for the end points of a spectrum, between which lie an infinite number of investment instruments, each differing from its nearest neighbors in barely perceptible ways. At one end of the spectrum is what is sometimes called "straight" or "classic" debt—"an unqualified obligation to pay a sum certain at a reasonably close fixed maturity date along with a fixed percentage in interest payable regardless of the debtor's income or the lack thereof."[18] At the other end of the spectrum is equity, which has not generated a similarly classic definition, but which connotes an unlimited claim to the residual benefits of ownership and an equally unlimited subjection to the burdens thereof. "The stockholder's intention," it has been said, "is to embark upon the corporate adventure, taking the risks of loss attendant upon it, so that he may enjoy the chances of profit."[19] Moving toward the center of the spectrum, away from both the classic definition of debt and the vaguer concept of equity, one encounters such financial phenomena as debentures that are entitled to a share of the issuing corporation's profits and are subordinated to the claims of general creditors, preferred stock that are entitled to receive a fixed return if earned and to be redeemed on demand at a specified price, and a host of other instruments with similarly blended characteristics.

Before we turn to the criteria used by the Service and the courts to classify these hybrid instruments, the following threshold points deserve attention:

1. Occasions for litigation. Because the distinction between debt and equity is relevant in applying scores of different tax provisions, the litigated cases are similarly diverse; but disputes arise with particular frequency in three circumstances: (1) on the receipt of a hybrid instrument in exchange for property, an event that raises the issue of recognition of gain or loss to the transferor and basis to the transferee if the transaction, as is often the case, occurs in the context of an incorporation under §351;[20] (2) during the term of the instrument, when interest is paid or accrued and deducted by the corporation; and (3) at maturity, when the holder collects the face amount

---

[18] Gilbert v. CIR, 248 F2d 399, 402 (2d Cir. 1957); see also infra note 39.

[19] US v. Title Guarantee & Trust Co., 133 F2d 990, 993 (6th Cir. 1943) (extract italicized in original). For an explicit recognition of the fact that risk per se is not a discernable boundary line, see American Processing & Sales Co. v. US, 371 F2d 842, 856 (Ct. Cl. 1967) ("In the final analysis all loans to a company depend for their repayment on the success of the borrower, and this is, of course, equally true of salvaging equity investments"); see also Motel Co. v. CIR, 340 F2d 445, 446 (2d Cir. 1965) ("the advance was a contribution to risk capital, not merely a risky-loan—an elusive categorization, to be sure, but one that is required by the fact that while [interest is deductible] returns on or of capital are not").

[20] See supra ¶¶ 3.03 and 3.14.

of the instrument or writes it off as worthless.[21] In these situations, both the corporation and its shareholders ordinarily prefer debt classification, while the government usually seeks to classify a disputed instrument as stock; but their roles are sometimes reversed.[22] Moreover, taxpayers and the government may take inconsistent positions in different years, depending on the context in which the issue arises; and the holders of a particular class of hybrid instruments may disagree with the issuer and each other about its proper classification.[23]

2. Shareholder vs. third-party creditors. When a corporation's debt is held by its shareholders in substantial proportion to their stock ownership, the courts know the facts of life, namely, that the shareholders usually subordinate or extend their claims rather than insist on payment if that action would trigger a bankruptcy proceeding. For this reason, as explained in more detail below, even the straightest of shareholder-held debt may be reclassified as equity; and shareholder-held hybrid instruments are a fortiori vulnerable.[24] On the other hand, if ostensibly straight debt is held by unrelated third parties, the courts almost always accept the documents as true debt, since the holders are themselves likely to be hard-nosed about enforcing their rights, even if this pushes the shareholders under water. Third-party holders of hybrid instruments, however, do not necessarily get the classification they seek; the favorable factors are not likely to be brushed aside as camouflage, but they may not outweigh the unfavorable ones.

3. Effects of reclassification. If purported debt obligations are held to constitute equity, it may become necessary to determine whether the reclassified instrument represents common or preferred stock or a capital contri-

---

[21] For an analysis of the litigated cases, comparing the facts in each case in tabular form, see 1987 Fed. Taxes (P-H) ¶ 13,096.

[22] For an example of role reversal in this area, see Zilkha & Sons, 52 TC 607 (1969) (acq.) (Service unsuccessfully argued that purported stock was disguised debt in order to disallow deductions under §243, relating to dividends received by one corporation from another).

[23] See Irving Bartel, 54 TC 25 (1970) (estoppel to deny debt status); §§1311–1314, mitigating the statute of limitations for certain inconsistent position cases; supra ¶¶ 3.10 and 3.11. See generally Walter & Strasen, Innovative Transactions, 64 Taxes 234 (1986) (discussing a public issue of preferred stock that, according to the prospectus, the issuer intended to treat as debt, although there was substantial authority supporting equity classification, virtually an invitation to corporate investors to report the dividends as such and claim the dividends-received deduction).

[24] See infra ¶ 4.03.

bution. Preferred stock is a plausible label, but the investment may be held to constitute merely an additional capital contribution by the shareholders.[25]

4. Changes in status. The classification of a particular instrument is ordinarily determined as of its date of issue, but on occasion the investment may turn out to be a chameleon. Thus, obligations initially held to constitute debt may, over the years, take on the color and character of equity; conversely, hybrid instruments that are held to constitute stock should not necessarily be permanently condemned to that status, although judicial examples of transformation into indebtedness have yet to be found.[26] Moreover, in the litigated cases, classification is routinely treated as an all-or-nothing question, so that instruments have rarely been fragmented between equity and debt.[27] There is nothing in the relevant taxonomic criteria to forbid a bifurcated outcome, but it may be more appealing as a method of settling a case at the administrative level than as a judicial resolution of the dispute.

5. Classification: Question of fact or of law? The Service does not ordinarily issue advance rulings on whether an interest in a corporation is to be treated as stock or debt on the ground that this issue "is primarily one of fact," like the market value of property.[28] Of course, in the absence of statu-

---

[25] For contributions to capital, see generally supra ¶ 3.13; see also infra ¶ 6.02, text at notes 15–17 (S corporation's purported debt reclassified as contribution to capital rather than as second class of stock terminating election).

[26] See Tampa & G.C.R.R. v. CIR, 469 F2d 263 (5th Cir. 1972) (per curiam) (initial debt status changed to equity); Cuyuna Realty Co. v. US, 382 F2d 298 (Ct. Cl. 1967) (same); Fin Hay Realty Co. v. US, 398 F2d 694 (3d Cir. 1968) (original equity status continued despite changes in circumstances). See generally Plumb, supra note 1 at 499–503.

[27] But see Farley Realty Corp. v. CIR, 279 F2d 701 (2d Cir. 1960) (second mortgagee entitled to receive 13–15 percent stated interest plus share in appreciation; held, borrower can deduct stated interest as such but not mortgagee's share of appreciation; latter was not interest on indebtedness, but equity interest in underlying property in nature of joint venture); Paulsen v. CIR, 469 US 131 (1985) (dissenting opinion of Justice O'Connor, asserting that majority in effect fragmented hybrid security in ruling that equity portion of entire value was too insubstantial to satisfy continuity-of-interest doctrine in applying tax-free reorganization provisions). See also infra text at note 61 and ¶ 14.11; Madison, The Deductibility of "Interest" on Hybrid Securities, 39 Tax Lawyer 465 (1986).

[28] Rev. Proc. 87-3, §4.02(1), 1987-1 IRB 27. The phrase "not ordinarily" means that "unique and compelling reasons must be demonstrated to justify a ruling or determination letter." Id. at §2.01. For convertible securities issued with a put entitling the holders to require the corporation to redeem 35 percent of their holdings if the Service asserts on audit that the instruments constitute an equity investment, see Debentures Redeemable Upon Adverse IRS Audit, 64 J. Tax'n 382 (1986).

tory rules, the courts prescribe the legal criteria that govern this question of fact, and, even in the application of the criteria, the proper classification of a particular transaction seems to be ultimately a matter of law.[29] Some of the governing criteria, however, look to factual matters (e.g., the intent of the parties and whether a maturity date is reasonably close) that, once determined by a jury or a trial judge sitting without a jury, are rarely reviewed by appellate courts, although a finding on such a question may be disregarded as immaterial in particular circumstances.[30]

6. Precedential value of case law. Because so many factors may be relevant to the ultimate decision in debt-equity cases, which arise in factual contexts that routinely overlap but never precisely coincide, judicial opinions regularly announce that earlier decisions, although suggestive, are not dispositive.[31] Since the area is devoid of black-letter law, the courts may find

---

[29] See Austin Village, Inc. v. US, 432 F2d 741, 744 (6th Cir. 1970) (earlier conclusion that debt-equity classification is a question of fact abandoned because "on conceptual analysis the better view may be that this issue is a question of law"); but see Roth Steel Tube Co. v. CIR, 800 F2d 921 (6th Cir. 1986) (question of fact reviewable under clearly erroneous standard; *Austin* not mentioned). See also US v. Snyder Bros., 367 F2d 980 (5th Cir. 1966) (opinion on reh'g), cert. denied, 386 US 956 (1967) (whether "debentures on their face constitute indebtedness" depends on interpretation of contract, and hence is a question of law); but see Bauer v. CIR, 748 F2d 1365, 1367–1368 (9th Cir. 1984) (primary issue is intent of parties, which is a question of fact).

[30] See Texas Farm Bureau v. US, 725 F2d 307 (5th Cir. 1984), cert. denied, 469 US 1106 (1985) (jury finding that certain advances constituted debt rejected because no factual issues were present; issue was for court, which should have found that advances were contributions to capital), which cites the principal cases both pro and con, on this fact law problem; see also Ragland Inv. Co. v. CIR, supra note 5 (government should not "blow hot or cold" on whether debt-equity classification is a question of fact or of law), which analogized this issue to the gift-income issue that the Supreme Court held was a question of fact in CIR v. Duberstein, 363 US 278 (1960). As to the relevance of the parties' subjective intent, see infra text at notes 77–80.

In John Kelley Co. v. CIR, 326 US 521, 529 (1946), the Court observed that the debt-equity issue "might be said to be a question of law as to whether the primary facts adduced made the payments [in two cases before it] dividends or interest," but it held that the Tax Court was entitled to the last word by virtue of its expertise, citing Dobson v. CIR, 320 US 489 (1943), reh'g denied, 321 US 231 (1944), which had ruled that Tax Court decisions were entitled to greater finality than decisions of the Federal District Courts. This distinction was subsequently rejected by the enactment of the statutory predecessor of §7482. See Rice, Law, Fact, and Taxes: Review of Tax Court Decisions Under Section 1141 of the [1939] Internal Revenue Code, 51 Colum. L. Rev. 439 (1951).

[31] See, e.g., American Processing & Sales Co. v. US, supra note 19 (earlier cases "offer tentative clues . . . but in the final analysis each case must rest and be decided

themselves in agreement with Justice Stewart's observation about hard-core pornography: "Perhaps I could never succeed in intelligibly [defining it], but I know it when I see it."[32]

7. Treasury authority under §385. The House version of the 1954 Code defined the terms "participating stock," "nonparticipating stock," and "securities" in an effort to clarify the rules governing corporate reorganizations and certain other transactions by distinguishing between stock and debt.[33] The definitions were dropped by the Senate, however, on the recommendation of the Senate Finance Committee, which observed: "Your committee believes that any attempt to write into the statute precise definitions which will classify for tax purposes the many types of corporate stocks and securities will be frustrated by the numerous characteristics of an interchangeable nature which can be given to these instruments."[34]

Having dropped the hot potato in 1954, Congress decided in 1969 to pass it on to the Treasury. Without explaining why precise definitions that could be frustrated if written into the Code would not succumb to the same fate if promulgated by regulations, Congress enacted §385, authorizing the Treasury to define corporate stock and debt by regulations for all purposes of the Code. Section 385 lists five factors that may be considered in the regulations: (1) whether there is a written unconditional promise to pay, on demand or on a specified date, a fixed amount in money in return for an adequate consideration and to pay a fixed rate of interest; (2) whether there is a subordination to, or a preference over, other debt; (3) the ratio of debt to equity; (4) whether there is convertibility of debt into stock; and (5) the relationship between stockholdings and holdings of the interest in question.

Eleven years after §385 was enacted, the Treasury issued proposed, then final regulations (with a delayed effective date that was extended several

---

upon its own unique factual flavor, dissimilar from all others"); see generally Plumb, supra note 1, at 407–410 and note 21.

[32] The authors owe this comparison to Judge Dillin, Sansberry v. US, 25 AFTR2d 620, n.4 (S.D. Ind. 1970) (not officially reported); the comparison is accentuated by the reference to "a corporation's hard core of equity capital" in Stone, Debt-Equity Distinctions in the Tax Treatment of the Corporation and its Shareholders, 42 Tul. L. Rev. 251 (1968).

[33] H.R. Rep. No. 1337, 83d Cong., 2d Sess. A-98–A-99 (1954).

[34] S. Rep. No. 1622, 83d Cong., 2d Sess. 42 (1954). For discussion of similar definitional efforts by other groups, see Committee on Reorganization Problems, N.Y. State Bar Association, Tax Section, Recommendations as to Federal Tax Distinction Between Corporate Stock and Indebtedness, 25 Tax Lawyer 57 (1971); Surrey, Income Tax Problems of Corporations and Shareholders: American Law Institute Tax Project–American Bar Association Committee Study on Legislative Revision, 14 Tax L. Rev. 1, 43 (1958).

times), and then issued new proposed regulations, which were in turn withdrawn in 1983.[35] As Mark Twain commented regarding reports of his death, reports of §385's life proved to be greatly exaggerated. If it has now been permanently relegated to the dustbin of history, perhaps the most fitting epitaph was pronounced in 1957, 12 years before its enactment:

> One might say that this is one of those areas of the tax law where the virtues of vagueness exceed its vices; that courts must look to all the facts and circumstances of each case to see what is really "intended" or what has "substantial economic reality"; and that it is salutary to tell taxpayers only that there is a danger zone which they enter at their peril.[36]

Life goes on.[37]

8. Involuntary reclassifications vs. voluntary conversion. The preceding discussion has concentrated on instruments sailing under false or ambiguous colors and whose credentials are challenged (usually by the Service, but occasionally by taxpayers). The instruments may be reclassified from debt to equity or vice versa. These involuntary reclassifications should be distinguished from the *voluntary* conversion of instruments that, for good business reasons, combine debt and equity features such as conventional convertible debentures. These instruments, whose dual features are openly avowed, are usually entitled to one status until converted by the holder, at which point

---

[35] TD 7920, 1983-2 CB 69. For a summary of the various phases of these regulations, see the 1983 supplements to the 4th Edition of this treatise. For discussion of the now-defunct final regulations, see Stone & McGeehan, Distinguishing Corporate Debt From Stock Under Section 385, 36 Tax L. Rev. 341 (1981); Kaplan & Yoder, New Variations On An Old Enigma: The Treasury Department's Debt-Equity Regulations, 1981 U. Ill. L. Rev. 567 (1981); Beghe, An Interim Report on the Debt-Equity Regulations Under Code Section 385, 59 Taxes 203 (1981); Natbony, Cleaning the Augean Stables: The Debt-Equity Regulations, 8 J. Corp. Tax'n 185 (1981); Levin & Bowen, The Section 385 Regulations Regarding Debt Versus Equity: Is the Cure Worse than the Malady? 35 Tax Lawyer 1 (1981). These articles cite many earlier discussions. (It can only be hoped that the authors of any articles not listed here either billed clients for their time or got tenure at their law schools, although some noble souls may have learned that virtue is its own reward.) See also Manning, Hyperlexis and the Law of Conversation of Ambiguity: Thoughts on Section 385, 36 Tax Lawyer 9, 15 (1982) (wondering whether historians will record that the best and the brightest of America's lawyers "dedicated their creative energies to the production of great works like 110 single-spaced page regulations defining the distinction between equity and debt"); the author of this derisive comment acknowledges (boasts?) that his only expertise is that of the usual corporate practitioner.

[36] Lyon, Federal Income Taxation, Surv. Am. L. 123, 142 annot. (1957).

[37] See infra ¶¶ 4.03–4.04.

their status changes. This ability to move from one rightful status to another (which generates tax issues that are examined later in this chapter[38]) sometimes causes convertible instruments to be described as "hybrid securities." This is a confusing label, since it erroneously implies that they are routinely candidates for reclassification.

¶ 4.03   HYBRID SECURITIES

Investors and corporations wishing to attain a creditor-debtor relationship can ordinarily achieve this objective for tax purposes with classic debt, i.e., "an unqualified obligation to pay a sum certain at a reasonably close fixed maturity date along with a fixed percentage in interest payable regardless of the debtor's income or the lack thereof."[39] Such a firm commitment is not likely to be reclassified as equity unless the obligations are held pro rata by the shareholders or the amount owed is so large, relative to the corporation's current and prospective assets, that the purported creditors are unprotected by an equity cushion.[40] The reference in this classic definition to "a reasonably close" maturity date reflects the fact that creditors whose right to get back their contribution is inordinately postponed may be subjected to the risks of the underlying enterprise to virtually the same extent as shareholders.[41] (In the long run, we are all dead, and perhaps we leave behind only shareholders, not creditors.) If, by contrast, an invulnerable equity status is desired, conventional common or preferred stock is virtually certain to establish the investor's intention "to embark upon the corporate adventure, taking the risks of loss attendant upon it, so that he may enjoy the chances of profit."[42]

---

[38] Infra ¶ 4.61.

[39] Gilbert v. CIR, supra note 18. For similar formulations, see §385(b)(1) ("a written unconditional promise to pay on demand or on a specified date a sum certain in money in return for an adequate consideration in money or money's worth, and to pay a fixed rate of interest"); §1361(c)(5)(B) (straight debt safe harbor for Subchapter S purposes), infra ¶ 6.02.

[40] See infra text at notes 70–74 (thin capitalization). In unusual circumstances, an equity cushion may seem superfluous; for example, if a corporation invests solely in government-guaranteed mortgages and its bonds are collateralized by the mortgages, the bondholders are subject to about the same risk as holders of government securities, even if they are not protected by an equity cushion contributed by the corporation's shareholders.

[41] See Rowan v. US, 219 F2d 51, 55 (5th Cir. 1955) (inordinately postponed maturity date as evidence of contribution to capital rather than debt); but note that §385(b)(1) refers only to a "specified maturity date," not a reasonably close one.

[42] US v. Title Guarantee & Trust Co., supra note 19.

As suggested earlier,[43] these two extremes mark the far ends of a spectrum that has room for an infinite number of hybrid securities that must be classified first by lawyers advising their clients, then by the Service, and finally, if the issue is litigated, by the courts. Some of these hybrid instruments reflect attempts to exploit the tax advantages of debt without being burdened by its nontax restrictions (e.g., impairment of the corporation's future borrowing capacity), but in recent years these experiments in ambiguity have been overshadowed by financial arrangements that combine debt and equity features for good business reasons. As lenders have contemplated inflation and the spectacular growth in the value of real estate and some other equities, they have increasingly sought to share in the earnings and appreciation that historically inured exclusively to the benefit of their borrowers. Conversely, even in a go-go financial environment, some entrepreneurial investors have attempted to cut their risks by bargaining for some of the protections that have traditionally been the hallmarks of the lender. To satisfy these conflicting appetites for risk and security, financial planners have devised a bewildering variety of fence-straddling securities (a/k/a "innovative financial products") that, although by no means innocent of tax motivations, seek to meet genuine business objectives achievable only by abandoning the historic distinction between the terms "pure debt" and "pure equity."[44]

In classifying these hybrid instruments, tax advisers, revenue agents, and judges must do their best with criteria that are difficult to apply for four reasons: (1) They were distilled from a vast body of case law, which almost never identifies any single criterion as either necessary or sufficient to establish debt or equity status;[45] (2) they were generated primarily to grapple with debt held by shareholders in substantial proportion to their stock, a circumstance that breeds skepticism about the economic reality of the purported debt; (3) they are numerous and are not accompanied by a point system or

---

[43] Supra ¶ 4.02.

[44] See, e.g., Walter & Strasen, Innovative Transactions, 64 Taxes 13, 147, 234 (1986); Taylor, Debt/Equity and Other Tax Distinctions: How Far Can We Go? 62 Taxes 848 (1984); Madison, supra note 27. For a similar blurring of the debt-equity distinction in the area of real-estate finance, where reclassification of the lender's status, under criteria that are still veiled in mystery, may result in co-ownership or partnership status, see generally Feder, "Either a Partner or a Lender Be": Emerging Tax Issues in Real Estate Finance, 36 Tax Lawyer 191 (1983); Fisher, Real Estate Financing Techniques: Equity Aspects of Debt Arrangements, 60 Taxes 1040 (1982). For preferred stock issued by public corporations in unusual circumstances, with provisions similar to debt instruments, see Jassy, Issuances of Floating Rate Preferred Stock by Special Purpose Subsidiaries of Loss Corporations, 39 Tax Lawyer 519 (1986).

[45] See John Kelley Co. v. CIR, supra note 30, at 530 ("no one characteristic, not even exclusion from management . . . can be said to be decisive in the determination of whether the obligations are risk investments in the corporation or debts").

hierarchical rating;[46] and (4) there are surprisingly few satisfying explanations of why any particular criterion is important or should be significant.

In determining whether hybrid securities should be classified as debt or equity, the courts customarily refer to a checklist of relevant items, as indicated by this extract from a much-cited decision of the Court of Appeals for the Third Circuit:

> In attempting to deal with this problem, courts and commentators have isolated a number of criteria by which to judge the true nature of an investment which is in form a debt: (1) the intent of the parties; (2) the identity between creditors and shareholders; (3) the extent of participation in management by the holder of the instrument; (4) the ability of the corporation to obtain funds from outside sources; (5) the "thinness" of the capital structure in relation to debt; (6) the risk involved; (7) the formal indicia of the arrangement; (8) the relative position of the obligees as to other creditors regarding the payment of interest and principal; (9) the voting power of the holder of the instrument; (10) the provision of a fixed rate of interest; (11) a contingency on the obligation to repay; (12) the source of the interest payments; (13) the presence or absence of a fixed maturity date; (14) a provision for redemption by the corporation; (15) a provision for redemption at the option of the holder; and (16) the timing of the advance with reference to the organization of the corporation.[47]

In starting with the premise that the security being classified "is in form a debt" and in referring to the holder's relative position as to *other* creditors, this checklist seems to be circular; but these references merely reflect the fact that most hybrid security disputes have involved claims by shareholders that advances to their corporations cast in the form of debt should be recognized as such, not that a different list of factors is controlling in determining the proper status of an instrument purporting to be equity.

A shorter list of evidentiary factors appears in an exhaustive analysis of the case law by the leading commentator on the debt-equity distinction, which is particularly useful because this study examines in detail the reasons for and against treating the individual items as significant. This compendium groups the factors mentioned in the cases into four categories: (1) those involving the formal rights and remedies of the parties; (2) those bearing on the genuineness of the alleged intention to create a debtor-creditor

---

[46] See Tyler v. Tomlinson, 414 F2d 844, 848 (5th Cir. 1969): "The object of the inquiry is not to count factors, but to evaluate them."

[47] Fin Hay Realty Co. v. US, supra note 26, citing earlier cases with similar lists; see also In re Lane, 742 F2d 1311 (11th Cir. 1984) (detailed application of 13-factor list to facts of case); Roth Steel Tube Co., supra note 29 (application of 11-factor test to facts).

relationship (especially relevant in classifying shareholder-held securities); (3) those bearing on the reasonableness or economic reality of the intention (similarly focusing on whether purported shareholder-held debt should be recognized as such); and (4) those that are merely rhetorical expressions of the result, having no proper evidentiary weight in themselves.[48]

At the risk of oversimplification, the conclusions in this analysis regarding the factors in category (1) can be summarized (with minor qualifications) as follows:

1. Maturity date. Perpetual debt is not unknown (e.g., British Consols), but a fixed or ascertainable maturity date is virtually essential to debt classification,[49] although alone it is not necessarily sufficient, since preferred stock may be subject to mandatory redemption at specified times. Thus, the absence of a fixed maturity date is more damaging to debt status than its presence is favorable. Moreover, the maturity date must not be too far in the future, taking into account the nature of the enterprise; the greater the risk of default when the day of reckoning finally arrives, the more the purported creditor is locked into the corporation's fortunes as a shareholder is.[50]

2. Remedies for default. On default, creditors ordinarily have the right to sue for the amount owing and if necessary to force the debtor into bankruptcy, although in the case of bonds, the creditors as a group may be bound by majority vote or by the judgment of an indenture trustee. Disappointed shareholders, however, can ordinarily exercise only their voting rights to replace the board of directors. As taxonomic criterion, however, the remedies available to the holder of the disputed security may at times be circular; it may be necessary to look to local law to determine whether the holder is entitled to the remedial rights of a creditor, and local law may employ criteria similar to the tax law in making this determination.[51]

---

[48] Plumb, supra note 1, at 411–412. For discussion of categories (2) and (3) (intention and economic reality), see infra ¶ 4.04.

[49] For a rare exception, see Helvering v. Richmond, F. & P. R.R. Co., 90 F2d 971 (4th Cir. 1937) (guaranteed stock with characteristics of both debt and equity; held to constitute debt, although holders could not demand payment of principal so long as annual guaranteed dividends were paid).

[50] See Plumb, supra note 1, at 415–416, citing cases suggesting that for the average business, a period of more than 20 years may, viewed realistically, put purported creditors at substantially the same risk as shareholders; but also citing cases allowing much longer periods. See also Monon R.R., 55 TC 345, 359 (1970) (acq.) (on facts, 50-year life not excessive).

[51] For example, even if subordination is not explicitly required by the agreement, it may be judicially imposed in the event of corporate insolvency if the debt is

3. Subordination. Subordination to the claims of general creditors is an adverse factor because it "tends to wipe out a most significant characteristic of the creditor-debtor relationship," and is practically an admission that the advances were considered equity capital, or "is indicative of equity investment."[52] On the other hand, if the disputed instrument, despite subordination to the claims of general creditors, ranks ahead of the preferred and common stock, it is not automatically denied the status of debt. Indeed, a holding company's debt is necessarily subordinated to *all* debt claims against its operating subsidiaries. Moreover, if the purported debt can be paid while senior claims are outstanding so that subordination is triggered only by a default in payment of the senior claims or by bankruptcy, this subordination is less damaging to debt status than if the subordinated claimants cannot be paid until all other claims have been discharged. The courts sometimes play down the significance of subordination when forced on a reluctant corporation by a regulatory agency or institutional lender; but, far from buttressing *debt* status, this may be evidence that the corporation needed additional *equity* capital to conduct its operations responsibly.[53]

4. Certainty of return. While shareholders are entitled to receive dividends only if the corporate earnings and surplus are adequate and the board of directors decides to make a distribution, the right of creditors to receive the interest specified in their contract is either unconditional or, if contingent on adequate corporate earnings, becomes absolute when the condition

---

held by the controlling shareholders, under the *Deep Rock* doctrine; see Taylor v. Standard Gas & Elec. Co., 306 US 307 (1939); Annotation, 51 A.L.R.2d 989 (1957). The relevance of the bankruptcy principles has been acknowledged in tax cases; see, e.g., Kentucky River Coal Corp. v. Lucas, 51 F2d 586, 588 (W.D. Ky. 1931), aff'd, 63 F2d 1007 (6th Cir. 1932) (concluding that local law would not allow so-called debenture stock to be redeemed if certain creditors would be injured, notwithstanding corporate agreement for redemption at par at specified time); see generally Campbell & Lynn, Creditors' Rights Handbook (Clark Boardman Co., Ltd., 1985).

[52] For these and other formulations, see Plumb, supra note 1, at 422; see also supra note 51 (status of shareholder-held debt if bankruptcy ensues).

[53] See Jones v. US, 659 F2d 618 (5th Cir. 1981) (surplus capital notes issued by insurance company to satisfy state reserve requirements; held, debt despite subordination to claims of policyholders); Rev. Rul. 85-119, 1985-2 CB 60 (same result for bank holding company's subordinated notes, with 12-year maturity, payable only with stock or proceeds of sale of stock; caveat against application of determination to instruments issued under other facts and circumstances); Estate of Mixon v. US, 464 F2d 394 (5th Cir. 1972) (no-interest shareholder advance to bank forced on parties by bank examiners). Compare Universal Castings Corp., 37 TC 107, 117 (1961), aff'd, 303 F2d 620 (7th Cir. 1962) (business necessity established that business needed additional equity). See also Federal Express Corp. v. US 645 F. Supp. 1281 (D. Tenn. 1986) (subordination to senior debt only; parity with trade debt; held debt).

is satisfied. Thus, if purported interest is payable only from such amounts as are left after the board has exercised a discretionary power to replenish the corporation's working capital or to establish reserves for contingencies, the instruments resemble stock rather than debt. A fortiori, the failure to provide for interest is ordinarily fatal, since true creditors do not permit their debtors to subject their funds to the risk of its business without appropriate compensation.[54]

   5. Participation in gains. The right of investors to share in the success of the enterprise is ordinarily not inconsistent with a creditor-debtor relationship, whether the participation takes the form of a right to receive a portion of earnings as a return on their advances or an option to convert debt into equity, as in the case of convertible debentures. Since participation in the debtor's earnings or growth is also consistent with equity status, it is at most a neutral factor rather than a dispositive criterion. If, however, exercise of a conversion privilege is virtually certain because the specified ratio provides an opportunity that cannot be refused, the debt features of the instrument may be brushed aside as camouflage.[55] Moreover, if the purported debt is excessive when measured against the assets from which it can be satisfied, payment may be so dependent on the upside potential of the assets that the holder cannot be properly distinguished from a shareholder.[56]

   6. Participation in gains and losses. Debt status has occasionally been claimed for securities that, for practical purposes, are wholly at the risk of the venture, because the corporation can discharge the purported debt by

---

   [54] See National Carbide Corp. v. CIR, 336 US 422, 435, n.16 (1949) (failure to provide for interest shows that alleged loans "were identical, except in name, with contributions to capital"); see also Rev. Rul. 83-98, 1983-2 CB 40 (adjustable variable-interest convertible notes held equity because, among other features, guaranteed return of $60 annually was unreasonably low for comparable debt and conversion into equity was highly probable); for analysis of this ruling, see Madison, supra note 27, at 492. If the purported creditor and debtor are related parties, however, the absence of an explicit provision for interest may be remedied by the imputation of interest under §482. See generally infra ¶ 15.03. Moreover, the Service in some circumstances may accept purported debt as such in order to apply the provisions of §7872 (imputation of interest on below-market shareholder-corporation loans).

   [55] See Rev. Rul. 83-98, 1983-2 CB 40.

   [56] For the disregard of purported debt incurred (almost always on a nonrecourse basis) on the acquisition of tax-shelter property for more than its true value, see, e.g., Brountas v. CIR, 692 F2d 152 (1st Cir. 1982), cert. denied, 462 US 1106 (1983), and cases there cited; see also Estate of Baron v. CIR, 83 TC 542, 548–550 (1984), aff'd, 798 F2d 65 (2d Cir. 1986) (obligations issued in tax shelter situations found too contingent to be included in basis).

transferring a specified number or par value of its shares (regardless of current market value) or by paying the holders a prescribed percentage of its gross sales. However, in these situations, the principal amount of the purported debt is not a sum certain, but an uncertain amount that can range from zero in the event of failure to a positive amount that may be either greater or less than the amount of cash or property advanced to the alleged debtor. Moreover, there is no maturity date in a realistic sense, since at the corporation's option the holder can be forced into an investment that ends only if and when the corporation is dissolved. The verdict on such securities: equity, either pure and simple, or impure and complex, but equity nevertheless.[57]

7. Participation in control. Voting rights are normally vested solely in the corporation's shareholders by charter provisions and local law; but it is not unusual for bonds and other loan agreements to impose restrictions on such financial matters as the payment of dividends, the creation of senior debt, and major acquisitions; and creditors sometimes are accorded representation on the board of directors. Thus, while managerial or voting rights are often cited as indicia of equity status, they are rarely, if ever, more than a marginal factor in determining the proper classification of the instruments in question.[58]

8. Label applied by parties. Hybrid securities often have hybrid names (e.g., debenture stock or guaranteed stock); but even unambiguous labels are not controlling, especially if it is the Service that seeks reclassification.[59] The courts, however, are sometimes reluctant to allow the parties to repudiate the label chosen by them, which may be viewed as akin to an admission against interest; but judicial references to the name given to the instrument,

---

[57] See Lanova Corp. v. CIR, 17 TC 1178 (1952) (notes payable with debtor's newly issued stock at par value equal to their face amount); Covey Inv. Co. v. US, 377 F2d 403 (10th Cir. 1967) (notes treated as equity even after corporation's right to convert them into stock expired); Knollwood Memorial Gardens, 46 TC 764 (1966) (sale of land for percentage of buyer's gross sales); see also Chazen & Ross, Conversion-Option Debentures, 79 Yale L.J. 647 (1970) (arguing that debentures convertible at corporation's option into stock should be classified as debt if, despite conversion, holders are better off than shareholders who bought same stock at issue price). Compare Rev. Rul. 85-119, 1985-2 CB 60.

[58] See Plumb, supra note 1, at 447.

[59] See Helvering v. Richmond, F. & P. R.R. Co., supra note 49, at 973, quoting an earlier nontax case: "The question in such [debt-or-equity] cases is not, what did the parties call it? But, what do the facts and circumstances require the court to call it?" Consistent treatment of the security in accordance with its label, however, may tip the scales; Zilkha & Sons, supra note 22, at 617 and cases there cited.

even if the parties had conflicting tax interests, seem more often to be rhetorical than dispositive.[60]

Once a disputed instrument's equity and debt features have been classified as such, it becomes necessary to determine which is the dominant group. An unusual approach to this process was employed by the Supreme Court in *Paulsen v. CIR*, decided in 1985, which involved hybrid securities of an unusual type: the shares of a federally chartered mutual savings and loan association, which constituted the only ownership interest in the association's goodwill and other assets, but which also evidenced passbook accounts and certificates of deposit that could be withdrawn in cash without regard to the claims of creditors.[61] In applying the tax-free reorganization provisions to an exchange of the shares of a state-chartered stock savings and loan association for shares of the federal institution when the two were merged, the Court held that the debt and equity aspects of the latter's shares should be considered separately, that their equity features "had almost no value," and that they must be disregarded in determining whether the shares represented a continuing equity interest in the federal association.

Although this decision may stimulate judicial attempts to separately quantify the equity and debt characteristics of hybrid securities more precisely than in the past, it seems more likely that *Paulsen* will be applied only to comparable situations, where the realities of the market demonstrate that investors do not pay for or expect any benefit from the equity side of the investment because the debt side is virtually riskless and carries a face amount equal to the cash paid in. These characteristics of mutual savings institutions have no counterpart in ordinary business corporations, where equity interests almost always have growth potential unless the corporation is so hopelessly undercapitalized that the stock is little more than a cheap lottery ticket.

Paulsen can thus be viewed as having nothing to say about the classification of an ordinary business corporation's hybrid securities, because they can never combine in a single indivisible instrument both ultimate ownership of the corporation's assets and the right to be paid off in full ahead of its creditors. On the other hand, it is also arguable that *Paulsen* is less unique than familiar—that is, it did not really break new ground, but instead merely followed, in an obviously unusual context, the conventional practice of weighing the relevant features of a hybrid security in determining whether its debt or equity characteristics predominate.

---

[60] See Plumb, supra note 1, at 450.

[61] Paulsen v. CIR, supra note 27; for the continuity of interest aspects of this decision, see infra ¶ 14.11.

¶ 4.04   SHAREHOLDER AND OTHER NON-ARM'S-LENGTH DEBT: INTENTION AND ECONOMIC REALITY

In addition to classifying hybrid securities, the courts are sometimes called upon—usually by the Service—to reclassify instruments as equity, even though they possess the formal indicia of debt (e.g., a fixed maturity date, interest payable without regard to corporate earnings, and seniority over shareholder distributions on liquidation, and, conversely, lack the formal characteristics of equity (e.g., participation in gains and losses, subordination to all creditors, and the right to receive all net liquidating proceeds regardless of amount). These efforts to reclassify nonhybrid securities are most likely to occur if the debt is held by the corporation's shareholders in substantial proportion to their stock, so that the formal terms of the instrument are not negotiated at arm's length and are not likely to be enforced by the shareholder-creditors with the same single-minded zeal characteristic of debt owed to institutional lenders or other outside investors. Other situations similarly suggesting that a transaction's superficially pure form may not be consistent with its substance are advances between brother-sister and other related corporations, loans to corporations owned by members of the creditor's immediate family, advances to corporations that are so seriously undercapitalized that they are wholly dependent on the continued financial support of the creditors, and advances by creditors to a corporate borrower that is so close to bankruptcy that its shareholders are no longer the real parties in interest.[62] Another situation involving ostensibly straight debt is a purported sale of property on credit by a nonshareholder to an undercapitalized corporation in circumstances assuring that the lion's share of any appreciation in the value of the property will be needed to pay off the alleged debt.[63]

In approaching cases of these types, the courts recognize that when "the same persons occupy both sides of the bargaining table, form does not nec-

---

[62] See, e.g., Merlo Builders, Inc., ¶ 64,034 P-H Memo. TC (1964) (corporate notes issued to nonshareholder financier with face amount equal to three times amount of cash advanced in circumstances requiring substantial additional financing); In re Indian Lake Estates, Inc., 448 F2d 574 (5th Cir. 1971) (advances by bondholders exercising day-to-day control over bankrupt corporation); Foresun, Inc. v. CIR, 348 F2d 1006 (6th Cir. 19965) (note issued to individual by corporation owned by her daughter and son-in-law); Old Dominion Plywood Corp., ¶ 66,135 P-H Memo. TC (1966) (advances by corporation to another corporation owned by overlapping but not identical shareholding group).

[63] See, e.g., Sherwood Memorial Gardens, Inc. v. CIR, 350 F2d 225 (7th Cir. 1965) (cemetary corporation not allowed to deduct payments on notes issued to acquire land from nonshareholders where sale price was measured by proceeds to be received on resale by corporation). For more on these creditors' corporations, see Stone, supra note 32, at 277–288; Plumb, supra note 1, at 480.

essarily correspond to the intrinsic economic nature of the transaction, for the parties may mold it at their will with no countervailing pull"; and this "power [of the related parties] to create whatever appearance would be of tax benefit to them despite the economic reality of the transaction" sometimes leads the courts to reclassify purported debt as equity even if "the instruments involved are entirely conventional in form and contain no ambiguity on their face."[64] A fortiori, the ambiguities of securities drafted by parties who are bargaining with themselves are likely to be resolved against them.

To classify securities whose authenticity is not attested by arm's-length bargaining, the courts look to (1) the genuineness of the parties' asserted intention to create a debtor-creditor relationship and (2) the reasonableness or economic reality of their intention[65] in an investigation that usually turns primarily on the following matters:

1. Pro rata holding of stock and debt. Although it is not fatal per se to debt classification, the fact that debt is owed in proportion to stockholdings tends to poison the atmosphere and to invite special scrutiny by the courts.[66] Conversely, a substantial disproportion in holdings of debt and stock aids in establishing that the debt is what it purports to be; but in determining this disproportion, family and economic solidarity is usually taken into account.[67] The debt of a publicly held corporation is rarely held by its shareholders in proportion to their stock, but the intercompany debt of such cor-

---

[64] Fin Hay Realty Co. v. US, supra note 26, at 697 ("both sides of the bargaining table" and "power to create"); Kraft Foods Co. v. CIR, 232 F2d 118, 123 (2d Cir. 1966) ("no ambiguity on their face"); see also Tyler v. Tomlinson, supra note 46, at 849 (combining the roles of shareholder and creditor "so undermined the traditional dichotomy between debtor and creditor that exercise of the demand [for repayment of purported debt] under any normal circumstances was extremely unlikely"); P.M. Fin. Corp. v. CIR, 302 F2d 786, 789 (3d Cir. 1962) (sole shareholder-creditor's control of corporation "will enable him to render nugatory the absolute language of any instrument of indebtedness"). But see Federal Express Corp. v. US, supra note 53 (arm's-length deal).

[65] For discussion, including citations, of these criteria, see Plumb, supra note 1, at 457–503 (intention) and 503–537 (economic reality).

[66] See Gilbert v. CIR, supra note 18; Gooding Amusement Co. v. CIR, 236 F2d 159 (6th Cir. 1956), cert. denied, 352 US 1031 (1957); US v. Haskel Eng'r & Supply Co., 380 F2d 786 (9th Cir. 1967).

[67] Disproportion in their holdings of stock and debt was helpful to the taxpayers in Bauer v. CIR, supra note 29 (substantially disproportionate advances by two related shareholders to their wholly owned corporation); Green Bay Structural Steel, Inc., 53 TC 451 (1969); and Charles E. Curry, 43 TC 667 (1965) (acq. and nonacq.). But family solidarity and other legal or economic affiliations can neutralize the significance of individual-by-individual disproportion. See Liflans Corp. v. US, 390 F2d

porations may have a pro rata character (e.g., the debt of a subsidiary to its parent) and have to run the gauntlet of judicial inspection[68] as does the intercompany debt of other members of an affiliated group.[69]

2. Excessive debt-equity ratio ("thin capitalization"). Some corporations are so unconcerned with their credit standing that they can issue seemingly orthodox debt securities in amounts that overwhelm the equity investment (e.g., bonds in the amount of $99,000 plus common stock, against assets valued at $100,000). Here the problem is whether the bonds, although containing ironclad formal indicia of debt, may be treated as the equivalent of stock for tax purposes, because anyone purchasing such instruments would regard himself, in light of the corporation's trivial equity, as a stockholder or potential stockholder so far as risk is concerned. Moreover, if the bonds participate in growth or if the assets are actually worth substantially less than the face amount of the bonds,[70] the holders also share in the corporation's profit potential, and this enhances the equity character of their economic status.

---

965 (Ct. Cl. 1968); C.M. Gooch Lumber & Sales Co., 49 TC 649 (1968), remanded, 406 F2d 290 (6th Cir. 1969); Motel Co. v. CIR, supra note 19.

[68] For parent-subsidiary advances that were treated as true debt, see Kraft Foods Co. v. CIR, supra note 64; Malone & Hyde, Inc., 49 TC 575 (1968) (open-account advances to finance subsidiary's inventory); Byerlite Corp. v. Williams, 286 F2d 285 (6th Cir. 1960); Georgia-Pacific Corp., 63 TC 790 (1975) (debt despite changed conditions rendering repayment increasingly improbable); Litton Bus Sys., Inc., 61 TC 367 (1973) (acq.) (advances to subsidiary to finance acquisition of another corporation; absence of formalities not fatal); Wagner Elec. Co. v. US, 529 F2d 533 (Ct. Cl. 1976) (advances for working-capital needs and to purchase plant and equipment; intercompany receivables for materials shipped and personnel loaned to subsidiary also qualified as debt).

For advances held to be capital contributions by the parent to the subsidiary, see Roth Steel Tube Co. v. CIR, supra note 429 (capital contribution even though only 62 percent ownership); American-La France-Foamite Corp. v. CIR, 284 F2d 723 (2d Cir. 1960), cert. denied, 365 US 881 (1961); Cuyuna Realty Co. v. US, supra note 26; Uneco, Inc. v. US, 532 F2d 1204 (8th Cir. 1976) (capital contributions despite parties' intent to create debt).

For the possibility that in unusual circumstances a parent's advances to a subsidiary might be treated as a debt because the parent obtained the funds from an outside lender that looked primarily to the subsidiary for repayment, see Jack Daniel Distillery v. US, 379 F2d 569 (Ct. Cl. 1967); but see National Farmers Union Serv. Corp. v. US, 400 F2d 483 (10th Cir. 1968) (*Jack Daniel* conduit theory rejected on facts).

[69] See C.M. Gooch Lumber & Sales Co., supra note 67; American Processing & Sales Co. v. US, supra note 19; Northeastern Consol. Co. v. US, 406 F2d 76 (7th Cir.), cert. denied, 396 US 819 (1969), and cases cited therein.

[70] See supra note 56.

In an important early case involving the debt-equity issue, the Supreme Court said of the facts before it: "As material amounts of capital were invested in stock, we need not consider the effect of extreme situations such as nominal stock investments and an obviously excessive debt structure."[71] This dictum started the courts on a search for acceptable debt-equity ratios, generating a number of holdings that the corporation's equity was too "thin" to support the purported debt superstructure.[72] In computing the ratio of debt to equity, the use of market values for the assets (including goodwill), rather than their cost or book value, is well established, and "outside" debt is generally counted as such, especially if guaranteed by the stockholders; however, there are still many unresolved questions in this area.[73]

As to the ratio itself, the courts have not laid down any mathematical formula, recognizing that what is excessive in one industry may be normal in another and that corporations' financial requirements vary even within the same industry. It is usually assumed, however, that a ratio of debt to equity that does not exceed 3 to 1 will withstand attack. A less favorable ratio is likely to invite attention, but there is a general judicial tendency to regard even an excessive ratio as no more than a factor to be considered rather than as an independent test of the purported debt's validity; and there are a few cases in which it is regarded as virtually irrelevant.[74]

---

[71] John Kelley Co. v. CIR, supra note 30, at 526.

[72] E.g., Dobkin v. CIR, 15 TC 31 (1950), aff'd per curiam, 192 F2d 392 (2d Cir. 1951). Compare the bankruptcy cases subordinating stockholder debt to the claims of outside creditors when the corporation is inadequately capitalized, supra note 51.

[73] See Kraft Foods Co. v. CIR, supra note 64; Gooding Amusement Co. v. CIR, supra note 66; Sheldon Tauber, 24 TC 179 (1955); Estate of Miller v. CIR, 239 F2d 729 (9th Cir. 1956); Liflans Corp. v. US, supra note 67, and cases cited therein; Bauer v. CIR, supra note 29 (evidently using book values but primarily for current assets; evidence showed that bank would have been willing to make equivalent loans if requested).

[74] See Bradshaw v. US, 683 F2d 365 (Ct. Cl. 1982) ("very high ratio of debt to equity" not fatal; "reasonable assurance of repayment" regardless of business success); Bauer v. CIR, supra note 29; Rowan v. US, supra note 41; Byerlite Corp. v. Williams, supra note 68; Baker Commodities, Inc., 48 TC 374 (1967), aff'd on another issue, 415 F2d 519 (9th Cir. 1969), cert. denied, 397 US 988 (1970) (700-to-1 ratio not fatal where cash flow and earning power of business could cover payments); Piedmont Corp. v. CIR, 388 F2d 886 (4th Cir. 1968) (thinness not fatal); Lots, Inc., 49 TC 541 (1968) (acq.) (assets equaled debt to shareholder-creditor).

Cases emphasizing the corporation's thinness in holding that shareholder loans did not constitute true debt include Ambassador Apartments, Inc. v. CIR, 406 F2d 288 (2d Cir. 1969); Northeastern Consol. Co. v. US, supra note 69; Tyler v. Tomlinson, supra note 46; US v. Henderson, 375 F2d 36 (5th Cir.), cert. denied, 389 US 953 (1967). See generally Plumb, supra note 1, at 507–519.

3. Debt issued for essential assets. Courts have sometimes suggested or held that debt is not bona fide if issued to shareholders in exchange for the core assets needed to get the business under way (e.g., machinery, plant, equipment, and so forth), at least in the absence of a business reason for using debt rather than equity for this purpose. The leading exponent of this view is *Schnitzer v. CIR,* decided by the Tax Court in 1949; but, because the court found other infirmities in the instruments as well, it is not clear whether the inability of the corporation to function without the assets for which the debt was issued was a controlling feature of the decision.[75] Since loans from outsiders would be honored as such even if used to purchase essential assets, a similar use of shareholder advances is not a satisfactory reason for treating them as equity investments. Moreover, even if the core assets concept came into vogue, it could often be avoided by having the shareholders purchase (or, on the incorporation of an existing enterprise, retain) the property and lease it to the corporation.

The highly leveraged tender offers and management buy-outs that became common in the mid-1980s involve debt that some target corporations may be unable to service with their normal cash flow, in which event they may have to sell off entire divisions to ward off financial disaster.[76] Despite this possibility, the Service has not suggested that the debt should be reclassified as equity because the corporation's core assets may have to be liquidated to pay off the debt. Moreover, any such rationale for reclassifying otherwise acceptable debt instruments would strike at the financial foundation of the real estate industry, since most realty-holding corporations incur mortgage debt that can be paid at maturity only by selling or refinancing the mortgaged property.

4. Intent to create a creditor-debtor relationship. At one time, the Tax Court came close to holding that loans by shareholders to their corporation could not be bona fide because shareholders could never be psychologically equivalent to outside lenders. In *Gooding Amusement Co.,* for example, the Tax Court held that notes issued by a corporation to its shareholders did not

---

[75] Schnitzer v. CIR, 13 TC 43 (1949), aff'd per curiam, 183 F2d 70 (9th Cir. 1950), cert. denied, 340 US 911 (1951); see also Morgan v. CIR, 30 TC 881 (1958) (corporation's ability to operate without assets for which debt was issued cited as favorable circumstance), rev'd on other issues, 272 F2d 936 (9th Cir. 1959); Santa Anita Consol., Inc., 50 TC 536, 551 (1968) (fact that funds were used for assets necessary to corporation's business must be weighed against "basic rule that, unless the debt is a mere sham or subterfuge, taxpayers are not foreclosed from financing a transaction in a manner to provide a minimum exposure of their assets to the risks of the venture"); Covey Inv. Co. v. US, 377 F2d 403 (10th Cir. 1967); Plumb, supra note 1, at 520–525.

[76] See, e.g., Canellos, The Overleveraged Acquisition, 39 Tax Lawyer 91 (1985).

create a debtor-creditor relationship, although they were normal both in form and amount, because the dominant shareholder and his family owned all the notes, and he had no "intention at the time of the issuance of the notes ever to enforce payment of his notes, especially if to do so would either impair the credit rating of the corporation, cause it to borrow from other sources the funds necessary to meet the payments, or bring about its dissolution"; although the judgment in this case was affirmed on the ground that "the findings of fact of the Tax Court are supported by substantial evidence and are not clearly erroneous,"[77] the finding of fact that the shareholder did not intend to enforce the notes resembled an irrebuttable presumption or inference inherent in the shareholder-corporation relationship rather than a conclusion based on evidence.

On the whole, however, a more traditional view of the intent necessary to uphold the validity of shareholder debt has carried the day. Thus, in *Gilbert v. CIR*, the Court of Appeals for the Second Circuit held that, in determining whether the lenders had a reasonable expectation of repayment, it was necessary to resort to such objective criteria as the ratio of debt to equity, pro rata holdings of debt and stock, use of the borrowed funds, whether outside investors would have made such an advance on similar terms, and conduct generally consistent with that of a creditor.[78] By focusing on objective circumstances of this type, the courts avoid giving excessive weight to the parties' "self-serving assertions."[79] The question thus boils down to whether the loan was so risky that it should be regarded as venture capital. Although this standard ("substantial economic reality," as phrased in a later decision of the Court of Appeals for the Second Circuit[80]) does not lend itself to mechanical application, it is as good a generalization as can be drawn from the fact-oriented case law involving a myriad of situations that differ only imperceptibly from each other.

5. Hypothetical third-party loans. In determining whether a purported loan by insiders should be respected as such, evidence that the corporation

---

[77] Gooding Amusement Co., 23 TC 408, 418–419 (1954); Gooding Amusement Co. v. CIR, supra note 66.

[78] Gilbert v. CIR, supra note 18.

[79] Texas Farm Bureau v. US, supra note 30, at 314 ("In a land of hard economic facts, we cannot root important decisions in parties' pious declarations of intent"); for problems in determining whether intention is a question of fact or of law, see supra text at notes 28–30.

[80] See Nassau Lens, Inc. v. CIR, 308 F2d 39 (2d Cir. 1962); see also Uneco, Inc. v. US, supra note 68 (advances to subsidiaries and affiliates were capital contributions; objective criteria of debt-equity cases controlled over subjective intent of the parties); see generally Plumb, supra note 1, at 457–461, Canellos, supra note 76.

could have borrowed on comparable terms from banks or other outside lenders is at least relevant and may go far towards establishing that the insider debt is economically viable.[81] Conversely, if the corporation is forced to turn to its shareholders for financing because funds cannot be obtained from outsiders or because existing outside loans are already in default, the shareholder advances may well be viewed as capital contributions.[82]

6. History of relationship. Some debt-equity cases must be decided before a course of dealings between the parties has illuminated the relationship, but many do not get to the courts until there is a record that includes not only the documents executed when the purported debt was created, but also a history of payments, extensions of time, forbearances, subordinations, and, in some cases, additional advances. Although the parties' actions over the years do not conclusively establish what they intended or should have expected when the relationship was created, the courts understandably often use hindsight in reaching their conclusions.[83] Thus, if an alleged debt was not paid at maturity or if other defaults were tolerated, these factors may suggest that the obligation was not bona fide when made or that it was tacitly converted into equity by forbearance.[84] On the other hand, meticulous compliance with all of the terms of the purported obligation, although helpful to the taxpayer's case, does not conclusively establish that the obligation was a genuine debt; for example, periodic payments, viewed objectively, may be tantamount to dividends even though labeled "interest" by the documents.[85]

---

[81] See Estate of Mixon v. US, supra note 53 (shareholder advance made before corporation had exhausted its line of credit with bank; no unsuccessful efforts to obtain outside financing); Bauer v. CIR, supra note 29 (evidence that bank loan could have been obtained). See generally Plumb, supra note 1, at 530–535. The concept of a comparable third-party lender, however, is difficult to apply to purported loans by creditors who are willing to accept subordination or other disabilities in return for a slice of the equity pie (e.g., in a leveraged buyout). See Canellos, supra note 76.

[82] See Towne Square, Inc., ¶ 83,010 P-H Memo. TC (1983) (corporation unable to raise substantial working capital from financial institutions; existing creditor threatening foreclosure, and so forth); see also Fin Hay Realty Co. v. US, supra note 26, at 699 (no evidence of ability to raise funds except from insiders).

[83] See generally Plumb, supra note 1, at 490–499 and cases there cited.

[84] See, e.g., Foresun, Inc., supra note 62 (repeated extensions of maturity date); Ambassador Apartments, Inc., supra note 74 (default followed by extension, followed by failure to enforce at new maturity date); Cuyuna Realty Co. v. US, supra note 26 (debt changed to equity by virtue of repeated defaults by insolvent debtor). But see Bordo Prods. Co. v. US, 476 F2d 1312 (Ct. Cl. 1973) (shareholder forbearance to enforce debt explained by unexpected financial reverses; not inconsistent with intent to create bona fide creditor-debtor relationship).

[85] See Isidor Dobkin, supra note 72; see also Motel Co. v. CIR, supra note 19 (transfer of property to creditor by quit-claim three years after default discounted as

---

PART B.   DEBT VS. EQUITY: MAJOR INCOME TAX CONSIDERATIONS

¶ 4.20   CAPITAL GAIN/LOSS TREATMENT ON SALES

In the hands of an investor, stock and debt instruments are almost always "capital assets" as defined by §1221, so that gain or loss on a sale or exchange is capital gain or loss under §1222.[86] This is generally also true for debt claims that are not evidenced by written instruments (e.g., open-account claims). There are, however, a number of exceptions to this general capital gain/loss regime that either deny capital asset status to the security or, without altering its status as such, treat gains and/or losses generated by the security as ordinary in nature rather than as capital gains or losses. The principal exceptions of this type are the following:

(1) Securities held by dealers who hold stock or debt instruments primarily for sale to customers in the ordinary course of business within the meaning of §1221(1). By complying with §1236, however, even dealers may hold securities in a segregated investment account and thus qualify them for capital gain or loss treatment.[87]

(2) Exclusions under §1221(4), which eliminates from the category of capital assets accounts or notes receivable acquired in the ordinary course of trade or business for services rendered or from the sale of stock in trade or similar property.[88]

(3) Bonds and other evidence of corporate debt issued after 1954 at a discount, that are subject to the original issue discount rules of

---

evidentiary factor, since this action occurred on eve of Service audit). But see Gordon Lubricating Co., ¶ 65,132 P-H Memo. TC (1965) (occasional defaults in periodic payments were cured by payments prior to taxable years before the court).

[86] The importance of capital gain was drastically reduced by the repeal in 1986 of former §1202, which had allowed individual taxpayers other than corporations to deduct 60 percent of their net capital gains; but the distinction between capital gains and ordinary income continues to be operative for a variety of purposes (e.g., the taxpayer's right to offset capital gains by capital losses without dollar limit, whereas ordinary income can be offset by only $3,000 of capital losses per year). In addition, exchange treatment for debt claims permits the taxpayer to offset the basis of the claim against the amount received; as explained infra ¶ 4.21, when stock is redeemed, the entire proceeds may have to be included in gross income with no offset for the basis of the redeemed shares.

[87] See Van Suetendael v. CIR, ¶ 44,305 P-H Memo. TC (1944) (pre-§1236), aff'd per curiam, 152 F2d 654 (2d Cir. 1945); Frank v. CIR, 321 F2d 143 (8th Cir. 1963); Nielsen v. US, 333 F2d 615 (6th Cir. 1964).

[88] See Burbank Liquidating Corp., 39 TC 999 (1963); Merchants Acceptance Co., ¶ 64,149 P-H Memo. TC (1964).

§§1271-1275.[89] Section 1286 imposes analogous rules on stripped bonds and coupons if purchased after July 1, 1982.[90] Similar but less drastic rules tax gain realized on the disposition of certain market discount bonds (bonds purchased for less than their stated redemption price) as ordinary income rather than capital gain.[91]

(4) Gain from stock of a collapsible corporation governed by the special rules of §341.[92]

(5) Gain from "section 306 stock" governed by the special rules of §306.[93]

(6) Stock or debt acquired and held as an integral part of a regular business transaction under the uncertain criteria of the *Corn Products Refining Co.* and *Bagley & Sewall* cases.[94] Here the business function of the security imposes ordinary income status on the ultimate gain or loss despite the property's literal qualification as a capital asset under §1221. Not surprisingly, the Service is attracted or repelled by the *Corn Products* doctrine, depending on whether its application in a particular case will turn capital gain into ordinary income or capital loss into ordinary loss; taxpayer allegiances are equally fickle, mutatis mutandis.[95]

---

[89] See infra ¶ 4.40.

[90] See infra ¶ 4.43. For the definition of stripped bonds and coupons, see §§1286(e)(2) and 1286(e)(3).

[91] See §1276, discussed infra ¶ 4.44.

[92] See infra ¶¶ 12.02–12.03.

[93] See infra ¶¶ 10.03–10.04.

[94] Corn Prods. Ref. Co. v. CIR, 350 US 46 (1955), reh'g denied, 350 US 943 (1956); CIR v. Bagley & Sewall Co., 221 F2d 944 (2d Cir. 1955).

[95] The principal cases include CIR v. Steadman, 424 F2d 1 (6th Cir.), cert. denied, 400 US 869 (1970) (ordinary loss when stock purchased by attorney to protect position as corporate general counsel became worthless); Schlumberger Technology Corp. v. US, 443 F2d 1115 (5th Cir. 1971) (ordinary deductions); Chemplast, Inc., 60 TC 623 (1973), aff'd per curiam, 506 F2d 1050 (3d Cir. 1974) (advances to affiliate to secure source of supply); Midland Distribs., Inc. v. US, 481 F2d 730 (5th Cir. 1973) (advances to 50 percent subsidiary; *Corn Products* not applicable because of investment motives); Campbell Taggart, Inc. v. US, 744 F2d 442 (5th Cir. 1984) (*Corn Products* applied to unusual facts: taxpayer originally planned to acquire target company as investment, abandoned that plan on learning of target's financial problems, but consummated purchase to protect its reputation as acquirer of other corporations; loss on disposition held ordinary, not capital; extensive analysis).

The Tax Court held that *Corn Products* does not apply if the taxpayer had a substantial investment motive in acquiring the securities; see W.W. Windle Co., 65 TC 694 (1976), appeal dismissed, 550 F2d 43 (1st Cir.) cert. denied, 431 US 966 (1977) (stock purchased with a substantial but not dominant investment motive; held, capital asset); Rev. Rul. 78-94, 1978-1 CB 58 (same); Wright v. CIR, 756 F2d 1039 (4th Cir. 1985) (*Windle* followed; capital loss because substantial investment motive); Union Pac. R.R. v. US, 524 F2d 1343 (Ct. Cl. 1975), cert. denied, 429 US

(7) Stock, securities, and debt claims that are flavored with an ordinary income character by assignment-of-income principles.[96]

(8) Losses on "section 1244 stock" of a so-called small business corporation that can qualify as ordinary rather than capital losses in prescribed circumstances.[97]

(9) Gain on the disposition of registration-required obligations that is taxed by §1287 as ordinary income if the security is not in registered form.[98]

¶ 4.21 PAYMENT OF DEBT VS. REDEMPTION OF STOCK

As indicated previously, it is often necessary to determine whether a taxpayer's investment in a corporation constitutes debt or equity in order to decide the tax consequences of amounts paid by the corporation to liquidate or discharge the investment.[99] The principal events requiring borderline instruments to be classified are:

1. Retirement of debt. Amounts received by the holder on the retirement of any corporate debt instrument are considered under §1271(a)(1) to be amounts received in exchange for the instrument, with the result that the receipt is a nontaxable return of capital to the extent of the holder's basis in the retired instrument.[100] For this purpose, "debt instrument" is defined by

---

827 (1976) (*Corn Products* applied to stock of subsidiaries whose operations were integrated with parent's business); Arkansas Best Corp., 83 TC 640 (1984) (partial capital loss under *Windle*, and partial ordinary loss under *Corn Products* for holding company's forced sale of subsidiary stock; mixed motives), but rev'd, 800 F2d 215 (8th Cir. 1986) (narrow reading of *Corn Products*; Court refused to extend beyond facts and would not apply doctrine to corporate stock), cert. granted, March 23, 1987.

See generally Bittker, Federal Taxation of Income, Estates and Gifts (Warren, Gorham, & Lamont, Inc., 1981), ¶ 51.10.3; Lee, Capital Gains Exception to the House's General Utilities Repeal: Further Indigestions From Overly Processed Corn Products, 30 Tax Notes 1375 (1986).

[96] See Eustice, Contract Rights, Capital Gain and Assignment of Income—The Ferrer Case, 20 Tax L. Rev. 1 (1964); Lyon & Eustice, Assignment of Income: Fruit and Tree as Irrigated by the P.G. Lake Case, 17 Tax L. Rev. 293 (1962). For transformation of fruit into a tree after its purchase, see Jamison v. US, 297 F. Supp. 221 (N.D. Cal. 1968), aff'd per curiam, 445 F2d 1397 (9th Cir. 1971).

[97] See infra ¶ 4.24.

[98] See supra text at note 16.

[99] See supra text at notes 6–9.

[100] This provision does not apply to noncorporate obligations; see §1271(b).

§1275(a)(1) as a bond, debenture, note, certificate, or other evidence of indebtedness. In providing for return-of-capital treatment on the retirement of debt instruments, §1271(a)(1) merely overlaps the result that would be reached under general tax principles; but, regardless of its foundation, this treatment sharply distinguishes retirements of debt instruments from stock redemptions, since, as explained subsequently, a redemption of stock is often taxed as a dividend in its entirety without any offset for the shareholder's investment in the redeemed stock.[101]

Exchange treatment under §1271(a)(1) also enables the holder of a retired debt instrument to claim capital gain or loss treatment if the instrument is a capital asset in the holder's hands and if the amount received exceeds (or is less than) its basis.[102] By suggesting an analogy between retirements and sales, §1271(a)(1) avoids an unwarranted capital-gain/ordinary-income distinction between those debt instruments that are sold by the holder just before maturity and those that are held until retirement.[103] Like the offset of basis already described, exchange treatment also distinguishes the retirement of debt from the redemption of stock, since amounts received on the redemption of stock may be treated as ordinary income in full if covered by corporate earnings and profits.[104]

The capital gain/loss status of amounts received on the retirement of debt instruments, however, must be qualified in two important respects. First, amounts attributable to OID must be reported as ordinary income, since they are tantamount to deferred interest. As explained later in this chapter, under current law, OID must ordinarily be reported periodically during the life of the debt instrument so that there is usually little, if any, unamortized OID to be reported at retirement.[105] Second, gain on the retire-

---

[101] Infra text at note 108.

[102] In the absence of §1271(a)(1), the retirement of debt does not qualify as a sale or exchange within the meaning of §1222; see Fairbanks v. US, 306 US 436 (1939); see generally Bittker, supra note 95, at ¶ 52.1.4.

[103] Because §1271(a)(1) applies only to debt instruments, however, a disparity between payment at maturity and sales before maturity can arise for debt not evidenced by bonds or other instruments such as open account obligations, as well as for obligations owed by individuals, since they are not covered by §1271(a)(1); see supra notes 100 and 102. A similar problem can arise if a debt is compromised or settled rather than retired. On the meaning of "retirement," see McClain v. CIR, 311 US 527 (1941) ("retirement" includes but is broader than "redemption"); see also Ogilvie v. CIR, 216 F2d 748 (6th Cir. 1954) (gain on settlement of judgment debt for more than its cost taxed as ordinary income; no sale or exchange); Jamison v. US, supra note 96.

[104] See infra text at note 108.

[105] See infra ¶ 4.40.
For the possibility of ordinary income when the issuer intends to call a debt instrument before maturity, see §1271(a)(2); see also Bolnick v. CIR, 44 TC 245

ment of bonds must be reported under §1276 as ordinary income rather than capital gain to the extent of any accrued market discount. As explained in a later section, §1276 applies to gain on bonds purchased from a prior holder for less than their stated redemption price (e.g., a $1,000 bond purchased for $950).[106]

Although the term "debt instrument," the focus of the preceding discussion, is broadly defined by §1275(a)(1), it does not encompass all forms of corporate debt. Thus, debt that is not evidenced by any written instrument, such as an open account debt, is not subject to §1271(a)(1). This means that the amount collected by a creditor from a debtor at maturity is not attributable to a sale or exchange of the obligation within the meaning of §1222 and hence does not qualify for capital gain or loss treatment.[107]

2. Redemptions of stock. In contrast to the favorable tax regime that ordinarily governs the retirement of debt instruments (i.e., return-of-capital treatment for the amount invested by the creditor, capital gain/loss for any excess or deficiency), stock redemptions (including the repayment of purported loans that are treated as equity) run a substantial risk of being taxed as dividends without any offset for the shareholder's basis in the redeemed shares. However, as explained in detail later in this work, some redemptions escape this fate and are instead treated as sales of the redeemed shares—that is, the shareholder's basis is offset against the amount received, and any excess or shortfall is treated as capital gain or loss.[108] The principal instances of this favorable sale-exchange treatment are non-pro rata redemptions, such as transactions that terminate the shareholder's interest in the corporation or that substantially alter a shareholder's proportionate interest relative to the retained interests of the other shareholders.[109]

One of the principal reasons for issuing debt securities at the time of incorporation is to set the stage for the future extraction of corporate earnings tax-free or, if the repayment exceeds the taxpayer's adjusted basis for the obligations, as capital gain. Moreover, the time of incorporation may be

---

(1965) (acq.) (gain on bond redeemed before maturity qualifies for capital gain in absence of intent to redeem early); Rev. Rul. 80-143, 1980-1 CB 19 (accord).

[106] See infra ¶ 4.44.

[107] See Fairbanks v. US, supra note 102. But see Prop. Regs. §1.1275-1(b)(1) (the term debt instrument includes "all rights to deferred payment under a contract whether or *not* evidenced by a formal instrument").

[108] Infra ¶ 9.02.

[109] For other redemptions qualifying for sale treatment, see §303 (certain redemptions from an estate to pay death taxes and funeral and administrative expenses) and §302(e) (partial liquidations) discussed infra ¶¶ 9.11 and 9.08 respectively.

the only opportunity to achieve such favorable results because, if bonds are issued to the shareholders at a later time, the distribution itself may well be taxed as a dividend.[110] In contrast, while a distribution of preferred stock by a profitable corporation can ordinarily be received tax-free, its later redemption is ordinarily taxed as a dividend under §306.[111]

¶ 4.22   CHARACTER OF INVESTOR'S LOSS ON SALE OR WORTHLESSNESS

The tax consequences of investment losses are governed by a variety of intricate statutory provisions and judicial doctrines, the precise interrelationship of which remains unclear at best. In general, the amount and timing of a loss deduction is a function of three elements: (1) adjusted basis, (2) amount realized (if any), and (3) the event that causes the loss to be sustained (e.g., sale, partial collection, or total worthlessness). The character of the loss (as capital or ordinary) is controlled in turn by a combination of factors: (1) the capital asset status of the claim, (2) the existence of a sale or exchange (actual or constructive), (3) the form of the investment (e.g., stock, security, or nonsecurity debt claim), (4) the relationship of the loss to the taxpayer's business, if any, (5) the taxpayer's holding period for the property, (6) the taxpayer's status as an individual or a corporation, and (7) the control relationship of the taxpayer to the corporation. As discussed later, the investor's loss may be treated as an ordinary loss, a long-term capital loss, a short-term capital loss, or an unrecognized loss, depending on the way these various elements are combined in a particular case. The principal combinations are the following:

1. Noncorporate shareholders: Loss on stock. The losses of an individual or other noncorporate shareholder, whether arising from the sale, redemption, liquidation, or total worthlessness of stock normally receive long-term capital loss treatment if the stock is a capital asset[112] and has been held for more than six months. Thus, §165(g)(1) (the worthless security loss provision) creates an artificial sale for stock that becomes totally worthless in the hands of the taxpayer. The reason for this provision is that a sale of the stock just before its value disappears would create a capital loss (unless the sale is for a nominal amount and hence can be disregarded as a sham);

---

[110] See infra ¶ 7.40.

[111] See infra ch. 10.

[112] See supra ¶ 4.20.

and there is no good reason to treat the taxpayer differently if the stock is held a little longer until its value completely evaporates.

Section 165(g)(1), however, does not always achieve complete parity between stock that is sold and stock that is held until it becomes worthless because in the latter instance the stock is deemed to be sold on the last day of the taxable year, presumably because of difficulties in pinpointing the exact day of worthlessness. Thus, a short-term loss may be turned into a long-term one—for example, if stock purchased on December 1, 1986 becomes worthless in fact on May 15, 1987, the loss would be short-term except for §165(g)(1), which requires it to be treated as realized on December 31, 1987. Had the taxpayer been able to realize the loss by a *sale* in May 1987, however, §165(g)(1) would not apply; the loss would have been short-term.

Section 165(g)(1) comes into play only if the security "becomes worthless during the taxable year," and thus does not preclude the government from arguing that the taxpayer's deduction is either premature or should have been taken in an earlier year.[113] To avoid an argument over the year of worthlessness, therefore, the taxpayer may be well advised to sell the security if a bona fide buyer can be found.[114]

Liquidations are also treated as the equivalent of a sale or exchange of the stock so that shareholders are entitled to a capital loss if they receive less for their stock than its adjusted basis.[115] This is also true of a redemption unless it is treated as the equivalent of a dividend under §302.[116]

Special rules applicable to losses on "section 1244 stock" are discussed later in this chapter.[117]

2. Noncorporate creditors: Loss on debt evidenced by corporate security. If an individual or other noncorporate taxpayer's debt claim against a corporation is evidenced by a security that has been held for more than six months, a loss from sale, retirement, or worthlessness is a long-term capital loss.[118] Of course, the loss must also satisfy such general provisions as

---

[113] An extended statute of limitations, §6511(d)(1), offers some protection against an attempt by the government to assign the loss to a year on which the statute has run.

[114] See generally Boehm v. CIR, 326 US 287 (1945), reh'g denied, 326 US 811 (1946); De Loss v. CIR, 28 F2d 803 (2d Cir. 1928), cert. denied, 279 US 840 (1929).

[115] See §331, discussed infra ¶ 11.03.

[116] Infra ¶ 9.02.

[117] See infra ¶ 4.24.

[118] See §§1221 and 1222 for sales; §§1221 and 1271 for retirements; §§165(g)(1) and 1221 for worthlessness. If the security has been held for six months or less, a sale or retirement for less than its adjusted basis generates a short-term capital loss, while

§165(c)(2) (transaction entered into for profit) and §267 (losses between related persons) to qualify for a deduction of any kind. Moreover, no deduction is allowed for a registration-required obligation that is not in registered form.[119]

3. Noncorporate creditors: Loss on debt not evidenced by security. If an individual or other noncorporate creditor's claim against the corporation is not evidenced by "a bond, debenture, note, or certificate or other evidence of indebtedness . . . with interest coupons or in registered form,"[120] a loss on worthlessness is not governed by §165(g)(1) (worthless securities), but by §166 (bad debts). This fact is of particular importance to investors in closely held corporations because their advances are frequently open-account loans or are evidenced merely by simple promissory notes.

The general rule of §166(a) allows an ordinary loss deduction for worthless debts, but this principle is subject to an important exception: By virtue of §166(d), an individual or other noncorporate taxpayer is confined to a short-term capital loss if the uncollectible claim is a nonbusiness debt. Moreover, §166(a) permits a partially worthless claim to be written off pro tanto even though the balance retains some value; debts subject to §166(d), however, cannot be deducted in installments but only when the unpaid balance becomes wholly uncollectible.

Section 166(d) was enacted in 1942; its stated purpose was to combat the practice of deducting as bad debts loans intended as gifts to friends and relatives. Because of the difficulty in determining whether such a loan was bona fide, the Treasury recommended that the taxpayer be limited to a capital loss.[121] The language in §166(d) is broader than necessary to achieve this purpose, however, and the courts have given it its full sweep, partly because they have perceived another purpose for the legislation. This, said the Supreme Court in *Putnam*, is "to put nonbusiness investments in the form of loans on a footing with other nonbusiness investments" (i.e., to confine the

---

a loss on worthlessness is treated by §165(g)(1) as occurring on the last day of the taxable year and thus may become a long-term capital loss; the same phenomenon as to stock has been noted, supra text at note 113.

See also John P. Gawler, 60 TC 647 (1973), aff'd per curiam, 504 F2d 425 (4th Cir. 1974) (contingent right to acquire stock was equity interest resulting in capital loss under §165(g)(1)).

[119] Section 167(j); see supra text at note 16.

[120] Section 165(g)(2)(C).

[121] See H.R. Rep. No. 2333, 77th Cong., 2d Sess. (1942), reprinted in 1942-2 CB 372, 408–409. In an analogous area, losses on sales between certain related parties, the statutory remedy was more drastic: disallowance of the deduction. See §267(a)(1).

creditor to a capital loss whether the worthless investment took the form of open-account advances, bonds, or shares of stock.)[122]

The term "nonbusiness debt" is defined in §166(d)(2) by indirection; it means a debt other than (1) a debt created or acquired in connection with a trade or business of the taxpayer, or (2) a debt the loss from the worthlessness of which is incurred in the taxpayer's trade or business.[123] Because of the imprecision in this definition and because open-account advances by investors to closely held corporations often turn sour, there have been scores of cases on the status of particular loans under this provision. The typical pattern involves a shareholder who owns most or all of the stock of a corporation by himself or with his family and who provides additional funds as loans in the early stages of the corporation's life. If the corporation fails, the government usually insists that the debt is a nonbusiness debt, resulting from the shareholder-creditor's investment activities rather than from a trade or business.[124]

Taxpayer hopes for ordinary deduction treatment in this area suffered a serious blow in *Whipple*, in which the Supreme Court denied business-debt status to loans made by a shareholder to one of several controlled corporations through which he conducted a variety of business activities.[125] The Court was not persuaded by the fact that the taxpayer devoted all his time to the business of his corporate enterprises, holding that this did not establish a business distinct from that of a shareholder attempting to increase the return on his investments. A series of later shareholder-investor cases indicates that

---

[122] See Putnam v. CIR, 352 US 82 (1956). If this was one of the purposes of the 1942 legislation, Congress neglected to say so; and it failed to establish complete parity, since §166(d)(1) establishes short-term capital loss treatment, while worthless securities (including stock) usually give rise to long-term capital losses.

[123] The latter part of the definition dates from 1942; the former part was added in 1954 to overrule Regs. §118, §39.23(k)-6(c), holding that a debt that arose in the taxpayer's business was a nonbusiness debt if he was no longer in business when it became worthless. Section 166(d)(2)(A) was further amended in 1958 to preclude the argument that the former language ("in connection with *a* taxpayer's business" [emphasis added]) embraced a debt created or acquired in connection with a trade or business of a taxpayer other than the one claiming the deduction.

[124] This argument is often coupled with an alternative argument: The advance did not create a debt but was a contribution to capital, deductible only as a capital loss and only when the stock became worthless. See supra ¶ 4.04.

[125] Whipple v. CIR, 373 US 193, reh'g denied, 374 US 858 (1963). In Stahl v. US, 441 F2d 999 (D.C. Cir. 1970), an ordinary loss was allowed under §165(c)(2) for securities pledged by the taxpayer with a brokerage firm in return for an interest in its profits on the ground that the transaction constituted a bailment rather than a loan, and thus was not subject to the business motive test of *Whipple*. For later cases restricting similar taxpayers to a capital loss because of differences in the subordination agreement, see Meisels v. US, 732 F2d 132 (Fed. Cir. 1984), and cases there cited.

short-term capital loss treatment under §166(d) is the general rule[126] and that taxpayers will be able to qualify for ordinary loss deductions only if the loan arises (1) in a business of moneylending; (2) in a business of organizing, promoting, financing, and selling corporate enterprises;[127] (3) in an effort to protect or advance the taxpayer's business as an employee of the debtor;[128] or (4) in some other commercial relationship with the debtor that can be characterized as a business rather than an investment, such as leasing property to the corporation or protecting a source of supply.[129] It may be that

---

[126] For selected post-*Whipple* cases denying business bad-debt treatment, see Estate of M.M. Byers, 57 TC 568 (1972), aff'd per curiam, 472 F2d 590 (6th Cir. 1973) (officer-shareholder's loan to corporate customer); Miles Prod. Co. v. CIR, 457 F2d 1150 (5th Cir. 1972) (individual shareholder's advances created nonbusiness bad debts); Robert E. Imel, 61 TC 318 (1973) (acq.) (investment motive for officer-shareholder's loans and guarantees); David Shinefeld, 65 TC 1092 (1976) (taxpayer loans to parent corporation to preserve business of subsidiary). See also Henry J. Benak, 77 TC 1213 (1981) (worthless note issued on redemption of §1244 stock held non-business bad debt short-term capital loss).

Nonshareholder loans, however, may have an easier time under *Whipple* if the creditor can show a reasonable business motive for the loan. See Maurice Artstein, ¶ 70,220 P-H Memo. TC (1970); Estate of A.M. Saperstein, ¶ 70,209 P-H Memo. TC (1970). But see Alfred H. Tolzman, ¶ 81,689 P-H Memo. TC (not dominant business motive; taxpayer was a 25 percent partner in partnership that owned 50 percent of debtor).

[127] For post-*Whipple* cases in which the taxpayer failed to qualify under the promoter theory, see Millsap v. CIR, 387 F2d 420 (8th Cir. 1968); US v. Clark, 358 F2d 892 (1st Cir.), cert. denied, 385 US 817 (1966); Townshend v. US, 384 F2d 1008 (Ct. Cl. 1967); and Eugene Mohr, 45 TC 100 (1966). But see Ralph Biernbaum, ¶ 63,210 P-H Memo. TC (1963) (taxpayer satisfied test); Samuel R. Milbank, 51 TC 805 (1969) (acq.) (direct loans and voluntary payments on moral guaranty of debts of corporation of which taxpayer was prime promoter).

[128] For the job protection route to business status, see Trent v. CIR, 291 F2d 669 (2d Cir. 1961). The Court in *Whipple* noted that this exception would play a limited role in the case of controlling shareholder-employees, a point on which the lower courts subsequently relied to find investor status in Weddle v. CIR, 325 F2d 849 (2d Cir. 1963). See also Kelson v. US, 503 F2d 1291 (10th Cir. 1974) (purpose of loans was to protect investment position, not employee status); David Shinefeld, supra note 126.

For taxpayer successes in getting ordinary loss treatment for job protection or job-related loans under *Trent*, see Philip W. Fitzpatrick, ¶ 67,001 P-H Memo. TC (1967); Lundgren v. CIR, 376 F2d 623 (9th Cir. 1967); Rev. Rul. 71-561, 1971-2 CB 128; see also James O. Gould, 64 TC 132 (1975) (shareholder's payment of debts of his defunct corporation; held deductible business expense because made primarily to preserve employment by another corporation rather than for investment motive). For employee guarantees of employer's debt to third parties, see Alfred M. Tolzman, supra note 126 (capital loss); Estate of Norma F. Allen, ¶ 82,303 P-H Memo. TC (1982) (ordinary loss).

[129] In *Whipple*, the Supreme Court remanded the case to the trial court to consider the impact of the taxpayer's status as a landlord of property rented to the cor-

Whipple and *Corn Products*[130] can be viewed as opposite ends of a spectrum, with a tension in classification between the predominantly investment-motivated transactions of *Whipple* (where the loss was capital) and the "integrally related to regular business functions" situation of *Corn Products* (where ordinary loss treatment applied).

The degree of proximity that the loan must have to the taxpayer's business in order to qualify as a business bad debt, formerly a matter of some dispute, was resolved by the Supreme Court in *US v. Generes*, which held that the taxpayer's business motivation must be dominant, not merely a significant factor.[131]

4. Corporate investors: Losses on debt and stock. Although the tax consequences of investment losses incurred by corporations are not free of some ambiguities, the pattern is less complex than for individual investors:

> (1) Worthless bad debts, if not evidenced by securities within the meaning of §165(g)(2)(C), are deductible as ordinary losses under

---

poration to which loans were made. See also Maloney v. Spencer, 172 F2d 638 (9th Cir. 1949) (shareholder in business of acquiring and leasing plants to corporate debtor); J.T. Dorminey, 26 TC 940 (1956) (acq.) (loans to corporation to facilitate acquisition of necessary business supplies); Estate of Lawrence M. Weil, 29 TC 366 (1957) (acq.) (loans to corporate sales agent of business operated by taxpayer as proprietorship); Tony Martin, 25 TC 94 (1955) (acq.) (entertainer's loan to corporation formed to produce motion picture to reestablish taxpayer's reputation); Wilfred J. Funk, 35 TC 42 (1960) (author-shareholder's loan to corporation formed to publish his writing); CIR v. Moffat, 373 F2d 844 (3d Cir. 1967) (taxpayer in business of leasing properties to controlled corporation); Bowers v. CIR, 716 F2d 1047 (4th Cir. 1983) (loan to client to maintain taxpayer's income level as employee of his corporation). See also Comment, Bowers v. Commissioner: Expanding the Scope of the Section 166 Bad Debt Deduction, 38 Tax Lawyer 251 (1984).

[130] Corn Prods. Ref. Co. v. CIR, supra note 94.

[131] US v. Generes, 405 US 93, reh'g denied, 405 US 1033 (1972); see also Odee Smith, 60 TC 316 (1973) (acq.) (on remand, part of loan held deductible as a non-business bad debt, having been made to recoup an investment, and part was held deductible as business bad debt, having been made to preserve the taxpayer's credit); French v. US, 487 F2d 1246 (1st Cir. 1973) (dominant motive test applied at time of advances, not when guarantor had to pay; court found investment motive as a matter of law, reversing jury verdict to contrary). But see Adelson v. US, 737 F2d 1569 (Fed. Cir. 1984) (lower court decision remanded for further evidence on whether advances were to further taxpayer's consulting business or to obtain equity interests in clients; on remand, 1984-2 USTC ¶ 9787 (Cl. Ct. 1984) (dominant motive was business), appeal after remand, 782 F2d 1010 (Fed. Cir. 1986). Compare Lorch v. CIR, 605 F2d 657 (2d Cir. 1979) (capital loss on securities in stockbroker's subordinated account); Henry J. Benak, supra note 126 (substantial investment motive); Alfred H. Tolzman, supra note 126 (business motive not dominant).

§166(a); the nonbusiness debt rules of §166(d) do not apply to corporations.[132]

(2) Worthless securities (including shares of stock as well as debt claims) give rise by virtue of §165(g)(1) to a capital loss as of the last day of the taxable year in which they become worthless. The term "security" is defined for this purpose by §165(g)(2)(C); it does not include stock, bonds, notes, etc., when issued by an "affiliated corporation," as defined in §165(g)(3).

(3) Worthless securities of an affiliated corporation (owned by the taxpayer to the extent of at least 80 percent of each class of stock[133] and more than 90 percent of whose gross receipts consist of operating income as distinguished from dividends, royalties, and similar passive income) give rise to an ordinary loss deduction by virtue of §165(g)(3).[134] (Because the stock ownership rule of §165(g)(3)(A) speaks of direct ownership, Regs. §1.165-5(i), Example (1), limits its application to first-tier subsidiaries.) The purpose of this exception to §165(g)(1) is to approximate roughly the treatment that would have been accorded to the loss if it had been incurred directly by the taxpayer-parent. If the subsidiary was engaged primarily in investment or trading activities, however, its worthless securities would produce a capital loss under §165(g)(1), conforming to the tax result that would have followed if the parent had carried on such operations in its own right.

These rules give way in the case of subsidiaries to (1) a judge-made principle allowing an ordinary loss in the case of securities acquired for such business purposes as assuring a source of supply for the parent corporation,[135] and (2) special statutory rules governing losses incurred on the liquidation of subsidiaries.[136]

---

[132] This virtual certainty of ordinary deduction treatment for corporate-held debts that turn sour adds fuel to the stock versus debt controversy over the status of such advances. See supra ¶¶ 4.02 and 4.04.

[133] See Hunter Mfg. Corp., 21 TC 424 (1953) (disregarding tax-motivated purchase of worthless stock to acquire requisite stock control); Northeastern Consol. Co. v. US, supra note 69 (§165(g)(3) ordinary-loss rule applicable only to total worthlessness); Textron, Inc. v. US, 561 F2d 1023 (1st Cir. 1977) (parent allowed deduction for worthless stock and debt of subsidiary despite its later reactivation with profitable business using net operating loss carry-over). See also Natbony, Twice Burned or Twice Blessed—Double Deductions in the Affiliated Corporation Context, 6 J. Corp. Tax'n 3 (1979).

[134] Rev. Rul. 75-186, 1975-1 CB 72 (for 90 percent test, gross receipts from subsidiary's entire existence must be aggregated).

[135] See supra note 95.

[136] See infra ¶¶ 11.41–11.42.

¶ 4.23　OUTSIDE LOANS GUARANTEED BY SHAREHOLDERS

When a loan made by an individual shareholder to his corporation becomes worthless, the shareholder is ordinarily confined to a capital loss by §165(g)(1) (if the debt is evidenced by a security) or by §166(d)(1) (if the debt is not evidenced by a security but is a nonbusiness debt). The shareholder is able to deduct the loss from ordinary income as a bad debt under §166(a) only by establishing that it is not a nonbusiness debt, and this phrase has been construed by the courts, as noted above, to bar a deduction under §166(a) in most cases of shareholder loans. [137]

What if the corporation borrows the funds it requires from a bank or other outside lender on notes endorsed by its shareholders, and the shareholders pay off the loan upon the corporation's failure? At one time, it appeared that this technique would assure a deduction from ordinary income for the shareholder who had to make good on a defaulted loan, since several courts of appeals held that payment on the guarantee (if not reimbursed by the corporation) gave rise to a loss on a "transaction entered into for profit" under §§165(a) and 165(c)(2) rather than to a bad debt that might be subject to the restriction of §166(d). In 1956, however, the Supreme Court pointed out in *Putnam v. CIR* that the guarantor, on paying the corporation's debt to the bank, was subrogated to the bank's claim against the corporation; and it concluded from this principle of private law that "the loss sustained by the guarantor unable to recover from the debtor is by its very nature a loss from the worthlessness of a debt." [138] This holding, treating the loss as a bad debt, relegates the guarantor to a short-term capital loss if the debt is a nonbusiness debt under §166(d) and the *Whipple* investor-motive test. Just as in the case of a direct loan to the corporation, therefore, guarantors can now ordinarily deduct their loss from ordinary income under §166(a) only if they can escape the nonbusiness debt label of §166(d). [139]

---

[137] See generally supra text at notes 125–131.

[138] Putnam v. CIR, supra note 122, at 85 (earlier cases cited in n.5 of the Court's opinion); see also Regs. §§1.166-8(b) and 1.166-8(c), Example (4); Rev. Rul. 60-48, 1960-1 CB 112; Nelson v. CIR, 281 F2d 1 (5th Cir. 1960) (*Putnam* applied to interest and principal of corporate loan guaranteed by a shareholder, so payment of interest gave rise to nonbusiness bad-debt deduction rather than to interest deduction), cert. denied, 439 US 892 (1978); Alfred H. Tolzman, supra note 126 (guarantor's payment of interest on guaranteed debt that accrued *after* his liability became primary and fixed held deductible under §163); infra note 139; Horne v. CIR, 523 F2d 1363 (9th Cir. 1975) (guaranty and indemnity obligations treated alike; taxpayer's indemnification payments, however, were nondeductible currently because debt not yet sour); Henry J. Benak, supra note 126 (guaranty payment nonbusiness bad debt); Brown, Comment: Putnam v. Commissioner–The Reimbursable Outlay Under the Tax Law, 6 Buffalo L. Rev. 283 (1957).

[139] For this possibility, see supra notes 127–129. For the status of interest accruing and paid by the guarantor after the corporate obligor's bankruptcy, see Statmore

There remain, however, some subtle distinctions in the law of surety-ship that in special circumstances may enable taxpayers who have acted as guarantors to bring themselves within the ordinary loss ambit of §§165(a) and 165(c)(2). Thus, it has been held that *partial* payments under guaranty or indemnity obligations and payments to be released from such obligations are deductible as ordinary losses under §§165(a) and 165(c)(2) rather than as bad debts under §166 because subrogation rights did not arise from the payment; thus, no debt became worthless.[140] But other decisions have held that even without the existence of a technical subrogation, the taxpayer's loss is in the nature of a creditor's bad debt loss, and thus must satisfy the business-versus-nonbusiness requirement of *Whipple* in order to be deductible as an ordinary item. These decisions rested on the ground that *Putnam* held broadly that "payments in discharge of a guaranty are normally to be treated as bad debt losses."[141] In still other decisions, bad debt classification for the loss has been avoided, but the deduction under §165(c)(2) nevertheless has been held to constitute a capital loss under §165(f), since the taxpayer's loss had its origin in, and derived its essential character from, a capital investment rather than from an ordinary business transaction.[142]

The *Putnam* doctrine is ordinarily disadvantageous to individual taxpayers, since it usually requires the loss to be deducted as a capital loss rather than an ordinary one. If the guarantee is given as an accommodation to a relative or friend, however, *Putnam* may be helpful; this is because bad debts are deductible, even though they arise out of a personal context,[143] while a nonbusiness loss incurred by an individual can be deducted only if it meets the standards of §165(c)(2) (transaction entered into for profit) and hence is nondeductible if its motivation is wholly personal.

---

v. CIR, 785 F2d 419 (3d Cir. 1986) (interest deductible from ordinary income) and cases there cited.

[140] See cases cited (but not followed) by In re Vaughn, 719 F2d 196 (6th Cir. 1983).

[141] Bert W. Martin, 52 TC 140, 144 (1969), aff'd per curiam, 424 F2d 1368 (9th Cir.), cert. denied, 400 US 902 (1970); followed by In re Vaughn, supra note 140 (necessary "to look beyond [the] linguistic facade" to "the essence of the payments"); Celanese Corp. v. US, 1985-2 USTC 9517 (Cl. Ct. 1985) (accord).

[142] See Estate of McGlothlin, 44 TC 611 (1965), aff'd, 370 F2d 729 (5th Cir. 1967) (shareholder's payment pursuant to indemnity agreement executed in connection with tax-free acquisition of taxpayer's corporation; held not deductible as ordinary loss; payment added to cost basis of acquired stock); Federal Bulk Carriers, Inc. v. US, 558 F2d 128 (2d Cir. 1977) (capital loss under *Arrowsmith* doctrine); J. Meredith Siple, 54 TC 1 (1970). For losses from subordinated loans to brokerage firms effected by subjecting the lender's securities to claims by the firm's customers, see supra note 125.

[143] But see E.J. Ellisberg, 9 TC 463 (1947) (on facts, transaction tantamount to bank loan to taxpayer and gift by him to son rather than as a bank loan to son guaranteed by taxpayer).

The use of corporate loans guaranteed by shareholders is sometimes suggested as a method of avoiding the thin capitalization problem.[144] The theory is that if the corporation is organized with a minimum of equity capital and borrows whatever funds it may need from a bank or other outside lender on notes endorsed by its shareholders, the interest paid by the debtor corporation to the lender is deductible under §163 and the repayment of the borrowed funds at maturity does not constitute a dividend to its shareholders. This recommendation of guaranteed loans as a solution to the problems of the thin corporation underestimates the perspicacity of the courts. Just as a bond is not necessarily a bond, so a lender is not necessarily a lender, and a guarantor is not necessarily a guarantor. *In form*, the bank may have lent money to the corporation upon the guaranty of the shareholders; but *in substance*, the bank may have made the loan to the shareholders, who in turn passed the funds on to the corporation as—perish the thought—a capital contribution.[145]

If the transaction is recast in this fashion, the payments by the corporation to the bank (whether labeled "interest" or "repayment of loan") would serve to discharge obligations of the shareholders to the bank and thus would be disguised dividends.[146] If the corporation became insolvent, however, the shareholders would suffer capital losses under §165(g) rather than short-term capital losses under §166(d) as interpreted by the *Putnam* case.[147]

¶ 4.24 LOSSES ON "SECTION 1244 STOCK"

The preceding sections of this chapter show that when an investment in a corporation becomes worthless, the investor's loss is usually treated as a capital loss rather than as an ordinary loss.[148] If the investment is evidenced by stock or securities, capital loss treatment is dictated by §165(g); if an open-account loan or a promissory note is used and the investor is not a

---

[144] Supra ¶ 4.04, text at notes 70–74.

[145] For cases holding that a loan guarantee may be tantamount to a capital investment by the shareholder-guarantor, see Casco Bank & Trust Co. v. US, 544 F2d 528 (1st Cir. 1976), cert. denied, 430 US 907 (1977) and cases there cited; In re Lane, 742 F2d 1311, 1320 (11th Cir. 1984) (guarantees used as "substitutes for infusion of more capital"). For a case treating the corporation as the true debtor, see J. Paul Smyers, 57 TC 189 (1971) (fact that bank loan would not have been made without guaranty of shareholder does not, per se, make bank loan equity when corporation not otherwise thin); Murphy Logging Co. v. US, 378 F2d 222 (9th Cir. 1967) (corporation not thin); Falkoff v. CIR, 605 F2d 1045 (7th Cir. 1979) (corporation true borrower). Compare Joseph Creel, 72 TC 1173 (1979); Selfic v. US, 778 F2d 769 (11th Cir. 1985).

[146] See generally infra ¶ 7.05.

[147] Supra note 138.

[148] Supra ¶¶ 4.20, 4.22, and 4.23.

corporation, the investor is ordinarily restricted to a capital loss by §166(d), relating to nonbusiness debts. In contrast to this capital loss treatment of most investments in a corporation, an individual proprietor or a partner who invests in a losing venture usually is entitled to deduct the expenses and losses incurred in the business from any outside income that may be received.[149] For this reason, investors in speculative enterprises sometimes operate in partnership form during the early years when the risk of loss is greatest, and incorporate only after success seems likely.

This disparity is reduced by §1244, under which losses incurred by individuals on "section 1244 stock," whether arising on a sale of the stock or on worthlessness, can be deducted from ordinary income, subject to a ceiling of $100,000 (for married couples filing a joint return) or $50,000 (for other taxpayers) in any taxable year.[150] Losses in excess of the applicable ceiling are subject to normal capital loss treatment. The announced purpose of §1244, which was enacted in 1958, was to "encourage the flow of new funds into small business" and to place shareholders in small corporations "on a more nearly equal basis with . . . proprietors and partners."[151]

1. Qualifying taxpayers. Section 1244 applies only to individual taxpayers; §1244(d)(4) explicitly disqualifies trusts and estates. Moreover, the stock must have been issued to a partnership or the individual claiming the loss, with the result that purchasers, donees, and other transferees of "Section 1244 stock" do not qualify.[152] This original-investor rule should embrace

---

[149] But see §469 imposing special limitations on the deduction of losses from "passive activities."

[150] For a more comprehensive tax regime under which the corporation's operating losses are currently passed through to the shareholders and reported on their individual returns, see the discussion of Subchapter S, infra ch. 6.

[151] H.R. Rep. No. 2198, 85th Cong., 1st Sess. (1958), reprinted in 1959-2 CB 709, 711. See generally Schoenfeld, Small Business Stock, Tax Mgmt. Portfolio (BNA) No. 98-4th (1987); Johnson & Cochran, Looking a Gift-Horse in the Mouth: Some Observations and Suggestions for Improving Internal Revenue Code Section 1244, 39 Sw. L.J. 975 (1986); Barrack & Dodge, Section 1244: Is the Intent of Congress Fianlly Achieved? 6 J. Corp. Tax'n 283 (1980); Moore & Sorlien, Adventures in Subchapter S and Section 1244, 14 Tax L. Rev. 453 (1959); Nicholson, Section 1244 Stock, 38 Taxes 303 (1960).

For special rules applicable to stock issued on or before November 6, 1978, see McGuffie, supra, at A-11.

For a pre-1978 requirement that "section 1244" stock be issued pursuant to a plan, see Russell L. Short, ¶ 86,360 P-H Memo. TC (1986), and cases there cited.

[152] Under Regs. §§1.1244(a)-1(b)(2) and the example at 1.1244(a)-1(c)(2), this disqualification extends even to stock issued to a partnership if it was distributed to a partner before the loss was sustained, although the statute itself seems to require only that (1) the stock was issued either to an individual or to a partnership and (2) the

issues of treasury stock as well as the issue of previously unissued stock.[153] The regulations provide that stock acquired through an underwriter can qualify if the underwriter was only a selling agent (i.e., a best-efforts underwriting) but not if the underwriter purchased the stock from the corporation and resold it to the investor (i.e., a firm-commitment underwriting).[154]

2. Corporate status when stock was issued. When the stock was issued, the corporation must have been a small business corporation. The corporation meets this requirement if the aggregate amount of money and other property received by the corporation for stock as a contribution to capital and as paid-in surplus does not exceed $1 million. This determination (in which property is valued for ascertaining gain at its adjusted basis as of the time received, reduced by liabilities that were assumed or to which the property was subject[155]) is made at the time of issuance of the stock in question but includes amounts received for all previously issued stock as well.[156] Purported debt that should be regarded as stock or a contribution to capital under the principles discussed earlier in this chapter[157] presumably is also charged against the statutory limit.

3. Corporate status when loss was sustained. In addition to being a small business corporation when the stock was issued, the corporation must meet the test of §1244(c)(1)(C) when the loss was sustained. Thus, it cannot be said with certainty when stock is issued that it will qualify for §1244 treatment. For the five taxable years immediately preceding the year when the loss was sustained (or for a specified shorter period if the corporation was not in existence for the entire five-year period), the corporation must have derived more than 50 percent of its aggregate gross receipts from sources other than royalties, rents, dividends, interest, annuities, and sales or exchanges of stock or securi-

---

loss was sustained by an individual. The regulations are based on a statement in H.R. Conf. Rep. No. 2632, infra note 160, at 43. See also Jerome Prizant, ¶ 71,196 P-H Memo. TC (1971) and supra ¶ 3.18.

Regs. §1.1244(a)-1(b)(2) also provides that a partner can qualify under §1244 only if he was a partner when the partnership acquired the §1244 stock.

[153] But see Firestone Tire & Rubber Co., 2 TC 827 (1943) (acq.) (treasury stock not issued).

[154] Regs. §1.1244(a)-1(b)(2).

[155] Section 1244(c)(3)(B).

[156] See §1244(c)(3). If the dollar limitation is exceeded, the corporation must designate which shares are to be treated as "section 1244 stock" under §§1.1244(c)-2(b)(2)–1.1244(c)-2(b)(4). Otherwise, §1244 treatment is allocated under a formula. For application of the $500,000 limit imposed by prior law, see Frantz v. CIR, 784 F2d 119 (2d Cir. 1986).

[157] Supra ¶ 4.04.

ties. This restriction is evidently designed to prevent a shareholder from enjoying a deduction from ordinary income under §1244 if the corporation was primarily engaged in investment activities that, if carried on by the taxpayer as an individual, would have produced capital losses.[158] The gross-receipts limitation is not applicable to a corporation whose deductions for the specified period, other than deductions under §172 (net operating loss carryover) and §§243 through 245 (dividends received), exceeded its gross income.

4. Qualifying stock. Before enactment of the Tax Reform Act of 1984, §1244 applied only to common stock, but this restriction was eliminated (prospectively only) by 1984 amendments to §§1244(c)(1) and 1244(d)(2).

5. Qualified consideration. Section 1244(c)(1)(B) provides that stock can qualify only if it was issued for money or other property, excluding stock issued for services, securities, or other stock.[159] This limitation is in turn subject to an exception: The Treasury is given authority by §1244(d)(2) to provide by regulation that stock will qualify if received in exchange for "section 1244 stock" in a reorganization under §368(a)(1)(F) (mere change in identity, form, place, or organization) if its basis is determined by reference to the taxpayer's basis for qualified stock. Exercising this authority, the Treasury has provided in Regs. §1.1244(d)-3 that common stock received as a stock dividend or in a recapitalization will qualify if received with respect to "section 1244 stock."

6. Qualifying losses. Under §1244(a), any loss on "section 1244 stock" that would otherwise "be treated as a loss from the sale or exchange of a capital asset" qualifies for transformation into ordinary loss. Although there is some shilly-shallying in the committee reports in describing the transactions to which §1244 applies,[160] Regs. §1.1244(a)-1(a) provides that §1244

---

[158] See Regs. §1.1244(c)-1(g)(2) (§1244 limited to largely operating company), approved in H.L. Davenport, 70 TC 922 (1978); Regs. §1.1244(c)-1(e)(2) (same).

Similar tainted sources of income may convert a corporation into a personal holding company (see infra ¶ 8.21) or deny Subchapter S status (infra ¶ 6.04).

[159] See Hollenbeck v. CIR, 422 F2d 2 (9th Cir. 1970) (stock issued to cancel alleged debt that was properly classified as equity; §1244 not applicable); Marcia B. Kaplan, 59 TC 178 (1972) (same); J. Paul Smyers, supra note 145 (same as to part of stock, but some stock qualified because issued for cash used to pay off guaranteed bank loans); see also R.G. Hill, 51 TC 621 (1969) (stock issued for cash to enable insolvent corporation to pay debts to purchasers did not qualify; merely an attempt to convert capital loss into ordinary deduction).

[160] Compare H.R. Rep. No. 2198, supra note 151 at 4 (sale or exchange) and 8 (losses on the sale, exchange or worthlessness), with H.R. Conf. Rep. No. 2632, 85th Congress, 2d Session 43 (1958) (sales and other dispositions).

covers a loss on a sale or exchange "including a transaction treated as a sale or exchange, such as worthlessness." This statement presumably embraces losses on complete and partial liquidations and stock redemptions, as well as losses incurred when the stock is sold or becomes worthless.

7. Limitation on deductible amount. Section 1244(b) provides that the aggregate amount treated by the taxpayer as an ordinary loss for any taxable year should not exceed $50,000 or, in the case of husband and wife filing a joint return, $100,000.[161] This annual limit applies regardless of the number of corporations qualifying under §1244 or when the stock was issued.

If the ordinary loss allowance cannot be employed in full in the taxable year in which the loss is sustained because of a shortage of income in that year, it becomes part of the taxpayer's net operating loss by virtue of §1244(d)(3). If the net operating loss is then carried to a taxable year in which the taxpayer is using his full allowance because of a loss on *other* "section 1244 stock," the regulations permit the net operating loss carry-over to be deducted from that year's ordinary income, even though the carry-over includes a §1244 loss sustained in another year.[162] In effect, the $50,000 or $100,000 ceiling for the carryover year is pierced, but only to the extent that the taxpayer was short of income in the year in which the carry-over loss was sustained.

8. Adjustments to stock's basis. In computing the taxpayer's loss on the sale or exchange of stock, the adjusted basis of the stock is ordinarily compared with the amount realized. Under §1244(d)(1)(A), however, the adjusted basis of the stock must be reduced in computing the amount of loss for purposes of §1244 if (1) the stock was received in exchange for property; (2) the basis of the stock is determined by reference to the taxpayer's basis for the property; and (3) the adjusted basis of the property (for determining loss) immediately before the exchange exceeded its fair market value.[163] In the absence of such a protective restriction, a taxpayer holding a depreciated capital asset could transfer it to a controlled corporation under §351 and then sell the stock (which under §358 would have the same basis as the property) in order to enjoy an ordinary loss under §1244. It should be noted that the tainted portion of the loss in such a case is not disallowed; it is simply

---

[161] The ceiling applies to joint returns even if the loss was sustained by only one of the spouses. Regs. §1.1244(b)-1. This regulation also provides that, in the case of a partnership, the limitation is determined separately as to each partner.

[162] See Regs. §1.1244(d)-4(a) (unmarried taxpayer with $15,000 net operating loss for 1980 that includes loss on "section 1244 stock" and no 1980 taxable income can use carry-over in 1981 in full, even though he also has §1244 loss for 1981 of $50,000).

[163] See Rev. Rul. 66-293, 1966-2 CB 305.

4-47 DEBT VS. EQUITY IN CAPITAL STRUCTURE ¶ 4.25

excluded from §1244, with the result that the shareholder is pro tanto relegated to a capital loss.

A second limitation is imposed by §1244(d)(1)(B), under which any increase in the basis of "section 1244 stock" (through contributions to capital or otherwise) is excluded in computing the loss under §1244. By virtue of this provision, a loss qualifies under §1244 only to the extent of the money or property paid for the stock when it was originally acquired by the taxpayer from the corporation. The purpose of §1244(d)(1)(B) is not given in the committee reports; it may have been designed to prevent an evasion of the $1 million limit of the statutory predecessor of §1244(c)(3)(A) by an offer of stock up to the full amount permitted, to be followed by contributions to capital of additional assets.

¶ 4.25 CORPORATE DEBTOR'S GAIN ON REDEMPTION OR RETIREMENT OF SECURITIES

On redeeming or repurchasing its own stock, a corporation recognizes no gain, even if the amount paid is less than the stock's par or stated value or the amount received when it was issued; any gain on the transaction is instead treated as a tax-free capital contribution under §118(a), as a distribution covered by §311(a)(2), or simply as a nontaxable capital adjustment.[164]

Contrasting sharply with redemptions of stock, the retirement of debt for less than its face amount ordinarily generates cancellation-of-indebtedness income under general tax principles, subject to an intricate web of judicial and statutory qualifications and exceptions.[165] So far as corporate debt

---

[164] For §118, see generally supra ¶ 3.13; for gain or loss if the redemption is effected with appreciated or depreciated property rather than with cash, see infra ¶ 7.21; for §311 generally, see infra ¶ 7.21; see also infra ¶ 5.04, and for a discussion of §162(1), disallowing deductions for stock redemption expenses, see ¶ 5.04, para. 4.

[165] See generally Regs. §§1.61-12(a) and 1.61-12(b); Eustice, Cancellation of Indebtedness and the Federal Income Tax: A Problem of Creeping Confusion, 14 Tax L. Rev. 225 (1959); Eustice, Cancellation of Indebtedness Redux: The Bankruptcy Tax Act of 1980, 36 Tax L. Rev. 1 (1980); Bittker, Federal Taxation of Income, Estates and Gifts, supra note 95, ¶ 6.4; Bittker & Thompson, Income From the Discharge of Indebtedness: The Progeny of *United States v. Kirby Lumber Co.*, 66 Calif. L. Rev. 1159 (1978).

For problems in distinguishing between discharges of debt and similar transactions having different tax consequences, see Carolina, Clinchfield & O. Ry., 82 TC 888 (1984) (cancellation of old debt as opposed to substitution of new debt); OKC Corp., 82 TC 638 (1984) (debt-discharge gain was ordinary income from settlement of lost profits claim, not §108 item); Colonial Sav. Ass'n, 85 TC 855 (1981) (payments by depositors as penalties for early withdrawals did not discharge any debt owed by tax-

is concerned, the major limitations to the basic rule that income is realized when debt is discharged for less than its face amount are the following:

(1) If the debt discharge qualifies as a capital contribution by a shareholder (e.g., a principal shareholder's cancellation of a debt owed to the shareholder, in order to improve the corporation's financial position), the debtor corporation is treated by §108(e)(6) as having satisfied the debt with cash equal to the shareholder's adjusted basis for the debt.[166]

(2) With certain limited exceptions, if a solvent debtor corporation transfers its stock to a creditor in discharge of a debt, it is treated by §108(e)(10)(A) as having satisfied the debt with cash equal to the stock's fair market value.[167]

(3) The obligations of a liquidating corporation may be paid off as part of the liquidating process, but often the shareholders assume the debt or take the corporate property subject to it. In that event, as explained later in this work, the corporation does not realize any debt-discharge income.[168]

(4) Insolvent and bankrupt debtors do not realize current income on the cancellation of debt under principles examined in detail later in this work, but their tax attributes (e.g., net operating loss and capital loss carryovers) are correspondingly reduced.[169]

Because it decorated the tax landscape for many years, former §108(d)(4) deserves mention here. Together with §108(c), it permitted debtors to exclude income from the discharge of certain qualified business debt on condition that the excluded amount was deducted from the corporation's basis for its depreciable assets; however, this deduction was repealed by the Tax Reform Act of 1986.[170]

---

payer bank); Vukasovich v. CIR, 790 F2d 1409 (9th Cir. 1986) (*Kerbagh-Empire* overall transaction loss doctrine no longer the law). See also infra ¶ 14.55 for a distinction between debt discharges and assumptions of debt in corporate acquisitions.

[166] See supra ¶ 3.13, text at note 142. Nonshareholder contributions to capital are governed by §118, discussed supra ¶ 3.13, text at note 136.

[167] See supra ¶ 3.12. For the practice at which §108(e)(10) is aimed, see Note, Debt-Equity Swaps, 37 Tax Lawyer 677 (1984); Bryan, Cancellation of Indebtedness by Issuing Stock in Exchange: Challenging the Congressional Solution to Debt-Equity Swaps, 63 Tex. L. Rev. 89 (1984).

[168] See infra ¶ 11.09.

[169] See generally §§108(a)(1) and 108(e)(10)(B); but see §382(*l*)(5)(C); infra ¶¶ 14.17, 14.20, 14.58, and 16.25, para. 6.

[170] See Pub. L. No. 99-514, §822, 100 Stat. 2373. (1986).

¶ 4.26 DISALLOWANCE OF CORPORATE INTEREST ON DEBT INCURRED TO FINANCE ACQUISITIONS

Responding in 1969 to public unease about a wave of corporate acquisitions in the 1960s, Congress enacted §279 to disallow corporate deductions for interest in excess of $5 million per year on certain debts incurred to acquire the stock or at least two thirds of the assets of another corporation.[171] Section 279, however, can be characterized as a two-time loser: (1) It was enacted after the conglomerate fever of the 1960s had already subsided, so its intended targets were no longer much in evidence; and (2) it tracks the financing techniques of its day so closely that it was easily sidestepped when the next wave of corporate acquisitions began in the 1980s.[172]

Section 279 applies to interest paid or incurred on "corporate acquisition indebtedness," defined by §279(b) as any corporate obligation evidenced by a bond, debenture, note, certificate, or other evidence of indebtedness that is issued after October 9, 1969 and that meets a four-part test:

1. Purpose. The obligation is issued to provide consideration for the acquisition of another corporation's stock or another corporation's assets under a plan for acquisition of at least two thirds (in value) of the target corporation's business assets (excluding money).

2. Subordination. The obligation is subordinated either to the claims of the issuing corporation's trade creditors or to a substantial amount of its unsecured debt, whether outstanding or subsequently issued.

3. Equity participation. The obligation either is convertible into the issuing corporation's stock or is part of an investment unit or other arrangement that includes an option to acquire stock of the issuing corporation.

4. Financial ratio. The issuing corporation's debt-to-equity ratio exceeds 2 to 1, or its projected earnings do not exceed three times the interest to be paid or incurred on the debt.[173]

---

[171] For extended analysis, see Kaplan & Jahns, Corporate Acquisition Debt—Interest Deduction—Section 279, Tax Mgmt. (BNA) No. 287 (1973). See generally 44 St. John's L. Rev. (special issue 1970), Vol. 44, Conglomerate Mergers and Acquisitions: Opinion and Analysis (exhaustive collection of articles on all aspects of this problem, including tax consequences); FTC Staff Report on Corporate Mergers to Antitrust Subcomm. of Senate Judiciary Comm., 91st Cong., 1st Sess. (1969).

[172] See Canellos, supra note 76; Allen, A Leveraged Buyout Checklist after Tax Reform, 32 Tax Notes 1151 (1986); Bowen, Structuring Leveraged Buyouts—Selected Tax Problems, 63 Taxes 935 (1985); Sheppard, supra note 1.

[173] The key concepts in computing these ratios are defined at length by §279(c).

Interest on debt meeting these requirements (which are elaborated and qualified in various respects by §279) is disallowed if and to the extent that it exceeds $5 million per year. The allowable amount, however, is reduced by interest on debt issued after 1967 if it meets the first of the four tests set out above, even though it does not itself constitute corporate acquisition indebtedness because it does not satisfy one or more of the other three tests. The disallowance applies not only to the issuing corporation itself, but also to any other corporation that guarantees or assumes the tainted debt.

There is a number of escape hatches from the disallowance mandated by §279, including (1) transactions involving the acquisition of less than 5 percent or more than 80 percent of the target corporation's stock; (2) transfers within an affiliated group of corporations; (3) acquisitions of foreign corporations, (4) post-acquisition improvements in the issuing corporation's financial ratios; and (5) certain nontaxable transactions. Moreover, §279 is entirely inapplicable to acquisitions effected with the issuing corporation's stock (since no interest deduction is claimed) or to efforts to acquire the issuing corporation's stock or to debt that does not satisfy the subordination or equity participation tests summarized above.

Thus, when the stock market heated up in the 1980s and hostile tender offers and leveraged management buyouts mushroomed, §279 could be easily sidestepped (e.g., by issuing nonconvertible junk bonds to the shareholders of the target company, or, in the case of management buyouts, because the acquisition debt is incurred to acquire the issuing corporation's own stock, not the stock of another corporation.)[174] For legislators seeking to discourage these acquisitions, therefore, it was back to the drawing board and to the likelihood that, once again, the barn would be empty before the door could be locked.

PART C.   ORIGINAL ISSUE AND MARKET DISCOUNT

¶ 4.40   ORIGINAL ISSUE DISCOUNT IN GENERAL

The use of debt rather than equity to finance a corporation's business needs is encouraged, as explained earlier, by the fact that interest on indebtedness can be deducted, but dividends paid on stock cannot.[175] For many years, this preference for debt was accentuated for both the debtor corporation and its bondholders by the tax rules governing the treatment

---

[174] See note 172 supra.

[175] See generally supra ¶ 4.02, which also notes other tax allowances favoring the use of debt over equity.

of original issue discount (OID). The attractions of OID (prior to the enactment of the statutory changes examined below) can be illustrated by assuming that a corporation issues 30 year bonds with a face value of $1,000 each, paying 10 percent annually, but sells the bonds for $850 each because 10 percent is too low a rate to attract investors. The $150 of OID serves the same function as the stated annual interest of $100—that is, it is an additional cost to the corporation of borrowing $850 from the bond-holder, and it is additional compensation to the bondholder for lending that amount to the corporation.[176] The only difference to the parties is that the corporation is not required to pay the OID of $150 until the bond matures, and that the bondholder does not receive the discount in cash until then unless the bond is sold in the interim.

To put current law in context, the major stages in the increasingly restrictive, and economically realistic, tax treatment of OID can be divided as follows:

1. Before 1969. Before 1969, corporations issuing debt with OID were allowed to accrue the discount on a straight-line basis over the life of the bonds. Thus, the $150 of OID on the 30-year bonds described above was accrued at $5 per year, and this amount, plus the $100 of stated interest, was deducted annually. Cash-basis bondholders, however, were not required to report the OID as it was earned year by year, but could instead wait until the amount was paid at maturity or was realized by an earlier sale of the bond.

Moreover, before 1956, there was some authority for reporting the earned discount as capital gain even though it resulted from the mere passage of time and not from the economic changes that ordinarily give rise to capital gains. In 1956, however, the Supreme Court held in *US v. Midland-Ross Corp.* that earned OID realized on a sale of the bond did not qualify for capital-gain treatment but must instead be reported as ordinary income.[177]

2. 1969 to 1982. Although it rejected the bondholder's capital-gain claim, *Midland-Ross* did not question either the cash basis bondholder's

---

[176] See US v. Midland-Ross Corp., 381 US 54, 57 (1965) ("earned original issue discount serves the same function as stated interest"—it is simply compensation for the use or forbearance of money); CIR v. Nat'l Alfalfa Dehydrating & Milling Co., 417 US 134, 145 (1974) ("An additional cost incurred in borrowing money").

[177] US v. Midland-Ross Corp., supra note 176. The case involved sales of bonds at gains attributable solely to earned OID, unaffected by changes in the market rate of interest or in the borrower's credit rating; see id. at n.4. For legislation enacted in 1954 covering the same ground, as well as gains realized on repayment of the bond at maturity (but limited to bonds issued after enactment of the 1954 Code), see id. at n. 5; S. Rep. No. 1622, 83d Cong., 2d Sess. 112 (1954).

right to postpone reporting earned discount until realized in cash on a sale or retirement of the bond or the accrual-basis corporation's right to amortize the earned discount on a straight-line basis over the life of the bond. This mismatch between the issuing corporation's current deductions and the bondholder's delayed reporting of the income evoked corrective action by Congress in 1969, when the predecessor of §1272 was enacted. This provision required the bondholder to report OID as ordinary income in equal annual installments over the life of the bond in a manner paralleling the issuing corporation's amortization of the discount. The holder's basis for the bond was increased by the amount taxed as income so that the same amount would not be taxed a second time on a sale of the bond or on its redemption at maturity.[178]

By taxing bondholders on amounts not currently received by them in cash, the 1969 legislation reduced the appeal of debt with OID; but this effect was not substantial if the discount was minor in amount or if, as was often the case, the holders were tax-exempt entities.[179] By the same token, however, the smaller the amount at stake, the smaller the revenue reward for the increase in complexity required to put cash-basis taxpayers on an accrual basis in this limited area. As will be seen, however, the increase in interest rates in the 1970s, as well as increased sophistication in the financial markets, led to a dramatic increase in the use of OID, including the issuance of deep-discount and zero-coupon bonds by corporate borrowers seeking to generate large current deductions by amortizing OID on bonds with far-off maturity dates.[180]

3. 1982 and after. The 1969 legislation tacitly assumed that the straight-line amortization of OID by the borrowing corporation and the corresponding ratable accrual of the same amounts by the bondholder were justified. From the perspective of both parties, however, OID does not accrue in equal annual installments (like simple interest), but instead compounds over the life of the loan, as explained subsequently in more detail.[181] This fact of financial

---

[178] For analysis of the 1969 legislation and of its exceptions to the accrual principle, see Landis, Original Issue Discount After the Tax Reform Act of 1969, 24 Tax Lawyer 435 (1971); N.Y. State Bar Association, Comm. on Corporate Taxation, Comments on Proposed and Final Regulations on Treatment of Corporate Debt Issued At Discount, 50 Taxes 274 (1972).

[179] Moreover, the 1969 law contained a de minimis exemption; for its counterpart in current law, see infra text at note 193.

[180] Infra ¶ 4.41.

[181] Id. See N.Y. State Bar Association, Tax Section, Report of Ad Hoc Committee on Proposed Original Issue Discount Regulations, 34 Tax Notes 363 (1987) (cited hereafter as New York State Bar Report); see also Halperin, Interest in Disguise: Taxing the "Time Value of Money," 95 Yale L.J. 506 (1986); Lokken, The Time

life was codified in 1982 by the enactment of §163(e) and the statutory predecessor of §1272, which allocated OID on debt instruments issued after July 1, 1982 over the life on the debt on a so-called constant-interest basis. This method of allocation attributes smaller amounts of discount to the debt's earlier years, as compared with the straight-line method, and larger amounts to later years. The amount so allocated to each year is deductible by the issuer under §163(e) and taxable to the holder under §1272.

The 1982 rules applied not only to debt instruments issued for money, but also to instruments issued for property if the debt itself was publicly traded or was issued for publicly traded stock or securities. In 1984, coverage was extended to debt-for-property transactions, even if neither the debt nor the property were publicly traded, subject to exceptions summarized below.[182]

Another 1984 innovation was the enactment of §1276, a characterization rule requiring gain on the disposition of so-called market discount bonds to be reported as ordinary income rather than as capital gain to the extent allocable to accrued market discount.[183] A bond is subject to this provision if it is purchased on the secondary market at a price less than its face, usually because the issuing corporation's credit rating declined or the market rate of interest increased after the bond was issued. In these circumstances, the bond's stated interest becomes inadequate, and the bond must be sold for less than its face in order to compensate the buyer adequately for his investment; and the appreciation over time of the resulting market discount, being tantamount to interest from the buyer's perspective, is so treated by §1276. The interest is not taxed to the bondholder, however, until the bond is sold or retired, as was OID during the period 1954 through 1969.

The current rules for both OID and market discount bonds are examined in detail subsequently.[184] Concerned as it is with the capital structure of private business corporations, however, this chapter does not deal with the tax treatment of OID on obligations issued by individuals or federal, state, or local governmental bodies, or on obligations maturing within a year of the date of issue.

Value of Money Rules, 42 Tax L. Rev. 1 (1986); Garlock, A Practical Guide to the Original Issue Discount Regulations, Prentice-Hall (1987); Canellos & Kleinbard, The Miracle of Compound Interest: Interest Deferral and Discount After 1982, 38 Tax L. Rev. 565 (1983).

[182] Infra ¶ 4.42.

[183] Infra ¶ 4.44.

[184] See generally infra ¶¶ 4.41, 4.42, 4.44. For transition rules governing debt instruments issued after May 27, 1969 and before July 2, 1982, see §1272(b); for instruments issued earlier, see Regs. §1.1232-1.

¶ 4.41   OID OBLIGATIONS ISSUED FOR CASH

1. Allocation of OID on constant-interest basis. Under §§163(e) and 1272(a) of current law, OID is allocated on a constant interest (or economic accrual) basis over the life of debt instruments issued after July 1, 1982.[185] In comparison to the pre-1982 allocation of OID on a straight-line basis, OID accrues under current law in steadily increasing amounts over the term of the obligation. In 1982, recommending adoption of the constant-interest method of amortizing OID, the Senate Finance Committee pointed out the distortions produced by the straight-line method, especially when applied to long-term deep discount and zero coupon bonds issued in the high interest rate environment of the late 1970s and early 1980s:

> Assume a 15-percent rate. Suppose a business wants to borrow $1 and then borrow at the end of the year to pay all interest charges for the year, and repeat this sequence each year for 30 years. Its interest payments would be 15 cents in the first year, 17.3 cents the second year (15 percent interest on the outstanding balance of $1.15), and so on, and would grow exponentially, eventually equalling $8.64 in the 30th year. At the end of 30 years, the overall debt would mount up to $66.21. A total of $65.21 in interest would be paid, and deducted, over the period, but the deductions would start small and grow.
>
> The taxpayer could achieve the same substantive result by issuing a zero-coupon bond at a price of $1 redeemable for $66.21 in 30 years. However, by using the OID bond, the taxpayer can obtain [under pre-1982 law] a deduction of $2.17 each year ($65.21 divided by 30). Thus, the OID bond allows larger interest deductions in early years than borrowing the same amount with ordinary loans. In this example, the taxpayer deducts in the first year more than twice the amount borrowed and more than 14 times the real interest. Conversely, the purchaser of the OID bond includes more interest in his income in early years than the purchaser of an ordinary bond.[186]

The distortions noted in this extract from the committee report are so glaring that it may be hard to understand how the straight-line method of amortizing OID came to be accepted in the first place. The explanation is that OID was traditionally used by investment bankers to make minor last-minute adjustments to rising interest rates. For example, a borrower, after exe-

---

[185] See generally N.Y. State Bar Report (on proposed OID regulations), supra note 181. See also Lokken, supra note 181, and Garlock, supra note 181. For instruments issued on or before July 1, 1982, see §1272(b) (instruments issued between May 27, 1969 and July 2, 1982 remain subject to straight-line allocation rules of pre-1982 law); for certain earlier obligations, see §§1271(c)(1) and 1271(c)(2).

[186] S. Rep. No. 494 (1982), 97 Cong., 2d Sess. 210. For the allocation mechanics, see Prop. Regs. §1.1272-2 (1986).

cuting the documents and printing the certificates for an issue of 30-year 8 percent bonds, might be advised by its underwriters that sales would be sluggish or even impossible unless the bonds were priced to yield 8.25 percent to maturity. This market adjustment could be easily accomplished without revising the documents by selling the bonds at an appropriate discount from their par value (i.e., for $972 rather than the originally contemplated $1,000 per bond). Although straight-line amortization by the issuer of the resulting OID of $28 in principle created the distortion noted above, the amounts were so small as to be negligible.[187]

The same was ordinarily true of bond premiums, which are the opposite of original issue discount—that is, if the stated interest rate is too high relative to the market when the bonds are floated, the excess can be eliminated by selling the bonds for more than their face amount. The holder is allowed by §171 to amortize the premium over the life of the bond, since it reduces the effective rate of interest; the issuer is similarly required by Regs. §1.61-12(c)(2) to take the premium into income.[188] For example, if the bonds described in the preceding paragraph were priced at too high an interest rate relative to the market rate when offered because the going rate for similar risks was only 7.75 percent, the disparity could be eliminated by selling the bonds at $1,029 (i.e., at a premium of $29).

This arcane subject came to public attention when financial planners, building on the dramatic increase in interest rates in the 1970s, began to market deep discount and zero coupon obligations whose interest was largely or even entirely buried in the spread between the offering price at issue and the amount to be paid at maturity.

The 1982 remedy, the so-called constant interest (or economic accrual) method of amortizing original issue discount, is embodied in §1272(a)(3), whose rationale has been explained as follows by the Senate Finance Committee:

> The premise of the OID rules is that, for Federal income tax purposes, an obligation issued at a discount should be treated like an obligation issued at par requiring current payments of interest. Accordingly, the effect of the OID rules is to treat the borrower as having paid semiannually the lender the interest accruing on the outstanding principal balance of the loan, thereby permitting the borrower to deduct as interest expense and requiring the lender to include in income such interest which has accrued but is unpaid. The lender is then deemed to

---

[187] For the status of de minimis discounts under current law, see infra text at note 193.

[188] Under §171(b)(3), as amended in 1986, bond premium is amortized on the constant interest method, compounded in the manner used to compute OID under §1272. For the treatment of premium on convertible bonds, see infra ¶ 4.60.

have lent the accrued but unpaid interest back to the borrower, who in subsequent periods is deemed to pay interest on this amount as well as on the principal balance. This concept of accruing interest on unpaid interest is commonly referred to as the "economic accrual" of interest, or interest "compounding."[189]

This method of accounting for OID can be illustrated by assuming that a corporate borrower sells an issue of $1,000 bonds, due at the end of five years, for $621 per bond—a price that will yield the investor 10 percent compounded annually for the bond's five-year life.[190] The OID of $379 ($1,000 to be received at maturity, less $621 paid) is allocated over the bond's life in installments as shown in Column A of the following table, the amount for each year being 10 percent of the Column B balance at the end of the preceding year. That balance, plus the OID allocated to the year in question, becomes the Column B balance on which the next year's interest is computed (at the constant rate of 10 percent).

Amortization of OID—Constant Interest vs. Straight-Line Method ($1,000, 10 year bond issued for $621 to yield 10 percent compounded annually to maturity)

End of Year	A. OID (constant-interest basis)*	B. Principal Plus Earned OID**	C. OID (straight-line basis)
0	0	$ 621.00	0
1	$ 62.00	683.00	$ 75.80
2	68.00	751.00	75.80
3	75.00	827.00	75.80
4	83.00	909.00	75.80
5	91.00	1,000.00	75.80
	$379.00		$379.00

*10 percent of Col. B balance at end of prior year, rounded off.
**This is the bond's adjusted issue price as described by §1272(a)(4).

Columns A and B can be likened to the results that would be achieved by borrowing $621, depositing it in a bank account subject to a 10 percent interest rate, allowing the deposit and accumulated interest to grow for five

---

[189] Sen. Rep. No. 83, (1985), 99th Cong., 1st Sess. 5, n.4; see generally Prop. Regs. §1.1272-1 (1986); New York State Bar Report, supra note 181; Harvey, How the New Original Issue Discount Regulations Will Affect Investment Decisions, 4 J. Tax'n Inv. 3 (1986).

[190] In the interest of simplicity, annual compounding is used in the example; but §§1272(a)(3) and 1272(a)(5) provide for semiannual compounding, since bond interest is ordinarily paid or credited semiannually. For examples, see Prop. Regs. §1.1272-1(k).

years until the balance in the account is $1,000, and then using that amount to pay off the $621 loan with interest at 10 percent compounded annually for the five-year period. The amounts shown in Column A are deductible by the issuer under §163(e) and are includable in the holder's gross income under §1272. Column C of the table shows how the pre-1982 straight-line method of amortizing OID produced larger allocations in the earlier years compared with the constant interest method now mandated by §1272 and lower amounts in later years. The disparities in the example are modest because of the bond's short life; but, as illustrated by the numbers in the extract from the Senate Finance Committee's 1982 report quoted previously,[191] the spreads are dramatically greater for long-term bonds with higher interest rates.

The 1982 shift from the straight-line method to the constant-interest method of allocating OID reduced the deductions allowed to the issuer in the early years of the bond's life, but it improved the position of bondholders by correspondingly reducing the amount to be included in income. For individuals, however, this mitigation of the pre-1982 inclusionary rules is of minor importance; the inclusion of OID in gross income is usually anathema, even when computed on the more favorable post-1982 constant-interest basis, since the taxable amounts are not received currently in cash. A few individual investors, however, may be willing to accept the current inclusion of amounts not received currently if they anticipate a decline in interest rates and want to lock in the current rate for the life of a zero coupon bond; they cannot get the same guarantee from ordinary bonds, since the semiannual interest payments will have to be reinvested at the rates prevailing from year to year as the payments are received.

In practice, therefore, the principal purchasers of deep discount and zero coupon bonds are tax-exempt organizations and deferred-tax accounts (such as IRAs and Keogh plans), which are not taxed currently on the steadily increasing amounts of amortized OID, whether it is allocated on the 1969 straight-line basis or the 1982 constant-interest method. In the end, therefore, the 1982 changes were of more importance to issuers than to investors in the OID instruments.

2. Computation of OID. The inclusion and deduction rules of §§1272 and 163(e) generally apply to any "debt instrument," defined by §1272(a)(1) as a bond, note, or other evidence of indebtedness, except for certain annuity contracts. Debt instruments are included in the definition whether or not the obligation is a capital asset to the holder or is publicly traded; but the income-inclusion rules do not apply to (1) debt instruments of a state or

---

[191] See text at note 186.

local government if interest on the instrument is exempt under §103; (2) U.S. savings bonds; and (3) instruments due within one year of issue.[192]

A debt instrument, as defined, is subject to the operative rules of §§1272 and 163(e) only if there is OID on the instrument (i.e., if its stated redemption price at maturity exceeds its issue price). A de minimis exception provides that OID is deemed to be zero if this excess is less than one quarter of one percent, multiplied by the number of complete years from issue to maturity. For example, on a 10-year bond paying $1,000 at maturity, there is no OID if the issue price exceeds $975 (i.e., $1,000 less 10 times 0.0025 of $1,000). The de minimis rule usually exempts holders of debt instruments from the OID rules if the discount is a pricing adjustment to an increase in the market rate of interest between the time the issuer decides on the terms of the instrument and the time the instrument is sold.[193]

The phrase "stated redemption price at maturity" means the sum of all amounts payable as interest and principal on the instrument (whether payable at maturity or at an earlier time), excluding only so-called stated or explicit interest that is payable unconditionally, at a fixed rate, and at least annually.[194] Interest meeting these conditions is disregarded in computing OID because, under rules of general applicability, it is deductible by the borrower and taxable to the lender when paid and received, and it does not

---

[192] These exemptions, along with the rules relating to debt issued by noncorporate persons, are outside the scope of this work and are not examined further. See Prop. Regs. §1.1275-1(b).

[193] Section 1273(a)(3) states that a de minimis discount "shall be treated as zero." If the introductory phrase of §1273(a)—"for purposes of this subpart [i.e., §§1271–1275]"—applies to §1273(a)(3) and means for *all* such purposes, the *Midland-Ross* case is evidently superseded, in which event a de minimis discount need not be reported as ordinary income when realized, even though it is clearly the functional equivalent of interest. But see the market discount rules of §1276, infra ¶ 4.44, which might treat this spread as ordinary gain but have their own de minimis rule.

The de minimis exception of §1273(a)(3) does not apply to the issuer, which can amortize the discount in the manner described supra in text at notes 185–190, by virtue of §163(e)(2)(B). See Prop. Regs. §§1.1273-1(a)(3) and 1.1273-2(f); New York State Bar Report, supra note 181.

[194] Section 1273(a)(2). Interest is considered payable unconditionally only if the failure to pay such interest results in consequences typical of defaults in normal commercial lending transactions (e.g., acceleration of all amounts due under the instrument). See Senate Finance Committee Explanation, S. Rep. No. 169, 99th Cong., 2d Sess. at 254–255 (Comm. Print 1984); Prop. Regs. §1.1273-1(b)(1)(iii); N.Y. State Bar Report, supra note 181.

For the treatment of deferred, contingent, and variable interest, see N.Y. State Bar Report, supra note 181; Garlock, supra note 181; Lokken, supra note 181; Walter & Strasen, Innovative Transactions—Eli Lilly Acquisition of Hybritech—Contingent Payment Units, 64 Taxes 488 (1986); Fisher & Norris, The Ins and Outs of the New OID/Imputed Interest System of Real Estate: Is the Partnership an Alternative?, 63 Taxes 877 (1985); Land, Contingent Payments and the Time Value of Money, 40 Tax Lawyer 237 (1987); Prop. Regs. §§1.1275-4 and 1.1275-5.

have the manipulative potential of interest that will not be paid until a distant future date.

The status of stated interest not meeting the unconditional-fixed-annual requirements, such as interest payable every two years, is unclear. Any nonconforming interest payable at maturity is included in computing the bond's stated redemption price at maturity by §1273(a)(2), which refers to "interest . . . payable *at that time*" (emphasis added); but this language would have to be stretched to encompass nonconforming interest payable during the life of the bond. Yet if such stated interest is not included in the bond's stated redemption price at maturity, it is taxable only when and if paid or payable and is free of the OID inclusionary rules.

The issue price of a debt instrument sold for money (which is subtracted from its stated redemption price at maturity to determine the amount, if any, of OID) is determined under §1273(b)(1) and (2).[195] Unless the instrument is publicly offered, the price is the amount paid by the first buyer. If the instrument is part of a publicly offered issue, however, this bond-by-bond pricing principle gives way, and the price is the initial offering public price (excluding bond houses and brokers) at which a substantial amount of the instruments was sold. For example, if a bond with a stated redemption price at maturity of $1,000 is sold by the issuer to a bond house for $890 and is then resold to the public for $900, the issue price is $900, even though the issuer receives only $890. Thus, commissions and underwriters' profits do not create OID.

If a debt instrument is issued as part of an investment unit that includes an option, security, or other property, the issue price for the unit is determined as though it were a debt instrument. The resulting aggregate amount is allocated to the components in proportion to their relative fair market values; the amount thus allocated to the debt instrument is its issue price.

3. Allocation of OID to proper period. In determining the OID to be reported each year, total OID is first allocated among accrual periods and is then prorated on a daily basis within each accrual period. For each taxable year, a holder usually must include in gross income the OID assigned to those days within the taxable year on which the instrument was held.

The first step in the allocation of OID among accrual periods is to determine under §1272(a)(3)(A) the instrument's yield to maturity. The yield to maturity is a constant interest rate that, when applied twice each year to the sum of the issue price and the previously accrued OID, yields aggregate OID accruals equal to the total OID. Expressed in another way, the yield to maturity is the discount rate under which the present value of the payments

---

[195] See Prop. Regs. §1.1273-2(b). For debt issued for property rather than cash, see infra ¶ 4.42. See generally N.Y. State Bar Report, supra note 181; Garlock, supra note 181; Lokken, supra note 181.

of principal and interest under the instrument equals the issue price. If a 10-year non-interest-bearing bond in the principal amount of $1,000 is issued for $400, for example, the yield to maturity is 9.38 percent, compounded semiannually, this being the annual rate (compounded semiannually) at which $400 must grow to reach $1,000 10 years hence. By the same token, it is the discount rate that, applied to $1,000 receivable in 10 years, produces a present value of $400.

Interest is computed under §1272(a)(3) on a semiannual basis to conform to prevailing financial customs, under which interest is ordinarily paid or accrued on bonds and other publicly held debt instruments every six months.[196] Each year for the life of the instrument, one accrual period ends on the day of the year corresponding to the day in the year of maturity on which the instrument will mature, and the other accrual period ends six months earlier. Assume that a bond issued on March 1, 1986 will come due on January 31, 1996. Each accrual period is six months long, except the first, which runs from March 1 through July 31 of 1986.

The OID allocated to a particular accrual period is determined in the following manner: (1) The adjusted issue price at the beginning of the period is computed (this is the sum of the issue price and the OID that accrued in all prior periods[197] and is the issuer's economic debt during the period); (2) The adjusted issue price is multiplied by the yield to maturity[198] (this product being the economic yield for the accrual period); (3) From this amount is deducted any interest payable during the accrual period, since such interest is independently deductible by the issuer and taxable to the holder.[199] The remaining amount is the OID for the period, or, to use the language of §1272(a)(3), "the increase in the [instrument's] adjusted issue price for [the relevant] accrual period."

> *To illustrate:* Assume that a 10-year non-interest-bearing bond in the principal amount of $1,000 is issued for $500. OID is $500, and the

---

[196] As originally enacted in 1982, the constant-interest rules used annual periods. This departure from custom was rectified in 1984 but with a grandfather clause under which the accrual periods for obligations issued after July 1, 1982 and before January 1, 1985 were one-year periods beginning each year on the anniversary of the date of original issue. Pub. L. No. 98-369, §44(i)(1), 98 Stat. 561 (1984); Prop. Regs. §1.1272-1(d).

[197] See Column B of table, supra text at note 190; Prop. Regs. §1.1272-1(e).

[198] If any period is less than six months (e.g., the initial period for the bond described in the text following note 196), the yield to maturity must be adjusted to take account of the shorter period; see §1272(a)(3)(A)(ii). See generally Prop. Regs. §1.1272-1(f).

[199] Section 1272(a)(3)(B); note that this applies to all interest payments, whether or not they meet the unconditional fixed annual requirements of §1273(a)(2); Prop. Regs. §§1.1272-1(a)(3) and 1.1273-1(b); N.Y. State Bar Report, supra note 181.

semiannual yield to maturity is 7.05 percent. For the first six-month accrual period, the OID accrual is $17.60 (i.e., one-half of 7.05 percent of $500); for the second period, the accrual is $18.30 (one-half of 7.05 percent of the sum of $500 and $17.60); for the third period, OID is $18.90 (one-half of 7.05 percent of the sum of $500, $17.60, and $18.30); and so on for the life of the bond.

Since the bond's various accrual periods do not necessarily coincide with the holder's holding period (e.g., because the bond is bought and sold during a single accrual period) or with the bondholder's taxable year (e.g., because the taxpayer reports on a calendar-year basis but owns a bond with accrual periods ending on January 31 and July 31, it is necessary to allocate the OID *within* the bond's accrual periods. Under §1272(a)(3), the intraperiod allocation is achieved by prorating each accrual period's OID on a daily basis among the days of that period. The resulting per-day allocations enable holders of an OID instrument to compute the OID that must be reported for each taxable year and also enable the issuer to compute its deduction for interest under §163(e)(1).

To illustrate: Assume that an individual buys a discount bond on July 1 and sells it on September 15 of the same year. If the accrual periods with respect to the bond end on January 31 and July 31, the holder must include daily portions from two accrual periods in gross income: (1) For the period ending July 31, the daily portions of OID for the period July 1 through July 31 must be included; and (2) for the period ending on the succeeding January 31, it is necessary to include the daily portions for August 1 through September 15.[200]

A holder's basis for a debt instrument is increased under §1272(d)(2) by all OID included in gross income under these rules. A holder who buys at original issue and holds to maturity thus has no gain or loss when the instrument is paid, since the OID will already have been taken into account. The holder similarly has no gain or loss on a sale before maturity, provided the sale price equals the issue price of the bond plus the accrued OID. This condition may be satisfied if there is no change in the issuer's credit rating or in the market rate of interest for similar risks between the issue date and the sale. If, however, these conditions are not satisfied, the holder ordinarily realizes capital gain or loss on the sale.[201] Profits from such market value

---

[200] For simplified counting conventions, see Prop. Regs. §1.1275-2(e).

[201] This assumes that the debt is a capital asset in the holder's hands. For gains realized by subsequent holders of market discount bonds, see infra ¶ 4.44. Capital gain can also be realized if debt is retired early at a premium either pursuant to a call

fluctuations are treated as capital gain to the original holder of the instrument rather than as interest because they are not received from the issuer (or from anyone else) as compensation for the use of the holder's money.

4. Subsequent holders. If an OID instrument is transferred by the original holder during its term, the OID is not recomputed to reflect the premium paid by the buyer for the increase in the bond's value since issue; instead, the transferee steps into the original holder's shoes and continues to report the OID as originally determined. (Although a recomputation of OID to take the premium into account would reflect economic reality more accurately, it would be more cumbersome than the method actually prescribed.) The taxable amount, however, is reduced if the purchaser's cost exceeds the sum of the issue price of the instrument plus the OID that was includible in the gross income of earlier holders. This reduction for the holder's acquisition premium is spread over the term of the instrument, commencing with the date of purchase and ending with its maturity date, as provided in §1272(a)(6) and Prop. Regs. §1.1272-1(g).

To illustrate: Assume that an individual purchases the 10-year bond described earlier (with a face amount of $1,000 and an issue price of $500) on the first day of the third accrual period for $600. The acquisition premium is $64.10 ($600 less the sum of $500 plus the OID of $17.60 and $18.30 for the first two periods). This acquisition premium is allocated among the third and succeeding periods, and the amount allocated to each period reduces the buyer's OID inclusion for that period.

The reduction just described is personal to the holder; if the bond is sold to another person, the latter must include the full amount of OID accruing during his ownership in gross income unless his price also includes an acquisition premium. If an instrument is purchased for an amount equalling or exceeding its stated maturity value, the resulting acquisition premium under §1272(a)(6) necessarily offsets all OID accruing during the purchaser's ownership, even if it is held until maturity. Through inadvertence or an excess of caution, §1272(c)(1) covers the very same ground by providing that §1272 will not apply to any holder purchasing the instrument at a premium, a term that is not defined, but that evidently means a price in excess of the instrument's stated redemption price at maturity.

The fact that some of the OID is not taxed to these subsequent holders does not negate the issuer's right to deduct the full amount of the OID under

option or by negotiation; but note the requirements of §1271(a)(2) (ordinary income if there was an intention when instrument was issued to exercise call option before maturity).

§163(e), since the issuer must pay that amount as compensation for use of the borrowed funds, whether the holders are taxed on it or not.

5. Term loans below market: Overlap with §7872. A below-market term loan made by a shareholder (or by any other lender if one of the principal purposes of the interest arrangement is the avoidance of any federal tax) is subject to §7872 and, unless shielded by an exception, may generate OID under §7872(b).

To illustrate: If *A* purportedly loans $100,000 to *XYZ*, *A*'s wholly owned corporation, receiving in exchange a $150,000 bond payable without interest in 10 years (reflecting an ostensible yield to maturity of about 4.1 percent) and the applicable federal rate is 9 percent, §7872(b) recharacterizes the advance as (1) a loan to *XYZ* of $62,196 (the present value of $150,000, discounted at 9 percent) and (2) an imputed cash transfer to *XYZ* of $37,804 ($100,000 less $62,196) presumably as a contribution to *XYZ*'s capital, the imputed transfer being treated as OID. The result, as shown below, is that *A* must take $87,804 of OID—$50,000 under §1272 and $37,804 under §7872(b)(2)—into gross income on an economic accrual (or constant interest) basis.

	Transaction as Represented	Transaction as Recharacterized
(1) Amount received by borrower		
(a) Loan	$100,000	$ 62,196
(b) Contribution to capital	–	37,804
(c) Total	$100,000	$100,000
(2) Amount payable at maturity		
(a) Loan	$100,000	$ 62,196
(b) Stated OID (subject to §1272)	50,000	50,000
(c) Imputed OID (subject to §7872)	–	37,804
(d) Total payable	$150,000	$150,000
(3) Yield to maturity (i.e., annual rate of growth required for line (1)(a) amount to reach line (2)(d) amount)	4.1%	9%

¶ 4.42   OID OBLIGATIONS ISSUED FOR PROPERTY

1. Introductory. When debt instruments are issued for property, the OID rules covering debt-for-money exchanges discussed previously could be applied merely by treating the value of the property received by the issuer (determined, if necessary, by appraisal) as the issue price of the instrument and then subtracting this amount from its stated redemption price at maturity in testing for the existence of OID. In the absence of bona fide market transactions, however, the appraised values of assets like real property and patents could be manipulated to create or eliminate OID; and the statutory rules address this tax-avoidance problem by prescribing one method of testing for OID for transactions that can be verified by market quotations and another method of testing for private transactions. [202] In addition, the imputed interest rules of §483 apply to those debt-for-property exchanges that are not covered by the OID rules.

2. Publicly traded transactions: §1273(b)(3). If debt instruments issued for property are traded on an established securities market and/or are issued for stock or securities that are traded on such a market, the issue price of the debt, as prescribed by §1273(b)(3), is the fair market value of the property. [203] Thus, if bonds are issued for shares of a publicly traded corporation, the issue price of the bonds is the quoted price of the shares. [204] If publicly traded bonds are issued for Blackacre, the fair market value of the bonds is controlling; and assuming an arm's-length exchange, the value of Blackacre is equal to the quoted price of the bonds. [205]

Once the issue price of the debt is determined, the OID rules of §1272 can be applied in the same manner as they are to debt-for-money exchanges. [206]

---

[202] For the use of market values in potentially abusive situations, see infra text at note 215. See generally N.Y. State Bar Report (on proposed OID regulation), supra note 181; Garlock, supra note 181; Lokken, supra note 181.

[203] Section 1273(b)(5) and Prop. Regs. §1.1273-2(a)(1) define "property" to include services and the right to use property in applying §1273(b), which prescribes rules for determining an instrument's issue price; but Prop. Regs. §1.1274-1(a)(1) makes §1274 inapplicable and refers to §§404 and 467 for the treatment of payments for services.

[204] The publicly traded condition is satisfied if the shares are part of a publicly traded issue, even if the shares exchanged are unregistered and cannot themselves be traded. See Rev. Rul. 75-117, 1975-1 CB 273 (analogous situation under prior law); Prop. Regs. §1.1273-2(c)(1). If both the bonds and the property are traded securities, Prop. Regs. §1.1273-2(c)(1) uses the value of the *issued* bonds to determine their issue price.

[205] For this equal-value concept, see US v. Davis, 370 US 65 (1962), reh'g denied, 371 US 854 (1962); Bittker, supra note 95 at ¶ 41.2.4. If the transaction is not at arm's length, any disparity in value may require the transaction to be realigned; for example, if the bonds are worth more than the property and the transferor of the property is employed by the issuer, the excess may constitute compensation to the transferor. But see Prop. Regs. §1.1273-2(c)(1) (if values distorted, issue price is determined under §1274 rules). See also Prop. Regs. §1.1012-2.

[206] See supra ¶ 4.41.

3. Private transactions: §1274. If the debt instruments are not publicly traded and are issued for property other than publicly traded stock or securities, their issue price must be computed under §1274, which uses the interest rates on federal debt as an objective benchmark in determining whether OID exists and, if so, its amount. Section 1274, enacted in 1984, is thus a compromise between (1) the older imputed interest rules of §483, relating to deferred payment sales, which impute interest if the stated interest is inadequate relative to an outside standard, but remedy the inadequacy only when payments are actually made to cash basis sellers; and (2) §1272, which requires agreed-upon OID to be reported currently even though unpaid.[207]

Instruments given as consideration for the sale or exchange of property[208] and payable in whole or in part more than six months after the sale or exchange[209] are tested under §1274(c) as follows:

(1) The present value of all payments due under the instrument (whether labeled "principal" or "interest")[210] is computed as of the date of the sale or exchange using the applicable federal rate of interest on Treasury obligations, as promulgated by the Treasury, compounded semiannually.[211]

---

[207] See generally N.Y. State Bar Report, supra note 181; Land, supra note 194; Schler, The Sale of Property for a Fixed Payment Note: Remaining Uncertainties, 41 Tax L. Rev. 209 (1986); Sheffield, Debt Issued for Traded and Nontraded Property, 62 Taxes 1022, 1027 (1984); Harris & Dentino, Section 1274–The Application of the OID Provisions to Debt Instruments Issued for Property, 9 Rev. Tax. Individuals 353 (1985); Wolf, Pisem & Graham, Time Value of Money, 32 Tax Notes 691 (1986); articles supra note 181; see also Prop. Regs. §§1.1274 and 1.1274A.

[208] For the meaning of "property," see supra note 203.

[209] Although §1274(c)(1)(B) uses six months as the benchmark for applying §1274, §1272(a)(2)(C) provides for current inclusion of OID only if the instrument has a fixed maturity date more than 12 months after issue.

[210] In making this computation, assumption of debts and acquisitions of property subject to a debt instrument are not taken into account unless there is a modification of the terms or a change "in the nature of the transaction." See §1274(c)(4) and Prop. Regs. §1.1274-7; see also 28 Tax Notes (1985) (wraparound debt does not qualify as assumption of debt); Prop. Regs. §1.1274-7(c) (same); N.Y. State Bar Report, supra note 181, at 408.

For problems in determining whether there is adequate stated interest if a seller-financed transaction provides for an equity kicker, see Wiesner & Smith, Equity Participation Loans: Uncertainty Increases Under the New OID Rules, 62 J. Tax'n 330 (1985); Prop. Regs. §1.1274-3(d); Land, supra note 184.

[211] Section 1274(d)(2). There are three federal rates, determined monthly: short-term, for instruments whose term is not over three years; mid-term, for terms over three but not over nine years; and long-term, for terms over nine years. See §1272(d)(1). In addition, the Treasury can authorize use of a lower rate if appropriate. See §1272(d)(1); see also §1272(d)(2) (applicable rate is lowest rate prevailing during three-month period ending with first calendar month in which

(2) This amount (the imputed principal amount) is compared with the instrument's stated principal amount.

(3) If the stated principal amount is less than or equal to the imputed principal amount, there is adequate stated interest, and if, as is usually the case, the stated redemption price at maturity does not exceed the stated principal amount, the issue price of the instrument under §1274(a)(2) is its stated principal amount.

(4) However, if the stated principal amount exceeds the imputed principal amount—that is, if the stated principal amount is greater than the amount that would be payable if the instrument grew at the applicable federal rate, compounded semiannually—the instrument's issue price under §1274(a)(2) is its imputed principal amount. In effect, this latter amount is treated as the true principal, and the balance of the stated principal amount is recharacterized as interest. As such, it is deductible by the obligor and cannot be included in the basis of the property for such purposes as computing depreciation and gain or loss on a sale; and it is includable as OID in the bondholder's gross income.

To illustrate: Assume that *XYZ* Corporation purchases Blackacre for $5 million, making a down payment of $1 million and issuing its mortgage bond in the amount of $4 million, payable in 5 years, with interest of 10 percent per year, payable annually. Assuming that the applicable federal rate is 8 percent (Example A) or 11 percent (Example B), and that the present value of the payments is $4,292,628 (Example A) or $3,808,901 (Example B), the following present values result:

---

there is a binding written contract for sale or exchange); §1274(d)(3) (options to renew or extend taken into account in determining term of instrument). For a typical monthly announcement of the relevant rates, see Rev. Rul. 85-190, 1985-2 CB 186. See generally Prop. Regs. §1.1274-6; N.Y. State Bar Report, supra note 181, at 406.

Section 1274(e) subjects debt instruments arising from sale-leaseback transactions to a more stringent test by discounting payments thereunder at 110 percent of the applicable federal rate. For discussion, see Pollack, Sale-Leaseback Transactions Adversely Affected by a Variety of Recent Developments, 64 J. Tax'n 151 (1986); Prop. Regs. §1.1274-3(e)(1)(iii).

From 1984 through 1985, a two-tier interest rate procedure was employed, involving a test rate to determine if OID existed and a higher imputation rate to correct the deficiency. The test rate thus provided a safe harbor from the higher imputation rate. For a description of this procedure, see S. Rep. No. 83, 99th Cong., 1st Sess. 1 (1985), reprinted in 1985 U.S. Code Cong. & Admin. News 410; see also Pub. L. No. 98-612, 98 Stat. 3180 (1984) (transitional rule for certain sales before July 1, 1985); Prop. Regs. §§1.1274-3(e)(2) and 1.1274-4(b)(2).

		*Present Value**		
End of Year	*Payment Due*	*Example A (8%)*	*Example B (11%)*	*Example C (15%)***
1	$ 400,000	$ 369,822	$ 359,381	$ 346,133
2	400,000	341,922	322,887	299,520
3	400,000	316,126	290,098	259,185
4	400,000	292,276	260,640	224,281
5	4,400,000	2,972,482	2,575,895	2,134,853
Total		$4,292,628	$3,808,901	$3,263,972

*Computed by compounding the applicable rate semiannually.
**For Example C, see infra text at note 215.

In Example A, there is adequate stated interest and the issue price of the debt is its stated principal amount of $4 million. The chain of reasoning leading to this conclusion is as follows: (1) the stated principal amount ($4 million) is less than the imputed principal amount ($4,292,628), and there is therefore adequate stated interest under §1274(c)(2); (2) the stated redemption price at maturity ($4 million, the interest payment of $400,000 due at maturity being excluded by virtue of §1274(a)(2) because the interest is based on a fixed rate and is payable unconditionally at least annually) does not exceed the stated principal amount ($4 million); and (3) the issue price is the stated principal amount under §1274(a)(1).[212]

In Example B, by contrast, (1) the stated principal amount ($4 million) exceeds the imputed principal amount ($3,808,901), and the stated interest is therefore inadequate under §1274(c)(2); (2) the stated redemption price at maturity ($4 million) exceeds the imputed principal amount ($3,808,901); (3) Section 1274 applies by virtue of §1274(c)(1)(A)(ii); (4) the issue price under §1274(a)(2) is the imputed principal amount; and (5) there is OID under §1273(a)(1) of $191,099 ($4 million less $3,808,901).

Once the issue price of debt-for-property instruments subject to §1274 has been determined, it is necessary to return to the general rules of §1273 to determine the amount of OID (if any), and to §1272 for the allocation of the OID among the relevant accrual periods.[213]

---

[212] Two statutory provisions compete for jurisdiction on these facts but reach the same result: (1) Section 1274(a)(1), providing that the issue price is the *stated principal amount* ($4 million, in this example) if there is adequate stated interest; and (2) §1274(c)(1)(A)(i), which renders §1274 inapplicable and therefore seemingly cedes jurisdiction to §1273(b)(4), which provides that the issue price is the *stated redemption price at maturity* (again, $4 million).

[213] Supra ¶ 4.41.

4. Cap of 9 percent on applicable discount rate. The discount rate used to determine the present value of payments under an instrument cannot exceed 9 percent by virtue of §1274A, provided that the principal amount of the instrument does not exceed $2.8 million and the property is not "new §38 property." (This term is defined by §48(a), which is retained in the Code even though its primary function, relating to the investment tax credit, was eliminated by the repeal of the credit in 1986.) In applying this dollar limit (which is to be adjusted upward for inflation after 1989), all sales and instruments arising from the same transaction or a series of related transactions are aggregated under §1274A(d)(1). If interest rates continue to decline, the 9 percent cap may soon be functus officio; but sharp future rises in interest rates would obviously give the cap a new lease on life.

5. Potentially abusive situations: §1274(b)(3). Use of the applicable federal rate to compute the present value of the payments due under a debt-for-property instrument insures objectivity but not economic realism. The credit standing of the issuer may be substantially inferior to the Treasury's (even given the national deficit), so that there may be adequate stated interest as measured by §1274(c); but the rate may be woefully inadequate by the standards of the market place. Thus, the stated interest of 10 percent is adequate in Example A of the earlier illustration[214] because the applicable federal rate is 8 percent; but if a hard-nosed banker demanded a yield to maturity of 15 percent, compounded semiannually, for a similar loan to the issuer, the $4 million bond would have to be priced at about $3.3 million (see Example C in the previous text), which implies that Blackacre is worth only about $4.3 million (i.e., the value of the bond plus the $1 million down payment) and that the spread (about $700,000) is OID.

Recognizing that an inflated sale price can be used to conceal OID when the relatively low federal discount rate is used to test the adequacy of stated interest, §1274(b)(3) permits the Service by regulations to require use of the fair market value of the property (Blackacre, in the preceding illustration) as the imputed principal amount of debt-for-property instruments issued in potentially abusive situations such as tax shelters, nonrecourse financing, or "recent sales transactions" (a phrase that presumably refers to the churning of property among related parties to create an inflated price to justify the amount of debt issued in the final exchange).[215] Applied to Blackacre, §1274(b)(3) substitutes $3,263,972 (see Example C) for $4 million as the imputed principal amount; the stated interest is not adequate under §1273(c)(2) because the stated principal amount ($4 million) exceeds the

---

[214] Supra para. 3, text at note 212.

[215] For other examples of potentially abusive situations, see Fisher & Norris, supra note 194; Sheffield, supra note 207; Prop. Regs. §1.1274-4(g); N.Y. State Bar Report, supra note 181, at 406.

imputed principal amount as determined under §1273(b)(3); the issue price as determined under §1274(a)(2) is $3,263,972; and there is OID under §1273(b)(1) of $736,028.

Given the legislative decision to use the federal interest rates as an objective standard in applying §1274 because taxpayer appraisals are subject to manipulation, it may seem ironic to revert to fair market value in situations of potential abuse. But since taxpayers are not likely to announce that they are parties to such situations, there will be a battle of appraisers only when and if the Service takes the initiative by rejecting the federal rate standard.

6. Exceptions to §1274. Section 1274(c)(3) exempts the following transactions and instruments from the rules of §1274:

(1) certain sales of farms for less than $1 million;

(2) debt instruments arising from the sale or exchange of a principal residence as defined by §1034;

(3) certain sales involving total payments of $250,000 or less;

(4) debt instruments that are publicly traded or issued for publicly traded stock or securities as provided by §1273(b)(3);[216]

(5) amounts contingent on the productivity, use, or disposition of certain patents transferred under §1235(a); and

(6) sales of land between related persons if subject to §483(e).

7. Elective use of cash method reporting. Section 1274A permits the borrower and lender to account for interest (including OID) on a debt-for-property instrument using the cash receipts and disbursements method (i.e., reporting and deducting payments when made), if (1) the borrower and lender make a joint election to do so; (2) the stated principal amount does not exceed $2 million; (3) the property is not new §38 property (impossible after 1986); (4) the lender does not use an accrual method and is not a dealer with respect to the property; and (5) §1274 would otherwise apply. The effect of such a cash-cash election (which binds their successors as well as the parties themselves) is that the instruments (so-called cash-method debt instruments) become subject to §483; thus, when payments are received, they are taxable as ordinary income to the extent of any imputed interest.[217]

---

[216] See supra text at notes 203–206; see generally Prop. Regs. §1.1274-1(b); N.Y. State Bar Report, supra note 181, at 404.

[217] See also §1274A(c)(4), providing that §483 be applied as though it contained remedies for potentially abusive situations similar to those authorized by §1274(b)(3), supra text at note 215.

8. Recharacterization of deferred sale payments under §483. The 1984 extension of the OID rules of §§1272 through 1274 to debt instruments issued for property, even if neither the property nor the instruments are publicly traded, severely curtailed the jurisdiction of the long-standing rules of §483, which characterize deferred payments on sales of capital assets as ordinary income if and to the extent that the stated interest on the buyer's obligations is inadequate when measured by an objective outside standard.[218] This reduction in the importance of §483 results from the fact that the OID rules, when applicable, require the seller of property to include in gross income amounts that under §483 would not be taxed until actually received. In this situation, §483(d)(1) explicitly cedes jurisdiction to §1272.

Section 483 remains applicable, however, to transactions that are exempted from §1272, particularly sales shielded by the $2.8 million ceiling, elective cash method debt instruments with stated principal amounts of $2 million or less, and farms sold for less than $1 million. As amended in 1985, §483 tests for the existence of unstated interest by a discounting method that is similar to the method used by §1274, and it allocates the unstated interest (if any) over time on an economic accrual basis. Unlike §§1272 and 1274, however, §483 does not put cash-method taxpayers on an accrual basis by requiring them to report currently an allocable portion of the earned but unpaid unstated interest; instead, part of each payment is characterized as interest *when received*, to reflect the unstated interest properly allocable thereto.[219]

¶ 4.43　STRIPPED BONDS

Section 1286, enacted in 1982, imposes the OID rules on so-called stripped bonds (i.e., bonds issued with interest coupons if there is a separation of ownership of the bond and any coupon not yet payable).[220] For this

---

[218] From 1964–1984, the benchmark rate was fixed by §483 itself; in 1984, §483 was amended to incorporate the applicable federal rate as prescribed by §1274(d); see supra note 211.

[219] For a more detailed analysis of §483, see Bittker, supra note 95, at ¶ 54.6.1. See also N.Y. State Bar Report, supra note 181, at 411.

For the intricate relationship between §§483, 1274, and 7872 (relating to certain shareholder-corporation and employer-employee loans if the interest rate is below market as tested by the applicable federal rate), see Moore, Analyzing the Complex New Proposed Regs. on Imputed Interest and Original Issue Discount, 65 J. Tax'n 14 (1986); Kohl, The Uncertain Interplay of the Code's Time Value of Money Provisions, 26 Tax Notes 827 (1985); Orbach, Fireman, & Levenson, Planning for Tax Advantages Under Proposed Below-Market Regs., 64 J. Tax 144 (1986).

[220] See generally McGrath, Coupon Stripping Under Section 1286: Trees, Fruits, and Felines, 38 Tax Lawyer 267 (1985); Preliminary Report by the N.Y. State Bar

purpose, "coupon" is defined by §1286(e) to include any right to receive bond interest, whether or not evidenced by a coupon. Stripped bonds and their coupons (as thus defined) are subject to the OID rules, even if the instrument was issued at face amount with adequate interest, because split ownership converts them into the equivalent of OID instruments.

> *To illustrate:* Assume that *XYZ* Corporation issued a 20-year bond with a face amount of $1,000 and a 10 percent interest rate, evidenced by formal detachable coupons. If the original owner immediately strips the coupons from the bond and sells the bond, the buyer gets an instrument that (1) will pay $1,000 at maturity without interest—the functional equivalent of a zero coupon bond—and (2) if discounted at 10 percent compounded annually, should sell for about $149. The retained coupons, taken collectively, account for the remaining $851 of the $1,000 paid for the complete instrument. Each coupon, in turn, is analogous to a mini-bond, paying $100 at maturity without interest. Discounted at 10 percent, the first coupon is worth about $91; the second, about $83; and so on. [221]
>
> Thus, the buyer of the stripped bond realizes OID of $851 over its 20-year life as it grows in value from $149 to $1,000, its redemption price at maturity. In the same vein, a person buying the first coupon for $91 would realize $9 of discount ($100 paid at maturity less cost of $91) during its one-year life; a person buying the second coupon for $83 would realize OID of $17 during its two-year life; and so on for each coupon.

To bring the tax results of bond stripping into closer conformity with economic reality, §1286(a) treats the purchaser of a stripped bond or coupon as though the instrument were a bond originally issued on the purchase date with OID equal to the excess of the amount payable at maturity over the instrument's ratable share of the purchase price. The OID as thus computed must be reported on the constant-interest basis described earlier in this chapter. [222]

In the preceding illustration, the bond was stripped immediately after it was issued, before any interest had accrued; but §1286 also applies if a bond is stripped at a later time. In this situation, §1286(b) requires the stripper to include in income any interest that has accrued before the disposition to the

---

Association's Ad Hoc Committee on Original Issue Discount and Coupon Stripping, 22 Tax Notes 993 (1984); Walter, Tax Aspects of Recent Innovative Financing—Strategies for Existing Discount Debt and for New Securities, 60 Taxes 995, 1008–1009 (1982).

[221] See §1286(a).

[222] Supra ¶ 4.41. But see §1281 for special treatment of the discount on the first coupon, which is a short-term obligation by virtue of ¶ 1283(a)(1)(A).

extent not already reported. The basis of the bond and coupons, increased by the amount of the accrued interest, is then allocated between the items retained and those disposed of; and the stripper is treated as having purchased each retained item for an amount equal to its allocated basis. The result is that each retained item can generate OID, which the stripper must include in income as though the item were a separate OID instrument.

¶ 4.44   MARKET DISCOUNT

Before 1982, investors purchasing previously issued bonds at a discount below face value (e.g., because the prevailing rate of interest at the time of purchase was higher than when the bond was issued or because the issuer's credit rating had declined in the interim) could report their profits as capital gains if they later sold the bonds at a profit or collected the face amount at maturity.[223] These changes in the value of the bond do not affect the amounts that the issuer must pay to the holder as interest or at maturity, since these obligations were fixed when the bond was originally issued; but from the holder's perspective, a so-called market discount bond is similar to a bond with OID, since it gradually increases in value as its maturity date approaches.[224] (There may be offsetting decreases or accentuating increases in value as a result of post-purchase changes in the market rate of interest or the issuer's credit rating; but these changes can also occur in the case of OID bonds.) Thus, like the appreciation in the value of an OID bond, the appreciation in a market discount bond's value between its acquisition and maturity is a supplement to the stated interest actually received by the holder.

On the theory that "from the standpoint of the holder of a bond, market discount is indistinguishable from OID,"[225] Congress enacted §§ 1276 and 1278 in 1984, requiring gain on the disposition of market discount bonds (if issued after July 18, 1984) to be reported as ordinary income to the extent of the accrued market discount.[226] The two types of discount may be indistinguishable, but their tax treatment is significantly different, since (1) market discount is taxed only when the debt is disposed of, while OID must

---

[223] See H.R. Rep. No. 98-861, 98th Cong., 2d Sess., reprinted in 1984-3 CB 59, Vol. 2, 59.

[224] In contrasting market discount with OID in US v. Midland-Ross Corp., supra note 176, at 58, n.4, the Supreme Court seemed to assume that only the latter is earned through the "mere passage of time"; in point of fact, this is true of both types of discount.

[225] Joint Comm. on Taxation, General Explanation of the Revenue Provisions of the Tax Reform Act of 1984, 98th Cong., 2d Sess. 93 (1985).

[226] Deductions for certain interest expenses attributable to debt incurred to purchase or carry market discount bonds may be deferred or disallowed by § 1277. See also § 1278(b) (election to avoid § 1277 by including market discount currently in gross income); Joint Committee on Taxation, supra note 225, at 97–98.

be reported currently as earned; and (2) market discount is taxed only if and to the extent that the holder realizes gain, while OID is taxed regardless of gains and losses.

Sections 1276 and 1278 apply to any "market discount bond," defined as a bond, debenture, note, certificate, or other evidence of indebtedness (excluding certain short-term and tax-exempt obligations, U.S. savings bonds, and installment obligations to which §453A applies), if its stated redemption price at maturity exceeds its basis immediately after acquisition by more than a de minimis amount.[227] The discount is allocated on a straight-line basis to the period during which the taxpayer held the bond (unless the taxpayer elects to use a constant-interest basis as required by §1272 for OID debt instruments); the gain, if any, realized on a disposition is taxable as ordinary income rather than capital gain, to the extent of the accrued market discount. The term "disposition" is not limited to sales and exchanges, but is defined by regulations to encompass transactions subject to the disposition rules of §1245(b) (with some exceptions, such as gifts, which are dispositions by virtue of §1276(d)(1)(A), but are not dispositions under §1245(b))[228]; and, on dispositions other than sales, exchanges, and involuntary conversions, the bond's fair market value is treated as the amount realized.

PART D.   CONVERTIBLE AND OTHER EQUITY-FLAVORED SECURITIES

¶ 4.60   CONVERTIBLE DEBT: PREMIUM AND DISCOUNT ON ISSUE AND RETIREMENT

1. Introductory. Convertible debt is ordinarily treated as pure debt until conversion, after which the investment becomes an equity interest.[229] In effect, until conversion, debt genes are treated as dominant and equity genes as recessive. Despite its dual characteristics, however, the instrument

---

[227] The Tax Reform Act of 1986 modified this definition by adding §1278(a)(1)(C), which generally excludes bonds acquired at original issue. In computing market discount, §1278(a)(2)(B) makes an adjustment for any OID that accrues between the taxpayer's acquisition of the instrument and its maturity. Thus, if a $1,000 bond with $100 of unaccrued OID is purchased for $850, the OID is included in the holder's gross income over the remaining term of the bond, and, if the holder holds it until maturity, the gain of $50 on retirement ($1,000 received, less the sum of $850 cost and $100 of OID included in income) is ordinary income under §1276.

[228] Section 1276(d)(1); for dispositions in nonrecognition transactions, see §1276(c). However, by virtue of §1276(d)(1)(C) (added in 1986), the transfer of a market-discount bond in a §351 exchange is a taxable event.

[229] See generally Willens, Corporate Finance Vehicles, 3 J. Tax'n Inv. 347 (1986); see also Regs. §1.1244(c)-1(b) (convertible securities not common stock);

is a single nonseverable security, since the holder must forfeit his creditor position if he wishes to become a shareholder. The conversion feature provides growth potential, since the value of the shares may rise above the conversion price; but protection from risk is afforded by the debt feature, which supplies a floor for the investment.

The following discussion focuses on two groups of tax issues generated by convertible debt: (1) the treatment of premium and discount when the securities are issued or retired, and (2) the tax effects of conversion into stock. Further issues created by the use of convertible debt and other equity-flavored instruments (such as warrants and stock purchase rights), which are discussed elsewhere in this work, include treatment of expenses incurred on issuing the instruments[230]; classification as debt or equity[231]; and classification as "stock or securities" under various nonrecognition provisions such as §351 and 361(a), relating to the tax-free organization and reorganization of corporations.[232]

2. Issue for cash. The tax treatment of premium and discount on convertible debt securities issued for cash is relatively well established:

(1) If the security is issued at a premium (i.e., for cash in excess of the face amount payable on retirement), the creditor may amortize the premium over the life of the bond under §171 (using a compound-interest method similar to OID, as a result of 1986 amendments), while the debtor corporation must include the premium in income ratably over the life of the debt under Regs. §1.61-12(c)(2) (no

---

Rev. Rul. 69-91, 1969-1 CB 106 (convertible debt not stock); Rev. Rul. 77-437, 1977-2 CB 28 (realization of income on discharge of indebtedness by exchange of outstanding convertible bonds with new convertible bonds with lower face amount): supra notes 54 and 55.

In the rare case to which §279 applies (denying the interest deduction for certain corporate acquisition indebtedness (see supra ¶ 4.26)), the normally recessive equity genes may be regarded as taking control even before conversion.

[230] See infra ¶ 5.04, para. 7.

[231] See supra note 229. If a convertible obligation is reclassified as equity, the usual characteristics of equity apply, including the nondeductibility of purported interest payments, the need to test payments at retirement (including premiums and discounts) under the stock redemption rules of §302, and the treatment of any difference between issue price and par or stated value as a nontaxable capital transaction; moreover, despite the equity nature of the reclassified security, it is not "voting" stock within the meaning of §368(a)(1)(B) and 368(a)(1)(C), relating to Type B and C tax-free reorganizations. On the other hand, exercise of the conversion privilege is a tax-free event, whether the security is classified as debt or equity; see infra ¶ 4.61 (convertible debt) and ¶ 14.17 (stock-for-stock conversions).

[232] For §§351 and 361(a), see supra ¶ 3.03 and infra ¶ 14.31 respectively.

mention was made of the *issuer's* income in the 1986 legislation). For both purposes, the amount, if any, attributable to the conversion feature is deducted from the issue price in computing the premium. Under §171(e), as amended in 1986, the deductible premium is treated as interest.

(2) If the security is issued for cash at a price below face, the creditor must accrue the OID in income over the life of the debt under §1272, while the debtor may deduct the amount as additional interest over the life of the debt under §163(e). In computing OID (as contrasted with premium), no allowance is made for the value of the conversion privilege.[233] As explained earlier in this chapter, OID must be reported on an economic or compound-interest basis.[234]

(3) If the security is retired at a premium, defined as more than its "adjusted issue price" (original issue price increased by any discount previously deducted by the issuer or decreased by any premium previously included in its income), §249 limits the amount deductible by the debtor corporation to a normal call premium on nonconvertible debt. Thus, redemption payments attributable to the value of the conversion feature are not deductible upon retirement.[235] The holder's gain in this situation ordinarily constitutes capital gain under.[236]

(4) Retirement at a discount (i.e., for less than the issue price of the debt plus the issuer's previously amortized discount or minus its previously included premium) results in cancellation of indebtedness income to the debtor corporation under Regs. §1.61-12(c)(3), unless the debtor is entitled to exclude the income under §§108 and 1017.[237]

---

[233] See Chock Full O'Nuts Corp. v. US, 453 F2d 300 (2d Cir. 1971) (no part of issue price attributed to conversion feature in computing OID); Honeywell, Inc., 87 TC 624 (1986) (same for debt issued by subsidiary and exchangeable for parent stock); Hunt Foods, Inc., 57 TC 633 (1972), aff'd per curiam, 496 F2d 532 (9th Cir. 1974) (accord); AMF, Inc. v. US, 476 F2d 1351 (Ct. Cl. 1973), cert. denied, 417 US 930 (1974); Prop. Regs. §1.1273-2(e) (continuing the rule of prior regulations).

[234] See supra ¶¶ 4.40 and 4.41; the same is true of post-1986 premium deductions, but not of premium income.

[235] See also Regs. §1.163-3(c).
For deductibility for premiums paid on retirement of convertible debt to the extent not prohibited by §249, see Rev. Rul. 74-210, 1974-1 CB 48; cf. Jim Walter Corp. v. US, 498 F2d 631 (5th Cir. 1974) (repurchase of stock warrants not deductible because transaction not a cancellation of indebtedness); §1032(a) (no gain or loss on corporation's purchase of its own stock options).

[236] See §1271(a)(1).

[237] See Rev. Rul. 68-288, 1968-1 CB 53; Rev. Rul. 70-368, 1970-2 CB 39 (retirement discount income not offset by retirement premium deduction on purchase of other bonds); see generally Eustice, Cancellation of Indebtedness and the Federal

3. Issue for property. Under §1273 of current law, convertible debt securities issued for property are subject to the same rules with respect to OID as securities issued for cash if the debt itself is part of an issue that is traded on an established securities market or if it is issued for publicly traded stock or securities. In other cases (i.e., where there is no public market price that can be compared with the stated redemption price of the instrument in order to determine whether any original issue discount exists), the applicable federal rate for Treasury obligations is used as a proxy for this purpose. The governing principles are discussed in detail earlier in this chapter.[238]

Although §§1273 and 1274 prescribe methods to determine whether OID arises on a debt-for-property exchange, the Code contains no comparable computational rules for bond premiums if property is acquired by issuing debt securities whose face amount is less than the property's fair market value; and the case law is similarly deficient. It is not clear, therefore, whether the excess of the value received over the face amount of the debt can be treated as bond premium or if it is the fruit of a profitable bargain that will be harvested over the life of the property.[239]

4. Examples. These principles can be illustrated by the following examples in which C is a cash-basis creditor and X Corporation is an accrual-basis debtor, assuming in each case that X issues a 20-year bond with a face amount of $1,000 and a conversion privilege worth $100.

Example A (Issue at par): If the bond is issued for $1,000 in cash, there is no OID, because Prop. Regs. §1.1273-2(e) allocates the entire issue price to the debt for this purpose.

Example B (Issue at discount): If the bond is issued for $800, the issue discount is just $200, even though only $700 was paid for the debt component (the other $100 being for the conversion feature). The discount is deductible and reportable by X Corporation under §163(e) and by C

Income Tax: A Problem of Creeping Confusion, 14 Tax L. Rev. 225 (1959); supra ¶ 4.25.

[238] See supra ¶ 4.42; New York State Bar Report (on proposed OID regulations), supra note 181, at 419.

[239] See Honeywell, Inc., supra note 233, and cases cited; but see §171(b)(4) (added in 1986), under which §171 bond premium is limited to market value of the acquired bond in a substituted basis exchange (unless the exchange is a §368 reorganization). Before enactment of the statutory predecessors of §§1273–1274, there was comparable uncertainty regarding whether debt-for-property exchanges could give rise to OID; see CIR v. National Alfalfa Dehydrating & Milling Co., supra note 176 (citing cases and leaving issues open); Gulf Mobile & Ohio R.R. v. US, 579 F2d 892 (5th Cir. 1978); Microdot, Inc. v. CIR, 728 F2d 593 (2d Cir. 1984). See also §1275(a)(4) and Prop. Regs. §1.1275-2(a); infra ¶ 14.17.

under §1272 using compound interest principles as explained earlier in this chapter.[240]

If this bond is retired by X Corporation for $1,000 after eight years and if the OID properly deducted by X during this period is $50, X incurs and may deduct the retirement premium of $150, the retirement price of $1,000 less adjusted issue price of $850 (i.e., issue price of $800 plus previously deducted issue discount of $50), provided that this premium does not exceed a normal call premium for a comparable non-convertible bond.[241]

If at the end of eight years, X Corporation retires the bond at $750, it realizes $100 of cancellation of indebtedness income (excess of adjusted issue price of $850 over $750 retirement price).

Example C (Issue at premium): If the bond is issued for $1,200 in cash, the amortizable premium is $100—i.e., the issue price ($1,200) less the amount attributable to the conversion value ($100) and the retirement price ($1,000). C can deduct the premium under §171 at a rate determined under compound interest principle as a result of 1986 amendments to §171(b)(3); but X apparently still includes a level annual amount in income (i.e., $5 per year), unless the regulations under §1.61-12(c)(2) are amended to provide for a compound interest inclusion method.

If X Corporation retires this bond after five years for $1,400, it is entitled to deduct the $225 retirement premium (the excess of the $1,400 retirement price over the adjusted issue price of $1,175—i.e., $1,200 less issue premium income of $25), unless this amount exceeds a reasonable call premium for nonconvertible debt.[242]

Retirement at $1,100 creates $75 of cancellation of indebtedness income to X Corporation (the excess of the adjusted issue price of $1,175 over the retirement price of $1,100).

Example D (Issue for property): If the bond is issued for property worth $800, the transaction creates $200 of OID if the bond or the property for which it is issued is traded on an established securities exchange. Otherwise, the existence and amount of OID is ordinarily determined by use of the applicable federal interest rate pursuant to §1274.[243]

---

[240] See supra ¶ 4.41.

[241] For this limitation, see §249(a).

[242] Id.

[243] For §1274, see supra ¶ 4.42. When §1274 is inapplicable (because, for example, the transaction is below the $250,000 floor prescribed by §1274(c)(4)(C)), the imputed interest rules of §483 may apply; see supra text at notes 218–219. For limits on the transferor's right to report gain on the transferred property on the installment basis, see §§453(f)(3)–453(f)(5) (publicly traded debt treated as payment, precluding defer-

¶ 4.61 CONVERTIBLE DEBT: EXERCISE OF CONVERSION PRIVILEGE

If convertible debt securities are not held until maturity but are instead converted into stock, the holder's exercise of the conversion privilege is treated as a nontaxable event by regulations and rulings running as far back as 1920, even though the value of the stock received exceeds or is less than the basis of the securities surrendered.[244] The conventional theory is that gain or loss is not realized on the conversion, but the same result can also be justified on several nonrecognition theories, including the "open" transaction theory (i.e., that the holder is merely acquiring stock at a bargain by exercising an option that was acquired simultaneously with, and as an inherent component of, the convertible security).[245]

Whatever the validity of the underlying theory, tax-free treatment to the holder on exchanges of convertible debt for stock or of convertible stock for stock of another class is well established[246]; and the holder's basis and holding period for the old instruments carry over into the new securities, as in the case of other nonrecognition transactions. For the issuing corporation, nonrecognition results from §1032, providing that amounts received for stock are not taxable to the issuing corporation.[247]

The treatment of unamortized issue discount and premium and of the expenses of issue upon a tax-free conversion of debt into stock has not been searchingly explored, but apparently the following results occur:

---

ral of gain); see also §453(k)(2) (added in 1986 and denying §453 deferral on the *sale* of publicly traded property).

[244] See Rev. Rul. 72-265, 1972-1 CB 222; but see Rev. Rul. 69-135, 1969-1 CB 198 (conversion into stock of a corporation other than the issuer is a taxable exchange under §1001); Rev. Rul. 69-265, 1969-1 CB 109 (same). For the effects of a conversion on the corporation, see Committee on Taxation of International Finance and Investment, N.Y. State Bar Association, Report on International Finance Subsidiaries, Tax Section, 28 Tax L. Rev. 439 (1973). See also New York State Bar Report, supra note 181, at 419.

[245] Other nonrecognition theories that may apply to the exercise of conversion rights, based on Regs. §1.1001-1(a) (exchange for property not "differing materially in kind or extent") are discussed infra ¶ 14.01 (mere refinancing or modification of the same continuing investment); ¶ 14.17 (§368(a)(1)(E) recapitalizations); supra ¶ 3.01 (bargain purchase investment transaction); and infra ¶ 7.41 (transaction in nature of stock dividend). See Fleischer & Cary, The Taxation of Convertible Bonds and Stock, 74 Harv. L. Rev. 473 (1961); Willens, supra note 229.

[246] Supra note 244. If, however, the converted securities are installment obligations under §453, the Service has taken the position that conversion is a disposition, triggering recognition of gain, including the excess (if any) of the value of the stock over the face amount of the debt. See Rev. Rul. 72-264, 1972-1 CB 131.

[247] For §1032, see supra ¶ 3.12.

(1) Unamortized issue premium is evidently not deductible by the holder or taxable to the issuer upon conversion, but is instead treated as part of the amount paid for the stock.[248]

(2) Unamortized issue discount and other unamortized issue expenses are not deductible by the debtor upon conversion, but are treated as adjustments to the amount paid for the stock.[249]

(3) Under §1272, the holder must accrue OID income currently, with a corresponding increase in basis. Unaccrued and unreported OID is presumably not taxed to the holder on conversion, although there appear to be no holdings squarely on this point.[250]

¶ 4.62   STOCK PURCHASE RIGHTS

Stock purchase rights (variously designated as warrants, options, or rights) are contractual agreements entitling the holder to acquire a designated number of shares of stock at a stipulated price at any time during the term of the contract. These rights can be created in a variety of situations. For example, a corporation may issue options to purchase its stock to its own shareholders, to creditors, other investors, or to employees; such options may also be issued by a parent or affiliated corporation, or they may be written by outside shareholders, as in the case of publicly traded short-

---

[248] See Albert Ades, 38 TC 501 (1962), aff'd per curiam, 316 F2d 734 (2d Cir. 1963) (holder); §1032 (issuer).

[249] See TD 4603, XIV-2 CB 58 (1935) (declared obsolete by Rev. Rul. 68-674, 1968-2 CB 609, presumably on procedural rather than substantive grounds); Rev. Rul. 72-348, 1972-2 CB 97 (expenses are capital expenditures); Chicago, M. St. P. & Pac. R.R. v. US, 404 F2d 960 (Ct. Cl. 1968); Chicago No. Shore & M. Ry. v. US, 326 F2d 860 (7th Cir. 1964), cert. denied, 377 US 964; reh'g denied, 374 US 872 (1964); Fleischer & Cary, supra note 245, at 499–522.

For the corporate debtor's treatment of interest on convertible debt that would have accrued and been paid but for the conversion, see Tandy Corp. v. US, 626 F2d 1186 (5th Cir. 1980) (deduction denied), and cases there cited; Husky Oil Co., 83 TC 717, 730–735 (1984) (same result for conversion into parent's stock).

For securities convertible into stock of the issuer's parent corporation, see Honeywell, Inc., supra note 233, and cases there cited (no §171 bond premium deduction); compare ITT & Cos., 77 TC 60 (1981), aff'd per curiam, 704 F2d 252 (2d Cir. 1983) (parent gets cost basis for subsidiary's bonds on conversion into parent stock).

[250] See Albert Ades, supra note 248; Rev. Rul. 60-37, 1960-1 CB 309 (bond-for-bond recapitalization exchange; issue discount not taxable, but taint carries over into the new bonds). See also infra ¶ 14.17; Prop. Regs. §1.1275-2(a)(1); N.Y. State Bar Report, supra note 181, at 419; supra note 244.

term options.[251] The tax issues discussed subsequently arise when a corporation issues stock purchase rights for cash or other consideration to investors, who are often, but not always, creditors of the issuing corporation.

It is well settled that a corporation does not realize taxable income from the receipt of property on the grant or exercise of options to purchase its own stock. The proceeds are viewed as nontaxable capital receipts, protected from tax by either §118 or §1032.[252] Moreover, the consideration received on issuing the option remains tax-exempt even if the option lapses without exercise,[253] while amounts paid to buy back the corporation's warrants are not deductible by virtue of §1032(a).

If warrants or options are issued as part of an "investment unit" (consisting of debt obligations and stock-purchase option rights), §1273(c)(3) requires allocation of the issue price between the debt and option elements in the package in proportion to their relative values, with the result that OID income and deductions can arise if the amount allocable to the debt component is less than its face.[254]

The treatment of stock-purchase rights acquired as part of a debt-and-option investment unit is as follows:

---

[251] For compensation possibilities, see §§421–425 (qualified stock options); Regs. §§1.421-6, 1.61-15 (nonqualified compensatory stock options); §83 (restricted property transferred for services).

For the status of warrants distributed to shareholders, see Rev. Rul. 70-521, 1970-2 CB 72 (distribution of transferable rights to buy portfolio securities of distributing corporation a taxable distribution of property under §317); infra ¶¶ 7.41–7.44.

For puts, calls, and other options, see §1234; Rev. Rul. 58-234, 1958-1 CB 279; Rev. Rul. 65-31, 1965-1 CB 365 (declared obsolete, Rev. Rul. 78-182, 1978-1 CB 265); Rev. Proc. 65-29, 1965-2 CB 1023; Rev. Rul. 63-225, 1963-2 CB 339; Rev. Rul. 70-521, 1970-2 CB 72.

See also Reiling, Warrants in Bond-Warrant Units: A Survey and Assessment, 70 Mich. L. Rev. 1411 (1972); Pesiri, Untangling the Warrant Web, 23 Tax Notes 525 (1984).

[252] See Chrysler Corp., 42 BTA 795, 806 (1940) (acq.) (forefeitures on stock subscriptions and sales are nontaxable capital receipts); for §§118 and 1032, see supra ¶¶ 3.12 and 3.13.

[253] Section 1032(a) (second sentence, enacted in 1984). For earlier Service rulings holding that a lapse was a taxable event by virtue of §1234(a), see Rev. Rul. 72-198, 1972-1 CB 223; Rev. Rul. 80-134, 1980-1 CB 187, declared obsolete (in view of 1984 amendment) by Rev. Rul. 86-9, 1986-1 CB 290.

[254] Regs. §§1.163-3 and 1.163-4; compare the situation of convertible debt securities, discussed supra ¶ 4.61, where the debt and equity components are not severed. See also Prop. Regs. §1.1273-2(d)(2)(iv) permitting the issuer and holder to agree upon a discount rate based on the yields on comparable instruments; cf. Regs. §1.1232-3(b)(ii)(b) (agreements relating to pre-1969 transactions).

To illustrate: L, an individual investor, paid $1,000 for X Corporation's 5-percent 20-year bond, with a principal amount of $1,000, together with a five-year warrant entitling the holder to purchase 10 shares of X Corporation stock at $100 a share. On the date of issue, the bond was worth $880, the warrant $120, and X's stock $90 per share.

(1) Under §1273(b)(2) and §1273(c)(2) respectively, X Corporation is treated as issuing, and L as purchasing, the bond for $880 and the warrant for $120. Hence, there is $120 of OID on the bond, which X may deduct under §163(e) and L must report as ordinary income under §1272(a) (both using compound-interest principles, as explained earlier in this chapter, to compute the amount properly attributable to each taxable year[255]).

(2) L's inclusion of the OID in income entitles L to increase pro tanto the basis for the bond. If L holds the bond to maturity, L will have included $120 of issue discount in income, resulting in a basis of $1,000 ($880 plus $120), and thus will realize neither gain nor loss on its collection.

(3) As to the warrants, L does not realize gain or loss on exercise, and takes $1,120 as the basis for the X stock ($1,000 exercise price plus $120 basis for the warrants). If L sells the warrants rather than exercising them, L will realize capital gain or loss under §1234 on the difference between the $120 basis and the amount realized on the sale. Lapse of the warrants results in a $120 capital loss to L under §1234.

X Corporation does not have any gain or loss on the issue, exercise, repurchase, or lapse of the warrants.

If a corporation acquires property in exchange for its own warrants in a taxable transaction, a 1972 Service ruling holds that the basis of the property received is its fair market value (which, assuming an arm's-length exchange, is also the value of the warrants); but the ruling was based at least in part on the theory that if the warrants lapsed without exercise, the corporation was required by §1234 to recognize income equal to the value of the property and hence of the warrants.[256] In 1984, however, §1032(a) was amended to provide that no gain or loss is recognized by the issuing corporation on a lapse (or repurchase) of a stock option; this suggests that the Service would refuse to apply the 1972 ruling to post-1984 acquisitions lest the corporation get a depreciable basis for property without any assurance that stock will actually be issued for it. Moreover, a 1975 Tax Court decision implies that

---

[255] See supra ¶ 4.41.

[256] Rev. Rul. 72-198, 1972-1 CB 223.

no basis should be assigned to the property unless and until the stock option is exercised.[257] The decision leaves room for a different result if the option "could have been valued with fair certainty" when issued;[258] but this is seldom possible in the case of long-lived options granted by closely held corporations. Moreover, the court declined to decide whether the value of the options when issued could be determined by valuing the property itself, because the value of the property in the case before the court was equally uncertain and, more important so far as other cases are concerned, because of doubts as to whether the tit-for-tat approach is valid if the value of the warrants can be fixed with certainty only at a later date.[259]

The basis of property received in a tax-free transaction, such as a corporate merger, is ordinarily the same as the transferor's basis, adjusted for any gain recognized on the exchange, as explained in detail in a later chapter.[260] Any warrants issued by the transferee in such a transaction constitute boot to the transferor, resulting in the pro tanto recognition of any realized gain; and this amount will in turn increase the transferee's basis for the property.[261] If, however, it is not feasible to value the warrants, the transaction may be held open for both the transferor and the transferee until the warrants are exercised, at which time the transferor will recognize the deferred gain and the transferee's basis will presumably be correspondingly increased.

In comparing the status of a holder of stock-purchase rights with that of other stock or security holders of a corporation, the following features should be noted:

(1) In order to become a full-fledged shareholder (with voting, dividend, and liquidation rights), the optionee must pay additional consideration on the exercise of the option. In the view of the Service, the optionee's rights in the interim do not constitute a security in applying the nonrecognition rules governing corporate reorganizations and similar transactions.[262]

---

[257] Simmonds Precision Prods., Inc., 75 TC 103 (1975).

[258] Id. at 120.

[259] Id. at 123–124.

[260] Infra ¶ 14.33.

[261] See infra ¶ 14.31 (warrants as boot); §§358(a)(1)(B)(ii) and 362(b) (adjustment for recognized gain); infra ¶ 14.56.

[262] See generally infra ¶ 14.31; see also Rev. Rul. 67-269, 1967-2 CB 298 (options, warrants, and convertible debentures do not have attributes of immediate stock ownership such as right to vote and receive dividends; hence they do not violate §1361(b)(1)(D), allowing Subchapter S corporations to have only one class of stock).

(2) The investor in a bond and warrant investment unit has two separate security interests; thus, there is a choice of either selling or maintaining one's creditor position with respect to the bond and also of exercising one's options and becoming a shareholder, selling those options on the market, or permitting them to lapse. The holder of a convertible bond, by contrast, has only a single security interest, since at some point a choice must be made between creditor and shareholder status.

(3) If held by shareholders pro rata, debt securities are a convenient device for bailing out earnings at the capital gain rate while maintaining an undiminished equity interest in the corporation. Stock-purchase options do not ordinarily offer the same opportunity because a sale of the options carries with it a transfer of the seller's inchoate equity interest represented by the optioned stock unless the underlying stock is Section 306 stock; but in the latter situation, the bailout potential is inhibited by §306.[263]

---

[263] See infra ¶ 10.02.

CHAPTER 5

The Corporation Income Tax

¶ 5.01   CORPORATE TAX RATES

1. Lower corporate rates. For taxable years starting on or after July 1, 1987,[1] §11(b) will tax a corporation's taxable income at the following rates:

Taxable Income	Rate
Up to $50,000	15%
Over $50,000 but not over $75,000	25
Over $75,000	34

The rate advantages of the first two brackets, however, are phased out by a surtax of 5 percent on taxable income between $100,000 and $335,000, resulting in marginal rates as follows:

---

[1] If July 1, 1987 falls within a corporation's taxable year, the rates set out here are blended with the rates in force before enactment of the Tax Reform Act of 1986. Under §15, the two sets of rates are applied to the taxable income for the entire year in

Taxable Income	Rate
Up to $50,000	15%
Over $50,000 but not over $75,000	25
Over $75,000 but not over $100,000	34
Over $100,000 but not over $335,000	39
Over $335,000	34

The top corporate rate of 34 percent breaks with tradition in two important respects: It is the lowest top corporate rate in at least 50 years; but, despite that fact, it is higher than the top personal rate (28 percent), which for most of the last fifty years has been at least 22 and sometimes as much as 49 percentage points higher than the corporate rate.[2]

A corporation computes its taxable base in much the same manner as any other taxpayer—that is, taxable income is defined by §63(a) as gross income (under §61) less the deductions allowed by Chapter 1 of the income tax title of the Code. Among the topics discussed in this chapter are the differences between an individual's gross income and a corporation's gross income; the differences in deductions; certain special deductions and related issues that are unique to the corporate-shareholder relationship; the corporation's method of accounting and taxable year requirements; the corporate alternative minimum tax, which was substantially revised by the Tax Reform Act of 1986; and certain distinctions between large and small corporations.

2. Corporate capital gains. Before 1987, corporations, like individuals, were subject to lower rates on their long-term capital gains; but this rate differential was eliminated by the Tax Reform Act of 1986 for taxable years beginning on or after July 1, 1987. The rest of the statutory framework relating to capital gains and losses, however, was carried forward;[3] thus, the

---

proportion to the number of days before and after the rate change, respectively, without regard to when particular items of income or deductions were realized.

For computations, see Raineri, An Analysis of Blended Corporate Tax Rates, 34 Tax Notes 1107 (1987).

[2] For a history of the corporate rates, see Eustice, Kuntz, Lewis, & Deering, The Tax Reform Act of 1986: Analysis and Commentary, ¶ 2.02 (Warren, Gorham & Lamont, Inc., 1987).

For computations of effective tax rates on corporations and discussions of the conceptual difficulties in making such computations, see U.S. Treasury Department, Effective Tax Rates Paid by United States Corporations in 1972 (1978); Kaplan, Effective Corporate Tax Rates, 2 J. Córp. Tax'n 187 (1975); Clowery, Outslay & Wheeler, The Debate on Computing Corporate Effective Tax Rates—An Accounting View, 30 Tax Notes 991 (1986).

[3] See Conf. Comm. Rep. No. 841, 99th Cong., 2d Sess. II-106 (1986), stating that the current statutory structure for capital gains "is retained in the Code to facilitate reinstatement of a capital gains rate differential if there is a future tax rate increase."

deduction of capital losses continues to be restricted by §1211(a), capital loss carry-backs and carry-overs are treated differently by §1212 than operating loss carry-backs and carry-overs, and so forth.

3. Alternative minimum tax (AMT). Section 55 imposes a tentative tax of 20 percent on the corporation's AMT income (computed after a $40,000 exemption and certain other conditions and qualifications), which is payable if and to the extent that it exceeds the corporation's regular tax. The relationship of the AMT to the regular corporate income tax and the base on which it is imposed are examined in detail later in this chapter.

4. Specialized corporate taxes. Corporations may be subject to special tax rates and to certain penalty taxes if (1) they accumulate income beyond the reasonable needs of the business in order to avoid shareholder taxes (§531); (2) they are classified as "personal holding companies" (§541) or as "foreign personal holding companies" (§551); or (3) they are foreign corporations and derive investment income from sources within the United States (§881).[4] The penalty taxes of §531 or §541 are imposed in addition to the regular §11 tax, although the regular corporate tax reduces the taxable base on which these taxes are computed. The tax imposed by §881, however, is in lieu of the regular §11 corporate tax.

5. Collateral implications of 1987 rate regime. The rate inversion effected by the Tax Reform Act of 1986 (under which the top corporate rate exceeds the top individual rate, contrary to prior custom), coupled with the Act's repeal of the rate differential for corporate and individual long-term capital gains, will have far-reaching planning implications for corporations and their shareholders. Foremost among these will be pressure to ameliorate the higher effective corporate tax by extracting funds from the corporation on a tax deductible basis, thus exacerbating the thin capitalization problem, the reasonable compensation issue, and situations where shareholders lease or license property to their corporation on non-arm's length terms for an excessive rent or royalty.[5]

---

[4] For §531, see infra ¶¶ 8.01–8.09; for §541, see infra ¶¶ 8.20–8.24; for §551, see infra ¶ 17.22; for §881, see infra ¶ 17.03; for the taxation of foreign corporations engaged in U.S. trade or business, see §§882 and 884, discussed infra ¶ 17.04.

[5] For the thin capitalization issue, see supra ¶ 4.01; for excessive compensation, rent, and royalties, see infra ¶ 7.05; for arrangements to refund amounts found by the Service to be excessive, see infra ¶ 7.05, notes 77 and 81; for the allocation of gross income, deductions, and other items under §482 if the Service finds this action necessary to clearly reflect income, see infra ¶ 15.03.

Avoidance of the corporate tax altogether by electing Subchapter S (see Chapter 6) is the simplest and most effective escape route, but a Subchapter S election is not always available (e.g., because the corporation has outstanding preferred stock or has impermissible shareholders, such as another corporation, a partnership, or a discretionary trust). If available, however, a Subchapter S election eliminates not only the §11 tax, but also the penalty taxes of §§531 and 541; in addition, S corporations are not subject to the corporate AMT, as discussed later in this chapter.

More drastic than a Subchapter S election would be a conversion of the corporation to a partnership, since, as a result of the Tax Reform Act of 1986's changes in §336 (see Chapter 11), both liquidating corporation and their shareholders are taxable on any appreciation in their assets or stock. If the corporation's basis for its assets is relatively high, however, avoidance of the corporate tax on the future income stream of the business may be worth the double tax cost of liquidating.

Apart from these planning options, the tax cost of receiving dividends will drop significantly, since by 1988 the top individual rate will be 28 percent. Further pressure to pay dividends will be exerted by §531 (which now has the highest rate in the Code, 38.5 percent) and §541 (even though its rate is the same as the top individual rate of 28 percent—lower than the §531 rate for the first time).

The 1986 rate changes will also have important ramifications, as explained later in this treatise, in a variety of specialized areas, including the treatment of collapsible corporations, "section 306 stock," market discount, integrated liquidation-reincorporations, and stock redemptions.[6] In all of these situations, the statutory imposition of ordinary income status on transactions that would otherwise generate capital gains will ordinarily be a paper tiger unless the taxpayer has offsetting capital losses. If, however, the loss of capital gain status also entails a loss of the right to offset the taxpayer's stock basis against the amount received or the right to report gain on the installment method under §453, the penalty will continue to be a matter of concern unless the basis is trivial in amount or acceleration of income is a matter of indifference.

¶ 5.02 CORPORATE TAXABLE INCOME

Corporations, like individuals, are taxed on their "taxable income," which is defined for corporations by §63(a) as "gross income minus the

---

[6] See generally infra ¶¶ 12.01 (collapsible corporations), 10.01 ("section 306 stock"), 4.44 (market discount), 11.05 (liquidation-reincorporations), and 9.02 (stock redemptions). For conversion to partnership status via the master limited partnership technique, see supra ¶ 2.04, note 53. See also Faber, Capital Gains vs. Dividends in Corporate Transactions: Is the Battle Still Worth Fighting? 64 Taxes 865 (1986); Bogdanski, Using Corporations for Tax Savings—A Reappraisal, 14 J. Corp. Tax'n 160 (1987).

deductions allowed by this chapter."[7] In defining "gross income," §61(a) does not explicitly distinguish between corporations and individuals, but there are nevertheless some differences between them as respects particular items, as explained later; and there are also important differences between corporations and individuals in the tax treatment of deductions.

Although §61(a) defines "gross income" in the same way for corporations and individuals,[8] some items listed in §61(a) are rarely or never received by corporations (e.g., alimony and income in respect of a decedent); while a few statutory exclusions from gross income by their terms apply only to corporations (e.g., §118, relating to contributions to capital, and §110, relating to payments by a corporate lessee of its corporate lessor's tax liabilities), and many other statutory exclusions involve items that by their nature could not be received by corporations, such as combat pay, social security benefits, and employee fringe benefits. An item of this type might be collected by a corporation following an assignment by the individual originally entitled to receive it; but its tax status would almost certainly be transformed in the process—that is, an amount that would constitute a scholarship in the hands of a student would be characterized as a contribution to capital or repayment of a loan in the hands of the assignee-corporation, depending on the reason for the assignment.

¶ 5.03   CORPORATE DEDUCTIONS

The Code allows individuals to take a number of deductions that are not allowed to corporations, including the standard deduction, the deduction for personal exemptions, and the additional itemized deductions for individuals for such items as medical expenses, alimony, moving expenses, and retirement savings, which are set out in Part VII of Subchapter B (§§211–220). The other principal differences between corporations and indi-

---

[7] As amended in 1986, §63(a) treats the standard deduction specially, but this does not affect corporations, since the standard deduction is confined to individuals.

[8] A few specific inclusionary sections apply only to corporations or only to individuals; for example, §78 (gross-up in computing derivative foreign tax credits) applies only to certain domestic corporations; §79 (inclusion of group term insurance premiums in excess of certain amounts) probably, although not explicitly, applies only to individuals; and §80 (recovery of a previously deducted worthless security loss from foreign government expropriation) applies only to domestic corporations.

Section 74(b), relating to tax-exempt prizes and awards, may have been intended to apply only to individuals, but corporations are not explicitly excluded. The use of the word "his" in §74(b)(1) should not in itself exclude corporations, since "his" is used elsewhere to avoid the more cumbersome form "his, hers, or its" (e.g., §§75 and 1221).

viduals vis-à-vis deductions are set out below.[9] As will be seen, some statutory provisions do not distinguish between individuals and corporations as such, but instead draw a line separating individuals and closely held corporations from other corporations in order to prevent restrictions aimed primarily at individuals from being sidestepped by a transfer of the restricted activities to a closely held corporation.

1. Deductibility of losses. Section 165(a) provides that any loss sustained during the taxable year, if not compensated for by insurance or otherwise, may be deducted. In the case of an individual, however, §165(c) goes on to restrict the breadth of §165(a) by allowing the deduction only if the loss was incurred in a trade or business, a transaction entered into for profit, or a casualty. The restrictions of §165(c) are not applicable to corporations, presumably on the theory that all corporate transactions arise in trade or business. On several occasions, however, corporations have been denied deductions under §162(a) (business expenses) and §167 (depreciation) on the ground that the property in respect of which the items arose was held for the personal convenience of the corporation's shareholders rather than for corporate business purposes, and losses incurred on such property might well be treated as personal rather than corporate items even in the absence of a specific provision.[10]

2. Bad debts. In the case of bad debts, a taxpayer other than a corporation is confined by §166(d) to a capital loss on nonbusiness debts. Since this restriction is by its terms inapplicable to corporations, in *Cooper-Brannan Naval Stores Co.*, the court allowed a corporation to deduct an uncollectible loan made to the son-in-law of the principal shareholder, stating that

---

[9] For restrictions on deductions for certain transactions between related parties (e.g., a sale of property by a corporation to its controlling shareholder or vice versa), see infra ¶ 5.04.

[10] See Greenspon v. CIR, 229 F2d 947 (8th Cir. 1956) (corporate expenditures to maintain "unique horticultural showplace" at sole shareholder's farm disallowed as business expenses and taxed as constructive dividends to shareholder); Black Dome Corp., ¶ 46,130 P-H Memo. TC (1946) (country estate); Savarona Ship Corp., ¶ 42,596 P-H Memo. TC (1942); International Trading Co. v. CIR, 275 F2d 578 (7th Cir. 1960). But see International Trading Co. v. CIR, 484 F2d 707 (7th Cir, 1973) (§165(a) does not limit deductibility of corporation's losses); cf. W.L. Schautz Co. v. US, 567 F2d 376 (Ct. Cl. 1977) (corporate nonbusiness loss denied under §274).

On the more general question of whether a holding company is engaged in business, see Campbell Taggart, Inc. v. US, 744 F2d 442 (5th Cir. 1984). Compare Arkansas Best Corp. v. CIR, supra ¶ 4.20, note 95.

For cases treating corporate payments of this type as constructive distributions to the shareholders benefitted thereby, see infra ¶ 7.05.

"it is not proper for this Board to go into the question of the motive of petitioner's officers in making the ... loan ... nor into the question of whether or not such loan was an ultra vires act."[11] Although the Service acquiesced in the decision,[12] it would be perilous to assume that such a transaction could never be regarded as a personal rather than a corporate transaction.

3. Charitable contributions. The deduction for charitable contributions is computed differently for corporations than for other taxpayers. Under the general rule of §170(a)(1), the contribution must be paid within the taxable year, regardless of the taxpayer's mode of accounting; but §170(a)(2) mitigates this requirement as to corporations on the accrual basis. They may elect to treat a contribution as paid during the taxable year if it is authorized by the board of directors during the year and paid within the first two and one-half months of the following taxable year. The ceiling on the deduction for charitable contributions is, in the case of individuals, 30 percent of adjusted gross income (increased to 50 percent for certain contributions); but for corporations the ceiling is 10 percent of taxable income (computed with certain adjustments). Contributions by a corporation in excess of this amount may be carried forward for five years, and deducted (together with any other contributions made in those years) subject to the 10 percent ceiling for those years.

4. Limitation on capital losses. A corporation may deduct its capital losses only to the extent of capital gains under §1211(a); it does not enjoy the privilege granted to other taxpayers by §1211(b) of applying the excess against a limited amount of ordinary income.

Individuals can carry unused capital losses forward for an unlimited period, while corporations are granted a carry-back period of three years and a carry-forward of five years, subject to special qualifications for foreign expropriation losses, S corporations, and a few other specialized categories.

5. Net operating losses. There are several differences between corporations and other taxpayers in computing the net operating loss deduction, but they merely reflect other differences in computing taxable income for corporations and other taxpayers.[13]

---

[11] Cooper-Brannan Naval Stores Co., 9 BTA 105 (1927) (acq).

[12] VII-1 CB 7 (1928).

[13] See §§172(d)(2)–172(d)(6).

6. Expenses for production of income. Section 212 was enacted in 1942 to permit the deduction of nonbusiness expenses (expenses paid or incurred for the production of income or for the management, conservation, or maintenance of property held for the production of income), and was enlarged in 1954 to embrace expenses incurred in the determination, collection, or refund of taxes. Section 212 is restricted to individuals, presumably on the theory that §162(a) covers the same ground for corporations that §§162(a) and 212 in combination cover for other taxpayers. Thus, if a corporation engaged in manufacturing holds some securities as an incidental investment, the cost of a safe-deposit box, investment advice, bookkeeping, and so forth, incurred with respect to the securities would be deductible under §162(a) as trade or business expenses, even though an individual proprietor holding such securities would have to resort to §212 as authority for deducting such expenses.[14]

7. Dividends-received deduction. Sections 243–246 permit corporations to deduct certain dividends received from other corporations. Of these provisions, the most important is §243, providing for a deduction of 80 percent or more of dividends received from domestic taxable corporations.[15]

8. Organizational expenditures. Section 248 permits a corporation to amortize its organizational expenditures over a period of 60 months or more.[16]

9. Dividends paid by public utilities on certain preferred stock. Although dividends paid by a corporaton are not normally deductible, §247 grants a limited deduction for dividends paid by public utility corporations on certain preferred stock.[17]

10. Shareholder's taxes paid by corporation. Section 164(e) permits a corporation to deduct a tax imposed on a shareholder on his interest as a

---

[14] During the 1942 hearings on §212, a taxpayer representative recommended its enlargement to include corporations. See Hearings on Revenue Act of 1942 before the Senate Finance Comm., 77th Cong., 2d Sess. 1733 (1942). The recommendation was not adopted, probably because it was thought to be unnecessary. At any rate, it has been generally assumed since 1942 that a corporation can deduct under §162(a) any expenses that could be deducted under §212 by an individual proprietor or partnership. See generally Bittker, Federal Taxation of Income, Estate and Gifts (Warren, Gorham & Lamont, Inc., 1981), ¶ 20.5.1.

[15] See generally infra ¶ 5.05.

[16] See generally infra ¶ 5.06.

[17] See infra ¶ 5.05 text at note 64.

shareholder if the corporation pays the tax and is not reimbursed by the shareholder. The taxes in question are imposed by some states on the capital stock of banks and some other corporations.[18]

11. Section 465 at-risk rules. Section 465, which limits the current deductibility of losses incurred in various business activities to the amount the taxpayer has at-risk (as defined), originally applied only to a short list of activities; but the rules have been expanded to cover all business and income-producing activities, including real estate placed in service after 1986.[19] Although aimed primarily at individuals, §465 applies to C corporations meeting the stock ownership requirements of §542(a)(2) (i.e., a corporation more than 50 percent in value of whose stock is owned directly, indirectly, or constructively by not more than five individuals).[20] Section 465 does not apply to S corporations, but their tax shelter losses are passed through to their shareholders, who are subject to §465 in their personal capacities.

12. Percentage cutbacks in corporate tax preferences. Section 291 imposes specified percentage limits on certain otherwise allowable corporate tax preferences. This provision was enacted in 1982 because, according to the Senate Finance Committee, "there is increasing concern about the equity of the tax system, and cutting back corporate tax preferences is a valid response to that concern."[21] The nature and severity of the cutbacks mandated by §291 vary, but the affected items are: (1) the ordinary income component of gain on the disposition of certain §1250 property (primarily real property subject to accelerated depreciation); (2) percentage depletion on iron ore and coal; (3) certain tax preferences of financial institutions; (4) the exempt foreign sales income of certain closely held foreign and possessions corporations; (5) amortization of pollution control facilities,; and (6) intangible drilling costs and mineral exploration and development costs.

---

[18] On §164(e), see General Motors Corp. v. US, 283 F2d 699 (Ct. Cl. 1960); Rev. Rul. 92, 1953-1 CB 39; Hillsboro Nat'l Bank v. CIR, 460 US 370 (1983) (no tax benefit income to corporation on recovery by shareholders of taxes previously deducted by corporation under §164(e)); see also Ferguson v. Fidelity Union Trust Co., 24 F2d 520 (3d Cir. 1928) (deductibility for years preceding enactment of §164(e)).

[19] In the case of real estate, the taxpayer's at-risk investment includes nonrecourse financing meeting the conditions of §465(b)(6)(B).

[20] For §542(a)(2), see infra ¶ 8.23. The passive activity loss limitations of §469, as added by the Tax Reform Act of 1986, apply to corporations subject to the at-risk rules of §465. See infra note 22.

[21] Senate Finance Comm. Rep. 494, 97th Cong., 2d Sess. 119 (1982).

13. Other restrictions. Other statutory remedies for tax shelter and similar tax-avoidance arrangements that apply not only to individuals, but also to some corporations, include the following: (1) §469, enacted in 1986, which imposes restrictions on the current deduction of so-called passive activity losses incurred by individuals, corporations meeting the stock ownership rules of §542(a)(2), and personal service corporations defined by §269A(b)(1), as modified by §469(j)(2);²² (2) §464, requiring farming syndicates to capitalize certain otherwise deductible expenditures for feed, seed, and other supplies, which defines "syndicate" to include partnerships and certain S corporations; (3) §183, relating to hobbies and other activities not engaged in for profit, which applies to S corporations as well as to individuals; and (4) §280A, relating to home offices, which also applies to both individuals and S corporations.²³

On the other hand, §447, requiring certain large-scale farming enterprises to use the accrual method of accounting, exempts individuals, S corporations, and certain specially defined family corporations.

¶ 5.04 SPECIAL DEDUCTION PROBLEMS ARISING FROM CORPORATE-SHAREHOLDER RELATIONSHIP

The relationship between corporations and their shareholders often generates questions about the deductibility of expenditures incurred by both groups and of losses incurred in their dealings with each other. The corporation's right to deduct shareholder-connected expenditures is governed by §162 (ordinary and necessary business expenses), whereas the individual shareholder's right to deduct corporate-connected outlays can be governed by either §162 or §212 (investment expenses); but in either case, account must also be taken of §§262 and 263(a)(1), denying deductions for personal expenses and capital expenditures respectively. The application of these statutory provisions depends so heavily on principles growing out of noncorporate contexts that a full discussion of this area is beyond the scope of this treatise; but mention may be made of a few areas of special interest.²⁴

---

²² For §269A, see supra ¶ 2.07. See generally Eustice, Kuntz, Lewis, & Deering, supra note 2, at ¶ 3.02; Shapiro, Your Tax Reform PAL, 33 Tax Notes 757 (1986); Lipton, Fun and Games With Our New PALs, 64 Taxes 801 (1986).

²³ In a few cases, restrictions that originally applied only to individuals and closely held corporations have been expanded by Congress to encompass all corporations (e.g., §267(a)(3) requiring that payments to foreign persons, whether or not related, are subject to the matching rules of §267(a)(2), infra note 27). See infra ¶ 5.09.

²⁴ On the definition of trade or business, see generally CIR v. Groetzinger, 55 USLW 4175 (US Feb. 24, 1987). On the treatment of a shareholder's expenditures to promote the corporation's business, see Deputy v. du Pont, 308 US 488 (1940);

1. Related party transactions. Section 267(a)(1) provides that losses from sales or exchanges of property, directly or indirectly, between certain related persons may not be deducted.[25] The relationships causing losses to be disallowed are specified by §267(b); they include (1) an individual and a corporation of which he owns, directly or indirectly, more than 50 percent in value of the outstanding stock; (2) a fiduciary of a trust and a corporation if the trust or a grantor thereof owns, directly or indirectly, more than 50 percent in value of the corporation's outstanding stock; (3) a corporation and a partnership if the same persons own more than 50 percent in value of the corporation's stock and more than 50 percent of the capital or profits interest in the partnership; and (4) an S corporation and another corporation (whether S or C) if the same persons own more than 50 percent in value of the stock of both corporations. In all of these situations, the ownership of stock is determined by reference to the constructive ownership rules of §267(c).

In addition, losses from the sale or exchange of property (except in liquidation or on certain sales of inventory in the ordinary course of business between two members of the same controlled group of corporations, as defined by §267(f)) are deferred rather than disallowed until realized by a sale or other transfer of the property outside the controlled group.[26]

Taxpayers subject to the related party loss rules of §267(a)(1) are also subject to the matching rules of §267(a)(2) if an expense or item of interest[27]

James M. Rawkins, 20 TC 1069 (1953) (deduction denied); Tom C. Connally, ¶ 61,312 P-H Memo. TC (1961) (same); Fischer v. US, 490 F2d 218 (7th Cir. 1973) (bargain sale of stock by corporate officer to convertible bondholders to settle their claim against corporation held not deductible by seller because not his expense); Bautzer v. US, AFTR2d 6227 (Ct. Cl. 1975) (shareholder expense for benefit of corporation held nondeductible capital expense). Compare James O. Gould, 64 TC 132 (1975) (shareholder payment of corporation's debts deductible business expense because purpose was to protect his employment with another corporation).

See generally Wilberding, An Individual's Business Investigation Expenses: An Argument Supporting Deductibility, 26 Tax Lawyer 219 (1973); Fleischer, The Tax Treatment of Expenses Incurred in Investigation for a Business or Capital Investment, 14 Tax L. Rev. 567, ns.42, 43, 111 (1959).

[25] Losses on liquidating distributions are exempt from this restriction; see generally infra ¶ 9.31.

[26] See generally Gardner, Disallowed or Deferred Losses, Expenses and Interest: Related Party Transactions and IRC Section 267, 44 NYU Inst. on Fed. Tax'n ch. 29 (1986); infra ¶ 15.04.

[27] The operational language of §267(a)(2) embraces any payment that is deductible by one party and includable in the related recipient's gross income, but the heading refers explicitly to "the case of expenses and interest," as did the heading of §267(a)(2)'s statutory predecessor; see also §267(a)(3), added in 1986, imposing the matching rule of §267(a)(2) on amounts payable to foreign persons, whether or not related (as provided by regulations).

owed by one party (on the accrual method of accounting) to the related party (if he is on the cash method) is not includable in the latter's gross income until it is paid. When originally enacted, §267(a)(2) was primarily concerned with the deduction of unpaid salaries owed by accrual-basis corporations to their cash-basis dominant shareholders (although it could also apply to other items such as unpaid rent or interest); and the statutory remedy was the complete disallowance of the corporation's deduction, unless the payment was made within two and one-half months after the close of the corporation's taxable year. Under the current version of §267(a)(2), however, the deduction is deferred until the item is includable in the payee's gross income (ordinarily as a result of payment); it is not disallowed, no matter how long the delay in payment.

2. Acquisition expenses: Proxy fight costs and related problems. Expenses incurred in connection with the acquisition of stock in a corporation ordinarily constitute nondeductible capital expenditures to be added to the basis of the acquired stock (as would the buyer's comparable costs of acquiring any other type of property[28]), whether the acquisition is a negotiated purchase or a hostile takeover via the tender offer or proxy contest route. In two decisions, the Supreme Court reemphasized the capital character of costs originating in the acquisition process, denying deductibility for the acquiring party's legal expenses of stock appraisal litigation brought by dissenting shareholders to determine the value of their stock.[29] Similar capital treatment is imposed on the selling expenses of transferor shareholders; these expenses constitute an offset against the sale proceeds and thus reduce the shareholder's gain or increase his loss.[30]

---

[28] Regs §§1.263(a)-2(a), 1.263(a)-2(c), 1.263(a)-2(e); Regs. §1.212-1(k); Dwight Williamson, 17 BTA 1112 (1929); Grossman, Tax Treatment of Professional Fees Related to Asset Acquisitions and Changes in Business Entities, 45 Taxes 880 (1967).

[29] Woodward v. CIR, 397 US 572 (1970); US v. Hilton Hotels Corp., 397 US 580 (1970); see also McGlothlin v CIR, 370 F2d 729 (5th Cir. 1967); Mountain Paper Prods. Corp. v. US, 287 F2d 957 (2d Cir. 1961); Locke v. CIR, 568 F2d 663 (9th Cir. 1978) (expenses of defending suit for fraud in sale of stock held nondeductible capital expenditures); William Wagner, 78 TC 910 (1982) (same).

See generally Cohen, The Deductibility of Stock Redemption Expenses, 24 Case W. Res. 431 (1973); Wilberding, supra note 24.

[30] Regs. §§1.263(a)-2(e) and 1.453-1(b)(1); Third Nat'l Bank in Nashville v. US, 427 F2d 343 (6th Cir. 1970); Helgerson v. US, 426 F2d 1293 (8th Cir. 1970). For borderline decisions on whether expenses were incurred in the disposition of property or for the collection of income, see CIR v. Doering, 335 F2d 738 (2d Cir. 1964); Petschek v. US, 335 F2d 734 (3d Cir. 1964); see also Estate of Meade v. CIR, 489 F2d 161 (5th Cir. 1974) (shareholder expense of collecting open liquidation claim held capital expenditure; attributable to disposition of stock); Estate of Baier v. CIR, 533 F2d 117 (3d Cir. 1976) (legal fees in collecting proceeds from sale of property;

There are, however, certain limited exceptions to the general rule of non-deductibility for these costs. Several decisions have allowed insurgent share-holders to deduct the expense of soliciting proxies from their fellow shareholders where their purpose was to alter the business policies of the incumbent management in order to increase their dividend income or the value of their stock.[31] Efforts to acquire mere voting power or control, as distinguished from the underlying property (stock) itself, will apparently escape the capital expenditure taint, at least if these efforts are sufficiently related to the production of income or the conservation of income producing property. Conversely, expenses incurred by a corporation in resisting the insurgents have been held deductible, at least where the management believed in good faith that the resistance was in the best interests of all shareholders;[32] and one case permitted a corporate business expense deduction for reimbursement of the proxy expenses of both the winning and losing shareholder groups.[33]

Acquisition expenses incurred in a tender offer, on the other hand, may stand on a different footing, at least with respect to the acquiring party. Here, the purchaser goes beyond merely soliciting votes, as in a proxy contest, and actually acquires the stock of the target corporation; accordingly, the expenses of planning and executing a successful tender offer seem clearly

---

capital expense). But see Sharples v. US, 533 F2d 550 (Ct. Cl. 1976) (*Woodward* and *Hilton Hotels* doctrine not applicable to §212(3); tax advice expenses deductible, even though connected with corporate liquidation).

See generally Schenk, Arrowsmith and Its Progeny: Tax Characterization by Reference to Past Events, 33 Rutgers L. Rev. 317 (1981).

[31] Graham v. CIR, 326 F2d 878 (4th Cir. 1964); Surasky v. US, 325 F2d 191 (5th Cir. 1963); Rev. Rul. 64-236, 1964-2 CB 64 (expenses deductible if proximately related to production of income or conservation of income-producing property); Alleghany Corp., 28 TC 298 (1957) (acq.) (controlling shareholder's expenses in defending against a proxy fight deductible); see also Dyer v. CIR, 352 F2d 948 (8th Cir. 1965) (expenses of shareholder crusading for particular point of view; nondeductible because not reasonably related to dividend income or stock value); Jean Nidetch, ¶ 78,313 P-H Memo. TC (1978), (deduction for costs of preparing for anticipated proxy contest to change corporate policies); Dolese v. US, 605 F2d 1146 (10th Cir. 1979) (fight for control in divorce litigation; some expenses paid by corporation nondeductible personal expenses, but some held deductible for preservation of corporate assets; proxy fight analogy applied).

See generally Note, Proxy Fight Expenses: Problems of Tax Deduction, 43 Va. L. Rev. 891 (1957); Note, CA-5 in Allowing Proxy Fight Costs Eases "Nonbusiness Expense" Definition, 20 J. Tax'n 104 (1964).

[32] Locke Mfg. Cos. v. US, 237 F. Supp. 80 (D. Conn. 1964); Rev. Rul. 67-1, 1967-1 CB 28 (accord if expenses were primarily concerned with questions of corporate policy rather than for benefit of particular individuals); Dolese v. US, supra note 31 (expense deductible to extent related to preservation of corporation's business; not deductible to extent expense was personal to divorce proceeding between husband and wife shareholders).

[33] Central Foundry Co., 49 TC 234 (1967) (acq.).

to fall within the category of costs incurred in the process of acquisition, required to be capitalized under the *Woodward* and *Hilton Hotels* decisions.[34] Expenses paid by the corporation in resisting a tender offer, however, should probably be deductible on the same basis as the cost of defending a proxy fight—that is, the expenses are incurred primarily to protect rather than acquire property and are primarily concerned with questions of corporate policy.[35]

While costs of effecting a *successful* acquisition are capital expenditures that must be added to the basis of the acquired property, expenses of unsuccessful bids or aborted acquisitions apparently are deductible either as business or investment expenses under §§162 and 212 or as business or investment losses under §165.[36] Capitalization is not appropriate in this situation, since the preliminary activities did not culminate in the acquisition of a specific property interest by the offeror taxpayer.

3. Corporate-shareholder disputes: Shareholder derivative suits, indemnity agreements, and so forth. Payments by a corporation or its officers and directors to resist or settle claims arising in shareholder derivative suits for breach of an officer's or director's fiduciary duty in the conduct of the corporation's business affairs have generally been held deductible as an ordinary and necessary outgrowth of the corporation's, the officer's, or the director's trade or business.[37] Courts apparently treat expenses for the

---

[34] Woodward v. CIR, supra note 29; US v. Hilton Hotels Corp., supra note 29; see also Rev. Rul. 73-580, 1973-2 CB 86 (legal and accounting expenses of in-house corporate acquisition department must be capitalized); Ellis Banking Corp. v. US, 688 F2d 1376 (11th Cir. 1982) (fees for investigation of potential target corporation held part of the cost of acquisition of the stock). See generally Capitalization of In-House Legal and Accounting Costs—Rev. Rul. 73-580, Tax Mgmt. Memo. (BNA) No. 74-09 (April 29, 1974).

[35] The Service initially so ruled in TAM 8516002, which was withdrawn in 1986 for reconsideration. See generally Rosenberg, The Reluctant Bride: Tax Treatment of Costs of Resisting Corporate Takeovers, 13 J. Corp. Tax'n 114 (1986); Bowen, Defenses Against Takeovers—Selected Tax Problems, 64 Taxes 835 (1986).

[36] Rev. Rul. 67-125, 1967-1 CB 31; Johan Domenie, ¶ 75,094 P-H Memo. TC (costs of abandoned business acquisition plan deductible §165 loss); Rev. Rul. 73-580, 1973-2 CB 86 (costs of abandoned acquisition plans deductible).

If the preliminary activities ripen into a successful acquisition, capitalization of start-up expenses may be required; see, e.g., Richmond Television Corp. v. US, 345 F2d 901 (4th Cir. 1965); see also §195, providing an election to amortize start-up costs, business investigation costs, and pre-opening costs (but not acquisition costs) of a new business over five years, commencing in the case of acquisitions with the date thereof under §195(c)(2)(B).

[37] See Larchfield Corp. v. US, 373 F2d 159 (2d Cir. 1966) (expenses by corporation as neutral party in derivative suit deductible; reimbursement of defendant-

defense or settlement of such suits as an ordinary and necessary cost of doing business in the corporate form. Since the corporation usually pays the entire cost of defending these suits, either under the court decree, the settlement agreement, or an indemnification bylaw, the issue of deductibility typically involves only the corporate payor, although occasionally directors and officers are also involved. The fact that the suit is settled or even that the corporation loses is generally no bar to a deduction. Deductions have been allowed for corporate reimbursement of both the shareholder-plaintiff's and the director-defendant's litigation expenses in a derivative action if the suit challenged the conduct of the corporation's business affairs.

Deductibility for derivative suit expenses is not automatic, however. If the suit relates to the recovery of or the defense of title to specific property, the litigation expenses will have to be capitalized as costs incurred in defending or perfecting title to property.[38] In some cases, an allocation between capital and noncapital expenditures may be appropriate.[39]

It is commonplace in many corporations for key executives and directors to seek protection against liability for the improper conduct of their business duties by indemnity agreements, reimbursement bylaws, or business liability insurance.[40] The Service has ruled that premiums paid by a corporation for group liability insurance indemnifying its officers for the expenses of defending lawsuits alleging misconduct in their official capaci-

---

directors' liabilities under indemnification bylaw deductible; reimbursement of plaintiffs' costs deductible except to extent attributable to recovery of specific property), and cases there cited; Ingalls Iron Works v. Patterson, 158 F. Supp. 627 (N.D. Ala. 1958) (reimbursement of shareholders' expenses in derivative suit deductible); Hochschild v. CIR, 161 F2d 817 (2d Cir. 1947) (director's legal fees in successful defense of suit alleging breach of corporate opportunity doctrine deductible); Graham v. CIR, supra note 31 (payment by director in settlement of suit alleging waste of corporate assets deductible); Mitchell v. US, 408 F2d 435 (Ct. Cl. 1969) (principal shareholder-officer's expenses in defense of suit for alleged fraud in sale of stock; deductible as expense of carrying on business as corporate officer).

[38] Larchfield Corp. v. US, supra note 37; Iowa S. Utils. Co. v. CIR, 333 F2d 382 (8th Cir.), cert. denied, 379 US 946 (1964); Pennroad Corp., 21 TC 1087 (1954), aff'd, 228 F2d 329 (3d Cir. 1955) (acq.); see also Galewitz v. CIR, 411 F2d 1374 (2d Cir.), cert. denied, 396 US 906 (1969) (legal expenses of shareholder in defending groundless suit challenging right to hold stock; nondeductible expense of defending title to stock).

[39] Larchfield Corp. v. US, supra note 37. At the least, allocation will not be permitted unless the taxpayer claiming the deduction proves the relationship of the litigation expenses to the various elements of the suit; thus, there is a premium on accurate recordkeeping.

[40] See Larchfield Corp. v. US, supra note 37 (payment to one of defendant-directors pursuant to an indemnity bylaw held deductible as compensatory fringe benefit, even though that director could not have deducted all of such payments individually if he had personally paid them).

ties were deductible §162 expenses of the corporation and that such payments did not constitute gross income to the officers.[41]

The litigation expenditures of plaintiff-shareholders may be either deductible expenses under §162 or §212 or capital outlays to be added to the basis of their stock under §§263(a)(1) and 1016(a)(1) (or partly one and partly the other), depending on the nature of their claims and the outcome of the suit.[42]

4. Redemption of stock. The corporate take-over movement of the early 1980s led Congress in 1986 to enact §162(*l*), which disallows otherwise allowable deductions for "any amount paid or incurred by a corporation in connection with the redemption of its stock." The corporation's right to deduct amounts paid to reacquire its stock was extremely doubtful even before the enactment of §162(*l*), although some hopes had been built on a 1966 decision of the Court of Appeals for the Fifth Circuit, allowing a deduction for amounts paid to purchase stock of a 50 percent dissenting shareholder in order to settle a lawsuit.[43] The decision was substantially undermined, however, by the Supreme Court's later decisions in *Woodward* and *Hilton Hotels*,[44] and still later the Court of Appeals for the Fifth Circuit itself confined the decision to expenditures "made to save the corporation from dire and threatening consequences";[45] but, because the management of a publicly held corporation naturally views almost any stock purchase by a

---

[41] Rev. Rul. 69-491, 1969-2 CB 22; Rev. Rul. 76-277, 1976-2 CB 41 (deductible if paid by officer).

See generally Mooney, The Indemnification Dilemma—Tax Problems in Protecting the Corporate Officer and Director From Liability, 51 Taxes 498 (1973).

[42] See Galewitz v. CIR, supra note 38; cf. Larchfield Corp. v. US, supra note 37; Mitchell v. US, supra note 37; Naylor v. CIR, 203 F2d 346 (5th Cir. 1953); Third Nat'l Bank in Nashville v. US, supra note 30; Newark Morning Ledger Co. v. US, 539 F2d 929 (3d Cir. 1976) (parent corporation's legal fees in litigation against its subsidiary alleging diversion of earnings and of corporate business opportunity; held deductible); US v. Brown, 526 F2d 135 (6th Cir. 1975) (shareholder's derivative suit had origin in buyout offer from other shareholder, hence litigation expenses nondeductible capital costs under *Woodward* and *Hilton Hotels*, even though suit resulted in increased price for stock and larger future income flow); see also cases supra notes 29 and 30.

[43] Five Star Mfg. Co. v. CIR, 355 F2d 724 (5th Cir. 1966).

[44] Woodward v. CIR, supra note 29; US v. Hilton Hotels Corp., supra note 29.

[45] Jim Walter Corp. v. US, 498 F2d 631, 639 (5th Cir. 1974); cf. Markam & Brown, Inc. v. US, 648 F2d 1045 (5th Cir. 1981) (repurchase under buy-sell agreement was "clearly capital," despite removal of animosity between shareholders); see also §1032, amended in 1984 to deny a loss deduction on a corporation's repurchase of options to buy or sell its own stock. Section 162(*l*) applies to payments on or after March 1, 1986; its enactment carries no implications for the deductibility of prior payments. See Conf. Comm. Rep. No. 841, 99th Cong., 2d Sess. II-169 (1986).

so-called corporate raider as presaging dire and threatening circumstances, the hope of deducting greenmail payments continued to spring eternal in the executive breast.

Rather than leave the deduction of such payments to case-by-case resolutions, §162(*l*) flatly disallows any deductions for the amounts paid for the stock, for related expenses (e.g., legal, brokerage, and accounting fees), and for payments under so-called standstill agreements by which the recipient agrees not to purchase any additional shares.[46] On the other hand, §162(*l*) explicitly exempts (1) interest, if otherwise deductible under §163; (2) dividends deductible under §561, relating to dividends paid in computing the accumulated earnings tax and in a few other circumstances;[47] and (3) expenses incurred by mutual funds all of whose stock is redeemable on the shareholder's demand.

Moreover, being confined to payments "in connection with the redemption of [the corporation's] stock," §162(*l*) leaves room for the deduction of payments, if otherwise allowable, that occur "in a transaction that has no nexus with the redemption other than being proximate in time or arising out of the same general circumstances."[48] Thus, a lump sum payment to a departing employee may be split between a nondeductible payment for his stock and a deductible payment in discharge of the corporation's obligations under an employment contract.

5. Golden parachute payments. The corporate take-over movement that led Congress to enact §162(*l*) in 1986 was also the impetus for the enactment in 1984 of §280G, which disallows certain payments to a "disqualified individual" if the payment is (1) contingent on a change in the ownership or effective control of a corporation or in the ownership of a substantial portion of a corporation's assets, provided the present value of the payment exceeds three times a defined base amount, or (2) paid pursuant to an agree-

---

[46] See generally Eustice, Kuntz, Lewis and Deering, supra note 2 at §2.07[2]; for pre-1986 law, see Resnick, The Deductibility of Stock Redemption Expenses and the Corporate Survival Doctrine, 58 So. Cal. L. Rev. 895 (1985).

Although the statutory language refers to payments to redeem its stock, the conference report on the Tax Reform Act of 1986 states that §162(*l*) includes amounts paid "indirectly, e.g., by a controlling shareholder, commonly controlled subsidiary or other related party." H.R. Rep. No. 841, 99th Cong., 2d Sess. II-168 (1986).

Since greenmail payments are essentially capital in character, they ought not to be fully chargeable to earnings and profits either, infra ¶ 7.03; but see §312(n)(7), infra ¶ 9.35. Query deductibility of these payments against book income for purposes of the AMT, infra ¶ 5.08.

[47] For §561, see infra ¶ 8.09.

[48] H.R. Rep. No. 841, 99th Cong., 2d Sess. II-168 (1986). For a description of an alternative to greenmail payments, see Walter & Strasen, Innovative Transactions— Sonat Inc.'s Purchase of the Coastal Debentures, 64 Taxes 77 (1986).

ment violating any generally enforced securities laws or regulations. If an agreement is entered into within one year of a change of ownership or control, it is presumed to be contingent on the change unless the contrary is established by clear and convincing evidence.[49] The term "disqualified individual" is defined by §280G(c) to include an officer, shareholder, or highly compensated individual (including a personal service corporation or similar entity), as well as any employee, independent contractor, or other person who performs personal services for the corporation and is specified in regulations to be issued. A disqualified individual's "base amount" is defined by ¶ 280G(b)(3) by reference to his average annual taxable compensation for a five-year base period preceding the change of control or ownership, after an allowance for amounts established as reasonable compensation for personal services that were rendered before the change (if not already compensated for) or that are to be rendered after the change.

The impetus for §280G was the much-criticized use of so-called golden parachutes to cushion the departure of the management of publicly traded corporations following a hostile take-over or to deter the take-over itself by increasing the cost; but §280G applies whether a change in ownership or control is friendly or hostile and whether the corporation is closely held or publicly traded. There are, however, two important exceptions to §280G's coverage, both added in 1986: It does not apply to (1) a "small business corporation" as defined by §1361(b) as a corporation that is eligible to elect S corporation status[50] or (2) a corporation whose stock is not readily tradeable (on an established securities market or otherwise), provided the payment is approved by the owners of more than 75 percent of the corporation's voting stock after adequate disclosure of all material facts.

Even with these exceptions, §280G can raise questions about the deductibility of payments in a variety of unexpected circumstances—e.g., payments under a contract not to compete, entered into on the sale of a family corporation that does not qualify for the §1361(b) exemption because it has two classes of stock and does not meet the shareholder-approval exemption because the transfer was authorized by the dominant share-

---

[49] See generally Staff of Joint Comm. on Taxation. General Explanation of the Revenue Provisions of the Deficit Reduction Act of 1984 199 (1984); N.Y. State Bar Association, Tax Section Report, The "Golden Parachute" Provisions of TRA '84, 27 Tax Notes 949 (1985), Krueger, Opportunities and Pitfalls in Designing Executive Compensation: The Effect of the Golden Parachute Penalties, 63 Taxes 846 (1985); Moore & Tilton, Golden Parachute Restrictions Require Planning on Existing and Proposed Arrangements, 61 J. Tax'n 234 (1984).

Although nondeductible for regular tax purposes, parachute payments ought to reduce earnings and profits (infra ¶ 7.03) and book income for AMT purposes (infra ¶ 5.08).

[50] For §1361(b), see infra ¶ 6.02. See generally Eustice, Kuntz, Lewis, & Deering, supra note 2, ¶ 2.07[5].

holder-employee, who has customarily made all business and financial decisions but who owns less than 75 percent of the stock. In situations like these, the corporation's principal protection may prove to be the three-fold cushion of §280G(b)(2)(ii), which allows a substantial margin for error in fixing the amount to be paid under a bona fide contract not to compete, separation agreement, or post-retirement consulting arrangement.

In their zeal to penalize genuine golden parachutes, the drafters of §280G may well have been simultaneously over- and under-inclusive: over-inclusive by raising problems for run-of-the-mill sales of closely held corporations and under-inclusive by defining the crucial term "parachute payment" as a "payment in the nature of compensation," thus opening the door to the argument that *real* golden parachutes are unjustified handouts of corporate assets, objectionable because they are *non*compensatory. Presumably, however, the courts will rescue §280G from this construction by ruling that excessive payments to departing corporate managers are in the nature of compensation if they *purport* to be compensatory.

Unfortunately, a disallowance of the corporation's deductions under §280G increases the loss suffered by the shareholders, who bear the ultimate burden of both the golden parachute payments and the additional corporate tax attributable to §280G. As if recognizing that §280G penalizes the wrong party to an abuse, Congress enacted §4999 as a companion provision, imposing a 20 percent excise tax on the recipient of a golden parachute payment. Query, however, whether in the future, canny insiders will require the corporation to reimburse them if they bail out and are caught by this tax.

6. Securities law violations. The tax implications of fines, penalties, civil damages, and legal expenses incurred by corporate officers, directors, shareholders, attorneys, accountants, and underwriters in criminal prosecutions and civil suits for violations of the federal securities laws are beyond the scope of this treatise; but comments on certain aspects of this area are in order at this point. The Supreme Court held in 1966 that legal expenses incurred in the unsuccessful defense of a criminal prosecution arising out of the taxpayer's business activities were deductible as business expenses and did not run afoul of the "frustration of public policy" doctrine; and this conclusion was later codified by legislation that, in effect, eliminated the ad hoc frustration doctrine by explicitly disallowing deductions for fines, penalties, bribes, and certain other payments.[51]

Thus, under §162(f), fines and penalties paid for violations of securities and other laws cannot be deducted, but legal expenses incurred by the cor-

---

[51] CIR v. Tellier, 383 US 687 (1966) (securities law fraud prosecution); Rev. Rul. 68-662. 1968-2 CB 69 (tax fraud prosecution); infra note 52. See generally Bittker, Federal Taxation of Income. Estates and Gifts, supra note 14, ¶ 20.3.3.

poration or its officers in defending against either criminal or civil charges are deductible.[52] Moreover, premiums paid for business liability insurance policies indemnifying corporate officers and directors (or attorneys, accountants, underwriters, and so forth) for expenses and liabilities incurred in connection with alleged securities law violations are deductible under §162(a), as applied by a 1969 revenue ruling.[53]

If a corporate insider repays so-called short-swing profits under §16(b) of the Securities Exchange Act of 1934, a deduction is allowable, but, in line with *Arrowsmith v. CIR,* it constitutes a capital loss rather than a deduction from ordinary income if, as would almost always be true, the insider's profit qualified as capital gain.[54]

7. Stock issuance expenses and related problems. Expenditures incurred by a corporation in issuing or reselling its own stock (whether upon initial organization or pursuant to a stock dividend, recapitalization, acquisitive reorganization, public offering, or private placement) are capital outlays that can be neither amortized nor deducted when the stock is ultimately retired or the corporation is liquidated.[55] These costs reduce the capital proceeds (if any) received by the corporation for its stock. The costs of registering stock

---

[52] Supra note 51. See also J.C. Bradford, 70 TC 584 (1978) (damages paid for fraudulent use of inside information held nondeductible capital expenditure); Rev. Rul. 80-119, 1980-1 CB 40 (legal expenses and out-of-court settlement payments by shareholder-director accused of violating §10(b) of Securities Exchange Act of 1934 held nondeductible capital expenditure attributable to acquisition of his stock). See Taggart, Fines, Penalties, Bribes, and Damage Payments and Recoveries, 25 Tax L. Rev. 611 (1970); S. Rep. No. 552, 91st Cong., 1st Sess. 273 (1969).

[53] Rev. Rul. 69-491, 1969-2 CB 22; see also Rev. Rul. 76-277, 1976-2 CB 41 (business liability insurance premiums deductible by corporate executives from adjusted gross income rather than from gross income).

[54] See Arrowsmith v. CIR, 344 US 6 (1952); Brown v. CIR, 529 F2d 609 (10th Cir. 1976), and cases there cited.

See generally Schenk, supra note 30; Note, Tax Treatment of Section 16(b) Payments, 27 Stan. L. Rev. 143 (1974).

[55] See generally McCrory Corp. v. US, 651 F2d 828 (2d Cir. 1981) (capitalized merger costs attributable to the issue of acquiring corporation's stock not deductible on subsequent disposition of acquired properties; such costs are never deductible); Pacific Coast Biscuit Co., 32 BTA 39 (1935); Van Keuren, 28 BTA 480 (1933); General Bancshares Corp. v. CIR, 326 F2d 712 (8th Cir.), cert. denied, 379 US 832 (1964) (stock dividend expenses); Rev. Rul. 67-125, 1967-1 CB 31.

See also Skaggs Co., 59 TC 201 (1972) (fee paid to investment banking group to insure that taxpayer would not have to redeem preferred stock during pendency of attempts to force conversion of preferred into common; held not §162 business expense, not deductible retirement premium, and not amortizable cost; rather, fee was nondeductible stock-issue related cost); Quality Brands, Inc., 67 TC 167 (1976) (costs of corporate name change; held nondeductible capital expenditure); Walton

with the Securities and Exchange Commission, either at or after original issuance, are similarly nondeductible capital structure costs, as are the costs of listing the stock on a stock exchange.[56] While the costs of equity financing are nondeductible capital items, the cost of issuing debt can be amortized over the term of the indebtedness,[57] thus adding yet another tax incentive for the use of debt instead of equity in the capital structure.

This discussion assumes that the stock is issued as planned. If, however, a proposed stock offering or change in the corporate capital structure is called off and the plan is abandoned, there is authority permitting a deduction for the preliminary costs.[58] The line separating abandonment from mere deferral, however, is easier to state than to draw.[59]

Hewett, 47 TC 483 (1967) (shareholder's payment of corporation's expenses of issuing stock to public; held nondeductible as not related to business of shareholder).

But see Rev. Rul. 73-463, 1973-2 CB 34 (right of shareholders of mutual fund to demand redemption makes company's capital-raising efforts, after its initial stock offering, a part of day-to-day operations; hence, expenses after 90-day initial stock offering period are deductible; same for expenses during and after 90-day period starting with post-effective statements relating to additional shares).

For further discussion, see infra ¶¶ 5.06, 11.08; and infra note 56.

[56] Rev. Rul. 69-330; 1969-1 CB 51 (registration); Dome Mines Ltd., 20 BTA 377 (1933) (listing on exchange); Davis v. CIR, 151 F2d 441 (8th Cir. 1945), cert. denied, 327 US 783 (1946) (shareholder's registration expenses for secondary public offering); Consumers Water Co. v. US, 369 F. Supp. 939 (D. Me. 1974) (stock registration costs nondeductible capital expenditure; extensive discussion); Affiliated Capital Corp., 88 TC No. 65 (1987) (updating registration).

But annual fees for maintaining stock exchange listings were held deductible in Chesapeake Corp. of Va., 17 TC 668 (1951) (acq.). The Service also allowed deductions for stock transfer fees paid to the corporation's registrar and transfer agent in Rev. Rul. 69-615, 1969-2 CB 26. Other corporate housekeeping expenses should similarly be deductible under §162 (e.g., annual reports, shareholder relations, proxy solicitation costs, and the like).

[57] See, e.g., Denver & R.G.W.R.R., 32 TC 43 (1959), aff'd on other issues, 279 F2d 368 (10th Cir. 1960), and cases cited therein; Rev. Rul. 70-353, 1970-2 CB 39 (bond issue discount deductibility); Rev. Rul. 70-359, 1970-2 CB 103; Rev. Rul. 70-360, 1970-2 CB 103 (method of amortizing bond issue expenses); Duncan Indus., Inc., 73 TC 266 (1979) (stock issue discount held deductible on facts as amortizable loan origination fee because stock issue tied into loan transaction).

[58] Rev. Rul. 67-125, 1967-1 CB 31; Sibley, Lindsay & Curr Co., 15 TC 106 (1950); Rev. Rul. 79-2, 1979-1 CB 98 (shareholder expenses of abandoned public stock offering deductible as ordinary loss).

If several capital adjustment plans are considered that are separate and distinct rather than merely alternative routes for the same transaction, the *Sibley* case permits the costs attributable to the abandoned plans to be deducted, but deduction will be denied where the taxpayer is unable to prove that the services rendered and the fees paid were divisible. See Arthur T. Galt, 19 TC 892 (1953), aff'd on other issues, 216 F2d 41 (7th Cir. 1954).

[59] See Denver & R.G.W.R.R., supra note 57; Chicago, M., St. P. & Pac. R.R., 404 F2d 960 (Ct. Cl. 1968). See generally Rev. Rul. 73-580, 1973-2 CB 86.

8. Organization, reorganization, and liquidation expenses. The tax treatment of these expenses is examined later in this chapter.[60]

¶ 5.05 DIVIDENDS-RECEIVED DEDUCTION AND RELATED PROBLEMS

Dividends received by a corporate taxpayer ordinarily qualify for the dividends-received deduction provided by §243 (generally 80 percent of dividends received from a domestic corporation subject to federal income taxes), §244 (at 1988 rates, about 47 percent of dividends received on certain preferred stock of public utilities), or §245 (80 percent of a specified portion of the dividends received from certain foreign corporations), all subject to the limitations imposed by §246.

Of these provisions, §243 is of principal importance.[61] By permitting the corporate taxpayer to deduct 80 percent (or more) of dividends received from other corporations, §243 reduces the effective maximum tax rate on dividends received by a corporation to 6.8 percent; that is, the top corporate tax rate of 34 percent is imposed on only 20 percent of the dividends received. If the corporation's taxable income is below $75,000 (the start of the 1988 top rate bracket), the effective tax rate on dividends received can range from a low of 3 percent (15 percent of 20 percent of dividends received) to 5 percent (25 percent of 20 percent of dividends received.)[62]

The salient features of §§243–245 are discussed in the following text.

1. Dividends from domestic corporations. Section 243(a)(1) provides generally that 80 percent of the amount received as dividends from a domes-

---

[60] See infra ¶ 5.06.

[61] From 1917–1935, corporations were not taxed on dividends received from other corporations in order to prevent the multiple taxation of corporate earnings as they passed from one corporation to another, possibly within the same chain of beneficial ownership. The law was revised in 1935, however, to exempt only 85 percent of the dividends received in order to discourage the use of multiple entities for tax avoidance and as a part of the New Deal program that pressed for the simplification of elaborate corporate structures. The 85 percent benchmark, adopted in 1935, was controlling until 1986, when it was lowered to 80 percent.

See generally Schaffer, The Income Tax on Intercorporate Dividends, 33 Tax Lawyer 161 (1979); Francis, The Tax on Intercorporate Dividends: Current Problems and Proposed Reforms, 64 Taxes 427 (1986).

[62] For the effect of the AMT on dividends, see infra notes 147 and 148. (The effective tax cost on dividends under AMT can increase to 12 percent if included in the book income preference and 16 percent under the adjusted current earnings preference.)

tic corporation that is subject to federal income taxation may be deducted.[63] The requirement that the paying corporation be subject to income taxation reflects the fact that the purpose of the deduction is to mitigate the multiple taxation of corporate earnings. In harmony with this principle, §243(c)(1) excludes amounts deductible by the paying corporation under §591 (relating to dividends paid by mutual savings banks and domestic building and loan associations, loosely referred to as "'interest"), and §243(c)(2) limits the deductibility of certain dividends received from a regulated investment company.

2. Dividends of affiliated groups. Section 243(a)(3) was enacted in 1964 as part of a general revision of the treatment of affiliated corporations; it permits a 100 percent deduction for certain intracorporate dividends paid from earnings accumulated during the period of affiliation, subject to an election under which all members of an affiliated group of corporations must consent to divide among them a single $100,000 exemption from the top 34 percent rate of §11(b) and the $250,000 minimum accumulated earnings credit. The election must also cover the foreign tax credit and certain other matters set out in §243(b). The treatment of multiple corporations, and affiliated groups in general, is considered in greater detail in Chapter 15.

3. Dividends on public utility preferred stock. Public utility corporations are allowed by §247 to deduct a portion of dividends paid by them on certain preferred stock.[64] Since (at 1988 rates) 14/34 of the dividend paid is deductible by the paying corporation, §244 requires the recipient corporation to take only the remaining 20/34 into account in computing its dividends-received deduction. The 80 percent deduction is applied against this residue, with the net result that 47.059 percent (i.e., $80/100 \times 20/34$) of the entire dividend received is deductible.

4. Dividends from certain foreign corporations. Dividends paid by a 10 percent owned foreign corporation qualify for the dividends-received deduction under §245 if (1) the paying corporation is not a foreign personal holding company or a passive foreign investment company,[65] (2) it is subject to federal income taxation; and (3) at least 10 percent (by voting power and

---

[63] In the case of a small business investment company (supra ¶ 1.06), the deduction is 100 percent of the dividends received, and the limit of §246(b) is inapplicable under §243(a)(2). In the case of certain electing affiliated groups, the deduction is also 100 percent by virtue of §243(a)(3), enacted in 1964. Infra ¶ 15.02.

[64] Supra ¶ 5.03, note 17.

[65] Infra ¶¶ 17.21 and 17.25.

value) of its stock is owned by the recipient corporation. If the dividends qualify under these tests, the 80 percent deduction is applied to a portion of the dividends, determined by reference to the ratio of the payor's post-1986 net earnings from sources within the United States to total post-1986 net earnings. By virtue of these complex limitations, the 80 (or 100) percent deduction is applicable to dividends paid by a foreign corporation only to the extent that, roughly speaking, they reflect income that has been subjected to U.S. taxation. Thus, if 60 percent of the foreign corporation's earnings are from business sources within the United States, 60 percent of its dividends will be eligible in the hands of a recipient corporation for the 80 percent deduction.[66]

If the foreign corporation is wholly owned by the U.S. corporate shareholders and if all of the subsidiary's gross income is effectively connected with a U.S. business, its dividends qualify for a 100 percent deduction under §245(b); in this situation, the foreign subsidiary is the economic equivalent of a U.S. enterprise.

5. Dividends from 10 percent owned foreign corporations: The deemed-paid foreign tax credit. Whereas intercorporate dividends between domestic corporations are substantially relieved from double taxation by the deduction mechanism of §243, relief from international double taxation is generally accomplished through the foreign tax credit rules of §§901–906. One of these provisions, the so-called deemed-paid foreign tax credit of §902, allows a domestic parent corporation that owns 10 percent or more of a foreign corporation and receives a dividend therefrom to elect to claim a so-called derivative foreign tax credit for taxes paid by the foreign corporation.[67]

6. Deductions by foreign corporations. A foreign corporation not engaged in trade or business in the United States is not allowed the 80 percent dividends-received deduction, or, for that matter, any other deductions, by virtue of §882; foreign corporations with a domestic business situs, however, are allowed to deduct items that are effectively connected with the U.S. business, including the §243 deduction if the dividends constitute U.S. business income.[68]

---

[66] The Tax Reform Act of 1986 extended the §245 deduction to corporations earning U.S. effectively connected income and to dividends from U.S. subsidiaries; the deduction is available only to U.S. 10 percent corporate shareholders and is calculated on a net basis. Moreover, any amount eligible for the deduction is treated as U.S. source income. See S. Rep. No. 313, 99th Cong., 2d Sess. 374–378 (1986).

[67] These provisions are considered in greater detail infra ¶ 17.11.

[68] These matters are considered infra ¶¶ 17.03 and 17.04.

7. Definition and amount of "dividend." As discussed in Chapter 7, the term "dividend," as used in §§243–245, is defined by §316. Although §§243–245 do not say so explicitly, dividends should not qualify for the dividends-received deduction unless they are includable in gross income. For this reason, stock dividends that are excluded from gross income under §305 should not give rise to a dividends-received deduction.[69] For the same reason, if a distribution is made in property other than money, the dividends-received deduction should be calculated on the property's fair market value, since §301(b) prescribes this method of determining the amount of the distribution. The regulations explicitly adopt this position with respect to the dividends-received deduction under §243,[70] but it seems equally applicable to the deduction authorized by §244.[71] Similarly, a distribution in partial or complete

---

[69] For §305, see infra ¶ 7.41. The Service takes the position that ordinary income is realized on a sale of stock rights (infra ¶ 7.44); it was held in Tobacco Prods. Export Corp., 21 TC 625 (1954) (nonacq.), that the income thus realized qualified for the dividends-received credit of the 1939 Code. See TSN Liquidating Corp. v. US, 624 F2d 1328 (5th Cir. 1980) (dividend in kind of unwanted portfolio securities, consisting of 78 percent of corporation's assets, followed by sale of stock by corporate shareholder, followed by buyer's capital contribution to its newly purchased corporation; held, alleged dividend not part of selling price, hence qualified for §243 deduction in hands of seller); Stranahan v. CIR, 472 F2d 867 (6th Cir. 1973) (sale of dividend rights currently taxable as dividend substitute); see also Rev. Rul. 82–11, 1982–1 CB 51 (sale of stock after record date but before ex-dividend date; held, corporate purchaser not entitled to §243 deduction, has no income on collection of dividend, and basis for shares is portion of purchase price not attributable to accrued dividend right, so no capital loss on resale of stock; corporate seller got §243 deduction because in effect it sold dividend right per *Lake* and *Horst* dividend substitution principles, infra ¶ 7.07, notes 123 and 124); Silco, Inc. v. US, 591 F. Supp. 480 (N.D. Tex. 1984) (owner on record date the taxable person); but reversed, 779 F2d 282 (5th Cir, 1986) (Rev. Rul. 82–11 was change in Service position and can only be applied prospectively). For similar results under amendments by the Tax Reform Act of 1984, see infra para. 9 of this section.

See generally Willens, Merger Arbitrage: The IRS Seeks to Terminate a Time-Honored Tradition, 2 J. Tax'n of Inv. 275 (1985); McKenna & Chudy, Tax Leveraged Investments: Section 246A; Section 7701(f), and Other Recent Developments, 13 J. Corp. Tax'n 3 (1986).

[70] Regs §1.243-1(c). For reasons explained infra ¶ 7.23, the valuation method specified by §301(b)(1)(B)(ii)—adjusted basis to the distributing corporation plus gain recognized on the distribution—is tantamount to using the property's fair market value. As noted in infra ¶ 7.23, however, property dividends to corporate shareholders will always be valued at market as a result of amendments in 1984. See H.R. 26–36, the Technical Corrections Act of 1987, §106(e)(10), providing for a single rule, fair market value under §301(b)(1).

[71] As to dividends received from foreign corporations, §245(c) provides that the amount of a property distribution that qualifies for treatment under §245 is to be determined under the rules of §301(b)(1)(B). Under §301(b)(1)(C), other property distributions from foreign corporations are to be taken into account at fair market

liquidation, since it is treated as the proceeds of a sale of the stock rather than as a dividend (see Chapters 9 and 11), would not qualify for the dividends-received deduction; the same should be true of a stock redemption if it escapes dividend treatment (see Chapter 9).[72] Likewise, other nondividend receipts should not be entitled to the dividends-received deduction of §243.[73] Reorganization boot dividends, however, have been held by the courts to qualify for the §243 dividends-received deduction, and the Service agrees.[74]

8. Overall restrictions on deductions. Although there are technically three separate dividends-received deductions (§243, for dividends paid by domestic corporations; §244, for preferred dividends paid by public utilities; and §245, for dividends paid by certain foreign corporations), they are aggregated by §246 for the purpose of imposing certain limitations:

(a) Certain distributing corporations excluded. Section 246(a) provides that the dividends-received deductions of §§243–245 do not apply to dividends paid by corporations that are exempt from tax under §501 (charitable corporations, federal instrumentalities,[75] mutual telephone companies, and

---

value. If the distribution is only partly under §245, proration is required in accordance with §§301(b)(1)(C)(i) and 301(b)(1)(C)(ii). But see the Technical Corrections Act of 1987, supra note 70.

[72] See §331(b); Roberts Gage Coal Co., 2 TC 488 (1943) (acq.); Fostoria Glass Co. v. Yoke, 45 F. Supp. 962, 965 (N.D. W. Va. 1942); Rev. Rul. 77–226, 1977–2 CB 90 (corporate purchaser of shares, following tender offer by issuer, sought to treat redemption of part of block as equivalent of dividend; held contemporaneous sale of remaining shares under prearranged plan inconsistent with dividend equivalency theory; §243 deduction denied). For application of Rev. Rul. 77–226, see GCM 39290 (Oct, 15, 1984), 23 Tax Notes 238 (1984); see also Willens, supra note 69; McKenna & Chudy, supra note 69. Since 1982, corporate shareholders can no longer qualify for partial liquidation treatment; infra ¶ 9.08.

For a related problem under the deemed-paid foreign tax credit provision of §902, see Associated Tel. & Tel. Co. v. US, 306 F2d 824 (2d Cir. 1962), cert. denied, 371 US 950 (1963) (distribution in complete liquidation not a dividend under §902); Fowler Hosiery Co. v. CIR, 301 F2d 394 (7th Cir. 1962) (same for partial liquidation).

[73] See Liston Zander Credit Co. v. US, 276 F2d 417 (5th Cir. 1960) (alleged dividends were refunds of insurance premiums, not eligible for §243 deduction); US v. Georgia R.R. & Banking Co., 348 F2d 278 (5th Cir. 1965) (§243 deduction belongs to beneficial owner of stock on which dividends were paid); CIR v. Waterman S.S. Corp., 430 F2d 1185 (5th Cir. 1970), cert. denied, 401 US 939 (1971) (alleged dividend held part of selling price for stock); infra ¶ 7.07; supra note 69.

[74] See infra ¶ 14.34; see also King Enter., Inc. v. US, 418 F2d 511 (Ct. Cl. 1969); American Mfg. Co., 55 TC 204 (1970); Rev. Rul. 72–327, 1972–2 CB 197; Willens, supra note 69.

[75] But see Rev. Rul. 56–510, 1956–2 CB 168 (dividends paid by Federal National Mortgage Association qualify; although exempt, it makes payments to Treasury in lieu of taxes).

so forth) or §521 (farmers' cooperative associations). These corporations are disqualified because their earnings are wholly or partially tax-exempt; §246(a) thus buttresses, and in part overlaps, the rules set out in §§243–245.

In the case of corporations under §§501 and 521, the disqualification of §246(a) is operative if the forbidden status exists during the year in which the distribution is made or existed in the preceding taxable year.

(b) Ceiling on aggregate deduction. Unless the taxpayer corporation has incurred a net operating loss in the taxable year, the aggregate deduction under §§243–245 may not exceed 80 percent of taxable income computed without regard to the deduction under §172 (net operating loss carry-over from another year), §§243–245, or §247 (dividends paid on public utility preferred stock.)[76]

(c) Sales of stock ex-dividend. Before 1958, the dividends-received deduction held out to the corporate taxpayer the possibility of buying stock just before a dividend became payable and selling it immediately thereafter in order to deduct the loss on the sale (presumably equal to the amount of the dividend, assuming no other market fluctuations), while paying income tax on only 15 percent (under then-applicable law) of this amount. A similar manipulative device was the maintenance of both long and short positions in the stock over the dividend payment date in order to deduct the amount of the dividend paid to the lender of the short stock from ordinary income while reporting only 15 percent of the dividend received on the long stock. To close these loopholes, §246(c) was enacted in 1958 and was strengthened in 1984. This provision denies any deduction under §§243–245 if the stock is not held for more than 45 days (90 days in the case of certain preferred stock), the holding period being tolled if the taxpayer substantially diminished its risk of loss from holding the stock.[77] Section 246(c) also denies the deduction if the taxpayer maintained a short position (or was subject to a similar obligation with respect to the dividend) in substantially identical stock or securities.[78]

---

[76] For this complex but rarely encountered restriction, see Graichen, The Net Operating Loss, 16 NYU Inst. on Fed. Tax'n 865, 867 (1958); Rev. Rul. 56–151, 1956–1 CB 382.

[77] See S. Rep. No. 1983, 85th Cong., 2d Sess. 28–29, 139–140 (1958). But cf. CIR v. Waterman S.S. Corp., supra note 73; Rev. Rul. 80-238, 1980-2 CB 96 (writing call on stock held by corporate shareholder did not shorten holding period for §246(c) purposes). But see restrictions imposed by §263(h), infra note 78.

[78] Section 263(h), enacted in 1984, also requires payments in lieu of dividends on stock sold short to be capitalized unless the short sale is held open for at least 46 days (more than one year in the case of extraordinary dividends), thus reversing the holding in Rev. Rul. 62-42, 1962-1 CB 133. See also §7701(f), also enacted in 1984, authorizing regulations to prevent the use of related parties to avoid provisions that deal with the linking of borrowing to investment or diminishing risks.

(d) Debt-financed portfolio stock dividends. Section 246A, enacted in 1984, deals with the tax rate arbitrage effects created by the use of leveraged portfolio stock, under which interest on debt incurred to finance the investment was fully deductible, while the associated dividend income on the acquired stock was taxed at a low effective rate because of the dividends-received deduction. Section 246A reduces the recipient corporation's §243 deduction to the extent of the debt financed percentage of the stock. Thus, if half of the stock basis is debt financed, half of the §243 deduction can be denied; the reduction, however, is not to exceed the amount of deductible interest.[79]

This provision does not apply, however, if the taxpayer acquired at least 50 percent of the stock (or owned at least 20 percent, and 5 or fewer corporate shareholders owned at least 50 percent of the paying corporation); neither does it apply if the taxpayer is entitled to the 100 percent dividends-received deduction; see §§246A(b)(1) and 246A(c)(2).

9. Basis reduction for extraordinary dividends. Section 1059, also enacted in 1984 (and strengthened in 1986), imposes a special basis reduction rule that requires a corporate shareholder to reduce its basis for stock owned by it to the extent of the nontaxed portion of any "extraordinary dividend," defined by §1059(c) as a dividend equaling or exceeding a prescribed "threshold percentage" (5 percent for preferred stock, 10 percent for other stock) of the underlying stock unless the stock was held for more than two years before the dividend announcement date or satisfies certain other conditions.

To illustrate: If *P* Corporation purchased stock of target *T*, which then distributed a dividend equal to or greater than 10 percent of *P*'s basis for its *T* stock, *P* would reduce the basis of the *T* stock (but not below

---

See generally Eustice, The Tax Reform Act of 1984, ¶¶ 3.02[3] (dividend-received deduction limitations), 3.04[3][c] (§7701(f) regulations), 5.05[6][c] (short-sale expenses) (Warren, Gorham & Lamont, Inc., 1984); Willens, supra note 69; McKenna & Chudy, supra note 69.

[79] See Eustice, supra note 78, ¶ 3.02[3][b]; Willens, supra note 69; McKenna & Chudy, supra note 69; Committee on Corporations, N.Y. State Bar Association, Tax Section, Report on Suggested Section 246A Regulations, 27 Tax Notes 203 (1985). The linkage between borrowing and investment is a tighter nexus under §246A than that under a similar provision, §265(2), since the statute requires *direct* attribution. See also §§7701(f), supra note 78, and 246A(f) (regulations authorized to reduce interest deduction in lieu of §243 deduction).

For proposals to expand the approach of §279 to take account of the tender offer movement of the 1980s, see Sheppard, Should Junk Bond Interest Deductions be Disallowed?, 34 Tax Notes 1142 (1987).

zero) by the amount of its §243 deduction unless the transaction satisfied one of §1059's exceptions. On a later sale or exchange of the stock, *P*'s gain or loss would be computed by reference to its basis as reduced by §1059; if the reduction was not fully absorbed by the stock's basis, the remainder would be treated as gain at that time.

Section 1059 does not apply to dividends that qualify for the 100 percent dividends-received deduction of §243(b) or, according to the Conference Report,[80] to dividends included in a consolidated return.[81]

¶ 5.06   ORGANIZATION, REORGANIZATION, AND LIQUIDATION EXPENDITURES

1. **Organization expenses.** Before 1954, a corporation's organization expenditures, such as legal fees for drafting the charter, bylaws, and stock certificates, could not be deducted when paid or incurred, but were treated as investments to be deducted as a loss on dissolution or, in the unusual case of a corporation of limited duration, to be amortized over the life specified in its charter.[82] For the stated purpose of conforming "tax accounting more closely with general business accounting for these costs,"[83] §248 was enacted

---

[80] H.R. Conf. Rep. No. 841, 99th Cong., 2d Sess. 166 (1986). The consolidated return regulations prescribe their own basis reduction under the investment basis adjustment rules, infra ¶ 15.23, so the statutory rule of §1059 is not needed here.

[81] See Eustice, Kuntz, Lewis, & Deering, supra note 2, ¶ 2.05[4]; see also Silco v. US, supra note 69. The conference report, supra note 80, notes that the §1059 basis will *not* apply in computing earnings and profits on the later sale of the stock; infra ¶ 7.03. See also §106(c) of the Technical Corrections Act of 1987, supra note 70.

[82] See Shellabarger Grain Prods. Co. v. CIR, 146 F2d 177, 185 (7th Cir. 1944); Hershey Mfg. Co. v. CIR, 43 F2d 298 (10th Cir. 1930).

See generally Weissman, Allowable Deductions on the Formation, Reorganization, and Liquidation of a Corporation, 53 Nw. U.L. Rev. 681 (1959) (re pre-1954 Code case law); Cohen, supra note 29; Grossman, Tax Treatment of Professional Fees Related to Asset Acquisitions and Changes in Business Entities, supra note 28; Maier, Deduction of Expenses Incurred in Corporate Reorganizations and Liquidations, 1968 So. Cal. Fed. Tax'n Inst. 253; N.Y. State Bar Association, Tax Section, Report on the Ancillary Tax Effects of Different Forms of Reorganizations, 34 Tax L. Rev. 477 (1979).

For the deductibility of organizational expenditures by a liquidating corporation, see infra ¶ 11.08; Weiss, Income Tax Deductions on Corporate Termination, 9 Tax L. Rev. 490 (1954).

[83] According to Paton, Accountants' Handbook 128 (Ayer, reprinted 1976), however, accountants agree that early amortization of organization costs is proper, but a more reasonable view is to treat these expenses as an asset to be amortized only when the corporation contracts or liquidates. See also American Inst. of Accountants, 43

in 1954 to permit the corporation to elect to amortize its organizational expenditures over a period of 60 months or more from the month in which the corporation begins business.[84] The regulations state that the date a corporation begins business is a question of fact and that ordinarily it is the date when the corporation "starts the business operation for which it was organized," not the date when it comes into existence.[85]

The term "organizational expenditures" is defined by §248(b) to mean any expenditure that is

(1) Incident to the creation of the corporation;

(2) Chargeable to capital account; and

(3) Of a character that, if expended incident to the creation of a corporation having a limited life, would be amortizable over such life.

The regulations list as examples of expenditures that will qualify under §248 "legal services incident to the organization of the corporation, such as drafting the corporate charter, bylaws, minutes of organizational meetings, terms of original stock certificates, and the like; necessary accounting services; expenses of temporary directors and of organizational meetings of directors or stockholders; and fees paid to the State of incorporation."[86]

The regulations go on to exclude expenditures connected with issuing or selling stock, such as commissions, professional fees, and printing costs.[87] This exclusion of the expense of raising capital is in harmony with *Surety Finance Co. v. CIR*, holding that such expenses are the equivalent of selling the stock at a discount and that they do not create an asset that is exhausted over the life of the corporation.[88] Similar expenses in selling debt securities are also excluded from §248 by the regulations, but these costs may be amortized over the term of the loan on the theory that they increase the interest expense on the borrowed funds.[89] The regulations also state that expendi-

---

Accounting Res. Bull. (1951) recommending that certain intangibles (including organization costs) be amortized only if they will not continue to have value during the entire life of the enterprise. But see Rev. Rul. 67-15, 1967-1 CB 71 (corporation can elect §248 amortization, even though expenditure capitalized on books).

[84] S. Rep. No. 1622, 83d Cong., 2d Sess. 37 (1954).

[85] Regs. §1.248-1(a)(3).

[86] Regs. §1.248-1(b)(2).

[87] Regs. §1.248-1(b)(3)(i), discussed supra ¶ 5.04, para. 7.

[88] Surety Fin. Co. v. CIR, 77 F2d 221 (9th Cir. 1935) (endorsed by S. Rep. No. 1622, supra note 84, at 224); see also Affiliated Capital Corp., supra note 56.

[89] Helvering v. Union Pac. Ry., 293 US 282 (1934); Molloy, The Ambiguous Tax Nature of the Various Costs of Borrowing Capital, 11 Tax L. Rev. 373 (1956); Denver & R.G.W.R.R., supra note 57.

tures connected with the transfer of assets to a corporation do not qualify for amortization under §248; no examples are given, but presumably the reference is to the cost of title searches, recordation, transportation, and so forth, which would be added to the basis of the assets themselves, to be depreciated over the life of the assets or offset against the proceeds when the assets are sold. Finally, the regulations state that expenditures connected with a corporation's reorganization, unless "directly incident to the creation of a corporation," do not qualify under §248, echoing a statement in the Senate report on the 1954 Code.[90] Some reorganizations include the creation of a new corporation (e.g., some consolidations and transfers to controlled corporations), however, and this part of the expenses can be amortized under §248.[91]

The election to amortize organization expenditures under §248 must be made on or before the date for filing the tax return for the taxable year in which the corporation begins business (§248(c)). The election must specify an amortization period of 60 months or longer that must commence with the month in which the taxpayer begins business and may not be altered, and the expenditures are to be deducted ratably over the specified period.[92] The regulations state that an election "shall apply" to all of the corporation's organization expenditures, thus prohibiting a partial election, but that only expenditures incurred before the end of the taxable year in which business begins will qualify.[93] This statement leaves ambiguous the status of subsequently incurred organization expenditures; it may be the position of the

---

[90] S. Rep. No. 1622, supra note 84, at 224.

[91] As to the possibility of deducting the balance of organization expenses on a later dissolution of the reorganized corporation, see Weissman, supra note 82, at 709; Weiss, supra note 82, at 492; Kingsford Co., 41 TC 646 (1964) (acq.) (organization expenses deductible on liquidation of corporation in Type C reorganization); infra ¶ 5.06, para. 2.

See generally Reef Corp., ¶ 65,072 P-H Memo. TC (1965), aff'd on other issues, 368 F2d 125 (5th Cir. 1966) (organization expenses of creating a new corporation in the context of a Type D reorganization amortizable under §248); Rev. Rul. 70-241, 1970-1 CB 84 (organization expenses of new corporation, created incident to a Type F reorganization, amortizable under §248); Deering Milliken, Inc., 59 TC 469 (1973) (taxpayer formed by consolidation of several existing corporations; legal fees and related expenses incurred in connection with appraisal proceeding by dissenting shareholders not deductible organization expenses under §248 because not functionally related to creation of new corporation, per *Woodward* and *Hilton Hotels*).

[92] In Bay Sound Transp. Co. v. US, 20 AFTR2d 5418 (S.D. Tex, 1967), aff'd in part and rev'd in part on other issues, 410 F2d 505 (5th Cir. 1969), it was held that filing of a return that erroneously claimed a full current deduction for organization expenses constituted a binding nonelection under §248.

[93] Regs. §1.248-1(a)(2).

Treasury that they are not only outside §248 but also disqualified for deduction on dissolution.

Failing an election, organizational expenditures may be deducted only on dissolution (except for a corporation of limited life) under the judicial rules developed before the enactment of §248.[94] If a corporation that elects under §248 is dissolved before its expenditures have been fully amortized, it should be entitled to deduct the balance at that time, but §248 is silent on this point.[95] Deductibility in such a case should be sustained, however, on the ground that organizational expenses represent an investment in the corporate shell, which is in effect abandoned as worthless on liquidation.

Not all expenditures of organizing a corporation will be amortizable under §248 or deductible upon its liquidation; some expenditures, usually those associated with the issuance, sale, registration, and listing of the corporation's own stock, are never deductible, as these costs are treated as permanent charges to capital rather than deferred expenses.[96] Moreover, organization costs incurred by the shareholders (as opposed to those incurred by the new corporation) do not qualify for amortization under §248 but must ordinarily be capitalized as part of the transferors' stock basis under the *Woodward* and *Hilton Hotels* principle that costs originating in the acquisition process constitute capital expenditures.[97]

Expenses incurred in amending the corporation's charter, although similar to organizational expenses, cannot satisfy the requirements of §248(b)(1), since they are usually incurred after the enterprise has gotten under way.[98] Exclusion from §248, however, should not bar a deduction when the corporation liquidates.

When a corporation with unamortized organization expenses undergoes a reorganization (see Chapter 14) that does not terminate its corporation existence (e.g., a recapitalization, or the acquisition of all of its stock solely in exchange for the voting stock of the acquiring corporation in a Type B reorganization), the corporation's deferred organization expense account is unaf-

---

[94] Shellabarger Grain Prods. Co. v. CIR, supra note 82; Liquidating Co., 33 BTA 1173 (1936); Koppers Co. v. US, 278 F2d 946 (Ct. Cl. 1960); Hollywood Baseball Ass'n, 42 TC 234 (1964); Kingsford Co., supra note 91.

[95] See infra ¶ 11.08.

[96] Supra ¶ 5.04, para. 7.

[97] Supra ¶ 5.04, para. 2.
Individual incorporator's expenses for tax advice in connection with the corporate organization may, however, be deductible under §212(3); see Kaufman v. US, 227 F. Supp. 807 (E.D. Mo. 1963) (cost of getting tax ruling on a merger deductible).

[98] See, e.g., Borg & Beck Co., 24 BTA 995 (1931) (acq.). But see Rev. Rul. 63-259, 1963-2 CB 95 (expenses of renewing charter amortizable under §248). Also see, e.g., US v. General Bancshares Corp., 388 F2d 184 (8th Cir. 1968) (expenses of changing corporation's name a nondeductible capital expenditure).

fected. But if the taxpayer corporation is acquired by another corporation in a Type A (merger or consolidation) or a Type C reorganization (assets are transferred to the acquiring corporation in exchange for its stock), or if the taxpayer corporation reincorporates into another corporate shell (in a Type F or in certain nondivisive Type D reorganizations), matters are less clear. It is likely, but not certain, that the transferor corporation's unamortized organization expense account passes over to the acquiring corporation by virtue of §§381(a)(2) and 381(c)(4) and can be amortized by it.[99] Carry-over treatment under §381 should be compared with the confusion under pre-1954 Code case law, under which deductibility of the transferor corporation's capitalized organization expenses depended on whether its legal existence terminated in the reorganization or survived; deduction was permitted if the taxpayer dissolved but was denied if the merger resulted in continued corporate existence.[100] The vitality of these decisions after the passage of §381 is doubtful, but their effects can still be felt if the reorganization does not constitute a §381(a) transaction or if it is held that capitalized organization expenses do not constitute a §381(c) carry-over item.

2. Expenses of reorganization. The well-established rule in this area is that amounts incurred to effectuate a corporate "reorganization" (in the broad sense of a rearrangement resulting in a restructuring of the corporate entity or enterprise, even if not a technical "reorganization" as defined by §368(a) (see Chapter 14) are not currently deductible as business expenses under §162 by the person incurring such costs.[101] The reasons given for

---

[99] See Regs. §1.381(c)(4)-1(a)(1)(ii), which provides that an acquiring corporation in a §381 transaction takes into account the acquired corporation's dollar balances that, because of its method of accounting, were not required or permitted to be deducted in full prior to the acquisition. See also infra ¶ 16.13.

See Rev. Rul. 70-241, 1970-1 CB 84 (unamortized §248 expenses carried over to successor corporation in a Type F reorganization; presumably, same result would occur in Types A and C reorganizations); see also McCrory Corp. v. US, supra note 55.

[100] Citizens Trust Co., 20 BTA 392 (1930) (merger preserved identity; no deduction); Motion Pictures Capital Corp. v. CIR, 80 F2d 872 (2d Cir. 1936) (same); Kingsford Co., supra note 91; Koppers Co. v. US, supra note 94 (§332 liquidation of controlled subsidiary; deduction allowed); see also Vulcan Materials Co. v. US, 446 F2d 690 (5th Cir.), cert. denied, 404 US 942 (1971), (deduction denied for previously capitalized organization and reorganization expenses upon a statutory merger of the taxpayer into another corporation following *Citizens Trust* and distinguishing *Kingsford* as a true dissolution); accord, Canal-Randolph Corp. v. US, 568 F2d 28 (7th Cir. 1977); see also articles cited supra note 82.

[101] See articles cited supra note 82. See also Rev. Rul. 73-580, 1973-2 CB 86 (expenses of in-house merger and acquisition staff must be capitalized; costs of abandoned acquisition plans deductible in year of abandonment). See Tax Mgmt. Memo.

denying deductibility of these costs vary from case to case. Most cases hold that they are capital in nature, resulting in a continuing benefit to the reorganized or successor corporation, so that they either should be capitalized in the basis of a separate asset or added to the basis of other property if related thereto. Other cases have implied that, while necessary, the expenses of a reorganization are unusual in a corporation's life and thus are not ordinary within the meaning of §162(a), a conclusion that now seems highly questionable in light of actual corporate practice. Still other cases have suggested that such costs constitute a reduction, or discount, in the value of the property acquired in the transaction and hence cannot be deducted even upon liquidation, by analogy to the stock issue expense cases.[102] Finally, it has been argued that the policy of nondeductibility for those expenses is based on a desire to put reorganization acquisitions on a par with regular taxable purchases, where acquisition costs are treated as part of the property's basis.[103]

Like all general rules, however, these are subject to important exceptions. The tax treatment of reorganization expenses mirrors the complexity and variety of the problems one encounters in the tax-free reorganization area generally (see Chapter 14). In the final analysis, deductibility of a particular expense turns on the mix of such factors as (1) the nature of the expense; (2) its relationship and proximity to the reorganization transaction; (3) the person who incurred it (transferor corporation, transferee corporation, or the shareholders and security holders of the reorganizing companies); (4) the form and structure of the particular transaction (i.e., merger, consolidation, stock-for-stock exchange, stock-for-assets exchange, transfer of assets to a controlled corporation, reincorporation, recapitalization, corporate division, or insolvency reorganization); (5) whether the transaction is actually consummated; and (6) the ability of the taxpayer claiming deductibility to identify with reasonable exactitude the functional steps in the reorganization proceedings to which the costs relate and the parties for whose benefit they were incurred.

(BNA) No. 74-09, supra note 34; Rev. Rul. 77-204, 1977-1 CB 40 (bankruptcy reorganization expenses nondeductible §263 capital expenditures; but bankruptcy liquidation expenses deductible, and expenses of operating business during bankruptcy deductible whether proceeding is a reorganization or a liquidation).

[102] Supra ¶ 5.04, para. 7.

[103] Supra ¶ 5.04, para. 2. See generally McCrory Corp. v. US, supra note 55 (court adopted bifurcated approach to capitalized merger costs; merger costs attributable to acquisition of target's assets were deductible on subsequent disposition of those assets by acquiring corporation; but expense attributable to issuance of the stock used to effect the acquisition never deductible).

See also §195 (election to amortize start-up costs of new business over five years); supra ¶ 5.04, note 36.

The expenses that can arise in effecting a reorganization are many and varied, including preliminary investigation and negotiation expenses; costs of preparing legal documents required to effect the reorganization; finder's fees; appraisal expenses; legal and accounting fees for preparation of SEC registration statements; fees for audit and preparation of financial statements; costs of proxy statements and the solicitation of shareholders; costs of shareholders' meetings; costs of amending the terms of existing indentures, mortgages, and loan agreements; costs of amending the corporate charter; expenses in selling or disposing of unwanted assets; expenses incident to the transfer of assets; legal research bearing on corporate law, tax law, or other legal problems presented by the reorganization plan; costs of obtaining a tax ruling; costs of listing the issued securities on an exchange; charges made by transfer agents; and court costs and other litigation expenses arising out of the reorganization. In addition to costs directly associated with the reorganization transaction itself, collateral expenses may be incurred in organizing new corporations and/or in liquidating corporate parties to the reorganization. These amounts, if sufficiently identifiable, may stand on a different footing from the pure reorganization expense items.

If any of these costs are to be deductible, accurate records of who sustained them and the proceedings to which they relate are essential; a failure to allocate costs contemporaneously will not foreclose a later allocation by the courts, but the chances of losing on burden-of-proof grounds are increased by lack of attention to itemization,[104] especially since these expenses are difficult to apportion under the best of circumstances.

In acquisitive reorganization transactions (whether the form is an acquisition of assets or of stock and whether the corporate fusion is by merger, consolidation, or practical merger in a Type C reorganization), expenses of the *acquiring* corporation would seem to be the most vulnerable to capital expenditure classification. Here, the Supreme Court decisions in *Woodward* and *Hilton Hotels*[105] that costs originating in the acquisition process (whether the transaction is taxable or tax-free) must be treated as nondeductible capital items are probably conclusive of the capitalization question. Even here, however, some of the expenses may be deductible or amortizable. For example, where a new subsidiary is created to act as the acquiring vehicle, its nativity expenses may qualify as amortizable organization expenses under Regs. §1.248-1(b)(4) to the extent that they are attributable to its initial creation. Where two corporations consolidate to form a new corporation, the costs attributable to the newly created corporation may

---

[104] Compare Sibley, Lindsay, & Curr Co., supra note 58, with Arthur T. Galt, supra note 58. See generally National Starch & Chem. Corp., ¶ 86,512 P-H Memo. TC (question of fact; no summary judgment for taxpayer or government).

[105] Supra ¶ 5.04, para. 2.

be amortizable under §248.[106] Conversely, some of the costs of the acquiring corporation (or of a subsidiary, if that is the vehicle utilized) may be attributable to the issuance of its own stock and neither deductible nor amortizable. If the proposed acquisition is abandoned, however, the Service agrees with decisions allowing the potential suitor to deduct its preliminary costs as an abandonment loss under §165, and one case allowed a deduction for reorganization plans that were discarded by the parties, even though an alternate plan was in fact consummated.[107]

If the acquiring corporation's expenses of effecting the reorganization are treated as capital expenses, as is usually the case, it is not clear how such expenses are to be capitalized. If they can be allocated to the acquisition of specific assets, an addition to the basis of such property seems in order, but if an allocation is not feasible, the costs presumably should be capitalized as a separate asset on the books of the acquiring company. Expenses of setting up a new subsidiary or of transferring the acquired assets to a new or existing subsidiary should be added to the parent's basis for its stock in the subsidiary.[108]

The *acquired* corporation's reorganization expenses in an acquisitive reorganization transaction likewise are generally not deductible currently,[109] although the proper treatment of these expenses is unclear. If capitalized, do these items pass over to the acquiring corporation via the carry-over basis rules of §362(b) or the tax attribute carry-over rules of §381? Do they represent part of the transferor corporation's cost of acquiring the transferee's stock (under *Woodward* and *Hilton Hotels*) to be added to its §358 basis for the acquired stock? Or do they evaporate into thin air? If the transferor corporation liquidates as part of the reorganization plan, can the liquidation and dissolution expenses be severed from the reorganization expense category and deducted?[110]

---

[106] Infra note 114.

[107] Rev. Rul. 67-125, 1973-2 CB 86, Rev. Rul. 73-580, 1967-1 CB 31, Sibley, Lindsay, & Curr Co., supra note 58.

[108] But see McCrory Corp. v. US, supra note 55 (costs attributable to asset acquisition via merger added to asset basis and deductible on later disposition of acquired assets; costs attributable to stock issued by acquiring corporation never deductible); but cf. §195 (election to amortize start-up, investigation, and preopening costs of new business over five years); supra note ¶ 5.04, note 36.

[109] See National Starch & Chem. Corp., supra note 104 (target's expenses in a reverse cash merger); Motion Pictures Capital Corp., supra note 100; articles cited supra note 82.

[110] In Kingsford Co., supra note 91, the Tax Court allowed the liquidating transferor corporation to deduct its capitalized organization expenses, even though the dissolution occurred as part of a Type C reorganization. The theory of this decision would seem to permit the transferor corporation to deduct its own regular liquida-

The few authorities that have focused on these problems are not illuminating. Most likely, the transferor's capitalized reorganization costs should carry over as an asset or as a corporate attribute to the acquiring corporation. Some of these costs should probably be added to its §358 basis for the stock or securities received in the exchange if it continues in existence holding the transferee corporation's stock or securities.[111] However, allocating costs to the stock acquisition component of the reorganization will not be an easy matter. Where the transferor corporation liquidates in a practical merger Type C reorganization, the Tax Court has permitted its liquidation expenses and capitalized organization expenses to be deducted.[112] If, however, dissolution of the transferor occurs pursuant to a statutory merger or consolidation (a Type A reorganization), the courts so far have denied deduction for the transferor's liquidation expenses and capitalized organization expenses on the ground that the transferor corporation's existence continues and carries over into the successor corporation.[113] The line between an existence-terminating liquidation and a continuity-preserving reorganization is at best technical, and the attempt to draw it has been properly criticized. The acquired corporation ought to be able to deduct its liquidation and dissolution expenses whether the acquisition is cast in the form of a Type C or a Type A reorganization,[114] but the courts have shown no signs of abandoning their emphasis on formalities in this area.[115]

---

tion expenses if they can be adequately identified and severed from the costs of participating in the reorganization.

[111] If the transferor liquidates as part of the reorganization (as it does in a merger or consolidation, and as it must (after 1984) in a Type C practical merger reorganization) (infra ¶¶ 14.12 and 14.14), its basis for the transferee corporation's stock or securities becomes irrelevant, since the liquidating corporation's distributee-shareholders derive their basis for the distributed stock or securities from their basis in their stock or securities of the transferor corporation (infra ¶ 14.34).

[112] Kingsford Co., supra note 91.

[113] See cases supra note 100.

[114] Even as to Type A reorganizations, there is apparently a further distinction between the statutory merger of one corporation into another corporation and a consolidation of two or more corporations into a newly created corporation; in the latter situation, the expenses of creating the new corporation ought to be amortizable under Regs. §1.248-1(b)(4) as organizational expenditures (at least where the costs do not relate to the issuance of its stock or to the transfer of assets to the new corporation). This distinction is a slender reed on which to hang deductibility for part of the reorganization costs, and it places a considerable premium on form over economic substance. But the reorganization area is so fraught with technicalities that one more is probably not fatal. See Rev. Rul. 70-241, 1970-1 CB 84 (organization expenses of corporation created pursuant to Type F reorganization; held amortizable under §248).

[115] See, e.g., Vulcan Materials Co. v US, supra note 100; see also National Starch & Chem. Corp., supra note 104.

Expenses of divisive reorganizations (see Chapter 13), although also generally nondeductible under the principles discussed above,[116] raise an additional set of problems that merit comment. Several decisions have allowed the transferor distributing corporation to deduct the expenses of effectuating a divisive reorganization where the costs were not incident to the issuance of its own stock or the creation of a new corporation.[117] Favorable decisions in these cases rested on the theory that the taxpayers did not acquire a capital asset or change their capital structure as a result of the transaction, but merely preserved or protected existing assets and rights or contracted the scope of their activities. As the court stated in *General Bancshares*, the dominant aspect of the plan of divestment was in the nature of a partial liquidation, and any technical reorganization of the taxpayer's corporate structure was merely incidental to liquidation: The court tested deductibility of the expenses by reference to the effects of the transaction at the corporate level, not at the shareholder level; expenses incurred by the parent in organizing the controlled corporation would, however, be nondeductible capital expenditures to be added to its basis for its stock in the newly created subsidiary.[118] If the corporate division takes the form of a split-up (whereby assets are transferred to two or more controlled corporations and the transferor corporation then liquidates) rather than a spin-off or split-off (see Chapter 13), the *General Bancshares* approach presumably would allow deduction of the liquidation expenses rather than require their capitalization as reorganization expenses.

Expenses of recapitalizing a corporation generally are capital expenditures for the acquisition of an intangible capital asset (i.e., the altered corporate structure) and, hence, are not currently deductible.[119] This leaves open

---

[116] See articles cited supra note 82.

[117] US v. General Bancshares Corp., supra note 98 (spin-off); US v. Transamerica Corp., 392 F2d 522 (9th Cir. 1968) (spin-off); E.I. du Pont & Co. v. US, 296 F. Supp. 823 (D. Del. 1969) (non-pro rata split-off, with taxpayer continuing to own the corporate shell), rev'd, 432 F2d 1052 (3d Cir. 1970) (capital per *Woodward* and *Hilton*); El Paso Co. v. US, 694 F2d 703 (Fed. Cir. 1982) (non-organizational expenses of forced divestiture proceedings incurred by parent corporation attributable to successful plan, and abandoned plans are generally deductible §162 expenses; transaction in substance a partial liquidation because of contraction effects; no continuing benefit for taxpayer or its subsidiaries).

[118] US v. General Bancshares Corp., supra note 98; see also El Paso Co. v. US, supra note 117 (divestiture proceeding expenses deductible; but no deduction for organization of subsidiary divestiture vehicle, start-up costs of new subsidiary's business, and costs of obtaining ruling on tax consequences of reorganization transaction). But see Bilar Tool & Die Corp. v. CIR, 530 F2d 708 (6th Cir. 1976) (expenses of non-pro rata split-off; held nondeductible capital structure adjustment costs); E.I. du Pont & Co. v. US, supra note 117 (same).

[119] See. e.g., Mills Estate, Inc. v. CIR, 206 F2d 244 (2d Cir. 1953); Gravois Planing Mill Co. v. CIR, 299 F2d 199 (8th Cir. 1962); Farmers Union Corp. v. CIR, 300

the possibilty of a loss deduction on liquidation of the corporation, but the possibility that at least some of these costs may be allocated to the issuance of new stock and, hence, permanently disallowed under the stock issue expense cases should not be overlooked. Moreover, the cost of effecting a recapitalization exchange of debt securities, as opposed to an exchange of equity instruments, will presumably be amortizable over the life of the new securities, since these costs have a definite and limited useful life.[120]

Shareholder expenses incurred pursuant to a reorganization or recapitalization of their corporation also ordinarily constitute nondeductible capital expenditures to be added to the basis of the stock or securities distributed to them in the reorganization transaction.[121] In one decision, a shareholder was permitted to deduct expenses incurred in obtaining a tax ruling from the Service on a proposed reorganization, but not the cost of determining the tax basis of new stock received in the reorganization, which was treated as a capital expenditure by the court.[122]

3. Liquidation expenses. The tax results of partial and complete liquidation expenses are considered in detail later in this treatise.[123]

F2d 197 (9th Cir.), cert. denied, 371 US 861 (1962); Jim Walter Corp. v. US, supra note 45 (payments to cancel warrants in connection with public issue of stock; held not deductible); cases cited supra note 55.

[120] Denver & R.G.W.R.R. and rulings cited supra note 57. See also infra ¶ 14.17, para. 3, on the difficulties of distinguishing between currently deductible retirement premium and amortizable issue discount (or currently taxable retirement discount and deferrable issue premium) when the principal amounts of the old and new securities differ at the time of the exchange: §249, denying a deduction for retirement premium attributable to the conversion feature of convertible securities, discussed supra ¶ 4.60; Rev. Rul. 74-210, 1974-1 CB 48 (premium to retire convertible debt deductible to extent not disallowed by §249); Rev. Rul. 77-204, 1977-1 CB 40 (bankruptcy reorganization expenses nondeductible §263 capital expenditures; but bankruptcy liquidation expenses deductible; and expenses of operating business during bankruptcy deductible whether proceeding is a reorganization or a liquidation).

[121] Rev. Rul. 67-411, 1967-2 CB 124 (shareholder expenses in a Type C reorganization a capital expenditure to be added to the basis of stock received in the reorganization); Regs. §1.263(a)-(2)(f); Edwards v. US, 25 AFTR2d 526 (W.D. Pa. 1970); McGlothlin v, CIR, supra note 29; Third Nat'l Bank in Nashville v. US, supra note 30 (dissenting shareholder's legal fees in appraisal proceeding held nondeductible); see aso El Paso Co. v. US, supra note 117 (divestiture proceeding expenses incurred by parent corporation deductible; but costs of reorganization, start-up of new subsidiary, and obtaining tax ruling nondeductible capital expenses).

[122] Kaufmann v. US, supra note 97; see also Sharples v US, supra note 30.

[123] Infra ¶ 11.08. See also articles supra note 82. See generally Gerli & Co, 73 TC 1019 (1980) (attorney fees for obtaining §367 ruling on liquidation of foreign subsidiary under §332 held capital expenditure), rev'd on other grounds, 668 F2d 691 (2d Cir. 1982).

4. Special problems in corporate asset acquisitions with assumed liabilities: current expense vs. capital cost treatment. As noted previously, property acquisition costs are not currently deductible by the acquiring party but instead must be capitalized as part of the cost basis of the acquired stock or properties.[124] Liabilities of the acquired party that are taken over by the buyer likewise are subject to this general rule of capitalization (and this includes expense-type obligations that would otherwise ordinarily be deductible).[125] Like all seemingly well-settled principles of taxation, however, numerous problems and ambiguities can arise here, depending upon the type of liability assumed, its maturation (i.e., the extent to which it is a past, present, or future obligation), the form of the acquisition (i.e., stock or assets, taxable or tax-free), and the details of the parties' business bargain.[126]

Thus, assumed potential or contingent liabilities generally ought not to be treated as part of the purchase price and should only be deducted when actually incurred by the acquiring party (although the line between accrued and potential liabilities is not always a bright one). Assumed expense liabilities in the context of a §351 incorporation are given special treatment by §357(c)[127] and liabilities assumed in a tax-free reorganization likewise operate under a special statutory regime.[128] These problems are dealt with throughout this treatise in the context where they arise and are mentioned here merely as a guide for the reader in a search for their treatment.[129]

¶ 5.07   THE CORPORATION'S TAXABLE YEAR AND METHOD OF ACCOUNTING

Under §§441 and 446, a corporation, like any other taxpayer, must report its taxable income on a taxable year basis and use a method of accounting that clearly reflects its income. Ordinarily, a newly organized corporation is free to adopt either a fiscal year (i.e., one ending on the last day of any month other than December) or a calendar year as its annual

---

[124] Supra ¶ 5.04, para. 2.

[125] See, e.g., GCM 39274 (Sept. 3, 1984), 24 Tax Notes 944 (1984), and cases cited. See generally Landis, Liabilities and Purchase Price, 27 Tax Lawyer 67 (1973). See also Fisher Cos., 84 TC 1319 (1985) (assumption of lessee's obligation to repair leased property held part of lessee's amount realized on sale of its leasehold interest and also part of buyer's purchase price).

[126] Landis, supra note 125.

[127] Supra ¶ 3.06, para. 3; see also supra ¶ 3.11, note 118.

[128] Infra ¶¶ 14.55 and 16.13, para. 4.

[129] In addition to the references in notes 127 and 128, see infra ¶¶ 11.08, 11.11, and 11.45, para. 2. See also supra ¶¶ 4.40 and 4.60.

taxable year, and can use either the cash method or an accrual method of accounting. These choices are made during the first year of the corporate taxpayer's existence and, once made, are binding thereafter unless the Service consents to a change or forces the taxpayer to change its accounting method in order to clearly reflect income.

The Tax Reform Act of 1986 modified these accounting elections in several important respects. Thus, under §441(i) a "personal service corporation" (defined in §269A as a corporation the principal activity of which is the performance of personal services by its shareholders)[130] is required to use the calendar year unless it establishes, to the Service's satisfaction, a business purpose for using a fiscal year (and for this purpose, *any* deferral of shareholder income will not be so considered). Similarly, an S corporation (see Chapter 6) is required to use the calendar year unless it can satisfy the Service that its natural business year is a fiscal year.

Moreover, §448 mandates the use of the accrual method of accounting for all C corporations subject to its provisions for years beginning after 1986. Corporations engaged in the farming business[131] and qualified personal service corporations, however, are exempted from this provision, as are corporations whose average annual gross receipts for the three-year period preceding the taxable year do not exceed $5 million. Qualified personal service corporations are defined by §448(d)(2) as those substantially all of whose activities involve the performance of services in the fields of health, law, engineering, accounting, architecture, actuarial science, performing arts, or consulting, and substantially all of whose stock is held by its employees (active or retired), their estates, or their heirs (but only for the two-year period after death). Special rules in §448(d)(4) exclude stock held by §401 plans and disregard community property laws in determining qualified owners. If use of the accrual method is required, §448(d)(5) allows the corporation to accrue its receivables on the basis of collection experience unless interest is payable on such amounts or penalties are imposed for late payment.

On the other hand, the matching rules of §267(a)(2)[132] were expanded in 1986 to cover *any* shareholder-employee of a personal service corporation regardless of the amount of stock ownership; in effect, this provision places the accrual-method payor corporation on the cash-basis method of accounting with respect to payments to its cash-method employee-shareholders by deferring deductions until the item is includable in the payee's gross income.

---

[130] Supra ¶ 2.07.

[131] But see §447 (added in 1976), supra ¶ 5.03, para. 13

[132] Supra ¶ 5.04, para. 1.

As a general rule, however, the principles governing accounting periods and methods of reporting income and deductions do not distinguish between corporate and noncorporate taxpayers in any systematic manner. However, corporations (especially larger enterprises) more typically tend to make use of the accrual method of accounting, while individuals generally tend to report on the cash basis, calendar year method.[133]

¶ 5.08 CORPORATE ALTERNATIVE MINIMUM TAX

1. Introductory. A centerpiece of the corporate tax provisions of the Tax Reform Act of 1986 is the repeal of the prior add-on corporate minimum tax and the enactment of a comprehensive alternative minimum tax with a broader base, a higher rate, and far greater complexity than its predecessor.[134] The AMT was designed, according to the Senate Finance Committee, to "serve one overriding objective: to ensure that no taxpayer with substantial economic income can avoid significant tax liability by using exclusions, deductions, and credits because, however worthy their goals, they become counterproductive when taxpayers are allowed to use them to avoid virtually all tax liability."[135] Measured on this standard, the pre-1987 corporate add-on tax and its counterpart for individuals were found wanting:

The committee believes that the minimum taxes under present law do not adequately address the problem of tax avoidance, principally for two reasons. First, the corporate minimum tax, as an add-on rather than an alternative tax, is not presently designed to define a comprehensive income base. Second, the present minimum taxes on both indi-

[133] See Bittker, supra note 14, ¶¶ 105.1.5 and 105.2.1, 105.3.1.

[134] For prior law, see generally Hevener, Minimum Tax and Alternative Minimum Tax—Computation and Application, Tax Mgmt. Portfolio (BNA) No. 288-3d (1987) (covering both pre- and post-1986 rules). See also Hobbet, Minimum Tax on Preference Items: An Analysis of a Complex New Concept, 32 J. Tax'n 194 (1970); Schenk, Minimum Tax for Tax Preferences, 48 Taxes 201 (1970); Mansfield, Galvin, & Craig, Minimum Tax and Tax Burden Adjustments, 23 Tax Lawyer 591 (1970).

In addition to replacing the prior corporate add-on tax with the corporate AMT, the Tax Reform Act of 1986 tightened the preexisting individual AMT, which shares many, but not all, of the features of the new corporate AMT. This represents the fifth phase of the minimum tax, a "toll charge" process begun in the Tax Reform Act of 1969 (a veritable tap on the wrist in its impact compared to the most recent legislation), successively strengthened by amendment in 1976, 1978, and 1982, and completely overhauled in 1986. Needless to say, the regulations have not kept pace with the statutory evolution and are for the most part woefully out of date.

[135] Senate Finance Comm. Rep. No. 313, 99th Cong., 2d Sess. 518–519 (1986).

viduals and corporations do not sufficiently approach the measurement of economic income. By leaving out many important tax preferences, or defining preferences overly narrowly, the individual and corporate minimum taxes permit some taxpayers with substantial economic incomes to report little or no minimum taxable income and thus to avoid all tax liability. [136]

In brief outline, [137] the corporate AMT imposed by §§55–59 as amended in 1986 has these features:

(1) A tentative minimum tax of 20 percent is computed on the corporation's alternative minimum taxable income (AMTI) to the extent that AMTI exceeds an exemption of $40,000 (which phases out at $310,000) reduced by a modified credit for foreign income taxes as restricted by §59(a).

(2) If the corporation's tentative minimum tax exceeds its "regular tax"—defined as the normal income tax, excluding such special levies as the accumulated earnings tax, the PHC tax, and so forth (which means in effect that these extra taxes accumulate on top of AMT)—for the taxable year, the *excess* amount (less a limited allowance for investment tax credits) is the AMT due.

(3) AMTI, on which the tentative minimum tax is based, is defined by §55(b)(2) as the taxpayer's taxable income (i.e., the base on which the regular tax is imposed), adjusted as provided by §§56 and 58, and increased by the tax preferences listed in §57. These modifications of taxable income are examined in more detail below.

(4) The AMT sometimes has the effect of a down payment on the regular tax because AMTI includes some income items that are deferred for regular tax purposes (e.g., gains on installment sales) and disallows some accelerated deductions (e.g., the excess of accelerated over straight-line depreciation). Recognizing that the taxpayer's regular tax liability will eventually reflect these timing differences, §53 protects the taxpayer against double counting by allowing the AMT allocable to such items to be credited against the

[136] Id. at 519.

[137] For more detailed analysis, see Hevener, supra note 134; Gould, The Corporate Alternative Minimum Tax: A Search For Equity Through a Maze of Complexity, 64 Taxes 783 (1986); Eustice, Kuntz, Lewis, & Deering, supra note 2, ¶ 3.05; Haspel & Wertlieb, New Law Makes Sweeping Changes in Corporate Minimum Tax, 66 J. Tax'n 22 (1987). See generally Sunley, Thinking About Senator Packwood's Alternative Minimum Tax for Corporations, 31 Tax Notes 395 (1986); N.Y. State Bar Association, Tax Section Report, The Senate's Proposed Book Income Tax Preference, 32 Tax Notes 569 (1986); Lucke, Eisenach, & Dildine, The Senate Alternative Minimum Tax: Does It Snare Only the Tax Abuser?, 32 Tax Notes 681 (1986).

taxpayer's regular tax in the appropriate later years. For credit purposes, the taxpayer's AMT can be carried forward indefinitely (until used), but no carry-back is allowed. Moreover, a credit is not allowed for the AMT allocable to so-called exclusion preferences (i.e., items involving permanent exclusions rather than timing differences, such as charitable contributions of appreciated property, the excluded portion of dividends,[138] and percentage depletion in excess of basis), since these items will never generate any regular tax liability.

As items (1) and (2) of the preceding summary indicate, if a corporation's tentative minimum tax for a given year is $1.2 million and its regular tax is $1 million, it must pay $1.2 million to the Treasury; this leads to the unwarranted conclusion that the taxpayer must pay *either* the AMT *or* the regular tax, whichever is greater, an error that is fostered by the fact that the minimum tax bears the label "alternative." Despite this label, the AMT is not a true alternative to the regular tax; in the preceding example, the AMT is $200,000, not $1.2 million, as the taxpayer will eventually discover when computing its credits under §53, which cannot exceed $200,000. Thus, the AMT is as much an add-on tax as its statutory predecessor, since the taxpayer pays either the regular tax or *both* the regular tax *and* the misnamed "alternative tax," never just the alternative tax (unless the regular tax happens to be zero). On the other hand, AMTI, the *base* on which the AMT is imposed, deserves the "alternative" label, since it diverges in many important ways from the taxable income base on which the regular tax is imposed.

2. AMTI: Section 57 tax preferences. In converting a corporation's taxable income to AMTI, the simplest adjustment is the addition of the tax preferences listed in §57 (i.e., the excess of percentage depletion over the adjusted basis of the property, certain intangible drilling costs, tax-exempt interest on certain private activity bonds, excess deductions by financial institutions for bad debt reserves, the appreciated portion of property deducted as a charitable contribution, and accelerated depreciation on pre-1987 property). These add-backs are computed after taking into account the percentage reductions already imposed by §291 on the amounts deducted in computing taxable income.[139]

The tax preference adjustments in computing AMTI involve a few complexities, but they are relatively straightforward. From here on, however, the process is uphill all the way.

---

[138] Supra ¶ 5.05.

[139] Section 59(f); for §291, see supra text at note 21.

3. AMTI: Sections 56 and 58 adjustments (other than for book income). Continuing the process of converting taxable income into AMTI, §56 mandates a series of adjustments that (1) stretch out the corporation's deductions for depreciation on personal and real property placed in service after 1986, as well as for mining exploration and development costs and pollution control facilities; (2) require income from long-term contracts to be computed under the percentage of completion method prescribed by §460; (3) deny dealers (as well as many others) the right to use the installment method of reporting income from sales; and (4) recompute net operating losses to reflect AMTI and limit the deductible portion to 90 percent of AMTI. Personal service and some other closely held corporations are required by §58 to make some additional adjustments for certain farm and passive activity losses in computing their AMTI.[140]

Because these §56 adjustments affect the basis of property and/or have other ongoing consequences, AMTI is best regarded as a parallel taxable base that must be computed for every taxable year even if the taxpayer incurs no actual AMT liability for a particular year or a series of consecutive years. Moreover, the timing differences between taxable income and AMTI in computing depreciation and amortization can have surprising consequences when the underlying property is disposed of. For example, if property with an original cost of $1 million qualifies for depreciation deductions of $600,000 in computing taxable income but for only $250,000 of AMTI deductions, its basis will be $400,000 for the regular tax and $750,000 for the AMT; if it is sold for $500,000, the sale will generate a gain of $100,000 for regular tax purposes but a loss of $250,000 for AMT purposes.

4. AMTI: Section 56(f) adjustment for book income (1987–1989). The most dramatic, novel, and intricate adjustment required to transmute taxable income into AMTI is the adjustment for the corporation's book income under §56(f). The book income adjustment, which is a creature of the Tax Reform Act of 1986, was explained as follows by the Senate Finance Committee:

> The minimum tax cannot successfully address concerns of both real and apparent fairness unless there is certainty that whenever a company publicly reports substantial earnings (either pursuant to public reporting requirements, or through voluntary disclosure for substantial non-

---

[140] Losses from farming and passive activities are also limited in computing taxable income for regular tax purposes, but §58 imposes somewhat more severe limits for AMTI purposes; for example, the PAL restrictions of §469 are applied by §58 without regard to the percentage phase-in schedule of §469(*l*), and farm losses are disallowed by §58(a)(1)(A) on an activity-by-activity basis, without any offset of losses from one activity against income from another. For the passive activity loss limitations, see supra ¶ 5.03, para. 13.

tax reasons), that company will pay some tax (unless it has sufficient net operating losses to offset its income for the year).

Thus, the committee believes that it is important to provide that the alternative minimum taxable income of a corporation will be increased when book income for the year exceeds alternative minimum taxable income. Such a provision will increase both the real and the perceived fairness of the tax system, eliminate the highly publicized instances in which corporations with substantial book income have paid no tax, and further broaden the minimum tax base to approach economic income more closely. [141]

The real and perceived fairness issue that troubled the committee arises because book income often reflects items that are included neither in the corporation's taxable income nor in its AMTI, even after it is increased for the tax preferences and other adjustments summarized above. The committee did not supply a list of the offending items, and an exhaustive list could probably not be compiled; but presumably it was concerned about items such as tax-exempt interest, unrecognized gains on exchanges, and accrued income earned by cash-basis taxpayers that swell a corporation's reported book income without generating any current regular tax liability.

Despite the committee's reference to both real and perceived fairness, it is hard to escape the conclusion that the book income remedy is concerned solely with perceptions, since the adjustment depends on what the corporation reports, not on the underlying naked facts. For example, assume that (1) the financial history and operations of corporations A and B are identical in every respect; (2) both have taxable income and AMTI (before the book income adjustment) of zero; (3) both receive $500,000 of tax-exempt interest and are advised of a potential tort claim of $1 million; (4) A reports zero book income because it creates a contingency reserve for the tort liability of $500,000 that offsets its $500,000 of tax-exempt interest; and (5) B reports book income of $500,000 because it chooses not to set up a reserve for the contingent tort liability. On these facts, A incurs no AMT liability, while B does, solely because of the difference in their reported book income. Of course, B's financial report may create a public perception of unfairness—no tax liability despite financial prosperity—that is not created by A's financial report. If the book income adjustment is a response to this perception rather than to reality, then—and only then—the difference in tax treatment between A and B can be defended.

The starting point in computing the book income adjustment is the net income or loss reported on the taxpayer's "applicable financial statement," a term that is defined by §56(f)(3)(A) in a hierarchical fashion as (1) a statement required to be filed with the SEC; (2) a certified audited income statement to be used for credit, shareholder, or any other substantial nontax

---

[141] Supra note 135 at 520 (footnote omitted).

purpose; (3) an income statement required to be filed with a federal, state, or local government or agency thereof; or (4) an income statement to be used for credit, shareholder, or any other substantial nontax purpose. If the corporation has more than one financial statement, the highest on this list is controlling; if the corporation has no statement (or has only a class (4) statement and elects accordingly), its net income or loss is treated as equal to its current earnings and profits without diminution for distributions.

Section 56(f)(2)(B) requires book income to be adjusted to eliminate any deductions for federal and foreign income taxes (since AMTI is a pretax amount), and it prescribes other adjustments for dividends (without the §243 deduction), consolidated reporting, and overlapping tax and book periods; but it does not require that the "applicable financial statement" conform to generally accepted accounting principles or, indeed, to any other quality standards. Thus, the Senate Finance Committee's report states that it does not intend "to establish the Secretary of the Treasury as an arbiter of acceptable accounting principles" and that the taxpayer's choice of a "reasonable" accounting method is controlling unless it results in the omission or duplication of items of income or expense.[142] If, however, the taxpayer's chosen method is too bizarre—e.g., if income is recognized only after all expenditures, including capital outlays, have been recovered from cash receipts (a product of so-called Yankee storekeeper accounting, or "don't count your chickens before they are hatched")—the resulting document may not qualify as a financial statement, in which event the adjustment would be based on the earnings and profits alternative of §56(f)(3)(B)(i).

Once the corporation's adjusted net book income has been ascertained, 50 percent of the excess of this amount over AMTI (computed before this adjustment and without regard to the alternative tax net operating loss deduction, if any) is added to AMTI. The excess of adjusted net book income over AMTI is informally termed BURP for "business untaxed reported profit."[143] Since the tax rate on AMTI (after the $40,000 exemption) is 20 percent, the effective rate on the corporation's BURP is 10 percent. This suggests that the

---

[142] Senate Finance Comm. supra note 135 at 534. For the Service's regulatory authority to require adjustments to prevent the omission or duplication of items, see §56(f)(2)(H), discussed in Eustice, Kuntz, Lewis, & Deering, supra note 2, at ¶ 3.05[4][c]. Temporary regulations on the book income preference were released on Apr. 23, 1987, TD 8138, issuing Temp. Regs. §1.56-1T.

[143] Professor Michael Graetz has been credited with the original suggestion that Congress could deal with the perception of unfairness created by high-reported, low-taxed corporate income by taxing the otherwise untaxed portion of book income, thus confirming the maxim: "When Big Mike burps, Wall Street trembles." See Sheppard, The Book Income Preference in the Corporate Minimum Tax, 33 Tax Notes 616 (1986); see also Spector, The AMT on Exempt Interest—Is It Escapable?, 33 Tax Notes 493 (1986).

book income "preference" was viewed by Congress as only half as unfair as the other preferences and adjustments included in AMTI.

5. AMTI: Adjusted current earnings (1990 and thereafter). The BURP adjustment described above is prescribed by §56(f)(1) for taxable years beginning in 1987, 1988, or 1989, and it is to be replaced for taxable years beginning after 1989 by an adjustment based on adjusted current earnings (ACE), defined by §56(g), as a hybrid account with features resembling both traditional earnings and profits (see Chapter 7) and taxable income. Recognizing that the ACE adjustment will require novel computations and records, the Tax Reform Act of 1986 directs the Treasury to "conduct a study of the operation and effect of §§56(f) and (g)." [144] If ACE dies before becoming effective, its coffin will probably generate more merriment than a Mardi Gras float.

If, however, ACE becomes effective as scheduled, AMTI will be increased by 75 percent of the excess (if any) of a corporation's ACE over its AMTI (as computed before the ACE adjustment and the alternative tax net operating loss deduction). [145] (The reason for using a 75 percent adjustment for ACE as compared with the 50 percent adjustment for BURP is unclear, since both BURP and ACE are pretax amounts; the Conference Report sheds no light on this matter, suggesting that ACE is viewed by Congress as only three fourths as unfair as other preferences but more unfair than BURP by half). Unlike the BURP adjustment for 1987–1989, the ACE adjustment can *reduce* AMTI; subject to the limit set out in §56(g)(2)(B), if AMTI (computed as explained previously) exceeds ACE, AMTI is reduced by 75 percent of the excess.

6. Examples. In the following examples, assume that *T* Corporation has regular §63 taxable income of $400, tax preferences (after §291 cutbacks) of $100, and financial book income of $900. (For purposes of the examples, these and subsequent figures have been divided by 1,000.) On these facts

---

[144] Pub. L. No. 99-514, §702, 100 Stat. 2345 (1986).

[145] The computation of ACE under §56(g)(3) starts with AMTI, which then is adjusted under §56(g)(4) (to include earnings and profits income items, to deny deductible earnings items (e.g., the §243 deduction), and to make the §312(n) adjustments). Depreciation is also computed for ACE purposes under the lowest and slowest of various designated methods. Section 56(g)(4) does not contain any adjustment to allow deductions otherwise allowable in computing earnings and profits (e.g., various deductions that are disallowed for tax purposes such as fines, penalties, bribes, excess capital losses, and the like). Thus, ACE is not a true earnings and profits account but rather a hybrid version that is based on both earnings and profits and taxable income.

(and disregarding the $40,000 exemption of §55(d)(2), which is assumed to have phased out), T's §11 regular tax liability for 1988 would be $136 (a flat 34 percent of $400), and its §55 tentative AMT liability would be $140 (20 percent of the $700 AMTI base, figured as $400 taxable income, plus $100 of preference, plus the special $200 book income preference of §56(f) (i.e., 50 percent of the $400 excess of book income over AMTI)). Thus, T's total tax for 1988 consists of $136 of regular tax and $4 of AMT.[146]

> *Example 1.* T also derives another $100 of §103 tax-exempt bond interest. AMTI increases by $50 (half of the increase in book income), and an additional AMT liability of $10 arises under §55.
>
> If the bonds are private activity bonds, the interest is also a preference in full in its own right under §57(a)(5)(A), resulting in an increase in AMT of $20. The book income preference is unchanged at $200, since the AMTI threshold was raised by the same amount as the book income figure, so the excess is still $400. Note, however, that half of the $100 interest arguably is also in the book income preference as a double-counted item if it is considered to be included in book at the top margin—that is, if the interest was excluded from book income because it was already included in the AMTI base, the book preference would only be $150 ($900 less $600 × 50 percent); whether §56(f)(2)(H) regulations will act to eliminate this item from book income is, however, unclear).
>
> *Example 2.* T also receives a $100 dividend from its wholly owned but unconsolidated subsidiary, S. The book income preference is increased by $50, and AMT goes up by $10.[147]
>
> *Example 3.* T sells dealer property for a gain of $400 that it defers under §453 but not for book purposes. AMTI first goes up by $400 to $900, since §56(a)(6) requires full inclusion of the gain in AMTI. (The book income preference remains at $200 because book income still exceeds AMTI by $400 (i.e., because the threshold went up along with

---

[146] The §55(a) tax is the excess of tentative minimum tax (in this case the $140 tax under §55(b) on AMTI) over the regular tax under §11(b) (in this case $136). As a practical matter, however, T's tax liability is simply the greater of the two taxes (except for purposes of §53 credit, which uses the excess figure).

[147] AMT liability increases by $10 here under §55(a), the excess of tentative minimum tax of $10 on the dividend over the zero regular tax thereon (because of the 100 percent §243 deduction), supra note 146; thus the effective tax cost is 10 percent on the dividend. If the dividend doesn't qualify for the 100 percent §243 deduction, the effective tax cost is 12 percent (i.e., 20 percent of the included portion of the dividend, which is in AMTI, plus 10 percent of the excluded portion, which is, however, included in the BURP account).

the increase in book income); but the double-counting argument in Example 1 applies here as well). AMTI thus is $1,100 (resulting in AMT of $220) or an increase of $80 in tax.

Example 4. *T* realizes a gain of $500 on the exchange of all the stock of a wholly owned subsidiary. The gain is not recognized for tax purposes, although it is reported currently for book purposes. *T*'s AMTI increases by $250, and *T*'s AMT liability increases by $50. (The same result would apply to any nonrecognition exchange gain that generates financial statement income.)

Example 5. *T* receives $200 of prepaid income that it defers for book purposes until "earned" in the following year. *T* is taxable in the year of receipt on such income (resulting in an increase in regular tax of $68 and thereby moving *T* out of AMT for that year); but the $200 book income could create AMT liability in the following year when booked for financial reporting purposes, even though it already has been fully subjected to regular tax. Moreover, the §53 credit is no help in these reverse timing cases since no credit carry-back is permitted.

Example 6. *T* establishes a $500 book reserve for an asserted tort liability that it pays in the following year. *T* has no book preference for the first year that it sets up the reserve, since the reserve book deduction lowered book income below the AMTI threshold of $500; but to the extent that book income is higher in the year of actual payment (when *T* obtains the tax deduction under §§461(f) and 461 (h)(2)(C)), AMT liability could arise. This same effect can be created by other book write-downs that are chargeable against financial earnings but are not deductible for tax purposes until the loss is actually realized in a closed transaction. Moreover, as in Example 5, the §53 credit is no help, since no credit carry-back is permitted.

Example 7. *T* has a net operating loss carry-over deduction of $500 (that eliminates regular taxable income and hence regular tax liability). The alternative net operating loss deduction of §56(d) can only offset 90 percent of AMTI, which amount is now only $500, consisting of the $100 of preferences and a $400 book income preference (i.e., $900 of book income less AMTI of $100 × 50 percent) that is computed without the special AMT net operating loss deduction. As a result, $50 of AMTI still exists. *T* thus has an AMT liability of $10. Similar results would occur if *T* had foreign tax credits, which are limited by §59(a) to 90 percent of gross AMT liability (resulting in a 2 percent bottom line AMT regardless of the size of *T*'s net operating loss deductions or foreign tax credits).

Assuming that the taxable year in the preceding example is 1990, when the ACE preference of §56(g) will replace the book income preference, T's tentative AMT liability would increase to $160 from $140, since 75 percent of the $400 excess of ACE over AMTI is the amount of the ACE preference. Similarly, T's AMT liability in Examples 1 and 2 would increase by $15, since the ACE preference would be $75 in both cases.[148] In Example 3, the ACE preference would be $300, and AMT would go up by another $20; but, because nonrecognition transactions are excluded from ACE by §312(f)(1), no additional AMT should result in Example 4. Similarly, Examples 5 and 6 would create different results under the ACE rules, since earnings and profits timing rules generally follow taxable income rather than financial accounting principles.[149] In Example 7, AMTI would increase by $200 to $700 (i.e., the $100 preference, plus 75 percent of the $800 ACE amount, or $600), resulting in a $200 AMTI base after allowing for the special §56(d) net operating loss deduction offset (assuming that this deduction was $500).

It should be noted, however, that §56(g)(2) allows for negative adjustments to AMTI (for 75 percent of the excess of AMTI over ACE), unlike the book income preference rules of §56(f). Negative adjustments might arise in cases where a sizeable ACE income item is accelerated for AMT purposes (e.g., a §453 gain that is included in full when sold for ACE, but taxed when collected). However, ACE, like BURP, is a pretax figure, so that §11 taxes and any other tax (e.g., §§531 and 541) will not reduce ACE, although they do reduce regular earnings and profits. Nondeductible expenses also do not reduce ACE, even though such amounts would reduce regular earnings and profits. Thus, the ACE amount is not a true earnings and profits computation, but instead is a hybrid figure based selectively on earnings and profits and ACE.

¶ 5.09   CORPORATE SIZE: "SMALL BUSINESS" VS. "BIG BUSINESS"

1. In general. The Code has long distinguished between large and small corporations, not as a systematic policy, but on an ad hoc basis in response to specific problems.[150] It is clear, however, that the corporate tax regime is

---

[148] Thus, T's effective tax rate on the $100 dividend in Example 2 would be 15 percent rather than 10 percent, supra note 147. If the §243 deduction is only 80 percent, the effective tax cost is 16 percent.

[149] See infra ¶¶ 7.03 and 7.04.

[150] For the taxation of closely held corporations, see Ness & Vogel, Taxation of the Closely Held Corporation (Warren, Gorham & Lamont, Inc., 1986).

multifaceted, with an impact that varies dramatically depending on the size of the corporate enterprise.

"Size" is defined in different ways for this purpose. Thus, effective tax rates are determined by annual income levels; the progressive effects of the §11(b) rates begin to phase out at $100,000 of taxable income and disappear at $335,000.[151] Other special tax benefits (or burdens) depend on the corporation's value, its annual gross receipts, or the character of its activities, while still others depend upon the number of its shareholders or the degree of concentration of shareholder ownership. Yet other Code provisions depend upon whether the corporation's stock is publicly traded.

Many of these matters are considered elsewhere in this treatise. For example, Subchapter S small business corporations are dealt with in Chapter 6; losses on §1244 small business stock are considered supra ¶ 4.24; the penalty taxes of §§531 and 541 (unreasonable accumulations and personal holding companies, respectively) are considered in Chapter 8;[152] foreign personal holding companies and controlled foreign corporations are dealt with in Chapter 17; affiliated corporation issues are treated in Chapter 15; and redemptions under §303 to pay death taxes are considered infra ¶ 9.11. Various instances where the Code distinguishes in some significant manner, between the tax consequences applicable to small, closely held corporations and to large, publicly traded companies, are noted here.

Tax rates. Perhaps the most evident tax distinction between various corporations is based on the size of their taxable incomes; §11(b), discussed earlier in this chapter, taxes income of less profitable companies at progressive rates up to $75,000 of taxable income and switches over to a purely flat tax regime once taxable income reaches the $335,000 level. Moreover, as noted in the previous section, the $40,000 exemption amount from the corporate AMT phases out when AMTI reaches $310,000. If the corporation is able to qualify for Subchapter S, eligibility for which is limited to corporations with a limited number (35) of shareholders and a restricted type of shareholder group (generally U.S. individuals only), corporate tax liability can be eliminated altogether. While denominated as a small business corporation, however, an S corporation has no other size limitations save the number (and type) of its shareholders; thus, it can be large economically but

---

[151] Supra ¶ 5.01.

[152] Although §531 clearly does (since 1984) apply to publicly owned corporations, in practice it continues to be a problem principally for closely held corporations; §541 specifically requires concentrated stock ownership in individual shareholders. The Technical Corrections Act of 1987, supra note 70, in §101(a)(2)(A), would reduce the §531 rate to 28 percent (the same as the PHC rate, discussed in Chapter 8).

still qualify for the relief of these provisions if its shareholder family is sufficiently concentrated and acceptably constituted.

The penalty tax provisions of §541 likewise focus on concentrated shareholder ownership (characterized by five or fewer individuals owning more than 50 percent of the corporation's stock and complex ownership attribution rules), but are only triggered if the corporation's activities also are essentially passive in character. (This is not a Code provision one strives to qualify for, since the 28 percent tax of §541 is levied on top of the §11 tax.) Until 1984, there was some authority to the effect that publicly held corporations were immune from the accumulated earnings tax of §531,[153] but the Tax Reform Act of 1984 specifically included publicly held corporations as §531 candidates (although, as a practical matter, this tax still seems to be a potential problem primarily for closely held corporations).

Finally, the low bracket rate benefits of §11(b) are restricted if the corporation is a member of an affiliated corporate group as defined by §§1561–1563.[154]

3. **Accounting methods and taxable year.** As noted previously,[155] the Tax Reform Act of 1986 mandated the use of the calendar year for S corporations and personal service corporations. Conversely, S corporations and most (but not necessarily all) personal service corporations are exempted from the mandatory accrual accounting method rules of §448,[156] as are small corporations whose average annual gross receipts for the three-year period prior to the taxable year do not exceed $5 million. Similarly, farming corporations are exempted from the mandatory accrual method rules of §447 (added by the Tax Reform Act of 1976) if they are family-controlled or have annual gross receipts of $1 million or less. Likewise, the capitalization rules of §263A, added by the Tax Reform Act of 1986,[157] do not apply to retailers whose average annual gross receipts for the three-year period preceding the taxable year are $10 million or less; a similar exception to the 1986 restrictive long-term contract rules of §460[158] is provided in §460(e) in cases where average annual gross receipts do not exceed $10 million.

The at-risk rules of §465 apply only to closely held C corporations that meet the concentrated stock ownership tests of §542(a)(2) (ownership of more than 50 percent by five or fewer individuals). Moreover, the passive activity loss limitation rules of §469, added by the Tax Reform Act of

---

153 See infra ¶ 8.02, supra note 152.

154 See infra ¶ 15.02.

155 See supra ¶ 5.07.

156 See Eustice, Kuntz, Lewis, & Deering, supra note 2, ¶ 6.05[1].

157 Id., ¶ 6.02[2].

158 Id., ¶ 6.02[4].

1986,[159] apply only to closely held C corporations (using the §542(a)(2) personal holding company definition) and to personal service corporations described in §269A(b)(1)[160] (although the §469 limitations apply more leniently to closely held regular C corporations than to personal service corporations, the latter being treated as individuals for purposes of these provisions).

Finally, the Tax Reform Act of 1986, in §474, provides a simplified dollar-value LIFO inventory method for certain small businesses, defined by §474(c) as those whose average annual gross receipts for a three-year period do not exceed $5 million.

4. Other special provisions. The Tax Reform Act of 1986 repeal of the *General Utilities* doctrine in §§336 and 337[161] contains a special grandfather transition rule in Act §633(d) that provides limited relief to certain small corporations that liquidate prior to 1989. A qualified small corporation is defined for this purpose as one whose stock value does not exceed $10 million (although such relief phases out between $5 and $10 million) and has more than 50 percent of its stock owned by 10 or fewer qualified persons (generally persons who could be shareholders of S corporations).

The 1986 Act also exempts certain closely held corporations from the golden parachute payment rules of §280G,[162] these being corporations that would be entitled to elect Subchapter S or whose shares are not publicly traded (as to the latter, more than 75 percent of its shareholders must approve the payment upon full disclosure of all material facts); see §280G(b)(5).

Shareholders of publicly traded corporations are no longer able to use §453 to defer gain on the sale of the corporation's publicly traded stock or debt securities by virtue of §453(k)(2), as added by the Tax Reform Act of 1986 (the Tax Reform Act of 1969 denied use of §453 for the *receipt* of readily tradeable debt in what is now §453(f)(4)(B)). Moreover, the original issue discount rules of §§1273 and 1274 operate differently, depending upon whether the debt instruments (or the property for which such instruments are issued) are publicly traded.[163]

---

[159] Id., ¶ 3.02.

[160] Supra ¶ 2.07.

[161] Infra ¶ 11.06, ¶ 11.60.

[162] Supra ¶ 5.04, para. 5.

[163] See supra ¶ 4.42.

CHAPTER 6

Corporate Elections Under Subchapter S

¶ 6.01 INTRODUCTORY

Over the years, it was often suggested that the Code be amended to permit (or even require) the shareholders of closely held corporations to be taxed as if they were carrying on their activities as partners—i.e., to relieve the corporation of taxation on condition that each stockholder report his share of the corporation's income on his individual income tax return, whether or not that income was distributed to him. Such a proposal was passed by the Senate in 1954 to permit "small corporations which are essentially partnerships to enjoy the advantages of the corporate form of organization without being made subject to possible tax disadvantages of the corporation" and to "eliminate the influence of the Federal income tax in the selection of the form of business organization which may be most desirable under the circumstances." The 1954 proposal was eliminated by the conference committee; but the idea was revived in 1958 and enacted into law as Subchapter S of the Code (now §§1361–1379) for the announced purposes of allowing business to select their legal forms free of undue tax influence, aiding small businesses by taxing the corporation's income to shareholders (who may be likely to be in lower brackets than their corporations), and permitting the shareholders of corporations that are suffering losses to offset the losses against their personal income from other sources.[1]

The principal features of Subchapter S, which was extensively revised by the Subchapter S Revision Act of 1982,[2] are outlined briefly below and are discussed in more detail later in this chapter, along with certain features of prior law that are of continuing importance.[3]

1. Eligibility. Subchapter S is applicable only to a "small business corporation," defined by §1361(b)(1) as a domestic corporation that does not have more than 35 shareholders (all of whom must be individuals, estates, or certain types of trusts) or more than one class of stock. The corporation may not be a member of an affiliated group (as defined in §1504, relating to the privilege of filing consolidated returns (see Chapter 15)); it may not have any nonresident alien shareholders; and it must not be an "ineligible corporation" described in §1361(b)(2).

2. Election. A small business corporation can bring Subchapter S into play by filing an election, which is valid only if all shareholders consent. Once made, the election becomes effective for the taxable year when made or for the immediately succeeding year and remains effective for all succeeding taxable years unless it is terminated (a) by revocation by holders of

---

[1] For the 1954 proposal, see S. Rep. No. 1622, 83d Cong., 2d Sess. 119 (1954); for the 1958 version as enacted, see S. Rep. No. 1983, 85th Cong., 2d Sess. 87 (1958), reprinted in 1958-3 CB 922, 1137. As a result of 1986 legislation, shareholders will often be in lower brackets; see ¶ 5.01.

Although the 1954 proposal for permitting corporations to elect noncorporate treatment was not enacted, a companion provision allowing certain unincorporated businesses to elect to be taxed as corporations found favor in legislative eyes; but after a period of trial, it was found wanting or unnecessary, and it was repealed in 1966.

For extensive analysis of the Subchapter S rules, see Eustice & Kuntz, Federal Income Taxation of S Corporations (Warren, Gorham & Lamont, Inc., rev. ed. 1985). See also Ness & Vogel, Taxation of the Closely Held Corporation (Warren, Gorham & Lamont, Inc., 4th ed. 1986); Coven & Hess, The Subchapter S Revision Act: An Analysis and Appraisal, 50 Tenn. L. Rev. 569 (1983).

[2] For this legislation, see S. Rep. No. 640, 97th Cong., 2d Sess. 1, reprinted in 1982-2 CB 718; for extensive analysis, see Eustice & Kuntz, supra note 1. For further reform proposals, see Coven, Making Subchapter S Work, 32 Tax Notes 271 (1986).

[3] For a detailed examination of prior law, see Eustice & Kuntz, Federal Income Taxation of Subchapter S Corporations (Warren, Gorham & Lamont, Inc., 1st ed. 1982).

more than one-half of the shares, (b) by disqualification (e.g., acquisition of its stock by a corporation or other ineligible shareholder, issuance of a second class of stock, and so forth), or (c) in certain situations, by the receipt of an excessive amount (as defined in the Code) of passive investment income for three consecutive taxable years.

Once an election has been terminated, the corporation (or any successor corporation) is ineligible to make another election under Subchapter S for five years unless the Treasury consents.

3. Corporate income. While the election is in effect, the corporation is not subject to the corporate income tax, the corporate alternative minimum tax,[4] the accumulated earnings tax, or the personal holding company tax; and the corporate income, whether distributed or not, is taxed to the shareholders.[5] (Not having been subjected to a tax at the corporate level, the income under pre-1986 law was ineligible for the dividends-received exclusion in the hands of the shareholder, but this penalty is now meaningless in view of the 1986 repeal of that provision.)[6]

4. Adjustments to basis. The shareholder's basis for his S corporation stock is increased to reflect the fact that he was taxed on his share of the corporation's undistributed income, and it is decreased if this previously taxed income is distributed to him. If there are excess corporate losses and deductions, the shareholder must reduce the basis of the stock (and, if necessary, of any corporate debt obligations he may hold) to reflect the fact that these amounts have been passed through for use on his individual tax return.

5. Corporate status. While an election is in effect, the corporation—known as an S corporation by virtue of §1361(a)—is treated substantially as a partnership in the sense that it is not taxed as a separate entity, but instead passes its income, deductions, and other tax items through to its shareholders, but it remains a corporation for many important purposes. Thus, even while the election is in effect, corporate redemptions, liquidations, reorgani-

---

[4] See ¶ 5.18.

[5] As a conduit, the S corporation bears comparison with a number of other business and investment arrangements that receive similar treatment under other provisions of the Code (e.g., Subchapter K (partnerships); Subchapter J (trusts); §§551–558 (foreign personal holding companies); §§851–855 (mutual funds); §§856–860 (real estate investment trusts); and §§951–964 (controlled foreign corporations).

See Eustice, Subchapter S Corporations and Partnerships: A Search for the Pass-Through Paradigm, 39 Tax L. Rev. 345 (1984); infra ¶ 6.09.

[6] See ¶ 7.06.

zations, and many other transactions are governed by the tax law applicable to corporations rather than by the law of partnerships, and, if the election is terminated, the corporate income tax once again becomes fully applicable.

¶ 6.02 ELIGIBILITY TO ELECT UNDER SUBCHAPTER S

To make an election under Subchapter S, a corporation must be a "small business corporation," defined by §1361(b) as a domestic corporation meeting the conditions discussed below.

1. Number of shareholders. The corporation may not have more than 35 shareholders.[7] In applying this restriction, a husband and wife (and their estates) are treated as one shareholder by §1361(c)(1) whether the stock is owned by them as separate individuals or as co-owners (e.g., in joint tenancy or as community property). Other joint tenants and tenants in common, however, are treated by the regulations as separate shareholders in applying the 35-shareholder limit.[8] The regulations also provide that if stock is held by a nominee, agent, guardian, or custodian, the beneficial owner is generally treated as the shareholder.[9] On the other hand, stock owned by a partnership is not imputed to the partners, but is instead treated by the regulations as owned by the partnership itself,[10] precluding an election under Subchapter S because partnerships are not eligible shareholders by virtue of §1361(b)(1)(B).

2. Types of shareholders. An election can be made only if all shareholders are individuals, estates,[11] or trusts as described by §1361(c)(2). To qual-

---

[7] When enacted in 1958, Subchapter S imposed a limit of 10 shareholders; the limit was liberalized on several occasions and was raised to 35 effective for taxable years beginning in 1983.

[8] Regs. §1.1371-1(d)(1).

[9] See Harold C. Kean, 51 TC 337 (1968) (beneficial ownership test of regulations for shareholder status valid; taxpayer's argument for "record" ownership rejected), aff'd on this issue, 469 F2d 1183 (9th Cir. 1972). For a less liberal view, see Friend's Wine Cellars, Inc., ¶ 72,149 P-H Memo. TC (stock held by nominee trust, which filed the consent; held that if trust was the shareholder, it was an ineligible shareholder; if not, wrong person filed consent); Wilson v. CIR, 560 F2d 687 (5th Cir. 1977) (nominee record owner ignored).

[10] Regs. §1.1371-1(d)(1) (last sentence).

[11] But see Old Va. Brick Co. v. CIR, 367 F2d 276 (4th Cir. 1966) (election invalidated when existence of estate terminated because of unreasonably prolonged administration). See also Rev. Rul. 76-23, 1976-1 CB 264 (estate holding Subchapter

ify, a trust must fit into one of four classes: (1) a trust treated by §§671-678 (relating to revocable and other grantor trusts) as owned in its entirety by an individual citizen or resident of the United States; [12] (2) a trust of the type just described that continues in existence after the deemed owner's death, but only for the 60-day period following the death or, if the entire corpus is includable in the deemed owner's gross estate, for the two-year period following death; (3) a trust receiving stock pursuant to a will, but only for the 60-day period following receipt of the stock; and (4) a voting trust. [13] In applying the 35-shareholder limit of §1361(b)(1)(A) and the prohibition on nonresident alien shareholders imposed by §1361(b)(1)(C), shares held by these qualified trusts are allocated by §1361(c)(2)(B) to the deemed owner in the case of class (1) trusts, to the deemed owner's estate in the case of class (2) trusts, to the estate of the testator in the case of class (3) trusts, and to each beneficiary in the case of class (4) trusts. Stock held by a custodian under the Uniform Gifts to Minors Act is treated by the Service as owned by the minor, and hence need not be qualified under the trust rules. [14]

3. One class of stock. The corporation may not have more than one class of stock. The regulations state that a class of stock is to be counted for this purpose only if it is issued and outstanding; thus, treasury stock or authorized but unissued stock of a second class does not disqualify the corporation. The term "class of stock" is not defined by the statute; the regulations state that if the outstanding shares "are not identical with respect to the rights and interest which they convey in the control, profits, and assets of the corporation," the corporation is considered to have more than one class. [15] Problems in applying this standard, especially to stock with divergent voting rights, led to the enactment in 1982 of §1361(c)(4), which provides that a corporation shall not be treated as having more than one class of stock merely because there are differences in voting rights among the shares of common stock.

S stock solely to facilitate payment of federal estate tax continues to be eligible shareholder while estate complies with §6166).

[12] Under §1361(d)—a highly specialized provision that bears all the earmarks of special legislation designed for the benefit of a single family—the income beneficiary of a trust meeting specified conditions can elect to qualify the trust under §1361(c)(2)(A)(i) and to be treated as the owner of the S corporation stock.

[13] For prior law, which was more restrictive regarding ownership in specifying the trusts that could own stock of an S corporation, see Eustice & Kuntz, supra note 3 at ¶ 2.03.

[14] TIR 113 (Nov. 26, 1958), 1958 Fed. Tax Serv. (P-H) ¶ 55,211.

[15] Regs. §1.1371-1(g); see also Rev. Rul. 85-161, 1985-2 CB 191 (shareholder agreement restricting transfers by one shareholder did not create second class of stock).

A source of anxiety in the early days of Subchapter S was whether purported debt instruments would be treated as a second class of stock (resulting in a corporation's ineligibility to elect under Subchapter S or in the termination of a prior election) if the obligation was treated as equity for such purposes as disallowing interest deductions.[16] After losing a series of cases in this area, the Service announced that it would not continue to litigate the issue; the regulations now provide that purported debt obligations, if held in substantially the same proportion as the nominal stock, are to be treated as contributions to capital rather than as a second class of stock.[17]

In addition, §1361(c)(5) was enacted in 1982 to create a safe harbor for "straight debt," defined as any written unconditional promise to pay a sum certain in money either on demand or on a specified date, provided that (1) the interest rate and payment dates are not contingent on profits, the borrower's discretion, or similar factors, (2) the obligation is not convertible directly or indirectly into stock, and (3) the creditor is an individual (other than a nonresident alien), an estate, or a trust qualified to be a shareholder of an S corporation. Even if debt meeting these conditions is treated as equity for other purposes (e.g., if interest deductions are disallowed because the corporation is undercapitalized), it is not treated as a second class of stock in applying §1361(b)(1)(D). The Treasury is authorized to prescribe regulations to coordinate the treatment of straight debt for purposes of Subchapter S and other income tax provisions. (In view of the experience under §385, such regulations are not likely to be swiftly forthcoming.[18])

4. No nonresident alien shareholders. The corporation may not have any nonresident alien shareholders. This restriction reflects the fact that corporate income is exempt from tax under Subchapter S on the assumption that it will be subjected to the graduated individual income tax rates, whereas most nonresident aliens are taxed under §871(a)(1) at the flat rate of 30 percent.[19] Moreover, it would be difficult to apply to undistributed corporate income the withholding system used to insure the collection of income taxes from nonresident aliens.

---

[16] For further discussion of this problem, see generally supra ¶ 4.02.

[17] Regs. §1.1371-1(g). See generally James L. Stinnett, 54 TC 221 (1970); Portage Plastics Co. v. US, 486 F2d 632 (7th Cir. 1973), and cases cited therein; for the Service announcement, see TIR 1248 (July 27, 1973), 1973 Fed. Tax Serv. (P-H) ¶ 55,385. See also TD 7920 (1983), reinstating the above regulations; supra ¶ 4.02.

[18] For §385, see supra ¶ 4.02, para. 7.

[19] See Ward v. US, 661 F2d 226 (Ct. Cl. 1981) (nonresident alien spouse treated as part owner of stock under community property law of foreign country; election not valid).

5. Ineligible corporations. The corporation may not elect under Subchapter S if it is a member of an "affiliated group," as defined by §1504, relating to consolidated returns.[20] Section 1361(c)(6) lifts this restriction, however, if the corporation is designated a member of an affiliated group only because of its ownership of stock in a second corporation that has not engaged in business and has no gross income for a specified period. This exception permits a Subchapter S election by a corporation that has subsidiaries in other states for the sole purpose of protecting its corporate name against appropriation.

Four other classes of corporations are also ineligible to make elections under Subchapter S: (1) financial institutions to which §585 or §593 (relating primarily to banks) apply; (2) insurance companies; (3) corporations electing under §936 (allowing credits for certain income from Puerto Rico and U.S. possessions); and (4) former or current domestic international sales corporations.[21]

¶ 6.03 MAKING A SUBCHAPTER S ELECTION

Under §§1362(a) and 1362(b), an eligible corporation may become an S corporation for a particular taxable year by filing an election,[22] which is valid only if all persons who are shareholders on the date of the election consent thereto. An election made on or before the fifteenth day of the third month of the current taxable year is effective for that year, provided that the corporation meets all eligibility requirements for the entire current year and that, in addition to all persons owning stock in the corporation at the time of the election, all persons owning stock during that year and prior to the election consent to it. If these conditions are not satisfied, the election is treated

---

[20] For this purpose, affiliated group status is determined without the exceptions of §1504(b); see generally infra ¶ 15.21. See also Rev. Rul. 72-320, 1972-1 CB 270 (election not terminated where S corporation acquired stock of subsidiary as transitory step in divisive reorganization); Rev. Rul. 73-496, 1973-2 CB 313 (same for acquisition of subsidiary, followed promptly by liquidation). But see Haley Bros. Constr. Corp., 87 TC 498 (1986) (presence of subsidiary terminated election per se under plain meaning of statute; opinion casts doubt on validity of transitory subsidiary rulings).

[21] Sections 1361(b)(2)(B)–1361(b)(2)(E). For the tax treatment of DISCs, see infra ¶ 17.14.

[22] Herbert Levy, 46 TC 531 (1966) (bankrupt corporation; trustee proper party to file election). See generally Rev. Rul. 86-141, 1986-49 IRB 6 (must be qualified corporation when election filed).

as applicable to the following taxable year, as is any election made after the fifteenth day of the third month of the current year.

In applying the unanimous shareholder-consent requirement of §1362(a)(2), the regulations state that the consent of a minor must be granted by the minor himself, his legal guardian, or his natural guardian if no legal guardian has been appointed; the Service has ruled that this requirement is applicable even if the stock is held by a custodian.[23] The regulations also provide that a shareholder's consent may not be withdrawn once a valid election is made by the corporation.[24]

¶ 6.04 EVENTS TERMINATING THE ELECTION

1. Revocation. A corporation may terminate its election if, but only if, shareholders holding more than one-half of the shares of stock on the day of the revocation consent thereto.[25] The revocation can specify its effective date (either the day of the revocation or a later date); otherwise, a revocation made on or before the fifteenth day of the third month of a taxable year is effective as of the first day of that year, while a revocation made thereafter becomes effective on the first day of the following taxable year.

The power to terminate the election by a revocation is fundamental to tax planning in closely held corporations. It permits shareholders to use Subchapter S to deduct net operating losses incurred in the early years of a

---

[23] See Regs. §1.1372-3(a); Rev. Rul. 66-116, 1966-1 CB 198 (custodian holding stock for minor cannot consent to election unless he is also minor's legal or natural guardian).

[24] Regs. §18.1362-2(a). For various problems in the consent procedure, see William Pestcoe, 40 TC 195 (1963) (late filing, although perhaps excusable, prevented valid election); Joseph W. Feldman, 47 TC 329 (1966) (election put in mailbox on last day for election but not postmarked until following day; held too late); Mitchell Offset Plate Serv., Inc., 53 TC 235 (1969) (acq.) (evidence of timely mailing in properly addressed envelope created presumption of delivery); McClelland Farm Equip. Co. v. US, 601 F2d 365 (8th Cir. 1979) (premature filing of election held effective); Thos. E. Bone, 52 TC 913 (1969) (corporate existence began when assets acquired from predecessor partnership, not when stock issued; hence, election not timely); Nick A. Artukovich, 61 TC 100 (1973) (corporation came into existence when it acquired assets (cash); election not timely; taxpayer's argument that existence started only when corporation acquired *operating* assets rejected); Rev. Rul. 69-591, 1969-2 CB 172 (de facto existence of new subsidiary began before formal issue of shares).

[25] Under prior law, elections could be revoked voluntarily only if all shareholders consented; but the election terminated if any new shareholder refused or failed to consent within a specified period. This new shareholder provision (repealed in 1982) seemed to invite evasion of the unanimous consent requirement by a rigged transfer of stock to a member of the transferor's family or other compliant transferee who, by prearrangement, would refuse to consent and thus terminate the election.

new venture (or in a poor year of an older company) and to terminate the election when the venture becomes profitable if the shareholders do not want to report the corporation's undistributed income on their personal returns. Revocations also play a role in the use of Subchapter S by corporations realizing substantial capital gains (e.g., on the sale of an industrial plant or other real estate) that are to be passed on to shareholders; however, such arrangements are inhibited to a significant extent by §1374, as explained later in this chapter.[26]

2. Disqualification. The election is terminated under §1362(d)(2) if the corporation ceases to be a "small business corporation" as defined by §1361(b) (i.e, by the acquisition of shareholders exceeding the limit of 35, a nonresident alien shareholder, or a shareholder who is not an individual, estate, or qualified trust, or by the issuance of a second class of stock).[27] At least on its face, §1362(d)(2) terminates the election if a single shareholder transfers a single share of stock to an unqualified shareholder, even if the transferee is a corporation that is wholly owned by the transferor or a taxpayer-dominated family partnership. A decent respect for the legislative pattern, however, requires some restraint on such attempts to terminate the election by a meaningless gesture; otherwise, the requirement of majority consent for a voluntary revocation under §1362(d)(1) would be nullified.[28]

3. Passive investment income. Under prior law, a Subchapter S election terminated if the corporation received foreign or passive investment income in excess of specified limits.[29] In 1982, the foreign income restriction was repealed, and the passive investment income restriction was modified to apply only if the corporation has Subchapter C earnings and profits at the close of each of three consecutive post-1981 election years, and then only if more than 25 percent of its gross receipts for each of these years consists of passive investment income as defined by §1362(d)(3)(D).[30]

An S corporation formed after December 31, 1981 rarely violates this restriction, since, if it has been an S corporation continually since its inception, it does not have any Subchapter C earnings and profits except by

---

[26] See infra ¶ 6.07.

[27] See generally Regs. §1.1372-4(b).

[28] For an analogy, see CIR V. Day & Zimmerman, Inc., 151 F2d 517 (3d Cir. 1945); see also T.J. Henry Assocs. Inc., 80 TC 886 (1982) (acq.) (intentional termination by transfer of one share to nonconsenting new shareholder held effective under prior law).

[29] See Eustice & Kuntz, supra note 3 at ¶¶ 4.05 and 4.06.

[30] For the taxation of the passive investment income during the three-year period, see infra ¶ 6.07, para. 2.

inheritance (e.g., by merger) from another corporation. Older S corporations, however, may have earnings and profits either from prior nonelection years or from pre-1982 election years.[31] If such a corporation also realizes excessive amounts of passive income, its Subchapter S election will terminate; or in less egregious cases, as explained later, it may be subject to the special tax imposed by §1375.[32] These statutory measures restrict attempts to use S corporations as incorporated pocketbooks for their shareholders by investing their retained earnings in marketable securities and other passive investments of a type that the shareholders would have purchased had the earnings been paid out as dividends. The passive income investment limitation can also be viewed as a rough-and-ready offset to the fact that a C corporation can be converted to S status without subjecting its accumulated earnings to tax at the shareholder level as if they were distributed in a quasi-liquidation.

In applying §1362(d)(2) to an S corporation with earnings and profits, it is necessary to compare its passive investment income with its gross receipts to determine whether the election is terminated. "Passive investment income" is defined by §1362(d)(3)(D) to mean gross receipts derived from royalties, rents, dividends, interest, annuities, and sales or exchanges of stock or securities (but only to the extent of net gains), except for interest on obligations acquired in the ordinary course of business from the sale of inventory and a few other special items.[33] In classifying rents, Regs. §1.1372-4(b)(5)(vi) distinguishes between passive rental income and receipts from an active business where significant services are rendered to the lessee, the latter category not being considered rent. Thus, amounts received from operating a hotel or motel, a warehouse storage business, or a parking lot do not constitute rent if significant services are rendered; on the other hand, where

---

[31] See infra ¶ 6.08.

[32] See infra ¶ 6.07, text at notes 65 and 66. See also Ginsburg, Subchapter S and Accumulated E&P: A Different View, 17 Tax Notes 571 (1982).

[33] See Rev. Rul. 72-457, 1972-2 CB 510 (corporation whose sole activity is buying and selling commodity futures contracts for own account does not have passive investment income from such activities; contracts not stock or securities); Rev. Rul. 79-294, 1979-2 CB 305 (computation of gross receipts from commodity futures transactions; gross receipts equal net gain from closing transaction; no gross receipts if corporation takes delivery or sustains loss), codified by §1362(d)(3)(C) of the 1982 law; New Mexico Timber Co., 84 TC 1290 (1985) (contra under pre-1982 law); John D. Thompson, 73 TC 878 (1980) (discount income from collections of purchased tax refund claims not passive investment income); Bradshaw v. US, 683 F2d 365 (Ct. Cl. 1982) (collections on installment notes from sale of land not passive investment income).

For special rules enacted in 1984 applicable to options and commodities dealers, see §1362(d)(3)(D)(v) (to be renumbered and clarified as §1362(d)(3)(E) by §106(f)(4) of the Technical Corrections Act of 1987, H.R. 2636).

mere rental of space is the principal activity (e.g., leasing of apartments or offices in an office building), rental income would result.[34]

It should be noted that §1362(d)(3)(A) compares the corporation's passive investment income to its gross receipts rather than to its gross income, apparently to facilitate use of Subchapter S by corporations operating at a loss, which might be disqualified if gross income were the relevant standard. "Gross receipts" is defined by Regs. §1.1372-4(b)(5)(iv) as the total amount received or accrued from sales, services, or investments, depending on the corporation's method of tax accounting. These amounts are not reduced by items of cost, returns, and allowances or other allowable deductions. However, the term does not include amounts received from nontaxable sales or exchanges, or to borrowed funds, repayments of a loan, or contributions to capital.[35]

---

[34] See Rev. Rul. 61-112, 1961-1 CB 399 (crop-share agreement where material participation in crop production was present); for the significant services issue, see Stover v. CIR, 781 F2d 137 (8th Cir. 1986) (mobile home park; services not significant), and cases there cited; Rev. Rul. 64-232, 1964-2 CB 334 (equipment rental business); Rev. Rul. 65-91, 1965-1 CB 431 (warehousing, storage, and parking lot businesses); Rev. Rul. 65-83, 1965-1 CB 430 (payments for the use of various types of personal property); Rev. Rul. 76-48, 1976-1 CB 265 (tennis and handball court receipts); Rev. Rul. 76-469, 1976-2 CB 252 (receipts from long-term leases of vehicles); Rev. Rul. 75-349, 1975-2 CB 349 (motion picture distribution); Rev. Rul. 81-197, 1981-2 CB 166 (distinction between "rents" and "service fees" in the case of airplane charters; rents where mere passive lease; service fee where lessor performs significant services).

See also House v. CIR, 453 F2d 982 (5th Cir. 1972) (active versus passive distinction applied to interest); Doehring v. CIR, 527 F2d 945 (8th Cir. 1975) (same); Marshall v. CIR, 510 F2d 259 (10th Cir. 1975) (contra); Zychinski v. CIR, 506 F2d 637 (8th Cir. 1974), cert. denied, 421 US 999 (1975) (no statutory basis for active/passive distinction as to gains on sales of securities by corporation in active business); Rev. Rul. 75-349, 1975-2 CB 349.

[35] See generally Valley Loan Ass'n v. US, 258 F. Supp. 673 (D. Colo. 1966) (repayments of loan constitute gross receipts; regulations to the contrary invalid); Marshall v. CIR, supra note 34 (contra); Branch v. US, 20 AFTR2d 5302 (N.D. Ga. 1967) (gross receipts included payment for option to purchase corporate property, even though not includable in gross income until following year); Rev. Rul. 68-364, 1968-2 CB 371 (assumption of liabilities constitutes gross receipts); Rev. Rul. 71-455, 1971-2 CB 318 (distributive share of gross receipts from a joint venture used in applying passive investment income test); Alfred M. Sieh, 56 TC 1386 (1971), aff'd per curiam, 31 AFTR2d 694 (8th Cir. 1973) (method of accounting controls computation of gross receipts; held cash-basis taxpayer's gross receipts include only actual collections on loan principal and interest); US v. 525 Co., 342 F2d 759 (5th Cir. 1965) (receipts from reserved oil payment not includable in gross income); Swank & Sons v. US, 362 F. Supp. 897 (D. Mont. 1973) (oil and gas lease bonus receipts not passive investment income), aff'd per curiam, 522 F2d 981 (9th Cir. 1975); Opine Timber Co., 64 TC 700 (1975) (delay rentals under oil and gas lease were passive investment income); Steadwell Johnston, ¶ 76,142 P-H Memo. TC (1976) (purported

4. Inadvertant terminations. Terminations under §1362(d)(2) or §1362(d)(3) (relating to supervening disqualifications and excess passive investment income respectively) can be forgiven under §1362(f) if (1) the Service determines that the termination was inadvertent, (2) the disqualifying event is corrected within a reasonable period after discovery, and (3) both the corporation and the shareholders agree to be treated as if the election had been in effect for the terminated period. The Senate Finance Committee admonished the Service to be "reasonable" in applying this amnesty provision where no tax avoidance would result from continued Subchapter S treatment; examples of inadvertent terminations cited in the Committee's report are (1) violation of the passive income test where a corporation in good faith, albeit erroneously, determined that it had no accumulated earnings and (2) breach of the one-class-of-stock rule where no tax avoidance resulted.[36] The termination waiver of §1362(f) can be retroactive for all years or merely retroactive to the period in which the corporation again became eligible for Subchapter S treatment.

5. Short taxable periods. Under §1362(e), if an S corporation's status terminates for less than its entire taxable year, there are two short taxable-year periods, one in which the corporation is treated as an S corporation and one in which it is taxed as a C (i.e., a regular) corporation.[37] The income for the regular corporation year is taxed on an annualized basis, and all items of income, deduction and credit are allocable between the two periods on a daily basis (unless all shareholders elect to apply normal accounting rules to both periods).

Thus, §1362(e)(1)(A) provides that the S short year ends on the day before the effective date of termination of S corporation status (although §1362(e)(6)(B) extends the due date of the corporation's final S short-year return to the due date of the C short-year return, including extensions), while the C short-year period commences with the date when S status terminated under §1362(e)(1)(B). The income allocation rules are found in §1362(e)(2) (the daily allocation rule), and §1362(e)(3) (election to allocate income under normal accounting rules). The annualization requirement for

---

installment sale of rent receipts disregarded as mere anticipatory assignment of income; hence, Subchapter S status terminated because of excessive rentals).

[36] S. Rep. No. 640 97th Cong., 2d Sess. 12–13 (1982), reprinted in 1982-2 CB 718, 723. See Rev. Rul. 86-110, 1986-38 IRB 4 (inadvertent termination waived); Note, When Can Inadvertent Termination of S Corporation Be Waived?, 65 J. Tax'n 116 (1986).

[37] For the effect of a termination resulting from the acquisition of an S corporation's stock by another corporation that elects under §338 (infra ¶ 11.47), see Eustice & Kuntz, supra note 1, at ¶¶ 5.08[1](b) and 13.04(9).

the C short-year period is provided by §1362(e)(5). Finally, §1362(e)(6)(A) provides that the short years created by §1362(e) count as only one year in determining corporate carry-overs and carry-backs.

¶ 6.05 ELECTION AFTER TERMINATION

If an election is terminated under §1362(d), the corporation may not make a new election for any year before the fifth taxable year beginning after the first year for which the termination was effective. This period of disqualification, which is equally applicable to any successor corporation of the electing corporation, as discussed later in this chapter, may be shortened by the Service under §1362(g). The Code lays down no standards for the exercise of judgment under §1362(g), but the regulations state that (1) the corporation has the burden of persuasion; (2) a transfer of more than 50 percent of the stock to outsiders tends to establish that consent should be granted; and (3) otherwise, consent is ordinarily denied unless the termination was involuntary so far as the corporation and its major shareholders were concerned.[38] An example of a termination that might evoke favorable action by the government under §1362(g) is a transfer to an ineligible shareholder by a minority shareholder in an effort to induce the others to buy him out.

The Service's power to shorten the waiting period does not alter the effect of §1362(b), which provides that an election must be made during the first two and one-half months of the taxable year for which it is to be effective or during the preceding year. This means that a termination, unless it occurs during the first two and one-half months of a taxable year, renders Subchapter S inapplicable for at least one year,[39] no matter how generously and rapidly the Service may wish to exercise its discretion to shorten the normal five-year waiting period of §1362(g).

The five-year waiting period of §1362(g) is applicable not only to the corporation whose election was terminated, but also to any "successor corporation." This term is defined by the regulations as a corporation that

---

[38] Regs. §1.1372-5(a); see also Rev. Rul. 67-382, 1967-2 CB 298 (consent to reelect not given where shareholders intentionally caused termination of Subchapter S status); Versitron, Inc. v. US, 38 AFTR2d 6119 (Ct. Cl. 1976) (not an abuse of discretion to deny reelection before five-year waiting period expired where previous election had been terminated by Type B reorganization). See also Rev. Rul. 86-141, 1986-49 IRB 6 (blanket amnesty under §1362(g) to enable terminated corporations to reelect in order to qualify for 1986 law transition relief rules).

[39] Such a termination not only revives the corporate income tax for the years of disqualification, but may also break the period during which previously taxed income can be distributed tax-free. See Regs. §1.1375-4(d); infra ¶ 6.08.

acquires a substantial part of the electing corporation's assets or whose assets were in substantial part owned by the electing corporation, provided that 50 percent or more of its stock is owned directly or indirectly by persons who owned 50 percent or more of the stock of the electing corporation when the termination became effective.[40]

Since §1362(g) can be construed to forbid an election only if it occurs *after* a termination,[41] the assets of a corporation whose election has terminated may evidently be transferred to another corporation that has *previously* made a valid election, even though it is controlled by the same or substantially the same shareholders without necessarily terminating the second corporation's election. This suggests that the shareholders of an electing corporation who foresee a termination of its election because of some transitory condition (e.g., passive investment income) may organize a new corporation before the disqualifying event occurs, cause it to elect under Subchapter S, and then transfer the assets of the disqualified corporation to the awaiting vehicle immediately after the first corporation's election terminates, hoping thereby to avoid the five-year waiting period. If the attempt to circumvent §1362(g) is too blatant, however, the election by the second corporation might be regarded as a new election by a successor corporation, even though it was made before the first corporation's election was terminated and its assets transferred.

¶ 6.06　PASS-THROUGH OF CORPORATE INCOME AND LOSSES TO SHAREHOLDERS

1. Background. From its enactment in 1958, Subchapter S has exempted electing corporations from the corporate income tax because the corporate income, whether distributed or not, is taxed to the shareholders. Until 1982 this result was achieved by requiring the shareholders to include in gross income not only any dividends received during the taxable year, but also the amounts they would have received as dividends if the corporation's undistributed taxable income had been distributed to them on the last day of the corporation's taxable year. This year-end principle made it possible for stock to be transferred to members of a shareholder's family at the last minute for income-splitting purposes, subject to the assignment-of-income

---

[40] Regs. §1.1372-5(b); see also Rev. Rul. 77-155, 1977-1 CB 264 (corporation purchased all stock of S corporation, terminating its status; parent then liquidated subsidiary; held parent not a successor corporation and hence not subject to five-year waiting period).

[41] See Regs. §1.1372-5(a), referring to a new election.

doctrine and similar principles.[42] Moreover, the constructive dividend principle required shareholders to treat their hypothetical receipts of the undistributed income as ordinary income, regardless of its nature when viewed at the corporate level.

Both of these features of prior law were eliminated in 1982 in favor of a broader conduit or pass-through approach based on the partnership model, under which income, losses, deductions, and credits retain their corporate-level character and are allocated to the S corporation's shareholders on a per-share, per-day basis (by virtue of §§1366 and 1377(a)(1) respectively) and are treated by shareholders as if attributable directly to the source from which they were generated. The 1982 rules are examined in subsequent paragraphs, first in respect to the S corporation itself and then as they affect shareholders. As discussed later, the pre-1982 rules continue to have certain residual consequences, especially for corporations that filed Subchapter S elections before 1983.[43]

2. Taxation of S corporations. Under §1363(a), S corporations are not subject to income taxes[44] except for the tax on built-in gains and the special tax on excess passive investment income imposed by §§1374 and 1375 respectively.[45]

Despite the tax exemption accorded by §1363(a) to S corporations, §1363(b) provides that their taxable income must be computed in the same manner as the taxable income of an individual except for the disallowance of personal exemptions, itemized personal deductions allowed to individuals, charitable contribution and NOL deductions, and a few other items; on the other hand, organizational expenses authorized by §248 can be deducted. It

---

[42] See generally infra ¶ 7.07; see also Henry D. Duarte, 44 TC 193 (1965) (purported transfers of S corporation stock to shareholder's minor children lacked economic reality; income allocable to children's shares held taxable to taxpayer).

For more on pre-1982 law, see Briskin, Use of Subchapter S Corporations to Shift Income Among Family Members, 59 Taxes 557 (1981).

[43] See infra ¶ 6.08, text at note 74.

[44] Section 1363(a) provides for exemption from "the taxes imposed by this chapter," which include not only the corporate income tax of §11 and the alternative minimum tax of §55, but also the accumulated earnings tax of §531 and the personal holding company tax of §541. In theory, an electing corporation is also relieved of the more exotic taxes imposed by §802 (insurance companies), §852 (regulated investment companies), §594 (certain mutual savings banks), and §881(a) (certain foreign corporations), but the first two classes could rarely, and the second two could never, qualify as electing corporations under Subchapter S.

Although tax-exempt, the electing corporation is required by §6037 to file an annual information return.

[45] For these taxes, see infra ¶ 6.07.

is necessary, however, to compute separately, as explained later, various income items, losses, deductions, and credits, because they retain their corporate-level status when passed through pro rata to the S corporation's shareholders; it is not clear why an S corporation's taxable income, as distinguished from its *gross* income, needs to be computed.[46] Moreover, in keeping with the conduit approach, S corporations are treated by §1371(a)(2) as individuals with respect to any stock they may hold in a C corporation (although *not* in another S corporation); thus, an S corporation receiving dividends from a C corporation is not entitled to the dividends-received deduction allowed by §243.

Most elections (e.g., depreciation and accounting methods) are made at the corporate level despite the conduit approach; but this one-for-all principle does not encompass the elections under §§163(d), 617, and 901, relating respectively to the limitation on interest on investment debt, the deduction and recapture of certain mining expenses, and the deduction or credit of foreign income taxes. Each shareholder is allowed by §1363(c)(2) to make these elections for himself.

The character of each separately computed item is determined under §1366(b) "as if such item were realized directly from the source from which [it was] realized by the corporation, or [was] incurred in the same manner as [it was] incurred by the corporation." Thus, if the shareholders of an S corporation use it to engage in a hobby, sport or recreation (such as the operation of a country estate), the income and deductions incurred in the activity must be treated by the shareholders as if attributable to the underlying activity; the items attain no greater dignity from being passed through the corporation. This point is reinforced by §183 (activities not conducted for profit) and §280A (home offices, vacation homes, and so forth), both of which are explicitly made applicable to S corporations as well as to individuals. Moreover, the passive activity limitation rules of §469, which were enacted in 1986, apply to S corporations in the same manner as to general partnerships.

Section 1378, enacted in 1982, restricts S corporations' election and change of their taxable years; in general, they must report on a calendar year basis (as do most individuals) unless a business purpose for a different accounting period is established to the satisfaction of the Service.[47] As a "pass-through entity" under §267(e), an S corporation is in effect placed on the cash method of accounting in deducting business expenses and interest

---

[46] For computation of an S corporation's taxable income in applying §§1374 and 1375, relating to the special taxes on certain built-in gains and on excessive passive income, see §1374(d)(4).

[47] For application under prior law of the taxable year requirement to S corporations on a change in stock ownership, see §1378(c)(2) (repealed by the Tax Reform Act of 1986); see also August, New Taxable Year Conformity Rules Under Tax Reform: Application to S Corporations, 3 J. Partnership Tax'n 370 (1987).

owed to related cash-basis taxpayers, including shareholders who own, directly or by attribution, any of its stock.[48]

3. Pass through of S corporation's tax items to shareholders. In determining the tax liability of an S corporation's shareholders, §1366(a) requires them to take into account their pro rata shares of (1) the corporation's income, losses, deductions, and credits whose separate treatment "could affect the liability for tax of any shareholder," and (2) the corporation's "nonseparately computed income or loss," defined as the corporation's gross income less its allowable deductions after excluding all separately stated items.[49] Thus, tax-exempt interest, long- and short-term capital gains, charitable contributions, foreign income taxes, and other items that are combined with similar items derived from the shareholder's personal activities, subjected to percentage or dollar limits or otherwise specially treated on individual income tax returns must be stated separately and allocated pro rata to the shareholders under §1366(a); each item retains its special character in the hands of the shareholder. (The list of such items will change from year to year as the Code is amended.) On the other hand, business profits (and losses) usually fall into the nonseparately computed category unless they are derived from activities that are themselves segregated at the individual level, such as income from oil and gas production, from foreign sources, and from passive activities.

A shareholder's pro rata share of these items is determined under §1377(a) by allocating an equal portion of each item to each day of the corporation's taxable year and dividing that amount by the shares outstanding on that day. If, however, a shareholder's interest is terminated during the taxable year, the allocation can be made as if the taxable year consisted of two short taxable years, the first of which ended on the day of the termination, provided all persons who were shareholders during the entire year agree to this treatment.

The shareholders then consolidate their allocated shares of these items with any similar items arising from their individual activities, reporting the aggregated amounts on their individual returns subject to any pertinent restrictions or elections. For example, the shareholder's share of the S corpo-

---

[48] For details, See Eustice & Kuntz, supra note 1 at ¶ 7.04[18].

[49] For prior law, under which NOLs (but not other losses or excess deductions) were passed through to the S corporation's shareholders, see Eustice & Kuntz, supra note 3, at ¶ 6.05.

Under current law, the S corporation's NOL, if computed, must be disaggregated to permit its constituent items of income, deduction, and loss (such as passive activity, oil and gas production, and foreign source income) to be computed separately when required by §1366(a)(1).

ration's short- and long-term gains are combined with his individual gains in determining his "net capital gain" under, §1222(11); similarly, his share of the S corporation's capital losses is combined with the individual's capital losses in determining the amounts that are currently deductible and/or carried forward to later years. This consolidation at the individual level of allocated and personally generated items may affect shareholders differently. For example, one shareholder's share of the corporation's charitable contributions may be used currently because, when added to that shareholder's personal contributions, it does not exceed the percentage limit imposed by §170(b)(1); on the other hand, a fellow shareholder whose taxable income is lower or who is more generous may be unable to make use of the corporate contribution currently or even in the later years to which excess contributions can be carried under §170(d)(1). In the same vein, shareholders may go their separate ways in dealing with their respective shares of foreign income taxes paid by the S corporation; one may elect to deduct these taxes (after combining the allocated amount with any foreign income taxes paid at the personal level), while the other shareholders may elect to take the foreign tax credit allowed by §901.

4. Adjustments to basis of shareholder's investment in S corporation's stock and debt. Under §1367(a)(1), the shareholders of an S corporation increase the basis of their shares by the amount of income passed through to them, substantially as if the income had been distributed and reinvested as a contribution to the corporation's capital; thus, they are not taxed a second time if they sell the stock at a price reflecting the corporate income that they reported on their individual returns but that was retained and accumulated by the corporation. (By virtue of §1367(b)(1), basis increases are contingent on inclusion of the income item in shareholders' gross income as adjusted for any redetermination of the shareholder's tax liability.)

On the other hand, shareholders are required by §§1367(a)(2)(B) and 1367(a)(2)(C) to reduce the basis of their stock (but not below zero) by their pro rata shares of the S corporation's deductions and losses;[50] since shareholders take advantage of these items on their personal returns, the reduc-

---

[50] If a shareholder's investment becomes worthless during the year, §1367(b)(3) provides for the reduction in basis before application of the worthless stock and securities rules of §§166(d) and 165(g); this may give the shareholder the benefit pro tanto of an ordinary loss rather than a capital loss. For prior law, see Abdalla v. CIR, 647 F2d 487 (5th Cir. 1981).

In the case of stock or debt received by gift, the shareholder's basis for determining gain may be different from his basis for determining loss (see §1015(a)), but §1366(d)(1) (which limits the amount of loss passed through to stock and debt basis) does not state which basis is to be used. The shareholder's basis for computing loss should probably be controlling.

tion in basis is necessary to prevent the same items from being used to reduce the shareholder's gain (or increase the loss) on selling the stock. For the same reason, the basis of the stock must be reduced under §1367(a)(2)(A) if the shareholder receives any tax-free distributions from the corporation; since these receipts ordinarily consist of previously taxed corporate income, the adjustment offsets the earlier increase in the basis of the stock under §1367(a) when the income was passed through to the shareholder.

If the basis of a shareholder's stock is reduced to zero by virtue of these adjustments (and the more specialized basis-reduction items listed in §1367(a)(2)), any additional downward adjustments are applied to the basis of any loans that the shareholder may have made to the corporation, as prescribed by §1367(b)(2).[51] If the deductions and losses allocated to the shareholder exceed the basis of both his stock and debt investment in the corporation, §1366(d)(1) prevents him from using the excess on his individual return. This barrier is imposed because the disallowed amount exceeds the shareholder's economic investment in the corporation, and, because of the limited liability accorded to shareholders, the amount does not have to be paid. The disallowed losses and deductions, however, do not evaporate into thin air; they can be carried forward indefinitely under §1366(d)(2), for use when and to the extent that the shareholder acquires a basis against which they can be applied (e.g., if the shareholder buys more stock or lends additional funds to the corporation, or the corporation generates taxable income). Moreover, §1366(d)(3) provides a mechanism for recognizing the carryforward, even if the S corporation loses its status as such. Finally, shareholders whose basis is insufficient to absorb the S corporation's current deductions and losses do not have to rely on the carryforward allowed by §1366(d); if they are willing and financially able to do so, they may increase

---

[51] For problems in identifying the shareholder-held debt against which deductions and losses can be applied, see Perry v. CIR, 392 F2d 458 (8th Cir. 1968) (corporate debts guaranteed by shareholder not debt whose basis is taken into account for loss pass-through purposes); Joe E. Borg, 50 TC 257 (1968) (cash-basis shareholder had zero basis for corporate notes issued, but not taxed, for compensation claims of taxpayer); Rev. Rul. 75-144, 1975-1 CB 277 (shareholder payment of corporate debt pursuant to guaranty created corporate obligation to shareholder by subrogation, giving shareholder basis under §1376 of prior law to allow pass-through of losses; same result if shareholder gives note to creditor in substitution for corporate debt); Selfie v. US, 778 F2d 769 (11th Cir. 1985) (shareholder gets basis if loan in fact made to him); E. J. Frankel, 61 TC 343 (1973), aff'd by order, 506 F2d 1051 (3d Cir. 1974) (shareholders not entitled to count loans to S corporation by their partnership, even though individual loans would have qualified).

For priority restoration of the basis of the shareholder's debt (before restoration of stock basis) to reflect later corporate earnings, see §1367(b)(2)(B) (which overruled prior law).

the basis of their investment immediately by such tactics as bona fide capital contributions, stock purchases, and extensions of additional credit.[52]

5. Distributions to shareholders. Distributions by S corporations to their shareholders, ordinarily reflecting corporate income that was previously passed through to them and was reported on their individual tax returns, are usually received tax-free and applied in reduction of the basis of their stock, with any excess treated as gain on the sale of property. This principle, however, is applied differently to S corporations with earnings and profits than to those without earnings and profits, as explained later in this chapter.[53]

6. Reallocation within the family. To curb the use of Subchapter S as a detour around the family partnership rules of §704(e),[54] §1366(e) provides that the corporate items taken into account by a shareholder may be apportioned or allocated among members of his family if they are shareholders and the Service finds this action necessary to reflect the value of services or capital rendered to the corporation by them.[55] The definition of family applicable to family partnerships (§704(e)(3)) is adopted for this purpose. Unlike §704(e), however, §1366(e) permits an allocation or apportionment

---

[52] For discussion of these and other basis-increasing tactics, see Eustice & Kuntz, supra note 1, at ¶ 10.03[2]. For unsuccessful attempts to receive a step-up in basis without a current outlay, see Rev. Rul. 81-187, 1981-2 CB 167 (shareholder's unsecured, unpaid demand note); Underwood v. CIR, 535 F2d 309 (5th Cir. 1976) (shareholder assumption of corporate note); Silverstein v. US, 349 F. Supp. 527 (E.D. La. 1973) (sham note). But see Selfie v. US, supra note 51.

[53] See infra ¶ 6.08.

[54] Under §704(e)(2), a partner reports his distributive share of the partnership income; however, if he acquired his partnership interest by gift, appropriate allowance must be made for reasonable compensation for services rendered (or capital supplied) to the partnership by the donor. See generally McKee, Nelson, & Whitmire, Federal Taxation of Partnerships and Partners (Warren, Gorham & Lamont, Inc., 1977), ¶ 14.05; Willis, Pennell, & Postlewaite, Partnership Taxation, pt. 17 (Shepard's/McGraw-Hill, 1971–1985).

[55] See generally Pat Krahenbuhl, ¶ 68,034 P-H Memo. TC (1968) (allocation required); Charles Rocco, 57 TC 826 (1972) (acq.) (contra; salaries were reasonable); Edwin D. Davis, 64 TC 1034 (1975) (no allocation where taxpayer did not perform substantial services for the corporation, even though he referred all business to corporation); Louis G. Horn, ¶ 82,741 P-H Memo. TC (S corporation conducting X-ray activities for related professional service corporation disregarded as sham; income allocated to personal service corporation).

For a more limited reallocation rule under pre-1982 law, involving distributions of dividends other than in proportion to intrafamily ownership, see Johnson v. CIR, 720 F2d 963 (7th Cir. 1983) (reallocation allowable only on initiative of Service, not on request of taxpayers); Eustice & Kuntz, supra note 3, at ¶ 13.05.

to reflect the value of a shareholder's services or capital not merely if the other members of his family acquired their stock from him but also if their stock was acquired from outsiders in an arm's-length transaction. In another respect, however, §1366(e) is narrower than §704(e); the latter permits a reallocation between donor and donee regardless of their relationship, but §1366(e) permits allocation or apportionment only within a family.

7. **Examples.** The pass-through rules of Subchapter S are illustrated by the following examples, in which X Corporation is wholly owned by individual A and reports its income on the calendar year, and A has a basis of $100 for his stock in X.

Example 1. X earns $400 of taxable income in year 1 and distributes $300 to A in December of that year. X is not taxed and, by virtue of §1371(c)(1), realizes no current earnings and profits; A is taxed on the $400 of X's income under §1366(a); the $300 distribution is tax-free under §1368(b); and A's basis for his X stock is increased by $100 to $200 under §1367(a) to reflect the undistributed $100 taxed to A. If X had instead distributed the $300 in year 2 (and had broken even that year), the tax results to A and X would be the same.

Example 2. If the $300 distribution in Example 1 consisted of property (e.g., a capital asset with a basis to X of $100) rather than cash, X would recognize a capital gain of $200 under §1363(d) that would pass through and be taxed as such to A under §1366(b). A's $100 stock basis would be increased by $300 (i.e., $400 of passed-through ordinary income and $200 capital gain less a $300 tax-free §1368 distribution) to $400. If the distributed property was depreciable in X's hands, §1239 would convert the recognized gain from capital to ordinary. Moreover, X might have been taxable on the $200 of capital gain under §1374.[56]

Example 3. If X incurred a $200 loss (rather than the gain hypothesized in Example 1) and made no distribution, the loss would pass through to A but would be limited by §1366(d)(1) to A's $100 stock basis in X. The excess would carry over indefinitely to future years under §1366(d)(2) and would be available to A when he obtained enough stock or debt basis to absorb it.

Example 4. Continuing with the facts of Example 3, if A loaned $100 to X in December of year 1, the $200 loss could be used in full by A, whose basis for his X stock ($100) and for his loan to X ($100) would be reduced to zero as a result of the loss pass-through. If X earned $150 in

---

[56] See infra ¶ 6.07, para. 1.

year 2, A's basis for the debt would be restored to $100 first, and the remaining $50 would then be applied to increase the basis of the stock from zero to $50 by virtue of §1367(b)(2)(B).

Example 5. If the loss in Example 3 was half capital and half ordinary, each type of loss would pass through as such under the conduit rule of §1366(b); and presumably the same 50-50 ratio would apply both to the $100 loss used currently by *A* and to the $100 loss carried forward for later use.

¶ 6.07 BUILT-IN GAINS AND EXCESS NET PASSIVE INVESTMENT INCOME

Although S corporations are not subject to the regular income tax, they are subject to the special taxes on built-in gains and on excessive net passive income imposed by §§1374 and 1375 respectively, both enacted to curb the use of Subchapter S elections as a tax-avoidance tactic.

1. Tax on built-in gains. Before 1966, when the statutory predecessor of §1374 was enacted, the pass-through of long-term capital gains authorized by Subchapter S encouraged "one-shot" elections by corporations that were about to realize a substantial capital gain on the sale of real estate or other assets and that wished to distribute part or all of the proceeds to their shareholders. Absent a Subchapter S election, the corporation realized capital gain on the sale, and the distribution to its shareholders was ordinarily a taxable dividend to the extent of earnings and profits. Subchapter S, on the other hand, offered the advantage of a single capital-gain tax to the shareholders, with no additional tax on the distribution of the sales proceeds up to the amount of the passed-through gain. After the pass-through and distribution, the corporation's Subchapter S election would be revoked and the corporation would resume its prior tax status.[57]

Section 1374 discouraged this tactic by imposing a tax at the corporate level[58] (coupled with a pass-through of the capital gain, less the corporate tax thereon, to the shareholders), if three conditions were met: (1) the excess of net long-term capital gain over net short-term capital loss exceeded

---

[57] For background, see S. Rep. No. 1007, 89th Cong., 2d Sess. 6 (1966), reprinted in 1966-1 CB 527, 531.

[58] The imposition of a capital gains tax under §1374 could formerly trigger liability for the corporate minimum tax imposed by §56 of prior law; see §§1363(a) and 58(a) of prior law; see also Eustice & Kuntz, supra note 1, at ¶ 7.05[3] for extended analysis of §1374 and the minimum tax associated with it.

The Tax Reform Act of 1986, however, removed S corporations from minimum tax exposure (because of the repeal of the capital gain preference rate).

$25,000 and also exceeded 50 percent of the corporation's taxable income;[59] (2) the corporate taxable income exceeded $25,000; and (3) the corporation was not subject to Subchapter S for the three immediately preceding taxable years or since its inception.[60]

The Tax Reform Act of 1986, as part of its repeal of the *General Utilities* doctrine,[61] retooled §1374 as well, extensively expanding this provision to cover *all* built-in gain property held by a C corporation at the time its S election becomes effective and recognized by the corporation at any time within the 10-year recognition period after Subchapter S status begins. Such gains are to be taxed under §1374(b)(1) at the maximum rate prescribed by §11(b), but in computing the corporate-level tax under §1374(b), the corporation is permitted to use its former C-year tax attributes (e.g., unexpired carryovers and credits). Section 1374 applies asset by asset, but the amount of taxable gain is subject to an overall limitation in §1374(c)(2) equal to the aggregate net built-in gain at the beginning of the election period under §1374(d)(1). Thus, if the corporation has potential gain assets of $100 and potential loss assets of $40, only $60 of net gain is subject to tax during the 10-year recognition period.

The Service announced subsequently[62] that regulations would be issued under §1374 to provide the following rules:

(1) Recognized built-in gains under §1374(d)(2) will include not only sales or exchanges but also any other income-recognition event that effectively realizes on the corporation's right to receive income (e.g., collection of accounts receivable by a cash-method taxpayer, or the receipt of §453 installments);

(2) In tracing and identifying pre- and post-election inventory property gains, the inventory method used by the taxpayer (FIFO, LIFO, and so forth) will control;

---

[59] Taxable income was defined for this purpose by former §1374(d), currently §1374(d)(4), without change in substance; compare 1363(b).

[60] Section §1374(c)(2). Although primarily directed against one-shot, tax-motivated elections, §1374 applied even if the corporation's election continued in force after the property sale. See Paramont Land Co. v. US, 727 F2d 322 (4th Cir. 1984); see also Warrensburg Board & Paper Corp., 77 TC 1107 (1981).

[61] See ¶¶ 7.20–7.22, 11.06.

[62] Ann. 86-128, 1986-51 IRB 22; see also Rev. Rul. 86-141, 1986-49 IRB 6 (prescribing rules for election prior to 1987 in order to avoid the effect of new §1374; the filing date is key for grandfather treatment here, but only if the corporation is an eligible corporation on such date (supra ¶¶ 6.02 and 6.03)).

The Technical Corrections Act of 1987, H.R. 2636, §106(f)(3), generally codifies most of the principles of Ann. 86-128 in new §1374(d)(5)-(7) (retroactively to Jan. 1, 1987).

See generally August, Corporate-Level Taxes on S Corporations After the Tax Reform Act of 1986, 4 J. Partnership Tax'n 91 (1987).

(3) Assets acquired in a carryover basis transfer from a C corporation (e.g., by merger) will be subject to the built-in gain rules of §1374 as of the time of their receipt (the 10-year recognition period also will commence at that point for those assets);

(4) Assets acquired from another S corporation that is subject to a §1374 limitation in a carryover basis transfer also will be subject to §1374 in the hands of the transferee, but the 10-year period will "tack" from the transferee in this case;

(5) Assets acquired in a substituted basis transaction (e.g., a §1031 exchange) will tack the holding period of the transferred assets; and

(6) Built-in loss assets contributed to the corporation in anticipation of the election in order to reduce the aggregate net built-in gain for purposes of §§1374(c)(2) and 1374(d)(1) will be subject to "anti-stuffing" principles similar to the rules of §336(d)(2),[63] under which built-in loss on property contributed within two years of the start of the S period (or the filing of the election, if earlier) will not reduce built-in gain unless the taxpayer establishes a clear and substantial business purpose for the contribution.

Section 1374 does not apply to a corporation that has always been an S corporation by virtue of §1374(c)(1) (except, as noted above, in cases where the aged S corporation acquires assets in a carryover basis transaction from a C corporation and is thus subjected to the anti-brokering restriction of regulations to be issued). Nor does this provision apply to post-election appreciation if the taxpayer can establish either that the assets were acquired after the election or that they subsequently increased in value. However, asset appreciation and potential income rights generated during years that the corporation was a regular C corporation can no longer escape the two-tier tax regime, established by the 1986 amendments, through an election of Subchapter S (unless the corporation is extraordinarily patient and willing to wait out the 10-year recognition period of amended §1374).

2. Tax on excess net passive income. As noted earlier, Subchapter S elections are terminated if the corporation has passive investment income exceeding the limits specified by §1362(d)(3).[64] Even if that drastic remedy is avoided, an S corporation is subject to a special tax if it has any Subchapter

---

[63] See ¶ 11.06. Built-in loss assets contributed after the election will not be effective, since §1374 applies asset by asset, and the aggregate cap of §1374(c)(2) is determined at the start of the election period.

[64] See supra ¶ 6.04, text at note 30.

C earnings and profits (regardless of amount) at the close of a taxable year[65] and more than 25 percent of its gross receipts consist of passive investment income. The tax is imposed on the corporation's "excess net passive income," defined as the amount that bears the same ratio to net passive income for the taxable year as the excess of passive investment income over 25 percent of gross receipts bears to total passive investment income for the same year.[66] The amount subject to tax, however, is limited by §1375(b)(1)(B) to the corporation's taxable income for the same year, as defined by §1374(d)(4). The tax is computed at the highest rate specified by §11(b), which prescribes the rates applicable to the regular corporate income tax. For example, if an S corporation with Subchapter C earnings and profits has net passive income of $100, gross passive income of $200, and gross receipts of $400, the excess net passive income is $50 ($100 × $100/$200) and the tax thereon under the 1988 rate schedule is $17 (34 percent of $50).

The Service is authorized by §1375(d) to waive the tax if the S corporation establishes to the satisfaction of the Service that it determined in good faith that it had no Subchapter C earnings and profits at the close of the relevant taxable year and that, within a reasonable period after this determination was found to be erroneous, it distributed those earnings and profits. Moreover, §1375(c)(2) provides that gains subject to the §1375 passive income tax will not be taxed again under the built-in gain tax provisions of §1374.

¶ 6.08 DISTRIBUTIONS OF PREVIOUSLY TAXED INCOME

1. Introductory. Since the heart of Subchapter S is its allocation of an S corporation's income to the shareholders when realized by the corporation, whether it is distributed to them or not, a mechanism is needed to permit the undistributed income to be received by them in later years without being subject to a second round of taxation. This is accomplished by §1368 (enacted in 1982 to replace an earlier, more complex system that, as explained later,[67] continues to apply to some distributions). The rules distinguish among corporations, depending on whether they do or do not have any accumulated earnings and profits; consequently, a preliminary explanation of this dividing line is necessary.

---

[65] For situations in which an S corporation can have earnings and profits, see infra ¶ 6.08, para. 1.

[66] For the terms "gross receipts" and "passive investment income," see §1362(d), discussed supra ¶ 6.04, para. 3.

[67] Infra text at note 74.

First, although S corporations are subject to the earnings and profits concept of Subchapter C by virtue of §1371(a)(1), their own business operations do not generate any *current* earnings and profits for post-1982 years by virtue of §1371(c)(1). Second, the only sources of accumulated earnings and profits for an S corporation are (1) the corporation's own history as a C corporation before electing S status; (2) its history as an S corporation before 1983; and (3) the inheritance of earnings and profits as the result of an event described in §1371(c)(2), such as a merger with a C corporation, a liquidation of a C corporation subsidiary (which would be rare, if not impossible, in light of §1361(b)(2)(A), or a spin-off, split-off, or split-up from a C corporation.

2. S corporations having no accumulated earnings and profits. Distributions by S corporations having no accumulated earnings and profits (including all S corporations created after 1982 that maintain S status continually from their inception and do not inherit earnings and profits from another corporation by virtue of a corporate adjustment under §1371(c)(2)) are governed by §1368(b). The distribution is excluded from the shareholder's gross income up to the adjusted basis of the stock (and it reduces basis pro tanto);[68] the excess, if any, is treated as gain from the sale or exchange of property.[69] Although §1368(b) does not say so explicitly, the gain should qualify as long- or short-term capital gain if the shareholder is an investor, but as ordinary income for dealers in securities who hold the stock for sale to customers in the ordinary course of business.[70]

These principles apply whether the distribution consists of cash or of property; however, a distribution of appreciated property ordinarily triggers the recognition of gain at the corporate level by virtue of §1363(d). The gain passes through to the shareholder and results in an increase in the basis of the stock; this in turn ordinarily insures that the distribution itself is tax-free to the shareholder. If, however, the gain is not only recognized at the corporate level but is also subjected to the special built-in gain tax imposed by §1374(a), the amount passed through is the gain reduced by the allocable tax.[71]

3. S corporations with accumulated earnings and profits. The rules applicable to distributions by S corporations with accumulated earnings and profits are more complex, primarily to prevent a C corporation with accumulated earnings and profits that have not been taxed to its shareholders

---

[68] See supra ¶ 6.06, paras. 4 and 5.

[69] This treatment is comparable to the result under §§301(c)(2) and 301(c)(3)(A) when distributions are made by a C corporation without current or accumulated earnings and profits; see infra ¶ 7.02.

[70] See infra ¶ 7.02 regarding similar language in §301(c)(3)(A).

[71] See §1374, imposing a tax in the circumstances summarized supra ¶ 6.07, para. 1; for the amount passed through, see §1366(f)(2).

from electing under Subchapter S and then distributing these profits to the shareholders as tax-free returns of capital or as capital gains. To prevent such a bailout, §1368(c) assigns distributions to three tiers:

(a) Tier 1. Up to the corporation's accumulated adjustments account, the distribution is treated as prescribed by §1368(b) (i.e., as a tax-free return of capital up to the adjusted basis of the stock, and as gain from the sale or exchange of property thereafter.)[72] An S corporation's "accumulated adjustments account" is defined by §1368(e)(1) as a record of adjustments for the corporation's Subchapter S period (the most recent continuous period during which it has been an S corporation, excluding taxable years beginning before 1983), similar to the basis adjustments prescribed by §1367 in determining a shareholder's basis for his stock and debt in the S corporation. For practical purposes, the balance in the accumulated adjustments account is usually the net amount of the income (except tax-exempt income), deductions (except nondeductible expense items), and losses passed through to the S corporation's shareholders less previous tax-free (and, probably, other nondividend) distributions to them.[73] This amount presumably can be negative following amendments to §1368(e)(1) in 1984.

(b) Tier 2. The balance, if any, of the distribution is treated as a dividend up to the amount of the distributing corporation's accumulated earnings and profits. This is the crucial part of §1368(c), since it ensures that distributions of accumulated earnings and profits are taxed as dividends, even though paid out by an S corporation.

(c) Tier 3. The remainder of the distribution, if any, qualifies for §1368(b) treatment and is treated the same as the Tier 1 portion (i.e., as return of capital and/or gain from a sale or exchange, as the case may be).

4. Old S corporations. In recognition of the fact that the rules prescribed by §1368 were enacted in 1982 and replaced an earlier set of rules governing distributions of corporate income taxed to shareholders under old Subchapter S but not distributed to them at the time of taxation, §1379(c)

---

[72] For an election to waive application of Tier 1 treatment in order to purge the corporation's accumulated earnings and profits (e.g., to avoid the tax imposed on the net passive income of S corporations with accumulated earnings and profits), see §1368(e)(3).

[73] For a more detailed examination of this new concept, see Eustice & Kuntz, supra note 1, ¶ 9.04[7]; Sharp & Webster, Accumulated Adjustments Account: Woe Is "S," 2 J. Partnership Tax'n 259 (1985). Unlike a comparable concept of prior law (i.e., the previously taxed income account), this account exists at the corporate level, is assignable with the transfer of a shareholder's stock, and, by virtue of §1371(e), can even survive termination for the period described in §1377(b).

See generally Rowland, Distributions of Cash and Property by S Corporations Require Careful Planning, 4 J. Partnership Tax'n 34 (1987).

carries forward the pre-1983 rules for corporations that qualified under Subchapter S for their last taxable year beginning before 1983. The pre-1983 rules, although more complex than the rules prescribed by §1368, similarly result in return of capital and gain treatment for distributions of so-called previously taxed income.[74] Given its purpose, the ambiguous reference in §1379(c) to "distributions of undistributed taxable income *for* any taxable year beginning before January 1, 1983" (emphasis added) is clearly intended to refer to the year when the income is realized by the corporation, not the year when it is distributed to the shareholders; thus, this transitional provision should apply to post-1982 distributions for the indefinite future.

¶ 6.09 COMPARISON OF C AND S CORPORATIONS AND PARTNERSHIPS

While the 1982 revision of Subchapter S went a long way toward conforming the treatment of S corporations and partnerships, it did not go all the way to the Subchapter K partnership model. For that matter, neither did it completely sever its ties with the Subchapter C rules governing ordinary business corporations. Subchapter S is closest to the partnership rules in its treatment of ordinary operations and distribution; but it differs markedly from Subchapter K as to the eligibility rules for Subchapter S status (there are no such limitations for partnerships other than the requirement of partnership status, but extensive eligibility restrictions attach to electing Subchapter S status).[75]

On the other hand, when an S corporation engages in various extraordinary transactions (e.g., stock redemptions, stock dividends, recapitalizations, partial and complete liquidations, divisive and acquisitive reorganizations, and so forth), the Subchapter C rules emerge as the dominant body of governing law (although special aspects of the Subchapter S provisions can apply here as well).

Table 6-1 illustrates the principal points of divergence between Subchapters C, S, and K.[76]

---

[74] For details, see the fourth edition of this treatise; Eustice & Kuntz, supra note 3, at ¶¶ 9.01–9.03.

[75] Supra ¶ 6.02.

[76] See generally Eustice & Kuntz, supra note 1, at ¶ 1.03; Eustice, Subchapter S Corporations and Partnerships: A Search for the Pass-Through Paradigm, 39 Tax L. Rev. 345 (1984); August & Schwimmer, Integration of Subchapter C With Subchapter S After the Subchapter S Revision Act—Part I, 12 J. Corp. Tax'n 107 (1985); August, Integration of Subchapter C With Subchapter S After the Subchapter S Revision Act—Part II, 12 J. Corp. Tax'n 269 (1985); Id., Part III, 12 J. Corp. Tax'n 323 (1985).

TABLE 6-1
Comparison of C, S, and K Entities

	C Corporation	S Corporation	K Partnership
Eligibility limitations			
Number of owners (limits)	None	35 (70)	At least 2
Owner identity limits	None	Yes	None
Affiliate limits	None	Yes	None
Capital structure limits	None	Yes	None
Income character limits	None (cf. §541)	Yes	None
Other limits	None	Eligibles	None
Status electivity			
Affirmative election	None	Yes	None
Owner consents	None	Yes	None
Voluntary status termination			
• Election	Elect S	Elect C (revoke)	None (cf. §761)
• Transactional	Liquidate/merge	Liquidate/merge	Merge/incorporate
Involuntary status termination	None	Yes	None
Entity treatment			
Entity taxability			
• Operations	Yes (§11)	No (except §1375)	No
• Asset sale	Yes	No (except §1374)	No
• Asset distribution gain	Yes (§§311, 336)	No (except §1363(d))	No
• Asset distribution loss	No (§311 unless §336)	No (except §336)	No
Taxable year	Any	Limited (§1378)	Limited (§706)
Accumulations	E&P (§§531,541)	Irrelevant	Irrelevant
Taxable income and elections	Entity level	Entity level (with exceptions) §§1363(b), 1363(c), 267(f)	Entity level (with exceptions)

(continued)

TABLE 6-1 (continued)

	C Corporation	S Corporation	K Partnership
Entity treatment (cont'd)			
Distributions			
• Cash or debt	E&P (§§535, 545)	No effect	No effect
• Property	§§311, 336 taxable gain	§1363(d) (except §368)	No effect
Inside asset basis	Inside events only	Same as C	§§753, 734, 743, 755
Sales of interests	No effect (unless §338)	No effect (unless revoked or tainted buyer)	Terminate if 50 percent (§708(b)(1)(B))
Conversion of status			
• Inbound	S to C/K to C	C to S/K to S	C to K/S to K
• Outbound	C to S/C to K	S to C/S to K	K to C/K to S
Reorganizations	§368	§368	§§708(b)(2)(A), 708(b)(2)(B)
Treatment of equity owner			
Undistributed income	No tax	Current tax	Current tax
Current losses			
• General	No deduction	Current deduction	Current deduction
• Limit		Outside basis (carry-over)	Outside basis (carry-over)
Character conduit	No	Yes (§1366(b))	Yes
Owner's basis			
• General	Constant	Adjusted Annually	Adjusted annually
• Effect of entity debt	None	None	Basis affected (§752)
Ordinary distributions			
• Cash or debt	Dividend (if E&P)	Basis recovery (gain)	Basis recovery (gain)
• Property	Dividend and basis (FMV)	Same as C	Nonrecognition and substituted basis (§732(a))
Redemptions and liquidations			
• Treatment in general	§§302, 331, 341 §334(a)	Same as C	§§731–736, 751(b)
• Basis	§§1221, 341	Same as C	§732(b), substituted
Sales of interests	§§354, 355, 356	Same as C	§§708, 741, 751(a), 743, 754
Reorganizations	§§381, 382	Same as C	§708(b)(2)
Attribute carry-overs		Same as C	No provision

CHAPTER 7

Dividends and Other Nonliquidating Distributions

PART A.   DISTRIBUTIONS IN CASH

¶ 7.01   INTRODUCTORY

As noted in Chapter 1, the corporation is a separate taxable entity under the Code, so that corporate income is taxed to the corporation and dividends paid by the corporation are taxable to the shareholders. In this chapter, we examine in more detail the taxation of corporate distributions, a subject of wonderful complexity.

A framework for the taxation of corporate distributions is provided by §§301(a), 301(c), and 316. By virtue of these provisions, a corporate distribution is a dividend that must be included in the recipient's gross income under §§301(c)(1) and 61(a)(7) if and to the extent that it comes out of either earnings and profits of the corporation accumulated after February 28, 1913 or earnings and profits of the taxable year. Most distributions of most corporations fall well within this category of taxable dividends and hence are taxed as ordinary income to the shareholder.[1] To the extent that a distribution by a corporation is not covered by current or post-1913 earnings and profits, however, it is treated by §301(c)(2) as a return of capital to the shareholder and is to be applied against and in reduction of the adjusted basis of his stock. If the distribution exceeds the adjusted basis of the stock, the excess is ordinarily taxed as capital gain, with the exception, of minor importance, of distributions out of an increase in the value of corporate property accrued before March 1, 1913.[2]

Assuming a corporation is newly organized with cash, the reason for gearing the taxability of its distributions to its record of earnings and profits is clear enough. Until the corporation has engaged in profitable operations, any distribution to its original shareholders is a return of their investment rather than income. Once the corporation has realized profits, however, its distributions may pro tanto be fairly regarded as income to the shareholders.

The equity of §§316 and 301(c) is far less clear, assuming that after a period of corporate profits, the stock changes hands and that before additional earnings arise (the next day, if you will) there is a distribution to the new stockholder. Has *he* not received a return of *his* capital? The economist might say that a distribution in these circumstances ought to be regarded as a return of capital, but §§301(c) and 316 are inescapable, so, to the extent of

---

[1] Before 1987, dividends paid to individual shareholders were ordinarily eligible for a $100 dividends-received exclusion under §116, but this provision was repealed by the Tax Reform Act of 1986. See infra ¶ 7.06. If the shareholder is a corporation, the 80 (or 100) percent dividends-received deduction of §§243–246 ordinarily is applicable. See supra ¶ 5.05.

[2] §§301(c)(3)(A), 301(c)(3)(B).

his share of the corporation's earnings and profits, the surprised stockholder has realized income. This "miracle of income without gain"[3] was attested long ago by the Supreme Court in U.S. v. Phellis:

> In buying at a price that reflected the accumulated profits, [the share-holder] of course acquired as a part of the valuable rights purchased the prospect of a dividend from the accumulations—bought "dividend on," as the phrase goes—and necessarily took subject to the burden of the income tax proper to be assessed against him by reason of the dividend if and when made. He simply stepped into the shoes, in this as in other respects, of the stockholder whose shares he acquired, and presumably the prospect of a dividend influenced the price paid, and was dis-counted by the prospect of an income tax to be paid thereon.[4]

In point of fact, however, the purchaser of stock must bid against many other potential buyers who would be affected in varying degrees by the income tax on a dividend and some of whom might be tax-exempt organiza-tions, so the price could rarely, if ever, be accurately "discounted by the prospect of an income tax to be paid" on dividends that may be declared immediately after the stock is purchased. Moreover, the distribution will be a dividend under §316 only if it is paid from the corporation's earnings and profits, and, since the calculation of earnings and profits may be a complex operation,[5] the purchaser often would not know the proper discount to apply (except possibly in the case of a closely held corporation), even if he were so foresighted as to anticipate the problem.

Just as the concept of earnings and profits may be unfair to a share-holder who buys stock before a corporate distribution, so on occasion it may, with equal irrationality, shower the shareholder with riches. If the cor-poration into which he buys is a deficit corporation, distributions by the corporation may be treated as wholly or partly tax-free returns of capital to the shareholder, even though they reflect earnings by the corporation after he buys his stock. This bonanza can occur if the corporation has neither post-1913 nor current earnings and profits and if (to reverse the discount theory of the *Phellis* case) the shareholder did not pay a premium when he bought his shares for the tax advantage lurking in the corporation's deficit.

Despite these shortcomings, the existing system of relating the tax sta-tus of corporate distributions to the corporation's earnings and profits is responsive to the felt need for a method of protecting returns of capital from the tax on dividends, and, while a better response to this need could no

---

[3] Powell, Income From Corporate Dividends, 35 Harv. L. Rev. 363 (1922).

[4] 257 US 156, 171–172 (1921).

[5] See infra ¶ 7.03.

doubt be devised, Congress has shown no disposition to depart from the present method.[6]

Before turning to the details of the general rule set out above, under which a distribution by a corporation is a dividend if it comes out of current or post-1913 accumulated earnings and profits but is a return of capital to the extent of any excess, it should be noted that special rules are provided for certain categories of distributions, among which are the following:

(1) Distributions in kind (i.e., property other than money);[7]

(2) Distributions of the corporation's own obligations;[8]

(3) Distributions of the corporation's own stock or of rights to purchase its stock;[9]

(4) Distributions in redemption of stock, including partial liquidations and complete liquidations (see Chapters 9 and 11); and

(5) Distributions in corporate reorganizations and similar transactions (see Chapters 13 and 14).

¶ 7.02 "DIVIDEND": A TERM OF ART

Under §301(c), a distribution is includable in a shareholder's gross income to the extent that it is a "dividend" as defined in §316; the balance of the distribution, if any, is a return of capital under §§301(c)(2) and 301(c)(3). The term "dividend," as defined for income tax purposes by §316(a), does not correspond to the term "dividend" under state law, with

---

[6] For proposals to eliminate earnings and profits as a benchmark and to use simpler methods of identifying returns of capital, see Staff Report, Senate Finance Committee, 99th Cong., 1st Sess., The Reform and Simplification of the Income Taxation of Corporations (1985); Sheppard, Eliminating Earnings and Profits, 28 Tax Notes 711 (1985); Colby, Blackburn & Trier, Elimination of Earnings and Profits From the Internal Revenue Code, 39 Tax Lawyer 285 (1986); Blum, The Earnings and Profits Limitation on Dividend Income: A Reappraisal, 53 Taxes 68 (1975); Andrews, "Out of Its Earnings and Profits": Some Reflections on the Taxation of Dividends, 69 Harv. L. Rev. 1403 (1956).

The growing tendency to consider eliminating the earnings and profits concept was reversed, at least for the foreseeable future, by the adoption in 1986 of this assertedly obsolete benchmark in computing alternative minimum taxable income under §56(f)(3)(B) as a substitute for book income in limited situations for 1987–1989, and in general under §56(g)(4) thereafter. See supra ¶ 5.08.

[7] See infra ¶ 7.20.

[8] See infra ¶ 7.40.

[9] See infra ¶ 7.41.

the result that a corporate distribution may be a "dividend" under §316(a) even if it impairs capital or is otherwise unlawful under state law. As pointed out by Rudick: "[W]hat the distributing corporation may call a dividend, or what the state law may call a dividend, or even what the recipient thinks of without question as a dividend, is not necessarily a 'dividend' for federal income tax purposes."[10] Conversely, it is possible for a distribution to constitute a lawful "dividend" under state law without qualifying as a "dividend" under §316(a).

The definition of "dividend" in §316 is two-fold: A distribution by a corporation to its shareholders is a "dividend" if it is made out of (1) earnings and profits accumulated after February 28, 1913, or (2) earnings and profits of the taxable year. "Earnings and profits" is a term of art that will be examined in detail,[11] but it must be pointed out here that it is *not* identical with "earned surplus," nor is it represented by a bank account or other specific corporate assets. A distribution is "out of" earnings and profits if the corporation operated profitably in the period under consideration, and no tracing or earmarking of funds or assets is required.

The first part of §316(a), which provides that a distribution is a "dividend" if it comes from earnings and profits accumulated since February 28, 1913, looks to the financial success of the corporation over the long haul. If the corporation has operated profitably since 1913 (or since organization, if it was incorporated after 1913), distributions will be taxed to the shareholders as "dividends." The exemption of earnings and profits accumulated before February 28, 1913 (the date of the first federal income tax imposed after the adoption of the Sixteenth Amendment) is a matter of legislative grace rather than constitutional right. It affects only corporations organized before 1913 and their successors; and since even a corporation that belongs to this select group is likely to keep its distributions to shareholders well within its current or recent earnings and profits, the complicated network of law built on the 1913 benchmark is of interest to very few shareholders.[12]

The second part of §316(a) provides that a distribution is a "dividend" if it comes from earnings and profits of the taxable year. Section 316(a)(2)

---

[10] Rudick, "Dividends" and "Earnings or Profits" Under the Income Tax Law: Corporate Non-Liquidating Distributions, 89 U. Pa. L. Rev. 865, 866 (1941). On state law, see Kriedmann, Dividends–Changing Patterns, 57 Colum. L. Rev. 372 (1957).

If the distribution is a "dividend" for federal tax purposes, it will ordinarily be taxable to the stockholder under the claim of right doctrine, notwithstanding any potential liability to creditors under state law. See US v. Lesoine, 203 F2d 123 (9th Cir. 1953). But see Knight Newspapers, Inc. v. CIR, 143 F2d 1007 (6th Cir. 1944).

[11] See infra ¶ 7.03.

[12] See Lynch v. Hornby, 247 US 339 (1918); see also Helvering v. Canfield, 291 US 163 (1934), holding that pre-1913 earnings and profits are wiped out by post-1913 losses and need not be restored from later earnings.

has a curious ancestry. It was enacted in 1936 as a relief measure when the undistributed profits tax was in effect. That tax was imposed on the undistributed part of corporate income, computed by deducting "dividends" from total income. Unless a deficit corporation could treat distributions out of current earnings as "dividends" for this purpose, it would be unable to avoid the undistributed profits tax no matter how large its distributions to stockholders were. To enable such corporations to obtain a credit for distributions out of current earnings, §316(a)(2) was enacted. Apparently, no thought was given to the effect of the new subsection apart from the undistributed profits tax, and it was left intact when the undistributed profits tax was repealed in 1939. The effect of §316(a)(2) can sometimes be avoided by postponing the distribution until the next year. If the corporation has no earnings in that year and still has a deficit, the distribution will be receivable tax-free, since it will fall under neither §316(a)(1) nor §316(a)(2), as in Example 2 at the end of this section.

Since most distributions are made by corporations that are currently profitable, §316(a)(2) often makes it unnecessary to compute the corporation's post-1913 accumulated earnings and profits. This makes for simplicity, but it also means that a distribution may be a taxable "dividend," even though the corporation has a deficit; if the concept of earnings and profits serves any useful purpose, it is partly undermined by §316(a)(2). For the original shareholders of a corporation, there is no economic difference between a distribution before the corporation has had any earnings, which is not a "dividend" under either §316(a)(1) or §316(a)(2), and a distribution after it has suffered a loss. But the latter is a "dividend" under §316(a)(2) if there are current earnings, even though they are insufficient to repair the deficit. For shareholders who acquire their stock after the deficit but before the earnings, §316(a)(2) is more defensible, to be sure; but here §316(a)(2) does not go far enough, since its impact can be avoided if the distribution can be postponed until a year in which the corporation has no earnings and profits.

If the corporation has neither post-1913 accumulated earnings and profits nor current earnings and profits, a distribution cannot be a "dividend." It is instead subject to §§301(c)(2) and 301(c)(3). Under §301(c)(2), the distribution is applied against and reduces the adjusted basis of the shareholder's stock. If the distribution is greater than the adjusted basis of the stock, the excess is subject to §301(c)(3). In this event, it will be treated as gain from the sale or exchange of property (and thus as capital gain if the stock is a capital asset), unless it is out of a pre-1913 increase in the value of the corporation's property, in which event it will enjoy an exemption from tax.[13]

---

[13] See Higginson v. US, 81 F. Supp. 254 (Ct. Cl. 1948), modified, 101 F. Supp. 763 (Ct. Cl. 1952); Ernest E. Blauvelt, 4 TC 10 (1944) (acq.); CIR v. Gross, 236 F2d

Several aspects of the return-of-capital distribution rules of §§301(c)(2) and 301(c)(3) deserve special comment. The sale gain created by §301(c)(3) will be entitled to capital gain treatment only if the stock is a capital asset in the shareholder's hands. The gain will be long- or short-term, depending upon his holding period for the stock. In computing gain under §§301(c)(2) and 301(c)(3), however, it is not clear whether the shareholder is entitled to recover his aggregate stock basis before reporting gain. If he must instead consider the distribution to have been made on a share-by-share basis, gain may be recognized on low-basis shares, even though his basis has not been fully recovered on high-basis shares.[14] When stock is redeemed under §302[15] and when corporate assets are distributed in complete liquidation,[16] gain or loss is generally computed on a share-by-share basis, and, presumably, the same approach should be applied to the computation of shareholder gain under §§301(c)(2) and 301(c)(3). A plausible argument could be made for aggregate treatment under §301(c)(2), however, on the ground that, since no partial loss deduction is permitted in this situation (unlike redemption and liquidation transactions), the shareholder's aggregate basis should be fully recovered before he is required to recognize any gain.

The second sentence of §316(a) lays down an irrebuttable presumption that every distribution is out of earnings and profits to the extent thereof and that it comes from the most recently accumulated earnings and profits. This prevents earmarking a distribution to control its tax status; for example, a corporation having current earnings and profits, post-1913 accumulated earnings and profits, and pre-1913 accumulated earnings and profits, cannot make a distribution from the pre-1913 earnings and profits until the current and post-1913 earnings and profits have been exhausted. After its current, post-1913, and pre-1913 earnings and profits have been exhausted, however, the corporation may be able to earmark a distribution so as to

---

612 (2d Cir. 1956); see also Falkoff v. US, 604 F2d 1045 (7th Cir. 1979); Rufus K. Cox, 78 TC 1021 (1982) (§301(c)(3) gain cannot be reported as installment sale transaction under §453).

The capital gain element, if any, is no longer entitled to a differential rate (because of the repeal in 1986 of former §1202), but capital gain, unlike ordinary income, can be offset to an unlimited extent by capital losses.

[14] See Johnson v. US, 435 F2d 1257 (4th Cir. 1971) (aggregate basis recovery method in reporting gain under §§301(c)(2) and 301(c)(3) rejected in favor of block-by-block method); see generally Note, Aggregation of Bases Under Sections 301(c)(2) and (3), 33 Tax Lawyer 937 (1980), and cases cited therein; see also Fink v. CIR, 789 F2d 427 (6th Cir. 1986), rev'd on another issue,−US−(1987) (same where there is capital contribution of stock, discussed supra at ¶ 3.13).

[15] See infra ¶ 9.02.

[16] See infra ¶ 11.03.

qualify it for the exemption conferred by §301(c)(3)(B) (pre-1913 increase in value) and thus protect its shareholders against a capital gain tax under §301(c)(3)(A).[17]

In determining whether a distribution is out of earnings and profits of the taxable year, §316(a)(2) provides that the earnings and profits for the year are to be computed as of the close of the taxable year without diminution by reason of distributions during the year. This means that a distribution will be a "dividend" if the corporation has earnings and profits at the end of the taxable year, even though it had none when the distribution occurred; conversely, a distribution that seemed to be a "dividend" when made may turn out to be a return of capital because the corporation has no earnings and profits at the end of the year. If the distributions for the year exceed in amount both the earnings and profits of the taxable year and the post-1913 accumulated earnings and profits, the regulations prescribe a method of allocating the two categories of earnings and profits to the various distributions in order to ascertain the "dividend" component of each one.

> *Example 1.* Assume that X Company has only individual shareholders and that all parties are on the cash-basis, calendar-year method of accounting. X Company has a deficit of $20,000 in its earnings and profits at the beginning of Year 1, has earnings and profits of $10,000 during Year 1, and distributes $10,000 to its shareholders on July 1 of that year. Under §316(a)(2), the year 1 distribution is a taxable dividend, notwithstanding X Company's deficit.

> *Example 2.* If, however, X Company in Example 1 waits until Year 2 to make this distribution and has no current earnings and profits in that year, the distribution will be treated as a return of capital under §§301(c)(2) and 301(c)(3), since X Company's Year 1 earnings and profits will be absorbed by its deficit, leaving no accumulated earnings to support dividend treatment in Year 2.

> *Example 3.* Y Company has accumulated earnings and profits of $15,000 on January 1 of Year 1, has earnings and profits of $10,000 during Year 1, and distributes $20,000 to its shareholders in April and $20,000 in September of that year. Regs. §§1.316-2(b) and 1.316-2(c) provide that the April distribution is a dividend in its entirety ($5,000 from current earnings and $15,000 from accumulated earnings), while only $5,000 of the September distribution is a dividend ($5,000 from

---

[17] For examples illustrating the foregoing principles, see Regs. §1.301-1(f), Examples (1)–(3).

current earnings, the accumulated earnings having been exhausted by the April distribution). [18]

Example 4. Z Company has accumulated earnings of $20,000 at the start of Year 1, incurs a current operating deficit of $16,000 in Year 1, and distributes $20,000 to its shareholders on July 1 of that year. The regulations suggest that the current deficit is prorated throughout the year if it cannot specifically be allocated to a part of the year. If the deficit is prorated, accumulated earnings at the date of the distribution will be reduced by $8,000 (one-half of the deficit) to $12,000, and the distribution will be a dividend to this extent; but if the deficit can be traced and allocated in full to the first half of Year 1, accumulated earnings will be reduced by $16,000, and the dividend portion of the distribution will be only $4,000. [19]

¶ 7.03   EARNINGS AND PROFITS

It is a curious fact that the Code, ordinarily so prodigal in the use of words, does not specifically define the phrase "earnings and profits." This omission is especially troubling because the phrase has no counterpart in the field of corporation law. [20] The phrase entered the federal tax law in 1916,

---

[18] See also Rev. Rul. 69-440, 1969-2 CB 46 (distributions on preferred stock absorb available current earnings and profits before distributions on common stock). These dividend source rules usually have significance only where there are changes of stock ownership during the year of distribution or where the corporation and its shareholders report on different taxable years.

For the effect of stock redemptions, see Baker v. US, 460 F2d 827 (8th Cir. 1972); Anderson v. CIR, 67 TC 522 (1976) (exhaustive analysis), aff'd per curiam, 583 F2d 953 (7th Cir. 1978); see also Rev. Rul. 74-338, 1974-2 CB 101, applying these principles where dividend and redemption distributions occur in the same year; Edelstein, Eighth Circuit's *Baker* Decision: Filling a Statutory Gap by Judicial Pragmatism, 38 J. Tax'n 66 (1973).

[19] See Regs. §1.316-2(b) (last sentence); Rev. Rul. 74-164, 1974-1 CB 74; see Steel Improvement & Forge Co. v. CIR, 36 TC 265 (1961), rev'd on other grounds, 314 F2d 96 (6th Cir. 1963); Rev. Rul. 69-447, 1969-2 CB 153.

[20] See generally Edelstein, Earnings and Profits: General Principles and Treatment of Specific Items, Tax Mgmt. Portfolio (BNA) No. 175-3d (1982); Edelstein, Earnings and Profits—Effect of Distributions and Exchanges, Tax Mgmt. Portfolio (BNA) No. 189-3d (1982); McDaniel, Earnings and Profits: More Than a Cold Accounting Concept: Additions to and Subtractions From, 32 Inst. on Fed. Tax'n 445 (1974). Two landmark articles on earnings and profits are outdated at certain points but are still useful. Rudick, supra note 10; Paul, Ascertainment of "Earnings or Profits" for the Purpose of Determining Taxability of Corporate Distributions, 51 Harv. L. Rev. 40 (1937), reprinted with revisions in Paul, Selected Studies in Federal

but until 1940 it was given meaning solely by judicial and administrative construction. In 1940, the effect of a few transactions on a corporation's earnings and profits was prescribed by statute, and Congress has intervened on many occasions since then. However, a comprehensive definition is still lacking. To compute a corporation's earnings and profits is often no simple task, especially if it has gone through a series of corporate reorganizations or other adjustments. It may be necessary to go back many years to decide how a transaction should have been treated under a long-interred statute because of its effect on earnings and profits.[21]

The computation of earnings and profits is not appreciably simplified when we find that in all probability the term had little or no meaning to the Congress that coined it. The phrase first appeared in the Revenue Act of 1916. The Revenue Act of 1913 had taxed "dividends" simpliciter, and, by failing to define the term, Congress apparently intended to adopt its meaning in common parlance. The Treasury was quick to give it the broadest possible meaning, including, among other things, distributions from corporate surplus accumulated before the adoption of the Sixteenth Amendment. This construction was upheld by the Supreme Court in *Lynch v. Hornby* on the ground that the word "dividends" was used in the 1913 Act "as descriptive of one kind of gain to the individual stockholder; dividends being treated as the tangible and recurrent returns upon his stock, analogous to the interest and rent received upon other forms of invested capital."[22]

In the meantime, however, Congress had expressly provided in the Revenue Act of 1916 that "the term 'dividends' as used in this title shall be held to mean any distribution made or ordered to be made by a corporation ... out of its earnings or profits accrued since March first, nineteen hundred

---

Taxation 149 (2d Ser. 1938). The Rudick article is supplemented by Albrecht, "Dividends" and "Earnings or Profits," 7 Tax L. Rev. 157 (1952). See also Emmanuel, Earnings and Profits: An Accounting Concept? 4 Tax L. Rev. 494 (1949), and articles cited supra note 6.

Earnings and profits questions are a no-ruling area; see Rev. Proc. 87-3, §3.01(22), 1987-1 IRB 27. For guidelines in determining earnings and profits, see Rev. Proc. 75-17, 1975-1 CB 677. For modified earnings and profits computations under the alternative minimum tax rules, see §56(g)(4), supra ¶ 5.09.

[21] Because there is no statute of limitations governing the effect of prior transactions on accumulated earnings and profits, the permanent retention of corporate records is advisable. For a graphic illustration of the timeless quality of earnings and profits questions, see Union Pac. R.R. v. US, 524 F2d 1343 (Ct. Cl. 1975), cert. denied, 429 US 827 (1976) (claim that earnings and profits were affected by accounting errors between 1900 and 1907, Issue III); see also Jacob M. Kaplan, 43 TC 580 (1965) (nonacq.); Alderson v. Healy, 15 AFTR2d 536 (D. Mont. 1965) (estoppel bars taxpayers from adopting inconsistent position on effect of prior transactions on earnings and profits).

[22] Lynch v. Hornby, supra note 12, at 344–345.

and thirteen. . . ."[23] It is thus reasonably clear that the phrase "earnings or profits" crept into the federal income tax law by accident when Congress was establishing March 1, 1913 as a dividing line between taxable distributions and nontaxable distributions.

In the first regulations issued under the 1916 Act, the Treasury seemingly regarded earnings and profits as identical with surplus.[24] It was inevitable, however, that the existence of a corporate surplus could not serve to differentiate between taxable and nontaxable distributions, unless the surplus was first adjusted almost beyond recognition. For example, a distribution of common stock by a corporation having only common stock outstanding decreases its surplus, although it does not subject the stockholders to tax;[25] if surplus were the criterion of taxability, a corporation could sweep its surplus account clean by a tax-free stock dividend and then distribute cash free of tax. This might be done even if the distribution of cash would be improper under local law, since in practice, and often even by their terms, state dividend statutes penalize the stockholders or directors only if creditors are injured by the distribution.

Another defect in using corporate surplus as a criterion of taxability is that it can be reduced by reserves for contingencies; if these were taken into account, the floodgates would be opened to a stream of tax-free cash distributions for as long as the corporation's directors could conjure up contingencies that would warrant the creation of reserves. It is not surprising, therefore, that surplus has been rejected as a criterion and that the phrase "earnings and profits" has acquired a meaning more in keeping with its function.

When one searches for the meaning of "earnings and profits," then, one is in reality asking how a corporate transaction *should* affect the stockholder who receives a distribution of cash or property from the corporation after the transaction has occurred. To take a simple illustration, assume that during the first year of a corporation's life it earns $10,000, pays a federal income tax of $2,000, and distributes $9,000 to its shareholders. If other facts were ignored, it would probably be agreed that $8,000 should be taxed to the shareholders as a dividend and that the remaining $1,000 should be treated by them as a return of capital.

Not all problems in the computation of earnings and profits, however, are solved so easily. Suppose, in the example just given, the corporation's business earnings amounted to $10,000, but in addition to this it had

---

[23] 39 Stat. 757 (1916).

[24] See Regs. §33 (revised), and Arts. 106–107 (1918). For the modern revival of this notion, see the book income preference of §56(f), supra ¶ 5.08, which is based on income reported in the applicable financial statement.

[25] See infra ¶ 7.42.

received $500 of tax-exempt interest on state and municipal bonds. Should the $9,000 distribution to the stockholders be treated as a dividend to the extent of $8,500, with only $500 treated as a return of capital? Or should the bond interest be excluded from earnings and profits as well as from taxable income? One might argue that the interest, which would not have been taxed to the shareholders if they had held the bonds in their personal capacities, should not become taxable as income to them merely because it was filtered through the corporate entity. Despite this argument, the regulations have long taken the position that tax-exempt bond interest increases earnings and profits, presumably on the theory that the corporation's capital is not invaded by a distribution of such income.[26]

What if the corporation creates a revaluation surplus or deficit by writing the value of its assets up or down to correspond with changes in their market value? Although one might argue for taking such adjustments into account in computing earnings and profits, since the market value rather than the cost of the corporation's assets is what realistically determines whether a distribution invades its capital or not, it is quite clear that appreciation or depreciation in value that has not been realized in the income tax sense does not affect earnings and profits.[27] A contrary rule would require the Treasury to appraise the assets with each distribution or, at least, with each revaluation by the directors.

It should be apparent by now that a corporation's accumulated earnings and profits are not necessarily equal to its surplus (despite occasional loose use of the terms, even in tax cases); nor are they equal to total taxable income. There is, however, a distinct relationship among all three. Starting with taxable income, for example, one can derive both earnings and profits and surplus by going through the corporation's books and records and adjusting for items and transactions that are treated one way in computing taxable income and another way in computing either earnings and profits or surplus. By a similar process, with surplus as a starting point, one can derive taxable income and earnings and profits; alternatively with earnings and profits as a base, taxable income and surplus can be computed. Indeed, the corporation income tax return contains a schedule on which the taxpayer reconciles taxable net income with the increase or decrease in surplus for the taxable year. In a similar manner, the increase or decrease in earnings and profits for the same year could be computed.

---

[26] Regs. §1.312-6(b) (last sentence).

[27] See Elton Hoyt, 2d, 34 BTA 1011 (1936); see also CIR v. Gross, supra note 13; Falkoff v. CIR, supra note 13 (borrowing against appreciated assets did not create earnings and profits). Unrealized depreciation will affect earnings and profits, however, when reflected in the valuation of the corporation's inventory by a writedown from cost to market.

Although earnings and profits can be derived by adjustments to surplus, it is more common to start with taxable income, and, to the extent that the Code and regulations define earnings and profits, both ordinarily take taxable income as the point of departure. The regulations state, for example, that "the amount of the earnings and profits in any case will be dependent upon the method of accounting properly employed in computing taxable income," so if the corporation computes taxable income on the cash-receipts or disbursements basis, it may not use the accrual method for computing earnings and profits.[28] Although they are not intended to provide a comprehensive account of the computation of earnings and profits,[29] the principal categories of adjustments required to convert taxable income into earnings and profits are set out below:

1. Certain items excluded from taxable income must be included in computing earnings and profits. Regs. §1.312-6(b) states:

> Among the items entering into the computation of corporate earnings and profits for a particular period are all income exempted by statute, income not taxable by the Federal Government under the Constitution, as well as all items includable in gross income under section 61 or corresponding provisions of prior revenue acts.[30]

In referring to "income not taxable by the Federal Government under the Constitution," the regulations no doubt mean interest on state and municipal obligations (though the constitutional immunity of such interest is far from clear). The quoted extract is followed by an explicit statement that such interest is taxable when distributed to shareholders as dividends. The reference in the regulations to "all income exempted by statute" is ambiguous; taken in its broadest sense, it would require all income items excluded from gross income by Part III of Subchapter B to be included in earnings and profits.[31] Although authority is scant, the leading commentators have agreed with the regulations in including in earnings and profits (1) the pro-

---

[28] Regs. §1.312-6(a). See infra ¶ 7.04 for more detailed discussion of accounting matters.

[29] See supra note 20.

[30] The converse (i.e., items of gross income that do not increase earnings) rarely arises. But see Regs. §1.78-1(a) (gross-up dividend attributable to deemed-paid foreign tax credit of §902(a)(1) does not increase earnings and profits).

[31] Among the items listed in Part III that might be received by a corporation are the following:

(1) Life insurance proceeds under §101(a);
(2) Gifts and bequests under §102;
(3) Interest on certain governmental obligations under §103;

ceeds of life insurance exempt from taxable income under §101(a); (2) interest on federal, state, and municipal obligations exempt under §103; and (3) compensation for injuries or sickness exempt under §104(a).[32] On the other hand, the commentators have thought that contributions to capital, gifts, and bequests received by a corporation should be excluded from earnings and profits as well as from taxable income, partly on the theory that gifts and bequests cannot be "earned" and are not thought of as profits, and partly on the theory that such gratuitious receipts are not income at all.[33]

There are, however, a number of realized income items that are exempted from income by statute only in the limited sense that income is recognized not at the outset of a transaction but at a later time (either through lower depreciation deductions or when the property eventually is sold). Since 1940, the Code has provided, in what is now §312(f)(1), that such gains and losses do not enter into earnings and profits until they are recognized;[34] thus, as to these items, the corporation's earnings and profits and its taxable income are computed in a similar manner. Nonrecognition transactions within the purview of §312(f)(1) include: §1031 (like-kind exchanges); §1033 (replacements of involuntarily converted property); §351 (transfers to a controlled corporation, discussed in Chapter 3); §361 (reorganization transfers, discussed in Chapter 14); and §1091 (wash sale losses). In all of these transactions, unrecognized gain or loss is deferred through the

---

(4) Compensation for injuries or sickness under §104 (see Castner Garage, Ltd., 43 BTA 1 (1940) (acq.));
(5) Income from discharge of indebtedness under §108;
(6) The value of a lessee's improvements on the lessor's property under §109;
(7) Income taxes paid by a lessee corporation under §110;
(8) Recovery exclusions under §111; and
(9) Capital contributions under §118.

[32] For the effect of distributions of property on earnings and profits, see §312(b), discussed in text infra at note 199.

[33] See supra note 20. Rev. Rul. 54-230, 1954-1 CB 114, states that the excess of life insurance proceeds (from a policy insuring the life of a stockholder) over the aggregate premiums paid is includable in earnings and profits. The reduction for premiums would be appropriate if the premiums had not been deducted from earnings and profits, but not otherwise. See infra note 51, suggesting that earnings and profits should be reduced by the excess of premiums paid but disallowed under §264 over the cash-surrender value of the policy. As to bequests, A.J. Diebold, ¶ 53,052 P-H Memo. TC (1953), holds that they constitute contributions to capital and do not increase earnings and profits. See also Rev. Rul. 66-353, 1966-2 CB 111 (contributions by customers do not increase earnings and profits), modified on other grounds by Rev. Rul. 75-557, 1975-2 CB 33.

[34] The Supreme Court, in CIR v. Wheeler, 324 US 542, reh'g denied, 325 US 892 (1945), held that Congress had merely codified existing law on this question. *Wheeler* involved property acquired by the corporate transferee in a tax-free §351 exchange.

operation of substituted basis rules, and it seems appropriate to carry through this deferral policy in the earnings and profits account as well.[35]

In line with this approach, courts have extended the principle of §312(f)(1) to transactions that are so similar in character to nonrecognition exchanges as to justify nonrecognition treatment in computing earnings and profits.[36] An example is income from a bargain discharge of the corporation's indebtedness where the corporation exercised its option under §108 to exclude such income when realized. Since the basis of its assets must be reduced under §1017, the income will be reflected in taxable income when the assets are depreciated or sold, and it has been held that earnings and profits are to be increased not when the debt is canceled but subsequent to cancelation.[37]

---

[35] Although §312(f)(1) is primarily concerned with realized gain or loss that will be recognized at a later date, its language is broad enough to exclude gains on the sale of Treasury shares from earnings and profits, since these gains are not recognized by virtue of §1032 (see supra ¶ 3.12). See Sprouse, Accounting for Treasury Stock Transactions: Prevailing Practices and New Statutory Provisions, 59 Colum. L. Rev. 882 (1959); United Nat'l Corp. v. CIR, 143 F2d 580 (9th Cir. 1944) (gain on retirement of preferred stock did not increase earnings and profits).

[36] But see Henry C. Beck Co., 52 TC 1 (1969), aff'd per curiam, 433 F2d 309 (5th Cir. 1970) (gain on intercompany transaction, eliminated on consolidated return of affiliated group, held to create current earnings). Later regulations applying a deferral approach for such gains also defer earnings and profits. See infra ¶ 15.23. The *Beck* decision seems inconsistent with the principle that nonrecognition transactions do not create current earnings and profits.

[37] See Bangor & A.R.R. v. CIR, 193 F2d 827 (1st Cir. 1951), cert. denied, 343 US 934 (1952); Alabama By-Prods. Corp. v. US, 137 F. Supp. 252 (N.D. Ala. 1955), aff'd per curiam, 228 F2d 958 (5th Cir. 1956); see also CIR v. Wheeler, supra note 34 (earnings and profits not increased to reflect excess of fair market value over basis of property contributed to corporation, where corporation takes carry-over basis); Meyer v. CIR, 383 F2d 883 (8th Cir. 1967) (debt cancellation resulting from bankruptcy reorganization did not create earnings and profits, even though cancelled debts exceeded downward basis adjustment); Rev. Rul. 75-515, 1975-2 CB 117 (Service will not follow *Meyer*); §312(*l*), enacted in 1980 (excluding debt cancellation income from earnings and profits only to extent applied to reduce basis under §1017; any deficit in earnings and profits is reduced by the capital account of shareholders whose interests are eliminated in bankruptcy proceeding).

If the corporate debtor does not elect to exclude cancellation of indebtedness income under §§108 and 1017 (or, as a result of 1986 amendments, cannot exclude such gain because it is solvent), earnings and profits should be increased by the gain on debt cancellation, unless it qualifies for one of the exceptions to cancellation of indebtedness income. See Annis V.N. Schweppe, 8 TC 1224 (1947), aff'd per curiam, 168 F2d 284 (9th Cir. 1948). See generally Eustice, Cancellation of Indebtedness and the Federal Income Tax: A Problem of Creeping Confusion, 14 Tax L. Rev. 225 (1959); Eustice, Cancellation of Indebtedness Redux: The Bankruptcy Tax Act of 1980 Proposals—Corporate Aspects, 36 Tax L. Rev. 1 (1980).

The effect on earnings and profits of nontaxable contributions to capital[38] is less clear, but it would seem that they should be treated as nonrecognition transactions by analogy to the principles of §312(f)(1), since the basis rules of §362 require the transferee to carry over the transferor's basis for the property or, in the case of nonshareholder capital contributions, to use a zero basis.[39] Similarly, a lessor corporation ought not to be required to increase earnings and profits by the value of improvements made by its lessee when §109 is applicable; taxable income, and hence earnings and profits, will be greater in later years because the basis of the property will not reflect the lessee's improvements. These rules can be reconciled with Regs. §1.312-6(b) by reading the reference to income exempted by statute as embracing items that are permanently excluded from income but not items whose taxable recognition is merely postponed.[40]

On the other hand, Regs. §1.312-6(b) probably requires an amount excluded from taxable income under the tax benefit rule of §111 (recovery of amounts whose deduction did not reduce income in a prior year) to be included in earnings and profits if the deduction served to reduce earnings and profits in an earlier year.[41] Similarly, if depreciation in excess of the amount allowable under §167 was deducted by the taxpayer, earnings and profits should be adjusted upward when the property is sold, even though the taxpayer is able to take advantage of §1016(a)(2)(B) in computing taxable income because the excess deductions were of no tax benefit.

2. Certain items deducted in computing taxable income may not be deducted in computing earnings and profits. This category consists of "artificially created deductions, or credits which are allowed for purposes of computing taxable net income, but which do not represent actual expenses or expenditures, i.e., there is no outlay by the corporation for the deductions or credits represented by such items."[42] Thus, in computing earnings and profits, depletion must be based on cost, even though percentage depletion is employed in computing taxable income.[43] Dividends received from another corporation must be included in full in computing the recipient corporation's earnings and profits, without regard to the 80 (or 100) percent deduc-

---

[38] See supra ¶ 3.13.

[39] See Annis V.N. Schweppe, supra note 37; Rev. Rul. 66-353, 1966-2 CB 111.

[40] For an analogy, see the cases involving the deductibility under §265 of expenses attributable to nonrecognized gain. See, e.g., CIR v. McDonald, 320 F2d 109 (5th Cir. 1963); CIR v. Universal Leaf Tobacco Co., 318 F2d 658 (4th Cir. 1963).

[41] The Service so ruled in Rev. Rul. 58-546, 1958-2 CB 143, but see the doubtful contrary result in Estate of Lasater v. Scofield, 74 F. Supp. 458 (W.D. Tex. 1947).

[42] Rudick, supra note 10, at 885.

[43] Regs. §1.312-6(c).

tion allowed by §243 in computing taxable income. The net operating loss deduction of §172 cannot be used to reduce earnings and profits, since it is simply a carry-back or carry-over of losses that reduced earnings and profits in the year they occurred. The same is true of the capital loss carry-back and carry-over of §1212.

3. Timing differences: Deferred income, accelerated deductions, and so forth. The method of accounting a taxpayer uses in computing taxable income is ordinarily controlling in computing earnings and profits,[44] but Congress has enacted some exceptions to this uniformity rule, primarily to require earnings and profits to be determined without the benefit of various income-deferral and deduction-acceleration rules allowed in computing taxable income. These limited assaults on certain tax accounting rules preserve the rules for the corporation itself but prevent them from creating tax-sheltered income for the shareholders, especially so-called return-of-capital distributions by public utility and real estate corporations.

The earliest of these restrictions, which is still the most important one of general interest, is §312(k), requiring straight-line depreciation to be used in computing earnings and profits for taxable years beginning after June 30, 1972, even though more rapid depreciation or amortization methods are used in computing taxable income.[45]

This approach was extended in 1984 to miscellaneous other tax accounting provisions by §312(n) in order "to ensure that a corporation's earnings and profits more closely conform to its economic income."[46] Thus, income from installment sales must be included in earnings and profits without the benefit of deferral under §453; taxpayers using the completed contract method of accounting for taxable income purposes must compute earnings and profits on the percentage of completion method; and intangi-

---

[44] See infra ¶ 7.04.

[45] Section 312(k) was enacted as §312(m) in 1969, but it was redesignated by the Tax Reform Act of 1976, Pub. L. No. 94-455, 90 Stat. 1520. See Regs. §§1.312-15; 1.312-7(c)(1); 1.312-7(c)(2), Example (3); and §312(f)(1) (third sentence). These sections provide that when §312(k) limits depreciation deductions for earnings and profits computations, straight-line depreciation should also be used in determining basis in computing gain or loss (for earnings and profits purposes) on later sales. See also Rev. Rul. 76-12, 1976-1 CB 91 (must use same useful life in computing taxable income and earnings and profits; tax choice controls); Rev. Rul. 79-20, 1979-1 CB 137 (each corporate member of a partnership must make the §312(k) adjustment). For detailed analysis of the complex operations of §312(k), see Edelstein, Tax Mgmt. Portfolio (BNA) No. 175-3d, at A-32 (1982).

[46] Staff of the Joint Comm. on Taxation, General Explanation of the Revenue Provisions of the Tax Reform Act of 1984, 98th Cong., 2d Sess. 177 (1984); see also §56(g)(4) (special earnings and profits preference for alternative minimum tax, supra ¶ 5.08).

ble drilling costs and mineral exploration and development costs—although deductible in computing taxable income under §263(c), §616(a), or §617— must be capitalized in computing earnings and profits but may be deducted ratably over a prescribed period of 60 or 120 months. In the same vein, construction period carrying charges must be added to the basis of the underlying property and depreciated rather than deducted currently in computing earnings and profits, and circulation expenses and trademark expenditures cannot be deducted under §173 or §177 but can presumably be deducted as business expenses or losses, if the facts so warrant, on a case-by-case basis. Various more specialized adjustments are prescribed to reflect certain LIFO inventory adjustments, and certain capital gain redemptions of the taxpayer corporation's stock.

The resulting increases in the corporation's current earnings and profits are not reduced by the income taxes allocable to the increases that will be paid in subsequent years when the deferred items are actually taken into account in computing taxable income. Thus, the earnings and profits account reflects the corporation's current economic income with respect to the deferred items but not its taxable income with respect to the corporation's federal income taxes.

Finally, §301(f) makes the earnings and profits adjustments mandated by §312(n) inapplicable to certain distributions to corporations owning at least 20 percent of the stock of the distributing corporation, provided the distributee would be entitled to a deduction under §§243–245 (relating to intercorporate dividends) with respect to the distribution (but solely for the purpose of computing the *amount* of that shareholder's dividend income).[47]

To illustrate: X Corporation has two shareholders, A, an individual, and C, a corporation, each owning 50 percent of X's stock. X has no current or accumulated earnings and profits in Year 1, except as generated by the sale of a capital asset (with adjusted basis of $20) for $100, payable in Year 2. X reports its $80 gain in Year 2 under §453. Under §312(n)(5), X has $80 of earnings and profits available for any Year 1 distributions made to individual shareholder A but no earnings and profits for dividend consequences to corporate shareholder C. Thus, if X distributes $80 ratably to A and C in Year 1, A will have a $40 dividend, while C will have a $40 return of stock basis under §301(c)(2) and, if such basis is exceeded, a gain under §301(c)(3). X's earnings and profits are reduced by $80 (i.e., to zero but not below), while C will have an increase of $40 in its earnings and profits.

---

[47] This special limitation is aimed at a manipulative device described in H.R. Rep. No. 861, 98th Cong., 1st Sess. 842 (1984). The Technical Corrections Act of 1987, H.R. 2636, §106(e)(12), would redesignate §301(f) as §301(e).

4. Certain items that cannot be deducted in computing taxable income may be deducted in computing earnings and profits. This category "consists of expenses and losses which are not allowed as deductions in computing taxable net income, but which clearly deplete the income available for distribution to the stockholders." [48] They must be deducted in computing earnings and profits to prevent distributions of the corporation's capital from being taxed as "dividends" to the stockholders. Among the items that require such a downward adjustment of earnings and profits are the following:

(1) Dividend distributions in prior years (because under §316(a)(2), current distributions do not reduce current earnings and profits, and, under §312(a), distributions cannot create a deficit in current or accumulated earnings and profits);

(2) Federal income taxes, net of credits such as the general business credit of §38 and the foreign tax credit of §27; [49]

(3) Expenses and interest incurred in earning tax-exempt interest, even though nondeductible under §265;

(4) Excess charitable contributions (i.e., amounts not deductible in computing taxable income because of the 10 percent ceiling of §170(b)(2)); [50]

(5) Premiums on term life insurance that are disallowed in computing taxable income by §264; [51]

---

[48] Rudick, supra note 10, at 887.

[49] See Rev. Rul. 63-63, 1963-1 CB 10 (investment credit (repealed in 1986) must be applied against tax liability in computing earnings and profits). Foreign taxes, however, should serve to reduce earnings and profits, even though claimed as a credit in computing the corporation's tax liability, since they represent an actual expenditure of funds. See also Rev. Rul. 66-336, 1966-2 CB 110 (amplifying Rev. Rul. 63-63), modified by Rev. Rul. 75-153, 1975-1 CB 106 (effect of investment credit, carry-backs, carry-overs, and basis adjustments on earnings and profits); Rev. Rul. 64-146, 1964-1 CB 129 (tax refund from net operating loss carry-back increases earnings and profits for accrual-basis corporation for taxable years in which right to refund arises).

[50] But see Rev. Rul. 78-123, 1978-1 CB 87 (charitable contribution of appreciated property is deductible only to the extent of basis, even though §170 deduction is based on value); Jacob M. Kaplan, supra note 21 (contra).

[51] The practice with respect to premiums paid for ordinary life policies is evidently to reduce earnings and profits by the excess of the premiums paid over the increase in the policy's cash surrender value. See Sidney Stark, 29 TC 122 (1957) (nonacq.) (stipulated computation of earnings and profits). It is at least arguable that the premiums should be deductible in full from earnings and profits on the ground that the increase in the policy's cash surrender value is unrealized appreciation (see supra note 27); but the contrary view is more harmonious with the fact that earnings and profits are not reduced by investment outlays. To the extent that the premiums have been deducted in computing earnings and profits, Rev.

(6) The excess of capital losses over capital gains, nondeductible by virtue of §1211; [52] and

(7) The bargain element arising on the exercise of qualified stock options. [53]

Earnings and profits should probably also be adjusted for certain other corporate outlays that are not deductible in computing taxable income, such as lobbying expenses and political contributions. [54] There is little reason to think that Congress would have wanted such items to be disregarded in determining whether a distribution to stockholders came out of earnings or capital. More debatable, however, is the proper treatment of expenses that are disallowed by §162(c) in computing taxable income on grounds of public policy, such as fines, bribes, over-ceiling price and wage payments, and the like. Although these items might be classed with penalties for federal income tax fraud, which have long been allowed by the Service itself as deductions in computing earnings and profits, [55] the "frustration of public policy" doctrine (as codified by §162) might be applied to the computation of earnings and profits, as well as to the computation of taxable income. [56]

Rul. 54-230, 1954-1 CB 114, is overly generous in including only the excess of the proceeds over the premiums in earnings and profits. Possibly this is based on the unstated assumption that the premiums were not deducted from earnings and profits when paid.

[52] See Regs. §1.312-7(b)(1). These same regulations allow a deduction for losses disallowed by §267(a)(1), but other §267 transactions were converted to a *deferral* regime in 1984. See supra ¶ 5.04, para. 1. The earnings charge for such items presumably will track the timing of their deductibility as well.

[53] See Luckman v. CIR, 418 F2d 381 (7th Cir. 1969) (bargain element constitutes economic expense for earnings and profits computation); Devine v. CIR, 500 F2d 1041 (2d Cir. 1974) (same); see also Anderson v. CIR, supra note 18 (employer-subsidiary corporation's earnings and profits reduced, rather than earnings and profits of parent-issuer of stock).

[54] See Cammarano v. US, 358 US 498 (1959); see also §162(e) regarding the limited deduction for lobbying expenses. But see §312(m) (no charge to earnings for interest paid on "registration required" debt under §163(f)).

[55] See Rev. Rul. 57-332, 1957-2 CB 231. But see Bernstein v. US, 234 F2d 475 (5th Cir.), cert. denied, 352 US 915 (1956), reh'g denied, 352 US 977 (1957), suggesting a contrary result; see also infra ¶ 7.04.

[56] See Tank Truck Rentals, Inc. v. CIR, 356 US 30 (1958) (overweight fines not deductible as ordinary and necessary business expenses under §162); CIR v. Sullivan, 356 US 27 (1958) (wages, rent, and so forth that are paid by an illegal business deductible under §162). These cases might be distinguished as resting on the "ordinary and necessary" requirement of §162, but *Tank Truck Rentals* was hostile to any tax concession that might reduce the sting of a fine for violating state or federal law. The *Sullivan* case, on the other hand, suggests that earnings and profits should be

5. Corporate distributions and changes in capital structure. In addition to the preceding adjustments, the calculation of earnings and profits must take account of a great variety of financial transactions that may occur only occasionally in the life of any one corporation. Among these transactions, most of which are discussed elsewhere, are the following:

(1) The receipt of tax-free distributions from other corporations, such as stock dividends,[57] nondividend distributions of cash and property,[58] and so forth;

(2) Distributions of property,[59] the corporation's own stock,[60] and its own obligations;[61]

(3) Distributions by a corporation in partial liquidation or in redemption of its stock;[62]

(4) Distributions by a corporation that is obligated on a loan made, guaranteed, or insured by the U.S. (or its agencies or instrumentalities), if the amount of the loan exceeds the adjusted basis of the property constituting security for the loan;[63]

(5) An election under Subchapter S (see Chapter 6); and

(6) Mergers, consolidations, liquidations, transfers of property, spin-offs, and other transactions by which one corporation succeeds to the assets and tax attributes of another corporation.[64]

---

reduced by corporate expenditures in order to achieve a result in accord with economic reality as far as the shareholder is concerned. See also §964(a), denying a charge to earnings and profits of a controlled foreign corporation to the extent such corporation pays bribes or kickbacks, for example, of the type described in §162(c). But see Rev. Rul. 77-442, 1977-2 CB 264 (pre-1976 bribes do reduce earnings and profits of a controlled foreign corporation). Compare §312(m) (no reduction for interest paid on registration-required debt, a result that is more punitive than classifying debt as equity (see supra ¶ 4.01), since dividends reduce earnings under §312(a)).

[57] See infra ¶¶ 7.42 and 7.43.

[58] See supra ¶ 7.02.

[59] See infra ¶ 7.20.

[60] See infra ¶¶ 7.42 and 7.43.

[61] See infra ¶ 7.40.

[62] See infra ¶ 9.35.

[63] Section 312(i). See CIR v. Gross, supra note 13; Alexander, Some Earnings and Profits Aspects of the Internal Revenue Code of 1954, 7 Hastings L.J. 285, 297–300 (1956). For a later illustration of the successful use of the mortgaging-out technique to pay tax-free dividends, see Falkoff v. US, supra note 13.

[64] See supra ¶ 2.10, and infra ch. 16.

¶ 7.04 TAX ACCOUNTING PRINCIPLES IN COMPUTING EARNINGS AND PROFITS AND DIVIDEND INCOME

Although ordinary tax accounting principles are applicable at many points in the computation of earnings and profits, there are a number of divergences. There are also some special rules governing the time when a shareholder is required to take dividends into account in computing taxable income.

1. Accounting for earnings and profits. Regs. §1.312-6(a) provides generally that the method of accounting used in computing earnings and profits is to follow that used for determining the corporation's taxable income. Thus, if the corporation computes taxable income on the cash-basis method of accounting, it cannot use the accrual method for computing earnings and profits. In addition, this requirement of accounting consistency probably applies to such special items as inventory methods, the treatment of bad debt under §166, special deductions for research and experimental expenses (§174), soil and water conservation expenses (§175), and other items that are specially treated in computing taxable income.[65] Similarly, items such as reserves for future expenses, even if proper under nontax accounting pinciples, should not reduce earnings and profits if they are not deductible for tax purposes; conversely, if an advance receipt is includable in taxable income, it likewise should be reflected in earnings and profits, even though nontax accounting practice would sanction deferral.[66]

As to certain items that are not taken into account in computing taxable income (e.g., federal income taxes and fraud penalties), however, variations from tax accounting principles have on occasion been permitted in the determination of earnings and profits, although this question is still a matter of some controversy. Thus, cash-basis corporations have been allowed to

---

[65] Deductions required to be deferred by §267(a)(2) (see supra ¶ 5.04) since 1984 should be deferred for earnings purposes as well. See Rev. Rul. 79-68, 1979-1 CB 133 (no earnings adjustment for accrual basis corporation's advance receipts that are properly deferrable); Rev. Rul. 79-69, 1979-1 CB 134 (cash-basis corporation charges earnings for estimated taxes paid, regardless of ultimate tax liability, which is to be reflected by adjustment when determined); see also supra text at notes 45 and 46 for provisions computing earnings and profits on a different tax accounting basis than taxable income, in order to reduce the disparity between earnings and profits and economic income.

[66] See Corinne S. Koshland, 33 BTA 634 (1935), aff'd, 298 US 441 (1936) (depreciation); Benjamin Siegel, 29 BTA 1289 (1934) (bad debts); IT 3543, 1942-1 CB 111 (amortization of emergency facilities); Paulina du Pont Dean, 9 TC 256 (1947) (acq. and nonacq.) (reserves); Regs. §1.312-6(a) (installment sales); CIR v. South Tex. Lumber Co., 333 US 496, reh'g denied, 334 US 813 (1948) (same). But see §312(n)(5) (1984 amendment denying §453 deferral).

accrue federal taxes and fraud penalties in computing earnings and profits;[67] and accrual-basis corporations have been allowed to accrue contested tax deficiencies for the year to which the tax related and fraud penalties for the year in which the fraudulent return was filed, although in computing taxable income, disputed liabilities are normally deductible only when the contest is settled.[68] These departures from normal tax accounting principles add to the complexity of this area, without making any offsetting contribution to rationality.

2. Accounting for dividends. The time when a distribution must be taken into account is important for two purposes: to fix the time when earnings and profits must be measured in order to determine whether it is a taxable dividend, and to determine the year in which it must be reported by the recipient. In Rev. Rul. 62-131, the Service ruled that the date of payment rather than the date of declaration is controlling in determining whether a distribution comes out of earnings and profits.[69] Similarly, Regs. §1.301-1(b) provides that if property other than money is distributed as a dividend, its fair market value (and hence its dividend status) is determined as of the date of the distribution, even if this is different from the date on which the distribution is includable in the recipient's gross income. The date of distribution, however, could be (1) the duty-to-pay date; (2) the actual transfer date (i.e., when the property passes beyond the distributing corporation's control); (3) the constructive payment date (i.e., when it could have been transferred); or

---

[67] See Demmon v. US, 321 F2d 203 (7th Cir. 1963); Thompson v. US, 214 F. Supp. 97 (N.D. Ohio 1962). Contra Helvering v. Alworth Trust, 136 F2d 812 (8th Cir.), cert. denied, 320 US 784 (1943); Rev. Rul. 70-609, 1970-2 CB 78; Joseph B. Ferguson, 47 TC 11 (1966) (cash-basis corporation could not accrue tax liabilities in computing its earnings and profits); William C. Webb, 67 TC 1008 (1977) (same).

[68] See Demmon v. US, supra note 67; Thompson v. US, supra note 67; Rev. Rul. 57-332, 1957-2 CB 231. But see Sidney Stark, supra note 51 (interest on contested tax liabilities accrues year by year); William H. Kenner, ¶ 75,118 P-H Memo. TC (1975) (contested tax deficiency is deductible for year to which deficiency relates, interest on deficiency is deductible ratably as it accrues, penalty for failure to file is deductible in year when return should have been filed, and interest on penalty is deductible only after assessment and notice and demand).

Section 461(f), added in 1964 to overrule US v. Consolidated Edison Co., 366 US 380, reh'g denied, 368 US 884 (1961), relates only to the accrual of contested deductible taxes and seems inapplicable to this area.

[69] Rev. Rul. 62-131, 1962-2 CB 94; see also Mason v. Routzahn, 275 US 175 (1927); supra ¶ 7.02 (regarding allocation of earnings and profits when less than corporation's distributions). But see CIR v. Goldwyn, 175 F2d 641 (9th Cir. 1949) (prior year's dividend reduced accumulated earnings and profits at the time of declaration rather than when paid). This failure to apply a uniform rule for determining the effect of earnings on distributions and of distributions on earnings is criticized by Albrecht, supra note 20, at 173–176.

(4) the actual receipt date. Of these four dates, the second is probably the correct one theoretically, but some support for the last one may exist as well.

Similarly, in determining when distributions are includable in the recipient's gross income, five points in time might theoretically be relevant: (1) the declaration date; (2) the record date; (3) the date on which the distribution is payable; (4) the date on which the corporation is willing and able to pay; and (5) the date on which the distribution is received by the shareholders. The Service's position on this question is set out in Regs. §1.301-1(b), which provides that distributions are includable in gross income "when the cash or other property is unqualifiedly made subject to [the shareholders'] demands." This language seems to eliminate the first two of the five possible dates, and probably the third as well, so that a choice must be made between the fourth and fifth dates. Elsewhere in the regulations, it is provided that year-end dividends that are paid by checks mailed in December but received by the shareholders in January, are not constructively received in the earlier year.[70] Despite this acceptance of the fifth possible date (actual receipt) as controlling in the case of year-end distributions, the doctrine of constructive receipt (the fourth date, in the foregoing scheme) is applied if the shareholder deliberately turns his back on a distribution that he could have had for the asking.[71] It has been held that these rules apply equally to accrual-basis taxpayers, who are thus placed on a cash basis for distributions, even though they acquire a claim against the payor corporation under local law on the declaration or record date.[72]

---

[70] See Regs. §1.451-2(b) (third sentence), evidently based on Avery v. CIR, 292 US 210 (1934); see also Rev. Rul. 64-290, 1964-2 CB 465, and Rev. Rul. 65-23, 1965-1 CB 520, relating to the reporting of distributions by the paying corporation under §6042(a) and pointing out the distinction between the year for determining the taxable status of distributions and the year they are to be included in the recipient's income.

See also Rev. Proc. 75-17, 1975-1 CB 677, for guidelines in determining earnings and profits.

[71] See Aramo-Stiftung v. CIR, 172 F2d 896 (2d Cir. 1949); A.D. Saenger, Inc. v. CIR, 84 F2d 23 (5th Cir.), cert. denied, 299 US 577 (1936); Bay Ridge Operating Co., ¶ 70,019 P-H Memo. TC (1970). But see CIR v. Fox, 218 F2d 347 (3d Cir. 1954) (no constructive receipt where taxpayer received dividend check by mail in January, even though check could have been picked up on December 31 at corporation's office); Bush Bros. & Co., 73 TC 424 (1979), aff'd, 668 F2d 252 (6th Cir. 1982) (no constructive receipt on facts; shareholders did not have unqualified right to distribution on earlier asserted date).

[72] See Rev. Rul. 78-117, 1978-1 CB 214; CIR v. American Light & Traction Co., 156 F2d 398 (7th Cir. 1946). Regs. §1.301-1(b) makes no reference to the shareholder's accounting method, and §§301, 116, and 243 all speak of distributions or dividends received by the shareholder, implying no distinction between cash-basis and accrual-basis taxpayers. See Dynamics Corp. of Am. v. US, 392 F2d 241 (Ct. Cl. 1968).

¶ 7.05 CONSTRUCTIVE DISTRIBUTIONS

The rules of §301(c) (under which corporate distributions are to be treated as dividends or returns of capital, depending upon the amount of the corporation's current and post-1913 earnings and profits) come into play only if a corporation makes a distribution to a shareholder "with respect to its stock." According to Regs. §1.301-1(c), §301 "is not applicable to an amount paid by a corporation to a shareholder unless the amount is paid to the shareholder in his capacity as such." Thus, if a corporation transfers property to a shareholder who is also a creditor of the corporation in satisfaction of his claim, the transaction is not governed by §301. Other examples include payments to a shareholder-employee as compensation for services, to a shareholder-vendor as payment for property, and to a shareholder-lessor as rent for the use of property.[73] Even if such transfers are regarded as "distributions,"[74] they are not made to a shareholder "with respect to [his] stock," as required by §301(a), and hence their tax consequences are governed by other sections of the Code.

A distribution to a shareholder in his capacity as such, however, is subject to §301 even though it is not declared in a formal fashion. Instances of constructive or disguised distributions are commonly encountered in the context of closely held corporations, whose dealings with their shareholders are more often than not characterized by informality. Although publicly held corporations rarely engage in this practice, some railroad and public utility corporations are parties to leases requiring the lessee to pay a fixed annual amount directly to the lessor's shareholders, an arrangement that is equivalent to a payment of rent to the lessor, coupled with a distribution by the lessor to its shareholders.[75]

Informal distributions can assume many forms;[76] a transfer need not constitute a distribution under state law to be treated as such for federal

---

[73] See example in S. Rep. No. 1622, 83d Cong., 2d Sess. 231 (1954); see also CIR v. Fender Sales, Inc., 338 F2d 924 (9th Cir. 1964), cert. denied, 382 US 813 (1965).

[74] The label seems inappropriate if the consideration received by the corporation is equal to the value of the amount paid by it, despite Palmer v. CIR, 302 US 63, 69 (1937) ("a sale of corporate assets to stockholders is, in a literal sense, a distribution of its property"). But see Citizens Bank & Trust Co. v. US, 580 F2d 442 (Ct. Cl. 1978) (no constructive distribution where corporation purchased at fair market value property that shareholder was under a binding obligation to buy). Compare Singleton v. CIR, 569 F2d 863 (5th Cir.) (dividend in form treated as such, although it arguably may not have been one in substance), reh'g denied, 572 F2d 320, cert. denied, 439 US 940 (1978).

[75] See US v. Joliet & C.R.R., 315 US 44 (1942); CIR v. Western Union Tel. Co., 141 F2d 774 (2d Cir.), cert. denied, 322 US 751 (1944).

[76] For classification of an alleged charitable contribution by an operating subsidiary to its parent corporation (a charity) as a nondeductible dividend, see Crosby

income tax purposes. Nor do all shareholders need to participate, although disproportionate transfers are less vulnerable than pro rata ones.[77] An economic benefit may constitute a constructive distribution, even though no money or property is transferred to the shareholder; but this possibility is clouded by the countervailing principle that shareholders and their corporations are separate taxable entities and that not every corporate action that is beneficial to shareholders will generate taxable income to them.

The characterization of an amount received by a shareholder directly or indirectly from a corporation may be important in determining whether (1) the corporation may deduct it; (2) it reduces the corporation's current earnings and profits in computing taxability of current distributions or merely reduces the earnings available for future distributions; (3) the recipient must treat it as ordinary gross income under §61(a) or may treat it in whole or in part as a return of capital under §301(c); and (4) the recipient is entitled to the intercorporate dividends-received deduction of §243. These classification difficulties can become acute in the case of payments that might in appropriate cases be treated as compensation to shareholder-employees (such as reimbursed shareholder expenses, travel and entertainment expenses, diversions of corporate income, and rent-free use of corporate property), rather than distributions. Some of the most frequently encountered transactions that may be treated as constructive or disguised distributions by a corporation to its shareholders are examined in the following paragraphs. This discussion uses the term "constructive dividend," even though the constructive or disguised distribution concept is not limited to distributions that constitute "dividends," the same principles being equally applicable to constructive nondividend distributions. The litigated cases, however, have ordinarily involved corporations with accumulated or current earnings and profits, and the term "constructive dividend" is therefore commonly used. Moreover,

---

Valve & Gage Co. v. CIR, 380 F2d 146 (1st Cir. 1967), cert. denied, 389 US 976 (1967); C.F. Mueller Co. v. CIR, 479 F2d 678 (3d Cir. 1973); see also Nissho Iwai Am. Corp., ¶ 85,578 P-H Memo. TC (1985) (cancellation of shareholder's burdensome contract held a dividend to extent of economic relief).

[77] See Estate of Chism v. CIR, 322 F2d 956 (9th Cir. 1963) (state law adjudication not controlling); Lengsfield v. CIR, 241 F2d 508 (5th Cir. 1957) (disproportionate distribution); see also Paramount-Richards Theaters, Inc. v. CIR, 153 F2d 602 (5th Cir. 1946); Lester E. Dellinger, 32 TC 1178 (1959); Ernest H. Berger, 37 TC 1026 (1962) (shareholders could not deduct amounts repaid to their corporation on theory that original payments (excessive salaries) were improper under local law). Compare Vincent E. Oswald, 49 TC 645 (1968) (acq.) (repayment of excessive salaries by shareholder-officer pursuant to binding corporate bylaw held deductible); see also Van Cleave v. US, 718 F2d 193 (6th Cir. 1983) (repayment qualifies for §1341 benefits, resulting in no-lose arrangement).

See generally Harley, Dealings Between Closely Held Corporations and Their Stockholders, 25 Tax L. Rev. 403 (1970).

constructive distributions are usually received by the shareholder himself, but a transfer by the corporation to relatives of the shareholder may qualify for this status and be taxed as though distributed directly to the shareholder.[78] Many of the transactions giving rise to constructive distribution disputes are driven by shareholder desires to extract dollars from their corporations on a tax-deductible basis, a goal that assumed even greater significance as a result of 1986 legislation raising the top corporate tax rate to a level above that of noncorporate taxpayers for the first time.[79]

1. **Excessive salaries paid to shareholders or their relatives.** Under §162(a), the corporation is entitled to deduct "a reasonable allowance for salaries or other compensation for personal services actually rendered." If compensation paid to a shareholder-employee is found to exceed a reasonable allowance, the corporation is denied a deduction for the excess amount, but the Service ordinarily has no reason to make any adjustment at the shareholder-employee level, since both the reasonable and the unreasonable portions of the compensation will have been reported as salary income.[80] If, however, compensation paid to spouses, children, or other relatives of a shareholder exceeds the value of their services, the excess amount (or the entire amount, if the recipients are no-shows) may be treated as a disguised distribution to the shareholder, who may be in a higher income tax bracket than the recipients.[81]

---

[78] See, e.g., Harry L. Epstein, 53 TC 459 (1970) (bargain purchase of corporate property by shareholder-created trust held to be taxable constructive dividend to shareholders); Green v. US, 460 F2d 412 (5th Cir. 1972) (bargain sale to children of taxpayer-shareholder constituted a taxable dividend to him despite his minority status, since he exercised substantial influence over transaction as director and president).

See generally Kingson, The Deep Structure of Taxation: Dividend Distributions, 85 Yale L.J. 861 (1976).

[79] See supra ¶ 5.01.

[80] Another example of such treatment is Olton Feed Yard, Inc. v. US, 592 F2d 272 (5th Cir. 1979), holding that fees paid by a corporation to its shareholders for guaranteeing payment of certain corporate loans were constructive dividends; the amounts presumably were included in the shareholders' gross income when received, and the only effect of characterizing them as dividends was to deny corporate deductions. For a decision allowing such payments to be deducted, see Tulia Feedlot, Inc. v. US, 3 Cl. Ct. 364 (Cl. Ct. 1983).

[81] In blatant cases involving alleged salaries paid to no-show relatives, negligence or fraud penalties might be in order. For payments to spouses of deceased shareholders, see Rubber Assocs., Inc. v. CIR, 335 F2d 75 (6th Cir. 1964) (corporation permitted to deduct payments made to spouses of deceased officer-shareholders, since they constituted additional compensation for officer-shareholders' services); Montgomery Eng'g Co. v. US, 230 F. Supp. 838 (D.N.J. 1964), aff'd per curiam, 344

If recharacterized as a distribution to the shareholder, the purported compensation should also be viewed as a tax-free gift by him to the recipients, who in turn should be entitled to a refund if the amount was included in taxable income when received. This analysis might be refined further, however, in order to allocate purported compensation among three categories: (1) compensation, which is deductible by the corporation under §162 and taxable to the recipient as compensation; (2) unreasonable compensation, which is not deductible by the corporation under §162 but nevertheless is taxable to the recipient as compensation; and (3) distributions disguised as compensation, which are not deductible by the corporation and are taxable to the shareholder (who is not necessarily the recipient) only to the extent of the corporation's earnings and profits and thereafter applicable to the basis of the stock, as provided by §301(c).[82]

Because the issue ordinarily arises under §162 rather than as an aspect of the constructive distribution problem, this is not the place to examine the criteria determining whether compensation is reasonable; however, the following much-quoted judicial summary of the relevant factors may be of interest:

> Although every case of this kind must stand upon its own facts and circumstances, it is well settled that several basic factors should be considered by the Court in reaching its decision in any particular case. Such factors include the employee's qualifications; the nature, extent and scope of the employee's work; the size and complexities of the business; a comparison of salaries paid with the gross income and the net income; the prevailing general economic conditions; comparison of salaries with distributions to stockholders; the prevailing rates of compensation for comparable positions in comparable concerns; the salary policy of the taxpayer as to all employees; and in the case of small corporations with a limited number of officers the amount of compensation paid to the particular employee in previous years. The action of the Board of Directors of a corporation in voting salaries for any given period is entitled to the presumption that such salaries are reasonable

---

F2d 996 (3d Cir. 1965) (widow owned no stock in corporation; payment held to be constructive dividend to unrelated controlling stockholder, who felt moral obligation to correct injustice done to widow by her deceased husband); Hardin v. US, 461 F2d 865 (5th Cir. 1972) (*Montgomery* followed in taxing controlling shareholder who directed payment to widow of deceased officer).

For the effect of an agreement to refund any compensation paid to a controlling shareholder, for example, if and to the extent that it was disallowed for deduction purposes, see Pahl v. CIR, 67 TC 286 (1976) (after-the-fact agreement not effective); see also Vincent E. Oswald, supra note 77. Van Cleave v. US, supra note 77.

[82] For the constructive distribution rationale, see Regs. §1.162-8; Quarrier Diner, Inc., ¶ 63,069 P-H Memo. TC (1963). Compare Sterno Sales Corp. v. US, 345 F2d 552 (Ct. Cl. 1965).

and proper. . . . The situation must be considered as a whole with no single factor decisive.[83]

Note should also be taken of a few cases holding compensation nondeductible, even though reasonable in amount, because it was a constructive distribution, usually due to the fact that the corporation had rarely if ever paid any dividends as such to its shareholders.[84] If the amounts were included in gross income by the recipients, however, such a recharacterization of the amounts as disguised dividends does not ordinarily alter their tax status.

2. Bargain purchases or rentals of corporate property by shareholders. The regulations state that a sale of property by a corporation to its shareholders for less than fair market value is a "distribution" under §301;[85] thus, if a corporation sells property worth $100 to its shareholders for $60, the $40 spread will be treated as a distribution under §301.[86] This rule ordinarily does not apply, however, to bargain sales by a corporation of its own shares, including distributions of stock rights, for reasons to be discussed subsequently.[87]

Instead of selling property to shareholders at a bargain price, corporations sometimes distribute options entitling their shareholders to purchase

---

[83] Mayson Mfg. Co. v. CIR, 178 F2d 115, 119 (6th Cir. 1949). See also East Tenn. Motor Co. v. US, 27 AFTR2d 452 (ED Tenn. 1970) (not officially reported) (jury instructions), aff'd, 453 F2d 494 (6th Cir. 1971); R.J. Kremer Co. v. CIR, ¶ 80,069 P-H Memo. TC (1980) (detailed examination of facts; limited relevance of comparisons in judging salaries paid by small businesses); IRS Audit Techniques Handbook for Internal Revenue Agents, ¶ 672(4)1 (1976) (IRM 4231). For more extensive discussion, with citations, see Bittker, Federal Taxation of Income, Estates and Gifts, ¶ 22.2.2 (Warren, Gorham & Lamont, Inc. 1981).

[84] See, e.g., Nor-Cal Adjusters, ¶ 71,200 P-H Memo. TC (1971), aff'd, 503 F2d 359 (9th Cir. 1974); Northlich, Stolley, Inc. v. US, 368 F2d 272, 278 (Ct. Cl. 1966) ("even a payment that is reasonable is not deductible if it was actually a distribution of earnings"; bonuses paid to shareholder-employees held to constitute dividends, even though corporation had previously declared dividends). For discussion and rejection of the automatic dividend rationale for disallowing deductions by corporations with poor dividend records, see Elliotts, Inc. v. CIR, 716 F2d 1241 (9th Cir. 1983), appeal after remand, 782 F2d 1051 (9th Cir. 1986).

[85] Regs. §1.301-1(j). For examples, see *Epstein* and *Green*, supra note 78; Honigman v. CIR, 466 F2d 69 (6th Cir. 1972) (shareholder bargain purchase a constructive dividend, even though sale resulted in partially deductible loss at corporate level).

[86] The text example assumes that the shareholder is an individual. For the special rules governing distributions of property by one corporation to another, see infra text at notes 196–198.

[87] See infra ¶¶ 7.42 and 7.43.

corporate assets (e.g., portfolio securities or real estate) at a fixed price at any time within a specified period. Under *Palmer v. CIR*,[88] a 1937 Supreme Court decision, it was possible that the shareholders would not be taxed on either the value of the options when distributed or the spread when they were exercised. The statutory foundation for *Palmer*, however, was later amended, and, in 1968, the Supreme Court seemed to treat taxability as a foregone conclusion, leaving open only the proper time, by saying that "it has not ... been authoritatively settled whether an issue of rights to purchase at less than fair market value itself constitutes a dividend, or the dividend occurs only on the actual purchase."[89] Later cases support the reasonable proposition that if the option can be valued when issued, that amount is includable in the shareholder's gross income as a dividend (assuming adequate earnings and profits), but that if valuation at that time is not feasible, the taxable amount is the spread between the option price and the fair market value of the underlying property when the option is exercised.[90]

In the same way as a bargain purchase, a bargain lease or uncompensated use of corporate property by a shareholder is a constructive distribution to the extent of the spread between the property's fair rental value and the amount paid by the shareholder.[91] Rather than estimate the rental value

---

[88] 302 US 63 (1937).

[89] CIR v. Gordon, 391 US 83, 90 n.4 (1968).

[90] See Redding v. CIR, 630 F2d 1169 (7th Cir. 1980), cert. denied, 450 US 913 (1983) (extensive analysis); Baumer v. US, 580 F2d 863 (5th Cir. 1978) ("open transaction" doctrine applied to option of indeterminate length to acquire real estate from issuing corporation and value at issue was not ascertainable; case remanded to determine spread at exercise). For a later installment in this litigation, see Baumer v. US, 685 F2d 1318 (11th Cir. 1982) ("law of the case" applied to prevent taxpayer effort on remand to introduce evidence of option's value when issued, since same evidence was available when case was first tried); Rev. Rul. 70-521, 1970-2 CB 72 (short-term transferable rights to acquire purchase portfolio securities; value when issued was controlling). See generally Jassy, Dividend Treatment of Distributions of Options to Acquire Assets of the Distributing Corporation, 34 Tax L. Rev. 607 (1979); Gann, Taxation of Stock Rights and Other Options: Another Look at the Persistence of *Palmer v. Commissioner*, 1979 Duke L.J. 911.

For the treatment of shareholders of one corporation on receiving a distribution consisting of warrants to buy a second corporation's stock from the latter corporation, see Louis A. Weigl, 84 TC 1192 (1985) (divided court) (value of warrants taxable on distribution if value is ascertainable at that time; §421 valuation principles applicable to distributing corporation, which received warrants as compensation for services, but not to distributee shareholders).

[91] See Rev. Rul. 58-1, 1958-1 CB 173; 58th St. Plaza Theatre, Inc. v. CIR, 195 F2d 724 (2d Cir.), cert. denied, 344 US 820, reh'g denied, 344 US 882 (1952) (lease to shareholder's wife); International Artists, Ltd., 55 TC 94 (1970); Nicholls, North, Buse Co., 56 TC 1225 (1971) (dominant shareholder received taxable constructive dividend from personal use of corporate yacht by son, a minority shareholder, measured by fair rental value of such use).

of such property, however, the courts occasionally treat the corporation's depreciation charges and maintenance expenses as a constructive distribution to the extent that they exceed the rent paid by the shareholder.[92] Although it may be easily administered, this approach must be regarded as a second-best alternative that is justified only if the benefit to the shareholder cannot be valued directly.[93] On the other hand, if the corporation's costs exceed the value of the benefit to the shareholder, the latter amount should probably be controlling, unless the property is maintained primarily for the shareholder's personal use, in which event the arrangement is better analyzed as an expenditure of corporate funds for the shareholder's benefit than as a mere use of corporate property by the shareholder.[94]

3. Excessive payments by corporation on purchasing or leasing shareholder's property. This category of constructive distributions is the converse of the preceding one; here, the shareholders receive too much from the corporation on a sale or lease of *their* property rather than pay too little for the corporation's property. In either event, the crucial test is whether the parties arrived at arm's-length terms in their purported sale, lease, or license transaction; if not, the arrangement will be treated as a device for the payment of an informal dividend.[95] Some cases in this area involve the added feature of

---

See Kohla, Dividend Income From Personal Use of Business Assets, 60 A.B.A. J. 1431 (1974).

[92] See Challenge Mfg. Co., 37 TC 650 (1962) (acq.). But see J. Simpson Dean, 9 TC 256 (1947), aff'd on other grounds, Dean v. CIR, 187 F2d 1019 (3d Cir. 1951) (rent-free use of corporation's riding horses not a constructive distribution because exercising them was beneficial to corporation); Peacock v. CIR, 256 F2d 160 (5th Cir. 1958) (difference between fair rental value and rent paid was intended as tax-free gift by corporation to shareholder).

[93] See Loftin & Woodward, Inc. v. US, 577 F2d 1206 (5th Cir. 1978) (fair market value controlling where corporate facilities were used for land-clearing operation benefitting related partnership; extensive discussion); Ireland v. US, 621 F2d 731 (5th Cir. 1980) (charter fare controlling in valuing shareholder benefit from personal use of company plane); Marcus W. Melvin, 88 TC 63 (1987) (personal use of corporation's luxury cars taxed as dividend at value of benefit).

[94] See Walker v. CIR, 362 F2d 140 (7th Cir.), cert. denied, 385 US 865 (1966) (constructive distribution not limited to fair market value of economic benefits conferred on shareholders; corporation's out-of-pocket cost of maintaining hunting lodge used by shareholders for personal recreation was proper measure of dividend income). But see CIR v. Riss, 374 F2d 161 (8th Cir. 1967) (fair rental value, rather than out-of-pocket cost, used to measure amount of constructive dividend); see also International Trading Co. v. CIR, 275 F2d 578 (7th Cir. 1960) (corporation's deduction for expenses attributable to property rented at fair value to shareholders is limited to rental income; excess expenses not "ordinary and necessary" under §162).

[95] See, e.g., Goldstein v. CIR, 298 F2d 562 (9th Cir. 1962) (excess portion of amount paid by corporation to shareholder for property must be reported as con-

a distribution in kind of corporate property to the shareholders, followed by a leaseback to the distributing corporation, in the hope of generating a corporate rental expense deduction under §162. The courts have not hesitated to find a lack of business reality in these transactions, treating the "rental" payments as constructive dividends. The mere fact that the lessor and lessee are related, however, does not require recharacterization of the payments if the transaction comports with reasonable economic standards.[96]

4. Corporate advances to shareholders. If corporate funds are loaned to a shareholder but there is no intent to create a bona fide creditor-debtor relationship, the withdrawals may be treated as constructive or disguised distributions. The intent of the parties is to be gleaned from an examination of all the facts. The use of interest-bearing notes and a history of actual payments on account of principal and interest create a presumption of bona fide debt; conversely, open-account loans with no provision for interest and no ascertainable maturity date are quite vulnerable.[97] Loans that were genuine when made are not immunized in perpetuity, since it may be found in a

---

structive dividend, not as capital gain on sale); Albert Crabtree, 22 TC 61 (1954), aff'd per curiam, 221 F2d 807 (2d Cir. 1955) (taxpayer transferred franchise to controlled corporation for stock and promise to pay half its profits for 10 years; payments were held to be disguised dividends); see also Ray E. Omholt, 60 TC 541 (1973) (excessive royalties constituted constructive dividend to shareholder-licensor when paid, not when demand notes therefor were distributed). Compare Edwin W. Stuchell, ¶ 78,236 P-H Memo. TC (1978) (long-term timber-cutting contract was reasonable when entered into in 1955; payments in 1968 and later years were held not to be subject to recharacterization, despite changes in value).

For disallowance of rents and royalties at the corporate level in such transactions, see Potter Elec. Signal & Mfg. Co. v. CIR, 286 F2d 200 (8th Cir. 1961). But see Ransom W. Chase, ¶ 65,202 P-H Memo. TC (1965) (license of shareholder-owned patents to controlled corporation upheld, with discussion of effect of tax motive).

[96] See Armston Co. v. CIR, 188 F2d 531 (5th Cir. 1951) (denying corporate deductions); see also Ingle Coal Corp. v. CIR, 174 F2d 569 (7th Cir. 1949) (shareholders liquidated corporation and immediately transferred assets to new corporation; royalties paid to them by new corporation were held to be constructive dividends). But see Alden B. Oakes, 44 TC 524 (1965) (deductions allowed). See generally Oliver, Income Tax Aspects of Gifts and Leasebacks of Business Property in Trust, 51 Cornell LQ 21 (1965).

[97] See James K. Pierce, 61 TC 424 (1974) (advances upheld as true loans in close case), and cases cited therein; Alterman Foods, Inc. v. US, 611 F2d 866 (Ct. Cl. 1979) (advances by subsidiaries to parent recharacterized as dividends). For an officer's unauthorized withdrawals from a public corporation, see Gilbert v. CIR, 552 F2d 478 (2d Cir. 1977) (withdrawals held to be true loan on facts because of intent to repay; proceeds not used for taxpayer's personal benefit). See generally Werner, Stockholder Withdrawals—Loans or Dividends?, 10 Tax L. Rev. 569 (1955).

later year that the corporation has forgiven the debt, an action that constitutes a constructive distribution.[98]

In determining whether a debatable advance is a true loan or a taxable distribution, the principles used to distinguish between debt and equity in the converse situation of advances by shareholders to their corporations are usually relevant.[99] In either situation, the failure to provide for interest on the alleged loan or providing a below-market rate points toward equity classification.[100] Under §7872, enacted in 1984, interest is imputed on certain loans between related persons if the stated rate (if any) is less than the applicable federal rate of interest, determined under §1274(d).[101] Does this mechanism for imputing interest cure the parties' failure to provide explicitly for interest and thus render this deficiency irrelevant in deciding whether a borderline advance is a tax-free loan or a taxable distribution? The answer should be no, since §7872 applies only to a below-market loan, not to distributions disguised as loans (in other words, §7872 comes into play only after a transfer of funds has been properly classified as a loan).

Once this issue is resolved in favor of loan status, however, §7872 has the following effect if the loan exceeds the $10,000 de minimis floor of §7872(c)(3) and the stated rate of interest thereon is below the statutory federal benchmark: (1) the corporation realizes imputed interest income equal to the disparity; (2) the shareholder is treated as paying the same amount (which can be deducted as interest, subject to the usual restrictions on the deduction of interest paid by the taxpayer);[102] and (3) the shareholder realizes dividend income equal either to the spread between the principal amount of a term loan and the present value of such amount (computed by discounting at designated market rates compounded semiannually) or, in the case of demand loans, to the amount of the annually imputed interest.

---

[98] Regs. §1.301-1(m); Shephard v. CIR, 340 F2d 27 (6th Cir.), cert. denied, 382 US 813 (1965); Eustice, supra note 37.

If the government relies on an alleged forgiveness as the crucial event, the taxpayer may counter by asserting that the original withdrawal was a constructive distribution, even though it was not reported as such, especially if the statute of limitations has run out on that year. Such inconsistencies may be remedied by the equitable doctrines of estoppel or recoupment, or by application of §§1311–1314 (mitigating statute of limitations).

[99] See supra ¶ 4.02.

[100] See supra note 99; ¶¶ 4.02–4.04.

[101] For discussion of §1274(d), see supra ¶ 4.40 (original issue discount). For pre-1984 cases holding that interest-free loans were not taxable distributions to shareholders, see Hardee v. US, 708 F2d 661 (Fed. Cir. 1983), and cases cited therein. Section 7872 applies to below-market loans between shareholders and their corporations. See Prop. Regs. §§1.7872-2(a)(2)(iii) and 1.7872-4(g)(1). For interest imputations under §482, see infra ¶ 15.03.

[102] See §§163(d) and 163(h); see also §§265 and 267.

To illustrate: A 10-year loan without interest by X Corporation to its shareholder A would result in OID treatment to X and A, accruable ratably over the ten-year term by X and A,[103] but A's current dividend would be the full amount of such discount. A demand loan, by contrast, would result in annual dividend income to A equal to the imputed interest amount.

Instead of advancing funds to its shareholders, a corporation may assist them by guaranteeing or assuming liability for their bank or other loans. It has been held that a constructive distribution occurs not when a shareholder's debt is assumed by the corporation but only if and when the corporation actually pays off the assumed obligation.[104] Much could be said for treating the guarantee or assumption itself as a distribution to the extent of a reasonable guarantor's fee, but valuation would ordinarily be a tough nut to crack.[105]

5. Corporate payments on loans by shareholders. As pointed out earlier, if an alleged loan by a shareholder to his corporation is found to be an equity investment in the nature of stock or a contribution to capital, payments of interest or principal by the corporation will be treated as distributions to him comparable to dividends or distributions in redemption of his stock.[106]

6. Corporate payments for shareholder benefit. This category of informal distributions ranges from borderline expenditures (e.g., for travel and entertainment), where an allocation between the shareholder and the corporation may be in order, to the blatant payment of personal expenses in an aura of fraud. The underlying principle is found in the landmark decision in *Old Colony Trust Co. v. CIR*,[107] holding that an employee realized income when his legal obligations were discharged by his employer. The basic issue

---

[103] For a fuller discussion of the treatment of OID, see supra ¶ 4.41; see also Prop. Regs. §§1.7872-4(d)(1), 1.7872-7(a)(1), and 1.7872-7(a)(3)(ii), Example.

[104] See Maher v. CIR, 469 F2d 225 (8th Cir. 1972) (taxpayer remained secondarily liable on debt after assumption and hence did not derive sufficient present economic benefit from assumption); accord, Rev. Rul. 77-360, 1977-2 CB 86 (Service will follow *Maher* on timing point, at least if assumption does not work a novation); see Rev. Rul. 78-422, 1978-2 CB 129.

[105] But see Tulia Feedlot, Inc. v. US, supra note 80 (in converse situation, corporation allowed to deduct 3 percent fee paid to directors for guaranteeing payment of its loans).

[106] See supra ¶ 4.21.

[107] 279 US 716 (1929).

is whether the corporate expenditure was incurred primarily to benefit the corporation's trade or business, or primarily for the personal benefit of the shareholders.[108] In cases of the latter type, the Service in former years was often content with disallowing deductions at the corporate level, but its current practice is to couple this disallowance with an assessment against the shareholder on a constructive distribution theory.[109]

The line between shareholder benefit and corporate benefit is not always clear, however, because some expenditures embody both elements, and an indirect benefit to the shareholder should not by itself be treated as a distribution to him.[110] Corporate contributions to a controlling shareholder's favorite charity can create this tension between corporate and shareholder

---

[108] See Herbert Enoch, 57 TC 781 (1972) (constructive dividend where corporation discharged shareholder's personal liability on debt; shareholder was true borrower, rather than corporation); see also Joseph Creel, 72 TC 1173 (1979), aff'd on other grounds sub nom. Martin v. CIR, 649 F2d 1133 (5th Cir. 1981). Compare Falkoff v. US, supra note 13. See also Rev. Rul. 75-421, 1975-2 CB 108 (corporate payment of shareholder's expenses for financial and accounting services to determine value of his stock in pending reorganization exchange held to be taxable dividend); Dolese v. US, 605 F2d 1146 (10th Cir. 1979), cert. denied, 445 US 961 (1980) (payment of costs of shareholder divorce litigation partly personal, and hence a dividend, and partly for corporate business purpose); Tennessee Sec., Inc. v. CIR, 674 F2d 570 (6th Cir. 1982) (corporation's payment of shareholders' personal guaranty liability held constructive dividend to shareholder-guarantors).

[109] See American Properties, Inc., 28 TC 1100 (1957), aff'd per curiam, 262 F2d 150 (9th Cir. 1958) (expenses of speed boats, paid by one-person corporation, held not to be deductible by corporation but taxable as disguised dividends to shareholder); Greenspon v. CIR, 229 F2d 947, 953–956 (8th Cir. 1956) (corporation's payments for erecting and maintaining "a unique horticultural show place" at stockholder's farm were disallowed and taxed as constructive dividends); Sachs v. CIR, 277 F2d 879 (8th Cir.), cert. denied, 364 US 833 (1960) (corporate payment of fine imposed on stockholder-president for filing fraudulent corporate return taxed as constructive dividend); Alan B. Larkin, 48 TC 629 (1967), aff'd, 394 F2d 494 (1st Cir. 1968) (corporate reimbursement of officer-shareholders' medical expenses held to be nondeductible dividend and taxable income to shareholder-employees); John L. Ashby, 50 TC 409 (1968) (corporate travel and entertainment expenses disallowed for lack of substantiation, but only part were dividends to 90 percent shareholder).

[110] An example of this is a payment by the corporation to discharge its own debts where the shareholder is only secondarily liable. See Rev. Rul. 69-608, 1969-2 CB 42. Cf. Jewell v. US, 330 F2d 761 (9th Cir. 1964) (corporation assumed shareholder's liabilities in connection with transfer of property to corporation under §112 of 1934 Act, precursor of §351; no constructive dividend because liability was related to subject matter of §112 transfer); Wolf v. CIR, 357 F2d 483 (9th Cir. 1966) (contra); see also US v. Smith, 418 F2d 589 (5th Cir. 1969) (corporate payment of contingent shareholder liabilities held not to be a constructive distribution if corporation assumed liabilities; otherwise, payment would be constructive dividend); Maher v. CIR, supra note 104. See also infra ¶ 9.07.

benefits, which led in 1968 to a ruling (later revoked) holding that a corporate contribution to a charitable foundation created by its sole shareholder was a constructive distribution to the shareholder and a contribution by him to the foundation.[111]

A capital outlay or other investment by the corporation for its *own* purposes is rarely treated as a constructive distribution to its shareholders, since the transaction changes the character of the assets held by the corporation (usually from cash to property) without affecting its net worth or bringing the shareholder any closer to personal enjoyment of the enterprise's earnings. In two areas, however, the benefits indirectly derived by a shareholder from a corporate investment have sometimes led the courts to regard it as a constructive distribution. The redemption by a corporation of the shares of one or more shareholders may be treated as a distribution to the remaining shareholders if they are thereby relieved of a binding personal liability to pay for the shares; this troublesome subject is discussed in a subsequent chapter.[112] Similarly, when a corporation pays the premiums on key-employee life insurance policies owned by its shareholders, the economic benefit to them amounts to a constructive distribution,[113] while, if the corporation owns the policies, premium payments will not result in taxable income to the shareholders.[114]

---

[111] Rev. Rul. 68-658, 1968-2 CB 119; Henry J. Knott, 67 TC 681 (1977) (acq.) (contra, in absence of personal benefit to shareholders or their families); Rev. Rul. 79-9, 1979-1 CB 125 (Rev. Rul. 68-658 revoked in conformity with acquiescence in *Knott*). See also Robert A. Wekesser, ¶ 76,214 P-H Memo. TC (1976) (shareholder gift of stock to charity in satisfaction of pledge, followed shortly by corporate redemption of donated stock, held not to be taxable as constructive dividend to shareholder because pledge not a debt, per Rev. Rul. 55-410, 1955-1 CB 297).

Rev. Rul. 79-9 is analyzed in Davis & McGill, Jr., Corporate Charitable Contributions and the Constructive Dividend Problem, 8 J. Corp. Tax'n 323 (1982).

[112] See infra ¶ 9.07. Rev. Rul. 69-608, 1969-2 CB 42.

[113] See Paramount-Richards Theatres, Inc. v. CIR, supra note 77 (policies owned by shareholders held to be constructive distribution); Howard Johnson, 74 TC 1316 (1980) (corporate payment of premium on split-dollar life insurance policies held by trust for benefit of taxpayer-shareholder's family was held to be constructive dividend to taxpayer); see also Arthur Genshaft, 64 TC 282 (1975) (acq.) (shareholder-officer taxed on economic benefit from corporate payment of insurance premiums on policies owned by corporation but payable to beneficiaries named by taxpayer; measure of tax is value of pure insurance protection provided to each beneficiary).

[114] As to the treatment of a shareholder-beneficiary of policies owned by the corporation, see Ducros v. CIR, 272 F2d 49 (6th Cir. 1959) (payment exempt under §101(a) rather than constructive dividend), which will not be followed by the Service (Rev. Rul. 61-134, 1961-2 CB 250); Prunier v. CIR, 248 F2d 818 (1st Cir. 1957), where the court went to some length to find that the corporation was the equitable

7. Unlawful diversion of corporate income by shareholder. Fraudulent devices by which shareholders intercept payments by customers before they reach the corporate treasury, collect kickbacks from suppliers, and so forth, are often treated as constructive distributions, although the courts have sometimes relied on §61(a) rather than §301 in order to uphold deficiencies assessed against the shareholders without regard to the corporation's earnings and profits account.[115] While *CIR v. Wilcox*, holding that embezzled funds were not taxable to the embezzler, was in force, the government sought to avoid this decision in unlawful diversion cases by proceeding on a constructive distribution theory under §301.[116] With the overruling of *Wilcox* by *James v. U.S.*, this strategy became unnecessary; instead, the government preferred an assessment under §61(a) because taxability under that section is not dependent upon the corporation's earnings and profits account.[117] Despite the authority upholding this approach, much can be said for the contrary view that an unlawful diversion of corporate funds is a constructive distribution, pure and simple. Diversions of corporate funds have much in common with corporate payments of the shareholder's personal

---

owner and beneficiary of the policies; see also Casale v. CIR, 247 F2d 440 (2d Cir. 1957); Sanders v. Fox, 253 F2d 855 (10th Cir. 1958); Edward D. Lacey, 41 TC 329 (1963) (acq.) (shareholder's estate was named beneficiary of policies purchased by corporation, but corporation was held to be beneficial owner); Rev. Rul. 59-184, 1959-1 CB 65 (acquiescing in *Prunier, Casale*, and *Sanders*; notwithstanding acquiescence, cautious advisors are not likely to use these cases in planning future transactions); Estate of Horne, 64 TC 1020 (1975) (payment of insurance proceeds to shareholder-beneficiary of corporation that owned policy on beneficiary's husband who was also a shareholder and officer, and that had paid all the premiums, was held not a dividend to beneficiary); M. Lucile Harrison, 59 TC 578 (1973) (proceeds collected by corporation from key-employee insurance policy were not taxable receipts in payment of claim but were exempt under §101(a)).

[115] See DiZenzo v. CIR, 348 F2d 122 (2d Cir. 1965) (diverted funds constitute ordinary income only to extent of earnings and profits). But see US v. Miller, 545 F2d 1204 (9th Cir. 1976), cert. denied, 430 US 930 (1977) (existence of earnings and profits not necessary in criminal fraud proceeding against diverting taxpayer), reviewing the earlier cases; see also James G. Schmidt, ¶ 67,195 P-H Memo. TC (1967), where shareholder diversions of corporate funds were taxed as dividends. The shareholder repaid diverted funds, and the corporation then reimbursed the shareholder for this amount. The court held that the reimbursement was also a dividend.

If the diversion is treated as a constructive distribution, the earnings and profits account must be adjusted to reflect any deficiencies, penalties, and interest for which the corporation is liable. See supra ¶ 7.04.

For an exhaustive analysis of the problems arising from shareholder diversions of corporate funds, see Gardner, The Tax Consequences of Shareholder Diversions in Close Corporations, 21 Tax L. Rev. 223 (1966).

[116] 327 US 404 (1946).

[117] 366 US 213 (1961).

expenses, but they may involve more concealment, since the funds never even pass through the corporation's hands.

8. Corporations under common control: triangular distributions. Constructive distributions ordinarily involve a receipt or use of money or other corporate property by the shareholder personally, but transactions between two corporations under common control can result in constructive distributions to their controlling shareholder, even though nothing passes directly to him.

> *To illustrate:* Assume that *A* owns all the stock of both *X* Corporation and *Y* Corporation and that *Y* is in financial distress and may default on a bank loan endorsed by *A*. *A* shores up *Y* by arranging for it to purchase property from *X* for less than its fair market value or to borrow funds from *X* in circumstances suggesting that repayment is unlikely.

Unsurprisingly, transactions like this one may be realigned by the Service and the courts, given the absence of any business reason for the accommodating corporation (*X*) to shower *Y* with riches. Thus, the benefit ostensibly moving directly from *X* to *Y* would be treated as having been distributed first by *X* to *A* and then transferred by *A* to *Y* as a contribution to *Y*'s capital.[118] (Modifying the adage that a given result at the end of a straight path does not achieve a different result if it was reached by following a devious path, one might say that a two-party transaction can be recharacterized as triangular in nature to reflect economic reality.)

---

[118] See, e.g., Gilbert L. Gilbert, 74 TC 60 (1980), and cases cited therein. In *Gilbert*, the issue was a transfer of funds as a purported loan by one controlled corporation to another to enable the latter to redeem part of its stock. The advance was held not to be a true loan. The shareholder controlling both corporations received a constructive dividend, since the purpose of the redemption was to increase his proportionate ownership of the second corporation; George W. Knipe, ¶ 65,131 P-H Memo. TC (1965), aff'd per curiam sub nom. Equitable Publishing Co. v. CIR, 356 F2d 514 (3d Cir. 1966), cert. denied, 385 US 822 (1966); Tirzah A. Cox, 56 TC 1270 (1971), modified, 58 TC 105 (1972) (payment by brother corporation to sister corporation; payment was used by latter to discharge bank loan on which major shareholder of both corporations was personally liable, which resulted in constructive dividend to shareholder); Sparks Nugget, Inc. v. CIR, 458 F2d 631 (9th Cir. 1972), cert. denied, 410 US 928 (1973) (nondeductible portion of excessive rental payments by one corporation to another; constructive dividend to controlling shareholder of both corporations); Rev. Rul. 78-83, 1978-1 CB 79 (diversion of income from one subsidiary to another was held to be constructive dividend to parent and capital contribution to recipient corporation); Gulf Oil Corp., 87 TC 548 (1986) (accord); see also Prop. Regs. §1.7872-4(g)(1) (application of below-market-rate loan rules) and supra note 101.

Distributions involving three or more parties often arise in the context of a §482 allocation among affiliated corporations, as explained later in this work.[119] However, it should be noted at this point that a constructive distribution to the common parent does not result automatically from a transaction that cannot be justified by reference to fair market values; in addition to the pricing error, which can be corrected by an allocation under §482, there must be a benefit to the parent.[120] Moreover, the courts have been reluctant to find the requisite personal benefit when advances from one corporation to another create valid debt obligations or when the transfer moves downstream from parent to subsidiary (thus remaining within a single line of descent) rather than laterally between sibling corporations.[121]

¶ 7.06   DIVIDENDS-RECEIVED EXCLUSION FOR INDIVIDUALS

From 1954 through 1986, the double taxation of corporate earnings was slightly mitigated for individual shareholders by an exclusion from gross income (and, in the early years, a credit) for a specified amount of qualifying dividends.[122] Under §116, the governing provision until its repeal by the Tax Reform Act of 1986, the exclusion was limited to $100 per taxable year, or, in the case of joint returns, $200.

---

[119] See infra ¶¶ 15.03 and 15.04; see also Prop. Regs. §1.7872-2(a)(2)(iii) (overlap of §7872 with §482).

[120] Sammons v. CIR, 472 F2d 449 (5th Cir. 1972) (twofold test: objective test is whether transfer caused funds or other property to leave transferor corporation's control so that shareholder could exercise control over property; subjective test is whether primary purpose was to benefit common shareholder); Gulf Oil Corp., supra note 118 (applying *Sammons*); Gilbert L. Gilbert, supra note 118 (fact that advance did not create valid debt and served no business purpose was not ipso facto determinative on constructive distribution issue); Stinnet's Pontiac Serv., Inc. v. CIR, 730 F2d 634 (11th Cir. 1984) (advances between brother-sister corporations held to be equity; constructive dividend to controlling shareholder).

[121] See Joseph Lupowitz Sons, Inc. v. CIR, 497 F2d 862 (3d Cir. 1974) (bona fide debt created by transfer of funds between corporations under common control; existence of debt, even though interest-free, precluded constructive distribution); Sammons v. CIR, supra note 120 (no cases since *Sammons* have involved Service attempts to impose constructive dividend treatment on purely downstream transfers of funds).

[122] For the policy issues, see Smith, Two Years of Republican Tax Policy: An Economic Appraisal, 8 Nat'l Tax J. 2 (1955); Shoup, The Dividend Exclusion and Credit in the Revenue Code of 1954, 8 Nat'l Tax J. 136 (1955). For renewed interest in this area, involving proposals to integrate the corporate and personal income taxes, see supra ¶ 1.08.

¶ 7.07 ASSIGNMENT OF DIVIDEND INCOME AND RELATED PROBLEMS

1. In general. On a gift, sale, or other transfer of stock, it is often necessary to determine whether dividend income on the transferred shares is to be reported by the transferor or transferee. This question can be answered only in the context of broad assignment-of-income principles, an area that is beyond the scope of this work;[123] little more can be done here than to suggest some of the issues and possible solutions.

As far as gifts are concerned, it is well established that the assignment of the right to receive a future dividend without an accompanying transfer of the underlying stock will not shift taxability of the dividends to the donee.[124] If the stock itself is transferred, however, the record date ordinarily is the relevant cutoff point for assignment-of-income purposes. If the gift occurs after the record date, the donor is taxable on the assigned dividend income, but if the gift precedes this date, the dividend income is taxed to the donee.[125] Unconditional gifts of stock followed by redemption of the stock

---

[123] See generally Lyon & Eustice, Assignment of Income: Fruit and Tree as Irrigated by the P.G. Lake Case, 17 Tax L. Rev. 295, 362 (1962); Eustice, Contract Rights, Capital Gain, and Assignment of Income: The *Ferrer* Case, 20 Tax L. Rev. 1 (1964); Bittker, supra note 83, ch. 75.

For the treatment of bond interest if the right to receive the interest is separated (or "stripped") from ownership of the underlying security, see §1286, discussed supra ¶ 4.43.

[124] See Margaret G. Dunham, 35 TC 705 (1961) (acq.); Overton v. CIR, 162 F2d 155 (2d Cir. 1947) (assignment of stock whose only effect was, or was thought to be, a shifting of dividend income to taxpayers' wives ignored as sham); Choate v. CIR, 129 F2d 684 (2d Cir. 1942) (assigned stock rights taxable to donor when exercised by donee). In situations where the stock is transferred in trust, however, the dividend income is not taxed to the grantor if the statutory rules of §§671–678 (as revised in 1986) do not so require, even though ownership of the stock may revert to him at some future date. A transfer of the right to dividends for a long period of years (e.g., more than 10 years) might have been effective in shifting tax liability under pre-1987 law on the ground that the transfer was comparable to a long-term trust, but that analogy became outmoded when the grantor trust rules were revised in 1986. See generally Helvering v. Horst, 311 US 112 (1940); Rev. Rul. 55-38, 1955-1 CB 389; see also US v. Georgia R.R. & Banking Co., 348 F2d 278 (5th Cir. 1965), cert. denied, 382 US 973 (1966) (lessee of stock for 99-year term held taxable on dividends).

For the converse situation, where the stock is transferred, but the right to the dividends is reserved, see Willard S. Heminway, 44 TC 96 (1965) (transfer of stock with reservation of dividend income by transferor for life; dividends held to be taxable to transferor).

[125] For transfers after the record date, see IT 4007, 1950-1 CB 11, superseded by Rev. Rul. 74-562, 1974-2 CB 28; Lillian M. Newman, 1 TC 921 (1943). Compare Matchette v. Helvering, 81 F2d 73 (2d Cir.), cert. denied, 298 US 677 (1936). For transfers before the record date, see Bishop v. Shaughnessy, 195 F2d 683 (2d Cir. 1952) (gift of preferred stock with dividend arrearages); Estate of Smith v. CIR, 292

from the donee generally have been respected by the courts, at least where the donee was not under a binding obligation to redeem.[126] Gifts of stock during the course of a complete liquidation, however, have fared less well; here, the more recent decisions have taxed the donor on the liquidation proceeds where the liquidation process was irreversible, as a practical matter, at the time of the gift.[127] Finally, death of a shareholder during the pendency of a dividend distribution or a sale of his stock raises problems under the "income in respect of a decedent" rules of §691.[128]

On occasion, a corporation's controlling shareholders waive their dividend rights for a period of time to strengthen the corporation's financial position; although this action is not likely to be treated as a constructive assignment of dividend income to the nonwaiving minority shareholders if it serves a bona fide business purpose, it is vulnerable if the beneficiaries of the waiver are members of the controlling shareholder's family.[129] Rev. Proc.

F2d 478 (3d Cir. 1961), cert. denied, 368 US 967 (1962) (contra; gift of stock after dividend declared but before record date; donor held taxable on theory that declaration of dividend created vested right in donor, under state corporate law); Rev. Rul. 60-331, 1960-2 CB 189 (unsuccessful attempt to transfer tax liability on deficiency dividend paid by personal holding company).

For sales, see Regs. §1.61-9(c); Rev. Rul. 82-11, 1982-1 CB 51 (corporation purchasing stock after record date not entitled to dividends received deduction, despite agreement with seller allowing buyer to receive and retain dividend; amount received is partial refund of purchase price paid for stock); Silco, Inc. v. US, 779 F2d 282 (5th Cir. 1986) (Rev. Rul. 82-11 inapplicable to purchases before ruling was promulgated). See generally Cutler, Dividend Arrearages, 37 Taxes 309 (1959).

[126] See Grove v. CIR, 490 F2d 241 (2d Cir. 1973), and cases cited therein; Robert A. Wekesser, supra note 111; Rev. Rul. 78-197, 1978-1 CB 83. For gifts to charity followed by an anticipated sale by the charity, see Blake v. CIR, 697 F2d 473 (2d Cir. 1982) (sale imputed to donor, despite more lenient approach of *Grove* case and Rev. Rul. 78-197).

For assignability of "section 306 stock," see Robert L. Fox, ¶ 68,205 P-H Memo. TC (1968) (charitable gift of "section 306 stock" followed by expected redemption did not result in taxable gain to donor). See infra ¶ 10.04.

See generally Galant, Planning Opportunity: The Gifting of Closely Held Stock to Charitable Organizations, 51 Taxes 645 (1973); Note, Charitable Donations of Stock–Grove v. CIR, 40 Brooklyn L. Rev. 1410 (1974).

[127] See Jones v. US, 531 F2d 1343 (6th Cir. 1976), and cases cited therein; Dayton Hydraulic Co. v. US, 592 F2d 937 (6th Cir.), cert. denied, 444 US 831 (1979) (applying *Jones*); Horace E. Allen, 66 TC 340 (1976) (extensive discussion).

[128] See Estate of Henry C. Bickmeyer, 84 TC 170 (1985) (extensive analysis with citations to earlier cases).

[129] See Rev. Rul. 65-256, 1965-2 CB 85, citing earlier rulings; Rev. Rul. 71-164, 1971-1 CB 108 (bank director did not constructively receive dividends waived by him). But see Bagley v. US, 348 F. Supp. 418 (D. Minn. 1972) (controlling shareholder, but not his wife, who was only minority shareholder, was taxable on ratable share of dividends waived in favor of other family members of closely held corporation); see also Green v. US, 460 F2d 412 (5th Cir. 1972) (constructive dividend to

67-14 contains guidelines on when the Service will rule with respect to dividend waiver plans. In brief, the following tests must be met: (1) there must be a bona fide business purpose; (2) the relatives of waiving shareholders must not receive more than 20 percent of the dividends paid; (3) the waiver term is limited to three years; and (4) a ruling will be conditioned on no changes in stock ownership that would enable relatives to receive more than 20 percent of the dividends paid.[130]

An attempt to convert anticipated dividend income into capital gain by selling the right to receive the dividend after the record date but before the payment date was rejected in *Estate of Rhodes v. CIR*.[131] A sale of stock dividend-on, however, generally produces capital gain or loss to the seller.[132] This approach, which differs from the practice of requiring the seller of a bond to report the interest accrued to the date of sale under Regs. §1.61-7(d), seems largely a matter of administrative convenience, and it would not prevent the Service, in an extreme case, from invoking assignment-of-income principles to require part of the proceeds from a sale of stock just before the record date to be allocated to dividend arrears, or even to dividends about to vest in the record owner.[133]

---

minority shareholder who exercised substantial influence over transaction); Estate of Hodgkins, ¶ 65,225 P-H Memo. TC (1965).

See generally Note, Income and Gift Tax Treatment of a Waiver of Rights to Future, Undeclared Dividends by a Corporate Shareholder, 32 Vand. L. Rev. 889 (1979).

[130] Rev. Proc. 67-14, 1967-1 CB 591.

[131] 131 F2d 50 (6th Cir. 1942).

[132] See Regs. §1.61-9(c); see also Stanley D. Beard, 4 TC 756 (1945) (acq.) (capital gain on sale of stock after adoption of plan of redemption, although latter would have resulted in ordinary income to seller). The same principle governs the transfer of stock with dividend arrearages. See Cutler, supra note 125, at 320. But see Rev. Rul. 82-11, 1982-1 CB 51.

In Mathis Estate, 47 TC 248 (1966), the court held that the redemption of preferred stock with dividend arrears qualified in full for capital gain treatment under §302(a). See also Rev. Rul. 69-131, 1969-1 CB 94 (premium paid for early redemption of preferred stock and in lieu of dividends accruing on later expected redemption date were held to be part of redemption proceeds). But see Rev. Rul. 69-130, 1969-1 CB 93 (dividends declared prior to call of preferred stock and included in total redemption payments were held taxable as separate §301 dividends); Arie S. Crown, 58 TC 825 (1972), aff'd, 487 F2d 1404 (7th Cir. 1973) (on redemption of preferred stock, part of proceeds were taxed as dividend because legal right to dividend existed at time of redemption, even though dividend had not been formally declared); Victor E. Gidwitz Family Trust, 61 TC 664 (1974) (accord); Rev. Rul. 75-320, 1975-2 CB 105 (portion of redemption proceeds taxed as dividends where shareholders had legal right to dividend at time of redemption; rest of redemption price treated as sale proceeds).

[133] See Brundage v. US, 275 F2d 424 (7th Cir.), cert. denied, 364 US 831 (1960); see also Rev. Rul. 82-11, 1982-1 CB 51.

On occasion, taxpayers have desired to use assignment-of-income principles as a sword for example, in order to accelerate income in order to make use of expiring deductions that could not otherwise be availed of. The technique adopted in this situation is to sell the taxpayer's future income rights for a present lump-sum consideration, taking the position that such amounts are immediately taxable when received. Courts, however, have not always accepted this device at face value, holding instead that the transaction should be treated as a nonrecourse loan,[134] although at least one circuit has agreed with the taxpayer's characterization of the transaction as a present taxable sale.[135]

2. Bootstrap sales—Taxability of dividends credited against, or used to finance, the purchase price. Identification of the proper taxpayer is often troublesome in the case of a bootstrap sale of corporate stock, in which dividends are credited against the purchase price. Regs. §1.61-9(c) provides that such dividends are taxable to the purchaser, even though he is not the legal owner of the stock and does not receive the dividends, if the seller retains legal title to the stock solely to secure payment. In such a case, the sales proceeds, including the portion defrayed by the dividends, will enter into the calculation of the seller's capital gain or loss.[136] If, however, the dividends are paid to the seller as the legal and equitable owner of the underlying stock, he is taxable even though the parties abate the price of the stock to take account of the distribution. Still, in *Waterman S.S. Corp. v. CIR*, a distribution was treated as part of the sales proceeds realized by the seller,

---

[134] J.A. Martin, 56 TC 1255 (1971), aff'd per curiam, 30 AFTR2d 5396 (5th Cir. 1972) (sale of future rents for present lump-sum payment constitutes nonrecourse loan); see also Mapco, Inc. v. US, 556 F2d 1107 (Ct. Cl. 1977) (short-term carve-out sale of future pipeline revenues to make use of expiring net operating loss held to be mere nonrecourse financing device); Stedwell Johnston, ¶ 76,142 P-H Memo. TC (1976).

[135] Stranahan v. CIR, 472 F2d 867 (6th Cir. 1973); see also Rev. Rul. 82-11, supra note 125. For a similar situation, see also McGrath, Coupon Stripping Under Section 1286: Trees, Fruits, and Felines, 38 Tax Lawyer 267 (1985).

Another way to accelerate the receipt of dividend income without currently depleting the corporation's cash or other liquid assets is the so-called consent dividend procedure sanctioned by §565, discussed infra at ¶ 8.09. Although intended primarily as an adjunct to §§531 and 541, relating to the special taxes on accumulated earnings and personal holding companies, §565 is not limited to this function. See Regs. §1.565-3(b), Examples (1) and (2).

[136] Steel Improvement & Forge Co. v. CIR, 314 F2d 96 (6th Cir. 1963); De Guire v. Higgins, 159 F2d 921 (2d Cir.), cert. denied, 331 US 858 (1947); Grayck, Taxing Income That Is Applied Against the Purchase Price, 12 Tax L. Rev. 381 (1957); Comment, Taxation of Pre-Sale, Intercorporate Dividends: Waterman S.S. Corp., 118 U. Pa. L. Rev. 622 (1970). See generally infra ¶ 9.07.

primarily on the ground that the various steps constituted a single transaction amounting in substance to an all-cash sale of the stock.[137]

The *Waterman* case was concerned with a dividend paid to the seller of the transferred corporation in anticipation of the sale. It should be noted that (1) the buyer of the stock, if also a corporation, often causes the acquired corporation to pay a dividend immediately *after* the sale, thus enabling the acquiring corporation to finance part of the purchase price, and (2) the dividend can be received at little or no tax cost because it qualifies for the §243 dividends-received deduction.[138]

---

[137] 430 F2d 1185 (5th Cir. 1970), cert. denied, 401 US 939 (1971) (distribution consisted of corporate note, which was promptly discharged with funds supplied by purchaser following acquisition of stock); see also O'Brien Co. v. CIR, 301 F2d 813 (3d Cir.), cert. denied, 371 US 820 (1962) (dividend taxable as such to seller, but allowed as credit against purchase price by sales contract); Casner v. CIR, 450 F2d 379 (5th Cir. 1971) (distribution of unwanted cash to seller before execution of binding stock-purchase contract held to be a dividend to buyer, not seller); Rev. Rul. 75-493, 1975-2 CB 108 (Service will not follow *Casner*, ruling instead that anticipatory distributions to seller are dividends to seller; *Waterman* distinguished because there the cash was actually supplied by purchaser of stock in effort to disguise true substance of transaction). For similar strip-out problems in the tax-free reorganization area, see infra ¶ 14.52.

Other decisions have tended to tax the transferor on anticipatory distributions, but not uniformly so. See, e.g., Percy A. Reitz, 61 TC 443 (1974), aff'd, 507 F2d 1279 (1975) (dividend followed by gift of stock, followed by liquidation of corporation; held dividend taxed to donor, even though he could have structured transaction in another manner); Thomas L. Perry, ¶ 76,381 P-H Memo. TC (1976) (dividend held part of selling price on facts); Walker v. CIR, 544 F2d 419 (9th Cir. 1976) (seller taxed on dividend declared and paid to him when he was beneficial owner of stock; dividend held to be neither part of sales proceeds nor constructive dividend to buyer); Pacific Coast Music Jobbers, Inc. v. US, 457 F2d 1165 (5th Cir. 1972) (purchase of stock of S corporation, but buyer did not elect; held, §1371 status terminated, and buyer was taxed on dividends used to pay off liability for purchase price).

[138] See supra ¶ 5.05. Compare Basic, Inc. v. US, 549 F2d 740 (Ct. Cl. 1977), in which the parent planned to sell a two-tier chain of subsidiaries, *S-1* and *S-2*. The parent first had *S-1* pay a dividend in kind of its *S-2* stock and then sold the stock of both subsidiaries to the buyer; the dividend of *S-2* stock was ignored as a transitory step without business purpose. The parent's capital gain was increased by the amount of the *S-2* dividend. The case seems inconsistent with Rev. Rul. 75-493, 1975-2 CB 108, and Rev. Rul. 69-608, 1969-2 CB 42. See also TSN Liquidating Corp. v. US, 624 F2d 1328 (5th Cir. 1980) (dividend in kind of unwanted portfolio securities, constituting 78 percent of target corporation's assets, followed by sale of stock by corporate shareholder to new buyer at scaled-down price, followed by capital infusion of cash into corporation by new owner; threshold dividend treated as true dividend, not part of selling price; taxpayer entitled to §243 deduction; mere infusion of assets into target after acquisition not enough to invoke *Waterman* principle). But see Blake v. CIR, supra note 126 (court applied step doctrine approach of *Basic, Inc.* case to tax donor on proceeds of donated stock used to buy other property from donor at inflated price; transactions linked by parties' "understandings").

If the buyer issues bonds or debentures in payment for the acquired stock, it can cause the subsidiary to pay dividends (taxed at a low rate by virtue of §243) and use these funds to pay deductible interest on the debt. This interplay between the §163 interest deduction and the §243 dividends-received deduction was the tax catalyst for many acquisitions by conglomerates in the late 1960s, and it led, in 1969, to a statutory limitation on the interest deduction in such cases. [139]

The §243 deduction was restricted in 1984 by the enactment of §246A (reducing the §243 deduction for dividends received from certain debt-financed portfolio stock investments) and §1059 (reducing the corporate shareholder's stock basis for the untaxed portion of extraordinary dividends (as defined) on stock held one year or less *after* the dividend; the tainted period was lengthened to two years and refocused to the period *preceding* the dividend by the Tax Reform Act of 1986). [140]

PART B.   DISTRIBUTIONS IN KIND

¶ 7.20   INTRODUCTORY

When a corporation distributes cash to its shareholders, the tax consequences to both the recipient and his corporation can be easily determined if the corporation's earnings and profits are known. The distribution is a "dividend" to the extent of the corporation's current and accumulated post-1913 earnings and profits; the balance, if any, is applied against and reduces the adjusted basis of the shareholder's stock under §301(c)(2); and any excess is subject to §301(c)(3). The shareholder, having received cash, has no problem of basis. As to the corporation, the distribution itself is not a taxable event; and the corporation's earnings and profits are reduced to the extent that the distribution is a "dividend" to the shareholders.

When we turn from a corporate distribution of cash to a distribution in kind, [141] however, the problems quickly proliferate. Does the mere distribution

---

For analysis of this area, see Kingson, supra note 78; Ditkoff, Intercorporate Dividends and Legitimate Tax Avoidance, 4 J. Corp. Tax'n 5 (1977); Schaffer & Gordon, Taxing Intercorporate Dividends Received as Part of the Sale of a Subsidiary, 30 Tax Lawyer 727 (1977); Lang, Dividends Essentially Equivalent to Redemption: The Taxation of Bootstrap Stock Acquisitions, 41 Tax L. Rev. 309 (1986).

[139] See supra ¶ 4.26.

[140] See supra ¶ 5.05, paras. 8 and 9.

[141] The term "distribution in kind" is used here to mean a distribution of property other than money or the distributing corporation's own stock or obligations. See §317(a).

of appreciated property create corporate income or earnings and profits? Does the distribution of depreciated property produce a corporate loss? If the distribution itself does not produce corporate gain or loss, is a prompt sale of appreciated or depreciated property by the distributees to be treated as a corporate transaction so that the gain or loss will be imputed to the corporation? Does a distribution of property come out of current or post-1913 earnings and profits (so as to constitute a "dividend") if the earnings and profits exceed the adjusted basis of the property but are less than its fair market value? Are the corporation's earnings and profits to be reduced by the fair market value of the distributed property or by its adjusted basis? What is the basis of the distributed property in the hands of the shareholders?

Before 1954, in the absence of statutory rules governing this area, the Treasury on a number of occasions advanced the theory that a corporation, on distributing appreciated property to its shareholders, realizes taxable income just as though it had sold the property for its fair market value or used it to satisfy an obligation in that amount. The courts consistently rejected the Treasury's argument, usually with a citation to *General Utilities & Operating Co. v. Helvering.* [142] In fact, although the government had argued for the recognition of taxable income upon a distribution of appreciated property in *General Utilities & Operating Co.*, the Supreme Court did not find it necessary to pass on this issue, [143] but even though the question was

---

[142] 296 US 200 (1935); see generally Mintz & Plumb, Dividends in Kind—The Thunderbolts and the New Look, 10 Tax L. Rev. 41 (1954), and their postscript, id. at 405 (discussing both pre- and post-1954 law); Raum, Dividends in Kind: Their Tax Aspects, 63 Harv. L. Rev. 593 (1950); Johnson, Corporation and Stockholder—Dividends in Kind, 1 Tax L. Rev. 86 (1945); Wallace, A Dissent, 1 Tax L. Rev. 93 (1945).

For articles discussing the post-1954 legislative action codifying and then restricting the nonrecognition rule of §311(a)(2), see infra note 143.

[143] The government's argument on this point was as follows:

In making [the appreciation] available to its own stockholders the corporation is realizing the appreciation, and nothing more is necessary. It is our view that the addition to surplus on account of the increased value and the distribution of this increased value in satisfaction of the company's general liability to its stockholders, are [sic] the evidence that the gain has been realized, for it is incomprehensible how a corporation can distribute to its stockholders something which it has not itself received. . . . It is clear that petitioner used the increased value for a corporate purpose, and was thereby enabled to pay its stockholders $1,071,426.25 [i.e., the fair market value of the distributed property]. Thus was petitioner serving the principal end for which it was organized—to earn profits which it would distribute to its stockholders—and we submit that in so justifying the hopes of its organizers this economic entity, called a corporation, truly derived an economic gain. (Respondent's Brief, at 18–19, 25.)

The Supreme Court refused to consider this issue, which was not raised in the lower courts. The only government argument it addressed (and rejected) was that the corporation's dividend resolution created an indebtedness to the shareholders that was

not foreclosed by that case, the result reached by the lower courts was endorsed, at least for the future, by the 1954 enactment of the statutory predecessor of §311(a)(2).

As originally enacted, §311(a)(2) in effect codified what had come to be called the *General Utilities* doctrine, namely, that a corporation does not recognize gain or loss on a distribution of appreciated or depreciated property to its shareholders with respect to their stock. This statutory rule covered what might be described as mere distributions, but the status of distributions to shareholders who did not hold the property but instead sold it shortly after the distribution was open to debate, especially if the sale was anticipated or prearranged. Several pre-1954 cases had required the corporation to recognize the gain or income realized by shareholders on such post-distribution, shareholder-level transactions;[144] and these judicial exceptions to the *General Utilities* doctrine survived the 1954 legislation.[145] The scope of these cases was uncertain, however, since they rested on such pervasive but

---

satisfied by the use of appreciated property. For the effect of dividend resolutions under current law, see infra text following note 155.

The *General Utilities* literature is unusually voluminous. See generally Federal Income Tax Project: Subchapter C (American Law Institute 1982) at 102–119 Wolfman, Corporate Distributions of Appreciated Property: The Case for Repeal of the *General Utilities* Doctrine, 22 San Diego L. Rev. 81 (1985); Nolan, Taxing Corporate Distributions of Appreciated Property: Repeal of the *General Utilities* Doctrine and Relief Measures, 22 San Diego L. Rev. 97 (1985); Shube, Corporate Income or Loss on Distributions of Property: An Analysis of *General Utilities*, 12 J. Corp. Tax'n 3 (Spring 1985); ABA Section of Taxation Task Force Report, Income Taxation of Corporations Making Distributions With Respect to Their Stock, 37 Tax Lawyer 625 (1984); Beck, Distributions in Kind in Corporate Liquidations: A Defense of *General Utilities*, 38 Tax Lawyer 663 (1985); Hawkins, A Discussion of the Repeal of *General Utilities*, 37 Tax Lawyer 641 (1984). Additional citations may be found in Yin, General Utilities Repeal: Is Tax Reform Really Going to Pass It By? Tax Notes (June 16, 1986), at 1111 n.6.

[144] See CIR v. First State Bank of Stratford, 168 F2d 1004 (5th Cir.), cert. denied, 335 US 867 (1948) (bank taxed on collections by shareholders from notes previously written off as worthless and distributed by bank to its shareholders); US v. Lynch, 192 F2d 718 (9th Cir. 1951), cert. denied, 343 US 934 (1952) (distribution of inventory property; corporation taxed on sale); see also CIR v. Transport Trading & Terminal Corp., 176 F2d 570 (2d Cir. 1949), cert. denied, 338 US 955, reh'g denied, 339 US 916 (1950) (distributing corporation taxed on sale of noninventory property because distribution served no business purpose and was made in anticipation of immediate sale by distributee shareholders); Hines v. US, 477 F2d 1063 (5th Cir. 1973) (contra; extensive analysis with citation of cases). See generally Bush Bros. & Co. v. CIR, 668 F2d 252 (6th Cir. 1982); Loengard & Cobb, Who Sold the Bush Brothers' Beans?, 35 Tax L. Rev. 509 (1980).

[145] S. Rep. No. 1622, supra note 73, at 247. See also Regs. §1.311-1(a) (§311 does not preclude imputing shareholder sales to the distributing corporation or taxing latter if distribution is in effect an anticipatory assignment of income). Compare Hines v. US and Bush Bros. & Co. v. CIR, supra note 144.

imprecise principles as business purpose, form as opposed to substance, and anticipatory assignment of income.

The 1954 statutory nonrecognition principle was qualified not only by this judicial practice of imputing some shareholder sales and other dispositions to the corporation but also by several explicit statutory exceptions that required the corporation to recognize gain on certain distributions of appreciated LIFO property and of other appreciated property if subject to a liability in excess of its basis.[146] Moreover, over the course of time, Congress created more and more exceptions to the ostensible general rule of nonrecognition, as far as distributions of appreciated property were concerned, while preserving intact the nonrecognition principle for the corporation's losses on depreciated property.[147] This legislative trend reached its zenith in 1986, when the general nonrecognition rule of §311(a)(2) was in effect repealed for all nonliquidating distributions of appreciated property, unless they qualified for nonrecognition under various transitional exceptions.

The discussion of the decline and fall of the *General Utilities* doctrine that follows concentrates first on current law governing corporate gain or loss on nonliquidating distributions of appreciated and depreciated property, which generally applies to distributions (including stock redemptions) in 1987 and thereafter;[148] next, the text discusses the rules governing nonliquidating distributions under pre-1987 law, which will be encountered in litigation for some years to come and which continues even after 1986 to apply to a few beneficiaries of "grandfathered" effective dates.[149]

¶ 7.21 CORPORATE GAIN OR LOSS ON POST-1986 DISTRIBUTIONS OF PROPERTY

1. Introductory. Section 311(a)(2) states that "no gain or loss shall be recognized to a corporation on the distribution, with respect to its stock, of . . . property." This self-styled general rule, enacted in 1954 to codify the *General Utilities* doctrine,[150] is truly general as to losses on the distribution

---

[146] See infra ¶ 7.22.

[147] See infra ¶ 7.22.

[148] See infra ¶ 7.21. For distributions in complete liquidation of the distributing corporation, see infra ¶ 11.06.

For analyses of the Tax Reform Act of 1986 amendments, see Eustice, Kuntz, Lewis, & Deering, The Tax Reform Act of 1986, ¶ 2.03 (Warren, Gorham & Lamont, Inc., 1987); Heigel & Schler, Repeal of the *General Utilities* Doctrine, 33 Tax Notes 961 (Dec. 18, 1986); Bonovitz, Impact of the TRA Repeal of *General Utilities*, 65 J. Tax'n 388 (1986).

[149] See infra ¶ 7.22.

[150] See supra text following note 143.

of depreciated property. But regarding gains on the distribution of appreciated property, it was subjected to an ever-increasing number of exceptions in the years after its enactment,[151] and it was in effect repealed in 1986, except as to distributions in tax-free reorganizations and similar transactions.

Before examining the current rules, a preliminary comment on the scope of §311(a)(2) may be useful. First, §311(a)(2) is applicable only if the corporation makes a distribution "with respect to its stock." The regulations expand on this language by stating: "Section 311 does not apply to transactions between a corporation and a shareholder in his capacity as debtor, creditor, employee, or vendee, where the fact that such debtor, creditor, employee, or vendee is a shareholder is incidental to the transaction."[152] Thus, if the corporation sells property to one of its shareholders in the ordinary course of business, the corporation's gain or loss is recognized in the usual manner, since the fact that the buyer is a shareholder is incidental to the transaction.[153] Gain or loss is also recognized if a corporation uses appreciated or depreciated property to pay compensation to an employee-shareholder, since the distribution is not made "with respect to its stock," even though the employee also happens to be a shareholder. The same principle applies if property is transferred to pay a debt owed to a shareholder.[154]

The debt-discharge situation, however, creates a special problem if the underlying obligation was created by a corporate decision to distribute the property as a dividend to its shareholders. In several pre-1954 cases, corporations were held to realize gain or loss on the distribution of appreciated or depreciated property to their shareholders as a dividend because the resolution authorizing the distribution created an enforceable obligation in a specified dollar amount and because this debt was satisfied by the distribution of property with a fair market value equal to the amount owing but with an adjusted basis to the corporation that was either less than or greater than its

---

[151] See infra ¶ 7.22.

[152] Regs. §1.311-1(e)(1). For attempts to circumvent the nonrecognition of loss on distributions of depreciated property by disguising the transaction as a sale or other normally taxable event, see infra text following note 157.

[153] See Owens Mach. Co., 54 TC 877 (1970). For the disallowance of losses between related parties, including a corporation and a shareholder owning (directly, indirectly, and constructively) more than 50 percent in value of its outstanding stock, see §267(a)(1), discussed supra at ¶ 5.04, para. 1.

[154] See Northern Coal & Dock Co., 12 TC 42 (1949) (acq.); Rev. Rul. 70-271, 1970-1 CB 166; Five Star Mfg. Co. v. CIR, 355 F2d 724 (5th Cir. 1966) (corporation allowed a deduction for business-related redemption of its stock); Harder Servs., Inc., 67 TC 585 (1976), aff'd, 77-2 USTC 9743 (1977) (contra); see also Arlington Metal Indus., Inc., 57 TC 302 (1971) (corporation's receipt of its own stock in satisfaction of corporation's claim against shareholder held to be ordinary income not protected by §311(a)); S. Rep. No. 1622, supra note 73, at 247.

value. [155] These cases may be viable under current law on the ground that it is not the distribution but the satisfaction of the debt that produces the gain or loss. On the other hand, the nonrecognition of losses mandated by §311(a)(2) would become a dead letter if dividend resolutions covering depreciated property were routinely accepted by the courts at face value. This suggests that they should be viewed with great skepticism.

2. Losses. The nonrecognition of losses on nonliquidating distributions of depreciated property, mandated by §311(a)(2) since 1954, was carried forward in 1986, even though Congress virtually repealed the *General Utilities* doctrine regarding appreciated property and for the first time allowed losses to be recognized when depreciated property is distributed in complete liquidation of the distributing corporation. [156] Despite these dramatic changes in the rules governing both liquidating and nonliquidating gains and liquidating losses, the legislative reports offer no explanation for perpetuating the 1954 rule for nonliquidating distributions of depreciated property; presumably, it was thought that they are more open than liquidating distributions to manipulation with respect to both their timing and their bona fides. [157]

Corporations wishing to transfer depreciated property to their shareholders in order to recognize the losses will no doubt seek to circumvent §311(a)(2) by a variety of tactics, such as sales to the shareholders or to third persons who then resell the same property to the shareholders. Sales directly to shareholders, however, must run the gauntlet of §§267(a)(1) and 267(b)(2), which disallow any deduction for losses on the sale of property by a corporation to a person owning more than 50 percent (by value) of the seller's outstanding stock. [158] Because stock ownership for this purpose

---

[155] This argument was made by the Service in *General Utilities*, supra notes 142, 143, but it was rejected on the ground that the dividend resolution in that case did not create a dollar indebtedness. For other cases, see Bacon-McMillan Veneer Co., 20 BTA 556 (1930); Callanan Rd. Improvement Co., 12 BTA 1109 (1928) (acq.) (loss on distribution of depreciated property); Natural Gasoline Corp. v. CIR, 219 F2d 682 (10th Cir. 1955) (ambiguous resolution did not create liability of fixed amount in dollars).

[156] See infra ¶ 11.06.

[157] As explained infra ¶ 11.06, the recognition of losses on liquidating distributions is subject to several statutory safeguards designed to prevent manipulative transactions, but the relevant committee report does not explain why these or similar protective provisions would not have been equally adequate for manipulative nonliquidating distributions.

For problems in determining whether a particular transaction is an isolated nonliquidating distribution, on which loss is not recognized, or an integral step in a liquidating distribution on which loss is recognized by §336(a), see infra ¶¶ 11.02 and 11.06.

[158] For discussion of §267, see generally ¶ 5.04, para. 1.

includes stock owned by specified members of the buyer's family, closely held corporations will usually find that sales are not a feasible way of avoiding §311(a)(2). Moreover, even if stock ownership is sufficiently dispersed to avoid application of §267(a), a purported sale may be brushed aside as a sham or recharacterized as a mere distribution coupled with a functionally unrelated contribution by the shareholders to the corporation's capital of the amounts ostensibly paid by them for the property.[159] Indeed, this approach is potentially more damaging to the shareholders than a simple application of §267(a), since losses disallowed under §267(a) may be taken into account when the shareholder ultimately disposes of the property; no comparable relief is available under §311(a)(2).[160]

An attempt to avoid the application of §311(a)(2) by a purported sale of the depreciated property by the corporation to an outsider may be attacked by the Service as a sham or a step transaction if the property is resold by the ostensible buyer to the shareholders, especially if the two steps are prearranged or occur in such rapid succession that prearrangement can be inferred. If, however, the depreciated property does not end up in the hands of the corporation's shareholders, §311(a)(2) will not ordinarily pose any threat to the corporation's right to recognize the loss, since it applies only to a distribution of property "with respect to [the distributing corporation's] stock."

In unusual circumstances, however, an ostensible corporate-level sale might be recharacterized as a distribution to the shareholders followed by a sale by them to the purchaser. For example, if a distribution-cum-shareholder sale is planned but called off at the last minute in favor of a sale by the corporation and a distribution by it of the proceeds, the Service might succeed in imputing the sale to the shareholders by analogy to the *Court Holding Co.* case, which involved the converse situation, namely, a shareholder sale of distributed property that was imputed to the corporation because at the last minute and without any business purpose the plan was changed to an ostensible shareholder sale.[161] Such a recharacterization of the transaction would result in nonrecognition of the loss at the corporate level on the theory that in substance the corporation did not sell the property but instead distributed it to its shareholders within the meaning of §311(a)(2). The shareholders, whose basis for the property would be its fair market value when received by them,[162] would then realize no loss on their sale to the ultimate purchaser.

---

[159] For an analogy, see supra ¶ 3.14 (ostensible sales recharacterized as §351 transactions).

[160] See §267(d), recognizing the shareholder's gain on a later sale of the property only if and to the extent that it exceeds the seller's disallowed loss.

[161] See CIR v. Court Holding Co., 324 US 331 (1945), discussed infra at ¶ 11.07.

[162] See §301(d)(1), discussed infra at ¶ 7.23, para. 1.

3. Gains. Although the nonrecognition rule of §311(a)(2), as enacted in 1954, remains in full force as far as losses are concerned, it was repeatedly eroded from 1954 to 1986 regarding gains on nonliquidating distributions of appreciated property,[163] and it was virtually eliminated by the enactment of current §311(b) in 1986. In taking this step, which was less a break with tradition than the culmination of a gradual process, Congress offered this rationale:[164]

> [T]he *General Utilities* rule tends to undermine the corporate income tax. Under normally applicable tax principles, nonrecognition of gain is available only if the transferee takes a carryover basis in the transferred property, thus assuring that a tax will eventually be collected on the appreciation. Where the *General Utilities* rule applies, assets generally are permitted to leave corporate solution and to take a stepped-up basis in the hands of the transferee without the imposition of a corporate-level tax.* Thus, the effect of the rule is to grant a permanent exemption from the corporate income tax.
>
> ---
> *The price of this basis step up is, at most, a single shareholder-level capital gains tax (and perhaps recapture, tax benefit, and other similar amounts). In some cases, moreover, payment of the capital gains tax is deferred because the shareholder's gain is reported under the installment method.

To correct the deficiencies that Congress perceived in pre-1986 law, §311(b)(1) provides for the recognition of gain if a corporation distributes property (other than its own obligations) to a shareholder in a distribution to which §§301–304 apply, i.e., distributions subject to the dividend rules of §301, stock redemptions, and partial liquidations.[165] Section 311(b), however, does not require gain to be recognized on distributions subject to other provisions of the Code, such as the rules governing complete liquidations and tax-free reorganizations and spin-offs.[166]

---

[163] See infra ¶ 7.22.

[164] H.R. Rep. No. 426, 99th Cong., 1st Sess. 282 (1985). The report also asserted that a pre-1986 discrepancy between the treatment of liquidating and nonliquidating distributions may have artificially encouraged corporate mergers and acquisitions, despite economic reasons for a different course of action.

See also Senate Finance Committee Staff Final Report, The Subchapter C Revision Act of 1985, 99th Cong. 1st Sess., S. Prt. No. 47, at 42–44 (1985), for additional criticisms of *General Utilities*.

[165] Section 311(b)(1) refers more broadly to a "distribution to which subpart A [of Part I of Subchapter C] applies," which includes §§301–307, but of these provisions, §§305–307, dealing with distributions of stock and stock rights, are rendered inapplicable by §317(a), which excludes these items from the term "property." Thus, the distributions affected by §311(b)(1) are those described by §§301–304.

[166] For distributions in complete liquidation of the distributing corporation, see

When applicable, §311(b) requires the corporation to recognize gain as though it had sold the distributed property to the distributee at its fair market value. Section 311(b)(1) says nothing about whether the hypothetical sale generates capital gain or ordinary income, but this issue (including the impact of any applicable recapture rules) is no doubt governed by the same principles that would apply to an actual sale. In borderline situations, however, it may be that a §311(b)(1) gain will qualify as capital gain because distributions are not effected with the aid of advertising, whereas an actual sale might have required enough advertising or similar activities to tip the scales in favor of ordinary income. On the other hand, on a corporate distribution of a mixed bag of assets, §311(a) and §311(b)(1) together may produce an unappetizing combination of recognized gains and nonrecognized losses, while an actual sale of the entire batch would permit the gains and losses to be offset against each other, resulting in a recognized net gain or loss.

Although it does not explicitly supersede it, the breadth of §311(b)(1) renders obsolete the case law under which shareholder gains on the sale of distributed property were sometimes imputed back to the corporation.[167] It is possible, however, that such an imputation may be appropriate in unusual situations, such as a shareholder sale of the property for more than its fair market value when distributed, if the sale is effected with the use of corporate facilities or with corporate participation.

Section 311(b)(1) is buttressed by §311(b)(2), which incorporates by reference rules similar to those prescribed by §336(b), relating to liabilities in excess of basis. Section 336(b) provides that if a corporation distributes property subject to a liability or if a corporate liability is assumed by a shareholder in connection with the distribution, the fair market value of the property shall be treated as not less than the amount of the liability.[168] Thus, if property with a basis of $90,000 in the hands of the distributing corporation and a fair market value of $100,000 is distributed subject to a liability of $125,000, the distributing corporation's gain is $35,000 ($125,000 minus $90,000). Section 336(b), and hence §311(b)(2), does not distinguish between recourse and nonrecourse liabilities, so the same result would be reached if the shareholder assumed the $125,000 liability rather than took the property subject to it.

---

infra ¶ 11.06; for distributions pursuant to tax-free and spin-off reorganizations, see generally infra ¶¶ 13.2 and 14.32, respectively.

[167] See supra note 161.

[168] For the tax treatment in other contexts of liabilities that are in excess of basis, see generally Bittker, supra note 83, at ¶ 43.5; see also §7701(g).

Presumably, §311(b)(2) applies asset-by-asset, as was the case under former §311(c). See infra note 176.

¶ 7.22 CORPORATE GAIN OR LOSS ON PRE-1987 DISTRIBUTIONS OF PROPERTY

Before its revision by the Tax Reform Act of 1986, §311 provided that as a general rule, no gain or loss was to be recognized by a corporation on the distribution of property with respect to its stock,[169] but as to gains, the ostensible general rule was subject to so many exceptions that it shielded only a few distributions.[170] Because pre-1987 distributions of appreciated property will no doubt continue to generate litigation for some years to come, and also because a transitional exemption for distributions in 1987 and 1988 by certain small, closely held corporations (which was proposed but not enacted in 1986) may be revived,[171] these pre-1987 statutory exceptions to the nonrecognition principle are summarized below.[172]

---

[169] For the meaning of "distribution [by a corporation] with respect to stock," as used in §311(a), see supra text at notes 73–74.

[170] For the evolution of §311 from a nearly unqualified codification of the *General Utilities* doctrine to a much-restricted provision, see supra text at notes 141–145, and articles cited in note 143. See also the Fourth Edition of this treatise, ¶¶ 7.21 and 9.64.

For a flow chart tracing the tax impact of pre-1987 distributions of appreciated property, see Bloom & Calvert, Corporate Changes Wrought by the Tax Reform Act of 1984, 11 J. Corp. Tax'n 299, 358 (1985); see also Javaras, Corporate Distributions of Property: Recent Judicial and Legislative Changes, 62 Taxes 587 (1984).

[171] See H.R. Con. Res. 395, 99th Cong., 2d Sess., Item 75 of which would have added §633(d)(9) to the effective date rules of the Tax Reform Act of 1986, preserving old §311 and certain other provisions for nonliquidating distributions by qualified corporations. For discussion of qualified corporations, see infra ¶ 11.61 (effective date grandfather clause for certain complete liquidations). The resolution was passed by the House (see Cong. Rec. H8453 (daily ed. Sept. 25, 1986)). The Senate also passed the resolution with some additional provisions, but the differences were not resolved and the resolution died when the 99th Congress adjourned. See Teubor, Battle Over Enrolling Resolution Continues, 33 Tax Notes 230 (1986) see currently §106(g)(6) of the Technical Corrections Act of 1987.

Even as enacted, however, the Tax Reform Act of 1986 offers limited protection for some distributions in kind. First, §633(d)(1) makes certain amendments (including the changes in §311) inapplicable to certain small corporations that are completely liquidated before 1989. For this transitional exemption, see infra ¶ 9.34, note 216. Distributions of appreciated property before this date are presumably protected if they are an integral part of the complete liquidation, even though they occur after the normal effective date of the corporate provisions of the 1986 Act. Second, it is possible that this protection applies even if the 1987 or 1988 distribution is not part of the complete liquidation, since §633(d)(1) provides for a delayed effective date if the corporation liquidates, without explicitly limiting this relief to the liquidating distributions. Compare the delayed effective date specified by §633(c)(1)(A), which applies only to distributions and sales "made pursuant to a plan of liquidation."

[172] Textual references to "old §311" refer to that provision as in force immediately before enactment of the Tax Reform Act of 1986.

1. Installment obligations. Old §311(a) explicitly cited §453B, relating to installment obligations, as an exception to the nonrecognition principle. This cross-reference ensured that a §311 distribution of installment obligations would constitute a "distribution, transmission, or disposition" within the meaning of §453B(a)(2), which would result in the recognition of gain or loss to the extent of any difference between the obligation's basis to the corporation and its fair market value when distributed. [173]

2. LIFO inventory. On a distribution of LIFO inventory, old §311(b) required the distributing corporation to recognize gain to the extent (if any) that the basis determined by a non-LIFO method (e.g., FIFO) exceeded the LIFO value. The difference between the LIFO and non-LIFO values was thus taken into income if the corporation disposed of the property by distributing it to its shareholders. Old §311(b) did not stand in the way of attributing additional income to the corporation on a later sale of the property by the shareholders. [174] The profit at that time would be calculated on the non-LIFO value. Since the 1954 Senate report on old §311 refers to the "attribution of income," however, it was not clear whether a loss could be claimed by the corporation if the sales price was less than the non-LIFO value. [175]

3. Liability in excess of basis. On a distribution of property that was subject to a liability, or if the shareholder assumed a liability in connection with the distribution, old §311(c) required the corporation to recognize gain if and to the extent that the liability exceeded the adjusted basis of the property. [176] In effect, the distribution was treated as a sale of the property for the amount of the liability, with the proceeds being applied to satisfy the liability, for which the corporation was thereafter only secondarily liable. The statute did not expressly so state, but if the liability was not paid by the shareholder or was not satisfied out of the property by which it was secured, upon payment the corporation was presumably entitled to a deductible loss or a bad debt.

Old §311(c) provided that if the liability was not assumed by the distributee shareholder, the recognized gain was not to exceed the excess of the property's fair market value over its adjusted basis. But this limitation may

---

[173] See generally Rev. Rul. 74-337, 1974-2 CB 94.

[174] For an analogy, see, e.g., US v. Lynch, supra note 144.

[175] S. Rep. No. 1622, supra note 73.

[176] See Rev. Rul. 80-283, 1980-2 CB 108 (§311(c) computations if the distribution involves two or more properties). See supra note 168.

have been rendered nugatory by the enactment in 1984 of §7701(g), deeming the value of property transferred subject to nonrecourse debt to be not less than the amount of the debt.

4. Recognition of gain under §311(d). Old §311(d)(1) provided that if a corporation distributed property (other than its own obligations) with a fair market value in excess of its adjusted basis, the distributing corporation recognized gain as though the property had been sold at the time of the distribution. At first blush, this deemed-sale provision seems wholly inconsistent with the nonrecognition principle announced as the general rule by old §311(a). On closer inspection, however, old §311(d)(1) turns out to have been narrower than old §311(a), so that both provisions could co-exist (which is not to say, however, that the statutory language would win a prize for draftsmanship).

First, old §311(d)(1) did not apply to losses; thus, old §311(a) continued to reign supreme over distributions of depreciated property. Second, old §311(d)(1) was limited to distributions to which Subpart A (§§301–307) applied, while old §311(a) applied more broadly to any distribution "with respect to [the distributing corporation's] stock."[177] Thus, old §311(d) did not affect distributions whose tax effects were prescribed by provisions other than §§301–307—e.g., distributions in the course of a spin-off under §355, a complete liquidation under §331, or a corporate reorganization as defined by §368. Finally, old §311(d)(1) was subject to a series of exceptions that returned the affected transactions to the nonrecognition regime of old §311(a)(2).

These exceptions, which appeared in old §311(d)(2), involved the following:

(1) Distributions in partial liquidation of the distributing corporation;

(2) Distributions constituting qualified dividends (as defined);

(3) Distributions of the stock or obligations of the distributing corporation's subsidiaries;

(4) Distributions qualifying under §303 (relating to death taxes, funeral and administration expenses, and so forth);

(5) Distributions to private foundations to redeem certain excess stock holdings; and

---

[177] For discussion of the comparable scope of current §311(b)(1), see text supra at note 165.

(6) redemptions by mutual funds on the demand of shareholders.

See Paragraph 5 following for discussion of the first three of these exceptions.

The second sentence of old §311(d)(1) provided that §311(d) was to be applied after the application of §§311(b) and 311(c), relating to LIFO inventory and liabilities in excess of basis, respectively. This order-of-battle ensured that old §§311(b) and 311(c) would apply even if the distribution was covered by one of the exceptions listed in old §311(d)(2); however, if only part of the distributing corporation's gain was taxed by old §311(b) or 311(c), the remainder would qualify for protection under old §311(d)(2).

5. Distributions with respect to qualified stock. The three most important exceptions to old §311(d)—for partial liquidations, "qualified dividends" as defined, and distributions of stock or obligations of a subsidiary— were subject to the nonrecognition rule of old §311(a)(2) so that the distributing corporation did not recognize gain if it used appreciated property to effect a qualifying transaction.

These three exceptions shared two major features. First, they covered distributions only if the stock was held by persons other than corporations, except that stock held by an S corporation was treated as though it were held by its shareholders pro rata. Second, the exceptions all involved distributions of a going business or its assets or, if the business itself was conducted by a subsidiary of the distributing corporation, distributions of the subsidiary's stock or obligations. Appreciated investment assets, like portfolio securities, did not ordinarily qualify for tax-free distribution, although they could slip through the filter if they accompanied a qualifying distribution of operating assets.

Because all three of these exceptions to the recognition of gain under old §311(d)(1) applied only to distributions with respect to "qualified stock," the meaning of this term was crucial. Roughly speaking, its function was to require recognition of gain on run-of-the-mill distributions by publicly held corporations (reflecting legislative discontent with some much-publicized royalty trust distributions by listed oil companies) while exempting distributions by closely held corporations to their substantial long-term noncorporate shareholders.

This bifurcated approach was achieved by defining "qualified stock" by reference to the characteristics of its holder rather than to features inherent in the shares themselves. First, the shareholder had to have held at least 10 percent in value of the distributing corporation's stock (or its predecessor's stock) throughout the five-year period ending on the date of the distribution or, if shorter, for the period during which the distributing corporation or a predecessor corporation was in existence.[178] In determining ownership of stock for this purpose, the constructive ownership rules of §318 applied[179]— one of relatively few occasions on which attribution could be beneficial to taxpayers. Thus, if A and A's daughter each owned 5 percent of the distributing corporation's stock for the requisite period, they both satisfied the 10 percent benchmark. It was not clear, however, if the daughter would qualify if she acquired her stock from A during the five-year period. But a strong case could be made for attributing the stock to her during the early part of the period, even though she was not then an actual shareholder in her own right, since A's stock would be attributed to her if she owned so much as a single share throughout the period.

Second, if stock was held by a "pass-through entity"—an S corporation, a partnership, a trust, or an estate—old §311(e) applied the five-year and 10 percent tests by treating the distribution as made directly to the shareholders, partners, or beneficiaries in proportion to their interests in the entity. Thus, some of an S corporation's stock in the distributing corporation could be qualified stock, while the rest was not.

Finally, stock held by a corporation (other than an S corporation) could not constitute qualified stock. This prohibition ensured that nonrecognition of gain by the distributing corporation would be allowed only if the recipient was required (assuming adequate earnings and profits) to include the full value of the distribution in gross income. This requirement was satisfied by individuals but not by corporations because before 1987 the amount included by corporations in income was limited to the property's adjusted basis in the hands of the distributing corporation, as explained in a subsequent section of this chapter.[180]

On a distribution of appreciated property with respect to qualified stock, the distributing corporation's gain was exempted by old §311(d)(2) from the recognition rule of §311(d)(1)—and hence it qualified for nonrecognition under the general rule of old §311(a)(2)[181]—in the following three situations:

(a) Partial liquidations. Old §311(d)(2)(A)(i) shielded distributions on qualified stock if §302(b)(4) applied to the distribution. Because §302(b)(4)

---

[178] If the stock ownership requirement was satisfied, additional stock acquired during the five-year period could ride piggyback on the status of the qualifying shares, even if the new shares were not taken into account in determining whether the threshold condition was met.

[179] Note, however, old §311(e)(1)(B)'s change in the meaning of "family." For discussion of §318, see infra ¶ 9.03.

[180] See §301(b)(1)(B), discussed infra at ¶ 7.23.

[181] This assumes that (1) the gain was not taxed under old §§311(b) or 311(c), which, as explained supra at text at end of para. 4, were applied before §311(d); and (2) the recapture rules (see infra text at para. 6) did not apply.

is examined in detail later in this treatise,[182] its requirements are not repeated here.

(b) Qualified dividends. Old §311(d)(2)(A)(ii) exempted "qualified dividends," if distributed with respect to qualified stock. To qualify, (1) the distribution had to be a dividend (i.e., covered by earnings and profits and thus includable in the distributee's gross income under §301(c)(1)); (2) the property must have been used by the distributing corporation in the active conduct of a trade or business; and (3) the property could not be described in §1221(1) (stock in trade, inventory, and so forth) or §1221(4) (accounts receivable acquired in the ordinary course of business for services rendered or from the sale of stock in trade, inventory, and so forth). Thus, distributions of investment property did not qualify.

(c) Stock or obligations of operating subsidiary. Under old §311(d)(2)(B), a distribution of appreciated stock or obligations of a controlled corporation (as defined) qualified for nonrecognition of gain if the following requirements were satisfied:

(1) The distribution was made with respect to "qualified stock," as previously defined;

(2) Substantially all of the assets of the controlled corporation consisted of the assets of one or more "qualified businesses," as defined by old §311(e)(2)(B)(i);

(3) No substantial part of the controlled corporation's nonbusiness assets was acquired from the distributing corporation in specified transactions within the five-year period ending on the date of the distribution;[183] and

(4) More than 50 percent by value of the controlled corporation's outstanding stock was distributed with respect to qualified stock.

6. Recapture and similar provisions. In 1962 and 1964, Congress cut back on the nonrecognition principle of old §311(a) by treating most corporate distributions of property as dispositions in applying the recapture rules of §§1245 and 1250 (involving depreciable personal and real property respectively) and §47 (relating to premature dispositions of investment tax credit property). This stream of exceptions quickly became a tidal wave, as

---

[182] See infra ¶¶ 9.08–9.10.

[183] For an analogous requirement applicable to tax-free spin-offs and similar transactions, see infra ¶ 13.06.

Congress added the following more specialized recapture provisions (listed here in order by Code numbers rather than chronologically):

(1) §341(f) (certain inventory-type property held by collapsible corporations); [184]

(2) §386 (corporate distributions of certain partnership and trust interests); [185]

(3) §617(d) (mining properties benefitting from deduction of certain mining exploration expenditures);

(4) §§897(d) and 897(f) (certain distributions involving foreign investments in U.S. real property);

(5) §1248 (dispositions of stock of certain foreign corporations); [186]

(6) §1252 (farmland held for less than 10 years if deductions were allowed under §175 or 182, relating to soil and water conservation expenditures and expenditures for clearing land, respectively); and

(7) §1254 (oil, gas, and geothermal property that gave rise to deductions for intangible drilling and development costs).

In applying these limitations (which did not appear in old §311 itself but were and continue to be scattered throughout the Code) on the nonrecognition principle of old §311(a), attention must always be given to the statutory language of the specific recapture provision, since they do not treat all distributions alike. Section 1245, for example, exempts certain distributions if the distributees carry over the distributing corporation's basis for the depreciable property; §341(f)(3) contains an exemption that is similar but conditioned on a consent by distributees; §47(b) exempts certain transfers involving a mere change in the form of conducting the trade or business; and there are other variations among the provisions. Moreover, some of these provisions apply only if the distributing corporation realizes gain on the transfer, in which event it is sometimes converted from capital gain to ordinary income, and some provisions compute gain in a special way for this purpose, while others (e.g., §47) apply even if no gain is realized.

---

[184] See infra ¶ 12.07.

[185] For a decision applying a similar approach under prior law, see Holiday Village Shopping Center v. US, 773 F2d 276 (Fed. Cir. 1985). See generally Eustice, The Tax Reform Act of 1984, ¶ 3.02[1][c] (Warren, Gorham & Lamont, Inc., 1984); Jones & Limberg, Corporate Transfers of Partnership Interests: An Analysis of New Section 386, 1 J. Partnership Tax'n 291 (1985). See also proposed §311(b)(3) (by the Technical Corrections Act of 1987).

[186] See infra ¶ 17.34.

7. Distributions by S corporations. Except for complete liquidations and certain tax-free reorganizations, S corporations were required under old §311 to recognize their gain on the distribution of appreciated property.[187]

8. Reallocations of income under §482. Finally, the Service's broad authority to reallocate income and other tax allowances under §482 among two or more organizations, trades, or businesses "in order to prevent evasion of taxes or clearly to reflect the income [of the parties]" allowed it, under a 1977 ruling and several judicial opinions, to sidestep the nonrecognition principle of old §311 in circumstances that remain to be clarified.[188] When the distribution involved affiliated corporations, §482's prerequisite of two or more organizations, trades, or businesses was usually satisfied easily; even in the case of distributions to individual shareholders, shareholder activities could be characterized as a trade or business if they disposed of the property over a period of time, as in *U.S. v. Lynch* and *CIR v. First Bank of Stratford.*[189] In this situation, however, §482 added little if anything to the case law, and if the distribution involved only a single asset and no continuing association among the shareholders as in *General Utilities* itself, §482's prerequisite of a separate organization, trade, or business was not likely to be satisfied.

¶ 7.23 TAXABILITY OF DISTRIBUTIONS TO INDIVIDUAL AND CORPORATE DISTRIBUTEES

The tax treatment of shareholders receiving a corporate distribution of property is prescribed by §301(b)(1)(A) for noncorporate distributees (i.e., individuals, estates, and trusts) and by §301(b)(1)(B) for corporate distributees. Although the results are virtually always the same under current law, this was not always true; and the discussion below accordingly distinguishes between corporate and noncorporate distributees in order to track the divergent statutory language.

1. Noncorporate distributees. If the fair market value of property distributed to noncorporate shareholders is fully covered by the corporation's current or post-1913 earnings and profits, the distribution is a taxable "dividend"

---

[187] See §§1363(d) and 1363(e); supra ¶ 6.08.

[188] Rev. Rul. 77-83, 1977-1 CB 139; see also Southern Bancorp., 67 TC 1022 (1977); Note, Section 482 and the Nonrecognition Provisions: Resolving the Conflict, 77 Nw. U.L. Rev. 670 (1982). For a more detailed analysis of §482, see infra ¶ 15.03.

[189] See supra note 144.

to the extent of its fair market value under §§301(b)(1)(A), 301(c), and 316.[190]
If, however, the value of the distributed property exceeds the corporation's
current and post-1913 earnings and profits, the regulations provide that the
distribution is a "dividend" only to the extent of the earnings and profits.[191]

> *To illustrate:* If *A* Corporation, with earnings and profits of $10,000,
> distributes property having a fair market value of $16,000 to its sole
> shareholder, *B*, the distribution is a taxable dividend to *B* in the amount
> of $10,000. The remaining $6,000 is applied against the basis of *B*'s
> stock under §301(c)(2), and the excess over basis (if any) generates capi-
> tal gain under §301(c)(3).[192] This calculation takes no account of *A*'s
> basis for the distributed property, which by itself is irrelevant to the
> outcome. If, however, the basis is less than $16,000, and if the gain is
> taxed to *A* under §311(b)—as will ordinarily be the case[193]—*A*'s earnings
> and profits will be increased by the gain recognized and reduced by the
> resulting corporate tax. This adjustment to the earnings and profits will,
> of course, alter the calculation set out above.[194] For example, if *A*'s
> earnings and profits are increased by $4,000 to $14,000, the distribution
> will be a dividend to *B* in that amount, and the remaining $2,000 will be
> subject to §§301(c)(2) and 301(c)(3).
>
> *B*'s basis for the distributed property is its fair market value, deter-

---

[190] Section 301(b)(1)(A) provides that in the case of a noncorporate distributee,
the amount of a distribution in kind is its fair market value, adjusted under
§301(b)(2) for liabilities (if any) assumed by the shareholder or to which the distributed property is subject. By virtue of §301(b)(3), fair market value is to be determined "as of the date of the distribution." This date may differ from the date when
the distribution is includable in gross income, according to Regs. §1.301-1(b). But if
the date of inclusion in gross income precedes the date of distribution, and the property increases in value between the two dates, query whether the higher value can
properly be included in computing income on the earlier date.

For valuation problems, see Baumer v. US, supra note 90 (open transaction
doctrine applied to option of unascertainable value when distributed); Louis A.
Weigl, supra note 90 (judgment reserved on whether §421 principles, relating to compensatory stock options, apply in valuing stock warrants distributed to shareholders); Cordner v. US, 671 F2d 367 (9th Cir. 1982) (dividend in kind of rare U.S. coins
taxable at market value, not face value); Rev. Rul. 80-213, 1980-2 CB 101 (dividends
on stapled stock); see also Corry, Stapled Stock—Time For a New Look, 36 Tax L.
Rev. 167 (1981).

[191] Regs. §1.316-1(a)(2).

[192] See Regs. §1.316-1(a)(3), Example. For an almost forgotten debate about the
validity of this regulation, see Harry H. Cloutier, 24 TC 1006, 1009–1015 (1955)
(acq.); and the Fourth Edition of this treatise, ¶ 7.22.

[193] See supra ¶ 7.21.

[194] See §316(a)(2) (earnings and profits computed as of end of year in which
distribution occurs); see also supra text following note 17.

mined as of the date of the distribution.[195] If *B* assumes (or takes the distributed property subject to) a liability of the distributing corporation, the amount of the distribution is reduced pro tanto (but not below zero) by §301(b)(2). This will affect the amount to be taken into income by *B*, but it will not affect *B*'s basis for the property, which remains its full fair market value under §301(d)(1).

2. Corporate distributees. In contrast to §301(b)(1)(A), which provides that a distribution of property to a noncorporate distributee is to be valued at its fair market value, §301(b)(1)(B) values a distribution to a *corporate* distributee at the lesser of (1) the property's fair market value or (2) its adjusted basis in the hands of the distributing corporation plus any gain recognized on the distribution. Under current law, however, these two amounts are the same, since the distributing corporation is required by §311, as amended in 1984, to recognize gain on all distributions of appreciated property to corporate shareholders.[196] Having determined the amount of the distribution under §301(b)(1)(B) (i.e., the property's fair market value, which becomes its basis under §301(d)(2)[197]), the distributee corporation must report the part that is covered by earnings and profits as a dividend and the balance, if any, as a distribution of capital subject to the rules of §§301(c)(2) and 301(c)(3). The distributee's holding period for the property, determined under §301(e)(1), begins with the date of the distribution.

This roundabout method of valuing distributions of property to corporate shareholders is a vestige of an earlier day, when the gain on a distribution of appreciated property ordinarily qualified for nonrecognition under the statutory predecessor of §311(a)(2).

To illustrate: Assume that *X* (the distributing corporation) was wholly owned by *C*, another corporation, and that *X*, having earnings and profits of $100,000, distributed property to *C* with a value of $100,000 and an adjusted basis in its hands of $10,000. Had it not been for §301(b)(1)(B), *C* would have had $100,000 of dividend income on receipt of the property, but by virtue of the 85 (or 100) percent deduc-

---

[195] Section 301(d)(1). But see §897(f) (distributions by domestic corporations of U.S. real property to foreign shareholders take carryover basis increased by gain recognized to distributing corporation and taxes paid by distributees).

[196] See supra text at notes 164–168. The Technical Corrections Act of 1987, H.R. 2636, §106(e), recognizes the new realities of property distributions by combining §§301(b)(1)(A), 301(b)(1)(B), and 301(d)(1)-(4) into a single rule for corporate and individual distributees (fair market value) and also repeals §301(e).

[197] For an adjustment to basis if the distribution is an extraordinary dividend, see §1059, discussed supra at ¶ 5.05, para. 9.

tion for intercorporate dividends provided by pre-1987 §243, only $15,000 (or zero) would have been subject to tax.

Thus, at little or no tax cost, C could have obtained a $100,000 stepped-up basis for computing depreciation and gain or loss on the distributed property, even though the gain qualified for nonrecognition (under prior law) as far as X was concerned. The "lower of value or basis" rule of §301(b)(1)(B) was enacted to prevent this result, with its attendant possibilities for manipulation, by providing that the amount of the distribution to C in the preceding example was only $10,000, the property's adjusted basis to X. Similarly, §301(d)(2) provides that C's basis for the property in the preceding example was $10,000, its basis in the hands of X. However, this protective mechanism is obsolete under current law because X in such situations is now required to recognize its gain in full on the distribution itself.[198]

3. Earnings and profits. The effect of a distribution of property on the distributing corporation's earnings and profits was clouded in obscurity for many years, but the subject was clarified and simplified by the enactment in 1986 of current §312(b). On a distribution of property whose fair market value exceeds its adjusted basis (basis for this purpose is the earnings and profits basis of the property), earnings and profits are first increased by the amount of the excess, and then decreased by the property's fair market value (but not below zero). Thus, if the earnings and profits amount is zero at the beginning of the taxable year and the corporation's only transaction is a distribution of property with an adjusted basis of $100 and a fair market value of $1,000, the earnings and profits account is increased by $900 (so that the distribution is a "dividend" to the extent of the appreciation), and is then reduced to zero (distributions do not create a deficit) at the end of the year.

Section 312(b) has no application to distributions of depreciated property. By virtue of §311(a)(2), (1) the loss on such a distribution is not recognized and does not reduce earnings and profits; (2) the distribution is a dividend to the extent of the property's fair market value up to the amount of any earnings and profits the corporation may have from other transactions; and (3) earnings and profits are decreased under §312(a)(3) by the adjusted basis of the property. Thus, if property with an adjusted basis of $15,000 and a fair market value of $10,000 is distributed by a corporation

---

[198] For §243, see supra ¶ 5.05. For years after 1986, the §243 deduction is generally 80 percent. For special rules applicable to foreign corporations whose distributions do not qualify for the deduction by virtue of §245, see §§301(b)(1)(C) (fair market value) and 301(d)(4); for distributions to foreign corporations, see §301(b)(1)(D) (property valued at fair market value if not effectively connected with U.S. trade or business) (both of these are slated for repeal by the Technical Corrections Act of 1987, supra note 196).

with $15,000 of earnings and profits, the distribution is a dividend of only $10,000, but it wipes out the corporation's earnings and profits account.

If the basis for earnings and profits purposes differs from regular adjusted basis (e.g., because of lower §312(k) depreciation), the former figure is to be used for purposes of §§312(a)(3) and 312(b) as well. Thus, if the §312 basis in the two preceding situations was $600 and $16,000, respectively, the amount of the dividend in the first example would be $400 ($1,000 fair market value minus $600 basis), and the earnings charge in the second would be $16,000 (§312 basis) or earnings and profits, if lower.[199]

PART C.   DISTRIBUTIONS OF CORPORATION'S OWN OBLIGATIONS, STOCK, AND STOCK RIGHTS

¶ 7.40   DISTRIBUTIONS OF CORPORATION'S OWN OBLIGATIONS

In lieu of distributing cash or property, a corporation may make a distribution to its shareholders of its own obligations, ordinarily (but not necessarily) evidenced by notes, bonds, debentures, or other securities. The Code seems to assume that such a distribution will have the same tax consequence as a distribution of other types of property, but the regulations depart from this assumption at certain points in the interest of simplicity.

In the case of a noncorporate distributee, it is reasonably clear that the distribution of a corporation's own obligations is a distribution of property under §301(b)(1)(A), even though the Code is not explicit on this point,[200] so that the amount of the distribution is the fair market value of the obliga-

---

[199] For prior law, see the fourth edition of this treatise at ¶ 7.24; Edelstein, Tax Mgmt. Portfolio (BNA) No. 189-3d (1982); see also §312(n)(4), added by the Tax Reform Act of 1984 but repealed in 1986 and superseded by §312(b). In computing the charge to earnings and profits for distributed property, current §312(b) also provides that the basis for earnings and profits purposes is to be used. For these basis rules, see supra note 45.

[200] Both §301(b), relating to the amount of a distribution, and §301(d), prescribing the basis of distributed property, speak of property without explicitly mentioning the distributing corporation's own obligations. Section 317(a), defining "property," is equally laconic; the regulations under §317(a) state that the term "property" includes "indebtedness to the corporation," but they say nothing about indebtedness *of* the corporation. Despite these unsatisfactory gaps, a distribution of the corporation's own obligations almost certainly is to be treated as a distribution of property, and the regulations under §301 so assume. See also §312(a)(2), which explicitly includes the corporation's own obligations within the term "property."

tions.[201] It follows from this and from §§301(c)(1) and 316 that the distribution is a "dividend" to the extent of current and post-1913 earnings and profits, and that any excess is to be treated as a return of capital under §§301(c)(2) and 301(c)(3). Furthermore, under §301(d)(1), the basis of the distributed obligations in the hands of the distributee is their fair market value. In these respects, there is no difference between a distribution of the corporation's own obligations and a distribution of other types of property.[202]

Recall, however, that if the distributee is another corporation, the "amount" of a distribution of property is either the property's fair market value or its adjusted basis in the hands of the distributing corporation (plus any gain recognized on the distribution), whichever is the less.[203] Although the Code itself does not state that a distribution of the corporation's own obligations is to be treated differently, the regulations provide that the fair market value of the obligations is controlling, thus confining the operation of §301(b)(1)(B) to distributions of property other than the corporation's own obligations or stock.[204] Similarly, §301(d)(2) provides that the basis to a corporate distributee of property is its fair market value or its adjusted basis in the hands of the distributing corporation, whichever is less, but the regulations confine this provision to distributions of property other than the cor-

---

[201] For the valuation of debt obligations, see Allan S. Vinnell, 52 TC 934 (1969); Wiseman v. US, 371 F2d 816 (1st Cir. 1967); Rose A. Coates Trust, 55 TC 501 (1970), aff'd, 480 F2d 468 (9th Cir.), cert. denied, 414 US 1045 (1973); Maher v. CIR, supra note 104; Rev. Rul. 77-360, 1977-2 CB 86; Thomas C. Stephens, 60 TC 1004 (1973), aff'd mem., 506 F2d 1400 (6th Cir. 1974) (installment payment agreement held to be mere open-account debt, not distribution of a corporate obligation). But see Rufus K. Cox, 78 TC 1021 (1982) (no installment-sale reporting for §301(c)(3) gain; notes taxable currently at fair market value).

For open transaction treatment, see Fehrs Fin. Co. v. CIR, 487 F2d 184 (8th Cir. 1973), cert. denied, 416 US 938 (1974) (dividend-equivalent redemption for an annuity payment obligation taxable only when received under open transaction theory).

[202] See supra ¶ 7.20.

[203] See supra text at note 196; see also old §311(d)(1) (corporation's own obligations excluded from rule requiring gain to be recognized on distribution of appreciated property), and new §311(b)(1)(A) (same). House Con. Res. 395, 99th Cong., 2d Sess., Item 223, proposed to insert the same provision in new §312(b) in order to correct a technical oversight in the Tax Reform Act of 1986, but the 99th Congress adjourned without passing this proposal. See supra note 171. But see §118(d)(3) of the Technical Corrections Act of 1987, which does do so.

[204] Regs. §1.301-1(d). In most instances, of course, the letter of §301(b)(1)(B) could not be applied to the corporation's own obligations, which have no adjusted basis. But it is possible for a corporation to issue securities and reacquire them, and, in this event, the obligations might possibly be regarded as having an adjusted basis that could be controlling under §301(b)(1)(B) if they were later distributed to shareholders.

poration's own obligations and provide that the basis of such obligations is their fair market value. [205]

Although the *fair market value* of the corporation's obligations controls both the amount of the distribution and the basis of the obligations, as just indicated, §312(a)(2) provides that the distributing corporation's earnings and profits are to be reduced by the *principal amount* of the obligations. In many cases, these amounts will be identical. If there is a difference because the obligation entails OID, §312(a)(2) substitutes the aggregate issue price for the principal amount. [206] If the difference is attributable to some other feature of transaction (e.g., bond premium), however, the principal amount is controlling.

¶ 7.41 STOCK AND STOCK RIGHTS: INTRODUCTORY AND CHRONOLOGY

The provisions relating to stock dividends in the 1954 Code, as amended by the Tax Reform Act of 1969, are the outgrowth of a long history of confusion and conflict that cannot be ignored in the interpretation of current law. [207] The Revenue Act of 1913 said nothing about stock dividends, and an attempt by the Treasury to tax such dividends under the catchall language of what is now §61(a) was rejected by the Supreme Court in *Towne v. Eisner* [208] on the ground that a stock dividend did not constitute "income" as that term was used in the statute. The Revenue Act of 1916, however, explicitly provided that a "stock dividend shall be considered income, to the amount of its cash value." But in *Eisner v. Macomber*, one of the most celebrated cases in the annals of federal income taxation, the Supreme Court held that the distribution of common stock by a corporation having only common stock outstanding could not be taxed constitutionally as income to the shareholders:

> We are clear that not only does a stock dividend really take nothing from the property of the corporation and add nothing to that of the shareholder, but that the antecedent accumulation of profits evidenced

---

[205] See Regs. §1.301-1(h)(2)(i); see also Denver & R.G.W.R.R. v. US, 318 F2d 922 (Ct. Cl. 1963), involving a distribution of obligations of an unusual type to a corporate shareholder.

[206] For OID, see §1275(a)(5); supra ¶ 4.40; see also Prop. Regs. §1.1275-2(c).

[207] This discussion is concerned with distributions by a corporation of its own shares, or of rights to acquire its own shares. Distribution of shares of another corporation is treated as a distribution in kind and is governed by the principles discussed supra at Part B; see Rev. Rul. 70-521, 1970-2 CB 72.

[208] 245 US 418 (1918).

thereby, while indicating that the shareholder is the richer because of an increase of his capital, at the same time shows he has not realized or received any income in the transaction.[209]

Although the constitutional theory of *Eisner* has few defenders today, its practical importance to corporate practice and to the collection of revenue may well have been exaggerated. Had the case gone the other way, stock splits would probably have been used as a substitute for stock dividends, coupled if necessary with periodic increases in par value or in stated capital. If a method of taxing stock splits had been developed, fractional shares might have been used to serve the principal functions of stock dividends without adverse tax consequences.

In later years, the Court qualified *Eisner* by ruling that it protected a distribution of stock only if the distribution did not alter the proportionate interests of the shareholders, so that Congress was free to tax disproportionate distributions. Thus, in *Koshland v. Helvering*,[210] involving a corporation with both common and nonvoting preferred stock outstanding, the Court held that a distribution of common stock as a dividend on the preferred stock (but not on the common stock) could be taxed. Subsequently, the Court held in *Strassburger v. CIR*[211] that a distribution of nonvoting preferred stock by a corporation having only common stock outstanding was not taxable because "the distribution brought about no change whatever in [the shareholder's] interest in the corporation [because] both before and after the event he owned exactly the same interest in the net value of the corporation as before." Similarly, in *Helvering v. Sprouse*,[212] involving a corporation with both voting and nonvoting common stock outstanding, the Court held that a distribution of nonvoting common stock pro rata to the holders of the voting and the nonvoting common stock was not taxable: "[T]o render the dividend taxable as income, there must be a change brought about by the issue of shares as a dividend whereby the proportional interest of the stock-

---

[209] 252 US 189, 212 (1920). See generally Powell, Stock Dividends, Direct Taxes, and the Sixteenth Amendment, 20 Colum. L. Rev. 536 (1920); Seligman, Implications and Effects of the Stock Dividend Decision, 21 Colum. L. Rev. 313 (1921); E.R.A. Seligman, Studies in Public Finance 99–123 (1925); Magill, Taxable Income 31 (rev. ed. 1945); Lowndes, The Taxation of Stock Dividends and Stock Rights, 96 U. Pa. L. Rev. 147 (1947); Rottschaefer, Present Taxable Status of Stock Dividends in Federal Law, 28 Minn. L. Rev. 106, 163 (1943).

[210] 298 US 441 (1936), reh'g denied, 302 US 781 (1938). For basis problems under *Koshland*, see Helvering v. Gowran, 302 US 238 (1937); Alvord & Biegel, Basis Provisions for Stock Dividends Under the 1939 Revenue Act, 49 Yale L.J. 841 (1940).

[211] Strassburger v. CIR, aff'd sub nom. Helvering v. Sprouse, 318 US 604, 607 (1943).

[212] 318 US 604, 608 (1943).

holder after the distribution was essentially different from his former interest."

With the proportionate interest test of these cases as their guide, the lower courts struggled with but did not solve the problem of separating taxable stock dividends from nontaxable ones.[213] These decisions left so much uncertainty in the taxation of stock dividends under the 1939 Code that the draftsmen of the 1954 Code essayed a new approach to the problem. As will be seen, however, the relatively simple statutory approach adopted in 1954[214] was superseded in 1969 by a far more complex network of rules.[215] Despite this substitution by Congress of statutory solutions in 1954 and again in 1969, the pre-1954 case law remains of continuing importance because it governs the basis of the original and dividend shares and the earnings and profits of the distributing corporation if the stock dividend was distributed before June 22, 1954.[216] For the same reasons, the 1954–1969 statutory rules remain significant as to stock dividends distributed during the 1954–1969 period, as well as some subsequent distributions subject to delayed effective dates for the 1969 legislation. Moreover, the 1969 legislative rules place great emphasis on whether stock distributions are proportionate or not, thus reviving to some extent the "disproportionate interest" concept of the pre-1954 case law.

¶ 7.42 STOCK DISTRIBUTION RULES, 1954–1969

The stock distribution rules laid down by §305 of the 1954 Code, which remained in force until superseded in 1969 by §305 of current law and whose continuing importance has already been mentioned, consisted of a broad general rule and two comparatively narrow exceptions. The general rule provided that distributions of stock or stock rights that were made by a corporation with respect to its stock were not includable in gross income. The first exception was for distributions discharging preference dividends for the corporation's current or preceding taxable year. The second exception provided that a distribution was taxable if it was payable either in stock or in property

---

[213] See, e.g., Tourtelot v. CIR, 189 F2d 167 (7th Cir. 1951), cert. dismissed, 343 US 901 (1952); Wiegand v. CIR, 194 F2d 479 (3d Cir. 1952); Schmitt v. CIR, 208 F2d 819 (3d Cir. 1954); John A. Messer, 20 TC 264 (1953); Pizitz v. Patterson, 183 F. Supp. 901 (N.D. Ala. 1960); see also Union Pac. R.R. v. US, 524 F2d 1343 (Ct. Cl. 1975), cert. denied, 429 US 827 (1976) (historical discussion of pre-1954 Code law). See generally Lyon, Old Statutes and New Constitution, 44 Colum. L. Rev. 599 (1944).

[214] See infra ¶ 7.42.

[215] See infra ¶ 7.43.

[216] See §§307(c), 312(d)(2), 391, and 1052(c).

at the election of any of the shareholders, whether the election was exercisable before or after the distribution was declared.[217]

This optional distribution rule obviously would have been ineffective if it did not embrace options granted to the shareholder and exercised before the declaration, as well as those that arise and are exercised after the declaration. But how far back before the declaration was the rule intended to reach? This question was posed in acute form by the so-called Citizens Utilities Plan, under which corporations issued two classes of stock, one paying cash dividends, and the other paying stock dividends. If a shareholder could freely exchange shares of one class for an equivalent number of shares of the other class, he would enjoy the financial advantages of an election to receive distributions either in cash or in stock, even though when the distribution was declared and made he had to accept whatever type of distribution was required by the class of stock he then owned.

In 1956, the Treasury promulgated proposed regulations announcing that a taxable optional distribution occurred if (1) there were two classes of stock outstanding; (2) some shareholders received cash dividends while others received stock dividends; and (3) at some point in time, a shareholder exercised the choice that created the severance of cash and stock dividend effects.[218] If the shareholder could freely convert one class into the other, much could be said for the theory of the proposed regulation. As applied to nonconvertible shares, it was rather drastic. Even if the two classes of stock were identical except for their dividend rights and were equal in value, the shareholder owning shares that were entitled only to stock dividends did not have an option to take cash currently, except by selling his stock (at the cost of taxes and brokerage commissions) and buying shares of the other class.

---

[217] See Regs. §1.305-2(a) (option in one shareholder is fatal to all); Lester Lumber Co., 14 TC 255, 261 (1950) (corporate law requires all stockholders to be treated alike; hence, corporation may not offer cash to some stockholders and require others to accept stock dividends). But see Rinker v. US, 297 F. Supp. 370 (S.D. Fla. 1968) (stock dividend that could be "cashed at the request of stockholders" held to be tax-free under §305(a); on facts, no election to take cash in lieu of stock); Frontier Sav. Ass'n, 87 TC 665 (1986) (no cash election where corporation had discretion not to redeem, even though its general policy was to redeem). Compare J. Robert Fisher, 62 TC 73 (1974) (stock received in lieu of cash dividend on shares acquired in exchange for taxpayer's stock in Type B reorganization held to be taxable stock dividend under optional distribution rule).

[218] See 21 Fed. Reg. 5104; see also TD 6476, 1960-2 CB 111, stating that the proposal "will be given further consideration before final action is taken thereon." The long delay in acting on the proposal suggested a lack of confidence in its theory. See IRS Attempts to Stop 2-Classes-of-Common Tax-Saving Plan; Legality Questioned, 5 J. Tax'n 178 (1956); Rev. Rul. 65-256, 1965-2 CB 85 (receipt of nondividend stock in statutory merger will not cause dividend income to the holder when distributions are made on other stock).

The 1956 proposal remained in limbo until 1969, when it was withdrawn and a much more elaborate set of regulations were issued, which contained the same rules for the Citizens Utilities Plan of two classes of stock but which also reached many more complex arrangements under which some shareholders receive distributions of stock and others get cash or other property. Briefly summarized, the 1969 regulations taxed escalating conversion ratio common stock issued as consideration in a tax-free reorganization on the ground that the periodic increase in the conversion ratio constituted a taxable distribution of stock rights on a second class of stock (but presumably only if the increase was related to or tied to cash dividends on other stock in some manner). In addition, decreasing conversion ratio stock issued in a reorganization resulted in taxable stock dividend income to the *other* shareholders of the acquiring corporation to the extent that their relative equity interests were increased thereby.[219]

By the time the 1969 regulations were issued in final form,[220] and before their validity under the 1954–1969 statute was tested, Congress was poised for action on the Tax Reform Act of 1969, which gave §305 its present form. This legislative action accepted the main features of the 1969 regulations and provided the Treasury with a firm statutory foundation for action thereafter against the diverse devices encompassed by the 1969 regulations.

¶ 7.43   STOCK DISTRIBUTION RULES, 1969 AND LATER YEARS

Against this background, Congress amended §305 in 1969. Straightforward pro rata distributions of stock or rights to acquire stock to a corporation's common shareholders are ordinarily tax-free, especially if no other classes of stock are outstanding, but the 1969 rules are a threat to many distributions of a more complex nature. Especially suspect are stock distributions or other devices used to preserve (or increase) the equity interests of one class of shareholders when cash or property is distributed to holders of another class of stock.

To forestall evasion of the 1969 rules, §305(c) authorizes the Treasury to issue regulations determining when changes in conversion ratios, changes

---

[219] See TD 6990, 1969-1 CB 95; TD 7004, 1969-1 CB 97. See generally Levin, New 305 Regs. Limit Tax Advantages of 2-Class Common Stock, But Alternatives Exist, 30 J. Tax'n 2 (1969); Ray, Stock Dividends; Section 305(b) and the Conglomerates, 21 S. Cal. Tax Inst. 341 (1969).

[220] It is worth noting that the regulations under the 1969 legislation treat the Citizens Utilities Plan, involving two classes of stock, as taxable under §305(b)(2) as enacted in 1969, rather than under §305(b)(1), the 1969 counterpart of the optional distribution provision of the 1954–1969 statute. See Regs. §1.305-3(e), Example (1).

in redemption prices, differences between redemption prices and issue prices, recapitalizations, and other transactions with similar effects are treated as distributions to shareholders whose proportionate interest in the corporation's earnings and profits or assets is increased by these events. Thus, transactions that are not normally viewed as distributions can trigger application of §305. If Eisner and Macomber[221] were dealing with today's Code, they might well ask, "What hath the Treasury wrought?" Despite its complexity, however, the 1969 legislation has evoked virtually no litigation in the nearly 20 years of its existence. It is not clear whether this is because taxpayers have been too overawed to move aggressively into uncharted waters or because the Service has been unable, for want of expertise or time, to enforce the intricate statutory provisions and accompanying regulations.

As amended in 1969, §305 consists of a general rule, five statutory exceptions, the previously mentioned grant of regulatory authority to the Treasury, and a definition stating that "stock" includes rights to acquire stock and that "shareholder" includes holders of rights to acquire stock and holders of convertible securities.[222]

1. General rule. Section 305(a) carries forward the 1954–1969 general rule that gross income does not include distributions of stock (or rights) of the distributing corporation with respect to its stock,[223] unless otherwise pro-

---

[221] See supra note 209.

[222] For analysis of the 1969 legislation, see Stone, Back to Fundamentals: Another Version of the Stock Dividend Saga, 79 Colum. L. Rev. 898 (1979) (stressing policy issues); Eustice, Corporations and Corporate Investors, 25 Tax L. Rev. 509 (1970); Bacon, Share Redemptions by Publicly Held Companies: A New Look at Dividend Equivalence, 26 Tax L. Rev. 283 (1971); Del Cotto & Wolf, The Proportionate Interest Test of Section 305 and the Supreme Court, 27 Tax L. Rev. 49 (1971); Metzer, The "New" Section 305, 27 Tax L. Rev. 93 (1971); Andrews & Wilson, Stock Dividend Taxation Under the Tax Reform Act of 1969: Expansion of an Ominous Past, 13 Ariz. L. Rev. 751 (1971); Bashian, Stock Dividends and Section 305: Realization and the Constitution, 1971 Duke L.J. 1105; Rustigan, Stock Distributions—Section 305, 49 Taxes 787 (1971); Stanger, The Interplay of Section 83 and Section 305, 54 Taxes 235 (1976).

For analysis of the regulations, see deKosmian, Taxable Stock Dividends Under New Section 305, 28 Tax Lawyer 57 (1974); Note, Discounted Preferred Stock Under the New Section 305 Treasury Regulations: On Confusing Debt and Equity, 84 Yale L.J. 324 (1974); Saltzman, The New Section 305 Regulations: Planning, Problems and Pitfalls, 27 S. Cal. Tax Inst. 41 (1975); Walter, Section 305, Its Implications in Reorganizations and Corporate Capital Structures, 54 Taxes 888 (1976); see also Committee on Corporate Taxation, Internal Revenue Code of 1954, Comments on Proposed Regulations Under Section 305 of the N.Y. State Bar Association, Tax Section, 49 Taxes 460 (1971).

[223] Concerned as it is with distributions by a corporation "with respect to its stock," §305 does not apply to transfers of stock to creditors, vendors, employees,

vided in §305(b). The heart of the 1969 legislation, however, lies in its exceptions rather than in the basic rule.

2. Optional distributions. The first exception, §305(b)(1), continues the rule of 1954–1969 law that a stock dividend is taxable if it is payable in lieu of money or other property at the election of any shareholder. If any shareholder has such an election, *all* shareholders are tainted thereby. This reenactment of prior law endorses the broad approach of the 1969 regulations, which, generally speaking, found a tainted taxable election in every case where a corporation had two classes of common stock outstanding, one receiving cash dividends and the other receiving stock dividends.[224]

---

and so forth who happen to be shareholders as well. For analogous interpretations of identical statutory language, see Regs. §§1.301-1(c) and 1.311-1(e).

For decisions taxing shareholders on the receipt of stock in a nonshareholder capacity, see CIR v. Fender Sales, Inc., supra note 73 (stock received in cancellation of claims for salary by two 50 percent shareholders); Rev. Rul. 67-402, 1967-2 CB 135 (accord); James C. Hamrick, 43 TC 21 (1964) (acq.) (settlement of dispute with other shareholders and the corporation). But see Deloss E. Daggitt, 23 TC 31 (1954) (acq.) (contra for pre-1954 taxable years); Joy Mfg. Co. v. CIR, 230 F2d 740 (3d Cir. 1956) (same). See Note, Application of Eisner v. Macomber to Pro Rata Stock Distributions in Payment of Salaries: An Opportunity for Tax Manipulation, 64 Yale L.J. 929 (1955).

Distributions of treasury stock and of rights to acquire treasury stock are covered by §305. See Regs. §1.305-1(a). For the rules governing distributions of debt instruments, including purported stock that is reclassified as debt, see supra ¶ 7.40. For distributions of stock of corporations other than the distributing corporation, see supra Part B.

[224] See Rev. Rul. 76-53, 1976-1 CB 87 (dividend reinvestment plan whereby cash dividends, at election of shareholders, could be used to buy corporation's stock at 5 percent discount below market was held to be taxable); Rev. Rul. 78-375, 1978-2 CB 130 (same). Compare Rev. Rul. 77-149, 1977-1 CB 82 (dividend reinvestment plan where cash dividends used to purchase stock on market at full value were taxed as §301 dividends; §305 held not to be applicable because election is to take cash or to use cash to buy stock); Rev. Rul. 76-258, 1976-2 CB 95 (distribution of preferred stock that is immediately redeemable at option of shareholder is taxable under §305(b)(1) as elective cash or stock transaction); Rev. Rul. 79-42, 1979-1 CB 130 (similar plan to Rev. Rul. 76-53; Rev. Rul. 77-149 distinguished); Rev. Rul. 83-68, 1983-1 CB 75 (principle of Rev. Rul. 76-258 followed, even though not all shareholders had right to redeem distributed stock); but contra to Rev. Rul. 83-68 is Frontier Sav. Ass'n, 87 TC 665 (1986) (first decision under 1969 law; taxpayer won because corporation had discretion to redeem, although it never exercised such discretion); Rev. Rul. 80-154, 1980-1 CB 68 (purported cash dividend in which shareholders had no choice but to use cash to pay for additional stock was held to be tax-free §305(a) stock dividend); Rev. Rul. 82-158, 1982-2 CB 77 (stock issued in an acquisitive reorganization not a §305(b) or 305(c) distribution).

3. Distributions of common and preferred. Section 305(b)(3) provides that if the distribution results in the receipt of preferred stock by some common shareholders and the receipt of common stock by other common shareholders, *all* the shareholders will be taxable on the receipt of their stock. The purpose of this rule is not immediately apparent, but presumably it was based on a fear that §306 bailout stock could be used as a substitute for regular cash dividends in order to avoid the disproportionate distribution rules of §305(b)(2).[225]

4. Distributions on preferred. Section 305(b)(4) provides generally that all stock dividends on preferred stock—whether they are actual or constructive stock dividends under §305(c) and regardless of whether the distribution has a disproportionate effect—are taxable.[226]

This general rule is subject to two limited exceptions: (1) certain conversion ratio adjustments applicable to convertible preferred,[227] and (2) reasonable call premiums (that is, the excess of the redemption price over the issue price of preferred stock does not constitute a constructive taxable stock dividend if reasonable).[228]

---

[225] See Rev. Rul. 86-25, 1986-1 CB 202 (recapitalization exchange, on facts, did not trigger application of §305(b)(3), even though direct stock distribution would have).

[226] See Rev. Rul. 84-141, 1984-2 CB 80 (constructive receipt of taxable §305(b)(4) stock dividend on preferred stock where holder of preferred stock had right to elect to receive common stock equal to cash dividends that had been passed for two consecutive quarters). For the meaning of "preferred stock," see Regs. §§1.305-5(a) and 1.305-5(d); Walter, "Preferred Stock" and "Common Stock": The Meaning of the Terms and the Importance of the Distinction for Tax Purposes, 5 J. Corp. Tax'n 211 (1978). See generally Rev. Rul. 83-119, 1983-2 CB 57.

[227] See Regs. §§1.305-5(a), 1.305-3(d), and 1.305-7(b); Rev. Rul. 77-37, 1977-1 CB 85 (adjustment of conversion ratio of convertible preferred stock to prevent dilution because of §355 spin-off distribution to common stock shareholders was held not to trigger taxable stock dividend); Rev. Rul. 83-42, 1983-1 CB 76 (actual distribution on convertible preferred stock to compensate for dilution caused by stock dividend on common stock taxable under §305(b)(4); antidilution exception limited to deemed distributions resulting from conversion ratio adjustments).

[228] Preferred stock retirement premiums bear a close functional relation to the debt issue discount rules of §1272 (see ¶ 4.40), and their treatment can be viewed as a backstop to protect avoidance of those provisions. This is the approach adopted by the regulations. See Regs. §§1.305-5(b); 1.305-7(c); 1.305-5(d), Examples (4) (reasonable call premium) and (5) (excessive call premium); and 1.305-5(d), Example (7) (excessive call premium can be generated by stock dividend if fair market value of distributed preferred stock is less than its redemption price); Rev. Rul. 83-119, 1983-2 CB 57.

For call premiums deemed reasonable even though they are outside the 10 percent safe-harbor zone, see Rev. Rul. 75-179, 1975-1 CB 103; Rev. Rul. 75-468, 1975-2

Recapitalizations to remove dividend arrears on preferred stock (whether for current or prior years) are specifically taxable under §§305(b)(4) and 305(c) to the extent that the arrears are discharged in the exchange.[229]

5. Distributions of preferred. Section 305(b)(5) provides that a distribution of convertible preferred stock will be taxable (even though pro rata), unless it is established that it will not have a disproportionate result. The committee reports use a likelihood-of-conversion test for this purpose, stating that if substantially full conversion is likely to occur, no disproportion will result, so that the distribution will be tax-free.[230] The example given in the committee reports shows that a four-month conversion term is unlikely to result in substantially full conversion, while 20 years would most likely result in substantially all the preferred stock being converted into common stock.[231]

6. Disproportionate distributions. The most important part of the restrictive treatment of stock dividends in the Tax Reform Act of 1969 is the

---

CB 115 (adjustment upward because of market decline after agreement on 5 percent premium). The principle of Rev. Rul. 75-468 was followed and extended in Rev. Rul. 81-190, 1981-2 CB 84 (unanticipated value fluctuations occurring after it was too late to change terms of tender offer).

See generally Note, Discounted Preferred Stock Under the New Section 305 Treasury Regulations: On Confusing Debt and Equity, 84 Yale L.J. 324 (1974); Minasian & Welz, Guidelines for Determining When Discount On Preferred Stock Will Create Taxable Income, 53 J. Tax'n 2 (1980). For a digest of private rulings that no taxable call premium exists if the preferred stock is immediately callable, see Shoptalk, 61 J. Tax'n 445 (1984).

[229] See generally Regs. §§1.305-5 and 1.305-7(c); see also Cong. Rec. 37902 (daily ed. Dec. 9, 1969) (statement of Sen. Long disclaiming any intent to alter the tax-free status of recapitalizations in which older stockholders exchange some or all of their common stock for preferred stock and retire from the business, while younger stockholders exchange preferred stock for additional common stock and continue to be active in the business (see ¶ 14.17), except to the extent preferred dividend arrears are discharged thereby); Regs. §1.305-3(e), Example (12); Rev. Rul. 75-93, 1975-1 CB 101 (disporportionate recapitalization exchange that resulted in increase in equity interest of exchanging shareholders did not trigger §305(b)(2) because recapitalization was not part of plan to periodically step up equity interests; the Service noted that this conclusion was consistent with the isolated redemption situations in Regs. §1.305-3(e), Examples (10), (11), and (13)). But see Rev. Rul. 83-119, 1983-2 CB 57.

[230] See infra note 236.

[231] For interpretations of §305(b)(5) and examples illustrating its scope, see Regs. §§1.305-6(a)(2) and 1.305-6(b).

disproportionate distribution rules of §305(b)(2), as amplified by §305(c). A distribution of stock or rights will be taxable if the distribution, or a series of distributions of which such distribution is one, has the result of a receipt of cash or property (other than stock of the distributing corporation) by some shareholders and an increase in the proportionate residual equity interests (i.e., interests in earnings or assets) of other shareholders. In testing for disproportion, each class of stock must be considered both separately (i.e., for disproportion within the class) and in conjunction with other classes (i.e., for disproportion between one class and another).

The requisite relationship between the two distributions is addressed in broad terms by Regs. §1.305-3(b), which provides that the stock and property distributions contemplated by §305(b)(2) need not be pursuant to a plan if they occur within 36 months of each other. If the distributions are not linked together by a plan, however, a separation of more than 36 months gives rise to a presumption that they were independent transactions. The regulations also point out that the property distribution must be one to which §301 applies, and that isolated redemptions do not constitute prohibited property distributions even if they result in §301 treatment to the redeemed shareholders.[232]

The scope of the disproportionate distribution rule of §305(b)(2) is broad but not limitless: One should not focus so intently on the hole as to miss the doughnut. Thus, the prohibited increase in equity must occur as the result of two separate transactions: a distribution of property and a distribution of stock (actual or constructive), presumably to different groups of shareholders. There must also be some connection between these transactions, although the relationship required by the statutory language is much less distinct than that embodied in the regulations.[233] While the regulations make plain that a property distribution to one group of shareholders can trigger a taxable stock divi-

---

[232] See generally Regs. §§1.305-3(b)(3) (last sentence); 1.305-3(e), Examples (10), (11), and (13); see also Rev. Rul. 77-19, 1977-1 CB 83 (20 isolated redemptions during previous three years from retiring or deceased shareholders, together with redemptions from public minority group when corporation went private, held not to be a periodic redemption plan); Rev. Rul. 78-115, infra note 237. For illustrations of periodic redemption plans, compare Rev. Rul. 78-60, 1978-1 CB 81; Regs. §1.305-3(e), Examples (8), (9); Rev. Rul. 78-375, 1978-2 CB 130.

The isolated redemption rationale should protect conventional stock buyout agreements triggered by the retirement or death of a key shareholder, even though the redemption brings about an increase in the equity interest of the continuing shareholders.

[233] See generally Regs. §§1.305-3(b)(4) (36-month benchmark for linking distributions of cash and property); 1.305-3(b)(3) (last sentence) (isolated redemptions will not trigger §305(b)(2)); Rev. Rul. 77-19, 1977-1 CB 83 (isolated redemptions); Regs. §1.305-3(e), Examples (10), (11), and (13) (same); Rev. Rul. 75-93, 1975-1 CB 101 (same).

dend to another group of shareholders,[234] it would seem that the same property distribution should not also trigger taxable stock dividend consequences to its distributees.[235] Moreover, the increase in equity interest required by the statute (i.e., an increase in earnings or assets) refers to an increase in the residual equity holders' interest in common stock or the like, rather than the type of equity participation represented by senior securities such as preferred stock, at least if the preferred stock is not convertible. Thus, the committee reports[236] state that disproportion will not result from a distribution of common stock on a corporation's only class of common stock, even though a class of cash-dividend-paying preferred stock (not convertible) is also outstanding; the stock dividend is pro rata in this situation because the interest of the preferred stock in earnings or assets is unaffected by the common stock dividend. This would be true even if the distributions are periodic rather than sporadic.[237] Likewise, a pro rata distribution of nonconvertible preferred stock by a corporation with only common stock outstanding would not be taxable; otherwise, §306 would have no application, since this example is the prototype §306 stock situation. (See Chapter 10 for further discussion of §306.) Finally, the regulations clarify the status of earn-out provisions under which additional stock or stock rights are issued, or conversion ratios are altered, in order to permit selling shareholders to benefit from a corporation's post-sale earnings record.[238] These changes are treated as adjustments of the price to be paid for the consideration received by the selling shareholders, not as distributions subject to §305.

7. Constructive distributions—escalating redemption prices, antidilution clauses, call premiums, recapitalizations, and so forth. The Treasury is empowered by §305(c) to issue regulations treating a wide variety of transactions as

---

[234] See Regs. §1.305-3(e), Examples (8), (9).

[235] But see Rev. Rul. 78-60, 1978-1 CB 81 (periodic redemption plan; shareholders whose stock was redeemed had constructive §305(c) distribution because their interests increased, despite redemption, since other shareholders redeemed a larger percentage of their holdings).

[236] See S. Rep. No. 552, 91st Cong., 2d Sess. (1969). See generally Regs. §1.305-3(e), Examples (1), (2). But see Regs. §1.305-3(e), Example (3) (equity increase must result in increase to one class of shareholders at expense of another class). Thus, in Example (3), a distribution of preferred stock on common stock (where another class of preferred stock is outstanding) will be taxable, unless the new preferred stock is junior or subordinate to the old; if the new preferred stock is equal or senior, the distribution will result in a prohibited equity increase to the distributees at the expense of the preferred shareholder class. See also Regs. §1.305-3(e), Example (15) (taxable stock dividend supplied property distribution to make another stock dividend taxable to other shareholders).

[237] See, e.g., Rev. Rul. 78-115, 1978-1 CB 85; Regs. §1.305-3(e), Example (14) (even though periodic, redemption plan had effect of mere financing arrangement).

[238] Regs. §1.305-1(c); see also Rev. Rul. 82-158, 1982-2 CB 77.

constructive distributions with respect to any shareholder whose proportionate interest in the corporation's earnings and profits or assets is increased thereby. The suspect transactions include changes in conversion ratios, changes in redemption prices, unreasonable call premium provisions, dividend equivalent periodic redemption plans,[239] and any other transactions, including recapitalizations, having a similar effect on the relative equity interests of any shareholder or holder of stock purchase rights or convertible securities. For this purpose, holders of convertible bonds and warrants are treated as shareholders under §305(d)(2)[240] and warrants constitute stock under §305(d)(1). It should be noted that any disproportion, however trivial, can trigger taxability under §305(b). The Senate Finance Committee had provided for a de minimis exception, but it was rejected in conference.[241]

The regulations issued pursuant to this grant of authority largely restate the statutory language of §305(c), but they also make clear that a deemed distribution under §305(c) is only a constructive *stock* distribution, that it will create dividend income to the constructive distributee only if it had one of the results described in §305(b), and that it will be taxable only to the person whose proportionate equity interest is increased thereby. The regulations also note that the constructive stock distribution is considered to have been made in a particular *class* of stock, common or preferred, depending upon the facts of that case. Regs. §1.305-7(b) deals with adjustments under antidilution provisions as deemed stock distributions under §305(c), providing that adjustments in conversion ratios, or prices, of convertible stock or debt under a bona fide reasonable adjustment formula (including, but not limited to, market price or conversion price formulas) to prevent dilution will not result in a deemed distribution of stock. Adjustments to compensate

---

[239] Regs. §1.305-7(a) requires that the redemption must be "equivalent to a dividend" to trigger application of §305(b)(2); see also supra notes 232–234 (regarding periodic and isolated redemption plans).

[240] See S. Rep. No. 552, supra note 236, at 152 (stock dividend is taxable if paid on common stock by corporation simultaneously paying interest on its convertible debentures). Despite §305(d), warrants and convertible bonds are treated by the Service as boot rather than as stock in the reorganization area. For discussion of stock in the reorganization area, see infra ¶ 14.31. See also Regs. §1.305-3(e), Example (4) (distribution of rights on common stock is taxable where convertible debt or stock is not subject to full antidilution protection); Rev. Rul. 75-513, 1975-2 CB 114 (cash dividend to common shareholders and compensating upward adjustment of conversion ratio of convertible debentures was held to be taxable constructive stock dividend to bondholders).

For collateral consequences of constructive stock dividends, see Rev. Rul. 76-186, 1976-1 CB 86 (convertible bondholders can step up basis of debt by amount of constructive stock dividend, which also reduces earnings and profits).

For taxable conversion ratio adjustments, see Regs. §1.305-3(e), Examples (6) and (7).

[241] S. Rep. No. 552, supra note 236, at 521.

for cash dividends paid to other shareholders, however, do not qualify for this exception.[242]

As for recapitalizations, the regulations provide that they constitute constructive distributions under §305(c) if (1) they are pursuant to a plan to periodically increase a shareholder's proportionate interest in the assets or earnings of the corporation, or (2) a preferred shareholder owning stock with dividend arrears exchanges such stock and as a result increases his interest in the corporation's earnings or assets.[243]

8. Treatment of tax-free stock distributions. Upon receiving a distribution of stock that is exempt from tax under §305(a), the shareholder is required by §307(a) to allocate the basis of the old stock between the old and the new stock as prescribed by the regulations. Pursuant to §307(a), the Treasury requires an allocation of basis in proportion to the fair market values of the old and new stock on the date of distribution.[244] The holding period of the new stock, in determining whether capital gain or loss on a sale or exchange is long-term or short-term, includes the period for which the shareholder held the old stock, by virtue of §1223(5). Ordinarily, therefore, the shareholder will report any gain or loss recognized on a sale, redemption, or other disposition of his dividend shares as long-term capital gain or loss. If the dividend shares are "section 306 stock" (primarily preferred stock distributed as a tax-free dividend by a corporation having earnings and profits),

---

[242] Regs. §1.305-3(d) deals with the effect of antidilution adjustments to conversion ratios of convertible stock and debt securities to take account of stock dividends paid on other shares. These provisions spell out various formulas for effecting the necessary "full antidilution adjustments" in order to prevent taxability of the stock dividend under §305(b)(2).

[243] See Regs. §1.305-7(c); infra ¶ 14.17; Rev. Rul. 83-119, 1983-2 CB 57 (in control shift recapitalization, which also purported to freeze equity value of retiring shareholder, redemption price of preferred stock was found to exceed its value, thereby creating a taxable §305(b)(4) dividend over life expectancy of holder, or when stock is redeemed at his death). For general valuation principles in equity freeze recapitalizations, see Rev. Rul. 83-120, 1983-2 CB 170; Rev. Rul. 86-25, 1986-1 CB 202.

[244] Regs. §1.307-1. If the stock on which the stock dividend is distributed was acquired at different times and for different prices, and if the shareholder can adequately identify each separate lot of the underlying stock, the basis and holding period of each old lot can be allocated to the new stock in proportion to the relative fair market values of the old lots. Otherwise, the shareholder must use the FIFO tracing approach; use of the average cost of all lots for basis and holding-period allocation purposes is not permitted. See OD 735, 3 CB 40, restated in Rev. Rul. 71-350, 1971-2 CB 176; Rev. Rul. 56-653, 1956-2 CB 185; Keeler v. CIR, 86 F2d 265 (8th Cir. 1936), cert. denied, 300 US 373 (1937).

however, the taxpayer may realize ordinary income on their disposition (under rules discussed in Chapter 10).

The distributing corporation does not reduce its earnings and profits when it makes a nontaxable distribution of its stock (§312(d)(1)(B)) and the recipient, if a corporation, does not increase its earnings and profits on receiving such a distribution (§312(f)(2)).[245]

9. Treatment of taxable stock distributions. When stock dividends are subject to §305(b), the distribution is to be treated as a distribution of property to which §301 applies. In a taxable election transaction under §305(b)(1), the amount of the distribution depends upon whether the shareholder takes the stock or rights in the distributing corporation or chooses to take other property instead. In the former case, Regs. §§1.305-2(b), Example (1) and 1.301-1(d) provide that the fair market value of the stock or rights is the amount of the §301 distribution, regardless of whether the distributee is an individual or a corporation.[246] In this respect, taxable stock dividends are treated as distributions by a corporation of its own obligations,[247] or, alternatively, they are analogous to cash dividends (measured by the fair market value of the stock). The distributing corporation's charge to earnings and profits for such distributions is, under Regs. §1.312-1(d), the fair market value of the stock or rights. Similarly, the basis of the distributed stock or rights in the hands of the shareholders, individual or corporate, is fair market value under §301(d)(1). The holding period of stock or rights received in a taxable distribution commences with the date of acquisition; there is no provision in §1223 for tacking in this case.

If, however, a shareholder exercises his election to receive money or other property in lieu of stock rights, Regs. §1.305-2(b), Example (1) provides that the normal dividend rules govern taxability of the distribution, i.e., if property other than money is received after 1986, both individual and corporate distributees use the value of the property in measuring the amount of their distribution under §301(b)(1), their basis for the property is determined by its value under §301(d), and the charge to earnings and profits is governed by the rules discussed previously. If the elected property consists

---

[245] The expense of issuing a stock dividend cannot be deducted under §162. See supra ¶ 5.04. This rule, which seems applicable whether or not the stock dividend is taxable to the recipients, would also preclude a reduction in earnings and profits to reflect the expense.

[246] Both §§317(b) and 1032 can be cited in support of the Treasury's decision to disregard basis in the case of a distribution of stock. See Bittker, Stock Dividends, Distributions in Kind, Redemptions, and Liquidations Under the 1954 Code, 1955 S. Cal. Tax Inst. 349, 354–355. But see Rev. Rul. 70-521, 1970-2 CB 72; infra ¶ 7.44, para. 2; see also Rev. Rul. 76-53, 1976-1 CB 87; Rev. Rul. 78-375, 1978-2 CB 130.

[247] Supra ¶ 7.40.

of obligations of the distributing corporation, the principles discussed previously[248] presumably would apply, although the regulations are not specific on this point.

Other taxable stock distributions under §305(b) (e.g., disproportionate distributions) generally are taxed in the same manner as the distribution of stock in the optional distribution case, that is, the value of the distribution will measure the amount of the §301 dividend (both to individual and to corporate shareholders), the basis of the distributed stock under §301(d), and the §312 charge to earnings and profits of the distributing corporation.[249]

10. Convertible securities and warrants. The treatment of convertible preferred stock and convertible debt securities under revised §305 merits additional comment. It seems clear that fancy forms of convertible preferred stock are severely inhibited; thus, §305(b)(4), in conjunction with the constructive stock dividend rules of §305(c), will create taxable dividend income to the shareholders (without the necessity of a conjunctive distribution of property) if the instrument provides for increasing redemption prices, excessive call premiums, or escalating conversion ratio features.[250] Moreover, the distribution of convertible preferred stock itself will be taxable under §305(b)(5) unless substantial likelihood of conversion can be proved. Convertible debenture holders, in addition to suffering indignities at the hands of the §279 corporate acquisition indebtedness rules,[251] are also to be treated as shareholders for purposes of the §305 stock dividend rules by virtue of §305(d)(2). In addition, the presence of such convertible debentures functions as a spoiler for other equity shareholders. The Senate report indicates that payment of interest on the debentures apparently will trigger taxability for stock dividends paid to the common stockholders.[252]

Section 305 creates comparable problems for the holders of warrants. Rights to purchase stock are classified as stock under §305(d)(1), and their holders are defined as shareholders by §305(d)(2). Thus, if a warrant to purchase common stock provides for periodic decreases in the exercise price to keep pace with cash dividends paid to the common shareholders, the result-

---

[248] See discussion in text supra at notes 200–206.

[249] See Regs. §1.305-1(b)(1) (1973) (as a general rule, use optional distribution method); Regs. §1.305-1(b)(3) (for §305(c) distributions, cross-reference to Regs. §1.305-3(e), Examples (6), (8), (9), and (15)); Rev. Rul. 76-186, 1976-1 CB 86.

[250] For antidilution clauses, see supra notes 227, 242–244. See generally Regs. §§1.305-3(e), Examples (4), (6), (7), and (15) and 1.305-5(d), Examples (2), (3), and (6).

[251] See supra ¶ 4.20.

[252] See S. Rep. No. 552, supra note 236, at 152.

ing increase in the warrant holder's share of the corporate earnings and profits, coupled with the parallel distribution of cash to the common
shareholders, could generate dividend income for the warrant holders under
§305(b)(2). Moreover, the holder of a warrant to acquire preferred stock presumably would be treated as a preferred stockholder under §305, which
could increase his exposure to taxability under such provisions as
§305(b)(4), where disproportion is unnecessary.

11. Effective date and transition rules. Section 421(b)(1) of the Tax
Reform Act of 1969 provides that §305, as amended in 1969, applies generally to all distributions, actual or constructive, after January 10, 1969. Section 421(b)(2) of the Act, however, sets forth extraordinarily intricate
transition rules, which can delay application of the 1969 statutory rules until
as late as 1991.[253]

¶ 7.44 STOCK RIGHTS

1. Nontaxable rights. Section 305 lumps together distributions of stock
rights and distributions of the stock itself, providing in §§305(d)(1) and
305(a) that a distribution by a corporation of "rights to acquire its stock" is
not includable in the shareholder's gross income, unless the distribution is
subject to one of the exceptions of §305(b).[254] Even though §305 does not
discriminate between stock and stock rights, however, a distribution of
rights presents certain peculiar problems.[255]

---

[253] See Regs. §1.305-8 for these delayed effective dates and note that if the 1969
statutory rules do not apply, the 1954–1969 statutory rules (see supra ¶ 7.42) apply to
distributions made or considered as made after January 10, 1969.

[254] See supra ¶ 7.43.

[255] By providing explicitly that a distribution of stock and stock rights shall be
treated as a distribution of property unless exempted, these provisions supersede pro
tanto the definition of "property" in §317(a), which excludes the distributing corporation's own stock and rights to acquire such stock. See Rev. Rul. 72-71, 1972-1 CB
99, for an extensive ruling on the tax consequences of the AT&T rights offering of
1970 (holding that the issue of rights to purchase a package of debentures and warrants where the warrants were equal in value to the rights at the date of the distribution of the rights resulted in a tax-free distribution of the rights under §305(a), since
the value of the rights was attributable solely to the warrants, which constituted stock
under §305(d)); see also Rev. Rul. 74-501, 1974-2 CB 98 (rights distribution when
value exceeded 15 percent, but stock price subsequently dropped and rights either
lapsed or corporation refunded subscriptions from prior exercise in same year; held,
no basis adjustment on lapse and no basis adjustment on refunds if exercise and
refund occurred in same year).

In the case of a nontaxable distribution of rights, basis is to be allocated under §307. The general rule prescribed by §307(a) and the regulations issued thereunder is an allocation of basis between the old stock and the stock rights in proportion to their fair market values as of the date of distribution.[256] The regulations also state that basis is to be allocated only if the rights are exercised or sold. In the case of exercise, the amount allocated to the rights is added to the cost of the stock acquired by exercising the rights; in the case of a sale, the amount allocated to the rights is used in determining the shareholder's gain or loss on the sale.[257] The effect of this limitation is that the shareholder realizes no loss if the rights expire without exercise or sale, and the allocated basis presumably reverts to the underlying shares.

The rule of allocation is subject to an exception. Section 307(b) provides that if the fair market value of the rights is less than 15 percent of the fair market value of the old stock at the time of distribution, the basis of the rights shall be zero, unless the shareholder elects to allocate basis under the method of allocation provided by §307(a). (The method of making an election is set out in Regs. §1.307-2.) The purpose of §307(b) is to avoid the necessity for trifling basis adjustments on a distribution of rights of little value; unless the shareholder elects to allocate his basis, he uses a zero basis for the rights whether they are exercised (in which case the basis of the new stock is its actual cost) or sold (in which case the entire proceeds of sale will be taxable gain), leaving the basis of the old stock intact.

If the shareholder sells his rights, §1223(5) permits the holding period of the underlying shares to be tacked on in determining the holding period of the rights if their basis "is determined under section 307"; this embraces rights with a zero basis under §307(b) as well as rights with an allocated basis under §307(a).[258]

2. Taxable rights. When a distribution of rights is taxable because the shareholders have an option to take property instead of rights or because the distribution falls within some other exception to the general rule of §305(a), §305(b) provides that "the distribution shall be treated as a distribution of property to which section 301 applies." The result is that the distribution itself is taxable, assuming that the rights can be valued and that there are adequate earnings and profits to the extent of the fair market value of the rights, whether they are subsequently sold, exercised, or allowed to lapse. Lapse would give rise to deductible loss, unless all shareholders allowed

---

[256] Regs. §§1.307-1(a) and 1.307-1(b).
[257] Regs. §§1.307-1(a) and 1.307-1(b).
[258] Rev. Rul. 56-572, 1956-2 CB 182.

their rights to lapse so that the economic relationships to the corporation and to each other were unchanged.

It also seems clear that *Choate v. CIR*,[259] likening a distribution of stock rights to a distribution of rights to purchase the distributing corporation's shares in another corporation, should not be applied to §305(b). Among other things, *Choate* held (under the pre-1954 statute) that a distribution of rights was taxable only if the corporation intended to distribute earnings and profits and, even then, only if the rights are exercised or sold. These are requirements that cannot properly be read into §§305(b) and 305(d)(1), which state that taxable *distributions* of stock are subject to §301 and that the term "stock" includes rights to acquire the corporation's own stock. Moreover, the analogy accepted in *Choate* would have the astonishing result under §311(b)(1) of current law of taxing the distributing corporation on the appreciation in the rights, since they could be said to have a zero basis in the hands of the distributing corporation.[260]

---

[259] 125 F2d 684 (2d Cir. 1942).

[260] For the fundamentally different issues raised by distributions of rights to acquire stock owned by the distributing corporation, see text supra at notes 87–90.

CHAPTER 8

Penalty Taxes on Undistributed Corporate Income

PART A.　THE ACCUMULATED EARNINGS TAX

¶ 8.01　INTRODUCTORY

For many years, the top tax rate applicable to individuals was 20 or more percentage points higher than the top corporate rate, and this disparity tempted individual taxpayers to form or use corporations as a shield against the individual income tax. To be sure, after-tax corporate income is not immediately available to shareholders for personal consumption, but this may not be critical: They may be satisfied to sell the stock (reporting the accumulated income as long-term capital gain), exchange it for the marketable stock of a publicly held corporation in a tax-free merger, or hold it for ultimate transfer to their heirs at death, with a stepped-up basis equal to its value at that time. After 1982, however, the highest top individual tax rate was no longer substantially higher than the top corporate rate, and in 1988 the top rates are scheduled to invert—that is, the top corporate rate of 34 percent will exceed the top noncorporate rate of 28 percent. Thus the incentive to *organize* corporations for tax-avoidance purposes is significantly reduced.

Once a corporation is in existence (whether its creation was motivated by tax avoidance or other purposes), however, the relationship between the individual and corporate rates is no longer of prime importance; what does matter is that the after-tax corporate income is taxed a second time if and when distributed to the individual shareholders. This provides a continuing incentive to retain and reinvest the corporate earnings instead of paying them out as dividends, particularly if the shareholders wish to dispose of the stock in a tax-free merger when a promising opportunity arises or if they plan to pass the stock on to their heirs at death (when it will acquire a new basis, equal to its fair market value at that time). For many years, the incentive to accumulate earnings rather than distribute them was enhanced by the traditional large rate differential between ordinary income and long-term capital gains, which enabled shareholders to realize gain on a corporation's accumulated earnings by selling their stock and paying a capital gains tax that could be as little as a third of the tax that they would have paid had the earnings been withdrawn as dividends; but this additional stimulus to accumulations is scheduled for elimination in 1988.

The Service is armed with two important weapons to combat tactical accumulations: (1) the accumulated earnings tax imposed by §531 on the accumulated taxable income (as defined) of corporations that accumulate their earnings in order to avoid the income tax on their shareholders (the subject of Part A of this chapter); and (2) the penalty tax imposed by §541 on personal holding companies (the subject of Part B). Three other sets of statutory provisions discouraging the use of corporations to allow shareholders to avoid taxes (the special treatment of shareholders in foreign personal holding companies, controlled foreign corporations, and collapsible corporations) are examined in later chapters.[1]

The accumulated earnings tax of §531 can trace its lineage to the Revenue Act of 1913,[2] which provided that if a corporation was "formed or fraudulently availed of" for the purpose of escaping the individual income tax by permitting gains and profits to accumulate in the corporation, each shareholder's ratable share of the corporate income was taxable to him whether distributed or not. The fact that the corporation was "a mere holding company" or that its accumulations were "beyond the reasonable needs of the business" was prima facie evidence of "a fraudulent purpose to escape [the individual income] tax." The references to fraud were dropped in 1916, and doubts about the constitutionality of taxing the shareholders on undistributed corporate income, engendered by *Eisner v. Macomber,*[3] led the Congress in 1921 to abandon this mechanism in favor of a tax on the offending corporation itself. The constitutionality of the revised tax was upheld, against a variety of objections, in *Helvering v. National Grocery Co.*[4]

The principal features of the accumulated earnings tax as presently constituted are the following:

(1) The tax is imposed on "every corporation [except personal holding companies, foreign personal holding companies, and tax-exempt corporations] formed or availed of for the purpose of avoiding the income tax with respect to its shareholders ... by permitting earnings and profits to accumulate instead of being divided or distributed" (§532).

(2) The fact that the corporation is "a mere holding or investment company" is prima facie evidence of the purpose to avoid the income tax on its shareholders (§533(b)).

(3) The fact that earnings and profits are allowed to accumulate "beyond the reasonable needs of the business" is determinative of the purpose to avoid income tax on its shareholders unless the corporation proves to the contrary by the preponderance of the evi-

---

[1] Ch. 12 and parts C and D of ch. 17 respectively.

[2] 38 Stat. 166.

[3] Eisner v. Macomber, 252 US 189 (1920).

[4] Helvering v. National Grocery Co., 304 US 282, reh'g denied, 305 US 669 (1938). In its opinion, the Supreme Court said, "Kohl [sole shareholder of the corporate taxpayer], the sole owner of the business, could not by conducting it as a corporation, prevent Congress, if it chose to do so, from laying on him individually the tax on the year's profits," citing the Revenue Act of 1913. The Court thus suggested that the 1921 change, which laid the tax on the corporation, was an unnecessary precaution by Congress, at least as to a one-person or other closely held corporation.

dence (§533(a)). The term "reasonable needs of the business" includes the "reasonably anticipated needs of the business" (§537(a)(1)).

(4) If a notice of deficiency is based on an alleged unreasonable accumulation, the burden of proof in any Tax Court proceeding depends in part on whether the taxpayer has been so notified by the government and has submitted an answering counterstatement with regard to this question (§534).

(5) When applicable, the tax is levied at the rate of 27.5 percent of the first $100,000 of "accumulated taxable income" (as defined) and at the rate of 38.5 percent of any "accumulated taxable income" above $100,000 (§531) (but the tax rate is proposed to be reduced to 28 percent after 1987).

(6) In computing the amount subject to tax, corporations are allowed to accumulate free of tax a minimum of $250,000 ($150,000 in the case of certain service corporations), and sometimes more, except for mere holding and investment companies (§535(c)).

¶ 8.02 THE FORBIDDEN PURPOSE

The accumulated earnings tax is designed to discourage the use of a corporation as an accumulation vehicle to shelter its individual shareholders from the personal income tax rates. The rule is phrased in terms of what the statute is designed to prevent (i.e., the forming or availing of a corporation *"for the purpose* of avoiding the income tax with respect to its shareholders ... by permitting earnings and profits to accumulate instead of being divided or distributed" (emphasis added). Thus, liability for the tax turns on the state of mind or intent of the corporation, primarily a question of fact. This essentially factual nature of §531 cases gives special weight to the trial court's decision and is an important consideration in litigation strategy. Since each case depends on its own facts, moreover, the decided cases, although numerous, are not very useful as precedents.[5]

---

[5] The principal looseleaf services contain tabulations of the litigated cases by reference to their separate specific facts (e.g., 1987 Fed. Taxes (P-H) ¶ 21,334). For general discussion, see Lewis, Accumulated Earnings Tax, Tax Mgmt. Portfolio (BNA) No. 35-6th (1987); Cunningham, More Than You Ever Wanted to Know About the Accumulated Earnings Tax, 6 J. Corp. Tax'n 187 (1979); articles by Altman, Crampton, Liles, Gannet, Winokur et al., on Improper Accumulation of Earned Surplus and Personal Holding Companies, 24 NYU Inst. on Fed. Tax'n. 805–993 (1966); Ziegler, The "New" Accumulated Earnings Tax: A Survey of Recent Developments, 22 Tax L. Rev. 77 (1966). For discussion of the current status of §531, see Kwall, Subchapter G of the Internal Revenue Code: Crusade Without a Cause? 5

In determining whether corporate earnings have been accumulated for the tainted purpose, the following issues require special attention.

1. Corporations subject to tax. Since personal holding companies and the U.S. shareholders of foreign personal holding companies are subject to special penalty taxes on undistributed income (discussed later in this chapter and in Chapter 17), corporations of these types are exempted from the accumulated earnings tax of §531, as are tax-exempt corporations (§532(b)). An accumulation for the purpose of sheltering *corporate* shareholders against income tax is within the literal scope of §532(a); but since tax avoidance is nominal in this instance because of the 80 or 100 percent deduction for intercorporate dividends allowed by §243,[6] it would be difficult to establish the forbidden purpose.[7]

Attention has therefore focused on accumulations for the purpose of shielding *individual* shareholders against income tax, and the regulations explicitly require avoidance of the individual income tax.[8] The tax can be imposed, however, if the purpose is to avoid income tax on the shareholders *of another corporation* (i.e., if the accumulating corporation's stock is owned by a second corporation and the purpose of the subsidiary's accumulation is to protect the individual shareholders of the parent corporation against the tax they would have to pay if the subsidiary distributed its earnings to the parent corporation and it in turn paid dividends to its shareholders).[9]

As a historical matter, the accumulated earnings tax has been imposed almost solely on closely held corporations, and this long-standing practice

---

Va. Tax Rev. 77 (1985). Earlier works of continuing interest are Cary, Accumulations Beyond the Reasonable Needs of the Business: The Dilemma of Section 102(c), 60 Harv. L. Rev. 1282 (1947); Rudick, Section 102 and Personal Holding Company Provisions of the Internal Revenue Code, 49 Yale L.J. 171 (1939); for discussion of the 1954 changes, see Cohen, Phillips, Surrey, Tarleau & Warren, The Internal Revenue Code of 1954: Carry-Overs and the Accumulated Earnings Tax, 10 Tax L. Rev. 277, 299–306 (1955).

[6] Supra ¶ 5.05.

[7] For the application of the accumulated earnings tax to corporations filing consolidated returns, see infra ¶ 15.23, text at para 8.

[8] See Regs. §1.532-1(a)(1). For accumulations by foreign corporations, see infra ¶ 17.25.

[9] See Regs. §1.532-1(a)(2). For the history of this provision, see Mead Corp. v. CIR, 116 F2d 187 (3d Cir. 1940). For applications, see US v. McNally Pittsburgh Mfg. Co., 342 F2d 198 (10th Cir. 1965); Hedberg-Freidheim Contracting Co. v. CIR, 251 F2d 839 (8th Cir. 1958); Inland Terminals, Inc. v. US, 477 F2d 836 (4th Cir.), on remand, 32 AFTR2d 5933 (D. Md. 1973) (subsidiary may accumulate for reasonable needs of parent). But see Wilcox Mfg. Co., ¶ 79,092 P-H Memo. TC (1979) (subsidiary liable for tax where accumulation was unreasonable on facts).

led to a 1974 decision of the Court of Appeals for the Ninth Circuit holding that the tax could not be properly applied to publicly held corporations.[10] The foundation for this determination—an inferred legislative prohibition—was eliminated in 1984 when Congress enacted §532(c), providing that tax liability must be determined without regard to the number of shareholders. However, the conferees recommending enactment of this provision simultaneously took away most of its bite by observing that "as a practical matter it may be difficult to establish [a tax-avoidance] purpose in the case of a widely-held operating company when no individual or small group of individuals has legal or effective control of the company."[11] The legislators might have added that the threat of stockholder pressure, including possible lawsuits if the corporation improperly accumulates its surplus, may constitute a greater incentive for corporate managements to declare dividends than §531 itself.[12] A rare instance of the §531 tax being imposed on a publicly held corporation is the *Trico Products* litigation.[13] There, however, six shareholders controlled about two thirds of the shares so that the courts were able to determine that the accumulations were motivated by the individual interests of this group. A stockholder's derivative action against the directors, who were also the principal shareholders, was settled by their personal payment of almost $2.5 million to the corporation for subjecting it to the §531 penalty.

2. **Tax-avoidance purpose in general.** The naked language of §532(a) could be interpreted to impose the penalty tax whenever the prohibited purpose exists, whether it is successfully consummated or not. However, courts may well hesitate to adopt this draconian construction of the statutory language and may require instead a showing of actual, rather than hoped-for, avoidance of shareholder income taxes. Thus, if the corporation is formed for the purpose of tax avoidance but abandons its plans, or

---

[10] Golconda Mining Corp. v. CIR, 507 F2d 594 (9th Cir. 1974).

[11] H.R. Rep. No. 861, 98th Cong., 2d Sess. 829 (1984), reprinted in 1984-3 CB 1, 84 (Vol. 2).

[12] These suits may take the form of an action to compel payment of dividends (e.g., Dodge v. Ford Motor Co., 204 Mich. 459, 170 N.W. 668 (1919); Kales v. Woodworth, 32 F2d 37 (6th Cir.), cert. denied, 280 US 570 (1929)), or a shareholder's derivative action on behalf of the corporation to recover from the directors the amount of any §531 tax paid (see Mahler v. Trico Prods. Corp., 296 N.Y. 902, 72 N.E.2d 622 (1947); Note, Derivative Actions Arising From Payment of Penalty Taxes Under Section 102, 49 Colum. L. Rev. 394 (1949)).

[13] Trico Prods. Corp. v. CIR, 137 F2d 424 (2d Cir.), cert. denied, 320 US 799 (1943), reh'g denied, 321 US 801 (1944); Trico Prods. Corp. v. McGowan, 169 F2d 343 (2d Cir.), cert. denied, 335 US 899 (1948); Mahler v. Trico Prods. Corp., supra note 12.

if the directors accumulate for the purpose of shielding shareholders against tax but their action turns out to be a brutum fulmen because the shareholders are in fact tax exempt, or if for some other reason the forbidden purpose fails to achieve its intended result, it is unlikely that the tax will be asserted or upheld.[14] Even if reduction of the shareholders' income tax liability is not indispensable, however, it can obviously be extremely important to the government's case. Here, as elsewhere in the law, a purpose can be inferred from the results. Hence, it is common practice in §531 cases for courts to consider, as evidence of the forbidden purpose, the tax effect that a dividend distribution would have had on the shareholders. On the other hand, courts have been quick to point out that the mere fact that shareholders would have paid more taxes if the earnings had been distributed as dividends rather than accumulated is not fatal on the question of tax avoidance.[15]

Several courts have been faced with the question of whether an honest, although mistaken, belief that accumulations were necessary for a purpose other than shareholder tax avoidance will protect the corporation from the penalty tax of §531. In a concurring opinion in *Casey v. CIR,* Judge Learned Hand expressed the view that it should do so:

> I believe that the statute meant to set up as a test of "reasonable needs" only the corporation's honest belief that the existing accumulation was no greater than was reasonably necessary. Section 532(a) was a penal

---

[14] In Helvering v. National Grocery Co., supra note 4, the taxpayer argued that the tax was unconstitutional because, inter alia, "the liability is laid upon the mere purpose to prevent imposition of the surtaxes, not upon the accomplishment of that purpose." If the court in fact accepted this construction of the statute, it was only for the purpose of argument; the facts were far more favorable to the government. The same may be said of other cases, such as De Mille v. CIR, 31 BTA 1161 (1935), aff'd, 90 F2d 12 (9th Cir.), cert. denied, 302 US 713 (1937), to the extent that they imply that liability can be imposed if the forbidden purpose exists but is not achieved.

[15] See Trico Prods. Corp., 46 BTA 346, 364–365 (1942) (findings as to additional income taxes that would have been paid by the shareholders had the corporation distributed its earnings); Apollo Indus., Inc., 44 TC 1 (1965) (limited importance of offsetting capital gains on a later sale of corporation's stock), rev'd on other grounds, 358 F2d 867 (1st Cir. 1966); R. Gsell & Co. v. CIR, 294 F2d 321 (2d Cir. 1961) (shareholder liability not conclusive); Florida Iron & Metal Co., ¶ 42,408 P-H Memo. TC (1942) (tax not imposed because accumulation resulted from bookkeeper's mistake, unknown to the directors, in understating earnings); Simons-Eastern Co. v. US, 354 F. Supp. 1003 (N.D. Ga. 1972) (no prohibited purpose because shareholders' income tax liability would not be reduced); see also Stevenson v. US, 378 F2d 354 (2d Cir. 1967), holding that the §531 tax applied even though no tax savings resulted because of dividend distributions during the following year; if accepted, this defense would have been a do-it-yourself deficiency dividend procedure, which is not available under §531 (infra ¶ 8.09).

statute, designed to defeat any plan to evade the shareholders' taxes, and there can be no doubt that it presupposes some deliberate purpose to do so and is not satisfied by proving that the corporation was mistaken in its estimate of its future "needs." [16]

Accordingly, it would seem that a corporation should not be liable for the accumulated earnings tax if it accumulates for reasons other than the forbidden purpose of §532(a), and this should be true even though the directors may have accumulated earnings out of caprice, spite, miserliness, or stupidity rather than for good business reasons. Consequently, if dividends are withheld to freeze out a minority shareholder or because of the controlling person's obsessive fear of future economic collapse, for example, rather than for the purpose of sheltering stockholders against income tax, the conditions of §532 are not satisfied, and the tax should not be imposed. [17]

Another aspect of the forbidden purpose issue should be noted at this point—that is, must tax avoidance be the *primary* or *dominant* purpose for accumulation, or is the statute satisfied if it is merely *one* of the determining purposes? Resolving a conflict in the cases, the Supreme Court held in *US v. Donruss Co.* that tax avoidance need be only one of the purposes for an unreasonable accumulation. [18] The Court stopped short (but just barely) of saying that mere knowledge of the tax consequences of accumulating would satisfy the prohibited purpose test; but the decision clearly downgrades the pure motives defense, thus confirming the customary focus on an analysis of the reasonable needs of the business. [19]

---

[16] Casey v. CIR, 267 F2d 26 (2d Cir. 1959); see also Duke Laboratories, Inc. v. US, 337 F2d 280 (2d Cir. 1964), where the government conceded that a corporation's honest, although mistaken, belief that its earnings were not excessive may exempt it from liability under §532(a); Bremerton Sun Publishing Co., 44 TC 566 (1965); James W. Salley, Inc. v. US, 38 AFTR2d 5076 (W.D. La. 1976).

In T.C. Heyward & Co. v. US, 18 AFTR2d 5775 (W.D.N.C. 1966), it was held that the accumulation was unreasonable but that there was no tax-avoidance purpose; a mistaken good-faith belief in the need for accumulation prevented imposition of the tax. The court stated, "The taxpayer's accumulations of income were fantastic. I do not believe that one bent upon tax evasion would have the unmitigated gall to attempt it in such an obvious manner."

[17] But see Smoot Sand & Gravel Corp. v. CIR, 274 F2d 495 (4th Cir.), cert. denied, 362 US 976, reh'g denied, 363 US 832 (1960) (reasonable purpose required); for an earlier installment in this litigation, see infra note 42. See generally Starman Inv., Inc. v. US, 534 F2d 834 (9th Cir. 1976) (accumulation due to caution); Myron's Ballroom v. US, 382 F. Supp. 582 (C.D. Cal. 1974) (questionable theory that reducing oral plans to writing for purchase of business premises evidenced shareholder's tax-avoidance motive), rev'd on other grounds, 548 F2d 331 (9th Cir. 1977).

[18] US v. Donruss Co., 393 US 297, reh'g denied, 393 US 1112 (1969).

[19] Infra ¶ 8.03.

3. Whose purpose? Although the statute does not specify the person or persons whose purpose is crucial in the determination of liability for the tax, the reference is presumably to those who control the corporation through stock ownership or otherwise. Unless the person with tax avoidance in mind can exercise control over the corporate dividend policy, his purpose hardly meets the statutory requirement.[20] Moreover, the existence of a substantial minority stock interest that would have objected to an unreasonable accumulation of earnings might negate a tax-avoidance purpose for the accumulation. The charge of improper purpose might also be rebutted by evidence that the shareholders were deadlocked on policy decisions and that a tax-avoidance intent held by one group could not have been put into force.[21]

4. Factors evidencing the prohibited purpose. The regulations provide that the following facts, among others, are to be considered in determining whether the tax-avoidance purpose was present: (1) dealings between the corporation and its shareholders, including loans to shareholders and expenditures of corporate funds for the personal benefit of the shareholders; (2) investments of undistributed earnings in assets having no reasonable connection with the corporation's business; and (3) the corporation's dividend history. It should be noted that these factors are not controlling on the tax-avoidance issue; rather they are merely evidence of whether the accumulation was for the prohibited purpose.[22] Thus, corporations have escaped the penalty tax of §531 despite poor dividend records, unrelated investments, and loans to shareholders, on establishing that the purpose of the accumulation was not to avoid shareholder tax; conversely, corporations with good dividend records and with no loans to shareholders or unrelated investments have nevertheless been held subject to the tax where the prohibited purpose existed.[23]

---

[20] See the *Trico Products* cases, supra note 13; Pelton Steel Casting Co. v. CIR, 251 F2d 278 (7th Cir.), cert. denied, 356 US 958 (1958), in which the Tax Court (28 TC 153, 173) said that "the corporation's intent will be considered to be that of those responsible for its acts." See also Regs. §1.341-2(a)(2) (infra ¶ 12.03), for a similar problem under the collapsible corporation provisions.

[21] For cases involving a minority stock interest, see Carolina Rubber Hose Co., ¶ 65,229 P-H Memo. TC (1965); Mountain State Steel Foundries, Inc. v. CIR, 284 F2d 737 (4th Cir. 1960); Ted Bates & Co., ¶ 65,251 P-H Memo. TC (1965), modified by ¶ 66,904 P-H Memo. TC (1966). For shareholder deadlocks, compare Casey v. CIR, supra note 16, with Hedberg-Freidheim Contracting Co. v. CIR, supra note 9, and Atlantic Properties, Inc. v. CIR, 519 F2d 1233 (1st Cir. 1975).

[22] Regs. §1.533-1(a)(2).

[23] See Thompson Eng'g Co. v. CIR, 80 TC 672, 704 (1983), rev'd on other grounds, 751 F2d 191 (6th Cir. 1985), and cases there cited; Snow Mfg. Co., 86 TC

Corporate loans to, or expenditures on behalf of, shareholders tend to show that the corporation had the capacity to distribute these funds as dividends. If there is a pattern of such transactions, it is but a short step to the conclusion that the loan is a substitute for a dividend, and it shows that corporate earnings were unreasonably diverted from corporate business needs. A similar inference may arise if the corporation has invested its funds for purposes that are not reasonably related to its business. Such unrelated investments may evidence not only the liquidity and dividend-paying capacity of the corporation but the forbidden purpose as well, since the diversion of corporate funds to uses not connected with its business supports an inference that the failure to distribute such funds as dividends was for the purpose of avoiding shareholder taxes. Here again, however, these adverse inferences may be rebutted by countervailing evidence.[24]

Finally, the corporation's dividend and earnings history is relevant to the question of whether funds were accumulated for the prohibited purpose. A failure to distribute dividends (or, in the case of an owner-managed business, to pay substantial salaries to shareholder-officers) suggests that earnings may have been accumulated to avoid shareholder taxes.[25] A good dividend or salary record, on the other hand, suggests that accumulations were not for the prohibited purpose.[26] An important aspect of the corpora-

---

260 (1986), Bardahl Mfg. Corp., ¶ 65,200 P-H Memo. TC (1965) (some loans showed tax-avoidance purpose; others were bona fide and hence did not constitute unreasonable diversion of corporate funds); Vuono-Lione, Inc., ¶ 65,096 P-H Memo. TC (1965) (tax not imposed despite loans to shareholders); Sterling Distribs., Inc. v. US, 313 F2d 803 (5th Cir. 1963) (same); Cataphote Corp. of Miss. v. US, 535 F2d 1225 (Ct. Cl. 1976) (loans to taxpayer's sole shareholder were adverse factors).

Of course, if the loans to shareholders are found to be constructive distributions under the principles discussed supra ¶ 7.05, liability under §531 will be avoided pro tanto but at the cost of tax assessments at the shareholder level.

[24] Compare Smith, Inc. v. CIR, 292 F2d 470 (9th Cir.), cert. denied, 368 US 948 (1961), and Cataphote Corp. of Miss. v. US, supra note 23, with Sandy Estate Co., 43 TC 361 (1964). For discussion of what constitutes "the" business of the taxpayer and the relationship of its investments to that business, see infra ¶ 8.06.

[25] For the effect of a temporary anti-inflation wage-price freeze order, issued in 1971 and followed by official guidelines restraining the payment of dividends, see Estate of Lucas v. CIR, 71 TC 838, 855–867 (1979), aff'd by court order, 657 F2d 841 (6th Cir. 1981) (accumulations justified to extent within guidelines); Doug-Long Inc., 72 TC 158 (1979). For an earlier Service policy of giving special audit attention to corporations failing to distribute at least 70 percent of their earnings, see S. Rep. No. 1622, 83d Cong., 2d Sess. 69 (1954); TD 6378, 1959-1 CB 680.

[26] See generally Bremerton Sun Publishing Co., supra note 16; Henry Van Hummell, Inc., 364 F2d 746 (10th Cir. 1966), cert. denied, 386 US 956 (1967); Cataphote Corp. of Miss. v. US, supra note 23; American Trading & Prod. Corp. v. US, 362 F. Supp. 801 (D. Md. 1972), aff'd per curiam, 474 F2d 1341 (4th Cir. 1973) (dividends paid even in years when taxpayer operated at tax loss).

tion's dividend record is its legal and financial ability to distribute earnings and profits to its shareholders. If a distribution would illegally impair the corporation's capital under local law or violate a bona fide loan agreement, a failure to distribute earnings and profits should not, absent special facts, trigger liability under §531.[27]

5. Relation of tax-avoidance purpose to reasonable needs of the business. Sections 531 and 532, which impose the tax on corporations formed or availed of for the forbidden purpose, must be considered in conjunction with §533(a), relating to accumulations beyond the reasonable needs of the business, and §533(b), relating to mere holding or investment companies. But §533 is a mere procedural buttress to §532(a); the latter is the basic operative provision of the statute. The ultimate question, in other words, is not whether the corporation had business needs for the accumulation but whether it was formed or availed of for the prohibited purpose.

Many cases, however, have been presented and decided as if an accumulation necessarily stems *either* from a purpose to provide for the reasonable needs of the business *or* from a purpose to reduce shareholders' taxes. This false dichotomy probably arises from §533(a), which provides that the fact that earnings are permitted to accumulate beyond the reasonable needs of the business shall be determinative of the purpose to avoid shareholder income taxes unless the corporation proves to the contrary by a preponderance of the evidence. By virtue of this provision, most of the cases have been won or lost on the battleground of reasonable business needs.

Thus, where business needs for the accumulation have been established, the government has ordinarily conceded or suffered defeat, despite the theoretical possibility that the accumulation was in fact motivated by a tax-avoidance purpose rather than by business needs.[28] Conversely, when an accumula-

---

[27] Note, however, the consent dividend procedure of §§561 and 565 (infra ¶ 8.09), avoiding the necessity of an actual distribution. A self-imposed restriction (e.g., a freezing of surplus by the distribution of a tax-free stock dividend) should not serve as an excuse in a §531 case; see infra ¶ 8.05; R.L. Blaffer & Co., 37 BTA 851 (1938), aff'd, 103 F2d 487 (5th Cir.), cert. denied, 308 US 576, reh'g denied, 308 US 635 (1939) (statutory prohibition against distribution of dividends did not justify an investment company's accumulation); Trico Secs. Corp., 41 BTA 306 (1940) (nonacq.) (loan agreement restriction); Stevenson v. US, supra note 15.

[28] See R. Gsell & Co. v. CIR, supra note 15, to the effect that a finding of business needs "amounts to a finding favorable to the taxpayer on the most persuasive fact, which would show that the corporation was not availed of for the purpose of preventing the imposition of a surtax upon its shareholders"; see also, to the same effect, Electric Regulator Corp. v. CIR, 336 F2d 339 (2d Cir. 1964).

The theoretical, and never very substantial, possibility that the accumulation in such cases was in fact motivated by a tax-avoidance purpose is diminished still further by §535(c)(1), which provides a credit in computing the §531 tax for such cur-

tion is found to be unreasonable, taxpayers can rarely rebut the inference that tax avoidance motivated the accumulation, especially since the Supreme Court held in *US v. Donruss Co.* that tax avoidance need be only one of the purposes, not the sole or dominating purpose, for the accumulation.[29]

¶ 8.03 REASONABLE NEEDS OF THE BUSINESS: IN GENERAL

As stated above, although a corporation is subject to the penalty tax only if formed or availed of for a tax-avoidance purpose, the issue that is by far the most important question and the one that is ordinarily most bitterly contested is whether a corporation's earnings have accumulated beyond the reasonable needs of the business. Resolution of this issue is critical not only because §533(a) provides that such an accumulation is determinative of the proscribed purpose (unless the corporation, by the preponderance of the evidence, proves to the contrary), but also because the accumulated earnings credit used in computing the tax under §535(c) grants the taxpayer an allowance for current earnings retained for the corporation's business needs.[30]

Before turning to the specific items that may constitute business needs for an accumulation, two preliminary points should be mentioned. First, the courts frequently state that the existence of reasonable business needs is a matter for the officers and directors of the corporation to decide, and that courts should hesitate to substitute their judgments and attribute a tax-avoidance motive unless the facts and circumstances clearly warrant the conclusion that the accumulation was unreasonable in amount and was retained for the prohibited purpose.[31] Second, in determining whether current earn-

---

rent earnings as are retained for business needs (infra ¶ 8.09); although this language does not explicitly exclude a government claim that current earnings were retained for tax avoidance rather than to meet a business need, it was held in John P. Scripps Newspapers, 44 TC 453 (1965), that a showing of business needs made it unnecessary to consider whether the corporation was availed of for the forbidden purpose. See also Vuono-Lione, Inc., supra note 23; Freedom Newspapers, Inc., ¶ 65,248 P-H Memo. TC (1965); Magic Mart, Inc., 51 TC 775 (1969) (acq.); American Trading & Prod. Corp. v. US, supra note 26 (relation between tax-avoidance purpose and reasonable needs of business); Snow Mfg. Co., supra note 23 (relation of business needs to net liquid assets and accumulated earnings).

[29] US v. Donruss Co., supra note 18; see also Ted Bates & Co., supra note 21; I.A. Dress Co. v. CIR, 273 F2d 543 (2d Cir.), cert. denied, 362 US 976 (1960); Bremerton Sun Publishing Co., supra note 16 (burden carried by taxpayer); Duke Laboratories, Inc. v US, supra note 16 (same in jury case).

[30] See infra ¶ 8.09, text at note 98.

[31] See, e.g., Thompson Eng'g Co. v. CIR, supra note 23 at 672–704, and cases there cited.

ings were accumulated for reasonable business purposes, the regulations and most courts require a determination of whether *prior* accumulations were, in fact, already sufficient to meet the taxpayer's current needs.[32] In making this determination, it is necessary to examine the character of the corporate assets, since earnings used for the expansion of business plant and equipment, inventories, or accounts receivable cannot be readily distributed to the shareholders, no matter how large the earned surplus may be.[33] The business needs issue, therefore, invites a thorough analysis of the corporation's business and financial status, including (1) its balance sheet position (i.e., the size, character, and relationship of its various asset, liability, and surplus accounts); (2) its profit and loss statements; (3) its liquidity and cash flow positions; (4) its working capital needs and operating cycle; (5) the type of business; (6) the economic conditions prevailing in the taxpayer's business; and (7) any other relevant facts (e.g., technology, abnormal industry risks, industry cycles). In addition, it is usually necessary to go behind the formal books and records of the taxpayer to its contracts, correspondence, and business policies in preparing a defense based on reasonable business needs. Accountants, business analysts, investments bankers, and loan officers are often used as expert witnesses to present this type of evidence.[34]

The following specific grounds, most frequently encountered in business needs cases, are listed in Regs. §1.537-2(b).

1. Bona fide expansion of business or replacement of plant. These are probably the most commonly asserted grounds for accumulating earnings and profits. The decisions are clear that financing replacements and expansion by reinvesting retained earnings, rather than by selling additional stock or borrowing, does not give rise to an adverse inference.[35] If earnings are immediately translated into an expansion of the taxpayer's business or replacement of its plant and equipment, the accumulation will not ordinarily be challenged by the government. However, as is more often the case, when actual expenditures will not be necessary until some time in the future, the Service may claim that current accumulations for these purposes are not

---

[32] Regs. §1.535-3(b)(1)(ii).

[33] See Smoot Sand & Gravel Corp. v. CIR, supra note 17; Electric Regulator Corp. v CIR, supra note 28; John P. Scripps Newspapers, supra note 28; Snow Mfg. Co., supra note 23.

[34] See generally Case, Accumulated Earnings Tax Aspects of Business Expansion and Investments, 32 Tax L. Rev. 1 (1976), for an exhaustive analysis of this area.

[35] See, e.g., Faber Cement Block Co., 50 TC 317 (1968); John P. Scripps Newspapers, supra note 28; Electric Regulator Corp. v. CIR, supra note 28; Duke Laboratories, Inc. v. US, supra note 16; Simons-Eastern Co. v. US, supra note 15. But see infra ¶ 8.05.

justified. This problem is complicated by §537 (enacted in 1954), which provides that the phrase "reasonable needs of the business" includes reasonably anticipated needs.[36]

Several decisions have considered the relationship between depreciation reserves and accumulations of surplus to finance replacement of plant and equipment. Since depreciation deductions are current charges against earnings, an additional reserve for the purpose of replacing plant or equipment will have to be justified by proof of the inadequacy of the taxpayer's depreciation reserves (e.g., because replacement costs will exceed the reserves). Otherwise, there would be, in effect, a double accumulation for replacing the same equipment or plant.[37]

Another difficult problem is the determination of whether earnings are being accumulated to expand or diversify "the" business of the taxpayer, or, instead, are being diverted to an unrelated business or investment purpose.[38]

2. Acquisition of a business enterprise through purchasing stock or assets. This ground for an accumulation is stated without qualification by Regs. §1.537-2(b)(2) so as to suggest that diversification, however unrelated to the taxpayer's existing line of business, will constitute a reasonable business need.[39]

3. Retirement of bona fide business indebtedness. An accumulation for the purpose of retiring bona fide business indebtedness (especially debt held by nonstockholder creditors) has long been recognized as a reasonable business need. Debt held by shareholders, on the other hand, may be another matter; some courts have exhibited less tolerance for accumulations to retire this type of obligation.[40] To the extent that shareholder-held indebtedness qualifies, this is yet another inducement to the use of thin corporations.[41]

---

[36] Infra ¶ 8.04.

[37] See Smoot Sand & Gravel Corp. v. CIR, supra note 17; Henry Van Hummell, Inc., supra note 26; see also Ted Bates & Co., supra note 21, which extends this principle to promotional expenses normally deducted by the taxpayer as incurred; Rev. Rul. 67-64, 1967-1 CB 150 (corporation cannot include a fund equal to its depreciation reserves, escalated for the increased replacement costs, in the reasonable needs of its business).

[38] See infra ¶ 8.06 for discussion.

[39] Id.

[40] See, e.g., Smoot Sand & Gravel Corp. v. CIR, supra note 17. See also the caveat infra ¶ 8.05.

[41] See ¶ 4.02.

4. Working capital for inventories. This ground for accumulating earnings, often associated with business expansion, is concerned with a revolving fund of liquid assets to finance the recurring operations of a business during its typical operating cycle. If relied on, this justification for accumulating earnings must be supported by an analysis of the corporation's cash flow, which in turn is a function of operating expenses, cost of goods sold, inventory size, rate of inventory turnover, credit policies, accounts receivable, collection rates, availability of credit, and other relevant matters.[42]

The operating cycle test, first enunciated by the Tax Court in the *Bardahl* case in 1965 and refined by later decisions, permits accumulations of current earnings to cover reasonably anticipated costs of operating a business for a single operating cycle.[43] This cycle may be described as the time needed to convert cash into raw materials, raw materials into finished goods, inventory into sales and accounts receivable, and any accounts receivable

---

[42] See Smoot Sand & Gravel Corp. v. CIR, 241 F2d 197 (4th Cir. 1957), cert. denied, 354 US 922 (1957), reh'g denied, 354 US 943 (1957); John P. Scripps Newspapers, supra note 28; Sandy Estate Co., supra note 24; Bardahl Mfg. Corp., supra note 23; Vuono-Lione, Inc., supra note 23; Henry Van Hummell, Inc., supra note 26; Apollo Indus., Inc., supra note 15; R. Gsell & Co. v. CIR, supra note 15; The Kirlin Co., ¶ 64,260 P-H Memo. TC (1964), aff'd per curiam, 361 F2d 818 (6th Cir. 1966); Ted Bates & Co., supra note 21; Sears Oil Co. v. CIR, 359 F2d 191 (2d Cir. 1966) (need to analyze inventory requirements of business); Oman Constr. Co., ¶ 65,325 P-H Memo. TC (1965) (accumulation reasonable to cover working capital needs, business risks); Faber Cement Block Co., supra note 35 (expansion, working capital needs, reinvested earnings financing allowable; held no §531 tax); Magic Mart, Inc., supra note 28 (accumulation reasonable for (1) working capital needs determined by operating cycle test, (3) future expansion since plans were sufficiently real, (4) possible flood damage reserve; since accumulation reasonable, intent immaterial because of §535(c)(1) credit).

[43] See Bardahl Mfg. Corp., supra note 23; Bardahl Int'l Corp., ¶ 66,182 P-H Memo. TC (1966); Snow Mfg. Co., supra note 23; James H. Rutter, ¶ 86,407 P-H Memo. TC (1986) (extensive computations with formula); Apollo Indus., Inc. v. CIR, supra note 15; Faber Cement Block Co., supra note 35; Magic Mart, Inc., supra note 28; Doug-Long, Inc., 72 TC 158 (1979) (estimated tax payments count as current expense); Grob, Inc. v. US, 565 F. Supp. 391 (E.D. Wis. 1983) (general application of *Bardahl*; use of peak operating cycle, inflation factor, estimated tax needs, and product liability self-insurance reserve).

Even the earnings of service corporations whose inventories are the skills of highly trained employees have been measured by the operating cycle standard (e.g., Simons-Eastern Co. v. US, supra note 15 (engineering and architectural firm)); C.E. Hooper, Inc. v. US, 539 F2d 1276 (Ct. Cl. 1976) (market research and radio survey); Central Motor Co. v. US, 538 F2d 470 (10th Cir. 1978) (finance companies and auto rental companies). But cf. EMI Corp., ¶ 85,386 P-H Memo. TC (1985) (no recurring business cycle).

See generally Libin, Accumulations After *Bardahl:* Developments Affecting the Accumulated Earnings Tax, 30 NYU Inst. on Fed. Tax'n 1143 (1972); Livsey, A Proposed Operating Cycle Test for Sec. 531 Working Capital Accumulations, 46 Taxes 648 (1968); Ziegler, supra note 5.

into cash. Under *Bardahl*, the length of the period is determined by three components: (1) the production cycle, or average inventory turnover period, computed by dividing the annual cost of goods sold for the year into the peak period (or average) inventory; (2) the collection cycle, or average accounts receivable turnover period, computed by dividing the annual sales for the year into the peak period (or average) accounts receivable; and (3) the credit cycle, or average accounts payable turnover period, computed by dividing annual purchases into average (or peak period) accounts payable. Each of these calculations yields a decimal figure representing part of a year; the first two are then added together and the third subtracted, the result being the average length of the operating cycle expressed as a decimal part of a year. This figure is then multiplied by the corporation's cost of goods sold and its operating expenses (excluding noncash expenses—such as depreciation—and federal income taxes) for the year in question, and the result is the amount of cash theoretically needed to cover the reasonably anticipated costs of operating the business for a single operating cycle.

Despite the impression of mathematical precision conveyed by the operating cycle test, its exactitude is largely illusory, and many difficult questions exist as to its scope and application.[44] For example, "net liquid assets" as used in *Bardahl* includes inventory and accounts receivable, items that are hardly liquid enough to support dividend distributions. However, the Second Circuit, in *Electric Regulator*, apparently viewed this term in the technical sense of quick assets.[45] Another debatable issue is whether the averages of prior years or only the year at issue should be used in computing the length of the operating cycle. Some commentators have even suggested that averages for the following year should be estimated and used, since that is the year for which working capital is required. The Tax Court has typically looked to the taxpayer's *peak* rather than average operating cycle needs on the ground that a business ought to be able to make provision for the heaviest demands on its funds.[46] Despite

---

[44] See generally Delaware Trucking Co., ¶ 73,029 P-H Memo. TC (1973) (*Bardahl* rule not to be rigidly applied); James H. Rutter, note 43; Dielectric Materials Corp., 57 TC 587 (1972) (acq.) (accumulated earnings tax not imposed on corporation that accumulated approximately $21,000 more than amount determined by application of the *Bardahl* formula; formula only an approximate guideline, so substantial compliance is adequate). See also Cheyenne Newspapers, Inc. v. CIR, 494 F2d 429 (10th Cir. 1974); Ready Paving & Constr. Co., 61 TC 826 (1974) (marketable warrants received as payment for work performed considered current liquid assets available for payment of dividends); Thompson Eng'g Corp. v. CIR, supra note 23 (only a guide, not a general rule); see also the service corporation cases, supra note 43; Snow Mfg. Co., supra note 23.

[45] Electric Regulator Corp. v. CIR, supra note 28.

[46] See Bardahl Int'l Corp., supra note 43; Magic Mart, Inc., supra note 28;

these difficulties, which are increased by changes in the level and nature of the taxpayer's business operations, the *Bardahl* formula is a useful guide to the determination of a ballpark figure for working capital needs.

5. Investments in and loans to suppliers or customers. The regulations state that investments in or loans to suppliers or customers, if necessary to maintain the business of the corporation, are reasonable business needs. Such investments and loans have not played an important role in the litigated cases, but in a few industries it may be essential to accumulate earnings for this purpose.

6. Other grounds for accumulations. The list of grounds for accumulation mentioned in Regs. §1.537-2(b) is expressly stated to be nonexclusive. Accumulations may be justified by a range of business needs as diversified as the character of modern business itself. Among the reasons for accumulating earnings that have received a sympathetic judicial response (although the taxpayer was not always successful in establishing that its accumulation was in fact so motivated) are the following: the need to meet competition; the need to fund pension or profit-sharing plans for employees; reserves for various business risks and contingencies such as self-insurance against casualties, potential liability from litigation, and unsettled industrial conditions, including threatened strikes or fear of depression; possible loss of a principal customer and need to move a plant to new location; self-insurance for key personnel; and special surety bonding needs in the taxpayer's business.[47] This list was augmented by

---

James H. Rutter, supra note 43; Kingsbury Inv., Inc., ¶ 69,205 P-H Memo. TC (1969); Alma Piston Co., 579 F2d 1000 (6th Cir. 1978); Doug-Long, Inc., supra note 43 (peak needs); Grob, Inc. v. US, supra note 43 (same); Central Motor Co. v. US, supra note 43; Snow Mfg. Co., supra note 23 (credit cycle; nontrade payables considered).

[47] See John P. Scripps Newspapers, supra note 28 (meeting competition); Bremerton Sun Publishing Co., supra note 16 (pension plan); Smoot Sand & Gravel Corp. v. CIR, supra note 17 (reserves against risks); Magic Mart, Inc., supra note 28 (flood damage reserve); Casey v. CIR, supra note 16 (litigation), Steelmasters Inc., ¶ 76,324 P-H Memo. TC (1976) (trademark litigation); Smokeless Fuel Co., ¶ 43,425 P-H Memo. TC (1943) (acq.) (threat of strikes); L.R. Teeple Co., 47 BTA 270 (1942) (loss of major customer; relocation); Bradford-Robinson Printing Co. v. US, 1 AFTR2d 1278 (D. Colo. 1957) (self-insurance); Simons-Eastern Co. v. US, supra note 15 (bonus plan; deductible portion of employees' personal liability insurance); Vuono-Lione, Inc., supra note 23 (surety bond requirements); Thompson Eng'g Co. v. CIR, supra note 23 (construction company's bonding needs); Rev. Rul. 70-301, 1970-1 CB 138 (satisfaction of proposed §531 tax deficiency); Alma Piston Co., supra note 46 (asserted tax deficiency).

the enactment in 1979 of §537(b)(4), sanctioning accumulations for the payment of reasonably anticipated product liability losses (as defined), pursuant to regulations to be issued by the Treasury.[48]

After listing some of the grounds that may constitute reasonable business needs, the regulations go on to list some indications that earnings are being accumulated beyond the reasonable needs of the business. Among those indications are (1) loans to shareholders and the expenditure of corporate funds for the personal benefit of shareholders; (2) loans to relatives or friends of shareholders, or to other persons if the loans have no reasonable relation to the conduct of its business; (3) loans to another corporation, the business of which is not that of the taxpayer corporation, if both corporations are under common control; (4) investments in properties or securities that are unrelated to the corporation's business;[49] and (5) retention of earnings to provide against "unrealistic hazards."[50] It should be noted that the foregoing transactions are not necessarily inconsistent with an accumulation for business needs, nor do they establish that the corporation's purpose is to shield shareholders against the individual income tax. Thus, funds that will be required for working capital or expansion might properly be temporarily invested in marketable securities or lent to shareholders. Such transactions serve as signals to the government, however, and may bring on a searching inquiry as to the corporation's reasons for accumulating its earnings.[51]

For the application of §531 to professional service organizations, see Earnest Booth, M.D., P.C., ¶ 82,423 P-H Memo. TC (1982) (rejecting claims that accumulation was warranted to meet malpractice liability in excess of insurance limits and that corporation needed to prepare for possible termination of contract with hospital); Brumer, Moss & Cohen, P.A. v. US, 37 AFTR2d 802 (S.D. Fla. 1975) (incorporated law firm found by jury to have retained one year's earnings for reasonable needs, but §531 tax imposed on amount accumulated in following year).

For more comprehensive compilations, see supra note 5; on accumulations to redeem stock, see infra ¶ 8.07.

[48] For such an allowance despite the absence of regulations, see Grob, Inc. v. CIR, supra note 43; see also Regs. §1.537-1(f); EMI Corp., supra note 43.

[49] On defining "the" business of the corporation, see infra ¶ 8.06.

[50] Regs. §1.537-2(c). The unreasonableness of such an accumulation is self-evident; the more interesting and relevant question is whether it negates rather than establishes the tax-avoidance purpose required by §531. See supra ¶ 8.02; T. C. Heyward & Co. v. US, supra note 16; Estate of Goodall v. CIR, 391 F2d 775 (8th Cir.), cert. denied, 393 US 829 (1968); Cataphote Corp. of Miss. v. US, supra note 23; Case, supra note 34.

[51] If a corporation accumulates earnings beyond the reasonable needs of the business, its portfolio securities of other corporations are valued at current net liquidation value, not historical cost. Ivan Allen Co. v. US, 422 US 617 (1975) (three dissents).

¶ 8.04   REASONABLE NEEDS OF THE BUSINESS: ANTICIPATED NEEDS

Section 537, providing that the term "reasonable needs of the business" includes "the reasonably anticipated needs of the business," was enacted in 1954. The Senate Report on the 1954 Code states that

> it is intended that this provision will make clear that there is no requirement that the accumulated earnings and profits be invested immediately in the business so long as there is an indication that future needs of the business require such accumulation. In any case where there exists a definite plan for the investment of earnings and profits, such corporation need not necessarily consummate these plans in a relatively short period after the close of the taxable year. However, where the future needs of the business are uncertain or vague, or the plans for the future use of accumulations are indefinite, the amendment does not prevent application of the accumulated earnings tax.[52]

The Senate Report goes on to state that §537 will eliminate "the so-called [pre-1954] immediacy test, under which there must be an immediate need for the funds in order to justify the retention of earnings." Section 537, however, is not inconsistent with the theory of an important pre-1954 case, *World Publishing Co. v. US*, holding that the reasonableness of an accumulation for expenditures that cannot be made until a later year is dependent, in part, on whether the corporation is likely to enjoy substantial earnings during the waiting period.[53]

The regulations state that the corporation's plans, in order to constitute a reasonably anticipated business need, must be specific, definite, and feasible. As a practical aid to demonstrating the concreteness of such plans, book entries (e.g., specific reserve accounts) may be helpful, although courts have been quick to note that they are not controlling.[54] Where the future business

---

[52] S. Rep. No. 1622, supra note 25, at 318.

[53] World Publishing Co. v. US, 169 F2d 186 (10th Cir. 1948), cert. denied, 335 US 911 (1949), reh'g denied, 336 US 915 (1949); KOMA, Inc. v. CIR, 189 F2d 390 (10th Cir. 1951); see also Frank H. Ayres & Son, ¶ 54,278 P-H Memo. TC (1954); according to the court,

> '[I]mmediate need' is a label used in cases where there was an unreasonable accumulation of earnings either because the need or plan of the corporation was so vague, tentative or indefinite that it did not justify the accumulation or ... for some reason the contemplated expenditures could not be made during the period under review or in the ascertainable future.

[54] See Regs. §1.537-1(b); Smoot Sand & Gravel Corp. v. CIR, supra note 42; Ted Bates & Co., supra note 21; Faber Cement Block Co., supra note 35; Motor Fuel Carriers, Inc. v. CIR, 559 F2d 1348 (5th Cir. 1977) (plans for expansion sufficiently definite, specific, and feasible; lack of dividends not fatal if good reason to accumu-

needs are uncertain or vague, or the plans for future use of an accumulation are inchoate and nebulous, suggesting an afterthought on the part of the taxpayer, the tax has ordinarily been imposed, since the needs for the accumulation were not reasonably anticipated.[55] The regulations provide that subsequent events will not vitiate an accumulation if all the elements of reasonable anticipation are present at the close of the accumulation year.[56] Thus, it has been held that current accumulations for future needs were reasonable when made, even though the plans were abandoned at a later date or a long delay was justified.[57] But an unexplained delay in carrying out the plans or an indefinite postponement may be considered in determining whether the taxpayer actually intended to carry out its alleged plans. The regulations also state that failure to consummate the plans may be considered in determining the reasonableness of *subsequent* accumulations.[58]

The general rule of §537(a) is buttressed by four special rules of §537(b), sanctioning the accumulation of amounts needed or reasonably anticipated as needed for (1) the redemption of stock under §303, relating to redemptions from a decedent's estate to pay estate taxes, etc. (2) redemptions of so-called excess business holdings, involving stock held by certain private foundations; (3) the discharge of obligations to make either of the foregoing types of redemptions; and (4) the payment of product liability losses as defined by §172(j) and by regulations.

---

late, as here); Chaney & Hope, Inc., 80 TC 263 (1983) (future needs definite; accumulation for purpose of meeting expected needs of pending merger).

[55] See Snow Mfg. Co., supra note 23 ("specificity requirements were written into the regulations because a loosely run corporation presents a high potential for post hoc, unsupported rationalizations for the prohibited hoarding of profits"); American Metal Prods. Corp. v. CIR, 287 F2d 860 (8th Cir. 1961); I.A. Dress Co. v. CIR, supra note 29; Dixie, Inc. v. CIR, 277 F2d 526 (2d Cir.), cert. denied, 364 US 827 (1960); Barrow Mfg. Co. v. CIR, 294 F2d 79 (5th Cir. 1961), cert. denied, 369 US 817 (1962); Bahan Textile Mach. Co. v. US, 453 F2d 1100 (4th Cir. 1972) (plans vague and indefinite); Cheyenne Newspapers, Inc. v. CIR, supra note 44 (plans too indefinite); Hardin v. US, 461 F2d 865 (5th Cir. 1972), citing Smoot Sand & Gravel, supra note 42 ("bare possibilities do not amount to reasonable business needs"). Compare Myron's Ballroom v. US, supra note 17 (plans sufficiently definite).

[56] Regs. §1.537-1(b)(2).

[57] See Sterling Distribs., Inc. v. US, supra note 23; Carolina Rubber Hose Co., supra note 21; Myron's Ballroom, supra note 17.

[58] Regs. §1.537-1(b)(2); see also Faber Cement Block Co., supra note 35 (no formal blueprints for action needed as long as expansion a real expectation and not a mere afterthought); Novelart Mfg. Co., 52 TC 794 (1969), aff'd, 434 F2d 1011 (6th Cir. 1970), cert. denied, 403 US 918 (1971) (acquisition plans vague and indefinite; accumulation unreasonable); Magic Mart, Inc., supra note 28 (expansion plans sufficiently real); Vulcan Steam Forging Co., ¶ 76,029 P-H Memo. TC (1976) (actions pursuant to plans for relocation justified accumulations for three years but not for fourth); Herzog Miniature Lamp Works, Inc. v. CIR, 481 F2d 857 (2d Cir. 1973) (no convincing evidence of taxpayer's intent to automate); Motor Fuel Carriers v. CIR, supra note 54.

¶ 8.05   REASONABLE NEEDS OF THE BUSINESS: METHODS OF FINANCING

The reasonable needs of the business can be satisfied, in many cases, either with equity capital or with borrowed funds. Despite this fact, the cases under §533 have almost invariably assumed that working capital, replacement of plant, and expansion will be financed in full with retained earnings and not with borrowed funds. Similarly, it has usually been assumed that funds to pay off indebtedness at maturity, or perhaps even earlier, constitute a business need, even though the debt might be refinanced. In *Helvering v. Chicago Stock Yards Co.*, however, the Supreme Court suggested that an accumulation to pay off debt that could be refinanced might be unreasonable.[59] If so, debt held pro rata by stockholders would seem to be especially vulnerable.[60]

Even if an accumulation to pay off corporate indebtedness or to purchase property without resorting to borrowing is found to be beyond the reasonable needs of the business, thus bringing §533(a) into play, the corporation might still rebut the existence of a tax-avoidance purpose by showing that the directors' excessive caution or childhood training in thrift was the sole motivation for the accumulation. Such a defense is easily advanced but less easily proved, however, so the status of equity financing under §533(a) remains exceedingly important.

A related problem arises from the fact that earnings do not necessarily have to be retained by a corporation with business needs for funds, since it could pay a dividend and the stockholders could reinvest the amounts thus received by them. This possibility was suggested in the *Chicago Stock Yards Co.* case;[61] but the suggestion has not been picked up for use in later cases for the reason that, rigorously applied, it would always prevent the use of retained earnings for business needs in circumstances where the shareholder's after-tax receipts would be sufficient to meet them if reinvested.[62]

---

[59] Helvering v. Chicago Stock Yards Co., 318 US 693 (1943).

[60] Cases assuming or holding that business needs may be properly financed by retained earnings rather than with outside funds include Duke Laboratories, Inc. v. US, supra note 16; Electric Regulator Corp. v. CIR, supra note 28; John P. Scripps Newspapers, supra note 28; Gazette Tel. Co. v. CIR, 19 TC 692 (1953) (acq.), aff'd, 209 F2d 926 (10th Cir. 1954); Faber Cement Block Co., supra note 35; Adolph Coors Co., ¶ 68,256 P-H Memo. TC (1968). But see Nemours Corp., 38 TC 585 (1962), aff'd, 325 F2d 559 (3d Cir. 1963) (future acquisitions could be financed by borrowing); Smoot Sand & Gravel Corp. v. CIR, supra note 42 (corporation's sole shareholder could have extended time to pay bonds held by him).

[61] Helvering v. Chicago Stock Yards Co., supra note 59, at 701–702.

[62] See discussion in Smoot Sand & Gravel Corp. v. CIR, supra note 42.

The consent dividend procedure of §565 (infra ¶ 8.09) amounts to a constructive distribution coupled with a reinvestment. As a mode of financing business needs, it is open to the same objection as an actual distribution followed by a reinvestment.

One aspect of internal financing that bears special note is the effect of stock dividends. Under §312(d), the distribution of a nontaxable stock dividend has no effect on earnings and profits. Hence, the fact that surplus has been capitalized by a stock dividend should not be relevant in determining whether earnings have been unreasonably accumulated for purposes of the §531 tax.[63]

¶ 8.06   REASONABLE NEEDS OF THE BUSINESS: WHAT IS "THE" BUSINESS?

Section 533(a) speaks of the reasonable needs of "the" business, and the regulations contain the sweeping statement that the business of a corporation "is not merely that which it has previously carried on but includes, in general, any line of business which it may undertake."[64] This statement, as well as the cases, validates an accumulation of earnings and profits to finance natural growth, including both vertical and horizontal integration.[65] If a single corporation is engaged in two entirely separate businesses, their needs can probably be considered in the aggregate, so that the earnings of one enterprise may be accumulated to feed the other. This seems to follow a fortiori from cases allowing a corporation to accumulate earnings to finance a subsidiary engaged in an unrelated business.[66]

The reference in the regulations to "any line of business which [the corporation] may undertake" seems to endorse an accumulation to finance any business that the corporate charter permits it to enter, a sweeping suggestion in these days of omnibus charters, relaxed charter amendment rules, and

---

[63] E-Z Sew Enters., Inc. v. US, 260 F. Supp. 100 (E.D. Mich. 1966) (stock dividends have no effect on earnings and profits for §531 tax purposes); accord Atlantic Commerce & Shipping Co. v. CIR, 500 F2d 937 (2d Cir. 1974); Rev. Rul. 65-68, 1965-1 CB 246.

[64] Regs. §1.537-3(a).

[65] See, e.g., Ted Bates & Co., supra note 21 (extension of business operations to Europe); Metal Office Furniture Co., ¶ 52,313 P-H Memo. TC (1952) (new line of merchandise); Lion Clothing Co., 8 TC 1181 (1947) (acq.) (department store buying out leased department); Defiance Lumber Co., ¶ 53,246 P-H Memo. TC (1953) (lumber manufacturer buying retail outlet); Smoot Sand & Gravel Corp. v. CIR, supra note 42 (possible entrance into ready-mix concrete business by sand and gravel company; however, in later proceedings cited supra note 17, this proposal was found not to be a reasonable possibility); Freedom Newspapers, Inc., supra note 28 (accumulation to build up newspaper chain); Lane Drug Co., ¶ 44,131 P-H Memo. TC (1944) (retail drug chain).

[66] See Sandy Estate Co., supra note 24 (one corporation, two businesses); Lannom Mfg. Co., ¶ 52,043 P-H Memo. TC (1952); see also Latchis Theatres of Keene, Inc. v. CIR, 214 F2d 834 (1st Cir. 1954).

conglomerate acquisitions. Moreover, the regulations also state that an accumulation "to acquire a business enterprise through purchasing stock or assets" is permissible.[67] To test these broad statements, let us assume that a corporation engaged in publishing a newspaper in New York City accumulates its earnings and profits primarily for the purpose of acquiring a cement factory in Colorado. If we take at face value the reference to "any line of business which [the corporation] may undertake," the accumulation is within the corporation's business needs and cannot be regarded as an investment in properties unrelated to the activities of the business.[68] The statutory presumption of §533(a) would then be inapplicable. Without relying on §533(a), however, the government might argue that the radical change in the character of the corporation's activities was evidence of a purpose to avoid tax on its shareholders. If on all the evidence the tax was applicable, the accumulated earnings credit of §535(c)(1) would immunize the accumulation to the extent that it was required to purchase the cement factory, but any excess would be subject to the penalty tax.

Although the regulations do not bring the distinction to the fore, it seems essential that "business" be differentiated from "investment" in determining if an accumulation is beyond the reasonable needs of "the" business. If our New York City newspaper publisher accumulated its earnings and profits in order to purchase oil royalties or mining claims, intending to hold them as investments, §533(a) would presumably be brought into play just as it would by an accumulation to purchase marketable securities or to increase idle cash balances. As to an accumulation to acquire rental real estate (e.g., apartment houses), the relevant line may be that drawn under §355 between rental property held for investment and that held as part of an active conduct of a trade or business.[69] Although §533(a) does not speak of active conduct of the business, as does §355, this concept seems implicit in the statutory purpose.[70]

What if a corporation accumulates its earnings and profits for investment in another corporation (in the form of a contribution to capital, a purchase of stock, or a loan evidenced by securities or on open account)? According to the regulations, the business of the second corporation "may

---

[67] Regs. §§1.537-2(b)(2) and 1.537-3(a). For a less tolerant earlier version, see Regs. §118, §39.102-3(b) ("radical change of business . . . may afford evidence" of tax-avoidance purpose).

[68] Regs §1.537-2(c)(4).

[69] Infra ¶ 13.04.

[70] See Henry Van Hummell, Inc., supra note 26; Kerr-Cochran, Inc. v. CIR, 253 F2d 121 (8th Cir. 1958); Jacob Sincoff, Inc. v. CIR, 20 TC 288, 292, aff'd, 209 F2d 569 (2d Cir. 1953); Smith, Inc. v. CIR, supra note 24; Atlantic Commerce & Shipping Co. v. CIR, supra note 63 (real estate business only a passive investment).

be considered in substance, although not in legal form, the business of the first corporation," if the second corporation is "a mere instrumentality" of the first.[71] This relationship may be established, according to the regulations, if the first corporation owns at least 80 percent of the second corporation's voting stock. If less than this amount is owned, the particular circumstances of the case will determine whether the first corporation is accumulating for a business of its own or not. The 80 percent benchmark is not to be found in the Code; it derives from a congressional committee report on the 1954 Code, where it is expressed as the opinion of the committee.[72] The regulations also echo the 1954 committee reports in stating that the first corporation's business does not include the business of a second corporation if the latter is a personal holding company, an investment company, or a corporation not engaged in the active conduct of a trade or business. Although the subsidiary may thus be regarded as an extension of the parent corporation in some circumstances, presumably the parent may accumulate to finance the subsidiary's activities only if the subsidiary's own resources are insufficient.[73]

The regulations focus on accumulations by parent corporations for the business needs of their subsidiaries and say nothing about the propriety of an accumulation by brother-sister corporations to meet each other's needs. Regs. §1.537-2(c)(3) states that loans to another corporation under common control with the taxpayer may evidence an unreasonable accumulation if the business of the borrowing corporation "is not that of the taxpayer corporation."[74]

---

[71] Regs. §1.537-3(b).

[72] H.R. Rep. No. 1337, 83d Cong., 2d Sess. 53 (1954); see also S. Rep. No. 1622, supra note 25, at 70.

[73] See Olin Corp. v. CIR, 42 BTA 1203, 1216 (1940), aff'd, 128 F2d 185 (7th Cir. 1942); Automotive Rebuilding Co., ¶ 58,197 P-H Memo. TC (1958); Meads Bakery, Inc. v. CIR, 364 F2d 101 (5th Cir. 1966) (advances to subsidiary did not cause accumulations to become unreasonable; taxpayer's plans for expansion and improvement satisfied anticipated needs test); see also Inland Terminals, Inc. v. US, supra note 9 (although regulation refers only to downstream investments, same principle authorizes subsidiary to accumulate to assist parent).

[74] See also Chaney & Hope, Inc., supra note 54, at 283 (1983) (accumulation for needs of sister corporation not reasonable), and cases there cited; Fine Realty, Inc. v. US, 209 F. Supp. 286 (D. Minn. 1962) (multiple real estate development corporations); John P. Scripps Newspapers, supra note 28; Bremerton Sun Publishing Co., supra note 16 (loans to sister corporations engaged in the same line of business as the taxpayer did not constitute unrelated investments).

See generally Harris et al., Improper Accumulation of Surplus and Personal Holding Companies: A Functional Presentation, 24 NYU Inst. on Fed. Tax'n 927, 950–958 (1966).

¶ 8.07   REASONABLE NEEDS OF THE BUSINESS: STOCK REDEMPTIONS

Sections 537(b)(1) through 537(b)(3) provide that the term "reasonable needs of the business" includes accumulations needed or reasonably anticipated to be needed to redeem the corporation's stock under §303 (relating to redemptions from a decedent's estate to pay death taxes, administration expenses, and funeral and administration expenses) and to redeem stock constituting so-called excess business holdings in the hands of certain private foundations. The status of redemptions that are not shielded by these special rules is cloudy, however, despite a substantial body of litigated cases.

Since a pro rata redemption of stock from all shareholders is ordinarily taxable as a dividend to the extent of the corporation's earnings and profits,[75] an accumulation of earnings to effect such a redemption is no different from an accumulation of current earnings to pay dividends in later years. Unless the distribution is delayed for an unreasonable period or is designed to give the shareholders the benefit of an anticipated lower effective tax rate when payment is made, the accumulation seems to raise no §531 problem. On the other hand, redemptions that are not pro rata (and even some pro rata redemptions) are treated as sales of the stock, with the result that the shareholder can offset the basis of the stock against the amount realized in computing gain or loss;[76] hence, if earnings are accumulated to effect such a nondividend redemption, the anticipated tax-free recovery of basis may be evidence of a tax-avoidance intent.[77]

A redemption of the stock of one or more shareholders is frequently employed as a method of shifting partial or complete control of the corporation to the remaining shareholders without depleting their personal funds in the process. An accumulation of corporate earnings for this purpose hardly seems to provide for the reasonable needs of the business within the meaning of §533(a); however, there are several cases in which a business nexus was found, usually because the shareholders who were bought out constituted a dissenting minority or because the remaining shareholders were key employees whose increased proprietary interest was regarded as helpful to the corporation's business. Because the importance of the redemption to the corporation's business activities is often tenuous or debatable, while the success of the remaining shareholders in achieving an increase in their propor-

---

[75] See infra ¶ 9.02.

[76] Id.

[77] See GPD, Inc. v. CIR, 508 F2d 1076 (6th Cir. 1974) (pattern of gifts to charities of taxpayer's stock, which was later redeemed, demonstrated prohibited purpose); see also Apollo Indus., Inc., supra note 15 (accumulations not excused by possibility of future tax at capital gain rate).

tional control is ordinarily obvious, other courts have viewed with less tolerance the accumulation of corporate earnings to effect a non-pro rata
redemption. The unsettled state of the law[78] suggests caution in relying on
the pro-taxpayer decisions, especially if the contemplated redemption is not
likely to occur until a distant future date or if it does not involve the elimination of a cantankerous minority shareholder but rather a buyout of a majority shareholder who wishes to liquidate his interest at the capital gain rate.[79]

A redemption seems even more vulnerable if it does not respond to a
clear and present business danger, but it is required by a conventional shareholder agreement to retire the shares of any party thereto upon his death or
retirement. The retention of shares after retirement (or their transfer to a
deceased shareholder's heirs) does not necessarily threaten any harm to the
business. Instead, the dominant motive for such agreements is usually the
desire of active shareholder-employees to keep others from sharing in the
earning capacity of the business and in its management, neither of which
possibilities automatically endangers the business. In a particular case, of
course, a shareholder's death or retirement may create the kind of business

---

[78] See John B. Lambert & Assocs. v. US, 38 AFTR2d 6207 (Ct. Cl. 1976) (per
curiam) (redemption of stock of uncontentious shareholder not justified; wife's stock
redeemed for personal rather than corporate purpose); compare EMI Corp., supra
note 43 (business need for buy-sell redemption plan). For earlier decisions, see Dill
Mfg. Co., 39 BTA 1023 (1939) (nonacq.) (redemption of 49 percent interest justified); Gazette Publishing Co. v. Self, 103 F. Supp. 779 (E.D. Ark. 1952) (same where
25 percent minority threatened sale to outsiders); Pelton Steel Casting Co. v. CIR,
251 F2d 278 (7th Cir.), cert. denied, 356 US 958 (1958) (§531 applied to accumulations to redeem 80 percent interest); Ted Bates & Co., supra note 21 (redemption to
permit sale of stock to key executives; §531 tax held inapplicable); KOMA, Inc. v.
CIR, supra note 53 (stock retired for noncorporate reason); see also Penn Needle Art
Co., ¶ 58,099 P-H Memo. TC (1958) (tax inapplicable where accumulation for other
business purposes was used to redeem stock of 50 percent shareholder to end a serious and unexpected dispute); Hedberg-Freidheim Contracting Co. v. CIR, supra
note 9 (shareholder deadlock; §531 tax upheld); Five Star Mfg. Co. v. CIR, 355 F2d
724 (5th Cir. 1966) (payment for dissenting shareholder's stock deductible as business expense; but see §162(l), added in 1986); Oman Constr. Co., supra note 42
(redemption of minority shareholder stock; valid business purpose under §531). For
the possibility of using a tax-free split-off under §355 to settle a shareholder dispute,
see infra ¶ 13.10.

See generally, Rudolph, Stock Redemptions and the Accumulated Earnings
Tax—An Update, 4 J. Corp. Tax'n 101 (1977); Herwitz, Stock Redemptions and the
Accumulated Earnings Tax, 74 Harv. L. Rev. 866 (1961); Goldstein, Tax Aspects of
Corporate Business Use of Life Insurance, 18 Tax L. Rev. 133, 207 (1963).

[79] See Lamark Shipping Agency, Inc., ¶ 81,284 P-H Memo. TC (1981) ("the fact
that a majority stock interest was redeemed made it unlikely that the redemptions
were motivated by anything other than a desire on the part of the redeeming shareholders to liquidate their interest at capital gain rates . . . [T]he redemption served no
reasonable business purpose, but instead provided proof of the existence of the proscribed purpose").

danger that has led some courts to regard a redemption as a reasonable need of the business; but it is a long step from this possibility to the conclusion that accumulating earnings to eliminate such hypothetical dangers is always responsive to an actual or reasonably anticipated need of the business. Moreover, an *option*, rather than an *obligation*, to retire the shares of retiring or deceased stockholders would usually protect the corporation adequately. It could then accumulate or not, according to its business judgment from time to time; and if insurance policies were procured, the proceeds could be retained or paid out, depending on the circumstances.

Whatever may be the status of the redemption itself, subsequent accumulations to meet business needs (e.g., expansion) are less vulnerable, even though they would not have been necessary if the corporate assets had not been depleted by the redemption. In such a case, the pre-redemption accumulations might have been improper, but the government's failure to attack them does not mean that the post-redemption accumulations exceed the reasonable needs of the business. The status of post-redemption accumulations to pay off a debt incurred to finance the redemption itself is more debatable; if the discharge of such a debt is treated as a bona fide business need, corporations contemplating a redemption could sidestep the risk of a pre-redemption accumulation by redeeming first and accumulating later.[80]

¶ 8.08 PRESUMPTIONS AND BURDEN OF PROOF PROBLEMS

Under procedural principles generally applicable to income tax litigation, the Service's determination of additional tax liability is presumptively correct. The burden of proving the determination wrong by a preponderance of the evidence, together with the corresponding burden of going forward with the evidence, is on the taxpayer. Thus, the taxpayer ordinarily is the moving party in civil tax litigation and bears the risk of nonpersuasion if the evidence is in equipoise.

1. Statutory presumption as to business needs. In addition to this presumption of correctness in favor of the government, §533(a) provides that the fact that earnings are permitted to accumulate beyond the reasonable needs of the business is determinative of the forbidden purpose to avoid shareholder taxes unless the taxpayer corporation proves to the contrary by

---

[80] However, "redeem now, pay later" was upheld as a corporate way of life in Mountain State Steel Foundries, Inc. v. CIR, 284 F2d 737 (4th Cir. 1960).

a preponderance of the evidence.[81] The regulations state that the presumption created by §533(a) adds still more weight to the Service's determination of a §531 tax liability.[82] In practice, this last clear chance to prove that the unreasonable accumulation was not motivated by a desire to avoid shareholder taxes is rarely availed of.[83]

2. Burden of proof in Tax Court cases: Section 534. If a notice of deficiency is based in whole or in part on an allegation that earnings were permitted to accumulate beyond the reasonable needs of the business, §534(a)(1) shifts the burden of proof to the government unless, before the notice of deficiency is mailed to the taxpayer, the corporation is notified that the proposed deficiency includes an accumulated earnings tax. If the corporation is given such a notification, it may, under §534(a)(2), submit a statement of the grounds on which it relies to establish that the accumulation is not beyond the reasonable needs of the business, together with facts sufficient to show the basis thereof. Such a statement shifts back to the government the burden of proof with respect to the grounds set out in the statement. To be effective, however, the taxpayer's §534(a)(2) statement must constitute more than mere notice of an intent to prove the reasonableness of the accumulation. Rather, the taxpayer must show its hand by stating clearly and specifically the grounds on which it will rely to prove reasonable business needs and by setting out the facts (not the evidence, but more than conclusions of law) that, if proven, support the alleged business needs for the accumulation.[84]

Under Rule 142 of its Rules of Practice, the Tax Court ordinarily rules on timely pretrial motions filed pursuant to §534(c). Thus, the taxpayer need not formulate its trial strategy until the burden of proof issue is settled. If the issue is resolved in the taxpayer's favor, the determination may be controlling in computing the accumulated earnings credit of §535(c)(1) as well

---

[81] Supra notes 28 and 29; infra note 98.

[82] Regs. §1.533-1(b).

[83] See supra note 29.

[84] For decisions on the adequacy of the taxpayer's §534 statement, see Bremerton Sun Publishing Co., supra note 16, and cases there cited; Herzog Miniature Lamp Works, Inc. v. CIR, supra note 58 (taxpayer's statement inadequate); Motor Fuel Carriers, Inc. v. CIR, supra note 54 (statement adequate to shift burden); see also James H. Rutter Mfg. Co., 81 TC 937 (1983) (Servic e opportunity for discovery has no effect on scope of facts that must be included in a §534(c) statement to shift burden of proof).

See generally Comment, Accumulated Earnings Tax: Burdens of Proof of Reasonableness and Purpose, 54 Calif. L. Rev. 1050 (1966); Goldfein, Tax Court in Chatham Corp. Clarifies Timing of Shift of Burden in §531 Cases, 27 J. Tax'n 2 (1967).

as under §533(a), although this question has not yet been answered by the courts.[85]

3. Presumption applicable to holding and investment companies. Section 533(b) provides that the fact that a corporation is a mere holding or investment company is prima facie evidence of the purpose to avoid the income tax on its shareholders. The regulations state that a "holding company" is a corporation "having practically no activities except holding property and collecting the income therefrom or investing therein" and that an "investment company" is a corporation whose activities consist substantially of buying and selling stock, securities, real estate, or other investment property "so that the income is derived not only from the investment yield but also from profits upon market fluctuations."[86] As in the case of a business corporation that has accumulated earnings beyond its reasonable needs, a holding or investment company may refute, with appropriate evidence, the inference that its accumulations were motivated by the purpose to avoid tax on its shareholders.

Section 533(b) must be considered in conjunction with §§532(b)(1) and 532(b)(2), exempting personal holding companies (PHCs) and foreign personal holding companies (FPHCs) from the accumulated earnings tax.[87] These exemptions are not animated by charity; rather, they reflect the fact that the undistributed income of PHCs and of FPHCs subject to a special system of taxation, whether the accumulation was motivated by a tax-avoidance purpose or not. Because §§532(b)(1) and 532(b)(2) exempt most closely held holding or investment companies, few targets are left in the holding company area for the accumulated earnings tax to hit, although the 1984 enactment of §532(c), stating that §531 is to be applied "without regard to

---

[85] Without discussing the question, the Tax Court may have assumed that a statement under §534(a)(2) could have this double effect in John P. Scripps Newspapers, supra note 28.

[86] See Regs. §1.533-1(c). H.C. Cockrell Warehouse Corp., 71 TC 1036 (1979) (held a mere holding company, as only activity a net-leased warehouse and two vacation homes leased to sole shareholder; fact that notice of deficiency did not specify grounds for §531 tax did not prevent Service from invoking holding company issue); Golconda Mining Corp., supra note 10 (taxpayer not a holding company, even though registered with the Securities and Exchange Commission as an investment company); Alex Brown, Inc., 60 TC 364 (1973), aff'd per curiam, 496 F2d 621 (6th Cir. 1974) (taxpayer determined to be holding or investment company when it remained dormant the last five months of its taxable year after having sold its operating assets); JJJ Corp. v. US, 576 F2d 327 (Ct. Cl. 1978) (corporation not a mere holding company on facts); see also Rhombar Co. v. CIR, 386 F2d 510 (2d Cir. 1967) (filing of §534 statement does not shift burden of proof under §533(b) where corporation is a mere holding company).

[87] For PHCs, see infra ¶ 8.20; for FPHCs, see ¶ 17.21.

the number of shareholders" of the affected corporation,[88] may stimulate the Service to pursue publicly held corporations that accumulate their investment income.

¶ 8.09　COMPUTATION OF ACCUMULATED EARNINGS TAX

The accumulated earnings tax is imposed by §531 on the corporation's accumulated taxable income, the rate being 27.5 percent of the first $100,000 of accumulated taxable income and 38.5 percent of any accumulated taxable income over $100,000.[89] The tax, which is imposed in addition to the regular corporate income tax, falls on the accumulated taxable income of the year or years for which the forbidden purpose is found, not on the entire accumulation of earlier years. The latter amount, however, is of course relevant to the issues of tax avoidance or reasonable business needs.

The term "accumulated taxable income" is defined by §535 to mean the corporation's taxable income with certain adjustments, minus the sum of (1) the dividends-paid deduction of §561 and (2) the accumulated earnings credit of §535(c). "Accumulated taxable income" is not to be confused with "current earnings and profits," for the accumulated earnings tax may be applied to a corporation that, for the year or years in issue, had no increase in its earnings and profits.[90]

1. **Adjustments to taxable income.** The corporation's taxable income, defined by §63(a), is subjected to certain adjustments, primarily for the purpose of deriving an amount that corresponds more closely to economic reality and thus measures more accurately the corporation's dividend-paying capacity for the year. Thus, taxable income is reduced by corporate income taxes accrued by the corporation during the taxable year,[91] charitable contri-

---

[88] Supra note 11.

[89] Section 6601(a)(4), enacted in 1986, provides for interest on a §531 tax from the due date of the return; for prior law, see Rev. Rul. 72-324, 1972-1 CB 399 (interest runs from notice and demand for payment; agreement to follow several cases that so held).

[90] See GPD, Inc. v. CIR, supra note 77 reversing a contrary holding by the Tax Court; see also Lamark Shipping Agency, Inc., supra note 79 (*GPD* issue not decided because taxpayer did not argue it).

[91] See generally Estate of Goodall v. CIR, supra note 50 (*Dixie Pine Products* rule applies in computing accrued tax deductions); Rev. Rul. 68-632, 1968-2 CB 253 (mere filing of tax return no longer considered a contest, in determining accumulated taxable income base, §531 deficiency accrues in year to which it relates). As to what constitutes a contest, see Rev. Rul. 68-631, 1968-2 CB 198; Rev. Rul. 72-306, 1972-1

butions disallowed by the 10 percent limitation of §170(b)(2), and certain capital losses. Conversely, the net operating loss deduction, capital loss carry-over, and 80 percent dividends-received deduction are disallowed. The taxpayer's net capital gain for the taxable year (adjusted for taxes) is eliminated from taxable income, and a few other adjustments of a minor nature are also made.[92]

2. Dividends-paid deduction. Taxable income, as thus adjusted, is then reduced by the dividends-paid deduction of §561. This deduction is the sum of two amounts:

(a) Dividends paid during the taxable year. This amount must obviously be taken into account in computing the accumulated earnings tax, which is fundamentally a tax on undistributed income. The term "dividend" means a distribution from current earnings and profits or from post-1913 accumulated earnings and profits, as under §316,[93] so that, in general, the corporation gets a deduction in computing its accumulated earnings tax only if the shareholder must report the distribution as ordinary income. There is an exception for amounts distributed in liquidation, however, that permits the corporation to deduct some distributions that may be treated by the shareholder as capital gain or even as a return of capital.[94] Because of the diffi-

---

CB 165 (notice of appeal or proposed deficiency at district conference is a "contest"); Doug-Long, Inc., 73 TC 71 (1979) (protest of deficiency is a contest and Regs. §1.535-2(a)(1) valid); Mariani Frozen Foods, Inc., 81 TC 448 (1983), aff'd per curiam sub nom. Melinda L. Gee Trust v. CIR, 761 F2d 1410 (9th Cir. 1985).

[92] These adjustments resemble, but are not identical with, those required to convert taxable income to earnings and profits (supra ¶ 7.03); see Ted Bates & Co., supra note 21. See also Rev. Rul. 70-497, 1970-2 CB 128 (tax-exempt income excluded from §535 base, but counts in determining reasonableness of accumulation); Rev. Rul. 78-430, 1978-2 CB 181 (accumulated taxable income base may be increased by §482 reallocation).

[93] See ¶ 7.02.

[94] Amounts distributed in liquidation (including redemptions to which §302 applies) qualify for the dividends-paid deduction of §561 (if the distribution is pro rata among the shareholders) to the extent "properly chargeable to earnings and profits." See §§562(b)(1)(A) and 562(c). Moreover, if a complete liquidation occurs within 24 months after the adoption of a plan of liquidation, all pro rata distributions during this period constitute dividends to the extent of the liquidating corporation's *current* earnings for the year of such distribution. Hence, a liquidating corporation can obtain as many as three taxable years of immunity from §531 by carefully timing its distributions. But see Rev. Rul. 75-139, 1975-1 CB 168 (denial of §561 deduction to a corporation that was liquidated as a step in a plan of reorganization).

Distributions in which shareholders of the same class are treated differently do not qualify for the §561 dividends-paid deduction; §562(c). See Estate of Fred W. Lucas, 71 TC 838 (1979) aff'd, 657 F2d 841 (6th Cir. 1981) (for triple-tax exposure

culty of determining a corporation's undistributed income with exactitude before the taxable year comes to a close, §563(a) provides that the dividends-paid deduction for a particular year includes dividends paid within the first two and one-half months of the following year.[95]

(b) Consent dividends for the taxable year. The consent dividend procedure found in §565 permits the shareholders of a corporation to agree to treat a specified portion of the corporation's earnings and profits as a dividend, even though no actual distribution is made. This enables a corporation that has earnings and profits but does not wish to make an actual distribution to avoid possible liability for the accumulated earnings tax. The consent dividend (which must be allocated pro rata among the shareholders in accordance with §565(b)(1)) is treated as if it had been distributed to the shareholders in money on the last day of the corporation's taxable year and had been turned back by them to the corporation as a contribution to capital.

3. Accumulated earnings credit. The final step in the computation of "accumulated taxable income" is to deduct the "accumulated earnings credit" of §535(c).[96] This credit was created to permit small companies to accumulate a minimum amount of earnings and profits, free of any risk that the accumulation will be found unreasonable, as well as to exempt, in the

---

here); H.H. King Flour Mills Co. v. US, 325 F. Supp. 1085 (D. Minn. 1971) (§302(b)(3) redemption does not qualify); GPD, Inc., supra note 77; Dielectric Materials Corp., supra note 44 (Service argued that unreasonable compensation disallowed as §162 deduction was a preferential dividend); W.T. Wilson, 10 TC 251 (1948) (acq.) aff'd, 170 F2d 423 (9th Cir. 1948), cert. denied, 336 US 909 (1949). See generally, Doernberg, The Accumulated Earnings Tax: The Relationship Between Earnings and Profits and Accumulated Taxable Income in a Redemption Transaction, 34 U. Fla. L. Rev. 715 (1982).

An in-kind dividend will be valued at its adjusted basis to the corporation at the time of the distribution (presumably even for loss assets); see Regs. §1.562-1(a). The regulation was held valid in Fulman v. US, 434 US 528 (1978); see also Gulf Inland Corp. v. US, 570 F2d 1277 (5th Cir. 1978) (*Fulman* applied retroactively); see Axelrod, The Accumulated Earnings Tax and the Deduction for Dividends in Property: Market Value or Basis? 4 J. Corp. Tax'n 208 (1977). But see ¶ 7.21 (since distributing corporation now has taxable gain here, perhaps market value is the proper measure; it would seem that either the regulation should be changed to reflect this fact or that the *Fulman* issue could possibly be relitigated successfully).

See also Joseph K., Inc., 51 TC 584 (1969) (no carry-back deduction allowed for distributions in excess of current earnings; only allowed currently for year of distribution).

[95] See generally Rev. Rul. 68-409, 1968-2 CB 252 (distribution within specified period qualified, even though recipient was not shareholder of taxpayer at end of prior taxable year).

[96] Although labeled a credit, this allowance functions as a deduction, since it reduces the base that is subject to the accumulated earnings tax, not the tax itself.

case of operating companies, such portion of the taxable year's accumulation as is retained for any reasonable business needs. Operating companies are allowed to accumulate, free of tax under §531, the greater of (1) a minimum credit of $250,000 ($150,000 in the case of a corporation whose principal function is the performance of health, legal, engineering, accounting, or certain other services),[97] or (2) such part (if any) of the taxable year's earnings and profits as are retained for the reasonable needs of the business.[98] Because the $250,000 (or $150,000) minimum credit is a lifetime allowance, however, it is reduced by any accumulated earnings and profits that are already on hand at the beginning of the taxable year.

To illustrate: Assume that a corporation has accumulated earnings and profits of $100,000 at the beginning of a taxable year in which it is subject to §531. Its current earnings and profits for the taxable year amount to $500,000, and the portion of the $500,000 retained for reasonable business needs is either $300,000 (Example *A*) or $25,000 (Example *B*). On these facts, the accumulated earnings credit is $300,000 in Example *A* and $150,000 in Example *B*, computed as follows:

	Example A	Example B
1. Earnings and profits, end of preceding year	$100,000	$100,000
2. Minimum credit ($250,000 less line 1)	$150,000	$150,000
3. Current earnings and profits		
a. Retained for business needs	$300,000	$ 25,000
b. Excess ($500,000 less line 3a)	$200,000	$425,000
4. Accumulated earnings credit (greater of line 2 or line 3a)	$300,000	$150,000

If the principal functions of the corporation in the preceding examples were the performance of health, legal, or other services listed in §535(c)(2)(B), its lifetime minimum credit would be $150,000 rather than $250,000; line 2 for both Example *A* and Example *B* would be $50,000; and

---

[97] See Rev. Rul. 84-101, 1984-2 CB 115 ($150,000 limit applies only to personal service companies that are specifically enumerated in §535(c)(2)(B); insurance broker entitled to $250,000 minimum credit).

[98] On the retention of current earnings for business needs, see supra note 28. For illustrative computations of the credit, see Regs. §1.535-3(b)(3); Shaw-Walker Co. v. CIR, 390 F2d 205 (6th Cir. 1968) (Tax Court denied credit, even though some current earnings reasonable, because prior accumulations unreasonable; the Sixth Circuit directed the Tax Court to reconsider this view); Rev. Rul. 73-139, 1973-1 CB 295; Snow Mfg. Co., supra note 23 (comparison of reasonable needs to net liquid assets reflected in accumulated earnings).

line 4—the credit allowable—would be $300,000 in Example *A* but only $50,000 in Example *B*.

In computing the credit for holding and investment companies, §535(c) does not take account of current accumulations for the corporation's reasonable needs, presumably because it is difficult, if not impossible, to fix a limit on such an enterprise's financial ambitions and appetite. Thus, the credit allowed to such companies is $250,000 less the accumulated earnings and profits on hand at the close of the preceding taxable year.

PART B.   THE TAX ON PERSONAL HOLDING COMPANIES

¶ 8.20   INTRODUCTORY

Since 1934, the Code has imposed a special tax on the undistributed income of so-called personal holding companies—corporations controlled by a limited number of shareholders and deriving a large percentage of their income from specified sources. PHCs were singled out for this punishment after extensive investigations in 1934 and again in 1937 led Congress to conclude that they were often vehicles by which their shareholders could avoid the graduated income tax imposed on individuals and that the traditional weapon against such a use of the corporation, the accumulated earnings tax of §531, could be avoided if the forbidden purpose was not detected or proved. Three of the most common devices were:

(1) Incorporated pocketbooks, in which an individual would organize a corporation to hold investment securities, so that the dividends and interest received would be taxed at the (then) relatively flat and low corporate rate, rather than at the (then) more steeply graduated individual rate.

(2) Incorporated talents, in which a film actor (or other highly compensated person) would organize a corporation and agree to work for it for a relatively modest salary. The corporation would then contract out the performer's services at their fair value, so that the difference between the amount received by it and the amount paid would be taxed only at the (then relatively lower) corporate rate. [99]

---

[99] See CIR v. Laughton, 113 F2d 103 (9th Cir. 1940), holding that the validity of such a device (apart from the PHC provisions) depended on "whether [Charles] Laughton's hiring of himself to his wholly owned corporation for a salary substantially less than the compensation for which the corporation supplied his services as its employee to various motion picture producers, constituted, in effect, a single transaction by Laughton in which he received indirectly the larger sum paid by the

(3) Incorporated yachts, country estates, and so forth, consisting, in the device's simplest form, of transferring a yacht, country estate, or similar property to a corporation, together with income-producing property, in the hope that the corporation could deduct operating expenses and depreciation from the income yielded by the other property. Another version, more modest but also more sophisticated, depended on proof that the yacht could not be rented to an outsider for as much as its operating expenses and depreciation. The corporation would then charter the yacht for this arm's-length amount to its sole shareholder, who would transfer to the corporation enough income-producing property to make up the deficit between the rent received by the corporation and the operating expenses and depreciation. In either form, the arrangement was dependent on establishing that the corporation's expenses in operating the yacht were ordinary and necessary business expenses; but the second version offered a greater hope of success.

To provide a more automatic penalty for these and similar practices, Congress created a new taxable entity—the personal holding company—which is subject not only to the normal corporate income tax but also to a special penalty tax (38.5 percent for taxable years beginning in 1987, 28 percent thereafter) imposed by §541 on the corporation's undistributed PHC income (but subject to refund if the corporation avails itself of the deficiency dividend procedures provided by §547).[100]

To constitute a PHC, a corporation must meet both an income test and a stock ownership test. That is, at least 60 percent of its adjusted ordinary gross income must be PHC income (primarily passive investment income plus personal service income in the case of incorporated talents[101]) and more

---

producers." See also Fontaine Fox, 37 BTA 271 (1938); Rev. Rul. 77-336, 1977-2 CB 202 (shareholder taxed on income earned by him and assigned to his 100 percent owned corporation); Charles Johnson, 78 TC 882 (1982), aff'd without op., 734 F2d 20 (9th Cir. 1984), cert. denied, 469 US 857 (1984) (shareholder taxed as earner of income under §61). For later cases and rulings in this area that tend to rely more on readjustments under §482 than on the assignment of income doctrine, see ¶ 1.05 and ¶ 15.03. See also ¶ 2.07.

[100] For computation of the tax, see infra ¶ 8.24; Schedule PH, which must be filed by PHCs with their regular income tax returns; and Mathison, Personal Holding Companies (Domestic)—Taxation and Relief, Tax Mgmt. Portfolio (BNA) No. 114-3d (1982). If Schedule PH is not filed, the statute of limitations on assessment of the PHC tax is extended by §6501(f) from the usual three years to six years. Should a PHC tax deficiency be assessed, interest commences on the date the return is due. Hart Metal Prods. Corp. v. US, 38 AFTR2d 6118 (Ct. Cl. 1976).

For the deficiency dividend procedure, see infra ¶ 8.24.

[101] Infra ¶ 8.22.

than 50 percent of its stock (by value) must be owned—directly or indirectly, actually or constructively—by five or fewer individuals. [102]

Certain corporations are exempt from the PHC category—primarily tax-exempt corporations, banks, life insurance companies, surety companies, certain finance companies, FPHCs, [103] and certain foreign corporations. [104]

PHCs are not subject to the accumulated earnings tax of §531 (27.5 percent to 38.5 percent under current law), whatever comfort this may confer. At the same time, they are subject to some special disabilities, in addition to the tax imposed by §541: (1) The at-risk rules of §465 and the passive activity loss restrictions of §469—both aimed primarily at individuals—are applicable to corporations meeting the stock ownership rules of §542(a); (2) a few more tax preferences are taken into account in computing the alternative minimum tax on PHCs than on other corporations; [105] and (3) many PHCs are subject to §368(a)(2)(F), disqualifying certain investment companies from reorganization treatment if the transaction involves two or more such companies. Moreover, these disabilities apply even if the corporation has no undistributed PHC income and hence is not liable for a PHC tax.

The PHC tax is not a major revenue factor in the taxation of corporations and shareholders, with respect to either the number of PHC returns filed or the amount of penalty taxes actually paid. This may be due to the fact that many of the incorporated pocketbooks at which Congress aimed the PHC provisions either operate under the close and constant scrutiny of attorneys and accountants, who see to it that substantially all their income is distributed, or have been liquidated or sold by their shareholders. In other instances, however, the practices that led to the enactment of the tax may be pursued in more sophisticated form, since PHC status can be avoided if care is taken to arrange a corporation's affairs so as to fall outside the definitional rules of thumb. Today's equivalent of the 1930 model PHC, in other words, may be satisfactorily disguised as a manufacturing or mercantile company whose only risk in this area is the possible application of §531 to its undistributed income. [106]

Moreover, there is some reason to believe that at least part of the revenue raised by the PHC tax is contributed by corporations that have become PHCs only by accident, so to speak. One litigated case involved a closely held manufacturing corporation that was in the process of liquidation. Its assets had

---

[102] Infra ¶ 8.23.

[103] For FPHCs, see infra ¶ 17.20.

[104] For these exemptions, see §542(c). But see Rev. Rul. 85-140, 1985-2 CB 172 (no exemption for domestic corporation wholly owned by foreign shareholders).

[105] See §56(b)(2)(C), relating to circulation expenditures, and §57(a)(7), relating to pre-1987 property; supra ¶ 5.08.

[106] See supra ¶ 8.01.

been sold on credit, and more than 80 percent of its income in the taxable year consisted of interest on the sales price. The tax was held applicable,

> But, urges the petitioner, the personal holding company surtax was enacted to remedy the evil of the "incorporated pocketbook," deliberately created to reduce the personal taxes of those who created them, and therefore, to impose the tax upon a corporation in petitioner's position is a perversion of the Congressional purpose. . . . It is, however, abundantly clear that Congress, in correcting an evil, is not narrowly confined to the specific instances which suggested the remedy. . . . In enacting the very section being applied here, Congress was attempting to foreclose the defense available under [the accumulated earnings tax] that the accumulation of profits was responsive to a legitimate business need.[107]

Thus, the fact that a corporation does not have a Wall Street address or that its assets do not consist of inherited wealth does not immunize it against PHC tax liability. As a consequence, these provisions are of wider interest than many attorneys and accountants realize.[108]

¶ 8.21   PERSONAL HOLDING COMPANY INCOME: THE 60 PERCENT OF INCOME TEST

For a corporation to be classifed as a PHC, both the stock ownership test of §542(a)(2)[109] and the tainted income test of §542(a)(1) must be satisfied. Because almost all closely held corporations (as well as some others) meet the stock ownership test, the income requirement is ordinarily the acid test of PHC status. This requirement is that at least 60 percent of the corporation's adjusted ordinary gross income for a taxable year constitutes PHC

---

[107] O'Sullivan Rubber Co. v. CIR, 120 F2d 845, 847–848 (2d Cir. 1941). See also 320 East 47th St. Corp. v. CIR, 243 F2d 894 (2d Cir. 1957) (interest on condemnation award; held PHC income); McKinley Corp. of Ohio, 36 TC 1182 (1961) (attempts to avoid the frying pan of §531 resulted in exposure to the fire of §541); Karon Corp., ¶ 75,283 P-H Memo. TC (1975) (no state of mind defense); Jerome S. Lachinski, ¶ 86,334 P-H Memo. TC (1986) (incorporated liquor store became PHC by inadvertence; no exemption for passive investment income as such, where income meets statutory requirements).

[108] See generally Nasuti & Sutherland, Personal Holding Companies (Domestic)–Definition, Tax Mgmt. Portfolio (BNA) No. 53-4th (1986); Mathison, supra note 100; Kwall, supra note 5; Morgan, The Domestic Technology Base Company: The Dilemma of an Operating Company Which Might Be a Personal Holding Company, 33 Tax L. Rev. 233 (1978). For the early history of these provisions, see Rudick, supra note 5; Paul, The Background of the Revenue Act of 1937, 5 U. Chi. L. Rev. 41 (1937).

[109] Infra ¶ 8.23.

income. Adjusted ordinary gross income was adopted in 1964 as the relevant measuring rod in an attempt to distinguish more precisely than did prior law between the corporation's active business income and its passive investment income.[110] Certain categories of income, such as rents, royalties, and interest, could in many cases be either active or passive depending on the circumstances; the adjusted ordinary gross income definition was designed to effect a more realistic classification of these items.

Briefly stated, "adjusted ordinary gross income" is defined by §543(b) to mean gross income less gains from the sale or other disposition of capital assets or §1231(b) assets,[111] less depreciation, taxes, interest, and rent incurred in connection with certain rental income and mineral royalties. The latter adjustments are designed to determine whether these specially treated activities are significant elements in the corporation's economic function or merely tax-avoidance operations to disguise the importance of its PHC income. The adjustments, however, do not prevent the use of businesses producing high amounts of gross income but little, if any, net operating income (e.g., bowling alleys, telephone-answering services, automatic laundries, and so forth) as a way of shielding tainted investment income.

It should be noted that a bona fide manufacturing or mercantile corporation whose cost of goods sold in a given year approaches its gross receipts from sales, resulting in little or no gross operating income, may become a PHC if it receives any dividends, interest, or other PHC items. Note also that the corporate tax return itself does not contain an entry for gross income, and §61, which purports to define this term, encompasses many penumbral receipts that are not explicitly listed in the statutory language. Similarly, the line between expenditures that enter into the computation of

---

[110] For corporations filing a consolidated return, adjusted ordinary gross income and PHC income are ordinarily computed on a consolidated basis, thus eliminating intragroup dividends and interest. See §542(b); Regs. §1.1502-14(a)(1); infra ¶ 15.23. For other aspects of this subject, see Rev. Rul. 74-131, 1974-1 CB 145; Rev. Rul. 79-60, 1979-1 CB 211; Rev. Rul. 74-432, 1974-2 CB 175; and Rev. Rul. 76-320, 1976-2 CB 181.

See generally Emory, The Personal Holding Company Tax and Inter-Company Transactions With Members of an Affiliated Group—New Difficulty With an Old Misconception, 30 Tax L. Rev. 283 (1975) (extensive analysis of PHC consolidated return relationship in §542(b)).

[111] Because capital gains are excluded from adjusted ordinary gross income, they constitute a neutral category of income, counting neither for nor against the taxpayer when the 60 percent test is applied. This category evidently embraces income that is treated as capital gain under such provisions as §§301(c)(3), 302, 331, 1234, and 1241, as well as §1231 capital gain regardless of the outcome of the §1231 hotchpot. On the other hand, gain on the sale of a capital asset is included in adjusted ordinary gross income if it is taxed as ordinary income under such provisions as §§1245, 1250, 1239, 1246, and 1231(b). See H.R. Rep. No. 749, 88th Cong., 1st Sess. 75 (1964), reprinted in 1964-1 CB (pt. 2) 125, 347.

gross income and those that are deductible only in computing taxable income is not always clear.[112]

¶ 8.22 DEFINITION OF "PERSONAL HOLDING COMPANY INCOME"

In applying the 60 percent test of §542(a)(1)[113] the following items of adjusted ordinary income are taken into account by §543(a), which defines PHC income:

1. Dividends, interest, royalties, and annuities. Dividends are included in PHC income whether they come within the normal rule of §316 or attain that status by reason of such special rules as §1248 (sale of stock of controlled foreign corporation), §78 (gross-up of foreign tax paid by foreign subsidiary), or §551 (undistributed foreign personal holding company income).[114]

The term "interest" is defined by Regs. §1.543-1(b)(2) as "any amounts, includible in gross income, received for the use of money loaned." Aside from the troublesome subject of original issue discount,[115] this definition is not ordinarily difficult to apply.[116] It should be noted that the imputed inter-

---

[112] See Levine, Gross Income in the Personal Holding Company, 9 Tax L. Rev. 453 (1954); Holleman, U.S. Taxation of Foreign Income: The Overseas Construction Industry, 23 Tax L. Rev. 155 (1968).

For purposes of the extended statute of limitations, applicable if the taxpayer omits more than 25 percent of gross income, the term "gross income" is given a meaning virtually equivalent to gross receipts by §6501(e)(1)(A)(i), but this provision is not controlling in applying §542(a)(1).

[113] Supra ¶ 8.21.

[114] See Mariani Frozen Foods, Inc., supra note 91 (regarding §551 dividends). Constructive distributions seem clearly embraced by §543(a)(1); see McKinley Corp. of Ohio, 36 TC 1182 (1961) (acq.).

[115] Compare Regs. §1.61-7(c), stating that original issue discount is interest except as otherwise provided by law, and Prop. Regs. §1.1272-1(a)(1), stating that OID is taxable as interest, with §1271(a)(1), providing that amounts received on the retirement of debt instruments must be considered as amounts received in exchange therefore; but note that OID is increasingly taxed currently as interest income on an accrual basis. See also §§483 and 7872. Moreover, §1276(a)(3) classifies "market discount" as interest for most purposes (including §543(a)(1)). See also US v. Midland-Ross Corp., 381 US 54 (1965), equating OID income with stated interest income; Jaglom v. CIR, 303 F2d 847 (2d Cir. 1962) (allocation between principal and interest required where bonds with defaulted interest were purchased and resold "flat"); Lubin v. CIR, 335 F2d 209 (2d Cir. 1964).

[116] See Western Credit Co. v. CIR, 325 F2d 1022 (9th Cir. 1963) (contract changes imposed by lender held interest); Gunderson Bros. Eng'g Corp., 42 TC 419

est provisions of §§483 and 1274 generate interest income where none would have existed under prior law. Two types of interest are excluded from adjusted ordinary gross income, and hence from PHC income, by §543(b)(2)(C): (1) interest on condemnation awards, judgments, and tax refund claims and (2) interest earned by certain dealers in U.S. securities.[117]

"Royalties," as the term is used in §543(a)(1), generally includes periodic receipts from licenses to use various kinds of intangible property rights (such as patents, trademarks, trade names, franchises, goodwill, or technical know-how) but not computer software royalties received in the active conduct of a software business that meets the intricate conditions of §543(d), as enacted in 1986. Mineral, oil, and gas royalties are specially treated, as described later, and so are copyright royalties. In some circumstances, moreover, royalties constitute rents and are subject to the special rules of §543(a)(2).[118] The principal classification problem concerns transactions in which it is not clear whether the transferor of property has granted a license on which it is receiving royalty payments or has sold the property and is receiving installment payments on the sale price.[119] Another troublesome area is the agreement that combines a license of property with an undertak-

---

(1964) (finance charges treated as interest); The Krueger Co., 79 TC 65 (1982) (interest imputed under §482 constituted PHC interest income); Lake Gerar Dev. Co., 71 TC 887 (1979) (interest on purchase-money mortgage is PHC interest); Investors Ins. Agency, Inc. v. CIR, 677 F2d 1328 (9th Cir. 1982) (payment held to be interest, even though no underlying debt; since parties intended payment to be interest and treated it as such, they were bound by their labels). But see Joseph Lupowitz & Sons, 497 F2d 862 (3d Cir. 1974) (advances were contributions to capital, not loans; hence accrued interest did not constitute true interest).

[117] See also the complete exemption granted by §§542(c)(2), 542(c)(6), and 542(c)(8) to certain finance companies and other commercial lenders.

[118] See infra text at note 121; Rev. Rul. 70-153, 1970-1 CB 139 (delay rentals under an oil and gas lease held to constitute rents rather than royalties); Johnson Inv. & Rental Co., 70 TC 895 (1978) (mineral payments, not being fixed and certain but contingent on extraction, constituted royalties rather than rent); Dothan Coca-Cola Bottling Co., v. US, 745 F2d 400 (11th Cir. 1984) (receipts were rent for lease of tangible assets, not royalties for use of franchise). Compare Pleasanton Gravel Co., 85 TC 839 (1985) (analysis of distinction between rent and royalties).

[119] See E.I. du Pont de Nemours & Co. v. US, 288 F2d 904 (Ct. Cl. 1961) (disclosure of information held a license); Dairy Queen of Okla., Inc. v. CIR, 250 F2d 503 (10th Cir. 1957) (subfranchise agreement held a sale); US v. Wernentin, 354 F2d 757 (8th Cir. 1966); §1253 (franchise transfers with retained interests taxed as ordinary gain); James O. Tomerlin Trust, 87 TC 876 (1986) (§1253 ordinary gain not PHC royalty; court found a true sale); Rev. Rul. 64-56, 1964-1 CB 133 (transfer of know-how), amplified by Rev. Rul. 71-564, 1971-2 CB 179; Rev. Rul. 75-202, 1975-1 CB 170 (transfer of exclusive rights to copyright, subject to contingent reversion; held a sale).

ing by the licensor to perform services, so that the payments received must be allocated between royalties and compensation for services.[120]

2. Rents. To discourage the acquisition of rental property that throws off large amounts of gross income in order to shield passive dividends, interest, and other investment income from the PHC tax, §543(a)(2) takes into account only the taxpayer's adjusted income from rents rather than its gross receipts from these sources, in computing adjusted ordinary gross income.[121] The corporation's adjusted income from rents is PHC income, unless (1) it constitutes 50 percent or more of the corporation's adjusted ordinary gross income; and (2) dividends paid for the taxable year equal or exceed the amount (if any) by which its nonrent PHC income for that year exceeds 10 percent of its ordinary gross income. Thus, a corporation engaged predominantly in rental activities may escape PHC status, but if its nonrental PHC income is substantial, it must make taxable distributions thereof.

The term "rents," as used in §§543(a)(2) and 543(b)(3), excludes (1) amounts that constitute PHC income by virtue of §543(a)(6) (compensation for use of corporate property by a shareholder); (2) copyright royalties, as defined in §543(a)(4); and (3) produced film rents, as defined in §543(a)(5)(B). Interest on the sales price of real property sold to customers in the ordinary course of business, however, is treated as rent by §543(b)(3) in order to permit real estate dealers receiving interest on purchse-money mortgages to avoid PHC status.

3. Mineral, oil and gas royalties. The taxpayer's "adjusted income" from these sources, as defined by §§543(a)(3), 543(b)(2)(B), and 543(b)(4)[122]

---

[120] See Portable Indus., Inc., 24 TC 571 (1955) (acq.); Irving Berlin Music Corp. v. US, 487 F2d 540 (Ct. Cl. 1973), cert. denied, 419 US 832 (1974) (receipts were royalties for use of copyright property, not compensation for services as exclusive agent).

See generally Morgan, supra note 108.

[121] "Adjusted income from rents" is defined by §543(b)(3). For classification of various items as rent or nonrent gross income, see Hilldun Corp. v. CIR, 408 F2d 1117 (2d Cir. 1969) (e.g., lessee payment of landlord's expenses; lessee improvements; security deposits; imputed rent); Bayou Verret Land Co. v. CIR, 450 F2d 850 (5th Cir. 1971); Johnson Inv. & Rental Co., supra note 118; see also Rev. Rul. 67-423, 1967-2 CB 221 (soil bank payments received under crop-sharing lease were not rents because the lessor materially participated in farming operations); Walt E. Eller, 77 TC 934 (1981) (rents from shopping center and mobile home park includable despite taxpayer's active managerial services; extensive analysis), discussed by Cook & Allen, *Eller* Considered: Are Substantial Services Irrelevant in Determining Personal Holding Company Rents? 10 J. Corp. Tax'n 139 (1983).

[122] In addition to production payments and overriding royalties, which are expressly mentioned by §543(b)(4), cash bonuses are includable, even if not covered

is included in PHC income, unless (1) the royalties constitute 50 percent or more of the taxpayer's adjusted gross income, (2) its personal holding company income from other sources is not more than 10 percent of ordinary gross income, and (3) its trade and business deductions under §162 (except for compensation for personal services rendered by shareholders and certain other deductions) equal or exceed 15 percent of adjusted ordinary gross income.

The 15 percent business expense test is designed to separate operating companies from holding companies by demanding a minimum level of business activity, but the statute does not expressly require that these expenses be related to the production of royalty income. The 10 percent test, like that for rents, ensures that mineral royalties cannot be used to shelter an excessive amount of other passive income. Finally, although income from working interests in oil and gas properties is not treated as PHC income, it must be reduced by depletion and certain other items under §543(b)(2)(B) in computing adjusted ordinary gross income, thereby making it more difficult to use this kind of income to avoid PHC status if the corporation receives tainted income from other sources.

4. Copyright royalties. Copyright royalties constitute PHC income under §543(a)(4), but publishers and other active business firms are exempted by virtue of rules similar to those applicable to rental income and mineral royalties. To qualify for the exemption, the corporation's copyright royalties (except for shareholder-created works) must constitute 50 percent or more of its ordinary gross income; its other PHC income must not exceed 10 percent of its ordinary gross income; and its §162 deductions allocable to its copyright royalties (other than for personal services rendered by shareholders and certain other items) must meet a complex text designed to ensure a substantial level of business activity.[123]

5. Produced film rents. Produced film rents (defined as amounts derived from film properties acquired before substantial completion of production) are subject under §543(a)(5) to the treatment formerly accorded to rents—that is, such amounts are PHC income unless they constitute 50 percent or more of the corporation's ordinary gross income. This test is rela-

---

by production; see Bayou Verbet Land Co. v. CIR, supra note 121; Rev. Rul. 72-148, 1972-1 CB 170 (restoration of previously deducted depletion on lease bonus not royalty income); see also §636, classifying certain production payments as loans "for purposes of this subtitle" (which includes the PHC provisions).

[123] See generally Irving Berlin Music Corp. v. US, supra note 120 (taxpayer received copyright royalties, not compensation). See also Cohen, Personal Holding Companies—Entertainment Indus., 1962 So. Cal. Tax Inst. 651.

tively easy to satisfy and should usually protect bona fide film production companies. Income from film properties acquired after substantial completion of production, however, is treated as copyright royalty income and is subject to the more stringent rules of §543(a)(4).

6. **Compensation for use of corporate property by shareholders.** Compensation for the use of tangible corporate property constitutes PHC income under §543(a)(6)(A) if the person entitled to use it owns (directly, indirectly, or constructively) 25 percent or more (by value) of the corporation's stock at any time during the taxable year. This provision was enacted primarily to reach the rent paid by shareholders for the use of incorporated yachts, country estates, and similar property.

Taken by itself, however, §543(a)(6)(A) would not have put an end to the practice of incorporating yachts and country homes in order to offset an operating loss against the corporation's investment income, since the corporation, although a PHC, would have no income and hence no undistributed income on which the penalty tax could be levied. But §543(a)(6)(A) must be examined in conjunction with §545(b)(6), which closes the gap by providing that, in computing the corporation's undistributed PHC income, deductions for expenses and depreciation allocable to corporate property are allowable only to the extent of the rent or other compensation received for the use of the property unless the Service is satisfied that (1) the rent was the highest obtainable (or, if none was received, that none was obtainable); (2) the property was held in the course of a business carried on bona fide for profit; and (3) either the property was necessary to the conduct of business or its operation could reasonably be expected to yield a profit.[124] Applied to an incorporated yacht rented from a corporation by its sole shareholder, §543(a)(6)(A) would require the rent to be treated as PHC income, and §543(a)(1) would have the same effect on the corporation's income from dividends and interest. Assuming no other income, the corporation would be a PHC. Under §545(b)(6), its deductions for expenses and depreciation incurred in operating the yacht would be limited to the amount of the rent, and the

---

[124] Although §545(b)(6) was enacted primarily to limit the corporation's deductions for maintenance and depreciation on incorporated yachts, estates, and similar property used by the shareholders, it is more broadly applicable to all corporate property, whether used by shareholders or not; see Wilson Bros. & Co. v. CIR, 170 F2d 423 (9th Cir. 1948), cert. denied, 336 US 909 (1949) (cargo vessels). Indeed, the language of §545(b)(6)(A) seems to forbid any deduction for maintenance or depreciation on corporate business property used by the corporation in the course of its own business activity unless the corporation shows that no rent was obtainable (i.e., that the property could not have been rented out). But literalness should not be carried this far, even for purposes of penalizing the despised PHC.

excess (or loss) could not be applied against the dividend and interest income. If not distributed, therefore, these items would be subject to the PHC tax.

As stated earlier, the function contemplated for §543(a)(6)(A) was to taint rent received by the corporation for yachts, country estates, and similar property used by an individual owning 25 percent or more of its stock. By its terms, however, §543(a)(6)(A) reaches rent for *any* property of the corporation if such a shareholder is entitled to its use, even though the property is used by the shareholder in a bona fide income-producing business. To avoid subjecting the corporation to the PHC tax in this situation, §543(a)(6)(B) taints the rental income only if the corporation has personal holding income from other sources (as specially defined) in excess of 10 percent of its ordinary gross income. If, however, the corporation does have an excess of other PHC income, the rents from shareholder-used property can generate a PHC tax even if the shareholder uses the property for business purposes rather than for pleasure or recreation.[125] Conversely, in the absence of other PHC income in excess of the 10 percent benchmark, not even the rent from incorporated yachts and estates falls afoul of §543(a)(6).

Section 543(a)(6) is applicable under the circumstances stated, to amounts received as compensation for the use of corporate property, regardless of designation and whether paid by the shareholder himself or not. Thus, rent received by a lessor corporation from a lessee corporation can be included if the property is subleased by the lessee to an individual owning more than 25 percent in value of the lessor's stock.[126]

7. Personal service contracts. Amounts received under a personal service contract constitute PHC income if (1) the individual who is to perform the services is designated (by name or by description) in the contract or can be so designated by some person other than the corporation; and (2) the designated person owns (directly, indirectly, or constructively) 25 percent or more (by value) of the corporation's stock at some time during the taxable

---

[125] See Hatfried, Inc. v. CIR, 162 F2d 628 (3d Cir. 1947) (no implied exemption for rents from property used by shareholders for business purposes), which was partially rejected by the later enactment of §543(a)(6)(B) but is otherwise still controlling.

[126] See Randolph Prods. Co. v. Manning, 176 F2d 190 (3d Cir. 1949) (lease to partnership of which shareholder was a member); American Valve Co. v. US, 137 F. Supp. 249 (S.D.N.Y. 1956) (same). For leases between brother-sister and parent-subsidiary corporations, see Rev. Rul. 84-137, 1984-2 CB 116 (leases do not create PHC income, despite ultimate individual shareholder ownership of both corporations, provided property is used by lessee corporation solely in its own business and not for individual or personal benefit of shareholder), and cases there cited.

See Rudolph, Shareholder Rent as PHC Income—A Misguided Missile Now Partially Disarmed, 8 J. Corp. Tax'n 118 (1981).

year. Amounts received from the sale or other disposition of such a contract are also included in PHC income.

This type of income is included in order to reach actors, producers, and other flamboyant incorporated talents.[127] Section 543(a)(7) is equally applicable, however, to corporations performing engineering, financial, or technical services of a more sober nature, although such corporations ordinarily are safe because they, rather than the other contracting party, usually designate the person or persons to perform the services. Although §543(a)(7) may have been drafted on the implicit assumption that the shareholder would not be designated in the contract unless his talents were of a special or unique character, so that the services contracted for could not have been supplied with equal skill by a nonshareholder employee of the corporation, no such requirement is explicit; and evidence that a designated shareholder's talents were not unique seems irrelevant to the operation of §543(a)(7). On the other hand, even if the 25 percent shareholder's skills are unique, it has been held that the compensation does not come within §543(a)(7) merely because of an expectation, not embodied in the contract, that he will perform the services.[128] It should be noted that if the corporation's personal service income is allocated and taxed to the shareholder on assignment of income grounds, under §482 or because the corporation is found to be a sham,[129] the income will not constitute PHC income under §543(a)(7).

---

[127] See supra ¶ 8.20; Regs. §1.543-1(b)(8), Example (1); see also Kenyatta Corp. 86 TC 171 (1986), aff'd, 812 F2d 577 (9th Cir. 1987) (incorporated former professional basketball star), and ¶ 2.07.

[128] See S.O. Claggett, 44 TC 503 (1965) (acq.). Before too much reliance is placed on this decision, it should be noted that §543(a)(7) does not require the contract to be in writing. See Rev. Rul. 69-299, 1969-1 CB 165 (oral contract sufficient); Kenyatta Corp., supra note 127 (taxpayer designated by name in various contracts); Thomas P. Byrnes, Inc., 73 TC 416 (1979) (shareholder-officer acted as sales representative but was not designated by contract as person obligated to do so). As to the effect of an expectation falling short of a contract that a shareholder will perform the services supplied by a corporation, see Rev. Rul. 75-67, 1975-1 CB 169 (PHC income not created merely because patient solicits and expects services of physician-shareholder of medical service corporation); Rev. Rul. 75-249, 1975-1 CB 171 (same for musician-shareholder); Rev. Rul. 75-250, 1975-1 CB 172 (same for certified public accountant); see also Rev. Rul. 71-372, 1971-2 CB 241 (stockbroker's services not unique); Frederick H. Foglesong, ¶ 76,294 P-H Memo. TC (1976) (novation successfully shifted from shareholder to corporation the contractual obligation to perform services for PHC purposes); reversed on other grounds (following intermediate appeal and remand), Foglesong v. CIR, 691 F2d 848 (7th Cir. 1982).

In an important ruling, Rev. Rul. 75-67, supra, the Service held that a one-person medical service corporation was not a PHC, (1) in the absence of contracts between the corporation or physician and its patients that the physician personally perform the services or (2) unless the services were so unique as to preclude substitution; see also Rev. Rul. 75-249, supra; Rev. Rul. 75-250, supra. See generally ¶ 2.07.

[129] For these possibilities, see ¶¶ 1.05, 2.07, and 15.03; Kenyatta Corp., supra note 127.

If the contract designates a 25 percent shareholder to perform services but contemplates that other employees will assist or work with him, does all, none, or part of the compensation received by the corporation for their joint services fall under §543(a)(7)? Several early cases held that the entire amount was within or outside the statutory provision, depending on whether the services of the other employees were incidental or important.[130] The Treasury accepted the no-allocation principle for menial or incidental services by non-shareholder employees but amended the regulations to provide for an allocation if their services are important and essential.[131] It has been held that this does not permit an allocation unless the contract explicitly requires the performance of important services by other employees.[132]

8. Income from estates and trusts. If the corporation is a beneficiary of a trust or estate, amounts includable in its income by virtue of the provisions of Subchapter J are treated as PHC income.

¶ 8.23 DEFINITION OF "PERSONAL HOLDING COMPANY": STOCK OWNERSHIP

As stated earlier, a corporation is a PHC if both its stock ownership and its gross income meet certain mechanical tests. The stock ownership test is met if, at any time during the last half of the taxable year, more than 50 percent in value of the corporation's outstanding stock is owned, directly or indirectly, by or for not more than five individuals.[133] The term "individual" presumably has the same meaning as in §1 of the Code, except that §542(a)(2) provides that some tax-exempt organizations and trusts are to be

---

[130] See General Management Corp. v. CIR, 135 F2d 882 (7th Cir.), cert. denied, 320 US 757 (1943) (services of auxiliary employees compared to "the trowel of the mason, the plane of the carpenter, the nurse assisting the physician"); Allen Mach. Corp., 31 TC 441 (1958) (acq.).

[131] See Regs. §1.543-1(b)(8)(ii), Example (2); see also Portable Indus., Inc., supra note 120 (allocation between royalties and compensation for services).

[132] Kurt Frings Agency, Inc., 42 TC 472 (1964), aff'd per curiam, 351 F2d 951 (9th Cir. 1965); Kenyatta Corp., supra note 127.

[133] See Coshocton Secs. Co., 26 TC 935 (1956) (taxpayer a PHC by reason of its stock ownership and gross income, although it could not have determined this fact for itself because some of its stock was owned by another corporation that would not have disclosed its beneficial ownership). Hybrid securities and the debt of thin corporations may be treated as stock for this purpose, at least to make the corporation a PHC. Query whether the corporation can escape this status by impeaching its own debt instruments? See Washmont Corp. v. Hendricksen, 137 F2d 306 (9th Cir. 1943) (corporation's label important, although not controlling).

treated as individuals, evidently on the theory that they may be dominated by the other shareholders of the corporation.

If all the corporation's outstanding stock is owned by fewer than 10 individuals, the stock ownership requirement of §542(a)(2) will automatically be satisfied, since more than 50 percent of the stock will necessarily be owned by five individuals or fewer. If the stock is more widely dispersed, however, or if some of it is owned by corporations, trusts, estates, or other entities, a closer examination of the facts will be required, since the ownership of stock is to be determined by the constructive ownership rules of §544. The principal features of these constructive ownership rules are as follows:

(1) Stock owned by corporations, partnerships, estates, or trusts is attributed proportionately to the shareholders, partners, or beneficiaries of these entities.

(2) An individual is considered as owning the stock owned by his brothers, sisters, spouse, ancestors, and lineal descendants.

(3) A member of a partnership is considered as owning the stock owned by his partners.

(4) A person having an option to acquire stock is considered as owning the stock itself.

(5) Certain securities convertible into stock are treated as outstanding stock.[134]

¶ 8.24   COMPUTATION OF PERSONAL HOLDING COMPANY TAX

If the corporation is found to be a PHC, a tax (in addition to the regular corporate income tax) is imposed by §541 at the rate of 28 percent in 1988 and thereafter (38.5 percent for 1987) on its undistributed PHC income. In the interest of brevity (and on the theory that any corporation that finds itself subject to this tax will have ample leisure to work out the details of the computation), only the highlights of the computation will be set out here.[135]

There are two steps in computing the taxable base (undistributed PHC income).

---

[134] For a more detailed discussion, see Ringel, Surrey & Warren, Attribution of Stock Ownership in the Internal Revenue Code, 72 Harv. L. Rev. 209 (1958); see also infra ¶ 9.03.

[135] For a more detailed explanation, see Mathison, supra note 100, at A-2.

1. Adjustments to taxable income. The corporation's taxable income is adjusted in the manner prescribed by §545(b). These adjustments transform taxable income into an amount that more closely resembles the corporation's net economic gain for the year. Thus, federal income taxes are deducted; the 80 percent dividends-received deduction of §243 is eliminated; the deduction for charitable contributions is not limited to 10 percent of taxable income but is allowed up to the percentage limits applicable to individuals; net capital gains (less the taxes allocable thereto) are eliminated from taxable income (so that, in effect, the corporation may accumulate long-term capital gains); the limitation on business expenses and depreciation of §545(b)(6) is applied, and the net operating loss deduction is severely limited, creating the possibility of an unexpectedly large PHC tax; and certain other adjustments are made.[136] It should be noted that the base on which the tax is imposed differs in many respects from PHC income, the concept used in determining whether a corporation is to be classified as a PHC.[137]

In addition to these generally applicable adjustments, §545(c) authorizes corporations that became PHCs by virtue of statutory changes in 1964 to deduct certain amounts paid or irrevocably set aside to discharge preexisting indebtedness,[138] and §546(d) limits the tax base of certain foreign corporations to amounts qualifying as personal service income from contracts described by §543(a)(7).

2. Dividends-paid deduction. From taxable income as thus adjusted there is deducted the dividends-paid deduction of §561. This deduction is the sum of (1) the dividends paid during the taxable year,[139] (2) the consent

---

[136] See Rev. Rul. 72-306, 1972-1 CB 165 (deduction of federal income taxes); Ellis Corp., 57 TC 520 (1972) (attribution of taxes to net capital gains); Rev. Rul. 79-59, 1979-1 CB 209 (loss carry-overs and carry-backs generally denied except for loss of preceding year, which is allowed in computing PHC tax, even though also allowed as carry-back in computing §11 tax); Kluger Assocs. v. CIR, 617 F2d 323 (2d Cir. 1980) (contested taxes not accruable); LX Cattle Co. v. US, 629 F2d 1096 (5th Cir. 1980) (same); Mariani Frozen Foods, Inc., supra note 91.

[137] See generally Friedman, Liquidation of Corporations Becoming Domestic Personal Holding Companies Under the Revenue Act of 1964, 20 Tax L. Rev. 435 (1965); Feder, Relieving the Impact of the Revenue Act of 1964 on "New" Personal Holding Companies, 23 NYU Inst. on Fed. Tax'n 723 (1965).

[138] See supra ¶ 8.22.

[139] The term "dividend" is defined by §562, which looks primarily to the standard definition of §316(a) as modified by §316(b)(2)(A), providing that certain distributions by PHCs are taxable to the shareholders as dividends, notwithstanding an absence of earnings and profits. Section 316(b)(2)(A) was intended as a relief measure; before its enactment, a PHC might be unable to make a dividend distribution of its PHC income because it had no earnings and profits. Thus, §316(b)(2)(A) is

dividends for the taxable year as provided in §565, and (3) the dividend carry-over of §564. Items (1) and (2) were described earlier, in conjunction with the accumulated earnings tax. Item (3) is the excess of dividends paid during the two preceding taxable years over the corporation's taxable income, as adjusted under §545, for those years.

Since the PHC tax is imposed on the corporation's *undistributed* PHC income, it is often said that a PHC can ward off liability for this tax by distributing its entire income for the taxable year. This general rule, however, is not precise enough as a guide to action. What is required is not a distribution of the corporation's taxable income, earnings and profits, or economic gains but a distribution of such an amount as will leave behind no undistributed PHC income. Thus, a corporation with a substantial amount of taxable income may not need to make any distribution if it has a §564 dividend carry-over that will eliminate its PHC income for the year. On the other hand, a corporation with little taxable income may find it necessary to make a substantial distribution because its taxable income reflects a dividends-received deduction under §243 that is not allowed in computing undistributed personal holding company income.

3. Deficiency dividend procedure. Because the prime purpose of the PHC tax is not to raise revenue but to force such corporations to distribute earnings to their shareholders (in whose hands the distributed earnings will be subject to the personal income tax), and in recognition of the PHC tax's punitive rate, §547 provides a locus poenitentiae in the form of the deficiency dividend procedure. Briefly stated, this procedure permits the corporation, after its liability for a PHC tax has been established, to make a dividend distribution to its shareholders and to take this distribution into account in retroactive reduction of its tax liability. In effect, the shareholders

---

similar in its purpose and effect to §316(a)(2) (supra ¶ 7.02). See Morris Inv. Corp. v. CIR, 156 F2d 748 (3d Cir.), cert. denied, 329 US 788 (1946); H.R. Rep. No. 2333, 77th Cong., 1st Sess. 136, 185 (1942), reprinted in 1942-2 CB 372, 473.

Under §§563(b) and 563(c), dividends paid within two and one-half months after the close of the year can be treated as paid on the last day of the year to a limited extent. When applying §§563(b) and 563(c), the failure of the PHC to distribute any dividends during the taxable year precludes the benefits of a purgative distribution made within the following two and one-half months. See Kenneth F. Darrow, 64 TC 217 (1975); Rev. Rul. 72-152, 1972-1 CB 272.

Regarding in-kind dividends, see supra note 94. Regarding §562(c) preferential dividends, see Henry Schwartz Corp., 60 TC 728 (1973) (acq.) (travel and entertainment expenses of husband and wife, equal owners of corporation, disallowed to corporation as §162 deductions; as constructive dividends to the shareholders, they qualified for dividends-paid deduction because pro rata).

For analysis of the intricate rules applicable to liquidating distributions, see Mathison, supra note 100 at A-12; Rev. Rul. 86-27, 1986-1 CB 248.

will be taxed currently by virtue of the distribution, and the corporation will thereby become entitled to a partial or complete refund of its PHC tax.[140] The corporation's liability for interest on the PHC tax is not eliminated, however, nor is its liability for penalties, additions for late filing or negligence, and so forth. Moreover, deficiency dividends do not negate the corporation's status as a PHC for such purposes as the alternate minimum tax and application of the at-risk rules of §465.

---

[140] The deficiency dividend procedures are strictly construed. See Leck Co. v. US, 32 AFTR2d 5891 (D. Minn. 1973) (taxpayer made distribution before §547(c) determination; despite good faith, distribution was not a §547(d)(1) deficiency distribution); Fletcher v. US, 674 F2d 1308 (9th Cir. 1982) (distribution before §547 determination of PHC liability not qualified); Rev. Rul. 86-104, 1986-34 IRB 14 (no extension of time to distribute). See generally Baumann, Jr., Deficiency Dividends and Other Solutions for Avoiding Personal Holding Company Tax, 59 J. Tax'n 202 (1983).

For attempts by shareholders to avoid tax on ripe deficiency dividend distributions by transferring their stock on the threshold of the distribution, see Rev. Rul. 60-331, 1960-2 CB 189 (§351 exchange not effective); George Cukor, ¶ 68,017 P-H Memo. TC (1968) (contra). Estate of Smith v. CIR, 292 F2d 478 (3d Cir. 1961), cert. denied, 368 US 967 (1962) (gift; not effective). See generally supra ¶ 7.07.

CHAPTER 9

Stock Redemptions and Partial Liquidations

PART A. EFFECT ON SHAREHOLDERS: SALE VS. DIVIDEND

¶ 9.01 PRE-1954 BACKGROUND

When a shareholder transfers stock to the issuing corporation in exchange for money or other property, the transaction may resemble either an ordinary sale of stock to an outsider in an arm's-length bargain or the receipt by the shareholder of a dividend from the corporation. The sale analogy is appropriate, for example, when the owner of preferred stock instructs a broker to sell the stock, and the broker, by chance, effects a sale to the corporation, which happens to be buying up its preferred stock at the time. The preferred shareholder ought to be able to treat the transaction in the same manner as any other sale, reporting the difference between the adjusted basis and the sales price as capital gain or loss.

On the other hand, when the owner of a one-person corporation having only common stock outstanding forgoes dividends for a period of years and then "sells" some shares to the corporation for cash, the transaction is more like a dividend than a sale. Although the shareholder has surrendered some of his stock, his interest in the corporation's assets and his control of the corporation's fate are undisturbed. If the transaction were not taxed as a dividend, moreover, the shareholder could enter upon a long-range program of intermittent transfers of stock to his corporation, employing tax-free stock dividends if necessary to replace his shares and to restore the corporation's stated capital for the benefit of nervous creditors. For shareholders who could adopt such a plan of intermittent "sales" of stock, the tax on dividend income would become a dead letter.

It should not be surprising, then, that a "sale" of stock by a shareholder to his corporation is sometimes taxed as a dividend instead as a sale. The knotty problem that has faced Congress, the Treasury, and the courts over the years—to which there can never be a universally acceptable solution—is the determination of which transfers of stock are to be classified as dividends and which as sales. For a period of more than 30 years ending in 1954, the general rule was that such transactions were sales unless the transaction was "essentially equivalent to the distribution of a taxable dividend" within the meaning of §115(g) of the 1939 Code,[1] in which event the entire distribution was taxed under §115(g) of the 1939 Code as a dividend to the extent of current and post-1913 earnings and profits. Although current law, as

---

[1] For a more extended account of §115(g) and pre-1954 law, see Bittker & Redlich, Corporate Liquidations and the Income Tax, 5 Tax L. Rev. 437, 470–473 (1950); Darrell, Corporate Liquidations and the Federal Income Tax, 89 U. Pa. L. Rev. 907 (1941).

explained below, is much more elaborate, it preserves this ancient and troublesome phrase, and thus a few words of history are necessary before we turn to the statutory language of the 1954 Code.

When the "essentially equivalent to the distribution of a taxable dividend" language first appeared, the courts were reluctant to tax redemptions as dividends unless the redeemed shares had been issued as tax-free stock dividends or in anticipation of a later redemption. Later, however, the courts viewed §115(g) more literally in that they increasingly started with the assumption that any pro rata redemption was equivalent to a taxable dividend, casting on the taxpayer the burden of establishing that it ought to be treated as a sale instead. If the redemption was not pro rata, however, it was ordinarily treated as a sale of stock by the shareholder, on which capital gain or loss would be realized. This exemption for disproportionate redemptions was based on the regulations, which provided for sale treatment if all of a particular shareholder's stock was redeemed,[2] and on the theory that a redemption of part of a shareholder's stock could be equally efficacious in changing "his interest in the corporation in the same way that redemption of all of his stock would do."[3]

As §115(g) of the 1939 Code came to be the norm rather than the exception by which all pro rata redemptions were tested, taxpayers found that the most promising escape was a judicial doctrine that a redemption resulting from a corporation contraction (or a "legitimate shrinkage") in the corporation's business activities was not essentially equivalent to a dividend.[4] The courts also agreed that a redemption for legitimate business purposes was not taxable under §115(g), without, however, agreeing on the meaning of that phrase. Even less helpful was the solemn announcement that the true test was whether the net effect of the redemption was the distribution of a dividend. In its infancy, this test was an attempt to escape an inquiry into the motives and plans of the shareholder and his corporation.[5] Since virtually all pro rata redemptions have the net effect of a dividend, however, the courts finally succeeded in converting this test into a restatement of the essentially equivalent language of the statute or, sometimes, into a pseudo-

---

[2] Regs. §118, §39.115(g)-1(a)(2). For an interpretation of this requirement, see Rev. Rul. 54-408, 1954-2 CB 165.

[3] Ferris v. US, 135 F. Supp. 286, 288 (Ct. Cl. 1955). As to pre-1954 Code redemptions that were superficially non-pro rata, but were pro rata in reality either because the loss of the redeemed shares did not seriously affect the shareholder's relative position or because the shareholder was closely related to the remaining shareholders, see J. Natwick, 36 BTA 866, 876 (1937); Pullman, Inc., 8 TC 292, 297 (1947) (acq.).

[4] See Joseph W. Imler, 11 TC 836 (1948) (acq.); for the continuing importance of this case and the corporate contraction doctrine, see infra ¶ 9.09.

[5] See Flanagan v. Helvering, 116 F2d 937 (D.C. Cir. 1940).

nym for the business purpose doctrine that this test was created to avoid.[6] The upshot was that in applying §115(g) of the 1939 Code, there was no escape from an inquiry into all the facts and circumstances of each case, and predictions were hazardous.[7]

The drafters of the 1954 Code hoped to bring order to this messy area by distinguishing between distributions that "may have capital-gain characteristics because they are not made pro rata among the various shareholders" and distributions "characterized by what happens solely at the corporate level by reason of the assets distributed."[8] The first of these two categories, which carries forward the non-pro rata concept of pre-1954 law, is governed by §§302(b)(1), 302(b)(2), and 302(b)(3) of current law (relating respectively to redemptions that are "not essentially equivalent to dividends," substantially disproportionate redemptions, and redemptions terminating the shareholder's entire interest in the corporation); the second category, which preserves the corporate contraction doctrine of pre-1954 law (but only for the benefit of noncorporate distributees), is embodied in §302(b)(4), relating to partial liquidations.

The balance of this chapter deals with the treatment of redemptions, partial liquidations, and certain related problems in the following order:

(1) Disproportionate redemptions, including the constructive ownership rules and the treatment of bootstrap acquisitions;

(2) Partial liquidations;

(3) Redemptions to pay death taxes;

(4) Redemptions of stock by affiliated corporations; and

(5) Collateral problems (i.e., computation of the shareholder's gain or loss; the mystery of the disappearing basis; the shareholder's basis for property received in redemption of stock; recognition of income or loss by the redeeming corporation; and the effect of a redemption on the corporation's earnings and profits).

¶ 9.02　SALE VS. DIVIDEND TREATMENT

Section 302(a) provides that a redemption of stock "shall be treated as a distribution in part or full payment in exchange for the stock" if the transaction fits into any one of the following four categories:

---

[6] See Keefe v. Cote, 213 F2d 651 (1st Cir. 1954).

[7] See generally Treusch, Corporate Distributions and Adjustments: Recent Case Reminders of Some Old Problems Under the New Code, 32 Taxes 1023, 1037 (1954); Bittker & Redlich, supra note 1.

[8] S. Rep. No. 1622, 83d Cong., 2d Sess. 49 (1954).

(1) A redemption that is not essentially equivalent to a dividend under §302(b)(1);

(2) A substantially disproportionate redemption under §302(b)(2);

(3) A redemption of all the shareholder's stock under §302(b)(3); and

(4) A partial liquidation under §302(b)(4) (applicable only if the redeemed shareholder is not a corporation).[9]

By virtue of §302(d), a redemption that does not fall within any of these categories is to be treated as a distribution under §301 (i.e., as a dividend to the extent of current and post-1913 earnings and profits, and a return of capital to the extent of any balance). Exchange treatment is almost always more advantageous to noncorporate shareholders than distribution treatment, since the former means that the amount includable in income is not the full amount received but that amount less the adjusted basis of the stock. Furthermore, although this is of lesser importance now that the pre-1987 capital gains deduction has been repealed, the gain or loss on the redemption is capital gain or loss if the stock is a capital asset in the shareholder's hands. (If the redemption is on credit, sale treatment also may entitle the selling shareholder to defer his gain under §453 if the stock is not publicly traded.) For corporate shareholders, however, dividend treatment may be preferable because then the amount received qualifies for the 80 or 100 percent dividends received deduction of §243 or is excluded from income if the corporations file consolidated returns.[10]

The term "redemption" is defined by §317(b) as a corporation's acquisition of its stock from a shareholder in exchange for property whether or not the stock is canceled, retired, or held as treasury stock.[11] This definition, as

---

[9] See generally Bacon, Corporate Stock Redemptions–Definitions; Basic Categories, Tax Mgmt. (BNA) No. 343-2d (1986); Chirelstein, Optional Redemptions and Optional Dividends: Taxing the Repurchase of Common Shares, 78 Yale L.J. 739 (1969); Thurston, The Considerations of Tax Reform: A Study of the Taxation of Nondividend Distributions, 32 Tax Notes 357 (1986); for special rules governing the redemption of stock of a collapsible corporation, see infra ¶ 12.02; for redemptions of "section 306 stock" (primarily, preferred stock issued as a tax-free stock dividend), see infra ¶ 10.02.

[10] For §243, see supra ¶ 5.05; for consolidated returns, see infra ¶ 15.20. For the reversal of roles that may occur in these circumstances, see Pacific Vegetable Oil Corp. v. CIR, 251 F2d 682 (9th Cir. 1957), where the corporate taxpayer successfully argued that a redemption was essentially equivalent to a dividend, while the government argued that it was not; see also Waterman S.S. Corp. v. CIR, 430 F2d 1185 (5th Cir. 1970), cert. denied, 401 US 939 (1971).

See generally Faber, Capital Gains v. Dividends in Corporate Transactions: Is the Battle Still Worth Fighting?, 64 Taxes 865 (1986).

[11] See Casco Prods. Corp., 49 TC 32 (1967) (transaction a reorganization in form but held to be in substance an indirect method of redeeming dissident minority inter-

well as §302 itself, presupposes that the redeemed instrument is properly classified as stock; as explained earlier, purported stock is sometimes reclassified as debt (in which event §302 is inapplicable), and vice versa. [12]

Of the four categories of redemptions that are treated as exchanges by §302(b), the most important in planning financial transactions are §302(b)(2) (substantially disproportionate redemptions) and §302(b)(3) (complete termination of shareholder's interest); [13] their rules, if complied with carefully, provide safe conduct passes to the promised land of sale treatment. Taxpayers who cannot bring transactions within these requirements can try to avail themselves of §302(b)(1) by establishing that the redemption is not essentially equivalent to a dividend; this, however, is a treacherous route, to be employed only as a last resort. [14] Section 302(b)(4), relating to partial liquidations, is useful only if the redeeming corporation carries on two or more qualified trades or businesses (as defined) or is, by reason of extraneous circumstances, able to effect a bona fide contraction of its business; it applies only to noncorporate shareholders. [15]

In determining whether a redemption qualifies as an exchange under these provisions, the constructive ownership rules of §318(a) must be taken into account. These rules apply to any transaction within the ambit of Sub-

---

est); Harry F. Cornwall, 48 TC 736 (1967) (acq.) (reduction of association member's interest held a redemption); Rev. Rul. 73-427, 1973-2 CB 301, and Rev. Rul. 78-250, 1978-1 CB 83 (reverse cash merger with transitory subsidiary treated as §302 redemption); Estate of A.J. Schneider, 88 TC No. 50 (1987) (purported sale in substance a redemption).

As to whether amounts received constitute redemption proceeds taxable as capital gain if §302(a) applies, or instead are payments of accrued dividends, see Arie S. Crown, 58 TC 825 (1972), aff'd mem., 487 F2d 1404 (7th Cir. 1973) (redemption of preferred stock with dividend arrears; held taxable under §301 to extent that corporation was legally obligated to pay dividends); Rev. Rul. 69-130, 1969-1 CB 93 (dividend declared prior to call of preferred stock included in redemption payments; taxable as §301 dividend); Rev. Rul. 75-320, 1975-2 CB 105 (redemption of preferred stock with dividend arrears; held taxable in part as capital gain and in part as §301 dividend to extent shareholders had legal right to dividend at time of redemption); Estate of Mathis, 47 TC 248 (1966) (acq.) (redemption of preferred stock with cumulative dividend arrears held taxable as capital gain); Rev. Rul. 69-131, 1969-1 CB 94 (premium paid for early redemption of preferred stock and amounts paid for undeclared dividends accruing on redemption date held taxable as redemption proceeds).

[12] See supra ¶ 4.21.

[13] For §§302(b)(2) and 302(b)(3), see infra ¶¶ 9.04 and 9.05 respectively. See also Rev. Proc. 86-18, 1986-1 CB 551 (procedure for requesting rulings under §302).

[14] See infra ¶ 9.06.

[15] See infra ¶¶ 9.08–9.09; Rev. Proc. 81-42, 1981-2 CB 611 (partial liquidation ruling procedure).

chapter C to which they are expressly made applicable and thus are by no means confined to stock redemptions.[16] But they have taken on special importance in the area of redemptions and are thus conveniently discussed at this point. As will be seen, these constructive ownership rules are expressly made applicable to §§302(b)(2) and 302(b)(3) redemptions by the statute itself; and Regs. §1.302-1(a) provides that they are also applicable to §302(b)(1) redemptions.[17] Because of the pervasive effect of constructive ownership on the redemption of the stock of family and other closely held corporations, §318 is examined here in some detail before consideration of the substantive rules of §302(b).

¶ 9.03   CONSTRUCTIVE OWNERSHIP OF STOCK

By virtue of §318(a), a taxpayer is considered as owning any stock that is (1) owned by certain members of his family; (2) owned by partnerships, estates, certain trusts, and certain corporations in which he is interested; or (3) subject to an option held by him. Conversely, entities in which he is beneficially interested (partnerships, estates, trusts, and corporations) are treated, subject to certain limitations, as owning stock that is owned directly by him. The attribution rules create, but do not destroy, ownership;[18] for example, if *A* owns 85 percent of a corporation's stock, and *B*, a person unrelated to *A* under §318, owns the other 15 percent and has an option to increase his percentage of ownership to 25 percent by acquiring unissued shares, *B*'s constructive ownership of 25 percent of the stock does not reduce *A*'s percentage of ownership from 85 to 75 percent.

Section 318(a) applies to transactions governed by Subchapter C (i.e., §§301-383, covering most, but not all, of the transactions discussed in this book), but only if expressly made applicable by the relevant statutory provi-

---

[16] For a list of provisions subject to §318(a), see the cross references in §318(b).

Pre-1954 law did not explicitly attribute stock owned by one person to another in the application of §115(g) of the 1939 Code, but both the courts and the Service at times regarded the relationship between a shareholder whose stock was redeemed and the remaining shareholders as significant in applying §115(g). See Rev. Rul. 55-373, 1955-1 CB 363; Rev. Rul. 55-547, 1955-2 CB 571; William H. Grimditch, 37 BTA 402, 412 (1938); 16 Fed. Reg. 10,312 (1951) (proposed regulation regarding tax effect of relationship between shareholders). But see Estate of Lukens, 246 F2d 403 (3d Cir. 1957).

[17] For the application of §318(a) to §302(b)(4), relating to partial liquidations, see infra ¶ 9.08.

[18] See Northwestern Steel & Supply Co., 60 TC 356, 362 (1973); see also Complete Fin. Corp., 766 F2d 436 (10th Cir. 1985) (family attribution rules of §1563). But see §382(l)(3)(A)(ii)(II), infra ¶ 16.24.

sion. Although intricately devised, §318 is only one of several sets of constructive ownership rules prescribed by the 1954 Code that differ among themselves in such details as the degree of family relationship warranting the attribution of stock from one person to another and in the way stock owned by a trust is allocated to its beneficiaries.[19] Although appropriate variations in the concept of attribution to suit the transaction under review are theoretically conceivable or even praiseworthy, the differences in the statutory provisions as actually prescribed by the Code are frequently trivial and almost always inexplicable.[20]

The types of attribution prescribed by §318 may be divided into attribution (1) from one member of a family to another (sometimes called collateral attribution); (2) from an entity, such as a trust or corporation, to persons beneficially interested therein, or vice versa (vertical or direct attribution, where the entity's stock is attributed to its owners or beneficiaries, and back attribution where their stock is attributed to the entity); and (3) from an entity to its owners or beneficiaries and from them to members of their family (or, conversely, from family members to beneficiaries and thence up to the entity), a combination of (1) and (2) that is sometimes called chain or double attribution, or reattribution.

Before 1964, a fourth category of attribution was possible, since stock owned by one beneficiary of an entity could be attributed to the entity and thence to another beneficiary. This type of reattribution is now prevented by §318(a)(5)(C).[21] Stock owned by the entity and attributed to a beneficiary thereof, however, is reattributed to the members of his family (and family stock attributed to a beneficiary is reattributed to the entity). This form of reattribution was unaffected by the 1964 change, and it causes much of the complexity and most of the confusion in applying §318.

Stated in greater detail, the constructive ownership rules of §318 are as follows:

---

[19] See, e.g., §341(d) (collapsible corporations), which adopts the constructive ownership rules of §544 applicable to personal holding companies; §267(c), supra ¶ 5.04.

[20] See generally Coven, The Affinity Provisions of the IRC: A Case Study in Nonsimplification, 45 Tenn. L. Rev. 557 (1978); Loeb, What Constitutes Ownership of Stock, 21 NYU Inst. on Fed. Tax'n, 417 (1963); Ringel, Surrey & Warren, Attribution of Stock Ownership in the Internal Revenue Code, 72 Harv. L. Rev. 209 (1958); Reilly, An Approach to the Simplification and Standardization of the Concepts "The Family," "Related Parties," "Control," and "Attribution of Ownership," 15 Tax L. Rev. 253 (1960).

[21] For an example of the type of attribution eliminated by the 1964 change, see S. Rep. No. 1240, 88th Cong., 2d Sess. 6 (1964), reprinted in 1964-2 CB 701, 705; see also Baker Commodities, Inc. v. CIR, 415 F2d 519 (9th Cir. 1969), cert. denied, 397 US 988 (1970). Note that the 1964 changes did *not* cover reattributions via the option rule of §318(a)(4).

1. Family attribution. Under §318(a)(1), an individual is deemed to own stock owned by his spouse, children, grandchildren, and parents. (Unlike §§267(c)(4) and 544(a)(2), §318(a)(1) does not attribute stock from one brother or sister to another.) Stock attributed from one family member to another under §318(a)(1) is not reattributed from the latter to members of *his* family.

> *To illustrate:* If *H*, his wife *W*, their son *S*, and their grandson, *G* each owns 25 shares of *X* Corporation, *H*, *W*, and *S* are each deemed to own 100 shares of *X* by virtue of §318(a)(1); *G*, on the other hand, is deemed to own only 50 shares (25 directly and 25 constructively from his father *S*). If *G* had a brother, *B*, no stock would be attributed from *G* to *B* through their father, *S*, because of §318(a)(5)(B).

A fortiori, §318(a)(5)(B) insures that stock owned by Bittker will not be attributed to his parents and then from them to *their* parents, and so on back to Adam and Eve, and then down through the family of man to Eustice.

2. Entity-to-beneficiary attribution. Under §318(a)(2), stock owned, directly or indirectly, by partnerships, estates, trusts, and corporations is attributed to the beneficial owners in the following manner: Section 318(a)(2)(A) provides that stock owned by or for a partnership or estate[22] is considered as owned by the partners or estate beneficiaries[23] in proportion to their beneficial interests. Section 318(a)(2)(B) provides that stock owned by a trust (other than a §401(a) trust for employees) is considered to be owned by the beneficiaries in proportion to their actuarial interest in the trust (regardless of how small, remote, or contingent it may be)[24] or, in the case of a trust described in §§671-679, to the person taxable on its income.

---

[22] Regs. §1.318-3(a) provides that stock is owned by an estate, for this purpose, if it is subject to administration, notwithstanding that legal title to the stock under local law vests in the heirs immediately upon death. It also defines the term "beneficiary of an estate"; see also Rev. Rul. 60-18, 1960-1 CB 145 (residuary legatee of an estate remains a beneficiary until the estate is closed).

[23] See Regs. §1.318-3(a) (person ceases to be beneficiary of estate when all property to which he is entitled has been received by him and there is only remote possibility that it will be necessary for estate to seek return of property or contribution to satisfy claims); see also Estate of Webber v. US, 404 F2d 411 (6th Cir. 1968) (debtor-beneficiary concept of regulations upheld); Estate of Weiskopf, 77 TC 135 (1981) (on facts, certain trusts were no longer beneficiaries of estate for attribution purposes).

[24] Compare the treatment of estate beneficiaries, where future interests do not confer beneficiary status; see §318(a)(3)(B)(i), which does not attribute stock from a beneficiary of a trust to the trust if the beneficiary's interest is both contingent and remote; see also Rev. Rul. 71-211, 1971-1 CB 112 (trust's stock not attributed to contingent beneficiary who renounced interest in trust).

Section 318(a)(2)(C) provides that stock owned by a corporation is attributed pro rata to those shareholders (if any) who own 50 percent or more by value of its stock.[25]

3. Beneficiary-to-entity attribution. Under §318(a)(3), stock owned, directly or indirectly, by partners, beneficiaries, and shareholders is attributed to a partnership, estate, trust, or corporation as follows: Section 318(a)(3)(A) provides that stock owned by partners or beneficiaries of an estate[26] is attributed (in full) to the partnership or estate. Section 318(a)(3)(B) states that stock owned by a beneficiary of a trust (other than a §401(a) employees' trust) is attributed to the trust unless the beneficiary has only a remote and contingent interest, as defined,[27] and that stock owned by a person taxable on trust income under §§671–679 is attributed to the trust. Section 318(a)(3)(C) provides that stock owned by a shareholder owning 50 percent or more of the value of a corporation's stock is attributed to the corporation.

As noted previously, however, by virtue of the 1964 amendments of §318(a)(5)(C), stock attributed from a beneficiary to an entity is not reattributed to other beneficiaries of the same entity.

4. Option attribution. Under §318(a)(4), a person who has an option to acquire stock is deemed to own the optioned stock (but not other stock owned by the optionor). The relation of §318(a)(4) to contingent options (e.g., an option exercisable on a merger, pursuant to a conversion privilege in a bond or note, or on a shareholder's death) and to options on unissued (or treasury) stock is unclear; the cases and rulings to date are conflicting.[28]

---

[25] Regs. §1.318-1(b)(3) provides that stock owned actually and constructively by the shareholder shall be aggregated in applying the 50 percent requirement; see also Regs. §1.318-2(a), Example (2). But the amount of stock owned by the corporation allocated to such a 50 percent shareholder may arguably be based on his actual, rather than constructive, ownership percentage; the statute and regulations are not clear on this point.

[26] For beneficiary status, see supra notes 22–24; see also Rev. Rul. 67-24, 1967-1 CB 75 (testamentary trust treated as in existence even though property will not be transferred to it until estate administration is completed). This ruling also notes that a beneficiary's stock is attributed to a trust and from it to an estate of which the trust is a beneficiary; this is not inconsistent with §318(a)(5)(C) because the reattribution from the trust to the estate is mandated by §318(a)(3)(A) rather than by §318(a)(2).

[27] See Regs. §1.318-2(c), Examples (2) and (3).

[28] See Sorem v. CIR, 334 F2d 275 (10th Cir. 1964) (employee stock options on unissued stock are to be taken into account); Regs. §1.302-3(a) (disregarding unissued stock); see also Rev. Rul. 68-601, 1968-2 CB 124, holding that warrants and convertible debentures are options within the meaning of §318(a)(4); but, contrary to

If both the option attribution and family attribution rules can apply, the option rule takes precedence by virtue of §318(a)(5)(D). A reattribution of the optioned stock to another member of the option holder's family is thus permitted. Similarly, if a partnership, estate, trust, or corporation has an option on stock owned by a partner, beneficiary, or shareholder, the stock can be reattributed to other beneficiaries of the entity.[29]

5. Other aspects of §318. Two ambiguities in the language of §318 are clarified by Regs. §1.318-1(b): A corporation is not deemed to own its own stock,[30] and stock is not to be counted more than once—for example, stock owned by a beneficiary of a trust is not attributed to the trust and then reattributed to the beneficiary. In determining constructive stock ownership, however, the stock is to be attributed in such a way as to maximize the taxpayer's ownership. Thus, if a 50 percent trust beneficiary has an option on all the stock of X Corporation owned by the trust, he is charged with all rather than only 50 percent of the stock, since the option rules result in greater constructive ownership.

Although the attribution rules of §318 are ordinarily disadvantageous to taxpayers, they may occasionally be used affirmatively to qualify a particular transaction for favorable treatment.

To illustrate: H owns 40 shares of X, W (his wife) owns 10, and A (unrelated) owns 50. A redemption of 23 of H's shares and 2 of W's shares will qualify both H and W for the favorable treatment accorded to substantially disproportionate redemptions by §302(b)(2),[31] since

---

Sorem, that stock subject to options is outstanding only for purposes of individual holder's ownership computation; Patterson Trust v. US, 729 F2d 1089 (6th Cir. 1984) (contra to Rev. Rul. 68-601, optioned stock treated as outstanding for denominator in computing dividend equivalent effect); §305(d), treating options as stock and option holders as stockholders for purposes of the stock dividend rules; Rev. Rul. 67-269, 1967-2 CB 298 (holder of warrant or convertible debenture not a shareholder for Subchapter S purposes, supra ¶ 6.02); infra note 36. See also §382(l)(3)(A)(iv), infra ¶ 16.24.

See generally Bloom & Willens, How to Treat Option Shares Held by Third Parties in Planning for a Redemption, 62 J. Tax'n 80 (1985); Winston, Attribution of Stock Ownership From Stock Options Under the Internal Revenue Code, 44 U. Chi. L. Rev. 482 (1977).

[29] Section 318(a)(5)(C), forbidding attributions from a beneficiary to an entity and thence to another beneficiary, does not apply to attributions of optioned stock. But see infra note 30.

[30] See also Rev. Rul. 69-562, 1969-2 CB 48 (corporation's option to acquire its own stock from one of its shareholders not subject to §318(a)(4) because on acquiring stock, corporation will not obtain voting or other shareholder rights).

[31] See infra ¶ 9.04.

both will be treated by §318 as owning 50 shares out of 100 before the redemption, and only 25 out of 75 thereafter. Were it not for §318, the change in W's ownership (from 10 out of 100 to 8 out of 75) would not be sufficiently disproportionate for favorable treatment under §302(b)(2).

6. Examples. The provisions of §318 may be illustrated by the following examples, in which it is assumed that the parties are unrelated unless otherwise stated:

Example 1. A, an individual, owns 50 percent of X Corporation's stock. The other 50 percent is owned by a partnership in which A has a 20 percent interest. The partnership is considered as owning 100 percent of X, and A is considered as owning 10 percent in addition to the *50* percent he actually owns.

Example 2. X Corporation's 100 shares of stock are owned as follows: Twenty shares each by *A, B,* and *C*, who are brothers, and 40 shares by a trust in which the interests of *A, B,* and *C*, computed actuarially, are 50 percent, 20 percent, and 30 percent, respectively. The trust is considered to own all of the stock in X, whereas *A, B,* and *C*, in addition to the 20 shares each owns directly, respectively own 20, 8, and 12 shares constructively.

If *C*'s interest in the trust was both remote (i.e., worth 5 percent or less) *and* contingent, his stock would not be attributed to the trust, but its stock would be attributed proportionately to him. [32]

Example 3. A and *B* own 70 percent and 30 percent, respectively, of *X* Corporation's stock. *A* and *X* Corporation each own one-half of *Y* Corporation's stock. *X* is deemed to own 100 percent of *Y* Corporation, while *A* is deemed to own 85 percent thereof. *Y*, on the other hand, is deemed to own 70 percent of *X* Corporation.

If *A* and *B* are related family members, *B* is deemed to own 100 percent of *Y* Corporation (85 percent by attribution from *A* and 15 percent by virtue of his 30 percent interest in *X*). (Another route to this result would be to attribute 50 percent of *Y* from *A* to *B* under family attribution, 35 percent from *X* to *A* to *B* by a combination of corporate and family attribution, and 15 percent from *X* to *B* by corporate attribution, *B* being subject thereto because he owns 30 percent of *X* directly and 70 percent by attribution from *A*.) *A* also owns 100 percent of *Y* (50 percent directly, 35 percent by attribution from *X*, and 15 percent by attri-

---

[32] See supra note 24.

bution from related family member B). Y is considered as owning 100 percent of X Corporation (30 percent from B to A, then 100 percent from A to Y).

Example 4. A and B each owns 50 percent of X Corporation and of Y Corporation. X is considered to own 100 percent of Y, and Y is considered to own 100 percent of X. By virtue of §318(a)(5)(C), however, A and B each owns only 50 percent of each corporation; the stock that is attributed from A to X and Y is not reattributed to B, or vice versa.

Example 5. X Corporation has 100 shares outstanding, W owns 30 shares, S (W's son), owns 20 shares, and E, an estate, owns 50 shares (W being the life beneficiary of the property administered by the estate, and S the remainderman). E owns 100 shares of X, 50 directly, 30 by attribution from W, and 20 from S to W (by family attribution) and thence from W to E (by beneficiary to estate attribution). W also owns 100 shares of X, 30 directly, 50 from E (W is considered to be the sole beneficiary, since she has the direct present interest in estate assets or income);[33] and 20 from S by family attribution. S likewise owns 100 shares of X, 20 directly, 30 from W, and 50 from E to W to S.

If S and W were unrelated, however, the estate would own only 80 shares of X (those owned directly, plus those attributed from W, S not being considered a beneficiary), as would W; S would own only 20 shares, the number owned directly.

Example 6. B has an option on stock owned by his sister, S; S's stock is attributed to B by the option rule, and is reattributed to any children of B and to the wife of B under the family rule. Although S's stock is also attributed to her parents, it would not be reattributed from them to B except for the option.

¶ 9.04 SUBSTANTIALLY DISPROPORTIONATE REDEMPTIONS

An ordinary dividend typically effects a distribution of money or property to the corporation's shareholders without disturbing their relative interests in the assets and earning capacity of the corporation. For this reason, a stock redemption was most likely to be treated as "essentially equivalent to a dividend" under §115(g) of the 1939 Code if it was pro rata among the

---

[33] See Regs. §1.318-3(a), Example (1)(b) (last sentence) and Example (2).

shareholders.[34] Conversely, a non-pro rata redemption ordinarily escaped the clutches of §115(g). Section 302(b)(2) of the 1954 Code carries forward this distinction by providing that a "substantially disproportionate" redemption is to be treated as a sale of the stock rather than as a distribution under §301.[35]

In order to qualify as substantially disproportionate under §302(b)(2), the redemption must meet three requirements:

(1) Immediately after the redemption, the shareholder must own (directly and constructively) less than 50 percent of the total combined voting power of all classes of outstanding stock entitled to vote;

(2) His percentage of the total outstanding voting stock immediately after the redemption must be less than 80 percent of his percentage of ownership of such stock immediately before the redemption; and

(3) His percentage of outstanding common stock (whether or not voting) after the redemption must be less than 80 percent of his percentage of ownership before the redemption.[36]

These tests are applied shareholder by shareholder, so that a redemption may be substantially disproportionate as to one but not as to others. The constructive ownership rules of §318 are applicable in determining whether a redemption is substantially disproportionate under §302(b)(2), and these rules materially reduce the feasibility of such redemptions by closely held family corporations.

The 50 percent restriction in §302(b)(2)(B) is presumably based on the theory that a reduction in the shareholder's proportionate ownership is not significant if he continues to own (directly or constructively) stock representing 50 percent or more of the voting power. The two 80 percent tests envision substantial shareholder-level contractions in the redeemed shareholder's equity and voting interest in the corporation.

---

[34] Supra ¶ 9.01.

[35] For a redeemed shareholder's disproportionate redemption coupled with a sale of the rest of the stock to a third party, see infra note 38; see also Rickey v. US, 592 F2d 1251 (5th Cir.), reh'g denied, 599 F2d 1054 (5th Cir. 1979) (single transaction, combination of sales and gifts, resulted in disproportionate redemption).

[36] Stock with contingent voting rights (e.g., preferred stock with a power to vote only if dividends are passed) is generally excluded from the term "voting stock." See Regs. §1.302-3(a)(3); see also Harry F. Cornwall, supra note 11 (reduction of association member's interest did not satisfy 80 percent voting interest test because voting on certain management functions was not by percentage interest).

If the corporation redeems only nonvoting stock (whether common or preferred), the redemption cannot qualify under §302(b)(2) because it will not reduce the shareholder's proportionate ownership of voting stock. A redemption of such stock can qualify, however, if it is coupled with a redemption of voting stock that would qualify if it stood alone.[37]

Regs. §1.302-3(b) sets out the following example to illustrate the application of §302(b)(2)(C):

Corporation *M* has outstanding 400 shares of common stock of which *A, B, C* and *D* each owns 100 shares or 25 percent. No stock is considered constructively owned by *A, B, C* or *D* under §318. Corporation *M* redeems 55 shares from *A*, 25 shares from *B*, and 20 shares from *C*. For the redemption to be disproportionate as to any shareholder, such shareholder must own after the redemption less than 20 percent (80 percent of 25 percent) of the 300 shares of stock then outstanding. After the redemptions, *A* owns 45 shares (15 percent), *B* owns 75 shares (25 percent), and *C* owns 80 shares (26⅔ percent). The distribution is disproportionate only with respect to *A*.

This example can be recast in tabular form:

	Shares Owned After Redemption		Shares Owned Before Redemption		Ratio of Percentage Owned After Redemption to Percentage Owned Before*	
A	45	= 15%	100	= 25%	15/25	= 60%
B	75	= 25%	100	= 25%	25/25	= 100%
C	80	= 27%	100	= 25%	27/25	= 108%
D	100	= 33%	100	= 25%	33/25	= 132%
Total	300	= 100%	400	= 100%		

*Must be less than 80% to qualify under §302(b)(2).

In computing the percentage of stock owned by each shareholder after the redemption, care must be taken to reflect the smaller number of shares

---

[37] Regs. §1.302-3(a); Rev. Rul. 77-237, 1977-2 CB 88 (piggyback rule of Regs. §1.302-3(a) applied where corporation redeemed all of nonvoting preferred stock held by one shareholder and 22 percent of common stock held by a related shareholder; §302(b)(2) satisfied because common stock was constructively owned by redeeming preferred shareholder, hence redemption was substantially disproportionate).

A redemption of voting preferred can qualify even if the shareholder owns no common; see Rev. Rul. 81-41, 1981-1 CB 121 (second 80 percent test must be satisfied only if shareholder owns some common stock).

outstanding, In the table above, for example, *B* owns 25 percent after the redemption (75 shares out of 300), not 18.75 percent (75 out of 400).[38]

To prevent an obvious abuse of §302(b)(2), the statute explicitly provides that it does not apply to any redemption under a plan that contemplates a series of redemptions that, in the aggregate, will not be substantially disproportionate with respect to the shareholder. Thus, to return to the illustration above, if the redemption of the stock of *A, B,* and *C* was in accordance with a plan by which 75 of *D*'s shares would later be redeemed, the redemption of *A*'s shares would not meet the test of §302(b)(2). For after the second step, *A* would own 20 percent of the total outstanding shares (45 out of 225), an insufficient reduction in his percentage. The redemption of *D*'s shares, however, would apparently qualify, even though it was the occasion for disallowing the redemption of *A*'s shares.[39] It should not be assumed, however, that the explicit reference in §302(b)(2)(D) to a "series of redemptions" is the Service's only weapon against attempts to abuse §302(b)(2). If a redemption viewed in isolation is substantially disproportionate as to a shareholder but the other shareholders have agreed to sell enough stock to him after the redemption to restore the status quo, the redemption will probably not satisfy §302(b)(2).

Finally, the Service will not issue an advance ruling on a redemption if the corporation is to pay for the stock over a long future period, if payments are contingent on earnings or if the stock is held in escrow or as security so that the shareholder may reacquire it upon the corporation's default.[40] This

---

[38] A failure to take account of the reduced number of shares outstanding after a redemption produced two erroneous computations in the Senate Finance Committee's report explaining §302; see S. Rep. No. 1622, supra note 8, at 234–235; Bittker, Stock Redemptions and Partial Liquidations Under the Internal Revenue Code of 1954, 9 Stan. L. Rev. 39 n.97 (1956). See generally Freret, A Simplified Computation for Substantially Disproportionate Stock Redemptions, 37 Taxes 767 (1959).

If a redemption is integrated with a corporate sale of additional stock to outsiders, the newly issued stock should be considered outstanding stock for purposes of the disproportionate computation under §302(b)(2) but not if the two transactions are independent events. See Rev. Rul. 75-447, 1975-2 CB 113.

[39] *D* would drop from a 25 percent shareholder at the start of the redemption series to an 11 percent owner, enough to satisfy §302(b)(2).

See, e.g., Blount v. CIR, 425 F2d 921 (2d Cir. 1969); see also Rev. Rul. 85-14, 1985-1 CB 92 (redemption failed under series of redemptions rule, even in absence of formal plan or agreement, where first redeemed shareholder had knowledge of impending second redemption); but see Glacier State Elec. Supply Co., 80 TC 1047 (1983) (possible future redemption under buy-sell agreement on shareholder's death not part of plan for series of redemptions).

[40] Rev. Proc. 86-3, §§3.01(16), 3.01(17), and 4.01(12), 1986-1 CB 416 (superseded by Rev. Proc. 87-3 1987-1 IRB 27). Rev. Proc. 86-3 also states that no ruling will be issued under §302(b) if the redeemed shareholder leases property to the corporation and the rent is dependent on future corporate earnings or is subordinate to general

reluctance to rule is a warning that, in appropriate cases of abnormally long-term credit redemptions, the Service might argue that the redemption is not substantially disproportionate because the shareholder may recapture part or all of the redeemed stock or that the corporation's obligations are so much like stock that the transaction is not a redemption within the meaning of §317(b) (i.e., an acquisition of stock in exchange for *property*).[41]

¶ 9.05 TERMINATION OF SHAREHOLDER'S ENTIRE INTEREST

1. Introductory. Section 302(b)(3) provides that a redemption must be treated as a sale if it "is in complete redemption of all the stock of the corporation owned by the shareholder." If a corporation is owned by *A* and *B*, two unrelated persons, a redemption of all the stock of either *A* or *B* will qualify under §302(b)(3). A redemption of this type was similarly treated as a sale, rather than a dividend distribution, under pre-1954 law. The principal importance of §302(b)(3) lies in its waiver, in certain circumstances, of the family attribution rules of §318. This waiver provides an escape route for closely held corporations that cannot effect a substantially disproportionate redemption under §302(b)(2), because in applying that provision, the redeemed shareholder is charged with the stock owned by the remaining shareholders. If the redeemed shareholder in such a case is bought out completely, the redemption may qualify as a complete termination under §302(b)(3), even though it is not substantially disproportionate under §302(b)(2). Section 302(b)(3) is also of importance in two other situations that cannot be brought within §302(b)(2): a redemption of nonvoting stock alone (discussed in the previous section) and a redemption of "section 306 stock" (discussed in the following chapter).

In order to qualify for protection under §302(b)(3), a redemption must completely terminate the shareholder's *proprietary* interest in the corporation.[42] Such a termination is easy to identify if the shareholder is paid in

---

creditors; but rent will not be considered dependent on earnings merely because it is based on a percentage of receipts or sales.

[41] For the reclassification of purported debt as equity, see supra ¶ 4.02. Once it is decided that the transaction is not a redemption or that the corporation's obligations are not property, however, the next step is far from certain. The transaction might be regarded as a tax-free exchange under §1036 or §368(a)(1)(E), with any down payment in the form of cash being treated as boot; but it is also possible that a later payment of the obligations would be regarded as a redemption. See infra ¶ 14.17; Mary Duerr, 30 TC 944 (1958) (1939 Code case).

[42] On termination of interest problems generally, see CIR v. Brown, 380 US 563 (1965); Bryant v. CIR, 399 F2d 800 (5th Cir. 1968); Gardner & Randall, Distribu-

cash. If he takes notes or other credit instruments in exchange for his stock, however, the claim that he terminated his proprietary interest may be open to question. The Service has been reluctant to approve credit redemptions where there is a possibility of recapture of the redeemed stock upon default by the corporation or where the payout term is unreasonably long. The courts, however, have been more tolerant except where the debt obligations seem to represent a continued, though disguised, equity interest in the corporation.[43]

A §302(b)(3) termination can occur through the combination of redemption by the corporation of part of the stock and sale of the rest to third persons if both dispositions are parts of single transaction.[44]

---

tions in Redemption of Stock: Changing Definitions for a Termination of Interest, 8 J Corp. Tax'n 240 (1981).

A redemption qualifies under §302(b)(3) if it terminates the shareholder's proprietary interest in the corporation, even if the shareholder retains or acquires some other interest in the corporation. See Rev. Rul. 70-639, 1970-2 CB 74 (landlord); Rev. Rul. 76-524, 1976-2 CB 94 (officer and director); see also Claude J. Lisle, ¶ 76,140 P-H Memo. TC (1976) (redemption price payable in installments, with stock in escrow; held a §302(b)(3) termination). But see Rev. Proc. 86-3, supra note 40, regarding rent; Rev. Rul. 77-467, 1977-2 CB 92 (fixed rent lease by former shareholder not a proprietary interest; but if rent is dependent on future earnings or is subordinate to general creditors, it may be a proprietary interest under Regs. §1.302-4(d)).

[43] For the problem of determining whether an instrument represents debt or equity see supra ¶ 4.02. See also Estate of Mathis, supra note 11 (redemption price payable in installments, with stock in escrow; held a §302(b)(3) termination); Perry S. Lewis, 47 TC 129 (1966) (stock redeemed in installments; held not essentially equivalent to dividend); Estate of Milton S. Lennard, 61 TC 554 (1974) (nonacq.) (subordinated demand note, paid within three months, held true debt, not an equity participation, so interest terminated); Bernard E. Niedermeyer, 62 TC 280 (1974) (preferred stock not debt so no termination), aff'd per curiam, 535 F2d 500 (9th Cir.), cert. denied, 429 US 1000 (1976); Claude J. Lisle, supra note 42 (redemption effected complete termination under §302(b)(3), even though price payable over 20 years and shareholders retained their offices and directorships; stock escrowed to secure collection of price; redeemed shareholders were not active in management, and retained interests were merely collateral security); Gordon Erickson, 56 TC 1112 (1971) (acq). (where redemption price contingently adjustable up or down, depending on actual profits from work in process, transaction qualified under §302(b)(3)); Rev. Rul. 75-433, 1975-2 CB 118 (*Erickson* principle followed on redemption of stock by S corporation); William M. Lynch, 83 TC 597 (1984), rev'd on other grounds, 801 F2d 1176 (9th Cir. 1986) (note subordinated to bank loan and secured by pledge of remaining shareholder's stock held true debt, not retained equity interest); Alfred N. Hoffman, 47 TC 218 (1966), aff'd per curiam, 391 F2d 930 (5th Cir. 1968) (stock redeemed for notes; redemption terminated shareholder's ownership interest for Subchapter S purposes despite pledge of stock as security). For possible application of §§483 and 1274 to debt instruments issued on a redemption, see supra ¶ 4.42.

[44] See Zenz v. Quinlivan, 213 F2d 914 (6th Cir. 1954), discussed infra ¶ 9.07.

2. Waiver of family attribution. If all of the stock *actually* owned by a shareholder is redeemed by the corporation and no stock outstanding thereafter is attributed to him by §318, §302(b)(3) is easily applied, and the transaction will be treated as a sale. But if such a clean redemption is prevented by the family attribution rules, they nevertheless can be waived by §302(c)(2), and the transaction will then be treated as a sale. Waiver is permitted if the shareholder (1) retains no interest in the corporation after the redemption (including an interest as officer, director, or employee), other than an interest as a creditor; [45] (2) does not acquire any such interest (other than stock acquired by bequest or inheritance) within 10 years from the date of the distribution; [46] and (3) agrees to notify the Service of the acquisition of any forbidden interest within the 10-year period. [47] The regulations provide that an interest in a parent, subsidiary, or successor corporation is equally fatal. [48]

---

[45] See Bernard E. Niedermeyer, supra note 43 (no de minimis exemption in applying retained interest test); Lynch v. CIR, supra note 43 (creditor interest is the *only* interest that can be retained); Sutton & Blume, Waiving the Family Attribution Rules Under Section 302(c)(2): An Analysis, 1 Tax L.J. 45 (1982); Nuzum, Waiver of the Family Ownership Rules Under Section 302(c)(2)(A): Retention or Reacquisition of a Prohibited Interest, 11 J. Corp. Tax'n 19 (1984).

[46] Because of the waiver, the acquisition of an interest by a person whose ownership would ordinarily be imputed to the distributee by the family attribution rules does not violate this condition. See Rev. Rul. 71-562, 1971-2 CB 173. The condition *would* be violated, however, if an entity of which the distributee is a beneficiary, partner, or shareholder acquires an interest during the 10-year period (e.g., by purchasing stock or acquiring an option to purchase stock).

For calculation of the 10-year period, see Rev. Rul. 83-116, 1983-2 CB 264 (10-year period can expire on Sunday, despite extension for Saturdays, Sundays, and legal holidays by §7503 in analogous situation).

[47] For the filing date, see Regs. §1.302-4(a) (filing date of first return for taxable year in which distribution occurs subject to extension on specified conditions). For the efficacy of late-filed agreements, see Fehrs Fin. Co. v. CIR, 487 F2d 184 (8th Cir. 1973), cert. denied, 416 US 938 (1974) (late filing fatal); Fehrs v. US, 556 F2d 1019 (Ct. Cl. 1977) (late filing allowed); Robin Haft Trust v. CIR, 62 TC 145 (1974) denying motion for reconsideration of 61 TC 398 (1973), rev'd on other grounds, 510 F2d 43 (1st Cir. 1975); Bernard E. Niedermeyer, supra note 43 (substantial compliance; mere delay not fatal); Rickey v. US, supra note 35 (waiver filed five years late, after favorable court decision; not fatal); Regs. §1.302-4(a)(2).

To protect the government, the shareholder is required by §302(c)(2)(A)(iii) to retain "such records as may be necessary for the application of this paragraph" and the statute of limitations is extended to permit the assessment of a deficiency until one year after the taxpayer gives notice of the acquisition of a forbidden interest.

[48] Regs. §1.302-4(c). But see Rev. Rul. 76-496, 1976-2 CB 93 (taxpayer organized new corporation two years after redemption that then purchased a division of former corporation that constituted 15 percent of its assets; held not a forbidden acquisition).

It is important to note that §302(c)(2) waives only the family attribution rules, not the *entity-beneficiary* or *option* attribution rules.[49] Entities can waive the family attribution rules, but only in certain circumstances.[50] A look-back rule prescribed by §302(c)(2)(B) may bar a waiver if certain changes in stock ownership occurred during the 10-year period preceding the distribution.[51]

The theory of the family attribution rules and their waiver may be stated in this fashion: A redemption of all of a shareholder's stock is properly treated as a sale because it terminates his interest in the corporation as effectively as a sale to a third person. The sale analogy is not appropriate, however, if stock is owned after the redemption by members of the ex-shareholder's immediate family. It is sufficiently possible that he will thereby continue his interest in the corporation (without the interference from the outside that might have resulted from a sale to a third person) so that an attribution of his relative's shares to him is a reasonable rule of thumb. If he is willing, however, to forgo for a 10-year period any interest in the corporation (other than an interest retained as a creditor or acquired involuntarily by bequest), it is reasonable to waive the family attribution rules and treat the redemption as a sale. This exception is not made for the entity-beneficiary or option attribution rules, however, because they impute stock on the basis of an economic interest rather than because of a family relationship that does not necessarily bespeak an identity of economic interest.

3. Waivers by entities. By virtue of §302(c)(2)(C), enacted in 1982, partnerships, estates, trusts, and corporations can waive the family attribution rules on two conditions: (1) Both the entity itself and each related person must satisfy the normal requirements for a waiver (i.e., no post redemption interest in the corporation, no acquisition of an interest within 10 years from the date of the redemption, and filing of the notification agreement); and (2) each related person must agree to be liable for any deficiency (including interest and additions to tax) resulting from a tainted acquisition of an interest during the 10-year period.[52] "Related person" is specially defined for

---

[49] Note also that the family attribution waiver applies only to §302(b)(3) redemptions effecting a complete termination of the shareholder's interest, not to redemptions seeking protection under §302(b)(1), §302(b)(2), or §302(b)(4).

[50] See infra text at notes 52–54.

[51] See infra text at notes 58–62.

[52] Section §302(c)(2)(C)(i)(II) imposes joint and several liability, but the conference report expresses an intent that the Service should look first to the entity whose stock was redeemed; H.R. Rep. No. 760, 97th Cong., 2d Sess. 545 (1982). For detailed analysis of §302(c)(2)(C), see Owen, Waivers of Family Attribution by Entities May Present Problems Despite TEFRA, 58 J. Tax'n 202 (1983).

these purposes as any person to whom stock is attributable under §318(a) at the time of the distribution if the stock would be further attributable to the entity under §318(a)(3).

> *To illustrate:* Assume that the stock of *X* Corporation is owned equally by *A* and by *T*, a trust of which *A*'s daughter *B* is the sole beneficiary. *A* redemption of *T*'s shares on these facts does not completely terminate *T*'s stock interest in *X* because *A*'s shares are attributed to *B* under §318(a)(1)(A)(ii) and then are reattributed from her to *T* under §318(a)(3)(B)(i). If, however, *T* and *B* comply with the waiver conditions and execute the notification agreement, the redemption qualifies because *T* is not considered as owning *A*'s shares; the redemption is therefore a complete termination vis-à-vis *T*.

Section 302(c)(2)(C) requires related persons (*B* in the example above) to participate in the waiver process because a waiver by the entity alone—if permitted—would allow the related person to benefit from favorable tax treatment of the entity of which he is a beneficiary, partner, or shareholder, even though the beneficiary, partner, or shareholder might retain an interest in the corporation (e.g., as an officer or director) or acquire additional stock therein within the 10-year period.[53]

Section 302(c)(2)(C) applies only to stock that the entity's beneficiary owns constructively by attribution from a member of the beneficiary's family's family; it does not apply to stock that the beneficiary owns directly, is considered as owning by attribution from another entity, or holds an option to purchase. Thus, if the facts in the preceding example are revised to specify that *A* owned 50 shares of stock, *T* owned 25 shares, and *B* owned 25 shares, a waiver would be fruitless because it could apply only to *A*'s shares, leaving intact the attribution of *B*'s stock to *T*; the latter attribution would mean that the redemption of *T*'s own shares would not be complete within the meaning of §302(b)(3).[54] The same defect would exist if *A* were not *B*'s par-

---

[53] For the effect of entity-only waivers under pre-1983 law, see Rickey v. US, supra note 35 (estate allowed to waive attribution from its beneficiaries); Metzger Trust v. CIR, 693 F2d 459 (5th Cir. 1982), reh'g denied, 698 F2d 1216 (5th Cir.), cert. denied, 463 US 1207 (1983) (*Rickey* not applicable to trusts), and cases there cited; see also Rev. Rul. 68-388, 1968-2 CB 122 (estate could not avoid attribution rules by selling stock to its sole beneficiary, who obtained the requisite funds by simultaneous redemption by corporation; transaction was disguised redemption of stock from estate); compare Rev. Rul. 79-67, 1979-1 CB 128, infra note 61. The enactment of §302(c)(2)(C) was not intended to endorse or reject the pre-1983 case law; see H. Rep. No. 760, supra note 52 at 545–546.

[54] If, however, *X* redeemed *T*'s and *B*'s shares simultaneously, a waiver under §302(c)(2)(C) would evidently be efficacious for both *T* and *B*; see Rev. Rul 72-472,

ent, but a corporation in which *B* was a shareholder or an unrelated person whose shares *B* held an option to buy.

4. Tainted post-redemption interest in corporation. As stated previously, a waiver of the family attribution rules is allowed only if, among other conditions, the redeemed shareholder has no interest in the corporation immediately after the redemption and does not acquire any such interest (other than inherited stock) for 10 years thereafter, interest being defined by §302(c)(2)(A)(i) to include an interest as officer, director, or employee, but to exclude an interest as a creditor.[55] Although the prohibition of an "interest as officer, director, or employee" might be construed to bar such a relationship only if coupled with a profit-sharing or similar financial stake in the corporation, the Service has espoused the stricter view that the performance of services, with or without compensation, is fatal.[56] It would be more consonant with the purpose of §302(c)(2) to distinguish between conduct support-

---

1972-2 CB 202 (contrary result under pre-1983 law would seemingly be reversed if parties employed §302(c)(2)(C) waiver).

Note that a redemption of *T*'s shares without a concomitant redemption of *B*'s shares) not only fails to qualify as a complete redemption (because of the attribution to *T* of *B*'s shares), but it cannot qualify as substantially disproportionate under §302(b)(2); *A*'s shares are attributed to *B* and then to *T* both before and after the redemption, and family-attribution waivers are not allowed in applying §302(b)(2). Thus, *T* is considered as owning all of the outstanding stock both before and after the redemption.

[55] For the acquisition of stock by a member of the distributee's family, see Rev. Rul. 71-562, 1971-2 CB 173.

[56] See Rev. Rul. 56-556, 1956-2 CB 177 (modified on another issue by Rev. Rul. 57-387, 1957-2 CB 225); Rev. Rul. 59-119, 1959-1 CB 68; Rev. Rul. 70-104, 1970-1 CB 66 (paid consultantship under five-year contract); Lynch v. CIR, supra note 43 (Court of Appeals rules that performance of post-redemption services, whether as employee or independent contractor, constitutes prohibited "interest"); LaVerne v. Seda, 82 TC 484 (1984) (on facts, continued employment fatal; concurring opinion favored per se rule to avoid judicial "burden of inquiring into the level of employment"); Michael N. Cerone, 87 TC 1 (1986) (on facts, continued employment gave taxpayer financial stake in corporation); Jack O. Chertkof, 649 F2d 264 (4th Cir. 1981) (management contract with corporation controlled by distributee constituted forbidden interest; courts "are not restricted to a fairyland view of business"); but see Estate of Milton S. Lennard, supra note 43 (bona fide independent status as contractor supplying goods or services for reasonable compensation not fatal); Rev. Rul. 84-135, 1984-2 CB 80 (unfunded pension rights not tainted interest).

For stock held or acquired by the distributee in a fiduciary capacity, see Rev. Rul. 81-233, 1981-2 CB 83 (custodian of donated stock under Uniform Gifts to Minors Act; held tainted interest); Rev. Rul. 71-426, 1971-2 CB 173 (fiduciary of voting trust that owned stock of corporation; held fatal); Rev. Rul. 75-2, 1975-1 CB 99 (fiduciary of trust that owned stock was elected president of corporation; held fatal).

ing an inference that the ex-shareholder did not effectively terminate his financial interest in the corporation and conduct that is consistent with such a termination and to waive the family ownership rules if his conduct falls in the latter category.

Since §302(c)(2) permits the retention or acquisition of an interest as a creditor, the shareholder will be able to sell his stock to the corporation on credit rather than for cash. But the regulations warn that an obligation "in the form of a debt" may, in substance, give the owner a proprietary interest in the corporation. The regulations provide in this respect that (1) the ex-shareholder's rights must not be greater than necessary for the enforcement of his claim; (2) the debt must not be subordinate to claims of general creditors; (3) payments of principal must not be contingent on earnings as respects their amount or certainty; and (4) the enforcement of his rights as creditor upon a default by the corporation will not constitute the acquisition of a forbidden interest unless stock of the corporation, its parent, or (in certain cases) its subsidiary is thus acquired.[57]

5. Ten-year look-back rule. The waiver of the family ownership rules granted by §302(c)(2)(A) is denied in certain circumstances. Before examining these conditions, which are set out in §302(c)(2)(B), it may be well to give an illustration of their purpose. If A owns all the stock of a corporation and wishes to give his son a gift of cash, he can, of course, use funds that he received as dividends, but only after they have been reported as income. If he raises the funds by causing the corporation to redeem part of his stock, the redemption will probably be taxed as a dividend.[58] But what if A gives his son some stock in the corporation and then causes this stock to be redeemed? If the transaction can avoid being classified as a sham,[59] the son

---

The statuory exemption for stock acquired by inheritance was held by Rev. Rul. 72-380, 1972-2 CB 201, to protect a distributee who became executor of an estate holding stock; see also Rev. Rul. 75-2, supra (amplifying Rev. Rul. 72-380); Rev. Rul. 79-334, 1979-2 CB 127 (applying Rev. Rul. 72-380 to distributee named by will as successor trustee of inter vivos trust).

See generally Rose, The Prohibited Interest of Section 302(c)(2)(A), 36 Tax L. Rev. 131 (1981).

[57] See Regs. §§1.302-4(d), 1.302-4(e); H.A. Dunn v. CIR, 615 F2d 578 (2d Cir. 1980) (true debt); see also Mary Duerr, supra note 41; supra note 40.

[58] The redemption would not qualify under §302(b)(3), because only part of A's stock was redeemed, or under §302(b)(2), because A owns more than 50 percent of the common stock of the corporation after the redemption; and it would not meet the requirements of §302(b)(1) (infra ¶ 9.06) unless other significant facts were present.

[59] A blatant case could be treated as an anticipatory assignment of a dividend (i.e., as though the corporation had redeemed the father's stock and he had made a

can claim the shelter of §302(b)(3); by forgoing any interest in the corporation for 10 years, he can avoid the family attribution rules of §318, which, if applicable, would take the transaction out of §302(b)(3) by imputing *A*'s unredeemed shares to his son.

To frustrate plans of the type just described, §302(c)(2)(B) provides that the family attribution rules may *not* be waived

(1) If any part of the redeemed stock was acquired, directly or indirectly, within the previous 10 years by the distributee from a related person;[60] or

(2) If any related person owns stock at the time of the distribution and acquired any stock, directly or indirectly, from the distributee within the previous 10 years unless the stock so acquired is redeemed in the same transaction.

These limitations on the waiver of the family attribution rules are not applicable if the acquisition in the case of (1) above or the disposition in the case of (2) above did not have "as one of its prinicipal purposes the avoidance of Federal income tax." The regulations state that a transfer "shall not be deemed" to have the avoidance of federal income tax as one of its principal purposes merely because the transferee is in a lower income tax bracket than the transferor.[61] Moreover, a 1985 ruling suggests that acquisitions of stock during the 10-year look-back period are not fatal unless they manifest a tax-avoidance purpose of a limited type (i.e., an attempt to retain a continuing interest in the corporation despite the redemption).[62]

---

gift of the proceeds to his son). See Estate of Rhodes v. CIR, 131 F2d 50 (6th Cir. 1942), supra ¶ 7.07; Estate of A.J. Schneider, supra note 11.

[60] See Rev. Rul. 82-129, 1982-2 CB 76 (tax-free partition of community property stock not an acquisition for this purpose).

[61] Regs. §1.302-4(g). For applications of these principles to particular sets of facts, see Rev. Rul. 56-556, 1956-2 CB 177; Rev. Rul. 56-584, 1956-2 CB 179; Rev. Rul. 77-293, 1977-2 CB 91 (gift to son by retiring shareholder not for tax avoidance on facts, even though gift lowered father's capital gain tax on redemption of remaining shares; waiver allowed); Rev. Rul. 77-455, 1977-2 CB 93 (retiring father's sale of part of common stock and part of voting "section 306 stock" to son, sale of part of common to key employee, and redemption of balance of common and preferred; held, §302(c)(2) waiver valid; no tax avoidance); Rev. Rul. 79-67, 1979-1 CB 128 (transfer from estate to beneficiary to set stage for §302(c)(2) waiver and thereby allow control shift through redemption; not tax avoidance); William N. Lynch, supra note 43 (gift to son was solely to shift control; no tax avoidance and hence waiver of attribution effective). See generally Kuntz, Stock Redemptions Following Stock Transfers, An Expanding "Safe Harbor" Under Section 302(c)(2)(B), 58 Taxes 29 (1980).

[62] Rev. Rul. 85-19, 1985-1 CB 94 (tax avoidance not present if transfer "was not in contemplation of redemption of the balance of the transferee's stock nor of

Reviewing the historical progression in the treatment of redemptions terminating the shareholder's entire interest, we find that the 1954 Code implemented the administrative and judicial rule of §115(g) of the 1939 Code providing that such a redemption was not "essentially equivalent to a taxable dividend," but with a series of checks and balances as intricate as a fugue. The attribution rules prevent a merely formal termination of the interest of a shareholder who retains an indirect stake in corporate affairs through his family, but this restriction is mitigated by the waiver of the family attribution rules. The waiver, however, becomes retroactively invalid if an interest is acquired during the 10-year period following the redemption. This condition, in turn, is subject to an exception for an interest acquired by bequest. However, the 10-year good-behavior period is available only to shareholders who have not participated during the preceding 10 years in transfers to or from a related person. Finally, such a preredemption transfer is disregarded if not motivated by tax avoidance.

¶ 9.06   REDEMPTIONS NOT ESSENTIALLY EQUIVALENT TO DIVIDENDS

Section 302(b)(1), echoing the language of §115(g) of the 1939 Code, provides that a redemption will be treated as a sale of the redeemed stock if it is not "essentially equivalent to a dividend."[63] Because of this provision, a redemption that fails to qualify for exchange treatment under §302(b)(2) (substantially disproportionate redemption), §302(b)(3) (complete termination of shareholder's interest), or §302(b)(4) (partial liquidation) has a last clear chance—more accurately, as will be seen, a last cloudy chance—to qualify by meeting the vague standards of §302(b)(1).[64]

The Senate Finance Committee's report on the 1954 Code stated that "the test intended to be incorporated in the interpretation of [§302(b)(1)] is in general that currently employed under section 115(g)(1) of the 1939

---

the stock transferred to the transferee;" ruling also based on fact that net effect of transfer was to return to status quo ante, where distributee reacquired stock previously transferred to donee in contemplation of redemption of donee's other shares).

[63] For §115(g), see supra ¶ 9.01.

[64] See §302(b)(5) (in applying §302(b)(1), redemption's failure to satisfy requirements of §302(b)(2), §302(b)(3), or §302(b)(4) shall not be taken into account). For extensive analysis of §302(b)(1), see Bacon, supra note 9, at A-76; Postlewaite & Finneran, Section 302(b)(1): The Expanding Minnow, 64 Va. L. Rev. 561 (1978); Blumstein, When Is a Redemption "Not Essentially Equivalent to a Dividend"? 7 J. Corp. Tax'n 99 (1980); Zinn & Silverman, Redemptions of Stock Under Section 302(b)(1), 32 Tax Lawyer 91 (1978).

Code,"[65] but its concurrent statement that the sole question is "whether or not the transaction by its nature may properly be characterized as a sale of stock by the redeeming shareholder to the corporation" led the Supreme Court in *US v. Davis* to hold that neither the absence of a tax-avoidance motive nor the presence of a business purpose for the redemption would protect it against dividend treatment.[66]

The regulations, although stating that dividend equivalence depends upon the "facts and circumstances of each case," provide that the constructive ownership rules must be considered in making this determination.[67] The Supreme Court endorsed this principle in the *Davis* case. In addition, if the redeeming corporation has only one class of stock outstanding, the regulations state that a pro rata redemption generally will be treated as a distribution under §301,[68] and this position was also endorsed by *Davis*.[69] Similarly, if the corporation has more than one class outstanding, redemption of an entire class also generally will fall under §301 if all classes of stock are held in the same proportion. Finally, the only example of a qualified §302(b)(1) redemption given by the regulations is a redemption of one-half of the nonvoting preferred stock of a shareholder who owns no shares of any other class of stock.[70]

In the *Davis* case, the Supreme Court was faced with a redemption of preferred stock by a corporation of which the taxpayer directly owned 25

---

[65] S. Rep. No. 1622, supra note 8, at 234. For §115(g)(1) of the 1939 Code, see supra ¶ 9.01.

[66] US v. Davis, 397 US 301, reh'g denied, 397 US 1071 (1970).

[67] Regs. §1.302-2(b).

[68] Id.

[69] For distributions treated as dividends because they were pro rata (or nearly so) as a result of attribution under §318, see Fehrs Fin. Co. v. CIR, supra note 47; Bernard E. Niedermeyer, supra note 43; Rev. Rul. 81-289, 1981-2 CB 82; Rev. Rul. 77-218, 1977-1 CB 81; Rev. Rul 71-261, 1971-1 CB 108; Estate of A.J. Schneider, supra note 11.

For attempts to avoid family attribution where the distributee is independent of, and hostile to, the persons whose shares would be attributed to the distributee, see Robin Haft Trust v. CIR, 510 F2d 43 (1st Cir. 1975) (family hostility exception precluded attribution); Rev. Rul. 80-26, 1980-1 CB 66 (Service will not follow *Robin Haft Trust* case); Michael N. Cerone, supra note 56 (extensive analysis); see also Title Ins. & Trust Co. v. US, 484 F2d 462 (9th Cir. 1973) (issue reserved because not raised by facts in cases before court); Estate of Arthur H. Squier, 35 TC 950 (1961) (non acq.) (sharp cleavage between executor of distributee estate and its beneficiaries resulted in reduction of estate's control after redemptions; held redemptions not essentially equivalent to dividends even after applying beneficiary-to-estate attribution rules); infra note 71.

[70] Regs. §1.302-2(a); see also Rev. Rul. 77-426, 1977-2 CB 87 (redemption of any amount of nonvoting, nonconvertible, nonparticipating preferred stock is meaningful if taxpayer owns no common stock, directly or indirectly).

percent of the common stock and all of the preferred. His wife and two children each owned 25 percent of the common stock. In reversing a lower court decision in favor of §302(b)(1) qualification, the majority in *Davis* held that (1) the constructive ownership rules of §318 apply to dividend equivalency determinations under §302(b)(1);[71] (2) redemptions of stock of a sole shareholder, including a constructive sole shareholder, are "always essentially equivalent to a dividend" under §302(b)(1);[72] (3) a business purpose is irrelevant in determining dividend equivalency under §302(b)(1); and (4) in order to avoid dividend equivalency, the redemption must result in a "meaningful reduction of the shareholder's proportionate interest in the corporation."[73]

A dissenting opinion in *Davis* asserted that the majority opinion "effectively cancels §302(b)(1) from the Code."[74] As a prediction, this complaint has proved to be erroneous; the provision has played a real, albeit modest, role by conferring exchange treatment on redemptions that are not "substantially disproportionate" within the meaning of §302(b)(2) but that nevertheless result in a "meaningful reduction" in the shareholder's proportionate interest in the corporation. This standard, however, can no more be reduced to a mathematical formula than can the emotional ingredients of a "meaningful personal relationship."

The meaningful reduction principle has been especially important in the case of nonvoting stock, which through a quirk of draftsmanship cannot qualify for the protection accorded to substantially disproportionate

---

[71] For attempts to avoid the family attribution rules in applying the essentially equivalent test of §302(b)(1), see supra note 69. For a more limited use of the family hostility issue as a factor in determining whether a reduction in a shareholder's proportionate interest is meaningful as required by the *Davis* case, infra text at note 73, rather than a means of negating attribution, see Trust of Henry T. Patterson v. US, 729 F2d 1089 (6th Cir. 1984) (redemption at insistence of corporation's chief executive, who threatened to quit unless he could get control).

[72] US v. Davis, supra note 66, at 307.

[73] Id. at 313. For the possibility that a redemption will satisfy the *Davis* requirement of a meaningful reduction in the shareholder's proportionate interest if, despite its failure to do so when viewed in isolation, it is an integrated step in a plan of redemption that, taken as a whole, meets the requirements of §302(b)(1), see Mary Johnston, 77 TC 679, 685-689 (1981) (principle recognized but not applied in absence of showing that firm and fixed plan existed), and cases there cited. For statutory recognition of the converse of this concept, see §302(b)(2)(D) (redemption not substantially disproportionate in applying §302(b)(2) if made pursuant to plan for a series of redemptions that in the aggregate are not substantially disproportionate); see also supra text at note 39.

[74] US v. Davis, supra note 66, at 314; see also Albers v. CIR, 414 US 982 (dissent from denial of writ of certiorari, urging reconsideration of *Davis*), reh'g denied, 414 US 1104 (1973). Note that of the current members of the Court, only four have spoken on the *Davis-Albers* issue, two remaining in the majority and two in dissent.

redemptions by §302(b)(2).[75] Thus, the regulations continue to illustrate §302(b)(1)—as they did before *Davis* was decided—with an example of a shareholder owning only nonvoting preferred stock that is limited as to dividends and liquidating distributions, stating that a redemption of half of his stock will ordinarily qualify under §302(b)(1), even though it does not qualify under §302(b)(2); in addition, a 1977 ruling holds that the redemption of an even smaller amount of such stock from a shareholder owning no stock of any other class, directly or constructively, is a meaningful reduction under *Davis* because "the rights represented by the redeemed shares were yielded to the common shareholders of the corporation and could not be recovered through the taxpayer's continued stock ownership."[76]

The meaningful reduction principle has also been applied by the Service and the courts to protect redemptions of voting preferred and common stock, even in cases involving the attribution of shares to the distributee pursuant to §318. In determining whether a reduction is meaningful, attention has sometimes been given not only to the numerical change in the percentage of shares owned, but also to whether the change entailed the loss of a significant degree of power. For example, in Rev. Rul. 75-502, an estate and its sole beneficiary owned 57 percent of the corporation's common stock before, but only 50 percent after, the redemption; since the remaining shares were held by a single unrelated individual, the estate and its beneficiary could no longer between them elect the directors and otherwise control the corporation's policies.[77] In another ruling, involving a redemption that reduced a shareholder's owner-

---

[75] See §302(b)(2)(C)(i) (test is ratio of *voting* stock before and after redemption).

[76] Regs. §1.302-2(a) (third sentence); the reference to ownership in this example should no doubt be taken to mean constructive as well as actual ownership. See Rev. Rul. 77-426, 1977-2 CB 87 (ruling premised on shareholder's not owning stock of any other class, directly or constructively); see also Rev. Rul. 85-106, 1985-2 CB 116 (redemption of nonvoting preferred stock did not qualify where distributee continued to own constructively voting and nonvoting common stock); Karlin, Rev. Rul. 85-106: An Unsupported Attack on Section 302(b)(1) Redemptions, 64 Taxes 529 (1986).

[77] Rev. Rul. 75-502, 1975-2 CB 111. For the possibility that the loss of power to initiate and force through a merger or other major corporate change might constitute a meaningful reduction, see Wright v. US, 482 F2d 600 (8th Cir. 1973) (reduction from 85 to 61.7 percent in state requiring two-thirds vote for mergers, liquidations, charter amendments, and so forth). The Service, however, does not regard loss of control over corporate major changes as relevant if the distributee continues to own more than half of the voting stock and can, therefore, control the corporation's day-to-day affairs; see Rev. Rul. 78-401, 1978-2 CB 127 (reduction from 90 to 60 percent; held dividend); Rev. Rul. 77-218, 1977-1 CB 81 (no actual ownership after redemption, but continued constructive ownership of 55 percent of voting rights); Blanche S. Benjamin, 66 TC 1084, 1113 (1976), aff'd, 592 F2d 1259 (5th Cir. 1979) (continuing control stressed; extensive review of evolution of §302(b)(1)); Estate of A.J. Schneider, supra note 11 (same).

ship of a corporation's common stock from 27 to about 22 percent (the remaining stock being owned by three unrelated shareholders), the Service noted that the distributee lost his earlier power to control the corporation in cooperation with only one of the other shareholders.[78]

The latter ruling did not state whether the numerical change by itself would have been sufficient to qualify the redemption for sale treatment. An earlier ruling, holding that a reduction of the distributee's direct and constructive ownership of a corporation's only class of common stock from 30 percent to 24.3 percent was "meaningful," did not refer to any factors other than the loss of voting rights and of claims on current earnings and accumulated surplus that necessarily accompanies any percentage reduction of ownership in such a situation.[79] Carrying the numbers game further, another ruling held that a redemption of common stock effected by a public corporation's tender offer, reducing the distributee's percentage of ownership from .0001118 percent to .0001081 percent, qualified as a meaningful reduction under *Davis*.[80] One cannot quarrel with the result; but is "meaningful reduction" the proper label when an infinitesimal percentage is nudged infinitesimally closer to zero?

In holding that §302(b)(1) requires "a meaningful reduction of the shareholder's proportionate interest in the corporation," the Supreme Court in the *Davis* case did not define the term "interest in the corporation" or address the problem that arises if some of the shareholder's rights are reduced by the redemption, while others remain unchanged. If there is only one class of stock outstanding, a redemption necessarily reduces each stick in the entire bundle proportionately; but if the corporation has several classes of stock outstanding and redeems part or all of only one class, the redemption can have different effects on the shareholder's various rights, particularly if constructive ownership is taken into account. For example, the shareholder's voting power may be more (or less) seriously altered by the redemption than his right to participate in ordinary dividends and liquidat-

---

[78] Rev. Rul. 76-364, 1976-2 CB 91. But cf. Rev. Rul. 85-106, 1985-2 CB 116 (redemption did not reduce distributee's power (by attribution) to participate in control group by acting in concert with other shareholders; held dividend).

[79] Rev. Rul. 75-512, 1975-2 CB 112; see also Agway, Inc. v. US, 524 F2d 1194 (Ct. Cl. 1975) (reduction from 18 to 16 percent of ownership of preferred stock by person owning 6 percent of common stock); Rev. Rul. 56-183, 1956-1 CB 161 (reduction in group's ownership from 11 percent to 9 percent not equivalent to dividend); Rev. Rul. 55-462, 1955-2 CB 221 (redemption of preferred stock to equalize two unrelated shareholders' ownership).

[80] Rev. Rul. 76-385, 1976-2 CB 92; but see Rev. Rul. 81-289, 1981-2 CB 82 (redemption pursuant to tender offer by public corporation treated as dividend as to shareholder who tendered 40 out of 2,000 shares, or 2 percent, the same fraction of corporation's outstanding shares that was actually redeemed; no reduction in shareholder's proportionate interest in corporation).

ing distributions; the redemption will not necessarily have the same effect on the right to vote for directors as on the right to vote on such major changes as charter amendments and mergers.

In a 1985 ruling involving a redemption that reduced the distributee's percentage interest in current earnings, accumulated surplus, and net assets on liquidation without reducing his voting power, the Service held that §302(b)(1) did not apply because a reduction in voting power is a key factor in applying this provision.[81] In reaching this conclusion, the Service did not rule that control is invariably more important than the shareholder's continuing direct or constructive interest in current and liquidating distributions; but much can be said for giving special attention to control, at least in the case of closely held corporations, whose controlling shareholders can determine business and financial policies that in turn determine the corporation's risk/return ratio, and in addition can avail themselves of corporate perquisites that in theory are subject to a rule of reason but in practice can seldom be restrained by the minority shareholders. A more debatable feature of this 1985 ruling, however, is that the redeemed shareholder's status was derived from the fact that, by reason of the way the corporation's voting stock was dispersed, there was no reduction in the shareholder's "potential (by attribution from [its sole beneficiary]) for participating in a control group by acting in concert with two other major unrelated shareholders."[82] Such a continuing capacity for manoeuver is undoubtedly important in the real world; but, if taken into account for tax purposes, it could have far-reaching ramifications, since virtually any shareholder can—depending on how the other shares are divided—cast a decisive vote.[83]

---

[81] Rev. Rul. 85-106, 1985-2 CB 116; this ruling announced that the Service will not follow Himmel v. CIR, 338 F2d 815 (2d Cir. 1964), involving comparable facts but holding that a reduction in the shareholder's right to participate in earnings currently and on liquidation was more important than unchanged voting power; see also Mary G. Roebling, 77 TC 30 (1981) (§302(b)(1) protected redemption of preferred stock despite continued ownership of common stock; Himmel applied); Mary Johnston, supra note 73, at 684 (decrease in voting control considered by courts "to be the most significant indicator of a 'meaningful' reduction"); Estate of A.J. Schneider, supra note 11.

For earlier cases in this area, see CIR v. Estate of Antrim, 395 F2d 430 (4th Cir. 1968) (no dividend on partial redemption of preferred stock); CIR v. Berenbaum, 369 F2d 337 (10th Cir. 1966) (dividend equivalence on partial redemption of preferred stock held by majority stockholder); Blanche S. Benjamin, supra note 77 (dividend equivalence on partial redemption of voting stock); Brown v. US, 345 F. Supp. 241 (S.D. Ohio 1972), aff'd per curiam, 477 F2d 599 (6th Cir. 1973), cert. denied, 414 US 1011 (1973) (dividend equivalence on partial redemption of preferred stock).

[82] Rev. Rul. 85-106, 1985-2 CB 116.

[83] For an analogous problem in applying the concept of control when valuing stock of closely held corporations for gift or estate tax purposes, given the potential importance of even a small block of shares, see Bittker, Federal Taxation of Income, Estates and Gifts (Warren, Gorham & Lamont, Inc., 1984), ¶ 132.3.4.

¶ 9.07   REDEMPTIONS IN CONJUNCTION WITH BOOTSTRAP ACQUISITIONS OF STOCK AND SHAREHOLDER BUY-SELL AGREEMENTS

1. Introductory. On a sale of stock, especially if it involves all or a controlling block of the stock of a closely held corporation, the buyer often proposes to finance the acquisition in part with the corporation's excess cash or liquid assets. Such a bootstrap buyout can take a number of forms, of which the following (with variations examined later in this discussion) are the most common: (1) a sale-and-seller-redemption in which some of the seller's shares are sold to the buyer and the rest are redeemed by the corporation; (2) a seller-dividend-and-sale, comprising a distribution of the liquid assets to the seller as a dividend, coupled with a simultaneous sale of all of the seller's shares to the buyer; and (3) a sale-and-buyer redemption involving a sale of all of the shares to the buyer, followed either immediately or at a later time by a dividend of the liquid assets or by a redemption that, being pro rata, is treated as a dividend. If the buyer paid for the shares in cash, the distributed assets may be retained to replenish the buyer's capital or used to pay off a short-term loan employed to finance the purchase; if the purchase was on credit, the liquid assets may be used to make the deferred payments as they fall due. [84]

All three methods of effecting a bootstrap purchase have substantially the same financial consequences in that in each case (1) the seller receives the same amount for the shares; (2) the net amount paid by the buyer is the same; and (3) the same amount is withdrawn from the corporation's treasury. As discussed later, however, the tax consequences are different, [85] and

---

[84] See generally Lang, Dividends Essentially Equivalent to Redemptions: The Taxation of Bootstrap Stock Acquisitions, 41 Tax L. Rev. 309 (1986); Bucholz, Disposing of Unwanted Assets in Corporate Mergers and Acquisitions, 38 Tax Lawyer 161 (1984); Jassy, The Tax Treatment of Bootstrap Stock Acquisitions: The Redemption Route vs. the Dividend Route, 87 Harv. L. Rev. 1459 (1974); these articles cite many earlier discussions of this long-troubled subject. See also Kingson, The Deep Structure of Taxation: Dividend Distributions, 85 Yale L.J. 861 (1976).

For leveraged buyout transactions, see Allen, A Leveraged Buyout Checklist, 33 Tax Notes 1151 (1986); Bowen, Structuring Leveraged Buy-Outs, 63 Taxes 935 (1985).

[85] This section of the text focuses on whether the transaction generates dividend income or is treated as an exchange with an offset of the basis of the shares. For the basis of the transferred shares in the buyer's hands, see Lang, supra note 84, at 315–318; see also §1059, supra ¶ 5.05. For the effect of redemptions on the corporation's earnings and profits, see infra ¶ 9.35; Lang, supra note 84, at 313–315.

Because bootstrap redemptions are virtually always isolated transactions within the meaning of Regs. §1.305-3(b)(3) (last sentence), they normally raise no serious questions under §305, even if that provision could otherwise be applied; see supra ¶ 7.43; Lang, supra note 84, at 350–351.

the courts are sometimes called upon to determine whether a particular set of facts falls into one or another of the three categories.

In the following discussion, it is assumed for convenience (unless otherwise stated) that the transaction involves *all* of the outstanding stock of the corporation; however, similar tax principles govern transfers of only *part* of the shares, subject to the qualifications noted. It is also assumed that all of the stock is owned by a single taxpayer (whether an individual or a corporation), and that the buyer is also a single taxpayer; but similar principles govern if there is a group of sellers or of buyers. It is also assumed that the corporation's contribution to the financial package consists of cash, portfolio securities, or other liquid assets.[86] Finally, it is assumed that the buyer and seller are not related parties whose stock ownership is attributed from one to the other under §318 and that the transaction is effected under a newly negotiated contract. Special problems arise if the transfer is between related parties or pursuant to a previously executed contract, such as a conventional corporate buy-sell agreement under which a continuing shareholder is required to purchase the shares of a retiring or deceased shareholder.

2. Sale-and-seller redemption. If some of the seller's shares are sold to the buyer, and the rest are redeemed by the corporation as part of the same plan, both steps in the transaction generate capital gain or loss, depending on whether the seller's basis for the shares exceeds or is less than the sales price. The sale step achieves this result because it resembles an ordinary sale of stock; the redemption step also qualifies for exchange treatment because it is a complete termination of the seller's interest in the corporation as required by §302(b)(3).[87]

This result was not reached without litigation. In a celebrated case involving this type of a bootstrap acquisition of the stock of a one-person corporation, the Service asserted that the redemption part of the transaction resulted in a dividend under §115(g) of the 1939 Code on the ground that the redemption of part of the seller's stock would have resulted in a dividend if

---

For problems under pre-1980 law in electing installment method treatment for the shares sold to the buyer, see Farha v. CIR, 483 F2d 18 (10th Cir. 1973) (redemption and sale aggregated in computing amount received in year of sale; thus computed, amount exceeded 30 percent limit of pre-1980 law; installment method not allowable); compare Clarence J. Monson, 79 TC 827 (1982).

[86] If the distribution consists of the assets of a going business or of the proceeds of disposing of such a business, the special rules applicable to partial liquidations may be controlling; see infra ¶ 9.08.

[87] For §302(b)(3), see supra ¶ 9.05. For complications if the buyer's shares are attributed back to the seller under §318 (so that the redemption does not terminate the seller's constructive ownership) and for the possibility of a waiver of the family attribution rules, see also supra ¶ 9.05.

it had preceded the sale of the remaining shares and that the result should be the same where the redemption, by prearrangement, followed the sale. The Court of Appeals for the Sixth Circuit held to the contrary in *Zenz v. Quinlivan*, stating that the taxpayer intended a complete termination of his stock ownership so that the redemption did not occur in such a manner as to make the distribution essentially equivalent to a dividend.[88]

The Service acquiesced in *Zenz* with respect to the 1939 Code and subsequently announced that such a transaction is also entitled to exchange treatment under the 1954 Code because it terminates the shareholder's entire interest in the corporation within the meaning of §302(b)(3).[89] The Service also ruled that the redemption and sale elements of an integrated plan should be aggregated in determining whether a seller who retains some shares is entitled to exchange treatment under §302(b)(2), relating to substantially disproportionate redemptions.[90]

Although it is usually considered safer to have the sale precede or occur simultaneously with the redemption (so that the seller owns no shares immediately after the redemption), the government conceded in *US v. Carey* that a redemption could not properly be treated as a distribution even if it preceded the sale of the remaining shares, where the two steps were components of a single plan; and a 1975 ruling held that the sequence of events is irrelevant if both are "clearly part of an overall plan."[91] The retiring shareholder, therefore, is on safe ground in assuming that the combined sale-redemption, if properly planned and executed, will be treated as an exchange of the transferred shares, including both those redeemed by the corporation and those purchased by the third party. This means that the redemption will not be treated as a dividend, but rather as an exchange; the selling shareholder, therefore, can offset basis against the redemption proceeds, report the differ-

---

[88] Zenz v. Quinlivan, 213 F2d 914 (6th Cir. 1954).

[89] Rev. Rul. 54-458, 1954-2 CB 167 (1939 Code); Rev. Rul. 55-745, 1955-2 CB 223 (1954 Code); Rev. Rul. 75-447, 1975-2 CB 113 (same); see also Monson v. CIR, 79 TC 827 (1982); Bleily & Collishaw, Inc., 72 TC 751 (1979) (sufficient plan to terminate, even though not legally binding).

[90] Rev. Rul. 75-447, 1975-2 CB 113; for §302(b)(2), see supra ¶ 9.04. See generally Coven, The Relevance of Fresh Investment to the Characterization of Corporate Distributions and Adjustments, 38 Tax L. Rev. 419 (1983).

[91] US v. Carey, 289 F2d 531 (8th Cir. 1961); Rev. Rul. 75-447, 1975-2 CB 113; see also Arthur D. McDonald, 52 TC 82 (1969) (rejecting Service's effort to separate redemption from transfer of remaining shares in purportedly tax-free reorganization); Rev. Rul. 75-360, 1975-2 CB 110 (acknowledging Service's error in attempting to separate redemption from transfer in *McDonald* case; entire transaction should have been treated as a taxable sale or exchange, not redemption and separable reorganization); cf. Vahlsing Christina Corp., ¶ 85,273 P-H Memo. TC (1985) (redemption separate from reorganization); see also Estate of A.J. Schneider, supra note 11 (purported stock sale by dominant shareholder held instead to have been a dividend equivalent redemption).

ence as capital gain or loss, and, if otherwise qualified, defer installment sale gain under §453.

3. Seller-dividend-and-sale. If the seller is an individual, the sale-and-seller-redemption method of effecting a bootstrap acquisition is attractive; but a corporate seller may prefer to withdraw the corporation's liquid assets as a dividend either because it is entitled to an 80 or 100 percent dividends-received deduction or, if consolidated returns have been filed, because the dividend is excluded from income in its entirety.[92] If the seller is an individual, however, the dividend-sale route is to be avoided except in unusual circumstances (e.g., if the corporation has no earnings and profits (so that the distribution will be treated as a return of capital under §301(c)(2)[93]) or if the seller has an otherwise useless net operating loss carry-over to offset against the dividend).

4. Sale-and-buyer-redemption. Finally, the seller may sell all of the shares to the buyer, who can promptly or at a later time withdraw the liquid assets from the corporation as a dividend or by a redemption that, being pro rata, is treated as a dividend.[94] If the buyer is a corporation, the dividend is eliminated from gross income if the two corporations file a consolidated

---

[92] For the dividends-received deduction, see supra ¶ 5.05 and infra note 96; for consolidated returns, see infra ¶ 15.20.

For an ingenious effort to exploit the corporate dividends received deduction, see Rev. Rul. 77-226, 1977-2 CB 90, involving the purchase by Y Corporation of 4,000 shares of stock of X Corporation, which was offering to purchase stock tendered to it by its shareholders. Y purchased the 4,000 shares on the market at the tender offer price, tendered 800 shares for redemption, treated the proceeds as a dividend (on the ground that the redemption was not substantially disproportionate under §302(b)(2) and was therefore equivalent to a dividend), sold the remaining shares on the market at a price reflecting the reduction in X's net worth attributable to the redemption, claimed an 85 percent dividends-received deduction for the redemption proceeds, and reported a short-term loss on the 3,200 shares. The Service ruled that the redemption and sale together terminated Y's interest in X within the meaning of §302(b)(3), citing Zenz v. Quinlivan, supra note 88, so that Y realized no gain or loss because the aggregate amount received by it equaled its cost for the 4,000 shares. For a subsequently enacted comprehensive barrier to such transactions, see §246(c), supra ¶ 7.07, and §1059, supra ¶ 5.05.

[93] For §301(c)(2), see supra ¶ 7.02.

[94] Dividend treatment is virtually certain if the buyer acquires and continues to own all of the stock or if the distribution is pro rata among a group of buyers. If the distribution consists of a going business, however, the redemption may qualify as a partial liquidation under §302(b)(4); see infra ¶ 9.08. For unsuccessful efforts by corporations to recharacterize a pro rata redemption as a seller redemption and sale, see Television Indus., Inc. v. CIR, 284 F2d 322 (2d Cir. 1960) (1939 Code).

return;[95] otherwise, the dividend is largely offset by the 80 percent dividends-received deduction.[96] If the buyer is an individual, however, this method is to be avoided because the dividend is fully includable in gross income to the extent of the distributing corporation's earnings and profits.

5. Recharacterization of transactions. With meticulous attention to the details, a bootstrap acquisition can ordinarily be structured to fit into any one of these patterns and, conversely, to avoid the other two. The possibilities for bungling are many, however, and sometimes business exigencies require a plan to be modified in midstream (e.g., after a sale on credit, but before all deferred payments have been made). Not surprisingly, the Service seeks to fit ambiguous transactions into whatever pattern will produce the most revenue, while taxpayers seek to fit them into the least costly form.

Such a battle is most likely to arise if some or all of the shares are sold on credit to an individual buyer who later seeks to make the deferred payments with corporate funds.[97] If the funds are withdrawn as a duly declared dividend, the distribution is ordinarily treated as such; but what happens if the buyer uses a redemption rather than a dividend to achieve his objective? In a leading case under the 1939 Code, *Wall v. United States*, the taxpayer

---

[95] For reduction of the buyer's basis for the stock in consolidated return situations, see Regs. §1.1502-32(b)(2)(iii)(C).

[96] See supra note 92. The 100 percent dividends-received deduction provided by §243(a)(3) applies only to distributions of earnings and profits arising in a taxable year after the acquisition. See §243(b)(1)(B)(i), discussed supra ¶ 5.05; see also §1059, supra ¶ 5.05, which reduces the buyer's stock basis. Because of the dividends-received deduction, a corporate seller may prefer dividend treatment. For examples of successful efforts to cast a redemption in the form of a dividend (e.g., by failing to surrender stock or by separating the distribution from the sale of the stock to the incoming shareholders), see TSN Liquidating Corp. v. US, 624 F2d 1328 (5th Cir. 1980); Steel Improvement & Forge Co. v. CIR, 314 F2d 96 (6th Cir. 1963); Merrill C. Gilmore, 25 TC 1321 (1956); Regs. §1.61-9(c). For contrasting cases in which the desired treatment was denied and an alleged dividend was taxed as part of the sales price of stock, see Waterman S.S. Corp. v. CIR, supra note 10; Rev. Rul. 77-226, 1977-2 CB 90; supra ¶ 7.07.

For the possibility that dividend income resulting from such a transaction may convert the parent corporation into a personal holding company, see McKinley Corp. of Ohio, 36 TC 1182 (1961) (acq.); supra ¶ 8.22.

See generally Lang, supra note 84; Bucholz, supra note 84.

[97] Attempted recharacterizations by the taxpayer are common if shares held by a corporation are redeemed and the corporate shareholder then sells its remaining shares. If the redemption can be separated from the sale, it generates dividend income qualifying for the 80 or 100 percent dividends-received deduction or for exclusion from income if consolidated returns are filed; but if the redemption and sale are integrated steps in a single transaction, they may generate taxable capital gain. See supra note 96.

See also Estate of A.J. Schneider, supra note 11 (purported stock "sale" held instead to be a dividend equivalent redemption and reissue of shares to buyers).

contracted to purchase stock from a co-shareholder on the installment plan.[98] After the sale was executed, he caused the corporation to discharge his purchase money obligation to the seller by redeeming the stock for which he was personally obligated to pay. The court held that the redemption was equivalent to a payment by the corporation of the taxpayer's personal debt:

> The controlling fact in this situation was that Wall [the buyer] was under an obligation to pay Coleman [the seller] $5,000 in the tax year and that [the corporation] paid this indebtedness for Wall out of its surplus. It cannot be questioned that the payment of a taxpayer's indebtedness by a third party pursuant to an agreement between them is income to the taxpayer. . . . The transaction is regarded as the same as if the money had been paid to the taxpayer and transmitted by him to the creditor; and so if a corporation, instead of paying a dividend to a stockholder, pays a debt for him out of its surplus, it is the same for tax purposes as if the corporation pays a dividend to a stockholder, and the stockholder then utilizes it to pay his debt.[99]

If, however, the corporation agrees to redeem some of the seller's shares and pays for the redeemed shares in installments over time, the payments do not discharge any obligation of the buyer and therefore do not constitute constructive distributions to the buyer.[100] This is true even if the buyer guarantees performance by the corporation, pledges his shares as security for the deferred payments, or agrees to buy the shares if the corporation defaults.[101] On the other hand, if the buyer is subject to a primary and unconditional obligation to purchase the shares but causes the corporation to redeem them, the redemption is a constructive distribution to the buyer because it discharges that obligation.[102] On rare occasions, however, a shareholder obli-

---

[98] Wall v. US, 164 F2d 462 (4th Cir. 1947).

[99] Id., at 464.

[100] Arthur J. Kobacker, 37 TC 882 (1962) (acq.); Ray Edenfield, 19 TC 13 (1952) (acq.), see also Cromwell Corp., 43 TC 313 (1965) (acq.); compare Wolf v. CIR, 357 F2d 483 (9th Cir. 1966).

[101] Ray Edenfield, supra note 100; Rev. Rul. 69-608, 1969-2 CB 42, Situation 5.

[102] See Sullivan v. US, 363 F2d 724 (8th Cir. 1966), cert. denied, 387 US 905 (1967) (taxpayer received constructive dividend when he caused controlled corporation to redeem shares of employee (who was required to sell them to taxpayer on terminating employment) because redemption relieved taxpayer of personal obligation to purchase the shares); see also Adams v. CIR, 594 F2d 657 (8th Cir. 1979) (taxpayer purchased bank stock under arrangement calling for redemption of some shares; plan approved by state banking authorities on condition redeemed shares were reissued to taxpayer as stock dividend; held redemption was constructive dividend); Skyline Memorial Gardens, Inc., ¶ 85,334 P-H Memo. TC (1985). Compare Citizens Bank & Trust Co. v. US, 580 F2d 442 (Ct. Cl. 1978).

gated to pay for shares has successfully established that he was acting as agent for the corporation, with the result that a redemption was treated as a payment by the corporation of its own, rather than the shareholder's, obligation.[103]

A 1969 ruling confirms these principles and applies them to a variety of situations.[104] Two examples involve conventional corporate buy-sell agreements under which continuing shareholders are required to purchase the stock of a retiring or deceased shareholder; the ruling holds that a redemption of the shares is a constructive distribution to the continuing shareholders if it occurs after their obligation is triggered by retirement or death.[105] Another example, however, reaches a contrary conclusion if the original agreement is rescinded in favor of a new agreement requiring the shares to be redeemed by the corporation, provided the rescission occurs before the triggering event occurs.[106] The ruling also holds that there is no constructive distribution if the buyer agrees to purchase the shares but intends from the outset to assign the contract to a corporation, provided the contract permits such an assignment and relieves the buyer of personal liability if the assignee agrees to be bound by its terms.[107] Still another situation involves shares subject to a put, under which the owner could require the taxpayer to purchase the shares or to cause them to be purchased. The ruling holds that if the taxpayer does not buy the shares personally but instead causes the corporation to do so, the corporate payment is not a constructive distribution to the taxpayer, since at that time the taxpayer was not subject to an unconditional obligation to purchase the shares and had no fixed liability to pay for them.[108]

---

[103] See CIR v. Decker, 286 F2d 427 (6th Cir. 1960); Fox v. Harrison, 145 F2d 521 (7th Cir. 1944); Frank Ciaio, 47 TC 447 (1967) (acq.); State Pipe & Nipple Corp., ¶ 83,339 P-H Memo. TC (1983); Rev. Rul. 80-240, 1980-2 CB 116; but see Glacier State Elec. Supply Co., supra note 39 (redeeming shareholder real owner, not mere agent or conduit).

[104] Rev. Rul. 69-608, 1969-2 CB 42.

[105] Id., Situations 1 and 2.

[106] Id., Situation 7. For discussion of the possibility of amending or rescinding troublesome agreements, see Lang, supra note 84, at 336–340.

[107] Rev. Rul. 69-608, 1969-2 CB 42. Situation 4; see also Arthur J. Kobacker, supra note 100; Holsey v. CIR, 258 F2d 865 (3d Cir. 1958); S.K. Ames, Inc., 46 BTA 1020 (1942) (acq.).

[108] Rev. Rul. 69-608, 1969-2 CB 42, Situation 4; S.K. Ames, Inc., supra note 107; see also Arthur C. Smith, Jr., 70 TC 651, 669–672 (1978), in which the taxpayer was required to purchase the shares of a deceased shareholder from his estate (and the estate was required to sell), and was also required to purchase certain other shares if the owners so desired; the court held that the redemption of the estate's shares was a constructive dividend to the taxpayer, but that the redemption of the other shares was not; Sullivan v. US, supra note 102, holding that the taxpayer received a con-

Another source of potential trouble in this area is a hasty agreement by the new investors to purchase all the stock, later called off when a more complete financial or legal analysis suggests the advisability of using corporate assets to pay for part of the stock. If a sale-and-buyer-redemption is substituted at the last minute for the original binding obligation of the investors to buy all the stock, a court might find that the transaction was in reality a shareholder transaction under principles analogous to *CIR v. Court Holding Co.*[109] The theory would be that the corporation was merely a conduit through which the shareholder obligated himself to acquire the stock. Although this theory has not yet played a significant role in the area of redemptions, the careful advisor will seek to avoid any occasion for putting it to the test.

¶ 9.08 PARTIAL LIQUIDATIONS: INTRODUCTORY

Section 302(b)(4) mandates exchange (rather than dividend) treatment for redemptions of stock provided (1) the stock is held by a person other than a corporation and (2) the distribution is in partial liquidation (as defined) of the distributing corporation.[110] Section 302(b)(4) differs from §302(b)(1) (redemptions not essentially equivalent to dividends), §302(b)(2) (substantially disproportionate redemptions), and §302(b)(3) (termination of shareholder's entire interest) in three important respects: First, it is available only to individuals, partnerships, estates, and trusts but not to corporations (except by virtue of §1371(a)(2), S corporations); second, qualification depends on the nature of the assets distributed rather than on the effect of the redemption on the redeemed shareholder's relative position vis-à-vis the

---

structive dividend when he caused his controlled corporation to redeem the shares of an employee who was required to sell them to the taxpayer on terminating his employment, because the redemption relieved the taxpayer of his personal obligation to purchase the shares. Compare Citizens Bank & Trust Co. v. US, supra note 102 (*Wall* not applied where shareholder's obligation to buy was taken over by corporation, but did not involve stock of the purchasing corporation; transaction did not have effect of a distribution, since equivalent values were transferred).

[109] CIR v. Court Holding Co., 324 US 331 (1945), discussed infra ¶ 11.07. See Milton F. Priester, 38 TC 316 (1962); compare Wolf v. CIR, supra note 100.

[110] See generally Cook & Marans, Partial Liquidation, Tax Mgmt. (BNA) No. 37-4th (1987); Golden, Thinking Small? Problems and Opportunities Presented by Partial Liquidations, 58 Taxes 887 (1980); Ward, The TEFRA Amendments to Subchapter C: Corporate Distributions and Acquisitions, 8 J. Corp. L. 277 (1983); Ginsburg, Taxing Corporate Acquisitions, 38 Tax L. Rev. 171 (1983); deKosmian, Partial Liquidations, Section 311(d) Redemptions and Section 304 Under TEFRA, 61 Taxes 918 (1983).

other shareholders; and third, the redemption can be pro rata among the shareholders without adverse consequences.

Section 302(b)(4) owes its origin to the pre-1954 judge-made corporate contraction doctrine, which was one way of establishing that a redemption was "not essentially equivalent to the distribution of a taxable dividend" within the meaning of §115(g) of the 1939 Code.[111] This doctrine was codified by §346 of the 1954 Code, which in 1982 was modified and renumbered as §302(b)(4) of current law. Aside from stylistic changes without substantive importance, §302(b)(4) differs from its 1954 predecessor in the following respects:

(1) Corporate shareholders (other than S corporations) of the distributing corporation do not qualify.[112]

(2) An ostensibly partial liquidating distribution that is one of a series of distributions in complete liquidation of the corporation no longer qualifies as a partial liquidation but is instead subject to §331(a), relating to complete liquidations.[113]

(3) Section 302(e)(1)(A) provides that whether a distribution is "not essentially equivalent to a dividend" is determined at the corporate rather than shareholder level. This explicit statutory language codifies the pre-1983 case law,[114] under which partial liquidations were "characterized by what happens solely at the corporate level by reason of the assets distributed."[115]

(4) The constructive ownership rules of §318 apply by virtue of §302(c)(1). This change, which resulted automatically from the transfer of the partial liquidation rules from §346 to §302, may have been inadvertent. Moreover, it seems to have no operational

---

[111] See supra ¶ 9.01.

[112] Corporations receiving distributions in partial liquidation were denied exchange treatment in 1982 on the ground that prior law allowed unwarranted advantages when one corporation acquired control of another; this was because carefully selected distributed assets qualified for a stepped-up basis with little or no immediate tax consequences to the acquiring corporation (since its basis for the redeemed shares ordinarily equaled the value of the distributed assets), and the acquired business continued with no significant changes. See Staff of Joint Comm. on Taxation, 97th Cong., 2d Sess., General Explanation of the Revenue Provisions of the Tax Equity and Fiscal Responsibility Act of 1982, at 125 (Joint Comm. Print 1982).

[113] See §346(a), discussed infra ¶ 11.02. For a more extended examination of the anamolous pre-1983 treatment of this subject, see the Fourth Edition of this work, ¶ 9.51.

[114] See H.R. Rep. 760 (1982), supra note 52, at 530.

[115] S. Rep. No. 1622, supra note 8, at 49; see also infra text at notes 141–143.

consequences, since §302(e)(4) (like the final sentence of §346(b), its statutory predecessor) provides that a partial liquidation qualifies as such even if the distribution is pro rata among the shareholders; the same disregard for the relative position of the shareholders vis-à-vis each other follows from the fact, noted previously, that §302(e)(1)(A) looks only to the corporate level in applying the dividend-equivalence standard.

(5) An overlap issue was resolved by a concurrent amendment to §302(b)(5). If a distribution qualifies both as a partial liquidation and as a complete termination of the shareholder's interest, and if the distributee relies on §302(c)(2) for a waiver of the family attribution rules, the distributee is not subject to the 10-year prohibition on the acquisition of an interest in the corporation.[116] Thus, distributees who are not sure that a distribution qualifies as a partial liquidation can file a §302(c)(2) waiver agreement without losing the right to rely on §302(b)(4) if they reacquire an interest in the corporation within the 10-year postredemption period.

Under current law, a distribution qualifies for exchange treatment under §302(b)(4) if it (1) is in redemption of stock held by a shareholder other than a non-S corporation;[117] (2) is pursuant to a plan; (3) occurs within the taxable year in which the plan is adopted or within the succeeding taxable year;[118] and (4) is not essentially equivalent to a dividend, as determined at the corporate rather than shareholder level.[119] The first of these requirements is formal in nature. The fourth, which carries forward the corporate contraction doctrine of prior law (augmented by a statutory safe harbor for corporations actively conducting two or more qualified businesses), is examined in detail in subsequent sections.[120] The second and third requirements are relatively simple but they raise a few issues, as indicated in the following paragraphs.

1. Redemption pursuant to plan. To qualify as a partial liquidation, a distribution must, among other things, constitute a redemption of stock pursuant to a plan. Under §317(b), stock acquired by a corporation from its

---

[116] For a similar but less explicit provision under prior law, see §346(c) of pre-1983 law.

[117] Section 302(b)(4)(A).

[118] Section 302(e)(1)(B).

[119] Section 302(e)(1)(A). For Service authority to issue regulations to prevent circumvention of §302(b)(4), see §346(b); Joint Comm. on Taxation, General Explanation of the Revenue Provisions of the Tax Equity and Fiscal Responsibility Act of 1982, at 127.

[120] See infra ¶¶ 9.09 (corporation contraction concept) and 9.10 (statutory safe harbor).

shareholders in exchange for property is treated as redeemed whether it is canceled, retired, or held as treasury stock.[121] Moreover, a transaction can qualify as a redemption even if there is no formal surrender of shares, as in the case of a distribution in partial liquidation of a closely held corporation, where the niceties of form are not observed.[122] By the same token, an otherwise qualifying distribution, coupled with a reduction in the stock's stated or par value, should also be construed as a redemption, although pre-1954 case law was to the contrary.[123]

Section 302(e)(1)(B) requires the corporation to redeem its stock pursuant to a plan, but "plan" is not defined in either the Code or the regulations. Perhaps an informal plan will suffice, as in other areas where a corporate adjustment must occur under a plan,[124] but careful counsel will not want to trust to luck.

2. Distribution in the year the plan is adopted or within the succeeding year. Since neither the Code nor the regulations defines the term "plan," it is not surprising that neither states how the year of its adoption should be determined. Presumably, the time will ordinarily begin to run from the formal action by the shareholders authorizing the redemption, but the Service

---

[121] Before 1982, when the partial liquidation rules were moved from §346 to §302, §317(b) was not applicable, since it applies only to Part I of Subchapter C (§§301–318). But there is no evidence that this restrictive principle was followed under the 1954 Code, despite some pre-1954 case law rulings that treasury stock had not been redeemed. See Boyle v. CIR, 187 F2d 557 (3d Cir.), cert. denied, 342 US 817 (1951), and cases there cited.

[122] See Rev. Rul. 81-3, 1981-1 CB 125 (constructive redemption deemed to occur where "there was a genuine contraction of business and the surrender of stock by the shareholders would have been a meaningless gesture"), endorsed by H.R. Rep. No. 760, supra note 52 at 530; Fowler Hosier Co. v. CIR, infra note 124. But see Rev. Proc. 87-3, §5.10, supra note 40 (Service will not rule on application of Rev. Rul. 81-3 to corporations with complex stock structure). See also Oscar Baan, 51 TC 1032 (1969) (redemption required for pre-1983 §346(a)(2) treatment where redistribution was non-pro rata), aff'd on other grounds sub nom. Gordon v. CIR, 424 F2d 378 (2d Cir. 1970), cert. denied, 400 US 848 (1970), and Baan v. CIR, 450 F2d 198 (9th Cir. 1971).

[123] See Sheehan v. Dana, 163 F2d 316, 319 (8th Cir. 1947); Beretta v. CIR, 141 F2d 452, 455 (5th Cir.), cert. denied, 323 US 720 (1944). The House version of the 1954 Code provided that a reduction of par value was a redemption, but this provision was omitted by the Senate, which stated "no inference is to be drawn by the elimination of this provision . . . as to the status of existing law in this area" (S. Rep. No. 1622, supra note 8, at 252). The proposed regulations under the 1954 Code took the position that a reduction in par value qualified (Prop. Reg. §1.317-2, 19 Fed. Reg. 8254 (1954)), but this provision was omitted from the final regulations.

[124] Fowler Hosiery Co. v. CIR, 301 F2d 394 (7th Cir. 1962); but see Blaschka v. US, 393 F2d 983 (Ct. Cl. 1968) (no formal or informal plan). See also Rev. Rul. 65-80, 1965-1 CB 154 (partial liquidation treatment will not be denied because corporation fails to file Form 966, the corporate information return).

might on occasion be justified in determining that the plan was adopted by informal action at an earlier date and in disqualifying a distribution as too late under §302(e)(1)(B). [125]

¶ 9.09　PARTIAL LIQUIDATIONS: THE CORPORATE CONTRACTION DOCTRINE

Section 302(e)(1)(A) provides that a distribution must be treated as a partial liquidation if it "is not essentially equivalent to a dividend (determined at the corporate level rather than at the shareholder level)" and if it satisfies the formal plan and timing requirements set out above. [126] By itself, this dividend-equivalence and corporate-level language is hopelessly murky; it can be understood only in the light of history, as explained in the rest of this section, and even then many uncertainties remain. These residual difficulties can be sidestepped, however, if the corporation is actively engaged in the conduct of two or more qualified businesses (as defined) and if the distribution satisfies the safe harbor requirements of §302(e)(2). [127]

1. Dividend equivalence. In using the phrase "not essentially equivalent to a dividend," §302(e)(1)(A)—like its statutory predecessor, the 1954–1982 version of §346(a)(2)—echoes the language of §115(g) of the 1939 Code and carries forward, to some degree at least, the corporate contraction doctrine developed in the pre-1954 law decisions. [128] Thus, the Senate Report on the 1954 Code states that the term "partial liquidation" as used therein primarily "involves the concept of 'corporate contraction' as developed under existing law." [129] At another point, the 1954 Senate report states:

The general language of the proposed draft would include within the definition of a partial liquidation the type of cases involving the contraction of the corporate business. Such as for example, cases which

---

[125] For a similar problem in determining when a plan of liquidation was adopted in applying former §337, see infra ¶ 11.61. See also infra ¶ 11.02 on the problem of determining whether a distribution is an ordinary dividend or part of a partial or complete liquidation; Rev. Rul. 77-468, 1977-2 CB 109 (intentional delay in distribution until after period specified by statutory predecessor of §302(b)(4) disqualifies distribution as partial liquidation, even though it otherwise constituted a genuine contraction).

[126] Supra text at notes 121–125.

[127] See infra ¶ 9.10.

[128] See supra ¶ 9.01, text at note 4.

[129] S. Rep. No. 1622, supra note 8, at 262.

hold that if the entire floor of a factory is destroyed by fire, the insurance proceeds received may be distributed pro rata to the shareholders without the imposition of a tax at the rates applicable to the distribution of a dividend, if the corporation no longer continues its operations to the same extent maintained by the destroyed facility. Voluntary bona fide contraction of the corporate business may of course also qualify to the same extent as under existing law. [130]

The 1939 Code decisions on corporate contraction embraced not only the well-known "contraction-by-fire" case of *Joseph W. Imler*, [131] but other situations where the reasons for capital gain treatment were at best obscure. Thus, redemptions attributable to (1) a reserve for expansion that was no longer needed, (2) a shift in the scale or nature of the corporation's operations causing a decline in its need for working capital, (3) an effort to shield property from the claims of corporate creditors, or (4) the liquidation of an unprofitable department were at times successful in claiming the mantle of corporate contraction, although not without exceptions. [132]

Notwithstanding the references to existing law in the 1954 Senate Report, the drafters of the statutory predecessor of §302(b)(4) gave at least two indications that the pre-1954 concept of corporate contraction was not ratified in every respect: First, the report states flatly that "a distribution of a reserve for expansion is not a partial liquidation;" second, it implies that redemptions qualify only if they "terminate a part of the business of the

---

[130] Id. at 49.

[131] Joseph W. Imler, supra note 4.

[132] As to reserves for expansion, see CIR v. Champion, 78 F2d 513 (6th Cir. 1935); Samuel A. Upham, 4 TC 1120 (1945) (acq.); contra, McGuire v. CIR, 84 F2d 431 (7th Cir.), cert. denied, 299 US 591 (1936).

For declines in working capital needs, see Clarence R. O'Brion, ¶ 51,373 P-H Memo. TC (1951); Edwin L. Jones, ¶ 42,555 P-H Memo. TC (1942); CIR v. Quackenbos, 78 F2d 156 (2d Cir. 1935); John P. Elton, 47 BTA 111 (1942) (acq.); contra, Dunton v. Clauson, 67 F. Supp. 839 (D. Me. 1946).

For protection against creditors, see CIR v. Sullivan, 210 F2d 607 (5th Cir. 1954); see also L.M. Lockhart, 8 TC 436 (1947).

For liquidation of a department, see CIR v. Babson, 70 F2d 309 (7th Cir.), cert. denied, 293 US 571 (1934); Heber Scowcroft Inv. Co., ¶ 45,235 P-H Memo. TC (1945). But see Estate of Chandler, 22 TC 1158 (1954), aff'd per curiam, 228 F2d 909 (6th Cir. 1955)

See generally Chommie, Section 346(a)(2): The Contraction Theory, 11 Tax L. Rev. 407, 417-422 (1956).

Because the courts rarely, if ever, found it necessary to base a decision on a single factor, it cannot be said with confidence that the element of contraction was the sole foundation for any of the foregoing decisions, although it appears to have been at least persuasive, if not the turning point, in all. It is entirely possible, however, that some of the earlier cases would not pass the more rigorous judicial examination that subsequently became customary.

corporation." [133] These remarks reject or cast doubt on pre-1954 cases holding that distributions of reserves for expansion or of excess working capital could qualify as partial liquidations. [134] Moreover, the intent to carry forward existing law should not be interpreted as a blanket approval of every judicial decision previously rendered or as preventing further evolutionary developments in what is at best a flexible concept rather than a frozen body of rules. In this respect, the *Imler* case itself, explicitly described and approved by the Senate Report, [135] states:

> The issue here raised presents a question of fact depending on the circumstances of the particular case. . . . No sole or universally applicable test can be laid down. . . . Though decided cases are not controlling, they are helpful as indicating what elements have been considered important, viz., the presence or absence of a real business purpose, the motives of the corporation at the time of distribution, the size of the corporate surplus, the past dividend policy, and the presence of any special circumstances relating to the distribution. [136]

The difficulty with corporate contraction as a standard for determining dividend equivalency stems from the fact that many distributions that contract the size of a corporation possess the major indicia of a dividend distribution (i.e., adequate earnings and profits, pro rata distribution, and continued operation of an active corporate enterprise). The resulting inadequacy of the corporate contraction concept to demarcate ordinary distributions from other distributions, except possibly in terms of an *unexpected* reduction of corporate activities, has been frequently noted by commentators, who have argued that the concept should be abolished or restricted. [137] Some courts have pointed out the possibility of abuse inherent in the contraction concept (e.g., a temporary investment in business assets is sold when convenient so that a distribution of the proceeds can be plausibly explained as a contraction of the business). [138] Recognizing its potential for disguising ordinary dis-

---

[133] S. Rep. No. 1622, supra note 8, at 262, 255.

[134] Supra note 132. See also Regs. §1.346-1(a); Rev. Rul. 78-55, 1978-1 CB 88 (distribution of cash reserve not a contraction because no significant reduction in business activities).

[135] S. Rep. No. 1622, supra note 8, at 262.

[136] Joseph W. Imler, supra note 4, at 840.

[137] See Cohen et al., Corporate Liquidations Under the Internal Revenue Code of 1954, 55 Colum. L. Rev. 37, 37–38 (1955); Surrey, Income Tax Problems of Corporations and Shareholders: American Law Institute Tax Project—American Bar Association Committee Study on Legislative Revision, 14 Tax L. Rev. 1, 5 (1958); Bittker & Redlich, supra note 1, at 472–473.

[138] See Trust of Edward L. Kraus, Jr., 6 TC 105, 120–121 (1946) (manufacturing company sold portfolio of securities and redeemed some of its stock with proceeds;

tributions as partial liquidations is the first step toward consciously policing the concept; [139] uncertainty as to its scope may be the most effective safeguard against abuse. The Service has not espoused a policy of total darkness, however, but has instead elucidated its approach to this area in numerous rulings. [140]

"liquidation of assets of the character we have here does not necessarily result in a liquidation of a business, nor does the fact that the $150,000 which was distributed was most of the proceeds from the sale of securities stamp them as liquidating distributions").

For a post-1954 case of like import, see Mains v. US, 508 F2d 1251 (6th Cir. 1975); see also Rev. Rul. 60-322, 1960-2 CB 118 (distribution of proceeds of investments and excess inventories; held not a qualified contraction of business), distinguished in Rev. Rul. 74-296, 1974-1 CB 80 (discontinuance of old business and change in character of remaining business constituted contraction).

[139] See generally Mains v. US, supra note 138 (sale of assets followed by reinvestment of part of proceeds and distribution of balance, representing insignificant percentage of distributing corporation's net worth; held not a qualifying contraction); Nord Krauskopf, ¶ 84,386 P-H Memo. TC (1984) (distribution of 4–6 percent of corporate assets; same result); Viereck v. US, 52 AFTR2d 6350 (Cl. Ct. 1983) (no substantial reduction in corporation's business activity); Cleveland v. CIR, 335 F2d 473 (3d Cir. 1964); Fowler Hosiery Co. v. CIR, supra note 124; Ballenger v. US, 301 F2d 192 (4th Cir. 1962); McCarthy v. Conley, Jr., 341 F2d 948 (2d Cir.), cert. denied, 382 US 838 (1965).

[140] See Rev. Rul. 71-250, 1971-1 CB 112 (temporary investment of proceeds from sale of business, followed by distribution; held a contraction, but profits component of proceeds taxable under §301), amplified in Rev. Rul. 76-279, 1976-2 CB 99; Rev. Rul. 79-275, 1979-2 CB 137 (distribution of unrelated assets not qualified; must distribute contracted business assets or proceeds of their sale); Rev. Rul. 74-296, supra note 138 (change from full-time department store to discount apparel store caused contraction); Rev. Rul. 75-223, 1975-1 CB 109 (parent's distribution of proceeds from liquidating sale of its subsidiary qualified as contraction but not distribution of stock of subsidiary; latter a separation, not a contraction), clarified by Rev. Rul. 77-375, 1977-2 CB 106 (amount of qualified partial liquidation distribution reduced by debt of subsidiary to parent that was canceled on subsidiary's liquidation into parent) and by Rev. Rul. 77-376, 1977-2 CB 107 (relative size of subsidiary's discontinued business irrelevant); Rev. Rul. 79-184, 1979-1 CB 143 (parent's sale of stock of subsidiary and distribution of proceeds was mere sale of investment asset by parent and distribution of dividend; subsidiary's business not attributed to parent; Rev. Rul. 75-223 distinguished); see also Rev. Rul. 76-429, 1976-2 CB 97 (13 days after subsidiary sold one of its two businesses and simultaneously distributed its other assets in complete liquidation, parent reincorporated second business; held a contraction); Rev. Rul. 76-526, 1976-2 CB 101 (distribution of passive real estate not a contraction); Rev. Rul. 76-289, 1976-2 CB 100 (tracing of distributed funds to discontinued business), expanding on Rev. Rul. 60-232, 1960-2 CB 115 (distribution of working capital attributable to the terminated business permitted); Rev. Rul. 78-55, 1978-1 CB 88 (no contraction of business activity).

For the Service ruling policy, see Rev. Proc. 87-3, §4.01(13), 1987-1 IRB 30 (contraction rulings not ordinarily issued unless distribution reduces gross revenues, net assets, or employees by at least 20 percent); Rose, Representations Required by IRS

2. Corporate level determination. The parenthetical language of §302(e)(1)(A) provides that dividend equivalence is to be "determined at the corporate level rather than at the shareholder level." This phrase makes explicit the long-established principle that partial liquidations are "characterized by what happens solely at the corporate level *by reason of the assets distributed*" (emphasis added)[141] or, as expressed by the 1982 conference committee report, that compliance with the definition of partial liquidation is to be made "with reference to the effect of the transaction on the distributing corporation and not with reference to its effect at the shareholder level."[142] The point is buttressed by §302(e)(4), providing that a distribution's redemption qualification as a partial liquidation must be determined without regard to whether or not the redemption is pro rata with respect to the shareholders. This concern with the nature of the assets distributed and the resulting effect on the corporation contrasts sharply with the significance of the very same language ("not essentially equivalent to a dividend") used in §302(b)(1), which as construed by the *Davis* case requires a meaningful reduction in the shareholder's proportionate interest in the corporation.[143]

¶ 9.10   SAFE HARBOR DISTRIBUTIONS OF QUALIFIED ACTIVE TRADE OR BUSINESS

The vagaries of the corporate contraction route to exchange treatment under §302(b)(4), relating to redemptions in partial liquidations of a corporation,[144] can be avoided if the distribution consists of the assets of a qualified trade or business (as defined) or is attributable to the corporation's ceasing to conduct such a business, provided that it is actively engaged in conducting another qualified trade or business immediately after the distribution. As with redemptions qualifying for exchange treatment under the more general standards for corporate contractions, this safe harbor for business terminations is available for both pro rata and non-pro rata redemptions, but is similarly restricted to noncorporate shareholders.[145] "Qualified

---

for Rulings on a Partial Liquidation of a Subsidiary's Business Go Further Than Necessary, 9 J. Corp. Tax'n 151 (1982).

[141] S. Rep. No. 1622, supra note 8, at 49.

[142] H.R. Rep. No. 760, supra note 52, at 530 (explicit statutory language codifies "present law").

[143] See supra text at notes 66–83; see also Rev. Rul. 82-187, 1982-2 CB 80.

[144] For the corporate contraction doctrine, see supra ¶ 9.09.

[145] See §302(e)(4) (qualification as partial liquidation determined without regard to whether redemption is pro rata); §302(b)(4)(A) (§302(a) applicable only to redemptions of stock held by noncorporate shareholders); see also §302(e)(5) (stock

trade or business" is defined by §302(e)(3) to mean a trade or business that (1) was actively conducted throughout the five-year period ending on the date of the redemption and (2) was not acquired by the distributing corporation within that period in a transaction in which gain or loss was recognized in whole or in part.[146]

This battery of requirements may be understood more easily if their purpose is recognized. Accepting the corporate contraction doctrine as an appropriate test, the drafters wanted to create an area in which capital gain or loss (and offset of basis) treatment would be assured without the necessity of justifying each distribution under the vague standards of the decided cases. They thought that if a corporation with two or more businesses wished to distribute one of them, the distribution should be treated as a partial liquidation. At the same time, they did not want to invite tax avoidance by allowing a closely held corporation to accumulate its earnings and profits, invest its surplus cash in assets that the shareholders would like to hold as individuals, and then go through the form of a corporate contraction by distributing the newly acquired assets and retaining the business assets.

In order to prevent avoidance of the tax on dividends by a corporate purchase of investment securities or real estate to be distributed in redemption of part of the stock of the corporation, §§302(e)(2)(A) and 302(e)(3)(B) grant a safe harbor to a distribution only if it consists of the assets of an actively conducted trade or business or is attributable to a termination of such a business (e.g., the proceeds of a sale). By itself, however, this requirement could be satisfied by reversing the transaction (i.e., by distributing the business and retaining the liquid assets); but this gambit is in turn barred by §§302(e)(2)(B) and 302(e)(3)(A), requiring the distributing corporation to be actively engaged in the conduct of a trade or business immediately after the distribution.

Taken in conjunction, these active conduct rules grant safe harbor treatment only to corporations with *two* actively conducted businesses, one of which (or the proceeds of which) is distributed and the other retained. The five-year rule, coupled with the prohibition on the acquisition of either of the trades or business by purchase,[147] is designed to prevent an accumulation of earnings and profits for investment in a business that the sharehold-

---

held by partnership, estate, or trust treated as if actually held proportionately by partners or beneficiaries). As to S corporation shareholders, see §1371(a)(2) (treated as individuals for purposes of Subchapter C).

[146] These requirements for safe harbor partial liquidations were originally enacted in 1954 as §346(b), which was revised in 1982 and renumbered as §§302(e)(2) and 302(e)(3), but these changes were not intended to have any substantive effect. See Staff of Joint Comm. on Taxation, supra note 112, at 126. For §346(b) as enacted in 1954, see S. Rep. No. 1622, supra note 8, at 262.

[147] See infra text at note 152.

ers would otherwise have used taxable dividends to acquire, with a view toward a prompt distribution in a purported business termination under §302(e)(2). It will not, however, prevent a similar plan for avoidance of the dividend tax if the shareholders are patient. After the acquired has been held and aged for five years (assuming its operation constitutes the active conduct of a trade or business), its distribution can qualify under §302(e)(2), with a possible exception for transactions that can be characterized as shams (an unlikely event in the case of an aged active business).

Section 302(e)(2) has much in common with §355, under which a divisive reorganization can be effected tax-free. If a corporation is conducting a five-year-old active trade or business and its subsidiary is conducting a second such business, §355 permits the parent to distribute the stock of the subsidiary to its shareholders in a tax-free redemption of part of the parent's stock (a so-called split-off), subject to conditions examined in Chapter 13.[148] Moreover, if both businesses are conducted by a single corporation, one can be transferred to a newly organized subsidiary as a prelude to a distribution of its stock to the shareholders of the parent.

Because §355 provides a tax-free route to such corporate separations, it has overshadowed §302(e)(2) and its statutory predecessor, §346(b). But §302(e)(2) may be the preferable (or even the only feasible) route in some circumstances. For example, if the fair market value of the assets to be transferred is less than the adjusted basis of the shares to be surrendered, a transfer of the business assets themselves under §302(e)(2) will permit the shareholder's capital loss to be recognized. Moreover, §355 permits the business assets to be distributed only if they are held in corporate form. If the shareholder wishes to conduct the distributed business as a sole proprietor or partner, §302(e)(2) is the route to follow; the shareholder will have to report his capital gain (if any), but this gain will permit a step-up in the bases of the distributed assets.

These differences between §§302(e)(2) and 355 affect tax planning, but the following underlying requirements of §302(e)(2) are virtually identical with the requirements of §355:

(1) The distributing corporation must be actively engaged in the conduct of a trade or business immediately after the distribution;[149]

(2) The distribution must similarly involve an actively conducted trade or business, since the distribution must either consist of the assets

---

[148] Another tax-free advantage of §355 is escape from the gain recognition rule of §311(b)(1), infra ¶ 9.34.

[149] Section 302(e)(2)(B). For discussion of the similar requirement under §355, see infra ¶ 13.04.

of, or be attributable to, the distributing corporation's ceasing to conduct such a trade or business; [150]

(3) Both businesses must have been actively conducted throughout the five-year period ending on the date of the redemption; [151] and

(4) The distributing corporation must not have acquired either business within the five-year period in a transaction in which gain or loss was recognized in whole or in part. [152]

The cases and rulings under §302(e)(2) and its statutory predecessor, §346(b), are relatively sparse compared with the cases and rulings construing the §355 counterparts of these requirements; the reader is therefore referred to the examination of §355 later in this treatise for analysis of the features that are common to §§302(e)(2) and 355. [153]

¶ 9.11   REDEMPTIONS UNDER §303

Section 303 provides that a redemption of stock, the value of which has been included in the gross estate of a decedent for federal estate tax pur-

---

[150] Section 302(e)(2)(A). For the phrase "a trade or business which has been actively conducted," see Kenton Meadows Co. v. CIR, 766 F2d 142 (4th Cir. 1985) (single integrated business, not two separate businesses; §355 cases allowing split of single business not applicable to partial liquidations); Nord Krauskopf, supra note 139 (terminated business not a separate business; merely an incident to taxpayer's main business activity); Blaschka v. US, supra note 124 (business not a separate, viable operation); Mains v. US, supra note 138 (operations that do not include every step in process of earning income not a separate business); H.L. Morgenstern, 56 TC 44 (1971) (ownership of subsidiary corporation's stock does not constitute actively conducting subsidiary's trade or business).

For discussion of the required distribution, see Gordon v. CIR, supra note 122 (full distribution of either proceeds or assets required; corporation's hold-back of some assets therefore prevented qualification as a partial liquidation), Kenton Meadows Co., supra (corporation did not distribute entire proceeds of sale of terminated business); Rev. Rul. 79-275, 1979-2 CB 137 (attributable interpreted to mean proceeds of sale of terminated business).

For discussion of similar requirements under §355, see infra ¶¶ 13.04 and 13.08.

[151] Section 302(e)(3)(A); see Rev. Rul. 71-473, 1971-2 CB 79 (period ends on sale of business); for a similar requirement under §355, see infra ¶ 13.06.

[152] Section 302(e)(3)(B). For the meaning of recognition of gain or loss in this context, see infra ¶ 13.06 at notes 55 and 56. It should be noted, however, that §302(e)(2) is not as explicit as §355(b)(2), which, in dealing with a similar problem, prohibits not only the acquisition of a trade or business during the five-year period but also the acquisition of a corporation conducting the trade or business; see infra ¶ 13.06.

[153] Infra ¶¶ 13.01–13.15.

poses, must in certain cases be treated as a sale of the stock, even though it would, but for §303, be taxed as a dividend under §301.[154] For example, if all the stock of a corporation is held by an estate, a redemption of part of the stock would not qualify for capital gains treatment under §302(b)(2) (substantially disproportionate redemptions) or §302(b)(3) (redemptions in termination of a shareholder's interest); nor, in the absence of other relevant facts, could it qualify under §302(b)(1) (redemptions not essentially equivalent to a dividend) or §302(b)(4) (partial liquidations).[155] When applicable, §303 permits the estate to offset its basis for the stock (ordinarily its fair market value at death) against the redemption proceeds, so that little if any gain or loss is realized.

Section 303 is an expanded version of a provision that was enacted in 1950 and whose purpose was then stated by the House Committee on Ways and Means as follows:

> It has been brought to the attention of your committee that the problem of financing the estate tax is acute in the case of estates consisting largely of shares in a family corporation. The market for such shares is usually very limited, and it is frequently difficult, if not impossible, to dispose of a minority interest. If, therefore, the estate tax cannot be financed through the sale of the other assets in the estate, the executors will be forced to dispose of the family business. In many cases the result will be the absorption of a family enterprise by larger competitors, thus tending to accentuate the degree of concentration of industry in this country. . . .

---

[154] For additional favorable features of a §303 redemption, see infra ¶ 9.34 text at notes 215–216 (corporation not taxed on distributing appreciated property under §303, under pre-1987 law that continues for transitional period); §537(a)(2) (in applying special tax on unreasonable accumulations of corporate surplus, §303 redemption requirements count as reasonable) (see supra ¶ 8.07); and former §382(a)(1)(C)(v) (in applying pre-1987 law limitations on net operating loss carryovers, decrease in outstanding stock was not counted if attributable to §303 redemption; current law §382(l)(3)(B)(i)(I) exempts all transfers *at death* from the change of ownership rules, but redemptions of stock will count whether or not §303 applies).

For redemptions by affiliated corporations, see §§304(a)(1) and 304(a)(2), discussed infra ¶ 9.12.

See generally Knickerbocker, Corporate Stock Redemption–Section 303, Tax Mgmt. (BNA) No. 91-5th (1986), and articles there cited; ABA, Tax Section Report, Overall Impact of the Tax Reform Act of 1976 on §303, 32 Tax Lawyer 257 (1979); Blum & Trier, Planning for Maximum Benefits of Section 303 Redemptions With Estate Tax Deferral, 53 J. Tax'n 236 (1980); Kahn, Closely Held Stocks–Deferral and Financing of Estate Tax Costs Through Sections 303 and 6166, 35 Tax Lawyer 639 (1982).

[155] For §302(b), see generally supra ¶ 9.02.

> Your committee is of the opinion that remedial action is desirable in order to prevent the enforced sale of the family businesses which are so vital and desirable an element in our system of free private enterprise.[156]

Despite its stated purpose of protecting against forced sales of family businesses, the danger of which may have been exaggerated and is in any event allayed by §6166 (permitting the federal estate tax to be paid in installments over a 10-year period if the estate includes an interest in a closely held business worth more than 35 percent of the adjusted gross estate[157]), §303 may be applied whether the estate is liquid or not and even if the distribution consists of illiquid corporate assets.

Section 303 contains the following conditions and limitations:

(1) The redeemed stock must be included in determining the value of the gross estate of the decedent for federal estate tax purposes. This requirement is satisfied, of course, if the stock was owned by the decedent at the time of his death. It is also satisfied if the stock, although not owned by the decedent at death, is included in his gross estate because (1) it was transferred in contemplation of death, (2) the decedent had a power of appointment over it, (3) it was held in joint tenancy with the decedent, and so forth.[158]

If stock was included in the gross estate and could have been redeemed under §303, the same privilege is extended by §303(c) to a redemption of new stock having a basis determined by reference to the basis of the stock that was actually included, such as stock acquired by the estate as a stock dividend or in a recapitalization or other tax-free exchange.[159]

---

[156] H.R. Rep. No. 2319, 81st Cong., 2d Sess. 63, reprinted in 1950-2 CB 380, 427–428.

[157] For §6166, see generally Bittker, supra note 83, at ¶ 135.5.

[158] In valuing a decedent's gross estate, §2035(d)(3)(A) preserves the old three-year gift in contemplation of death rule for purposes of §303(b). This estate tax rule was intended to preclude deathbed transfers in order to reduce the size of the estate so that its retained stock would be more likely to qualify for a §303 redemption; but §2035(d)(3)(A) also seems to permit stock to be counted toward §303's 35 percent requirement, even though transferred on the decedent's deathbed. For an attempt to prevent this perverse result, see Rev. Rul. 84-76, 1984-1 CB 91 (transferred stock does not qualify for §303 redemption because it does not generate any federal estate tax liability, even though it is counted in applying 35 percent requirement and hence may enable *other* stock to qualify). See also Prop. Regs. §1.303-1(a)(3).

[159] Regs. §1.303-2(d) provides that "section 306 stock" can be redeemed under §303; see also Rev. Rul. 82-72, 1982-1 CB 57 (charge to corporate earnings and profits when "section 306 stock" is redeemed under §303; but see §312(n)(7), added in 1984, limiting the charge to the redeemed stock's ratable share of earnings, infra ¶ 9.35); Rev. Rul. 73-177, 1973-1 CB 168 (application of §303 to stock received by estate in §333 liquidation); Prop. Regs. §1.303-1(f) (§303 overrides §306).

(2) The distributing corporation's stock included in the gross estate must exceed 35 percent of the excess of the gross estate over the amounts allowable as deductions under §§2053–2054 (funeral and administration expenses, claims, taxes, losses, and so forth). Corporations whose stock makes up 20 percent or more of the gross estate can be aggregated in satisfying the 35 percent requirement;[160] the 20 percent requirement can in turn be satisfied by treating stock that the decedent's surviving spouse holds as community property (or as joint tenant, tenant by entirety, or tenant in common) as if it were included in determining the value of the gross estate.

(3) The total application of §303 cannot exceed the sum of (1) the death taxes imposed because of the decedent's death and (2) the funeral and administration expenses allowable as deductions for federal estate tax purposes.[161]

(4) The benefits of §303 are available only to amounts distributed within a limited period after the death of the decedent.[162]

If only part of the redemption qualifies for §303 sale treatment, with the rest constituting a dividend under §301, part of the shareholder's basis for the redeemed stock should be allocated to that portion of the transaction constituting a sale.[163] One possibility, analogous to the part-gift-part-sale rules of Regs. §1.1001-1(e), would be to apply the total basis against the §303 sale proceeds in computing gain. If the basis is not fully recovered, loss would not be allowed under the part-sale analogy; the unrecovered basis would presumably stay with the stock retained by the redeeming shareholder, as would be the case in a §301(c)(2) distribution. Another method

---

[160] Estate of Byrd v. CIR, 388 F2d 223 (5th Cir. 1967) (stock owned constructively under §318 not counted in determining applicable percentage requirement); see also Rev. Rul. 69-594, 1969-2 CB 44 (two corporations that were separate at date of death treated as such, even though merged before optional valuation date); Prop. Regs. §1.303-1(a)(2).

[161] For a requirement that the redeemed shareholder bear the economic burden of death taxes and expenses, see §303(b)(3) and Prop. Regs. §1.303-1(d), infra note 165. Although §303(a) speaks of "a distribution," Rev. Rul. 67-425, 1967-2 CB 134 holds that a series of redemptions can qualify; see also Regs. §1.303-2(g) (§303 applied to multiple redemptions in their chronological order); Prop. Regs. §1.303-1(e)(1) (same).

[162] See §303(b)(1) (general rules) and §303(b)(4) (limit on distributions more than four years after decedent's death); see also Rev. Rul. 67-425, 1967-2 CB 134 (corporate notes treated as current distributions); Rev. Rul. 72-188, 1972-1 CB 383 (interrelationship of §§303 and 6166); Prop. Regs. §1.303-1(c) (distribution timing rules generally).

[163] See Rev. Rul. 71-261, 1971-1 CB 108.

would be to allocate the basis in proportion to the relative value of the sale and dividend portions of the distribution. Thus, if 25 percent of the distribution qualified for §303 treatment, the shareholder would be entitled to apply 25 percent of his basis to that part of the transaction. Substantially the same result would be achieved by allocating basis in proportion to the relative basis of the stock qualifying for §303 treatment, since the stock, having been inherited, would have a basis equal to its fair market value at the time of death by virtue of §1014.[164]

Although stock must be included *in* the gross estate to qualify for a §303 redemption, it does not have to be redeemed *from* the estate. Thus, §303 can apply to a distribution to a beneficiary of the estate to whom the stock was distributed; indeed, it can apply even if the estate never owned the stock, as in the case of stock transferred by the decedent during his lifetime, subject to a retained life estate or power to alter beneficial enjoyment. Distributions to shareholders other than the estate itself, however, qualify only to the extent that they reduce the shareholder's direct or indirect liability for the decedent's death taxes or the funeral and administration expenses allowable as deductions to the estate.[165] In determining whether this condition is satisfied, it is necessary to look to federal estate tax law (e.g., §2206–2207, relating to the liability of beneficiaries of life insurance on the decedent's life and recipients of property over which the decedent had a power of appointment), state probate and apportionment statutes, and the provisions of the decedent's will.

¶ 9.12   REDEMPTIONS BY AFFILIATED CORPORATIONS

Section 302(a), which determines whether a stock redemption must be treated as a sale of the stock rather than as a distribution, applies to a redemption by a corporation of its stock;[166] but what if the stock of one corporation is sold to another corporation? If the two corporations are not affiliated in any way, there is no reason for the transaction not to be taken at face value and treated as an ordinary sale of stock without regard to §302.

Should the same rule apply, though, if the two corporations are affiliated (e.g., if a shareholder sells part of his stock in a parent corporation to its subsidiary)? In answering this question, it should be noted that the net effect of such a transaction is comparable to a distribution of assets by the subsidi-

---

[164] For similar identification problems, see infra ¶¶ 9.31 and 11.03. See also Regs. §1.303-2(g) and Prop. Regs. §1.303-1(e).

[165] Section 303(b)(3). See H.R. Rep. No. 1380, 94th Cong., 2d Sess. 35 (1976), reprinted in 1976-3 CB, Vol. 3, at 769; Prop. Regs. §1.303-1(d).

[166] See generally supra ¶ 9.02.

ary to its parent followed by a redemption by the parent of its own stock; a transaction that takes the latter form is taxed as §301 distribution (i.e., taxable to the extent of the parent's earnings and profits) unless it qualifies for sale/exchange treatment under §302(b) (because, for example, it qualifies as a substantially disproportionate redemption or as a partial liquidation[167]). Brother-sister corporations can create a similar problem if their common owner causes one of them to purchase some of the stock of the other. The only difference between this transaction and the payment of a simple dividend by the first corporation is that the first corporation ends up with some stock of the second corporation, although this shift in formal ownership does not diminish their common owner's continuing control over both corporations.

If parent-subsidiary and brother-sister transactions such as these are taken at face value (i.e., as purchases by one corporation of the stock of another, rather as redemptions), the rules of §302(b) determining whether a redemption should be treated as a sale or as a dividend could be evaded by any closely held enterprise that could be conducted through two or more affiliated corporations.[168] For this reason, §304 subjects acquisitions of one corporation's stock by a related corporation to the redemption rules of §302 in the manner described below.[169]

1. Acquisitions by subsidiary corporation. If a subsidiary corporation (the "controlled" or "acquiring" corporation) acquires stock of its parent (the "issuing" corporation) from a shareholder thereof, §304(a)(2) provides that any money or other property paid for the stock must be treated as a distribution in redemption of the parent corporation's stock. Whether the

---

[167] For substantially disproportionate redemptions and partial liquidations, see supra ¶¶ 9.04 and 9.08 respectively.

[168] For §302, see supra ¶¶ 9.02–9.10.

For an unsuccessful Service effort (before enactment of remedial legislation) to treat a subsidiary's purchase of stock of its parent as a distribution by the latter, see CIR v. John Rodman Wanamaker, Trustee, 11 TC 365 (1948), aff'd per curiam, 178 F2d 10 (3d Cir. 1949); for an equally unsuccessful Service attempt to deal with a brother-sister transaction, see Trianon Hotel Co., 30 TC 156 (1950).

[169] See generally Gould, Stock Sales Subject to Section 304, Tax Mgmt. (BNA) No. 83-5th (1986); Tiger, Redemptions Through Use of Related Corporations: New and Old Problems Under Section 304, 39 Tax L. Rev. 77 (1984); Marans, Section 304: The Shadowy World of Redemptions Through Related Corporations, 22 Tax L. Rev. 161 (1967); addenda, id. at 721; Kempf, Section 304 of the Internal Revenue Code: Unmasking Disguised Dividends in Related Corporation Transactions 33 U. Chi. L. Rev. 60 (1965).

For special rules negating the application of §304(a) to certain distributions to minority shareholders incident to the formation of a bank holding company as defined by the Bank Holding Company Act of 1956, see §304(b)(3)(C).

transaction, so viewed, qualifies for sale/exchange rather than dividend treatment depends on the normal rules prescribed by §§302–303.[170] Since §304 transactions do not involve an actual redemption of the transferred stock, which instead remains outstanding in the hands of the acquiring corporation, all or part of the stock may be attributed back to the transferor shareholder in determining whether the substantially disproportionate or complete termination rules of §§302(b)(2) and 302(b)(3) apply.[171]

If the transferor shareholder is treated as receiving a distribution under §301 rather than as having sold the stock, the dividend component is determined by looking first to the earnings and profits of the acquiring subsidiary corporation and then to the earnings and profits of the issuing parent corporation.[172] Thus, by selling stock of one corporation to a related corporation, the shareholder may be worse off than with a conventional redemption by the issuing corporation, because under §304 the pool of earnings and profits is enlarged to include both corporations.

In applying §304(a)(2), the concept of control is crucial, since §304(a)(2) encompasses an acquisition of stock only if the issuing corporation controls the acquiring corporation. The term "control" is defined by §304(c)(1) as the ownership of stock possessing at least 50 percent of the total combined voting power of all classes of stock entitled to vote or at least 50 percent of the total value of all classes of stock. In computing these percentages, §304(c) incorporates by reference the constructive ownership rules of §318(a), with some modifications.[173]

---

[170] Supra ¶¶ 9.04–9.11. A *parent's* acquisition of its *subsidiary's* stock is governed by §304(a)(1) (the brother-sister rules) rather than by §304(a)(2), Rev. Rul. 70-496, 1970-2 CB 74; but see Rev. Rul. 74-605, 1974-2 CB 97 (§304 not applicable to acquisition of stock of second-tier subsidiary from first-tier subsidiary).

[171] For such an attribution in a brother-sister transaction, see Regs. §1.304-2(c), Examples (1) and (3). For a formula applicable to parent-subsidary transactions, see Tiger, Sales of Stock to Related Corporations: Current Problems Under Section 304, 40 J. Tax'n 86 (1974). Waiver of this attribution under §302(c)(2) (supra ¶ 9.05) is not available, since it involves an entity-to-shareholder attribution situation; but see Fehrs v. US, supra note 47 (waiver allowed in a §304 case where section applied only because of family attribution).

[172] Under prior law, when the dividend component of the distribution was determined by treating the property as distributed by the subsidiary to the parent and by it to the selling shareholder, the Service ruled that the parent received a taxable dividend. See Rev. Rul. 69-261, 1969-1 CB 94; Helen M. Webb, 67 TC 293 (1976) (rejecting Rev. Rul. 69-261); see also Rev. Rul. 80-189, 1980-2 CB 106 (revoking Rev. Rul. 69-261).

[173] For §318(a), see supra ¶ 9.03; the principal modification is the substitution of a 5 percent benchmark for the normal 50 percent test of §318(a) for attributing stock to and from corporations. Note that under §318(a)(3)(C), as modified by §304(c)(3)(B)(ii), stock of one corporation owned by a 50 percent or over shareholder of a second corporation is imputed in full to the second corporation; but if the share-

2. Acquisitions by related (but nonsubsidiary) corporations; brother-sister acquisitions. A remedial rule applicable only to a subsidiary's purchase of stock in its parent would, as noted earlier, permits taxpayers to avoid the rules of §302 by using brother-sister corporations instead of parent-subsidiary corporations.[174] To close this gap, §304(a)(1) provides that if one or more persons are in control of each of two corporations, one of which acquires stock in the other from a controlling person, then the money or other property paid for the stock must be treated as a distribution in redemption of the acquiring corporation's stock.[175] In determining whether or not the transaction is a sale or exchange under §302(b), however, §304(b)(1) provides that §302(b)'s rules are applied by reference to the issuing corporation's stock.

To illustrate: If A owns all of the stock of X and Y Corporations and sells half of his X stock to Y, he continues to own all of X's outstanding

---

holder owns between 5 and 50 percent of the second corporation, only a corresponding percentage of the stock is imputed to the second corporation.

Before 1984, the statutory predecessor of §304(c)(3) eliminated the 50 percent limit of §§318(a)(2)(C) (attribution from corporations) and 318(a)(3)(C) (attribution to corporations) without specifying any de minimis substitute. This had the draconic effect, at least in theory, of bringing §304 into force if a corporation sold stock of a subsidiary to the subsidiary of another corporation (or to the parent), even if the two parent corporations were publicly owned and were connected only because an individual, unknown to both of them, happened to hold one share of stock in each corporation.

To illustrate: Publicly held corporations X and Y each have a subsidiary, XS and YS. A owns one share of each parent company. If X sold some of its XS shares to YS, under pre-1984 law A's share of X would be attributed to Y under §318(a)(3)(C), whereupon all of Y's stock in Y-S would be attributed to X from its new constructive shareholder Y under §318(a)(3)(C) (which did not contain a proportionate share limit such as that in §318(a)(2)(C)), and the same process operated to make Y the owner of X-S.

For illustrations of prior law, see Rev. Rul. 77-427, 1977-2 CB 100, and Rev. Rul. 58-79, 1958-1 CB 177.

[174] See Rev. Rul. 59-97, 1959-1 CB 684, and cases there cited. The parent-subsidiary remedy of §304(a)(2) was enacted in 1950; the brother-sister remedy of §304(a)(1) in 1954.

[175] If two or more persons in the aggregate control both corporations, their sales are subject to §304(a)(1) if the transactions are related to each other (determined by looking to all of the facts and circumstances), whether they are simultaneous or not (Regs. §1.304-2(b)). See also Coyle v. US, 415 F2d 488 (4th Cir. 1968) (§304(a)(1) applies to sale to corporation owned by seller's sons, even though seller owned no stock therein directly); Rev. Rul. 71-563, 1971-2 CB 175 (same). Note that a §302(c)(2) attribution waiver apparently would not be available in the *Coyle* case transaction, even for a sale of all of the taxpayer's stock, since §302(c)(2)(C) applies only to *entity* redemptions, supra notes 52–54. But see Fehrs v. US, supra note 47 (waiver allowed where §304 applied only because of family attribution).

stock (half directly and the other half constructively by attribution from Y). Thus, the transaction is neither a substantially disproportionate redemption under §302(b)(2) nor, a fortiori, a complete redemption of A's stock in X under §302(b)(3). It must, therefore, be treated as a distribution rather than as a sale unless it can qualify as "not essentially equivalent to a dividend" under §302(b)(1)–virtually impossible under the *Davis* case.[176] Viewed as a distribution by Y, the amount received by A will be a dividend to the extent of the earnings and profits of Y Corporation and, if not fully covered thereby, to the extent that the shortfall is covered by X's earnings and profits.

The status of the X stock acquired by Y is harmonious with the treatment of the amount paid to A. Because the entire amount paid by Y is treated as a distribution to A, the stock is treated as if it had been transferred by A to Y as a contribution to capital; Y therefore holds it with a carry-over basis equal to its adjusted basis in A's hands.[177] If, on the other hand, a §304(a)(1) transaction such as this qualifies as a sale or exchange (because, for example, it satisfies the requirements of §302(b)(2), relating to substantially disproportionate redemptions[178]), the acquiring corporation treats the stock as if purchased by it, with the result that its basis is its cost.

In determining whether the brother-sister relationship required by §304(a)(1) exists—more precisely, whether one or more persons are in control of both corporations—"control" is defined by §304(c)(1) in the same manner as §304(a)(2), relating to the parent-subsidiary relationship; and the

---

[176] US v. Davis, supra note 66. It is awkward to apply §302(b)(4), relating to partial liquidations, to §304 transactions, since the assets are actually distributed by the acquiring corporation; but §304(b)(1) states that the sale vs. dividend determination is to be made by reference to the issuing corporation's stock. But see Blaschka v. US, supra note 124 (looking to acquiring corporation but finding no partial liquidation on facts).

For examples of §304(a)(1) transactions, see Rev. Rul. 70-496, 1970-2 CB 74; Rev. Rul. 77-427, 1977-2 CB 100; Fehrs Fin. Co. v. CIR, supra note 47; Fehrs v. US, supra note 47; Rev. Rul. 75-174, 1975-1 CB 252; Rev. Rul. 70-111, 1970-1 CB 184.

For the application of §303 (relating to redemptions to pay death taxes and the like) to §304(a)(1) transactions, see Rev. Rul. 71-527, 1971-2 CB 174 (percentage test of §303(b)(2)(A) applies to stock of acquiring corporation).

For the nonapplication of the §302(c)(2) family attribution waiver, see supra note 175.

[177] Section 304(a)(1) (second sentence), as amended by the Tax Reform Act of 1986. For the basis of property received by a corporation as a contribution to capital, see §362(a)(2), discussed supra ¶ 3.13.

[178] For an example of such a transaction, see Regs. §1.304-2(c), Example (3); for cost basis treatment as a result of changes in 1986, see supra note 177, overruling the contrary holding of Rev. Rul. 77-427, 1977-2 CB 100.

same constructive ownership rules apply. It should be noted, however, that if two or more persons control both corporations when their stock is combined, but no one alone controls both, §304(a)(1) does not encompass a transaction in which only one of them transfers stock. For example, if A and B, unrelated individuals, each own 45 percent of X Corporation and 45 percent of Y Corporation, and A transfers some of his X shares to Y, the transaction is not described by §304(a)(1)(B) because the X stock is not acquired "from the person (or persons) so in control" of both corporations.[179]

3. Overlap between parent-subsidiary and brother-sister relationships. Section 304(a)(1), relating to brother-sister corporations, provides that it applies only if §304(a)(2), relating to parent-subsidiary corporations, does not. Taken literally, this hierarchical proviso is inconsistent with the brother-sister examples in the Treasury Regulations, since the ostensible brother-sister relationship can be converted in each case into a parent-subsidiary relationship by the constructive ownership rule of §318(a)(3)(C). If A and B each owns one-half of X and Y Corporations (as hypothesized by one of the examples[180]), then X controls Y (because the Y stock owned by A and B is attributed to X) and Y, mirabile dictu, controls X (because their X stock is attributed to Y). The resulting problem of simultaneous triple incest (who did what and to whom?) is sidestepped by the regulations, which implicitly give precedence to an actual brother-sister relationship over a constructive parent-subsidiary relationship.[181]

The distinction between a parent-subsidiary pair and a brother-sister pair of corporations, however, is less significant now than it was before 1982, when the earnings and profits of both corporations were taken into account in computing dividend treatment only for a parent-subsidiary pair; since then, §304(b)(2) has done this for brother-sister pairs as well. In determining

---

[179] This assumes, of course, that the statutory language should not be construed as if it read "from the person (or from one or more of the persons) so in control." For a possible analogy, see Vogel Fertilizer Co. v. US, 455 US 16 (1982); see also Temp. Regs. §1.338-4T(c)(5).

[180] Regs. §1.304-2(c), Example (1).

[181] This approach may have been inspired by the pre-1982 predecessor of §304(b)(2)(B), which provided that a subsidiary's acquisition of its parent's stock should be treated, in computing the parent's earnings and profits, "as if the property [paid for the stock] were distributed by the acquiring corporation to the issuing corporation and immediately thereafter distributed by the issuing corporation," since this hypothetical distribution presupposes an unbroken upstream chain of corporations. See generally Broadview Lumber Co. v. CIR, 561 F2d 698 (7th Cir. 1977) (parent-subsidiary rule applicable only if parent has control of subsidiary without aid of constructive ownership rules); Stewart & Randall, A Proposed Solution to the Statutory Overlap of Sections 304(a)(1) and 304(a)(2), 9 J. Corp. Tax'n 125 (1982).

the acquiring corporation's basis for the redeemed stock, however, it still makes a difference whether the governing provision is §304(a)(1) or §304(a)(2).[182]

4. Application to more complex transactions. In its early years, the focus of §304 was on transfers of stock involving existing parent-subsidiary and brother-sister corporations, in which the only consideration received for the transferred stock was money or other property. Less clear was its application to transactions in which (1) some transferors received stock of the acquiring corporation instead of (or in addition to) money or other property,[183] (2) the acquiring corporation was newly created to acquire the transferred stock, or (3) the transferor or transferors did not control the acquiring corporation before the transfer but acquired control as part of the transfer plan. Because the effects of these factors under the pre-1982 version of §304 were ambiguous, it was not evident whether §304 covered a variety of complex transactions, including plans under which the shareholders of an existing corporation (1) borrowed against the stock and then transferred that stock to a newly organized corporation for all of its stock plus an assumption of the liability; (2) transferred the stock to a newly organized corporation for stock plus notes or securities; or (3) transferred the stock to an existing corporation for 80 percent or more of its stock plus notes, money, or other property.

In each of these transactions, the transferors got, immediately or over time, money or other property, possibly representing a substantial part of the value of the transferred stock, while continuing to control both the issuing and the acquiring corporation; but they could offer one or more defenses against the application of §304. First, it was arguable that §304 (until amended in 1982 as described below) did not apply to brother-sister transfers if the transferors did not control the acquiring corporation before the transfer, even though they acquired control as an integral part of the transfer plan.[184] Second, it was arguable that the nonrecognition principle of §351, which is literally satisfied in each of these cases, superseded §304.[185] Third, in the first two types of transactions, and possibly in the third as well, the acquiring corporation had no earnings and profits.

---

[182] See supra text at notes 177–178; Rev. Rul. 80-189, 1980-2 CB 106.

[183] See §317(a), defining "property" to exclude stock in the distributing corporation.

[184] Compare Regs. §1.304-2(a) (control must exist before the acquisition) with Rev. Rul. 72-569, 1972-2 CB 203 (control obtained by acquisition sufficient).

[185] Haserot v. CIR, 399 F2d 828 (6th Cir. 1968) (§351 trumps §304); Rev. Rul. 73-2, 1973-1 CB 171, and Rev. Rul. 78-422, 1978-2 CB 129, and cases there cited (contra).

Congress addressed the ambiguities and deficiencies of the pre-1982 version of §304 by amending it in 1982 in the following respects:

(a) Determining control. Section 304(c)(2) provides that stock of the acquiring corporation received for stock of the issuing corporation must be taken into account in determining whether the person who has control of the issuing corporation also controls the acquiring corporation.[186]

(b) Overlap with §351. Section 304(b)(3)(A) provides that §304 takes precedence over §351 if both would otherwise apply. If the acquiring corporation assumes (or takes subject to) liabilities, the liabilities generally count as property in applying §304 (and therefore in applying §302).[187] Under §304(b)(3)(B), however, a liability incurred by the transferor to acquire the transferred stock (including an extension, renewal, or refinancing of such a stock-acquisition liability) is not subjected to §304. This exception is allowed because the transaction is comparable to a debt-financed purchase of the stock by the acquiring corporation itself from the former owner, which would not bring either §302 or §304 into play; but the exception applies even if the debt was incurred in an unrelated transaction long before the transfer of the stock.[188] To forestall manipulative transactions, however, this acquisition-debt exemption does not apply to stock acquired from a related person unless his interest in both corporations is terminated.[189]

(c) Earnings and profits. When pre-1982 brother-sister transfers of stock were treated as distributions, the dividend component was limited to the earnings and profits of the acquiring corporation. This restriction permitted a profitable company's earnings to be bailed out by a transfer of its stock to a newly created controlled corporation or an existing controlled corporation with a zero or deficit earnings and profits account. Section 304 was amended in 1982 to amalgamate the earnings and profits of both corporations, and

---

[186] For problems in construing §304(c)(2)(B), see Tiger, supra note 169, at 88–92.

[187] See Rev. Rul. 78-422, 1978-2 CB 129; Peter Schaefers, ¶ 84,627 P-H Memo. TC (1984), and cases there cited; see also Maher v. CIR, 469 F2d 225 (8th Cir. 1972) (distribution occurred when assumed liabilities were paid); Rev. Rul. 77-360, 1977-2 CB 86 (accord with *Maher* on timing unless assumption works a novation).

[188] Rev. Rul. 80-240, 1980-2 CB 116 (same result before enactment of §304(b)(3)(B), where debt was incurred by shareholder and assumed by transferee corporation as steps in a single plan); see also Citizens Bank & Trust Co. v. US, 580 F2d 442 (Ct. Cl. 1978) (shareholder not taxed when corporation he controlled took over his obligation to buy stock of another corporation from estate of deceased co-shareholder; *Wall* principle, supra note 98, did not make shareholder of acquiring corporation the owner of purchased stock). For the Service's view before these amendments, see Rev. Rul. 78-422, 1978-2 CB 129 (liability assumption triggered §304).

[189] Section 304(b)(3)(B)(iii) (added by technical amendment in 1984).

amended again in 1984 to require each corporation's earnings and profits to be applied separately.[190] The 1984 rule prevents netting the two accounts if one corporation has a positive account and the other has a deficit.

5. Overlap with reorganization provisions. Section 304(b)(3)(A), as enacted in 1982, was not limited to §351 transactions, but referred more broadly to Part III of Subchapter C, which includes not only §351, but such other provisions as §368, relating to tax-free corporate reorganizations. To eliminate the resulting implication that §304 takes precedence over all non-recognition rules included in Part III of Subchapter C, §304(b)(3)(A) was amended in 1984 to refer solely to §351 transactions.[191]

PART B.   COLLATERAL PROBLEMS ARISING FROM STOCK REDEMPTIONS AND PARTIAL LIQUIDATIONS

¶ 9.30   INTRODUCTORY

The preceding sections of this chapter have been primarily concerned with one question: Is the shareholder whose stock has been redeemed entitled to treat the transaction as a sale of the stock so that the difference between the amount realized and the adjusted basis of the stock is includable in gross income and potentially deferrable under §453 if redeemed for untraded notes (or, if the comparison is negative, deductible as a loss), or is the transaction instead a distribution in full under §301, taxable currently as a dividend to the extent of the corporation's earnings and profits and applicable against the basis of the stock if and to the extent that it exceeds the earnings and profits? In addition to this primary shareholder-level issue, however, redemptions and partial liquidations have the collateral consequences for both the shareholder and the corporation that are discussed in the following section.

¶ 9.31   COMPUTATION OF SHAREHOLDER'S GAIN OR LOSS

As explained earlier, §302(a) provides that a redemption "shall be treated as a distribution in part or full payment in exchange for the stock"

---

[190] Section 304(b)(2).
[191] See infra ¶ 14.13.

if it qualifies under §§302(b)(1)–302(b)(4), relating to redemptions that are not essentially equivalent to a dividend, substantially disproportionate, complete terminations of the shareholder's stock ownership, and partial liquidations.[192] The same is true of a redemption qualifying under §303, relating to redemptions to pay death taxes and the like[193] and to sales of stock of one corporation to a related corporation if the transaction satisfies one of the tests of §§302(b)(1)–302(b)(4) or of §303, after applying the rules of §304.[194]

If the redemption qualifies for sale/exchange treatment under one of these provisions, the shareholder's gain or loss is computed as if the stock had been sold to an unrelated third party. Thus, if the shareholder owns shares purchased at different times and for different prices, he may select as he chooses the shares to be surrendered to the corporation for redemption and use shares with a high or low basis and a short or long holding period.[195]

Yet, although the shareholder may be able to control the tax consequences of the transaction by shrewdly selecting the shares to be surrendered, he should not be able to manipulate the gain or loss to be recognized by surrendering more shares than would be called for in an arm's-length transaction. If the redemption is not pro rata, market value will ordinarily govern the number of shares surrendered. If the transaction is not effected at market value, it may be in part a method of paying compensation or making a gift. Thus, if the shareholder receives more than his shares are worth, the excess may represent compensation or a gift paid to him by the remaining shareholders. Conversely, if he receives less than the value of his shares, the difference may represent compensation or a gift paid by him to them.[196]

If the redemption is pro rata, however, the number of shares to be surrendered will usually be a matter of indifference to the shareholders. Thus, if X Corporation's net worth is $100,000, represented by 100 shares of common stock, owned one-half by A and one-half by B, and it distributes $40,000 in partial liquidation, one would expect A and B to surrender 20 shares each for redemption, but A and B could just as well surrender 25 shares each. Can they minimize their capital gain or create capital losses by doing so? In Rev. Rul. 56-513, the Service said of a distribution in partial liquidation:

---

[192] Supra ¶ 9.02.

[193] Supra ¶ 9.11.

[194] Supra ¶ 9.12.

[195] For installment distributions in complete liquidation (as contrasted with nonliquidating distributions), see Rev. Rul. 85-48, 1985-1 CB 126, and earlier rulings there cited.

[196] See Rev. Rul. 58-614, 1958-2 CB 920.

In determining the amount of the gain or loss, regardless of the actual number of shares surrendered for redemption by the stockholders, the total number of shares deemed to have been surrendered is that number which bears the same ratio to the total number of shares outstanding as the [amount] distributed bears to the total fair market value of the net assets of the corporation immediately prior to the distribution.[197]

The ruling does not state how the basis of the shares "deemed to have been surrendered" is to be computed. It would seem reasonable to use an appropriate fraction of the total basis of all shares held by the shareholder in question. Despite this ruling, there have been a number of litigated cases in which stock was redeemed at par value, original cost, book value, or other artificial prices, and the shareholder's gain or loss was apparently computed accordingly rather than by recasting the transaction as provided by Rev. Rul. 56-513.[198]

Although Rev. Rul. 56-513 is applicable by its terms whether the shareholder realized gain or loss on the transaction, a caveat should be interposed with respect to gains. If the shareholder surrenders too few shares so that the amount distributed to him exceeds the value of the shares he gives up, it is not inconceivable that the transaction will be treated as a sale only to the extent of the fair value of the shares, with any excess being subject to §301, taxable as a dividend to the extent of the corporation's earnings and profits. Rev. Rul. 54-408,[199] holding that a certain redemption constituted a partial liquidation "to the extent that the distribution does not exceed the fair market value of the stock being redeemed," suggests by negative inference that any excess would be a §301 distribution. This approach conflicts with Rev. Ruls. 56-513 and 68-348,[200] and the issue cannot be regarded as closed.[201]

Still another problem is the deductibility of a loss if the shareholder receives less than the adjusted basis of the shares redeemed. Section

---

[197] Rev. Rul. 56-513, 1956-2 CB 191, 192; Rev. Rul. 74-544, 1974-2 CB 108 (same); Rev. Rul. 77-245, 1977-2 CB 105 (clarifying Rev. Rul. 56-513).

[198] See Joseph W. Imler, supra note 4 (par value and cost); Sam Rosania, Sr., ¶ 56,116 P-H Memo. TC (1956) (par and cost); CIR v. Snite, 177 F2d 819 (7th Cir. 1949) (redemption at somewhat below market value); Keefe v. Cote, 213 F2d 651 (1st Cir. 1954) (minority shareholder paid substantially more than majority holder); J. Paul McDaniel, 25 TC 276 (1955) (acq.) (varied prices; aggregate proceeds equal to cost); see also Rev. Rul. 68-348, 1968-2 CB 141 (gain or loss on partial liquidations computed separately for different blocks of stock, distribution being allocated in proportion to number of shares in each block); Rev. Rul. 85-48, 1985-1 CB 126.

[199] Rev. Rul. 54-408, 1954-2 CB 165.

[200] Rev. Rul. 56-513, 1956-2 CB 191; Rev. Rul. 68-348, 1968-2 CB 141; see also Rev. Rul. 85-48, 1985-1 CB 126.

[201] See also Rev. Rul. 59-97, 1959-1 CB 684; Samuel S. Schahet, ¶ 59,051 P-H Memo. TC (1959); Bittker, supra note 38, at 51–53.

267(a)(1) disallows losses on the sale or exchange of property between an individual and a corporation of which he owns directly or indirectly more than 50 percent of the stock. [202] It goes on, however, to make an exception for a loss "in case of a distribution in corporate liquidation." A loss incurred in a partial liquidation would thus come within the exception and would not be disallowed by §267. [203] Even so, it is not necessarily deductible. *Higgins v. Smith* is still to be contended with, [204] and it might lead to the disallowance of a loss on a partial liquidation of a one-person corporation, especially if the transaction was tax motivated. Where there are a number of shareholders, however, *Higgins v. Smith* should not imperil the deduction if control is dispersed or if the shareholders are affected unequally by the redemption.

¶ 9.32 THE MYSTERY OF THE DISAPPEARING BASIS

When the redemption of stock is treated as a sale, either because the transaction is a partial liquidation or because it is a nondividend redemption, the taxpayer can offset the basis of his stock against the proceeds of the redemption in computing his gain or loss. But if the redemption is taxed as a dividend, the mystery of the disappearing basis presents itself. For example, if A holds all of the stock of X Corporation with a basis of $100,000, and half of the stock is redeemed for $150,000 in a transaction that constitutes a taxable dividend, does the basis of the redeemed shares disappear? If A had received an ordinary dividend of $150,000 without any surrender of shares, his cost basis of $100,000 for his shares would remain intact. There is no reason why he should be worse off when the dividend of $150,000 is distributed in redemption of some of his stock.

Although no statutory provision addresses this subject, the Regulations have provided for many years that if a redemption is treated as the distribution of a dividend, "proper adjustment of the basis of the remaining stock will be made with respect to the stock redeemed." [205] If the

---

[202] See McCarthy v. Conley, 341 F2d 948 (2d Cir. 1965) (loss on §302(b)(3) redemption, terminating shareholder's stock ownership, disallowed).

[203] Before 1982, as explained supra ¶ 9.08, partial liquidations were governed by §§331 and 346; the 1982 amendments, which included moving the partial liquidation rules to §302, should have no effect on the status of a partial liquidation as a distribution in corporate liquidation under §267(a)(1). But see H.R. 2636, §106(e)(9) of the Technical Corrections Act of 1987 (nonapplication of §267(a)(1) limited to *complete* liquidation losses).

[204] Higgins v. Smith, 308 US 473 (1940) (disallowing deduction for loss on sale by sole shareholder to controlled corporation before enactment of statutory predecessor of §267); the cases on this point, collected in Bittker, supra note 38, at 54, are inconclusive.

[205] Regs. §1.302-2(c); see also Levin v. CIR, 385 F2d 521 (2d Cir. 1967) (citing regulation to rebut taxpayer's claim that loss of basis would result in unconstitu-

redeemed shareholder retains any shares, their basis is increased by the basis of the redeemed shares, an adjustment that will reduce the gain or increase the loss otherwise incurred by the shareholder on a later disposition of the retained shares.[206] If the shareholder retains no shares after the redemption, the regulations sanction a transfer of his basis to the shares of a related taxpayer, at least if they were attributed to the redeemed shareholder and were therefore responsible for his inability to offset the basis of the redeemed shares against the amount received for them.[207] Ordinarily, the transfer of the redeemed shareholder's basis to shares owned by a related person is a reasonable adjustment; but in some circumstances it can add insult to injury—if, for example, the beneficiary of the adjustment is a hated relative. In such a case, the redeemed shareholder is first taxed as if he owned his relative's shares[208] and then is told that the basis of those shares—the source of his trouble—will be augmented for the benefit of that relative. Indeed, the hapless redeemed shareholder is subjected to a third indignity; if he reads the regulations, he will find that the transfer of basis is described as a "proper" adjustment![209]

¶ 9.33   THE BASIS OF DISTRIBUTED PROPERTY

If the shareholder receives property rather than money in redemption of stock, he must assign a basis to it for computing depreciation, gain or loss on a sale, and so forth. If the property is received in a nondividend redemption under §302(a) or §303, the Code does not state explicitly how its basis to the shareholder is to be determined, so that the general rule of §1012—"the basis of property shall be the cost of such property"—is controlling. Cost for this purpose is the fair market value of the redeemed stock, the same amount

---

tional tax). See generally Brodsky & Pincus, The Case of the Reappearing Basis, 34 Taxes 675 (1956); Katcher, The Case of the Forgotten Basis: An Admonition to Victims of Internal Revenue Code Section 115(g), 48 Mich. L. Rev. 465 (1950).

[206] Regs. §1.302-2(c), Examples (1) and (3); for an allocation of the basis of redeemed shares to shares in another corporation held by the redeemed shareholder, where the amount received was treated as a dividend under §304, see Regs. §1.304-2(c), Example (1); see also Regs. §1.304-3(a) (last sentence); Coyle v. US, supra note 175 (noting this possibility before §304 regulations were issued).

For a §304 transaction in which the basis of redeemed shares was permanently lost, not merely transferred, see Rev. Rul. 70-496, supra note 170.

[207] See Regs. §1.302-2(c). Example (2); see also Levin v. CIR, supra note 205 (transfer of basis to shares owned by taxpayer's son).

[208] For the effect of family hostility on attribution, see supra ¶ 9.06, note 69.

[209] Regs. §1.302-2(c).

that is used by the shareholder in computing the gain or loss realized on exchanging the stock for the distribution.[210]

If, however, the redemption is treated as a distribution under §301 rather than as a sale of the stock, the shareholder's basis for the property received is determined under §301(d), which distinguishes between corporate and noncorporate shareholders. For noncorporate shareholders, the basis of the property is its fair market value. For corporate shareholders, the basis, as determined under §301(d)(2), is fair market value or the distributing corporation's adjusted basis (adjusted for gain recognized to the distributing corporation), whichever is lower. If the corporation distributes depreciated property, §301(d)(2) requires a meaningless comparison, since by hypothesis the fair market value of such property is less than its adjusted basis (and, of course, there is no gain to be recognized). The comparison is also meaningless in the case of appreciated property, provided the distribution is subject to §311(b) as amended in 1986, since the distributing corporation must always recognize gain on the distribution; thus the comparison is between two identical amounts (fair market value and adjusted basis plus the recognized gain).[211] If, however, appreciated property was distributed before the 1986 amendment to §311, it would not ordinarily have resulted in the recognition of the gain; and the comparison mandated by §301(d)(2) in such cases is a real one.

¶ 9.34　RECOGNITION OF CORPORATE GAIN OR LOSS ON DISTRIBUTIONS IN REDEMPTION OF STOCK

Under §§311(a) and 311(b) as amended in 1986, corporations recognize gain on the distribution of *appreciated* property in redemption of their stock, but do not recognize loss if they use *depreciated* property for this purpose. As applied to losses, this nonrecognition rule carries forward the so-called *General Utilities* doctrine, which stems from a 1935 decision of the Supreme Court that was codified in 1954.[212] For gains, however, current law rejects the *General Utilities* doctrine, thus completing a process of erosion that began on a small scale in 1954 and grew in force from time to time thereafter. The evolution and extinction—at least for the forseeable future—of the

---

[210] There may be a discrepancy between the value of the stock redeemed and the value of the property received; see Rev. Rul. 56-513, 1956-2 CB 191, 192, on the possibility that the transaction will be recast to bring these values into harmony.

[211] For §311(b) as amended, see supra ¶ 7.21. See the Technical Corrections Act of 1987, H.R. 2636, §106(e)(11) (repealing the above distinction for distributions subject to 1986 law).

[212] General Util. & Operating Co. v. Helvering, 296 US 200 (1935), discussed supra ¶ 7.20.

General Utilities doctrine as to gains and its preservation as to losses are examined in detail earlier in this treatise.[213]

The bifurcated approach of current law, under which gain but not loss is recognized, applies to all redemptions, whether treated as dividends under §301 or as sales of the stock under §302(a).[214] Before the 1986 amendments to §311, however, corporations distributing appreciated property to redeem their stock in certain transactions qualifying under §302(b)(4) or §303, relating respectively to partial liquidations and redemptions to pay death taxes, were not required to recognize their gain.[215] Under a transitional rule, it is possible, although not certain, that these pre-1987 rules continue to apply to certain small business corporations, provided the corporation liquidates completely before 1989.[216]

¶ 9.35   EFFECT OF REDEMPTION ON CORPORATION'S EARNINGS AND PROFITS

Redemptions of stock affect a corporation's earnings and profits in two ways: First, the distribution creates earnings and profits if the corporation uses appreciated property (rather than money or depreciated property) to effect the redemption; second, whether the distribution consists of money or of appreciated or depreciated property, the earnings and profits account must be properly reduced to reflect the distribution. As will be seen, the amount of the reduction depends on whether the redemption is treated as a taxable dividend under §301 or as a sale of the stock under §302(a).[217]

Thus, the corporation's earnings and profits account is tied to the effect of the redemption on the corporation's shareholders, even if the corporation cannot readily determine whether the distribution was properly treated as a dividend or a sale by particular shareholders because it is unable to ascertain either the identity of its shareholders or whether any of them is the constructive owner of shares registered in another name. Moreover, this issue may not be susceptible to determination until many years after the redemption. For example, if a shareholder relies on §302(c)(2) for relief from the constructive ownership rules, a distribution that appears to qualify for sale treatment under §302(a) may turn out to be a §301 dividend if the distribu-

---

[213] Supra ¶¶ 7.20–7.22.

[214] For this distinction, see supra ¶ 9.02.

[215] See supra ¶ 7.22.

[216] See §633(d) of the Tax Reform Act of 1986 (Pub. L. No. 99-514), which is not part of the Code; see also supra ¶ 7.22, note 171, for a proposed but unenacted broader exemption for certain 1987 and 1988 redemptions; reproposed in §106(g)(6) of the Technical Corrections Act of 1987.

[217] For this distinction, see generally supra ¶ 9.02.

tee acquires a disqualifying interest in the corporation within the following 10 years.[218]

1. Increase of earnings and profits on distribution of appreciated property. Under §312(b), as amended in 1986, the distribution of appreciated property creates earnings and profits equal to the excess of its fair market value over its basis.[219] This explicit provision may be superfluous, since §311(b), as amended in 1986, requires the corporation to recognize gain on a distribution of appreciated property "as if such property were sold to the distributee at its fair market value,"[220] and the courts might have ruled that this hypothetical sale creates earnings and profits in the same manner as an actual sale; §312(b), however, leaves no room for doubt on this score (although a double counting will surely *not* be called for).

2. Redemption treated as dividend. If the redemption is treated as a distribution of property under §301, the corporation's earnings and profits are adjusted under §312(a) in the same way as for any other dividend—that is, earnings and profits are reduced by the amount of money, the principal amount of any obligations, and the adjusted basis of any other property distributed or, in the case of appreciated property, its fair market value.[221]

3. Redemption treated as sale/exchange. If the redemption is treated as a sale or exchange under §302(a) (relating to substantially disproportionate redemptions, partial liquidations, and so forth) or §303 (redemptions to pay death taxes, and so forth),[222] §312(n)(7) provides that the reduction in the corporation's earnings and profits must not exceed the redeemed stock's ratable share thereof.[223]

---

[218] For this possibility, see supra ¶ 9.05.

[219] Section 312(b) was presaged by the enactment in 1984 of §311(n)(4), increasing earnings and profits by any appreciation untaxed under former §311(d)(2); but this limited provision was repealed in 1986 when §312(b) was enacted.

[220] For §311(b) as amended in 1986, see supra ¶ 7.21.

[221] See §312(b)(2). For this purpose, the earnings and profits basis of the distributed property is to be used; see supra ¶ 7.23.

[222] For §§302(b) and 303, see supra ¶¶ 9.02 and 9.11 respectively.

[223] The ratable share principle adopted by §312(n)(7) (enacted in 1984) resolved uncertainties that had long existed under prior law, which provided that a distribution did not reduce earnings and profits to the extent that it was "properly changeable to capital account." See generally Estate of Uris v. CIR, 605 F2d 1258 (2d Cir. 1979), and Ronald D. Anderson, 67 TC 522 (1976) (acq.) (extensive discussion); Edelstein & Korbel, The Impact of Redemption and Liquidation Distributions on

To illustrate: Assume that X Corporation is owned one-half by A and one-half by B, unrelated individuals. X has \$50,000 of earnings and profits, and its net worth is \$100,000. X redeems all of A's shares for \$50,000, their fair market value, in a transaction qualifying under §302(b)(3), relating to complete terminations of the shareholder's stock ownership.[224] Since the distribution is treated as a sale by A of his stock, it might appear at first blush that this should not reduce earnings and profits to any extent, since no part of the distribution will be taxed as a dividend to A. That result, however, would saddle B with potential dividend income of \$50,000, even if the earnings were attributable to operations during the period when both A and B owned their stock. On the other hand, the opposite extreme—reducing the earnings and profits by the full amount distributed to A—would mean that neither A nor B would ever report any dividend income to reflect the corporation's earnings and profits.

Section 312(n)(7) adopts a middle course, reducing the earnings and profits by \$25,000, the amount fairly attributable to A's shares.[225] The reduction, however, may not exceed the amount distributed.[226] Thus, if X Corporation had earnings and profits of \$120,000, the reduction would be limited to \$50,000—the amount distributed to A—even though A's ratable share of the earnings and profits would be \$60,000.

Earnings and Profits: Tax Accounting Aberrations Under Section 312(e), 20 Tax L. Rev. 479 (1965); Note, Rev. Rul. 79-376: Effect of Section 312(e) Redemption Distribution on Earnings and Profits, 34 Tax Lawyer 817 (1981).

Under a leading case construing this murky provision, it was formerly possible to sweep a corporation's earnings and profits clean without generating any dividend income for the redeemed shareholder. See Helvering v. Jarvis, 123 F2d 742 (4th Cir. 1941); Rev. Rul. 79-376, 1979-2 CB 133 (acquiescing in *Jarvis* and revoking an earlier contrary ruling, Rev. Rul. 70-531, 1970-2 CB 76). For more extensive discussion of this problem, see ¶ 9.65 of the Fourth Edition of this treatise.

[224] For §302(b)(3), see supra ¶ 9.05.

[225] For problems in allocating earnings and profits when applying §312(n)(7) to corporations with several classes of stock outstanding, see Staff of Joint Comm. on Taxation, 98th Cong., 2d Sess., General Explanation of the Revenue Provisions of the Tax Reform Act of 1984, at 181 (Joint Comm. Print 1984); see also Rev. Rul. 82-72, 1982-1 CB 57 (allocation between preferred and common stock under old §312(e), which was repealed in 1984).

[226] This qualification appears in the legislative history of §312(n)(7) (supra note 225). It could conflict with the relevant statutory provisions, §§312(a)(3) and 312(n)(7), if the redemption is effected with depreciated property whose value is less than the shareholder's rateable share of the earnings and profits; for example, if the rateable share is \$25,000, the adjusted basis of the property is \$20,000, and its value is \$18,000, the statutory provisions appear to reduce earnings and profits by \$20,000 (the lower of ratable share and adjusted basis), but the statement in the committee report restricts the reduction to \$18,000.

CHAPTER 10

Preferred Stock Bailouts

¶ 10.01 INTRODUCTORY

One of the most urgent problems before Congress when the 1954 Code was being drafted was the preferred stock bailout, an ingenious but simple plan that allowed shareholders to withdraw corporate earnings and profits as long-term capital gains. A corporation with substantial earnings and profits and liquid assets would distribute a dividend of preferred stock to its shareholders, who would receive the stock tax-free[1] and promptly sell it to an insurance company or other institutional investor. Shareholders would compute their gain on the sale by subtracting the adjusted basis of the dividend shares (an allocated portion of each shareholder's basis for the original shares) from the proceeds of sale; and this difference would be reported as long-term capital gain. The corporation would subsequently redeem the preferred stock from the purchaser at a modest premium, either under a sinking fund schedule provided in the preferred stock contract or when deemed advisable by the corporation. The net result to both the corporation and its shareholders would be the equivalent of a cash dividend, except for the obligations imposed by the preferred stock contract during the time the shares

---

[1] For the circumstances in which stock dividends were tax-free under pre-1954 law, see supra ¶ 7.41; for current law, see the discussion of §305 supra ¶¶ 7.42–7.43.

remained outstanding. But the tax consequences, it was hoped, would be vitally different.[2]

For several years prior to 1954, the Treasury Department was able to dampen the enthusiasm of most tax advisers for this bailout device by refusing to rule that a dividend of preferred stock was receivable tax-free if an early sale of the dividend shares was intended.[3] Not all advisers were so timid, however, and boldness was finally rewarded. In *Chamberlin v. CIR*,[4] the Court of Appeals for the Sixth Circuit held that a dividend of preferred stock distributed by a corporation having only common stock outstanding was not rendered taxable by a prearranged plan for its sale, despite a provision in the plan for mandatory retirement of the preferred shares over a period of seven years. Unless rejected by other courts or by legislation, the *Chamberlin* case might have made taxable distributions virtually obsolete, at least for closely held corporations, since preferred stock distributions with periodic redemptions could have become a substitute for annual cash dividends.

¶ 10.02 BAILOUTS UNDER CURRENT LAW

The 1954 Code met the challenge of the preferred stock bailout by creating a new category of stock—"section 306 stock"—the sale, redemption, or other disposition of which generally gives rise to ordinary income rather than capital gain. Section 306 consists of (1) a definition of "section 306 stock"; (2) a set of rules providing that the disposition of "section 306 stock" will produce ordinary income rather than capital gain; and (3) a series of exceptions to these punitive rules.[5] Interpretation and application of §306 can become quite complex in a given case, but one should keep in mind the specific evil at which the provision was aimed: the conversion of potential dividend income into capital gain (with an offset of basis) without dilution

---

[2] Unlike preferred stock, a corporation's debt securities do not have a high bailout potential, since the distribution itself is ordinarily taxable as a dividend. See supra ¶ 7.40 (ordinary distributions of corporation's own obligations) and infra ¶ 14.17 (distributions of debt in recapitalizations).

[3] See De Wind, Preferred Stock "Bail-Outs" and the Income Tax, 62 Harv. L. Rev. 1126 (1949).

[4] 207 F2d 462 (6th Cir. 1953), cert. denied, 347 US 918 (1954); see also Estate of Rosenberg, 36 TC 716 (1961) (bailout via recapitalization; Tax Court, rejecting *Chamberlin*, held for taxpayer under pre-1954 law); §306(h) (§306 not applicable to pre-1954 transactions even if disposition occurs after enactment of §306).

[5] For exhaustive reviews, see Lischer, Section 306 Stock, Tax Mgmt. (BNA) No. 85-3d (1981); Lowe, Bailouts: Their Role in Corporate Planning, 30 Tax L. Rev. 357 (1975); Rowland; Section 306: Its History and Function as a Bailout Preventer (Including Bailouts That May Never Occur), 39 Tax Lawyer 121 (1985).

of the shareholders' underlying equity investment in and control of the corporation.

Of course, during the formative years of §306, the top tax rate on ordinary income realized by individuals was far higher than the rate applicable to long-term capital gain (70–91 percent, as opposed to 25 percent). A substantial, although less dramatic, rate differential continued until the enactment of the Tax Reform Act of 1986, under which this differential will be eliminated as of 1988. Despite so marked a change in the tax environment, however, §306 was preserved intact by the 1986 Act, even though the provision's actual effect on taxpayers will be significantly different once the rate differential is eliminated: The principal adverse result of falling afoul of §306 will then be that the taxpayer will not be allowed to offset the basis of the "section 306 stock" against the amount realized on a sale or redemption, a denial that under prior law, was exacerbated by the statutory conversion of favorably taxed long-term capital gain into ordinary income. Although the conversion continues under the 1986 Act, it will no longer entail the loss of a rate differential; nevertheless, it will be disadvantageous to taxpayers with capital loss carry-overs, which can be applied against the ordinary income generated by a sale or redemption of "section 306 stock" only to the extent of the $3,000 limit imposed by §1211(b)(2)(B).

¶ 10.03 THE DEFINITION OF "SECTION 306 STOCK"

The definition of "section 306 stock" is concerned primarily with what might be termed the classic arrangement of *Chamberlin*, i.e., with preferred stock held by persons who received it as a tax-free dividend from a corporation with earnings and profits. Because variations on the *Chamberlin* arrangement are possible, however, the statutory definition is broad enough to reach a variety of transactions that might be used, either deliberately or incidentally, as a substitute for a preferred stock dividend. The result is the elaborate definition of §306(c), which embraces the four categories of stock discussed below.

1. Stock received as tax-free dividend. Stock (other than common stock issued with respect to common stock) held by the distributee is "section 306 stock" by virtue of §306(c)(1)(A), if any part of the distribution was not includable in gross income by reason of §305(a).[6] The preferred stock dividend in *Chamberlin* is typical of what is being defined here.

---

[6] The language of §306(c)(1)(A) suggests that no matter how small a part of the distribution is tax-free under §305(a), the whole distribution is "section 306 stock." Until amended in 1973, Regs. §1.306-3(c) provided that an allocable portion of each

The exception for common stock issued as a dividend on common stock recognizes that such stock is not ordinarily a promising instrument for effecting a bailout, since the shareholders to whom it is issued cannot dispose of it without a loss in both their voting control and their interest in the unrestricted growth of the corporation, and because a later pro rata redemption of the common stock would ordinarily constitute a dividend, taxable as ordinary income, to the shareholders. Although common stock is not defined by either §306 itself or by the regulations, the Service has ruled that "if a stock . . . is nonvoting and is limited in *either* the right to dividends or the right to assets upon liquidation, then it is considered to be other than common stock [the disposition of which] may result in the bailout abuse that Congress intended to preclude."[7]

In other rulings, however, the Service has held that voting rights do not necessarily immunize the stock against the §306 taint. Thus, a 1979 ruling denied common stock classification to a corporation's so-called Class A common stock because such stock's right to current dividends was limited to 6 percent of its par value in any taxable year. This was held even though it was the only class of stock entitled to vote and it could participate in liquidating distributions with the Class B common stock in proportion to their par values.[8] This ruling pushed the §306 concept to its limit, if not beyond: If the Class B shareholders sold their Class A stock, they would give up their previously unlimited interest in the corporation's future growth, since the purchasers of the Class A stock could use their voting control to hold down the level of current dividends and could ultimately vote to distribute the accumulated profits in liquidation.[9] Other rulings, however, have reserved

---

share was "section 306 stock" to the extent the distribution was tax-free under §305(a), and that an allocable portion of each share would be untainted to the extent the distribution was taxable. This language was deleted in 1973.

For discussion of §305(a), see generally ¶ 7.43.

[7] Rev. Rul. 82-191, 1982-2 CB 78, summarizing Rev. Rul. 76-387, 1976-2 CB 96 (nonvoting stock is common stock where not limited and preferred as to dividend or liquidation rights and not by its terms redeemable; stock not suitable for bailout because sale would cause loss of equity position).

Even if stock is not ostensibly limited in its right to receive dividends and liquidating distributions, it can be classified as "section 306 stock" if it is subject to redemption at a fixed price at the corporation's option, since the redemption price imposes a cap on its growth potential. See Rev. Rul. 57-132, 1957-1 CB 115 (nonvoting common stock redeemable at 110 percent of book value held "section 306 stock"); but see Rev. Rul. 76-386, 1976-2 CB 95 (stock was common stock, even though corporation had right of first refusal at net book value if shareholder desired to dispose of stock; stock could not be used to effect bailout).

[8] Rev. Rul. 79-163, 1979-1 CB 131 (Situation 2).

[9] Rev. Rul. 79-163, 1979-1 CB 131 (Situation 2), does not state whether the nonvoting Class B stock was entitled under state law to vote on an extraordinary event,

the §306 taint for shares that seem more suited, as a practical matter, to the effectuation of a bailout.[10]

Section 306(c)(1)(A) comes into play if the dividend shares are excluded from the recipient's gross income under §305(a), and that exclusion is now much narrower than it was when §306 was enacted.[11] If stock with a bailout potential is taxed when distributed, there is, of course, no need for the after-the-fact taint imposed by §306 on tax-free dividends. However, §305(a)—even in its current, restrictive form—ordinarily permits conventional preferred stock to be distributed as a tax-free dividend to holders of the corporation's common stock. Consequently, §306 continues to be required as a barrier against the type of bailout achieved in *Chamberlin*.

    2. Stock received in a corporate reorganization or division. Stock (other than common stock) received in certain wholly or partly tax-free corporate reorganizations and separations is "section 306 stock" if the effect of the transaction is substantially the same as the receipt of a stock dividend, or if the stock is received in exchange for "section 306 stock." This branch of the "section 306 stock" definition is designed to cope with stock suitable for use in a bailout if it is distributed in a partly or wholly tax-free transaction (such as a recapitalization) that may serve the same function as a tax-free stock dividend. In applying the "effect of a stock dividend" test, the regulations promulgate a so-called cash substitution

---

such as a liquidation. If it could block a liquidation, the corporate accumulations could be kept in limbo indefinitely, unless the two classes of shareholders reached a settlement.

[10] See Rev. Rul. 75-236, 1975-1 CB 106 (Class A stock distributed pro rata in recapitalization not common stock because limited and preferred as to dividends, even though it was only class of voting stock outstanding); Rev. Rul. 81-91, 1981-1 CB 123 (so-called preferred stock was entitled to annual cumulative dividend equal to 6 percent of par value and to repayment of par value on liquidation, but thereafter current dividends and liquidating proceeds were shared with common stock and both classes had equal voting rights; held, preferred stock was not "section 306 stock"); Rev. Rul. 75-222, 1975-1 CB 105 (Class B stock received in recapitalization was common stock, even though it had a greater right to receive cash dividends than did other class of common stock).

For the classification of stock in a related context, see Regs. §1.305-5(a) (preferred stock has limited rights and privileges, generally associated with dividend and liquidation priorities, and "does not participate in corporate growth to any significant extent"). See also Regs. §1.1244(c)-1(b); Carnahan v. US, 188 F. Supp. 461 (D. Mont. 1960) (common stock defined for purposes of §1036). See generally Walter, "Preferred Stock" and "Common Stock": The Meaning of the Terms and the Importance of the Distinction for Tax Purposes, 5 J. Corp. Tax'n 211 (1978); Lowe, supra note 5.

[11] See supra ¶ 7.43.

standard, which imposes the §306 taint if cash received in lieu of the stock would have been taxed as a dividend.[12] The effect of §306 on stock distributed in corporate reorganizations and divisions is not easily examined, except in conjunction with the underlying transactions themselves, which are discussed in subsequent chapters.[13]

3. Stock received in a §351 exchange. A third situation that can evoke a §306 taint is the acquisition of stock (other than common stock) in a §351 exchange, such as (1) the transfer by *A*, the sole shareholder of *X* Corporation, of his *X* common stock to newly created *Y* Corporation, in exchange for *Y* common and preferred stock, or (2) *A*'s transfer of *X* common stock to previously created *Z* Corporation (whose common stock was already owned by *A*) in exchange for *Z* preferred stock. If *X* had any earnings and profits, a cash distribution by it to *A* would have been a taxable dividend pro tanto; under §304, the same result would follow if either *Y* or *Z* (rather than *X*) distributed cash to *A*.[14] *A*'s receipt of *Y* or *Z* preferred stock, however, would be a tax-free transaction by virtue of §351,[15] and, like the preferred stock dividend in *Chamberlin*, although less directly, it could serve as a way of bailing out cash from *Y* to *Z* (either of which can obtain the cash, if necessary, by causing *X*, its new subsidiary, to declare a dividend).

Section 306(c)(3), enacted in 1982, responds to this holding company gambit by imposing the §306 taint on stock (other than common stock) acquired in a §351 exchange, if a distribution of money, in lieu of the stock, would have been treated as a dividend to any extent. This determination is to be made by applying rules similar to those employed by §304(c)(2) in determining whether certain distributions of property constitute taxable dividends.[16] The operation of the §304(c)(2) rules is more fully examined in the discussion of §304 in the previous chapter;[17] however, their impact on §306 is suggested by the following example.

---

[12] Regs. §1.306-3(d).

[13] See infra ¶¶ 13.13 (corporate divisions) and 14.35 (reorganizations). See also Lischer, supra note 5, at A-8–A-19.

[14] For discussion of §304, see supra ¶ 9.12.

[15] For discussion of §351, see supra ¶ 3.01.

For a ruling holding that the *Y* or *Z* preferred stock is "section 306 stock" if the issuer has earnings and profits at the end of the year in which the stock is distributed, see Rev. Rul. 79-274, 1979-2 CB 131. See also Corry, Preferred Stock Issued in Tax-Free Exchanges: Does Section 306 Apply? 35 Tax L. Rev. 113, 141 (1979).

[16] In applying §306(c)(3), the attribution rules of §318(a) apply as modified by §304(c)(3)(B), which reduces the stock ownership prerequisite for attribution from 50 percent to 5 percent. For discussion of §318(a), see supra ¶ 9.03.

[17] See supra ¶ 9.12.

To illustrate: If *A* and *B* own *X* Corporation equally and transfer their *X* stock to new *Y* Corporation, taking back *Y* common and preferred stock ratably, the preferred stock will be tainted as "section 306 stock" if *X* has *any* current or accumulated earnings and profits (even if they arise later in the same taxable year) because a cash distribution by *Y* would have resulted in dividend treatment to *A* and *B* under §§304(a)(1) and 304(b)(2)(A). If, however, *A* took back the *Y* common stock, and *B* took the *Y* preferred stock, the preferred stock would not be tainted in *B*'s hands, since a cash distribution to *B* would not have been a dividend but would instead have been treated by §302(a) as payment for *B*'s stock, assuming that *A*'s stock is not attributed to *B* by §318.

4. Stock with a transferred or substituted basis. Section 306(c)(1)(C) pursues "section 306 stock" into the hands of a transferee if the transferee's basis is determined by reference to the basis of the transferor. Thus, "section 306 stock" continues to be tainted in the hands of a donee, a corporation receiving the stock in a tax-free §351 exchange,[18] or a partnership receiving the stock as a contribution from a partner. The taint terminates when the holder dies, however, since the stock passes to the shareholder's heirs with a new basis equal to its fair market value at the testator's death. In this instance, the evil that men do does not live after them, but is interred with their bones. A sale of "section 306 stock" also purges it insofar as the purchaser is concerned, although the sale ordinarily has adverse consequences to the seller.[19]

In addition to perpetuating the taint if "section 306 stock" passes to a transferee whose basis is determined by reference to the transferor's basis, §306(c)(1)(C) spreads the contagion to *other* stock whose basis is so determined. Thus, a wholly or partly tax-free exchange under §1036 (stock for stock of the same corporation) is subject to §306(c)(1)(C). If, however, §306(c)(1)(B)—relating to stock received in a corporate reorganization or division—is applicable to the same transaction, it takes precedence over §306(c)(1)(C). The principal significance of this grant of exclusive jurisdiction to §306(c)(1)(B) is that it exempts common stock from being classified as "section 306 stock."

---

[18] See Rev. Rul. 77-108, 1977-1 CB 86 (on tax-free §351 exchange of "section 306 stock" for preferred stock of transferee corporation, stock received by corporation retains §306 status, while stock issued by it to transferors acquires §306 status, since basis of both classes is determined by reference to transferors' basis for their "section 306 stock"; immaterial that transferee corporation has no earnings and profits).

[19] See infra ¶ 10.04, text following note 25.

The four-part definition of "section 306 stock" summarized in the preceding paragraphs is qualified and augmented by the four following rules:

1. No earnings, no taint. By virtue of §306(c)(2), stock distributed by a corporation having no current or accumulated earnings and profits for the year of distribution is not "section 306 stock."[20] Since a distribution of money in these circumstances would not have been taxed to the shareholders as dividend income, the stock is not regarded as an appropriate candidate for the punitive rules of §306. Even though the stock is not section 306 stock, however, its later redemption might be taxed as a dividend under §§301 and 302, unless the redemption terminates the shareholder's interest, is substantially disproportionate, or is not essentially equivalent to a dividend.[21]

2. Stock rights. To prevent evasion of §306 through the use of stock rights, §306(d) provides that stock rights shall be treated as stock, with the result that the rights will constitute section 306 stock when distributed if an alternative cash distribution would have been taxed as a dividend. Moreover, the exercise of such tainted rights will transfer their §306 character to the stock acquired thereby to the extent of the fair market value of the rights when distributed. When the holder disposes of "section 306 stock" acquired by exercising tainted rights, any cash amount paid when the rights were exercised is taken into account in determining the tax treatment of the proceeds received on the disposition.[22]

3. Changes in terms. Section 306(g) is designed to prevent the effectuation of a bailout by means of substantial midstream changes in the terms of stock that was innocent when issued. The statutory remedy is to examine the

---

[20] Section 306(c)(2) speaks of a stock distribution that "would [not] have been a dividend *at the time of the distribution* if money had been distributed in lieu of stock." (Emphasis added.) The cash-substitution standard of Regs. §1.306-3(a) impliedly denies the exemption if there are earnings and profits at the end of the distribution year, even if there were none at the time of the distribution itself, since distributions of money are dividends in this situation under the nimble dividend rule of §316(a)(2), discussed supra ¶ 7.02; see also supra note 15. Note also that the exemption is denied by Regs. §1.306-3(a) if the value of the stock is covered by earnings and profits in whole or *in part*. See also supra note 6.

Section 306(c)(2) exempts only stock that is *distributed* by the corporation; Rev. Rul. 77-108, 1977-1 CB 86, holds that the exemption does not apply to stock received in an *exchange* with the issuing corporation.

[21] For §§301–302, see generally supra ¶ 9.02. For the effect of a prearranged plan for the issuance, sale, and prompt redemption of such stock, see infra ¶ 10.07.

[22] See Regs. §1.306-3(b).

stock both when it is distributed and when the changes are made, and apply the §306 taint by reference to whichever date would produce, or increase, the taint.

4. Convertibility. Section 306(e) provides that if "section 306 stock" becomes common stock, whether pursuant to a conversion privilege or otherwise, the §306 taint does not attach to the common stock received in the exchange. On the other hand, common stock that is convertible into preferred stock or other property will not be treated as common stock; thus, such stock, if distributed pro rata, may be classified as "section 306 stock."[23]

¶ 10.04   DISPOSITIONS OF "SECTION 306 STOCK"

The sting of §306 is found in §306(a), which prescribes special rules to govern the redemption, sale, or other disposition of "section 306 stock": Roughly speaking, the amount received for the stock (not merely the excess over its basis) is taxable as ordinary income. In applying this punitive principle, however, §306(a) distinguishes between redemptions and other dispositions, as explained below.

1. Redemptions. If the stock is redeemed, §306(a)(2) provides that the amount received by the shareholder is to be treated as a §301 distribution. Thus, it is taxable as a dividend to the extent of the corporation's earnings and profits *at the time of redemption*; the balance, if any, is a return of capital under §§301(c)(2) and 301(c)(3).[24]

It is not entirely clear whether the nondividend portion of the redemption proceeds, if any, should be applied against the adjusted basis of the "section 306 stock" alone or against the basis of the original stock as well. Ordinarily, a §301 distribution is not taxed as capital gain under §§301(c)(2) and 301(c)(3)(A) until the shareholder has recovered the basis of the stock with respect to which the distribution was received; and it may well be that holders of "section 306 stock" are similarly entitled to recover the basis of their entire stock interest under §301(c)(2) before reporting capital gain under §301(c)(3). Since the redemption transaction is treated under §306(a)(2) as a §301 distribution, it seems appropriate to reassign the "sec-

---

[23] Depending upon the circumstances, however, the distribution of convertible stock may be a taxable dividend under §305(b) (see supra ¶ 7.43); if so, it will not become "section 306 stock," and §306(e) will not apply to a later conversion.

[24] For discussion of §301(c), see supra ¶ 7.02.

tion 306 stock" basis to the shareholder's original stock and allow a §301(c)(2) basis recovery thereof.[25]

2. Sales. If "section 306 stock" is sold or otherwise disposed of, §306(a)(1) splits the amount realized into two components: The part that would have been a dividend *at the time of the distribution* if cash had been distributed in lieu of the "section 306 stock" is treated as ordinary gain from the sale of a noncapital asset, and the balance is applied against the basis of the "section 306 stock," any excess being treated as capital gain if the stock qualifies as a capital asset. A loss is not recognized even if basis is not fully recovered.

The computation of ordinary gain for this purpose has several features that require special comment. Although §306(a)(1)(A)(ii) refers to hypothetical dividends *at the time of distribution* of the "section 306 stock," this determination should probably take into account the fact that "real" dividend income can result under §316(a)(2) if current earnings and profits arise after the date of a distribution but during the same taxable year.[26] This principle probably applies to the computation under §306(a)(1)(A)(ii), since the language of this provision (which measures the amount of ordinary gain by reference to the amount of a "would-have-been" cash dividend) shows no clear congressional intent to limit gain to the corporation's date-of-distribution earnings. The term "ratable share" in §306(a)(1)(A)(ii), however, should be contrasted with the more general terms of §316(a), in which the amount of dividend income is limited only by the earnings and profits of the distributing corporation.[27]

If §306(a)(1), which governs sales of "section 306 stock," had been in effect when the *Chamberlin* transaction occurred, the shareholders, upon selling the preferred stock, would have realized ordinary income equal to their ratable share of the corporation's earnings and profits measured as of the year the stock was distributed. The bailout would then have failed utterly. In fact, an ordinary dividend in cash may be preferable to a sale of "section 306 stock," since a dividend reduces the corporation's earnings and profits and thus reduces the likelihood that future distributions will be taxed as ordinary income to its shareholders. By contrast, a sale of "section 306 stock" is treated simply as a sale of a noncapital asset (to the extent of its ratable share of earnings and profits at the time of distribution), and hence it does not reduce the corporation's earnings and profits.

---

[25] See supra ¶¶ 7.02, 9.02, and 9.32.

[26] See supra note 20.

[27] For the possibility of dividend income under §316 that is disproportionate to a stockholder's "ratable share" of earnings, see ¶ 7.23. However, this result is less likely since the 1984 amendments to §311. See supra ¶ 7.21.

To illustrate: *A* owned 100 shares of *X* Corporation's common stock—which constituted all of the stock outstanding—with a basis of $6,000. During a year when its earnings and profits were $3,500, *X* issued preferred stock worth $5,000 as a dividend to *A*. Immediately after the distribution, *A*'s common stock was worth $10,000. The preferred stock dividend constituted "section 306 stock," since the issuing corporation had earnings and profits at the time of the distribution. Under §307(a), *A*'s basis for the newly acquired preferred stock was $2,000, and his basis for the common stock was $4,000.

Two years later, when *X*'s earnings and profits were $5,000, a hypothetical sale by *A* of preferred stock to an outsider for $5,000 would have been fragmented into two components, with the following results: (1) ordinary gain of $3,500 (that portion of the preferred stock dividend that would have been a taxable dividend two years earlier if cash had been distributed instead of stock) and (2) a $500 increase in the basis of *A*'s common stock to reflect the fact that the remaining sales proceeds of $1,500 were $500 less than the basis of the preferred stock. Since no loss can be deducted by virtue of §306(a)(1)(C), the stepup in the basis of the common stock would have compensated *A* for the denial of the loss by correspondingly reducing the gain (or increasing the loss) realized if and when *A* disposed of the common stock.[28] Under this scenario, there would have been no reduction in *X*'s earnings and profits.

If, however, *A*'s preferred stock had been redeemed by *X* for $5,000, *A* would have a dividend of $5,000, since *X*'s redemption year earnings and profits of $5,000 would have fully covered the amount distributed. In addition, the basis for *A*'s common stock would have been increased by $2,000 (the basis of the redeemed preferred shares). If, on the other hand, *X*'s earnings and profits that year had been only $3,500, *A*'s dividend would have been limited to $3,500, while the balance of $1,500 received by *A* would have been a nontaxable return of capital under §301(c)(2), and the basis of *A*'s common stock would have increased by the unrecovered portion ($500) of the basis for the preferred stock.

3. Other dispositions. Section 306(a)(1), treating as gain the proceeds from the sale of a noncapital asset, comes into play if a shareholder "sells or otherwise disposes of 'section 306 stock'" (other than by redemption). The regulations do not define the phrase "otherwise disposes of," except to say that it may include, "among other things," a pledge of the stock, "particularly where the pledgee can look only to the stock itself as its

---

[28] See Regs. §1.306-1(b)(2), Examples (2) and (3); see also supra ¶ 9.32 for discussion of similar adjustments when a redemption of stock generates ordinary income without any offset for the basis of the redeemed shares.

security."[29] Ordinarily, such a pledge does not constitute a disposition of property, so gain is not recognized, even though the amount borrowed exceeds the basis of the pledged property. However, a contrary rule for "section 306 stock" is hardly beyond the power of Congress. The regulations do not state whether the amount realized on such a pledge of the stock is its fair market value or the amount borrowed. If the latter is controlling, presumably any additional amount realized on selling the stock would also be taxed under §306(a)(1).

4. Charitable contributions and other gifts. In 1957, the Service ruled that the donation of "section 306 stock" to a tax-exempt charitable foundation did not constitute a disposition by the donor under §306(a)(1) at either the time of the gift or upon a later sale by the charity, even though the donor was entitled under 1957 law to deduct the fair market value of the stock as a charitable contribution.[30] The ruling noted that the stock retained its taint in the hands of the donee, and it concluded from this that the statutory plan was to tax the donee rather than the donor. Since the donee was tax-exempt, however, it would not be taxed on a sale or redemption of the stock,[31] moreover, a redemption would reduce the corporation's earnings and profits.

Such results were difficult to justify, and §170(e)(1)(A), enacted in 1969, ended this practice by requiring the donor to reduce the amount of the charitable contribution deduction by the ordinary income component of the "section 306 stock."[32] This provision, however, does not alter the basic rule that gifts are not income-triggering dispositions, and hence it does not prevent gifts of "section 306 stock" to younger members of the shareholder's family, whose taxes on disposition of the tainted stock may be lower than the taxes the donor would have incurred on similar dispositions.[33]

---

[29] See Regs. §1.306-(b)(1); see also S. Rep. No. 1622, 83d Cong., 2d Sess. 242 (1954). For comparable problems in the treatment of liabilities in excess of basis, see discussion of §§357(c) and 311(c) supra ¶¶ 3.06, 7.22; Bittker, Federal Taxation of Income, Estates and Gifts (Warren, Gorham & Lamont, Inc., 1981), ¶¶ 40.6.3 and 43.5.2. See also §7701(g).

[30] Rev. Rul. 57-328, 1957-2 CB 229.

[31] For retention of the taint in the hands of the donee, see §306(c)(1)(C). For successful examples of the contribution-redemption device, see Behrend v. US, 31 AFTR2d 406 (4th Cir. 1972) (not officially cited), and cases cited therein.

[32] For an application of §170(e)(1)(A) to "section 306 stock," see Rev. Rul. 76-396, 1976-2 CB 55; see also Walter Bialo, 88 TC No. 63 (1987).

[33] For discussion of gifts in anticipation of a prompt redemption, see infra note 49.

5. Tax-free exchanges. If "section 306 stock" is exchanged for other stock in a nontaxable transaction (such as a §351 transfer, reorganization, or exercise of conversion rights), the exchange is not a disposition of the stock within the meaning of §306(a), by virtue of §306(b)(3).[34] Relief is only temporary, however, if under §306(c)(1)(B) or 306(c)(1)(C) the stock received becomes "section 306 stock."[35]

¶ 10.05   RELIEF PROVISIONS

In four situations, §306(b) grants an exemption from the punitive rules of §306(a), which ordinarily treats the amount realized on a disposition of "section 306 stock" as a §301 distribution if the stock is redeemed, or as gain from the sale of a noncapital asset if the stock is sold or otherwise disposed of. These exemptions, covering dispositions of "section 306 stock" that are not suited to the bailout of corporate earnings and profits, are as follows:

1. Partial or complete termination of shareholder's interest in corporation. If "section 306 stock" is sold or otherwise disposed of in a transaction (other than a redemption) that terminates the owner's entire stock interest in the corporation, including stock attributed to the owner by the constructive ownership rules of §318(a), and if the transferee is not a person whose ownership of stock would be attributed back to the transferor under §318(a),[36] the disposition is immunized by §306(b)(1)(A) from the punitive rules of §306(a). The justification for this exemption is that there is no bailout of the corporate earnings if the shareholder disposes of his "section 306 stock" either simultaneously with or after a sale of his other stock, since the same result could have been achieved by selling the original shares before the "section 306 stock" was distributed to him. For the same reason, §306(b)(1)(B) grants an exemption if "section 306 stock" is redeemed in a transaction qualifying under §302(b)(3), relating to terminations of the redeemed shareholder's entire stock interest in the corporation.[37]

---

[34] See infra ¶ 10.05.

[35] See supra ¶ 10.03.

[36] This qualification, which is imposed by §306(b)(1)(A)(ii), seems to be redundant, since a disposition cannot terminate the shareholder's entire stock interest within the meaning of §306(b)(1)(A)(iii) if the shares are transferred to a person whose ownership would be attributed to the transferor. For discussion of §318(a), see supra ¶ 9.03.

[37] For discussion of §302(b)(3), see supra ¶ 9.05. Ordinarily, the redemption must encompass not only the shareholder's own stock, but also any shares that are attributed to the shareholder by §318(a); however, the family attribution rules can be

Redemptions qualifying as partial liquidations under §302(b)(4) are also exempted; they do not terminate the shareholder's entire stock interest, but they are nonetheless included in the amnesty because "a bona fide contraction of the corporate business is not considered a means of distributing corporate earnings to shareholders at capital gains rates."[38] This view of the corporate contraction doctrine rests on the debatable assumption that it will be strictly applied.

2. Complete liquidations. The rules of §306(a) are not applicable if "section 306 stock" is redeemed in a complete liquidation.[39] This exemption is parallel to the exemption of sales and redemptions of the shareholder's entire stock interest in the corporation: The same result (ordinarily, capital gain or loss on the liquidation) could have been achieved without the intervention of "section 306 stock." The corporation's earnings and profits account, of course, is wiped out by the liquidation, but this would be the case even if the corporation had no outstanding "section 306 stock."

3. Tax-free exchanges. A third exemption, §306(b)(3), negates an application of the rules of §306(a) to the extent that gain or loss is not recognized on the disposition of the "section 306 stock." This exception embraces, for example, dispositions of "section 306 stock" in transactions under §§351 and 1036. However, the relief is only temporary, since the stock received in exchange will become "section 306 stock" by virtue of §306(c)(1)(C). If the transferor of "section 306 stock" receives other property (i.e., "boot") in a §351 or §1036 transaction so that the exchange is only partly tax-free, the fair market value of the boot is subject to §306(a).[40]

---

waived in certain circumstances, as explained supra at ¶ 9.05. This waiver is not available if the "section 306 stock" is sold rather than redeemed.

[38] S. Rep. No. 1622, 83d Cong., 2d Sess. 243 (1954). For partial liquidations under §302(b)(4), see supra ¶ 9.08.

[39] Section 306(b)(3). For discussion of complete liquidations, see infra ¶ 11.02. The exemption of §306(b)(3) seems intended to protect persons who own "section 306 stock" of the liquidating corporation, but it may also protect the liquidating corporation *itself* if it owns "section 306 stock" in another corporation. If the "section 306 stock" was transferred to the liquidating corporation as part of a plan for a later purge under §306(b)(3), this protection may be denied on assignment-of-income or substance-over-form grounds. See Lyon & Eustice, Assignment of Income: Fruit and Tree as Irrigated by the P.G. Lake Case, 17 Tax L. Rev. 293, 423 (1962). But corporate-level liquidation sales become taxable under §336 as a result of 1986 amendments. See infra ¶ 11.61.

[40] See Regs. §1.306-3(e); see also §356(e) (receipt of boot in corporate reorganizations in exchange for "section 306 stock"). But see §306(e)(1) and Regs. §1.306-3(f)

4. Transactions not in avoidance of federal income tax. This exemption applies to transactions that in the opinion of the Treasury are not in pursuance of a plan that has federal income tax avoidance as one of its principal purposes. The regulations refer to "isolated dispositions of 'section 306 stock' by minority shareholders" as one example.[41] The fact that the regulations refer to isolated dispositions is worth noting. If a publicly held corporation were to adopt a plan of declaring and redeeming preferred stock dividends annually, this exemption from §306(a) might not be available even to minority shareholders.

Another area of potential application for this exception is a disposition by shareholders of a fraction of their "section 306 stock," along with an equal or larger fraction of their original shares, a transaction that ordinarily would not operate to avoid federal income tax.[42]

¶ 10.06 USES FOR "SECTION 306 STOCK"

Despite the taint imposed by §306, there are situations in which the distribution of a preferred stock dividend by a corporation with earnings and profits can help shareholders to achieve business or estate planning objectives. For example, on a bootstrap sale of a corporation, the sellers may transfer both their common stock and their "section 306 stock" to the buyers

---

(common stock is not "section 306 stock" if exchanged tax-free for "section 306 stock" of the same corporation). See also Rev. Rul. 77-108, 1977-1 CB 86.

[41] See Regs. §1.306-2(b)(3). For application, see Rev. Rul. 56-116, 1956-1 CB 164; Rev. Rul. 57-103, 1957-1 CB 113; Rev. Rul. 57-212, 1957-1 CB 114; Rev. Rul. 56-223, 1956-1 CB 162; Rev. Rul. 77-455, 1977-2 CB 93.

See Rev. Proc. 77-37, §5, 1977-2 CB 568, for ruling guidelines under §306(b)(4) when convertible preferred stock is received in a reorganization. See also infra ¶ 14.35.

[42] But see Fireoved v. US, 462 F2d 1281 (3d Cir. 1972) (redemption of "section 306 stock" following sale of part of shareholder's common stock not entitled to immunity under §306(b)(4)(B) because of retained control over corporate action); Rev. Rul. 75-247, 1975-1 CB 104 (sale of part of shareholder's common stock and pro rata amount of preferred "section 306 stock" not automatically entitled to exception of §306(b)(4)(B); shareholder must also negate tax avoidance plan); see also Rev. Rul. 77-455, 1977-2 CB 93 (shareholder retirement by combined sale-redemption; no tax avoidance); Rev. Rul. 80-33, 1980-1 CB 69, involving a charitable contribution of "section 306 stock," in which the Service ruled (citing *Fireoved*) that, despite the existence of a bona fide business purpose for issuing the stock, a dividend of bonds would have accomplished the same purpose. Since the taxpayer failed to establish that preferred stock was not used to avoid a dividend tax, the Service refused to exercise its discretion under §306(b)(4); Walter Bialo, supra note 42 (same).

For extended discussion of §306(b)(4), see Schneider, Internal Revenue Code Section 306 and Tax Avoidance, 4 Va. Tax Rev. 287, 310–330 (1985).

in a single transaction, thus gaining the protection of §306(b)(1)(A). The buyers may dispose of the preferred stock (now free of its prior §306 taint) to pay off loans incurred for the acquisition. A similar such situation would involve a sale of common stock to incoming shareholders, coupled with a simultaneous sale of preferred stock to investors willing to take a short-term position pending redemption of the preferred stock. Alternatively, the sellers might sell the common stock but retain the preferred stock under an arrangement calling for its redemption at a later date in circumstances complying with the exemption granted by §306(b)(1)(B). Of course, bootstrap sales can often be achieved, even though common stock is the only class of outstanding stock (by arranging to have the corporation buy part of the common stock in conjunction with a sale of the balance to the new owners).[43] However, a combination of common and preferred stock may offer more flexibility in structuring the transaction.

"Section 306 stock" can also be useful in making family gifts if the donees (who take the stock with the taint, by virtue of §306(c)(1)(C)) are likely to hold the stock indefinitely or dispose of it in a transaction qualifying for an exemption under §306(b), such as a sale in conjunction with a sale by the donors of their retained common stock. Such a gift enables the donors to maintain control of the corporation while reducing the potential value of their estates for estate tax purpose. Moreover, unlike the common stock of most family corporations, preferred stock can usually be valued for gift tax purposes with relative ease. Alternatively, the older shareholders may retain the preferred "section 306 stock" (which will be purged of its taint when they die) for fixed dividend income, while control of the corporation is transferred to younger members of their family or to active executives by gifts or sales of the common stock. This strategy may also serve to freeze the value of the older generation's interest in the corporation for estate tax purposes.[44]

¶ 10.07   IS §306 THE EXCLUSIVE REMEDY FOR ATTEMPTED BAILOUTS?

As stated previously, stock distributed—either at the time of organization or at a later date—by a corporation having no earnings and profits cannot be "section 306 stock," by virtue of §306(c)(2).[45] A redemption of such untainted

---

[43] For discussion of all-common-stock bootstrap sales, see ¶ 9.07.

[44] See generally Abbin, Have They Nuked the Freeze? Evaluating the Impact of Recent Decisions, Regulations and Rulings, 19 Inst. on Est. Plan. ¶ 500 (1985); Abbin, Bifurcation Is Alive and Well—Tax Court Nixes IRS Technical Advices, 35 Tax Notes 77 (1987).

[45] See supra text at note 20.

stock, therefore, will not be subject to the punitive rules of §306(a), even if it occurs when the corporation does have earnings and profits. The inapplicability of §306 will not assure the shareholders of capital gain or loss treatment on the redemption, however, since the transaction will be subject to §302, which ordinarily taxes a pro rata redemption as a dividend.[46]

What if the shareholders seek to avoid §302 by selling the untainted stock to a third person, and the corporation thereafter redeems it from the buyer? This question requires further attention to *Chamberlin*, where the court held on the facts before it that the distribution-sale transaction was not the equivalent of a taxable dividend.[47] Another court, of course, might not view such a transaction so leniently; but in relitigating the issue, the government would be met by the argument that Congress enacted §306 with *Chamberlin* before it and intended §306 to be the exclusive remedy for any attempted bailout through the medium of a distribution, sale, and redemption of preferred stock. In answering this theory, it might be argued that §306 was intended to be an automatic safeguard against bailouts and that Congress did not want to impose its drastic rules on stock issued when the corporation has no earnings and profits, but that §302 nonetheless remains unimpaired by the enactment of §306. This view of §§306 and 302 means that a purchaser of untainted stock might be regarded under §302(d) as a mere conduit through which the original shareholders receive a dividend if all the surrounding circumstances of the transaction warrant this conclusion.[48] To take an extreme case, if untainted preferred stock is sold under an agreement calling for its redemption within a few days, the government might properly argue that the transaction is in effect a redemption of stock from the original shareholders rather than from the buyer.[49] If the time between the sale and redemption is lengthened, however, the resulting intervention of business and legal risks for all parties makes it increasingly difficult to find that the transferees of the stock are merely conduits for the original shareholders. It may well be, then, that §306 has become the exclusive remedy for all but the most extreme sale-and-redemption cases.

---

[46] See generally supra ¶ 9.02.

[47] Chamberlin v. CIR, supra note 4.

[48] This view, of course, assumes that the original shareholders participate in the transaction on a pro rata basis, so none of the escapes provided by §302(b) is applicable. See supra ¶ 9.02. See e.g., Estate of A.J. Schneider, 88 TC No. 50 (1987).

[49] But see Rev. Rul. 78-197, 1978-1 CB 83 (gift of stock to charity followed by prearranged redemption; held, proceeds will be treated as income to donor "only if the donee is legally bound, or can be compelled by the corporation, to surrender the shares for redemption"); but compare Estate of A.J. Schneider, supra note 48 (purported stock sale in substance a redemption but was equivalent to dividend).

CHAPTER 11

Complete Liquidations

PART A.　THE GENERAL RULE: COMPLETE LIQUIDATIONS TREATED AS SALES OF THE LIQUIDATING CORPORATION'S STOCK

¶ 11.01　INTRODUCTORY

Section 331(a) provides that amounts distributed to a shareholder in complete liquidation of a corporation must be treated as "full payment in exchange for the stock"; and §331(b) reinforces this analogy to a sale by rendering §301, relating to dividends, inapplicable to amounts received in a complete liquidation. Thus, the shareholder computes gain or loss by subtracting the adjusted basis of the stock from the amount realized (the money, if any, plus the fair market value of any other property received), and reports the difference as capital gain or loss if, as is almost always the case, the stock is a capital asset in the shareholder's hands.

The approach embodied in §331 was adopted by Congress in 1924 on the theory that "[a] liquidating dividend is, in effect, a sale by the stockholder of his stock to the corporation; he surrenders his interest in the corporation and receives money in place thereof."[1] The analogy between a com-

---

[1] S. Rep. No. 398, 68th Cong., 1st Sess. 11 (1939), reprinted in 1939-1 CB 266, 274 (Part 2).

plete liquidation and a sale of the stock, however, is not a perfect one. A sale of shares merely substitutes one shareholder for another, leaving the corporation's earnings and profits account intact. The result is that the earnings and profits will be taxed as ordinary income if and when they are distributed to the new shareholder; he becomes a surrogate, as it were, for the outgoing shareholder, since the distributed corporate earnings will be subjected to the individual income tax rate. On a complete liquidation, however, no one steps into the shoes of the original shareholder. The earnings and profits account—representing income that has so far escaped the individual income tax because its distribution has been postponed—is wiped clean.[2]

A sale of shares, then, merely puts off the day of reckoning for the accumulated earnings and profits; by contrast a complete liquidation guarantees that there will be *no* reckoning other than a recognition of capital gain or loss. This is true even if the distributed assets consist of a going business that is subsequently conducted as a sole proprietorship or partnership by the distributees.[3]

The distinction between a taxable dividend of the corporation's earnings and profits and a liquidating distribution, however, is less dramatic under current law than it was before 1987, when long-term capital gains enjoyed a substantial tax rate differential. Under current law, the principal remaining advantage accorded to liquidating distributions over ordinary dividends (aside from the fact that a shareholder is allowed to set off his stock basis against the liquidation distribution proceeds) is that a taxpayer with capital losses can use them to offset any capital gain on a §331 liquidating distribution without dollar limit but can apply such losses against only $3,000 of ordinary income (including dividends).

To illustrate: Assume that A owns all of the stock of X Corporation, with an adjusted basis of $250,000, its value when recently inherited from A's mother. X has accumulated earnings and profits of $100,000 and a net worth of $250,000. X pays an ordinary dividend to A of $100,000, thus reducing its net worth (and hence the value of A's stock) to $150,000, and X also distributes its remaining assets to A in complete liquidation. Unfortunately for A, these transactions generate $100,000

---

[2] For the taxation of liquidating distributions by certain foreign corporations as dividends to the extent of earnings and profits, see §1248, discussed infra ¶ 17.34.

[3] See generally Bittker & Redlich, Corporate Liquidations and the Income Tax, 5 Tax L. Rev. 437, 448–451 (1950); Subchapter C Advisory Group, Revised Report on Corporate Distributions and Adjustments (and comments thereon), in Hearings Before House Comm. on Ways and Means, 86th Cong., 1st Sess. 473 (1959). For comparison with the partnership liquidation rules, see supra ¶ 1.07.

of ordinary income and a capital loss of $100,000, which together can be used to offset only $3,000 of ordinary income per year.[4]

This is an extreme and simplistic example, but it demonstrates that the 1986 repeal of the rate differential for long-term capital gains did not put capital gains and losses on a plane of complete equality with ordinary income and losses.[5] The example also shows that distributions in complete liquidation must be distinguished from other distributions, particularly ordinary dividends. Moreover, even if §331 does not affect the shareholder's ultimate tax liability for a particular tax year, complete liquidations differ from other distributions in their effect on the corporation itself. For example, the corporation is allowed by §336(a), as amended in 1986, to recognize losses on liquidating distributions of depreciated property but not on nonliquidating distributions.[6]

The discussion of complete liquidations that follows in this chapter is divided into three parts. Part A examines the basic rules applicable to complete liquidations, including such problems as distinguishing complete liquidations from other distributions, computation of the shareholder's gain or loss on liquidating distributions, the basis of the property received by shareholders in exchange for stock, the treatment of transactions in which a liquidation is coupled by prearrangement with the reincorporation of some of the distributed assets, and recognition by the liquidating corporation of its gain or loss on liquidating distributions of appreciated and depreciated property as a result of a fundamental reform enacted by Congress in 1986. Subsequent sections in Part A deal with assignment of income and related problems for the liquidating corporation, the liquidating corporation's deductions, indebtedness, and earnings and profits account, and special rules for allocating the purchase price in asset acquisitions.

Part B examines the special rules applicable to complete liquidations of subsidiary corporations into their parent corporation including the treatment of corporate acquisitions when the target company holds appreciated assets and the acquiring corporation wishes to increase the basis of these assets to their fair market value to reflect the amount paid by it to acquire the target company's stock.

---

[4] If the taxpayer could establish that the dividend was an integral step in a prearranged plan of complete liquidation, he would realize neither gain nor loss, since the amount received would be equal to the adjusted basis for the stock; for this possibility, see infra notes 12–13.

[5] See H.R. Conf. Rep. No. 841, 99th Cong., 2d Sess. II-106 (1986) ("current statutory structure for capital gains is retained in the Code to facilitate reinstatement of a capital gains rate differential if there is a future tax rate increase").

[6] See infra ¶ 11.06.

Finally, Part C describes the treatment of complete liquidations under certain nonrecognition provisions that were repealed in 1986, but that continue to be of interest because they are subject to a delayed effective date for certain small business corporations that completely liquidate in 1987 or 1988 and also because they will undoubtedly generate litigation for some years to come in light of their application to pre-1987 transactions. These otherwise obsolete nonrecognition provisions are former §337, under which a corporation did not recognize gain or loss on a sale of its assets within the 12-month period commencing with the adoption of a plan of complete liquidation, provided all assets (except amounts retained to meet claims) were distributed within the 12-month period; and former §333, which permitted certain individual shareholders to elect to postpone recognition of gain on certain complete liquidations occurring within one calendar month.

¶ 11.02   MEANING OF "COMPLETE LIQUIDATION"

The Code does not define the term "complete liquidation," nor do the regulations under §331. The regulations under §332, however, contain this statement, which probably applies equally to §331:

> A status of liquidation exists when the corporation ceases to be a going concern and its activities are merely for the purpose of winding up its affairs, paying its debts, and distributing any remaining balance to its shareholders. A liquidation may be completed prior to the actual dissolution of the liquidating corporation. However, legal dissolution of the corporation is not required. Nor will the mere retention of a nominal amount of assets for the sole purpose of preserving the corporation's legal existence disqualify the transaction.[7]

The cases support this pragmatic approach to the term "complete liquidation." For example, in *Kennemer v. CIR*, the court said:

> It is not material that the distribution was not specifically designated as a liquidating dividend or that no formal resolution to liquidate or dissolve the corporation had been adopted when the distribution was made. An intention to liquidate was fairly implied from the sale of all the assets and the act of distributing the cash to the stockholders. Permitting the forfeiture of its right to do business was an additional circumstance which the [Tax Court] properly considered with the other facts in evidence. The determining element was the intention to liqui-

---

[7] Regs. §1.332-2(c). For §332, see infra ¶¶ 11.40–11.41.

date the business, coupled with the actual distribution of the cash to the stockholders.[8]

Moreover, although this extract implies that a sale of the corporate assets is required, it is well established that a distribution in kind is equally efficacious.[9]

Although a complete liquidation is ordinarily effected by a dissolution under state law, it is not essential that the corporation dissolve for complete liquidation treatment to apply. Thus, in Rev. Rul. 54-518, the Service ruled that retention of the corporation's charter to protect the corporation's name against appropriation was not inconsistent with a complete liquidation under former §333; the ruling seems equally applicable to §331.[10] The prompt reactivation of an allegedly liquidated corporation, however, may retroactively vitiate the tax results of a normal complete liquidation.[11]

Although the courts and the regulations are willing to give effect to an informal liquidation, it is dangerous to make distributions to the shareholders before the intention to liquidate is evidenced by formal action. In the absence of such formalities, it may take a lawsuit to establish that the earliest distributions in a series were liquidating distributions, subject to §331(a), rather than ordinary distributions, taxable as dividends under §301 to the extent of the corporation's earnings and profits.[12] Similarly, it seems unwise

---

[8] Kennemer v. CIR, 96 F2d 177, 178 (5th Cir. 1938).

[9] See Rev. Rul. 63-107, 1963-1 CB 71. For other examples of informal complete liquidations, see Shore v. CIR, 286 F2d 742 (5th Cir. 1961); Joseph Olmsted, ¶ 84,381 P-H Memo. TC (1984) (complete liquidation found despite extended stretched-out liquidation process); Estate of William G. Maguire, 50 TC 130 (1968) (contra); see also Blawie, Some Tax Aspects of a Corporate Liquidation, 7 Tax L. Rev. 481, 488–496 (1952).

[10] Rev. Rul. 54-518, 1954-2 CB 142. For §333 (repealed in 1986), see infra ¶ 11.62.

[11] Rev. Rul. 76-429, 1976-2 CB 97 (13 days after subsidiary sold one of its two businesses and distributed its other assets in complete liquidation, parent reincorporated the second business; held partial rather than complete liquidation); see generally infra ¶ 11.05. For the possibility that a sale of stock coupled with a prearranged liquidation may be recharacterized as a liquidation and sale of the assets, see Estate of Weiskopf, 64 TC 78 (1975), aff'd without opinion, 538 F2d 317 (2d Cir. 1976) (sale of stock of corporation that was liquidated thereafter by purchaser; held liquidation by seller); Owens v. CIR, 568 F2d 1233 (6th Cir. 1977). But see Gray v. CIR, 561 F2d 753 (9th Cir. 1977) (Tax Court holding of constructive liquidation reversed; held true sale of stock and liquidation by buyer).

[12] The regulations under §332 contain this statement, which seems equally applicable to §331(a): "Where there is more than one distribution, it is essential that a status of liquidation exist at the time the first distribution is made." Regs. §1.332-2(c). See Joseph Olmsted, supra note 9 (serial liquidation over long period found to be liquidation). If the distributee is a corporation, the shoe may be on the other foot,

to leave the status of a distribution ambiguous by failing to adopt a plan of liquidation, even though §331(a) does not insist upon such action, or by neglecting to redeem the stock. The characterization problem can also be troublesome if the corporation distributes all of its assets in installments, since the early installments may be treated as severable events on which the taxpayer's gain or loss is computed distribution-by-distribution, rather than in the aggregate.

Section 346(a) provides that each distribution in a series of distributions in redemption of all of the corporation's stock pursuant to a plan is to be treated as a distribution in complete liquidation; [13] but it sheds no light on whether a distribution is or is not part of a series if the corporation does not adopt a formal plan or if the plan is ambiguous.

¶ 11.03 LIQUIDATING DISTRIBUTIONS AND SHAREHOLDER GAIN OR LOSS

1. General. Section 331(a) provides that amounts distributed in complete liquidation of a corporation must be treated as full payment in exchange for the shareholder's stock. [14] If the stock is a capital asset in the hands of the shareholder, as would normally be the case under §1221 (unless it is held by a dealer for sale to customers in the ordinary course of business), a complete liquidation will produce capital gain or loss, since §331(a) treats the liquidation transaction as an exchange of the stock. The amount of the gain or loss and its character as long-term or short-term capital gain or

---

since the tax on a nonliquidating distribution may be less painful by virtue of the dividends-received deduction of §243 (supra ¶ 5.05) than the capital gain tax on a complete liquidation.

[13] See generally Joseph Olmsted, supra note 9, which found liquidation status on the facts despite a long delay in the liquidation process; see also Rev. Rul. 85-48, 1985-1 CB 126. For the pre-1982 version of §346(a), treating such distributions as partial liquidations, see supra ¶ 9.08, text at note 113.

[14] But see Braddock Land Co., 75 TC 324 (1980) (distribution based on creditor status not subject to §331 treatment; shareholder-creditors' cancelation of their claims for accrued salaries in course of corporation's complete liquidation disregarded as sham). See also Dwyer v. US, 622 F2d 460 (9th Cir. 1980) (shareholder taxed on accrued interest when he canceled debt on complete liquidation, even though corporate-level deduction had been denied under §267). See generally Brod, Liquidations Involving Shareholder-Creditors—Tax Traps for the Unwary, 7 J. Corp. Tax'n 352 (1981).

See also Schaefer v. Welch, 252 F2d 175 (6th Cir. 1958), holding that pre-1913 appreciation in value is counted in computing the shareholder's capital gain on a complete liquidation even though it could be distributed tax-free in an ordinary distribution; Wallace v. US, 146 F. Supp. 444 (Ct. Cl. 1956) (contra).

loss in turn depend upon the shareholder's adjusted basis and holding period for the stock and the value of the liquidating distribution.

The regulations require the shareholder's gain or loss on liquidating distributions to be computed on a per-share basis, so that gain or loss is separately calculated for blocks of stock acquired at different prices and dates.[15] For example, if A acquired 100 shares of stock in X Corporation for $3,000 in year 1 and 100 shares for $6,000 in January of year two, a liquidating distribution of $50 per share in June of year two would produce $2,000 of long-term capital gain on the year 1 block, and $1,000 of short-term capital loss on the year 2 block.[16]

If a shareholder transfers stock to a donee or dies after the liquidation process has begun, there is some authority for taxing the donee or other transferee on post-assignment distributions. The weight of authority, however, requires the gain to be reported by the donor or treated as income in respect of a decedent.[17]

2. Problems of valuation and timing. Under §1001(a), a shareholder's gain or loss upon liquidation of the corporation is the difference between the adjusted basis of his stock and the fair market value of the liquidating distribution.[18] Calculating the value of the distributed assets is ordinarily feasible, although appraisals or estimates may be necessary; but disputed claims,

---

[15] Regs. §1.331-1(e).

[16] For the computation of gain or loss when the liquidation is effected by a series of distributions over a period of time, see Rev. Rul. 68-348, 1968-2 CB 141; supra ¶ 9.31. For non-pro rata distributions, see Rev. Rul. 79-10, 1979-1 CB 140; see also Rev. Rul. 85-48, 1985-1 CB 126, for amplification of Rev. Rul. 68-348 and Rev. Rul. 79-10.

In J.K. Downer, 48 TC 86 (1967), the shareholder's gain or loss on disposition of his stock was computed on a share-by-share basis; see also Johnson v. US, 435 F2d 1257 (4th Cir. 1971) (same for §301(c)(3) capital distribution gain even though a loss would not be allowable under that provision).

[17] See W.B. Rushing, 52 TC 888 (1969), aff'd on other grounds, 441 F2d 593 (5th Cir. 1971); Keck v. CIR, 415 F2d 531 (6th Cir. 1969); Jones v. US, 531 F2d 1343 (6th Cir. 1976) (en banc); Horace E. Allen, 66 TC 340 (1976); Dayton Hydraulic Co. v. US, 592 F2d 937 (6th Cir.), cert. denied, 444 US 831 (1979) (liquidation too ripe to shift shareholder tax burden thereon); CIR v. Court Holding Co., 324 US 331 (1945); Estate of Sidles, 65 TC 873 (1976) (acq.) (liquidation so advanced when corporation's sole shareholder died that liquidating distribution was income in respect of a decedent); Kinsey v. CIR, 477 F2d 1058 (2d Cir. 1973) (donor taxed on liquidation proceeds); Hudspeth v. US, 471 F2d 275 (8th Cir. 1972) (accord). But see supra ¶ 7.07 (for further discussion of gifts of stock).

[18] For the possibility of constructive receipt of funds that are readily available to the shareholder, see Rev. Rul. 80-177, 1980-2 CB 109; see also Lowndes v. US, 384 F2d 635 (4th Cir. 1967).

contingent contract rights, mineral royalties, business goodwill,[19] and other rights may be difficult if not impossible to value with reasonable accuracy. If the value of some or all of the assets received by the shareholder cannot be ascertained with reasonable accuracy, the computation with respect to these assets is held "open," under *Burnet v. Logan*, until they are sold, collected, or otherwise reduced to property of ascertainable value.[20] Such a delay will affect the year in which gain or loss is recognized by the shareholder, and it may also affect the characterization of the gain or loss. This is because the gain or loss ultimately realized on an open liquidation is part of the capital gain or loss generated by the exchange of the stock under §331(a); if the asset in question had been valued when received, however, any gain or loss realized on its later collection, sale, or other disposition (i.e., the difference between the amount ultimately realized and the asset's value at the time of distribution) would be ordinary or capital, depending on whether it was a capital asset in the shareholder's hands and on whether the latter transaction was a sale or exchange within the meaning of §1222.[21]

> *To illustrate: A*, the sole shareholder of *X* Corporation, receives in complete liquidation of *X* cash of $10,000, operating assets with an ascertainable value of $30,000, and a contingent claim against *Y* in the face amount of $50,000 (which may be valueless, depending on

---

[19] Goodwill is normally valued by reference to the earnings history and capacity of the business out of which it grows. Regarding whether corporate goodwill is distributed to a shareholder on liquidation if it was his personal efforts as an employee of the corporation that attracted the customers, see Ruth M. Cullen, 14 TC 368 (1950) (acq.); Frank J. Longo, ¶ 68,217 P-H Memo. TC (1968); see also Concord Control, Inc. v. CIR, 615 F2d 1153 (6th Cir. 1980) (purchase price premium allocable to "going concern value" despite absence of good will; remand for explanation of computation of going concern value), on remand, 78 TC 742 (1982) (acq.).

For timing of gain or loss generally, see John E. Byrne, 54 TC 1632 (1970) (gain taxable in year of distribution of corporate assets, not when technical title changed), aff'd per curiam, 449 F2d 759 (8th Cir. 1971); Ethel M. Schmidt, 55 TC 335 (1970) (no loss until final distribution); Rev. Rul. 72-137, 1972-1 CB 101 (shareholders taxed in year of distribution to trust in which they held beneficial interests).

See generally North Am. Serv. Co., 33 TC 677 (1960) (acq.); Rev. Rul. 66-81, 1966-1 CB 64; Harnack, The Commissioner Is Looking for Good Will, 40 Taxes 331 (1962); Henszey, Going Concern Value After *Concord Control, Inc.*, 61 Taxes 699 (1983).

[20] Burnet v. Logan, 283 US 404 (1931).

[21] See generally Farer, Corporate Liquidations: Transmuting Ordinary Income Into Capital Gains, 75 Harv. L. Rev. 527 (1962); Eustice, Contract Rights, Capital Gain, and Assignment of Income–The Ferrer Case, 20 Tax L. Rev. (1964); Note, "Open" Transactions in Federal Income Taxation, 38 U. Cin. L. Rev. 62 (1969); Schenk, *Arrowsmith* and Its Progeny: Tax Characterization by Reference to Past Events, 33 Rutgers L. Rev. 317 (1981).

later events beyond X's or A's control. A's basis for his stock in X is $50,000. If it is held that X's claim against Y has no readily ascertainable value under *Burnet v. Logan,* the liquidation computation is held open until the claim is finally reduced to money or other property with an ascertainable value. If A subsequently collects $40,000 on the claim (column A in following table,) this amount is deemed to have been received in exchange for his stock, and A's gain of $30,000 (aggregate liquidating distribution of $80,000, less $50,000 basis for stock) is taxable as capital gain. If A collected only $7,000 on the claim (column B), his loss of $3,000 ($50,000 basis for stock, less aggregate distribution of $47,000) would be deductible as a capital loss when the claim was settled.

These results may be compared with the consequences of a closed liquidation, based on the assumption that the claim against Y was valued at $30,000 when it was distributed to A. His gain on the liquidation would be $20,000 (liquidating distribution of $70,000, less $50,000 basis for stock). On collecting $40,000 on the claim (column C), A would realize gain of $10,000 ($40,000 received, less $30,000 basis for claim under §334(a)), and this gain would constitute ordinary income for want of a sale or exchange of the claim.[22] If he collected only $7,000 (column D), he would realize a loss of $23,000 (basis of $30,000, less $7,000 received), which might be an ordinary loss or a capital loss, depending on principles discussed in Chapter 4.

In tabular form, the four scenarios just described are as follows (dollar amounts in thousands):

	Open Liquidation		Closed Liquidation	
	A	B	C	D
(1) Amount realized—liquidation				
(a) Cash	$10	$10	$10	$10
(b) Operating assets	30	30	30	30
(c) Claim vs. Y	40	7	30	30
(d) Total	$80	$47	$70	$70
(2) Less: Adjusted basis of stock	50	50	50	50
(3) Gain (loss) on liquidation	$30	($ 3)	$20	$20
(4) Amount collected on claim vs. Y	$40	$ 7	$40	$ 7
(5) Less: Adjusted basis of claim vs. Y	40	7	30	30
(6) Gain (loss) on collection	0	0	$10	($23)

---

[22] Hale v. Helvering, 85 F2d 819 (D.C. Cir. 1936). For §334(a), see infra ¶ 11.04.

It will be noted that the same aggregate gain or loss will be reflected on *A*'s tax returns whether the liquidation is treated as open or closed when distribution is made, but the character of his gain or loss and the years of realization may differ. Thus, assuming ultimate collection of $40,000 on the claim, the open liquidation computation produces $30,000 of capital gain in the year the claim is settled; the closed computation produces $20,000 of capital gain in the year of liquidation, and $10,000 of ordinary income when the claim is settled. The revised assumption, (i.e., a settlement of the claim for $7,000) is reflected on *A*'s tax return in the year of settlement as a loss of $3,000, assuming an open liquidation; the closed liquidation approach produces capital gain of $20,000 in the year of distribution and a loss of $23,000 when the claim is settled. The way in which the shareholder's economic gain "nets out" as just described can be seen in the above table: The sum of line (3) and line (6) is the same for columns A and C (open and closed liquidations, assuming that $40,000 is collected on the claim), as well as for columns B and D (open and closed liquidations, assuming that $7,000 is collected).

Because of the deferral of tax that results from holding a liquidation open on a plea that the fair market value of assets is not ascertainable, together with the possibility of thus transmuting potential ordinary income into capital gain, the Service has ardently resisted taxpayer arguments that assets were not susceptible of valuation when distributed in liquidation. Thus, Rev. Rul. 58-402 states that the Service will "continue to require valuation of contracts and claims to receive indefinite amounts of income, such as those acquired with respect to stock in liquidation of a corporation, except in rare and extraordinary cases."[23] The shoe is on the other foot, however, if the shareholder claims a loss on the liquidation on the ground that assets of this type should be taken into account at a low or nominal value. Here the Service may argue that the difficulty of valuing such assets

---

[23] Rev. Rul. 58-402, 1958-2 CB 15. This resistance may moderate, however, when the repeal of the capital gain rate differential of §§1201 and 1202 by the Tax Reform Act of 1986 becomes fully effective (in 1988); see also Regs. §1.1001-1(a) (third sentence). If a fair market value can be ascribed to the stock surrendered, US v. Davis, 370 US 65 (1962), supports an assignment of this value to the assets received in exchange, although this would leave a troublesome allocation problem if there is more than one asset of unascertainable value.

The advantage to the shareholder of open liquidation treatment would be reduced if it brought §483 (imputed interest on delayed payments for capital assets), or §1274 (the original issue discount rules applicable to deferred payment sales of property), or §1276 (the market discount rules applicable to debt claims acquired at less than their face amount) into play, since a portion of the gain ultimately realized would then be taxed as ordinary income. Since this possibility is not peculiar to corporate liquidations, but would arise in the case of any taxable exchange of a capital asset if the amount realized did not have an ascertainable fair market value, an evaluation of it is beyond the scope of this work. See supra ¶¶ 4.40–4.44.

makes the shareholder's claim premature and that no loss should be allowed until the claims have been collected or sold.[24]

If the $50,000 claim against *Y* in the preceding example had been payable in five installments rather than in a single payment, subsequent collections by the distributee shareholder, *A*, in the closed liquidation situation raise still another timing problem: whether *A* is entitled to recover his $30,000 basis before reporting gain, or must instead report a ratable portion of each installment collection ($50,000 less $30,000 over $50,000, or 40 percent) as ordinary discount income. The cases generally allow the basis recovery approach if the claim is held to be speculative; otherwise, a ratable portion of each installment must be reported as ordinary income when collected.[25] The value of a distributed asset may be sufficiently ascertainable to require closing the liquidation, but at the same time may be speculative enough to allow a recovery of basis before further gain or loss must be reported thereon.

Another aspect of this problem is illustrated by *Warren v. US,* where the court held that a distribution in liquidation of an overriding royalty

---

[24] Open liquidation cases include CIR v. Carter, 170 F2d 911 (2d Cir. 1948) (oil brokerage commission contracts); Henry A. Kuckenberg, ¶ 60,281 P-H Memo. TC (1960) (partially completed construction contract); CIR v. Doering, 335 F2d 738 (2d Cir. 1964) (contested movie distribution contract rights); Stephen H. Dorsey, 49 TC 606 (1968) (patent royalty rights); Shea Co., 53 TC 135 (1969) (acq.) (contested corporate claims); Miller v. US, 235 F2d 553 (6th Cir. 1956) (liquidation in which speculative second mortgage notes were distributed held open because a fair market value could not be ascribed to them; but taxpayer held to realize ordinary income on collection because there was no sale or exchange of the notes), 262 F2d 584 (1958) (on remand); Cloward Instrument Co., ¶ 86,345 P-H Memo. TC (1986); Osenbach v. CIR, 198 F2d 235 (4th Cir. 1952); Rev. Rul. 58-402, 1958-2 CB 15. (seemingly assuming capital gain for open liquidation).

Closed liquidation cases include Campagna v. US, 290 F2d 682 (2d Cir. 1961) (second mortgage contracts); Chamberlin v. CIR, 286 F2d 850 (7th Cir. 1960) (patent royalty rights), cert. denied, 368 US 820 (1961); Grill v. US, 303 F2d 922 (Ct. Cl. 1962) (film distribution contract); Pat O'Brien, 25 TC 376 (1955) (acq.) (movie distribution contract); United Mercantile Agencies, 34 TC 808 (1960) (delinquent accounts receivable); Waring v. CIR, 412 F2d 800 (3d Cir. 1969) (patent royalty rights).

Cases involving losses claimed by shareholders are Charles A. Dana, 6 TC 177 (1946) (acq.); Palmer v. US, 1 AFTR2d 863 (D. Conn. 1958); see also Warren v. CIR, 193 F2d 996, 1001 (1st Cir. 1952); Ethel M. Schmidt, supra note 19; H.B. Grudberg, ¶ 75,142 P-H Memo. TC (1975) (open loss).

[25] Joseph J. Weiss, ¶ 65,020 P-H Memo. TC (1965) (installment collections on closed liquidation claim reportable partly as ratable discount income and partly as recovery of basis); General Ins. Agency, Inc., ¶ 67,143 P-H Memo. TC (1967), aff'd, 401 F2d 324 (4th Cir. 1968) (same); Neil S. McCarthy, ¶ 63,033 P-H Memo. TC (1963), (recovery of basis allowed); Judith Schneider, 65 TC 18 (1975) (acq.) (film contract rights in closed liquidation; basis to be recovered ratably under income forecast depreciation method); see generally Wingate E. Underhill, 45 TC 489 (1966).

interest in oil property was a closed transaction and that subsequent collections in excess of the property's basis were reportable as ordinary income.[26] The court noted that the shareholders acquired income-producing property from the liquidating corporation in exchange for their stock and that subsequent receipts of income from that property were not converted into deferred liquidation capital gain merely because the property interest was acquired in a liquidation distribution. In short, open liquidation treatment may be limited to distributions of claims representing potential income at the corporate level (i.e., corporate receivables, comparable to "income in respect of a decedent" items defined in §691,[27] as opposed to distributions of income-producing assets). The courts, other than in *Warren*, have not explicitly adopted this approach, however, in deciding whether a liquidation is open or closed.

3. Effect of liabilities on shareholder's gain or loss. If on a complete liquidation the shareholders assume (or take property subject to) liabilities, their gain or loss must be computed with this fact in mind. Thus, if property with a gross value of $100,000 is distributed in complete liquidation subject to a liability of $40,000 to a shareholder whose stock has a basis of $50,000, the gain realized on the distribution is $10,000; this is because the amount realized under §1001 on the liquidation exchange is the net value of the distribution.[28] Moreover, under §§336(b) and 7701(g), property transferred subject to recourse or nonrecourse debt must be valued at no less than the amount of the liability.

If the amount of the liability is unknown at the time of distribution or is so speculative or contingent that it is properly disregarded in computing the shareholder's gain or loss on the liquidation, a later payment of the debt by the shareholder will probably generate a capital loss under *Arrowsmith v. CIR*, rather than a deduction from ordinary income, on the theory that his capital gain on the liquidation was overstated.[29]

---

[26] Warren v. US, 171 F. Supp. 846 (Ct. Cl.), cert. denied, 361 US 916 (1959).

[27] See Ferguson, Income and Deductions in Respect of Decedents and Related Problems, 25 Tax L. Rev. 1 (1969).

[28] Ford v. US, 311 F2d 951 (Ct. Cl. 1963); see also infra ¶ 11.04, concerning the shareholder's basis for the encumbered property; Rev. Rul. 72-137, 1972-1 CB 101; M.Q. Petersen, ¶ 71,021 P-H Memo. TC (1971).

Alternatively, the shareholder could be viewed as realizing the full gross value of the property, and as paying consideration equal to the amount of the liabilities.

[29] Arrowsmith v. CIR, 344 US 6 (1952); see also Judith Schneider, supra note 25 (transferee liability disregarded in computing shareholders' gain in year of liquidation; taxpayer has *Arrowsmith* capital loss on payments in later years); Rev. Rul. 78-25, 1978-1 CB 270 (*Arrowsmith* capital loss for payor-shareholder; but §1341 also applies); Schenk, supra note 21; Note, Tax Treatment of Stockholder-Transferees'

4. Judicial exceptions to §331(a). No statute except a new one is innocent of judicial exceptions. Suppose a taxpayer acquires all the stock of a corporation for the sole purpose of liquidating the corporation in order to use its assets (e.g., a stock of merchandise in short supply) in his own business. If, by reason of market fluctuations, there is a difference between the cost to him of the shares and the value of the assets at the time he liquidates the corporation, is the gain or loss recognized?

On the ground that such a transaction is in substance no more than a purchase of assets, rather than a purchase of stock and a liquidation of the corporation, it was held in *H.B. Snively*[30] that no gain is recognizable. As to the income produced in the interim by the corporate assets, however, the court held that it should be taxed to the corporation, rather than to the stockholder, despite the plan to liquidate:

> The stock purchase coupled with the intent to dissolve the corporation and the taking of some steps to that end, in our opinion, did not *ipso facto* either destroy the existence of the corporation as a taxable entity or permit the petitioner to appropriate as his own income which would otherwise be taxable to the corporation.[31]

A purchase of stock was similarly treated as the equivalent of a purchase of assets in *Ruth M. Cullen*, where a shareholder of a corporation bought out the other shareholders, intending to liquidate the corporation and operate its business as a sole proprietorship.[32] Although the price paid for the stock (book value) exceeded the value of the liquidating distribution, the court held that the taxpayer had not sustained a deductible loss because at the conclusion of the plan, she had neither more nor less than she had paid for.

Strictly speaking, the *Snively* and *Cullen* cases need not be regarded as exceptions to §331(a), since that section neither taxes gain nor allows the deduction of losses. These functions are performed by §§61(a) and 165(a); §331(a) merely makes it clear that the stock of a liquidating corporation is to

---

Payments in Satisfaction of Dissolved Corporations' Unpaid Debts, 61 Yale L.J. 1081 (1952); Regs. §1.338(b)-3T (infra ¶ 11.48, text at note 211). The shareholder's payment of the debt may be treated as a constructive payment by the corporation, entitling the corporation to a deduction if a direct payment by it would have been deductible; see Royal Oak Apartments, Inc., 43 TC 243 (1964) (acq.).

[30] H.B. Snively, 19 TC 850 (1953) (acq.), aff'd on another issue, 219 F2d 266 (5th Cir. 1955); see also infra ¶ 11.44 (regarding *Kimbell-Diamond* doctrine); Lowndes v. US, supra note 18 (ordinary income on bargain purchase of stock of dormant corporation whose sole asset was cash); Estate of Weiskopf v. CIR, supra note 11; Owens v. CIR, supra note 11 (follows *Lowndes*); compare Gray v. CIR, supra note 11 (true stock sale and buyer liquidation).

[31] H.B. Snively, supra note 30, at 858; this holding was affirmed on appeal, supra note 30.

[32] Ruth M. Cullen, supra note 19.

be treated as if it had been sold or exchanged. For the same reason, §331(a) does not preclude application of the *Corn Products* doctrine,[33] with the result that a corporate liquidation that is intimately connected to the shareholder's regular trade or business might, in appropriate circumstances, produce ordinary, rather than capital, gain or loss. The business function of such stock overrides its technical definition as a capital asset and requires the gain or loss to be treated as an integral component of the shareholder's regular business income.

¶ 11.04 BASIS OF PROPERTY RECEIVED IN COMPLETE LIQUIDATION

Section 334(a) provides that the basis of property received in a complete liquidation must be its fair market value at the time of distribution if gain or loss was recognized on its receipt.[34] It will be noted that the basis of the stock given up in the liquidation, plus the gain or minus the loss recognized on the liquidation, will equal the fair market value of the property received. If no gain or loss is recognized on the liquidation, because the stockholder's basis for the stock he surrenders happens to coincide with the value of the liquidating distribution, the basis of the distributed assets is their cost (i.e., the value of the stock given up).[35]

---

[33] Corn Prods. Ref. Co. v. CIR, 350 US 46 (1955); see also CIR v. Bagley & Sewall Co., 221 F2d 944 (2d Cir. 1955); Arkansas Best Corp. v. CIR, 800 F2d 215 (8th Cir. 1986), cert. granted (1987); supra ¶ 4.20.

[34] "Recognized" as used in §334(a) probably means "recognizable," so that the failure to recognize gain or loss would not bar an application of the provision, although such an inconsistency may permit the statute of limitations to be opened up under §1311. But see CIR v. Estate of Goldstein, 340 F2d 24 (2d Cir. 1965) (refusing to open barred year of liquidation where taxpayer was not inconsistent, even though assets were later held susceptible of valuation). See also supra ¶ 3.10 for an analogous problem when gain should have been, but was not, recognized on the receipt of boot.

If the shareholders assume or take property subject to liabilities, their basis is the unencumbered fair market value of the assets. See Ford v. US, supra note 28; Crane v. CIR, 331 US 1 (1947); M.Q. Petersen, supra note 28 (if liabilities exceed value, basis is value of property, not face of debt); see also CIR v. Tufts, 461 US 300 (1983). But see §7701(g); Columbus & G. Ry. Co., 42 TC 834 (1964) (basis does not include hypothetical liability that is not expected to be paid), aff'd per curiam, 358 F2d 294 (5th Cir.), cert. denied, 385 US 827 (1966); see generally Regs. §1.1001-2 (1980).

For the possibility that the basis allocation rules of §1060 may be applicable in determining the basis of the assets received by the shareholders in complete liquidation of their corporation, see infra ¶ 11.11, text at note 109.

[35] See §1012. The values of the stock and the liquidating distribution are ordinarily identical; if a discrepancy exists, there is authority for letting the value of the

By tying the basis of the distributed property to its fair market value on distribution, §334(a) assures that the shareholder's economic profit or loss, measured from the time of his acquistion of the stock to his sale of the property received in the liquidating distribution, will be recognized in two steps. The difference between the cost of the stock and the value of the distribution is taxed on liquidation, and the difference between the latter amount and the proceeds of the property on an ultimate sale or other disposition is taxed when the property is sold. For examples, see columns C and D of the example in the previous section. As noted in connection with this illustration, the gain recognized on the liquidation ordinarily constitutes capital gain under §§331(a) and 1221, but the character of the income or loss recognized on the sale or other disposition of the property depends on the nature of the assets in the shareholder's hands and on whether the disposition qualifies as a sale or exchange under §1222. Assets constituting stock in trade when held by the corporation, for example, may be capital assets when held by the shareholder, or vice versa.[36]

It is important to note that the liquidation of a corporation that owns appreciated inventory assets gives the inventory a stepped-up basis at the cost of a capital gains tax, a possibility that may be of advantage if the shareholders intend to continue the business as partners. This opportunity to acquire a stepped-up basis often gives rise to disputes over the valuation of such assets. It also was an important incentive for the troublesome liquidation-reincorporation device.[37]

¶ 11.05 LIQUIDATION FOLLOWED BY REINCORPORATION

The concept of complete liquidation usually envisions a termination of the liquidating corporation as an entity, either by a sale of its assets to outsiders and a distribution of the proceeds to the shareholders or by a distribution of assets to the shareholders so that they may either sell them or operate

---

stock control. See Avco Mfg. Corp., 27 TC 547, 556 (1956) (acq.); Rev. Rul. 56-100, 1956-1 CB 624. But cf. Philadelphia Park Amusement Co. v. US, 126 F. Supp. 184 (Ct. Cl. 1954); Moore-McCormack Lines, Inc., 44 TC 745 (1965) (acq.); Amerada Hess Corp. v. CIR, 517 F2d 75 (3d Cir.), cert. denied, 423 US 1037 (1975).

[36] Greenspon v. CIR, 229 F2d 947 (8th Cir. 1956); Acro Mfg. Co. v. CIR, 334 F2d 40 (6th Cir.), cert. denied, 379 US 887 (1964); see also F.W. Drybrough, 45 TC 424 (1966) (acq.), aff'd per curiam, 384 F2d 715 (6th Cir. 1967).

[37] Berg v. US, 167 F. Supp. 756 (W.D. Wis. 1958); Morton Ollendorff, ¶ 59,055 P-H Memo. TC (1959); infra ¶ 11.05. But see §336 as amended by the Tax Reform Act of 1986, infra ¶ 11.06, which now taxes at the liquidating corporate level as well at the shareholder level.

the business in noncorporate form. Sometimes these possibilities are combined: Some assets are sold by the corporation, others are distributed in kind to the shareholders; and of the latter, some are sold by the shareholders and others are used in a noncorporate business.

Before enactment of the Tax Reform Act of 1986, however, the shareholders of a closely held corporation sometimes liquidated it in an attempt to acquire a stepped-up basis for the appreciated corporate assets at the favorable pre-1987 tax rate on long-term capital gains and/or to obtain money, portfolio securities, or other liquid assets at the same favorable rate, even though they intended to continue to conduct the business in corporate form. This gambit could take any of several guises, such as a complete liquidation of the original corporation followed by a prearranged tax-free transfer under §351 of all or part of the operating assets to a newly organized successor corporation.[38] Under the pre-1987 version of §336, the liquidation did not trigger recognition of gain by the first corporation on its distribution of the appreciated assets;[39] thus, if the plan succeeded, the only tax paid was on the shareholders' capital gain (which might be small if the stock had a high basis, because, for example, it was recently inherited). Not surprisingly, the Service sought to defeat these liquidation-reincorporation plans with a variety of weapons, as explained in more detail later in this work.[40]

As amended in 1986, §336(a) provides for the recognition of gain or loss on liquidating distributions of appreciated or depreciated property,[41] so that in the future, such liquidation-reincorporation attempts will be less likely to be encountered. The device is not dead, however, since a corporation with appreciated property may be liquidated because it has a supply of losses to apply against its §336(a) gain. In this residual situation, the Service will no doubt persist in its effort to recharacterize liquidation-reincorporations in a way that will defeat the taxpayers' rosy expectations.[42]

¶ 11.06 LIQUIDATING CORPORATION'S GAIN OR LOSS ON DISTRIBUTIONS OF APPRECIATED OR DEPRECIATED PROPERTY

1. Introductory. In a dramatic rejection of tax principles that were more than half a century old, Congress amended §336(a) in 1986 to provide for the recognition of gain or loss to a corporation on the distribution of its

---

[38] For §351, see supra ¶ 3.01.

[39] See infra ¶ 11.06.

[40] Infra ¶ 14.54.

[41] See infra ¶ 11.06.

[42] See generally infra ¶ 14.54.

property in complete liquidation "as if such property were sold to the distributee at its fair market value." This rule is subject to only a few exceptions[43] and supersedes the so-called *General Utilities* doctrine, as codified by the pre-1987 version of §336(a), under which a distribution in complete liquidation did not trigger a corporate-level recognition of gain or loss except for recapture items such as LIFO inventory and accelerated depreciation.[44] This 1986 revolution in the treatment of corporate gain and loss on complete liquidations was accompanied, as explained earlier in this work,[45] by important changes in the treatment of stock redemptions and other nonliquidating distributions; but these amendments were less dramatic, both because the nonrecognition principle was retained for corporate losses on the distribution of depreciated property and because the nonrecognition principle for gains on nonliquidating distributions had been substantially eroded even before it was abandoned in 1986.[46]

The practical effect of §336(a), as amended in 1986, can be illustrated by assuming that a closely held corporation is to be liquidated so that the shareholders can conduct the business in partnership form or as a prelude to a sale of its assets to outsiders; the corporation owns a mixed bag of appreciated and depreciated assets, with an aggregate fair market value of $2 million and an adjusted basis of $500,000; and the shareholders have an aggregate adjusted basis for their stock of $200,000. On these facts, the complete liquidation will generate a net gain of $1.5 million for the corporation if the gains and losses on the various items can be offset against each other;[47] if

---

[43] Gain and loss are not recognized on tax-free transactions subject to §§351–368, such as spin-offs and corporate reorganizations (infra text at note 54), or on certain parent-subsidiary transactions (infra text at note 55) and certain losses with a tax avoidance aroma are not recognized (infra text at notes 51–53).

[44] For these exceptions to the pre-1987 nonrecognition principle, see the Fourth Edition of this treatise at ¶ 11.61.

For the *General Utilities* doctrine and its repeal, see supra ¶¶ 7.20 and 9.34.

See generally, Sheppard, Enforcing *General Utilities* Repeal, 32 Tax Notes 1217 (1986): Hiegel & Schler, Repeal of the *General Utilities* Doctrine, 33 Tax Notes 961 (1986); Bonovitz, Impact of *General Utilities*, 65 J. Tax'n 388 (1986); Eustice, Kuntz, Lewis, & Deering, The Tax Reform Act of 1986, ¶ 2.03 (Warren, Gorham & Lamont, Inc., 1987); Brode, General Utilities Repeal: A Transactional Analysis, 66 J. Tax'n 322 (1987).

[45] See supra ¶¶ 7.20–7.21.

[46] For the treatment of nonliquidating distributions of appreciated property under pre-1987 law, see supra ¶ 7.22.

[47] See Williams v. McGowan, 152 F2d 570 (2d Cir. 1945) (gain and loss must be computed separately on assets, even though functionally interrelated in conduct of a going business).

Although losses on sales to certain related parties are usually not deductible under §267(a)(1), this provision contains an exemption for complete liquidations. (See §106(e)(9) of the Technical Corrections Act of 1987, amending §267(a)(1) to preclude its application to both the corporation and its shareholders in a *complete*

this is not the case, however, the result may be an unappetizing combination of taxable ordinary income and capital losses that cannot be used currently, cannot be carried forward because the corporation is terminating, and cannot be carried back because the corporation did not realize any capital gains during the carry-back period allowed by §1212(a)(1).

After §336(a) has imposed its toll on the corporation, the shareholders compute their gain or loss under §331(a) by subtracting the basis of their shares from the fair market value of their respective portions of the liquidating distribution, which amount reflects the corporation's own tax liability. Assuming a corporate tax liability of $500,000, the aggregate amount distributed to the shareholders will be $1.5 million, and if all shareholders realize gains, their aggregate taxable gain will be $1.3 million ($1.5 million received, less adjusted basis of $200,000).

Thus, the complete liquidation produces the same tax result at both the corporate and shareholder levels as that produced by a sale of the assets by the corporation and the corporation's distribution of the proceeds, less its tax liability, to the shareholders.[48] Assuming gains at both levels, §336(a) as amended in 1986 can be viewed as a buttress to the so-called double taxation of corporate earnings;[49] this treatment can be compared with the earlier system of taxing realized gains twice (first, when realized on a sale or other taxable disposition by the corporation, and then when distributed to the shareholders), but taxing unrealized potential gains only at the shareholder level.[50]

This double taxation of unrealized gains under post-1986 law reaches its zenith only if the corporation has a low basis for its assets and the shareholders also have a low basis for their stock. In some situations, the shareholders may realize losses even though the corporation has a gain (e.g., in the case of recently purchased or inherited stock), or vice versa; and it is also possible for losses to be realized at both levels. Gains at both levels are sufficiently frequent, however, to suggest caution in choosing between the corporate and unincorporated forms of doing business. Although corporations can be created tax-free under §351, termination of a corporation's life is another matter. This is especially true if the corporate activities create goodwill, since goodwill value must be taken into account by both the corpora-

---

liquidation.) For the possibility that the allocation principles rules of §1060, enacted in 1986, may be controlling in determining the liquidating corporation's gain or loss, see infra ¶ 11.11, text at note 109.

[48] Under §336(b), the fair market value of property must be treated as equal to any liability to which it is subject or any liability assumed by the shareholders in connection with the distribution; this provision partially overlaps §7701(g), which, however, applies only to nonrecourse debt.

[49] See supra ¶ 1.03.

[50] As noted supra ¶ 7.20, the practice of exempting unrealized gain at the corporate level began with the *General Utilities* case, but was subject to more and more qualifications in later years, supra ¶ 7.22.

tion itself and the shareholders in computing their gain if the corporation liquidates; the result may well be a valuation by the Service that is both high and difficult to disprove. Thus, the warning posed in Chapter 2 that a corporation, like a lobster pot, may be easy to enter but painful to get out of, applies with special force after the 1986 amendments to §336.

2. Losses on distributions to related persons. Recognizing that taxpayers might take advantage of the repeal of the *General Utilities* doctrine "to recognize losses in inappropriate situations or inflate the amount of losses actually sustained,"[51] §336(d)(1) provides for nonrecognition of losses on distributions to related persons (as defined by §267), if (1) the distribution was not pro rata among the shareholders or (2) the property was acquired by the corporation within the preceding five years in a §351 transaction or as a contribution to capital (modes of transfer that are tax-free as respects the transferor and that give the transferee corporation a carry-over basis for the property).

The ban on recognizing a corporate loss when depreciated property is distributed to related persons applies even if the distribution is made on a non-pro rata basis for bona fide business reasons, because, for example, widely divided ownership would make it difficult to deal with the property or would create risks that some of the shareholders do not want to accept. The five-year restriction is also broad: Although the targeted abuse was no doubt the transfer of depreciated property during the tainted five-year period in order to enable a prosperous corporation to deduct a built-in loss that the transferor of the property could not use, §336(d)(1) applies even if the property was worth *more* than its basis when it was transferred to the corporation (so that the decline in value occurred entirely during the period of corporate ownership) and even in the absence of a tax-avoidance purpose. However, if the loss property is sold to an unrelated buyer, §336(d)(1) does not apply, and the loss would thus be allowed.

3. Losses with tax-avoidance purpose. Section 336(d)(2) imposes another restriction on the recognition of losses. This restriction is broader than that of §336(d)(1) in that it applies whether the distributee is a related person or not, but narrower because it applies only to property acquired with a built-in loss and disallows only that amount.

This so-called anti-stuffing rule applies if (1) property was acquired by the corporation with a built-in loss in a §351 transaction or as a contribution to capital and (2) the acquisition of the property was part of a plan, a principal purpose of which was to enable the corporation to claim a loss on a liquidating sale or distribution of the property. Section 336(d)(2) can apply

---

[51] H.R. Conf. Rep. No. 841, 99th Cong., 2d Sess. II-200 (1986). For the general nonapplicability of §267 to complete liquidations, see supra note 47.

no matter how long the interval between the acquisition of the property and its distribution may have been; but if the period is two years or less, a tax-avoidance purpose is presumed unless the regulations provide otherwise. The Conference Report on the Tax Reform Act of 1986 expresses an expectation that the regulations (1) will not apply the two-year presumption unless "there is no clear and substantial relationship between the contributed property and the conduct of the corporation's current or future business enterprises," (2) will permit losses to be recognized on the disposition of any trade or business assets that are contributed to the corporation, and (3) will exempt from disallowance losses on property acquired by a corporation within its first two years of existence. [52]

When applicable, §336(d)(2) prevents recognition of the built-in loss by reducing the property's adjusted basis pro tanto. Thus, if property worth $200 was acquired under §351 with a carry-over basis of $1,000 and is distributed in complete liquidation when it is worth $150, its adjusted basis is reduced to $200 ($1,000, less built-in loss when acquired of $800), and the corporation recognizes loss of only $50 (revised adjusted basis of $200, less value when distributed of $150) (i.e., the portion of the loss that occurred during the corporation's ownership). [53]

4. Tax-free corporate exchanges. Section 336(c) provides that the general gain/loss recognition rule of §336(a) does not supersede the nonrecognition rules of §§351–368, relating to tax-free organizations of corporations under §351, spin-offs and similar transactions under §355, and corporate reorganizations under §§361 and 368. [54] Because the liquidating corporation's basis for the transferred property is not stepped-up in these situations (since the distributees take a substituted basis, as defined by §7701(a)(42), for the property), this exemption only defers recognition of the liquidating corporation's gain or loss rather than insuring that it will never be recognized. Distributions of taxable boot, however, are not protected by §336(c), so that gain (but not loss) will be recognized on the distribution of such property.

---

[52] Id. at II-201. See also Joint Committee Staff General Explanation of the Tax Reform Act of 1986, at 341–344.

[53] If the loss occurred and was deducted in a taxable year preceding the adoption of a plan of complete liquidation, §336(d)(2)(C) permits the Service to recapture the loss pursuant to regulations, in lieu of reopening the earlier year.

[54] See supra ¶ 3.01 (§351 transfers), infra ¶ 13.01 (§355 spin-offs and like reorganizations), and infra ¶ 14.01 (§361 reorganizations); see also §1363(e), supra ¶ 6.08, for a similar rule applicable to S corporations. Note, however, that this exception in §336(c) only applies to the extent that the distribution is tax-free to the recipient; distributions of taxable boot result in recognized gain to the distributing corporation, but losses are denied here by §361(c), infra ¶ 14.32. But see the Technical Corrections Act of 1987, §118(d)(4)(D) (§336(c) amended to merely cross reference to §361(c)(4), which is also amended to render §§336 and 337 inapplicable to reorganization distributions).

5. Parent-subsidiary transactions. Section 332, explained later in this chapter, permits parent corporations to liquidate their subsidiaries on a tax-free basis, but concomitantly requires the parent to take over the subsidiary's basis for the distributed assets; in harmony with this carry-over of the subsidiary's basis for the assets, the subsidiary does not ordinarily recognize gain or loss on §§332 and 334(b) distributions to its parent.[55]

6. Related statutory changes. The rejection of the nonrecognition principle of *General Utilities* would have sent shock waves throughout the corporate-shareholder provisions of the Code had it not been accompanied by a series of changes to reduce or eliminate certain potential statutory inconsistencies. Thus, gain is now recognized, as explained earlier in this work, on nonliquidating distributions of appreciated property, including stock redemptions and partial liquidations.[56] Losses, however, are not recognized on nonliquidating distributions; this residual disparity between nonliquidating and liquidating transactions evidently reflects a fear that the former, having less drastic business and other nontax consequences than the latter, are more likely to be used for the premature recognition of losses or other abuses.

Another important 1986 change, examined later in this chapter,[57] was the repeal of §337, whose function—to ensure that only one tax would be paid if a corporation sold its assets and promptly liquidated—was incompatible with §336(a), as amended in 1986, under which a complete liquidation generates taxable events at both the corporate and shareholder levels.

A similar harmonizing change was the repeal of §333, which had permitted certain corporations to be liquidated without tax at either the corporate or shareholder level.[58]

On the other hand, Congress did not repeal §341, relating to collapsible corporations, although the 1986 rejection of the *General Utilities* doctrine (and concurrent repeal of the capital gain rate differential) destroyed the infrastructure upon which §341 rests.[59]

7. Effective date and grandfather exemptions. Section 336, as amended in 1986, applies to distributions in complete liquidation after July 31, 1986,

---

[55] See infra ¶¶ 11.41 and 11.49 (new §337 now applies to the subsidiary's distributions).

[56] See supra ¶¶ 7.20 and 9.34.

[57] See infra ¶ 11.61.

[58] See infra ¶ 11.62.

[59] See infra ¶ 12.01. The repeal of both corporate and shareholder level capital gain rates can produce a combined tax burden of up to 52.48 percent on a liquidation (34 percent at the corporate level and 18.48 percent for the shareholders).

unless the liquidation is completed by the end of calendar year 1986. This general effective date, however, is subject to three types of grandfather clauses, which preserve the pre-1987 nonrecognition rule for:

(1) Small business corporations satisfying conditions summarized later in this chapter, if they liquidate completely by the end of 1988;[60]

(2) Corporations that took specified action (e.g., adoption of a plan of complete liquidation) before August 1, 1986, if the liquidation was completed by the end of 1987;[61] and

(3) Taxpayers qualifying under so-called targeted grandfather clauses, which identify their beneficiaries by specifying dates of incorporation or other vital statistics that, it was assumed by the drafters, would exclude all but the favored few.[62]

8. Examples. These provisions can be illustrated by the following examples, in which T is an operating company that owns two operating divisions, T-1 and T-2. T's sole shareholder is individual A, and any purchaser of T's assets or stock is corporate buyer, P.

Example 1: T liquidates, distributing all of its T-1 and T-2 properties in kind to A. If both businesses have built-in gains, T will be fully taxable on the distribution as if the assets had been sold at their fair market values for cash. If T sold T-1 and T-2 to P, the gains likewise would be fully recognized to T.

Example 2: If T's businesses in Example 1 had built-in losses instead of gains, the losses also would be recognized on the distribution or sale, subject to the limitations of §§336(d)(1) and 336(d)(2). (Loss would be denied if the assets had not been "aged" for five years in T, or if the tax-avoidance anti-stuffing rule of §336(d)(2) applied.)

Example 3: If T's assets were subject to liabilities in excess of the value of the T-1 and T-2 properties, §336(b) nevertheless mandates a deemed valuation at least equal to the amount of those liabilities assumed or taken subject to by A on the liquidation of T. Whether A is entitled to include the full face amount of those liabilities in his §334(a) basis, however, is unclear.

---

[60] Infra ¶ 11.60.

[61] Tax Reform Act of 1986, Pub. L. No. 99-514, 100 Stat. 2277, §633(c)(1).

[62] Id., §633(c)(2) and two other paragraphs, which were enacted as (e) and (f) but should read (f) and (g).

Example 4: T drops its two divisions into newly organized subsidiaries *S-1* and *S-2*, and distributes the stock of *S-1* and *S-2* to *A* in complete liquidation. If §355 applies, as it should here (see Chapter 13), no gain or loss results to *T* under §336(a) by virtue of §§336(c) and 361(c). If §355 does *not* apply, however, the distribution is taxable to *T* under §336.

Example 5: T merges into *P* for *P* stock and thereby liquidates. No gain or loss results to *T* on either the merger or the liquidation distribution of the *P* stock under §336(c) and §361 (see Chapter 14). No change occurred in the law here in 1986 except in cases where *T* distributes appreciated boot, in which event gain (but not loss) would be recognized to *T* on the distribution.

Example 6: P buys all of the *T* stock and does not elect §338. No tax results to *T* here, even if *T* liquidates upstream into *P* under §332 (as a result of new §337). Note also that if *P* has tax loss carry-overs, it subsequently can sell off parts of the *T* business and shelter any gains recognized with its loss carry-overs (see Chapter 16).

Example 7: T elects S status (see Chapter 6) in early 1987. No currently taxable event occurs to *A* or *T* as a result of this election. Under §1374, as amended in 1986, however, any built-in gains at the date of *T*'s S election will be taxable to *T* if recognized within 10 years of the election.

Additional examples illustrating application of the parent-subsidiary liquidation rules of §§332 and 337 appear at the conclusion of Part B.

¶ 11.07 ASSIGNMENT OF INCOME AND RELATED PROBLEMS FOR LIQUIDATING CORPORATION

1. Introductory. The adoption of a plan of complete liquidation does not terminate the corporation's existence. Under the regulations, death does not occur until the corporation "ceases business and dissolves, retaining no assets."[63] When the liquidating process is protracted, the corporation must

---

[63] Regs. §1.6012-2(a)(2); see also supra ¶¶ 2.09 and 11.02; Rev. Rul. 61-191, 1961-2 CB 251 (corporation may be dissolved de facto even though not dissolved de jure); US v. Joliet & C. R.R. Co., 315 US 44 (1942) (corporate existence continued after perpetual lease of property); Hersloff v. US, 310 F2d 947 (Ct. Cl. 1962), cert. denied, 373 US 923 (1963) (corporate existence preserved by continuing business activities despite technical dissolution); Sigurd N. Hersloff, 46 TC 545 (1966) (acq.).

continue to file tax returns and pay the corporate income tax on its sales, collections, commissions, and other income.[64] If the corporation winds up by selling all of its assets before making a liquidating distribution and terminating its corporate existence, it will have paid its debt to society, and no further tax problems are likely to arise. Frequently, however, some or all of the assets are distributed in kind to the shareholders, especially if a going business is to be continued. Such a midstream liquidation usually involves the transfer of appreciated assets, accounts receivable, claims for services rendered, and other sources of future income, some of which may be associated with expenses deducted by the liquidating corporation in past years.

Before 1987, the statutory provisions governing complete liquidations created a potential escape hatch for the untaxed appreciation in these potential-income items, since the liquidating corporation was not required to recognize gain on the distribution, while §334(a) gave the shareholders a basis for the distributed items equal to their fair market value. As amended in 1986, however, §336(a) requires the liquidating corporation to recognize gain or loss on distributed property as if it were sold to the distributee shareholders for its fair market value.[65] Thus, the pre-1986 escape hatch is closed if and to the extent that the potential income is reflected in the fair market value of the asset at the time of distribution. For example, if previously deducted supplies with a zero basis are distributed in liquidation, their fair market value is includable in the liquidating corporation's income under §336(a), and the same is true if a cash-basis corporation distributes its uncollected accounts receivable for services rendered.

However, the fair market value of a distributed asset may not adequately reflect its capacity to shift income from the liquidating corporation to the distributee shareholder, particularly if the corporation used an accounting method that did not adequately reflect income, or if the item's value is highly contingent. In these unusual situations, a variety of weapons developed by the Service, with judicial support, to close the pre-1987 escape hatch may continue to reach some post-1986 distributions.[66] Accordingly,

---

[64] Estate of Charles Fearon, 16 TC 385 (1951) (acq). (liquidation spread over more than 23 years); Joseph Olmsted, supra note 9 (same).

[65] See generally supra ¶ 11.06.

[66] See the Fourth Edition of this treatise, ¶ 11.62; Pat O'Brien, 25 TC 376 (1955) (acq.) (Service unsuccessful in taxing corporation; predecessor transaction to collapsible corporation provisions, infra ch. 12); see also Lyon & Eustice, Assignment of Income: Fruit and Tree as Irrigated by the P.G. Lake Case, 17 Tax L. Rev. 293 (1962); Eustice, supra note 21, at 51; Weiss, Corporate Contingent Income: A Case of Tax Planning, 12 Tax L. Rev. 73 (1956); Morrison, Assignment of Income and Tax Benefit Principles in Corporate Liquidations, 54 Taxes 902 (1976); Byrne, The Tax Benefit Rule as Applied to Corporate Liquidations and Contributions to Capital: Recent Developments, 56 Notre Dame L. Rev., 215 (1980).

these remedies are described in the paragraphs that follow. It is possible, however, that the courts will be less willing now to apply these remedies than in the past, on the ground that §336(a), as amended in 1986, provides a sufficient remedy to preempt the field except in the most egregious circumstances. Moreover, in a number of the cases cited below, if the post-1986 hypothetical sale requirement of amended §336(a) had been applicable, it would have produced substantially the same result, so that the Service would not have had to invoke these less direct remedies.

2. Anticipatory assignment of income. Corporations cannot escape the corporate income tax by an anticipatory assignment of income to shareholders, even though the assignment takes the form of a complete liquidation. This principle is simply an application of a pervasive doctrine of income tax law under which income is taxed to the one who earns it rather than to the person who happens to collect it. This doctrine is of such breadth and general application that it falls outside the scope of this treatise. An illustration of its use in the context of a complete liquidation is *J. Ungar, Inc. v. CIR*, in which a corporation was taxed on commissions for services performed by it, although the amounts in question were collected by a shareholder after the corporation's assets were distributed to him in complete liquidation.[67]

3. Clear reflection of income under §446(b). As a general rule, taxable income is computed under the accounting method regularly employed by the taxpayer; but the Service, under §446(b), may compel use of another method if the taxpayer's method does not clearly reflect income. A method of accounting that would clearly be permissible for a continuing business may not properly reflect income where the corporate taxpayer liquidates in midstream. For example, in the well-known *Jud Plumbing* and *Standard Paving* cases, construction companies using the completed-contract method of reporting income liquidated before certain construction contracts were fully completed, and they were in effect required to shift from the completed-

---

[67] J. Ungar, Inc. v. CIR, 244 F2d 90 (2d Cir. 1957); see also Williamson v. US, 292 F2d 524 (Ct. Cl. 1961) (cash-basis corporation taxed on accounts receivable for previously rendered services); Wood Harmon Corp. v. US, 311 F2d 918 (2d Cir. 1963) (condemnation award, liquidated in amount and paid after distribution to shareholders, taxable to corporation). For the relationship between the date of liquidation and the date the income is paid by the obligor, see Sol C. Siegel Prod., Inc., 46 TC 15 (1966) (acq.) (cash-basis corporation not taxed in year of distribution where it did not liquidate until a year later and payments were received by shareholders in subsequent year); see also Siegel v. US, 464 F2d 891 (9th Cir. 1972), cert. dismissed pursuant to agreement, 410 US 918 (1972); Shea Co., supra note 24 (contingent income claims not accruable); Judith Schneider, supra note 25.

contract method (under which income would not be recognized until the work was finished) to the percentage-of-completion method of reporting income.[68]

4. Effect of §482. In some pre-1987 cases, the Service relied on §482, permitting income and deductions to be reallocated among related businesses under common control, as a ground for requiring a liquidating corporation to report income realized in form by the distributees of the corporation's assets. This approach obviously has much in common with the assignment of income doctrine.[69]

5. Contingent or inchoate income items and the problem of corporate existence. Under pre-1987 law, a corporate level tax was sometimes avoided when a corporation in the process of complete liquidation distributed items of potential income that were too contingent to constitute current income under any ordinary accounting method. In a number of such cases, the courts refused to apply the assignment of income doctrine because the corporation either had not earned the potential income at the time of distribution or was not in existence at the later time when the uncertain income matured and became definite.[70]

Where corporate existence continues, however, the liquidating corporation may be taxed if it is found to have earned the income in question.[71] On the meaning of corporate existence, the regulations have long provided substantially as they do now:

---

[68] Jud Plumbing & Heating, Inc. v. CIR, 153 F2d 681 (5th Cir. 1946); Standard Paving Co. v. CIR, 190 F2d 330 (10th Cir. 1951), cert. denied, 342 US 860; see also CIR v. Kuckenberg, 309 F2d 202 (9th Cir. 1962) (cash-basis construction company required to accrue income on completed contracts); Susan J. Carter, 9 TC 364, 373 (1947) (acq.), aff'd on another issue, 170 F2d 911 (2d Cir. 1948) (brokerage contracts); Idaho First Nat'l Bank v. US, 265 F2d 6 (9th Cir. 1959) (accrued interest taxed to liquidating cash-basis bank); Storz v. CIR, 583 F2d 972 (8th Cir. 1978) (income earned for §61 purposes, even though not accruable); Judith Schneider, supra note 25 (part of income not accruable, part accruable); Louis S. Rotolo, 88 TC No. 85 (1987).

[69] See Jud Plumbing & Heating, Inc. v. CIR, supra note 68; General Elec. Co. v. US, 3 Ct. Cl. 289 (Cl. Ct. 1983); for §482, see generally infra ¶ 15.03.

[70] See Cold Metal Process Co. v. CIR, 247 F2d 864 (6th Cir. 1952) (income not earned); Shea Co., supra note 24 (income not accruable because contingent); see also Sigurd N. Hersloff, supra note 63 (corporate existence held to have terminated for the years in issue); Judith Schneider, supra note 25 and cases there cited.

[71] See J. Ungar, Inc. v. CIR, supra note 67; Wood Harmon Corp. v. US, supra note 67; Hersloff v. US, supra note 63; Sol C. Siegel Prod., Inc., supra note 67; Storz v. CIR, supra note 68.

Existence of corporation. A corporation in existence during any portion of a taxable year is required to make a return. If a corporation was not in existence throughout an annual accounting period (either calendar year or fiscal year), the corporation is required to make a return for that fractional part of a year during which it was in existence. A corporation is not in existence after it ceases business and dissolves, retaining no assets, whether or not under state law it may thereafter be treated as continuing as a corporation for certain limited purposes connected with winding up its affairs such as for the purpose of suing and being sued. If the corporation has valuable claims for which it will bring suit during this period, it has retained assets and therefore continues in existence. A corporation does not go out of existence if it is turned over to receivers or trustees who continue to operate it.[72]

6. Section 336(a) and the tax-benefit doctrine. If a liquidating corporation distributes assets that generated business deductions when acquired but that have not been fully consumed or amortized, the distribution raises the question whether the corporation must give back the prior tax benefits. Examples of such items include amounts paid for tools and supplies that were deducted rather than capitalized and the expenses of raising an agricultural crop that has not yet been harvested when the corporation liquidates. Deductions for additions to the corporation's bad debt reserves create a similar problem if the reserve is excessive at liquidation. Still other examples are amounts received by the corporation but not includable in gross income, such as customer deposits, overcharges held for refund, and prepaid subscription income, that are still held in suspense when the corporation liquidates.

Under the hypothetical sale approach of amended §336(a), some of these items (e.g., unconsumed supplies) generate corporate gain equal to the excess of their value over their basis. If, however, this excess is less than the amount deducted (because the value of the deducted item has declined), it may be that the amount not taxed by §336(a) will be taxed to the liquidating corporation by virtue of the tax benefit doctrine. In this connection, it should be noted that in 1983 the Supreme Court applied the tax benefit doctrine to a liquidating corporation's distribution of unconsumed but previously deducted supplies, even though the corporation did not recover anything in a technical sense.[73] In reaching this result, the Court held that the

---

[72] Regs. §1.6012-2(a)(2). See generally Shea Co., supra note 24, and cases cited supra notes 70 and 71.

[73] Hillsboro Nat'l Bank v. CIR, 460 US 370 (1983) (extensive analysis; divided court); the tax benefit issue arose in US v. Bliss Dairy, Inc., which was decided at the same time as, and under the caption of, the *Hillsboro Bank* case. See also Carlton L. Byrd, 87 TC 830 (1986); E.W. Gorton, ¶ 85,045 P-H Memo. TC (1985). See generally Blum, The Role of the Supreme Court in Federal Tax Controversies—*Hillsboro National Bank* and *Bliss Dairy, Inc.*, 61 Taxes 363 (1983); Cartano, The Tax Benefit Rule in Corporate Liquidations, 10 J. Corp. Tax'n 216 (1983).

tax benefit doctrine reaches an "event" if it is "fundamentally inconsistent with the premise on which the deduction was initially based."[74] The fundamentally inconsistent event in this situation is the corporate liquidation, since if it had occurred in the year in which the supplies were purchased, they could not have been deducted except to the extent actually used in that year; the excess would not have been properly allocable to the conduct of the corporation's trade or business.

Some of the other items mentioned earlier (e.g., customer deposits and overcharges held for refund) would not be candidates for the tax benefit doctrine, since they did not generate any deductions but were instead excluded from income because offset by liabilities. If and to the extent that the offsetting liabilities will continue after the liquidation, these items affect the fair market value of the distributed assets and hence should be taken into account in computing the corporation's gain on the hypothetical sale mandated by §336(a). If, however, the offsetting liabilities have become excessive (e.g., because it is reasonably clear that some former customers will never claim their deposits or overcharges), the excess ought to be included in the liquidating corporation's income because the earlier exclusion was based on the assumption that the corporation would be taxed in due course if the offsetting liability evaporated.

7. Imputation of shareholder sales to liquidating corporation. Finally, attention must be given to a common phenomenon that has generated an extraordinary body of judge-made and statutory law: the liquidation of a corporation in conjunction with a sale of its assets if the corporation's assets are worth substantially more than their basis in the hands of the corporation and its stock is similarly worth substantially more than its basis in the hands of the shareholders. If the corporation sells the assets, its gain is subject to a tax at the corporate level, and the liquidating distribution (the sales pro-

---

For the principal pre-1983 case, now rejected, holding that a "recovery" was essential to application of the tax benefit doctrine, see CIR v. South Lake Farms, Inc., 324 F2d 837 (9th Cir. 1963). But see also Louis S. Rotolo, supra note 68.

[74] Hillsboro Nat'l Bank v. CIR, supra note 73, at 383. In Rev. Rul. 85-186, 1985-2 CB 84, the Service ruled that under *Hillsboro*, a *sale* of technology created by expenditures that had been deducted under §174 did not trigger recapture of the deductions, because the legislative history of §174 indicated that Congress recognized that the deductions might produce an asset with a long-term value. Under §336(a), a *distribution* of zero-basis technology would require the recognition of gain measured by its fair market value, but if the amount deducted were greater than the technology's value when distributed, the rationale of Rev. Rul. 85-186 would evidently excuse the corporation from including the excess in income. See also Louis S. Rotolo, supra note 68 (shareholders' new basis under §334 for distributed inventory not inconsistent with allowing corporation to set off costs against associated income triggered by the liquidation).

ceeds, less the corporation's tax and other liabilities) is subject to a second tax at the shareholder level. On the other hand, before 1987 if the assets were distributed in liquidation to the shareholders and sold by them, the only tax was imposed on the shareholders; there was no corporate-level tax because, as explained earlier in this chapter, the pre-1987 version of §336(a) provided (with minor exceptions) that gain was not recognized by a corporation on a liquidating distribution of its assets in complete liquidation.[75]

This distribute-first method of avoiding a corporate level tax suffered from a serious practical deficiency: The shareholders had to pay the shareholder level tax even if they could not find a buyer for the assets at an acceptable price. It was not unusual, therefore, for the corporate officers to put the assets on the market, negotiate with buyers, and, on reaching an agreement on the terms of a sale, arrange for a liquidating distribution of the assets to the shareholders just before the closing so that the sale was made, at least in form, by the shareholders. In 1945, however, the Supreme Court held in *CIR v. Court Holding Co.* that the Tax Court had properly taxed the corporation on the gain from such a last-minute purported sale by its shareholders:

> The incidence of taxation depends upon the substance of a transaction. The tax consequences which arise from gains from a sale of property are not finally to be determined solely by the means employed to transfer legal title. Rather, the transaction must be viewed as a whole, and each step, from the commencement of negotiations to the consummation of the sale, is relevant. A sale by one person cannot be transformed for tax purposes into a sale by another by using the latter as a conduit through which to pass title.[76]

Five years later, however, in *US v. Cumberland Public Service Co.,* the Supreme Court upheld a Court of Claims decision that refused to attribute a shareholder sale of the assets to the corporation where the shareholders had first attempted to sell their stock to the buyer and then offered to liquidate the corporation and sell the assets.[77] *Court Holding Co.* was distinguished because the Tax Court had found in that case "that the corporation never really abandoned its sales negotiations, that it never did dissolve, and that the sole purpose of the so-called liquidation was to disguise a corporate sale through use of mere formalisms."[78]

---

[75] Supra ¶ 11.06.

[76] CIR v. Court Holding Co., 324 US 331, 334 (1945).

[77] US v. Cumberland Pub. Serv. Co., 338 US 451 (1950).

[78] Id. at 454. Although the corporation in the *Court Holding Co.* case did not dissolve, it seems unlikely that such action would have altered the Tax Court's conclusion that the sale was in substance made by the corporation rather than by the

In distinguishing the facts of these two cases, the Supreme Court acknowledged that "the distinction between sales by a corporation as compared with distributions in kind followed by shareholder sales may be particularly shadowy and artificial when the corporation is closely held".[79] This led Congress, in 1954, to enact old §337, which ordinarily eliminated a tax at the corporate level on liquidation-sale transactions, whether the sale was made directly by the corporation or was imputed to it under the *Court Holding Co.* doctrine.[80] After 32 years of faithful service, however, old §337 was repealed because its elimination of the corporate level tax was inconsistent with a fundamental feature of the corporate provisions of the Tax Reform Act of 1986 (i.e., the recognition of corporate gain or loss on liquidating distributions).[81] This legislative decision, embodied in the current version of §336(a),[82] in effect renders both *Court Holding Co.* and *Cumberland Public Service* virtually obsolete in the area of their birth, since appreciated corporate assets now trigger the recognition of gain at the corporate level whether they are distributed to the shareholders and sold by them or are sold by the corporation itself.[83]

It is possible, however, that the *Court Holding Co.* case will continue to play a marginal role in the liquidation-sale area if a sale negotiated by a corporation is called off at the last minute in favor of a distribution and the shareholders then manage to sell the assets for more than their fair market value at the time of the distribution (i.e., the amount used in computing gain under §336(a)).[84] If the additional gain realized by the shareholders in this situation can be imputed back to the corporation on a finding that the shareholders are merely a conduit for the corporation in effecting the sale, then it follows that the *Cumberland Public Service Co.* case is of continuing importance as well, since it points the way to a true sharcholder sale when the facts

---

shareholders; moreover, as noted earlier, a complete liquidation for tax purposes can occur without a dissolution under state law; see supra ¶ 11.02, text following note 9.

[79] US v. Cumberland Pub. Serv. Co., supra note 77, at 454–455.

[80] For old §337 (so-called because, upon its repeal in 1986, it was replaced by a provision with the same number but covering a different subject matter), see infra ¶ 11.61.

[81] See supra ¶ 11.06. For a transitional exemption to the repeal of old §337, applicable to certain small business corporations that completely liquidate in 1987 or 1988, see infra ¶¶ 11.60 and 11.61.

[82] For §336(a), see supra ¶ 11.06.

[83] The *Court Holding Co.* doctrine, however, has worked its way into the tax law as a principle of general importance; the case is sometimes cited as an independent force, at other times as an example of the form over substance or assignment of income principle.

[84] For the possibility of imputing additional gain to the corporation in this situation, see supra ¶ 11.05, text at notes 41 and 42.

are slightly different. This in turn means that the "shadowy and artificial" distinction between corporate and shareholder sales that was eliminated for 32 years by old §337 may have been revived, albeit in severely limited circumstances, by the Tax Reform Act of 1986.

¶ 11.08　THE LIQUIDATING CORPORATION'S DEDUCTIONS

Just as the process of liquidation creates a number of problems in determining the liquidating corporation's income, so it has ramifications in the area of corporate deductions. The principal issues are (1) whether any adjustment is required with respect to expenditures that would ordinarily be deductible, if the corporation liquidates before the economic benefit of the expenditures has been fully reflected in its income stream; (2) conversely, whether expenditures that were not fully deducted in past years because they were expected to have a continuing economic benefit can be deducted when the fact of liquidation terminates their usefulness; and (3) whether the expenses of effecting the liquidation itself can be deducted by the corporation and/or its shareholders.

1. Adjustment for expenditures with continuing economic benefit. As noted previously, the Service has endeavored to require a corporation liquidating in midstream to report its potential income by invoking assignment of income principles, §446(b) (requiring that the taxpayer's accounting method must clearly reflect income), and the tax benefit doctrine, and—with less success—by disallowing as deductions to the liquidating corporation those expenses that are attributable to its unreported potential income items, on the ground that they are not ordinary and necessary expenses of carrying on a trade or business.[85]

A related development is the attempt of the Service to apportion or allocate expenses incurred during the corporation's final tax period (if related to property distributed in kind to its shareholders) between the corporation and the shareholders, under the "clear reflection-of-income" language of §§446(b) and 482. For example, Rev. Rul. 62-45[86] holds that real estate taxes for the year of liquidation must be apportioned on a pro rata basis between the liquidating corporation and its distributee shareholders by virtue of §482, a result that is explicitly required by §164(d) if the property is sold. This approach was upheld in *Tennessee Life Insurance Co. v. Phinney;*

---

[85] Supra ¶ 11.07.

[86] Rev. Rul. 62-45, 1962-1 CB 27.

but in *Simon J. Murphy Co. v. CIR*, the liquidating corporation was allowed to deduct such taxes without apportionment.[87]

It is difficult to determine the extent to which deductions can be apportioned between the corporation and its shareholders under §482 on a distribution in kind or limited on a pro rata basis under §446(b) on a sale of the property for whose benefit the expenditure was incurred. Deductions that accrue ratably over a fixed period of time (such as interest, rent, property taxes, and the like) probably should be prorated to the date when the liquidating corporation's assets are distributed or sold, at least if the corporation uses the accrual method of accounting. This approach is somewhat less appropriate for cash-basis taxpayers, who can ordinarily deduct their expenses when paid. Proration may be appropriate even for cash-basis taxpayers, however, if the expenditure creates a benefit beyond the year of payment, since this would merely reflect the fact that the liquidating corporation has not sustained the entire burden of these expenses, having terminated its operations prior to completion of the period to which they relate.

2. Unamortized deferred deductions. Different considerations may apply, however, when the corporation has previously capitalized long-term expenses (such as prepaid rent, insurance premiums, or supplies) and is amortizing these items over the period to which they relate. In practice, these deferred expense items may be reflected on the corporate books as assets, although from a tax viewpoint it is more accurate to view them as deferred deductions. If the unexpired benefits of these expenditures inure to the benefit of the shareholders on a distribution in kind or to the purchaser on the sale of a going business, the unamortized cost should not be deductible by the transferor corporation, since it has been transferred as part of the assets. If, however, the unused benefits from such expenditures expire with the taxpayer's liquidation (e.g., if the taxpayer's leases or insurance policies are canceled without refund of the prepaid rent or premiums), deductions should be allowed for the unamortized portions of these expenses in the liquidating corporation's final return. In effect, this is the taxpayer's last chance to take account of the previous expenditure of funds for these items, which it was

---

[87] Tennessee Life Ins. Co. v. Phinney, 280 F2d 38 (5th Cir.), cert. denied, 364 US 914 (1960); Simon J. Murphy Co. v. CIR, 231 F2d 639 (6th Cir. 1956); see also Winer v. CIR, 371 F2d 684 (1st Cir. 1967); Bird Management, Inc., 48 TC 586 (1967); Tennessee Carolina Transp., Inc., 582 F2d 378 (6th Cir. 1978) (tax benefit recapture of previously expensed costs, measured by lower of fair market value at liquidation or portion of amount deducted attributable to remaining useful life); Rev. Rul. 78-278, 1978-2 CB 134. But see Louis S. Rotolo, supra note 68 (inventory costs allowed as offset against related income triggered by liquidation).

required to defer over a ratable period of time, but which nevertheless constituted a cost of doing business.

This principle was applied to corporate organizational expenses and similar items by *Koppers Co. v. US* on the ground that the corporation on liquidation "lost or abandoned something for which it had paid."[88] The liquidation antedated the enactment of §248, permitting the corporation to amortize such expenses over a 60-month period, but the principle is equally applicable if the corporation elects not to amortize or elects to do so but liquidates before the amortization period expires.[89] On the other hand, the liquidating corporation is not allowed to deduct the expenses incurred earlier on issuing its capital stock or stock dividends (e.g., legal fees, printing costs, and underwriters' commissions), although a retirement of its bonds or other debts at the time of liquidation entitles it to deduct any previously unamortized discount or a premium paid on a premature retirement.[90]

3. Liquidation expenses. The cost of preparing and effectuating a plan of complete liquidation and dissolution was held deductible in an early decision by the Board of Tax Appeals on the ground that the winding up is directly connected with the conduct of the business itself and is "in the nature of a final accounting of the results of the [corporation's] business rendered to its stockholders and the state."[91] If the liquidation transaction is part of a tax-free merger or other reorganization of the disappearing corporation, however, only the costs properly allocable to the liquidation aspect of

---

[88] Koppers Co. v. US, 278 F2d 946 (Ct. Cl. 1960); see also Louis Rotolo, supra note 68.

[89] For §248, see supra ¶ 5.06. See also Hollywood Baseball Ass'n, 42 TC 234 (1964), vacated 383 US 824 (1966) (deduction allowed for promotional shares issued for organization services); Frank J. Longo, supra note 19 (corportion allowed deduction for abandonment of goodwill on liquidation where business was not continued by shareholders). Compare George C. Carlson, ¶ 67,116 P-H Memo. TC (1967) (unamortized portion of expenses not deductible because of continuing benefit to distributee shareholder). It may be necessary to decide whether the corporation has been liquidated or merged, since in the latter case a deduction may be disallowed because the expenses inure to the benefit of a successor corporation and will be deductible only when the latter is liquidated. See Kingsford Corp., 41 TC 646 (1964) (acq.).

[90] See supra ¶¶ 5.04 and 5.06; see also Rev. Rul. 86-67, 1986-1 CB 238 (unamortized loan costs deductible in year debtor's existence terminates).

[91] Pacific Coast Biscuit Co., 32 BTA 39, 43 (1935) (acq.); see also Koppers Co. v. US, supra note 88 (§332 liquidation); Pridemark, Inc. v. CIR, 345 F2d 35 (4th Cir. 1965) (§337); Gravois Planing Mill Co. v. CIR, 299 F2d 199 (8th Cir. 1962), and cases there cited (partial liquidation); Connery v. US, 460 F2d 1130 (3d Cir. 1972) (complete liquidation); Rev. Rul. 77-204, 1977-1 CB 40 (expenses of bankruptcy liquidation deductible). These cases may be reinforced by the hypothetical sale approach of §336(a), as amended in 1986, treating the liquidating distribution as if the property had been sold for its fair market value.

the transaction are deductible.[92] Moreover, expenses related to sales of property by the liquidating corporation should be treated as selling expenses, which offset the proceeds received on the sale even though occurring in a liquidation context.[93]

Corporate expenses incurred in effecting a partial liquidation or similar contraction of the corporate enterprise have caused more difficulty. The more recent decisions, however, have shown a tendency to allow the deduction for those costs shown to be attributable to the partial liquidation feature of the transaction, as opposed to expenses attributable to a change in the corporate structure.[94] Accurate recordkeeping and itemized professional bills are essential to separate the deductible costs attributable to the partial liquidation feature of the transaction from the costs that are attributable to the nondeductible capital structure adjustment.

According to Rev. Rul. 67-125,[95] corporate expenses attributable to distributions in redemption of stock under §302 (which do not constitute a partial liquidation) are nondeductible capital structure adjustment expenditures. The distinction between a partial liquidation and a §302 stock redemption (see Chapter 9) as the touchstone for deductibility is dubious and contrary to the spirit, if not the holding, of *General Bancshares*[96] and other decisions allowing a deduction for similar expenses that did not add anything of value to the corporation's capital structure. As the court noted in *General Bancshares*, the distribution did not result in the creation of additional corporate rights or assets, nor did it add anything of value to its corporate structure. Instead, what was achieved by the distribution was a pro tanto contraction in the value of its shares. This language seems equally applicable to a §302 stock redemption distribution, or, for that matter, to an ordinary dividend distribution, whether of cash or property.

---

[92] See generally authorities cited supra ¶¶ 5.04 and 5.06; Kingsford Corp., supra note 89; Carruthers, How to Treat the Expenses of Organization, Reorganization, and Liquidation, 24 NYU Inst. on Fed. Tax'n 1055 (1966); Maier, Deductibility of Expenses Incurred in Corporate Reorganization and Liquidations, 20 S. Cal. Tax Inst. 253 (1968).

[93] See Page v. CIR, 524 F2d 1149 (9th Cir. 1975); Benedict Oil Co. v. US, 582 F2d 544 (10th Cir. 1978), and cases there cited.

[94] See Gravois Planing Mill Co. v. CIR, supra note 91 (dominant aspect of transaction a partial liquidation, not a recapitalization; expenses deductible); US v. General Bancshares Corp., 388 F2d 184 (8th Cir. 1968) (expenses of divesting unwanted nonbanking assets deductible as partial liquidation expenses, even though divestiture tax-free; expenses of changing corporate structure not deductible); US v. Transamerica Corp., 392 F2d 522 (9th Cir. 1968); du Pont de Nemours & Co. v. US, 432 F2d 1052 (3d Cir. 1970); Bilar Tool & Die Corp. v. CIR, 530 F2d 708 (6th Cir. 1976); El Paso Co. v. US, 694 F2d 703 (Fed. Cir. 1982) (§355 divesture expenses deductible).

[95] Rev. Rul. 67-125, 1967-1 CB 31.

[96] US v. General Bancshares Corp., supra note 94.

Shareholder expenses incurred in effecting a partial or complete liquidation of their corporation ordinarily constitute capital expenditures, which enter into the computation of gain or loss arising from the distribution,[97] although curiosities can be found even here.[98] Expenses of resisting liquidation, however, may be allowed as a deduction under §212(2) as an expense for the conservation of income-producing property.[99] Finally, the possibility of deducting under §212(3) any professional fees attributable to advice regarding the tax consequences of the transaction should not be overlooked.[100]

¶ 11.09 THE LIQUIDATING CORPORATION'S INDEBTEDNESS

The indebtedness of a liquidating corporation must either be paid off before the final distribution of its assets to shareholders or assumed by them or by some other person (e.g., a purchaser of its assets); failing a formal arrangement for a discharge or assumption of the debt, the shareholders are liable as transferees. Payment of the debt may generate a deduction for unamortized discount or a retirement premium; if appreciated or depreciated property is used instead of cash, the corporation will realize gain or loss under familiar principles.[101]

If the corporation's debt is assumed by a purchaser of the assets instead of being paid off, the amount thereof is taken into account in computing the gain or loss realized by the corporation on the sale. Although an assumption

---

[97] See, e.g., Rev. Rul. 67-411, 1967-2 CB 124; Third Nat'l Bank in Nashville v. US, 427 F2d 343 (6th Cir. 1970); Helgerson v. US, 426 F2d 1293 (8th Cir. 1970); Estate of McGlothlin v. CIR, 370 F2d 729 (5th Cir. 1967); Gerli & Co., 73 TC 1019 (1980), rev'd on another issue, 668 F2d 691 (2d Cir. 1982) (parent's expenses on obtaining §367 ruling for liquidating of foreign subsidiary, held capital); supra ¶ 5.06.

[98] See CIR V. Doering, supra note 24 (shareholder's expense of collecting a contingent corporate claim distributed in liquidation held deductible); Estate of Meade v. CIR, 489 F2d 161 (5th Cir.), cert. denied, 419 US 882 (1974) (contra).

[99] See Allied Chem. Corp. v. US, 305 F2d 433 (Ct. Cl. 1962) (stockholder's expenses in opposing Securities and Exchange Commission proceedings to dissolve corporation allowed as §162 business expense).

[100] See Kaufmann v. US, 227 F. Supp. 807 (W.D. Mo. 1963); see also Sharples v. US, 533 F2d 550 (Ct. Cl. 1976) (costs of tax contest deductible under §212(3) even though claim arose in context of complete liquidation). But see Gerli & Co., supra note 97.

[101] See supra ¶¶ 5.04 and 5.06. For the debt cancellation rules of §108, see supra ¶ 4.25, infra ¶ 14.58; Rev. Rul. 70-271, 1970-1 CB 166. See generally Eustice, Cancellation of Indebtedness and the Federal Income Tax: A Problem of Creeping Confusion, 14 Tax L. Rev. 225 (1959).

of corporate debt by the shareholders on a distribution of assets to them might have the legal effect of a discharge of the corporation's liability and thus might be regarded as a transfer pro tanto by the corporation of appreciated or depreciated property in payment of its debt, it is highly unlikely that this theory would be advanced by the Service or entertained by the courts. The transfer of assets by a liquidating corporation to its shareholders, under an agreement by which they assume its liabilities, is so customary that it is reasonable to regard it as a "distribution of property in complete liquidation" within the meaning of §336(a), both as amended in 1986 and as it existed previously.

Moreover, §336(b), as amended in 1986, provides that the value of property distributed in a liquidation must be treated as not less than any liability to which it is subject or any liability assumed by the shareholders in connection with the distribution (a provision that partially overlaps §7701(g), although §7701(g) applies only to nonrecourse debt). For example, if a corporation's assets are worth $80 and are subject to liabilities of $100, on distributing that property to its shareholders in a liquidation, the corporation will be treated as having sold the assets for $100 under §336(b), the amount of the debt; presumably, the shareholders should also be entitled to a $100 basis for the property under §334(a), although an $80 fair market value basis is more compatible with the statutory language.

¶ 11.10 EARNINGS AND PROFITS OF THE LIQUIDATING CORPORATION

In an ordinary complete liquidation, to which the general rule of §331(a) applies, it is not necessary to determine the effect of liquidation on the corporation's earnings and profits because the corporation has no successor and its earnings and profits do not affect the shareholder's tax on the liquidation. This is true even though any gain or loss recognized under §336(a), as amended in 1986, results in a pro tanto increase or decrease in earnings and profits.

When a subsidiary corporation is liquidated under §332, however, its earnings and profits must be determined because they are inherited by the parent corporation under §§381(a)(1) and 381(c)(2).[102] A liquidating corporation's earnings and profits can also be relevant if the corporation is subject to the alternative minimum tax book income or adjusted current earnings tax preferences, or to the controlled foreign corporation, foreign investment company, or passive foreign investment company provisions. In the latter

---

[102] For §332, see generally infra ¶ 11.40; for §381, see infra ¶ 16.10; see also Nesson, Earnings and Profits Discontinuities Under the 1954 Code, 77 Harv. L. Rev. 450 (1964).

three cases, the shareholder's gain may be taxed as ordinary income rather than capital gain to the extent of his ratable share of the corporation's post-1962 earnings and profits; alternatively, the shareholder may be charged with interest for the deferral of tax with respect to undistributed earnings. [103]

¶ 11.11　ASSET ACQUISITIONS: ALLOCATION OF PURCHASE PRICE IN COMPUTING BASIS

When an acquiring corporation purchases the stock of a target company, whether in a negotiated transaction or a hostile tender offer, its basis for the target's stock under §1012 is ordinarily the amount paid for the stock, regardless of the target's so-called "inside basis" (i.e., its basis for its assets), and the assets retain their basis even if the target distributes them to the new parent in complete liquidation. [104]

Instead of purchasing the target company's stock, however, the acquiring corporation sometimes purchases its assets, especially in the case of a closely held company. For the acquiring corporation, this alternative to a purchase of stock can reduce or even eliminate the business risk of subordination to unrecorded liens and undisclosed liabilities against the target company. While it is true that these risks can sometimes be minimized if the seller is willing to have its representations survive the closing, to guarantee the balance sheet and schedule of liabilities, or to put part of the purchase price into escrow pending the settlement of liabilities, the buyer often prefers to sidestep such devices by simply purchasing the assets. This mode of acquisition also ordinarily makes it easier to exclude unwanted assets from the transaction.

If an asset acquisition involves the payment of an agreed amount for all of the acquired assets rather than a separately bargained-for payment for each asset, both the seller and the buyer must allocate the lump sum among the transferred items. The seller must do this to compute separately its long-term and short-term capital gains and losses and its ordinary income and losses, [105] although the resulting separate results are now less consequential

---

[103] See infra ¶¶ 17.24, 17.25, and 17.34; for the alternative minimum tax impact, see supra ¶ 5.08. Note that grandfathered §337 nonrecognition sales, infra ¶ 11.61, still are subject to AMT rules under §56(f) or §56(g). But see Rev. Rul. 76-239, 1976-1 CB 90 (tax-free §337 gain did not increase earnings and profits).

[104] See generally infra ¶¶ 11.40 and 11.44. For elections under §338, which result in a step-up of the subsidiary's basis to the amount paid by the acquiring corporation for the subsidiary's stock, see infra ¶ 11.46.

[105] See Williams v. McGowan, 152 F2d 570 (2d Cir. 1945) (seller must allocate lump sum consideration; going business is not a single asset but a bundle of assets that must be disaggregated in computing gains and losses).

than they were before the 1986 repeal of the rate differential for long-term capital gains. The buyer must also allocate the amount paid in order to compute its capital gain or loss and ordinary income or loss when the acquired items are disposed of, as well as to compute its depreciation, amortization, and other allowances in the interim.

As a general rule, the tax interests of the seller and buyer in allocating a lump sum among a mixed bag of assets are adverse. The seller ordinarily wants to allocate as much as possible to long-term capital assets, such as goodwill and land, while the buyer prefers a small allocation for these nondepreciable assets; conversely, the seller prefers a low valuation for inventory, since inventory profits constitute ordinary income, while the buyer prefers a high value to reduce its income from future sales. In the absence of an agreed allocation, the self-interest of the parties stimulates inconsistent allocations that can leave the Service with the short end of two sticks. If, however, the parties have agreed on an allocation, the Service and the courts have been disposed to accept it on the theory that the tax polarity between buyer and seller insures that the agreed-upon values are reasonable and also because the resulting consistency protects the Service against being whipsawed.[106]

The legal context for the allocation of the purchase price of assets constituting a trade or business was changed in 1986 by the enactment of §1060, which prescribes statutory allocation rules if the transferee's basis in the assets is determined wholly by reference to the consideration paid for the assets (as distinguished, for example, from an acquisition in a nonrecognition transaction resulting in a substituted basis for the acquired assets). When §1060 applies, it has three results:

(1) The consideration received by the transferor must be allocated among the assets in the manner prescribed by §338(b)(5), which employs a hierarchical system that uses the residual method of valuing goodwill and going concern value;[107]

(2) The resulting allocation is controlling in determining both the transferee's basis for the assets and the transferor's gain or loss on the transfer; and

---

[106] See Ronald G. Landry, 86 TC 1284 (1986), and cases there cited; see also CIR v. Danielson, 378 F2d 771 (3d Cir. 1967) (strong proof required when one party seeks to set aside agreed allocation).

For deficiencies in the tax polarity theory, see Bittker, Federal Taxation of Income, Estates and Gifts (Warren, Gorham & Lamont, Inc., 1981), ¶ 4.4.4. See generally Rogers, Purchase Price Allocations in Taxable Acquisitions: New Frontiers—New Hazards, 62 Taxes 813 (1984); Fowler, Intangible Assets—Purchase Price Allocation and Amortization Deductions, 44 NYU Inst. on Fed. Tax'n ch. 28 (1986).

[107] For §338(b)(5), see infra ¶¶ 11.46 and ¶ 11.48. See generally Banc One Corp., 84 TC 476 (1985). For §1060, see Unger, Gain Recognition and Basis in Acquisitions, 45 NYU Inst. on Fed. Tax'n ch. 3 (1987).

(3) The Service is authorized to require the transferor and transferee to report the amount allocated to goodwill or going concern value and to supply other information specified by regulations.

The terse language of §1060 is augmented on two points by the relevant legislative committee report, which states that (1) a group of assets constitutes a business for §1060 purposes "if their character is such that goodwill or going concern value could under any circumstances attach to such assets" and (2) §1060 is not intended to restrict the Service's ability to challenge taxpayer determinations of fair market value by any appropriate method, such as an independent showing of the value of goodwill, in order to call into question the taxpayer's valuation of other assets.[108]

It remains to be seen whether §1060 will substantially change the status quo, particularly given the tendency of the Service and the courts to accept agreed allocations. If such an allocation is reported and adhered to by both the seller and the buyer, the objectives of §1060 will ordinarily have been served; and it may well be that agreements will usually be accepted by the Service, as in the past, because its audit facilities are stretched to the limit by other enforcement responsibilities.

Another question for the future is whether §1060 applies to transfers of assets by a liquidating corporation to its shareholders. Its language can be construed to encompass such a transfer, provided the assets constitute a trade or business, since the transferee-shareholder's basis for the assets under §334(a) is their fair market value, which is identical with the value of the "consideration [i.e., the stock surrendered] paid for such assets," as required by §1060(c)(2). Moreover, §336(a), as amended in 1986, requires the distributing corporation to recognize gain or loss "as if such property were sold to the distributee at its fair market value,"[109] an event that would bring §1060 into play. Finally, consistency in computing the distributing corporation's gain or loss and the distributee shareholders' basis for the assets, notice to the Service of the amount assigned to goodwill and going concern value, and use of the residual method of determining the value of these intangibles seem as appropriate for liquidating distributions as for actual sales. Nonetheless, it is unlikely that §1060 was drafted with liquidating distributions in mind.

---

[108] H.R. Conf. Rep. No. 841, 99th Cong., 2d Sess. II-208 (1986). See also S. Rep. No. 313, 99th Cong., 2d Sess. 251 (1986), for a more extensive explanation of §1060 (and the reasons for its proposed enactment), and Joint Comm. Staff General Explanation of the Tax Reform Act of 1986, at 355–360.

[109] For §336(a), see generally supra ¶ 11.06. Section 1060 originated in the Senate version of the 1986 Tax Reform Act, which preserved the *General Utilities* nonrecognition regime of §§336 and 337 and capital gain treatment for corporate taxpayers.

On an actual sale, if the buyer does not pay the entire purchase price in cash but instead issues its debt obligations for part or all of the amount owing, the original issue discount rules of §1274 and the imputed interest rules of §483[110] may turn part of the buyer's principal payment into currently deductible interest if the minimum interest test rates established by these provisions are violated. If, however, the price also includes stock of the buyer and the transaction does not qualify as a tax-free reorganization, the value of the buyer's stock generally constitutes its cost for the property, at least if the stock is traded;[111] and if stock purchase warrants also are used as part of the consideration, includability in the buyer's cost basis presumably depends upon whether the warrants have a readily ascertainable value.[112] Liabilities of the seller that are assumed (or taken subject to) by the buyer are included in cost basis at face (less any original issue discount or imputed interest inherent in the obligations), and this treatment also applies to expense obligations of the seller that are assumed and paid by the buyer; on the other hand, potential liabilities that are assumed by the buyer generally do not enter into basis (nor are they currently deductible) until the liability is actually incurred by the buyer, and the same is generally true with respect to contingent liabilities that are assumed in the transaction.[113]

If a buyer's purchase price is partially contingent upon certain specified events (e.g., achievement of designated levels of profitability), a portion of such payments will be subject to either the OID rules of §1274 or the imputed interest rules of §483.[114] The treatment of the remainder of such payments depends upon the underlying asset to which they relate (i.e., if made for franchises, trademarks, or trade names, §1253(d)(1) governs the buyer's treatment, permitting a deduction under §162(a) when paid;[115] other payments are excluded from basis until the contingency is fixed, and at that time the buyer obtains additional basis credit in the assets acquired[116]).

---

[110] Supra ¶ 4.42.

[111] See supra ¶ 3.12 and infra ¶ 14.33.

[112] Supra ¶ 4.62; Simmonds Precision Prods., Inc., 75 TC 103 (1980).

[113] Supra ¶ 5.06, para. 4; see also supra ¶ 4.42.

[114] See also infra ¶ 14.56 for the effect of contingent price terms on tax-free reorganization transactions.

[115] Rogers, supra note 106, at 829.

[116] Id. See also Holden Fuel Oil Co., ¶ 72,045 P-H Memo. TC (1972); Yates Indus., Inc., 58 TC 961 (1972), aff'd without opinion, 480 F2d 920 (3d Cir. 1973); Associated Patentees, Inc., 4 TC 979 (1945) (acq.); Liquid Paper Corp. v. US, 1983-1 USTC ¶ 9305 (Cl. Ct. 1983) (applying *Associated Patentees* to various contingent price payments); see also Temp. Regs. §1.338(b)-3T(g) (same) Lee & Bader, infra note 211.

PART B.　PARENT-SUBSIDIARY LIQUIDATIONS: GAIN, LOSS, AND BASIS

¶ 11.40　INTRODUCTORY

As has been seen, §331(a) establishes the rule that a complete liquidation of a corporation is to be treated by the shareholder as a sale or exchange of his stock, and §1001(c) establishes the principle that the entire amount of the gain or loss on the sale or exchange of property is to be recognized "except as otherwise provided in this subtitle." An important exception to the general rule that the shareholder's gain or loss is to be recognized on a complete liquidation is §332, which provides that under certain conditions, no gain or loss will be recognized by a parent corporation on the receipt of property distributed in complete liquidation of a subsidiary. This nonrecognition provision is coupled with a basis provision, §334(b), which ordinarily requires the parent corporation to take over the distributed assets at the subsidiary's basis.[117] In keeping with this carry-over of the subsidiary's basis, §337(a) (as amended in 1986) provides that the subsidiary does not recognize either gain or loss on a §332 distribution, a message that is reinforced as to the nonrecognition of losses by §336(d)(3).[118]

The prototype of §332 came into the Code in 1935. Congress hoped that it would encourage the simplification of complex corporate financial structures by permitting the liquidation of unnecessary subsidiaries without recognition of gain. Since statutory mergers can be accomplished tax-free, it is not surprising that Congress was willing to extend the same privilege to the practical, or upstream, merger that results when a subsidiary corporation is liquidated into its parent. Moreover, since the parent corporation ordinarily inherits its liquidated subsidiary's earnings and profits and other tax attributes under §381(a)(1),[119] the liquidation of a subsidiary is less appropriate as a taxable occasion than the liquidation of other corporations.

Since §334(b) provides that a parent corporation, on liquidating a subsidiary under §332, must take over the assets at the subsidiary's basis, a later sale of the assets by the parent will (assuming no change in values) require the recognition by it of the gain or loss that would have been recognized by the subsidiary had it made the sale. This result is in accord with §332's underlying assumption that the complete liquidation of a subsidiary works a

_____

[117] See generally Kurlander, Liquidation of Corporate Subsidiaries—General, Tax Mgmt. Portfolio (BNA) No. 238-4th (1986). See also Rev. Proc. 81-68, 1981-2 CB 723 (procedure for requesting rulings under §§332 and 334(b)).

[118] For treatment of the subsidiary in a §332 liquidation, see generally infra ¶ 11.49.

[119] See infra ¶ 16.11.

change of form rather than of substance. Note, however, that the parent's stock basis—representing its investment in the subsidiary—is not taken into account, either when the subsidiary is liquidated or when the assets thus acquired are ultimately sold by the parent. Thus, §332's assumption that the elimination of the corporate veil between parent and subsidiary should have no tax significance, though generally commendable, necessarily has the effect of obliterating forever the parent's gain or loss on its investment in the subsidiary.

Consider columns A and B below.

	A	B
Parent's basis for stock of subsidiary	$100,000	$100,000
Subsidiary's basis for its assets	40,000	135,000
Fair market value of subsidiary's assets	75,000	125,000

In column A, the parent has suffered a real loss of $25,000 (basis of stock less value of liquidating distribution), but this loss will go unrecognized; and on a sale of the assets (assuming no later change in value), the parent will recognize gain of $35,000. In column B, on the other hand, the parent's real gain of $25,000 will go unrecognized, and a sale of the assets by the parent will produce a tax loss of $10,000.[120]

Other combinations of basis and value are of course possible, but all would have in common a disregard of the parent's gain or loss on its investment in the subsidiary in order to treat the liquidation as a matter of form only. Most of the problems under §332 arise from attempts by the parent corporation or the government, as the case may be, to escape from §332—which at least in form is not an elective provision—so that the parent's gain or loss on its investment can be recognized when the subsidiary is liquidated.

As suggested earlier, §332 was originally enacted to encourage the simplification of complex corporate financial structures, and its non-recognition principle—adopted as a concession to the parent corporation—reflected the assumption that the provision's principal function would be to facilitate the tax-free elimination of existing subsidiaries. In the frenzied corporate take-

---

[120] These results under §§332 and 334(b)(1) may be somewhat mitigated by the fact that under §381(a)(1), the parent will inherit the tax attributes of the subsidiary. In Example A, there might be a loss carry-over from the subsidiary resulting from its earlier operations in which the investment of $100,000 was pared down to assets with a basis of only $40,000; in Example B there would probably be earnings and profits resulting from successful operations in the past. But it would be pure accident if these offsetting tax advantages counterbalanced the effects of §§332 and 334(b)(1) with even the roughest degree of accuracy. See Peerless Inv. Co., 58 TC 892 (1972). For characterization of the parent's gain or loss on a later sale, see Acro Mfg. Co. v. CIR, supra note 36.

over environment of the 1980's, however, §332 emerged from its traditional sleepy corner of the tax law and became a major stumbling block in the corporate acquisition movement. For the purchasing corporation, the problem created by §332 was the difficulty of obtaining a basis for the target's assets commensurate with the price paid for the stock; the low basis would persist whether the target was kept alive or was liquidated pursuant to §332. This problem was exacerbated by the Tax Reform Act of 1986, which repealed the *General Utilities* doctrine and required corporations distributing appreciated assets, whether in liquidation or otherwise, to recognize their gain, except in severely limited circumstances.[121] As will be seen later in this chapter, the purchasing corporation can sometimes get a stepped-up basis for the target's assets even though the target does not recognize its gain; but this best of both worlds outcome is hedged about by intricate restrictions.[122]

¶ 11.41 NON-RECOGNITION OF PARENT'S GAIN OR LOSS

Section 332 provides that no gain or loss shall be recognized on the receipt by a corporation of property distributed in complete liquidation of another corporation, provided (1) the corporation receiving the property owns a specified amount of the distributing corporation's stock; (2) there is a complete cancellation or redemption of all of the stock of the distributing corporation; and (3) the transfer of the property occurs within certain time limits. It has been held that the term "property" as used in §332 includes cash, so that a liquidation in which nothing but money is distributed is within §332.[123] Although §334(b)(1), requiring the parent to carry over the subsidiary's basis for the distributed assets, cannot be applied to a distribution of money, the cited cases point out that the subsidiary will have recognized gain or loss on disposing of its assets, so that the function of §334(b)(1) has already been discharged. If an all-cash distribution did not qualify under §332, there would be an unwarranted disparity between a liquidation that followed a sale of assets and one that preceded the sale.

If the parent corporation does not intend to continue the subsidiary's business (e.g., if the subsidiary's assets are sold by either the subsidiary or the parent, and the parent thereupon devotes the proceeds of the sale to a

---

[121] For the recognition of gain on distributions of appreciated property, see generally supra ¶¶ 9.34 and 11.06.

[122] See infra ¶¶ 11.44–11.48.

[123] Tri-Lakes S.S. Co. v. CIR, 146 F2d 970 (6th Cir. 1945); International Inv. Corp. v. CIR, 11 TC 678 (1948) (overruling an earlier Tax Court case to the contrary), aff'd per curiam, 175 F2d 772 (3d Cir. 1949); Rev. Rul. 69-379, 1969-2 CB 48; Rev. Rul. 74-54, 1974-1 CB 76 (cancellation of parent's debt to subsidiary not recognized under §332).

radically different line of business), the cases have divided on the applicability of §332. Judge Hand, in *Fairfield Steamship Corp. v. CIR*, said of the predecessor of §332 that its "underlying purpose was to permit the union in one corporate form of a single business or venture which had theretofore been managed by two corporations" and that "the privilege assumes that the business shall continue and that the liquidation shall not be merely a step in winding it up."[124] In the *International Investment Corp.* case, however, the Tax Court rejected the theory that there must be a continuation of the precise business of the liquidated subsidiary by the parent, although hinting that §332 might be inapplicable if (as in the *Fairfield Steamship Corp.* case) both the subsidiary and the parent were liquidated.[125]

If the subsidiary is insolvent, and its shareholder receives nothing on the liquidation, §332 is inapplicable, since there has been no "receipt by a corporation of property distributed in complete liquidation of another corporation."[126] In this event, the shareholder may deduct its loss on the worthless stock under §165(g). This principle was applied in *CIR v. Spaulding Bakeries, Inc.,* where a parent corporation that owned all the common and nonvoting preferred stock of a subsidiary received assets in liquidation with a value less than the liquidating preference of the preferred stock.[127] The court held that the 1939 Code predecessor of §332 was inapplicable, on the theory that nothing was received by the parent in respect of its common stock. An alternative approach would be to disregard the common stock

---

[124] Fairfield S.S. Corp. v. CIR, 157 F2d 321, 323 (2d Cir. 1946), cert. denied, 329 US 774 (1946). The court in this case erroneously assumed that §332 is applicable to the subsidiary's gain or loss, whereas it is confined to the parent's gain or loss; and an addendum to the opinion fails to clear up the confusion. In Acro Mfg. Co. v. CIR, supra note 36, where the parent corporation immediately sold the assets of its liquidated subsidiary, the court held that the character of those assets did not carry over from the subsidiary to the parent. If the court had applied the *Fairfield S.S. Corp.* principle, the liquidation would have been a taxable event, giving the parent a basis for the distributed assets under §334(a) equal to their fair market value. Moreover, Rev. Rul. 69-172, 1969-1 CB 99 (involving combined liquidations of a parent and its subsidiary), apparently assumed nonapplication of the *Fairfield S.S.* principle.

[125] International Inv. Corp. v. CIR, supra note 123; see also Rev. Rul. 70-357, 1970-2 CB 79 (§332 applies to liquidation in which parent discontinues subsidiary's business). Compare Kamis Eng'r Co., 60 TC 763 (1976) (§332 not applicable on liquidation of both subsidiary and parent pursuant to single plan); Rev. Rul. 76-429, 1976-2 CB 97 (reincorporation of one of liquidated subsidiary's two businesses held inconsistent with §332; transaction was partial liquidation of subsidiary). See generally Spurgeon, Avoiding the Waves From *Fairfield Steamship*, 56 A.B.A. J. 1005 (1970).

[126] Regs. §1.332-2(b).

[127] CIR v. Spaulding Bakeries, Inc., 252 F2d 693 (2d Cir. 1958); H.K. Porter Co., 87 TC 689 (1986) (*Spaulding Bakeries* principle reaffirmed).

because its equity was zero[128] and to treat the preferred stock as all the corporation's stock under §332(b)(3), in which event the parent's gain or loss on the preferred stock would go unrecognized under §332.[129]

The effect on the parent of receiving property from its subsidiary in payment of a debt, rather than in liquidation of its stock, is discussed later in this chapter.

Application of §332 is governed by several conditions, as discussed in the following paragraphs.

1. Eighty percent stock ownership. Section 332(b)(1) provides that §332 applies only if the parent corporation owns enough stock of the subsidiary to satisfy the requirements of §1504(a)(2) (relating to affiliated groups of corporations), which requires the parent to own (1) stock possessing at least 80 percent of the total combined voting power of all classes of stock entitled to vote, and (2) at least 80 percent of the total value of shares of all other classes of stock (except certain nonvoting stock that is limited and preferred as to dividends).[130] This amount of stock must be owned on the date that the plan of liquidation is adopted and at all times thereafter until the receipt of the property.

In view of this condition, can the parent avoid §332 (e.g., to recognize a loss, or to avoid inheriting the subsidiary's earnings and or profits) by selling some of the subsidiary's stock, either before a plan of liquidation is adopted or between that date and the receipt of the property, so as to reduce its ownership below the 80 percent benchmark? In *CIR v. Day & Zimmermann, Inc.,* such a sale by the parent for the sole purpose of avoiding §332 was held to be effective; the shares were offered for sale at a public auction after the liquidation had been decided on and were purchased by the parent corporation's treasurer at "a fair price under all the circumstances" with his own

---

[128] Cf. Helvering v. Alabama Asphaltic Limestone Co., 315 US 179 (1942) (creditor command over property equivalent to proprietary interest).

[129] Compare Norman Scott, Inc., 48 TC 598 (1967) (merger of insolvent brother corporation into solvent sister corporation qualified as valid Type A reorganization; parent-subsidiary liquidation cases distinguished). See infra ¶ 14.12; Rev. Rul. 68-602, 1968-2 CB 135; Inductotherm Indus., ¶ 84,281 P-H Memo. TC (1984) (subsidiary held to be solvent on finding that parent's advances were equity capital contributions; hence, §332 applied on liquidation, and §381 tax history carried over to parent); Textron, Inc. v. US, 561 F2d 1023 (1st Cir. 1977) (parent allowed §165(g)(3) deduction for worthless investment in defunct subsidiary, despite subsequent reactivation of subsidiary with new profitable business).

[130] The pre-1987 version of §332(b)(1) prescribed the 80 percent rule; but it was amended in 1986 to incorporate by reference the more detailed rules of §1504(a)(2). For the possibility that stock owned by two or more affiliated corporations may be aggregated in applying the 80 percent benchmark, see infra text at note 229.

funds and at his own risk and without "being directed by anyone to bid for the shares."[131] Since the subsidiary was about to be liquidated and the amount of the liquidating distribution (to be paid in cash) could be estimated with reasonable accuracy, it is surprising that the transaction was given effect for tax purposes; but the decision, rendered in 1945, now seems sanctified by the passage of time.[132]

If a corporation with 80 percent or more of the stock of another corporation can avoid §332 by reducing its holdings to less than 80 percent, does it follow that a corporation with less than 80 percent can bring itself within §332 by increasing its holdings? There is clearly no rule that the entire 80 percent must have been acquired at one time. However, what if some shares are acquired immediately before a liquidation solely to qualify? The requisite 80 percent ownership must exist "on the date of the adoption of the plan of liquidation." Neither §332 nor the regulations thereunder, however, define the term "date of the adoption of the plan." If the shareholders of the subsidiary adopt a resolution authorizing the directors to liquidate, the date of the resolution will probably be controlling in ordinary circumstances; but if the parent corporation has previously decided to liquidate the subsidiary and thereafter acquires additional shares solely in order to meet the 80 percent requirement, it may be held that the plan of liquidation was informally adopted before the additional shares were acquired. If the adoption of the plan is predated in this fashion, the acquisition of additional shares, even though it occurs before the formal meeting of the subsidiary's shareholders, will be too late.[133]

2. Complete cancellation or redemption of all the subsidiary's stock in accordance with a plan of liquidation. Section 332 is applicable only if the subsidiary distributes property "in complete cancellation or redemption of all its stock." Ordinarily this requirement is satisfied without any diffi-

---

[131] CIR v. Day & Zimmerman, Inc., 151 F2d 517 (3d Cir. 1945).

[132] See George L. Riggs, Inc., 64 TC 474, 488–489 (1975) (acq.).

[133] See generally George L. Riggs, Inc., supra note 132 (extensive analysis; on facts, adoption of plan of liquidation did not predate acquisition of 80 percent control despite general intent by parent to liquidate subsidiary after obtaining requisite 80 percent control); see also Rev. Rul. 75-521, 1975-2 CB 120 (purchase from other shareholders to get 80 percent control allowed); Crescent Oil, Inc., ¶ 79,026 P-H Memo. TC (1979) (§332 not applicable because parent did not own 80 percent when plan adopted); Rev. Rul. 70-106, 1970-1 CB 70 (redemption of 25 percent minority interest, giving parent 100 percent control), was part of single liquidation plan; parent did not have requisite control. But see infra note 156 (on backing into control prior to liquidation). For efforts to achieve nonrecognition of gain on the liquidation of a subsidiary of which the parent owns less than 80 percent of the stock, see infra ¶ 14.53, para. 4.

culty, since in most cases the corporation distributes all of its assets, calls in and cancels the stock certificates, and dissolves under state law. However, the regulations provide that a dissolution is not required, and even that the corporation may retain assets in a nominal amount to preserve its legal existence. Some informality in the liquidating process, although not to be recommended, may be tolerated, as under §331(a).[134] As to the requirement of a plan of liquidation, §332(b)(2) explicitly provides that a shareholder's resolution authorizing the distribution of all the corporation's assets in complete cancellation or redemption of all the stock "shall be considered an adoption of a plan of liquidation" if the transfer of all the property occurs within the taxable year, even though no time for completing the transfer is specified in the resolution. The term "plan of liquidation" is not necessarily restricted to a shareholders' resolution, however; the statutory requirement should be satisfied by a resolution of the directors if under state law they have the power to liquidate the corporation, and the government has on occasion argued that the term "plan" embraces a determination by the controlling shareholder to liquidate, even though it is not put into writing.[135]

3. Timing of the distribution. As already stated, §332(b)(2) provides that the shareholder's resolution authorizing the distribution will be considered an adoption of a plan of liquidation, even though it specifies no time for completing the transfer, if the transfer is in fact completed within the taxable year.[136] Otherwise, the plan of liquidation must provide for the transfer of all the property within three years from the close of the taxable year in which the first distribution is made, and the transfer must be completed during this period. If the transfer is not completed within this period, or if the parent corporation does not remain qualified until the transfer is completed, §332 is retroactively inapplicable to all distributions under the plan.[137] Because of this possibility, the Service may require the taxpayer to post a bond or waive

---

[134] See Regs. §1.332-2(c); supra ¶ 11.02; see also Rev. Rul. 54-518, 1954-2 CB 142 (similar position under 1939 Code). There appears to be a conflict between Regs. §1.332-2(c) and the requirement of §332(b) of a "complete cancellation or redemption of all the stock." But cf. Rev. Rul. 76-429, 1976-2 CB 97 (no §332 complete liquidation when liquidated subsidiary was reincorporated). Compare Rev. Rul. 84-2, 1984-1 CB 92 (reincorporation of nominal assets solely to protect corporate name did not vitiate §332).

[135] See Rev. Rul. 58-391, 1958-2 CB 139; supra note 133.

[136] See Rev. Rul. 71-326, 1971-2 CB 177 (§332 liquidation when all liquidating distributions were made within one year, even though distribution did not occur until three years after adoption of plan; delay for valid business reasons).

[137] In Rev. Rul. 76-525, 1976-2 CB 98, the Service ruled that the retention of any assets by the subsidiary for the purpose of engaging in an old or new business

the statute of limitations on assessment and collection, or both, in order to ensure assessment and collection of all income taxes attributable to the distributed property. [138]

The provisions of §§332(b)(2) and 332(b)(3) suggest the possibility of avoiding §332 when the taxpayer so desires by specifying no limit in the shareholders' resolution, spreading the transfers out over more than one taxable year, and adopting no other formal plan of liquidation. In *Burnside Veneer Co. v. CIR,* however, it was held that the statute was applicable if the liquidation was in fact completed within the three-year period, on the ground that the resolutions of the shareholders and directors and the local corporation law contemplated a prompt liquidation. [139] In another case, the Tax Court said: "There is no need for any formal plan of liquidation if one can be discovered from the circumstances surrounding the liquidation." [140] These were cases in which the taxpayer was seeking to avoid §332 on the ground that the arrangements for liquidation did not constitute a sufficiently formal plan of liquidation to meet the statutory requirements. Had the courts acceded to the taxpayers' arguments, §332 would have become an almost entirely optional provision. If the Service objects to the absence of a formal plan of liquidation, however, deficiencies in the paperwork may be taken more seriously.

What if the plan provides, in accordance with §332(b)(3), that the liquidation is to be completed within three years, but the distributions are deliberately spread out over a longer period? The final clause of §332(b)(3) states that if the transfer is not completed within the three-year period, none of the distributions will be considered distributions in complete liquidation. While this clause can be used by the government to disqualify a nonconforming transaction, it is not so clear that the taxpayer could avail itself of a deliberate delay that serves no purpose. The parent might be held, in such a case, to

---

will cause the transaction to flunk the §332 test; compare Rev. Rul. 84-2, 1984-1 CB 92.

In Cherry-Burrell Corp. v. US, 367 F2d 669 (8th Cir. 1966), the court held that an involuntary delay in the final distribution of assets (caused by litigation against the liquidating subsidiary) did not cause a forfeiture of the nonrecognition benefits of §332. This application of equitable considerations to the time limits of §332 was, to say the least, highly unusual; it is doubtful that similar flexibility applied to the time schedules of old §§333 and 337 (infra ¶¶ 11.61 and 11.62).

[138] Section 332(b), second sentence; Regs. §1.332-4.

[139] Burnside Veneer Co., v. CIR, 167 F2d 214 (6th Cir. 1948).

[140] International Inv. Co. v. CIR, supra note 123, at 685; see also Service Co. v. CIR, 165 F2d 75 (8th Cir. 1948) (parent corporation could not use its failure to comply with the record keeping provisions of Regs. §1.332-6 to avoid the application of §332; these requirements were "promulgated primarily for the protection of the revenue, not for the advantage of the taxpayer").

have received a constructive distribution despite its willingness to wait until after the prescribed three-year period for an actual distribution.[141]

¶ 11.42 EFFECT OF SUBSIDIARY INDEBTEDNESS TO ITS PARENT

Section 332 provides for nonrecognition of gain or loss when property is distributed to a parent corporation in complete liquidation of its 80 percent subsidiary. If the subsidiary is indebted to the parent at the time of the liquidation, its property may be transferred to satisfy indebtedness as well as in cancellation of its stock. As noted in the previous section, if the subsidiary is insolvent, so that there is no distribution with respect to its stock, the parent's loss is not subject to §332. Even in the case of a solvent subsidiary, however, a distribution to the parent in its capacity as creditor rather than as shareholder results in recognition of gain or loss thereon by the parent.[142]

Before 1954, the Service took the position that the subsidiary recognized gain or loss on such a transfer if it satisfied its indebtedness to the parent with appreciated or depreciated property.[143] Because of difficulties in determining which of the subsidiary's assets were used to satisfy its indebtedness and which were distributed in exchange for the stock, however, the

---

[141] Compare David T. Grubbs, 39 TC 42 (1962). For a related problem under old §337, see infra ¶ 11.61; see also Lowndes v. US, 384 F2d 635 (4th Cir. 1967); supra ¶ 11.02. But see Rev. Rul. 77-150, 1977-1 CB 88.

[142] See Regs. §1.332-7; Rev. Rul. 59-296, 1959-2 CB 87, amplified by Rev. Rul. 70-489, 1970-2 CB 53; see Brod, Liquidations Involving Shareholder-Creditors—Tax Traps for the Unwary, 7 J. Corp. Tax'n 352 (1981); supra ¶ 11.03, note 14.

If the subsidiary cannot satisfy its debt to the parent in full, the parent will have a bad-debt deduction under §166(a) or a worthless security deduction under §165(g), supra ¶ 4.22.

Query: Can the parent, if it wishes to bring the transfer of the subsidiary's assets under §332 (e.g., to inherit a loss carry-over), forgive the debt and thereby lay the foundation for a transfer of the subsidiary's assets in liquidation of the stock? Rev. Rul. 68-602, 1968-2 CB 135, answered this question in the negative under step-transaction principles. Another possibility, if the subsidiary is indebted to the parent (or to a third party) in an amount exceeding the value of its assets, is that the debt will be treated as the equivalent of stock (on the ground that the creditors would take over the corporation in the event of a bankruptcy reorganization), thus bringing §332 into play for the creditor (supra notes 128–129). But see Northern Coal & Dock Co., 12 TC 42 (1949) (acq.). Compare Rev. Rul. 78-330, 1978-2 CB 147 (parent cancellation of brother-subsidiary debt prior to merger into sister subsidiary in order to avoid §357(c) gain held not violation of §357(b)). See generally Stuetzer, Upstream Debts in Section 112(b)(6) Liquidations, 5 Tax L. Rev. 199, 209 (1950).

[143] IT 4109, 1952-2 CB 138 (gain); Northern Coal & Dock Co., supra note 142 (loss); see also Rev. Rul. 70-271, 1970-1 CB 166.

Service later ruled that it would not insist upon recognition of gain by the subsidiary if the parent executed a closing agreement agreeing to carry over the subsidiary's basis for all the transferred property. The 1954 Code adopted this approach by providing in the statutory predecessor of §337(b)(1) that the subsidiary recognizes neither gain nor loss on transfers of property in satisfaction of indebtedness to its parent; and §334(b)(2) provides that the parent's basis for such property must be the same as the subsidiary's (although this provision still refers inadvertently to §332(c), the statutory predecessor of §337(b)(1)).

Because §337(b)(1) applies only if the subsidiary is indebted to its parent "on the date of the adoption of the plan of liquidation," preplan transfers of appreciated or depreciated property in satisfaction of the subsidiary's debt to its parent result in recognition of gain or loss to the subsidiary, and also confer on the parent a basis for the property equal to its fair market value at the time of the transfer. If the subsidiary's anticipatory payment of its debts is an integral part of the plan of liquidation, however, it may result in a finding that the plan was adopted prior to the date of formal adoption.

¶ 11.43 MINORITY SHAREHOLDERS

Under §332, nonrecognition treatment applies only to the parent corporation's gain or loss on the liquidation. Minority shareholders must determine their gain or loss without regard to §332. Ordinarily, such amounts are recognized under §§331(a) and 1001(c), but these shareholders may be entitled to nonrecognition treatment by virtue of the reorganization provisions of the Code.[144] For example, if the liquidation of an 80 percent subsidiary takes the form of a statutory merger in which all of its assets are transferred to the parent, and the parent issues its stock to the subsidiary's minority shareholders as consideration for their ratable interest in the subsidiary's property, the transaction may constitute a tax-free reorganization under §368(a)(1)(A). In this event, neither the parent corporation nor the subsidiary's minority shareholders would recognize gain or loss.[145]

If the parent owns less than 80 percent of the subsidiary's outstanding stock, however, tax-free acquisitions of the subsidiary's assets by the parent and nonrecognition treatment for the minority shareholders face greater technical difficulties, with the tax results depending, it would seem, primar-

---

[144] Another nonrecognition possibility for minority shareholders, until its repeal in 1986, was §333, discussed infra ¶ 11.62.

[145] See §332(b), last sentence; Regs. §§1.332-2(d) and 1.332-2(e). For the possibility that the reorganization provisions do not apply to a §332 transaction in this situation, see infra ¶ 14.53, para. 1.

ily on the form of the transaction. Thus, in Rev. Rul. 54-396, the Service ruled that acquisition of all the assets of a 79 percent owned subsidiary in exchange for the parent's stock, followed by a liquidation of the subsidiary, did not constitute a reorganization under §112(g)(1)(C) of the 1939 Code, since the acquiring corporation, in substance, obtained only 21 percent of the subsidiary's assets in exchange for its stock, the balance being acquired as a liquidating distribution in exchange for the parent's 79 percent stock interest.[146]

¶ 11.44   PARENT'S BASIS FOR PROPERTY ACQUIRED BY LIQUIDATING RECENTLY PURCHASED SUBSIDIARY: BACKGROUND

Upon the liquidation of a subsidiary under §332, §334(b)(1) provides that the property received by the parent retains the basis that it had in the hands of the subsidiary. As already noted, this is one reason why parent corporations occasionally maneuver, sometimes successfully, to remove a liquidation from the clutches of §332.[147]

If the carry-over rule of §334(b)(1) were rigorously applied, it would create an unjustified dichotomy between two otherwise similar methods of acquiring the assets of another corporation: If the purchasing corporation purchased the assets from the second corporation, the former's basis would be its cost under §1012; but if it acquired the assets by purchasing the stock of the second corporation and liquidating it, it would have to carry over the second corporation's basis. This inherited (or inside) basis might, of course, be substantially greater or less than the price paid for the stock (the outside basis), because the price paid for the assets, although it may be adjusted up or down to some extent because of the potential gain or loss built into the subsidiary's assets, primarily reflects the market value of the corporate assets rather than their basis in the hands of the target.

For this reason, in a line of pre-1954 cases, the courts adopted the position that the purchase by one corporation of the stock of another corporation in order to obtain its assets through a prompt liquidation should be treated as a single transaction (i.e., a purchase of the assets), producing a basis equal to their cost rather than a carry-over of basis. In the leading case, *Kimbell-Diamond Milling Co. v. CIR*, the single transaction doctrine was

---

[146] Rev. Rul. 54-396, 1954-2 CB 147; see also infra ¶ 14.53, para. 4.

[147] In the case of high-basis assets, however, §334(b)(1) is advantageous, since the potential loss on such property shifts upstream to the distributee-parent. For possible application of §482 to reallocate the loss from the parent to the subsidiary, see General Elec. Co. v. US, supra note 69; for limitations under §382, see infra ¶ 16.25.

applied at the behest of the Service so as to deny the purchasing corporation the right to carry over an inside basis in excess of the price paid for the stock; but the *Kimbell-Diamond* principle was also applied to give the acquiring corporation the benefit of its cost, if cost exceeded the acquired corporation's inside basis.[148]

As the criterion to determine whether the parent's basis for assets acquired by liquidating a subsidiary was its outside basis for the stock or the subsidiary's inside basis for the assets, however, the single transaction principle enunciated in the *Kimbell-Diamond* case was unpredictable. Congress intervened in 1954 by enacting an exception to §334(b)(1). This exception treated the purchase and liquidation of a subsidiary as in substance a purchase of its assets (resulting in an outside basis) if a controlling stock interest in the subsidiary was acquired by purchase within a 12-month period and the subsidiary was liquidated pursuant to a plan of liquidation adopted under §332 within two years after the qualifying stock purchase was completed.[149]

This mandatory statutory rule reigned from 1954 to 1982, when an accumulation of objections led to its replacement by an elective provision, §338, which is still in force.[150] As will be seen, however, 1986 changes in related provisions—especially §336(a), which now requires a liquidating corporation to recognize gain on the distribution or sale of appreciated property—have greatly reduced the appeal of elections under §338.[151]

¶ 11.45   PARENT'S BASIS FOR PROPERTY ACQUIRED BY LIQUIDATING RECENTLY PURCHASED SUBSIDIARY: 1954-82 RULES

1. Introductory. As mentioned earlier, in 1954 Congress enacted §334(b)(2) to reduce the uncertainties resulting from the *Kimbell-Diamond* case while preserving its central concept. This provision, like *Kimbell-Dia-*

---

[148] Kimbell-Diamond Milling Co. v. CIR, 14 TC 74, aff'd per curiam, 187 F2d 718 (5th Cir.), cert. denied, 342 US 827 (1951); see also US v. M.O.J. Corp., 274 F2d 713 (5th Cir. 1960); US v. Mattison, 273 F2d 13 (9th Cir. 1959); Griswold v. CIR, 400 F2d 427 (5th Cir. 1968) (stock purchase, liquidation, and reincorporation held a tax-free reorganization with carry-over basis, infra ¶ 14.54). But see Security Indus. Ins. Co. v. US, 702 F2d 1234 (5th Cir. 1983) (stock purchase, liquidation, and reincorporation transfer held §334(b)(2) stepped-up basis liquidation; no mention in opinion of *Griswold*). See also Frederick Steel Co., 42 TC 13 (1964) (doctrine not applied where both corporations were under common control), rev'd, 375 F2d 351 (6th Cir. 1967), cert. denied, 389 US 901 (1967).

[149] See infra ¶ 11.45.

[150] See infra ¶¶ 11.46–11.48.

[151] For §336(a), see supra ¶ 11.06; for the effect of this and other 1986 changes on §338, see infra ¶ 11.46.

mond itself, treated the parent's purchase and prompt liquidation of a sub-sidiary as merely a roundabout way of purchasing the assets, resulting in a basis for the assets equal to the amount paid for the stock. Although §334(b)(2) was repealed in 1982 and replaced by §338,[152] the latter provision incorporates so many features of §334(b)(2) that they warrant attention before we turn to §338.

2. Old §334(b)(2): Stock purchase treated as purchase of assets. Section 334(b)(2) was enacted in 1954 to incorporate "rules effectuating principles derived from *Kimbell-Diamond Milling Co.*"[153] Section 334(b)(2) provided that the parent corporation's basis for property acquired in a §332 transaction was the cost of the stock (with certain adjustments), rather than the subsidiary's basis for the assets, if at least 80 percent of the stock was acquired by pur-chase, as defined in §334(b)(3),[154] during a period of not more than 12 months, and if the distribution was pursuant to a plan of complete liquidation under §332 adopted not more than two years after the purchase.[155] Of these

---

[152] See infra ¶ 11.46.

[153] S. Rep. No. 1662, 83d Cong., 2d Sess. 257 (1954). For more extensive treat-ment of §334(b)(2), see the Fourth Edition of this treatise and the 1987 Cumulative Supplement No. 2 thereto.

[154] On the meaning of "purchase," see Bijou Park Properties, Inc., 47 TC 207 (1966) (not a qualified purchase because stock was acquired from related seller within meaning of §318); Baker Commodities, Inc. v. CIR, 415 F2d 519 (9th Cir. 1969), cert. denied, 397 US 988 (1970) (stepped-up basis for assets acquired on liqui-dation of various subsidiaries denied for lack of qualified purchase); Stevens Pass, Inc., 48 TC 532 (1967) (qualified purchase, not a §351 transaction); Broadview Lum-ber Co. v. US, 561 F2d 698 (7th Cir. 1977) (not qualified because stock was acquired from related seller); DeWitt v. US, 503 F2d 1406 (Ct. Cl. 1974) (qualified purchase where parent bought stock from charity, even though a person related to the parent had contributed stock to charity with expectation that parent would buy it back); Rev. Rul. 57-296, 1957-2 CB 234 (because §351 applied, not a qualified purchase where parent exchanged subsidiary's notes for subsidiary's stock); Rev. Rul. 77-427, 1977-2 CB 100 (not a qualified purchase where stock acquired in §304(a)(1) transac-tion, even though selling shareholder gets sale treatment per §302(b)(2)), rev'd by statutory amendment in 1986; Rev. Rul. 58-79, 1958-1 CB 177, to contrary, revoked prospectively, but revived (by the 1986 amendment). Under §334(b)(3) as amended in 1966, if the acquired corporation itself owns a subsidiary, the acquiring parent could obtain §334(b)(2) treatment whether the acquired corporation was liquidated before or after the liquidation of its subsidiary.

See generally Note, Section 334(b)(2): The "Purchase" Requirement, 30 Tax Lawyer 188 (1976).

[155] Rev. Rul. 80-358, 1980-2 CB 111 (12-month period started with date parent first deemed to own subsidiary's stock via §318).

See Regs. §1.334-1(c)(3), stating that the two-year period began to run after the earliest date, which was the end of a period of 12 months or less within which the

conditions, the purchase requirement[156] caused the most trouble, since §334(b)(3) defined this term to exclude (1) transactions in which the basis of the stock carried over from the transferor (e.g., an acquisition by gift, contribution to capital, or tax-free reorganization) or was determined under §1014 (inherited property); (2) acquisitions of stock in exchanges to which §351 applied;[157] and (3) acquisitions from related persons within the meaning of §318(a).[158] Thus, the statutory *Kimbell-Diamond* rule applied primarily to one-shot purchases of stock by the parent corporation from unrelated persons in transactions that, as to the sellers, were taxable events (i.e., in which their gain or loss on the transfer was recognized).[159]

---

amount of stock required by §334(b)(2)(B) was acquired. In short, the time limits of §334(b)(2) prohibited creeping acquisitions.

For illustrations of situations where control was acquired through the grant and exercise of options, see Rev. Rul. 74-295, 1974-1 CB 78, which applies the principles of Regs. §§1.334-1(c)(6)(iii) and 1.334-1(c)(3) to seven situations.

[156] On the possibility of backing into the 80 percent purchase requirement via a combination of stock redemptions and market purchases of the stock, see Rev. Rul. 70-106, 1970-1 CB 70, holding that if the redemptions were part of the liquidation plan, §332 did not apply to the parent because it did not have 80 percent control. Several cases decided subsequent to Rev. Rul. 70-106, however, held that a combination of purchase and redemption of the subsidiary's stock could establish §334(b)(2) control. See Madison Square Garden Corp. v. CIR, 500 F2d 611 (2d Cir. 1974); George L. Riggs, Inc., supra note 132; cf. Rev. Rul. 75-521, 1975-2 CB 120 (50 percent parent purchased the 80 percent control from other shareholders on the market). Moreover, Joint Comm. Staff, General Explanation of TEFRA, 97th Cong., 2d Sess. 134 (1982), states that the 80 percent requirement of §338(d)(3) (the successor to §334(b)(3) "may be satisfied through the combination of stock purchases and redemptions," and the §338 regulations agree, infra ¶ 11.47.

[157] Chrome Plate, Inc. v. US, 614 F2d 990 (5th Cir. 1980), cert. denied, 449 US 842 (1980), (acquiring corporation dropped purchased stock into new subsidiary, which then liquidated acquired corporations; held §334(b)(3) not satisfied); see also Rev. Rul. 77-427, 1977-2 CB 100; Rev. Rul. 57-296, 1957-2 CB 234, Baker Commodities, Inc. v. CIR, supra note 154; Priv. Ltr. Rul. 80-21-001, 1980 Fed. Taxes (P-H) ¶ 55,115 (acquisition of additional stock by intervening capital contribution did not violate purchase requirement where parent had previously acquired requisite 80 percent by qualified purchase; Rev. Rul. 57-296, 1957-2 CB 234, distinguished).

[158] See cases supra note 154; supra ¶ 9.03.

[159] For the application of §334(b)(2) to a chain of subsidiaries, see Regs. §1.334-1(c)(7); Rev. Rul. 74-211, 1974-1 CB 76 (parent's acquisition of second-tier corporation's stock by qualified purchase). For illustrations of the wrong way to structure such transactions, see Chrome Plate, Inc. v. US, supra note 157 (form of transaction binding even though it could easily have been structured to meet §334(b)(3)'s requirements); New York Fruit Auction Corp., 79 TC 564 (1982) (parent downstream merger into purchased subsidiary); see also Rev. Rul. 80-358, 1980-2 CB 111 (delayed liquidation of first-tier subsidiary precluded application of §334(b)(2) to liquidation of second-tier subsidiary).

In keeping with the theory that a §334(b)(2) transaction was in substance a purchase of the assets, the acquiring corporation did not inherit the liquidating corporation's earnings and profits or other tax attributes, as it would in an ordinary liquidation of a subsidiary by its parent.[160] On the other hand, the purchase of assets theory was generally not carried to the point of holding that the liquidating corporation realized gain or loss on a hypothetical sale of its assets to the acquiring corporation.[161]

If the conditions of §334(b)(2) were satisfied, the parent corporation's adjusted basis for its stock in the subsidiary (including any stock that may have been acquired in an unqualified transaction) was allocated among the assets received in the liquidating distribution in accordance with the regulations.[162]

The application of §334(b)(2) was a relatively straightforward exercise if the liquidation occurred immediately after the subsidiary's stock was acquired. If, however, the liquidation was delayed,[163] computation of the parent's basis for the assets could be complicated by a variety of events between the date the stock was acquired and the date of the liquidating distribution, such as a sale by the subsidiary of some of the assets or its purchase of additional assets. The regulations described and illustrated various adjustments to take appropriate account of such post-acquisition events.[164]

---

[160] See Supreme Inv. Corp. v. US, 468 F2d 370 (5th Cir. 1972) (parent's §334(b)(2) basis not disallowed under §269(a)); Home Sav. & Loan Ass'n v. US, 514 F2d 1199 (9th Cir.), cert. denied, 423 US 1015 (1975).

[161] Dallas Downtown Dev. Co., 12 TC 114 (1949) (acq.) (no gain to liquidating corporation); CIR v. South Lake Farms, Inc., supra note 73; but cf. Idol v. CIR, 319 F2d 647 (8th Cir. 1963); Blueberry Land Co., 42 TC 1137 (1964), aff'd, 361 F2d 93 (5th Cir. 1966).

[162] See discussion infra para. 5. The parent's holding period for the subsidiary's stock could be tacked onto the parent's holding period for its assets, since, under §334(b)(2), the assets have the same basis as the stock for which they were exchanged; see §1223(1); Cabax Mills, 59 TC 401 (1972) (acq.); accord, Rev. Rul. 74-522, 1974-2 CB 271.

[163] The plan of liquidation had to be adopted within two years of the last qualifying acquisition of stock (§334(b)(2)(A)), and the liquidation itself could be spread over a three-year period after the plan was adopted (§332(b)(3)).

[164] For illustrations of the mechanics of Regs. §1.334-1(c), see First Nat'l Bank of N.J., 51 TC 419 (1968) (parent allowed to step up basis of liquidated subsidiary's assets to the extent that subsidiary's earnings and profits were increased by a bad-debt reserve income item, net of taxes thereon, required to be included in subsidiary's final return); accord R.M. Smith, Inc., 69 TC 317 (1977), aff'd 591 F2d 248 (3d Cir. 1979), cert. denied, 444 US 828 (1979); Boise Cascade Corp. v. US, 288 F. Supp. 770 (D. Idaho 1968), aff'd per curiam, 429 F2d 426 (9th Cir. 1970); Silverman, Leave It to Smith (or, "Refinements" on Section 334(b)(2)), 33 Tax L. Rev. 545 (1978); Yost, Delayed Section 334(b)(2) Liquidation: The *Smith* Case—A Pyrrhic Victory for the IRS, 5 J. Corp. Tax'n 263 (1978).

Unlike the *Kimbell-Diamond* doctrine as judicially formulated, §334(b)(2) applied without regard to the acquiring corporation's intent; the assets acquired a new basis if the liquidation satisfied the statutory conditions, even though it may not have been contemplated by the acquiring corporation when the stock was purchased.[165] The automatic application of §334(b)(2) to transactions meeting the statutory requirements, however, did not mean that *Kimbell-Diamond* had no continuing vitality when these statutory conditions were not satisfied. It might be applied to a prearranged liquidation if the time limits prescribed by §334(b)(2) for acquiring the stock or liquidating the acquired corporation were deliberately avoided. Even more clearly, the purchase of stock by an individual with an intent to liquidate the corporation in order to obtain its assets—a transaction outside of §334(b)(2) because the purchaser is not a corporation—might be treated as a purchase of assets.

3. Delayed liquidation problems. Because a purchased subsidiary did not have to be liquidated immediately in order for the parent to qualify for the basis benefits of §334(b)(2), adjustments to the parent's basis for its stock of the subsidiary were necessary to take account of the subsidiary's operations between the date of the parent's purchase of the stock and the liquidation, as well as its interim distributions, earnings and deficits, and other items. In prescribing the adjustments, Regs. §1.334-1(c)(4) attempted to put the par-

---

If the parent owned 80 percent of the subsidiary's stock but at the time of the subsidiary's liquidation was obligated to purchase the minority interest, the parent obtained a §334(b)(2) basis in all the subsidiary's assets, not just 80 percent of them. See Madison Square Garden Corp. v. CIR, supra note 156; cf. May B. Kass, 60 TC 218 (1973) (taxpayer was one of the minority shareholders), aff'd mem. (3d Cir. 1974); Yoc Heating Corp., 61 TC 168 (1973) (taxpayer a newly formed subsidiary of parent to which the acquired corporation's assets were transferred; §334(b)(2) not applicable, but taxpayer obtained cost basis in the acquired corporation's assets). See generally Mopsick, Yoc Heating Corp. and Two-Step Asset Acquisitions, 1 J. Corp. Tax'n 235 (1974); infra text at note 179; supra notes 148, 159, and 162.

[165] Supra ¶ 11.03; see also Rev. Rul. 60-262, 1960-2 CB 114 (formal steps controlling under §334(b)(2), regardless of purpose or intent). The Court of Claims, however, in the first reported decision on the issue, held that the *Kimbell-Diamond* doctrine survived the enactment of §334(b)(2). American Potash & Chem. Corp. v. US, 399 F2d 194 (Ct. Cl. 1968).

Contra to American Potash & Chem. Corp. v. US, however, are International State Bank, 70 TC 173 (1978); Broadview Lumber Co. v. US, supra note 154 (*Kimbell-Diamond* preempted by 1954 Code amendements); accord Chrome Plate, Inc. v. US, supra note 157.

See generally, Dubroff & Daileader, *Kimbell-Diamond* Revisited; A Critique of Judicial Analysis of the Exclusivity of Section 334(b)(2), 43 Alb. L. Rev. 739 (1979); Dolan, *Kimbell-Diamond, Chrome Plate* and Taxpayer Intent in the Liquidation of Subsidiaries: Should Congress Reexamine Section 334(b)(2)?, 8 J. Corp. Tax'n 281 (1982).

ent in essentially the same position, for basis purposes, as if the subsidiary had been liquidated immediately after the parent purchased its stock.

The adjustments required were the following:

(1) Regs. §§1.334-1(c)(4)(i)–1.334-1(c)(4)(iv) provided that the adjusted basis of stock in the subsidiary must be reduced by dividends distributed out of preacquisition earnings and profits, the theory being that these earnings were in effect purchased by the parent when it acquired the stock, so that distributions represent a return of investment to the parent, somewhat analogous to the flat purchase rules of Regs. §1.61-7(c) in the case of bonds purchased with defaulted interest arrears.

(2) Stock basis also had to be reduced (but not below zero) by liquidating distributions of cash or its equivalent under Regs. §1.334-1(c)(4)(v).

(3) Stock basis was increased by unsecured liabilities (including tax liabilities of the subsidiary) assumed or taken subject to by the parent upon liquidation.

(4) Stock basis was also increased by the post-acquisition earnings and profits account (or reduced by a deficit therein). This account was a mechanism to equalize the stock purchase transaction with a purchase of assets.[166] In computing this account, accrual accounting principles applied, and earnings or deficits were measured by using a hypothetical basis for the subsidiary's assets, determined as if the parent had promptly liquidated it at the time of the qualifying stock purchase. (See Regs. §1.334-1(c)(4)(iv).)

(5) Regs. §1.334-1(c)(4)(viii) denied a §334(b)(2) basis for property contributed by the parent, directly or indirectly, to the capital of the subsidiary during such period.

Once the adjusted stock basis was determined under these rules, it was allocated among the noncash assets of the subsidiary (net of specific liens on particular assets) in proportion to their relative values. Liens were then added to the basis of the assets to which they related. If more than one asset was covered by a lien, it was allocated among them in proportion to relative values.[167]

---

[166] For a similar stock basis adjustment in the consolidated return area, see discussion infra ¶ 15.23; First Nat'l State Bank of N.J., supra note 164; see also Knapp King-Size Corp. v. US, 1975-1 USTC ¶ 9461 (Ct. Cl.) (§334(b)(2) basis for inventory acquired after stock purchase while parent and subsidiary filed consolidated return), modified, 36 AFTR2d 5591, and modified opinion affirmed per curiam, 527 F2d 1392 (Ct. Cl. 1975).

[167] See Regs. §1.334-1(c)(4)(viii). For different treatment under §338(b)(5), see infra ¶ 11.48.

As the complexity of these regulations suggests, the wisest course of action was to liquidate the subsidiary immediately following the purchase of its stock, if possible. (As discussed later in this chapter, however, the successor regulations under §338 are even more complex.)

4. Contingent liabilities and related problems. The regulations provided that liabilities of the subsidiary that the parent assumed or took subject to were, upon liquidation of the subsidiary, added to the parent's basis for the assets of the subsidiary under §334(b)(2).[168] (The same is true of a direct purchase of assets under §1012.) The treatment of contingent liabilities, however, was less clear. One approach was to estimate the amount of such liabilities at the time of liquidation and to include this amount in the basis computation, adjusting the basis when subsequent events finally determined the exact amount of these liabilities. Support for this approach exists in Rev. Rul. 55-119, relating to the basis of property purchased in exchange for a private annuity.[169] Another approach, adopted by the Tax Court in *Pacific Transport Co.*, was to ignore contingent liabilities initially under §334(b)(2) but to allow the parent an expense deduction when the liability became fixed or was paid.[170] A third possibility, asserted by the Service in the *Pacific Transport* case but rejected by the lower court, was to hold the basis adjustment open (somewhat on the order of an open liquidation) until the liabilities were fixed, and then, prospectively, adjust the basis upward.[171]

---

[168] See generally Rev. Rul. 59-412, 1959-2 CB 108. But in Rev. Rul. 69-426, 1969-2 CB 48, the Service ruled that property received by the parent in satisfaction of the subsidiary's debt to the parent took a carry-over basis under §334(b)(1), even though the transaction otherwise qualified as a §334(b)(2) liquidation, since property received in the parent's capacity as creditor did not qualify for the benefits of §334(b)(2). Compare Rev. Rul. 70-271, 1970-1 CB 166, where the Service held that corporate debts assumed by the shareholders in the context of a reorganization-liquidation of the corporation could be added to the §358 basis of the stock received by the shareholders in the exchange.

See also R.M. Smith, Inc., supra note 164 (no adjustment for subsidiary's negligence penalty; not a liability assumed by parent as a result of the stock purchase and liquidation).

[169] Rev. Rul. 55-119, 1955-1 CB 352.

[170] Pacific Transp. Co., ¶ 70,041 P-H Memo. TC (1970), vacated and remanded, 483 F2d 209 (9th Cir. 1973) (per curiam), cert. denied, 415 US 948 (1974) (applying principles of *Woodward, Hilton Hotels,* and *Magruder v. Supplee*); see also Rev. Rul. 76-520, 1976-2 CB 42 (parent's payment of subsidiary's expenses, incurred before parent's purchase of stock paid by parent after §334(b)(2) liquidation, but held part of parent's basis for assets; post-liquidation costs deductible by parent).

[171] See, e.g., Rees Blow Pipe Mfg. Co., 41 TC 598 (1964) (nonacq.), aff'd per curiam, 342 F2d 990 (9th Cir. 1965); InterCity TV Film Corp., 43 TC 270 (1964). Compare Manuel Mayerson, 47 TC 340 (1966) (acq.) (99-year purchase money

A similar problem was created when the amount to be paid by the parent for the stock was contingent (e.g., on resolution of the subsidiary's contingent liabilities or achievement of a specified level of earnings in future years). The only alternatives appeared to be the estimated cost approach of Rev. Rul. 55-119[172] (subject to later prospective adjustments once the contingencies were resolved) or the open basis theory asserted by the Service in *Pacific Transport.* A deduction for the payments when made would be improper in this situation, since the amounts in question were paid for the acquisition of property.[173]

5. Valuation problems: cash equivalents; goodwill, and other noncash assets. The regulations under §334(b)(2) required the parent's stock basis, as adjusted, to be spread ratably among the liquidated subsidiary's noncash assets (including goodwill) in proportion to their relative values.[174] Attempts by the parent to assign specific values to assets in the stock purchase transaction were thus apparently foreclosed.[175] Debates over the relative mix of asset values could be considerable as a result of this approach, and two categories of property, cash equivalent assets and goodwill, caused much of the difficulty. In Rev. Rul. 66-290,[176] the Service defined cash to include currency, checking accounts, time deposits, drafts, checks, money orders, and certificates of deposit, all of which are valued at face. Accounts receivable, notes, inventory, and marketable securities, even if highly liquid in charac-

---

liability part of cost basis under §1012, even though there was no personal liability and no amortization of the debt was required); supra note 170; David Bolger, 59 TC 760 (1973).

[172] Rev. Rul. 55-119, 1955-1 CB 352.

[173] See generally Woodward v. CIR, 397 US 572 (1970); Hilton Hotels Corp. v. US, 397 US 580 (1970). But compare Associated Patentees, Inc., 4 TC 979 (1945) (acq.); Rev. Rul. 67-136, 1967-1 CB 58; supra ¶ 5.04; supra note 116; infra ¶ 11.48.

[174] If some of the assets cannot be assigned a reasonably accurate value when the liquidation occurs, the result may be an open liquidation under Burnet v. Logan, discussed supra ¶ 11.03, text at notes 20–27; Lee & Bader, infra note 211.

[175] For an illustration, see Boise Cascade Corp. v. US, supra note 164, in which the court held that securities, inventory, prepaid supplies and accounts receivable were not equivalent to cash but that debt of a parent to the subsidiary was. Also, the buyer could not overturn the regulation's allocation priorities on intent grounds; thus, the *Williams v. McGowan* principle was held not applicable to a stock acquisition. See also Ralph R. Garrow, 43 TC 890 (1965), aff'd per curiam, 368 F2d 809 (9th Cir. 1966) (relative value allocation mandatory).

See generally Rogers, Purchase Price Allocations in Taxable Acquisitions: New Frontiers—New Hazards, 62 Taxes 813 (1984); Banc One Corp., 84 TC 476 (1985), aff'd without opinion, 815 F2d 75 (6th Cir. 1987); supra ¶ 11.11, and infra ¶ 11.48.

[176] Rev. Rul. 66-290, 1966-2 CB 112.

ter, were excluded from this definition and entered into the basis allocation mechanism of §334(b)(2).[177]

Whether or not goodwill is present on the subsidiary's liquidation depends, in general, upon continuity of the acquired business as a viable entity. Fusion of the subsidiary's assets into the parent's general operations or liquidation of most of the properties through sales and the like would indicate the parent's lack of interest in preservation of the acquired enterprise as a going concern, and so precluded allocation of basis to goodwill as an asset. If goodwill existed, however, any purchase premium in excess of the value of the other properties had to be assigned to this item, rather than spread among the other assets in proportion to their values.[178]

6. Reorganization aspects. If the parent liquidated a recently acquired subsidiary and then reincorporated the assets, there was a possibility that the transaction would be recharacterized as a tax-free reorganization (resulting in a carry-over of basis), rather than as a §332-334(b)(2) liquidation followed by a §351 transfer, as explained later in this treatise.[179]

¶ 11.46 ELECTIVE TREATMENT OF CERTAIN STOCK PURCHASES AS ACQUISITIONS OF TARGET CORPORATION'S ASSETS: INTRODUCTORY

1. Background: Deficiencies in §334(b)(2). Nearly 30 years of experience with the intricacies of §334(b)(2) exposed a host of deficiencies in its

---

[177] R.M. Smith, Inc., supra note 164 (prepaid federal income taxes cash equivalent; but no allocation of basis to receivables in excess of face on facts here, even though receivables not cash equivalent); Rev. Rul. 77-456, 1977-2 CB 102 (allocation of basis to receivables can never exceed their *face*, although can have allocation of basis less than face); Boise Cascade Corp., supra note 164; see infra ¶ 11.48 for allocation rules under §338.

[178] On the problems of valuing various assets acquired in a §334(b)(2) liquidation, see Jack Daniel Distillery v. US, 379 F2d 569 (Ct. Cl. 1967) (valuation of bulk inventory and goodwill); see also Knapp King-Size Corp. v. US, 527 F2d 1392 (Ct. Cl. 1975) (per curiam) (inventory acquired after purchase of subsidiary's stock); for guidelines in determining value of inventory in a §334(b)(2) liquidation of bulk purchase, see Rev. Proc. 77-12, 1977-1 CB 569.

See also Banc One Corp., supra note 175 (excess price in bank acquisition nondeductible goodwill or going concern value; not depreciable intangible for either loan portfolio premium or core deposit base; goodwill determined under residual method here); see also Concord Control, Inc., supra note 19 (purchase price premium allocable to nonamortizable intangible asset called "going concern value" even though court found as a fact that no goodwill was present); VGS Corp., supra note 19 (same); see Henszey, Going Concern Value After *Concord Control*, 61 Taxes 699 (1983).

[179] See generally infra ¶¶ 14.53, 14.54, and 14.57.

operation, ranging from excessive complexity and discontinuities in its interim adjustment rules to the potential for creative manipulation inherent in the extended period during which the purchased subsidiary could be kept alive before liquidation.[180] The asset purchase theory of §334(b)(2) was seen as being inconsistent with the fact that continuation of the purchased subsidiary's life was allowed for as long as five years after its acquisition, since inclusion in the buyer's consolidated return during this period allowed the acquired company's tax attributes to be used by the consolidated group.[181] Moreover, recapture income generated on the eventual liquidation could be sheltered by losses of other members of the group, a result not available where assets are directly purchased. Finally, selectivity in tax results (stepped-up basis for some assets and survival of tax history for others) could be arranged through a variety of pre-acquisition or post-acquisition planning techniques.

2. Enactment of §338: Elective treatment of qualified stock purchases. Against this background, Congress repealed §334(b)(2) in 1982 and replaced it (along with any nonstatutory equivalent[182]) with §338. Under §338, in the case of a "qualified stock purchase" (defined by §338(d)(3) as, roughly speaking, the purchase of at least 80 percent of the target corporation's stock in one or more transactions within a 12-month acquisition period, which may, if the 80 percent block is purchased in a single transaction, be as short as one day), a purchasing corporation can elect to treat the target (1) as having sold all of its assets in a single transaction for their fair market value and (2) as if it were a new corporation purchasing the assets on the day after the acquisition. The effect of this deemed sale is that the target's assets acquire a new basis equal to their fair market value, which, assuming a pur-

---

[180] See generally Ginsburg, Taxing Corporate Acquisitions, 38 Tax L. Rev. 171 (1983); Bonovitz, Taxable Dispositions of a Corporate Business Before and After TEFRA, 60 Taxes 812 (1982); Battle, Section 338—Stock Purchases Treated as Asset Purchases for Tax Purposes, 60 Taxes 980 (1982); Ward, The TEFRA Amendments to Subchapter C: Corporate Distributions and Acquisitions, 8 J. Corp. L. 277 (1983); Bloom, The Stark Reality of the New Liquidation and Redemption Rules, 10 J. Corp. Tax'n 3 (1983); Silverman & Serling, An Analysis of the TEFRA Changes Affecting Corporate Distributions and Acquisitions, 59 J. Tax'n 274 (1983); Heinkel, Section 338—An Analysis and Proposals for Reform, 59 Notre Dame L. Rev. 158 (1983); N.Y. State Bar Association, Tax Section, Report of the Committee on Corporations on Section 338, 37 Tax Lawyer 155 (1983); Henderson, Planning Possibilities Under Section 338, 36 S. Cal. Tax. Inst. ch. 9 (1984); Indoe, IRC Section 338, 44 NYU Inst. on Fed. Tax'n ch. 26 (1986).

[181] See infra ¶ 15.24.

[182] E.g., any judge-made exception to the carry-over basis principle of §332(b)(1), such as the *Kimbell-Diamond* case (supra note 148).

chase of all of the target's stock, will normally be identical with the amount paid by the purchasing corporation for the stock plus the target's liabilities.

The hypothetical rebirth of the target as a new corporation at dawn on the day following the hypothetical sale of its assets does not affect its status under state law; the born again corporation is the same legal entity that it was on the previous day.[183] For tax purposes, however, the corporation is a new entity not only because of the statutory change in the basis of its assets, but also because, as explained subsequently, it is not burdened with any earnings and profits or other old tax attributes. In honor of this change, the regulations sometimes refer to the "old target" or the "new target," depending on whether pre- or post-acquisition tax attributes or other matters are involved, although there is only a single corporation so far as state law is concerned.

In 1982, when §338 was enacted, the target corporation recognized neither gain nor loss on the deemed sale, because by statutory fiat it satisfied the requirements of the then-current rules of §337.[184] Thus, although §338— like §334(b)(2) before it—was often described as treating the purchase of a subsidiary and its prompt liquidation as tantamount to a direct purchase of the assets, the analogy was valid only for the purchasing corporation. As to the target corporation, the analogy was invalid, since it would have recognized gain or loss on an actual sale of its assets but recognized neither under pre–1987 law if the transaction took the form of a purchase of the target's stock followed by liquidating distribution of its assets to the new parent.

The nonrecognition rules of §337, however, were repealed in 1986, and a concomitant change was made in §336(a), relating to distributions by the target corporation[185]. These changes had two interrelated effects. First, they converted the one-way approach of pre-1987 law, as described, into a two-way approach by allowing the purchasing corporation to treat the purchase of a target corporation's stock as a purchase of the assets only if the target recognizes its gain or loss on the deemed sale of its assets. Second, these changes deprived §338 elections of virtually all of their allure. Because of this dramatic alteration of the environment within which §338 operates, an election is now likely to be advantageous only if the target has losses to offset the gains on the deemed sale, holds primarily depreciated property, or

---

[183] Moreover, the hypothetical liquidation of the target occurs only at the corporate level; the shareholders of the target (both the purchasing parent and any unacquired minority shares) are unaffected by this event.

[184] For the pre-1987 version of §337, see infra ¶ 11.61. For the very different post-1986 provision bearing the same number—an inexcusably confusing drafting deficiency—see infra ¶ 11.49.

[185] For §336(a) as amended in 1986, see supra ¶ 11.06. For the repeal of pre-1987 §337, see infra ¶ 11.61. For a limited transitional preservation of old §337, see infra ¶ 11.60, text at note 234.

can profit from a stepped-up basis because it will support increased deductions for depreciation or amortization. An irony of this reduced importance of §338 is that the statutory changes bringing it about were enacted less than a year after the most voluminous regulations in history were promulgated by the Treasury to explain the operation of §338.[186] Although not exactly dead on arrival, these "temporary" regulations may prove truer to their label than their drafters imagined.

The hardy few who still contemplate an election under §338 have a primary choice: whether to make the election or not. Whatever decision is made, they then have a secondary choice: whether to keep the target alive or to liquidate it.

If the election is made, the target must recognize gain or loss on the deemed sale; the assets acquire a new basis (which, roughly speaking and disregarding complexities, is equal to their fair market value); and the target's tax history (including such attributes as loss carry-overs, earnings and profits, and accounting methods) are obliterated. The purchasing corporation then has the option either to keep the born-again target alive or to liquidate it.

(1) If the target is liquidated, the purchasing corporation acquires the assets with their new fair market value basis, but it does not inherit the target's old tax attributes, since they were eliminated by the election; thus, an election with a liquidation has substantially the same tax consequences as a simple purchase of the target's assets.

(2) If the election is not followed by a liquidation of the target, the results are comparable to a purchase of the assets coupled with their immediate transfer to a newly created subsidiary under §351. The no-liquidation procedure, however, permits the target corporation to be preserved as an entitiy for state law purposes, a privilege that may be useful if franchises, contracts, or other rights would be jeopardized by a liquidation; by contrast, under old §334(b)(2), the target had to be liquidated if the purchasing corporation wanted to step up the basis of its assets to the price paid by it for the stock.

If, on the other hand, the purchasing corporation does not make a §338 election, the tax transaction is treated as a purchase of the target's stock rather than as an acquisition of the target's assets. The target accordingly recognizes neither gain nor loss, and its tax attributes, including the basis of its assets, are unaffected by the change in ownership.

If the target is not liquidated, it simply becomes a member of the purchasing corporation's family. If, however, the target is liquidated, its assets pass to the parent with a carry-over basis; and its other tax attributes are

---

[186] Temp. Regs. §§1.338-1T–1.338-5T.

similarly inherited by the parent under §381(a)(1), although subject to disallowance under §269(b) if the subsidiary is liquidated pursuant to a plan adopted within two years after acquisition and tax avoidance is the principal purpose of the liquidation.[187]

3. Consistency requirements: Inadvertent elections. Because §338 is an elective provision, taxpayers can use it in those unusual situations when it will be beneficial—as just explained—but avoid an election when it will be disadvantageous, as is typically the case after 1986. This "heads I win, tails you lose" feature of §338, however, is qualified by two sets of so-called consistency rules, under which the purchasing corporation may be forced to use §338 even if it intended to avoid it. These consistency requirements, and a procedure for avoiding an inadvertent election by making a protective carry-over basis election, are explained in the following text.[188]

4. Elective recognition of gain or loss by target corporation: Sale of stock treated as sale of assets. A conventional election under §338 is made by the purchasing corporation, and this election does not affect the seller, since the target's hypothetical sale of its assets is deemed to take place at the close of the acquisition date. Thus, if the seller's basis for the target's stock is below its fair market value, the seller must recognize its gain on selling the stock, even though the target will also recognize gain if the purchaser makes a §338 election.

Section 338(h)(10), however, provides an alternative election, available if the target is a member of an affiliated group of corporations (whether the group files a consolidated return or not[189]), under which the target recognizes gain or loss as if it had sold its assets in a single transaction, and the selling corporation does not recognize gain or loss on its sale of the target's stock. If the seller has a substantial gain on its stock and the subsidiary also has a substantial gain on its assets, a §338(h)(10) election permits the seller to dispose of the subsidiary subject to only one tax (at the subsidiary's level), even though the purchasing corporation obtains the subsidiary with a

---

[187] For §381(a)(1), see generally infra ¶ 16.10; for the tax-avoidance proviso, see §269(b), explained in H.R. Rep. 432, 98th Cong., 2d Sess. 1623, Part 2 (1984). For §269 generally, see infra ¶ 16.21.

[188] See infra ¶ 11.47, text at notes 198–204. For protective carry-over basis elections, see infra text at notes 205–206.

[189] Before 1987, §338(h)(10) elections could be made only if the target's group filed a consolidated return; but the Tax Reform Act of 1986 permits the Service to lift this restriction by regulations, §338(h)(10)(B). See also §336(e), for a comparable election by a parent corporation that has made a taxable disposition of its subsidiary's stock under §336, supra ¶ 11.06.

stepped-up basis for its assets. Moreover, a §338(h)(10) election is advantageous if the subsidiary's inside asset gain is lower than the parent's outside stock gain.

By treating a sale of stock as a sale of assets, §338(h)(10) reaches substantially the same result, so far as basis is concerned, as would have been achieved if the selling corporation had liquidated the target subsidiary under §332, taken over the subsidiary's basis for its assets under §334(b)(1), and then sold the assets to the purchasing corporation. Like an election under §338(h)(10), moreover, such a liquidation-cum-sale also preserves the target's tax attributes (e.g., loss carry-overs) for the benefit of the selling parent corporation, which inherits those attributes in the actual (or deemed) §332 liquidation of the target-subsidiary. Similarly, a conventional sale of the target's stock also preserves its tax attributes, which are retained by the target if it is kept alive or, if it is liquidated, are inherited by the purchaser if it does not make an election under §338(a) or is able to ward off disallowance under §269(b) by establishing that tax avoidance was not the primary purpose for the liquidation.[190]

¶ 11.47   SECTION 338: THE ELECTION AND ITS EFFECTS

In order to examine the details of §338, the following discussion covers (1) the threshold requirement of a qualified stock purchase by the purchasing corporation of the target's stock; (2) the election itself; (3) the consistency rules, which may result in an inadvertent deemed election; (4) determination of the amount to be allocated among the target's assets; and (5) the allocation method. The rules of §338 are then illustrated by a series of examples.[191]

---

[190] For §269(b), see supra note 187.

[191] The final two topics on this list are considered infra ¶ 11.48. As of this writing, neither the published articles nor the temporary regulations take account of the 1986 changes in §§336(a) and 337 that, as noted supra text following note 185, have dramatically reduced the appeal of §338 elections. For pre-1987 law, see generally O'Hara & Schiffhouer, Stock Purchases Treated as Asset Acquisitions—Section 338, Tax Mgmt. Portfolio (BNA) No. 16-16th (1986); Wellen, A Revised Roadmap to Section 338, 32 Tax Notes 447 (1986); Wexler & Welke, Temporary Regs. Under Section 338—Consistency and Complexity, 63 Taxes 916 (1985); Silverman & Risinger, Temporary Regs. Under Section 338: An Analysis of the Consistency Provisions, 63 J. Tax'n 282 (1985); N.Y. State Bar Association, Tax Section, Report on the Temporary Section 338 Regulations, 30 Tax Notes 137 (1986); Henderson, Tax Planning for Taxable Stock Acquisitions Under the Section 338 Temporary Regulations, 38 S. Cal. Tax Inst. ch. 2 (1986); Faber, The Search for Consistency in Corporate Acquisitions, 13 J. Corp. Tax'n 187 (1987); Buchholz, The Consistency Requirements of Section 338—Inconsistencies and Incongruities, 13 J. Corp. Tax'n 283 (1987).

1. Qualified stock purchase. A "qualified stock purchase" is defined by §338(d)(3) as a transaction or series of transactions within a 12-month acquisition period in which the purchasing corporation purchases stock of the target corporation in the amount specified by §1504(a)(2) (i.e., stock possessing at least 80 percent of the total voting power and at least 80 percent of the total value of the target's stock, excluding certain nonvoting, nonparticipating, nonconvertible preferred stock).[192] As was true under §334(b)(2), a purchase for this purpose is essentially a cost-basis acquisition from an unrelated party.[193] Purchases by two or more members of an affiliated group of corporations can be amalgamated under §338(h)(8) in applying the 80 percent stock ownership requirements.[194] Purchases by individuals, partnerships, and trusts and estates are not taken into account; these disqualified purchasers can, however, lay the groundwork for an election under §338 by organizing a corporation and having it make the requisite purchases.

If the target corporation has a subsidiary, its stock is deemed to be acquired on the acquisition date of the target's stock, and the same is true of lower-tier subsidiaries. Thus, the assets of these corporations, like the assets of the target itself, qualify for a new basis on the theory that they are sold and repurchased immediately after the hypothetical sale and repurchase of the target's assets.[195]

In satisfying the 80 percent stock purchase requirement of §338(d)(3), stock acquired before the 12-month acquisition period begins is not taken into account, but the cost or other basis of this prematurely acquired stock—called "nonrecently purchased stock" by §338(b)(6)(B)—is included in the basis allocated to the target's assets by virtue of §338(b)(1)(B) if the purchasing corporation acquires enough additional stock within the 12-month period to make a valid election. If, however, the purchaser owns more than 20 percent of the target's stock before the 12-month period begins, subsequent purchases will not satisfy the 80 percent requirement unless an extra-

---

[192] These stock requirements are identical with those required to effect a §332 liquidation of the newly acquired subsidiary. See supra ¶ 11.41.

[193] Section 338(h)(3)(A) essentially tracks the purchase definition of old §334(b)(3); see supra notes 154–156. Similarly, §§338(h)(1) and 338(h)(2) define the acquisition time frame in the same manner as old §334(b)(2), supra note 155. See Temp. Regs. §1.338-4T(c)(1).

[194] For this purpose, an affiliated group has the same meaning as under §1504 but without the exceptions in §1504(b) (e.g., foreign corporations, possessions corporations, tax exempt corporations). See §338(h)(5); infra ¶ 15.21. For the aggregation of purchases, see Temp. Regs. §1.338-4T(h)(1) (stock considered purchased and held by parent if purchased or held by any member of parent's affiliated group).

[195] See S. Rep. No. 494, 97th Cong., 2d Sess. 194 (1982); §338(h)(3)(B); see also Temp. Regs. §§1.338-4T(c)(2) and 1.338-4T(c)(3). For prior law, which had a similar purchase rule for a chain of subsidiaries, see supra note 159.

neous event (e.g., an issue of additional stock) clears the way for a qualifying purchase.

2. The election. Under §338(g), the election must be made no later than the 15th day of the ninth month beginning after the month in which the acquisition date (i.e., the date within the 12-month acquisition period on which the requisite 80 percent ownership is acquired) occurs. Once made, the election is irrevocable under §338(g).

If all or part of the target's stock is transferred to other members of the purchasing corporation's affiliated group, the purchasing corporation presumably continues to be the member entitled to make the election.[196] If split acquisitions are made by a purchasing affiliated group (e.g., half of the target's stock is purchased by the parent and half by its subsidiary),[197] identification of the proper electing member is less clear, although the most likely candidate is the controlling parent.

3. Consistency requirements. A major theme of §338 is consistency of treatment when the purchasing corporation acquires two or more members of the same affiliated group or combines a purchase of assets from the target or an affiliate with a qualified stock purchase.[198] This all-or-nothing group-wide approach applies to actions during the "consistency period," defined by §338(h)(4) to consist of the one-year period beginning before the 12-month acquisition period, the acquisition period itself, and the one-year period immediately following the acquisition period (or longer if the Service determines under §338(h)(4)(B) that there was a plan to make a qualified stock purchase plus one or more other stock purchases or asset acquisitions[199]).

The stock purchase consistency rule, imposed by §338(f), applies to all qualified purchases of stock of members of an affiliated group during the consistency period. Under §338(f), a §338 election as to the first such purchase automatically applies to all later qualified purchases of the stock of the target's affiliates within the consistency period. Conversely, a failure to make a §338 election on the first purchase precludes an election for the sub-

---

[196] See H.R. Rep. No. 760, 97th Cong., 2d Sess. 538 n.2 (1982), noting that §338(h)(8) (treating acquisitions by affiliates of the purchasing corporation as an acquisition by the purchasing corporation) will prevent intragroup transfers of purchased stock from disqualifying a §338 election, citing Chrome Plate v. US, supra note 157.

[197] For the aggregation of purchases in this situation, see supra note 194.

[198] See articles listed supra note 191.

[199] For circumstances warranting such an extension of the consistency period, see Temp. Regs. §1.338-4T(g)(1), Question 1.

sequent acquisitions during the consistency period. A "target affiliate," for this purpose, is defined by §338(h)(6) as a member of the target corporation's affiliated group at any time from the beginning of the consistency period to the acquisition date.[200]

The asset acquisition consistency rule, imposed by §338(e)(1), provides that if the purchasing corporation acquires an asset of the target or a target affiliate at any time during the consistency period, the purchasing corporation is deemed to have made a §338(a) election for the target unless the acquisition is pursuant to a sale in the ordinary course of the seller's business,[201] the purchasing corporation's basis for the acquired property is determined wholly by reference to the transferor's basis (e.g., a §332, §361, or §351 acquisition),[202] or the acquisition meets conditions prescribed by regulations.[203]

To buttress the stock purchase and asset acquisition consistency rules, the Service is armed by §338(e)(3) with an antiavoidance weapon, authorizing it to treat a planned stock acquisition that meets the 80 percent requirements as a qualified stock purchase if necessary to carry out the purpose of the consistency rules.[204] Thus, if the purchasing corporation makes a qualified stock purchase of the target and, pursuant to a plan, purchases at least 80 percent of the stock of a target affiliate over a 15-month period, the normal 12-month acquisition period can be extended to transmute the second transaction into a "qualified stock purchase," with the result that the consistency rules of §338(f) apply.

4. Protective carry-over basis election. The regulations prescribe a procedure by which a corporation making a qualified stock purchase can protect itself against a deemed election under §338(e)(1), triggered by a tainted asset acquisition.[205] As its name implies, a "protective carry-over basis elec-

---

[200] For the meaning of "affiliated group," see §338(h)(5); for the exclusion of certain foreign and other corporations, see §338(h)(6)(B); for the stock purchase consistency regulations, see Temp. Regs. §1.338-4T(e).

[201] For this exception, see Temp. Regs. §1.338-4T(f)(3); the basis carry-over rules are §§334(b) and 362.

[202] For this exception, see Temp. Regs. §1.338-4T(f)(4).

[203] For this exception, which covers various transactions that do not involve a step-up in basis (such as dividends in kind of loss property), see Temp. Regs. §1.338-4T(f)(5); see also Temp. Regs. §1.338-4T(f)(7) (de minimis exception).

[204] For regulations extending the 12-month acquisition period under §338(e)(3), see Temp. Regs. §1.338-4T(g)(1), Question 2.

[205] See Temp. Regs. §1.338-4T(f)(6)(i)(A). See generally Bonovitz, Making the Protective Carryover Basis Election Under the Sec. 338 Temp. Regs., 63 J. Tax'n 10 (1985).

tion" requires the purchasing corporation to carry over the seller's basis for the tainted asset. The result, subject to limited relief provisions and other conditions, may be that the purchasing corporation will be taxed on disposing of the tainted property even though the seller was also taxed when it transferred that property to the purchasing corporation.

If a timely protective carry-over election is not filed, a tainted asset acquisition will be treated as an "affirmative action carry-over election" (a curious label, since the "election" is involuntary, but the "affirmative action" presumably is the acquisition of the tainted asset), which has substantially the same effect as an actual carry-over basis election, except that the district director can override the affirmative action carry-over election and impose a deemed election under §338(e)(1).[206]

¶ 11.48 ALLOCATION OF BASIS PURSUANT TO §338 ELECTION

1. Introductory. The mechanism provided by §338 to harmonize the tax treatment of qualified stock purchases and that of acquisitions of the target's assets involves a hypothetical sale of assets by the target and its hypothetical rebirth as a new corporation. More precisely, §338(a) provides that if the purchasing corporation makes a §338 election (or is treated as having done so by virtue of the consistency rules[207]), the target corporation must be treated as having (1) sold its assets at the close of the acquisition date at their fair market value in a single transaction and (2) as having become a new corporation that purchased all of the assets as of the beginning of the following day.

When §338 was enacted, the target's hypothetical sale of its assets was not ordinarily a taxable event (except for recapture property), because the sale qualified for nonrecognition of gain or loss under the pre-1987 version of §337. Old §337, however, was repealed by the Tax Reform Act of 1986 as a by-product of the Act's rejection of the *General Utilities* doctrine.[208] Under post-1986 law, the target's hypothetical sale ordinarily triggers the recognition of gain or loss.

The function of the target's hypothetical sale of its assets and its hypothetical repurchase of the same assets on the following day, along with §338's related basis-allocation rules, are illustrated in the following example.

---

[206] Temp. Regs. §1.338-4T(f)(6)(i)(A).

[207] For these rules, see supra text at notes 198–206.

[208] For old §337, see infra ¶ 11.61; for the *General Utilities* doctrine and its repeal, see supra ¶¶ 7.21, 9.34, and 11.06.

To illustrate: Assume that target corporation *T* owns a single asset with an adjusted basis of $300,000 and a fair market value of $1 million, that *T*'s business liabilities aggregate $400,000, and that a sale by *T* of its asset would generate a tax liability of $250,000. Purchasing corporation *P* buys all of *T*'s stock for its fair market value of $350,000 ($1 million less liabilities of $400,000 and less potential tax liability of $250,000) and makes an election under §338.

Under §338(b), as explained in more detail later, *T* is treated as selling and then repurchasing its assets for $1 million (i.e., the amount paid by *P* for *T*'s stock ($350,000), plus *T*'s liabilities of $650,000 (business liabilities of $400,000 plus tax liability of $250,000 arising from *T*'s hypothetical sale of its assets)). This amount is allocated to *T*'s only asset, with the result that a subsequent *actual* sale of the asset by *T* (or by *P*, if it acquires the asset through a tax-free liquidation of *T* under §332) will generate no additional gain or loss. For *P*, this result mirrors the result that would have been reached if *P*, instead of buying *T*'s stock for $350,000, had bought the asset for $1 million, either from *T* directly or from *T*'s parent corporation after the latter obtained it from *T* through a tax-free liquidation under §332.

In real life, the facts are virtually always more complicated than in the preceding example. Among the more commonly encountered problems is the determination of the aggregate amount to be allocated among *T*'s assets if, for example, *P* does not acquire all of *T*'s stock during the 12-month acquisition period, either because *P* acquired some of *T*'s stock before the period began or because some of *T*'s stock is owned by minority shareholders who refuse to sell. Problems can also arise in allocating the aggregate amount of basis among *T*'s assets, especially if goodwill or going concern value is involved. The regulations prescribe elaborate rules for these and other issues.

2. Aggregate basis to be allocated. As prescribed by §338(b), the basis of the assets in the hands of the reborn target corporation when it emerges from §338's womb consists of four elements, which are aggregated to produce what the regulations call "adjusted grossed-up basis."[209] These four components of AGUB are the following:

(a) The grossed-up basis of the purchasing corporation's recently purchased stock (i.e., stock purchased within the 12-month acquisition period). If there

---

[209] Temp. Regs. §1.338-4T(j)(l); see generally Bush & Mullaney, Basis Allocations for a Target's Assets Under the New Section 338 Temp. Regs., 64 J. Tax'n 328 (1986).

are no outside shareholders on the acquisition date, this amount is the basis of the recently purchased stock. If, however, some of the target's stock is owned by outsiders, the term "grossed-up basis" is defined by §338(b)(4) by reference to a fraction that, in effect, treats the stock of outsiders as having been purchased for the same average per-share price as the purchasing corporation's recently purchased stock in computing the basis to be allocated to the target's assets. For example, if P purchases 80 percent of T's stock during the 12-month acquisition period for $1 million and the other 20 percent is owned by minority shareholders, the grossed-up basis of P's stock as defined by §338(b)(4) is $1.25 million ($1 million $\times$ $^{100}/_{80}$).

(b) *The basis of the purchasing corporation's nonrecently purchased stock, if any.* This amount can be stepped up to an amount commensurate with the grossed up basis of the recently purchased stock by an election to recognize the gain under §338(b)(3). For example, if P owns 90 percent of T's stock (which was recently purchased with a grossed-up basis of $9 million) and 10 percent of nonrecently purchased stock (with a basis of $600,000), the latter amount can be stepped up for AGUB purposes to $1 million ($9 million $\times$ $^{10}/_{90}$), provided the purchasing corporation recognizes gain of $400,000 ($1 million less $600,000).

(c) *T's liabilities.* Under §338(b)(2), adjustments to AGUB are to be made to reflect the target corporation's liabilities, pursuant to regulations. Under the temporary regulations, AGUB includes the target's bona fide liabilities on the acquisition date if these would be included in basis had the target acquired the assets from an unrelated person and, as part of this hypothetical acquisition, the target had assumed (or taken the assets subject to) the liabilities.[210] Speculative or contingent liabilities do not initially qualify for inclusion in AGUB, but they can be taken into account if and when they become fixed and determinable.[211] Because an election under §338 results in a deemed sale by the target of its assets as of the close of the acquisition date, the tax liability resulting from this sale is included in AGUB. Section 338(a)(1) provides that the assets must be treated as having been sold "at fair market value in a single transaction," and one might infer from the lengthy regulations that "fair market value" was a newly minted phrase requiring an encyclopedic explanation. To compute the target's tax liability for purposes of AGUB, the regulations create a new concept—the "aggregate deemed sale price"—to be used in determining the target's gain or

---

[210] Temp. Regs. §1.338(b)-1T(f); see also Temp. Regs. §1.338(b)-3T(c).

[211] Id. For related problems under former §334(b)(2), see supra notes 168–173. See generally Lee & Bader, Contingent Income Items and Cost Basis Corporate Acquisitions: Correlative Adjustments and Clearer Reflection of Income, 12 J. Corp. Law 137 (1987).

loss, which in turn determines its tax liability.[212] ADSP can be determined either by a conventional appraisal of the target's assets or by use of an elective ADSP formula pursuant to §338(h)(11). The method of computing ADSP, which is elaborated in great detail by the regulations,[213] in effect treats the purchasing corporation's acquisition of the target's stock as establishing an arm's-length market value for its assets.

(d) Other relevant items. In addition to the target's liabilities, AGUB is adjusted for other relevant items, as prescribed by regulations. The vague statutory reference to "other relevant items" is clarified by the regulations, which limit its scope to (1) items arising solely from adjustment events occurring after the target's first taxable year (e.g., contingent payments, price rebates, or a liability that was contingent on the acquisition date but became fixed and determinable at a later time) and (2) items noted on the examination of a return that affect the cost to the purchasing corporation of its interest in the target's assets (e.g., distributions from the target to the purchasing corporation and postacquisition purchases of minority shares for less than the average price of the purchasing corporation's recently purchased stock).[214]

3. Allocation of AGUB among the target's assets. Section 338(b)(5) provides that the AGUB amount determined under §§338(b)(1) and 338(b)(2) must be allocated among the target's assets pursuant to regulations. For this purpose, the temporary regulations divide the target's assets into four classes,[215] which are dealt with in hierarchical fashion:

(1) Class I—cash, demand deposits, and similar accounts.

(2) Class II—certificates of deposit, U.S. government securities, readily marketable stock or securities, and foreign currency.

(3) Class III—tangible and intangible assets (other than Class I, II, and IV assets), whether or not depreciable, depletable, or amortizable.

(4) Class IV—intangible assets in the nature of good will and going concern value.

---

[212] Temp. Regs. §§1.338-4T(h)(1) and 1.338-4T(h)(2)(i).

[213] See generally Temp. Regs. §1.338-4T(h).

[214] See Temp. Regs. §§1.338(b)-1T(b)(2)(ii), 1.338(b)-1T(g), and 1.338(b)-3T(a)(1).

[215] Temp. Regs. §1.338(b)-2T(b). The same quadripartite division is used in allocating aggregate deemed sales price to the target's assets in computing its tax liability on the deemed sale; see Temp. Regs. §§1.338-4T(h)(2)(iii) and 1.338-4T(h)(2)(vi); see also supra ¶ 11.11 (use of same division in applying §1060, relating to certain direct acquisitions of assets involving goodwill or going concern value). For similar allocation rules under former §334(b)(2), see supra notes 174–178.

AGUB is reduced by the Class I assets (which do not thereby acquire a basis, since they are not bought or sold in the conventional sense and do not generate gain or loss when disposed of). This AGUB amount is then allocated among Class II assets in proportion to their fair market value at the beginning of the day following the acquisition date, but not in excess of their fair market values; the remaining AGUB is allocated in the same manner among Class III assets; and finally, any residual AGUB is allocated to the target's Class IV assets. This so-called residual method of allocating AGUB is more likely to assign high values to goodwill and going concern value, which cannot be amortized, than does the more conventional so-called two-tier allocation method, under which a lump sum purchase price is allocated to all assets to the extent of their separate fair market values, with any excess then being allocated among them in proportion to their first-tier values.

The regulations address in some detail a variety of special problems in the allocation of AGUB to the target's assets, including the effect of any nonrecently purchased stock and of such adjustment events as additional payments by (or refunds to) the purchasing corporation with respect to its stock in the target.[216]

4. Examples. The application of the §338 rules can be illustrated by the following examples, in which T is the target corporation and X and Y are wholly owned subsidiaries of T, P is the acquiring corporation and has one wholly owned subsidiary (S), and each group files consolidated returns.

Example 1: P (or S) purchases all of T's stock for cash and makes the §338 election.

Under the 1982 version of §338, P was deemed to have purchased the stock of X and Y as well as T's stock. Accordingly, the T group's taxable year closed, and each member was deemed first to have sold its assets under former §337 with no gain or loss (except for recapture) at a price equal to its allocable share of P's purchase price (plus any adjustment for recapture tax liability) and then to have repurchased these assets at the same price and entered P's consolidated group with a clean slate (each member having purged its tax history and stepped up or stepped down its asset bases prior to includability in P's consolidated return).

However, under the Tax Reform Act of 1984 amendment to §338(h)(3)(B), the X and Y *stock* is deemed to have been sold and repur-

---

[216] See Temp. Regs. §1.338(b)-2T(c)(3) (nonrecently purchased stock) and §1.338(b)-3T (subsequent adjustments to AGUB); for an application of the residual method under the statutory predecessor of §338, see Banc One Corp., supra note 175; R.M. Smith, Inc. v. CIR, supra note 164. See generally Bush & Mullaney, supra note 209.

chased by T (and thus is controlled as to T by P's election, or nonelection of §338, under the §338(f) consistency rules). In addition, §338(h)(15) allows a combined deemed sale return by the T, X, and Y group. See Temp. Regs. §1.338-4T(k)(6).

Finally, because the Tax Reform Act of 1986 repealed §337 and the reference to §337 in §338(a), T (and its subsidiaries, X and Y) will have full recognition of gain or loss on their deemed asset sales after 1986 (including, for T, gain or loss on its stock in subsidiaries X and Y).

Example 2: The same results occur as in Example 1 if, within the two-year consistency zone of §338(h)(4), P acquires assets from T, X, or Y, or if P buys X and Y stock in a series of stock purchases, regardless of the order. However, the provisions do not apply if T, X, and Y do not constitute an affiliated group under §1504.[217]

Example 3: If P acquires one or more of T's affiliates in a basis carryover reorganization, the consistency rule of §338(e) does not apply by virtue of §338(e)(2)(B).

Example 4: If P purchases only 80 percent of T's stock, the deemed §338(b) sale price would be grossed up to 100 percent.

Under the 1982 version of §338, T, X, and Y obtained §337 nonrecognition for only 80 percent of their gain by virtue of §338(c)(1), unless P acquired the rest of T's stock within one year by purchase or completely liquidated T, X, and Y within such period.[218]

However, after the Tax Reform Act of 1984 amendment to §338(h)(3)(B), X and Y could get *full* §337 protection because T was deemed to have sold and repurchased *all* of its X and Y stock.

Now, after the repeal of §337 (and §338(c)(1)) by the Tax Reform Act of 1986, all members of the T group have full recognition of gain or

---

[217] This would be the case, for example, if X and Y both had outstanding issues of *participating* preferred stock or nonvoting common stock owned by persons other than T. See infra ¶ 15.21. Substantial changes in the consolidated return eligibility rules of §1504 were effected by the Tax Reform Act of 1984, which make it considerably more difficult to attain affiliated status, and thus may have increased the opportunity of using various decontrol ploys.

[218] On the liquidation of T (and X and Y), P would inherit T's (and X and Y's) stepped-up basis that resulted from the §338 election by virtue of §334(b)(1). But after the Tax Reform Act of 1984, only T would have to be liquidated to avoid the §338(c)(1) tax; see infra Example (8). The Tax Reform Act of 1984 also added §338(h)(7), which requires that additional stock acquisitions must be by purchase or a §302(a) redemption by target. However, §338(c) was repealed by the Tax Reform Act of 1986.

loss on their deemed asset sales (including gain or loss on the stock of X and Y) if §338 is elected by P.

Example 5: If P already owns 20 percent of T's stock and buys the remaining 80 percent in a qualified purchase, the gross-up pricing rules of §338(b) formerly resulted in a 100 percent basis step up to T, X, and Y, which were presumably able to count P's preexisting ownership for applying the pre-1986 §337 nonrecognition rules under former §338(c)(1).

Under the gross-up basis rules of §338(b) after the Tax Reform Act of 1984 amendments, however, basis is not grossed up to the extent of P's potential gain in old and cold T stock unless P elects to recognize its gain on that stock. [219]

Example 6: P buys 20 percent of T's stock in January and 20 percent in each of March, May, July, and September. A qualified purchase results (for T, X, and Y stock), the acquisition date occurs with the July purchase (when 80 percent control is acquired), and the acquisition period ends 12 months after the January purchase. The fact that P had options to acquire any of T's stock is disregarded under §338(h)(3)(A)(iii).

The deemed sale price for the T group's assets is the full fair market value of T's assets, and the deemed asset sales occur as of the July control acquisition date. [220] Thus, any income to the T group as a result of its deemed asset sales is reportable in the T group's final return preceding the July acquisition date, and T (and its affiliates) enter P's con-

---

[219] While §338(c)(1) speaks of cases where P holds less than 100 percent of T's stock, by implication it would seem that if P held all of that stock as a result of both prior minority ownership and a qualified 80 percent control purchase, §337 would have applied in full to the deemed sale. But the Tax Reform Act of 1984 revised the deemed basis rules of §338(b) and now denies a basis step-up for any unrealized appreciation attributable to the previously held target stock unless P elects to be taxed on the gain attributable to its old and cold T stock. See Temp. Regs. §1.338-4T(j). In effect, the surrogate tax rules of former §338(c)(1) and the taxable gain election rules of §338(b)(3) were mutually exclusive. However, the Tax Reform Act of 1986 repealed §338(c)(1) as part of its repeal of the *General Utilities* doctrine, supra ¶ 11.06.

[220] By virtue of former §338(c)(1), T, X, and Y could get 100 percent §337 protection under pre-1986 law, since P acquired the rest of T's stock within one year of the July acquisition date. But see §338(h)(7), supra note 218 (such additional stock acquisitions must be by purchase or by a §302(a) redemption). However, §338(c)(1) was repealed by the Tax Reform Act of 1986.

T's deemed acquisition of X and Y also occurs on the July acquisition date under the Tax Reform Act of 1984 amendments to §338(h)(3)(B), even if X and Y were only 80 percent owned by T (see infra Example (8)).

solidated return immediately after such date (with a clean slate) as if their assets had been purchased by the *P* group.

The deemed purchase price also includes any tax liability generated in the *T* group as a result of these deemed asset sales. A statutory circle existed under pre-1984 law, however, since the deemed sale price included tax liability while tax liability depended on the deemed sale price. If consistency with asset sales is the goal, tax liability should be computed based on the actual (grossed up) stock sale price, and then adjusted upward for the resulting tax liability; the Tax Reform Act of 1984 achieved this result under the revised deemed sale and purchase rules of §§338(a)(1) and 338(b).

Example 7: If *P* makes additional investments in *T* (or *X* and *Y*) after acquiring control, such amounts are not reflected in asset basis because they occur with respect to the stock of new corporations *T, X,* and *Y*.[221]

Example 8: If *T* owns 80 percent of *X, X* owns 80 percent of *Y,* and *P* buys 80 percent of *T* stock and elects §338, the deemed purchase rules of §338(h)(3)(B) result in a qualified purchase of the *T* stock by *P,* of the *X* stock by *T,* and of the *Y* stock by *X.*

¶ 11.49 LIQUIDATING SUBSIDIARY'S RECOGNITION OF GAIN OR LOSS

1. In general. Section 332 provides that a parent corporation does not recognize gain or loss on liquidating a subsidiary, but it says nothing about the effect of the liquidating distribution on the subsidiary. As noted earlier, the Tax Reform Act of 1986 generally requires a liquidating corporation to recognize gain or loss on distributing its appreciated or depreciated assets;[222] but, consistent with the basis carry-over principle of §334(b), this requirement does not apply to distributions to an 80 percent distributee in a complete liquidation to which §332 applies. Section 337(a) as enacted in 1986 provides instead that the subsidiary does not recognize gain or loss on such distributions, including distributions to satisfy debts to its parent corpora-

---

[221] Similarly, any stock basis adjustments required by the consolidated return regulation investment basis rules are not considered here either.

Moreover, additional income generated in the acquiring corporation's consolidated return as a result of post-acquisition adjustments to the purchase price of the acquired corporation's stock is to be accounted for separately, according to the Committee Reports; see S. Rep. No. 494, supra note 195, at 194, and H.R. Rep. No. 760, supra note 196, at 537. Presumably, separate return limitation year-type computations will be made with respect to such amounts; see infra ¶ 15.24. Temp. Regs. §1.338(b)-3T(h)(2) so provides.

[222] See supra ¶ 11.06.

tion.[223] The term 80 percent distributee is defined by §337(c) as the parent corporation, whose ownership of 80 percent or more of the subsidiary's stock brings the nonrecognition principle of §332 into play.

The subsidiary, however, is not protected against the recognition of gain if the 80 percent distributee is a tax exempt organization unless the distributed property is used by the organization in an unrelated trade or business.[224] This limitation is imposed because the carry-over of the liquidating subsidiary's basis under §334(b), although technically applicable to a tax exempt parent, will not ensure ultimate recognition of gain on a disposition of property by the tax exempt distributee unless it uses the property in an unrelated business.

The nonrecognition of gain and loss on distributions of property to an 80 percent distributee applies only to the property actually distributed to the parent, not to the parent's pro rata share of the subsidiary's gain and loss. For example, if the subsidiary distributes Blackacre (fair market value of $800 and adjusted basis of $790) to its 80 percent parent and distributes Whiteacre (fair market value of $200 and adjusted basis of $10) to the shareholders owning the remaining 20 percent of its stock, the subsidiary's $10 gain on Blackacre is not recognized, but its $190 gain on Whiteacre must be recognized, even though the parent's share of the $200 aggregate gain is $160 ($200 × $80/100). Moreover, if Whiteacre's basis were $250, the subsidiary's $50 loss would not be recognized.[225] Regardless of the tax effect of distributing Whiteacre on the subsidiary, Whiteacre's basis in the hands of the minority shareholders would be $200, its fair market value, and this is also the amount used in determining the shareholders' gain or loss on surrendering their shares in exchange for the liquidating distribution.[226]

---

[223] See §§337(a) and 337(b)(1) (the latter of which provides the same rule as former §332(c) of pre-1986 law). Note also that §334(b)(2) (the parent's carry-over basis rule for property received in satisfaction of the subsidiary's debt) still refers (erroneously) to §332(c), the predecessor of §337(b)(1); but the Technical Corrections Act of 1987, in §106(e)(6), revises §334(b) to correct this error; see supra ¶ 11.42. Gains, if any, on distributions to minority shareholders are not covered by the nonrecognition principle of §337(a), but §336(d)(3) precludes the recognition of losses on such distributions.

[224] For recognition of gain (including any applicable recapture amount) if the property ceases to be used in the exempt organization's unrelated business, see Conf. Rep., supra note 51, at II-202.

See also §367(e)(2) (nonrecognition principle of §§337(a) and 337(b)(1) inapplicable to foreign corporations except as permitted by regulations); Notice 87-5, 1987-3 IRB 7 (regulations to be issued under §367(e), dealing with foreign-to-foreign liquidations).

[225] Section 336(d)(3). For Service acceptance of targeted distributions generally, see Rev. Rul. 83-61, 1983-1 CB 78.

[226] Section 334(a); see generally supra ¶ 11.04.

2. Qualified §332 liquidations and the mirror subsidiary technique. Section 334(b), requiring the parent to carry over the subsidiary's basis on a §332 liquidation, applies not only to liquidations of old subsidiaries but also to the liquidation of subsidiaries newly acquired in a tender offer or other recent acquisition, even if the price paid for the stock greatly exceeds the target company's basis for its assets.[227]

The carry-over of basis in the latter situation has given rise to the "mirror subsidiary" device, which can be best explained with an example.

To illustrate: Target company *T* owns both a hotel division (fair market value, $15 million; adjusted basis, $12 million) and a computer software division (fair market value, $5 million; adjusted basis, $1 million). Purchasing corporation *P* wants to acquire and operate *T*'s hotel business, but is not interested in the software division. *T*'s shareholders are willing to sell all of their stock for $20 million but will not agree to any arrangement to split off either division. *P* is prepared to buy the stock, believing that it can sell the software division for its proportionate share ($5 million) of the $20 million purchase price for *T*'s stock, provided this can be done without a tax on the unrealized appreciation in either the hotel or software division ($3 million and $4 million respectively).

If *P* does what comes naturally—a purchase of *T*'s stock, followed by a liquidation of *T*—the liquidation will be tax-free under §332, but *P* will have to take over *T*'s basis for the assets,[228] and this means that a sale of the software division will generate gain of $4 million (sale price of $5 million, less carry-over basis of $1 million).

Enter now the mirror subsidiary device. *P* creates two new subsidiaries: *MS-1*, with $15 million of capital, and *MS-2*, with $5 million of capital. *MS-1* and *MS-2* purchase 75 and 25 percent respectively of *T*'s stock; *T* liquidates by distributing the hotel division to *MS-1* and the software division to *MS-2*; *P* sells the stock of *MS-2* for $5 million, as anticipated. At first blush, the mirror subsidiaries do not seem to help because neither *MS-1* nor *MS-2* owns 80 percent of T, as required for a §332 liquidation; and if the liquidation is not subject to §332, *T*, as the liquidating corporation, must recognize its entire $7 million gain under §336(a). However, the consolidated return regulations contain a provision aggregating the stock ownership of affiliated corporations for certain purposes, including the stock ownership requirement of

---

[227] See supra ¶ 11.44.

[228] As explained supra ¶ 11.47, *P* could elect under §338 to use the fair market value of *T*'s assets as its basis, but this would require *T* to recognize its $7 million gain on all of its assets, both the hotel division and the software division.

§332(b)(1).[229] If this aggregation rule applies to mirror subsidiary transactions, then *T* would not recognize gain on its liquidating distributions to *MS-1* and *MS-2*. This would in turn mean that *MS-1* and *MS-2* take over *T*'s basis for its distributed assets; but *MS-2*'s low inside basis for the software assets might not be troublesome to the hypothetical purchaser of its stock (e.g., because the appreciation primarily reflects the value of the software division's good will, which is unlikely to be sold in the near (or even in the remote) future.

The effect of the Tax Reform Act of 1986 on the mirror subsidiary device, however, is not free from doubt: After the chairmen of the House Committee on Ways and Means and the Senate Finance Committee disagreed publicly on this question, the Treasury announced that it would not revise the consolidated return regulations or take other regulatory action before completing a general study of Subchapter C.[230] The announcement suggests, however, that if the sale of a mirror subsidiary is a prearranged part of the original acquisition, it might run afoul of the step transaction doctrine and be treated as a taxable sale of assets by the target company.

3. Examples. These provisions can be illustrated by the following examples in which *T* is an operating company that also owns two operating subsidiaries, *T-1* and *T-2; T-2*, in turn, owns all of operating subsidiary *T-3. T*'s sole shareholder is individual *A*.

Example 1: T liquidates completely. *T* will have full recognition of gain or loss on all of its assets, assuming that any loss assets have not been contributed within the five-year predistribution period, and that §355 does not apply to the distribution of the *T-1* and *T-2* stock (which it could not on these facts because *T* is not a mere holding company under §355(b)(1)). If §355 did apply, *T* would not be taxable on the distribution of its subsidiaries' stock. *T-1, T-2,* and *T-3* have no tax consequences as a result of *T*'s liquidation (unless *T* elected, under §336(e), to treat the taxable disposition of the *T-1* and

---

[229] Regs. §1.1502-34, infra ¶ 15.21.

[230] Letter signed by Secretary James Baker, Dec. 9, 1986, reprinted in 33 Tax Notes 1073 (1986); see also Treasury Punts on Mirror Transactions, 33 Tax Notes 988 (1986); and other discussions there cited; Peter L. Faber Letter, 32 Tax Notes 1022 (1986); Sheppard, The Prodigal Son of Mirror, 34 Tax Notes 444 (1987); Sheppard, The Mirror Cracked, 34 Tax Notes 538 (1987); Hiegel & Schler, supra note 44, at 966; Kliegman, Do Mirror Transactions Survive the 1986 Act?, 66 J. Tax'n 206 (1987); Sheppard, Mirror Transactions Go Forward, 35 Tax Notes 1057 (1987); Rev. Proc. 87-23; 1987-21 IRB 18 (no ruling).

T-2 stock as an asset sale at the first-tier subsidiary level, in which event the two subsidiaries, *T-1* and *T-2* (but presumably not *T-3*) would have recognized gain or loss on that portion of the transaction, but *T* would not).

Example 2: All of *T*'s subsidiaries are liquidated upstream into *T*. No gain or loss results to any entity here, since the assets stop at the parent level; but if assets are actually distributed to minority shareholders of *T-1, T-2,* or *T-3,* such distributing subsidiary will recognize gain, but not loss, on that distribution.

Example 3: *T-3* sells all of its assets to corporate buyer *P* and liquidates into *T-2*. *T-3* has full recognition, but *T-2* has none (the same result as under former §337(c)(2) of pre-1987 law).

Example 4: *T-2* sells all of its *T-3* stock to corporate buyer *P*. Full gain or loss results to *T-2* (unless §338 is elected by *P* and both *T-2* and *P* elect §338(h)(10) or unless *T-2* makes the new §336(e) election to treat the transaction as a *T-3*-level asset sale, with the same results as Example 3).

Example 5: *T* distributes the *T-1* stock, and §355 applies. No gain or loss results to *T* here, since §311(b)(1) does not apply to a §355 distribution (see Chapter 13).

Example 6: *T* merges into *P* Corporation for *P* stock and liquidates. No gain or loss results to *T* on either the merger or the liquidation distribution of *P* stock under §§336(c) and 361 (see Chapter 14); no change occurred in the law here, unless *T* distributes appreciated boot, in which case gain (but not loss) would be recognized to *T* under new §361(c) (infra ¶ 14.32).

Example 7: *P* Corporation buys all of the *T* stock and does not elect §338. No tax results to *T* or its affiliates, even if there are later upstream §332 liquidations into *P*. (Note that if *P* has tax-loss carry-overs, it can sell off parts of the *T* group and shelter any gains with its own loss carry-overs, as discussed in Chapter 16.)

Example 8: *P* Corporation creates mirror subsidiaries *P-1, P-2,* and *P-3,* which then jointly acquire all the stock of *T* with cash contributed by *P* equal to the value of the *T* stock; *T* is then liquidated into *P*'s three subsidiaries, with *T*'s operating assets going to *P-3* and the stock of *T-1* and *T-2* going to *P-1* and *P-2* respectively. Whether the mirror subsidiary device still works under the 1986 amendments is presently unclear, although the stock aggregation rules of Regs. §1.1502-34 indicate that §332 will apply in this case unless and until those regulations are amended.

PART C. NONRECOGNITION OF GAIN OR LOSS ON 1987-1988 LIQUIDATIONS OF CERTAIN SMALL BUSINESS CORPORATIONS

¶ 11.60 QUALIFICATION FOR 1987-1988 TRANSITIONAL EXEMPTIONS

When Congress amended §336(a) in 1986 to require corporations to recognize gain or loss on liquidating distributions, it granted a transitional exemption preserving the nonrecognition principle of pre-1987 law for certain small business corporations liquidating in 1987 or 1988.[231] This nonrecognition principle is, however, subject to the exceptions for gain or loss on §453B installment obligations and for gain on certain LIFO inventory that were set out in the pre-1987 version of §336(a).[232]

The 1986 change in §336(a) was also accompanied by the repeal of two provisions that were inconsistent with the new rules: (1) old §337, providing for the nonrecognition of corporate gain or loss on certain sales of assets after the adoption of a plan of complete liquidation if the corporation liquidated within 12 months thereafter and (2) §333, permitting certain shareholders of a corporation to elect not to recognize gain on a liquidating distribution, but requiring them to preserve their stock basis as the basis of the corporation's basis for the assets.[233] The repeal of these provisions, however, was subject to a transitional exemption for 1987 and 1988 liquidating distri-

---

[231] See §633(d)(1), Pub. L. No. 99–514, 100 Stat. 2287 (1986), which is not part of the Code and which contains a reference to "this section" when "this subtitle" is evidently intended (a proposed amendment to this effect is pending in §106(g)(3) of the Technical Corrections Act of 1987).

For the application of the transitional exemption to corporations that completely liquidated in 1986, that took specified action before August 1, 1986 and completely liquidate before 1988, or that are covered by a so-called targeted (i.e., special beneficiary) grandfather clause, see supra text at notes 61 and 62.

[232] The pre-1987 version of §336(a) was also subject to assignment of income and similar qualifications (discussed supra ¶ 11.07), and to a variety of provisions, scattered through the Code, treating liquidating distributions as recapture events; see generally the Fourth Edition of this treatise, ¶ 11.61.

[233] See infra ¶ 11.61 for old §337, and infra ¶ 11.62 for old §333.

butions by certain small business corporations, identical with the §336(a) transitional exemption mentioned above.[234]

Eligibility for these transitional exemptions is limited to corporations satisfying three conditions:

(1) The fair market value of the corporation's stock when the plan of complete liquidation is adopted (or, if greater, its value on August 1, 1986) must not exceed $10 million;

(2) From August 1, 1986 to its complete liquidation, more than 50 percent by value of its stock must be held by 10 or fewer individuals, estates, or certain types of trusts;[235] and

(3) The liquidation must be completed before January 1, 1989.

In computing the number of shareholders and determining whether they qualify, stock held by corporations, trusts, or partnerships is treated as owned proportionately by the shareholders, beneficiaries or partners; and stock owned by members of the same family (directly or by attribution) is treated as owned by one person.[236]

Although the limit on qualifying for transitional relief is set at $10 million, full benefits are granted only to corporations with a value of less than $5 million, and the percentage of gain or loss covered by the exemption is reduced from 100 to zero proportionately for corporations with a value between $5 million and $10 million. Moreover, the nonrecognition rule does not encompass gains and losses on ordinary income items or short-term capital assets, nor does it cover gains on installment obligations subject to §453B.

Although the transitional exemption (for both liquidating distributions and liquidating sales) was enacted as a favor to qualifying corporations, it

---

[234] Section 633(d), Pub. Law No. 99–514, 100 Stat. 2278 (1986). Section 633(d) is not incorporated in the Code.

As explained earlier in this work, the transitional exemptions for qualified corporations are not explicitly limited to the gain or loss on liquidating distributions; hence, §633(d) also preserves pre-1987 law for corporate gains and losses on partial liquidations and §303 redemptions (relating to distributions to pay death taxes and the like), provided the corporation meets the value and stock ownership rules summarized in the text and completely liquidates by the end of 1988. See supra ¶ 9.34, text at note 216. See also §106(g)(6) of the Technical Corrections Act of 1987.

[235] The Conference Report, supra note 51, sets out a five-year holding period that does not appear in §633(d) as enacted but that was included in a corrective but unenacted concurrent resolution; see 132 Cong. Rec. H8447, §74 (daily ed., Sept. 25 1986); see currently §106(g)(5)(B) of the Technical Corrections Act of 1987.

[236] See §633(d)(6)(B), which incorporates by reference the definition of "family" in §318(a)(1). The shareholder ownership requirements generally track permissible shareholders in S corporations, supra ¶ 6.02.

See generally Schmehl, How Liquidations and S Elections May Avoid the Impact of TRA '86, 67 J. Tax'n 30 (1987).

applies to losses as well as to gains; and it is mandatory rather than elective. Thus, a qualifying corporation with an overall loss that would otherwise be recognized under §336(a) as amended in 1986 is willy-nilly subject to pre-1987 law. A possible escape hatch is to delay completion of the liquidation until after 1988. This gambit may fail if the delay serves no business purpose (for example, if a trivial amount is retained by the corporation instead of being distributed[237]), but there is some authority under old §337 for giving effect to the delay in an analogous situation.[238]

At best, however, this escape is available only to unusually knowledgeable or well-advised taxpayers. For others, a careful reading of the relevant provisions of the Code will not suggest—not even by a cross-reference—that the Tax Reform Act of 1986 contains a grandfather clause, intended as a boon to small business corporations, that can operate to disallow a loss that the current version of §336(a) explicitly sanctions.

¶ 11.61 NONRECOGNITION OF CORPORATE GAIN OR LOSS ON SALES WITHIN ONE-YEAR PERIOD FOLLOWING ADOPTION OF PLAN OF COMPLETE LIQUIDATION

1. **Introductory.** As explained earlier in this chapter, under pre-1954 law, corporations did not ordinarily recognize gain or loss on liquidating distributions of their assets; but if the corporation sold its assets instead of distributing them, the gain or loss was recognized even if the corporation subsequently distributed the proceeds of the sale to its shareholders in complete liquidation.[239] Moreover, this difference in tax results was complicated by the Supreme Court's 1945 decision in *CIR v. Court Holding Co.*, holding that an ostensible distribution of the corporate assets to the shareholders in complete liquidation followed by a prearranged sale by them could, on an analysis of all the facts, be recharacterized as a taxable sale by the corporation, coupled with a distribution of the sales proceeds to the shareholders.[240] The impact of the *Court Holding Co.* doctrine, however, was greatly restricted by the enactment in 1954 of old §337, providing for the nonrecog-

---

[237] See Rev. Rul. 80-177, 1980-2 CB 109 (applying constructive receipt doctrine to cash-basis shareholder who delayed surrendering shares, evidently to shift income to a later year).

[238] See infra ¶ 11.61, note 250, and text at notes 257–258.

[239] See supra ¶ 11.07, at para. 7.

[240] CIR v. Court Holding Co., supra note 76. For discussion of this case and of US v. Cumberland Pub. Serv. Co., supra note 77, which qualified its scope, see supra ¶ 11.07, para. 7.

nition of gain or loss on sale-liquidation transactions meeting the requirements summarized in the following text.

Although old §337 was repealed in 1986, it was preserved for corporations qualifying for the 1987–1988 transitional exemption described previously.[241] For this reason, it is referred to below in the present tense.

2. Adoption of plan of complete liquidation. The general rule of old §337(a) provides that if a corporation (1) adopts a plan of complete liquidation and (2) distributes all of its assets (less those retained to meet claims) in complete liquidation within the 12-month period beginning on the date of the adoption of the plan, it does not recognize gain or loss from the sale or exchange of property within the 12-month period.[242] The regulations provide that sales made on the same day that the plan is adopted are subject to §337 even if they precede adoption of the plan, and they also sanction preplan negotiations and executory contracts to sell the assets (as distinguished from an actual contract of sale).[243]

If no formal resolution was adopted at any time, the courts sometimes came to the taxpayer's rescue by holding that a plan of liquidation can be adopted without a document in writing and that the plan can be gleaned from all of the facts of a business transaction.[244] This pattern of behavior is obviously not to be recommended, however, since it may take a lawsuit to establish the applicability of §337; and the cases are in conflict.

Section 337 has the effect of changing the result in cases like *Court Holding Co.,* because even if a sale by the shareholders is imputed to the

---

[241] Supra ¶ 11.60, text at notes 234–236.

[242] For the application of §337 to insolvent corporations, see §337(g), which overruled Rev. Rul. 56-387, 1956-2 CB 189 (§337 cannot apply to insolvent corporations because assets are distributed to creditors, not to shareholders).

For a detailed analysis of old §337, see Rock & von Gal, Corporate Liquidations Under §337, Tax Mgmt. Portfolio (BNA) No. 18-16th 1986, and the Fourth Edition of this treatise, ¶¶ 11.63–11.67.

[243] Regs. §1.337-2(a). Note, however, that a transfer of title and possession and unconditional obligations by the seller and buyer may turn a purported executory contract to sell into a completed contract of sale. If this occurs before the plan is adopted, §337 does not apply.

For other problems in interpreting old §337(a)'s reference to a "sale or exchange . . . of property," particularly the status of such transactions as condemnations, collection of insurance proceeds after a fire, and discharges of debt for less than the face amount owed, see Rev. Rul. 64-100, 1964-1 CB 130 (casualty losses covered); §337(e) (special timing rule for involuntary conversions).

[244] See J.B. Mitchell, ¶ 72,219 P-H Memo. TC (1972), and cases there cited; Rev. Rul. 65-235, 1965-2 CB 88 (§337 applied to sale, where shareholders owning enough stock to approve corporate dissolution agreed before sale to complete liquidation). But see Intercountry Dev. Corp., ¶ 61,217 P-H Memo. TC (1961).

corporation on the ground that they acted merely as a conduit for a corporate sale, the gain is not recognized by the corporation under §337(a) if the sale occurs within 12 months following adoption of the plan of liquidation. This assumes, of course, that the corporation liquidates in 1987 or 1988 and thus qualifies for the postponed effective date described above.[245] Thus, the corporation itself can negotiate with potential buyers and make the sale; there is no need for the shareholders to liquidate the corporation before looking for a buyer for the assets or to employ the ritual endorsed by the *Cumberland Public Service Co.* case.[246]

3. Complete distribution within 12-month period. Section 337 requires all corporate assets to be distributed in complete liquidation within the 12-month period beginning on the date the plan is adopted[247] except for assets retained to meet claims. Although contingent and disputed claims may be provided for, as well as those that are fixed in amount, the amount retained must be reasonable and the arrangements for payment must be made in good faith.[248] The regulations state that the term "claims" does not embrace amounts set aside to meet claims of shareholders with respect to their stock; but the Tax Court may disagree on this point, at least if the claims are insignificant in amount. A safer way, however, to provide for payment to shareholders who cannot be located or whose rights are in dispute is the distribution of the net assets to an escrow agent or trustee for the shareholders.[249] This device may also be useful in providing for payment of contingent creditor claims against the corporation, since it may avoid the problem of proving that a retention of assets by the corporation itself is reasonable in amount.

---

[245] See generally CIR v. Court Holding Co., supra note 76; for the transitional exemption, see supra text at note 234.

[246] See US v. Cumberland Pub. Serv. Co., supra note 77.

[247] For problems in computing the elapsed time, see Rev. Rul. 79-3, 1979-1 CB 143; Rev. Rul. 83-116, 1983-2 CB 264 (no extensions for Saturdays, Sundays, or holidays); E.B. Grain Co., 81 TC 70 (1983) (contra).

[248] O.B.M., Inc. v. CIR, 427 F2d 661 (2d Cir. 1970) (reasonable excuse for failure to distribute within 12 months where taxpayer had contingent liabilities and contingent assets); but see Vern Realty, Inc., 58 TC 1005 (1972), aff'd mem. (1st Cir. 1973) (deposit of liquidating sales proceeds in bank account did not constitute §337(a) distribution; constructive receipt doctrine not applicable).

[249] See Rev. Rul. 80-150, 1980-1 CB 316 (liquidating trust); Jeanese, Inc. v. US, 341 F2d 502 (9th Cir. 1965) (inventory assets retained to meet claims); Regs. §1.337-2(b) (retention to pay shareholder claims not allowed; distribution to trustee for shareholders permissible); Mountain Water Co. of La Crescenta, 35 TC 418 (1960) (acq.) (small amounts retained to meet shareholder claims); Rev. Rul. 63-245, 1963-2 CB 144 (distribution of claim that could be readily transferred to trustee for shareholders for collection and distribution of proceeds; approved); Rev. Rul. 65-257, 1965-2 CB 89 (distribution to escrow agent for dissenting minority shareholders).

Introducing an elective element into ostensibly mandatory provisions, a Service ruling holds that §337 is inapplicable if distribution of the assets is deliberately delayed until the 12-month period expires, even if this is done to permit losses to be recognized.[250]

4. Inventory property and installment obligations. Section 337 is inapplicable to sales of the corporation's stock in trade, inventory, and most installment obligations. These items are excluded because §337 was aimed at winding up sales, rather than at sales in the regular course of business that happened to occur during the final months of the corporation's life. In keeping with this spirit, however, §337(b)(2) makes an exception for a bulk sale of substantially all the inventory property to one person in one transaction. Although the statute is silent on the time when the "substantially all" test is to be applied, Regs. §1.337-3(b) provides that this determination is to be made at the time of the bulk sale. Thus, a corporation can make taxable sales of inventory property in the regular course of business after adoption of its plan of liquidation, with a tax-free bulk sale of its remaining stock in trade just before distribution of its assets in liquidation. Moreover, because §337(b)(2) permits a bulk sale of stock in trade attributable to *a* business of the corporation, §337(a) applies to the bulk sale of inventory of one business, without regard to what the corporation does with the stock in trade of any *other* business in which it may be engaged.[251]

5. Relation of old §337 to assignment of income, clear reflection of income, and tax benefit principles. As noted earlier, a substantial body of case law and rulings evolved before 1987 in the complete liquidation area, under which a corporation that distributed its assets in kind was required to recognize the accrued or potential income inherent therein even though the distribution itself was not a taxable event under pre-1987 law.[252] Whether these authorities invoke assignment of income principles, the requirement of §446(b) that the taxpayer's accounting method must clearly reflect income, or the tax benefit doctrine, they must be reckoned with by corporations subject to old §337 by virtue of the 1987–1988 transitional exemption.[253]

---

[250] Rev. Rul. 77-150, 1977-1 CB 88.

[251] Because the complexities of §337's treatment of inventory and installment obligations are of significance only to the limited group of corporations qualifying for the 1987–1988 transitional exemption, readers are referred to the materials cited supra note 242 for a more detailed analysis of this subject. (In any event, transition relief is not available for this type of property; see supra text after note 236.)

[252] See supra ¶ 11.07.

[253] For special problems in applying these principles to liquidations under old §337, see materials cited supra note 242.

6. Deemed sales under §338. Before it was amended in 1986, §338 permitted certain purchases of stock to be treated as acquisitions of the target corporation's assets if the purchasing corporation elected to treat the target as having sold all of its assets on the date of acquisition and as having reincorporated on the following day as a new corporation.[254] Under §338(a)(1), this deemed sale was treated as a transaction subject to §337; thus, the target recognized neither gain nor loss on the deemed sale, even though it did not actually distribute its assets in complete liquidation, as §337 ordinarily required.[255]

7. Ineligible corporations. Even if they otherwise qualify under the transitional exemption for complete liquidations in 1987 or 1988, collapsible corporations, subsidiary corporations liquidating under §332, and corporations electing to liquidate under §333 are barred from employing old §337.[256]

8. Avoidance of §337 to recognize losses. Section 337 is not in form elective, and it provides for the nonrecognition of both gains and losses on sales by the corporation within the prescribed one-year period. If, however, a corporation wishes to avoid the application of §337 (e.g., to recognize losses that will generate refund claims when carried back and applied against taxable income reported in earlier years), it can either sell its assets before adopting the plan of liquidation or postpone the liquidation until 1989. Since these gambits require the recognition of both gains and losses on the sale, the corporation may try to take advantage of the best of both worlds by selling the depreciated property before the plan is adopted, adopting the plan, selling the appreciated assets, and then liquidating within the statutory transitional period. If the straddle is taken at face value, an otherwise eligible corporation can recognize its losses (because they will not be subject to §337), while using §337 to shield its gains from recognition.

The regulations seek to discourage straddles by stating that the plan of liquidation is ordinarily adopted when the shareholders adopt a resolution authorizing such action, but that if the corporation sells a substantial part of its assets before the resolution, "the date of the adoption of the plan of liquidation shall be determined from all the facts and circumstances."[257] The Ser-

---

[254] For the 1986 amendments to §338 that eliminate references to old §337 and thus require gain or loss to be recognized on the deemed sale, see supra ¶ 11.46.

[255] Id.

[256] For collapsible corporations, see §337(c)(1)(A) and infra ch. 12; for §332 liquidations, see §337(c)(2) and supra ¶ 11.40; for §333 liquidations, see §337(c)(1)(B) and infra ¶ 11.62.

[257] Regs. §1.337-2(b).

vice, however, has not been very successful in disallowing losses on the ground that a plan of liquidation was adopted by an oral agreement or understanding before the depreciated property was sold.[258]

¶ 11.62   NONRECOGNITION OF SHAREHOLDER GAIN ON ELECTIVE ONE-MONTH LIQUIDATIONS IN 1987 OR 1988

1. Introductory. Section 333—repealed in 1986 except for certain small business corporations (as defined) that completely liquidate before 1989[259]— provides that, under certain circumstances, a shareholder's gain on the complete liquidation of a corporation may go unrecognized if he and enough other shareholders so elect. Because of §333's transitional applicability to certain 1987–1988 transactions, it is referred to here in the present tense, despite its repeal in 1986.

The principal function of §333 is to permit a corporation holding appreciated property but having little or no earnings and profits or cash to be liquidated without the recognition of gain by its shareholders. If the corporation has any earnings and profits or if it distributes cash or stock or securities acquired by it after December 31, 1953, the shareholder's gain is recognized in whole or in part, depending upon certain conditions described hereafter. In return for the nonrecognition of gain under §333, the Code exacts the usual price of nonrecognition: The shareholder's basis for the assets received on the liquidation is the same as his basis for the stock surrendered (adjusted if any gain was recognized). On a later sale of the assets (and assuming no change in value), the shareholder will recognize the gain that went unrecognized at the time of the liquidation.

Despite the shareholder's exposure to tax when the distributed assets are sold, §333 lets the corporation off scot-free, no matter how much the assets may have appreciated in its hands. This regime was consistent with the *General Utilities* principle embodied in pre-1987 law, which did not tax corporations on a liquidating distribution of appreciated assets; but it became outmoded in 1986, when the *General Utilities* principle was

---

[258] See Virginia Ice & Freezing Corp., 30 TC 1251 (1958); City Bank of Wash., 38 TC 713 (1962) (nonacq. on this point, 1964-2 CB 8); see also Rev. Rul. 77-150, 1977-1 CB 88.

[259] For the conditions that must be satisfied to qualify for this transitional exemption, see supra ¶ 11.60, text at notes 234–236. For examples illustrating the exemption, see Rev. Rul. 87-4, 1987-2 IRB 6.

repealed,[260] and §333 was an ancillary victim of that change in legislative policy. Section 333, however, has been allowed to linger on for the benefit of the shareholders of specified small business corporations that liquidate in 1987 or 1988, and its requirements and tax consequences are accordingly summarized below.[261]

2. Scope of nonrecognition. Section 333 applies only to the gains of "qualifying electing shareholders" (as defined). It does not apply to losses, nonelecting shareholders, or collapsible or so-called excluded corporations.[262]

A qualified electing shareholder does not recognize any gain on shares owned by him when the plan of liquidation was adopted if the corporation has no post-1913 earnings and profits, *and* if he receives no money or stock or securities acquired by the liquidating corporation after December 31, 1953. Otherwise, the qualified electing shareholder must recognize gain, if any, to the extent of the greater of the following:

(1) His ratable share of the post-1913 earnings and profits (computed under accrual principles), or

(2) The sum of the money received by him and the fair market value of any stock or securities so received that were acquired by the liquidating corporation after December 31, 1953.

3. Basis of property received. If a shareholder takes advantage of §333, the basis of any property received (other than money) is prescribed by former §334(c). The underlying principle is that the basis of the shareholder's stock in the liquidating corporation is carried over and becomes the basis of the property received in exchange. More explicitly, §334(c) provides that the basis of the property received is the same as the basis of the stock, less any money received and plus any gain recognized under §333.

As is ordinarily the result when the basis of property given up in a nontaxable exchange is substituted for the basis of property received, §334(c) has as its purpose the recognition, when the assets are sold or other-

---

[260] See supra ¶¶ 7.21 and 11.06.

[261] For more detailed discussions of §333, see Schoenfeld, Tomasulo, Berlin & Nicholson, Corporate Liquidations Under Section 333, Tax Mgmt. Portfolio (BNA) No. 58-7th (1986), and the Fourth Edition of this treatise, ¶ 11.20. See also Rev. Rul. 87-1, 1987-2 IRB 4.

[262] For collapsible corporations, see infra ch. 12. For excluded corporations, see §333(b) (corporation owning 50 percent or more of total combined voting power of stock entitled to vote on plan). For earnings and profits aspects, see Rev. Rul. 87-1, 1987-2 IRB 4.

wise disposed of, of the gain that went unrecognized at the time of the liquidation. Because a §333 liquidation is a closed rather than open transaction,[263] however, the character of the gain or loss ultimately realized by the shareholder on the distributed assets depends upon whether they are capital or ordinary assets in his hands and on whether the disposition is a "sale or exchange" under §1222. Thus, in *Osenbach v. CIR*, gain realized by the shareholder on collecting claims that had been distributed to him in a §333 liquidation was taxed as ordinary income, although a substantial portion of it would have been taxed as capital gain at the time the claims were distributed to him had the transaction been a normal §331(a) liquidation.[264]

4. Qualified electing shareholders. To qualify for nonrecognition of gain under §333, the taxpayer must be a qualified electing shareholder, which requires satisfying these conditions:

(1) The shareholder must own stock when the plan of liquidation is adopted and must elect under §333 within 30 days thereafter.[265]

(2) The shareholder must not be an "excluded corporation"—one that, at any time between January 1, 1954 and the date the plan of liquidation is adopted, owned stock possessing 50 percent or more of the total combined voting power of all classes of stock entitled to vote on the adoption of the plan.

(3) If the shareholder is not a corporation, he will qualify only if elections are filed by noncorporate shareholders who, when the plan is adopted, own stock possessing at least 80 percent of the total combined voting power of the noncorporate-owned stock entitled to vote on the adoption of the plan.

(4) If the shareholder is a corporation, it will qualify only if elections are filed by corporate shareholders who, when the plan is adopted, own stock possessing at least 80 percent of the total combined voting power of the corporate-owned stock (other than stock owned by an excluded corporation) entitled to vote on the adoption of the plan.

5. Plan of liquidation. Section 333(a)(1) requires that the liquidation occur pursuant to a plan of liquidation.[266]

---

[263] For this distinction, see supra ¶ 11.03.

[264] Osenbach v. CIR, supra note 24.

[265] For the election, see Regs. §1.333-3. For revocation of an improvident election, see DiAndrea, Inc., ¶ 83,768 P-H Memo. TC (1983); Kulsrud, Escaping Improvident Election Under Section 333: Revocations After DiAndrea, 13 J. Corp. Tax'n 27 (1986).

[266] For the term "plan," see supra ¶¶ 11.02 and 11.41, text at notes 134–135.

6. Complete cancellation and redemption of stock. Section 333(a)(2) provides that the distribution must be "in complete cancellation or redemption of all the stock." Despite this requirement, Rev. Rul. 54–518 permits the retention of the liquidating corporation's charter (to protect the corporate name against appropriation), so long as the corporation distributes all of its assets and enters a state of quiescence.[267]

7. Transfer of all property in one calendar month. Section 333(a)(2) provides that the transfer of all the corporation's property under the liquidation must occur "within some one calendar month." No reason comes to mind for this insistence on haste, which is, however, somewhat alleviated by a tolerant attitude in the regulations toward arrangements for paying unascertained and contingent liabilities.[268] Some relief also results from the fact that the month of distribution need not be the month in which the plan of liquidation was adopted, as well as from the fact that dissolution under state law is not necessary.[269]

---

[267] Rev. Rul. 54-518, 1954-2 CB 142.

[268] Regs. §1.333-1(b)(1); see also supra ¶ 11.61 for a similar problem under old §337.

[269] Regs. §§1.333-1(b)(1) and 1.333-1(b)(2).

CHAPTER 12

Collapsible Corporations

¶ 12.01   INTRODUCTORY

In 1982, the American Law Institute described the collapsible corporation rules, set out in §341, as "characterized by a pathological degree of complexity, vagueness and uncertainty."[1] Four years later, the Tax Reform Act of 1986 added three new anomalies. First, the 1986 Act repealed the tax rule that spawned the collapsible corporation's tax avoidance potential.[2] Second, §341 was nevertheless preserved virtually intact by the 1986 Act (and, indeed, its reach was slightly expanded).[3] Third, however, the punitive remedy employed by §341 to discourage the use of collapsible corporations

---

[1] American Law Institute, Federal Income Tax Project: Subchapter C 111, (1982).

[2] I.e., the nonrecognition of gain on corporate distributions of appreciated property under the pre-1987 versions of §§311 and 336 (codifying the *General Utilities* doctrine). For this doctrine and its repeal in 1986, see supra ¶ 7.20; for a transitional provision preserving the *General Utilities* doctrine for certain small business corporations that completely liquidate before 1989—and for whose shareholders, therefore, §341 may still be a menace—see supra ¶ 11.61.

[3] This is a case of "even though the reason has terminated, the law does not change." Its classical form (*ratione cessante, cessat lex ipsa*, i.e., the reason having terminated, so does the law) may be more pleasing, but the senior author has long thought that the claim is not supported by the history of the law.

became, at most, a slap on the wrist,[4] effectively neutralizing the first two anomalies.

A bit of background may provide some insight into this complex, vague, uncertain, and anomalous provision. The collapsible corporation first attracted attention in the motion picture industry in the late 1940s. A producer and a group of leading actors would organize a corporation for the production of a single motion picture. They would invest small amounts of cash and agree to work for modest salaries, and the corporation would finance the production with borrowed funds. When the motion picture was completed but before it was released for public exhibition, the corporation would be liquidated.

Under the *General Utilities* doctrine and the statutory predecessor of §311(a)(2), the corporation did not recognize gain on the liquidating distribution.[5] The shareholders would report the difference between the cost of their stock and the value of their proportionate shares in the completed film—established on the basis of previews—as long-term capital gain rather than as ordinary income (this, of course, at a time when there was a large disparity in the rates applicable to these two categories of income).[6] For example, if the shareholders' initial investment was $100,000 and the value of the film was determined to be $1.1 million, the shareholders' profit of $1 million was taxed at the capital gain rate (e.g., 25 percent, or

---

[4] The conversion of capital gains into ordinary income no longer deprives the taxpayer of the rate differential formerly enjoyed by long-term capital gains, although it may still be disadvantageous in other respects (primarily if the taxpayer has offsetting capital losses). Two ancillary disabilities imposed on collapsible corporations, disqualifying them under §§333 and 337 (relating to certain complete liquidations and to sales in conjunction with liquidations), were eliminated in 1986 when the underlying provisions were themselves repealed. See supra ¶¶ 11.62 and 11.61 for §§333 and 337 respectively.

[5] For the *General Utilities* doctrine and §311(a)(2), see supra ¶ 7.20. This part of the foundation on which the collapsible corporation rested was eliminated in 1986 by the enactment of §§336(a) (gain recognized by distributing corporation on liquidating distributions of appreciated assets) and 311(b)(1) (same result for nonliquidating distributions).

Section 121 of the proposed Subchapter C Revision Act of 1985 (unenacted) would have repealed §341 in conjunction with its proposed repeal of the *General Utilities* doctrine; see Senate Finance Committee Staff, Final Report on Subchapter C (S. Prt. 99-47, 99th Cong., 1st Sess. 3 (1985)). In addition, the Treasury's proposals for fundamental tax reform in November 1984 would have repealed §341 (since the Treasury recommended replacement of capital gain treatment with an indexing regime).

[6] In 1950, when the statutory predecessor of §341 was enacted, the maximum rates applicable to individual taxpayers on long-term capital gain and ordinary income were 25 percent and 91 percent respectively. (Under the Tax Reform Act of 1986, post-1987 capital gains are subject to the same rate as ordinary income.)

$250,000, when the practice first became popular). Under the statutory predecessor of §334(a), the basis of the film in the hands of the shareholders was $1.1 million; and if the net rentals received thereafter equaled that amount, the shareholders would have no further gain or loss, since the fair market value of the film could be amortized against the rentals.[7] In effect, the exhibition profit, which would have been taxed as ordinary income to the corporation (or to the producers if they had operated in noncorporate form from the outset) was converted into capital gain. Moreover, instead of two taxes (a corporate tax on the exhibition income and an individual tax at the capital gain rate on a sale or liquidation of the corporation), there was only one.

The collapsible corporation was also used by investors and builders constructing homes in residential subdivisions. A corporation created to construct the houses would be liquidated before the houses were sold; and the corporation would not recognize any gain on the liquidating distribution of the houses. The shareholders would report as long-term capital gain the difference between the cost of their stock and the value of the completed houses. The houses, which thus acquired a stepped-up basis equal to their fair market value at the time of distribution, would then be sold, ordinarily with no further gain or loss to be accounted for. Here again, only one tax would be paid instead of two, and it would be computed at the then favorable long-term capital gain rate.

Section 341, the original version of which was enacted in 1950, attacked the collapsible corporation by requiring the shareholder's gain on the liquidation of the corporation to be reported as ordinary income rather than as long-term capital gain and by applying the same remedy to sales and exchanges of the corporation's stock.[8] This extension to sales was a necessary buttress to the treatment of liquidations: Without it, shareholders of a collapsible corporation would have been able to sell their stock to outside investors, reporting their profit as long-term capital gain; and the purchasers of the stock could then liquidate the corporation without recognizing any

---

[7] If the proceeds exceeded or fell short of the estimated fair market value, the shareholders would have additional income or deductible loss. In Pat O'Brien, 25 TC 376 (1955) (acq.), it was held that receipts in excess of the film's basis were taxable as ordinary income.

[8] For unsuccessful attempts by the Service to attack collapsible corporations with nonstatutory remedies, see Herbert v. Riddell, 103 F. Supp. 369 (S.D. Cal. 1952); Pat O'Brien, supra note 7; see also CIR v. Gross, 236 F2d 612, 618 (2d Cir. 1956), upholding the Tax Court's refusal to impute a salary to corporate officers who preferred to take their profits on a business venture in the form of capital gain distributions on their stock; but see Jacobs v. CIR, 224 F2d 412 (9th Cir. 1955) (successful attack by Service). For further discussion of possible nonstatutory weapons, see Bittker & Redlich, Corporate Liquidations and the Income Tax, 5 Tax L. Rev. 437, 439–448 (1950).

gain, since the value of the liquidating distribution would ordinarily be substantially the same as the cost of their shares.[9]

Thus, although the term "collapsible corporation" originally implied the use of a temporary corporation that was to be dissolved as soon as its tax avoidance purpose had been accomplished, §341 as enacted was (and continues to be) much broader. Because it is not limited to liquidations but applies as well to sales and exchanges of the stock of a collapsible corporation, §341 may come into play even though the corporation is in fact kept alive for an indefinite period of time.[10]

¶ 12.02   THE FRAMEWORK OF §341

Although the details of §341 are quite intricate, its basic principle is simple: A shareholder who disposes of stock in a collapsible corporation in a transaction that would ordinarily produce capital gain must instead report the gain as ordinary income. As explained in the previous section, this rule applies not only to liquidating distributions, but also to sales and exchanges of the collapsible corporation's stock. Two less frequent transactions are also covered: partial liquidations under §302(b)(4) and distributions subject to §301(c)(3)(A), relating to distributions that are not covered by corporate earnings and profits and exceed the basis of the shareholder's stock.[11]

Section 341 is applicable only if the shareholder's gain would otherwise be capital gain[12] and is inapplicable to losses. In addition, §341 applies by

---

[9] This assumes that the liquidation was not effected until the sale was old and cold; otherwise, the liquidating distribution might be imputed to the selling shareholders, who would then be treated as selling the assets (rather than their stock) to the purchasers.

[10] See Burge v. CIR, 253 F2d 765, 767 (4th Cir. 1958) (statutory predecessor of §341 "was drawn in broad general terms to reach the abuse which had arisen, whatever form it might take"); see also Braunstein v. CIR, 374 US 65 (1963).

[11] Partial liquidations and §301(c)(3)(A) distributions resemble complete liquidations and sales of the corporation's stock in that they generate capital gain or loss at the shareholder level; see supra ¶¶ 7.02 (§301(c)(3)(A) distributions) and 9.08 (partial liquidations).

There is, however, one curious omission from this grouping; a distribution in redemption of stock that is treated as long-term capital gain under §302(a). The omission, however, may be neutralized by the fact that most redemptions by collapsible corporations will reflect a corporate contraction (see supra ¶ 9.09) and hence will constitute a partial liquidation, covered by §341(a)(2).

[12] Thus, if a corporate distribution of money or property is treated as dividend income to its shareholders under §301, §341 does not apply. Similarly, if the stock is not a capital asset because the shareholder holds it as dealer property, ordinary gain would result on its sale without resort to §341(a).

its terms to gain that otherwise would be considered as capital gain, but it does not of its own force make the gain taxable; thus, it has no effect on a tax-free exchange of stock in a collapsible corporation (e.g., under §351, §354, §355, §361, or §1036).[13]

Aside from the operative rules of §341(a), the statute consists of a definition of the term "collapsible corporation"; a statutory presumption in aid of the definition; three sets of limitations that moderate the rules of §341(a) in certain circumstances; an escape for transactions involving a limited class of property, particularly rental real estate; and a consent procedure that negates the application of §341 to a corporation's shareholders if the corporation waives the benefit of certain nonrecognition provisions on a later disposition of specified types of property. These aspects of §341 are examined in the remaining sections of this chapter.[14]

Before turning to a more detailed analysis, however, it is necessary to place §341 in proper context or, putting the point more bluntly, to cut it down to size. From 1950, when the statutory predecessor of §341 was enacted, until enactment of the Tax Reform Act of 1986, the operative remedy of §341(a) (i.e., taxing the shareholder's gain as ordinary income rather than as capital gain) was a bitter pill for taxpayers to swallow. For transactions after 1987, however, the elimination of the historic rate differential between ordinary income and long-term capital gains[15] means that taxpayers will fear application of §341 only in limited circumstances, primarily when they have a stockpile of capital losses that can be offset against only $3,000 of ordinary income but can be applied without dollar limitation against capital gains.

Thus, unless the historic rate differential is restored,[16] the Service will often have nothing to gain by applying §341. On the other hand, for the

---

Before 1986, §341 was also inapplicable to transactions producing short-term capital gains; but it was extended to encompass such transactions by §1804(i)(1) of the Tax Reform Act of 1986.

[13] See Rev. Rul. 73-378. 1973-2 CB 113 (stock received in a tax-free acquisitive reorganization of a collapsible corporation not tainted in hands of former shareholders of acquired corporation).

[14] Because of the greatly reduced importance of §341 following the Tax Reform Act of 1986, the analysis of its details here is somewhat condensed; for fuller discussions, see the corresponding chapter of the Fourth Edition of this treatise; Nicholson, Collapsible Corporations—General Coverage, Tax Mgmt. (BNA) No. 29-4th (1981); Ginsburg, Collapsible Corporations—Revisiting an Old Misfortune, 33 Tax L. Rev. 307 (1978).

[15] See supra note 6.

[16] See the conference report on the Tax Reform Act of 1986, H.R. Rep. No. 841, 99th Cong., 2d Sess. II-106 (1986) ("current statutory structure for capital gains is retained in the Code to facilitate reinstatement of a capital gains rate differential if there is a future tax rate increase").

same reason—and also because the corporation must now recognize gain on most distributions of appreciated property[17]—the collapsible corporation is no longer an appealing tax avoidance device.

¶ 12.03　THE DEFINITION OF "COLLAPSIBLE CORPORATION"

The term "collapsible corporation" is defined by §341(b)(1) to mean a corporation that is formed or availed of:

(1) Principally for the production of property (or for certain other activities discussed below); and

(2) With a view to (a) a sale, liquidation, or distribution before the corporation has realized two thirds of the taxable income to be derived from the property,[18] and (b) a realization by the shareholders of the gain attributable to the property.

If we take the extreme case of a corporation organized solely to produce one motion picture, which, by agreement among the shareholders at the time of its creation, is to be sold as soon as the film is completed and before the corporation has realized any taxable income from the film, the applicability of §341(b) is indisputable.[19] Moreover, the use of an existing corporation for these purposes will not escape §341(b), since it is applicable whether the corporation is formed or availed of for the specified purpose. Finally, although the collapsible corporation provisions are aimed primarily at attempts to convert untaxed corporate ordinary income into shareholder-level capital gain, the Supreme Court has held that there is no implied exception in §341 for profits that would have been taxed as capital gain if the

---

[17] See supra note 5.

[18] Before 1984, the statutory benchmark "was a substantial part" rather than two thirds of the taxable income; see infra note 38.

[19] Before 1987, a shareholder view toward *liquidating* the corporation before it realized two thirds of the potential income would have been as fatal as an intention to *sell* the stock. But, as explained supra ¶ 11.06, a liquidating distribution of the property is now treated by §336(a) as a corporate sale of the assets—that is, any appreciation must be recognized by the corporation. Thus, if the shareholders intend to liquidate the corporation before it has realized two thirds of the potential income, the intention will be frustrated by §336(a); their view, being self-destructive, ought not to count under §341(b)(1)(A). On the other hand, §341(b)(1)(A) continues to encompass an intention to *sell* the stock before corporate realization of at least two thirds of the income.

corporate assets had been owned and sold by the shareholders as individuals.[20] Accordingly, the operation of §341 may serve to convert what would otherwise be long-term capital gain into ordinary income solely because of the use of a corporation.[21]

The definition of "collapsible corporation" (which should be examined with a lively appreciation of the fact that the term is not confined to such classic collapsible patterns as the temporary corporations used in the motion picture or construction industries) contains the following elements:

1. Formed or availed of. Because §341 reaches corporations that are either formed or availed of for the proscribed purposes, it is not confined to a corporation that is specially created for the purpose or that is dissolved as soon as the purpose has been achieved.[22] Temporary corporations may be especially vulnerable, but a long life does not ensure immunity.

2. Principally for the manufacture, construction, or production of property. Early debate on this aspect of the definition in §341(b) centered on whether the word "principally" modified the language "manufacture, construction or production," or referred instead only to the collapsible view test, discussed in paragraph 4 below. If the latter was the correct interpretation, the statute would have been appreciably narrowed in scope; however, the regulations adopted the former construction from the outset, and the courts soon agreed.[23] The result of these cases is that the corporation need only be formed or availed of principally for the manufacture, construction, or production of property, a condition satisfied by most ordinary business corporations; the forbidden view need not be the principal reason for formation or use of the corporation.

Similarly, the definition of "manufacture, construction or production" has received an expansive interpretation by the courts and the Service. This definition has two elements: (1) whether the questioned activity itself constitutes production, and (2) the duration of the activity (a matter

---

[20] See Braunstein v. CIR, supra note 10; see also Bailey v. US, 360 F2d 113 (9th Cir. 1966) (no implied exception in §341 for shareholders whose intent had been to liquidate the corporation in tax-free liquidation); but see Rev. Rul. 56-160, 1956-1 CB 633.

[21] This phenomenon was largely responsible for the enactment in 1958 of the amnesty granted by §341(e), which is examined infra ¶ 12.06.

[22] See Regs. §1.341-2(a); Burge v. CIR, supra note 10; Glickman v. CIR, 256 F2d 108 (2d Cir,. 1958); King v. US, 641 F2d 253 (5th Cir. 1981).

[23] See Regs. §1.341-2(a)(1); Weil v. CIR, 252 F2d 805 (2d Cir. 1958); Burge v. CIR, supra note 10; Mintz v. CIR, 284 F2d 554 (2d Cir. 1960); King v. US, supra note 22.

that is significant not only in applying the view requirement but also in applying the three-year rule of §341(d)(3), summarized in the following section). The earlier opinions and rulings on this question suggested that practically any corporate activity that is materially related to a property-creating transaction would satisfy the statutory test,[24] but it has been held that the term "construction" does not include (1) minor alterations or corrections of an existing structure that did not change its character or increase its fair market value; (2) the drilling of dry holes and unsuccessful exploration activities; or (3) various preliminary activities by a real estate construction corporation.[25]

If the corporation goes beyond distinctly preliminary activities or mere maintenance of existing assets, however, it may be engaged in construction. It should not be forgotten that engaging in such activity to any extent suffices under §341(b)(2)(A). Thus, a conservative but useful rule of thumb is that construction has ended when "the last nail has been driven, the last brush stroke applied, and the last bush planted."

It would seem that any type of property that a corporation is capable of producing will meet the requirements of the statutory definition. Although most transactions that run afoul of §341 involve the construction or production of tangible property (buildings, motion pictures, and so forth), the creation of such intangibles as goodwill, secret formulas, industrial know-how,

---

[24] See, e.g., Abbott v. CIR, 28 TC 795 (1957), aff'd, 258 F2d 537 (3d Cir. 1958) (corporation owning unimproved land held to have engaged in construction by contracting to install streets, obtaining Federal Housing Administration mortgage commitment and depositing funds in escrow to ensure that improvements would be installed); Ellsworth J. Sterner, 32 TC 1144 (1959) (hiring mortgage broker and architect, application for FHA mortgage insurance, and negotiation of sales contract held construction); Rev. Rul. 56-137, 1956-1 CB 178 (rezoning of land from residential to commercial use held construction); Rev. Rul. 69-378, 1969-2 CB 49 (approval of lessee's construction plans and like actions is "construction"; "termination" is date following completion of physical construction); Manassas Airport Indus. Park, Inc. v. CIR, 66 TC 566 (1976), aff'd per curiam, 557 F2d 1113 (4th Cir. 1977) (preliminary activities were construction; post-liquidation construction also counted); but see Rev. Rul. 77-306, 1977-2 CB 103 (lessee construction not attributed to lessor who did not participate other than through higher rent). See also King v. US, supra note 22, for an expansive interpretation of "construction."

[25] See Rev. Rul. 72-422, 1972-2 CB 211; Rev. Rul. 64-125, 1964-1 CB (Part 1) 131; Calvin A. Thomas, ¶ 81,387 P-H Memo. TC (1981), and cases there cited (purchase of land and modification of zoning not construction); see also Computer Sciences Corp., 63 TC 327 (1974) (production of secret process completed when process ready for commercial use and production of income on commercial basis).

For the Service's conservative policy on advance rulings, see Rev. Proc. 87-3, §4.01-18, 1987-1 IRB 27 (ordinarily no ruling on §341(b) status, but request will be considered if corporation has been in existence 20 years, not more than 10 percent of its stock has changed hands, and it has conducted substantially the same business for that period).

and the like, even by a service business, seem to be within the reach of the section, and the few reported cases have so held.[26]

3. Purchase of §341 assets. Even if the corporation does not engage in the manufacture, construction, or production of property, it may fall within §341 by engaging in the purchase of section 341 assets, provided this is done with a view to a sale, liquidation, or distribution before the corporation has realized two thirds of the taxable income to be derived from such property. This portion of the definition is primarily aimed at the use of collapsible corporations to convert the profit on inventory property and stock in trade into capital gain:

> The procedure used is to transfer [an appreciated] commodity to a new or dormant corporation, the stock of which is then sold to the prospective purchaser of the commodity who thereupon liquidates the corporation. In this manner the accretion in the value of the commodity, which in most of the actual cases has been whiskey, is converted into a gain realized on the sale of stock of a corporation, thus creating the possibility that it might be taxed as a long-term capital gain.[27]

Under this part of the definition of "collapsible corporations," every corporation holding appreciated inventory or stock in trade would be a potential target for §341, and its fate would depend on whether the elusive view was present; but the regulations cut down the scope of §341(b)(2) by conferring immunity on the corporation if its inventory property—more precisely, the property described in §§341(b)(3)(A) and 341(b)(3)(B)—is normal in amount and if the corporation has a substantial prior business history involving the use of such property.[28]

---

[26] See King v. US, supra note 22, and cases there cited; F.T.S. Assocs., Inc., 58 TC 207 (1972) (acq.) (marketing rights to a secret process created or purchased by corporate taxpayer).

[27] S. Rep. No. 781, 82d Cong., 1st Sess. (1951), reprinted in 1951-2 CB 458, 481. For a possible nonstatutory attack on this practice, see Jacobs v. CIR, supra note 8.

For an application of §341(b)(3) to a one-shot purchase and sale of a single parcel of real estate, see Estate of Van Heusden v. CIR, 369 F2d 119 (5th Cir. 1966). But see Calvin A. Thomas, supra note 25 (property not held for sale; *Van Heusden* distinguished). See also King v. US, supra note 22 (one-shot sale of option to acquire tract of land held sale of "section 341 asset); Combs v. US, 655 F2d 90 (6th Cir. 1981) (co-op conversion resulted in §341 treatment for sale of stock because shareholders intended to profit from increased value of individual apartments).

[28] Regs. §1.341-5(c)(1); see also Rev. Rul. 56-244, 1956-1 CB 176 (inventory, although appreciated in value, was normal in amount for volume of sales and not in excess of average inventory over preceding several years; corporation held not collapsible).

The term "section 341 assets" embraces not only inventory and property held for sale to customers in the ordinary course of business, but also unrealized receivables and fees from the sale of "section 341 assets" and property described in §1231.[29] The latter category of property may have been brought within the aegis of §341 to prevent dealers in apartment houses or other rental property from converting ordinary income into capital gain through the use of a separate corporation for each parcel of property. The result of treating §1231(b) property as "section 341 assets" is that the typical real estate holding corporation, formed to purchase an apartment house or other rental property, may be collapsible if the requisite view is present, even though the shareholders are investors rather than dealers and would have been entitled to report their profit on the building as capital gain under §1231 in the absence of a corporation.[30]

The collapsible corporation provisions had thus come full circle: Designed to prevent the transmutation of ordinary income into capital gain, they could now convert capital gain into ordinary income. In recognition of this possibility, Congress enacted §341(e) in 1958 to provide an escape from collapsibility in cases where, roughly speaking, the taxpayers would have enjoyed capital gains had they not used the corporate form.[31]

4. With a view to collapse. Since many, if not most, ordinary business corporations are formed or availed of principally for the production or purchase of property (especially since these terms are broadly defined by §341), the major issue in a §341(b) case is usually the existence of the requisite view on the part of the shareholders to effect a sale, liquidation, or distribution before the corporation has realized two thirds of the income to be derived from the property. The classic collapsible corporation was one whose shareholders planned at the very outset to liquidate before any corporate income

---

[29] The term "section 341 assets" does not include §1231 property used in connection with the manufacture, construction, or production of inventory property or of property held for sale to customers in the ordinary course of business; see §341(b)(3)(D). On the troublesome question of dual purpose property held for either development or sale, see Malat v. Riddell, 383 US 569 (1966) ("primarily," as used in §1221(1), means "of first importance").

Regardless of the type of property involved, the term "section 341 assets" is limited to property held for less than three years, but (1) the tacking rules of §1223 apply in determining the holding period and (2) the period does not begin until manufacture, construction, and so forth is completed; see §341(b)(3) (last sentence).

[30] See Braunstein v. CIR, supra note 10 (no implied exception for transactions that would have generated capital gains if effected by shareholders as individuals).

[31] See infra ¶ 12.06.

was realized. The regulations, however, provide that §341(b) is satisfied if a sale, liquidation, or distribution before the corporation has realized a substantial part of the gain from the property "was contemplated, unconditionally, conditionally, or as a recognized possibility."[32]

This statement seems to suggest that the requisite view exists whenever the controlling shareholders can reasonably foresee that, for the right price, they may decide to sell their stock or liquidate the corporation before it realizes two thirds of the income from its collapsible property. If so, the recognized possibility test would be almost all-embracing; but the courts may be unwilling to go this far.[33]

The regulations go on to state that the persons whose view is crucial are those who are in a position to determine the policies of the corporation, whether by reason of majority stock ownership or otherwise. This approach may be hard on innocent minority shareholders, but without such a rule, §341 could be too easily avoided by keeping one such shareholder in the dark. Finally, the regulations provide that the collapsible view must exist at some time during construction, production, or purchase of the collapsible property. Some courts have felt that the regulations are overly generous to the taxpayer in this respect, asserting that the view need only be held when the corporation is availed of for the collapsible purpose, even if production of the property has been completed by then; other decisions, however, have questioned or rejected this interpretation.[34] In any event, determination of the time at which the view arose will of necessity be difficult, involving as it does a highly subjective issue of intent; and the chronological breadth of the term "production" makes it difficult to establish that a tainted view, if it existed, did not arise until after production was completed.

---

[32] Regs. §1.341-2(a)(2). For this outdated use of the term "substantial part" of the taxable income, rather than two thirds, see infra note 38.

[33] For a willingness to infer the tainted view in cases involving real estate operators, see August v. CIR, 267 F2d 829 (3d Cir. 1959); Carl B. Rechner, 30 TC 186 (1958); Edward S. Zorn, ¶ 76,241 P-H Memo. TC (1976) (distribution of excess mortgage proceeds taxable as ordinary gain because distribution was recognized possibility before completion of construction); Nordberg, "Collapsible" Corporations and the "View," 40 Taxes 372 (1962).

[34] See Regs. §1.341-2(a)(3). For a decision holding or implying that the regulation is too generous, see Glickman v. CIR, supra note 22 (dictum); Sidney v. CIR, 273 F2d 928 (2d Cir. 1960); Burge v. CIR, supra note 10; for a view more in accord with the regulations, see Jacobson v. CIR, 281 F2d 703 (3d Cir. 1960); Payne v. CIR, 268 F2d 617 (5th Cir. 1959); Tibbals v. US, 362 F2d 266 (Ct. Cl. 1966) (sale not foreseeable prior to completion of construction; regulations' approach referred to as settled law); see also Louis Kellner, ¶ 71,293 P-H Memo. TC (1971) (view to liquidate arose after construction due to unforeseeable change of conditions); F.T.S. Assocs., Inc., supra note 26 (view to liquidate arose after alleged collapsible activity); Computer Sciences Corp., supra note 25 (same).

It must be concluded, therefore, that the regulations bring within §341 any corporation that is formed or availed of for the production or purchase of property if the persons in control recognize (before production is completed) the possibility of selling or liquidating the corporation at a profit before it has realized two thirds of the income from its property. Moreover, the natural tendency of courts and administrators is to assume that what did in fact happen was intended, so that self-serving disclaimers of any tainted intent are likely to be less persuasive than the actual results. This emphasis on objective considerations is evident in Regs. §1.341-5(b), which states that a corporation ordinarily will be considered collapsible if (1) gain attributable to property produced or purchased by the corporation is realized by the shareholder on a sale of his stock or on a nondividend distribution; (2) the production or purchase of the property was a substantial corporate activity; and (3) the corporation has not realized the requisite portion of the taxable income to be derived from such property.[35]

Regs. §1.341-2(a)(3), however, mentions one avenue of escape: proof that the decision to sell, liquidate, or distribute was "attributable solely to circumstances which arose after the manufacture, construction, production, or purchase (other than circumstances which reasonably could be anticipated at the time of such [activity])." Among the post-production circumstances that have been held to qualify are illnesses of an active shareholder; unexpected changes in the law; dissents among the shareholders, especially if a minority interest is bought out; unexpected changes in the value of the property; and a shareholder's sudden need for funds to enter or expand another business.[36] This exception is less useful than might appear, however, because of the difficulty of proving that the cause of the sale could not ini-

---

[35] For Service practice with respect to requests for advance rulings, see supra note 25.

[36] See Charles J. Riley, 35 TC 848 (1961) (acq.) (illness); Maxwell Temkin, 35 TC 906 (1961) (acq.) (same); Regs. §1.341-5(d), Example (3) (same); Rev. Rul. 57-575, 1957-2 CB 236 (sale of property to United States under statute whose enactment was not anticipated); CIR v. Lowery, 335 F2d 680 (3d Cir. 1964) (buyout of minority shareholder who could not make additional investment); Jacobson v. CIR, supra note 34 (damage to property); Southwest Properties, Inc., 38 TC 97 (1962) (acq.) (change in property's value); Morris Cohen, 39 TC 886 (1963) (nonacq.) (same); but see Braunstein v. CIR, supra note 10 (change in value not controlling); Jack D. Saltzman, ¶ 63,080 P-H Memo. TC (1963) (need for funds); Stanley Stahl, ¶ 66,094 P-H Memo. TC (1966) (economic and business factors beyond taxpayer's control); George Freitas, ¶ 66,105 P-H Memo. TC (1966) (plan to sell arose after completion of construction); Computer Sciences Corp., supra note 25 (same); Joseph M. Crowe, 62 TC 121 (1974) (acq.) (no view where sale of stock did not occur with "freedom of choice" contemplated by §341(b) but was instead compelled by disagreement between equal shareholders).

tially have been anticipated as well as because the production process may extend beyond completion in a layman's sense.[37]

5. Corporate realization of two thirds of taxable income from the property. A corporation can escape the taint of collapsibility under §341(b)(1)(A) if, before the sale, exchange, or distribution, it realizes two thirds of the taxable income to be derived from its collapsible property.[38]

In theory, the amount *actually* realized is irrelevant, and the amount that the shareholders *intended* the corporation to realize is controlling. But this would make the corporation collapsible even if all the income had in fact been realized by it, provided that the shareholders had earlier entertained the view that the income should not be realized by the corporation. The regulations, perhaps treating the events as they occur as the best evidence of what was intended, clearly imply that actual—rather than intended—realization is controlling.[39]

If the collapsible property consists of fungible units in an integrated project (e.g., separate installments of a television or motion picture series or individual units in a housing project), the amount realized is determined by treating the aggregate of these properties as a single unit. Thus, if a corporation is engaged in constructing a housing project, the entire project constitutes a single property for realization purposes.[40] On the other hand, if the

---

[37] See King v. US, supra note 22 (minimal acts sufficient); Carl B. Rechner, supra note 33; Sproul Realty Co., 38 TC 844 (1962) (acq.).

[38] Before 1984, §341(b)(1)(A)'s escape hatch referred to realization of "a substantial part" of the taxable income to be derived from the property, rather than two thirds. In addition to the intrinsic vagueness of the word "substantial," there was a grammatical ambiguity in §341(b)(1)(A); it was not clear whether the corporation was collapsible if it was sold or liquidated when a substantial part of the taxable income *remained to be realized* or only if the sale or liquidation occurred before a substantial part *had been realized.* The latter interpretation was obviously more lenient; it would exempt the corporation if the shareholders planned to have it realize, for example, a third of the taxable income; on the other hand, the former interpretation would clearly not be satisfied on these facts, since two thirds of the income would remain to be realized. For competing views on this issue, compare CIR v. Kelley, 293 F2d 904 (5th Cir. 1961) (realization of about one third sufficient), with Abbott v. CIR, supra note 24 (corporation collapsible if substantial part remains to be realized); see also Rev. Rul. 72-48, 1972-1 CB 102 (acquiescing in *Kelley,* but stating that the Service was not precluded from applying unspecified other provisions of the Code in order to tax gain as ordinary income—presumably clear reflection of income, assignment of income, step transaction, and similar doctrines).

[39] See Regs. §§1.341-2(a)(4) and 1.341-5(c)(2). But see Payne v. CIR, supra note 34.

[40] See Regs. §§1.341-2(a)(4) and 1.341-5(d), Examples (2) and (3). But compare §341(d)(2), Regs. §1.341-4(c)(3), and infra ¶ 12.05 (re computation under 70-30 percent rule).

corporation constructs two unrelated office buildings, the sale of one will not protect it from collapsible treatment if the stock is sold before two thirds of the income from the second is realized.

Apparently the "taxable income to be derived from the property" means the taxable income that would be realized if the property were sold at the time the shareholder's gain arises.[41] This test seems appropriate in the case of property held for sale (e.g., inventory or residential home units); but if rental property is involved, some courts require an estimate of the projected net rental income to be realized over the economic life of the property, a measure that is considerably more difficult to apply.[42] In addition, the fact that the property has produced no net income or is losing money has not precluded a finding of collapsibility where the prohibited view was present.[43]

6. Realization by shareholders of gain attributable to the property. If the other elements of the collapsible definition are satisfied, the final element—realization by the shareholders of gain attributable to the collapsible property—will be satisfied almost automatically, since the appreciation will be reflected in the amount they receive for their stock.[44]

7. Scope of term "manufacture, construct, produce or purchase." To safeguard the statutory purpose, §341(b)(2) provides that a corporation "shall be deemed to have manufactured, constructed, produced, or purchased property" if any of the following conditions is satisfied:

(1) If the corporation engages in manufacture, construction, or production of property "to any extent." By virtue of this provision, the

---

[41] See Levenson v. US, 157 F. Supp. 244 (N.D. Ala. 1957); CIR v. Kelley, supra note 38.

[42] See Sidney v. CIR, supra note 34; Mintz v. CIR, supra note 23; Payne v. CIR, supra note 34. The *Mintz* and *Sidney* cases also held that premiums received from a lender, with which an FHA mortgage was placed, were not part of the net income to be derived from such property. See also Manassas Airport Indus. Park, Inc., supra note 24 (determination of estimated net income from the property; revenues unrelated to collapsible activity excluded; also, losses reduce numerator). In Estate of Van Heusden v. CIR, supra note 27, the court stated that "substantial realization" means realization of income from the *ownership* of property, not from its sale, a doubtful theory.

[43] See Spangler v. CIR, 278 F2d 665 (4th Cir.), cert. denied, 364 US 825 (1960); Short v. CIR, 302 F2d 120 (4th Cir. 1962).

[44] See, e.g., Payne v. CIR, supra note 34 (shareholder's view to collapse and realization of gain attributable to collapsible property go hand in hand). For problems in determining whether the shareholder's gain is attributable to the collapsible property, see infra ¶ 12.05 (70-30 exception of §341(d)(2)).

corporation need not have either originated or completed the process of manufacture, construction, or production; any interim contribution to the process is sufficient.

(2) If the corporation holds property having a basis determined by reference to the cost of such property in the hands of a person who manufactured, constructed, produced, or purchased it. This provision reaches such devices as the transfer of collapsible property by the manufacturer to an innocent corporation by a tax-free exchange under §351 or the use of a second corporation into which a collapsible corporation is merged.

(3) If the corporation holds property having a basis determined by reference to the cost of other property manufactured, constructed, produced, or purchased by it. This provision prevents an escape from §341 by a plan under which the corporation would manufacture property and transfer it for other property in a tax-free exchange (e.g., under §1031), following which the shareholders would liquidate the corporation or sell their stock before the corporation had realized income from the newly acquired property.

A further buttress to §341 is the inclusion of holding companies in the term "collapsible corporation." Where a corporation is employed to hold the stock of a manufacturer of collapsible property, the parent corporation will be a collapsible corporation by virtue of §341(b)(1) if it is formed or availed of with a view to a sale, liquidation, or distribution before the manufacturing subsidiary has realized at least two thirds of the taxable income from the property.[45]

¶ 12.04   THE REBUTTABLE PRESUMPTION OF COLLAPSIBILITY

Section 341(c) establishes a rebuttable presumption of collapsibility if the fair market value of the corporation's "section 341 assets" is (1) 50 percent or more of the fair market value of its total assets, and (2) 120 percent

---

[45] See Computer Sciences Corp., supra note 25, for a near miss under this provision (parent had view to sell stock of subsidiary created to hold developed computer programs, but view arose after completion of development; thus subsidiary was not collapsible); see also Rev. Rul. 56-50, 1956-1 CB 174 (holding company purged of collapsible taint when it sold subsidiary's stock and was taxed under §341 on resulting gain). See generally Del Cotto, The Holding Company as a Collapsible Corporation Under Section 341 of the Internal Revenue Code, 15 Buffalo L. Rev. 524 (1966).

or more of the adjusted basis of such "section 341 assets."[46] The theory of this presumption is that if the "section 341 assets" are substantial in amount and have risen in value to a level significantly above their basis, it is reasonable to place the burden of disproving collapsibility on the taxpayer.

In order to prevent manipulation, §341(c)(2) provides that cash, stock, and certain securities are to be disregarded in determining the corporation's total assets; otherwise, the shareholders of a corporation with substantially appreciated "section 341 assets" might attempt to avoid the statutory presumption by contributing liquid assets to the corporation's capital to dilute these "section 341 assets" to less than 50 percent of the total assets. Perhaps the business purpose doctrine could be used as an alternative Service weapon against attempts to drown a corporation's "section 341 assets" in a sea of other assets through contributions to capital that have no nontax purpose.

In applying the presumption of §341(c), appreciation in "section 341 assets" is measured against the basis of the assets, not against the shareholders' investment. Thus, if shareholders invest $15,000 in a corporation that constructs "section 341 assets" at a cost of $100,000 (represented by $15,000 of equity investment and $85,000 of borrowed funds), the presumption of §341(c) will not be applicable if the assets increase in value to only $115,000 (this being less than 120 percent of their basis), even though the appreciation ($15,000) represents a profit of 100 percent on the shareholders' investment. If the assets increased in value to $120,000, however, §341(c) would become applicable; and this would be true even if the shareholders had financed the entire cost of construction ($100,000) with their own funds and had enjoyed a gain of only 20 percent on their investment.

¶ 12.05   THE ESCAPE HATCHES OF §341(d)

Even though a corporation is collapsible under the preceding principles, §341(d) makes the punitive rules of §341 inapplicable if any one of the following three conditions—applied shareholder by shareholder[47]—is satisfied:

1. Not more than 5 percent of stock. A shareholder is not subject to §341 unless he owns (1) more than 5 percent in value of the outstanding

---

[46] Section 341(c) also provides that absence of these triggering conditions does not give rise to a presumption of noncollapsibility. For the scope of the term "section 341 assets," see §341(b)(3), discussed supra text at notes 27–30.

[47] Section 341(d) provides relief for the qualifying shareholder, but not for the corporation; see Leisure Time Enters., Inc., 56 TC 1180 (1971) (collapsible corporation not entitled to use the pre-1987 version of §337, even though shareholders were protected from §341(a) by §341(d)(3)); Rev. Rul. 63-125, 1963-2 CB 146.

stock or (2) stock that is attributed to another shareholder who owns more than 5 percent of the stock. The ownership of stock is determined under a set of constructive ownership rules,[48] and the specified amount of stock will be fatal if owned when the manufacture, construction, or production of property is begun, when "section 341 assets" are purchased, or at any time thereafter.

2. Not more than 70 percent of gain attributable to collapsible property. Section 341(d)(2) insulates a shareholder's gain on a sale, liquidation, or distribution from collapsible treatment unless more than 70 percent of the gain is attributable to the collapsible property. Thus, if 30 percent or more of the gain can be traced to noncollapsible property, the entire gain will qualify for capital treatment even though the corporation is collapsible under the general definition in §341(b).

The 70 percent rule of §341(d)(2) is of little relevance in the classic collapsible corporation situation, where the corporation purchases or constructs a single property. If that property is not a tainted asset (e.g., because over two thirds of the income from it has been realized), then the corporation is not collapsible under the general definition, and there is no need to look to §341(d)(2) for relief. If, on the other hand, the property is a collapsible asset because of insufficient realization, then of necessity more than 70 percent of the gain—indeed all of the gain—is attributable to that property, and §341(d)(2) offers no relief.

If a corporation holds two or more properties, however, it may be collapsible under the §341(b) definition because of insufficient realization on any *one* property, notwithstanding full realization on the others.[49] Thus, in the context of §341(b), a finding that there is more than one property may hurt but can never help the taxpayer. Under the 70 percent rule, however, just the opposite is the case, because a finding that there are two separate properties permits the shareholder to avoid §341 if 30 percent or more of his gain is attributable to the property on which there has been adequate realization, even though the greater part of the gain may be attributable to other properties that are collapsible.

> *To illustrate:* Corporation *X* (wholly owned by *A*) owns Property *Y* and Property *Z*, which have appreciated by $100,000 and $200,000 respectively. Of the appreciation on *Y*, $67,000 has been realized by the corporation, resulting in a tax of $14,000, and $33,000 is unrealized; none

---

[48] The constructive ownership rules applicable to personal holding companies (§544) are adopted for this purpose, except that the definition of "family" is expanded to include brothers, sisters, and their spouses, and spouses of lineal descendants.

[49] Regs. §§1.341-2(a)(4), and 1.341-5(d), Example 2.

of the Z appreciation has been realized. A sells his X stock at a gain of $286,000 (realized gain on Y of $67,000, unrealized appreciation on Y of $33,000, unrealized appreciation on Z of $200,000, less corporate tax paid of $14,000). Of A's gain, 30.07% ($86,000/$286,000) is attributable to a noncollapsible asset (Y). Thus, if the properties are treated separately in applying the 70 percent rule, the realization of approximately 23 percent of the pretax income ($67,000/$300,000) to be derived from the properties would protect the shareholder against §341.[50]

In computing the gain attributable to the collapsible property, the regulations adopt a "but for" approach—that is, it is the amount of the excess of the gain recognized by the shareholder over the gain he would have recognized if the collapsible property had not been constructed or purchased.[51] This determination takes into account not only the appreciation in value of the collapsible property but also any accumulation of income produced by the property.[52] Furthermore, consistent with this "but for" approach, gain may be attributable to the collapsible property even though it results from an increase in the value of property other than the property constructed or produced, if there is a causal relationship between the collapsible activity and the appreciation.[53]

3. Gain realized after expiration of three years. Section 341(a) treatment may also be avoided by a shareholder if gain on stock of a collapsible corpo-

---

[50] Before the 1984 substitution of the two-thirds rule for the prior substantial part requirement (supra note 38), the two-property rule could cut down even more drastically the percentage of appreciation that had to be realized. Recognizing that manipulation of the two-property principle was especially feasible in the case of fungible assets such as inventory, Congress in 1984 enacted the final sentence of §341(d) to authorize the Treasury to require all inventory assets to be aggregated in applying the 70 percent rule. See Prop. Regs. §1.341-4(c)(4).

[51] Regs. §1.341-4(c)(2).

[52] Regs. §1.341-4(c)(4); Regs. §1.341-5(d), Example (2).

[53] See Regs. §1.341-4(c)(3) (increase in value of property adjacent to collapsible property included because attributable to construction on latter property); see also Rev. Rul. 65-184, 1965-2 CB 91 (gain attributable to project completed more than three years before realization of gain by shareholder is nonetheless included in gain attributable to collapsible property for purposes of 70 percent rule); see also Spangler v. CIR, supra note 43 (gains arising from construction contract refunds, rentals, and off-site improvements included in gain attributable to collapsible property); Benedek v. CIR, 429 F2d 41 (2d Cir. 1970), cert. denied, 400 US 992 (1971) (shareholder's gain on distribution of excess mortgage proceeds attributable to constructed buildings, not to leaseholds of land); cf. Mintz v. CIR, supra note 23 (land and buildings constitute single unit in computing gain attributable to collapsible property); Payne v. CIR, supra note 34 (same).

ration is realized more than three years after the corporation completes production or purchase of the collapsible property.[54] (The shareholder's holding period for his *stock* is irrelevant; §341(d)(3) is concerned only with the corporation's holding period for the property.) Although the statute is not crystal clear on this point, it is evidently not necessary for all of the corporation's collapsible property to be held for three years to bring §341(d)(3) into play. Thus, if the corporation owns two collapsible projects, one of which has been held for more than three years, the portion of the shareholder's gain attributable to that project may qualify for relief under §341(d)(3), even though the rest of the gain, reflecting the value of the more recent project, is taxable as ordinary income.

Because the terms "manufacture, construction and production" have such an expansive meaning,[55] the three-year rule of §341(d)(3) is a treacherous exception: The waiting period commences only on completion—not partial or substantial completion—of the productive process. Moreover, production of "the" property must be completed; if the corporation is engaged in multiunit construction activities, it may be difficult to say whether there is only a single project on which work is continuing or several projects, one or more of which have been completed.

¶ 12.06   THE AMNESTY OF §341(e)

Section 341(e) ameliorates the rigors of the collapsible corporation provisions on a shareholder-by-shareholder basis by exempting a shareholder's gain from §341(a)(1) (thus allowing it to qualify as long-term capital gain) if the stock is sold or exchanged and specified conditions are satisfied.[56] These

---

[54] See Rev. Rul. 57-491, 1957-2 CB 232 (three-year period includes holding period of certain predecessor owners of the property); Rev. Rul. 79-235, 1979-2 CB 135 (inclusion of holding period for property exchanged under §1031).

[55] See supra text at notes 23–26.

[56] See §341(e)(11) (failure to qualify under §341(e) not relevant in determining whether corporation is collapsible). Before 1987, §341(e) applied not only to sales and exchanges, but also to the shareholder's gain on certain liquidating distributions, but §341(e)(2), the applicable provision, was repealed in 1986 because the distribution itself became a taxable event at the corporate level under the Tax Reform Act of 1986; see supra ¶ 11.06. Two other exemptions granted by §341(e)—relating to the status of the corporation itself under §§333 and 337—were also repealed by the 1986 Act, subject to certain transitional grandfather clauses; see supra ¶¶ 11.62 and 11.61 respectively. It is probably intended that the repealed provisions of §341(e) will continue to apply to complete liquidations before January 1, 1989 of certain small corporations that meet the transitional rules in Section 633(d) of the Tax Reform Act of 1986. For the application of §341(e) in situations not governed by the changes made by the 1986 Act, see the Fourth Edition of this treatise, at 12-32–12-35.

prerequisities to the application of §341(e), which are unusually complex even by Code standards, are best approached after their purpose is described.[57]

Under §341(b)(3)(D), which was enacted in 1954, a corporation formed or availed of to purchase rental property (e.g., an apartment house) may be collapsible even though the shareholders could, in the alternative, have acquired the property as individuals and reported their gain on a sale as long-term capital gain (unless they were dealers in such property).[58] Recognizing §341's potential for overkill in situations of this type, Congress enacted §341(e) in 1958. Its underlying theory is that the collapsible corporation provisions should not be applicable if the net unrealized appreciation in the corporation's "subsection (e) assets" (roughly speaking, property held by the corporation that would produce ordinary income if sold by the corporation itself or by its principal shareholders) amounts to no more than 15 percent of the corporation's net worth.

The term "subsection (e) assets" is used throughout §341(e) as the means of determining if there has been a significant appreciation in the value of the corporation's ordinary income assets. This term is defined by §341(e)(5)(A) to include the following categories of property:

(1) Property not used in the trade or business. Any such property is a "subsection (e) asset" if the corporation's gain on a sale would be taxed as ordinary income—i.e., if the property is neither a capital asset nor §1231(b) property. Moreover (and this is the unique innovation of §341(e)), property held by the corporation is brought into the "subsection (e) asset" category if, in the hands of any shareholder owning (directly or constructively) more than 20 percent in value of the corporation's stock, it would not be a capital asset or §1231(b) property. Thus, property held by the corporation constitutes a "subsection (e) asset" if, in the hands of the corporation, it is stock in trade, inventory property, or property held for sale to customers in the ordinary course of trade or business, or *if it would have this status were it held by any shareholder owning directly or constructively more than 20 percent of the corporation's stock.*[59]

---

[57] Because the Tax Reform Act of 1986 greatly reduced the importance of §341 itself (see supra text at notes 2–4 and 14–17), this description of §341(e) is abbreviated. For more extensive analysis, see the Fourth Edition of this treatise and the other discussions cited supra note 14.

[58] In Braunstein v. CIR, supra note 10, the Supreme Court refused to provide a judicial escape for property that would have constituted a capital asset in the shareholder's hands, but this decision came after the enactment of §341(e) and relied in part on the existence of this statutory escape.

[59] See King v. US, supra note 22 (more than 20 percent shareholder was dealer in similar property, so corporation's assets were "section 341(e) assets").

(2) Property used in the trade or business: net unrealized depreciation. Where there is net unrealized depreciation on assets used in the trade or business, they constitute "subsection (e) assets."

(3) Property used in the trade or business: net unrealized appreciation. Where there is net unrealized appreciation on assets used in the trade or business, they constitute "subsection (e) assets" if they would be neither capital assets nor §1231(b) assets in the hands of a more than 20 percent shareholder. This provision is crucial to the purpose of §341(e). If a corporation's sole property is an apartment house or other rental property that has appreciated in value, the property will constitute a "subsection (e) asset" only if a more than 20 percent shareholder is a dealer in such property.

(4) Copyrights and similar property. A copyright, literary composition, letter, memorandum, or similar property is a "subsection (e) asset" if it was created in whole or in part by the personal effects of an individual owning directly or constructively more than 5 percent of the corporation's stock, or, in the case of letters and memoranda, if it was produced for such a 5 percent shareholder.

The definition of "subsection (e) assets" is used by §341(e)(1), which makes §341(a)(1) inapplicable to the shareholder's gain on a sale or exchange of stock if the net unrealized appreciation in the corporation's "subsection (e) assets" does not exceed 15 percent of the corporation's net worth and if the shareholder does not own more than 5 percent of the corporation's stock. If the shareholder owns between 5 and 20 percent of the stock, a similar calculation is made, but it must take into account not only the corporation's "subsection (e) assets" but also any corporate assets that would produce ordinary income if held by the particular shareholder for whom the calculation is made. Finally, if the shareholder owns more than 20 percent of the stock, that shareholder's calculation must also take into account any corporate assets that would have produced ordinary income (1) if he owned them and (2) if he had held in his individual capacity the property of certain other corporations of which he owned more than 20 percent of the stock in the preceding three years. For all of these percentage computations, constructive as well as actual ownership is taken into account.

Thus, the corporate assets will be tainted by the dealer status of any shareholder owning more than 20 percent of the stock of the corporation; and this taint will affect all shareholders of the corporation, regardless of the size of their shareholdings. In addition, a shareholder owning more than 5 percent of the stock must take into account any other corporate assets that would be ordinary income assets if he held them in his personal capacity, but this taint will affect only that individual shareholder. Finally, as regards a more than 20 percent shareholder, any corporate assets will be tainted by the hypothetical dealer status he would have attained if he had engaged in certain transactions as an individual rather than in corporate form during the preceding three years.

These extraordinary statutory gyrations can be illustrated by assuming that Smith-Jones, Inc. is owned equally by Smith and Jones (who are unrelated); that its sole asset is an appreciated apartment house; that neither Smith nor Jones is a dealer in such property; and that Jones has owned more than 20 percent of the stock of certain other real estate corporations during the preceding three years.[60] In these circumstances, Smith-Jones, Inc. owns no "subsection (e) assets," either in its own right or by attribution from Smith or Jones. As regards Smith, the net unrealized appreciation under §341(e)(1) is zero. Thus, a sale or exchange of Smith's stock (except to the issuing corporation or to a related person) is exempt from the operation of §341(a)(1).

As regards Jones, it is necessary to determine whether more than 70 percent in value of the assets of any of his other corporations are similar or related in use or service to the property held by Smith-Jones, Inc. If so, Jones is to be treated as though any sale or exchange by him of stock in any such other corporation (while he owned more than 20 percent of its stock) had been a sale by him of his proportionate share of that corporation's assets.[61]

The mere fact that the Jones corporations were or were not dealers in the property in question is not revelant; the purpose of imputing sales to Jones is to determine *his* status based on both these hypothetical sales and any actual sales by him of similar properties held in his individual capacity. The number and frequency of sales, however, are usually only two of the factors determining whether the taxpayer is a dealer; and it is not clear whether §341(e)(1)(C) attributes to the shareholder not only his proportionate share of the corporation's assets but also his share of any corporate activity (use of agents, advertising, and so forth) that may have resulted in the sales. If, taking into account these hypothetical sales or exchanges by Jones, he would have been a dealer in the type of property held by Smith-Jones, Inc., he can make use of §341(e)(1) only if the net unrealized appreciation in the apartment building owned by Smith-Jones, Inc., does not exceed 15 percent of its net worth.

Finally, §341(e)(1) cannot be invoked if the stock is sold to the issuing corporation, nor does it apply to a more than 20 percent shareholder if the stock is sold to a "related person," as defined by §341(e)(8).

---

[60] For a more complex but less typical illustration of the operation of §341(e), see the Fourth Edition of this treatise at 12-30.

[61] Section 341(e)(1)(C)(ii) also takes into account for this purpose certain transactions under pre-1987 §337. The Tax Reform Act of 1986 replaced old §337 (subject to certain transitional grandfather clauses) with an identically numbered but totally different provision; see supra ¶ 11.49.

¶ 12.07   AVOIDANCE OF §341 BY A §341(f) CONSENT

Not content with the three original escape hatches of §341(d) and the labyrinthine escape route of §341(e), Congress provided further relief from §341 in 1964 by enacting the consent procedure of §341(f). This provision permits a shareholder to sell stock on the normal capital gain basis, free of any threat from §341(a), if the corporation consents to recognize gain on its "subsection (f) assets" (primarily real estate and noncapital assets) when, as, and if it disposes of them in certain transactions that would otherwise qualify for nonrecognition of its gain. The common characteristic of these transactions is that, prior to the enactment of the Tax Reform Act of 1986, the corporation would not have recognized gain on its disposition of the property, but the basis of the property in the hands of the transferee was stepped up to fair market value.[62] The rationale of the consent is that the shareholder should be protected against the application of §341(a) if the corporation *promises to recognize* its collapsible gain after he disposes of his stock, just as he has always been protected if the corporation *actually recognizes* the gain before he sells his stock.[63]

The impact of a §341(f) consent, however, was dramatically altered by the enactment of the Tax Reform Act of 1986, since the events to which the consent applies were deprived of their nonrecognition status, as explained in detail elsewhere in this work.[64] Thus, except in a few transitional situations, a consent is redundant, since it merely requires the consenting corporation to recognize gain on dispositions that are now taxable in any event by virtue of the 1986 changes.[65] While a pre-1987 consent entailed a loss of a corporation's opportunity to avoid the recognition of gain on certain liquidating and other distributions to its shareholders, a consent no longer requires the corporation to give up significant tax allowances unless it qualifies for transitional relief (or Congress revives the *General Utilities* doctrine). Consents, therefore, may become more common, even though §341(a) itself is far less threatening than it was before 1987. As a tactical gambit, a consent now

---

[62] For the *General Utilities* doctrine and the relevant pre-1987 statutory provisions, see supra ¶¶ 7.20, 9.34, and 11.60.

Under §341(f)(3), the consent does not apply to dispositions that entail no change in the basis of the property, such as tax-free reorganizations; see infra text at notes 68–69.

For use of a consent, see King v. US, supra note 22; for exhaustive analysis of the consent privilege, see Nicholson, Collapsible Corporations—Section 341(f), Tax Mgmt. (BNA) 49–2d (1983).

[63] See supra text at note 38.

[64] See §§311(b)(1) and 336(a), supra ¶¶ 7.21 and 11.06.

[65] A few unusual transactions, however, may trigger the recognition of gain under §341(f)(2) but not under the statutory rules repealing the *General Utilities* doctrine (e.g., abandonment, retirement, and gifts); see infra note 70.

accomplishes less than it formerly did, because the disparity between long-term capital gains and ordinary income is far less significant than formerly, as noted earlier,[66] but the cost of a consent is now disproportionately lower.

The relief granted by §341(f) applies only if the shareholder engages in a true sale of stock, not in a transaction that is assimilated to a sale for some purposes (e.g., a distribution in redemption of stock, a partial or complete liquidation, or a nonliquidating distribution).[67] To qualify for §341(f)(1) treatment, the corporation and any subsidiary (or chain of subsidiaries) connected by stock ownership of 5 percent in value must file a consent to the recognition of gain provisions of §341(f)(2).[68] A consent is not conditioned on a showing that the corporation is in fact collapsible; indeed, one of the advantages of §341(f) is that it permits avoidance of such a determination. If the consent is filed, however, it cannot be repudiated at a later time on the ground that it was an empty formality because the shareholder's gain was not within the scope of §341.

The consent becomes irrevocable as soon as any shareholder has effected a sale of his stock. Section 341(f)(2) then provides for recognition of gain at the corporate level on the ultimate disposition of all "subsection (f) assets," even in a transaction that would otherwise qualify for nonrecognition of gain[69]—subject to an exception for tax-free exchanges under §332 (liquidation of subsidiary), §351 (transfer to controlled corporation), §361 (corporate reorganization), §371(a) and §374(a) (bankruptcy reorganizations), provided that the basis of the assets carries over to the transferee and the transferee files a similar consent to recognize gain when it disposes of them.[70]

For six months after the filing of a consent, any shareholder may safely sell stock of the consenting corporation in one or a number of transactions. When the consent expires, a new one may be filed, similarly effective for a six-month period whether the shareholders have made sales under the prior consent or not; and this process may be continued indefinitely. The use of

---

[66] See supra notes 4 and 6.

[67] Regs. §1.341-7(a)(2)(i) narrows the term "sale" still more, limiting it to sales that would produce long-term capital gain but for §341. Query the result of this restriction of the expansion of §341(a) in 1986 to encompass short-term capital gains; see supra note 12.

[68] For the mechanics of the consent procedure, see Regs. §§1.341-7(b), 1.341-7(c), 1.341-7(d), and 1.341-7(j); see also §341(f)(8) (foreign corporation's consent not effective except as allowed by regulations).

[69] See Regs. §1.341-7(e)(7) (disposition includes abandonment, gift, sale and leaseback transaction, and so forth, but not borrowing on security of property).

[70] See generally Regs. §§1.341-7(e) and 1.341-7(f). See also §341(f)(8)(B) (exemption for tax-free transactions with carry-over basis inapplicable if transferee is a foreign corporation, except as allowed by regulations).

the privilege with respect to *one* corporation, however, precludes the same shareholder or any person related to him within the meaning of §341(e)(8)(A) from using it with respect to any other corporation for a five-year period.[71] There is a FIFO quality to this one-shot rule, in that a shareholder cannot disregard a consent applicable to his first sale of stock (either because he had no gain or because he is prepared to prove that the corporation was noncollapsible), in order to get the benefit of a consent filed by another corporation whose stock he sells at a later time.

"Subsection (f) assets" are defined in §341(f)(4) as noncapital assets that the corporation owns, or has an option to acquire, at the date of any qualified sale of stock by a shareholder. However, land, any interest in real property (except a mortgage or other security interest), and unrealized receivables or fees as defined by §341(b)(4) constitute "subsection (f) assets," without regard to whether they would otherwise constitute noncapital assets. This is also true of two other categories of property: (1) in the case of any assets in the above categories that are being manufactured at the time the stock is sold, the property resulting thereafter from the manufacturing process and (2) in the case of land or real property, any improvements resulting from construction commencing within two years after the stock is sold.[72] The character and amount of the corporation's gain on disposing of its "subsection (f) assets," however, depend on their status at the time of disposition, not on their status when the consent is filed or the stock is sold.

---

[71] Regs. §1.341-7(h); see King v. US, supra note 22.

[72] See Regs. §1.341-7(g).

CHAPTER 13

Corporate Divisions

¶ 13.01   INTRODUCTORY

This chapter is concerned with the tax consequences of corporate divisions: arrangements by which the shareholders of a single corporation split up their investment among several corporate shells. This has been a troubled area of the tax law and, although the statutory scheme was extensively revised in 1954, it is impossible to ignore the pre-1954 statutes and judicial doctrines. Before turning to the legal issues, it is important to note that the generic label "corporate division" embraces a broad spectrum of transactions, differing from each other in the following characteristics, among others:

1. Nature of assets. The shareholders of a corporation engaged in two or more separate businesses may wish to place the assets of one of the businesses in a separate corporation. At the opposite extreme, the assets to be segregated in a separate corporation may be cash or marketable securities. Between these two extremes, the shareholders or a corporation conducting an integrated business (e.g., manufacturing) may wish to place some of its business assets (e.g., real estate) or business functions (e.g., sales, research and development, or purchasing) in a separate corporation.

2. Purpose. The purpose of the division may be to comply with an antitrust decree (e.g., distributing some of the assets of an integrated business or the stock of a competitor or customer); to comply with state or foreign law (e.g., a prohibition on combining several business functions in the same corporation or a requirement that a local enterprise have a stated percentage of local shareholders); to separate a regulated enterprise from an unregulated one; to segregate a risky or speculative enterprise from a more stable one; to reduce federal income taxes (e.g., by qualifying both corporations for the reduced tax rates applicable to lower income levels[1]); to prepare for a sale, either prearranged or to be negotiated, of one or both of the corporations; to prepare for a liquidation of one of the corporations so its assets may be held or sold by the shareholders as individuals; and so forth.

3. Ratio of distribution. The distribution may be either pro rata or disproportionate. Thus, two equal shareholders of a corporation who are deadlocked on business policy may wish to divide the assets between two corporations so that each of them may become the sole owner of one. A corporation may wish to buy out the entire interest of a minority shareholder in exchange for all the stock of a subsidiary (the assets of which may be a separate business, cash or marketable securities, or a combination of such assets). On the other hand, the distribution may be entirely pro rata, and it may either remain so or become disproportionate by reason of sales by some of the shareholders. An intermediate possibility is a distribution under which two equal shareholders in a corporation wind up, after a divisive distribution, with the stock of two corporations, held in the proportion (for example) of 60-40 for the first corporation and 40-60 for the second.

---

[1] But see §§269, 1551, and 1561, infra ch. 15.

4. Form of distribution. When the shareholders of a corporation no longer wish to entrust their eggs to one basket, there are various ways of getting them into several baskets. The corporation may distribute some of its assets to the shareholders pro rata. This ordinarily constitutes a dividend if the corporation has post-1913 or current earnings and profits, and the tax cost may be prohibitive. Alternatively, the assets may be distributed to the shareholders in exchange for some of their stock. If the distribution is not pro rata, so that some of the shareholders are bought out entirely or suffer a substantial reduction in proportionate stockholdings, the transaction will produce capital gain or loss for these shareholders under §302(b) (see Chapter 9). But if the assets are to be distributed to all shareholders pro rata, each surrendering a proportionate amount of stock, the redemption may constitute a taxable dividend under §302(d) unless it can qualify as a partial liquidation under §§302(b)(4) and 302(e)(1) (corporate contraction) and/or §302(e)(2) (distribution of an active trade or business), in which event the transaction produces capital gain or loss (see Chapter 9). Finally, the distribution may be a complete liquidation, in which event capital gain or loss ordinarily results to the shareholders (see Chapter 11).

The methods of dividing the corporate enterprise just described have been discussed in earlier chapters. In this chapter, we will consider other methods of accomplishing this result, which, upon compliance with an intricate set of statutory conditions, permit the corporation to be divided on a wholly tax-free basis. These methods are known to tax lawyers as spin-offs, split-offs, and split-ups.

(1) **Spin-off (vs. dividend).** A spin-off is a distribution by one corporation of the stock of a subsidiary, either an existing subsidiary or a newly created one.

(2) **Split-off (vs. redemption).** The split-off is identical with the spin-off except that the shareholders of the parent corporation surrender part of their stock in the parent in exchange for the stock of the subsidiary.

(3) **Split-up (vs. liquidation).** In a split-up, the parent corporation distributes its stock in two or more subsidiaries (preexisting or created for the purpose) in complete liquidation.

Before 1954, the tax consequences of these three methods of dividing up a corporate investment were quite divergent, despite the fact that their economic consequences were ordinarily almost identical. This pre-1954 history was influential in shaping the 1954 statutory provisions. For this reason, as well as for its impact on later judicial attitudes and administrative practices, a historical note is essential. Following this note, the current provisions are discussed.

¶ 13.02 DIVISIVE REORGANIZATIONS BEFORE 1954

1. Spin-offs. The Revenue Act of 1924 permitted a spin-off to be accomplished tax-free by providing that (1) the transfer by a corporation of part or all of its property to a second corporation constituted a reorganization if the first corporation or its stockholders (or both) were in control of the second corporation immediately after the transfer and (2) no gain was to be recognized by the shareholders of the first corporation if stock of the second corporation was distributed to them as part of the reorganization plan.[2] This blanket tax exemption for the spin-off held out the possibility of undermining the tax on dividend income on a grand scale, since, at least so far as the letter of the statute was concerned, a corporation could transfer its excess funds or liquid assets to a newly organized corporation and distribute the stock of the new corporation to its shareholders, who could thereafter liquidate the new corporation in order to get its assets. By this device, it was hoped that the shareholders would avoid the tax on dividend income; although they would be taxed on liquidating the second corporation (on the difference between the value of the assets received in liquidation and the allocated basis of the stock), this tax would be at the capital gain rate; and not even a capital gain tax would be due if they kept the second corporation alive as a holding company.

In *Gregory v. Helvering*, however, the Supreme Court held that full compliance with the letter of the spin-off statute was not enough if the transaction was otherwise indistinguishable from an ordinary dividend:

> When [the statute] speaks of a transfer of assets by one corporation to another, it means a transfer made "in pursuance of a plan of reorganization" of corporate business; and not a transfer of assets by one corporation to another in pursuance of a plan having no relation to the business of either, as plainly is the case here. Putting aside, then, the question of motive in respect of taxation altogether, and fixing the character of the proceeding by what actually occurred, what do we find? Simply an operation having no business or corporate purpose—a mere device which put on the form of a corporate reorganization as a disguise for concealing its real character, and the sole object and accomplishment of which was the consummation of a preconceived plan, not to reorganize a business or any part of a business, but to transfer a parcel of corporate shares to the petitioner. . . .
>
> The whole undertaking, though conducted according to the terms of [the statute], was in fact an elaborate and devious form of conveyance masquerading as a corporate reorganization, and nothing else. The rule which excludes from consideration the motive of tax avoidance is not pertinent to the situation, because the transaction upon its face lies

---

[2] Section 203(c), 43 Stat. 256 (1924).

outside the plain intent of the statute. To hold otherwise would be to exalt artifice above reality and to deprive the statutory provision in question of all serious purpose.[3]

While the *Gregory* case was moving from the court of appeals to the Supreme Court, Congress enacted the Revenue Act of 1934, which eliminated the statutory provision on which Mrs. Gregory had relied. In recommending this change, the House Committee on Ways and Means said that, by employing spin-offs, "corporations have found it possible to pay what would otherwise be taxable dividends, without any taxes upon their shareholders" and that "this means of avoidance should be ended."[4] Had Congress withheld its legislative hand until after the Supreme Court's decision, it might have decided that the courts could be trusted to distinguish legitimate spin-offs from tax-avoidance devices. Instead, Congress reduced all spin-offs, whether serving business purposes or not, to the level of ordinary distributions, taxable as dividends to the extent of the corporation's earnings and profits. Although this legislative action in 1934 robbed the Supreme Court's decision in the *Gregory* case of some of its immediate importance, over the years the decision has so permeated every crevice of the tax law that it must always be in the forefront of the tax lawyer's mind. Moreover, the decision has had a special impact on the reorganization provisions of the Code,[5] and the later history of corporate separations has been constantly haunted by the fear that a dividend may be masquerading as a divisive distribution.

From time to time after 1934, there were proposals to reinstate the spin-off as a tax-free reorganization, with appropriate restrictions to prevent its use primarily for tax avoidance. These efforts finally bore fruit in 1951, when the 1939 Code was amended to provide in §112(b)(11) for the tax-free spin-off of the common stock of a subsidiary under a plan of reorganization unless it appears that (A) any corporation which is a party to such a reorganization was not intended to continue the active conduct of a trade or business after such reorganization, or (B) the corporation whose stock is distributed was used principally as a device for the distribution of earnings and profits to the shareholders of any corporation a party to the reorganization.[6]

---

[3] Gregory v. Helvering, 293 US 465, 469–470 (1935).

[4] See H.R. Rep. No. 704, 73d Cong., 2d Sess., reprinted in 1939-1 CB (Part 2) 554, 564.

[5] See infra ¶ 14.51.

[6] S. Rep. No. 781, 82d Cong., 1st Sess., reprinted in 1951-2 CB 458, 499. See generally Mintz, Divisive Corporate Reorganizations: Split-Ups and Split-Offs, 6 Tax L. Rev. 365 (1951); Mette, Spin-Off Reorganizations and the Revenue Act of 1951, 8 Tax L. Rev. 337 (1953); Bondy v. CIR, 269 F2d 463 (4th Cir. 1959); Estate of Parshelsky v. CIR, 303 F2d 14 (2d Cir. 1962) (extended historical review and discussion).

Condition (A) of §112(b)(11) was designed to prevent a corporation from separating its cash or investment property from its operating assets in order to spin off the stock of a new corporation holding one or the other, since the shareholders would thereby be enabled to liquidate or sell the inactive corporation at the capital gain rate. Condition (B) was probably intended to deny tax immunity if the distributing corporation's dividend history suggested that the spin-off was a belated substitute for ordinary dividends and there was some reason to think that a prompt sale of either corporation, especially if prearranged, would support an inference that the spin-off was such a device for distributing earnings and profits. These provisions did not have an opportunity to acquire a more definite meaning, however, because §112(b)(11) was supplanted only three years after its enactment by the more elaborate provisions of §355 of the 1954 Code, which will be discussed subsequently. For this reason, the 1951 legislation is notable mainly for its cautious reinstatment of the tax-free spin-off, with statutory restrictions that are reminiscent of the *Gregory* case and that in turn foreshadow, as will be seen, several limitations in §355 of current law.

2. Split-ups. The transfer of corporate assets to two new corporations, followed by a complete liquidation of the original corporation, was a tax-free reorganization as early as 1918. When Congress stripped all spin-offs—good, bad, or indifferent—of their tax immunity in 1934, however, it took no action on the split-up. This is strange, since the tax-free split-up could be used for the same purpose as the reviled spin-off: A corporation could transfer its business assets to one corporation and its unneeded liquid assets to another and distribute the stock of both corporations in a complete liquidation. This would enable the shareholders to carry on the business through the first of the new corporations and to liquidate the second in order to obtain the liquid assets that would otherwise have been distributed to them by the original corporation as a dividend. Whatever the reason for legislative abstinence, the Supreme Court's decision in *Gregory* operated thereafter as a safeguard against abusive split-ups.

3. Split-offs. The 1934 reformers also refrained from action on the split-off, although it too could be pressed into service as a substitute for the spin-off. So far as the language of the pre-1954 statute was concerned, the split-off met the literal requirements of a tax-free reorganization.[7] It was arguable, however, that a split-off was no more than a spin-off coupled with a surrender of stock in the original corporation that was a meaningless gesture if pro rata, and that it should therefore be taxed as a spin-off. In 1953, however, the Ser-

---

[7] See §§112(b)(3), 112(g)(1)(D), and 112(g)(2) (1939 Code).

vice, after some vacillation, ruled favorably on a pro rata split-off serving a business purpose.[8]

¶ 13.03 DIVISIVE CORPORATE DIVISIONS UNDER CURRENT LAW

The tax status of corporate divisions was drastically altered by §355 of the 1954 Code. This provision permits the tax-free distribution by one corporation (the distributing corporation) of stock or securities in another corporation (the controlled corporation) to shareholders with respect to their stock[9] or to security holders in exchange for their securities,[10] if the following conditions (discussed in more detail subsequently) are satisfied:

---

[8] Rev. Rul. 289, 1953-2 CB 37. For the pre-1954 case law, see Chester E. Spangler, 18 TC 976 (1952) (acq.); Riddlesbarger v. CIR, 200 F2d 165 (7th Cir. 1952). For the taxability of non-pro rata split-offs (on continuity-of-interest grounds), see Case v. CIR, 103 F2d 283 (9th Cir. 1939).

[9] See CIR v. Baan, 382 F2d 485 (9th Cir. 1967) (transfer of stock of transferor's subsidiary to transferor's shareholders on their exercise of stock rights was not distribution by transferor "with respect to its stock" within meaning of §355); see also Redding v. CIR, infra note 82 (same). Compare CIR v. Gordon, 382 F2d 499 (2d Cir. 1967) (involving the same transaction but another shareholder and holding that §355 applied). The *Baan* case was affirmed; the *Gordon* case was reversed and remanded by the Supreme Court, 391 US 83 (1968), but on another ground, i.e., the transactions giving the shareholders the requisite 80 percent control of the distributed corporation took place in two steps (occurring in 1961 and 1963), the first of which was independent in the sense that a further distribution, although contemplated, was not promised or required. For the *Gordon* case on remand, see infra note 145.

See generally O'Dell & Boyd, Using Stock Rights in a Corporate Spin Off: The *Redding* Case Offers Words of Warning, 8 J. Corp. Tax'n 140 (1981); Note, Redding v. Commissioner: Step Transaction Doctrine Applied to Distribution of Stock Warrants in a Section 355 Spin-Off, 35 Tax Lawyer 257 (1981).

[10] For possible taxability to the distributing corporation under §1001(c) if appreciated stock or securities are distributed in exchange for its own *debt* securities, see Rev. Rul. 70-271, 1970-1 CB 166, and Rev. Rul. 76-175, 1976-1 CB 92, since neither §311(a) nor §336(c) would apply here. But see §361(b)(3) and flush language, and §361(c) as amended in 1986, infra ¶ 13.12. See also the Technical Corrections Act of 1987, §118(d)(4), providing for nonrecognition at the distributing corporation level in revised §361(c)(3) and new §355(c).

If the distribution is made with respect to a capacity other than stockholder or security holder (e.g., employee or landlord), the transaction will be characterized in whole or in part by that status. See, e.g., Rev. Rul. 77-20, 1977-1 CB 91 (excess of value of distributed stock over value of stock surrendered by shareholder-landlord constituted rent owed by distributing corporation to shareholder and is taxable as such to distributee, notwithstanding §355); Regs. §1.356-5; S. Rep. No. 1622, 83d Cong., 2d Sess. 50 (1954) ("As in the case of the organization of a corporation [supra ¶ 3.08], a disproportionate distribution which has the effect of a gift or of the payment of compensation will be subject to tax as such.").

1. Control. Immediately before the distribution, the distributing corporation must control the corporation whose shares or securities are being distributed. The term "control" is defined by §368(c),[11] which requires the distributing corporation to own stock of the subsidiary possessing at least 80 percent of the total combined voting power and at least 80 percent of the total number of shares of all other classes of stock.[12]

2. Post-distribution active conduct of two or more businesses. Immediately after the distribution, both the distributing corporation and the controlled corporation (or corporations) must be engaged in the active conduct of a trade or business; or, if immediately before the distribution the distributing corporation had no assets other than stock or securities in the controlled corporations,[13] then each controlled corporation must be engaged, immediately after the distribution, in the active conduct of a trade or business. A corporation is treated as engaged in the active conduct of a trade or business if it is so engaged on its own account or if substantially all of its assets consist of the stock and securities of a controlled corporation that is so engaged.[14]

---

[11] See supra ¶ 3.07.

[12] For a checklist of items to be supplied in requests for rulings under §355, see Rev. Proc. 86-41, 1986-45 IRB 7, and 1986-46 IRB 24.

For transactions to obtain control of a partially owned subsidiary in preparation for a spin-off, see Rev. Rul. 63-260, 1963-2 CB 147 (contribution of stock to the distributing corporation by its sole shareholder disregarded as a transitory step); Rev. Rul. 69-407, 1969-2 CB 50 (recapitalization to acquire control held effective); Rev. Rul. 70-18, 1970-1 CB 74 (preliminary merger of two sister corporations, which gave survivor control of jointly owned subsidiary held valid); Rev. Rul. 71-593, 1971-2 CB 181 (transfer of assets for additional stock, putting transferor in control of transferee, held effective); Rev. Proc. 87-3, 1987-1 IRB 27 (§4.20) (rulings not ordinarily granted if distributing corporation obtained control by transfer of liquid assets in tax-free transaction). See also infra text at ¶ 13.06, note 58, Regs. §1.355-2(f)(2), Example (last sentence) (corporation owning 75 percent of the distributing corporation's stock purchased the remaining 25 percent; §355 held inapplicable, apparently because §355(b)(2)(D)(ii) prohibits an acquisition of control in a taxable transaction within five years of the distribution).

[13] The rule of no assets other than stock or securities in the controlled corporation imposed by §355(b)(1)(B) is subject to a de minimis rule. See Regs. §1.355-4(a)(2); Prop Regs. §1.355-3(a)(1)(i)(B) (Jan. 21, 1977).

[14] See Rev. Proc. 77-37, §3.04, 1977-2 CB 568 (for ruling purposes, "substantially all its assets" under §355(b)(2)(A) means 90 percent in gross value of stock and securities of controlled operating subsidiaries). For the application of §355(b)(2)(A) to holding companies, see Rev. Rul. 74-382, 1974-2 CB 120 (§355(b)(1)(B) satisfied where distributing corporation X owned two subsidiaries, Y and Z, and Z's assets consisted solely of stock of nine operating subsidiaries; Z treated as engaged in trade or business by virtue of §355(b)(2)(A)); for a pre-distribution maneuver by a holding

3. Five-year pre-distribution business rule. The foregoing requirement, relating to the active conduct of a trade or business, is satisfied only if the trade or business was (1) actively conducted throughout the five-year period ending on the date of distribution; (2) not acquired within the five-year period in a taxable transaction; and (3) not conducted by another corporation the control of which was acquired (directly or indirectly) during the five-year period in a taxable transaction.

4. Distribution of all stock and securities in controlled corporation. The distributing corporation must distribute either (1) all of its stock and securities in the controlled corporation or (2) enough stock to constitute control as defined by §368(c), *and* establish to the satisfaction of the Treasury that the retention of stock or stock and securities in the controlled corporation is not part of a tax-avoidance plan.

5. Not a device for distributing earnings and profits. The transaction must not be used principally as a device for the distribution of earnings and profits, but the mere fact that stock or securities of one or more of the corporations are sold after the distribution, unless under a pre-distribution arrangement, is not to be construed to mean that the transaction was used principally as such a device.

These conditions are equally applicable to spin-offs, split-offs, and split-ups. Moreover, the distribution need not be part of a reorganization by virtue of §355(a)(2)(C); thus, the stock and securities of an existing subsidiary may be distributed tax-free. In this respect, §355 departs from pre-1954 law, under which the creation of, or a transfer of, assets to the distributed subsidiary was an essential prerequisite to a tax-free distribution. Section 355 does not restrict the type of stock that can be distributed tax-free, but if preferred stock is distributed, it may constitute "section 306 stock" (see Chapter 10), whose later sale or redemption will produce ordinary income rather than capital gain, as discussed later in this chapter. Finally, a distribution can qualify under §355 whether or not it is pro rata with respect to the distributing corporation's shareholders.

Section 355 embraces the distribution of securities as well as stock. but if the principal amount of the securities received by a distributee exceeds the

---

company to qualify under §355(b)(1)(A), see Rev. Rul. 74-79, 1974-1 CB 81 (holding company X wishing to distribute controlled operating subsidiary N could not qualify under §355(b)(1)(B) because its assets included not only a second qualifying operating subsidiary M but also the stock of two other nonqualifying subsidiaries, O and P, and stock of M would not constitute substantially all of X's assets immediately after distribution; held, by liquidating M, parent would become an operating company within meaning of §355(b)(1)(A)).

principal amount of the securities surrendered by him, the fair market value of the excess principal amount is treated as boot; and if no securities are surrendered, the entire fair market value of the securities received is so treated. [15]

Since only the stock and securities of a controlled corporation can be distributed tax-free under §355(a)(1), any other property that may be distributed in conjunction with a corporate division will be treated as boot, taxable under §356. Moreover, if the value of the stock and securities received by any recipient exceeds the value of the stock and securities surrendered, the excess is not shielded by §355, but must be treated in accordance with its true character (e.g., as a gift or payment of compensation). [16]

As stated earlier, §355 does not require the distributing corporation to transfer part of its assets to the controlled corporation, as was required by pre-1954 law. If there is a transfer, however, it will constitute a reorganization under §368(a)(1)(D), and this in turn means that the transferor corporation will not recognize gain or loss on the transfer by virtue of §361(a) and that there will be a carry-over of basis from the transferor corporation to the transferee by virtue of §362(b). [17]

Finally §355, as summarized previously, is concerned with the impact of a corporate division on the persons receiving the distributed stock or securities, not with the impact of the distribution on the distributing corporation itself. These corporate level matters, such as the fate of the distributing corporation's earnings and the question of whether appreciation in the distributed stock and securities will be taxed to the distributing corporation, are examined later in this chapter and elsewhere in this work. [18]

¶ 13.04　THE ACTIVE BUSINESS REQUIREMENT

The most important innovation of the 1954 Code in the taxation of corporate divisions, and one of the most troublesome of §355's conditions, is its active business requirement, which, stripped of details, requires that:

　(1) Both the distributing corporation and controlled corporation (or, if the stock of more than one controlled corporation is distributed, each of the controlled corporations) must be engaged,

---

[15] See infra ¶ 13.11.

[16] See supra note 10.

[17] See infra ¶ 13.14.

[18] See infra ¶ 13.12, text at notes 126–132.

immediately after the distribution, in the active conduct of a trade or business.

(2) The relevant business must have been actively conducted throughout the five-year period ending on the date of the distribution (as discussed later,[19] this requirement has generated an important body of case law, resulting in the invalidation of an important part of the regulations and the promulgation in 1977 of proposed regulations, which, as of late 1987, had not yet been issued in final form).

(3) The relevant business must not have been acquired, directly or indirectly, by a purchase or other transaction in which gain or loss was recognized.

Before examining these requirements in detail, it should be noted that §355 itself does not define the term "active trade or business," but the regulations provide as follows:

For purposes of §355, a trade or business consists of a specific existing group of activities being carried on for the purpose of earning income or profit from *only* such group of activities, and the activities included in such group must include every operation which forms a part of, or a step in, the process of earning income or profit from such group. Such group of activities ordinarily must include the collection of income and the payment of expenses.[20]

The requirement that the trade or business be conducted actively, both immediately after the distribution and during the prescribed five-year period preceding that date, is not elaborated by the regulations. The naked term trade or business, of course, appears in many provisions of the Code (most notably in §162, relating to the deduction of trade and business expenses), but the concept of an *actively* conducted trade or business is less common, although that term has been adopted with increasing frequency in recent legislation.[21]

---

[19] Infra ¶ 13.06.

[20] Regs. §1.355-1(c); Rev. Rul. 82-219, 1982-2 CB 82 (active business continued, even though taxpayer received no income during one of the five pre-distribution years because of insolvency of sole customer); Prop. Regs. §1.355-3(b)(2)(ii) (Jan. 21, 1977) continues this general definition in substantially the same terms, but without the restrictive word "only."

[21] A similar phrase in §302(e)(2) ("actively engaged in the conduct of a trade or business") appears previously in this treatise (supra ¶ 9.10), but it too lacks a statutory definition, and the regulations under this provision adopt the definition of the §355 regulations. See Regs. §1.346-1(c) (relating to the predecessor of §302(e)(2), §346(b)). For other selected provisions (although not a complete list) requiring the

No matter how strictly the active business requirement may be construed, it should pose no difficulties for business firms, such as most conglomerate empires, consisting of separately managed and operated companies engaged in divergent commercial and industrial lines, or even for more modest companies engaged in two or more distinctly separate lines of business activity.[22] Moreover, as explained subsequently, the division of integrated companies is now often feasible as a result of the judicial invalidation of certain otherwise troublesome portions of the regulations.[23] A danger flag, however, continues to mark two other types of assets and activities that taxpayers would often like to separate from an existing business and distribute on a tax-free basis—(1) marketable securities and other passive investment assets and (2) owner-occupied real estate—as explained below. These two categories are singled out for special, and hostile, treatment in both the existing regulations and in the 1977 proposed regulations.

1. Investment property. The regulations state that holding stock, securities, land, or other property for investment, including casual sales thereof, does not constitute the active conduct of a trade or business.[24] As an example, the regulations refer to a manufacturing corporation that owns investment securities that it proposes to place in a new corporation to be spun off to its shareholders.[25] It is obviously necessary to exclude a transaction of this

---

active conduct of a trade or business, see §311(e)(3) (relating to certain corporate distributions), which was, however, repealed in 1986, supra ¶ 7.22; §367(a)(3) (transfer to foreign corporation); §936(a)(2)(B) (income from U.S. possessions); §904(d)(2)(A) (foreign tax credit); §865(f)(2) (source of gain); §954(c)(2)(A) (controlled foreign corporation's foreign personal holding company income definition); §465(c)(4)(A) (at-risk exception for leasing) and §465(c)(7) (exception to at-risk rules for active business, close corporations); and §469(h)(4)(B) (passive activity limitation for losses); and so forth.

[22] See, e.g., Rev. Rul. 56-655, 1956-2 CB 214 (retail appliance branch and retail furniture branch managed separately by two brothers; held separate businesses); Rev. Rul. 56-451, 1956-2 CB 208 (metal industry magazine a separate business from other magazines published to serve the electrical industry; query: Is each electrical industry magazine also a separate business?); Rev. Rul. 56-557, 1956-2 CB 199 (bank's management of real estate acquired by foreclosure qualified as active business); Rev. Rul. 68-407, 1968-2 CB 147 (wholesale drug division a separate business from retail division despite predominately interbusiness dealings); Rev. Rul. 57-190, 1957-1 CB 121 (sale of different brands of autos in different locations represented separate businesses, even though, on facts, one did not meet five-year test).

[23] Infra ¶ 13.05.

[24] Regs. § 1.355-1(c)(1); see also Prop. Regs. § 1.355-3(b)(2)(iv)(A), which is similar in import.

[25] Regs. § 1.355-1(d), Example (1). Prop. Regs. § 1.355-3(c), Example (1) continues this example.

kind (which is strikingly reminiscent of the *Gregory* case[26]) from §355, lest the provision become an open sesame to avoidance of the tax on dividends. Another illustration of this principle is a ranching corporation that owns land adjacent to property on which oil has been discovered. Before the corporation has engaged in any activity in relation to its mineral rights, it proposes to transfer them to a new corporation to be spun off to its shareholders.[27]

Both of these examples, however, might go the other way under different circumstances. A manufacturing corporation could be engaged in the trade or business of buying and selling securities; but this would be a rare combination of business activities, and if the corporation had been reporting its profits on the sale of securities as capital gains, a claim that it was in the securities business in order to permit a tax-free separation under §355 would unquestionably be vigorously resisted by the Service. It would probably be easier for the ranching corporation to establish that it was also engaged in the oil and gas business. The example in the regulations specifies that the corporation had "engaged in no activities in connection with the mineral rights," thus leaving open the possibility that exploration, drilling, production, and sales could in time rise to the dignity of a separate trade or business.[28] Whether a corporate partner in an active business partnership will be treated as itself being engaged in an active business has not as yet been authoritatively determined, but analogous authorities in the partnership area suggest at least that a general partner should be deemed to be engaged in the business of the partnership.[29]

2. Owner-occupied real property. The regulations also exclude from the concept of active trade or business under §355 the ownership and operation

---

[26] Supra note 3. See also Rev. Rul. 66-204, 1966-2 CB 113 (investment activities not an active business for §355 regardless of size or turnover); Rev. Rul. 68-284, 1968-1 CB 143 (leasing vacant land not an active business).

[27] Regs. §1.355-1(d), Example (7). Prop. Regs. §1.355-3(c), Example (3) is the same as old Example (7). See also Example (6) of Regs. §1.355-1(d) (vacant land not an active business), continued in Prop. Regs. §1.355-3(c), Example (2).

[28] See Rev. Rul. 57-492, 1957-2 CB 247 (involving a spin-off of subsidiary corporation engaged in marketing and refining operations), which held that these activities did not become "the active conduct of a trade or business" until oil was discovered in commercial quantities, on the grounds that prediscovery activities (investigations, negotiations for mineral rights, exploration, and drilling) did not independently produce income or contain all the elements necessary to the production of income.

[29] See Rev. Rul. 75-23, 1975-1 CB 290; Regs. §1.355-5(a)(1); Rev. Rul. 73-360, 1973-2 CB 293; George Butler, 36 TC 1097 (1961) (acq.); McKee, Nelson & Whitmire, Federal Taxation of Partnerships and Partners, ¶ 9.05 (Warren, Gorham & Lamont, Inc., 1977).

of land or buildings entirely or substantially used and occupied by the owner in the operation of a trade or business.

To illustrate this principle, the regulations give three examples of corporations engaged in a trade or business that wish to employ §355 to separate their owner-occupied real estate holdings from their other assets.[30] In one example, the real estate is the factory of a manufacturing corporation, and the regulations state that the operation of the factory is not a trade or business separate from the corporation's manufacturing activities. The other two examples both involve banks that wish to spin off the buildings in which their banking operations are carried on. In one case, 10 of the 11 floors of an office building are rented to tenants, the ground floor is occupied by the bank itself, and the bank's real estate department is in charge of the rental, management, and maintenance of the building. In the other case, only one half of the second floor of a two-story building is rented. The regulations state that the first bank's rental activities constitute a trade or business but that the second bank's rental activity is "only incidental to its banking business." It is not clear whether the first building could be spun off under §355 if the rental, management, and maintenance had been entrusted to a real estate agent or management corporation rather than conducted by the bank itself.

Prop. Regs. §§1.355-3(b) and 1.355-3(c) continue to wrestle with the problem of owner-occupied real estate, although the major focus of the proposed regulations on this question is under the device limitation[31] rather than the active business limitation. If the property is not actively managed by the owner (i.e., the owner does not perform significant services with respect to the operation and management of the leased property),[32] it cannot be successfully separated under §355. Thus, proposed Example (13) of the regulations denies active business status to a factory that is net-leased by a subsidiary to its operating parent, as does proposed Example (6) (net lease of land and building by subsidiary to parent). Moreover, proposed Example (5) is similar to old Example (4) but denies separability for net-leased property to be used by the distributing corporation; proposed Example (4) is similar to old Example (3), and the 10-story rental business is found to be an active one because of significant services rendered by the owner in the operation and management of the property.

On several occasions, the courts have refused to allow a tax-free separation of real estate that was predominantly owner-occupied on the ground that the activities connected with the outside rental income were too insig-

---

[30] Regs. §1.355-1(d), Examples (2), (3), and (4).

[31] See infra ¶ 13.07.

[32] Prop. Regs. §§1.355-3(b)(2)(iii) and 1.355-3(b)(2)(iv); see also Rev. Rul. 86-125, 1986-43 IRB 4; Rev. Rul. 86-126, 1986-43 IRB 5.

nificant to constitute an active business.[33] By implication, although not directly, the activity and income attributable to the continued occupancy of the premises by the distributing corporation were regarded as insufficient to create such an active business.[34] To an extent that is not clear, these decisions also rely on the fact that the pre-distribution ownership of the real estate was incidental rather than essential to the income-producing capacity of the existing business.

---

[33] See Rafferty v. CIR, 452 F2d 767 (1st Cir. 1971), cert. denied, 408 US 922 (1972) (property aged for five years in a separate subsidiary, which net-leased the property to its parent; court found no active business because the economic activities constituted a mere investment, and subsidiary had no significant indicia of corporate activity); see also Isabel A. Elliott, 32 TC 283 (1959); Appleby v. CIR, 35 TC 755 (1961), aff'd per curiam, 296 F2d 925 (3d Cir.), cert. denied, 370 US 910 (1962); Bonsall v. CIR, 317 F2d 61 (2d Cir. 1963). But see King v. CIR, 458 F2d 245 (6th Cir. 1972) (separately incorporated terminals owned by interstate trucking company qualified for tax-free distribution; concurring-dissenting judge would have remanded to determine whether distribution was a device to distribute earnings and profits within meaning of §355(a)(1)(B)).

Other rulings have also held that an active business requires substantial management and activities carried on directly by the corporation (disregarding activities carried on through independent contractors): Rev. Rul. 73-234, 1973-1 CB 180 (farming activities qualified because of substantial direct participation in management and operations); Rev. Rul. 86-126, 1986-43 IRB 5 (Rev. Rul. 73-234 distinguished, no active business where corporation's farming activities were supervisory and advisory rather than operational and managerial); Rev. Rul. 73-237, 1973-1 CB 184 (substantial management services as general contractor qualified, even though actual construction work was subcontracted out); Rev. Rul. 86-125, 1986-43 IRB 4 (Rev. Rul. 73-237 distinguished; corporation that owned office building, which was managed by independent real estate management company, not engaged in active business; its limited managerial or operational activities were comparable to those of a prudent investor); Rev. Rul. 73-236, 1973-1 CB 183 (real estate investment trust cannot be in active business; REIT provisions and §355(b) mutually exclusive; properties managed by independent contractors and hence not active business); see also Rev. Rul. 58-164, 1958-1 CB 185 (real estate rented to outsiders an active business on facts); Rev. Rul. 79-394, 1979-2 CB 141 (subsidiary held engaged in active business on facts, even though it had no paid employees of its own; corporation used employees of sister subsidiary under reimbursement arrangement; after distribution, it hired these employees directly to perform the services); Rev. Rul. 80-181, 1980-2 CB 121 (amplifying Rev. Rul. 79-394—not necessary that services be reimbursed; §482, infra ¶ 15.03, would accomplish same result in any event). See Lee, Section 355 Active Business Requirement: What Advice to Give Clients Today, 45 J. Tax'n 272 (1976).

[34] Prop. Regs. §§1.355-3(b)(2)(iii) and 1.355-3(b)(2)(iv)(B), requiring active and substantial management and operations functions for active business status generally and performance of significant services with respect to the operation and management of leased property (real or personal) essentially incorporate the rationale of the Rafferty case and of these rulings, as does Prop. Regs. §1.355-3(c), Examples (6) and (13); cf. King v. CIR, supra note 33 (motor freight terminals net leased to parent constituted active business by subsidiaries).

Whatever their rationale, these cases offer little hope of qualifying the ownership of real estate as an active business unless there is a five-year history of dealing on a substantial scale with occupants other than the owner.[35] Although these cases concerned real estate, the same principles would no doubt be applied to a transfer of vehicles or other equipment to a separate corporation, coupled with a leaseback to the distributing corporation.

¶ 13.05 DIVISIONS OF AN INTEGRATED BUSINESS

When issuing regulations under §355, the Treasury construed the active business requirement of §355 to preclude "the division of a single business."[36] Inspiration for this approach stemmed from the fact that §355(b)(1) requires the active conduct of two separate businesses *immediately after* the distribution; and, since §355(b)(2) demands a five-year pre-distribution history for such business, the Service reasoned that *the* business conducted before the distribution had to be the *same* business as that required to be conducted after the distribution. Despite this theory, the regulations from their inception have tolerated divisions of enterprises that were to some extent integrated before the distribution. Thus, Example (8) provides that a corporation manufacturing and selling ice cream at two plants, located in different states, can transfer one of the plants and related activities to a new corporation and distribute its stock without tax under §355.[37] Another example approves the tax-free separation of a suburban men's retail clothing store from a similar downtown store, but waters down its value as a guidepost by specifying that the stores do not share a common warehouse and that the manager of each store "directs its operations and makes the necessary purchases."[38]

These examples are useful in some cases, but they raise, without resolving, difficulties for companies with plants located in a single area rather than separated by state lines. Similar problems also exist for companies with separate stores or other outlets that are to be operated independently after a proposed distribution but that in the past were subject to unified rather than separate control over financial policies, advertising, hiring and firing, and other major business practices. Indeed, whenever two or more businesses are part of a single corporate group, there is bound to be *some* degree of paren-

---

[35] But see King v. CIR, supra note 33. See also Lee, "Active Conduct" Distinguished From "Conduct" of a Rental Real Estate Business, 25 Tax Lawyer 317 (1972).

[36] Regs. §1.355-1(a) (third sentence).

[37] Regs. §1.355-1(d), Example (8); see also Examples (9), (13), (14), and (15), involving somewhat similar divisions of activities carried on in different states.

[38] Id., Example (10).

tal surveillance and supervision unless the top management is asleep at the switch; and the examples in the regulations do not illuminate the boundary line between permissible and excessive integrated control of the two businesses. Thus, for practical purposes, the examples leave the prohibition on divisions of a single business largely intact, especially as a warning. Taxpayers seeking to use §355 to divide integrated enterprises, therefore, promptly attacked the rationale of this part of the regulations, and they achieved a substantial measure of success.

The leading case is *Coady v. CIR*, in which the Court of Appeals for the Sixth Circuit upheld a tax-free division of a construction company, owned by two equal shareholders, into two businesses, each owned 100 percent by one of them.[39] The division was effected by a transfer of a major construction contract together with an appropriate amount of cash and equipment to a new corporation, the stock of which was then transferred to one of the shareholders in return for all his stock in the distributing corporation (i.e., by a non-pro rata split-off). The latter corporation was left with a second major contract, together with the rest of the equipment and cash. In holding that §355 could be used to divide a single, functionally integrated predistribution business into two separate post-distribution businesses, the court invalidated Regs. §1.355-1(a) to the extent that it holds that §355 does not apply to such a transaction. *Coady* was followed by *US v. Marett*, a Fifth Circuit case upholding a similar division of a single business;[40] and the Service subsequently announced that it would dispose of cases involving the active business requirements of §355(b) in accordance with these pro-taxpayer cases and a third case in which the Service prevailed.[41]

The Service's acquiescence in these appellate cases was followed in 1977 by the promulgation of proposed regulations, which "provide for the separation of a single business consistent with the holdings" in the *Coady* and *Marett* cases.[42] Although still not yet issued in final form, the proposed regulations, and especially the examples illustrating the new approach, have been more influential in the disposition of current transactions than the inconsis-

---

[39] CIR v. Coady, 289 F2d 490 (6th Cir. 1961).

[40] US v. Marett, 325 F2d 28 (5th Cir. 1963) (manufacturing plant producing for a single customer spun off from two other plants producing for same customer and others); see also Rev. Rul. 64-147, 1964-1 CB 136; Patricia W. Burke, 42 TC 1021 (1964) (spin-off of branch store).

[41] Rev. Rul. 75-160, 1975-1 CB 112, citing *Coady, Marett*, and *Rafferty*, supra notes 39, 40, and 33 respectively.

[42] Prop. Regs. §1.355, Preamble published in 42 Fed. Reg. 2694 (1977).
See generally Helfand & Lafving, Filling the Serbonian Bog With Quicksand—Proposed Section 355 Regulations Further Obscure Corporate Separations, Part I, 5 J. Corp. Tax'n 345 (1979); Part II, 6 J. Corp. Tax'n 53 (1979); Part III, 6 J. Corp. Tax'n 133 (1979).

tent portions of the regulations themselves, even though the latter have not been formally revoked.

1. Vertical divisions of a single business under the proposed regulations. The proposed regulations have a particularly dramatic effect on "vertical" divisions of a single pre-distribution business (i.e., separations like the one in *Coady*, in which the distributing and controlled corporations each conduct a business that includes all of the stages or functions of the larger business as it was conducted before the distribution). Thus, one of the examples is modeled on the facts of *Coady* itself, in which a single construction company was split into two enterprises, each carrying on its own share of the pre-distribution business.[43] Another example permits a suburban department store to be separated tax-free from a downtown store, even though the stores "are operated as a single unit and have common advertising, bank accounts, billing, purchasing, and management"—features that presumably would have negated a tax-free division under the regulations that were invalidated by the *Coady* case.[44] Example (11) permits a company with three manufacturing plants to spin-off two of them without specifying that the retained and separated plants are not separated by state lines, a condition that was specified in similar examples in the old regulations.

2. Horizontal divisions of an integrated business. Instead of a vertical division resulting in brother-sister businesses that each carry the genes of the parent business from which they both stem, taxpayers sometimes wish to achieve a horizontal division of an integrated business along functional lines. The regulations, however, state that a group of activities that "are not themselves independently producing income" do not qualify as an active business;[45] in keeping with this theory, hypothetical spin-offs of a manufacturing company's research division, sales functions, and captive coal mines are disqualified in three separate examples.[46]

Although these functional divisions differ from the vertical all-function division upheld in *Coady*, the Tax Court in that case stated that the purpose of the active business requirement of §355(b) is "to prevent the tax-free sep-

---

[43] Prop. Regs. §1.355-3(c), Example (10); see also Example (11), which seems modeled on the facts in *Marett*.

[44] Id., Example (12); see also Example (7) (suburban and downtown stores with pre-distribution common warehouse and delivery trucks).

[45] Regs. §1.355-1(c)(3).

[46] Regs. §1.355-1(d), Examples (5) (research department of company engaged in manufacture and sales of wood products), (11) (sales functions of company processing and selling meat products), and (12) (steel company's captive coal mine). But see infra note 49 for Service change of heart.

aration of *active* and *inactive* assets into *active* and *inactive* corporate entities,[47] an explanation that would not condemn a functional division of a single business previously operated as an integrated entity; and in an influential dictum, the Court of Appeals for the First Circuit said flatly that "the *Coady* rationale is also applicable to functional divisions of existing businesses."[48] Against this background, it is not surprising to find that the 1977 proposed regulations delete the independent production of income requirement quoted above and reverse the results in all three of the functional division examples, although with some variations in the facts.[49]

The proposed regulations, however, do not explicitly reject the result reached in another example in the original regulations of a functional division—an executive dining room maintained by a manufacturing company—that is disqualified, even though it "is managed and operated as a separate unit and the executives are charged for their meals."[50] Yet, assuming that the function is economically viable in the sense that it can operate at a profit if separated from the original business, its separation seems no more objectionable than the separation of a more crucial function of the original business. This lame duck example, therefore, seems to qualify for favorable treatment under the spirit of the proposed regulations, even though it is not explicitly addressed therein.

Although the 1977 proposed regulations thus markedly liberalize the status of horizontal divisions of an integrated business, it should be noted that an activity with no customers or clients other than the original business itself offers a greater opportunity to siphon off the latter's earnings in the future (by a manipulation of intercompany transactions) than an activity that deals solely or primarily with outsiders. Recognizing this possibility, the 977 proposed regulations warn that post-distribution relationships between

---

[47] Edmund P. Coady, 33 TC 771, 777, aff'd per curiam, supra note 39.

[48] Rafferty v. CIR, supra note 33, at n.10; see also King v. CIR, supra note 33. Despite this endorsement of functional divisions, the Tax Court has usually avoided the issue in post-*Coady* cases by finding that the separated activities either constituted an independent five-year-old business or came within the geographical concept of the regulations. See Marne S. Wilson, 42 TC 914 (1964) (separation of credit and collection assets and activities of retail furniture store), rev'd on other ground (no business purpose); CIR v. Wilson, 353 F2d 184 (9th Cir. 1965); H. Grady Lester, Jr., 40 TC 947 (1963) (acq.) (warehouse distribution business separated from business of selling to jobbers); Albert W. Badanes, 39 TC 410 (1962) (same type of business in different cities of same state); Hanson v. US, 338 F. Supp. 602 (D. Mont. 1971) (division of auto dealership into separate financial and sales corporations).

[49] Prop. Regs. §1.355-3(c), Examples (14) (research department), (8) (sales activities), and (9) (captive coal mine). Example (14) specifies that the research department will contract with outside companies as well as with its former parent; but no such expansion of its customer list is specified for the captive coal mine in Example (9).

[50] Regs. §1.355-1(d), Example (16).

the distributing and transferee corporations may constitute evidence that the transaction was used principally as a device for the distribution of earnings and profits in violation of §355(a)(1)(B), which is examined in detail subsequently.[51] Of course, the Service has other tools, such as §482, permitting it to correct transactions that do not reflect the terms that would prevail if the parties had dealt with each other at arm's length; and if perfect enforcement of these remedial measures could be anticipated, there would be no warrant for disqualifying transactions in advance because of fears of later related-party misconduct. The proposed regulations, however, presuppose the uncertainties of enforcement in the real world; even so, the disqualification of any particular corporate divisions as a tainted device within the meaning of §355(a)(1)(B) ineluctably rests on guesswork.

¶ 13.06 THE FIVE-YEAR PRE-DISTRIBUTION BUSINESS HISTORY REQUIREMENT

As has been seen, §355's active business requirement is designed to prevent a tax-free separation of liquid assets as a substitute for current dividends. By itself, however, the active business requirement would not prevent a corporation from investing its surplus funds in a new business and spinning it off in preparation for a sale of the business by the shareholders—a scheme that would have substantially the same economic effect as a distribution of money. Or, if the shareholders desired to invest in a new business as individuals or partners, the corporation might build up the new business for them and then spin it off rather than paying ordinary dividends. To prevent such devices, §355(b)(2)(B) provides that both the distributed business and the retained business (or, in the event of a split-up, both of the distributed businesses) must have been actively conducted throughout the five-year period ending on the date of the distribution.[52]

The purpose underlying the requirement of a five-year history for each business is to prevent of the temporary investment of liquid assets in a new business preparatory to a spin-off or other tax-free corporate division under §355. If the business has been conducted actively for five years, it presumably was not created for the purpose of avoiding the tax on dividends. But, even though the business might not have been *created* for this purpose, it might have been *purchased* by the distributing corporation as a temporary investment in anticipation of a distribution. To forestall this possibility, two additional conditions must be met if the business (or the corporation con-

---

[51] Infra ¶ 13.07.

[52] See the comparable requirements of §302(e)(2), designed to serve a similar purpose, supra ¶ 9.10.

ducting it) has changed hands within the five-year period ending with the date of the distribution:

(1) Under §355(b)(2)(C), a trade or business is disqualified if it was acquired within the five-year period in a transaction in which gain or loss was recognized in whole or in part. As was indicated with respect to the comparable prohibition in §302(e)(2),[53] the statutory purpose was to exclude a business that was *purchased* by the distributing or controlled corporation within the preceding five years. Since the *purchaser* would not recognize gain or loss on such an acquistion of an existing business, the phrase "transactions in which gain or loss was recognized in whole or in part" must mean, at least primarily, transactions in which the *seller* recognized gain or loss. (It should also include the acquisition of a business from another corporation that avoided the recognition of gain or loss under former §337,[54] but whose shareholders recognized gain or loss on the liquidation.) Moreover, if the seller happens not to recognize gain or loss because it is a tax-exempt institution or because the sale price of the business is equal to its adjusted basis, the acquisition should be barred for the purpose of §355(b)(2)(C), although its language is far from satisfactory on this point.[55]

Section 355(b)(2)(C) permits the acquisition of a business in a tax-free transaction, such as the liquidation of a subsidiary under §332, a tax-free merger or consolidation under §§361 and 368(a)(1)(A), or an exchange under §351. But the use of boot in an otherwise tax-free exchange may disqualify the transaction, at least if the *transferor* realizes and recognizes gain, since §355(b)(2)(C) forbids the recognition of gain or loss "in whole or in part."[56]

---

[53] Supra ¶ 9.10.

[54] See supra ¶ 11.61. This provision was repealed, however, in 1986, supra ¶ 11.06.

[55] Prop. Regs. §1.355-3(b)(4)(i) adopt a carry-over basis versus cost-basis approach as the touchstone to §355(b)(2)(C), specifically noting that old §337 sales were not qualified acquisitions; moreover, Prop. Regs. §1.355-3(b)(4)(ii) incorporates the theory of Rev. Rul. 69-461, 1969-2 CB 52, that acquisitions within an affiliated group are not tainted acquisitions. See also Rev. Rul. 78-442, 1978-2 CB 143 (same for §357(c) gain).

[56] For discussion, see Oscar E. Baan, 45 TC 71 (1965), holding that an acquisition in which the transferor did not recognize gain because it was incurred on an intercompany transfer between members of an affiliated group of corporations filing a consolidated return did not violate the prohibition of §355(b)(2)(C). When *Baan* and a companion case went up on appeal (supra note 9), the Court of Appeals for the Ninth Circuit did not reach this issue, while the Second Circuit affirmed on the ground that §355(b)(2)(C) applies only to "the bringing of new assets within the combined corporate shells" of the distributing and the controlled corporations. See also supra note 55.

(2) Secondly, §355(b)(2)(D) strengthens §355(b)(2)(C) by prohibiting—for the five-year period before distribution—the acquisition of control of a corporation conducting the business unless the acquisition was a tax-free transaction. This requirement forestalls the purchase by one corporation of the stock of another corporation within the five-year period for the purpose of (1) spinning off the stock of the second corporation, or (2) acquiring its business in a tax-free liquidation in order to spin off the business.[57] Section 355(b)(2)(D), however, permits the acquisition of control during the five-year period by a transaction in which gain or loss was not recognized in whole or in part or by reason of such transactions coupled with other acquisitions before the five-year period.[58]

When the distributing or controlled corporation's acquisition of a business (or of a corporation conducting the business) is consistent with §§355(b)(2)(C) and 355(b)(2)(D) (i.e., in the case of a tax-free acquisition), the predecessor's business history is tacked on in computing the five-year period. Thus, if a business conducted by a partnership for three years was

---

If the transferor suffers a *loss* on the exchange, the transfer of boot will not result in the recognition of any part of the loss, because of §§356(c), 361(a), and 351(b)(2). Even so, such a transaction ought not to qualify under §355(b)(2)(C), at least if it is the functional equivalent of an ordinary purchase; but the clumsy statutory language may be construed so as to leave an unwarranted opening for such an acquisition. Even less clear is the result where the transferor's boot gain goes unrecognized because it completely liquidates, as it must in order to qualify the transaction as a tax-free reorganization; infra ¶ 14.32 (this problem is similar to the §337 acquisition case before its repeal in 1986, noted in the text); see also text supra note 55.

As noted infra ¶ 14.32, it is no longer possible for the transferor corporation in a qualified reorganization to recognize gain or loss *on the exchange* of its assets in the reorganization; see §361 as amended in 1986.

[57] See Regs. §1.355-4(b)(2), Example, continued in Prop. Regs. §1.355-3(b)(4)(iii); see also Rev. Rul. 74-5, 1974-1 CB 82 (indirect acquisition case—*P* buys stock of *T* and *T* distributes stock of *S* to *P*; valid §355 distribution by *T* to *P*, but not if *P* then distributes the *S* stock to its shareholders, because this would violate §355(b)(2)(D)).

[58] See Rev. Rul. 73-44, 1973-1 CB 182 (contribution of five-year-old division to subsidiary acquired within five years in a taxable transaction held a qualified spin-off of subsidiary under §355, even though "aged" business constituted less than half of subsidiary's assets); Rev. Rul. 76-54, 1976-1 CB 96 (Rev. Rul. 73-44 interpreted to mean that parent purchased business assets rather than stock of subsidiary that ran the unaged business); compare Rev. Rul. 57-144, 1957-1 CB 123 (backing into 80 percent control by redemption transaction within five years that brought parent above 80 percent line not qualified; hence, spin-off of other controlled subsidiary a taxable dividend). See GCM 39264 (Aug. 13, 1984), ruling that the acquisition described in Rev. Rul. 57-144 is irreversible and cannot be purged; thus, parent must wait five years to distribute).

acquired by the distributing corporation in a §351 transaction and was conducted by the distributing corporation for two more years, it has the requisite five-year history. A business acquired by purchase, however, must be conducted by the acquiring corporation itself for the full five-year period to meet the standard of §355(b)(2)(B).[59]

A problem that is especially troublesome in applying the five-year rule is to determine whether a group of activities constitutes a separate business, which must have its *own* five-year history, or is a separable part of a larger enterprise that can share in the latter's five-year history. Taxpayers may find themselves on a tightrope here, (i.e., asserting that the activities are sufficiently distinctive to constitute a separate active business after the distribution but that they were so closely associated with the original business before the distribution as to inherit its five-year history).[60] The more distinctive and independently viable the activities are, however, the weaker is their claim to an inherited history.

Application of the five-year rule is complicated by such problems as (1) whether the commencement of a business activity is an extension of an old business or constitutes entry into a new and separate business; (2) whether a change of location constitutes an abandonment of the old business and the start of a new one or merely a continuation of the old business at a new location; (3) whether a cessation of business activity followed by a resumption of activity constitutes a termination of the old business and the start of a new one or is a continuation of the old business after a temporary lull; (4) whether expansion constitutes an entry into a new business; and (5) whether the source of funds behind an expansion is significant. The regulations state that changes during the five-year period (e.g., the addition of new products or the dropping of old ones, changes in productive capacity, etc.) are consistent with the conduct of a continuing business, provided "the changes are not of such a character as to constitute the acquisition of a new business."[61]

---

[59] See Marne S. Wilson, supra note 48; see also W.E. Gabriel Fabrication Co., 42 TC 545 (1964) (acq.) (five-year history not broken by unusual loan of business to shareholder in anticipation of a §355 transaction); Edward H. Russell, 40 TC 810 (1963), aff'd per curiam, 345 F2d 534 (5th Cir. 1965) (dates of acquisition and of distribution determined).

[60] See Prop. Regs. §1.355-3(c), Example 12 (suburban department store constituted part of single integrated department store business, implying that it inherited latter's nine-year history, although this was not necessary to result because it had a six-year history even if viewed independently). See also Estate of Lockwood v. CIR, 350 F2d 712 (8th Cir. 1965).

[61] Regs. §1.355-4(b)(3); see also Prop. Regs. §1.355-3(b)(3); Estate of Lockwood, supra note 60.

This language has been interpreted by the Service in published rulings to permit a change in location or a temporary cessation of business activity by a corporation intending to resume the business without breaking the five-year chain.[62] The acquisition by a dealer holding a franchise for the sale and service of one brand of automobile tires of a similar franchise for another brand, however, was held to start a new five-year period running for the second franchise, to which the holding period of the first franchise could not be tacked on.[63]

The five-year rule is also troublesome in the case of a business that expanded rapidly during the five-year pre-distribution period. An increase in the size of its productive capacity, labor force, sales, and so forth, or a vertical expansion along functional lines should be treated as a continuation of the old business rather than the acquisition of a new one, even if the new assets are substantial in value relative to those that are over five years old. A point may be reached, however, at which the new assets so completely overshadow the old ones, especially if there has been a horizontal expansion into a new line of activity, that this new line of activity must be regarded as a new business. In effect, the continuity-of-business test of §355 requires more than the mere continuation of *a* business; rather, it is *the* business that must be continued for the five-year period in order to satisfy §355(b)(2)(B).

If two businesses can be identified but the earnings of one have been employed to finance substantial growth in the other during the five-year period, the Service may assert that §355 cannot be used to effect a separation. Thus, Rev. Rul. 59-400 held that §355 did not apply to the spin-off of a rental real estate business where the earnings of a separate hotel business were used to feed the growth of the rental business.[64] The precise basis for the ruling is unclear, but its emphasis on the translation of hotel earnings into marketable rental property implies that it was based on §355(a)(1)(B),

---

[62] See Rev. Rul. 56-344, 1956-2 CB 195 (change of location); Rev. Rul. 57-126, 1957-1 CB 123 (temporary cessation of activity in unusual circumstances); see also Estate of Lockwood, supra note 60.

[63] Rev. Rul. 57-190, 1957-1 CB 121; see also Lloyd Boettger, 51 TC 324 (1968) (§355(b)(2)(C) not satisfied where a business was purchased within five years of split-up, even though it was of same type as acquiring corporation's business and was integrated into acquiring corporation's operations). The distinction between mere expansion and a tainted purchase is not an easy line to draw. See Regs. §1.355-4(b)(3); Prop. Regs. §1.355-3(b)(3) (change of business vs. acquisition of business); Riener C. Nielsen, 61 TC 311 (1973) (§355 not applicable to other shareholders in *Boettger* case because acquired business was not sufficiently integrated with old business to share its business history). Compare Estate of Lockwood, supra note 60 (focus on type of business rather than geographical location).

See generally Emory, Tax Court Further Narrows Tax-Free Corporate Separations, 47 Taxes 219 (1969).

[64] Rev. Rul. 59-400, 1959-2 CB 114.

prohibiting a distribution that is "principally a device for the distribution of the earnings and profits of the distributing corporation" rather than on the theory that the rental activities did not constitute an active business. The source of the funds used to establish or expand a business may be relevant in applying the device rule, but it seems to shed little light on whether corporate activities constitute an active business or, if they do, on the age of the business. A 1964 ruling allowing a substantial capital contribution by a parent corporation to a subsidiary just prior to a distribution of the subsidiary's stock under §355 bears out this observation, although it does not wholly repudiate the notion that the use of earnings generated by the business to expand a second business may weaken the latter's claim to an independent five-year history.[65]

¶ 13.07 THE "DEVICE" RESTRICTION

To be tax-free under §355, a distribution must not be used "principally as a device for the distribution of the earnings and profits of the distributing corporation or the controlled corporation or both."[66] Following this prohibition, §355(a)(1)(B) provides that the mere fact that stock or securities in either corporation are sold or exchanged (other than pursuant to a predistribution arrangement) must not be construed to mean that the transaction was used principally as a device. The regulations, giving this clause the narrowest possible meaning, state that a sale of stock or securities that is not prearranged is not determinative that the transaction was a device, but that, whether prearranged or not, a sale is evidence of that taint.[67]

The theory that a postdistribution sale, especially if prearranged, is a method of bailing out earnings and profits is frequently advanced but infrequently examined. The problem reduces itself to a sale of common stock, since securities will be taxed as boot under §355(a)(3) unless securities in an

---

[65] Rev. Rul. 64-102, 1964-1 CB 136; see also Rev. Rul. 78-383, 1978-2 CB 142; Rev. Rul. 71-383, 1971-2 CB 180; Rev. Rul. 83-114, 1983-2 CB 66 (threshold capital contribution not per se a device to distribute earnings and profits; depends on facts). But see Rev. Rul. 86-4, 1986-1 CB 174 (is evidence of device regardless of size).

[66] This restriction was taken almost verbatim from the pre-1954 spin-off provision, §112(b)(11) of the 1939 Code (see supra text at note 6), where it seems to have been aimed mainly at prearranged sales of the stock of either corporation in addition to serving as a statutory business purpose rule and to strengthen the active business requirement of §112(b)(11); for current law, see generally Greene, Unraveling Part of the Tangled Web of Section 355: Uses, Abuses, and Alternatives to Corporate Separation, 1981 S. Cal. Tax Inst. ¶ 9.

[67] Regs. §1.355-2(b)(1); see also Rev. Rul. 55-103, 1955-1 CB 31 (distribution of subsidiary to pave way for sale of parent to buyer that did not want to acquire subsidiary; not qualified).

equal or greater principal amount are surrendered, while preferred stock will ordinarily be rendered harmless by §306(c)(1)(B).[68] The central question, then, is whether a sale of the common stock of either the distributing corporation or the controlled corporation is a device for bailing out earnings and profits. Such a sale spells a loss of control of one of the businesses (and a loss of the seller's share in the corporation's earning power and growth potential as well), whereas a bailout ordinarily means that earnings and profits have been drawn off without impairing the shareholder's residual equity interest in the corporation's or corporations' earning power, growth potential, or voting control.[69] This is why, except in rare cases, common stock is not brought under the aegis of §306.[70]

If immunity from taxation is being conferred by §355 only on the assumption that the original shareholders will continue to operate both businesses after the distribution, it would seem appropriate to require the stock of both corporations to be held for a specified period of time, or to "taint" the stock (as is done under §306). Instead, §355(a)(1)(B) attempts to distinguish between sales that are prearranged and those that are not, a distinction that is difficult to administer and meaningless in any event. In this connection, it should be noted that a partial liquidation is treated as a capital gain (or loss) transaction by §§302(e)(1) (corporate contractions) and 302(e)(2) (distribution of a separate trade or business), and that the distributees are thereafter free to dispose of either the distributed assets or the original stock.[71] This treatment of partial liquidations cannot be reconciled with the assumption of §355(a)(1)(B) that a prearranged sale demonstrates (or aids in

---

[68] See infra ¶ 13.13.

[69] See Rafferty v. CIR, supra note 33 (spin-off of subsidiary that leased real estate to parent constituted device because of high bail-out potential; "in the absence of any direct benefit to the business of the original company, and on a showing that the spin-off put salable assets in the hands of the taxpayers, the continued retention of which was not needed to continue the business enterprise, or to accomplish taxpayers' purposes . . . the distribution was principally a device to distribute earnings and profits."). Compare King v. CIR, supra note 33 (no device because separated assets essential to business and not suitable for bail-out).

See generally Lee, Functional Divisions and Other Corporate Separations Under Section 355 After Rafferty, 27 Tax L. Rev. 453 (1972).

[70] See supra ¶ 10.03.

[71] A corporate contraction can qualify under §302(e)(1) only if it is "not essentially equivalent to a dividend;" see supra ¶ 9.09. If a prearranged sale of distributed assets is a device for distributing earnings and profits, this part of §302(e)(1) would be violated. But it has ordinarily been assumed that a partial liquidation is not tainted by a subsequent sale of the distributed assets. Moreover, §302(e)(2), relating to the distribution of "a qualified trade or business," does not even contain the restriction that the transaction must not be essentially equivalent to a dividend.

demonstrating) that the distribution is a device for the distribution of earnings and profits.

Despite these shortcomings in the theory that a prearranged sale of either the distributing or the controlled corporation is a device for distributing earnings and profits, the 1977 proposed regulations state flatly that (1) a sale or exchange of 20 percent or more of the stock of either the distributing or controlled corporation "will be considered" to violate the anti-device rule provided the sale or exchange was negotiated or agreed upon before the distribution and (2) if a sale was discussed by the buyer and seller and was reasonably to be anticipated by both parties, it "shall ordinarily be considered" as made pursuant to such a predistribution arrangement.[72] Even if the prearranged sale or exchange involves securities rather than stock or falls below the 20 percent benchmark for stock, it will be considered "as substantial evidence" that the transaction was used principally as a device to distribute earnings and profits.[73]

Although §355(a)(1)(B) refers to a sale or exchange of stock *or* securities, a disposition of securities may be less objectionable to the Service than a sale of stock, at least if the distribution of the securities produced dividend income as boot under §356(a)(2). Moreover, a prearranged sale by a relatively minor distributee, especially one whose plans were not known to the others, would presumably be less important than a prearranged sale by a controlling shareholder.

Other aspects of the anti-device rule that deserve close attention are:

1. Contemporaneous tax-free transactions. As applied to prearranged sales of the stock of one of the corporations, the device clause serves to insure a continuity of interest on the part of the shareholders; they will be unable to cash in on their investment as part of the divisive transaction but will have to wait until the distribution itself is "old and cold." If the stock is transferred by them in a tax-free exchange, however, their pre-distribution proprietary interest will ordinarily continue, and it must then be decided if a §355 transaction can be combined with a tax-free reorganization (or similar transaction) without impairing the tax-free status of either event. An example is a §355 spin-off in anticipation of a tax-free merger of the distributing corporation into an acquiring corporation, the spin-off being used to rid the distributing corporation of a business that the acquiring corporation does not wish to take over.

As an initial matter, such a distribution-acquisition combination does not seem to violate the underlying policies of §355, nor should the device

---

[72] Prop. Regs. §1.355-2(c)(2); for examples, see Prop. Regs. §1.355-2(c)(4).

[73] Id.

clause of §355(a)(1)(B) necessarily be invoked to deny §355 treatment for the anticipatory division of the enterprise. The device clause refers to a distribution of earnings and profits, and, in this situation, earnings of both the distributing corporation and the controlled corporation remain in corporate solution. Moreover, the shareholders of the corporation whose stock is transferred in the reorganization maintain a continuing interest in the earnings of that corporation by virtue of the stock acquired in exchange for their former stock interest in the transferred corporation. The Service, however, at first regarded the contemplated disposition of the stock of one of the corporations in a merger as evidence that the §355 transaction was a device, and the cases on this point were conflicting; but in 1968, the Service agreed that §355 was not per se incompatible with a contemporaneous merger reorganization, and the 1977 proposed regulations now agree.[74]

2. Non-pro rata or non-dividend distributions. If a transaction would—absent §355—be taxed to the participating shareholders as a sale of their stock, giving rise to capital gain or loss rather than as a dividend, the Service has ruled that it does not constitute a device to distribute earnings and profits.[75] An example is a split-off in which a shareholder exchanges all his stock in the distributing corporation for all of the stock of the controlled corporation, which would be treated as a capital gain or loss event under §302(b)(3) (complete termination) if §355 did not apply. This stress on a lack of dividend equivalency is likely to be confined to split-offs and split-ups that are non-pro rata in character under §§302(b)(2) and 302(b)(3); pro rata transactions will ordinarily invite closer scrutiny.[76]

---

[74] Rev. Rul. 68-603, 1968-2 CB 148; Prop. Regs. §1.355-2(c)(2) (third sentence); see also CIR v. Morris Trust, 367 F2d 794 (4th Cir. 1966); Rev. Rul. 75-406, 1975-2 CB 125; Rev. Rul. 78-251, 1978-1 CB 89; Rev. Rul. 83-114, supra note 65; Samansky, Tax-Free Distributions of Stock Followed by a Merger With Boot: A Current Analysis, 49 J. Tax'n 12 (1978); and infra ¶ 14.52.

[75] See Rev. Rul. 71-383, 1971-2 CB 180 65 (substantially disproportionate split-off); Rev. Rul. 71-384, 1971-2 CB 181 (return of capital split-off distributions); Rev. Rul. 71-593, supra note 12 (non-pro rata split-off that terminated interest); Rev. Rul. 77-377, 1977-2 CB 11.1 (§303 qualified redemption not device, even though planned before the §355 distribution).

Prop. Regs. §1.355-2(c)(1) adopt the nondividend equivalence theory of these rulings, stating that the distribution "is ordinarily not considered to be a device" if the distribution, absent §355 protection, would qualify for exchange treatment under §302 (presumably with consideration of §318) or if the distribution would be a return of capital transaction under §301(c)(2) because of the absence of earnings in both corporations.

[76] See Prop. Regs. §1.355-2(c)(1), stating that pro rata distributions offer "the greatest potential" for a bail-out and hence are more likely to be undertaken as a device (unless neither corporation has any earnings and profits).

3. Excess nonbusiness assets. The regulations state that in determining whether a transaction was used principally as a device, consideration should be given "to all of the facts and circumstances of the transaction" and in particular "to the nature, kind and amount of the assets of both corporations (and corporations controlled by them) immediately after the transaction."[77] This statement is a warning that a distribution may be a device for the distribution of earnings and profits, even if the distributees do not sell the stock or securities. Thus, if a corporation with substantial earnings and profits owns two qualifying trades or businesses worth $100,000 each (including working capital), but also holds liquid assets valued at $1 million that are not required in the businesses, the Service may regard a corporate division as a device for the distribution of earnings and profits, even though the stock and securities of both corporations are to be retained by the distributees. The last sentence of Regs. §1.355-2(b)(3), moreover, could carry an unfavorable implication for a corporation holding excess liquid assets, especially if it had been miserly in declaring dividends in past years. Since the earnings are still in corporate solution, however, §531 may be a more suitable approach to this problem than §355(a)(1)(B).[78]

4. Intercorporate dealings. Finally, Prop. Regs. §1.355-2(c)(3)(iv) states that postdistribution intercorporate dealings can be evidence of a device, listing as examples the continued performance of services or supplying of research data or raw materials to the group in the same manner as existed prior to the separation transaction; thus, a captive coal mine (Example (9) in Prop. Regs. §1.355-3(c)) would be vulnerable to a device finding if it continued to supply the parent's needs on the same basis, and the separation of the manufacturing and sales functions in proposed Example (8) likewise would be questioned if the sales corporation continued to act as the exclusive sales agent for the manufacturing corporation after the transaction.

¶ 13.08   DISTRIBUTION OF ALL STOCK AND SECURITIES IN CONTROLLED CORPORATIONS

Section 355(a)(1)(D) requires the distributing corporation to distribute either (1) all of the stock and securities in the controlled corporation held by

---

[77] Regs. §1.355-2(b)(3); see also Prop. Regs. §§1.355-2(c)(1), 1.355-2(c)(3); Rev. Rul. 86-4, 1986-1 CB 174 (transfer of small percentage of investment assets before distribution is factor to be considered in applying device criterion).

[78] For §531, see ¶¶ 8.01–8.09. As to passive assets and passive activities generally, see §469, enacted in 1986.

it immediately before the distribution, or (2) an amount of stock constituting control under §368(c); but, in the latter event, the Treasury must be satisfied that the retention of stock (or stock and securities) in the controlled corporations was not pursuant to a plan having as one of its principal purposes the avoidance of federal income tax.

The committee reports on the 1954 Code do not explain this limitation on the retention of stock or securities by the distributing corporation, but presumably it was to prevent a parent corporation from making periodic distributions of small amounts of stock and securities in a subsidiary as a substitute for ordinary dividends.[79] It is not clear, however, why periodic distributions of small amounts of the controlled corporation's stock should be treated as a dividend once the basic policy decision to permit a tax-free distribution of *all* of its stock and securities under §355 was made. The theory that underlies §355, if valid at all, seems as applicable to a partial separation of the controlled corporation as to a complete separation. Perhaps the drafters of §355(a)(1)(D) were concerned about a distribution of part of the controlled corporation's stock or securities in anticipation of a sale by the distributees. But the device language of §355(a)(1)(B) serves as an independent restriction on sales, at least if they are prearranged;[80] no reason suggests itself for imposing a more severe restriction on sale of all the stock received in a partial separation than on a sale of part of the stock received in a complete separation. As to a distribution of preferred stock as a prelude to a bailout of earnings and profits, the danger seems no greater in a partial separation than in a complete separation, and §306 was evidently thought to be a sufficient safeguard in the latter instance.[81] An attempted bailout with the use of securities (notes, debentures, or bonds) would ordinarily be frustrated by §355(a)(3), under which securities constitute boot if no securities are surrendered or to the extent that their principal amount exceeds the principal amount of any securities surrendered.

---

[79] If this was its purpose, the distribution requirement overlaps and serves as a buttress to the device restriction of §355(a)(1)(B), discussed supra ¶ 13.07, which makes §355 inapplicable if the transaction is "used principally as a device for the distribution of the earnings and profits" of either corporation.

The regulations under the pre-1954 spin-off provision (supra notes 6 and 8) contained the following statement, upon which §355(a)(1)(D) of the 1954 Code was probably patterned: "Ordinarily, the business reasons (as distinguished from any desire to make a distribution of earnings and profits to the shareholders) which support the reorganization and the distribution of the stock will require the distribution of all of the stock received by the transferor corporation in the reorganization." Regs. §§118, 39.112(b)(11)-2(c).

[80] See supra ¶ 13.07.

[81] See infra ¶ 13.13.

Whatever the validity of the reasons for its existence, §355(a)(1)(D) must, of course, be complied with. Although §355(a)(1)(D)(i) requires the distributing corporation to distribute all the stock and securities in the controlled corporation held by it immediately before the distribution,[82] it does not explicitly require the distribution of any stock or securities that may be held by another controlled corporation rather than by the distributing corporation itself. Nor does it explicitly preclude a pre-distribution sale or other disposition of such stock or securities, although it is possible that such a transfer might be denied tax effect if made pursuant to the plan of distribution and as a device to defeat §355(a)(1)(D)(i).

Aside from such implied nonstatutory limitations on a predistribution transfer, it should be noted that such transfers of stock of the controlled corporation are inhibited to some extent by §355(a)(1)(A), requiring the distributing corporation to have control immediately before the distribution of the corporation whose stock or securities are to be distributed. Thus, at best only a limited amount of stock could be disposed of by the distributing corporation.

A degree of flexibility is introduced into the requirement under discussion by §355(a)(1)(D)(ii), providing that stock or securities[83] of the controlled corporation may be retained by the distributing corporation provided it (1) distributes enough stock to constitute control under the 80 percent definition of §368(c), and (2) establishes to the satisfaction of the Treasury that the stock or securities held back are not being retained in pursuance of a plan having as one of its principal purposes the avoidance of federal income tax. The regulations also state that ordinarily the business reasons for a corporate division, "as distinguished from any desire to make a distribution of earnings and profits," will require a distribution of all the stock and securities of the controlled corporation. A retention of stock or securities to meet bona fide business commitments (e.g., a stock option plan)

---

[82] For the status of a two-step distribution, see the Supreme Court's decision in the *Gordon* case, supra note 9 and the *Baan* case, supra note 9, both denying §355 treatment for creeping distributions. See also Gerald R. Redding, 71 TC 597 (1979) (distribution of controlled subsidiary via rights offering held a valid §355 transaction; rights merely a procedural device to effect the distribution and to permit distributing corporation to raise capital concurrently). On appeal, *Redding* was reversed, 630 F2d 1169 (7th Cir. 1980), cert. denied, 450 US 913 (1981) (distribution of control must be to shareholders of parent; requirement not satisified in case because some rights were exercised by persons who were not stockholders of parent); see O'Dell & Boyd, supra note 9.

[83] Section 355(a)(1)(D)(ii) permits a retention of stock or of stock and securities, but does not mention a retention of securities alone. The regulations, however, remedy this oversight. See Regs. §1.355-2(d), Prop. Regs. §1.355-2(d).

not undertaken in anticipation of the §355 division ought to evoke a favorable ruling from the Service.

The regulations go on to make the curious statement that the fact that the retained stock or securities would constitute taxable boot if distributed does not tend to establish the *absence* of a tax-avoidance plan.[84] This seems obvious; the real problem in this area is whether a retention of such stock or securities tends to establish the *existence* of such a plan. But there are few published rulings to aid in determining what circumstances will, in the eyes of the Service, justify a retention of stock or securities.

¶ 13.09　NON-PRO RATA DISTRIBUTIONS

A non-pro rata corporate division may be a useful method of settling a dispute among the shareholders of a closely held corporation. For example, a corporation owned equally by two shareholders who are at loggerheads might transfer part of its assets to a subsidiary and then transfer the stock of the subsidiary to one of the shareholders in exchange for all of his stock in the parent, with the result that the original corporation will be solely owned by one of the shareholders and the new corporation will be solely owned by the other. Section 355 explicitly provides in §355(a)(2)(A) that a corporate division (if otherwise qualified) will be tax-free "whether or not the distribution is pro rata with respect to all of the shareholders of the distributing corporation."[85] This permits stock of an existing subsidiary to be distributed in a non-pro rata division (e.g., transfer of a subsidiary's stock to buy out one of the shareholders of the parent). Moreover, if it is necessary to create a subsidiary (or to transfer additional property to an existing subsidiary) as part of the plan, this can be done tax-free under §368(a)(1)(D), which provides that a transfer by a corporation of part of its assets to another corporation will constitute a reorganization if, immediately after the transfer, the

---

[84] See Regs. §1.355-2(d), Prop. Regs. §1.355-2(d). See generally Rev. Rul. 75-321, 1975-2 CB 123 (retention of 5 percent of stock of spun-off subsidiary to meet collateral requirements of short-term financing for distributing corporation's other businesses held valid business purpose for retention, and thus §355(a)(1)(D) not violated); Rev. Rul. 75-469, 1975-2 CB 126 (retention of debt securities of split-off subsidiary did not violate §355(a)(1)(D) where securities were substituted as collateral for stock of subsidiary, which had been pledged to secure bank loans, the proceeds of which had been reloaned by the parent to the subsidiary for use in the latter's business).

For the circumstances in which the stock of a controlled corporation can constitute boot, see infra ¶ 13.11.

[85] For pre-1954 law, see Frank W. Williamson, 27 TC 647 (1957) (acq.); Case v. CIR, supra note 8; Lyons, Realignment of Stockholders' Interests in Reorganizations Under Section 112(g)(1)(D), 9 Tax L. Rev. 237 (1954).

transferor or one or more of its shareholders, *including persons who were shareholders immediately before the transfer*, or any combination thereof is in control of the transferee corporation. These statutory provisions permit shareholders to go their separate ways on a tax-free basis, whether the stock used to effect the separation is the stock of an existing subsidiary or that of a newly created one.[86]

There will be times, however, when taxpayers will regard this gift horse with some dissatisfaction, since a shareholder who is bought out with the stock of a subsidiary may realize a loss because his adjusted basis for the surrendered stock exceeds the fair market value of the stock or securities received. Since §355, if applicable, will deny recognition to this loss, the taxpayer may search for a way of avoiding §355, and the government, in its turn, may be in the unusual position of asserting with vigor that the manifold conditions of §355 were clearly satisfied. In this connection, it should be noted that such a shareholder who is bought out with *assets* rather than with stock will enjoy a deductible loss under §302(b)(3), at least if §267(a)(1) is inapplicable.[87]

Reliance on §355 to effect non-pro rata redemptions can create some tax distinctions between transactions having no significant business differences.

> *To illustrate:* Assume that *A* and *B* are equal owners of a department store and a radio station (for purposes of this example, both equal in value), and that because of disagreements about business policy they wish to go their separate ways, with *A* becoming the sole owner of the department store and *B* the sole owner of the radio station.
>
> In Case 1, assume further that both businesses are owned by *X* Corporation, the stock of which is owned 50-50 by *A* and *B*. In this situation, the parties can achieve their objective through a classic split-off under §355 by causing *X* first to transfer the radio station to newly created *Y* corporation in exchange for all of *Y*'s stock, and then to transfer the *Y* stock to *B* in exchange for *B*'s *X* stock. After these steps are taken, *A* will be the sole owner of *X*, which will own the department store, and *B* will be the sole owner of *Y*, which will own the radio station.
>
> This familiar route to a tax-free separation is not feasible, however, if the circumstances are altered by assuming that there are two separately incorporated businesses, *L* owning the department store and *M* the

[86] The judiciary's continuity-of-interest doctrine must bow to the amended definition of "reorganization" in §368(a)(1)(D), at least to a degree. See Regs. §1.368-1(b), third sentence.

[87] For treatment of the distributing corporation, see supra ¶¶ 7.21 and 9.34, and infra ¶ 13.12.

radio station, and that *A* and *B* are equal shareholders of both *L* and *M*. If *A* transfers his one-half interest in *M* to *B* in exchange for *B*'s one-half interest in *L, A* and *B* will become the sole owners of the department store and the radio station respectively, as intended. But *A* will realize and recognize gain on the exchange if the value of the *L* stock received by him exceeds the adjusted basis for the *M* stock transferred by him; the same will be true, mutatis mutandis, of B's exchange.

In Case 2, assume that *A* and *B* seek to avoid these shareholder-level taxable gains and to achieve a tax-free division by transferring their *L* and *M* stock to a newly created holding company, *HC*, and by then causing *HC* to split up through a transfer of all its *L* stock to *A* and all its *M* stock to *B*, in exchange for the *HC* stock of each. Not surprisingly, this transitory use of *HC* is disregarded by the regulations, which state that §355 does not apply "if the substance of the transaction is merely an exchange between shareholders . . . of stock . . . in one corporation for stock . . . in another corporation."[88] As such, it will be taxed as a shareholder-level exchange, the very result that *A* and *B* wish to avoid.

In Case 3, another attempt to avoid a shareholder-level taxable exchange, *A* and *B* do not create a holding company as in Case 2, but instead transfer their *M* stock to *L* as contributions to the latter's capital and then cause *L* to transfer the *M* stock to *B* in exchange for his *L* stock. This achieves their business objective, since *A* will own all the stock of *L*, and *B* will own all the stock of *M*, which in turn own the department store and radio station respectively. The case law on transactions of this type, however, indicates (although not unanimously) that Case 3 will be treated as "a straightforward, taxable stock swap," despite the effort to launder the *M* stock by passing it through *L* on its prearranged journey to *B*.[89] It should be noted, however, that both Cases 2 and 3 would qualify under §355 if the pre-distribution transactions (the transfer to the holding company in Case 2 and the contributions to capital in Case 3) were sufficiently old and cold before the divisions were effected.

---

[88] Regs. §1.355-3(a); see also Prop. Regs. §1.355-4; Portland Mfg. Co., 56 TC 58 (1971) (acq.), aff'd 35 AFTR 2d 1439 (9th Cir. 1975).

[89] See Kuper v. CIR, 533 F2d 152, (5th Cir. 1976), and cases there cited; Rev. Rul. 71-336, 1971-2 CB 299. But see Albert W. Badanes, supra note 48 (contra). See also Harry B. Atlee, 67 TC 395 (1976) (acq.) (transfer of individually owned property to corporation as contribution to capital, followed by transfer of property to newly created subsidiary to set stage for purported spin-off; not qualified under §355). Compare Rev. Rul. 77-11, 1977-1 CB 93 (§355 can be used in Case 2 and 3 patterns to divide corporate assets, *vertically*, as long as transaction does not have effect of indirect shareholder-level exchange).

¶ 13.10 JUDICIAL LIMITATIONS ON TAX-FREE CORPORATE DIVISIONS

Before 1954, spin-offs, split-offs, and split-ups could be effected tax-free only by complying with the reorganization provisions of the Code, under which for many years a literal compliance with the statutory language has been insufficient if the transaction did not satisfy the spirit of the law.[90] Although it is no longer necessary to have a tax-free reorganization as a prelude to a corporate division, the regulations under §355 require spin-offs, split-offs, and split-ups to satisfy the traditional judicial restrictions on the tax-free reorganization:

The distribution by a corporation of stock or securities of a controlled corporation to its shareholders with respect to its own stock or to its security holders in exchange for its own securities will not qualify under section 355 where carried out for purposes not germane to the business of the corporations. The principal reason for this requirement is to limit the application of section 355 to certain specified distributions or exchanges with respect to the stock or securities of controlled corporations incident to such readjustment of corporate structures as is required by business exigencies and which, in general, effect only a readjustment of continuing interests in property under modified corporate forms. Section 355 contemplates a continuity of the entire business enterprise under modified corporate forms and a continuity of interest in all or part of such business enterprise on the part of those persons who, directly or indirectly, were the owners of the enterprise prior to the distribution or exchange. All the requisites of business and corporate purposes described under Treas. Regs. §1.368 must be met to exempt a transaction from the recognition of gain or loss under this section.[91]

The historic relationship between corporate divisions and the reorganization provisions of the Code justifies the assumption that the judical doctrines worked out for corporate reorganizations will be applied with little modification to distributions under §355, even though effected without a technical reorganization.

1. Business purpose. Without attempting an exhaustive list of the business purposes that might support a tax-free distribution under §355, the following possibilities come to mind:

---

[90] For the pre-1954 status of divisive transactions, see supra ¶ 13.01; for the business purpose doctrine and other judicial limits on tax-free reorganizations, see infra ¶ 14.51.

[91] Regs. §1.355-2(c).

(1) Compliance with laws requiring two businesses to be separated; [92]

(2) Compliance with federal antitrust laws; [93]

(3) Separation of a business to permit its employees to share in profits of ownership; [94]

(4) Settlement of a shareholder dispute, by giving each group of shareholders control of ownership of one business; [95] and

(5) Expansion of access to credit or to equity funds. [96]

A major problem under Regs. §1.355-2(c), quoted earlier, that can arise in some of the above situations is whether a business purpose for the *distribution* must be established or whether it is sufficient to show a business purpose for carrying on the businesses in separate corporations. Thus, if an employee profit-sharing or stock-option plan is to be established for employees in a particular branch of the corporation's activities, it may be necessary to segregate that business in a separate corporation, but the plan would not necessarily require the stock of that corporation to be distributed to the orig-

---

[92] Rev. Rul. 83-23, 1983-1 CB 82 (spin-off to satisfy foreign decree requiring 60 percent direct ownership of local business by nationals); Rev. Rul. 75-321, 1975-2 CB 123 (distribution of bank by one-bank holding company to comply with banking law requirements).

[93] See Prop. Regs. §1.355-2(b)(2), Example (1).

[94] Rev. Rul. 85-127, 1985-2 CB 119 (giving key employee increased interest in split-off division); Rev. Rul. 75-337, 1975-2 CB 124 (split-off of stock of subsidiary to inactive shareholders of franchised auto dealership parent corporation to ensure that, after death of 70-year-old majority shareholder, only active shareholders would remain in the dealership as required by auto manufacturer for franchise renewal); see also Rev. Rul. 69-460, 1969-2 CB 51.

[95] See Prop. Regs. §1.355-2(b)(2), Example (2).

[96] Rev. Rul. 77-22, 1977-1 CB 91 (commercial credit); Rev. Rul. 83-114, 1983-2 CB 66 (attracting investment capital to distributed subsidiary that was required to be divested by antitrust decree); Rev. Rul. 82-130, 1982-2 CB 83 (spin-off of real estate subsidiary by parent in high-technology business to facilitate parent's public offering of stock); Rev.Rul. 85-122, 1985-2 CB 118 (spin-off to facilitate financing by parent); see also Rev. Rul. 76-527, 1976-2 CB 103 (spin-off to make subsidiary's stock more acceptable in a proposed merger).

For business purposes recognized in other cases and rulings, see Rev. Rul. 76-187, 1976-1 CB 97 (avoidance of state and local taxes being paid by parent); Rev. Rul. 78-383, 1978-2 CB 142 (to remove assets from foreign country to escape threat of confiscation); Sidney L. Olson, 49 TC 84 (1967) (to contain spread of union-organizing activities); Rev. Rul. 82-131, 1982-2 CB 83 (spin-off of unregulated subsidiary by regulated parent to justify parent's rate increase for its regulated business held a valid purpose); Spinoffs Can Be Used to Avoid a Hostile Takeover, 61 J. Tax'n 186 (1984) (to increase value of parent stock as defensive tactic to prevent hostile takeover attempt).

inal corporation's shareholders.[97] Similarly, a corporation carrying on both a risky or speculative business and a stable one could ordinarily protect the assets of the latter business by placing the risky business in a subsidiary corporation; if so, it could be argued that no business purpose is served by a distribution of the stock of the subsidiary.[98]

The 1977 proposed regulations, which are supported by the case law, require a showing that the *distribution*, not merely separate incorporation of the two businesses, serves a business purpose.[99] This requirement is likely to be most troublesome in spin-offs and other pro rata transactions. If the distribution is non-pro rata, its realignment of the shareholders' interests will ordinarily be of sufficient economic significance to pass muster unless the proportionate change is trivial or the reshuffling is between members of a family.

2. Shareholder-level vs. corporate-level purposes. An important issue in applying the business purpose doctrine, which is closely related to (and may overlap) the previously discussed problem of establishing a business purpose for the distribution, is whether a so-called shareholder purpose for the distribution (e.g., estate planning) will suffice, even though that purpose does not affect the welfare of the businesses as such.

The 1977 proposed regulations state that §355 will apply to the transaction "only if carried out for real and substantial non-tax reasons germane to the business of the corporations," adding that "a shareholder purpose for the transaction may be so nearly coextensive with a corporate business purpose as to preclude any distinction between them," but further cautioning that "if a transaction is motivated solely by the personal

---

[97] See Rev. Rul. 69-460, 1969-2 CB 51 (resolution of shareholder dispute and enabling parent's employees to acquire proprietary stake in parent without acquiring interest in subsidiary were valid business purposes; but enabling subsidiary's employees to acquire interest in subsidiary was not a valid business reason for spin-off, since distribution was not necessary to achieve this result). But see Rev. Rul. 85-127, 1985-2 CB 119.

[98] See Prop. Regs. §1.355-2(b)(2), Example (3) (separation of high-risk business could be accomplished by separate incorporation, but did not require distribution). Compare id., Example (4) (total separation required by lender in accordance with customary business practice). See also Prop. Regs. §1.355-2(c)(4) (presence of business purpose is not equivalent to absence of "device" to distribute earnings and profits); Rev. Rul. 82-130, 1982-2 CB 83, and Rev. Rul. 82-131, 1982-2 CB 83.

[99] Prop. Regs. §1.355-2(b)(1); Bonsall v. CIR, supra note 33 (dictum, echoing Estate of Parshelsky v. CIR, supra note 6, which invalidated a spin-off under pre-1954 law because there was no business purpose for the distribution); Gada v. US, 460 F. Supp. 859 (D. Conn. 1978); Wilson v. CIR, supra note 48 (same; also, absence of device not equivalent to a business purpose); see also Rev. Rul. 69-460, 1969-2 CB 51; Rafferty v. CIR, supra note 33, which takes a middle road on this point.

reasons of the shareholder" (e.g., personal planning), the distribution will not qualify.[100] This insistence on a corporate-level business purpose is consistent with the Service's long-held views and also finds some support in the case law.[101]

3. Continuity of interest. As to the requirement in the excerpt from the regulations quoted previously of a continuity of interest on the part of those persons who directly or indirectly owned the enterprise prior to the division, this provision stems from a line of cases holding that the tax-free reorganization provisions may not be used to confer tax exemption on a transaction that is, in essence, a sale.[102] Since it is "the owners of the enterprise" who must maintain a continuing interest, the requirement is more applicable to shareholders than to bondholders and other creditors.[103] Moreover, §355(a)(2)(A) expressly validates a distribution that is non-pro rata; thus, the continuity-of-interest requirement is not violated by a transaction that leaves ownership of the distributing corporation in the hands of one shareholder and ownership of the controlled corporation in the hands of another shareholder.

It may also be permissible for some of the shareholders to give up their proprietary interests entirely by exchanging stock for securities or other property, subject to the recognition of boot; the reorganization cases tolerate such a loss of interest to some extent so long as a substantial number of old shareholders retain a proprietary interest.[104] If the shareholders sell or exchange their securities immediately after the distribution, however, the Service may attack the transaction not only as violating the judicial doctrine

---

[100] Prop. Regs. §1.355-2(b)(1).

[101] Supra note 99. But see Rev. Rul. 75-337, 1975-2 CB 124.

[102] See Pinellas Ice & Cold Storage Co. v. CIR, 287 US 462 (1933); Le Tulle v. Scofield, 308 US 415 (1940), reh'g denied, 309 US 694 (1940); infra ¶ 14.11; see also Rena Farr, 24 TC 350 (1955), applying the continuity-of-interest requirement to a pre-1954 split-off and holding that it was satisfied despite a subsequent sale of stock by the distributee; Note, Developing an Independent Role for Business Purpose and Continuity of Interest in Section 355 Transactions, 44 U. Cin. L. Rev. 286 (1975).

[103] The regulations explicitly permit securities of a parent corporation to be exchanged for stock of a controlled corporation. But for potential taxability of the distributing corporation, see supra note 10 and infra ¶ 13.12.

[104] See infra ¶ 14.11; Rev. Rul. 69-293, 1969-1 CB 102 (conversion of distributing corporation to a nonproprietary tax-exempt organization following spin-off broke continuity of interest and rendered distribution taxable); Rev. Rul. 76-528, 1976-2 CB 103 (continuity existed where 60 percent shareholder of distributing corporation was partnership that dissolved and distributed the stock pro rata to its partners, after which there was a non-pro rata split-up of the distributing corporation).

of continuity of interest but also as a device for the distribution of earnings and profits under §355(a)(1)(B).[105]

¶ 13.11 "BOOT" UNDER §355

When its conditions are satisfied, §355(a)(1) provides that no gain, income, or loss shall be recognized on the receipt of stock or securities of a controlled corporation. If anything else is distributed, however, it will constitute boot, the tax treatment of which is prescribed by §356.[106] All of the following categories of property constitute boot:

(1) Money or other property (including stock or securities of a corporation that does not qualify under §355 as a controlled corporation);

(2) Securities of the controlled corporation, to the extent that their principal amount exceeds the principal amount of the securities that are surrendered in the distribution, and the full fair market value of such securities if no securities are surrendered;[107]

---

[105] See supra ¶ 13.07.

[106] See §355(a)(4)(A).

[107] As a result of amendments in 1980, §355(a)(3)(C) provides that the distribution will be taxable to the extent attributable to interest accrued on the parent's securities during the creditor's holding period.

The drafting of §355(a)(3)(A) is somewhat misleading. Section 355(a)(3)(A) states flatly that §355(a)(1)—which permits a tax-free distribution of stock or securities—"shall not apply" if the principal amount of securities received exceeds the principal amount of securities surrendered or if securities are received and none are surrendered. But §355(a)(4)(A) refers to the boot provision (§356) for the treatment of an excess principal amount, thus implying that §355 applies, but that the fair market value of the excess principal amount will constitute boot. This implication is confirmed by §356(d)(2)(C). There is, however, no reference in §355(a)(4)(A) to the case where securities are received and none are surrendered. This omission, presumably inadvertent, is remedied by the regulations, under which the application of §355 is not defeated by such a distribution, but the fair market value of the securities received is treated as boot. See Regs. §1.356-3(a), last sentence, illustrated by §1.356-3(b), Example (1); see also §356(d)(2)(B); S. Rep. No. 1622, 83 Cong., 2d Sess. 266 (1954).

Section 355(a)(3)(A) is inadequately drafted in another respect, since it seems to compare the aggregate principal amounts of securities received with the aggregate amount surrendered. It is quite clear that this comparison should be made separately for each distributee.

For examples of the treatment of securities constituting boot, see Regs. §1.356-3(b).

(3) Short-term notes and other obligations of the controlled corporation that do not constitute securities; [108]

(4) Stock rights or stock warrants, according to the regulations (§1.355-1(a)); and [109]

(5) Stock of a controlled corporation if it was acquired within five years of the distribution by reason of any transaction in which gain or loss was recognized in whole or in part (§355(a)(3)(B), second sentence). Thus, if the distributing corporation owned 85 percent of the stock of the controlled corporation throughout the five-year period but purchased the remaining 15 percent (directly or through a subsidiary) within the period, the latter portion would constitute "other property" on distribution. [110] The purpose of this restriction is to prevent the distributing corporation from investing its excess funds in additional stock of the controlled corporation as a prelude to a tax-free distribution. [111]

If boot is received in a §355 *exchange* (split-offs and split-ups), its tax results are prescribed by §356(a), while if boot is received in a §355 *distribution* (spin-offs), §356(b) is the operative provision.

For split-offs and split-ups, §356(a)(1) follows the usual principle of recognizing any gain that the recipient may have on the exchange but in an amount not in excess of the value of the boot. (If the taxpayer has no gain

---

Legislation proposed by the staff of the Senate Finance Committee to reform the provisions of Subchapter C would treat securities as boot per se (for purposes of gain).

[108] See the analogous problem under §351(a), discussed supra ¶ 3.03.

[109] But see Oscar E. Baan, supra note 9, and note the possibility that rights or warrants could be received tax-free under §305 (supra ¶ 7.44), even though distributed in conjunction with a §355 transaction. See also infra ¶ 14.31.

[110] For an example, see Regs. §1.355-2(f)(2) and Prop. Regs. §1.355-2(f)(2). But see Trust of E.L. Dunn, 86 TC 745 (1986) (tainted stock dropped into spun-off holding company did not infect holding company stock); Hoffman, The AT&T Divestiture: Tax Planning for Tax-Free Spin-Offs Which Involve Ineligible Businesses, 64 Taxes 619 (1986).

[111] Much the same effect, however, could be obtained by transferring the liquid funds to the subsidiary, either as a contribution to its capital or under §351; but such a transaction might be evidence that the later distribution was a device for distributing earnings and profits. For this issue, see Rev. Rul. 83-114, 1983-2 CB 66 (cancelation of subsidiary's debt to parent as contribution to capital not, in itself, a fatal device), and rulings there cited; see also Rev. Rul. 86-4, 1986-1 CB 174 (contribution is evidence of device, however).

But see Rev. Rul. 78-442, 1978-2 CB 143 (§357(c) gain on preliminary incorporation did not taint subsidiary's stock under §355(a)(3)); Trust of E.L. Dunn, supra note 110 (insulation of boot taint by preliminary drop-down of tainted stock to spun-off holding company).

because the aggregate value of the stock, securities, and boot received is less than the adjusted basis of the stock and securities surrendered, §356(a) is inoperative; but §356(c) prohibits the recognition of this loss). Having determined the portion of the gain that is to be recognized under §356(a)(1), the taxpayer turns to §356(a)(2) to ascertain whether it is to be treated as ordinary income or as capital gain. Section 356(a)(2) provides that if the exchange "has the effect of the distribution of a dividend," it must be so treated to the extent of the taxpayer's ratable share of post-1913 earnings and profits.[112] The balance, if any, of the recognized gain is capital gain.[113] There is some old authority for the proposition that §356(a)(2) automatically converted any recognized gain into a dividend to the extent of earnings and profits; but a more discriminating approach to the question has more recently been adopted. For example, if a minority shareholder receives bonds in exchange for all of his stock in a corporate division and realizes a profit on the transaction (i.e., the excess of the principal amount of the securities received over the adjusted basis of the stock surrendered), the exchange (which would give rise to capital gain if effected as a §302(b)(3) redemption) should not be automatically treated as a dividend under §356(a)(2).[114]

If boot is received in exchange for "section 306 stock," a special rule is applicable by virtue of §356(e): Regardless of whether the shareholder realizes gain or loss on the exchange, the fair market value of the boot is treated as a distribution of property under §301, which means that it will be taxed as a dividend to the extent of his ratable share of the parent corporation's current and post-1913 earnings and profits.[115]

¶ 13.12 ANCILLARY MATTERS: BASIS, HOLDING PERIOD, EARNINGS AND PROFITS, ETC.

1. Distributees' basis. The basis of property received by the shareholder or security holder in a §355 transaction is prescribed by §358. If no boot is distributed, the aggregate basis of the original stock and securities will be spread over both the distributed and the retained stock and securities in

---

[112] Section 356(a)(2) makes no reference to current earnings and profits; neither do the regulations.

[113] For an example, see Regs. §1.356-1(c).

[114] For application of the dividend-equivalence test rather than the earlier automatic-dividend rule doctrine to §355 transactions, see Rev. Rul. 74-516, 1974-2 CB 121. See generally, see infra ¶ 14.34. Compare the device test of Prop. Regs. §1.355-2(c)(11), supra note 75.

[115] See also Regs. §1.356-4.

proportion to their respective market values. If boot is distributed, the basis of the qualified (or nonrecognition) property must be adjusted to reflect the amount of money and the value of any other boot received, as well as any gain or income recognized; and the boot (other than money) takes a basis equal to its fair market value.[116]

Application of the distributee basis rules of §358 creates several difficult problems of interpretation. For example, when is the market value of the distributed property to be determined? The possibilities include the date of distribution by the transferor corporation, the date of actual or constructive receipt by the distributees, the effective date of the distribution plan, and the "ex-dividend" (i.e., record) date; but there is no clear statement by the Service or the courts as to which of these dates is controlling.[117] Comparable timing problems may exist in the case of dividends in kind, which bear a close functional relation to spin-off distributions.[118] If the stock on which the distribution is made was acquired at different times and for different prices, the rules developed for stock dividends should probably be followed in the case of spin-offs,[119] those developed in the redemption and partial liquidation areas apparently should be applied to split-offs,[120] and those developed in the liquidation area seemingly should be applied to split-ups.[121]

2. Holding period. By virtue of §1223(1), the taxpayer's holding period for any qualified (or nonrecognition) stock or securities received under §355 ordinarily includes the period he held the stock or securities surrendered (if the transaction was a split-off or a split-up) or retained (if it was a spin-

---

[116] See §358(b)(2) (split-offs and split-ups); §358(c) (spin-offs); Regs. §1.358-2. For the possibility of market discount being created via the substituted basis rules of §358 (e.g., where bonds of the parent are exchanged for bonds of the subsidiary), see §1278(a)(2)(A). But see §1278(a)(1)(C), added in 1986 (no market discount on bond acquired in original issue unless exchanged for old market discount bond in a §368 reorganization).

[117] For example, Regs. §1.358-1(a) values boot as of the "date of the transaction;" Rev. Rul. 56-557, 1956-2 CB 199 refers to the effective date of the distribution; Rev. Rul. 56-555, 1956-2 CB 210, speaks of the "time of distribution." See also Regs. §1.368-3(b)(2) (value as of date of the exchange).

The record date has the virtue of avoiding complicated recalculations of gain or loss if the stock is sold "ex-dividend" before actual receipt of the distributed property, but this approach has not been followed by the Service in its published rulings. Cf. Silco, Inc. v. US, 779 F2d 282 (5th Cir. 1986).

[118] See supra ¶ 7.04. See also the treatment of nontaxable stock dividend distributions, supra ¶ 7.43.

[119] Supra ¶ 7.43, note 244.

[120] Supra ¶¶ 9.02 and 9.08.

[121] Supra ¶ 11.03; see also infra ¶ 14.34, para. 3.

off).[122] The holding period of boot commences with the distribution, however, since its basis under §358(a)(2) is its fair market value, not an amount determined by reference to the basis of the original stock and securities.

3. Asset basis. If the distributing corporation transfers assets as a preliminary step to the corporate division, the transaction is a reorganization under §368(a)(1)(D), and the transferee corporation carries over the distributing corporation's basis and holding periods under §§362(b) and 1223(2).

4. Earnings and profits. Section 312(h) provides for proper allocation of the earnings and profits of the distributing and controlled corporations under regulations to be prescribed by the Treasury. In brief, the regulations provide that where the §355 transaction is a Type D reorganization,[123] earnings of the distributing corporation are allocated to the newly created controlled corporation in proportion to the relative values of the assets transferred and retained. The regulations also state, however, that "in a proper case," the allocation should be made in proportion to the net bases (after reduction for liabilities) of the properties transferred and retained, and that other allocation methods may be appropriate in certain cases, although no guidance is given as to when these other methods may be employed. Perhaps a useful analogy and general approach may be found in §482 (and, to some extent, in §446(b)),[124] permitting the Service to adjust a taxpayer's accounting practices and methods in order to "clearly reflect income." Where the §355 transaction does not involve a reorganization transfer (e.g., where a preexisting subsidiary is spun off), the regulations provide that the distributing corporation's earnings are decreased by the lesser of (1) the amount of the adjustment that would have been required had it transferred the stock of the controlled corporation to a new subsidiary and then distributed the latter pursuant to a Type D reorganization or (2) the net worth of the controlled corporation. Note that the controlled corporation apparently retains its *own* earnings account in such a case. In no event, say the regulations, will a deficit of the distributing corporation be allocated to the controlled corporation.[125]

---

[122] But see supra ¶ 3.10.

[123] Infra ¶ 14.16. A divisive Type D reorganization is not a §381 transaction, however, so the rules of §381(c)(2) do not apply here; infra ¶¶ 16.11 and 16.13. See text infra note 133.

[124] Infra ¶ 15.03.

[125] See Regs. §1.312-10; Bennett v. US, 427 F2d 1202 (Ct. Cl. 1970); infra ch. 16; Alexander, Some Earnings and Profits Aspects of the Internal Revenue Code of 1954, 7 Hastings L.J. 285, 302 (1956); Nesson, Earnings and Profits Discontinuities Under the 1954 Code, 77 Harv. L. Rev. 450, 474 (1964).

5. Effect of §355 distributions on the distributing corporation. The nonrecognition principle embodied in §355 applies only to the recipient of a qualifying distribution; but an important by-product of §355 is its effect on the distributing corporation, whose adjusted basis for the distributed stock or securities is almost always less or greater than their fair market value. Under §311(a), as amended in 1986, a distributing corporation does not recognize gain or loss on a nonliquidating distribution of property with respect to its stock.[126] This rule is qualified by §311(b)(1) as respects gain for distributions to which subpart A (i.e., §§301–307) applies; but since §355 is not within the scope of this exception, the general nonrecognition rule of §311(a) applies to nonliquidating distributions under §355 (i.e., to spin-offs and split-offs).

In the case of split-ups, however, the distributing corporation liquidates; this means that the controlling provision, so far as the distributing corporation is concerned, is §336 rather than §311.[127] The impact of §336, as amended in 1986, on the distributing corporation is far from clear.[128] Section 336 begins inauspiciously for split-ups by providing that, as a general rule, gain or loss must be recognized on a liquidating distribution as though the distributed property were sold to the distributee at its fair market value. This ominous rule, however, is qualified by §336(c), which exempts distributions from the recognition principle set out in the general rule of §336(a) "to the extent that there is nonrecognition of gain or loss with respect to such property to the recipient under part III [i.e., §§351–368]."[129]

In applying this exemption to split-ups, it is necessary to distinguish

---

As to an existing subsidiary's own earnings account, Regs. §1.312-10(b), last paragraph, states that the subsidiary's account is the greater of the parent's earnings adjustment for the distribution of the stock or the amount of its own earnings and profits account.

[126] For §311, see generally supra ¶¶ 7.21 and 9.34. See also supra note 10.

[127] But see §346(b), under which a split-up can be subjected to special rules under regulations to prevent circumventing the tax treatment of partial liquidations. See supra ¶ 7.22, infra ¶ 13.15.

[128] For §336, see generally supra ¶ 11.06.

For a clean-up of §§336(c) and 361 by the pending Technical Corrections Act of 1987, see §118(d)(4) of H.R. 2636; for background, see Eustice, A Case Study in Technical Tax Reform: Section 361, 35 Tax Notes 283 (1987).

[129] Section 336(c) is apparently the victim of a drafting error: It provides that "this section" shall not apply in specified circumstances; but this creates a vicious circle, since §336(c) seems to negate itself, because it is part of "this section" (a circularity that resembles a famous paradox: If a person says "I never tell the truth," is his statement believable?). Section 336(c) should obviously be applied as if it read: "Section 336, other than this subsection (c), shall not apply." The Conference Committee Report's reference to this provision (H.R. Conf. Rep. No. 99-841, 99th Cong., 2d Sess. II-199-200) is poorly drafted; it refers to "the tax-free reorganization provisions of the Code (part III of subchapter C)," although part III includes a number of provisions (e.g., §§351 and 355) that do not necessarily involve tax-free reorganizations.

between (1) a split-up that not only qualifies under §355 but also constitutes a tax-free reorganization (e.g., a Type D reorganization in which the distributing corporation transfers two or more operating divisions to two or more newly created subsidiaries, and then distributes the stock of the subsidiaries to its shareholders in complete liquidation)[130] and (2) a split-up that qualifies under §355 without being a tax-free reorganization (e.g., the liquidation of a holding company whose only assets are the stock and securities of two or more old and cold subsidiaries.)

For split-ups that are both §355 distributions and tax-free reorganizations (like the Type D transaction just suggested), §361(b)(1) ousts §336 from jurisdiction, and §361(b)(3) provides for the nonrecognition of gain or loss on the distributing corporation's distribution of stock and securities to its shareholders in pursuance of the plan of reorganization.

If the §355 split-up is not a Type D reorganization, however, its effect on the liquidating corporation is more problematical. The recognition-of-gain rule of §336(a) is rendered inapplicable by §336(c) (since §355 is included in part III, to which §336(c) refers); but §361 is also inapplicable, since it applies only to distributions pursuant to a plan of reorganizations.[131] Nonreorganization split-ups, therefore, fall between these two statutory stools, but where exactly do they land? There appears to be two safety nets, neither wholly reliable. The first of these is §311; although normally inapplicable to liquidating distributions because they are caught by §336, §311 on its face can apply to all distributions, including split-ups that are not subject to either §336 or §361. Second, there is our old friend, the *General Utilities* doctrine; although bruised and battered by the Tax Reform Act of 1986, it may remain valid where not explicitly overruled. If a split-up lands in either of these safety nets, the distributing corporation does not recognize gain or loss; this is a reasonable result, since spin-offs, split-ups, and reorganization-linked split-ups qualify for nonrecognition, and there seems to be no sensible reason to treat nonrecognition split-ups differently. A technical correction to clarify the nontaxability of the distributing corporation is, as of this writing, in the legislative process.

It should be noted also that gain can be triggered to the distributing corporation under §361(c), even though a reorganization distribution occurs, if the distribution results in taxable gain to the distributees (e.g., because

---

[130] For Type D reorganizations, see infra ¶ 14.16.

[131] Section 361(c) contains a parenthetical qualification exempting §355 and certain other distributions from its sweeping rule requiring gain to be recognized on distributions pursuant to a plan of reorganization; but since the general rule of §361(c) does not apply to §355 distributions that are not linked to a tax-free reorganization, its parenthetical exception is also inapplicable.

The Technical Corrections Act of 1987, supra note 128, rectifies this problem by adding new §355(c) (which makes §311(a) applicable to the parent's distribution of its subsidiaries' stock or securities).

securities of the subsidiary are distributed to the parent's shareholders, or securities of the subsidiary are distributed to security holders of the parent in an excess principal amount). It seems unlikely (one would hope) that Congress intended this result.[132]

6. Carry-over of distributing corporation's tax history. The carry-over rules of §381 (see Chapter 16) do not apply to divisive Type D reorganizations, with the result that the tax attributes of the distributing corporation (except for earnings and profits) will stay behind in that corporation at the conclusion of the transaction. If the division is a split-up, however, the tax history of the liquidated corporation disappears.[133]

If the division is by a non-pro rata split-off, §382 similarly could apply to limit either the distributing corporation's or the distributed corporation's loss carry-overs, since an ownership change occurs as a result of this transaction within the meaning of §382(g)(1) (i.e., the split-off is treated either as an ownership shift involving a 5 percent shareholder or as an equity structure shift). However, the resulting contraction in the distributing corporation's business is no longer a factor under the 1986 version of §382.[134]

¶ 13.13   CORPORATE DIVISIONS AND §306

The pre-1954 spin-off provision (§112(b)(11) of the 1939 Code) did not permit the distribution of preferred stock of the controlled corporation.[135] The reason for this restriction was a fear that a tax-free distribution of preferred stock, if permitted, could be used to bail out earnings and profits, since the shareholders could sell the preferred stock (perhaps under an arrangement for its prompt redemption) while retaining the common stock in both corporations. With the enactment of §306 of the 1954 Code as a safeguard against the preferred stock bailout in all of its aspects, it is not surprising that §112(b)(11)'s prohibition on distributions of preferred stock was not carried forward into §355 of the 1954 Code. Preferred stock can, therefore, be distributed with impunity under §355, provided its other conditions are met; but the preferred stock must run the gauntlet of §306.

Section 306(c)(1)(B) provides that stock received by a shareholder

---

[132] For further consideration of §361, see Eustice, supra note 128; and infra ¶ 14.32. But see proposed §355(c), supra note 131; see also the proposed revision of §361(c), supra note 131 (reorganization distributions of party stock or securities—including warrants—not taxable).

[133] Rev. Rul. 56-373, 1956-2 CB 217 (net operating loss carry-overs disappear in split-up), amplified by Rev. Rul. 77-133, 1977-1 CB 96 (regarding split-off).

[134] For §382, as extensively amended in 1986, see infra ¶¶ 16.23–16.25.

[135] Supra ¶ 13.02.

under §355 is "section 306 stock" in his hands if:

(1) It is not "common" stock;

(2) With respect to its receipt, the shareholder's gain or loss went unrecognized to any extent by reason of §355 or §356; and

(3) The effect of the transaction was substantially the same as the receipt of a stock dividend.[136]

Notwithstanding the foregoing, the stock cannot be "section 306 stock" if the corporation had no earnings and profits during the year it was distributed.[137]

If preferred stock is received in a spin-off or in a pro rata split-off or split-up, it would ordinarily seem entirely reasonable to find that "the effect of the transaction was substantially the same as the receipt of a stock dividend." To take a simple example, if a corporation transfers a five-year-old business to a second corporation in exchange for its common and preferred stock and spins off all the stock of the second corporation, the effect of the transaction is the same as a transfer of the business for the common stock of the second corporation, followed by a spin-off of the common stock and declaration by the second corporation of a dividend of preferred stock. Even if the transaction is not pro rata, it may be similar to a stock dividend. For example, if two shareholders of a corporation are deadlocked and they compose their differences by a split-off under which one shareholder retains all the stock of the distributing corporation and the second receives all the common and preferred stock of a newly created controlled corporation, the transaction has the same effect for the second shareholder as a split-off of the common stock of the controlled corporation followed by a preferred stock dividend.

On the other hand, some non-pro rata divisions do not have the effect of a stock dividend. An example would be a corporation with three unrelated shareholders[138] who arrange a split-up in which each of the first two shareholders receives all the common stock of a new controlled corporation while the third shareholder receives preferred stock of either or both controlled corporations. The conclusion that preferred stock in these circum-

---

[136] For the meaning of "common stock" as the term is used in §306, see supra ¶ 10.03. Even if the transaction did not have the effect of a stock dividend, the stock received will constitute "section 306 stock" if it was received in exchange for "section 306 stock."

For convenience, the term "preferred stock" is used in the text instead of the more accurate but cumbersome term "stock that is not common stock."

[137] Section 306(c)(2); supra ¶ 10.03.

[138] In determining whether a transaction has substantially the same effect as a stock dividend, it is necessary to consider the relationship of the distributees to each other. See §306(c)(4), applying the attribution rules of §318.

stances would not be "section 306 stock" is buttressed by §306(c)(2), which makes §306 inapplicable if a distribution of cash in lieu of the stock would not have been taxed as a dividend.[139]

Although the cash substitution test of §306(c)(2) is a method of determining when preferred stock is *not* "section 306 stock," the regulations have derived from it the inference that preferred stock *is* "section 306 stock" if a distribution of cash in lieu of the stock would have been a dividend. Although not compelled by the statutory language, this inference is not unreasonable in the light of §306's purpose: If a direct distribution of cash would have been taxed as a dividend, it is appropriate to taint the stock and compel shareholders to recognize ordinary income when they dispose of it.[140]

Whatever is ultimately decided about peripheral cases, however, it is a fair working hypothesis that preferred stock received in a spin-off or in a pro rata split-off or split-up will ordinarily be "section 306 stock" if gain goes unrecognized by virtue of §355 and if the corporation has earnings and profits. A sale or other disposition of stock, therefore, will be subject to the punitive rules of §306(a). It will be recalled, however, that these rules are subject to certain exceptions, one of which is §306(b)(1)(A), providing that a sale or other disposition that "terminates the entire stock interest of the shareholder in the corporation" is not subject to §306(a). If the preferred stock was issued by the controlled corporation, however, it is not clear whether the corporation under §306(b)(1)(A) is the distributing corporation, the controlled corporation, or both.[141] If a prearranged sale of the common stock of either corporation is a device for the distribution of earnings and profits, as is commonly suggested,[142] a sale of both the preferred and the common stock of one of the corporations should be entitled to no better treatment. This line of argument suggests that §306(b)(1)(A) should be available only if the shareholder sells his entire stock interest in both the distributing and the controlled corporation.

A similar problem arises under §306(b)(4), which is concerned with a disposition of "section 306 stock" that follows or occurs simultaneously with

---

[139] Section 306(c)(2) may have been intended to grant absolution only in cases where the corporation has no earnings and profits, as is suggested by its catchline, but its language is much broader.

[140] See Regs. §1.306-3(d). For discussion of the cash substitution test, see infra ¶ 14.35. See generally Rev. Rul. 77-335, 1977-2 CB 95 (parent's spin-off of subsidiary's common and preferred stock under §355; held, preferred was "section 306 stock" under cash substitution test).

[141] Rev. Rul. 77-335, 1977-2 CB 95, holds that testing for §306 stock status is made by reference to the distributing corporation (i.e., the parent) as if *its* stock had been distributed rather than that of the subsidiary.

[142] See supra ¶ 13.07.

a disposition of "the stock with respect to which the section 306 stock . . . was issued." It is not clear whether the underlying stock is the stock of the distributing corporation, the stock of the controlled corporation, or both.

One more point should be noted in this area: The device language of §355(a)(1)(B) may apply to a distribution of preferred stock, even though the conditions of §306 are not met. Thus, assume a plan for a corporate division under which shareholders receive preferred and common stock plus enough money or other property so that their gain would be fully recognized under §356(a)(1) or §356(b). There being no unrecognized gain, §306(c)(1)(B) will not intervene to taint the preferred stock. But if the purpose of the transaction is to enable the shareholders to sell their preferred stock under a *Chamberlin*-type plan calling for its early redemption, the distribution itself may be a device for the distribution of earnings and profits.[143] A similar theory might be employed by the government if preferred stock is received in a corporate division by shareholders who have suffered a loss, since here too the preferred stock would not be tainted. [144] Indeed, a prearranged sale or redemption may be a device that will take the transaction out of §355, even in cases where §306 would be an alternative weapon for the government.

¶ 13.14   THE MONOPOLY OF §355

In order to prevent the restrictions of §355 from being undermined, it was necessary to prevent divisive reorganizations from finding another route to tax-free status. The principal problem was that the term "reorganization" has long included a transfer by a corporation of all or part of its assets to a controlled corporation, and distributions in the course of a reorganization are normally receivable tax-free; indeed, it was only by virtue of these statutory provisions that corporate divisions were tax-free before 1954. The drafters of the 1954 Code, therefore, gave §355 a monopoly on divisive reorganizations by providing:

---

[143] This theory might not be acceptable in the Sixth Circuit, which decided in the taxpayer's favor in Chamberlin v. CIR, 207 F2d 462 (6th Cir. 1953), cert. denied, 347 US 918 (1954), supra ¶ 10.01, unless the redemption was to occur within a much shorter period of time; but other courts might not follow *Chamberlin*.

[144] See §306(c)(2). If the shareholder's basis for the stock surrendered in a split-off, for example, is $10,000, and the shareholder receives common stock of a controlled corporation plus preferred stock with an aggregate fair market value for both of $8,000, §306(c)(2) apparently ensures that the preferred will not be "section 306 stock," since, if cash was received in lieu of the preferred stock, the shareholder would have had no dividend income.

(1) In §368(a)(2)(A), that if a transfer of assets by one corporation to another could qualify as a reorganization under both §§368(a)(1)(C) and 368(a)(1)(D), it will be treated as qualifying only under subparagraph (D);

(2) In §368(a)(1)(D), that a transfer of assets by one corporation to another will constitute a reorganization only if stock or securities of the transferee corporation are distributed in a transaction qualifying under §354, §355, or §356; and

(3) In §354(b)(1), that §354(a) will apply to a Type D reorganization only if the transferee corporation acquired substantially all of the transferor corporation's assets and the transferor thereupon distributed all of its assets in pursuance of the plan of reorganization.

By virtue of the foregoing provisions, a divisive reorganization will not be able to qualify under §354, with the result that shareholders who wish to divide up their corporate investment in a tax-free transaction will have to resort to, and satisfy the requirements of, §355.[145]

¶ 13.15 NONQUALIFYING CORPORATE DIVISIONS

Section 355 is a nonrecognition provision: If its conditions are met, a taxpayer who receives stock or securities in a corporate division does not recognize gain or loss. Section 355 does not, however, lay down any rules for the taxation of distributions that do *not* meet its requirements. Consequently, for the treatment of nonqualifying corporate divisions, we must look to other statutory provisions, as well as to certain doctrines of judicial origin. It will be helpful to consider spin-offs, split-offs, and split-ups separately, since the form of a nonqualifying transaction may be important, even though §355 has endeavored to treat all qualifying transactions alike.

1. Nonqualifying spin-offs. If a spin-off fails to win tax immunity under §355, it seems clear that the distribution of stock or securities to a

---

[145] See infra ¶ 14.16. On remand of the *Gordon* case (supra note 9), it was held that the transaction (which failed to meet the standards of §355) was not entitled to tax-free treatment as a Type D or Type F reorganization and that stock rights do not constitute stock within the meaning of §354(a). See Gordon v. CIR, 424 F2d 378 (2d Cir. 1970), cert. denied, 400 US 849 (1970); see also Redding v. CIR, supra note 82. For an alternate device that has a divisive effect but that presumably avoids the strictures of §355, see Sheppard, GM's Class E Stock: Tax Planning in Second Gear, 36 Tax Notes 130 (1987); Walter & Strassen, General Motors Class E and Class H Common Stock, 64 Taxes 365 (1986).

shareholder of the original corporation will be treated as an ordinary distribution in kind under §301. This means that the distribution will be taxed as a dividend to the extent of the corporation's current and post-1913 accumulated earnings and profits and as a return of capital if it exceeds them.[146] If the spin-off is preceded by a transfer of part of the distributing corporation's assets to the controlled corporation, the distributing corporation will recognize neither gain nor loss by virtue of §351, and ordinarily none of its earnings and profits will be allocated to the controlled corporation.[147]

   2. Nonqualifying split-ups. The tax consequences of nonqualifying split-up are less clear. At least prima facie, the transaction is a complete liquidation of the distributing corporation, subject to §331(a)(1), so that the shareholders would recognize capital gain or loss, depending on whether the value of the liquidating distribution exceeds or is less than the adjusted basis of the stock given up. On this theory, any transfer of assets by the distributing corporation to a controlled corporation (e.g., if one or both of the controlled corporations were created as part of the plan) would apparently qualify under §351, so that no gain or loss would be recognized on the transfer.[148] In this respect, the transfer of assets would resemble a transfer in conjunction with a nonqualifying spin-off as discussed in the preceding paragraph, although the regulations may require an allocation of earnings and profits to the controlled corporations in certain instances.[149]

   But while the foregoing consequences seem reasonable enough if the division serves a business purpose and the transaction fails to qualify under §355 only because one of the businesses was conducted for less than five years, what if the division is simply a method of segregating liquid assets in one corporation and business assets in another, possibly preparatory to a liquidation or sale of the liquid-assets corporation? Should such a transac-

---

   [146] For further discussion of distributions of property, see supra ¶ 7.23; see also the *Baan* and *Gordon* cases (supra note 9); for taxability of the distributing corporation, see infra para. 4.

   [147] Ordinarily, gain or loss on a transfer preparatory to a spin-off goes unrecognized under §361(a). This provision would be inapplicable on the facts assumed in the text, however, since the transfer of assets would not constitute a reorganization under §368(a)(1)(D) (infra ¶ 14.16). But §351 would apply, as stated in the text, even though §361(a) would not; see §351(c), supra ¶ 3.09, infra note 148.
   On the allocation of earnings and profits, see Regs. §1.312-11(a).

   [148] Section 351's control requirement is not violated by the transferor corporation's distribution of the stock by virtue of §351(c), which seems as applicable to a distribution in complete liquidation as to any other kind of distribution. For taxability of the distributing corporation, see infra para. 4.

   [149] See Regs. §1.312-11(a), requiring allocation of earnings and profits in a nonqualifying split-up where the transferor corporation liquidates or effects a substantial §302 redemption of its stock.

tion be treated as a complete liquidation, giving rise to capital gain or loss, or as an ordinary distribution of the liquid assets, taxable as a dividend to the extent of earnings and profits? Under §368(a)(1)(F), the creation of the business-assets corporation might be regarded as a "mere change in identity, form, or place of organization, however effected," in which event the transfer of the business assets would be a reorganization under §368(a)(1)(F) of the 1954 Code,[150] and the stock of the liquid-assets corporation would then constitute boot, taxable as a dividend up to the amount of the shareholder's gain, if any.[151] Moreover, the earnings and profits and other tax attributes of the original corporation would be inherited by the business-assets corporation under §381 (see Chapter 16). This theory—that the transaction is a Type F reorganization—can be advanced only if the business-assets corporation is created as part of the plan of distribution. It would not be available if the business-assets and liquid-assets corporations are both existing subsidiaries of the liquidating corporation.[152]

An alternate attack on the use of a split-up to segregate liquid assets in a separate corporation is suggested by Regs. §1.301-1(1), providing that §301 is applicable to a distribution, "although it takes place at the same time as another transaction if the distribution is in substance a separate transaction whether or not connected in a formal sense." Although the language of the regulations is open to the objection that it requires an integrated transaction to be broken into two elements, it is only a short step from such cases as *Gregory* and *Bazley* [153] to the conclusion that the segregation of liquid assets in a separate corporation coupled with a distribution of its stock is the equivalent of a dividend.

One more point: What if the controlled corporations are both engaged in the active conduct of a five-year-old trade or business, but the distribution fails to qualify under §355 because (by reason of a prearranged sale of stock) it is treated as a device for distributing earnings and profits? Such a nonqualifying division would seem to be as fair game for dividend treatment as the blatant segregation of liquid assets in a separate corporation; if the distribution is really such a device, it ought to be taxed for what it is (or is thought by Congress to be)[154]—a distribution of earnings and profits.

---

[150] Infra ¶ 14.18.

[151] See §356(a)(2).

[152] For more on reincorporations, see infra ¶ 14.54; see generally Telephone Answering Serv. Co., 63 TC 423 (1974), aff'd per curiam, 546 F2d 423 (4th Cir. 1976), cert. denied, 431 US 914 (1977). See also §346(b), supra ¶¶ 7.21, 7.22 and 9.64.

[153] Supra ¶ 13.02; infra ¶¶ 14.17 and 14.54.

[154] As pointed out supra ¶ 13.07, it is not clear why a prearranged sale should mark the transaction as a device for the distribution of earnings and profits.

3. Nonqualifying split-offs. If a split-off fails to qualify under §355, it should, at least prima facie, be treated as a redemption of the distributing corporation's stock. In this event, the tax consequences of the distribution would be determined by §302: It would be a dividend (to the extent of available earnings and profits) unless it could meet the tests of §302(b)(1) (not essentially equivalent to a dividend), §302(b)(2) (substantially disproportionate redemption), §302(b)(3) (termination of the shareholder's interest), or §302(b)(4) (partial liquidation).[155] If the distributing corporation transferred part of its assets to the controlled corporation in preparation for the distribution, the transfer would be tax-free under §351 (§368(a)(1)(D) not being applicable[156]), and a portion of the distributing corporation's earnings and profits might be allocated to the controlled corporation by Regs. §1.312-11(a).[157]

4. Gain or loss to distributing corporation. If stock or securities are distributed in a spin-off or split-off that fails to qualify under §355, the distributing corporation must recognize any gain on the distribution by virtue of §311(b)(1), but §311(a)(2) forbids the recognition of any loss.

The status of a failed split-up is more complex. If the transaction does not qualify as a tax-free reorganization, it is subject to §336(a), which provides for the recognition of gain or loss on a liquidating distribution, subject to the limitations imposed by §336(d), relating to certain distributions to related persons and certain carry-over basis transactions. If, however, the failed split-up qualifies as some other type of tax-free reorganization (e.g, a nondivisive Type D or Type F reorganization), §336(c) renders §336(a) inapplicable. This brings into play §361(b)(3), which provides that the distributing corporation does not recognize gain or loss on its disposition of the stock or securities received by it pursuant to the plan of reorganization.[158]

---

[155] Although for practical purposes a split-off resembles a partial liquidation, the Tax Court has held that former §346 (currently §302(e)), relating to partial liquidations, does not apply to distributions of the stock of a controlled corporation, even though these rules would govern a distribution of the underlying business assets if owned directly by the distributing corporation. H.L. Morgenstern, 56 TC 44 (1971); see also Rev. Rul. 75-223, 1975-1 CB 109; and Rev. Rul. 79-184, 1979-1 CB 143. For taxability of the distributing corporation, see infra para. 4.

[156] Infra ¶ 14.16.

[157] See supra note 149.

[158] But see §346(b), under which a split-up might be treated as a partial liquidation under regulations to be issued by the Service, in which case §311 would be the governing provision.

See generally infra ¶¶ 14.16, 14.18, and 14.54 as to Type D and Type F reorganizations; for §361, see infra ¶ 14.32; see also supra text at notes 126–132.

¶ 13.16 FOREIGN CORPORATIONS

To qualify for nonrecognition treatment under §355, divisive transactions involving foreign corporations must satisfy the requirements of §367(a) if they have an expatriating effect (under which certain toll charges may be imposed), while nonexpatriating transactions may be subject to a toll charge under §367(b).[159]

---

[159] See infra ¶ 17.44.

CHAPTER 14

Corporate Reorganizations

PART A.   GENERAL CONSIDERATIONS

¶ 14.01   INTRODUCTORY

The federal income tax treatment of gains and losses from dispositions of property is controlled by a complex variety of statutory provisions. Section 61(a)(3) provides that the term "gross income" includes "gains *derived* from dealings in property," conversely, §165(a) allows, with certain limitations, deductions for losses *sustained*. Hence, a realizable event must occur with respect to the taxpayer's property before gain becomes taxable or loss deductible—that is, mere unrealized appreciation or depreciation in the value of property does not constitute a presently taxable transaction.[1] When

---

[1] There are minor exceptions (e.g., the valuation of inventory at cost or market value, whichever is lower, or, in the case of security dealers who elect to do so, at market value regardless of cost (see §1256); and reserves for bad debts).

a taxable disposition of property occurs,[2] the *amount* of gain or loss arising therefrom is determined under §1001, which provides that the taxpayer's gain or loss is the difference between the amount realized for the property and its adjusted basis and that the gain or loss thus determined must be recognized, unless otherwise provided by the statute.

There are many instances in which the Code does otherwise provide, and it is one group of such exceptions—the corporate reorganization provisions of §§354–368—to which this chapter is devoted.

The underlying assumption of the tax-free exchange provisions is that the new property is substantially a continuation of the old investment still unliquidated, and, in the case of reorganizations, that the new enterprise, the new corporate structure, and the new property are substantially continuations of the old still unliquidated. This continuity of investment principle lies at the heart of the nonrecognition provisions and is the reason why gain or loss, although realized, is not recognized at the time of exchange. (If, along with the qualified nonrecognition property, the taxpayer receives any cash or other boot, however, his gain must be recognized pro tanto.)

In an effort to ensure a recognition of the gain or loss at a more appropriate later time, however, the Code provides in general for continuity of adjusted basis, so that the taxpayer's basis for the property received in the exchange will reflect his basis for the property given up. Thus, the gain or loss that went unrecognized at the time of the exchange will be recognized

---

As to whether realization is a constitutional requirement or a principle of administrative convenience and economic policy, compare Surrey, The Supreme Court and the Federal Income Tax: Some Implications of the Recent Decisions, 35 Ill. L. Rev. 779 (1941), with Roehner & Roehner, Realization: Administrative Convenience or Constitutional Requirement, 8 Tax L. Rev. 173 (1953).

[2] If the property is disposed of by an exchange rather than a sale, account must be taken of Regs. §1.1001-1(a), stating that gain or loss is realized only "from the exchange of property for other property differing materially either in kind or extent." This language apparently reflects certain decisions holding that "refunding exchanges" of "virtually" identical securities do not give rise to presently taxable gain or deductible loss. See, e.g., Mutual Loan & Sav. Co. v. CIR, 184 F2d 161 (5th Cir. 1950); Motor Prods. Corp., 47 BTA 983 (1942), aff'd per curiam, 142 F2d 449 (6th Cir. 1944); Rev. Rul. 79-155, 1979-1 CB 153 (modifications in terms of debt assumed in merger substantial enough to create an exchange); Rev. Rul. 81-204, 1981-2 CB 157 (exchange of mortgage pools involving identical mass asset pots not a taxable §1001 exchange; properties did not differ materially in kind or extent); Rev. Rul. 85-125, 1985-2 CB 180 (same where series of concurrent sales and purchases of pools); infra note 4.

See also discussion of the convertible bond rule (infra ¶ 14.17) by virtue of which the conversion of bonds into stock of the debtor corporation does not cause recognition of gain or loss.

For other possible nonrecognition provisions that may apply to security exchanges, see §§267(a)(1) (loss sales to related persons), 1036, and 1091 (wash sales).

when (and if) he ultimately liquidates his investment. This principle is frequently breached, however, because stock held until death receives a new date of death basis in the hands of the heir.

In a sense, the corporate reorganization provisions are an analogue or extension of §1031, providing that gain or loss shall not be recognized on the exchange of investment or business property for other property of a like kind. Although stock and securities are explicitly excluded from §1031,[3] they may be exchanged tax-free if the transaction is a qualified corporate reorganization. The reorganization rules are considerably more complex than the terms of §1031, but both the underlying rationale and the basic statutory approach of these two provisions are similar (i.e., (1) continuity of investment and (2) deferral of realized gain or loss through substituted basis rules).

In approaching the taxation of corporate reorganizations, it is essential to grasp at once the simple but often elusive fact that the Code defines and uses the term "reorganization" in a special way. To the general practitioner, a reorganization ordinarily connotes the financial rehabilitation of a bankrupt enterprise. To the tax lawyer, however, the term embraces a much wider variety of corporate readjustments, most of which have the flavor of prosperity rather than depression. As will be seen, "reorganization" is defined for tax purposes by §368(a)(1) to include mergers, consolidations, recapitalizations, acquisitions by one corporation of the stock or assets of another corporation, and changes in form or place of organization. The statutory definition (which is exclusive for this purpose) looks primarily to the form rather than the substance of these transactions, since it embraces almost without discrimination one-person enterprises and publicly held corporations, business corporations and "incorporated pocketbooks," affiliated companies and previously unrelated corporations, big and little corporations, successful corporations and bankrupts.[4]

The common bond among these mismated transactions is that—subject to the inevitable refinements that will be discussed later—if the readjustment

---

[3] The exclusion of stock and securities from the scope of §1031 dates from 1923; the section was enacted to combat the establishment by brokerage firms of exchange departments, through which their customers could trade appreciated securities without recognizing gain. See Seidman Legislative History of Federal Income Tax Law: 1851–1938, at 798 (Prentice-Hall, 1959). Compare the swap fund device under §351, supra ¶ 3.15; infra ¶ 14.19.

[4] But see Emery v. CIR, 166 F2d 27 (2d Cir. 1948), holding that the reorganization provisions do not apply to a refunding of the obligations of a municipal corporation. Despite this, the investor does not necessarily recognize gain or loss: If the new obligations are sufficiently similar to the old ones, the transaction may be a mere extension rather than an exchange. See supra note 2; see also Rev. Rul. 81-169, 1981-1 CB 469 (municipal refunding exchange taxable); Rev. Rul. 87-19, 1987-11 IRB 20 (waiver of right to additional interest a deemed exchange under §1001).

qualifies as a reorganization, the corporation recognizes neither gain nor loss on the transfer of its property for stock or securities in another corporation that is a party to the reorganization, and the shareholders and creditors may exchange their stock or securities for new instruments without the recognition of gain or loss. Moreover, the tax attributes (loss carry-overs, earnings and profits, accounting methods, and so forth) of a corporation whose assets are acquired by another corporation in the reorganization are ordinarily inherited by the acquiring corporation (see Chapter 16).

The statutory definition of reorganization thus hauls in a most variegated catch but does almost nothing to segregate the transactions according to their economic consequences. Thus, the reincorporation of a corporation in another state, entailing no significant changes in the rights of the corporation's shareholders and creditors, is a reorganization, but so is the merger of an independent corner grocery store into a national food chain, although the local merchant who has exchanged his stock for the marketable stock of the surviving corporation may feel, quite rightly, that he has sold out. A recapitalization in which bondholders get new securities with different maturities and interest rates is a reorganization, but so is a recapitalization in which bondholders get common stock with an attendant shift in the ownership of the corporation.

The traditional theory of the reorganization provisions is that gain or loss should not be recognized on changes of form when the taxpayer's investment remains in corporate solution or when "a formal distribution, directly or through exchange of securities, represents merely a new form of the previous participation in an enterprise involving no change of substance in the rights and relations of interested parties one to another or to the corporate assets."[5] As suggested earlier, however, the statutory definition of reorganization takes in corporate adjustments that go far beyond changes of form only.[6] To some extent, the treatment of boot, especially since 1954, is a

---

[5] See Bazley v. CIR, 331 US 737, reh'g denied, 332 US 752 (1947) (infra ¶ 14.17). In point of fact, the transaction before the court in that case, involving a reshuffling of the capital structure of a family corporation with no change in ownership, met this specification more clearly than would most mergers and consolidations, although the court held that it was not a reorganization. This is not to say that the court failed to reach the right result, but the quoted language is an accurate description of very few corporate reorganizations.

[6] There may, of course, be valid economic or other reasons for the nonrecognition of gain or loss, even though Congress has failed to announce them. Compare Hellerstein, Mergers, Taxes, and Realism, 71 Harv. L. Rev. 254 (1957), and Sandberg, The Income Tax Subsidy to "Reorganizations," 38 Colum. L. Rev. 98 (1938), with Dane, The Case for Nonrecognition of Gain in Reorganization Exchanges, 36 Taxes 244 (1958). See also Surrey, Income Tax Problems of Corporations and Shareholders: American Law Institute Tax Project—American Bar Association Committee Study on Legislative Revision, 14 Tax L. Rev. 1 (1958); Cohen,

restraining influence; the courts have on occasion intervened to prevent some outright sales and dividends from disguising themselves as tax-free reorganizations, but the judicial restraints themselves are often matters of form rather than substance.

The reorganization provisions are extraordinarily complex, even for the Code. They endeavor to prescribe, in a few sentences, the tax treatment of a diversity of transactions that have little in common when viewed from the standpoint of business, financial, or economic purposes or results. They have been altered by Congress every few years, always ad hoc, and the earlier versions continue to govern the basis of assets and stock acquired in ancient reorganizations as well as to influence the administrative and judicial construction of today's statute.

There is a good deal of interplay, overlap, and conflict between the reorganization provisions and such other statutory provisions at §301 (distributions of cash and other property), §302 (redemptions of stock and partial liquidations), §305 (stock dividends), §306 (preferred stock bailouts), §331 (complete liquidations), and §355 (corporate divisions), since any of these events may accompany, be part of, or serve as a substitute for a reorganization. There is a similar conflict of jurisdiction within the reorganization provisions themselves, since—to take but one example—a statutory merger may be indistinguishable in results from an exchange by one corporation of its voting stock for all of the assets of another corporation; but different statutory rules are prescribed for these functionally equivalent reorganizations.

It should be noted that reorganization transactions often involve interdependent tax consequences, since the nonrecognition of gain that is ordinarily desired by transferor corporations and their shareholders carries with it a substituted basis for the property acquired by the transferee and possibly other disadvantages (e.g., an inherited earnings and profits account). This conflict in interest is not unusual in business transactions, of course, and the tax cost to each party is typically reflected in the business bargain to the extent that it can be anticipated and assured; but if the tax results are unpredictable and a binding ruling is not or cannot be obtained from the Service, the parties may take opposing forensic positions on the tax questions when they arise. This source of conflict among the participants to a corporate exchange may be heightened by differences among the transferors themselves; thus, some shareholders may wish to postpone the recognition

---

Conglomerate Mergers and Taxation, 55 A.B.A. J. 40 (1969); FTC Staff Report on Corporate Mergers to Antitrust Subcomm. of Senate Judiciary Comm. (Nov. 3, 1969); Conglomerate Mergers and Acquisitions: Opinion and Analysis, 44 St. John's L. Rev. 1 (1970, special ed.). More currently, see Joint Comm. Staff, Federal Income Tax Aspects of Mergers and Acquisitions (JCS-6-85), 99 Cong., 1st Sess. (1985), reprinted in DTR (BNA) No. 62 (April 1, 1985).

of gain on a merger, while their fellow shareholders, who bought their stock at a higher price, may wish to recognize their loss. Finally, the attitude of any one participant in an exchange may depend on whether the tax issue arises at the time of the exchange or when he disposes of the property received, possibly many years later.

Because the stakes are often very high and the sources of conflict among taxpayers and between them and the government are so numerous, almost all reorganization exchanges involving the shareholders of publicly held corporations, and many private transactions as well, are conditioned on a favorable ruling by the Service unless the exchange falls in a simple and well-worn pattern. For this reason, the legal form or business bargain is often adjusted to eliminate questions that will be decided adversely by the Service or—equally important—that it will not answer under its current policy. Rarely do the participants deliberately invite a test of strength in the courts, even if they feel a good deal of confidence in the outcome. As a result, the Service can make "law" in this area by a lifted eyebrow. It follows that the practitioner must not only examine with care the statute, regulations, decisions, and published rulings relating to a proposed transaction, but must also determine the informal administrative climate with respect to it.[7]

The Staff of the Senate Finance Committee submitted a preliminary report on the reform and simplification of Subchapter C on September 22, 1983, which proposed the replacement of the Type A, B, and C acquisitive reorganization rules of present law with a single elective nonrecognition carry-over basis system at the corporate level. Shareholders, in turn, would be permitted to receive stock tax-free in a qualified acquisition without regard to the treatment of the transaction at the corporate level or the terms of the exchange with other shareholders. Under this proposal, the limitations of present law now applicable to acquisitive reorganizations (i.e., continuity of interest, continuity of business enterprise, corporate-shareholder parallel treatment, the business purpose requirement, and the qualified consideration rules would be replaced.[8] The Staff's final report was issued on May 20, 1985 and contained draft statutory language of "The Subchapter C Revision

---

[7] See Rev. Proc. 86-42, 1986-45 IRB 12 (standardized representations in acquisitive reorganization ruling requests); Rev. Proc. 77-37, 1977-2 CB 568 (rules of thumb used by the Service in issuing rulings in this area dealing with such matters as "substantially all" under §368(a)(1)(c), continuity of interest under §368(a)(1)(A), and the treatment of delayed or contingent stock issue plans); Rev. Proc. 87-3, 1987-1 IRB 27 (listing of the various "no ruling" areas generally).

[8] Staff of the Senate Fin. Comm., Report on the Reform and Simplification of the Income Taxation of Corporations, 98th Cong., 1st Sess. (Comm. Print 1983), S. Rep. No. 85; see also Joint Comm. Staff, Federal Income Tax Aspects of Mergers and Acquisitions, supra note 6.

Act of 1985" as well as general and technical explanations of these proposals.[9] At this writing, these proposals have not been formally introduced.

¶ 14.02   THE STATUTORY PATTERN

Turning now to the statute, we find that §368(a)(1) defines "reorganization" to mean:

(1) A statutory merger or consolidation (Type A);

(2) The acquisition by one corporation solely in exchange for all or part of its voting stock (or the voting stock of a parent corporation) of stock of another corporation if the first corporation has control (as defined) of the second immediately after the acquisition (Type B);

(3) The acquisition by one corporation, in exchange for all or part of its voting stock (or the voting stock of a parent corporation), of substantially all the properties of another corporation (Type C). The consideration given by the acquiring corporation must be solely voting stock, except that liabilities of the acquired corporation may be assumed, property may be taken subject to liabilities, and a limited amount of money or other consideration may be paid;

(4) A transfer by a corporation of all or part of its assets to another corporation if, immediately after the transfer the transferor, its shareholders (including its former shareholders), or both in combination, are in control of the transferee corporation, but only if the stock or securities of the transferee corporation are distributed, under the plan, in a transaction that qualifies under §§354, 355, or 356 (Type D);

(5) A recapitalization (Type E);

(6) A mere change in identity, form, or place of organization, however effected (Type F); or

(7) Certain insolvency reorganizations (Type G).

---

[9] Staff of the Senate Fin. Comm., The Subchapter C Revision Act of 1985, A Final Report, 99th Cong., 1st Sess. (1985), S. Rep. No. 47.

For discussion of these proposals, see infra ¶ 14.21. In the Tax Reform Act of 1986, H.R. Rep. No. 3838, §634, the Treasury was directed to study these (and other) proposals and report back to Congress by January 1, 1988.

For a summary, see Eustice, Kuntz, Lewis & Deering, The Tax Reform Act of 1986: Analysis and Commentary, ¶ 2.08 (Warren, Gorham & Lamont, Inc., 1987).

In general, Types A and C are fusion- or acquisitive-type transactions, which are methods used to combine the assets of two or more corporations (whether previously independent or affiliated). Type B is used to acquire a subsidiary; Type D may be used to combine two affiliated corporations, to reincorporate, or to effect a corporate separation under §355. Types E and F reflect changes in the structure of a single corporation. However, Types A and C may also be used to combine an existing corporation with a newly organized corporate shell, achieving the net result of a Type E or F reorganization.

Type B seems to differ from the other types in that the acquired corporation becomes a subsidiary of the acquiring corporation, but the subsidiary may be liquidated as part of the reorganization, with results that often can hardly be distinguished from Type A or C reorganizations. In Type C, a pre-1985 transferor corporation might remain alive as a holding company; but after amendments in 1984, it must be liquidated, so that its shareholders become shareholders of the acquiring corporation, as they would in a Type B reorganization. As will be seen, these examples do not exhaust the areas of overlap between the various types of reorganization. Indeed, the statute itself recognizes that a reorganization may satisfy the requirements of both Types C and D, and prescribes in §368(a)(2)(A) which rules are to control.

The basic problems that arise in applying the statutory definition of the term "reorganization" are examined in Part B of this chapter, and special problems and aspects of that term are considered in Part D.

Although §368(a)(1) defines the term "reorganization," it docs not of its own force have any operative significance. Its definitions become important only as they are employed in other provisions of the Code, the most important of which are the following:

(1) Section 354, providing (with qualifications) that gain or loss will not be recognized if stock or securities in a corporation that is "a party to a reorganization," a term defined by §368(b), are exchanged solely for stock or securities in the same corporation or in another corporation that is a party to the reorganization;

(2) Section 361, under which a corporation that is a party to a reorganization recognizes neither gain nor loss if it exchanges property under the plan of reorganization for stock, securities, or other property with another corporation that is a party to the reorganization;

(3) Sections 356 and 357, providing for the treatment of boot and liabilities in reorganization exchanges;

(4) Sections 358 and 362(b), providing substituted basis rules in reorganization exchanges; and

(5) Section 381, providing for the transfer of a corporation's net operating loss carry-over, earnings and profits, and other tax attributes
to a successor corporation in certain reorganizations, subject to the
limitations of §382(b) (see Chapter 16).

These operative rules (except for §381) are discussed in Part C of this chapter.

Citations to the vast literature on the corporate reorganization provisions appear at appropriate points hereafter, but discussions of a general or
historical character are cited below.[10]

Proposals submitted by the Staff of the Senate Finance Committee in
1983 and 1985 to repeal the acquisitive reorganization rules of present
§§368(a)(1)(A), 368(a)(1)(B), and 368(a)(1)(C) and to replace these provisions with a single elective nonrecognition carry-over basis system at the
corporate level are considered later in this chapter.

¶ 14.03 JUDICIAL LIMITATIONS IN GENERAL

The reorganization provisions of the 1954 Code are the progeny of surprisingly primitive ancestors. For many years, for example, an acquisition by
one corporation of substantially all the properties of another corporation

---

[10] See generally Darrell, The Use of Reorganization Techniques in Corporate
Acquisitions, 70 Harv. L. Rev. 1183 (1957); McDonald & Willard, Tax-Free Acquisi-
tions and Distributions, 14 NYU Inst. on Fed. Tax'n 859 (1956); Merritt, Tax-Free
Corporate Acquisitions—The Law and the Proposed Regulations, 53 Mich. L. Rev.
911 (1955); Cohen et al., The Internal Revenue Code of 1954: Corporate Distribu-
tions, Organizations, and Reorganizations, 68 Harv. L. Rev. 393, 414–426 (1955);
Darrell, Corporate Organizations and Reorganizations Under the Internal Revenue
Code of 1954, 32 Taxes 1007 (1954); Greene, Proposed Definitional Changes in
Reorganizations, 14 Tax L. Rev. 155 (1959).

For the early history of reorganization provisions, see Paul, Studies in Federal
Taxation 165 (West, 3d Ser., 1940); Miller, Hendricks & Everett, Reorganizations
and Other Exchanges in Federal Income Taxation (1931); Baar & Morris, Hidden
Taxes in Corporate Reorganizations (1935).

For more recent discussions, see Committee on Reorganizations, N.Y. State Bar
Association, Tax Section, Report on Ancillary Tax Effects of Different Forms of
Reorganizations, 34 Tax. L. Rev. 477 (1979); McGaffey & Hunt, Continuity of
Shareholder Interest in Acquisitive Corporate Reorganizations, 59 Taxes 659 (1981);
materials supra notes 8 and 9; Sachs, Subchapter C Overlaps, 40 NYU Inst. on Fed.
Tax'n 48 (1982); Proceedings of the University of San Diego Corporate Tax Confer-
ence (articles on Subchapter C reform topics), 22 San Diego L. Rev. 1–345 (1985);
Posin, Taxing Corporate Reorganizations: Purging Penelope's Web, 133 U. Penn. L.
Rev. 1335 (1985).

For a useful summary, see Maloney & Brandt, Taxable and Nontaxable
Acquisitive Techniques: A Case of the Basics Not Being Basic, 14 J. Corp. Tax'n 203
(1987).

was a "reorganization," regardless (so far as the statutory definition was concerned) of the nature of the consideration paid. Faced by such a rudimentary statute, the courts not surprisingly felt called upon to protect the spirit of the legislation against its letter by segregating sales and disguised dividends from true reorganizations. The early statute also provided that a transfer by a corporation of part of its assets to a controlled corporation was a reorganization and that the shareholders of the transferor could receive the stock of the transferee without the recognition of gain. This set of provisions, taken literally, seemed to open the door to the tax-free distribution of dividends if the distributing corporation went through the ritual of putting the cash or property to be distributed into a newly organized subsidiary and then distributed the subsidiary's stock. Here again, the courts intervened to prevent the reorganization provisions from being used to undermine the statutory scheme for taxing corporate earnings upon distribution to the shareholders.

The rudimentary provisions that first evoked the protective instincts of the courts have been revised many times in the intervening years, and in some areas the amendments have taken over the watchdog function of the courts. However, Congress has never ousted the courts of this jurisdiction, so that the sophisticated reorganization provisions of the 1986 Code have not outgrown the judicial restrictions that were imposed in their childhood.

It remains true, therefore, that literal compliance with the reorganization provisions is not enough; a transaction will be governed by the statutory provisions only if it comes within their presuppositions as well as their language. The courts have driven this truth home with a variety of formulations, usually classified as the business purpose, step transaction, and continuity of interest doctrines. All of them have been encountered at earlier points in this work, and the first two (which often merge into a kind of substance over form approach) crop up at so many points in the law of federal taxation as to defy summary, at least in a guidebook. Their relevance at critical points in the reorganization area is discussed hereafter. A convenient summary of their import, which is quoted in almost every government brief in a litigated reorganization case, is to be found in Regs. §1.368-1(b):

> Under the general rule, upon the exchange of property, gain or loss must be accounted for it the new property differs in a material particular, either in kind or extent, from the old property. The purpose of the reorganization provisions of the Code is to except from the general rule certain specifically described exchanges incident to such readjustments of corporate structures made in one of the particular ways specified in the Code, as are required by business exigencies and which effect only a readjustment of continuing interest in property under modified corporate forms. Requisite to a reorganization under the Code are a continu-

ity of the business enterprise under the modified corporate form. . . . In order to exclude transactions not intended to be included, the specifications of the reorganization provisions of the law are precise. Both the terms of the specifications and their underlying assumptions and purposes must be satisfied in order to entitle the taxpayer to the benefit of the exception from the general rule.[11]

However, the proposals submitted by the Staff of the Senate Finance Committee for the reform of Subchapter C would drastically revise and simplify the acquisitive reorganization rules of present law and, in the process, repeal the judicially imposed business purpose, continuity of business enterprise, and continuity of proprietary interest limitations.

¶ 14.04 RELATION TO OTHER ACQUISITION TECHNIQUES

It should be noted that a tax-free reorganization is merely one method of acquiring stock or business assets; alternatively, they may be purchased in a transaction that is no more complex than the purchase of an automobile or acquired by one of the means discussed earlier in connection with stock redemptions (see Chapter 9) and complete corporate liquidations (see Chapter 11). If the reorganization route is chosen, the taxpayers must be prepared to prove that the substance of the transaction accords with its form. If the acquisition is found to be a taxable sale, the fact that the parties label it a tax-free reorganization will not control; conversely, an acquisition formally designated a sale may, in substance, constitute a tax-free reorganization.

The primary difference between a reorganization and a purchase acquisition is the character of the consideration paid by the acquiring corporation. In a reorganization, stock of the acquiring company constitutes the principal, if not sole, consideration for the acquired stock or properties; a purchase of stock or assets, by contrast, can be effected for cash, the buyer's debt securities, stock, or other property. Moreover, in a reorganization, it is ordinarily necessary to acquire all or substantially all of the acquired corporation's properties, while a purchase transaction can be more selective, leaving unwanted assets in the hands of the sellers to be held, or disposed of, as they see fit. Finally, a reorganization often, but not always, involves the extinction of the transferor or acquired corporation (either by operation of law, as in a statutory merger, or by voluntary liquidation), while a corporation that sells its assets may continue in existence after the sale and embark on a new venture with the proceeds.

---

[11] For similar statements, see Regs. §§1.368-2(g) and 1.1002-1(c).

In choosing between a tax-free reorganization and a taxable purchase, the following factors and stakes are ordinarily the most important:

	Reorganization	*Purchase*
(1) Recognition of gain or loss	Generally no current recognition	Generally taxable currently
(2) Basis and holding periods of assets and stock or securities	Substituted or derivative basis and holding periods	Cost or new basis and holding periods
(3) Character of recognized gain or loss	Dividend possibility	Generally capital gain or loss
(4) Survival of corporate tax attributes	Generally carry-over to transferee per §381	Generally extinguished (if seller liquidates)
(5) Other aspects:		
(a) Deductibility of payments on securities issued	Dividends on stock not deductible	Interest on debt securities generally deductible
(b) Effect of acquisition on equity, control, and earnings of buyer corporation	Equity and control diluted (but can use pooling accounting)	No dilution (but purchase accounting)
(c) Risk and growth potential	Continuing proprietory stake in affairs of buyer (risk of gain and loss continues)	Low or no risk, and no growth potential (sellers have cashed in)

The parties to a transaction sometimes try to straddle the fence with respect to these matters, hoping to obtain the most favorable benefits of both forms of acquisition. One such device, the debt financed acquisition, inspired some of the statutory changes in the Tax Reform Act of 1969, as discussed in Chapter 4; others (iiquidation-reincorporation transactions and quasi-reorganization transactions) are considered elsewhere in this chapter. The success of these plans is by no means a foregone conclusion, and they have generated a good deal of litigation. Most taxpayers, however, are content to avoid the outer fringes of tax maneuvering in this area and are willing, if not anxious, to cast their lot exclusively with either the tax-free reorganization rules or the taxable purchase rules.

¶ 14.05 OTHER GENERAL CONSIDERATIONS

1. Nontax factors as to form of reorganization. Assuming a decision to employ a tax-free reorganization for a proposed acquisition, a number of nontax factors may be relevant in determining the form of the transaction. The principal choice is between acquiring stock or assets; but even within these two basic categories, legal consequences may vary. The most important nontax matters[12] to be considered in most acquisitions are the following:

(1) The possibility of contingent or undisclosed liabilities (or other burdensome obligations) of the acquired corporation may make a Type C asset acquisition preferable to a Type B stock acquisition or a Type A merger;

(2) Conversely, if preservation of the corporate entity or other non-transferable rights or privileges of the acquired corporation is desired, a Type B stock acquisition (or its functional equivalent, the reverse merger) may be the only feasible route;

(3) A Type A merger usually requires the approval of the shareholders of both corporations, while the shareholders of the acquiring corporation may not have to approve a Type B or C transaction;

(4) The percentage of shareholders who must approve an exchange may vary, depending upon the type or reorganization chosen;

(5) Appraisal rights for dissenting shareholders of the transferor corporation are more easily avoided by a Type B stock acquisition than a Type A merger or a Type C asset acquisition; and

---

[12] See generally Darrell, The Use of Reorganization Techniques in Corporate Acquisitions, supra note 10; Woodside, SEC Merger Considerations, 36 Taxes 136 (1958).

See also Stark, Non-Income Tax Aspects of Corporate Reorganizations: A Check List of the Issues and Problems Involved, 24 NYU Inst. on Fed. Tax'n 1085 (1966); Schneider, Acquisitions Under the Federal Securities Acts—A Program for Reform, 116 U. Pa. L. Rev. 1323 (1968); Maloney & Brandt, supra note 10.

See articles by Englert, Podolin, & Oatway on Tax Accounting in Mergers and Acquisitions, 29 NYU Inst. on Fed. Tax'n 491–532 (1971); Harney & O'Connor, Tax Accounting and Financial Statement Principles Applicable to Business Combinations, 49 Taxes 864 (1971); Panel Discussion, Accounting Principles for Pooling of Interests, 25 Tax Lawyer 29 (1971); Stark, Corporate Reorganizations and SEC Rules 144, 133, and 145, Dissenter's Rights; Restructuring the Corporations for Public Offering; Use of Liquidation Trustees in Section 337 Liquidations, 31 NYU Inst. on Fed. Tax'n 1699 (1973); Perlmutter, Comparison of Tax, Accounting and Securities Aspects of Business Combinations, 2 J. Corp. Tax'n 305 (1975); Fiflis, Accounting for Mergers, Acquisitions and Investments in a Nutshell: The Interrelationships of, and Criteria for, Purchase or Pooling, the Equity Method, and Parent-Company-Only and Consolidated Statements, 37 Bus. Lawyer 89 (1981).

On transferee liability aspects, see Mathison, Donald & Barsky, Transferee Liability, Tax Mgmt. Portfolio (BNA) No. 158-3d (1983).

(6) The Securities and Exchange Commission, state blue sky, and stock exchange rules and regulations may depend upon the form of the transaction.

2. Special forms of reorganization. Because of their specialized character, reorganizations and exchanges governed by the following provisions are not discussed here:

(1) Section 1071, relating to sales and exchanges of property to effectuate a change in policy or the adoption of a new policy by the Federal Communications Commission with respect to the ownership and control of radio broadcasting stations;

(2) Sections 1081–1083, relating to exchanges and distributions in obedience to orders of the SEC under the Public Utility Holding Company Act of 1935; and

(3) Sections 1101–1103, relating to distributions under the Bank Holding Company Act of 1956.

3. Miscellaneous. A tax-free reorganization, like any complex commercial transaction, is often a costly affair, and the parties usually seek to deduct or amortize these costs if possible. Nondeductibility is the general rule for such costs, however, unless they relate (1) to the organization of a new corporation, in which event they can be amortized over a period of five years under §248; (2) to the liquidation of an existing corporation, in which event they may be deductible as liquidation expenses; or (3) to a determination of the tax consequences of the transaction, in which event they may be currently deductible under §162 or §212(3). The legal and financial costs of issuing and registering stock, of acquiring stock or assets of the absorbed company, of amending corporate charters, and of soliciting shareholder proxies and consents, on the other hand, constitute nondeductible capital expenditures. The expense of issuing *debt* securities, by contrast, can be amortized over the life of the indebtedness, since debt capital is considered to have a limited useful life. These matters have been considered in detail at other points in this work: Special corporate-shareholder deduction problems and organizational, reorganization, and liquidation expenses, for example, are discussed in Chapter 5.

Regs. §1.368-3 requires the corporate and individual participants in a tax-free reorganization to keep detailed records of the reorganization proceedings and to file with their returns for the year of the reorganization a complete statement, setting out the information prescribed by these regulations. For a corporate party to a reorganization, the material to be filed includes a copy of the plan (with a sworn statement showing the purpose of the plan and all transactions pursuant to it), the basis of the property (including stock or securities) transferred incident to the plan, the amount of stock or securities and other property received in the exchange (valued as of the date of the exchange), and the amount and nature of any liabilities assumed, or taken subject to, in the exchange. Individual participants must file similar statements with their returns but need not submit copies of the plan itself.

A final point: Although the federal income tax consequences tend to dominate the typical reorganization transaction, the state income tax consequences should not be overlooked, even if the state follows the federal system.

PART B.   REORGANIZATION DEFINED

¶ 14.10   INTRODUCTORY

As noted earlier, the term "reorganization" has a technical meaning for federal income tax purposes, and is defined by §368(a)(1) to mean seven (and only seven) forms of corporate adjustments: statutory mergers and consolidations (Type A), acquisitions by one corporation of the stock or assets of another corporation (Types B and C), transfers to controlled corporations (Type D), recapitalizations (Type E); changes in the form or place of organization (Type F), and insolvency reorganizations (Type G). In general, these categories can be classified into three functional patterns: (1) fusion, or acquisitive, reorganizations, whereby one corporate enterprise absorbs the stock or assets of another corporation (Types A, B, C, and, to some extent, D and G); (2) fission, or divisive, reorganizations, whereby a single corporate enterprise is divided into two or more separate entities through a process of corporate mitosis (Type D, taken in conjunction with the provisions of §355 (see Chapter 13)), and (3) internal readjustments or reshufflings in the capital structure of a single corporate enterprise (Types E and F).

In practice, however, these basic patterns may overlap, so that tax consequences may vary depending upon which statutory category of reorganization is deemed controlling. This, in turn, may depend on the form of the transaction, the amount and character of the consideration exchanged, and the change in the parties' legal and economic relationships to the properties involved and among themselves. In many cases, formal events control the tax results; in other instances, form is disregarded, so that a state of tension exists between the words of the statute and the economic or business substance.

In this portion of the chapter, matters relating to the general definition of reorganization will be examined, together with the judicial glosses that the statutory provisions have acquired. Other definitional problems, such as the meaning of party to a reorganization and plan of reorganization, will also be considered. Because of their fundamental importance to the concept of corporate reorganization, the continuity of interest doctrine and the plan of reorganization requirement are considered before discussion of the various categories of reorganization.

Note that proposals by the staff of the Senate Finance Committee for the reform of Subchapter C, released in 1985, would drastically overhaul and simplify the acquisitive reorganization rules of the Type A, B, and C reorganizations and replace them with a single elective nonrecognition carry-over basis system applicable to all qualified acquisitions of stock or assets, regardless of the type of consideration paid. These proposals are considered in a subsequent section.

¶ 14.11   CONTINUITY OF PROPRIETARY INTEREST AND PLAN OF REORGANIZATION

1. Continuity of interest in general. Like the business purpose and step-transaction doctrines, the requirement that the original owners retain a continuing interest in the reorganized corporation was born of a judicial effort to confine the reorganization provisions to their proper function. The business purpose and step-transaction doctrines, however, almost immediately found application throughout the tax law, while the continuity of interest doctrine has seemed relevant primarily in the area that gave it birth and the related area of transfers of property under §351 (see Chapter 3).

The continuity of interest doctrine has a multifaceted character, depending upon the context in which it arises. At the corporate level, the major focus is on the business enterprise and its continuation, under modified forms, following the corporate readjustment; at the investor level, the relevant factors are the nature and extent of their continued participation in the corporation's control, earnings, and assets, and the relationship of their interests to those of other shareholders and security holders after the transaction has been consummated. Thus, the nature of the consideration received in the transaction (stock, debt, or other property), the remoteness of the ownership interests from the underlying assets of the business, the proportion of old owners who continue their participation after the transaction, the length of time the investor interests continue (holding period aspects), and the special features and problems of debt securities all form important aspects of the continuity of interest concept.[13]

---

[13] See generally Hutton, Musings on Continuity of Interest—Recent Developments, 56 Taxes 904 (1979). For discussion of recent reform proposals by the ALI

2. Character of the consideration. The continuity of interest doctrine, set out in Regs. §§1.368-1(b) and 1.368-1(c), can be traced back to *Cortland Specialty Co v. CIR*, where substantially all the properties of one corporation were acquired by another corporation in exchange for cash and short-term promissory notes.[14] Although the transfer came within the literal language of the reorganization provisions, the court held that the term "reorganization" presupposes "a continuance of interest on the part of the transferor in the properties transferred" and that the transaction before the court was too much like a sale to satisfy this criterion. Moreover, the court held that the promissory notes received by the transferor (having serial maturities, of which the longest was 14 months) were not "securities" within the meaning of what is now §354. The following year, in *Pinellas Ice & Cold Storage Co. v. CIR*, the Supreme Court held as to a similar transaction that "the seller must acquire an interest in the affairs of the purchasing company more definite than that incident to ownership of its short-term purchase-money notes" if the transaction is to qualify as a reorganization as well as that the notes (all payable within four months) were not securities.[15] Two years later, the Supreme Court held in *Helvering v. Minnesota Tea Co.* that a transfer of substantially all the assets of a corporation for voting trust certificates representing common stock worth about $540,000, plus about $425,000 in cash, was a reorganization under the statute applicable to the year in question.[16] Referring to the statement in *Pinellas* that the seller must "acquire an interest in the affairs of the purchasing company," the Court said:

> And we now add that this interest must be definite and material; it must represent a substantial part of the value of the thing transferred. This much is necessary in order that the result accomplished may genuinely partake of the nature of merger or consolidation. . . .
>
> The transaction here was no sale, but partook of the nature of a reorganization in that the seller acquired a definite and substantial interest in the purchaser.
>
> True it is that the relationship of the taxpayer to the assets conveyed was substantially changed, but this is not inhibited by the statute. Also, a large part of the consideration was cash. This, we think, is permissible so long as the taxpayer received an interest in the affairs of the trans-

---

Subchapter C Project, see Wolfman, Continuity of Interest and the American Law Institute Study, 57 Taxes 840 (1979).

See also McGaffey & Hunt, supra note 10 (focusing on cash-option merger transactions).

[14] Cortland Specialty Co. v. CIR, 60 F2d 937 (2d Cir.), cert. denied, 288 US 599 (1932).

[15] Pinellas Ice & Cold Storage Co. v. CIR, 287 US 462 (1933).

[16] Helvering v. Minnesota Tea Co., 296 US 378 (1935).

feree which represented a material part of the value of the transferred assets.[17]

A further development came in *LeTulle v. Scofield*, in which all the assets of a corporation were transferred for $50,000 in cash and $750,000 in bonds of the acquiring corporation.[18] The Court held that the transaction was not a reorganization, despite compliance with the literal language of the statutory definition:

> Where the consideration is wholly in the transferee's bonds, or part cash and part such bonds, we think it cannot be said that the transferor retains any proprietary interest in the enterprise. On the contrary, he becomes a creditor of the transferee; and we do not think that the fact referred to by the Circuit Court of Appeals, that the bonds were secured solely by the assets transferred and that, upon default, the bondholder would retake only the property sold, changes his status from that of a creditor to one having a proprietary stake, within the purview of the statute.[19]

In *John A. Nelson Co. v. Helvering*, however, the Court found the requisite continuity of interest where assets were transferred for consideration composed of 38 percent in preferred stock and 62 percent cash.[20] The preferred stock was nonvoting (in the absence of dividend default) and was redeemable at stated intervals, but the Court held that the statute did not require participation by the transferor in the management of the transferee.[21] Finally, in *US v. Hendler*, the Court held that the assumption and payment by the transferee corporation of liabilities of the transferor corporation constituted taxable boot, although not enough boot was involved to destroy the status of the transfer as a reorganization.[22]

The continuity of interest test has been summarized in *Southwest Natural Gas Co. v. CIR*, as follows:

> While no precise formula has been expressed for determining whether there has been retention of the requisite interest, it seems clear that . . . [there must be] a showing: (1) that the transferor corporation or its shareholders retained a substantial proprietary stake in the enterprise

---

[17] Id. at 385–386.

[18] LeTulle v. Scofield, 308 US 415 (1940).

[19] Id. at 420.

[20] John A. Nelson Co. v. Helvering, 296 US 374 (1935).

[21] See also Helvering v. Watts, 296 US 387 (1935) (bonds and stock paid for assets; held a reorganization).

[22] US v. Hendler, 303 US 564 (1938).

represented by a material interest in the affairs of the transferee corporation, and (2) that such retained interest represents a substantial part of the value of the property transferred.[23]

The Court in this case refused to find the requisite continuity where less than one percent in value of the total consideration paid by the transferee consisted of its stock, even though substantial continuity existed *prior* to the transaction because of preexisting affiliation of the two corporations.[24]

Thus, the continuity of interest requirement, as developed in the above decisions, seemed to involve two distinct elements: (1) the qualitative nature of the consideration given by the transferee and (2) the proportion or amounts thereof that consisted of continuity-preserving interests. As to the former, the only type of consideration that carried the requisite continuity "genes" was an equity interest, evidenced by common or preferred stock, whether voting or nonvoting. Cash or its equivalent (e.g., short-term purchase money notes), long-term debt securities, and the assumption of liabilities all failed to meet the test of continuity, since the transferors, by the receipt of such consideration, were either cashing in their investment interest in the property or switching to a creditor status with respect thereto, rather than retaining a proprietary interest.

As to the relative amounts of equity and nonequity consideration that could be received by the transferors, matters were less clear. The *Minnesota Tea* case held that the equity mix must be a substantial or material part of the value of the transferred assets, and that a 56 percent equity interest was adequate by this standard; *Southwest Natural Gas*, on the other hand, held that less than one percent was not, even though substantial preexisting continuity was present there. It should be noted that the percentages in question represent the proportion of equity consideration to aggregate consideration received for the transferred assets, not the relation between the transferor's equity in the transferee and the total equity therein; a whale can swallow a minnow and satisfy the continuity of interest requirement.[25]

---

[23] Southwest Natural Gas Co. v. CIR, 189 F2d 332 (5th Cir.), cert. denied, 342 US 860 (1951).

[24] Infra ¶ 14.53.

[25] See generally Rev. Rul. 66-224, 1966-2 CB 114 (50 percent equity continuity of interest, by value, adequate); Rev. Proc. 77-37, 1977-2 CB 568 (50 percent continuity rule of thumb for ruling purposes, even if non-prorata; Service will consider contemporaneous sales and redemptions in making determination of continuity if part of plan); Rev. Rul. 75-95, 1975-1 CB 114 (stock in voting trust still owned for continuity of interest purposes); US v. Adkins-Phelps, Inc., 400 F2d 737 (8th Cir. 1968) (continuity satisfied where 99 percent shareholder received one sixth of stock of acquiring corporation in merger even though acquiring corporation had call on stock at par of only $997); May B. Kass, 60 TC 218 (1973), aff'd by court order, 491 F2d 749 (3d Cir. 1974) (16 percent not "tantalizingly high" enough); Yoc Heating

As noted previously (see Chapter 4), the distinction between debt and equity investor interests is not always easily determined. Where purported debt is treated as equity, the usual consequence is to confer reorganization status on an alleged taxable acquisition; but the converse is rarely encountered in practice, since alleged equity interests are not likely to be treated by the parties or the Service as disguised indebtedness. Hybrid equity interests, however, may also cause difficulty because they straddle the fence.[26] These interests are often used by savings and loan associations and certain cooperatives and have raised continuity of interest problems when a reorganization of such an enterprise has been attempted.[27]

Corp., 61 TC 168 (1973) (15 percent not enough); see also Superior Coach of Fla., Inc., 80 TC 895 (1983) (historic shareholders cashed out; no continuity of interest; stock of target purchased by shareholder of acquiring corporation who then merged target into acquiring corporation); Security Indus. Ins. Co. v. US, 702 F2d 1234 (5th Cir. 1983) (same; cash purchase of target stock by holding company, immediate liquidation of target; reincorporation of operating assets in another subsidiary).

[26] See generally Rev. Rul. 69-3, 1969-1 CB 103 (merger of two mutual savings and loan associations qualified as Type A reorganization where passbooks for identical cash deposits were issued by acquiring corporation to members of the acquired association); Rev. Rul. 69-6, 1969-1 CB 104 (merger of state capital stock savings and loan into federal nonstock savings and loan a sale and liquidation of transferor rather than reorganization; passbook interests issued for stock interests in acquired corporation; held equivalent to cash and hence no continuity); Rev. Rul. 70-298, 1970-1 CB 82; Rev. Rul. 78-286, 1978-2 CB 145 (merger of two mutual savings banks qualified despite absence of stock); Rev. Rul. 80-105, 1980-1 CB 78 (conversion of federal nonstock mutual savings and loan to state stock savings and loan held valid Type F reorganization).

See generally Soukup, The Continuity-of-Proprietary Interest Doctrine and Thrift Institution Mergers, 12 J. Corp. Tax'n 141 (1985).

[27] Westside Fed. Sav. & Loan Ass'n v. US, 494 F2d 404 (6th Cir. 1974) (merger of State mutual building and loan association into federal savings and loan association a valid reorganization; continuity of interest and business enterprise satisfied; court also held shareholder equity interests were voting stock); accord First Fed. Sav. & Loan Ass'n v. US, 452 F. Supp. 32 (N.D. Ohio 1978), 41 AFTR2d 78-1403, aff'd without opinion, 615 F2d 1360 (6th Cir. 1980).

But see Paulsen v. CIR, 469 US 131 (1985), which followed the holding of Rev. Rul. 69-6, 1969-1 CB 104 (no continuity of interest on exchange of target's stock for withdrawable passbook accounts of acquiring mutual savings and loan; instruments were predominately debt; equity features trivial when compared to debt features (i.e., were essentially equivalent to cash)). See also Home Sav. & Loan Ass'n v. US, 514 F2d 1199 (9th Cir.), cert. denied, 423 US 1015 (1975) (merger of two state mutual savings and loan associations not a valid Type A reorganization; member interests not equity and lacked continuity of interest).

For discussions of the Supreme Court's decision in *Paulsen*, see: Soukup, supra note 26; Friedrich, Recent Developments, 12 J. Corp. Tax'n 218 (1985); and Note, *Paulsen v. Commissioner:* The Continuity-of-Interest Doctrine and Tax-Free Mergers Involving Mutual Savings and Loan Associations, 79 Nw. U. L. Rev. 623 (1984).

3. Remote continuity: The *Groman* doctrine. In *Groman v. CIR*, the Court held that continuity of interest did not exist to the extent that the transferors received stock of the transferee corporation's parent in exchange for their property (although the transaction did constitute a reorganization).[28] The refusal to find a continuity of interest in such a triangular transaction[29] merely because a second corporate shell was interposed between the transferred property and the transferors reflected a surprisingly restrictive and formal view of the continuity doctrine's function.

A separable feature of the *Groman* transaction (i.e., the receipt by the transferors of stock in both the parent and the subsidiary, however, raised a somewhat different policy consideration, since the transferors thus acquired independent disposable interests in two corporations and could thus sell one interest while retaining the other. As will be seen, the former aspect of the *Groman* case has been modified by subsequent statutory developments; but the decision continues to have vitality where not altered by these amendments.[30]

4. Continuity of participation by the transferors. Another aspect of the continuity doctrine relates to the number of former owners who maintain a

---

[28] Groman v. CIR, 302 US 82 (1937).

[29] In *Groman*, shareholders of *T* Corporation transferred their *T* stock to *S* Corporation, a newly organized subsidiary of *P* Corporation, in exchange for cash and nonvoting preferred stock of *P* and *S*; *S* immediately liquidated *T*. The Supreme Court held that the stock of *P* received by the old shareholders of *T* did not give them a continuing interest in *T*'s assets, despite the fact that *P* owned all of the stock of *S*, which in turn owned the *T* assets. A companion case, Helvering v. Bashford, 302 US 454 (1938), also involved a triangular acquisition, except that the acquired properties were received by the parent itself and were then transferred by it to a subsidiary as part of a single plan. The Court held that *Groman* was applicable despite these variations in the facts. See also Anheuser-Busch, Inc. v. Helvering, 115 F2d 662 (8th Cir. 1940), cert. denied, 312 US 699 (1941); Hedden v. CIR, 105 F2d 311 (3d Cir.), cert. denied, 308 US 575 (1939); Mellon v. CIR, 12 TC 90 (1949) (nonacq.), aff'd on other issues, 184 F2d 157 (3d Cir. 1950). But cf. Robert Campbell, 15 TC 312 (1950) (acq.); Rev. Rul. 77-449, 1977-2 CB 110 (successive dropdowns to second-tier grandchild subsidiary valid §351 exchanges; each dropdown a separate §351, even though single plan to transfer assets to second-tier subsidiary), Rev. Rul. 83-34, 1983-1 CB 79 (same even where only 80 percent ownership of subsidiaries); see also Rev. Rul. 84-30, 1984-1 CB 114 (continuity not violated where target corporation passed acquiring corporation stock upstream to its grandparent).

See generally Lurie, Namorg–or *Groman* Reversed, 10 Tax L. Rev. 119 (1954); Schneider, Groman–or Namorg–Revisited: The Persisting Problem of Remote Continuity of Interest, 61 Den. U. L.J. 469 (1983); Murray, How to Avoid Loss of Continuity of Interest Through Stock Remoteness in a Reorganization, 59 J. Tax'n 8 (1983); Murray, IRS Revocation of "Stock Remoteness" Posture May Have Positive Effect on Reorganizations, 60 J. Tax'n 352 (1984) (discussion of Rev. Rul. 84-30).

[30] Infra ¶¶ 14.12, 14.15, and 14.53.

continuing proprietary interest in the transferred properties. For example, in a merger or consolidation, some shareholders of the transferor corporation may elect to take cash, securities, or other property rather than stock of the acquiring corporation. Is the merger vulnerable because some of the old shareholders have lost their proprietary interest while others have changed the relative proportions of their proprietary interest? The fact that some shareholders do not agree to the exchange and are paid off in cash was held irrelevant in *Miller v. CIR*, where the court stated that it "is an almost universal experience that some nonassenting stock must be acquired otherwise than through the consolidation plan."[31] (Those shareholders who take cash, however, would recognize their gain, if any, under §§354(a)(2) and 356 or §302). It cannot be assumed, however, that this tolerant attitude toward the common practice of paying off some shareholders in cash would be displayed toward an exchange in which only a small fraction of the participants received an equity interest in the transferee.[32]

This aspect of the continuity problem also has special features that are peculiar to Type D reorganizations and Type E recapitalizations.

Assuming that a sufficient number of stockholders of the transferor corporation acquire a proprietary interest in the transferee corporation, does the continuity of interest doctrine require that their participation arise solely from their status as stockholders of the transferor? Somewhat surprisingly, the courts have held that stock received by shareholder-creditors of the transferor can be counted in applying the continuity of interest doctrine whether it is received in their capacity of creditor or that of shareholder.[33]

---

[31] Miller v. CIR, 84 F2d 415 (6th Cir. 1936) (also held 25 percent continuity enough); see also Reilly Oil Co. v. CIR, 189 F2d 382 (5th Cir. 1951) (69 percent of the stockholders of transferor participated in a creditors' reorganization and secured control of the transferee; held sufficient continuity of interest); Western Mass. Theatres, Inc. v. CIR, 236 F2d 186 (1st Cir. 1956) (67 percent participation acceptable despite a shift in relative proportions). But see Maine Steel, Inc. v. US, 174 F. Supp. 702 (D. Me. 1959) (continuity broken by obligation to dispose of stock); Rev. Rul. 66-23, 1966-1 CB 67 (contra where stock would not have to be divested for seven years).

[32] See CIR v. Berghash, 361 F2d 257 (2d Cir. 1966) (control broken by drop from 100 percent to 50 percent); Reef Corp. v. CIR, 368 F2d 125 (5th Cir. 1966), cert. denied, 386 US 1018 (1967) (contemporaneous redemption of 48 percent of transferor's shareholders did not break continuity; redemption treated as severable transaction from the reorganization, even though part of the overall plan); see also Superior Coach of Fla., Inc., supra note 25, and Security Indus. Ins. Co. v. US, supra note 25 (continuity killed by cash purchase of target stock; historic shareholders terminated and continuity of interest failed; no reorganization); Warsaw Photographic Assocs., 84 TC 21 (1985).

[33] See Western Mass. Theatres v. CIR, supra note 31; see also CIR v. Huntzinger, 137 F2d 128 (10th Cir. 1934); Prairie du Chien-Marquette Bridge Co. v. CIR, 142 F2d 624 (3d Cir. 1944); US v. Adkins-Phelps, Inc., supra note 25; Norman Scott,

This conclusion may rest in part on the *Alabama Asphaltic* case, holding that creditors of an insolvent corporation, upon instituting bankruptcy proceedings, "had effective command over the disposition of the property" and that by this action, they stepped into the shoes of the old shareholders and succeeded to their former proprietary interest; since this interest was continued in the reorganized corporation, the continuity of interest requirement was satisfied despite elimination of the old stockholders.[34] If the transferor is not insolvent, however, the courts may be less ready to allow stock received in exchange for debt claims to be counted in determining whether shareholders have established a continuing interest in the transferred property.

5. Postacquisition continuity: How long? Does the continuity doctrine require that the shareholders of the acquired corporation retain their proprietary interest in the transferee corporation for some minimum period of time? Rev. Rul. 66-23[35] states generally that "unrestricted rights of ownership for a period of time sufficient to warrant the conclusion that such ownership is definite and substantial" will suffice, "notwithstanding that . . . the shareholder is required by a court decree to dispose of the stock before the end of such period," and that "ordinarily, the Service will treat five years of unrestricted . . . ownership as a sufficient period" for continuity of interest purposes.[36]

Inc., 48 TC 598 (1967) (merger of insolvent corporation into solvent sister corporation satisfied continuity of interest since shareholders had proprietary interest, either as stockholders or as creditors).

Stock received *solely* by creditors who are not also shareholders, however, may not carry the requisite continuity in some cases; see Helvering v. Southwest Consol. Corp., 315 US 194, reh'g denied, 315 US 194, reh'g denied, 316 US 710 (1942) (creditors not shareholders here; see infra ¶ 14.16).

[34] See Helvering v. Alabama Asphaltic Limestone Co., 315 US 179 (1942). For some of the ramifications of this decision, see Chicago Stadium Corp., 13 TC 889 (1949); San Antonio Transit Co., 30 TC 1215 (1958) (acq.); Scofield v. San Antonio Transit Co., 219 F2d 149 (5th Cir.), cert. denied, 350 US 823 (1955). See generally Atlas Oil & Ref. Corp., 36 TC 675 (1961) (acq.); Darrell, Creditors' Reorganizations and the Federal Income Tax, 57 Harv. L. Rev. 1009 (1944); supra ¶ 4.02 (as to classification of ambiguous instruments as stock or debt claims); infra ¶ 14.20. See also Tillinghast & Gardner, Acquisitive Reorganizations and Chapters X and XI of the Bankruptcy Act, 26 Tax. L. Rev. 663 (1971) (before amendments in 1980, see infra ¶ 14.20).

[35] Rev. Rul. 66-23, 1966-1 CB 67.

[36] See also John A. Nelson Co. v. Helvering, supra note 20 (callable preferred acceptable); Rev. Rul. 68-22, 1968-1 CB 142 (no adverse effect where stock subject to call at rate of 10 percent per year and no present intent to redeem); Schweitzer & Conrad, Inc., 41 BTA 533 (1940) (partial redemption of callable preferred shortly after the reorganization not an interdependent step and did not affect prior transaction); US v. Adkins-Phelps, Inc., supra note 25: Rev. Rul. 78-142, 1978-1 CB 111 (mandatory call after five years).

The ruling notes, however, that a preconceived plan or arrangement to dispose of the acquiring corporation's stock could cause trouble, at least if more than 50 percent of the stock is disposed of by the transferor's shareholders under the plan.[37] It seems to be generally accepted that shareholders of the transferor are relatively free to sell part or all of the stock received by them in the exchange if they are under no binding obligation to do so, without fear of breaking the reorganization, although it may be arguable that a preconceived plan for such a sale would be fatal even without a formal commitment.[38]

6. Securities and continuity of interest. As noted earlier, the principal function of the continuity of interest doctrine has been to separate sales from reorganizations; if the transferors received only debt obligations of the transferee in exchange for their property, continuity would be lacking under the *LeTulle* case,[39] since some form of proprietary interest (represented by common or preferred stock of the transferee) had to be retained by the

---

[37] In Rev. Rul. 69-265, 1969-1 CB 109, the Service ruled that an acquisition of assets by a second-tier subsidiary solely in exchange for voting preferred stock of a first-tier subsidiary that, after five years, was convertible into common stock of the parent of the first-tier subsidiary *was not* a valid Type C reorganization where the stock was convertible directly by exchange with the parent, but *was* a valid Type C reorganization where the parent contributed its stock to the first-tier subsidiary and the conversion would be effected by exchange directly with that corporation. Although the ruling does not discuss the continuity of interest issue, it obviously assumes that continuity would not be broken by the subsequent exchange. Note, however, that the final exchange would not completely terminate (although it would attenuate) the transferors' interest in the assets transferred in the original transaction, since they would receive thereby stock of the acquiring corporation's grandparent.

But see Rev. Rul. 77-479, 1977-2 CB 119 (prearranged sale of 80 percent of stock after recapitalization did not affect reorganization because continuity doctrine inapplicable to Type E).

[38] See McDonald's of Zion, Inc., 76 TC 972 (1981) (no postmerger holding period for acquiring company's stock so long as sale discretionary with target company shareholders; even though premerger intent to sell out, not fatal to reorganization; sale an independent transaction because reorganization and sale not mutually interdependent), rev'd, 688 F2d 520 (7th Cir. 1982) (continuity broken under step transaction principles where intended sale by target shareholders of acquiring corporation's stock; court imposed consistency of treatment on Service here; since Service required postacquisition continuity for favorable ruling, it could not deny that requirement where the tax stakes favored the buyer corporation, as here). Compare Robert A. Penrod, 88 TC No. 79 (1987) (continuity not broken by later sales).

For analysis of Tax Court decision in *McDonald's*, see Prusiecki, Continuity of Interest in Tax-Free Mergers: New Opportunities After *McDonald's of Zion*, 55 J. Tax'n 378 (1981).

[39] LeTulle v. Scofield, supra note 18.

transferors. If, however, sufficient proprietary continuity is maintained by the transferors so that the transfer qualified as a reorganization, it is then necessary to determine whether any additional consideration, such as debt obligations of the transferee, constituted securities, which could be received without recognition of gain under prior versions of §§361(a) and 354(a), or whether such consideration instead constituted taxable boot.

In *Helvering v. Watts* (involving a transfer of assets for stock and mortgage bonds), the Court held that the bonds were securities rather than boot;[40] the *Pinellas* case held that short-term notes did not constitute securities.[41]

In *Neville Coke & Chemical Co. v. CIR*, the court relied on the continuity of interest principle in holding that various creditor claims, exchanged by the taxpayer, did not constitute securities (hence, the exchange was ruled taxable even though the consideration *received* by the taxpayer concededly consisted of securities).[42] Pressed to its extreme, the approach of the *Neville Coke* decision could render many recapitalization exchanges and most creditor reorganizations taxable; this result cannot be reconciled with the implicit assumption that debt instruments constitute securities underlying such central reorganization provisions as §§354(a)(2), 356(d), and 361(a). Moreover, the general thrust of the continuity of interest doctrine is to prevent a shift from an ownership interest to a less permanent creditor interest; in the *Neville Coke* case, by contrast, the taxpayer was shifting from a less permanent (short-term creditor) to a more permanent (long-term creditor and shareholder) interest, a result which seems to accord with, rather than violate, the underlying policy of the continuity of interest doctrine.[43]

Another aspect of this problem is the apparent holding in *Bazley v. CIR* that long-term debt instruments received in a recapitalization exchange did not constitute securities; as pointed out in the discussion of *Bazley*, this dictum cannot be applied generally without serious conflict with the structure and presuppositions of the reorganization provisions, and it has not gained any momentum with the passage of time.[44] Despite *Neville Coke* and *Bazley*,

---

[40] Helvering v. Watts, supra note 21.

[41] Pinellas Ice & Cold Storage Co. v. CIR, supra note 15. For the relation of this issue to §351 exchanges, see supra ¶ 3.04. See also Regs. §§1.371-1(a)(5), 1.371-2(b) (withdrawn in 1982), and 1.374-1(a)(5).

[42] Neville Coke & Chem. Co. v. CIR, 148 F2d 599 (3d Cir.), cert. denied, 326 US 726 (1945).

[43] See generally Griswold, "Securities" and "Continuity of Interest," 58 Harv. L. Rev. 705 (1945); see also Rev. Rul. 59-222, 1959-1 CB 80; Prentis v. US, 273 F. Supp. 460 (S.D.N.Y. 1967) (six-month notes held securities because part of a single plan for delayed issue of preferred stock).

[44] Bazley v. CIR, supra note 5. See discussion infra ¶ 14.17.

then, it seems clear that long-term debt instruments ordinarily will constitute securities, even though they do not provide the transferor with a continuity of interest in the transferred property.

A final aspect is the relationship of the term "securities" to equity flavored instruments such as warrants, options, and convertible debentures. Although the term "securities" is usually restricted to debt interests rather than equity interests, corporate finance has spawned a variety of complex investor instruments that do not fit tidily into one or the other of the two statutory categories (stock and securities).[45]

7. Contingent consideration. A continuity of interest problem may arise if the parties keep a reorganization open for a period of time by providing for the payment of additional consideration (usually stock) if the earnings of the acquired corporation reach a stipulated level or if a similar contingency occurs. Mere delay in closing out the final payment for the acquisition, without more, should not affect the basic tax-free character of the transaction. An excessively tentative transfer, however, may fail to qualify as a present exchange on the theory that the parties merely entered into an executory agreement to reorganize at a future time. This result seems limited to extreme situations; the typical contingent consideration reorganization sails well within the zone of present transaction status. If the only consideration to be paid under the agreement is stock of the acquiring corporation, the continuity of interest doctrine should not be violated by the delayed issuance of that stock or by the fact that the right to receive stock is contingent.

8. Statutory evolution of the continuity doctrine. Most of the cases in which the continuity of interest doctrine was developed and applied related to transactions attempting to qualify as reorganizations under the pre-1934 statutory definition, which said nothing about the nature of the consideration which could be received by transferors. In 1934, however, the definition of "reorganization" was amended so that nothing but voting stock of the acquiring corporation could be used as consideration in an acquisition of the stock or assets of another corporation. (This limitation, somewhat modified since 1934, is to be found in §§368(a)(1)(B) and 368(a)(1)(C) of current law, governing Type B and C reorganizations.) In *Helvering v. Southwest Consolidated Corp.*, the Supreme Court drove home this restriction by holding that the transferor's receipt of stock warrants from the transferee prevented the exchange from qualifying as solely for voting stock, noting that the new stat-

---

[45] For a discussion of this problem, see infra ¶ 14.31.

utory test was much stricter than the judicially created continuity of interest doctrine.[46] Thus, in the case of Type B and C reorganizations, the continuity of interest doctrine is overshadowed by the statutory limits on the consideration that can be received, especially since most courts have served notice that "solely," as used in §368(a)(1), means exactly that.

Later statutory developments have somewhat relaxed the 1934 amendment to take care of several practical problems, but it continues to provide statutory assurance that the transferor will acquire a proprietary interest in Type B and C reorganizations. These post-1934 amendments, which are discussed subsequently, permit

(1) The assumption of liabilities, or the taking of property subject to liabilities in Types A and C reorganizations;

(2) The use of a limited amount of cash or other property in a Type C reorganization; and

(3) The use of voting stock of the acquiring corporation's parent in Type A, B, and C reorganizations.

Despite these statutory substitutes or buttresses for the judicially created continuity of interest requirement, it is still important in Types A and E reorganizations, where the statute is silent on the nature of the consideration which can be received by the transferors; in addition, it seems likely that continuity notions will still apply generally to other types of reorganizations[47] and may even have continuing relevance even under the Types B and

---

[46] Helvering v. Southwest Consol. Corp., supra note 33. But see C.E. Graham Reeves, 71 TC 727 (1979), rev'd sub nom. Chapman v. CIR, 618 F2d 856 (1st Cir. 1980) vacated, 618 F2d 856 (1st Cir. 1980), cert. dismissed, 451 US 1012 (1981).

See also Pierson v. US, 472 F. Supp. 957 (D. Del. 1979) (can pay 20 percent cash in a Type B), rev'd, 621 F2d 1227 (3d Cir. 1980).

[47] As to Type D reorganizations, the continuity doctrine raises special problems, discussed infra ¶ 14.16. It should be noted that it is described as generally applicable to all reorganization transactions by Regs. §1.368-1(b).

Like the 1934 change discussed in the text, the addition of §354(a)(2) in 1954 (infra ¶ 14.34) provides a statutory backstop to the continuity doctrine by making it more difficult for shareholders to upgrade their status to creditors in a reorganization exchange.

But Rev. Rul. 77-415, 1977-2 CB 311, holds that the continuity of interest doctrine does not apply to Type E recapitalizations. See also Rev. Rul. 77-479, 1977-2 CB 119 (same). Accord with Rev. Rul. 77-415 are Microdot, Inc. v. US, 728 F2d 593 (2d Cir. 1984) (no continuity of interest requirement in recapitalization), and Golden Nugget, Inc., 83 TC 28 (1984).

On the application of continuity principles to Type F reorganizations, see Aetna Casualty & Sur. Co. v. US, 568 F2d 811 (2d Cir. 1976); infra ¶ 14.18.

C rules, notwithstanding the statutory specificity as to permissible consideration in those provisions.

9. Limitations of continuity doctrine. Although the continuity of interest doctrine was devised and is applied as a means of denying tax-free status to sales that happen to meet the literal requirements of a reorganization, it works more as a blunt instrument than as a scalpel. Among its shortcomings are these:

(1) It assumes that the receipt of stock in exchange for stock necessarily ensures a continuing interest, without regard to the economic results of the transaction. In fact, however, the exchange may drastically alter the shareholder's rights and risks. If he gives up the common stock of a closely held corporation and gets back marketable stock of a national, publicly held corporation, the exchange may be substantially the same as a sale of the original stock followed by an investment of the proceeds in a totally different enterprise. Indeed, if the closely held company is merged into an investment company or other corporation with a broad spectrum of business activities, the exchange may be similar to a sale of the original stock coupled with an investment in a diversified portfolio of investments. Even if the acquiring corporation is not a national colossus, the shareholder's business risks may be fundamentally changed if he exchanges common stock for nonparticipating preferred, or vice versa.

(2) In applying the continuity of interest doctrine, the courts have employed the converse, but almost equally mechanical, assumption that bonds cannot represent a proprietary interest in the reorganized corporation.[48] Yet the size or financial status of the obligor may give the creditor good reason to worry about the safety of his investment and to follow the fate of the transferred assets with acute concern. Thus, the economic fortunes of the bondholders in *LeTulle v. Scofield*[49] may have continued to rest upon the value and income potential of the transferred assets, while the shareholder of a local business who receives stock of a national company in a merger may be virtually independent of fluctuations in the value of the assets in which he was formerly interested.

(3) The exchange of a proprietary interest for bonds may not represent much of an economic shift if the stock given up was nonparticipat-

---

[48] An exception presumably could be made for cases of thin capitalization (supra ¶ 4.04). See generally W.H. Truschel, 29 TC 433 (1957) (acq.); Reef Corp. v. CIR, supra note 32.

[49] LeTulle v. Scofield, supra note 18.

ing preferred or common stock of a corporation whose assets were not likely to fluctuate in value or yield. An example is *Roebling v. CIR*.[50] Here, the continuity of interest doctrine was applied to deny tax-free status to an exchange of common stock for bonds, although the exchange did not produce a substantial difference in the investor's financial position.[51]

(4) The continuity of interest test as it is presently understood presumably does not apply to the *acquiring* corporation or its shareholders, so that both the statutory and judicial limitations could be finessed by structuring the transaction as a reverse acquisition. Such a role reversal apparently enables the parties to avoid the literal strictures of the continuity doctrine because the acquired corporation and its shareholders receive only qualified consideration.[52]

10. The plan of reorganization. Another fundamental definitional aspect of the corporate reorganization concept is the plan of reorganization, pursuant to which the steps in the corporate readjustment are effected.[53] Unlike the continuity principle, which is of wholly judicial origin, a plan of reorganization is explicitly required by §§354 and 361, which grant tax-free treatment to exchanges only if they are made "in pursuance of the plan of reorganization." Regs. §1.368-3(a) provides that "the plan ... must be adopted by each of the corporations parties thereto; and the adoption must be shown by the acts of its duly constituted responsible officers, and appear upon the official records of the corporation." Regs. §1.368-2(g) defines the term as follows:

> The term "plan of reorganization" has reference to a consummated transaction specifically defined as a reorganization under Section 368(a). The term is not to be construed as broadening the definition of "reorganization" as set forth in Section 368(a), but it is to be taken as

---

[50] Roebling v. CIR, 143 F2d 810 (3d Cir. 1944), cert. denied, 323 US 773 (1944).

[51] See generally Brookes, The Continuity of Interest Test in Reorganizations—A Blessing or a Curse? 34 Calif. L. Rev. 1 (1946); Baker, Continuity of Interest Requirement in Reorganizations Re-examined—The Hickok Case, 18 NYU Inst. on Fed. Tax'n 761 (1960); Bloom & Sweet, How IRS Uses Continuity of Interest to Raise New Problems in Reorganizations, 45 J. Tax'n 130 (1976).

[52] But for an argument that the doctrine should apply on the acquiring side as well as the acquired side of the transaction, see Turnier, Continuity of Interest—Its Application to Shareholders of the Acquiring Corporation, 64 Calif. L. Rev. 902 (1976).

[53] See generally Manning, "In Pursuance of the Plan of Reorganization:" The Scope of the Reorganization Provisions of the Internal Revenue Code, 72 Harv. L. Rev. 881 (1959); Faber, The Use and Misuse of the Plan of Reorganization Concept, 38 Tax L. Rev. 515 (1983).

limiting the nonrecognition of gain or loss to such exchanges or distributions as are directly a part of the transaction specifically described as a reorganization in Section 368(a).[54]

While the plan of reorganization requirement may be viewed as an aspect of the broader step transaction doctrine (and there is a conceptual similarity between them), it also stands on its own as a discrete and independently essential element for a tax-free reorganization. Although informality is not fatal here, any more than in other comparable parts of the Subchapter C provisions, oral plans and handshake deals are the exception rather than the general rule in the reorganization area, especially when companies of any substantial size are involved. The central function of the plan is to separate those transactions making up the reorganization from other steps, however proximate in time, that are not part of the reorganization.

As noted above, the plan of reorganization requirement limits rather than expands the definition of reorganization, and it is invoked most frequently by the Service in an attempt to defeat rather than impose tax-free treatment for a particular transaction.[55] Without such a limitation, however, the concept of reorganization would have no clearly defined beginning or end; reorganizations, like other commercial events, must have a start and a finish.[56]

11. Current proposals. The report of the staff of the Senate Finance Committee on the reform and simplification of Subchapter C, submitted in 1983 and 1985, proposed to replace the present acquisitive reorganization provisions of §§368(a)(1)(A), 368(a)(1)(B), and 368(a)(1)(C) with an elective nonrecognition carry-over basis system at the corporate level. The type of consideration paid would be irrelevant under these proposals and, as a consequence, the continuity of interest limitation would be repealed.

---

[54] See also Regs. §1.383-3(c)(3) (date of the plan); Tax Reform Act of 1976 §806(g) (effective date of §382(b) amendments); Regs. §1.368-1(d)(1)(iii) (date of Type B reorganization acquisition is date that exchange of all stock under the plan of reorganization is complete).

[55] For an exception, in which the Service usually tries to establish that a transaction was a reorganization, see infra ¶ 14.54, relating to reincorporation cases; see also Simon v. CIR, 644 F2d 339 (5th Cir. 1981) (steps as a whole were a reorganization).

[56] For various judicial interpretations of the scope of the plan of reorganization concept, see CIR v. Gordon, 391 US 83 (1968); American Potash & Chem. Corp. v. US, 399 F2d 194 (Ct. Cl.), motion denied, 402 F2d 1000 (Ct. Cl. 1968); Dunlap & Assocs., 47 TC 542 (1967); Bruce v. Helvering, 76 F2d 442 (D.C. Cir. 1935); see also ITT & Cos., 77 TC 60 (1981), aff'd, 704 F2d 252 (2d Cir. 1983) (subsequent conversion of subsidiary bonds into parent stock following prior tax-free acquisition of subsidiary by parent not part of original plan of reorganization).

¶ 14.12   STATUTORY MERGERS AND CONSOLIDATIONS (TYPE A)

Under §368(a)(1)(A), a statutory merger or consolidation is the proto-type reorganization.[57] In a merger, one corporation absorbs the corporate enterprise of another corporation, with the result that the acquiring company steps into the shoes of the disappearing corporation as to its assets and liabilities. Consolidations typically involve the combination of two or more corporations into a newly created entity, with the old corporations going out of existence. In both of these transactions, however, shareholders and creditors of the disappearing transferor corporations automatically become shareholders and creditors of the transferee corporations by operation of law. It should be noted that the transferor corporation or corporations in a statutory merger or consolidation disappear as legal entities, with the result that this form of reorganization involves a technical dissolution of the acquired corporation. (Although in a Type C reorganization, often called a "practical merger," the transferor corporation formerly could be kept alive, the statute was amended in 1984 to require liquidation of the corporation here, as well.)

When two enterprises are to be combined, it is often purely a matter of form whether the parties employ a reorganization of Type A (statutory merger or consolidation), Type B (acquisition by one corporation of the stock of another corporation), or Type C (acquisition by one corporation of substantially all the properties of another corporation). As will be seen, however, §368(a)(1)(B) seems literally to permit the use of no consideration other than voting stock in a Type B reorganization, and §368(a)(1)(C) affords only slightly more freedom in a Type C reorganization; but §368(a)(1)(A)–quite unaccountably–imposes no restrictions on the type of consideration to be used in a statutory merger or consolidation.

Nonvoting stock and securities can be used with impunity, so far as the statutory language is concerned, in a Type A reorganization; the exchange can qualify as a reorganization even if money or other property changes hands. The money or other property will constitute boot of course, and so will securities in some circumstances, with the consequences discussed later in this chapter;[58] but they will not result in disqualifying the transaction in

---

[57] The statutory requirements of the applicable state law must be satisfied; see Edward H. Russell, 40 TC 810, 822 (1963), aff'd per curiam, 345 F2d 534 (5th Cir. 1965). But an exchange that fails to comply with state law or that takes place under foreign law may constitute a Type C or D reorganization, even though it is not a Type A reorganization. See Regs. §1.368-2(b); Rev. Rul. 57-465, 1957-2 CB 250.

But see Rev. Rul. 74-297, 1974-1 CB 84 (triangular merger into domestic subsidiary of foreign parent qualified under §368(a)(2)(D) if §367 ruling obtained).

[58] Infra ¶¶ 14.31, 14.32, and 14.34.

its entirety, as can occur when money, property, nonvoting stock, or securities are used in a Type B or C reorganization.

The greater flexibility of a Type A reorganization is not without its perils, however. It may lure the taxpayer into an excessive use of securities or other nonproprietary consideration, in violation of the continuity of interest doctrine, whereas the more rigid requirements of a Type B or C reorganization help to keep the taxpayer on the straight and narrow tax-free path. Thus, in *Roebling v. CIR*, a merger of two corporations was held to fall outside of §368(a)(1)(A) because the shareholders of the absorbed corporation received nothing but bonds of the continuing corporation; although there was a merger under state law, the old shareholders did not retain a continuing proprietary interest in the transferred assets.[59] A statutory merger may fail to qualify even if the shareholders get some stock in the continuing corporation if the stock represents only a small fraction of the total consideration received by them.[60]

Under §368(a)(2)(C), enacted in 1954, an otherwise qualified Type A reorganization will not lose its tax-free status merely because part or all of the assets acquired in the transaction are transferred to a subsidiary by the acquiring corporation.[61]

Aside from the continuity of interest problem relating to the proportion of nonproprietary consideration that can be paid by the acquiring corporation, statutory mergers and consolidations ordinarily cause little difficulty. The following special situations, however, require attention.

1. Mergers of affiliated corporations. If the shareholders of brother-sister corporations receive bonds, debentures, or other debt instruments in a merger or consolidation, the net effect of the transaction may be indistinguishable from the payment of a taxable dividend under the *Bazley* doctrine. Alternatively, the transaction might be viewed as a redemption of the stock

---

[59] Roebling v. CIR, supra note 50. See also W.H. Truschel, supra note 48; West-Shore Fuel, Inc. v. US, 598 F2d 1236 (2d Cir. 1979) (shareholders not entitled to use §453 in all debt mergers; transaction a corporate-level asset sale, not a shareholder level stock sale). But see §453(h), added by the Installment Sales Revision Act of 1980, which allows shareholder use of §453 in such cases.

[60] See Southwest Natural Gas Co. v. CIR, supra note 23.

[61] For the background of this provision, see supra ¶ 14.11, note 29. If assets are transferred to a subsidiary under §368(a)(2)(C), the transferor-parent is a party to the reorganization by virtue of §368(b) (third sentence), and the subsidiary seems to be a party to the reorganization by virtue of §368(b)(2) or, if newly created, §368(b)(1). See Regs. §1.368-2(f) (seventh sentence).

Moreover, Rev. Rul. 68-261, 1968-1 CB 147, allows the acquiring company to drop the acquired assets into more than one subsidiary under §368(a)(2)(C). See generally infra ¶ 14.15.

of the merged corporation by its surviving sister corporation, in which event its tax consequences will be governed by §304. Neither of these forbidding possibilities is brought into play, however, by a merger or consolidation of affiliated corporations in which the shareholders do not try to upgrade their status to that of creditors but instead content themselves with an exchange of stock for stock.[62]

The merger of a subsidiary into its parent, or vice versa (so-called upstream and downstream mergers, respectively) involves a potential conflict between the rules governing reorganizations and those governing liquidations, discussed later in this chapter.

2. Triangular mergers and subsidiary merger techniques. As noted above, §368(a)(2)(C) specifically allows part or all of the assets acquired in a Type A reorganization to be dropped into a controlled subsidiary of the acquiring corporation after the acquisition without affecting the tax-free status of the transaction. A variation on this technique is a triangular merger involving a direct transfer of assets by the acquired corporation to the acquiring corporation's controlled subsidiary in exchange for stock of the parent. Rev. Rul. 67-326 held that such a transaction could not qualify for tax-free treatment (even though it apparently constituted a Type A reorganization), however, because the parent was not a party to the reorganization, *but that it could* qualify for nonrecognition as a Type C reorganization if the conditions of that section were satisfied.[63]

In 1968, Congress enacted §368(a)(2)(D), specifically allowing this type of statutory merger into a newly created or preexisting controlled subsidiary of the acquiring corporation on certain limited conditions, thus creating a hybrid category of reorganization, discussed later in this chapter, that resembles both the Types A and C forms of acquisition, but that has its own requirements.

Instead of having the acquiring corporation's subsidiary emerge as the surviving corporation in the transaction, another triangular merger technique is to merge a newly created subsidiary (organized with voting stock of the parent corporation) into the acquired corporation, so that the latter is the surviving legal entity. In effect, the acquired corporation ends up as a controlled subsidiary of the acquiring parent corporation under this procedure.

In Rev. Rul. 67-448, the Service approved such a transaction,[64] but treated it as a constructive Type B reorganization rather than as a Type A

---

[62] See Norman Scott, Inc., supra note 33. For §304, see supra ¶ 9.12.

[63] Rev. Rul. 67-326, 1967-2 CB 143.

[64] Rev. Rul. 67-448, 1967-2 CB 144.

(statutory merger) reorganization. The transitory character of the subsidiary apparently justified looking through the form of the transaction to its substance, so that the acquisition was viewed as a constructive Type B reorganization (exchange of stock for stock), which had to satisfy the solely for voting stock limitation of that provision. In 1971, however, Congress enacted §368(a)(2)(E), specifically allowing this form of subsidiary merger on certain conditions, thus creating yet another hybrid category of reorganization that resembles both the Types A and B forms, but that has its own requirements.[65] The substantive differences between these variations on the triangular merger technique are slight, the identity of the surviving corporation being the principal technical distinction, so that form continues to play a dominant role in this corner of the reorganization area.

3. Creeping multistep mergers. A statutory merger is often merely the culminating step in a series of acquisition transactions, all looking to the ultimate absorption of the target company's properties when control has been obtained by the acquiring corporation. Whether the final fusion of the acquired corporation's assets into the acquiring corporation qualifies as a statutory merger Type A reorganization, or instead constitutes a liquidation (subject to the subsidiary liquidation rules of §332 and related provisions (see Chapter 11), is not always clear, since the tax results depend not only upon the form of the initial transactions (i.e., whether the acquisitions were for cash or stock of the acquiring company) but also on whether these steps were independent events or parts of a single, integrated transaction.

If, pursuant to a single plan, the acquiring corporation purchases all of the acquired company's stock for cash and promptly merges with its new subsidiary, reorganization treatment ought not to apply because the shareholders of the acquired corporation have sold out and, hence, lack a continuing interest in the old enterprise.[66] If the first step of the transaction is effected partly for cash and partly for stock of the acquiring corporation, however, the continuity of interest doctrine may be satisfied if the stock component of the consideration is substantial enough. Thus, the *King Enterprises* decision found a Type A reorganization upon the subsequent merger of the purchased corporation into the acquiring company in such a situation,

---

[65] See generally Shors, The Role of the Subsidiary in Corporate Reorganization, 18 Drake L. Rev. 175 (1968); Levin, The New Subsidiary-Merger Statute and Other Current Tax Problems in Acquisitions, 47 Taxes 779 (1969); Ferguson & Ginsburg, Triangular Reorganizations, 1972 S. Cal. Tax Inst. 1, and, in expanded form, 28 Tax L. Rev. 159 (1973).

For further discussion, see infra ¶¶ 14.15 and 14.53.

[66] Superior Coach of Fla., Inc., supra note 25, and Security Indus. Ins. Co. v. US, supra note 25, so held.

even though cash was paid for about 49 percent of the acquired corporation's stock and the first step of the acquisition (the purchase of stock for cash and stock), could not qualify as a Type B reorganization.[67] Moreover, if the initial steps are old and cold (i.e., separate from the subsequent merger of the acquired into the acquiring corporation), reorganization treatment of the second transaction probably should prevail.

Finally, if the first-stage stock acquisitions are effected solely for voting stock of the acquiring corporation, the initial acquisitions may themselves qualify as a Type B reorganization, discussed in the following section, in which event all exchanges would be tax-free to the respective parties.

Other aspects of the creeping acquisition problem are considered in greater detail in Part D.

4. Merger combined with §355 distributions. In preparation for a merger, one of the corporations may have to dispose of a separable business that the other corporation does not want to acquire; it may seek to do so in a tax-free distribution under §355. The possibility of thus combining two tax-free transactions, without an adverse impact on either one, is discussed in Part D.

5. Redemption of minority or dissenting shares. In conjunction with a statutory merger or consolidation, one of the corporations often wishes to redeem some of its shares, either as a convenient way of disposing of assets that the surviving corporation does not wish to acquire or to eliminate a dissenting group and thereby avoid the assertion of appraisal rights under state law. Does such a transaction endanger the status of the merger by weakening its compliance with the continuity of interest doctrine? As indicated earlier, if shareholders representing a substantial equity interest in the

---

[67] King Enters., Inc. v. US, 418 F2d 511 (Ct. Cl. 1969) (purchase of stock followed by preplanned merger of the newly acquired subsidiary into its new parent held a statutory merger); compare American Potash & Chem. Corp. v. US, supra note 56, holding that a two-step acquisition of stock for stock pursuant to a tender offer did not constitute a Type B reorganization because control was acquired over more than a 12-month period; on rehearing, however, the case was reconsidered on this point and remanded. See infra ¶ 14.13, notes 83 and 102.

See generally Levin & Bowen, Taxable and Tax-Free Two-Step Acquisitions and Minority Squeeze-Outs, 33 Tax L. Rev. 425 (1978); Henderson, Voting Stock in a Two-Step Asset Acquisition: The *Kimbell-Diamond* Reorganization, 25 Tax L. Rev. 375 (1970); Mopsick, *Yoc Heating Corp.* and Two-Step Asset Acquisitions, 1 J. Corp. Tax'n 235 (1974); Bruce, Liquidations and Reorganizations: *Madison Square Garden* and *Kass*, 30 Tax L. Rev. 303 (1975); Pugh, Combining Acquired and Acquiring Corporations and Their Subsidiaries: Some Anomalies of Form and Substance, 35 Tax L. Rev. 359 (1980).

transferor continue as shareholders of the surviving corporation, the continuity principle will be satisfied, even though the other shareholders are bought out.[68] At one time, the Service seemed ready to question such transactions if operating or business assets were used to pay for the redeemed shares under an amorphous continuity of business enterprise doctrine, but its doubts may have been laid to rest.[69]

6. Mergers that overlap with Type C or D reorganizations. A statutory merger may also fit the description of a Type C or D reorganization. If it does, must the restrictions imposed on the latter forms be complied with or can the exchange qualify if it meets the merger rules alone? Section 368(a)(2)(A) arbitrates one such conflict—between Type C and D reorganizations—by providing that an exchange described in both definitions must be treated as a Type D reorganization; but there is no such statutory direction for other instances of overlapping jurisdiction.[70] Legislative history, however, may supply the key: Mergers and consolidations have been tax-free transactions since 1918, and it is reasonably clear that the other types of reorganizations defined by §368(a)(1) were added to the law at later times to facilitate business adjustments rather than to restrict the tax-free status of mergers.[71] For this reason, it would be reasonable to resolve cases of overlapping definitions by allowing an exchange to qualify as a Type A transaction whether or not it meets the standards applicable to a Type C or D transaction.[72]

¶ 14.13 ACQUISITIONS OF STOCK FOR VOTING STOCK (TYPE B)

A Type B reorganization, as defined by §368(a)(1)(B), is the acquisition of stock of one corporation in exchange solely for part or all of the voting stock of either the acquiring corporation or its parent,[73] provided that the

---

[68] See Western Mass. Theatres v. CIR, supra note 31 and ¶ 14.11; infra ¶ 14.52.

[69] At least if a significant portion of the target's historic business activities or assets are continued by the acquiring corporation; see infra ¶ 14.51, para. 2.

[70] If a transaction is both a reorganization and a §332 liquidation, it is to be treated as a liquidation, at least so far as the parent corporation is concerned, by virtue of §332(b) (last sentence); see infra ¶ 14.53; Long Island Water Corp., 36 TC 377 (1961) (acq.). But see American Mfg. Co., 55 TC 204 (1970).

[71] See Paul, supra note 10, at 19–20.

[72] But see Rev. Rul. 67-326, 1967-2 CB 143.

[73] The use of stock of the acquiring corporation's *parent* as consideration in a Type B reorganization was authorized for the first time in 1964; at the same time,

acquiring corporation has control of the acquired corporation immediately after the acquisition (whether or not it had such control before the acquisition). "Control" is defined by §368(c) as the ownership of stock possessing at least 80 percent of total combined voting power, plus at least 80 percent of the total number of shares of all other classes of stock.[74] In a Type B reorganization, the sole consideration that can be used is voting stock[75] of either the acquiring corporation *or* its parent, but not a combination of both.

---

§368(a)(2)(C) was amended to permit stock acquired in a Type B reorganization to be transferred to a subsidiary of the acquiring corporation, and §368(b)(2) was amended to provide that the parent in such a triangular acquisition is a party to the reorganization. These statutory amendments limit the doctrine of the *Groman* and *Bashford* cases (supra ¶ 14.11, notes 28 and 29).

See Rev. Rul. 73-16, 1973-1 CB 186 (successive Type B reorganizations rearranged under step-transaction doctrine into simultaneous direct Type B reorganization and triangular Type B reorganization, both tax-free); Rev. Rul. 67-448, 1967-2 CB 144 (parent transferred its voting stock to newly formed subsidiary that merged into corporation the parent sought to acquire; after these steps, parent owned 95 percent of the acquired corporation; held Type B reorganization). See also §368(a)(2)(E) (added in 1971), making "reverse mergers" "hybrid" Type A reorganizations. See generally supra ¶ 14.12; infra ¶ 14.15.

See also Rev. Rul. 74-564, 1974-2 CB 124, and Rev. Rul. 74-565, 1974-2 CB 125 (transactions failing to qualify as reverse mergers under §368(a)(2)(E) because stock of grandparent rather than of parent was used nevertheless qualified under Rev. Rul. 67-448 as triangular stock acquisitions under §368(a)(1)(B), which permits use of parent's voting stock by acquiring subsidiary); Regs. §1.368-2(j)(7), Examples (4) and (5) (same).

[74] For discussion of the 80 percent control requirement, see supra ¶ 3.07; on the meaning of "immediately after" the acquisition, see the similar language in §351 (supra ¶ 3.09). For the effect on the control requirement of a contemporaneous redemption by the acquired corporation of one class of its outstanding stock (callable preferred), see Rev. Rul. 55-440, 1955-2 CB 226 (redeemed stock excluded in computing control); see also Rev. Rul. 76-223, 1976-1 CB 103 (threshold amendment of charter to give vote to nonvoting preferred so as to allow acquiring corporation to get 80 percent control of voting stock without acquiring the preferred; held valid Type B reorganization). The attribution rules of §318 do not apply in determining control in this context, Rev. Rul. 56-613, 1956-2 CB 212.

[75] For the meaning of "voting stock," see Forrest Hotel Corp. v. Fly, 112 F. Supp. 782, 789 (S.D. Miss. 1953) (common stock that could not vote at the time of the transaction because of arrearages on the preferred stock; held voting stock; preferred stock that was voting because of the arrearages also voting stock); Firestone Tire & Rubber Co., 2 TC 827 (1943) (acq.) (treasury stock held to be voting stock); Helvering v. Southwest Consol. Corp., supra note 33 (warrants not voting stock); Rev. Rul. 69-91, 1969-1 CB 106 (convertible debentures not voting stock); Rev. Rul. 66-339, 1966-2 CB 274 (voting agreement rights, warrants, options, stock rights, convertible debentures, and similar rights to purchase voting stock acquired in connection with a loan agreement; held not voting securities).

See also Rev. Rul. 70-108, 1970-1 CB 78 (convertible preferred stock with right to buy additional stock disqualified as equivalent to warrants); Rev. Rul. 71-83,

Although the voting stock may be either common or preferred, there apparently is scant room to maneuver in a Type B reorganization. The Supreme Court has said that the statutory phrase "solely for voting stock" leaves no leeway, not even for warrants to purchase additional voting stock of the acquiring corporation; this strict view has been applied in a number of cases.[76] Although the statutory requirement as thus interpreted assures that a continuity of interest will exist in a Type B reorganization, it has the effect of disqualifying an exchange if an inconsequential amount of boot is used. Moreover, unless a business purpose exception is to be added, it permits taxpayers to avoid tax-free status (e.g., so a loss will be recognized) almost at will (i.e., by larding an otherwise qualified Type B exchange with a little boot).[77]

1971-1 CB 268 (cumulative, nonvoting, convertible preferred stock not voting stock for purposes of the voting power computations with respect to consolidated return filing qualification under §1504); Everett v. US, 448 F2d 357 (10th Cir. 1971) (hybrid equity interests in federal savings and loan association; held voting stock; see, however, Paulsen v. CIR, supra note 27); Rev. Rul. 75-33, 1975-1 CB 115 (voting preferred with contingent right to additional cash dividends; held voting stock); Rev. Rul. 72-72, 1972-1 CB 104 (shareholder of acquiring corporation had irrevocable right to vote stock for five years; treated in hands of owner as nonvoting stock automatically convertible into voting stock after five years); compare Rev. Rul. 73-28, 1973-1 CB 187 (parent's acquisition of all stock of second-tier subsidiary from first-tier subsidiary in exchange for parent's voting stock a valid Type B reorganization, even though stock of parent could not be voted by subsidiary under local law).

See generally Dailey, The Voting Stock Requirement of B and C Reorganizations, 26 Tax L. Rev. 725 (1971).

[76] See Helvering v. Southwest Consol. Corp., supra note 33; see also Mills v. CIR, 39 TC 393 (1962) (no de minimis rule applicable to "solely"), rev'd on other grounds, 331 F2d 321 (5th Cir. 1964); Turnbow v. CIR, 286 F2d 669 (9th Cir.), aff'd on other issues, 368 US 337 (1961); infra ¶ 14.34, for discussion of related aspects of *Turnbow*.

See generally Rev. Rul. 75-123, 1975-1 CB 115, where the Service, following its longstanding practice, ruled that the purchase of 20 percent of the acquired corporation's stock for cash would destroy a Type B reorganization if it was part of the same transaction in which 80 percent is acquired for voting stock. Contra were the lower court decisions in *Graham Reeves* and *Pierson*, supra note 46, both of which, however, were reversed on appeal, id. and infra notes 78–81.

See also Vernava, The Howard and Turnbow Cases and the "Solely" Requirement of B Reorganizations, 20 Tax L. Rev. 387 (1965); Kanter, Cash in a "B" Reorganization: Effect of Cash Purchases on "Creeping" Reorganization, 19 Tax L. Rev. 441 (1964). For proposals to amend the definition of a Type B reorganization to permit the use of additional consideration, see Greene, supra note 10; XVIII ABA Tax Section Bull., No. 4 (July 1965).

[77] With the latter possibility, compare the fact that the receipt of boot in an otherwise tax-free exchange does not ordinarily permit a realized loss to be recognized (e.g., §351(b), §356(c)).

Judicial acceptance of *Southwest Consolidated*'s dictum that solely means solely was temporarily interrupted by a narrowly divided Tax Court decision in *C.E. Graham Reeves* where a plurality of six judges held that cash paid in a Type B reorganization did not per se violate the statute if the requisite 80 percent control was acquired in one transaction solely for voting stock.[78] The exchange in *Reeves* was held to satisfy this test, regardless of *prior* cash purchases by the acquiring corporation of 8 percent of the target company's shares (which purchases the court held to be irrelevant for this purpose). The plurality opinion's test for §368(a)(1)(B) was a narrow one, however, since the transaction in which the 80 percent stock control was acquired had to be one in which only voting stock was paid as consideration. Two concurring judges would have gone even further and allowed payment of up to 20 percent cash in the same transaction as the stock for stock control acquisition transaction (a view that was subsequently adopted by a Delaware district court decision in the same case[79]). Five judges dissented in *Reeves*, however, stating that the weight of precedent required a decision for the government on the "solely" question and that the majority's view created too much uncertainty in an area that had long been considered to be well settled; this view prevailed in the initial appeals,[80] before the case was ultimately settled.[81]

---

[78] C.E. Graham Reeves, supra note 46.

[79] Pierson v. US, supra note 46. The district court judge found the prior precedents to be either readily distinguishable or at best unpersuasive; instead, after analyzing the prior legislative history (which was found to be inconclusive) and the congressional policies of the reorganization provisions, payment of some cash in a Type B reorganization was held to be permissible under the existing statutory scheme. The government's inability to articulate any policy reason, save the literal language of §368(a)(1)(B), for taxing the transaction in the *Reeves* and *Pierson* decisions, seemed to strongly influence the majority judges in *Reeves* and the judge in *Pierson*.

[80] One of the principal effects of the lower court *Reeves* and *Pierson* decisions would be to ease the definitional pressures on the Type B provisions in the situations discussed infra in paras. 1–7. But in the appeals from these decisions, supra note 46, the lower court position was reversed, largely on the grounds of Judge Wilbur's dissent in *Reeves* that stare decisis was too well established on this question to tolerate any new judicial departures.

[81] The case was settled in May, 1981 upon payment by ITT of $18.5 million; the shareholders obtained tax-free exchange treatment if they treated basis consistently and were not deemed to have received additional income as a result of ITT's payment. In short, the "litigation" was settled, but the "law" is not.

See generally Silverman & Trow, Cash Consideration in a "B" Reorganization: Where Are *Reeves* and *Pierson* Taking Us? 51 J. Tax'n 2 (1979); Romano, Comment, The "Solely for Voting Stock" Requirement of B Reorganizations: Reeves v. Comm'r, 79 Colum. L. Rev. 774 (1979); Steines, Policy Considerations in the Taxation of B Reorganizations, 31 Hastings L.J. 993 (1980); Note, The "Solely for Voting Stock" Requirement in a (B) Reorganization After *Reeves v. Commissioner* and *Pier-*

Before 1954, the statutory language seemed to require that at least 80 percent of the acquired corporation's stock be acquired in the reorganization exchange itself. Hence, it was generally assumed that a corporation that had acquired over 20 percent of another corporation's stock in an unrelated prior transaction could not use a Type B reorganization to increase its ownership to 80 percent or more.[82] A 1954 change in the language of §368(a)(1)(B) makes it clear that control need not be obtained in one fell swoop, and that a creeping acquisition of control can qualify as well as an increase in ownership by a corporation that already has control. For example, if Y Corporation, in four successive and separate transactions, acquired (solely for its voting stock) 40 percent, 30 percent, 20 percent, and finally 10 percent of the stock of X Corporation, the last two acquisitions would qualify as Type B reorganizations under the amended definition, although the first two would not.

The 1954 change was not without its difficulties, however, mainly because the term "acquisition" is not defined. Thus, if the acquiring corporation purchases 50 percent of the stock of another corporation in January for cash and exchanges its voting stock for the rest of the stock in July, has it engaged in a single transaction that fails to qualify because it was not solely for voting stock or were there two separate acquisitions, one of which was an ordinary purchase and the other a Type B reorganization? The regulations permit a prior cash purchase to be disregarded if it was independent of the stock-for-stock exchange; conversely, stock-for-stock acquisitions in a series are to be aggregated if they occur "over a relatively short period of time such as 12 months."[83] This problem is especially troublesome in tender offer

---

son v. United States, 66 Va. L. Rev. 133 (1980); Fissel, Case Comment, Reeves v. Commissioner, 71 TC 727 (1979), 48 U. Cin. L. Rev. 1058 (1979); Thompson, Qualifying as a "B" Reorganization: The ITT-Hartford Cases: Alternatives to Use of a "B," 39 NYU Inst. on Fed. Tax'n ch 7 (1981); and McMahon, Defining the "Acquisition" in B Reorganizations Through the Step Transaction Doctrine, 67 Iowa L. Rev. 31 (1981).

[82] See Lutkins v. US, 312 F2d 803 (Ct. Cl.), cert. denied, 375 US 825 (1963); Kanter and Vernava, supra note 76.

[83] See Regs. §1.368-2(c), echoing the language of S. Rep. No. 1622, 83d Cong., 2d Sess. 273 (1954); see generally McDonald & Willard, supra note 10, at 871–876; American Potash & Chem. Corp. v. US; supra note 56; King Enters., Inc. v. US; supra note 67; supra ¶ 14.12; infra ¶ 14.53.

See also Rev. Rul. 69-585, 1969-2 CB 56 (valid Type B where corporation acquired 25 percent of the stock as a dividend in kind from wholly owned subsidiary); Rev. Rul. 72-354, 1972-2 CB 216 (can purge purchased stock of its taint by unconditional sale to unrelated buyer prior to offer to acquire balance of stock in exchange for acquiring corporation's stock).

See generally McMahon, supra note 81, on defining "the acquisition" for purposes of the Type B definition; and Henry, The Impact of Reeves v. Comm'r on the

acquisitions if the first step was effected for cash and the parties then want to complete the acquisition on a tax-free basis.

It should be noted that the definition of a Type B reorganization apparently focuses solely on the consideration paid by the acquiring corporation in exchange for the stock of the acquired corporation. Other consideration presumably can be paid by the acquiring company for debt instruments of the acquired corporation and for other properties owned by the acquired corporation or its shareholders if such payments are not made directly or indirectly for the acquired corporation's *stock*.[84] For example, it would seem that a Type B reorganization would not be affected by the fact that the acquiring corporation also (1) purchased the acquired corporation's debt securities or other property for cash; (2) paid off the acquired corporation's liabilities or assumed its indebtedness; (3) loaned money to the acquired corporation; (4) paid cash or other consideration to shareholders of the acquired corporation in a capacity other than their status as shareholders (e.g., as employees or creditors); or (5) purchased other assets owned individually by the shareholders.[85]

Creeping Control "B" Reorganization: The Need for Legislative Reexamination of Section 368(a)(1)(B), 10 J. Corp. Tax'n 195 (1983).

[84] See Arthur D. McDonald, 52 TC 82 (1969) (dominant shareholder of acquired corporation exchanged his common solely for voting stock of acquired corporation and redeemed his preferred out of funds supplied to acquired corporation indirectly by acquiring corporation pursuant to single plan; government counsel conceded that exchange of common was a Type B reorganization). But in Rev. Rul. 75-360, 1975-2 CB 110, the Service reversed its position in *McDonald*, stating that it should not have argued the redemption question but instead should have attacked the Type B reorganization because of the indirect payment of cash by the acquiring corporation.

[85] See Rev. Rul. 69-91, 1969-1 CB 106 (purchase of convertible debentures of acquired corporation; held not part of stock-for-stock exchange); Rev. Rul. 69-142, 1969-1 CB 107 (exchange of debentures of acquiring corporation for debentures of acquired corporation, held predominantly by nonshareholder creditors, did not affect tax-free reorganization status of stock-for-stock exchange); Rev. Rul. 70-41, 1970-1 CB 77 (acquisition of debt securities in exchange for voting stock; held severable from stock-for-stock exchange; but debt-for-stock exchange taxable); Rev. Rul. 70-269, 1970-1 CB 82 (substitution of acquiring corporation's stock options for those of acquired corporation; held severable from stock-for-stock Type B reorganization exchange); Rev. Rul. 78-408, 1978-2 CB 203 (warrants for warrants separate taxable exchange); J. Robert Fisher, 62 TC 73 (1974) (stock received in lieu of cash dividends on shares acquired in exchange for taxpayer's stock in Type B reorganization; held taxable as a stock dividend under §305(b)(1) and severable from Type B reorganization). But cf. Regs. §1.368-2(j)(5) (in reverse mergers, §354 applies to liability assumption exchanges).

See also Rev. Rul. 72-343, 1972-2 CB 213 (interim financing of target company by acquiring company in connection with pending merger; held taxable boot paid as part consideration for assets); compare Rev. Rul. 72-522, 1972-2 CB 215 (acquiring corporation acquired all of target company's stock from its shareholders solely for

A final point: Although a Type B reorganization ordinarily is effected by exchanges between the shareholders of the acquired corporation and the acquiring corporation, this need not be the case; for example, the acquiring corporation can obtain the requisite 80 percent control by issuing its voting stock to the acquired corporation in exchange for its newly issued stock or treasury stock, in which event the transaction would qualify as a §351 exchange (see Chapter 3) as well as a Type B reorganization.[86]

The other principal problems that arise in Type B reorganizations, stemming mainly from the solely for voting stock requirement, are discussed immediately below.

1. Minority or dissenting shares. Where stock of the acquired corporation is widely held, some of its shareholders may be unwilling to accept the acquiring corporation's stock and will insist on a cash payment for their shares. It is clear that the acquiring corporation cannot, directly or indirectly, make such a payment as part of the plan without the risk of destroying Type B reorganization status.[87] It is apparently permissible, however, for the acquired corporation to redeem the stock of these shareholders for cash

---

voting stock, but as part of the plan it also purchased additional stock directly from the target company for cash, none of which went to shareholders of the acquired corporation; held valid Type B reorganization because cash purchase severable from stock-for-stock exchange).

[86] See Rev. Rul. 70-433, 1970-1 CB 82 (§351 treatment allowed to avoid necessity for §367 ruling when transaction also a Type B reorganization); see also Rev. Rul. 79-274, 1979-2 CB 131 (overlap of B reorganization and §351; voting preferred received pro rata can be "section 306 stock" if transferee has earnings for its first year); for analysis, see Corry, Preferred Stock Issued in Tax-Free Exchanges: Does Section 306 Apply? 35 Tax L. Rev. 113 (1979). But see §306(c)(3), added by the Tax Equity and Fiscal Responsibility Act of 1982.

[87] If the requisite 80 percent can be obtained in a stock-for-stock transaction, however, it would not be infected by a later purchase of additional shares for cash if the two transactions are clearly separable. Nor would the reorganization be infected if the dissenters are willing to accept the acquiring corporation's shares but are later redeemed out by the latter, provided the redemption is not part of the original plan of reorganization. See Rev. Rul. 56-345, 1956-2 CB 206; Rev. Rul. 57-114, 1957-1 CB 122.

As to simultaneous transactions, it has been suggested that an acquisition of 80 percent of the acquired corporation's stock for voting stock and of part or all of the remaining 20 percent for cash would be consistent with §368(a)(1)(B). This theory is not easily reconciled with the cases cited supra note 76. See also §368(a)(2)(E) (infra ¶ 14.15); Rev. Rul. 75-123, 1975-1 CB 115, which specifically rejects this view. See generally supra notes 78–81.

See also Rev. Rul. 73-102, 1973-1 CB 186 (acquiring corporation's assumption and payment of acquired corporation's liability to pay dissenters in a Type C reorganization; held boot rather than liability assumption, because liability created in the reorganization).

or other property or for persons interested in effectuating the transaction to buy them out without infecting the Type B reorganization.[88]

2. Fractional shares. The exchange ratio in stock-for-stock acquisitions often gives the shareholders of the acquired corporation the right to receive fractional shares of the acquiring corporation. The issuance of fractional shares or of "scrip" evidencing such rights does not violate the solely for voting stock requirement.[89] To avoid the distribution of fractional shares, however, the acquiring corporation often makes arrangements with a bank under which a shareholder can purchase an additional fraction to make up a full share or, alternatively, sell his fractional interest. The Service does not regard such arrangements as constituting additional consideration in violation of the solely for voting stock requirement.[90]

3. Payment or assumption of liabilities. Unlike §368(a)((1)(C), which explicitly refers to the assumption of the acquired corporation's liabilities, §368(a)(1)(B) makes no mention of liabilities. In most Type B reorganizations, there is no need for any action with regard to the acquired corporation's liabilities, since its creditors simply ride through the reorganization, preserving their claims against the debtor despite the change in ownership of

---

[88] See Hoboken Land & Improvement Co. v. CIR, 138 F2d 104 (3d Cir. 1943); Howard v. CIR, 238 F2d 943 (7th Cir. 1956); San Antonio Transit Co., supra note 34; Rev. Rul. 55-440, 1955-2 CB 226; Rev. Rul. 56-184, 1956-1 CB 190; Rev. Rul. 68-285, 1968-1 CB 147 (valid Type B reorganization where acquired corporation paid dissenting shareholders from escrow account, even though payments made after stock exchanges); see also Rev. Rul. 79-100, 1979-1 CB 152 (shareholder-level stock purchases not boot; directors' qualifying shares in bank purchased by new directors per grant of nonassignable option); Rev. Rul. 68-562, 1968-2 CB 157 (valid Type B reorganization, even though majority shareholder of acquiring corporation purchased 50 percent of acquired corporation's stock before the reorganization in his individual capacity).

Compare Rev. Rul. 85-139, 1985-2 CB 123 (payment of cash by subsidiary of acquiring parent violated "solely" rule; thus, parent can pay for child under Rev. Rul. 68-562, but not vice versa).

See generally Kringel, Preventing a Dissenting Shareholder From Destroying a Tax-Free Reorganization, 31 J. Tax'n 138 (1969).

[89] See Rev. Rul. 55-59, 1955-1 CB 35.

[90] See Rev. Rul. 66-365, 1966-2 CB 116 (cash in lieu of fractional shares does not violate the "solely" requirement in Type B and C reorganizations if not bargained for as separate consideration); see also Mills v. CIR, supra note 76 (cash in lieu of fractional shares is not additional consideration); Rubenfeld, Handle Expenses, Fractional Shares, Escrows in Reorganization With Great Care, 15 J. Tax'n 66 (1961); Vernava, supra note 76, at 397, 413–415; Goldman, The C Reorganization, 19 Tax L. Rev. 31, 55, 61, 73 (1973).

its stock.[91] If the acquiring corporation prefers to assume or refund these obligations, however, the solely for voting stock requirement of §368(a)(1)(B) will be violated if the payment or assumption of the liabilities constitutes the payment of additional boot under the *Hendler* case.[92] It is arguable that any relations between the acquiring corporation and the acquired corporation's creditors are separable from the stock-for-stock transaction and that the assumption or payment of such liabilities is not additional consideration for the acquired stock, and the Service generally agrees with this view.[93] As assumption or payment of a shareholder's liabilities, on the other hand, would be vulnerable, since such action would ordinarily constitute additional payment for the stock.[94]

4. Employment agreements. Consideration paid by the acquiring corporation to shareholder-employees of the acquired corporation is currently taxable to the recipients, either as compensation income (if the payment is severable from the stock acquisition transaction) or as part of the selling price for the transferred stock. In the latter event, however, the entire transaction would be taxable if the consideration consisted of anything other than voting stock of the acquiring corporation.[95]

---

[91] If the acquired corporation is insolvent, however, its creditors may be in effect the sole owners of the proprietary interest therein, so that the acquisition of their claims for voting stock of the acquiring corporation is a Type B reorganization. See Rev. Rul. 59-222, 1959-1 CB 80.

[92] See supra ¶ 14.11, para. 2; infra ¶ 14.55; §357 does not cover this situation; see Rev. Rul. 73-102, 1973-1 CB 186; Rev. Rul. 73-54, 1973-1 CB 187; see also Rev. Rul. 79-4, 1979-1 CB 150 (acquiring corporation's payment of shareholder-guarantor's debt held boot; shareholder treated as true debtor, not mere guarantor of target corporation's debt). Compare Rev. Rul. 79-89, 1979-1 CB 152 (acquiring corporation's contribution of cash to target to enable it to pay debt guaranteed by shareholder not boot).

[93] The tax treatment of the creditors and the debtor corporation in such a case is unsettled; see Rev. Rul. 59-222, 1959-1 CB 80; supra note 85.
    See also Rev. Rul. 69-142, 1969-1 CB 107; Rev. Rul. 70-41, 1970-1 CB 77.

[94] See Rev. Rul. 70-65, 1970-1 CB 77 (assumption of one shareholder's liabilities inconsistent with Type B reorganization, even though the transaction qualified as a Type C reorganization for the corporate shareholder whose liabilities were assumed); Rev. Rul. 73-54, 1973-1 CB 187; Rev. Rul. 79-4, 1979-1 CB 150 (shareholder-guarantor held true debtor under debt-equity analysis principles so that acquiring corporation's discharge of such debt ruled boot to shareholder). Compare Rev. Rul. 79-89, 1979-1 CB 150 (acquiring corporation's contribution of cash to acquired corporation to enable it to pay off debt guaranteed by one of the two shareholders not boot).

[95] See Rev. Rul. 77-271, 1977-2 CB 116 (stock exchanged for stock of equivalent value in Type B reorganization held tax-free, while additional stock paid for services held separate from reorganization transaction and taxable as compensation under

5. Expenses. Although it is evidently the Service's practice to rule
that stock transfer taxes in a Type B exchange can be paid by the acquiring corporation on the theory that it is jointly liable therefor and hence is
not paying any additional consideration to the shareholders of the
acquired corporation, rulings often explicitly require the shareholders to
pay their own share of the reorganization expenses (e.g., attorneys' fees,
accounting expenses, commissions).[96] There seems to be scant authority
on the proper allocation of reorganization expenses for this purpose, however, and in practice it is often assumed that the shareholders are more or
less passive participants who incur no expenses unless they employ independent counsel, financial advisers, or otherwise intervene in the reorganization process.[97]

A once troublesome question—whether an agreement by the acquiring
corporation to bear the costs of registering the transferred stock with the
SEC constitutes forbidden additional consideration to the transferees of the
stock—was laid to rest by a published ruling, which states that these
expenses are properly borne by the acquiring corporation because they serve
to promote the orderly marketing of its stock[98] (a theory that would seem to
cover successive registration costs as well). The Service issued a comprehensive ruling on the treatment of reorganization expenses in 1973.[99]

---

§61); see also Jack F. Morrison, 59 TC 248 (1972) (acq.) (stock options issued to
shareholder-employees of acquired corporation in merger held compensatory and
taxable as ordinary income when issued because options although not traded had
readily ascertainable fair market value).

[96] See Rubenfeld, supra note 90.
As to whose expenses are whose in a reorganization, see supra ¶ 5.06.

[97] Rev. Rul. 75-421, 1975-2 CB 108 (acquired corporation's payment of sole
shareholder's financial and accounting expenses incurred to determine value of his
stock for Type B reorganization exchange offer; held taxable dividend); Rev. Rul.
76-365, 1976-2 CB 110 (acquiring corporation's payment of acquired corporation's
expenses of evaluating acquiring corporation's offer and other competing offers not
boot for Type C reorganization purposes).

[98] Rev. Rul. 67-275, 1967-2 CB 142.

[99] Rev. Rul. 73-54, 1973-1 CB 187 holds that assumption and payment by the
acquiring corporation of the acquired corporation's share of the reorganization
expenses will not constitute boot in a Type B or C reorganization if the expenses
were solely and directly related to the reorganization (e.g., legal and accounting
expenses, appraisal fees, and administrative costs of the reorganization such as printing, clerical work, security underwriting and registration costs, transfer taxes, and
transfer agent's fees). "Unrelated" expenses, however, cannot be paid by the acquiring corporation (e.g., investment and estate planning advice to shareholders, and
shareholder expenses for advice as to participation in the reorganization). Also, payment of state transfer taxes will constitute boot if liability is solely that of shareholders; moreover, payment of cash for use by the acquired corporation to pay expenses
will also constitute boot. See also Rev. Rul. 76-365, 1976-2 CB 142.

6. Transfer of additional shares. The number of shares to be paid by the acquiring corporation in a Type B exchange is sometimes contingent on future events (e.g., the settlement of a disputed claim against the acquired corporation or the level of its earnings); and shares may be put in escrow pending a determination of the transferor shareholders' right to receive them. The Service evidently concedes that this contingent right to receive additional shares does not violate the solely for voting stock requirement (unless evidenced by a negotiable instrument), but a portion of the shares, if and when received by the shareholder, may give rise to imputed interest income under §483. [100]

7. Contemporaneous dividends. The Service generally has permitted the acquired corporation to pay regular (and in some cases irregular) dividends on its stock more or less contemporaneously with the tax-free acquisition of its shares if the funds are not supplied directly or indirectly by the acquiring corporation. [101] By the same token, the payment of contemporaneous dividends by the acquiring corporation in the ordinary course to its shareholders should not be treated as disguised boot even though its new shareholders participate. A disguised boot problem could arise, however, if the distributions flow from the acquiring corporation to shareholders of the acquired corporation in disproportionate or unusual amounts.

8. Overlap problems. If a Type B stock-for-stock acquisition is followed by a prearranged liquidation of the newly acquired subsidiary corporation, these steps have substantially the same effect as a Type A statutory merger or a Type C acquisition of assets for voting stock. Since the stock acquisition is merely an interdependent step in a single plan to obtain the assets of the acquired corporation, it has been held that the transaction constitutes a Type C rather than a Type B reorganization. [102] The principal points at

---

[100] See generally infra ¶¶ 14.31 and 14.56.

[101] See Rev. Rul 68-435, 1968-2 CB 155; Rev. Rul. 69-443, 1969-2 CB 54; Rev. Rul. 70-172, 1970-1 CB 77; supra ¶ 7.07; Arthur D. McDonald, supra note 84; Rev. Rul. 75-360, 1975-2 CB 110.

[102] See CIR v. Dana, 103 F2d 359 (3d Cir. 1939); Goldman, supra note 90; see also Regs. §1.382(b)-1(a)(6). This approach is reminiscent of the *Kimbell-Diamond* doctrine (supra ¶ 11.44). As to the acquiring corporation, the liquidation of its newly acquired subsidiary would be tax-free under §332 (supra ¶ 11.40). But compare Rev. Rul. 74-35, 1974-1 CB 85 (distribution of unwanted investment assets, 30 percent of total assets, after stock acquisition did not taint tax-free status of Type B reorganization).

See generally South Bay Corp. v. CIR, 345 F2d 698 (2d Cir. 1965); Long Island Water Corp., supra note 70; Rev. Rul. 67-274, 1967-2 CB 141, specifically holding that such a transaction is, in substance, a Type C reorganization where plan exists to

which this difference is felt are (1) a limited amount of consideration other than voting stock can be used in a Type C reorganization, and there is explicit authority to assume the acquired corporation's liabilities, but (2) creeping acquisitions are not permitted. The Types B and C definitions also overlap when a holding corporation whose assets consist entirely of stock of a subsidiary transfers the stock to another corporation solely in exchange for the latter's voting stock. The regulations suggest that this would constitute a Type C reorganization. [103]

It should also be noted that a Type B reorganization may occur in the context of other reorganization transactions (e.g., where a corporation changes its domicile to a different state (in a Type F reorganization) and concurrently acquires the outstanding interests in a partially owned subsidiary in a stock-for-stock exchange. [104] Similarly, as previously stated, a Type B reorganization may also qualify as a §351 transaction if the acquiring corporation exchanges its voting stock directly with the acquired corporation and thereby obtains 80 percent control of the latter. [105]

---

liquidate newly acquired subsidiary following acquisition of its stock; see also American Potash & Chem. Corp. v. US, supra note 56; King Enterprises, Inc. v. US, supra note 67; infra ¶ 14.53.

For a decision applying Rev. Rul. 67-274, see Resorts Int'l, Inc., 60 TC 778 (1973), modified, 511 F2d 107 (5th Cir. 1975); Rev. Rul. 76-123, 1976-1 CB 94 (same in context of concurrent §351 exchange with another transferor; two shareholders transferred all the stock of their respective companies to a new corporation for its stock, after which one of the acquired corporations was liquidated into its new parent; ruling recharacterized stock acquisition-liquidation segment of transaction as an asset acquisition which qualified as a Type C reorganization).

[103] The suggestion arises by negative inference from Regs. §1.368-2(f) (last sentence): If P's stock was S's only asset, S would evidently be treated by the Service as a party to the reorganization, but this would be possible under §368(b)(2) only if the exchange is regarded as a Type C reorganization (i.e., "a reorganization resulting from the acquisition by one corporation of stock or properties of another").

See also Rev. Rul. 70-65, 1970-1 CB 77.

[104] See Dunlap & Assocs., supra note 56 (combination of Type B reorganization with Type A and/or F reorganization; reincorporation in new state followed by acquisition of minority interests in subsidiaries of old corporation). But cf. Bercy Indus., Inc., 70 TC 29 (1978), rev'd, 640 F2d 1058 (9th Cir. 1981) (triangular forward merger into shell subsidiary of acquiring corporation sufficient to allow postmerger carry-backs despite §381(b)(3); transaction not a Type F and no opinion as to whether it was a Type B, although court seemed to view it as the functional equivalent of a Type B). See §368(a)(1)(F), as amended by Tax Equity and Fiscal Responsibility Act of 1982, (Type F limited to single operating company), infra ¶ 14.18, para. 4.

[105] Rev. Rul. 70-433, 1970-1 CB 82. The result may create an identity crisis in determining which corporation acquired which; the answer to this question would not affect the tax-free status of the exchange of stock, but basis, holding period, and

At times, taxpayers are tempted to use a stock-for-stock Type B reorganization to accomplish indirectly what cannot be achieved directly through a Type A or C assets-for-stock reorganization (i.e., to exchange property (e.g., an unincorporated business) for stock on a tax-free basis by putting the property into a controlled corporate entity and then exchanging its stock for voting stock of the acquiring corporation). Although the transaction literally qualifies as a Type B reorganization, even a casual student of the step-transaction doctrine would refuse to insure such a device, especially if the newly created corporation is promptly put to death by the acquiring corporation after it obtains the stock. The Service will almost certainly recharacterize the transaction as a taxable exchange of *assets* for stock, and, unless the initial incorporation step is old and cold, this attack will be upheld. [106]

The extensive amendments to the stock dividend rules by the Tax Reform Act of 1969 (see Chapter 7) may cause collateral difficulties in some of the fancier forms of Type B reorganizations, such as those involving the delayed issuance of stock or the issuance of convertible equity securities with variable conversion ratios. As a general rule, however, an acquisitive reorganization exchange of stock for stock is functionally distinguishable from the transactions governed by the §305 rules, and the tax-free character of the reorganization should not be affected by these provisions. [107] Post-reorganization changes in the relative equity interests of the acquiring corporation's shareholders stemming from the terms of the stock used in the acquisition can run afoul of these new constructive stock dividend rules, however, and

---

the carry-over of corporate tax attributes are another matter, for which see infra ¶ 14.53.

See also Rev. Rul. 79-274, 1979-2 CB 113 (overlap of §351 and B reorganization; voting preferred issued pro rata as "section 306 stock"); for analysis of Rev. Rul. 79-274, see Corry, supra note 86; §306(c)(3), added by Tax Equity and Fiscal Responsibility Act of 1982, supra note 86.

[106] See West Coast Marketing Corp., 46 TC 32 (1966) (held a taxable exchange of assets for stock); Rev. Rul. 70-140, 1970-1 CB 73 (same, even though acquired corporation was not liquidated by the acquiring corporation); see also Rev. Rul. 70-225, 1970-1 CB 80; infra ¶ 14.52; supra ¶ 11.07 (*Court Holding Co.* doctrine). But see Maurice Weikel, ¶ 86,858 P-H Memo. TC (1986) (steps separate).

For discussion of the tax efficacy of such threshold §351 transactions to set the stage for later exchanges of stock, see supra ¶ 3.14.

Rev. Rul. 70-434, 1970-2 CB 83, approved a Type B reorganization, however, where unwanted assets first were distributed in a preliminary spin-off, and stock of the distributing corporation then was exchanged for stock of the acquiring corporation.

[107] Regs. §1.305-1(c) makes clear the statement in the text that acquisitive reorganizations with adjustable price terms are not within the purview of the §305 stock dividend rules; Rev. Rul. 82-158, 1982-2 CB 70; supra ¶ 7.43.

this possibility should be considered before adopting separate classes of stock through issuance of a hybrid form of acquisition currency.

¶ 14.14 ACQUISITIONS OF PROPERTY FOR VOTING STOCK (TYPE C)

A Type C reorganization, as defined by §368(a)(1)(C), is an acquisition by one corporation (the acquiring corporation) of substantially all the properties of another corporation in exchange solely for voting stock of the acquiring corporation or its parent or in exchange for such voting stock and a limited amount of money or other property. Although there are differences in form, a Type C reorganization may have economic consequences substantially the same as Type A (statutory merger or consolidation),[108] but the statute lays down more explicit rules for the Type C reorganization—notably, the fact that the consideration must be voting stock plus, in some instances, a limited amount of money or other property. Type C also has consequences similar to a Type B reorganization (stock-for-stock) followed by a liquidation of the acquired corporation but is slightly more flexible in allowing a limited amount of consideration to be used in addition to voting stock.[109] The salient features of §368(a)(1)(C) are the following:

(1) The acquiring corporation must acquire substantially all of the properties of another corporation.

(2) The acquisition must be either solely for voting stock of the acquiring corporation or its parent or solely for such voting stock plus, if certain conditions are met, a limited amount of money or other property.

(3) The acquiring corporation may transfer part or all of the acquired assets to a corporation controlled by it.

(4) As a result of an amendment in 1984, the transferor must liquidate under the plan, unless the Service waives this requirement.

---

[108] See William H. George, 26 TC 396 (1956) (acq.) (involving amalgamation of a Louisiana corporation and a Mississippi corporation into a new Louisiana corporation that was not a statutory consolidation (Type A) because of state law restricting the consolidation of domestic and foreign corporations; held, however, that transaction was a Type C reorganization); see also Rev. Rul. 56-345, 1956-2 CB 206, referring to a §368(a)(1)(C) reorganization as a practical merger.

[109] On the treatment of transactions that could qualify as either Type B or C exchanges, see supra note 102.

(5) If a transaction meets the requirements of a Type C reorganization but is also described in §368(a)(1)(D) (Type D), it is to be treated as a Type D reorganization.

These requirements are discussed in more detail hereafter.[110]

1. Acquisition of substantially all the properties of another corporation. The acquiring corporation must, under §368(a)(1)(C), acquire substantially all of the properties of another corporation. In many instances, the acquiring corporation takes over all of the transferor corporation's assets, without exception, and no problem arises in determining what constitutes "substantially all of the properties." When it becomes necessary to make this determination because the acquiring corporation does not take over all of the assets, it should be remembered that the Type C reorganization was made tax-free to accommodate transactions that had the effect of mergers but could not qualify under §368(a)(1)(A) because, for some business reason, a statutory merger or consolidation was not feasible. In the light of this history, transactions should not be allowed to qualify as Type C exchanges if they are essentially divisive in character; their proper route is a Type D transaction, which contains restrictions to prevent an end run around §355. Type C transactions, by contrast, should exhibit merger equivalence.

Although *CIR v. First National Bank of Altoona*[111] is frequently cited as establishing that 86 percent of total net worth is "substantially all" and *Arctic Ice Machine v. CIR*[112] as establishing that 68 percent is insufficient, a ruling espouses the sounder view that no particular percentage is controlling. Instead, "the nature of the properties retained by the transferor, the purpose of retention, and the amount thereof" are all to be considered; the ruling approved of a retention of cash, accounts receivable, notes, and 3 percent of total inventory, the aggregate value of which was approximately equal to the corporation's liabilities, even though the retained assets amounted (according to the headnote) to 30 percent of the total assets.[113] As a general rule, the

---

[110] See generally Goldman, supra note 90.

[111] CIR v. First Nat'l Bank of Altoona, 104 F2d 865 (3d Cir. 1939), cert. dismissed, 309 US 691 (1940).

[112] Arctic Ice Mach. Co. v. CIR, 23 BTA 1223 (1931).

[113] See Rev. Rul. 57-518, 1957-2 CB 253; see also Milton Smith, 34 BTA 702 (1936) (acq.); Cortland Specialty Co. v. CIR, supra note 14 (91 percent of net assets); Schuh Trading Co. v. CIR, 95 F2d 404 (7th Cir. 1938) (90.94 percent substantially all).

See Rev. Proc. 77-37, 1977-2 CB 586 (for ruling purposes, the transfer of 70 percent of gross assets and 90 percent of net assets will be deemed substantially all, but must consider "linked" threshold distributions).

percentages of transferred and retained assets are computed by reference to values net of liabilities rather than gross values.

Where the transferor continued in existence after the transfer (as it was entitled to do in a Type C reorganization until the 1984 amendment[114]) and operating assets were retained, either for the purpose of continuing in business or for sale to another purchaser, the substantially all requirement apparently was applied more strictly. Thus, the Service expressly noted in Rev. Rul. 57-518 that assets could be retained only to pay unassumed liabilities and that any other use (such as sale, investment, or business conduct) might be fatal.[115] The ruling also warned that operating assets could not be retained for the purpose of continuing in business, even though such assets were matched by liabilities. The same caveat would be justified if investment assets were retained rather than business assets, in view of the possibility that this would create the possibility of achieving a divisive reorganization without running the gauntlet of §§355 and 368(a)(1)(D).[116] Moreover, it would also be appropriate to take account of the *value* of the retained assets as well as the percentage they represent of the total assets, since a $100 million corporation that transfers even 90 percent of its net assets in a putative Type C reorganization still retains a lot of life and should not automatically be deemed to satisfy the substantially all requirement of §368(a)(1)(C). However, legislation enacted in 1984 requires complete liquidation of the transferor corporation pursuant to the plan of reorganization unless regulations waive this requirement; in such a case, a complete liquidation will be deemed to have occurred.[117]

---

[114] See Helvering v. Minnesota Tea Co., supra note 16; John A. Nelson Co. v. Helvering, supra note 20; Rev. Rul. 68-358, 1968-2 CB 156 (continuation of transferor as a holding company did not affect Type C reorganization status); World Serv. Ins. Co. v. US, 471 F2d 247 (8th Cir. 1973) (not necessary for transferor to liquidate in Type C reorganization; §382(b) not violated by failure to liquidate); see also Rev. Rul. 73-552, 1973-2 CB 116 (holdback of insubstantial liquid assets did not break Type C reorganization, even though transferor intended to reenter active business; acquiring corporation's stock distributed to shareholders in exchange for part of transferor's stock; full carry-over of transferor's tax history under §381).

But legislation enacted in 1984 now requires the complete liquidation of the transferor pursuant to the plan of reorganization; §368(a)(2)(G), added by the Tax Reform Act of 1984 (effective on date of enactment, July 18, 1984). The complete liquidation requirement is waivable by regulations, but the parties will be treated as if the acquired corporation had in fact been liquidated in such a case. See infra para. 4.

[115] Rev. Rul. 57-518, 1957-2 CB 253.

[116] A point of similar import is that the transferor's tax attributes pass over to the transferee in a Type C reorganization by virtue of §381 (infra ch. 16, Part B), thus leaving the transferor with a clean slate in its earnings and profits account and other tax characteristics as well.

[117] Infra para. 4.

Retention of assets primarily for the purpose of paying off the unassumed liabilities of the transferor, including its reorganization or liquidation expenses, ordinarily is permissible; this transaction is no different in substance from the case where all assets are transferred subject to liabilities and the transferee then pays off the liabilities with part of the acquired assets.[118] Where liabilities are so large, however, that the net assets constitute only a small fraction of the corporation's gross assets, the continuity of interest principle may prevent qualification as a Type C reorganization on the ground that the shareholders' equity is so thin that the creditors in substance own the proprietary interest in the corporation.[119]

Where the transferor corporation is liquidated as part of the reorganization transaction as it must now be after legislation in 1984 (1), the courts were less rigorous in their application of the substantially all requirement, especially where the properties retained consist of nonoperating assets. See, for example, *James Armour, Inc.*, holding that 51 percent of the corporation's assets (consisting of all of its operating assets) was substantially all within the meaning of §354(b)(1)(A), where the retained liquid assets were distributed in complete liquidation as part of the plan,[120] and *Gross v. CIR*, suggesting that the term "properties" is narrower than "assets," and that it does not include surplus cash that is not needed in the business, could have been paid out as an ordinary cash dividend, and is subsequently distributed as a liquidating dividend pursuant to the reorganization plan.[121]

---

[118] See Rev. Rul. 57-518, 1957-2 CB 253; Rev. Rul. 56-345, 1956-2 CB 206; see also Roosevelt Hotel Co., 13 TC 399 (1949) (acq.); Southland Ice Co., 5 TC 842 (1945) (acq.); Westfir Lumber Co., 7 TC 1014 (1946) (acq.). These cases involved retention of assets to pay claims of dissenting bondholders in a creditor's reorganization; whether they would be equally applicable to claims of dissenting shareholders is unclear. Rev. Rul. 57-518 implies that a distribution to shareholders is not a proper purpose for retention of assets; but where the claims of dissenting shareholders become creditor claims under local law, satisfaction of such obligations may be acceptable, and certain private rulings have implicitly sanctioned the retention of assets to pay dissenting shareholders' claims. Compare the problem of retaining assets to pay claims under former §337, before its repeal in 1986 (supra ¶ 11.61); note also Regs. §1.354-1(a) (last sentence).

[119] See Rev. Rul. 57-518, 1957-2 CB 253; Civic Center Fin. Co. v. Kuhl, 83 F. Supp. 251 (E.D. Wis. 1948), aff'd per curiam, 177 F2d 706 (7th Cir. 1949); Regs. §1.368-2(d)(1); see also Helvering v. Alabama Asphaltic Limestone Co., supra note 34; Wortham Mach. Co. v. US, 521 F2d 160 (10th Cir. 1975) (purported Type C reorganization failed because of lack of business purpose and continuity); infra ¶ 14.55 and notes 130 and 131.

[120] James Armour, Inc., 43 TC 295 (1965).

[121] Gross v. CIR, 88 F2d 567 (5th Cir. 1937); see also CIR v. First Nat'l Bank of Altoona, supra note 111, for a similar case. But see National Bank of Commerce of Norfolk v. US, 158 F. Supp. 887 (E.D. Va. 1958) (retention of 19 percent of operating assets for distribution to shareholders fatal); Rev. Rul. 57-518, 1957-2 CB 253.

Whether the acquiring corporation has received substantially all the properties of the acquired corporation is ordinarily determined as of the time of the transfer. If the acquiring corporation is not interested in acquiring some of the assets, however, and the unwanted assets are disposed of by the transferor corporation in anticipation of the Type C reorganization transfer, the comparison may be made as of the time the plan was put into action, especially if the anticipatory disposition was tax-free (in which latter case a divisive transaction has occurred).[122]

These principles may be illustrated by the following examples, in which it is assumed that X Corporation's assets consist of operating assets worth $90 and liquid assets (cash, short-term receivables, and investments) worth $30. X Corporation also has $20 of liabilities, so that its net worth is $100.

Example 1. If X transfers its operating assets to Y, retaining the liquid assets to discharge its liabilities, the Service probably will rule that the substantially all requirement is satisfied, since the assets transferred amount to 90 percent of X's net worth.

Example 2. If Y assumes X's liabilities in the above example, the substantially all requirement may arguably not be met, since 30 percent of net assets have been retained; in general, a transfer of less than 90 per-

---

For other examples of the operating asset test, see American Mfg. Co., supra note 70; Ralph C. Wilson, 46 TC 334 (1966); Moffatt v. CIR, 363 F2d 262 (9th Cir. 1966), cert. denied, 386 US 1016 (1967); see also Rev. Rul. 78-47, 1978-1 CB 114 (substantially all test applied to business assets in downstream transfer); Smothers v. US, 642 F2d 894 (5th Cir. 1981) (necessary operating assets the benchmark for substantially all test). See infra ¶ 14.54.

[122] See, e.g., Helvering v. Elkhorn Coal Co., 95 F2d 732 (4th Cir. 1937), cert. denied, 305 US 605, reh'g denied, 305 US 670 (1938), where a prior tax-free spin-off of unwanted assets was considered by the court, in a rather extreme situation, in determining whether the taxpayer had transferred substantially all of its properties under the predecessor of §368(a)(1)(C); see also Mellon v. CIR, supra note 29; Ralph C. Wilson, supra note 121; Rev. Proc. 77-37, 1977-2 CB 568 (§3.01 states that threshold payments to dissenters, redemptions, and extraordinary dividends will be considered in applying the 90 percent and 70 percent guidelines if they are part of the plan of reorganization).

Rev. Rul. 74-457, 1974-2 CB 122, holds that cash used by an acquired corporation to pay its regular dividends before the Type C reorganization transfer of assets will not be taken into account for computation of the substantially all test; but if payment of the dividend occurs after the asset transfer, both the cash used to pay the dividend and the liability therefor will be considered in applying the substantially all test.

For further discussion of this issue, and for the possibility that stripping the corporation of unwanted assets may be permissible in Type A and B reorganizations, see infra ¶ 14.52

cent of the net assets is questionable (although here there has been a *transfer* of 90 percent; but due to liability assumptions, the *retention* effect bulks larger).[123]

Example 3. If *X*'s liabilities amounted to $100 rather than $20, the transfer of $20 of operating assets, even though constituting 100 percent of *X*'s net worth, arguably would not be considered substantially all. Either the continuity of interest principle or the substantial size of the retained assets (which consist of operating properties as well) could, and probably should, defeat Type C reorganization status in this case due to the transaction's lack of resemblance to a merger or consolidation.

2. Consideration paid by the acquiring corporation. The consideration that can be paid by the acquiring corporation in a Type C reorganization must consist primarily of its own voting stock.[124] There are, however, three exceptions to this rule: (1) Since 1954, voting stock of a corporation that is in control of the acquiring corporation (i.e., its parent) may be given as alternative consideration for the acquisition; (2) an assumption of the transferor's liabilities by the acquiring corporation (or the acquisition of the properties subject to liabilities) is disregarded in determining whether the acquisition is solely for voting stock; and (3) by virtue of §368(a)(2)(B) (added in 1954), a limited amount of consideration other than voting stock may be given.

In permitting the use of a parent corporation's voting stock and in providing in §368(b) that the parent thereby becomes a party to a reorganization, the intention of the 1954 revisions was to modify the contrary rule of the *Groman* and *Bashford* cases.[125] It should be noted, however, that the regulations provide that voting stock of *either* the acquiring corporation *or* its parent may be used as consideration, but not both.[126] The Service has ruled

---

[123] But see James Armour, Inc., supra note 120 (51 percent satisfactory); and Rev. Proc. 77-37, 1977-2 CB 568 which seems to focus on the net worth percentage at *commencement* of the transaction.

[124] For the meaning of "voting stock," see supra note 75.

[125] Supra ¶ 14.11, note 29. The parent's status as a party to a reorganization becomes important under §§354 and 361 (infra ¶¶ 14.32 and 14.34).

[126] See Regs. §1.368-2(d)(1). Thus, *Groman* and *Bashford* remain controlling in split consideration transactions. But see Rev. Rul. 64-73, 1964-1 CB 142. For more on this problem, see infra ¶ 14.53; Lurie, supra note 29; and Schneider, supra note 29.

The regulations' statement that split consideration exchanges break the reorganization may be too broad, however. *Groman* found a reorganization but held that the parent's stock was boot; if the amount of parent stock is small enough to fit within

that the assets could be acquired by a wholly owned sub-subsidiary of the parent corporation whose stock was issued as consideration [127] on the ground that the 1954 amendments indicated that Congress desired "to remove the [*Groman-Bashford*] continuity of interest problem from the section 368(a)(1)(C) reorganization area." [128]

In determining whether the acquisition is solely for voting stock, §368(a)(1)(C) provides that the assumption of liabilities by the acquiring corporation or the acquisition of properties subject to liabilities must be disregarded. [129] Note that liabilities are disregarded only in determining whether the exchange is solely for stock and thus in determining whether the transaction constitutes a reorganization; the liabilities may become relevant in the computation of boot under §357(b). Moreover, the regulations state that §368(a)(1)(C) "does not prevent consideration of the effect of an assumption of liabilities on the general character of the transaction" and that an assumption may "so alter the character of the transaction as to place the transaction outside the purposes and assumptions of the reorganization provisions." [130] This warning may mean that if the net worth of the transferred properties is insignificant, so that the consideration paid is primarily the

---

the boot relaxation rule of §368(a)(2)(B), a Type C reoganization should still be possible here.

[127] Rev. Rul. 64-73, 1964-1 CB 142.

[128] See infra §14.53.

[129] Although the voting stock of the acquiring corporation's parent may be used in acquiring the properties, apparently the acquiring corporation is the only one that may assume the transferor's liabilities. But if the transferor corporation receives stock of *A* Corporation in exchange for properties that are transferred to *B* Corporation (a subsidiary of *A*), is the transaction to be viewed as (1) an acquisition by *B* in exchange for its parent's stock, so that *B* is the acquiring corporation; or (2) an acquisition by *A* in exchange for its own stock, followed by a transfer of the assets under §368(a)(2)(C) to *B*, so that *A* is the acquiring corporation? The same problem arises in applying §381 (infra ch. 16, Part B), under which the tax attributes of the transferor corporation are inherited by the acquiring corporation. See Regs. §§1.381(a)-1(b)(2) and 1.381(a)-1(b)(3)(ii); Rev. Rul. 70-107, 1970-1 CB 78; Rev. Rul. 70-224, 1970-1 CB 79; Rev. Rul. 73-257, 1973-1 CB 189.

For the background of this provision, see US v. Hendler, supra note 22; Surrey, Assumption of Indebtedness in Tax-Free Exchanges, 50 Yale L.J. 1 (1940); infra ¶ 14.55.

See also Rev. Rul. 73-102, 1973-1 CB 186 (assumption of acquired corporation's liability to pay dissenters in a Type C reorganization; held boot because liability created in the reorganization; but §368(a)(2)(B) saved reorganization status because 80 percent of assets acquired for voting stock). But see Rev. Rul. 76-365, 1976-2 CB 110 (assumption of acquired corporation's expenses of evaluating unsuccessful competing offers a valid liability assumption in a Type C reorganization; not boot because assumed liabilities were preexisting, not fixed or determined in the reorganization).

[130] Regs. §1.368-2(d)(1).

assumption of indebtedness with only a trivial amount of voting stock to sweeten the bargain, the transaction will fail to qualify as a reorganization for want of a continuity of interest on the part of the transferor corporation or its shareholders. [131]

In application, the terms "assumption" and "liabilities" as used in §368(a)(1)(C) raise a number of interpretative questions, which are considered later in this chapter.

Until 1954, voting stock was the sole consideration (aside from assuming liabilities or taking property subject to liabilities) that could be employed by the acquiring corporation in a Type C reorganization; any other consideration would prevent the exchange from qualifying. [132] In 1954, however, §368(a)(2)(B) was enacted to relax this restriction to a very limited degree. Under §368(a)(2)(B), the use of money or other property will not prevent the exchange from qualifying as a Type C reorganization if at least 80 percent of the gross fair market value of all of the property of the transferor corporation is acquired for voting stock. Thus, up to 20 percent of the property, by fair market value, may be acquired for money or other property. [133] There are, however, the following practical and legal restrictions on the use of §368(a)(2)(B):

(1) An error in computing value may be fatal. Thus, if all of the properties of the transferor corporation are thought to be worth $100,000, for which voting stock of the acquiring corporation plus $20,000 of cash is paid, the reorganization will fail to qualify if the properties turn out to be worth less than $100,000.

(2) Since at least 80 percent of the fair market value of *all* the properties of the transferor corporation must be acquired for voting stock, any property that is to be retained by it will reduce the amount of money or other property that may be paid by the acquiring corporation. Thus, assuming properties worth $100,000 of which $15,000 is to be retained, only $5,000 of the transferred assets may be acquired for money or other property.

---

[131] See supra note 119.

[132] See Helvering v. Southwest Consol. Corp., supra note 33: " 'Solely' leaves no leeway. Voting stock plus some other consideration does not meet the statutory requirement."

[133] For an illustration of the boot relaxation rule of §368(a)(2)(B) in a Type C reorganization, see Everett v. US, supra note 75 (examination of the facts of the case set forth in the district court opinion, however, indicates that the cash paid plus the liabilities assumed exceeded 20 percent of the transferor's properties, thus failing to satisfy the requirements of §368(a)(2)(B); all parties apparently ignored this situation). See also Rev. Rul. 73-102, 1973-1 CB 186, for illustration of successful utilization of §368(a)(2)(B) in a case of dissenting shareholder claims assumed and paid by the acquiring company. See generally Rev. Rul. 72-343, 1972-2 CB 213.

(3) Under the second sentence of §368(a)(2)(B), liabilities assumed by the acquiring corporation (or to which the acquired property is subject) are to be treated as money in determining whether 80 percent of all property is acquired for voting stock. Thus, if the transferor's properties are $100,000 and are subject to liabilities of $17,000, the acquiring corporation could not pay more than $3,000 in money or other property in addition to assuming the liabilities or taking the properties subject to them. In the absence of a ruling to the contrary, contingent liabilities should also probably be taken into account for this purpose.

(4) Any money or other property used under §368(a)(2)(B) will constitute boot to the transferor corporation, resulting in the possible recognition of its gain to the transferor's shareholders when distributed in the transferor's required liquidation. [134]

Because the consideration that may be used by the acquiring corporation in a Type C reorganization is so restricted, even under the 1954 amendment, the acquiring corporation may search for ways to avoid these restrictions. One device would be to acquire only the assets that are essential to its business needs, leaving behind in the transferor corporation cash, marketable securities, accounts receivable, and so forth. The problem here, as already stated, is that the acquisition might then fail to qualify as a reorganization because less than substantially all of the properties would have been acquired, or because the transferor fails to liquidate. Another possibility is for the transferor corporation to borrow against its properties just before the exchange and to distribute the borrowed funds; but this too might disqualify the transaction if the distributed funds are treated as part of the transferor's properties in applying the substantially all requirement or if the assumption of such liability is considered a mere substitute for cash boot. Alternatively, the acquiring corporation might buy some of the transferor's assets for cash and then, in an unrelated transaction, acquire the balance for voting stock, in the hope that the latter event would be a Type C reorganization. The step-transaction doctrine, discussed later in this chapter, obviously threatens the validity of the allegedly separate reorganization in such a case.

Where the acquiring corporation has purchased some of the transferor corporation's *stock* in earlier unrelated transactions (either from those shareholders who desired cash or pro rata from all shareholders), use of §368(a)(1)(C) to acquire the transferor's *properties* may be difficult. If the

---

[134] But see Regs. §1.361-1, stating that nonvoting stock and securities of the acquiring corporation used as consideration under §368(a)(2)(B) may be received tax-free by the transferor corporation. In view of the 1984 legislation mandating the transferor's liquidation, supra note 114, corporate-level taxability should no longer be possible in a qualified Type C reorganization; infra ¶ 14.32.

acquiring corporation has at least 80 percent control of the transferor, the latter's assets can be acquired tax-free under §332 (see Chapter 11); but where less than 80 percent control exists and where the transferor corporation is liquidated, as it now must under 1984 legislation, the acquiring corporation may be held to have acquired part of the transferor's assets in liquidation rather than solely for voting stock, so as to render §368(a)(1)(C) inapplicable.[135] This danger may be avoided by the interposition of a controlled subsidiary of the acquiring corporation.[136]

Finally, if the acquiring corporation owns 20 percent or less of the transferor's stock, its acquisition of the assets may qualify as a Type C reorganization on the ground that the other property (i.e., the previously purchased stock) used to acquire its proportionate share of the assets comes within the boot relaxation rule of §368(a)(2)(B).

3. Transfer of part or all of acquired assets to a subsidiary. Under §368(a)(2)(C), a transaction that is otherwise a Type C reorganization does not forfeit its status as such because the acquiring corporation transfers part or all of the assets to a corporation controlled by it. This provision was new in 1954, and it is a corollary of the 1954 change under which a parent corporation's stock may be used as the consideration in a Type C reorganization. It is now possible for a corporation to acquire assets in exchange for its parent's stock, for the parent to acquire the assets for its own stock and then transfer them to a subsidiary, or for a corporation to acquire assets for its parent's stock and transfer them to a subsidiary.[137]

---

[135] See Bausch & Lomb Optical Co. v. CIR, 267 F2d 75 (2d Cir. 1959), cert denied, 361 US 835 (1959); Grede Foundries, Inc. v. US, 202 F. Supp. 263 (E.D. Wis. 1962).

[136] These possibilities are discussed in more detail infra ¶ 14.53; see also Rev. Rul. 57-278, 1957-1 CB 124 (interposition of subsidiary as acquiring corporation); Rev. Rul. 69-48, 1969-1 CB 106 (distinguishing Rev. Rul. 57-278 on the facts); Rev. Rul. 85-138, 1985-2 CB 122 (extending Rev. Rul. 69-48 to payments by sister subsidiary of acquiring corporation); supra ¶ 14.12 (as to creeping acquisitions); ¶ 14.13 (same); Rev. Rul. 72-354, 1972-2 CB 216 (purge sale of tainted stock). See generally MacLean, "Creeping Acquisitions," 21 Tax L. Rev. 345 (1966), and articles cited therein.

[137] See also Rev. Rul. 68-261, 1968-1 CB 147 (drop into multiple subsidiaries); Rev. Rul. 58-93, 1958-1 CB 188 (§368(a)(2)(C) permits assets to be transferred directly to subsidiary, without passing through hands of parent corporation); §368(b) (third sentence) (acquiring corporation is a party to a reorganization, even though it transfers the assets to a subsidiary); Rev. Rul. 81-247, 1981-2 CB 87 (post-acquisition dropdowns under §368(a)(2)(C) do not violate continuity of business enterprise regulations); infra ¶¶ 14.51 and 14.53.

See supra note 129 on the problem of determining which of several corporations is the acquiring corporation.

4. Requirement that transferor liquidate. A transferor corporation that had exchanged its operating assets for stock in a Type C reorganization often preferred not to liquidate pursuant to the reorganization (which it did not have to do before the 1984 amendment). Since its tax history was stripped out by §381(a)(2),[138] passing over automatically to the acquiring corporation (see Chapter 16), the transferor could continue in existence as a holding company with a clean slate of earnings and profits. Alternatively, it could distribute out the acquiring corporation's stock tax-free to its shareholders under §354 and retain other untransferred assets (assuming they were not significant enough to violate the substantially all requirement), thereby avoiding the possible boot dividend consequences that would result to the shareholders if those assets were distributed in the reorganization.[139] Finally, if the corporation's asset bases were high enough to tolerate the receipt of boot (within the §368(a)(2)(B) amnesty zone) without significant corporate-level gain, it could likewise avoid shareholder boot dividend risks by retaining such property (with only a nominal recognition of gain, if any).

Because of these, and other, abuse possibilities, legislation was enacted in 1984 to require complete liquidation by the transferor pursuant to the plan of reorganization unless waived by regulations; any waiver, however, will be conditioned on the parties being treated as if complete liquidation had, in fact, occurred, eliminating any potential for manipulation.[140]

5. Overlap problems. A reorganization may qualify under both §§368(a)(1)(C) and 368(a)(1)(D) (e.g., a transfer by one corporation of all of its assets to a second corporation in exchange for all of the second corporation's voting stock) if the first corporation thereafter distributes the second corporation's stock pursuant to the plan of reorganization in a transaction under §354, §355, or §356. Under §368(a)(2)(A), such a reorganization is to be treated as a Type D reorganization. This provision, which is designed to preserve the integrity of §355 and presumably applies even if the transferor fails to make a qualified distribution of the controlled corporation's stock, is discussed subsequently.[141]

---

[138] See Rev. Rul. 73-552, discussed supra note 114; Rev. Rul. 76-188, discussed infra note 141.

[139] Rev. Rul. 73-552, 1973-2 CB 116.

[140] The Tax Reform Act of 1984, supra note 114, §368(a)(2)(G).

[141] See infra ¶ 14.16; see also Goldman, supra note 90, at 39; see Rev. Rul. 74-545, 1974-2 CB 122 (transaction described in §368(a)(1)(D) even though it does not qualify as reorganization distribution under §354 or §355); compare Rev. Rul. 76-188, 1976-1 CB 99 (parent's transfer of substantially all assets to new subsidiary, after which it stayed alive as a holding company; held §351 exchange and Type C reorganization; not a Type D because transferor did not distribute stock of subsidi-

Other instances of overlapping jurisdiction can arise where the acquisition also constitutes a Type A statutory merger; the Type A rules, as noted previously, presumably take precedence in such cases. On the other hand, the Service has ruled that the Type C reorganization rules can come into play if the transaction does not technically qualify as a Type A reorganization for some reason of local or federal law.[142] The Type C rules may also be imposed on an alleged Type B stock-for-stock acquisition if the acquired subsidiary is liquidated pursuant to an integrated plan.[143] Finally, it may be possible for a Type C reorganization to constitute, or coexist with, a tax-free §351 exchange (see Chapter 3); Rev. Rul. 68-357 specifically recognized this possibility,[144] holding that both §§351 and 368(a)(1)(C) applied to a transaction where a sole proprietor and three corporations transferred all their assets to a new commonly controlled corporation pursuant to a single plan of consolidation.[145]

¶ 14.15 MERGER WITH CONTROLLED SUBSIDIARY (HYBRID TYPE A)

1. General. Although state laws may permit a controlled subsidiary to consummate a triangular statutory merger with another corporation through the use of its parent's stock (i.e., the acquired corporation merges directly into the controlled subsidiary, and stock of its parent is given as consideration for the acquisition), the Service initially ruled that the parent was not a party to such a reorganization under *Groman*, so that its stock constituted taxable boot to the recipients (unless the transaction qualified as a Type C reorganization, in which event nonrecognition treatment could apply).[146] In

---

ary, so §368(a)(2)(A) not applicable; Rev. Rul. 74-545 distinguished); Rev. Rul. 78-130, 1978-1 CB 114 (not a Type D because no direct control of transferee, but transaction qualified alternatively as a triangular Type C); Rev. Rul. 84-30, 1984-1 CB 114 (valid type C even though target passed acquiring corporation's stock upstream to its grandparent; continuity of interest not violated).

[142] See Rev. Rul. 67-326, 1967-2 CB 143 (triangular statutory merger also qualified as a Type C reorganization); Rev. Rul. 57-465, 1957-2 CB 250 (merger of foreign corporations cannot qualify as Type A, but can be a Type D or presumably Type C reorganization); supra note 108; Aetna Cas. & Sur. Co. v. US, 403 F. Supp. 498 (D. Conn. 1975) (pre-1968 case; merger of 61 percent owned subsidiary into newly created 100 percent owned subsidiary; held valid triangular Type C reorganization), rev'd on other grounds, 568 F2d 811 (2d Cir. 1976) (held a Type F).

[143] Supra ¶ 14.13, note 102.

[144] Rev. Rul. 68-357, 1968-2 CB 144.

[145] See also Rev. Rul. 76-123, 1976-1 CB 94.

[146] Rev. Rul. 67-326, 1967-2 CB 143.

response to this problem, Congress amended the reorganization definition rules of §§368(a) and 368(b) in 1968 to allow three-party statutory mergers into controlled subsidiaries if the conditions of §368(a)(2)(D) were satisfied. The acquisition by a subsidiary, in exchange for stock of its parent, will qualify as a Type A reorganization under this provision if (1) substantially all the properties of the transferor are acquired by the subsidiary; (2) the transferor is merged (not consolidated) into the subsidiary; (3) the merger would have qualified under §368(a)(1)(A) had it been effected directly into the parent; and (4) no stock of the subsidiary is used in the transaction.[147]

In a similar development, §368(a)(2)(E) was added in 1971 to allow the so-called reverse merger type of acquisition, whereby the controlled subsidiary merges into the target company (which emerges as the surviving corporation) and shareholders of the latter exchange their stock for stock of the parent. The Service initially classified such a transaction as the functional equivalent of a Type B reorganization,[148] with the result that the acquisition had to be effected exclusively with voting stock.[149] Section 368(a)(2)(E) provides that the reverse merger will qualify as a Type A reorganization if (1) the surviving corporation holds substantially all of the properties of both corporations after the transaction and (2) former shareholders of the surviving corporation exchange stock constituting control (i.e., 80 percent) for *voting* stock of the parent. Section 368(b) was also amended to make the parent a party to the reorganization. A limited amount of other consideration (e.g., nonvoting stock or bonds) will not destroy reorganization status under the 1971 legislation, whereas it may have been fatal if the transaction had to

---

[147] See generally articles supra note 29; Shors, supra note 65; Levin, supra note 65; Ferguson & Ginsburg, Triangular Reorganizations, supra note 65; Freling, Current Problems in Subsidiary Mergers and Other Triangular Reorganizations, 29 NYU Inst. on Fed. Tax'n, 347 (1971).

For further discussions of the §368(a)(2)(E) provisions, see Flyer, An Analysis of the New A Reorganization: Its Operation and Planning Potential, 35 J. Tax'n, 30 (1971); see also Stutsman, Triangular Mergers, 50 Taxes 820 (1972); Pleasants, Practical Planning for the Reverse Triangular Merger Technique of Section 368 (a)(2)(E), 39 J. Tax'n, 66 (1973); Testa, The "A," "B," "C" Matrix of Triangular Reorganizations, 38 NYU Inst. on Fed. Tax'n, ch. 1 (1980).

[148] Rev. Rul. 67-448, 1967-2 CB 144.

[149] See Rev. Rul. 73-427, 1973-2 CB 301 (broken reverse merger by use of transitory subsidiary treated as taxable stock purchase transaction without gain or loss to acquiring corporations); see also Rev. Rul. 74-564, 1974-2 CB 124; Rev. Rul. 74-565, 1974-2 CB 125, Aetna Cas. & Sur. Co. v. US, supra note 142; Rev. Rul. 79-273, 1979-2 CB 125 (same as Rev. Rul. 73-427: cash reverse merger treated as taxable stock purchase and *Zenz* redemption where target distributed stock of unwanted subsidiary).

See Blanchard, The Effect of the Step-Transaction Doctrine on Reverse Subsidiary Mergers: An Analysis, 55 J. Tax'n 72 (1981) (discussion of nonqualified §368(a)(2)(E) deals).

meet the requirements of a Type B reorganization as indicated by the 1967 published ruling.

Amendments to the reorganization rules by the Bankruptcy Tax Act of 1980 generally extended the tax-free triangular rules of §§368(a)(2)(D) and 368(a)(2)(E) to bankruptcy reorganizations under §368(a)(1)(G). In addition, these provisions sanctioned asset dropdowns in bankruptcy reorganizations and also amended §368(b) to include the parent of an acquiring subsidiary as a party to the reorganization.

The 1968 and 1971 statutory changes acknowledge that essentially the same result could have been accomplished under prior law by a direct merger of the acquired corporation into the parent followed by a transfer of the acquired assets into one or more of its controlled subsidiaries under §368(a)(2)(C). Sections 368(a)(2)(D) and 368(a)(2)(E) do not alter the definition of a Type A reorganization, however; rather, they create a fourth and a fifth category of acquisitive reorganization, incorporating features of the Type A, B, and C patterns along with requirements uniquely their own. There are many problems in interpreting §§368(a)(2)(D) and 368(a)(2)(E), the more important of which are considered below.

2. Technical analysis. Section 368(a)(2)(D) requires that substantially all of the properties of the transferor corporation must be acquired by the subsidiary, reflecting the similar limitation in §368(a)(1)(C).[150] It is essential under §368(a)(2)(D) that the transferor be merged into the parent's subsidiary; hence, consolidations and reverse mergers are not permitted by this

---

[150] For §368(a)(1)(C), see supra ¶ 14.14. See also Rev. Rul. 72-405, 1972-2 CB 217 (triangular merger into newly organized subsidiary followed by planned liquidation of subsidiary into parent; held a direct Type C reorganization per step-transaction analysis of Rev. Rul. 67-274); Rev. Rul. 72-576, 1972-2 CB 217 (§368(a)(2)(D) triangular merger into subsidiary for stock of parent not spoiled by planned dropdown into second-tier subsidiary because §368(a)(2)(C) protects second step); Rev. Proc. 77-37, 1977-2 CB 568 (triangular mergers under §§368(a)(2)(D) and 368(a)(2)(E) included in "substantially all" ruling guideline); Rev. Rul. 81-247, 1981-2 CB 87 (dropdown does not violate continuity of business enterprise regulations, infra ¶ 14.51).

Regulations under §368(a)(2)(D) were adopted by TD 7422, 1976-2 CB 105 (1976), Regs. §1.368-2(b)(2). Their principal features are: (1) The "could have merged with the parent" test means only Type A mergability (e.g., continuity of interest, business purpose, and continuity of business enterprise), not legal nubility into the parent; (2) the substantially all test has the same meaning as for Type C reorganizations; (3) the parent, the subsidiary, or both, can pay boot, subject only to continuity of interest limitations; and (4) the parent can assume the liabilities (the example given is substitution of the parent's stock options for those of the acquired corporation). See Cook & Coalson, The "Substantially All of the Properties" Requirement in Triangular Reorganizations—A Current Review, 35 Tax Lawyer 303 (1982).

provision. However, §368(a)(2)(E)[151] governs reverse mergers[152] and similarly incorporates a substantially all limitation[153] (as in the Type C definition), as well as imposing a requirement that *voting* stock of the parent be used to acquire at least 80 percent of the stock of the surviving corporation.[154] This limitation provision smacks of the Type B definition, although

---

[151] Regulations under §368(a)(2)(E) were proposed on Dec. 29, 1980 as Prop. Regs. §1.368-2(j). Their principal features were (1) there must be a bulk acquisition of control in the transaction, Prop. Regs. §§1.368-2(j)(3)(i) and 1.368-2(j)(3)(ii); (2) the substantially all test applies to both the target company and the merging subsidiary, but, for this purpose, property transferred to the disappearing subsidiary that is used to pay boot to the target company, dissenters, creditors, or reorganization expenses is disregarded, Prop. Regs. §1.368-2(j)(3)(iii); (3) the parent can drop the target's stock into a controlled subsidiary under §368(a)(2)(C) (*but* the target can not drop more than 10 percent of *its* net assets into a controlled subsidiary), Prop. Regs. §1.368-2(j)(4); and (4) the parent can assume liabilities of the target, Prop. Regs. §1.368-2(j)(5). See generally, N.Y. State Bar Association, Tax Section, Comments on Report on Reverse Triangular Mergers and Basis-Nonrecognition Rules in Triangular Reorganizations, 36 Tax L. Rev. 395 (1981); see also Cook & Coalson, supra note 150.

Final regulations under §368(a)(2)(E) were issued in TD 8059, 1985-2 CB 123. The final regulations modified these proposals in the following manner: (1) While control must be acquired in the transaction (i.e., *P*'s prior stock ownership in *T* will not contribute to satisfaction of the control requirement), *P* can back into control where *T* redeems some of its stock in the acquisition (although *T*'s distributions will cut into the substantially all requirement), Regs. §1.368-2(j)(3)(i); (2) for purposes of the substantially all test, *T*'s distributions to its shareholders in the transaction cut into that amount, Regs. §1.368-2(j)(3)(iii); (3) the parent can drop *T*'s stock into a subsidiary after the acquisition, and, in a reversal from the proposed regulations, *T* can also drop down *its* assets into a new subsidiary, Regs. §1.368-2(j)(4); (4) *P* must control *T* immediately *after* the transaction, thus raising the possibility of a decontrol event if *P* disposes of some of its *T* stock or new investors acquire additional *T* stock as part of the overall transaction); (5) §368(a)(1)(B) can backstop a failed §368(a)(2)(E), Regs. §1.368-2(j)(7), Examples (4) and (5); and (6) *P*'s assumption of *T*'s liabilities is treated as a capital contribution to *T* (and exchange of *P* and *T* securities are governed by §§354 and 356), Regs. §1.368(j)(5).

[152] Rev. Rul. 84-104, 1984-2 CB 94 (no §368(a)(2)(E) for consolidations, but consolidation under the National Bank Act considered a merger because one of parties survivied, so valid reverse merger; Regs. §1.368-2(j)(2) not applicable to consolidations).

[153] Rev. Rul. 77-307, 1977-2 CB 117 (cash contributed by parent to new subsidiary for use in paying off dissenters, avoiding issuance of fractional shares, and paying organizational expenses not counted for substantially all test in reverse mergers); Regs. §1.368-2(j)(3)(iii) (same); see also Regs. §1.368-2(J)(7), Example (3).

[154] But Prop. Regs. §1.368-2(j)(7), Example (4), held that parent must acquire complete control of target *in* the acquisition (i.e., threshold redemption by target of its preferred stock (and less than 10 percent of total stock outstanding) violated §368(a)(2)(E) control acquisition requirement); note, however, that a similar transaction apparently does not spoil a Type B, since acquiring corporation only has to *end*

ameliorated with a boot relaxation rule similar to the Type C category of reorganization. It seems clear that a transaction that does not satisfy the requirements of §368(a)(2)(D) or §368(a)(2)(E) should still qualify as a Type B or C reorganization if these particular provisions are satisfied.[155] Other definitional aspects of §§368(a)(2)(D) and 368(a)(2)(E) are the following:

(a) Permissible consideration. The major importance of new §368(a)(2)(D) is that a wider range of consideration can be used to effect the acquisition (other than stock of the subsidiary); thus, nonvoting stock of the parent can be given in exchange for the properties (unlike Types B and C), as can cash and debt securities (of either the subsidiary or the parent), limited only by the general continuity of interest requirement that a substantial proportion of the consideration must consist of equity interests.[156]

The reverse merger rules of §368(a)(2)(E), by contrast, require that voting stock of the parent must be exchanged for at least 80 percent of the stock of the acquired corporation; the other 20 percent, however, can be acquired for other types of consideration.[157]

---

up in control of target. But the final regulations ignore target stock redemptions in testing whether control was acquired by *P* (although such redemptions do count for substantially all purposes), Regs. §1.368-2(j)(3)(i); see also Regs. §1.368-2(j)(7), Examples (2) and (3), illustrating "back in control" acquisitions).

[155] See rulings cited supra notes 146, 148, and 149. But see Rev. Proc. 82-50, 1982-2 CB 839 (no ruling on whether §368(a)(1)(B) or §351 applied via Rev. Rul. 67-448 if transaction structured as a §368(a)(2)(E) reverse merger but failed to qualify as such because it violated substantially all, or control requirements). But the final regulations, §1.368-2(j)(7), Examples (4) and (5), specifically allow §368(a)(1)(B) treatment to backstop §368(a)(2)(E).

See current ruling position, see Rev. Proc. 87-3, §5.18, 1987-1 IRB 27.

[156] Supra ¶ 14.16. The original version of the 1968 legislation provided that the acquisition had to be "in exchange solely for stock of the parent," similar to the language in §§368(a)(1)(B) and 368(a)(1)(C); the final version omitted this restriction, and the committee reports state that the continuity of interest standards applicable to the Type A reorganization are to apply here as well. See H.R. Rep. No. 1902, 90th Cong., 2d Sess. 2 (1968); S. Rep. No. 1653, 90th Cong., 2d Sess. 2 (1968). The literal language of §368(a)(2)(D) could be read to require the acquisition of substantially all of the properties for stock of the parent, but this seems an unnecessary restrictive interpretation of the provision in view of the above committee reports and was rejected by the regulations. See also Rev. Rul. 78-397, 1978-2 CB 150 (circular cash flow, to meet state law minimum capital requirement, disregarded as transitory step); Rev. Rul. 77-428, 1977-2 CB 118 (merger of parent into new second-tier subsidiary of new first-tier subsidiary a valid §368(a)(2)(D) reorganization; immaterial that both surviving subsidiary and its parent were newly created or that parties were related).

[157] See Rev. Rul. 74-564, 1974-2 CB 124 (freeze-out of 2 percent minority interest in second-tier subsidiary by having grandparent create a new subsidiary with its stock, which then merged into second-tier subsidiary; held not a good §368(a)(2)(E) reverse merger because stock of grandparent, rather than stock of first-tier subsidiary

(b) Liability assumption. Although the statute is silent on this point, assumption by the subsidiary of the transferor corporation's liabilities, which occurs by operation of law in a merger, should have no effect on the transaction. The joint assumption of liabilities by the parent with the subsidiary, however, could cause trouble, and taking over convertible debenture obligations of the transferor likewise creates substantial problems, both at the time of initial assumption and, later, upon conversion of the bonds into stock of the parent or its subsidiary.[158]

(c) The "could have merged with parent" test. If local or federal law forbids a direct merger into the parent corporation, it could be argued that the §368(a)(2)(D) route is not available under a strict reading of the statutory language. On the other hand, this requirement may mean only that the continuity of interest doctrine would have been satisfied had the transaction been structured as a merger into the parent. Although the latter view seems

---

parent, used as consideration and also because first-tier subsidiary did not acquire control in the transaction, since it already had 98 percent control; but transaction a valid triangular Type B reorganization under §368(a)(1)(B) because solely voting stock of grandparent used); Rev. Rul. 74-565, id. (not a good triangular §368(a)(2)(E) reverse merger because parties used stock of grandparent of acquiring corporation first-tier subsidiary; but was a valid §368(a)(1)(B) triangular Type B reorganization because solely voting stock of parent of acquiring corporation was used as consideration for the acquisition); Rev. Rul. 77-428, 1977-2 CB 118 (reverse merger of new second-tier subsidiary into grandparent, which survives as subsidiary of new first-tier subsidiary, a valid §368(a)(2)(E) reorganization; fact that ultimate parent a new corporation, or that parties related, immaterial).

See also Regs. §§1.368-2(j)(3)(i) and 1.368(j)(7), Example 4 (must acquire 80 percent control in the merger); but the final regulations disregard target redemptions of its stock for purposes of the control test (although not for purposes of the substantially all test), and also provide that the control test will not be flunked because P acquired additional T stock from T in the transaction or because P obtains T stock in exchange for its prior interest in a subsidiary (S) that is merged into T (although the receipt of such T stock will not contribute to satisfaction of the control test). See Regs. §1.368-2(j)(7), Examples (6), (7), and (9).

[158] See generally Levin, supra note 65, at 786, for discussion of these problems. See also infra ¶¶ 14.31–14.34, and 14.55.

Rev. Rul. 73-257, 1973-1 CB 189 held that both the subsidiary and the parent could simultaneously assume liabilities in a §368(a)(2)(D) reorganization without affecting the reorganization status; moreover, §357(a) protected the assumptions from boot treatment.

Final regulations under §368(a)(2)(D) in §1.368-2(b)(2) provide that the parent is a party to the exchange for purposes of §357(a); see also Regs. §1.368-2(j)(5) (parent can assume target's liabilities in a reverse merger); the final regulations treat the liability assumption as a capital contribution to target, and they also note that an exchange of target and acquiring corporation securities is governed by §§354 and 356 (but see rulings under Type B, supra note 85, which treat such an acquisition of target debt securities as a separate taxable exchange).

more sound from a policy standpoint, the statutory language could just as easily support the more restrictive interpretation. The fact that §368(a)(2)(E) contains no comparable limitation suggests that continuity of interest, rather than legal nubility, was Congress' major concern here.[159]

(d) The "no subsidiary stock" test. The use of even a small amount of the subsidiary's stock in addition to the parent's will disqualify the transaction under §368(a)(2)D). Perhaps such a transaction could qualify as a Type C reorganization under the boot relaxation rules of §368(a)(2)(B), but if the *Groman* doctrine still applies, the *parent's* stock is the boot, and hence even a Type C reorganization would fail. Conversely, if larger amounts of the subsidiary's stock (and relatively smaller amounts of the parent's stock) are used in the merger, it would seem that the acquisition could satisfy the traditional two-party merger rules of §368(a)(1)(A), without resort to §368(a)(2)(D); the parent's stock may be boot under *Groman*, but the continuity of interest doctrine tolerates a substantial amount of nonqualified consideration.

(e) Convertible debentures and warrants. If the subsidiary issues convertible debentures or warrants as part of the consideration, these securities ordinarily will constitute taxable boot to the recipients (at least under current Service views); a more serious issue is whether they constitute use of the subsidiary's stock, either on issue or on conversion or exercise so as to violate §368(a)(2)(D). Until this issue is clarified by ruling or regulation, the use of such instruments is risky.[160]

(f) Parent as a party. Under the last two sentences of §368(b), the parent is a party to a three-party merger only if the transaction qualifies under §368(a)(2)(D) or §368(a)(2)(E); thus, acquisitions that fail one or more of the special requirements of §368(a)(2)(D) or §368(a)(2)(E) are not covered by these rules, and unless the transaction can qualify as a Type B or C reorganization, the stock of the parent will not qualify under the nonrecognition provisions of §§354 and 361.

(g) Other reverse merger problems. The parent's basis for the acquired subsidiary stock in a §368(a)(2)(E) transaction is unclear (i.e., is it the carry-

---

[159] The House Committee Report to §368(a)(2)(D) seems clearly to support the conclusion in the text that the "could have merged with parent" test was concerned with tax law qualification of the merger, rather than legal ability to merge into the parent, and the regulations agree. See also Rev. Rul. 74-297, 1974-1 CB 84.

[160] Rev. Rul. 79-155, 1979-1 CB 153 (convertible debt assumed jointly by parent and subsidiary; debt convertible into stock of parent and into stock of subsidiary if parent disposed of subsidiary; held not stock of subsidiary yet, until conversion).

over basis of the acquired stock under §362(b) or a substituted basis determined by reference to the parent's stock under §358?).[161] Also, the relationship of §368(a)(2)(E) to the loss carry-over restrictions of §382 before their amendment in 1986 was not luminously apparent.[162] If the Type B reorganization analogy is adopted (which seems most appropriate where a phantom subsidiary is involved), the results could differ from situations where the merged subsidiary constituted a real corporation.[163]

3. Examples. The provisions of §§368(a)(2)(D) and 368(a)(2)(E) can be illustrated by the following examples, in which T is the acquired target corporation, P is the parent, and S is a wholly owned subsidiary of P.

Example 1. T merges into S under applicable state law solely in exchange for stock (common or preferred, voting or nonvoting) of P. The transaction qualifies as a Type A reorganization and would also qualify as a Type C if the P stock were voting stock.

Example 2. The consideration given by P consists of one-half nonvoting preferring stock and one-half bonds or cash. The transaction constitutes a Type A reorganization, but the bonds and cash are taxable boot to T's shareholders.

Example 3. S merges into T (using voting stock of P as the consideration for the exchange), so that T becomes a wholly owned subsidiary of P. The transaction constitutes a Type A reorganization under §368(a)(2)(E) if shareholders of T exchange at least 80 percent of its stock for voting stock of P. If this requirement is not satisfied, the transaction must be viewed as an attempted Type B reorganization, accord-

---

[161] See infra ¶ 14.33. But Prop. Regs. §1.358-6(c) (1980) allows use of target's net asset basis as the basis for its stock in the target in a tax-free reverse merger (as if the parent had acquired the target's net assets and retransferred them to the target).

[162] See infra ¶ 16.22. But under §382 as amended in 1986, the loss limitations of §382 are clearly triggered by a reverse merger change of ownership, infra ¶ 16.24.

[163] Regulations under §368(a)(2)(E) were proposed on Dec. 29, 1980, Prop. Regs. §1.368-2(j) (summarized supra note 151), and became final in TD 8059 on October 22, 1985 (supra note 151). Concurrently, regulations dealing with subsidiary-level nonrecognition and parent's basis for its subsidiary's stock in triangular acquisitions also were proposed on Dec. 29, 1980; Prop. Regs. §§1.1032-2 and 1.358-6 (which are considered infra ¶ 14.33).

For discussion of the mirror subsidiary acquisition technique, which combines triangular acquisitions with special rules in the consolidated return regulations, see infra ¶ 15.23, para. 5, and supra ¶ 11.49.

ing to Rev. Rul. 67–448.[164] Since voting stock apparently is the sole consideration that can be used in a Type B reorganization, the transaction may fail to so qualify.

If T redeems 10 percent of its stock as part of the transaction and P pays cash boot of 20 percent for the remaining T stock (through S), the transaction qualifies under §368(a)(2)(E), since the redeemed stock is not considered as outstanding for purposes of the 80 percent control test (although it does count for the substantially all test) under Regs. §1.368-2(j)(7), Examples (2) and (3). However, if P holds 21 percent prior old and cold ownership of T, the transaction cannot be done as a reverse merger under Regs. §1.368-2(j)(7), Examples (4), (5), although it can be done as a Type B.

Example 4. If T is considered (because of a preliminary spin-off or the like) to have held back significant amounts of its assets, §368(a)(2)(D) may not be satisfied because S must obtain substantially all of T's properties.[165] The same is true of a reverse merger under §368(a)(2)(E), which requires the surviving corporation to hold substantially all the properties of both corporations (other than stock of its parent) after the transaction.

Example 5. If 5 percent of the consideration consisted of S stock and 95 percent of T stock, neither §368(a)(2)(D) nor §368(a)(1)(C) would be satisfied, since they do not cover split-consideration acquisitions. Thus, under *Groman,* P's stock would not carry continuity and the reorganization would fail because of excessive boot. If the stock proportions were reversed, however (i.e., 95 percent S stock and 5 percent P stock), the transaction should be able to qualify as a two-party merger under §368(a)(1)(A), with the P stock treated as taxable boot to T's shareholders under *Groman.*

Example 6. If P owns 50 percent of T (old and cold) and S merges into T with the other T shareholders receiving P stock, the transaction does not qualify under §368(a)(2)(E) according to Regs. §1.368-2(j)(7), Example (9), because of the failure to acquire control in the transaction (P's prior interest in T will not add to the control test).[166]

---

[164] Rev. Rul. 67-448, 1967-2 CB 144; Regs. §1.368-2(j)(7), Examples (4) and (5) (Type B test for failed §368(a)(2)(E)).

[165] See supra ¶ 14.14; infra ¶ 14.52. For "substantially all" aspects in §368(a)(2)(E), see Regs. §1.368-2(j)(3)(iii).

[166] The transaction in Example 6 appears to constitute a Type D reorganization (after 1984) since P has 50 percent control of T (infra ¶ 14.16); but P's stock would not be party stock since there is no statutory provision for a triangular Type D (in

Example 7. *T* has operating division *X* and also wholly owns two subsidiaries, *T-1* and *T-2*. *P* creates three mirror subsidiaries, *P-1, P-2,* and *P-3*, which then jointly acquire all the *T* stock with cash (or stock debt) contributed to them by *P*. *T* is then liquidated into *P*'s three subsidiaries, with the *T-1* and *T-2* stock passing to *P-1* and *P-2*, and *T*'s operating assets passing to *P-3*. *P* can then sell the stock of *P-1, P-2,* or *P-3* with no further significant gain, [167] depending on its basis for the mirror subsidiaries' stock.

¶ 14.16   TRANSFER OF ASSETS TO CONTROLLED CORPORATIONS (TYPE D)

A Type D reorganization, as defined by §368(a)(1)(D), is a transfer by a corporation of all or part of its assets to a corporation controlled (immediately after the transfer) [168] by the transferor or its shareholders, but only if stock or securities of the controlled corporation are distributed in pursuance of the plan of reorganization by the transferor corporation in a transaction which qualifies under §§354–356. As will be seen, the principal transactions that will qualify as Type D reorganizations, as a result of changes in 1954, are the following:

---

which event *T*'s other shareholder would have a taxable exchange). Query, could the acquisition qualify as a triangular Type C or does §368(a)(2)(A) preempt the Type C since the transaction is described in §368(a)(1)(D)? In any event, it would seem that *S* would have nonrecognition under §361, *T* would take a carry-over basis for *S*'s assets under §362(b), and *P* would have no gain or loss under §354.

[167] See infra ¶ 15.23, para. 5. But if the acquisition is a tax-free reverse merger, *P*'s basis in the mirror subsidiaries may reflect built-in gain due to the lack of a step-up in its basis for that stock; supra note 161.

[168] For the meaning of the requirement that control exist immediately after the transfer, see supra ¶ 3.09; Ericsson Screw Mach. Prods. Co., 14 TC 757 (1950); Maine Steel, Inc. v. US, supra note 31; James C. Hamrick, 43 TC 21 (1964) (acq.); Burr Oaks Corp. v. CIR, 365 F2d 24 (7th Cir. 1966), cert. denied, 385 US 1007 (1967). Compare Rev. Rul. 59-222, 1959-1 CB 80; Rev Rul. 59-296, 1959-2 CB 94. See also the discussion supra ¶ 14.11. Where creditors are shareholders as well, courts have generally found the requisite control to be present: see Darrell, supra note 10.

See also Turner Constr. Co. v. US, 364 F2d 525 (2d Cir. 1966), remanded on other issues sub nom. Prentis v. US, supra note 43; Turner Advertising of Ky., Inc., ¶ 66.101 P-H Memo. TC (1966); Rev. Rul. 76-108, 1976-1 CB 103 (shareholder's binding obligations to transfer 51 percent of stock after transfer to controlled corporation killed "control immediately after" status; an integral transaction per *American Bantam* (American Bantam Car Co., 11 TC 397, aff'd per curiam, 177 F2d 513 (3d Cir. 1949), cert. denied, 339 US 920 (1950)).

(1) A transfer by one corporation of substantially all its assets to a controlled corporation, [169] followed by a complete liquidation of the transferor corporation or

(2) A transfer by one corporation of part of its assets to a controlled corporation, followed by a distribution of the controlled corporation's stock in a spin-off, split-off, or split-up under §355 (see Chapter 13).

1. Continuity of interest aspects. Section 368(a)(1)(D) permits the acquired assets to be transferred to a corporation controlled by the transferor corporation, by one or more of its shareholders (including persons who were shareholders immediately before the transfer), or by any combination thereof. The parenthetical clause of §368(a)(1)(D) was added in 1954 to permit the transfer of assets to a corporation as a preliminary to a non-pro rata split-off or split-up, under which the transferee corporation is controlled, after the division, by persons who were, but no longer are, shareholders of the transferor corporation. Regs. §1.368-1(b) takes note of this provision by implying that Type D reorganizations are not subject to the continuity of interest requirement in the same way as other reorganizations.

While the purpose of the 1954 change was to permit corporate divisions under §355 in which the shareholders of the old corporation part company and go their separate ways, it would be a mistake to assume that the continuity of interest requirement has been wholly obliterated in Type D reorganizations. Thus, assume a transfer by *T* Corporation (owned 99 percent by *A* and one percent by *B*) of all of its property to *P* Corporation (owned 100 percent by *B*) in exchange for bonds of *P*, followed by a complete liquidation of *T* Corporation. The transaction meets the literal requirements of a Type D reorganization in that assets were transferred by a corporation (*T*) to a second corporation (*P*), which was controlled, immediately after the transfer, by a person (B) who was previously a shareholder of the transferor (*T*), and securities of the transferee (*P*) were distributed by *T* in a transaction meeting the requirements of §§354(b) and 356. [170] Since A, who owned indirectly 99 percent of the assets of *T* Corporation, received nothing but

---

[169] This portion of the Type D reorganization definition was modified by the Tax Reform Act of 1984, which provided, in §368(c)(2), that "control" for purposes of §§354(b) and 368(a)(1)(D) is to be determined under §304(c) (supra ¶ 9.12) (i.e., 50 percent of vote or value (with modified §318 attribution)). This definition was moved to §368(a)(2)(H) in the Tax Reform Act of 1986 without change in substance. But see Baline, 32 Tax Notes 816 (1986).

[170] A possible infirmity arises under §356 from the fact that *T* did not distribute any nonrecognition property along with the boot (see Rev. Rul. 77-415, 1977-2 CB 311); this omission, if relevant, could be corrected if *P* gave *T* an insignificant amount of stock along with the bonds as consideration for the assets.

bonds of *P*, the transaction ought to be treated as a sale under *LeTulle v. Scofield*[171] rather than as a tax-free reorganization.

Even though the transferors *in the aggregate* maintain a continuing interest in the transferee, some of them may drop out of the proprietary category. Thus, some shareholders may receive stock in the continuing corporation, but others may receive securities, cash, or other property. Assuming that the old shareholders as a group receive or retain enough stock to satisfy the control requirement, is the reorganization vulnerable because some of the shareholders have lost their proprietary interest? As pointed out earlier in this chapter, the courts have been rather tolerant of exchanges in which dissenting shareholders are bought out, but a transaction in which only a few of the shareholders retain an interest in the continuing enterprise is more vulnerable than one in which only a few drop out.

When a financially distressed corporation is reorganized, the creditors may become the sole owners of the reorganized corporation; if so, the proprietary interest of the old shareholders is wiped out, not continued. In *Helvering v. Alabama Asphaltic Limestone Co.*, it was held that the creditors, upon instituting bankruptcy proceedings, "had effective command over the disposition of the property" and that this was the equivalent of a proprietary interest.[172] Since this interest was continued in the reorganized corporation, the continuity of interest doctrine was satisfied despite the elimination of the shareholders. Whether these creditors obtain the status of shareholders, so as to satisfy the control requirements of §368(a)(1)(D), however, is another matter; the *Southwest Consolidated Corp.* case specifically held that they do not.[173]

2. Distribution requirement. The definition of a Type D reorganization was changed in 1954, in another and even more important respect, by the addition of the requirement that stock or securities of the transferee corporation must be "distributed [by the transferor] in a transaction which qualifies under sections 354, 355 or 356."[174] If the distribution of stock or securities is to qualify under these provisions, it will have to meet one of the following sets of conditions:

---

[171] LeTulle v. Scofield, supra note 18.

[172] Helvering v. Alabama Asphaltic Limestone Co., supra note 34.

[173] Helvering v. Southwest Consol. Corp., supra note 33. For current law treatment of insolvency reorganizations, see infra ¶ 14.20.

[174] Ordinarily, the transferor will have received stock or securities of the transferee in the reorganization itself; but this does not seem essential, since §368(a)(1)(D) is broad enough to reach a contribution to the capital of the controlled corporation. If the reorganization takes this form, the stock or securities to be distributed will be those already owned by the transferor.

But see Warsaw Photographic Assocs., 84 TC 21 (1985) (failed Type D test because stock not passed from transferee to transferor and then to shareholders; percentages changed as well).

(1) To qualify under §354 (or under §354 in conjunction with §356), the transaction will have to satisfy the requirements of §354(b), also enacted in 1954, under which the transferee must acquire "substantially all of the assets of the transferor"[175] and the transferor in turn must distribute all of its properties (the stock, securities, and other property received in the reorganization, as well as its other properties) in pursuance of the plan of reorganization.[176]

Although §354(b) does not explicitly require a complete liquidation of the transferor, the requisite distribution of all of the transferor's properties will have the effect of a complete liquidation.[177] Moreover, since substantially all of the assets of the transferor will be held by the transferee corporation, the transaction is similar to a mere reincorporation (a Type F reorganization); if the capital structure of the transferee is different from that of the transferor, the transaction also will have the effect of a recapitalization (Type E).

(2) To qualify under §355 (or under §355 in conjunction with §356), the transaction will have to meet the standards of that section (see Chapter 13).

It will be noted that a Type D reorganization that meets the conditions of §354(b) will not be a vehicle for splitting the corporate assets between two corporations, and hence it cannot be used to circumvent the painfully worked out rules governing corporation divisions under §355. It was ironic that in amending §368 in 1954 in order to protect the integrity of §355, however, Congress materially reduced its effectiveness in combatting the reincorporation device, an oversight that was finally recognized and corrected 30 years later in the Tax Reform Act of 1984.[178]

---

[175] The phrase "substantially all of the assets" as used in §354(b) has been, somewhat surprisingly, interpreted more flexibly than the phrase "substantially all of the properties" in §368(a)(1)(C). See James Armour, Inc., supra note 120 (51 percent held substantially all for this purpose); Ralph C. Wilson, supra note 121; American Mfg. Co., supra note 70 (20 percent substantial because all operating assets); discussion supra ¶ 14.14; see also Rev. Proc. 77-37, 1977-2 CB 568 (70-to-90 ruling line); Rev. Rul. 75-383, 1975-2 CB 127 (transfer of all assets by a 100 percent owned foreign subsidiary to a 100 percent owned U.S. subsidiary without issue of additional stock a valid nondivisive Type D reorganization, so §367 ruling necessary); infra ¶ 14.54.

[176] In a sense, §§354(b) and 368(a)(1)(D) are circular, since a transaction is a reorganization under §368(a)(1)(D) only if the accompanying distribution qualifies under §354(b), but §354(b) applies only to "an exchange in pursuance of a plan of reorganization within the meaning of §368(a)(1)(D)." The two provisions are not in conflict, however, and a transfer of substantially all the assets of one corporation to a controlled corporation followed by a distribution by the transferor of all of its assets will satisfy both provisions simultaneously.

[177] Supra §11.02. But see David T. Grubbs, 39 TC 42 (1962), infra ¶ 14.54.

[178] Supra note 169, infra ¶ 14.54 (control definition for §368(a)(1)(D)/354(b) reorganization conformed to §304(c) line).

Section 368(a)(1)(D) speaks of a transfer by a corporation of "all or *a part* of its assets to another corporation." This language must be read in the light of the requirement of a distribution qualifying under §354 or §355, however, with the result that a transfer of part of the assets will be a reorganization only if there is a §355 division; if the distribution is to qualify under §354 rather than under §355, there must be a transfer of substantially all of the assets of the transferor. [179]

3. Overlap problems. Before 1954, there was a large area of overlap between §351 (see Chapter 3) and the Type D reorganization, in that a parent corporation's transfer of part of its property to a newly organized subsidiary was both a §351 exchange and a Type D reorganization. Now that a Type D reorganization requires a distribution under §354 or §355, however, the overlap has been much reduced; most transfers to subsidiary corporations will now qualify simply as §351 exchanges (although §351 continues to apply concurrently to Type D transactions).

Mention has already been made of §368(a)(2)(A), providing that a transaction described in both §§368(a)(1)(C) (Type C reorganizations) and 368(a)(1)(D) (Type D) are to be "treated as described only in" §368(a)(1)(D). The announced purpose of this provision, enacted in 1954, was "to insure that the tax consequences of the distribution of stocks or securities to shareholders or security holders in connection with divisive reorganizations will be governed by the requirements of section 355 relating to [the] distribution of stock of a controlled corporation." [180]

The abuse against which §368(a)(2)(A) is aimed seems obscure, however, since a Type C reorganization, in which substantially all of the properties of a corporation are placed in another corporation in exchange for voting stock, may not lend itself to a divisive reorganization any more readily than a Type D reorganization that meets the test of §354(b) (transfer of substantially all assets to a transferee corporation followed by a distribution in liquidation by the transferor of all of its property). The effect of §368(a)(2)(A) is equally obscure, since a Type C reorganization that does *not* meet the tests of Type D reorganization may be unaffected by §368(a)(2)(A), while one that does meet these tests does not seem to be restricted in any way by being treated as exclusively a Type D reorganization. [181] Possibly,

---

[179] See Rev. Rul. 57-465, 1957-2 CB 250.

[180] S. Rep. No. 1622, 83d Cong., 2d Sess. 274 (1954).

[181] Section 357(c) (taxing the excess of liabilities over adjusted basis as gain) is applicable to Type D reorganizations but not to other types. There is no reason to think that §368(a)(2)(A) was intended to have any bearing on this area; in any event, a reorganization meeting the requirements of both Types C and D would probably have been subject to §357(c) even in the absence of §368(a)(2)(A).

§368(a)(2)(A) was intended to exclude from Type C any transfer of assets by one corporation to a corporation controlled by the transferor or its shareholders (i.e., any transfer described in the first part of §368(a)(1)(D)), so that such a transaction could qualify as a reorganization only if it also satisfied the second part of §368(a)(1)(D); but the language was not well chosen to accomplish this result.

It is worthy of note that although §368(a)(1)(D) displaces §368(a)(1)(C) where they overlap, §368(a)(1)(D) may in turn be displaced by §368(a)(1)(F) if the reorganization qualifies both as a Type D and as a Type F transaction. [182]

4. Current reform proposals. The staff of the Senate Finance Committee, in its preliminary report on the reform and simplification of Subchapter C, recommended two significant changes in the nondivisive Type D reorganization definition: (1) the control threshold would be lowered from 80 percent to 50 percent and (2) §318(a) principles would apply in determining such control. Under these proposals, the scope of the Type D reorganization would expand materially, and thereby prove considerably more effective in combatting the liquidation-reincorporation device, which was the purpose of the proposal. This proposal was adopted by the 1984 tax reform legislation in slightly altered form. [183]

The staff's final report on the reform of Subchapter C proposed to drop the Type D reorganization altogether as unnecessary, since reincorporating Type Ds would be handled under the new acquisition rules, [184] while divisive

---

Compare Rev. Rul. 74-545 with Rev. Rul. 76-188, both summarized supra note 141. See also Rev. Rul. 78-130, 1978-1 CB 144 (overlap of §351, Type C, and Type D reorganizations; assets of first-tier subsidiary transferred to new second-tier subsidiary of sister first-tier subsidiary for stock of latter not a Type D because no direct control, but valid triangular Type C; assets of second-tier subsidiary transferred to new second-tier subsidiary for stock of transferor's parent a Type D because control test met here). See also Rev. Rul. 84-30, 1984-1 CB 114 (lateral asset transfer by second-tier "nephew" subsidiary to first-tier "aunt" subsidiary held valid Type C reorganization; presumably not a Type D because of lack of direct control of transferor).

[182] See Rev. Rul. 57-276, 1957-1 CB 126, infra ¶ 14.18.

[183] The Tax Reform Act of 1984, supra note 169. For analysis of the staff's acquisition proposals, see infra ¶ 14.21.

[184] These transactions would constitute qualified asset acquisitions under the proposed new regime, although they would be mandatory carry-over basis transactions because they occur between related parties. Moreover, the quantum of property acquired would be tested under a substantially all standard (rather than the proposed statutory test of 70 percent of gross and 90 percent of net), the intent being to retain the flexible approach to reincorporation transactions under current law; supra note 175.

Type Ds would be treated exclusively under §§351 (if a division is being spun off) and 355 (where stock of a subsidiary is being distributed). [185]

¶ 14.17   RECAPITALIZATIONS (TYPE E)

Although a recapitalization has been a form of reorganization since the latter term received its first statutory definition in the Revenue Act of 1921, the scope of "recapitalization" remains cloudy to this day. An early administrative ruling adopted the view of Cook on Corporations that a recapitalization is "an arrangement whereby the stock and bonds of the corporation are readjusted as to amount, income, or priority, or an agreement of all stockholders and creditors to change and increase or decrease the capitalization or debts of the corporation or both," and the Supreme Court said, more briefly, that the term connotes "reshuffling of a capital structure within the framework of an existing corporation." [186]

Although these definitions leave many questions unanswered, they seem to confine the term "recapitalization" to the readjustment of the financial structure of a single corporation; [187] and this in turn means that a characterization of the event for tax purposes is ordinarily important only to the persons who have exchanged their stock or securities for other stock or securities. The corporation itself does not ordinarily receive property (other than the surrendered stock or securities) in a recapitalization and hence is not confronted by any problems of basis; and, since its existence is not terminated, its tax attributes (e.g., earnings and profits, loss carry-overs, and

---

[185] If the spun-off corporation is an old and cold subsidiary, §355 alone applies to determine taxability; if a division is being spun off, a preliminary incorporation step is required, but it was felt that §351 could adequately carry the freight here and that the Type D provision thus was surplusage.

[186] See SM 3710, IV-1 CB 4 (1925), quoted with approval in United Gas Improvement Co. v. CIR, 142 F2d 216 (3d Cir.), cert. denied, 323 US 739 (1944); Helvering v. Southwest Consol. Corp., supra note 33. See generally Hanna, A Recapitalization: The E Reorganization of the Internal Revenue Code, 27 Tax Lawyer 447 (1974).

See also Rev. Proc. 81-60, 1981-2 CB 680 (guidelines and information to be included in ruling requests); Rev. Rul. 82-34, 1982-1 CB 59 (no business continuity requirement). But see Rev. Proc. 87-3, 1987-1 IRB 27, §3.82 (no ruling on whether transaction constitutes Type E, or §1036, except where recapitalization part of a larger transaction and not possible to determine tax consequences of larger transaction without determination of recapitalization status). See generally Microdot, Inc. v. US, 728 F2d 593 (2d Cir. 1984); Golden Nugget, Inc., 83 TC 28 (1984).

[187] An exception might be made for a liquidation followed by a prearranged reincorporation, which might be treated as a recapitalization (infra ¶ 14.54), but even here, the new corporation might be regarded not as a second entity but as a reincarnation of the original corporation.

accounting methods) are not affected by the exchange. This is why §381 (see Chapter 16) does not refer to a Type E reorganization; since there is no acquiring corporation in a recapitalization, there is no need to provide affirmatively for a preservation of tax attributes.[188]

A recapitalization can be a method of shifting the ownership of stock in the corporation, however, and it was therefore surprising that the limitations on the net operating loss carry-over imposed by §382 (change of stock ownership by purchase or reorganization) did not apply to recapitalizations until the statute was finally amended in 1986 to reach these transactions.[189]

The vague definitions of "recapitalization" that are quoted above have been filled in to some extent by the examples in Regs. §1.368-2(e), a number of litigated cases, and some rulings. For convenience, the exchanges that may (or may not) be recapitalizations are classified in the discussion that follows by reference to the type of instrument surrendered and the type received. Unless otherwise stated, it is assumed that the transaction serves a business purpose.

1. Exchanges of stock for stock. The regulations provide that the surrender for cancellation of 25 percent of a corporation's preferred stock in exchange for its no-par value common is a recapitalization. So is the converse, a surrender of common in exchange for preferred.[190] Thus, both downstream (senior to junior) and upstream (junior to senior) equity exchanges can qualify as tax-free recapitalizations.[191]

---

[188] Since the recapitalized corporation is not dependent upon §381, it retains all of its tax attributes, not merely those listed in §381(c). See Rev. Rul. 54-482, 1954-2 CB 148.

[189] Infra ¶¶ 16.22–16.25.

Before its amendment by the Tax Reform Act of 1986, old §382(a) only applied to a stock purchase transaction (i.e., a taxable cost basis acquisition, and a recapitalization generally did not constitute such an event unless it had the effect of a redemption (e.g., an exchange of common for preferred, which did not constitute stock under the prior version of §382)). The 1986 version of §382(g)(3)(A), however, now specifically covers ownership changes effected by a recapitalization; see infra ¶ 16.24.

[190] Regs. §§1.368-2(e)(2) and 1.368-2(e)(3); see also Regs. §1.368-2(e)(4).

[191] See generally J.J. Kaufman, 55 TC 1046 (1971) (acq.) (liquidation of corporation 18 months after recapitalization exchange of new common for old preferred did not bar tax-free treatment of prior exchange); Rev. Rul. 72-206, 1972-1 CB 105 (exchange of new preferred for old common a recapitalization and tax-free to shareholders under §354); Rev. Rul. 74-269, 1974-1 CB 87 (exchange of old common for new preferred a recapitalization, but, if values differ, transaction will have collateral tax consequences, such as a gift, compensation, satisfaction of debt, and so forth); Rev. Rul. 83-119, 1983-2 CB 57 (estate freeze recapitalization; value of new preferred less than value of old common and thus created §305(b)(4) taxable dividend). For valuation factors in determining values of common and preferred, see Rev. Rul. 83-

Since these transactions are recapitalizations under §368(a)(1)(E), the shareholder on exchanging his preferred stock for common (or vice versa) recognizes neither gain nor loss under §354, provided the exchange is in pursuance of the plan of reorganization. Ordinarily the requirement of a plan will create no difficulty. If preferred stock is issued with a conversion privilege, however, so that the exchange represents no more than an isolated decision by the shareholder to exercise his privilege, it may be that the transaction is not a recapitalization or that even if it is, the exchange is not in pursuance of the plan of reorganization.[192]

But the Service has ruled that the exchange of a bond for preferred stock of the same corporation, pursuant to a conversion privilege contained in the bond when it was issued, is not an occasion for recognizing gain or loss. Although the theory of the ruling (no closed transaction) is not entirely persuasive, it seems well entrenched; and the exchange of preferred stock for common should qualify a fortiori for nonrecognition of gain or loss.[193] If preferred is converted into common, the shareholder will hardly care whether the nonrecognition of gain or loss is premised on the reorganization provisions of the Code or on the rulings just cited. If common is exchanged for preferred under a conversion privilege,[194] however, some or all of the preferred received by the shareholder might be "section 306 stock" (see Chapter 10) by virtue of §306(c)(1)(B) (e.g., stock received in pursuance of a plan of reorganization) if the exchange is a recapitalization; if it is not a

---

120, 1983-2 CB 170; Friedman, New Ruling Requires Creative Planning in Structuring Recapitalizations, 60 J. Tax'n 146 (1984); supra ¶ 7.43.

[192] See Rev. Rul 54-65, 1954-1 CB 101. But see Rev. Rul. 77-238, 1977-2 CB 115.

[193] See Rev. Rul. 72-265, 1972-1 CB 222; Rev. Rul. 57-535, 1957-2 CB 513. But see Rev. Rul. 54-65, 1954-1 CB 101; Rev. Rul. 56-179, 1956-1 CB 187. Conversion into stock of another corporation, even though controlled, is a taxable event. See Rev. Rul. 69-135, 1969-1 CB 198; Rev. Rul. 69-265, 1969-1 CB 109; Levin, supra note 65, at 786. Rev. Rul. 69-135 was distinguished in Rev. Rul. 79-155, 1979-1 CB 153 (issuer of stock on conversion also an obligor on debt, even though not the only one, since both parent and subsidiary jointly assumed convertible debt in merger agreement and right to convert into parent stock granted in amended security pursuant to the initial reorganization transaction).

See also Rev. Rul. 77-238, 1977-2 CB 115 (conversion of common into preferred and conversion of preferred into common pursant to terms of certificate of incorporation permitting, or requiring, such conversions and in furtherance of a corporate business purpose; held valid Type E reorganization).

See generally Fleischer & Cary, The Taxation of Convertible Bonds and Stock, 74 Harv. L. Rev. 473 (1961); Reiling, Warrants in Bond-Warrant Units: A Survey and Assessment, 70 Mich. L. Rev. 1411 (1972); Lipton, Debt-Equity Swaps for Parent-Subsidiary: A Current Analysis of a Useful Technique, 59 J. Tax'n 406 (1983) (focus on Rev. Rul. 69-265).

[194] A privilege to convert common into preferred may be possible as a matter of corporate law, although it would be unusual. See §306(e)(2).

recapitalization, the preferred would be "section 306 stock" only if the exchange could be treated as a stock dividend under §306(c)(1)(A), which would require some stretching of the statutory language.[195]

Although the regulations are concerned mainly with exchanges of preferred for common and vice versa, an exchange of common for common or preferred for preferred could equally well qualify as a recapitalization.[196] Exchanges of this type may also come within §1036, providing that gain and loss go unrecognized if common stock is exchanged for common stock of the same corporation, or preferred for preferred. Although §1036 may have been intended primarily to apply to exchanges among shareholders, the regulations state that it is also applicable to exchanges between shareholders and the corporation and that it thus overlaps §368(a)(1)(E).[197]

The regulations formerly provided that an exchange could qualify as a recapitalization even though the shareholder gave up preferred stock with dividend arrearages and received stock in discharge of the arrears as well as in exchange for the stock surrendered.[198] This example was in harmony with a statement in the Senate Report on the 1954 Code, which in turn rested on case law.[199] Under the 1969 amendments to the stock dividend rules, however, such an exchange is taxable under §305(b)(4) (distributions on preferred stock) to the extent of the dividend arrears.[200] Moreover, the 1969 Act version of the stock dividend rules in §§305(b) and 305(c) can cause certain disporportionate recapitalization exchanges to be taxable if the transaction has the effect of a non-pro rata stock dividend, even though the exchange also qualifies as a reorganization. (However, a statement by Senator Long

---

[195] But see §306(e)(2).

[196] See Rev. Rul. 54-482, 1954-2 CB 148 (common for common); Rev. Rul. 56-586, 1956-2 CB 214 (preferred for preferred); Rev. Rul. 70-298, 1970-1 CB 82 (equity interests in a cooperative); James H. Johnson, 78 TC 564 (1982) (exchange of old common for new class of common a recapitalization).
See also Rev. Rul. 72-57, 1972-1 CB 103, modified by Rev. Rul. 78-351, 1978-2 CB 148 (reverse split exchange of old common for new common and cash in lieu of fractional shares effected to eliminate a one percent minority interest in subsidiary; held a recapitalization exchange and not a §1036 exchange; thus, parent had nonrecognition as to stock exchange and *Davis* boot dividend on the cash received, while minority shareholders, whose interests were terminated, had §302(b)(3) redemption treatment); Rev. Rul. 72-199, 1972-1 CB 228 (exchange among shareholders of one class of common for another; held tax-free under §1036, even though one class had preemptive rights, broader stock dividend rights, and presumably different voting rights).

[197] Regs. §1.1036-1(a).

[198] See Regs. §1.368-2(e)(5) (before amendment in 1973).

[199] See S. Rep. No. 1622, supra note 180, at 44; South Atlantic S.S. Line v. CIR, 42 BTA 705 (1940) (acq.); Skenandoa Rayon Corp. v. CIR, 122 F2d 268 (2d Cir.), cert. denied, 314 US 696 (1941).

[200] See Regs. §1.368-2(e)(5) (1973).

during the Senate floor debate on the bill[201] conceded that there was no intention to tax the classic recapitalization in which older executives switch from common to preferred and retire from the business, while younger executives exchange some or all of their preferred for additional common and continue to be active in the business except to the extent that stock is given in discharge of preferred dividend arrears.[202]) In any event, stock-for-stock recapitalizations must pay close attention to the §305 rules lest the recapitalization exchange inadvertently fall into the taxable net of these provisions.[203]

Regulations under amended §305 were proposed in 1971 and became final in 1973; both sets of regulations clearly envision the applicability of §305(b) to otherwise tax-free recapitalization exchanges in view of their frequently functional resemblance to stock dividend distributions. Applicability of §305(b)(4) to recapitalizations is especially likely, and both the proposed and final regulations contain examples of that result.

The proposed regulations, in their examples under §1.305-5(c), purported to distinguish between true exchanges, where the shareholder's rights, although altered, were not enlarged as a result of the exchange (and hence were not deemed subject to the §305(b)(4) rules), and those transactions that had the functional effect of a stock dividend and thus were governed by the rules of §305. The final regulations, however, shifted their focus from an exchange versus stock dividend effect analysis to an original issue discount approach,[204] in effect making the provisions of §305(b)(4) an equity-based backstop to the debt discount provisions of amended §1272.[205] Another pro-

---

[201] 115 Cong. Rec. 37902 (1969).

[202] See Regs. §1.305-3(e), Example (12), which incorporates this principle. But see Rev. Rul. 83-119, 1983-2 CB 57 (can have §305(b)(4)–§305(c) dividend here if excess redemption premium on new preferred and on facts).

[203] Supra ¶ 7.43; see also Rev. Rul. 75-93, 1975-1 CB 101 (disproportionate recapitalization exchange, which resulted in an increase of equity interests for the exchanging shareholders, did not trigger §305(b)(2) because the recapitalization was not part of a plan to periodically step up equity shares; this conclusion, said the Service, was consistent with the isolated redemption situation of Regs. §1.305-3(e). Examples (10), (11), and (13)); Rev. Rul. 75-179, 1975-1 CB 103 (call premium on preferred reasonable, even though greater than 10 percent safe haven, because purpose of call provision was to force convertibility into common; hence, §305(b)(4) constructive distribution on preferred not triggered by this provision); Rev. Rul. 83-119, 1983-2 CB 57 (excess redemption premium on new preferred issued for old common in estate freeze transaction resulted in §305(b)(4) dividend where value of preferred less than its redemption price; dividend taxable over life of holder, since not redeemable until death).

[204] See Note, Discounted Preferred Stock Under the New Section 305 Treasury Regulations: On Confusing Debt and Equity, 84 Yale L.J. 324 (1974); and Rev. Rul. 83-119, 1983-2 CB 57, for an example.

[205] Supra ¶ 4.40. See Regs. §§1.305-7(c) and 1.368-2(e)(5), defining "recapitalization" in the context of §305 and emphasizing the issue discount thrust of these provisions. See also Regs. §1.305-5(d), Examples (1), (2), (3), (6), and (7). These regula-

nounced theme of the final regulations is to inhibit senior equity interest step-ups, similar to the debt security bailout rules of §354(a)(2).

2. Exchanges of old bonds for new stock. Turning to downstream exchanges of debt securities for stock, we find that one of the examples given by the regulations to illustrate the meaning of recapitalization is a discharge by a corporation of outstanding bonds with preferred stock instead of cash.[206] The transaction would presumably qualify just as easily if common were issued for the bonds or if the instruments given up were debentures, long-term notes, or other securities.[207] However, the recapitalization is no longer tax-free in its entirety to the extent that interest is in arrears on the securities given up and part of the stock received is in discharge of the arrears; the courts at one time refused to divide the exchange into a tax-free recapitalization coupled with a taxable payment of interest or to treat the instrument surrendered as a security (to the extent of the principal amount) and as a separate claim that did not constitute a security (to the extent of the interest arrears), but the statute was amended in 1980 to overrule this result.[208] If the creditors control

---

tions are discussed in greater detail under the stock dividend materials; supra ¶ 7.43. See also Rev. Rul. 83-119, 1983-2 CB 57.

[206] Regs. §1.368-2(e)(1).

[207] Although the definitional section, §368(a)(1)(E), does not require the use of securities, so that theoretically a recapitalization could involve short-term notes or open account indebtedness, the operative provision, §354, is more restrictive (infra ¶ 14.34). See also the *Neville Coke* decision, supra note 42, and discussion in supra ¶ 14.11 of the continuity aspects of securities. See generally Lorch v. CIR, 605 F2d 657 (2d Cir. 1979), cert. denied, 444 US 1076 (1980) (bond for stock exchange as recapitalization).

See also possible nonrecognition under the convertible bond rule theory of Rev. Rul. 72-265, 1972-1 CB 222, unless the obligation is a §453 installment obligation, in which case, the Service ruled, conversion constitutes a §453(B) disposition with gain being recognized to the extent of the full value of stock received on the conversion, Rev. Rul. 72-264, 1972-1 CB 131. Compare Ltr. Rul. 80-52-018 (1981), Fed. Taxes (P-H) ¶ 54,976 (parent has no §171 amortizable bond premium for excess of value of its stock over face of subsidiary's debt on conversion of that debt into parent's stock; excess value attributable to conversion feature). Accord with Letter Ruling is National Can Corp. v. US, 687 F2d 1107 (7th Cir. 1982) (no §162 deduction either because of §1032); Honeywell, Inc., 87 TC 624 (1986). But see ITT & Cos., 77 TC 60 (1981), aff'd per curiam, 704 F2d 252 (2d Cir. 1983) (parent gets basis in subsidiary's bonds equal to value of parent's stock at date of conversion). Contra is National Can Corp. v. US, supra (parent has zero basis for bonds). See Lipton, supra note 193; see also §171(b)(4), added by the Tax Reform Act of 1986.

[208] See CIR v. Carman, 189 F2d 363 (2d Cir. 1951), affirming the Tax Court's decision in which the government acquiesced, 1954-2 CB 3, after losing Estate of Bernstein, 22 TC 1364 (1954) (acq.), and several other cases on this point; see also Rev. Rul. 59-98, 1959-1 CB 76. A comparable attempt to discharge preferred dividend arrears by a recapitalization would be unsuccessful because of the 1969 amend-

the corporation after the exchange, the transaction also may qualify under §351 (see Chapter 3).[209]

Legislation enacted in 1984 significantly expanded the scope of the OID rules (and concurrently downgraded the coverage of §483).[210] Moreover, this legislation also characterized accrued market discount as interest in the hands of the holder under an approach similar to the rules of the 1954 Code's §1232 before its amendment by the Tax Reform Act of 1969 (i.e., as ordinary income taxable only on disposition, rather than currently as accrued, to the extent that such discount accrued ratably during the taxpayer's holding period for the bond).[211] Thus, if bonds with accrued market discount (i.e., having an adjusted basis less than face) are exchanged for stock or securities in a recapitalization, such discount taint would carry over into the new stock or securities and be taxed as interest income to the exchanging creditor *when* that property is disposed of by sale, retirement, or other disposition.[212]

---

ment to §305(b)(4); see Regs. §§1.305-7(c), 1.305-5(d), Example (1), and 1.368-2(e)(5).

The Bankruptcy Act of 1980 overruled the *Carman* case principle and amended §354(a)(2)(B) to make property attributable to accrued interest (including any accrued but untaxed OID, which, however, should only occur for pre-1969 debt issues) on the exchanged debt securities taxable to the exchanging creditor as a separate item of interest. See infra ¶¶ 14.20 and 14.34. However, as a result of 1984 amendments (infra note 210), earned market discount is not taxable at such time (infra note 212). But it should be possible to successfully recapitalize out of unearned OID taint (and unearned market discount taint, as well) by issuing new stock for the old debt, because the OID taint should not carry over into the new stock (at least if such stock is common stock). If preferred stock were reissued to retire the debt, query whether the OID character would shift to the preferred as excessive call premium under §305(b)(4) and thus be accrued over the noncall term of the preferred as a constructive stock dividend under Regs. §1.305-5(d), Examples (5) and (7), and §1.305-7(c). Also, one must be wary of creating excessive call premium on the preferred in a recapitalization exchange if the call price of the preferred exceeds the value (or face) of the debt. See Note, Discounted Preferred Stock, supra note 204.

[209] But §351(d)(2), added by the Bankruptcy Tax Act of 1980, excluded non-security debts from the definition of property under §351.

[210] The Tax Reform act of 1984, adding §§1271–1278, supra ¶ 4.40. See Eustice, The Tax Reform Act of 1984, ¶ 3.03[5] (Warren, Gorham & Lamont, Inc., 1984); Lokken, The Time Value of Money Rules, 42 Tax L. Rev. 1 (1986).

[211] Under §1276(b)(1), market discount builds up ratably on a *straight-line* basis (unlike OID, which, after the Tax Equity and Fiscal Responsibility Act of 1982, was changed to an economic accrual method in what is now §1272). From 1969–1982, OID also accrued (and was currently taxed) ratably on a straight-line basis. Unlike issue discount, however, market discount is only taxed on "disposition" (i.e., sale, retirement, or gift, but not in a tax-free nonrecognition exchange transaction); supra ¶ 4.44.

[212] Sections 1276(a)(1), 1276(a)(3), 1276(c)(2)(B), and 1276(d)(1)(B); see also supra note 208 and ¶ 4.44.

The corporation, on recapitalizing, may be able to pay off its creditors with stock worth less than the principal amount of the securities surrendered by them. At one time, the government argued that the spread represented income on the cancellation of indebtedness, taxable to the corporation under §61(a)(12). But the Service subsequently ruled that the substitution of common stock for debentures and unsecured claims did not effect a cancellation, reduction, or discharge of indebtedness; instead, the transaction amounted to a transformation from a fixed indebtedness to a capital stock liability.[213] The House version of the bill that became the Bankruptcy Tax Act of 1980 proposed to modify this rule by subjecting exchanges of nonsecurity debt for stock to the cancellation of indebtedness rules of §§108 and 1017,[214] but the Senate refused to go along with this proposal, and its view prevailed in the final 1980 Act.[215] However, legislation enacted in 1984

---

[213] See Rev. Rul. 59-222, 1959-1 CB 80; see also Tower Bldg. Corp., 6 TC 125 (1946) (acq.); CIR v. Capento Secs. Corp., 140 F2d 382 (1st Cir. 1944). On the tax consequences to the corporation of a forgiveness of interest in the course of a recapitalization, see Rev. Rul. 58-546, 1958-2 CB 143. But compare Rev. Rul. 70-271, 1970-1 CB 166; Eustice, Cancellation of Indebtedness and the Federal Income Tax: A Problem of Creeping Confusion, 14 Tax L. Rev. 238 (1959).

The corporation would in any event have two other strings to its bow: §354 (although the court in the *Capento* case, supra, reserved judgment on whether this provision applies to the reorganized corporation or only to its shareholders and security holders) and §1032 (whose language might be applied to the transaction described, although it was enacted for quite a different purpose (supra ¶ 3.12)). It is also possible that the transaction would come within one of the exceptions to the general principle that income is recognized on the cancellation of indebtedness for less than its face amount. See Eustice, supra; see also, as to a discharge of indebtedness in bankruptcy proceedings, Regs. §1.61-12(b); infra note 214.

The inputed interest provisions of §483 must also be considered in assessing the tax consequences of a bond-for-stock recapitalization. While §483 could apply to an exchange of old stock for new bonds (and conceivably even to an exchange of old bonds for new bonds), it ordinarily would not apply to an exchange of old bonds for new stock (unless the issue of such stock was deferred for the statutory period), infra ¶ 14.56; Prop. Regs. §1.483-1(b); supra ¶ 4.42. For taxability of any accrued market discount on the exchanged bonds, see supra notes 208, 211, and 212.

[214] The House version of the Bankruptcy Tax Act of 1980, initially proposed to amend §§108 and 1032 to provide that stock issued to satisfy debt generally would not be subject to §1032 and that the transaction would be treated as if the debt were satisfied for cash equal to the value of the stock. This provision would not apply to registered security debt in a §354 transaction, however, except to the extent that there was an accrued interest on the debt. See infra ¶¶ 14.20 and 14.58, see also supra ¶ 4.25.

But this provision was subsequently modified to permit the debtor to elect to apply the amount of its debt discharge gain either first to reduce depreciable property basis or, alternatively, to reduce other tax attributes.

[215] The Senate Finance Committee dropped the equity-for-debt provisions of proposed §108(f)(1) and retained the rule that no tax consequences result to the debtor from the satisfaction of its debts with stock (unless only a de minimis amount

removed the exception for debt-equity exchanges by solvent corporations and subjected these transactions to the general cancellation of indebtedness regime, while the Tax Reform Act of 1986 completely removed debt cancellation gains of solvent corporations from the regime of §§108 and 1017,[216] thereby subjecting these gains to current taxation.

3. Exchanges of bonds for bonds. For a number of years, the Service held the view that a horizontal exchange of outstanding bonds (or other securities) for new securities, if not accompanied by a modification of the corporation's stock structure, was a refinancing rather than a recapitalization. This theory escaped challenge until 1941, perhaps because most such exchanges during the 1930s produced losses that, under the Service's view, could be deducted unless barred by §1091 (wash sales). In 1941, however, the Board of Tax Appeals rejected the Service's theory, and its judgment was affirmed by the Court of Appeals for the Second Circuit in *CIR v. Neustadt's Trust*:

> The Commissioner contends that only a change in authorized or outstanding capital stock of a corporation can properly be denominated a recapitalization or a reshuffling of the capital structure. He describes an exchange of old debentures for new debentures in the same corporation as a mere refinancing operation. . . . But in common financial parlance

---

of stock was issued). The Finance Committee also modified the House version of the bill by providing that if a package of stock and other property was issued to cancel debts, the other property will be deemed to have satisfied an equivalent amount of debt, and the stock will be deemed to have satisfied the balance. Finally, the Finance Committee version provided in §108(e)(7) for an ordinary income recapture rule to the creditor who subsequently sells the stock (to the extent of the creditor's prior ordinary loss or bad debt deduction). This version of the bill ultimately passed in December 1980.

[216] The Tax Reform act of 1984 provided for the creation of debt cancellation gain in cases where the exchange was effected by a solvent corporation under §108(e)(10). For description of the types of transactions that inspired this amendment, see Heng & Parker, Tax-Free Debt Repurchases Using Stock-for-Debt Exchanges, 60 Taxes 527 (1982). See also Walter, Tax Aspects of Recent Innovative Financings—Strategies for Existing Discount Debt and for New Securities, 60 Taxes 995 (1982) (analyzing equity-for-debt swaps); Note, Debt-Equity Swaps, 37 Tax Lawyer 677 (1984); and Bryan, Cancellation of Indebtedness by Issuing Stock in Exchange: Challenging the Congressional Solution to Debt-Equity Swaps, 63 Tex. L. Rev. 89 (1984).

The Tax Reform Act of 1986 made cancellation of indebtedness gains of *solvent* corporations currently taxable without exception by repealing the basis reduction election alternative; the 1986 Act also required that one-half of the gain on equity-for-debt swaps by *insolvent* corporations must reduce the debtor's loss carry-overs; infra ¶¶ 14.58 and 16.25, para. 6.

the long term funded debt of a corporation is usually regarded as forming part of its capital structure. . . . By changing the interest rate and
date of maturity of its old bonds and adding a conversion option to the
holders of the new, the corporation could strengthen its financial condition, while the bondholders would not substantially change their original investments by making the exchange. "Recapitalization" seems a
most appropriate word to describe that type of reorganization and it is
the very kind of transaction where Congress meant the recognition of
gain or loss to be held in suspense until a more substantial change in the
taxpayer's original investment should occur.[217]

After losing several other cases on this point, the Service acquiesced in *Neustadt's Trust* and revoked its earlier rulings to the contrary.[218]

It should be noted that if in an exchange of securities for new securities,
the principal amount of the securities received exceeds the principal amount
of those surrendered, the fair market value of the excess is boot under
§§354(a)(2)(A) and 356(d)(2)(B). The taxpayer's gain, if any, would be recognized to the extent of the boot and generally would be taxed as capital
gain, if the bonds are capital assets in his hands, under §§356(a)(1) and
356(a)(2), since the transaction does not have "the effect of the distribution
of a dividend."[219] If the excess principal amount is a method of discharging
arrears in interest (or accrued market discount and untaxed OID in the case
of pre-1969 issues) on the bonds, the bondholder's gain is taxable separately
(after amendments in 1980) as ordinary interest income; but unearned OID
and market discount presumably are taxable as capital gain under
§§356(a)(1) and 356(a)(2).[220] (Under the final Senate Finance Committee
staff proposals for the reform of Subchapter C,[221] the excess of the issue
price of securities received over the *basis* of securities surrendered would be

---

[217] CIR v. Neustadt's Trust, 131 F2d 528, 529–530 (2d Cir. 1942).

[218] See Rev. Rul. 77-415, 1977-2 CB 311. But see Emery v. CIR, supra note 4,
holding that bonds of municipal corporation do not come within §368(a)(1)(E), on
the ground that Congress could not have intended this result.

[219] See Rev. Rul. 71-427, 1971-2 CB 183 (creditor boot taxed as capital gain; no
dividend effect).
  Since 1980, the use of §453 also seems possible here in view of the abolition of
the two-payment rule and the 30 percent initial payment limitation; see §453(f)(6)
(bonds must not be tradable under §§453(f)(4) and 453(f)(5) limitations, however).
But the Tax Reform Act of 1986 repealed use of §453 for sales of traded stock or
securities in §453(k)(2)(A).

[220] Supra note 208. See infra ¶ 14.34; and note also §§483 and 1274 in this
regard. In Rev. Rul. 60-37, 1960-1 CB 309, the Service ruled that issue discount
income attributable to the old bonds preserves its character as such in the new bonds
after a tax-free recapitalization exchange.

[221] Released May 20, 1985; this proposal was not contained in the staff's preliminary report of September 1983; supra notes 8 and 9.

taxable boot, although loss would continue to be unrecognized. Thus, the receipt of securities would be boot per se for purposes of gain exchanges under this reform proposal).

The Tax Reform Act of 1969 amended the rules relating to OID income by requiring the creditor-holder of issue discount bonds to accrue issue discount income ratably over the life of the bonds (see Chapter 4), and this treatment would seem to apply to bonds issued in a recapitalization under the theory of Rev. Rul. 60-37.[222] By the same token, unamortized §171 bond issue premium on the old securities should be deductible over the life of the new bonds.[223]

Legislation enacted in 1984 materially revised and expanded the OID rules once again, extending the scope of these provisions to a significantly wider range of transactions (including reorganization exchanges, whether or not involving traded securities).[224] Under these amendments, issue discount can arise whether or not the bonds are traded. If the bonds are traded, then the issue price will be determined by the value of the traded property; if not traded, the new bonds' issue price would be their discounted present value, using a prescribed statutory rate keyed to federal securities (and using compound interest principles). Moreover, accrued market discount (i.e., the excess of face of the bond over the holder's adjusted basis for the bonds) generally will be characterized as interest and taxed as such to the holder on the disposition of the bond, except that such discount will carry over into new bonds received in exchange therefore in a tax-free transaction.[225]

---

[222] Rev. Rul. 60-37, 1960-1 CB 309. The Tax Equity and Fiscal Responsibility Act of 1982 added §1232A, currently §1272, which changed the straight-line ratable accrual method of the 1969 legislation to an economic accrual method based on a yield-to-maturity compound present value interest formula.

The principle of Rev. Rul. 60-37 was codified by Regs. §1.1232-3(b)(1)(iv); also, Regs. §1.1232-3A(a)(2)(iii) computes accrual of OID carry-over by reference to the term of the new obligation received. These principles continue to apply after the 1984 amendments to the OID rules (infra note 224); see §1275(a)(4), and Prop. Regs. §1.1275-2(a).

[223] Supra note 207. But see §171(b)(4), added by the Tax Reform Act of 1986, limiting bond acquisition premium where a bond is acquired in a tax-free exchange for property (and limiting the premium to the excess of the value of the bond over its face), except in cases of a §368 bond-for-bond reorganization exchange.

The 1986 Act also places the amortizable bond premium deduction on a compound interest calculation system similar to the OID rules, supra ¶ 4.40.

[224] The Tax Reform Act of 1984, replacing §§1232 and 1232A with §§1271–1275; supra ¶ 4.40. See Eustice, supra note 210, ¶¶ 2.02[2] and 3.03[5][b]; Lokken, supra note 210.

[225] The Tax Reform Act of 1984, adding §§1276–1278. Bond-for-bond recapitalization exchanges would not trigger current tax on accrued market discount income (at least if the face of the new bonds does not exceed the face of the old), by virtue of §§1276(c)(2)(A) and 1276(d)(1)(B); rather, the discount taint will carry over into the

At the corporate level, the OID statute was amended in 1969 to provide that bond issue discount did not arise on the issuance of bonds or other securities in a reorganization exchange under §368(a)(1) even though the *value* of the old securities was less than the principal amount of the new obligations.[226] On the other hand, unamortized issue discount on the old bonds (and unamortized issue costs of the old bonds) continued to be deductible ratably over the life of the new obligations.[227] (The decisions under the law prior to the 1969 amendments on these questions were numerous and conflicting.[228]) However, legislation adopted in 1982[229] eliminated

---

new bonds. See Eustice, supra note 210, ¶¶ 2.02[4], 3.03[5][a], and 3.03[5][b]; Lokken, supra note 210.

The Tax Reform Act of 1986 grandfathered pre-1984 Act market discount bonds exchanged for new bonds having the same term and the same interest rate in §1278(a)(1)(C)(iii).

[226] For the law applicable to this period (1969–1982), see Rev. Rul. 77-415, 1977-2 CB 311 (no OID created in bond-for-bond or bond-for-stock recapitalization exchanges; continuity doctrine not applicable to Type E reorganization; §354(a)(1) nonrecognition on the bond-for-bond exchanges; §302 redemption on bond-for-stock exchange); Regs. §1.1232-3(b)(2)(iii)(*d*).

See generally Walter, supra note 216. Accord with Rev. Rul. 77-415 is Microdot, Inc. v. US, supra note 186; and Golden Nugget, Inc., supra note 186.

But see §1232(b)(4), added by the Technical Corrections Act of 1982, infra note 229, which is currently found in §1275(a)(4).

[227] Husky Oil Co., 83 TC 717 (1984) (no deduction for unamortized issue costs of old debt where exchanged for new debt; instead, such costs are spread over life of new debt).

[228] As to whether the exchange created deductible OID to the debtor issuing corporation under pre-1969 law, see National Alfalfa Milling Co. v. CIR, 417 US 134 (1974) (no OID on exchange of new bonds for old stock, at least where face of debt did not exceed initial issue price of stock; Supreme Court followed theory that value of old preferred is irrelevant if less than issue price of old preferred).

But see Cities Serv. Co. v. US, 522 F2d 1281 (2d Cir. 1974), cert. denied, 423 US 827 (1975) (OID can be created where new debt is exchanged for old preferred stock if face of new debt exceeds initial issue price of preferred) (the case was reversed and remanded, however, on the measure of the OID), on remand, 443 F. Supp. 392 (S.D.N.Y. 1978), aff'd, 586 F2d 967 (2d Cir. 1978); contra Fed-Mart Corp. v. US, 572 F2d 235 (9th Cir. 1978) (no OID on redemption of 22 percent of common stock for debentures; market value of debentures speculative per *National Alfalfa*, and no additional cost of acquiring use of capital; *Cities Service* approach rejected). But see Gulf M. & O.R.R. v. US, 579 F2d 892 (5th Cir. 1978) (following *Cities Service*).

See generally Rockler et al., Status of Amortizable Bond Discount After *National Alfalfa Case*, 41 J. Tax'n 134 (1974); Wolf, Original Issue Discount: Before and After *National Alfalfa*, 28 Tax Lawyer 325 (1975); Lewis, Recognizing Discharge of Indebtedness Income on Bond-for-Bond Recapitalizations, 45 J. Tax'n 370 (1976); de Kosmian, Original Issue Discount, 22 Tax Lawyer 339 (1969); supra ¶¶ 4.60 and 4.42; Eustice, supra note 213.

[229] See §1232(b)(4), added by the Technical Corrections Act of 1982. Under this legislation, reorganization exchanges of *traded* debt-for-debt after December 13, 1982 can create OID if the face of the new obligations exceeds the fair market value of the

the reorganization exception to the OID rules, so that recapitalization exchanges of traded debt again could give rise to OID, but limited to the spread between the face of new bonds and the greater of the old bonds' value or adjusted issue prices (initial issue price plus accrued OID).[230] Amendments in 1984 further broadened the possibility for OID by extending coverage to exchanges of nontraded debt as well.[231]

Where the face amount of the new securities exceeds the principal amount of the old issue, however, the corporate debtor may be entitled to a current deduction for the excess principal amount as a retirement premium attributable to the redemption of the old issue (unless such premium is attributable to a conversion privilege, for which see §249); in the alternative, the excess principal amount may be considered as amortizable issue discount incurred with respect to the new securities to be deducted ratably over the life of the new obligations.[232] If, on the other hand, the principal amount of the old obligations exceeds the principal amount of the new securities, the corporate debtor may be in receipt of cancellation of indebtedness income by reason of its bargain retirement of the old obligations; alternatively, this spread in principal amounts could be considered as amortizable issue premium income with respect to the new securities.[233]

---

old bonds; such OID is limited, however, to the "adjusted issue price" of the old bonds (if greater than value), which term is defined as original issue price plus previously includable OID thereon; see Walter, Recent Innovative Financing Techniques—An Addendum, 61 Taxes 184 (1983). This provision currently is found at §1275(a)(4) after the 1984 amendments to the OID rules, supra note 224, but was expanded to cover reorganization exchanges of untraded debt as well as traded debt. See Prop. Regs. §1.1275-2(a) (1986).

[230] This rule continued as §1275(a)(4) after the 1984 Act revisions to the OID rules, supra note 224. For the treatment of market discount on recapitalization exchanges (which will give rise to taxable interest to the holder, although not an interest deduction to the corporate debtor), see supra note 225.

[231] The Tax Reform Act of 1984, adding §§1274 and 1275(a)(4). The amount of OID on exchanges of untraded debt is determined by the discounted present value of the new bonds, using a prescribed statutory rate, keyed to various federal securities and compounded semiannually; see Prop. Regs. §1.1275-2(a).

[232] But could not have OID in reorganization exchange between 1969 and 1982, supra note 226; see Rev. Rul. 77-415, discussed supra note 226. But see §1232(b)(4), added by the Technical Corrections Act of 1982, supra note 229 (can now have OID in bond-for-bond recapitalization if face of new exceeds greater of value of old or adjusted issue price of old (i.e., original issue price plus accrued OID)); and §1275(a)(4), added by the Tax Reform Act of 1984 (can also have OID on exchanges of untraded debt). See Walter, supra note 229.

[233] If the values of both sets of securities (assuming that they are equivalent) equal the face of the old debt, OID (or issue premium) classification should be the result; if the values equal the face of the new debt, however, cancellation of indebtedness (or retirement premium) should result. But see Alfalfa Milling Co. v. CIR, supra note 228.

4. Exchanges of old stock for new bonds. The most controversial problem in the recapitalization area is the upstream exchange of stock for bonds (or other securities), and the heart of the problem can be illustrated quickly. Assume a prosperous one-person corporation with only common stock outstanding. If the corporation declares a dividend of its own bonds, debentures, or other securities, the shareholder will realize ordinary income in an amount equal to the fair market value of the bonds, assuming sufficient earnings and profits. Can the same transaction be turned into a recapitalization by having the shareholder surrender his stock in exchange for a package consisting of new stock with a different par value (or with other changes) plus bonds? Even if the exchange is a recapitalization, of course, the bonds would constitute boot under §§354(a)(2)(A) and 356(d). But if the shareholder realizes no gain on the exchange (because his stock has a higher basis than the value of the stock and bonds received) or if his gain is relatively small,[234] the recapitalization—if it can be so characterized—will enable him to bail out earnings and profits at the capital gain rate by selling the bonds or causing the corporation to retire them under §1271.[235]

In *Bazley v. CIR*, the Supreme Court held that an exchange by the shareholders of a family corporation of all of its common stock (1,000 shares, with a total par value of $100,000) for 5,000 shares of new common stock with no par value but an aggregate stated value of $300,000 plus debenture bonds (payable in 10 years but callable at any time) of a principal

---

See also Rev. Rul. 77-437, 1977-2 CB (debtor corporation realizes cancellation of indebtedness income on recapitalization exchange of new convertible bonds having a face amount lower than that of old convertible bonds even though values were equivalent; interest rate on new bonds higher and more favorable conversion terms, but this did not prevent cancellation of indebtedness income to corporation). See supra ¶¶ 4.60 and 4.25.

If basis of the old debt exceeds face of the new debt, exchanging creditor arguably may get §171 bond purchase premium deduction over life of the new debt in view of §§171(b)(1)(A) and 171(b)(1)(B) definition of bond premium as excess of basis of the debt over face. But see supra notes 207 and 223.

[234] Before the enactment in 1954 of §354(a)(2)(A), gain would not have been recognized—*if* the transaction qualified as a reorganization—no matter how low the shareholder's basis for his stock was, because securities could be received tax-free under the predecessor of §354(a)(1).

[235] The advantages of using some bonds or other securities in the corporation's original capital structure were discussed in Chapter 4, Part C. The question now is whether a going concern can distribute bonds in a wholly or partly tax-free recapitalization so as to remedy the failure, deliberate or inadvertent, to issue bonds when it was organized. For a parallel, see Chamberlin v. CIR 207 F2d 462 (6th Cir. 1953), cert. denied, 347 US 918 (1954), discussed supra Chapter 10, which brought on the enactment of §306 to close off the use of preferred stock dividends for a bailout of earnings and profits.

See also supra ¶ 7.40 (bond dividends).

amount of $400,000 was not a recapitalization as that term is used in §368(a)(1)(E),[236] reasoning as follows:

> [Recapitalization] is one of the forms of reorganization which obtains the privileges afforded by [§368(a)]. Therefore, "recapitalization" must be construed with reference to the presuppositions and purpose of [§368(a)]. It was not the purpose of the reorganization provision to exempt from payment of a tax what as a practical matter is realized gain. Normally, a distribution by a corporation, whatever form it takes, is a definite and rather unambiguous event. It furnishes the proper occasion for the determination and taxation of gain. But there are circumstances where a formal distribution, directly or through exchange of securities, represents merely a new form of the previous participation in an enterprise involving no change of substance in the rights and relations of the interested parties one to another or to the corporate assets. As to these, Congress has said that they are not to be deemed significant occasions for determining taxable gain. . . .
>
> What is controlling is that a new arrangement intrinsically partake of the elements of reorganization which underlie the Congressional exemption and not merely give the appearance of it to accomplish a distribution of earnings. In the case of a corporation which has undistributed earnings, the creation of new corporate obligations which are transferred to stockholders in relation to their former holdings, so as to produce, for all practical purposes, the same result as a distribution of cash earnings of equivalent value, cannot obtain tax immunity because cast in the form of a recapitalization-reorganization. . . .
>
> What have we here? No doubt, if the Bazley corporation had issued the debentures to Bazley and his wife without any recapitalization, it would have made a taxable distribution. Instead, these debentures were issued as part of a family arrangement, the only additional ingredient being an unrelated modification of the capital account. The debentures were found to be worth at least their principal amount, and they were virtually cash because they were callable at the will of the corporation which in this case was the will of the taxpayer. One does not have to pursue the motives behind actions, even in the more ascertainable forms of purpose, to find, as did the Tax Court, that the whole arrangement took this form instead of an outright distribution of cash or debentures, because the latter would undoubtedly have been taxable income whereas what was done could, with a show of reason, claim the shelter of the immunity of a recapitalization-reorganization.[237]

Although the result in the *Bazley* case—dividend income in an amount equal to the fair market value of the debentures—is clear enough, the

---

[236] Bazley v. CIR, supra note 5.
[237] Id. at 740–743.

Supreme Court gave so many reasons for the result that the case's ambit is quite uncertain. The theory that the debentures produced "for all practical purposes, the same result as a distribution of cash earnings of equivalent value" would seem to condemn any recapitalization in which securities are received pro rata by shareholders if the securities are marketable or if the corporation's financial status permits an immediate retirement. The statement that the debentures "were virtually cash because they were callable at the will of the corporation which was in this case the will of the taxpayer"[238] seems to rest on the corporation's liquid asset position, coupled with a unity of interest that might not exist if the stock was widely held or divided evenly among two or more unrelated persons. The theory that the transaction was simply an ordinary distribution of debentures disguised as a recapitalization suggests the possibility that a business reason for the exchange of stock might have helped to validate the distribution of the debentures. This theory also seems applicable only if securities are received by holders of *common* stock, since an exchange of *preferred* for securities could not ordinarily be effected by the dividend route. Finally, the emphasis in *Bazley* on the pro rata character of the transaction suggests that a distribution that is not pro rata would be less vulnerable, at least if the shareholders are not bound together by family ties.[239]

Recapitalizations in which shareholders get securities on a pro rata basis have been on the decline since the *Bazley* case, not only because its rationale is menacingly uncertain, but also because an exchange that slips by *Bazley* must still run the gauntlet of §§354(a)(2)(A) and 356, under which the fair market value of the bonds is boot even if the transaction qualifies as a recapitalization.[240] Although boot is troublesome only if the taxpayer enjoys a gain on the exchange (see §356(a)(1)), this condition is ordinarily present

---

[238] It is not clear whether the Supreme Court meant that the debentures were not securities, a holding that would have important ramifications in such other areas as §351 exchanges (supra ¶ 3.03). It should be noted that there might be a recapitalization, even though the new claims against the corporation did not constitute securities under §354. See L. & E. Stirn, Inc. v. CIR, 107 F2d 390 (2d Cir. 1939).

[239] See Davis v. Penfield, 205 F2d 798 (5th Cir. 1953), involving an exchange of preferred stock for debentures, where *Bazley* was distinguished on various grounds, including the more public character of the corporation and the fact that the debentures were no more marketable than the preferred stock given up. To the same effect is Berner v. US, 282 F2d 720 (Ct. Cl. 1960).

[240] The *Bazley* opinion suggested, as an alternative basis for decision, that the debentures were boot under pre-1954 law. Since §354(a)(2) was not then in force, the Supreme Court must have meant that the debentures were the equivalent of cash. Even so, they would have been taxable as a dividend only to the extent that the taxpayer realized a gain on the exchange by virtue of §112(c) of the 1939 Code, and the Tax Court in Alice Bazley, 4 TC 897 (1945), did not determine the amount of the taxpayer's gain, if any; see also Lokken, supra note 210.

in the case of the closely held corporation that wishes to engage in this kind of recapitalization,[241] and earnings and profits are likely to be large enough to result in dividend treatment under §356(a)(2) for the entire value of the securities. Thus, *Bazley* and the 1954 statutory changes render the pro rata exchange of common stock for new common stock and bonds an unpopular method of recapitalizing corporations except where the shareholders of the recapitalized corporation are other corporations, for whom the dividends-received deduction of §243[242] virtually nullifies the pain of a *Bazley*-type dividend.

There may still be some room, however, for an exchange of stock for securities on a non pro rata basis. Thus, in *Daisy Seide*, the Tax Court held that *Bazley* did not apply to an exchange of preferred stock for debentures where the preferred was not held in proportion to the common[243] and where the debentures were not readily marketable or likely to be retired at an early date because of the corporation's poor earnings record and obsolete plant.[244] Such an exchange might be a recapitalization under the 1954 Code, but there are two obstacles to the tax-free treatment it enjoyed under the 1939 Code: (1) Since the shareholders received *only* securities for their stock, §354 would be inapplicable to the exchange[245] and (2) even if §354 is applicable, the

---

[241] The principal exception would be a corporation whose stock has been inherited recently so that the shareholder has a stepped up basis under §1014 equal to the stock's fair market value.

Different results can occur under the *Bazley* dividend approach and the boot dividend reorganization rules of §356(a)(2) in the following cases: (1) If the §1001 realized gain is less than the boot, §§301 and 316 would tax the full distribution of securities if covered by earnings, while §356(a)(2) limits recognition to the amount of the realized gain and (2) if earnings and profits are low or zero, *Bazley* and §301(c)(2) require application of the distributed securities against stock basis before reporting gain under §301(c)(3) once such basis is recovered, while the §356(a)(1) approach would recognize the top layer of realized gain from the exchange where boot is received.

[242] Supra ¶ 5.05.

[243] Daisy Seide, 18 TC 502 (1952). All the stock was held by two families; if each family was considered as a unit, the preferred shares (and hence the debentures received in exchange for the preferred) were held pro rata. The court, however, looked to individual ownership only, which was not pro rata. It is entirely possible that family ownership would receive more attention from another court, or even from the Tax Court if the family were small enough, despite the fact that the constructive ownership rules of §318(a) are not expressly made applicable for this purpose. Note the reference in the *Bazley* case to a family arrangement, and note also that the court referred to the will of "the" taxpayer, although the stock was divided between husband and wife.

[244] See also Wolf Envelope Co., 17 TC 471 (1951) (nonacq.).

[245] This position is adopted by Regs. §1.354-1(d), Example (3), presumably on the ground that §354 applies only if the taxpayer receives some nonrecognition prop-

debentures would constitute boot, with the result that the shareholder's gain (if any) would be recognized to the extent of their fair market value. It should be noted that if a non-pro rata exchange fails for any reason to qualify as a recapitalization, the participating shareholders do not necessarily realize dividend income: The transaction is in substance a redemption of their stock, which may produce capital gain or loss if the conditions of §302(b)(1), §302(b)(2), or §302(b)(3) are satisfied.[246]

Legislation enacted in 1984 extended the OID rules to debt dividends[247] and to other exchanges of stock (whether traded or not) for debt (whether traded or not), regardless of the status of the exchange as a recapitalization reorganization.[248] Moreover, if §483 or §1272 does not apply, then §7872

---

erty. This objection would disappear if the shareholders received some new stock, as well as the securities, in exchange for their old stock. See also Rev. Rul. 77-415, 1977-2 CB 311 (transaction is a recapitalization, but gain fully taxed; presumably loss would be deductible, since transaction a §302 redemption, not a §354 exchange). Accord with Rev. Rul. 77-415 is Microdot, Inc. v. US, supra note 186; Golden Nugget, Inc., supra note 186.

Moreover, the redeeming taxpayer could use §453 installment sale rules here, if the bonds (and, since amendments by the Tax Reform Act of 1986, the stock) are not traded per §§453(f)(4), 453(f)(5), and §453(k)(2)(A). However, §483, and §1273 or §1274, can apply here as well.

[246] Supra ¶ 9.02 and Rev. Rul. 56-179, 1956-1 CB 187. For treatment of the issuing corporation, see text supra notes 226 and 228–233; supra ¶ 9.34. For the possibility of creating OID deductions for the corporation by exchanging new bonds for old preferred stock, see Cities Serv. Co. v. US, supra note 228; §§1273 and 1274; supra ¶ 4.40; infra note 248.

See also §453 (as amended in 1980) for possible installment sale treatment if bonds not traded (no longer any two-payment rule). But see §453(k)(2)(A) (not usable if stock traded either).

[247] For the treatment of OID debt dividends before the 1984 amendments, see Claussen's Inc. v. US, 469 F2d 340 (5th Cir. 1972) (held no OID was created on the issue of new bonds for old common in a pro rata recapitalization exchange because the common shareholder's proportional interests were not affected by the transaction; query whether the exchange was merely a *Bazley* bond dividend because of the pro rata character of the transaction).

But after the Tax Reform Act of 1984, supra note 224, OID on debt dividends will now be created to the extent the face of the debt exceeds its discounted present value, §1274(a)(5). Moreover, this amendment modified the charge to earnings and profits under §312(a)(2) for debt dividends (limiting such charges to the value of the distributed debt), supra ¶ 7.40; see Prop. Regs. §1.1275-2(c). If neither §483 nor §1274 applies (e.g., because the debt is a demand debt), then §7872 will, with comparable results, although the shareholder's foregone OID interest element will also be a capital contribution to the corporation; see Prop. Regs. §§1.7872-2(a)(2)(ii) and 1.7872-4(d)(1); infra note 249.

[248] See §§1273(b)(3) (traded), and 1274 and 1275(a)(4) (untraded), supra note 224; supra ¶ 4.40.

(the below market interest rules) can apply, which in turn will trigger collateral tax consequences to the shareholder-creditor and corporate debtor. [249]

5. Continuity of interest in recapitalizations. The consideration that may be used in a Type E reorganization is left unregulated by the statutory definition, but there is authority for the proposition that continuity of interest is not required in the reorganization of a single corporation, and the Service has recently agreed. Thus, in *Alan O. Hickok*, a transaction in which a number of shareholders exchanged their stock for debentures was held to be a tax-free recapitalization, [250] despite their loss of a proprietary interest in the corporation. [251] It is not clear whether this principle would or should be followed in a Type A reorganization that was the functional equivalent of a recapitalization of a single corporation (e.g., the merger of a corporation into a newly organized corporate shell or into a wholly owned subsidiary) or in a merger of brother-sister corporations.

As to recapitalizations in which some of the shareholders lose their proprietary interest, in Rev. Rul. 56-179, the Service ruled that a transaction in which some preferred shareholders exchanged their stock for common stock, while others received either cash or a combination of bonds and common stock, constituted a recapitalization. [252] This ruling goes far beyond *Elmer W. Hartzel*, holding that an exchange in which some of a corporation's common stockholders exchanged their common for preferred stock was a tax-free recapitalization, [253] where the court rejected the government's theory that the transaction violated the continuity of interest requirement and that it was the equivalent of a pro rata distribution of the preferred stock followed by an independent and taxable exchange among the shareholders; [254] but in

---

[249] See Prop. Regs. §§1.7872-2(a)(2)(ii) (application of §7872 where §§483 and 1274 do not apply) and 1.7872-4(d) (capital contribution for foregone interest element in the case of corporate-shareholder loan transactions); supra ¶¶ 4.40 and 7.40.

[250] Alan O. Hickok, 32 TC 80 (1959) (acq.).

[251] Under §354(a)(2)(A) of the 1954 Code, however, the shareholders would have to recognize gain in full on such an exchange, since the transaction would be entirely outside the nonrecognition provisions of §§354 and 356; the character of this gain presumably would be tested under §302.

See also Davis v. Penfield, supra note 239; Rev. Rul. 77-415, 1977-2 CB 311 (new bonds for old stock a recapitalization, but transaction taxed as a redemption to exchanging shareholders under §302; no continuity of interest required here; Service agreed to follow Hickok); Rev. Rul. 77-479, 1977-2 CB 119 (planned shareholder resale not fatal).

[252] Rev. Rul. 56-179, 1956-1 CB 187.

[253] Elmer W. Hartzel, 40 BTA 492 (1939) (acq.).

[254] See also Alan O. Hickok, supra note 250; Marjorie N. Dean, 10 TC 19 (1948) (acq.). The type of recapitalization involved in the *Hartzel* and *Dean* cases was approved as tax-free under §305(b) as well as by final Regs. §1.305-3(e), Example (12).

Rev. Ruls. 77-415[255] and 77-479,[256] the Service conceded that continuity of interest is not required in a recapitalization exchange.

¶ 14.18　CHANGES IN IDENTITY, FORM, OR PLACE OF ORGANIZATION (TYPE F)

1. General. A Type F reorganization is "a mere change in identity, form, or place of organization of one corporation,[257] however effected" under §368(a)(1)(F). This provision of the statute is not explained further in the regulations and it received almost no administrative or judicial attention until recently.[258] In Rev. Rul. 57-276, it was applied to the reincorporation of a corporation in another state (effected by creating a new corporation in the other state and then merging into the new corporation),[259] and in *Helvering v. Southwest Consolidated Corp.*, it was held that "a transaction which shifts the ownership of the proprietary interest in a corporation is hardly 'a mere change in identity, form, or place of organization' within the meaning of [§368(a)(1)(F)]."[260] It may be that a reincorporation coupled with a

---

See generally Friedman & Silbert, Recapitalizations—Exchanges of Stock, Securities and Property of the Same Corporation Under the Internal Revenue Code of 1954, 13 NYU Inst. on Fed. Tax'n 533 (1955); Tarleau, Recapitalizations, 11 NYU Inst. on Fed. Tax'n 371 (1953); Golomb, Recapitalization: The Definition Problem, 7 Tax L. Rev. 343 (1952).

[255] Rev. Rul. 77-415, 1977-2 CB 311. Accord with Rev. Rul. 77-415 are Microdot, Inc., v. US, supra note 186; Golden Nugget, Inc., supra note 186.

[256] Rev. Rul. 77-479, 1977-2 CB 119; see also Rev. Rul. 82-34, 1982-1 CB 59 (continuity of business enterprise limitation, infra ¶ 14.51, also not applicable).

[257] The "one corporation" language was added to the Type F definition in 1982 to deal with the problems described in para. 4 of this section.

[258] See generally Cole & Brezak, Meeting the IRS' New F Reorganization Tests, 44 J. Tax'n 344 (1976); McManus, Judicial Law-Making: The Liquidation of a Corporation Treated as an F Reorganization. 2 J. Corp. Tax'n 273 (1975); Pugh, The F Reorganization: Reveille for a Sleeping Giant? 24 Tax L. Rev. 437 (1969); Comment, (F) Reorganizations and Proposed Alternate Routes for Post-Reorganization Net Operating Loss Carrybacks, 66 Mich. L. Rev. 498 (1968); Comment, Section 368(a)(1)(F) and Loss Carrybacks in Corporate Reorganizations, 117 U. Pa. L. Rev. 764 (1969); Metzer, An Effective Use of Plain English—The Evolution and Impact of Section 368(a)(1)(F), 32 Tax Lawyer 703 (1979); Solomon, The Judicially Expanded "F" Reorganization and Its Uncertain Operating Rules, 7 J. Corp. Tax'n 24 (1980).

[259] Rev. Rul. 57-276, 1957-1 CB 126; see also Rev. Rul. 80-105, 1980-1 CB 78 (conversion of federal nonstock mutual Savings and Loan into state stock Savings and Loan held Type F); Rev. Rul. 87-27, 1987-15 IRB 5 (change of *country* of incorporation an F).

[260] Helvering v. Southwest Consol. Corp., supra note 33.

change in the number of shares, par value, voting rights, and so forth, would be a Type F reorganization, at least if it did not materially change the rights of the shareholders inter se, but since this would also probably be a Type E recapitalization, §368(a)(1)(F) seems to add nothing to its status.[261] More recently, several decisions expanded the scope of the Type F reorganization to include fusions of multiple affiliated operating companies[262] and even to a situation where proprietary continuity was significantly diluted as a result of the transaction.[263]

2. Overlap aspects. In 1940, Randolph Paul said that the Type F reorganization "is so little relied upon by taxpayers that this part of the statute has indeed perished through lack of use,"[264] and in 1954 the House proposed

---

[261] See generally Marr v. US, 268 US 536 (1925), holding such a transaction to be a taxable exchange under the Revenue Act of 1916. See also Ahles Realty Corp. v. CIR, 71 F2d 150 (2d Cir. 1934), cert. denied, 293 US 611 (1934) (Type F reorganization, having effect of a recapitalization that would be vulnerable under the subsequently decided *Bazley* case, supra note 5, discussed supra ¶ 14.17); Rev. Rul. 66-284, 1966-2 CB 115 (where less than one percent of shares of publicly held corporation do not participate in a reincorporation-type statutory merger, the transaction qualified as a Type F reorganization); Dunlap & Assocs., Inc., supra note 56 (reincorporation by merger a Type F reorganization); Rev. Rul. 67-376, 1967-2 CB 142 (reincorporation as a business trust, taxable as an association, a Type F reorganization); Casco Prods. Corp., 49 TC 32 (1967) (merger of 91 percent owned subsidiary into newly formed 100 percent owned subsidiary to freeze out subsidiary's 9 percent minority interest; held in substance a redemption; issue of Type F qualification not decided); Rev. Rul. 72-206; 1972-1 CB 105 (change of name and issue of new stock in exchange for all of old stock held prior to transaction a Type F reorganization); Berger Mach. Prods., Inc., 68 TC 358 (1977) (merger of four active brother-sister corporations into new corporation not a Type F reorganization because of shifts in relative shareholder interests; majority also refused to find a Type F reorganization where fused corporations active); Rev. Rul. 75-561, 1975-2 CB 129, discussed infra para. 3, this section.

[262] Infra para. 3, this section. But see 1982 amendments that vitiate most (but *not* all) of these decisions, infra para. 4, this section.

[263] Aetna Cas. & Sur. Co. v. US, supra note 47 (pre-1968 merger of 61 percent owned subsidiary into newly organized 100 percent owned subsidiary to eliminate minority interest; found a Type F reorganization on a *Casco* analysis). On petition for rehearing (39 AFTR2d 1111), the court limited its holding on the Type F reorganization definition to the §381(b)(3) carry-back rules. Compare Bercy Indus., Inc., supra note 104; infra note 267.

See also Security Indus. Ins. Co. v. US, 702 F2d 1234 (5th Cir. 1983) (purchase of subsidiary stock, liquidation, and reincorporation of operating assets in another subsidiary not a Type F; no continuity of interest; continuity broken by cash purchase); Bogaard, Comment—Corporation Reorganization, 4 J. Corp. Tax'n 251 (1977).

[264] Paul, Studies in Federal Taxation 82 (West, 3d Ser., 1940).

its repeal. It was retained in the 1954 Code, however, and came to play an unexpectedly important role. In Rev. Rul. 57-276, the Service acknowledged that a Type F reorganization will often also constitute a Type A, C, or D reorganization.[265] In case of such an overlap, the Service ruled that the transaction should be treated as a Type F reorganization under §381(b), which distinguishes between Types A-D and Type F for purposes of closing the taxable year and carrying back a net operating loss.[266] One of the reasons for Type F's previous obscurity was that other types performing the same functions had the same tax results as a Type F exchange, so that it was not necessary to distinguish between them; under Rev. Rul. 57-276, however, it may be essential to determine whether a Type A, C, or D reorganization also meets the requirements of Type F. Several of the later Type F reorganization cases have involved this issue.[267]

The Type F provisions were also applied to a putative §351 exchange in Rev. Rul. 68-349.[268] There, an individual transferred appreciated property to a new corporation for its stock, while a corporation simultaneously transferred all of its assets to the new corporation (likewise in exchange for stock) and then liquidated. The Service ruled that the transaction constituted a taxable exchange of property by the individual for stock of an uncontrolled corporation, and that the alleged corporate transferor had merely reincorporated in a severable Type F reorganization.[269]

---

[265] Rev. Rul. 57-276, 1957-1 CB 126.

[266] If the transaction meets the requirements of *both* Types C and D, as well as Type F, however, it is arguable that §368(a)(2)(A) takes hold and requires it to be characterized as a Type D reorganization exclusively. See Gordon v. CIR, 424 F2d 378 (2d Cir. 1970), cert. denied, 400 US 848 (1970) (disqualified Type D transaction is not a Type F reorganization; §355 is exclusive in divisive reorganization area). See also Rev. Rul. 72-420, 1972-2 CB 473 (overlap of Type F and §1036); Rev. Rul. 79-289, 1979-2 CB 145 (overlap of Types D and F; held §357(c) not applicable to Type F).

See also §1244(d)(2) (successor corporation in a Type F reorganization to be treated as the same corporation as its predecessor, which will require a determination of when a reorganization of another type also meets the standards of Type F); and §382(g)(3)(A)(ii) (Type F is not an equity structure change, infra ¶ 16.24).

[267] See Dunlap & Assocs., Inc., supra note 56; Casco Prods. Corp., supra note 261; Bercy Indus., Inc., supra note 104; infra notes 271 and 272.

In *Bercy*, the Ninth Circuit reversed the Tax Court on the loss carry-back issue (postmerger carry-back allowed after forward triangular merger into new shell subsidiary even though transaction not a Type F or Type B; no tracing problems here, so §381(b)(3) limitation not applicable; transaction functional equivalent of a Type B stock acquisition, even though court did not decide whether transaction constituted a Type B).

[268] Rev. Rul. 68-349, 1968-2 CB 143.

[269] See generally supra ¶¶ 3.14 and 3.19.

3. Other special aspects. One of the more important roles for the Type F reorganization was its use as a weapon against the liquidation-reincorporation bailout device. Although the courts did not fully embrace the Type F provision as a solution to reincorporation problems, it continued to be a brooding presence in the area that could not be ignored.[270]

Whether the Type F reorganization could apply to the fusion of two or more active corporations (even though commonly owned) or was limited to transactions involving changes in the structure of a single corporate enterprise, was a subject of considerable controversy until 1982, when the matter was solved by an amendment to the statute, as discussed in the following paragraph. The Tax Court and the Service at first took the latter view,[271] but other courts applied the Type F definition to fusions of active affiliated companies if there was (1) identity of proprietary interest and (2) uninterrupted business continuity,[272] and the Service, in Rev. Rul. 75-561,

---

[270] See the discussion infra ¶ 14.54.

[271] Estate of Stauffer v. CIR, 403 F2d 611 (9th Cir. 1968), and Associated Mach. v. CIR, 403 F2d 622 (9th Cir. 1968), reversed the Tax Court on this issue; the Service first announced that it will not follow the appellate decisions (Rev. Rul. 69-185, 1969-1 CB 108), but Rev. Rul. 75-561, 1975-2 CB 129, revoked Rev. Rul. 69-185 and agreed to follow *Stauffer* and other decisions (infra note 272), which upheld Type F status in these situations; see Rev. Rul. 78-287, 1978-2 CB 146 (same for downstream merger of parent into subsidiary if tests of Rev. Rul. 75-561 are met).

See also Eastern Color Printing Co., 63 TC 27 (1974) (acq.) (liquidation of a wholly owned operating subsidiary by merger into its passive parent holding company, whose only asset was stock of the subsidiary, qualified as a Type F reorganization on facts so that post-fusion losses could be carried back to pre-fusion years of the subsidiary under §381, a narrow holding, since Tax Court did not overrule its position that merger of two operating companies is not a Type F reorganization); Berger Mach. Prods., Inc. supra note 261 (not a Type F); Romy Hammes, Inc., 68 TC 900 (1977) (same); Bercy Indus., Inc., supra note 104 (but *Bercy* was reversed, supra note 267); Mariani Frozen Foods, Inc., 81 TC 448 (1983), aff'd sub nom. Gee Trust v. CIR, 761 F2d 1410 (9th Cir. 1985) (merger of holding company subsidiary into its parent not a Type F where subsidiary's asset promptly resold by parent after merger; no business continuity).

[272] Home Constr. Corp. v. US, 439 F2d 1165 (5th Cir. 1971) (merger of 123 affiliated corporations a Type F reorganization, citing *Stauffer* and *Davant*; remanded to determine loss carry-back deductions under *Libson Shops* tracing principles); Performance Sys., Inc. v. US, 382 F. Supp. 525 (M.D. Tenn. 1973), aff'd per curiam, 501 F2d 1338 (6th Cir. 1974) (upstream merger of 100 percent operating subsidiary into parent held a Type F reorganization under authority of *Davant, Stauffer, Associated Machine*, and *Home Construction Corp.* cases; court felt parent-subsidiary fusion no different from brother-sister fusion for Type F reorganization purposes if business and proprietary continuity tests met); accord Movielab, Inc. v. US, 494 F2d 693 (Ct. Cl. 1974); see also Aetna Cas. & Sur. Co. v. US, supra note 47.

Compare Berger Mach. Prods., Inc., supra note 261; Romy Hammes, Inc., supra note 271 (not a Type F reorganization on fusion of active brother-sister corporations; no substantial identity of owners and different businesses). But see TFI Cos. v. US,

finally agreed to follow these decisions[273] under certain limited conditions.[274]

4. Type F reorganizations involving multiple operating companies under TEFRA. After nearly fourteen years of judicial expansions of the Type F reorganization definition in §368(a)(1)(F) to include fusions of active affiliated corporations if there was (1) identity of relative shareholder proprietary interest and (2) uninterrupted business continuity,[275] Congress overturned these decisions (including the limited concessions in Rev. Rul. 75-561) and adopted the Service's original views first expressed in Rev. Rul. 69-185 by adding the "three little words" "of one corporation" to §368(a)(1)(F). In keeping with the freewheeling Conference Committee legislative approach, no such provision existed in either the House or Senate bills; undeterred by this technicality, the Conference amended the Type F definition effective for transactions occurring after August 31, 1982.[276]

The Conference Report noted, however, that the new limitation "does not preclude the use of more than one *entity* to consummate the transaction provided only one *operating* company is involved."[277] It may well be that

---

40 AFTR2d 5688 (C.D. Cal. 1977) (valid Type F reorganization under Rev. Rul. 75-561).

[273] Rev. Rul. 75-561, 1975-2 CB 129; see also Rev. Rul. 78-287, 1978-2 CB 146; Rev. Rul. 78-441, 1978-2 CB 152 (de minimis rule applies to Rev. Rul. 75-561 Type Fs).

[274] These were that there be identity of shareholder interests, the same (or integrated) businesses, and uninterrupted business continuity (also loss carry-backs must be traceable to the same business). If these conditions existed, fusions of active brother-sister corporations and parent subsidiary corporations would qualify as Type F reorganizations. But see supra note 257 and infra para. 4.

See Rev. Rul. 79-71, 1979-1 CB 151 (post-fusion business continuity test of Rev. Rul. 75-561 satisfied where service corporation and corporation engaged in business of leasing facilities to service corporation were merged into a new corporation and leasing activities discontinued; previous integration of premerger activities, coupled with use of facilities by new corporation after merger, enough to satisfy business continuity). But see Mariani Frozen Foods, Inc., supra note 271; National Tea Co., 83 TC 8 (1984), aff'd, 793 F2d 864 (7th Cir. 1986) (post-reorganization loss not attributable to pre-fusion business and thus could not be carried back to transferor-subsidiary's prior year; loss-tracing rule of Rev. Rul. 75-561 a proper limitation and was not satisfied here).

See generally infra ¶¶ 16.12, 14.53 and 14.54.

[275] Supra para. 3, this section, notes 271 and 272.

[276] Prior law continued to apply, however, to plans adopted before such date and consummated by the close of 1982, Tax Equity and Fiscal Responsibility Act §225(b)(2).

[277] H.R. Rep. No. 760, 97th Cong., 2d Sess. 541 (1982). (The example given is the reincorporation of an operating company in a different state.)

fusion of an operating subsidiary with its passive holding company parent (as in the *Eastern Color* case[278]) can still be a Type F under the amended restrictive definition; on the other hand, fusions of multiple operating subsidiaries, or combinations of an operating parent and its operating subsidiary, can no longer be Type Fs.[279] Curiously, the new legislation may have failed to reach the decision in *Bercy Industries*, in which the court did not hold that the transaction was a true Type F reorganization.[280]

¶ 14.19   TRANSACTIONS INVOLVING INVESTMENT COMPANIES

Legislation passed by Congress as part of the Tax Reform Act of 1976 amended §368(a)(2) of the reorganization definition provisions by adding subparagraph (F), the general purpose of which is to restrict tax-free treatment for reorganizations involving two or more investment companies, which have the effect of diversifying investment assets in a manner similar to the exchange-fund device.[281] The term "investment company" is defined by §368(a)(2)(F)(iii) as a regulated investment company, a real estate investment trust, and a corporation more than 50 percent of whose assets (excluding cash and cash equivalents by virtue of §368(a)(2)(F)(iv)) consist of stock or securities (and for this purpose, the committee reports intend a very broad definition (e.g., rights, warrants, options, commodity futures contracts)), and more than 80 percent of such assets are held for investment.

The general effect of §368(a)(2)(F) is to deny tax-free reorganization treatment to the undiversified investment company (defined by implication in §368(a)(2)(F)(ii) as an investment company more than 25 percent of whose non-cash assets are invested in stock and securities of one issuer or more than 50 percent of the value of whose total assets are invested in the stock or securities of five or fewer issuers; that is, if a substantial portion of its assets are invested in a limited number of companies, the corporation will be subject to this provision if it affiliates with another investment company), and to its shareholders and security holders.

---

[278] Supra note 271.

[279] E.g., transactions like those involved in *Home Construction, Performance Systems,* and *MovieLab*, supra note 272.

[280] Supra note 267. *Bercy* involved a forward triangular merger into a newly created shell subsidiary. Moreover, reverse triangular mergers under §368(a)(2)(E) and Type B reorganizations still do not invoke the carry-back limitations of §381(b)(3). See Barbosa, An Analysis of "F" Reorganizations Involving a Single Operating Corporation After TEFRA, 11 J. Corp. Tax'n 3 (1984).

[281] Supra ¶ 3.15. See, e.g., Rev. Rul. 87-9, 1987-5 IRB 4.

A special lookthrough rule for 50 percent-owned subsidiaries is provided in §368(a)(2)(F)(iii)—that is the parent will be deemed to own its ratable share of such subsidiary's assets directly—and §368(a)(2)(F)(iv) further provides that acquisitions for the purpose of becoming diversified or ceasing to be an investment company can be disregarded. While §368 treatment is denied to such a transaction, the transferor corporation was presumably entitled to former §337 treatment (before its repeal in 1986), and its shareholders were governed by the liquidation rules of §§331 and 334.[282]

Section 368(a)(2)(F) does not apply if each investment company is owned substantially by the same persons in the same proportion (§368(a)(2)(F)(v)); but a special rule is provided in §368(a)(2)(F)(vi) to treat reverse acquisitions as constructive exchanges by the surviving company and its shareholders and security holders.

It should be noted that fusions of diversified investment companies are not affected by this proposal; nor are mergers, for example, of only one investment company (whether diversified or not) with an operating company covered by its provisions; it is only fusions of two undiversified investment companies (both of which will be taxed) or of an undiversified and a diversified investment company that are denied reorganization treatment by this amendment, with the result that such combinations should be treated as taxable purchases and sales under the general liquidation rules (see Chapter 11), effective for transfers after February 1, 1976.[283]

¶ 14.20   INSOLVENCY REORGANIZATIONS (TYPE G)

1. General. In order to reform and modernize the tax rules applicable to insolvency reorganizations, reflecting the general bankruptcy reform leg-

---

[282] See Rev. Rul. 69-6, 1969-1 CB 104. For the repeal of §337 by the Tax Reform Act of 1986, see supra ¶ 11.61.

[283] For analyses of this legislation, see Eustice, The Tax Reform Act of 1976: Loss Carryovers and Other Corporate Changes, 32 Tax L. Rev. 113 (1977); Bacon, TRA '76 Affects Parent-Subsidiary Liquidations, Investment Company Reorganizations, PHC Income, §1239, 46 J. Tax'n 264 (1977); see also Freeman, Leveraged Buy-Outs: Cash Company and Investment Company Reorganizations, 6 J. Corp. Tax'n 239 (1979). Regulations under §368(a)(2)(F) were proposed on December 30, 1980, Prop. Regs. §1.368-4. The Revenue Act of 1978 also subjected investment companies to the common control limitations of §267(b)(3) (which would deny recognition of loss).

In a related development, regulations were proposed on December 28, 1979 and became final on December 29, 1980, in Regs. §1.368-1(d), which restrict cash company mergers under continuity of business enterprise principles; see infra ¶ 14.51, para. 2.

The Finance Committee staff's proposals for reform of Subchapter C, supra note 9, would continue the investment company restrictions of present law; infra ¶ 14.21.

islation of 1978, the House Ways and Means Select Subcommittee introduced the Bankruptcy Tax Act of 1979. This bill represented the joint efforts of the tax and bankruptcy bars, working together with Congress, to draft legislation that would bring some order to the chaotic state of present law as it applied to insolvency proceedings. These proposals, in slightly revised form, ultimately were enacted as the Bankruptcy Tax Act of 1980 in December of 1980.

In general, Section 4 of this Act replaces former §§371 and 372 with a new set of specific reorganization provisions tailored to the special exigencies of insolvency reorganizations. A new category of reorganization (Type G) was adopted in §368(a)(1)(G), which provision strongly resembled the language and operation of the Type D reorganization. Moreover, triangular reorganizations involving insolvent corporations were greatly facilitated under the new Act. The new Type G reorganization also can be either acquisitive or divisive in character. Finally, the continuity of interest limitations of prior law were significantly eased for insolvency reorganizations, a feature of the new legislation that was one of its most notable characteristics. These provisions were generally effective for insolvency proceedings commencing on or after October 1, 1979, although the ultimately enacted version pushed this effective date forward to 1981 (unless taxpayers elect the earlier date).

The Economic Recovery Tax Act of 1981 amended §368(a)(3)(D) as to reorganizations involving economically distressed financial institutions, extending the Type G reorganization provisions to such transactions free of the continuity of interest requirement if (1) substantially all the transferor's assets are acquired, (2) substantially all its liabilities are assumed, and (3) the appropriate bank regulatory agency certifies that certain conditions exist or will exist in the near future in the absence of action by such agency.[284] These provisions apply to transfers after 1980 and expire after 1988.

2. Technical analysis. A Type G reorganization is defined by §368(a)(1)(G) as "a transfer by a corporation of all or part of its assets to another corporation in a title 11 or similar case; but only if, in pursuance of the plan, stock or securities of the corporation to which the assets are transferred are distributed in a transaction which qualifies under Section 354, 355, or 356." A "title 11 or similar case" is defined by §368(a)(3)(A) as a case under Title 11 of the Code (i.e., the Bankruptcy Act) or a receivership, foreclosure, or similar proceeding in a federal or state court. Section 368(a)(3)(B)

---

[284] See generally Soukup, supra note 26; Kliegman, Troubled Thrift Reorganizations—The Short, Happy Life of §368(a)(3)(D), 64 Taxes 281 (1986). See also Rev. Proc. 82-13, 1982-1 CB 447; supra note 27. The Tax Reform Act of 1986 repealed §368(a)(3)(D) for thrift reorganizations after 1988 in §382(*l*)(5)(F).

defines a qualified transfer of assets as one where the transfer is under the jurisdiction of a court in a bankruptcy proceeding and the transfer is pursuant to a plan of reorganization approved by the court. However, nondivisive Type G reorganizations must satisfy the tests of §354(b), which require a transfer of substantially all of the corporation's assets and its complete liquidation (although the committee reports suggest that the "substantiality" standard is less rigorous here in view of the special nature of insolvency proceedings). In the case of overlaps with other types of reorganizations or with §332 or §351, §368(a)(3)(C) gives the Type G reorganization provisions exclusive jurisdiction over the transaction. Moreover, §351(e)(2) denies §351 treatment for any transfer of property by a debtor corporation pursuant to a bankruptcy reorganization plan to the extent stock or securities received in the plan are used to satisfy a transferor corporation's debts.

Thus, transfers of assets and exchanges of stock and securities pursuant to a court approved insolvency reorganization plan constitute tax-free reorganizations to the transferor corporation under §§368(a)(1)(G) and 361 and to the exchanging stockholders and security holders under §§368(a)(1)(G) and 354 or §355. Moreover, §381(a)(2) was amended to provide that the tax history of the debtor corporation carries over to the transferee if the transaction constitutes a reorganization under §§368(a)(1)(G) and 354(b)(1) (i.e., is nondivisive), a result comparable to the present treatment of nondivisive Type D reorganizations. However, §§354(a)(2) and 355(a)(3) were amended to tax exchanging security holders to the extent that consideration received was attributable to interest accrued on their securities during the period they held such obligations.

Finally, triangular reorganization treatment was extended to Type G reorganizations by the following provisions:

(1) Section 368(a)(3)(E) allows the reverse merger treatment of §368(a)(2)(E) to apply for insolvency reorganizations if stockholders of the debtor corporation receive *no* consideration for their stock, and former creditors of the debtor corporation get voting stock of the acquiring corporation's parent equal to 80 percent of the total value of its debt (i.e., *creditors* of the debtor corporation are treated as its stockholders for purposes of the reverse merger rules);

(2) The subsidiary forward merger rules of §368(a)(2)(D) were extended to Type G reorganizations;

(3) Dropdowns in nondivisive Type G reorganizations were permitted under an amendment to §368(a)(2)(C); and

(4) The party definition of §368(b) was amended to include parent corporations in Type G asset acquisitions.

Recapitalization exchanges involving the same continuing corporate entity do not constitute Type G reorganizations; these transactions, however, will be affected by the amendments to the cancellation of indebtedness rules.[285]

3. Examples. In the following examples it is assumed that *D* Corporation is involved in a title 11 or similar case and that its assets are transferred pursuant to a court-approved plan in that proceeding.

Example 1. *D* transfers substantially all of its assets to *P* Company for *P* stock (voting and/or nonvoting) or for a combination of stock and debt securities, which consideration is distributed exclusively to *D*'s debt security holders (*D*'s former shareholders having been wiped out). *D* recognizes no gain or loss under §§368(a)(1)(G) and 361, and the exchanging security holders recognize no gain or loss under §354(a) (except to the extent that consideration received is attributable to accrued interest on their transferred securities). *D*'s tax history carries over to *P* under §381 (and §382 will be applied by including *D*'s historic (i.e., 18-month holding period before filing proceeding) creditors as well as its former stockholders in the testing process).

Example 2. *P* retransfers the *D* assets to *S*, a wholly owned subsidiary under the facts in Example 1, with the same results.

Example 3. *D* merges into *S*, a controlled subsidiary of *P* for consideration paid by *P*, under the facts in Example 1, with the same results.

---

[285] For an extensive analysis of this general area, see Henderson & Goldring, Failing and Failed Businesses, CCH Tax Transactions Library (1987).

For analysis of the House bill proposal, see Rabinowitz & Rubin, The Bankruptcy Tax Act of 1979–HR 5043: Proposals for New Tax Treatment of Debtors and Creditors, 57 Taxes 911 (1979). For analysis of final legislation, see Eustice, Cancellation of Indebtedness Redux: The Bankruptcy Tax Act of 1980–Corporate Aspects, 36 Tax L. Rev. 1 (1980); Scranton, Corporate Transactions Under the Bankruptcy Tax Act of 1980, 36 Tax L. Rev. 147 (1981); Watts, Corporate Acquisitions and Divisions Under the Bankruptcy Tax Act: The New "G" Type Reorganization, 59 Taxes 845 (1981); Bergquist & Groff, Reorganizing the Financially Troubled Corporation After the Bankruptcy Tax Act of 1980, 36 Tax L. Rev. 517 (1981); Plumb, The Bankruptcy Tax Act, 33 S. Cal. Tax Inst. 800 (1981); Asofsky, Reorganizing Insolvent Corporations, 45 NYU Inst. on Fed. Tax'n ch. 5 (1983); Bacon, Rescue Planning for the Failing or Bankrupt Company, 61 Taxes 931 (1983); and Henderson, Developing a Tax Strategy for the Failing Company, 63 Taxes 952 (1985).

For analysis of prior law dealing with insolvency reorganizations, see the Fourth Edition of this work, ¶ 14.05, note 11.

Example 4. S, a controlled subsidiary of *P*, is merged into *D*. Section 368(a)(2)(E) will apply if *D*'s shareholders get nothing and if the creditors of *D* get *P* voting stock equal to 80 percent of the value of *D*'s debts.

Example 5. D transfers one of its two businesses to new subsidiary *P* for *P* stock, which it distributes to its creditors, and transfers its other business (also substantial in size) to new subsidiary *Q* Company for *Q* stock, which it likewise distributes to its creditors. Even though the transaction is divisive in effect, it still qualifies as a Type G reorganization so that *D* has nonrecognition under §361 (and §351 will not apply), while the distributee creditors get nonrecognition under §355 rather than §354. (Query *D*'s nonrecognition rule where it distributes the *P* and *Q* stock to its creditors (under §361(c))).

Example 6. To the extent that *D*'s former stockholders participate in the transaction, the above results would be unchanged (except in Example 4 the reverse merger situation, where stockholders of *D* must not receive any consideration).

Example 7. To the extent creditors of *D* do not exchange securities in the transaction, the entire reorganization may be vulnerable, since §368(a)(1)(G) is conditioned on the distribution qualifying under §354 or §356 (and neither provision applies to the *transfer*, as opposed to the *receipt*, of nonsecurity debt). In such a case, *D* presumably would recognize gain or loss on its asset transfers (unless the transaction met one of the other reorganization definitions), and the creditors of *D* would similarly have immediate recognition of gain or loss on their respective exchanges.

Example 8. While *D* might have been entitled to former 1954 Code §337 nonrecognition treatment in the Example 7 transaction under §337(g), §337 was repealed by the Tax Reform Act of 1986 (see Chapter 11). Moreover, §382 will not be triggered to the extent that historic creditors of *D* receive stock in exchange for their claims under §382(*l*)(5)(A) (see Chapter 16).

4. Collateral aspects. The Bankruptcy Tax Act provisions also contained numerous other changes to the Subchapter C rules, including: (1) amendments to §118, which treat the satisfaction of debt by capital contribution as a cash payment by the debtor (see Chapter 3); (2) amendments to §337 (which, however, was subsequently repealed by the Tax Reform Act of 1986), extending nonrecognition treatment to liquidation sales by insolvent corporations (see Chapter 11); (3) modifications of §§381 and 382 to ease the tax history carry-over rules for insolvency reorganizations, although §382 was drastically revised and restricted, by the Tax Reform Act of 1986, (see Chapter 16); and (4) changes in §351 to eliminate nonsecurity debt of the transferee and accrued interest on the transferee's debt from the definition of property.

Moreover, a fundamental restructuring of the cancellation of indebtedness rules of §§108 and 1017 was effected by the Act, which matters are considered in greater detail in Part D.

5. Current reform proposals. The final report of the Senate Finance Committee staff for the reform of Subchapter C proposed to drop the special insolvency reorganization rules of current law and instead treat these transactions under the new proposed acquisition system, discussed in the following section. The staff felt that the Type G rules would be unnecessary under this regime.[286]

¶ 14.21 CURRENT REFORM PROPOSALS: CARRY-OVER BASIS ELECTION

1. General. On September 22, 1983, the staff of the Senate Finance Committee submitted its preliminary report on the reform and simplification of Subchapter C. The staff's final report, released May 20, 1985, contained a draft of specific statutory legislation as well as general and technical explanations of the proposed legislation.[287] A centerpiece of these reports was the staff's proposal to replace the acquisitive reorganization provisions of present §§368(a)(1)(A), 368(a)(1)(B), and 368(a)(1)(C) and the related triangular acquisition rules of §§368(a)(2)(C), 368(a)(2)(D), and 368(a)(2)(E) with a single elective nonrecognition carry-over basis system at the corporate level. The principal limitations of present law now applicable to acquisitive

---

[286] Query whether the definition of "qualified asset acquisition," which adopts a mechanical 70-to-90 test in determining whether a sufficient quantum of the target's assets have been acquired, will cause problems in the insolvency area? (Current law also requires the transfer of substantially all of the debtor's assets, but the Type G substantiality rule is less rigorous than its Type C counterpart.) It may be that special rules will have to be added to the staff proposals to deal with insolvency reorganizations if the proposals ever become law, since a truly insolvent corporation has *no* net assets to transfer. See H.R. Rep. No. 833, 96th Cong., 2d Sess. 31 (1980); S. Rep. No. 1035, 96th Cong., 2d Sess. 35 (1980) (liberal test for substantiality).

[287] While the final acquisition proposals underwent some modification in certain technical aspects, they did not change materially from the initial preliminary version. See supra notes 8 and 9.

reorganizations (i.e., qualifying consideration, continuity of interest, continuity of business enterprise, parallel treatment at the corporate and shareholder levels, and the business purpose requirement) would all be repealed.

In effect, the present system of transactional electivity would be replaced with an express election regime keyed to the parties' decision to preserve basis for the acquired corporate assets by electing carry-over basis treatment, in which case the transaction would be entitled to nonrecognition treatment regardless of the type of consideration paid for the acquired properties. If, on the other hand, cost-basis treatment is elected, full recognition of gain or loss by the corporate transferor would be required, again without regard to the form of consideration paid. Regardless of what happens at the corporate level, shareholders would be permitted to receive stock tax-free in a qualified acquisition.

The proposed elective nonrecognition carry-over basis system has residual elements of §§368, former 337 (before its repeal in 1986), and 338 of the 1954 Code law, principally in the definition of qualified acquisition. But it is clearly a new regime that is being proposed, and a system that is markedly simpler to apply than 1954 Code law, and that radically alters some longstanding principles that have existed in the reorganization sections since their inception over five decades ago.

The proposed acquisition rules would replace the reorganization, liquidation, and basis rules of present law; their dominant themes are electivity and flexibility. However, valuation of assets will be required in every cost-basis stock acquisition, and valuation questions will also arise in asset acquisitions where a premium price is alleged to have been paid for goodwill. The proposed system also is strongly flavored by §338 principles (except that corporate-level gain or loss now would be recognized in view of the 1986 repeal of §337, although only at one level in the case of corporate chains). Another major theme of these proposals is consistency of treatment to corporate sellers and buyers; the tax price for cost-basis treatment will be corporate-level recognition of gain or loss, regardless of the tax treatment at the shareholder level. Such treatment is expressly elective by the parties and hence should be negotiated as part of the overall acquisition terms. In the final Conference Report to the Tax Reform Act of 1986, the Treasury was instructed to study further proposals for the reform of Subchapter C and report back to Congress by 1988; presumably the staff's Subchapter C acquisition proposals will feature heavily in this study.

2. Qualified acquisition: Proposed §364. A qualified stock acquisition under §364(b) consists of an acquisition of 80 percent control (defined by reference to consolidated return eligibility under §1504(a) (i.e., 80 percent of vote *and* value, exclusive of pure preferred) within 12 months. A qualified asset acquisition under §364(c) consists of a merger or consolidation, or a transaction, in which substantially all the assets of one corporation are acquired by the acquiring corporation and/or its affiliates.[288] In applying the substantially all standard, however, pretransaction asset tailoring would be expressly permitted (i.e., the *Elkhorn Coal* doctrine would not apply here). Acquisitions of stock from related transferors (under §318) did not count for qualified stock acquisition treatment under the preliminary proposals, but the final report dropped this rule; instead, the final report adopted a §304 parity rule and imposed mandatory carry-over basis treatment for such related party stock acquisitions in proposed §365(d)(1). Similarly, asset acquisitions from corporations within a §304(c) related controlled group (i.e., where there was at least 50 percent common ownership) could be qualified asset acquisitions, although carry-over basis treatment would be mandatory under proposed §365(d)(1) in this situation as well.[289]

The various forms of triangular acquisition under present law (i.e., triangular Type C, forward mergers, and reverse mergers) were treated as stock acquisitions under the preliminary proposals, but only reverse mergers are so treated in the final revision. Moreover, two-step stock and asset acquisitions would be treated as stock acquisitions if stock control was acquired on the first step, regardless of whether assets were acquired as the ultimate step.

Several aspects of the qualified acquisition definition in proposed §364 should be noted:

(1) The type of consideration paid (i.e., stock, debt, or cash) is irrelevant; rather, the definition is transactionally focused.

(2) The qualified stock acquisition definition in §364(b) essentially returns to the 1939 Code definition of a Type B reorganization; that is, creeping acquisitions beyond the requisite one-year acquisition period are prohibited (in this respect, the stock acquisition definition more nearly resembles §338(d)(3) of current law):

(a) Control can be acquired by combined purchase and redemption back-in transactions;

(b) Reverse triangular mergers (under current law §368(a)(2)(E)) are treated as stock acquisitions by §364(f), but other asset triangulars are treated as asset acquisitions; and

---

[288] The final report dropped the substantially all test and replaced it with a mechanical test derived from the ruling guidelines of Rev. Proc. 77-37 (i.e., 70 percent of gross and 90 percent of net assets held immediately before the acquisition). Aggregation by affiliates would be permitted in proposed §365(a)(5) (similar to §338(h)(8) of current law).

[289] In the case of related party asset acquisitions, the mechanical 70-to-90 test, supra note 288, would not apply; instead, the more flexible substantially all standard would govern, as interpreted by the cases in the reincorporation area, infra ¶ 14.54.

(c) Under the special lookthrough rule of §364(d), a qualified stock acquisition of the target is deemed to constitute a qualified stock acquisition of any of the target's controlled subsidiaries (similar to the lookthrough rule under §338 of current law).

(3) Mandatory liquidation within 12 months of the acquisition is required by §364(c)(2) in order to constitute a qualified asset acquisition (current law, as amended by §368(a)(2)(G) in 1984, requires liquidation pursuant to the plan in order to constitute a Type C reorganization):

(a) Under §365(d)(2), however, failure to liquidate will not prevent mandatory carry-over basis treatment for related party asset acquisitions (although it *will* deny the other benefits of qualified asset acquisition treatment such as nonrecognition of gain to the target);

(b) Moreover, assets acquired by distribution (including a liquidation) will not qualify by virtue of §364(c)(3) (which provision apparently perpetuates remnants of the *Bausch & Lomb* creeping asset acquisition doctrine, although it may merely have been intended to exclude dividend, redemption, and §332 (or §331) liquidation distributions, or, in addition, to prevent a step-one stock acquisition from being treated as an asset acquisition on a step-two liquidation); and

(c) The pretailoring principle allows the substantially all standard to be satisfied by threshold distributions (and spin-offs), unlike current law, which tests substantiality under step-transaction principles (a companion rule permits a §351 dropdown of an active business, but without a five-year rule, followed by a qualified stock acquisition without breaking control under §351).

(4) Although the qualified acquisition definition of §364 generally intends to harmonize the rules for stock and asset acquisitions, several discontinuities remain:

(a) Stock control is 80 percent, while 70 percent of gross assets and 90 percent of net assets must be acquired for a qualified asset acquisition (thus, if *P* owns 21 percent of target *T, P* cannot do a qualified stock acquisition, although apparently it can do a qualified asset acquisition; but see (3)(b) above);

(b) Creeping stock acquisitions are prohibited, and asset acquisitions are not (if the consistency rules of §365(c) are satisfied); and

(c) Control can be acquired in a redemption back-in transaction, but assets cannot be acquired by distribution.

(5) Asset and stock acquisition overlaps are covered in §364(e), so that:

(a) Under §364(e)(1), where part of the target's acquired assets consist of stock of a controlled subsidiary, the acquisition is bifurcated and treated as separate stock and asset acquisitions, although the stock counts for purposes of the 70-to-90 test—for example, if operating company *T* also has a subsidiary, *S*, *P*'s acquisition of all of *T*'s assets will be treated as a qualified asset acquisition of *T*'s operating assets and a qualified stock acquisition of *S*; and

(b) Under §364(e)(2), where multiple asset-acquisitions occur, and *T-1* owns stock in *T-2*, *T-1*'s stock in *T-2* is disregarded in applying the 70-to-90 test to the *T-1* acquisition.

(6) Under §364(g), recapitalizations are treated as qualified stock acquisitions, and reincorporations (formerly Type F reorganizations) are treated as qualified asset acquisitions, but mandatory carry-over basis treatment for both is required by §365(e) because they are related party acquisitions.

3. The election: proposed §365 in general. Asset acquisitions are presumed to be carry-over basis acquisitions under proposed §365(a) unless the parties specifically elect cost-basis treatment under proposed §365(b); in a merger or consolidation, the surviving corporation makes the cost-basis election, while in other asset acquisitions, both the transferor and transferee corporations must jointly elect cost-basis treatment. Stock acquisitions likewise are presumed to be carry-over basis transactions unless the acquiring corporation specifically elects cost-basis treatment.

The election would be irrevocable, and the preliminary report suggested that it would have to be made within eight and one-half months after the acquisition month (paralleling the §338 election time frame); the final report specifically adopted this time frame in §365(g).

As noted above, however, §365(d) provides that stock or asset acquisitions from related parties (under §304(c) principles) cannot elect cost-basis treatment, and §365(e) provides similar results for Type F reincorporations. Conversely, if assets are acquired by a nontaxpaying entity (e.g., §501(c) organizations, foreign corporations, regulated investment companies), mandatory cost-basis treatment is required by §365(f) (and also would override §365(d)) in view of the last clear chance to extract an entity level tax on those assets. This provision does not apply, however, if both corporations are the same type. (Query, must a foreign corporation acquire only a foreign corporation to qualify for this exception, or can it acquire a §501 organization; in other words, does "same type" mean only same general type, or does it mean same specific type?)

The acquiring corporation is defined generally as the one that makes the qualified acquisition, but where the target's stock or assets are split among affiliates of an acquiring corporation (as is allowed under the aggregation rule of §366(a)(5)), the acquiring corporation is the common parent of the acquiring group (unless one member acquires enough of the target to qualify in its own right), §366(b)(1).

4. Consistency rules: Proposed §365(c). The choice between carry-over basis and cost-basis treatment is made on a corporation-by-corporation basis, not an asset-by-asset basis. In order to prevent avoidance of the prohibition against selective asset basis stepups, a limited consistency rule (less onerous, although by no means simpler, than those of §338) would be imposed by proposed §365(c) with respect to assets held directly by the acquired corporation at any time during the one-year period prior to its acquisition and acquired at any time within the consistency period (generally a two-year period bracketing the acquisition date). In such a case, the election governing the acquired corporate entity that first held that asset will also apply to that asset.

An exception to the consistency rules of §365(c) is provided for nonamortizable goodwill and the like in §365(b)(2),[290] where carry-over basis treatment can be elected for such property even though cost-basis treatment is elected for the target's other assets. The inconsistent treatment exception for goodwill and the like is tightly drawn, however, and heavy regulation delegations abound here (as they do in the case of the general consistency rules in §365(b)(2)(C)); moreover, inventory and securities are specifically excluded in §365(b)(2)(C).

The entity-by-entity consistency rules of proposed §365(c)(2) also provide for exceptions similar to those in §338(e)(2) (and the asset consistency regulations in §1.388-4T(f) have continued relevance under this provision, which is definitely not a happy prospect). Among these exceptions are carry-over basis acquisitions (or an election to treat a purchased asset as a carry-over basis acquisition on the buyer's side), purchases in the ordinary course of business, and others by regulation (e.g., §1.338-4T(f)(5) suggests a likely future list under this provision as well). The staff's Technical Explanation gives 15 examples of the consistency rules. Unlike the affiliated group consistency rules of §338, however, proposed §365(c) only requires entity-by-entity consistency.

5. Corporate-level treatment. If a carry-over basis election is made for the acquisition, no gain or loss is recognized to the corporate transferor, the asset basis carries over to the transferee, and all other tax attributes of the transferor likewise carry over to the transferee under §381 (see Chapter 16).

---

[290] For a creative, although unsuccessful, attempt to amortize various purchased intangibles of a target, see Banc One Corp., 84 TC 476 (1985); see generally supra ¶ 11.11.

In a stock acquisition, the acquiring corporation's outside basis for the stock would be conformed to the subsidiary's net inside asset basis under proposed §1020. This result would occur regardless of the type of consideration paid and without regard to the former judicially imposed continuity of interest, continuity of business enterprise, and business purpose limitations.

Unlike current law, however, the preliminary report provided that the transferor corporation in a qualified asset acquisition (the prototype of the former Type C reorganization) was required to completely liquidate within 12 months or be taxed on any boot received and any unrealized appreciation on retained assets (which provision was reminiscent of the former 1954 Code §337 rule).[291] Gain (but *not* loss) so recognized would be treated as long-term capital gain and would be computed by subtracting the aggregate basis of all the assets transferred from the value of all the consideration received. The staff's final report revised this approach and simply required the target to completely liquidate within 12 months in *all* cases (whether or not boot was received) in order to constitute a qualified asset acquisition; on such a liquidation, the target would recognize gain (or loss) on the distribution of any retained assets (but not on any consideration received from the acquiring corporation for its assets).

Election of cost-basis treatment for the acquisition would result in full gain or loss recognition at the corporate level, again regardless of the consideration paid by the acquiring corporation. Moreover, the target's tax attributes would not carry over to the acquiring corporation (in an asset acquisition, they would remain in the target or expire if the target liquidates; in a stock acquisition, they would be purged by the cost-basis election). Regardless of the corporate-level treatment, the target's shareholders could receive tax-free exchange treatment to the extent that they receive qualified consideration, generally stock of the acquiring corporation or its affiliates.

6. Shareholder-level treatment. Shareholder taxation would be determined independently of corporate-level treatment under the staff's proposed acquisition system, unlike under current law. Thus, shareholders who receive only qualified stock in a qualified corporate acquisition would be entitled to nonrecognition treatment in full on their exchange, even though other shareholders receive cash and even though cost-basis and recognition treatment is elected at the corporate level. If a shareholder receives both qualified stock

---

[291] For shareholder-level treatment under these proposals, see infra ¶ 14.34. For 1984 legislation adopting this requirement, see supra ¶ 14.14, note 114 (i.e., acquired corporation in a Type C reorganization must completely liquidate under the plan by virtue of new §368(a)(2)(G)). The final report requires complete liquidation of the target corporation within 12 months, regardless of the consideration received, in order for the transaction to constitute a qualified asset acquisition.

and boot, dividend equivalence is tested by assuming a full issuance of stock followed by a hypothetical redemption of such stock for the boot by the acquiring corporation; if dividend equivalence results, it will be taxed in full as such, regardless of the shareholder's realized gain or loss on the exchange and measured by the combined earnings of the target and acquiring corporations. (However, after the Tax Reform Act of 1986 repeal of §1202, boot dividend treatment will no longer involve a rate differential cost.) The proposal also would allow recognition of loss to a shareholder who receives only boot (i.e., unqualified consideration such as cash, debt, or property other than stock of a party to the acquisition) or to a security holder who receives no stock or securities of a party to the acquisition. Loss would still be unrecognized, however, if the security holder receives securities of a party.

7. Related developments: Tax Reform Act of 1986 amendments.[292] The 1986 legislation did not include the Finance Committee staff acquisition system, but did pick up on the staff's proposal to repeal the *General Utilities* doctrine, although in a somewhat different form than the staff version. Thus, the nonrecognition rules of §§336 and 337 were generally repealed, with no permanent exceptions at either the corporate or shareholder levels (the staff proposal provided for relief provisions at the shareholder level).[293] The demise of §§336 and 337 will probably tend to force most, if not virtually all, corporate acquisition transactions into the tax-free reorganization mold (unless corporate level gain or loss amounts are relatively insubstantial or can be sheltered by loss carry-overs of the target).

---

[292] H.R. Rep. No. 3838, §§631–633, which passed on October 22, 1986.

[293] Supra ¶¶ 11.06 and 11.61. For analysis of the staff's proposals, see Eustice, supra note 9.

The House bill of what became the Tax Reform Act of 1986 proposed the following corporate-level recognition exceptions: (1) §332 liquidations; (2) tax-free stock or security distributions in reorganizations; and (3) distributions of long-term capital gain property by active business corporations on "qualified stock" (i.e., stock held by noncorporate, 10 percent shareholders for at least five years), similar to §311(d)(2) of pre-Tax Reform Act of 1986 law, supra ¶¶ 9.34 and 7.22. The final Conference version, however, repealed all of the exceptions of §311 (except for losses and §355 distributions), and retained only the first two exceptions of the House bill proposal (i.e., tax-free reorganization distributions of stock or securities (§336(c)) and §332 distributions to a controlling parent (new §337); distributions to minority shareholders in a §332 liquidation will trigger gain, but not loss, to the subsidiary under new §337(a) and new §336(d)(3), however. New §§336(d)(1) and 336(d)(2) provide for special limitations on recognition of loss: Distributions to §267 related shareholders are denied recognition by §336(d)(1) if either the distribution is not pro rata, or it consists of property contributed within five years of the distribution; §336(d)(2) denies losses on property contributed within two years of the liquidation plan adoption date if the property had a built-in loss when contributed. See H.R. Rep. No. 841, 99th Cong., 2d Sess. 200–201. See supra ¶¶ 11.06, 11.49, and 11.61.

PART C. TREATMENT OF PARTIES TO A REORGANIZATION

¶ 14.30 INTRODUCTORY

1. General. Section 368(a) defines the term "reorganization" but does not, of its own force, have any operative effect. Its definitions become effective only insofar as they are employed in other provisions of the Code, of which the most important are the following:

(1) Section 354, providing (with qualifications) that gain or loss must not be recognized if stock or securities in a corporation that is "a party to a reorganization," a term that is defined by §368(b), are exchanged solely for stock or securities in the same corporation or in another corporation that is a party to the reorganization.

(2) Section 361, under which a corporation that is a party to a reorganization recognizes neither gain nor loss if it exchanges property under the plan of reorganization for stock, securities or other property with another corporation that is a party to the reorganization (and also under which gain is recognized on the distribution of appreciated boot property).

(3) Sections 356 and 357, providing for the treatment of boot and liabilities in reorganization exchanges.

(4) Sections 358 and 362(b), providing for substitutions and carryovers of basis in reorganization exchanges.

(5) Section 381, providing for the transfer of a corporation's net operating loss carry-over, earnings and profits, and other tax attributes to a successor corporation in certain reorganizations, subject to the limitations of §§269 and 382 (see Chapter 16).

These operating provisions deal with the tax treatment of various parties to a reorganization, (i.e., recognition of gain or loss realized on the respective exchanges, the character of gain required to be recognized, if any, and the basis of property received in the exchanges). All presuppose the existence of a reorganization under §368, and, in the material that follows, it will be assumed that the underlying transaction satisfies this statutory definition.

2. Party to a reorganization. For application of the nonrecognition provisions of §§354 and 361, the stock or securities involved in the reorganization exchanges must be issued by a party to the reorganization, and each corporate participant in the reorganization must also be "a party" thereto. This term is defined by §368(b) to include a corporation resulting from a reorganization and both corporations in the case of an acquisition by one corporation of stock or properties of another.[294] The statutory group of qualified parties has been expanded steadily since 1954 to keep pace with the growth of the various triangular reorganization techniques. Thus, the parent was made a party to triangular Type C reorganizations by the second sentence of §362(b) in 1954, and §368(a)(C) asset dropdowns would no longer affect the parent's party status by virtue of the third sentence of §368(b). The parent's stock in triangular Type B reorganizations (and stock dropdowns) was added to the party roster in 1964, while stock of the parent in §368(a)(2)(D) subsidiary mergers joined the list in 1968. Finally, the parent in a §368(a)(2)(E) reverse merger also was made a qualified party in 1971, and triangular insolvency reorganizations joined the guest list in 1980.

> *To illustrate:* If P Corporation owns all the stock of S Corporation and transfers it to Y Corporation in exchange for Y's voting stock in a Type B reorganization (P not being in control of Y), S and Y are parties, but P is not. If all of S's assets are transferred to Y in a Type A or C reorganization, party status remains unchanged.[295] But if the S stock had constituted substantially all the assets of P (so that the transaction would be a Type C reorganization), or if P controlled Y after the transaction (a Type D), P then would become a qualified party to the reorganization.[296] If the S stock or assets had been transferred to Z (a controlled subsidiary of Y) in one of the various types of triangular reorganizations (e.g., Type A, B, or C), Y would continue to be a party by virtue of the second and fifth sentences of §368(b), while if Y acquired the S stock or assets directly and then dropped S into Z in a §368(a)(2)(C) transfer, the third sentence of §368(b) would preserve Y's status as a party.[297]

---

[294] According to Groman v. CIR, supra note 28, discussed supra ¶ 14.11, the pre-1954 definition was not exclusive, and the 1954 changes, amplifying its scope, do not seem intended to exclude any corporation that would previously have qualified. See supra ¶ 14.15 for 1968 and 1971 amendments to §368(b), making the parent a party to certain triangular mergers.

See generally Hays Corp. v. CIR, 40 TC 436 (1963), aff'd, 331 F2d 422 (7th Cir. 1964), cert. denied, 379 US 842 (1964); Regs. §1.368-2(f), with examples illustrating the definition of §368(b).

[295] Had the transaction been cast in a somewhat different form, however, P would be a party. See §368(b) (second and third sentences), added in 1954.

[296] The Finance Committee staff's Subchapter C reform bill proposes to continue this rule in new §354(c); that is, where parent P's principal asset is stock of subsidiary S, the acquisition of the parent's assets (i.e., the S stock) would be treated as an asset acquisition, and thus the parent would become a party, so as to allow its shareholders to exchange their parent stock tax-free on its liquidation.

[297] It has been pointed out earlier that §368(a)(2)(C) permits property or stock to be transferred to a subsidiary of the acquiring corporation in a Type A, B, or C

3. Party to the acquisition. The Senate Finance Committee staff's final report on the reform of Subchapter C, released in 1985, proposed to completely revise the acquisition rules of current law and replace them with a new elective nonrecognition regime at the corporate level, as discussed earlier. For the target corporation, the type of consideration would be irrelevant; rather, taxability would depend upon whether cost or carry-over basis treatment was elected. For shareholders, however, only receipt of qualified consideration would be permitted on a tax-free basis, and the key to this term is stock of a party to the acquisition.

The staff's preliminary report defined an acquisition "party" as the acquiring corporation in a vertical chain of control above the actual acquiring corporation, but this rule was modified in the final report to include simply the common parent of the acquiring affiliated group and any member of the group designated by regulations. (One hopes that these regulations would once and for all put to rest any lingering vestiges of the *Groman-Bashford* doctrine.)[298]

¶ 14.31 STOCK OR SECURITIES VS. BOOT: IN GENERAL

The basic nonrecognition provisions relating to reorganization exchanges, §§354 and 361, require the receipt of stock or securities in order to qualify for nonrecognition treatment. The term "stock or securities" (construed by Regs. §1.368-2(h) to mean "stock and/or securities") is not defined in the Code.[299] As an initial matter, it should be noted that

---

reorganization. This can be done tax-free under §351, so far as the transaction between the acquiring corporation and its subsidiary is concerned; but if the subsidiary's stock or securities are to be used to compensate the original transferor of the assets or stock in a Type A, B, or C reorganization, they can be received tax-free under §354 only if the subsidiary is a party to the reorganization. It is curious that when the third sentence of §368(b) was added in 1954 to ensure that the acquiring corporation would not lose *its* status as a party to the reorganization by transferring the assets to a subsidiary, nothing was done to make it clear that the subsidiary was also a party. It is possible that the subsidiary is a party by virtue of §368(b)(2) (see supra note 129) or that, if newly created, it qualifies under §368(b)(1); see also supra notes 61 and 294; supra ¶ 14.15.

But see Rev. Rul. 69-413, 1969-2 CB 55 (parent corporation in a triangular Type F reorganization not a party because §368(b) not applicable to Type F reorganizations using parent's stock).

[298] But the staff Technical Explanation suggests examples for these regulations that require a per stirpes relationship between the stock issued and the assets acquired; will *Groman* never die?

[299] For the use of the term in §351, see supra ¶ 3.03; see also §385, added by the Tax Reform Act of 1969 (supra ¶ 4.02), authorizing the Treasury to define corporate "stock" and "indebtedness" by regulations.

§368(a)(1), defining the term "reorganization," imposes additional restrictions on the type and amount of consideration that can change hands. For example, presumably only voting stock[300] can be used in a Type B reorganization; a Type C reorganization similarly requires the use of voting stock, although it also tolerates a limited amount of other consideration. Moreover, the use of nonequity securities (e.g., in a Type A reorganization) may be restricted by the judicially created continuity of interest doctrine, even though the consideration to be used is not explicitly regulated by §368(a)(1)(A). However, Regs. §1.361-1 expressly notes that consideration that might infect qualification as a reorganization of one type under §368 (e.g., nonvoting stock or debt securities) nevertheless can be received tax-free under §361(a) if the transaction otherwise can qualify as a reorganization.

1. Definition of "stock." Ordinarily, a share of "stock" embodies the permanent proprietary ownership or equity interest in a corporation that entitles the holder to (1) share proportionately in the profits of the business; (2) vote on matters affecting the corporate enterprise; and (3) share ratably in the assets of the venture (after payment of debts) on liquidation. These rights typically are evidenced by a formal certificate registered in the name of the holder on the books of the corporation. However, various hybrid instruments may be created that lack one or more of these indicia of stock, and several cases have arisen under the provisions of §1032 (see Chapter 3) as to whether amounts had been received by a corporation in exchange for *stock*.[301]

Another aspect of the definition of "stock" relates to the thin capitalization problem (see Chapter 4). If a corporation is thinly capitalized, or if indebtedness held pro rata by shareholders is intended by the parties to constitute part of the corporation's permanent capital structure, courts may hold that the debt must be classified as stock under familiar principles that are equally applicable in the reorganization area.[302] The converse (conver-

---

300 For a definition of "voting stock," see supra note 75.

301 In rare cases, a single instrument may constitute stock but also embody rights of a nonstock character. To the extent of the value of the latter rights, the transaction may be outside the reorganization provisions. See, for an analogy, Corn Prods. Ref. Co. v. CIR, 350 US 46 (1955); see also Rev. Rul. 61-18, 1961-1 CB 5; supra ¶ 3.12; Rev. Rul. 68-22, 1968-1 CB 142 (5 percent preferred capital certificates of interest in a farmers' cooperative association held stock); Gordon v. CIR, supra note 266 (rights to acquire stock of a controlled subsidiary were not stock); supra ¶ 14.11, note 27; Paulsen v. CIR, supra note 27.

302 See Reef Corp. v. CIR, supra note 32 (notes issued by the acquiring corporation in an alleged "purchase" of assets held to constitute stock). But see Book Prod. Indus., Inc., ¶ 65,065 P-H Memo. TC (1965); W.H. Truschel, supra note 48 (debt

sion of purported equity into debt in order to render part or all of the reorganization taxable) rarely, if ever, occurs, however.[303]

Where contingent rights to acquire stock, rather than stock itself, are issued in connection with a reorganization, several decisions have rejected the Service's attempts to classify such instruments as boot. In *Carlberg v. US*, the court held that transferable certificates of contingent interest, representing reserved shares of stock held for the account of exchanging shareholders in a merger pending determination of contingent liabilities, constituted stock rather than boot.[304] The *Carlberg* rationale was followed by the Tax Court in *James C. Hamrick*, where the taxpayer acquired a contractual right to receive additional shares of stock of a corporation if a patent that he had transferred to the corporation in a §351 exchange proved profitable.[305] In both *Carlberg* and *Hamrick*, the courts held that the taxpayers' contingent rights to receive additional shares of stock were, in substance, equivalent to the stock itself, since the holders of these rights could receive nothing but stock under the agreement.[306] Interests of the type involved in the *Carlberg* and *Hamrick* cases satisfy the continuity of interest notion underlying nonrecognition treatment in this area; since the only interest that can be obtained by these rights is stock, there is no cashing in of the taxpayer's investment, which would justify present imposition of the tax.[307]

---

obligations were classified as such, thereby preventing reorganization status, over the Service's assertion that the debt instead constituted an equity interest).

[303] See supra ¶ 14.11, para. 2. But see Paulsen v. CIR, supra note 27.

[304] Carlberg v. US, 281 F2d 507 (8th Cir. 1960).

[305] James C. Hamrick, supra note 168.

[306] See Rev. Rul. 66-112, 1966-1 CB 68, acquiescing in *Hamrick*'s result as to a contingent contractual right to additional shares that is not assignable or readily marketable.

Rev. Proc. 77-37, 1977-2 CB 568, states that favorable rulings will be issued on contingent stock issue deals if (1) there is a five-year limit on the plan; (2) the rights to receive additional stock are not assignable; (3) the holder thereof is entitled to receive only stock of the acquiring corporation; (4) there is a valid business purpose for the plan; (5) there is a ceiling on the amount of additional stock that can be issued under the plan; and (6) at least 50 percent of the total amount of each class of stock that may be issued under the plan is issued in the initial distribution.

See also Rev. Rul. 67-90, 1967-1 CB 79 (additional stock issue contingent on future value of acquiring corporation's stock allowable where parties unable to agree on value of such corporation's stock, even though both corporations listed on national exchanges); Rev. Rul. 75-33, 1975-1 CB 115; Rev. Rul. 78-142, 1978-1 CB 111 (rescission rights not boot); Rev. Rul. 73-205, 1973-1 CB 188 (use of contingent stock payout based on adjustment in conversion ratio of voting convertible preferred stock issued in the reorganization did not involve boot; formula satisfied five-year term, ceiling, 50 percent down payment, nonassignability, solely voting stock, and business purpose tests). See generally infra ¶ 14.56, para. 2.

[307] Note that §483 could create imputed interest income if issuance of the stock is delayed for more than six months from the date of exchange, although Regs.

The receipt of rights, warrants, or options to purchase stock may be another matter, however. Regs. §1.354-1(e) states that stock rights or warrants are not included in the term "stock or securities." Inspiration for this treatment may have come from the *Southwest Consolidated Corp.* case, holding that warrants did not constitute *voting stock* within the meaning of §368(a)(1)(C),[308] a decision with continuing influence that goes beyond the precise issue there decided.[309]

2. Definition of "securities." The question of whether a debt obligation constitutes a security has long been shrouded in confusion, much of which stems from the holding in *Pinellas Ice & Cold Storage Co. v. CIR* that short-term notes received in exchange for property did not constitute "securities" within the intendment of the reorganization provisions.[310] Confusion was compounded when *Neville Coke & Chemical Co. v. CIR* applied the continuity of interest principle to hold that an exchange of debt instruments for stock did not qualify for nonrecognition treatment under §354;[311] the implication in *Bazley* that long-term debenture bonds received in a recapitalization exchange for stock did not constitute securities[312] did little to clarify the situation.[313]

Notwithstanding these difficulties in determining whether an instrument is a security, the courts have ordinarily focused on its maturity date: Notes with a five-year term or less seem to be unable to qualify as securities, while a term of ten years or more is apparently sufficient to bring them within the statute. Later decisions, however, seem to have adopted a continuity of creditor interest approach, stating that time alone is not decisive and that what is required is an overall evaluation of the nature of the debt, degree of participation and continuing interest in the affairs of the business, the extent of proprietary interest compared with the similarity of the note to a cash payment, and the purpose of the advances.[314]

---

§1.483-2(a)(2) states that such interest income will not destroy reorganization status. See Rev. Rul. 70-120, 1970-1 CB 124 (use of escrowed stock arrangement not subject to §483, i.e., stock issued if shareholders can vote escrowed stock and have right to dividends as paid); Rev. Rul. 70-300, 1970-1 CB 125 (application of §483, or formulas to avoid §483, in contingent stock issue reorganization); Jerrold L. Kingsley, 72 TC 1095 (1979), aff'd, 662 F2d 539 (9th Cir. 1981), and cases cited (deferred delivery of stock to cover contingent claims triggered §483); for the continuity of interest notion, see supra ¶ 14.11; see generally Walter & Strassen, Contingent and Adjustable Stock in a Public Contest, 65 Taxes 439 (1987).

[308] Helvering v. Southwest Consol. Corp., supra note 33.

[309] See discussion infra para. 3, this section.

[310] Pinellas Ice & Cold Storage Co. v. CIR, supra note 15.

[311] Neville Coke & Chem. Co. v. CIR, supra note 42.

[312] Bazley v. CIR, supra note 5.

[313] See discussion supra ¶¶ 14.11 and 14.17; Griswold, supra note 43.

[314] See discussion and cases cited supra ¶¶ 3.03 and 3.14; Rev. Rul. 59-98, 1959-1 CB 76 (secured bonds with an average life of six and one-half years constituted

Under the final report by the Senate Finance Committee staff on the reform of Subchapter C, released in 1985, the definition of securities would be rendered largely immaterial as a practical matter since the receipt of securities would be boot per se, even when exchanged for other securities. Thus, whether or not a particular debt instrument is, or is not, a security would have no effect under the staff's final proposals (gains would be recognized, even if the instrument is a security, while losses would not be, even if it is a nonsecurity boot).

It should be noted that §483 can apply to securities received in a nonrecognition exchange where maturity is more than six months from the date of the exchange if the securities do not carry interest or the stated interest rate is below the requisite applicable federal rate. The original issue discount provisions of §1272 must also be considered in this context.[315]

3. Equity-flavored securities (rights, warrants and convertible securities). While *Southwest Consolidated* holds that warrants and other call option rights are not voting stock,[316] and *Bateman* and *Gordon* hold they are not stock[317] (in effect, they represent merely a future interest in the stock, which,

---

securities under §354 when exchanged for stock); Rev. Rul. 59-222, 1959-1 CB 80 (exchange of debenture bonds for stock nontaxable, but exchange of unsecured general creditor claims for stock taxable). Rev. Rul. 59-98 also held that interest arrears form a part of the debt security and the fact that part of the stock was received in discharge of these arrears did not cause recognition of gain to the exchanging security holder; see discussion supra ¶ 14.17, note 208; Cutler, Dividend Arrearages, 37 Taxes 309 (1959).

See also Turner Constr. Co. v. US, supra note 168 (six-month note; held boot, not a security), remand, sub nom. Prentis v. US, supra note 43 (held securities because part of a single plan for delayed issue of preferred stock); Regs. §§1.371-1(a)(5) and 1.371-2(b) (short-term purchase-money notes not securities), withdrawn in 1982; Regs. §1.374-1(a)(5) (same).

For corporate law aspects of the securities definition question, see Lipton & Katz, "Notes" Are Not Always Securities, 30 Bus. Law. 763 (1975).

[315] See generally supra ¶ 4.40; Prop. Regs. §§1.483-1(b)(1), 1.1275-1(b)(1), and 1.1275-2(a) (1986).

[316] Helvering v. Southwest Consol. Corp., supra note 33.

[317] Wm. H. Bateman, 40 TC 408 (1963), holding in reliance on the *Southwest* case that warrants did not constitute stock when received in a merger. But see Estate of Nettie Miller, 43 TC 760 (1965) (nonacq.) (bearer warrants of a foreign corporation, entitling the holder to vote and to receive dividends, held to be stock); Gordon v. CIR, supra note 266 (rights to acquire stock of a controlled subsidiary; held did not constitute stock).

See also Estate of Charles A. Smith, 63 TC 722 (1975) (acq.) (warrants received by estate in merger held boot per *Bateman*, but no tax under §356(a) because estate got §1014 stepped up basis and hence no realized gain); Rev. Rul. 69-264, 1969-1 CB 102 (receipt of option right to redeem its own stock; held taxable boot).

while a valuable right, is not the same thing as the stock itself), this does not necessarily end the matter, since warrants were held to be securities, at least under pre-1954 Code law, in the *Raymond* case.[318] Even if warrants qualify as securities, however, it may be necessary to determine whether they are sufficiently infused with equity characteristics to escape the principal amount taxability rules of §§354(a)(2)(A) and 356(d)(2), which presumably are limited in their application to *debt* securities. It has been suggested that warrants should be classified as equity securities[319] which thus could be received tax-free by exchanging stockholders and security holders in Type A reorganizations (but not in Type B or Type C reorganizations, where only *voting stock* is allowed) on the ground that warrants look only toward further investment and increased equity participation in the corporation, while debt securities result in the ultimate receipt of cash and termination of the holder's economic interest in the company. In effect, warrants are similar to the type of potential equity interest represented by a contingent right to receive additional stock although the warrant holder must pay for the privilege of becoming a stockholder.

Whether warrants should be considered to carry continuity of interest or should be counted as stock for purposes of the 80 percent control definition of §368(c) would not have to be decided by this interpretation, since classification as equity securities would be enough to allow their tax-free receipt by the exchanging parties to the reorganization free of the debt security rules of §§354(a)(2) and 356(d). The unsuitability of warrants as a bailout device is a strong argument in favor of this treatment.[320]

---

[318] At the very least, warrants and rights would seem to constitute securities, as held in E.P. Raymond, 37 BTA 423 (1938); note, however, that if only *stock* is surrendered, the receipt of *debt* securities becomes taxable under §354(a)(2)(A), although not under §361(a) (infra ¶¶ 14.33 and 14.34).

[319] See Special Committee on Reorganization Problems, N.Y. State Bar Association, Tax Section, Report on Stock Warrants in Corporate Organizations and Reorganizations, (July 29, 1968). See also §305(d)(1), defining "warrants" as "stock" for purposes of the stock dividend rules (supra ¶ 7.43); §1504(a)(5)(A) (infra ¶ 15.21); supra ¶ 4.62. But see Rev. Rul. 67-269, 1967-2 CB 298 (warrant and convertible debenture holders not shareholders); Rev. Rul. 78-408, 1978-2 CB 203 (exchange of warrants for warrants taxable exchange; separate from stock-for-stock Type B reorganization transaction).

See generally Reiling, Warrants in Bond-Warrant Units: A Survey and Assessment, 70 Mich. L. Rev. 1411 (1972); Pesiri, Untangling the Warrant Web, 23 Tax Notes 525 (1984).

[320] See also Jack L. LeVant, 45 TC 185 (1965) (exchange of nonrestricted compensatory stock option for stock of acquiring corporation in a statutory merger did not qualify for nonrecognition treatment under §354(a), rev'd on other grounds, 376 F2d 434 (7th Cir. 1967); William H. Husted, 47 TC 664 (1967) (acq.); Jack F. Morrison, supra note 95; infra ¶ 14.34.

Debt obligations, as noted above, may or may not constitute securities, depending upon the continuity of creditor interest aspects of the instrument. Convertibility into stock of the issuing corporation would seem to make classification of the debt obligation as a security more likely because of the potential equity participation feature, although it would also ordinarily continue to be classified as a debt security until the holder terminates his creditor status through the exercise of the conversion privilege.[321]

Treating convertible debentures as debt until conversion may at first seem inconsistent with the argument for equity security classification of rights and warrants, but the former instruments do differ, in several respects, from stock purchase rights: Most important is the fact that the convertible debenture holder has downside protection through his election to continue as a creditor, a choice that will be exercised if the value of the stock fails to rise above the conversion price; moreover, the debentures have the normal characteristics of debt during the period preceding conversion (i.e., interest is usually, but not always, payable currently, regardless of earnings, and the debt claim takes priority over that of stockholders of the corporation).

The warrant holder's interest in the corporation, by contrast, is essentially a proprietary one, in that the warrant will have value only if the value of the stock is expected to appreciate above the purchase price (although warrants do not vote, cannot receive dividends, and have no current claim on assets of the corporation). Thus, while a convertible debenture has an equity feature through the possibility that the stock into which it is convertible will rise in value, it does not seem so heavily infused with a present proprietary interest as to merit classification with warrants as an equity security if the Service and courts ultimately adopt the treatment for warrants suggested above.

Convertible stock (usually preferred that is convertible into common, although the converse (i.e., upstream convertibility from common into preferred)) is at least theoretically possible) will of course be treated as stock, notwithstanding the convertibility feature, and it seems relatively clear that the value of the conversion privilege should not be treated as boot, severable from the underlying security to which it attaches. (The comparable problem under §1272 as to whether original issue discount arises from the conversion

---

[321] See Fleischer & Cary, The Taxation of Convertible Bonds and Stock, 74 Harv. L. Rev. 473 (1961); supra ¶ 4.61.

But see §279, added by the Tax Reform Act of 1969, restricting deductibility for interest paid on certain types of convertible securities on the ground that they are equity-type obligations (supra ¶ 4.26); §385 (supra ¶ 4.02), noting the equity characteristic of convertibility as a factor in the classification as stock or debt.

feature of a convertible debt security, answered in the negative by the Service, is discussed in Chapter 4.)

Where stock or debt securities are convertible into stock of *another* corporation, Rev. Rul. 69-265 holds that the conversion privilege is not boot if the conversion is to be effected directly with the *issuing* corporation, but that the right to convert is boot if the conversion is to be effected with the corporation *into* whose stock the stock or debt securities are convertible.[322] In the former situation, according to the ruling, the transaction is equivalent to a right to redeem the convertible stock, while in the second case, something extra is present (i.e., the right to receive property (stock) from another corporation).[323]

¶ 14.32 TREATMENT OF CORPORATE TRANSFEROR: SECTIONS 357, 358 AND 361

1. Nonrecognition: General background. The transferor corporation, under the 1954 Code version of §361(a), recognized neither gain nor loss on an exchange of property for stock or securities of a party to the reorganization if the exchange was pursuant to a plan of reorganization.[324]

---

[322] See Rev. Rul. 69-265, 1969-1 CB 109 (put-type option right to redeem stock of acquiring corporation after five years in exchange for other property; held not boot, and held a Type C reorganization; ruling further held that right to exchange acquiring corporation's stock with parent of acquiring corporation *was* boot).

See generally Eisenberg, IRS Position on Right to Convert Into Another Corporation's Stock Is Confusing, 33 J. Tax'n 25 (1970).

[323] See also Rev. Rul. 70-108, 1970-1 CB 78, holding that convertible stock that also gave the holder the right to purchase additional shares for a stated price at the time of conversion created taxable boot; the latter right was in the nature of a warrant, even though (unlike the typical warrant) the right was not severable from the underlying security.

With Rev. Rul. 70-108, compare Rev. Rul. 75-33, 1975-1 CB 115 (contingent dividend rights not boot), and Rev. Rul. 78-142, 1978-1 CB 111 (rescission rights not boot).

For other problems arising from the use of convertible stock or debt securities in a reorganization, see supra ¶¶ 4.60, 7.62, and 14.17.

[324] It should be noted that nonvoting stock and securities can be received tax-free under §361(a) if issued in a qualified reorganization (i.e., Type A statutory merger or in a Type C reorganization under the boot relaxation rule, even though they might not constitute permissible consideration in a different type of reorganization (i.e., a Type B exchange). See Regs. §1.361-1.

Unlike §354 (infra ¶ 14.34), §361(a) permits securities to be received tax-free, even though none are surrendered or the principal amount of those received exceeds that of those surrendered. But see infra note 335.

The nonrecognition rules of §361 applied only if the transferor corporation and the corporation whose stock or securities were received were both "a party to a reorganization." This term is defined by §368(b) to include a corporation resulting from a reorganization and both corporations in the case of an acquisition by one corporation of stock or properties of another.[325]

In addition to requiring that the stock or securities received must be those of a party to a reorganization and that the transferor of property likewise must be a party thereto, §361(a) required that the exchange be "in pursuance of the plan of reorganization."[326]

Nonrecognition of the transferor's gain under §361(a) applied only if the exchange was solely for stock or securities, but §361(b) intervened to moderate this strict rule. Under §361(b), the transferor did not recognize its gain if it distributed all of the boot in pursuance of the plan of reorganization; if it retained part or all of the boot, its gain (if any) was recognized up to an amount equal to the boot retained. Even if the boot exceeded the corporation's gain (e.g., boot worth $100,000, but gain of only $50,000), it was essential that the entire boot be distributed; §361(b)(1)(B) required the recognition of gain to the extent that boot was retained. Moreover, the boot had to be distributed to shareholders; its application to pay debts of the corporation did not qualify as a distribution under §361(b)(1).[327] The corporation was absolved from the recognition of gain by §361(b)(1) on the theory that it was a mere conduit for passing the consideration received in the reor-

---

[325] For discussion, see supra ¶ 14.30, para. 2.

[326] On this requirement, see Regs. §§1.368-1(g) and 1.368-3(a); see also Faber, supra note 53; Manning, supra note 53; Silberman, When Can an "Option to Purchase" Constitute a "Plan of Reorganization?" 23 J. Tax'n 136 (1965). Note also that the plan requirement has been involved in many of the cases arising under the step-transaction doctrine (especially as applied to the reincorporation area), for which see infra ¶¶ 14.51 and 14.54. See generally discussion supra ¶ 14.11, para. 10.

[327] See Liquidating Co., 33 BTA 1173 (1936) (nonacq.); Minnesota Tea Co. v. Helvering, 302 US 609 (1938) (corporation taxable where boot was distributed to shareholders in return for their assumption of corporate debts, since distribution to shareholders "was a meaningless and unnecessary incident in the transmission of the fund to the creditors"). The Tax Reform Act of 1986, however, overruled Minnesota Tea, and now allows distributions to creditors under §§368(a)(2)(G)(i) and 361(b)(3) of the Code.

See also Rev. Rul. 70-271, 1970-1 CB 166 (a distribution in kind to creditors of the transferor is a transaction resulting in recognized gain or loss to the debtor corporation); Rev. Rul. 75-450, 1975-2 CB 328 (distribution of acquiring corporation's stock to shareholders who assumed and paid acquiring corporation's liability to pay a finder's fee in that stock; held a taxable sale by the acquired corporation of the stock used to pay the fee, since the shareholders were a mere conduit for transfer of the stock under *Minnesota Tea*).

See generally Carlson, Boot at the Corporate Level in Tax-Free Reorganizations, 27 Tax. L. Rev. 499 (1972).

ganization to its shareholders,[328] but the boot was not necessarily taxable to the shareholder, who may have exchanged his stock in the distributing corporation for a liquidating distribution on which he realized no gain.[329] If the boot was not distributed, recognized gain was computed in the same manner as a partially taxable §351 exchange.[330]

Section 361(b)(1) came into play only if the corporation realized a gain on the reorganization. If it suffered a loss, §361(b)(2) provided that it could not be deducted even though boot was received.

If the transferor corporation was required to recognize gain on the disposition of part of its assets, either because boot received from the acquiring corporation was not fully distributed to shareholders or because part of its assets were sold to persons other than the acquiring corporation, it was nevertheless possible in 1986 to claim the nonrecognition benefits of former 1954 Code §337 before its repeal with respect to this gain.[331] Use of former §337 to obtain nonrecognition for gains realized on dealings with outsiders in the context of a reorganization cum liquidation of the transferor did not seem to be prohibited by any express provisions of the statute or by any compelling reasons of policy. Priority of the reorganization rules was probably justified where gain would be recognized under §361, absent applicability of §337, since §337 ought not to be allowed to function as a backstop to §361 where the two conflicted; but nonrecognition of gain under §337 from sales to outsiders (even though effected as part of the overall plan of reorganization) did not seem to be incompatible with the provisions of §361, whose focus was on dealings between the transferor corporation and the acquiring corporation. Even so, however, the Service, in Rev. Rul. 70-271,[332] and most (although not all) courts[333] denied use of §337 to a corporation that was also subject to the jurisdiction of §361.

---

[328] S. Rep. No. 398, 68th Cong., 1st Sess. 16, reprinted in 1939-1 CB (Part 2) 266, 277. The possibility of retained boot in a Type C reorganization was eliminated by the Tax Reform Act of 1984, however, which required, in §368(a)(2)(G), that the transferor liquidate "pursuant to the plan" in order to have a valid Type C reorganization, supra ¶ 14.14, note 114.

[329] See infra ¶ 14.34.

[330] See American Mfg. Co., supra note 70; supra ¶ 3.05.

[331] See Rev. Rul. 69-6, 1969-1 CB 104, for a holding that an all cash merger, while not a reorganization, nevertheless qualified as a §337 transaction at the corporate level and a §331 liquidation at the shareholder level; infra ¶ 14.57. But §337 (and §336) nonrecognition was repealed by the Tax Reform Act of 1986, supra ¶¶ 11.06 and 11.61.

[332] Rev. Rul. 70-271, 1970-1 CB 166.

[333] FEC Liquidating Corp. v. US, 548 F2d 924 (Ct. Cl. 1977), held that the reorganization provisions completely preempt the liquidation provisions, so that the transferor-corporation in a Type C reorganization could not rely on 1954 Code §337

If the transferor corporation was an S corporation, §1363(d) (enacted by the Subchapter S Revision Act of 1982), arguably could have caused recognition of gain on the distribution of the acquiring corporation's stock pursuant to the reorganization. Although the committee report stated that §1363(d) did not apply if the transferor completely liquidated, the Tax Reform Act of 1984 clarified this problem retroactively by exempting tax-free reorganization distributions from §1363(d) in §1363(e). Moreover, the restrictive §311(d) rules enacted by TEFRA and materially tightened once again in 1984 (see Chapter 7) did not cover tax-free reorganization distributions (nor did they cover complete liquidation distributions). However, the Tax Reform Act of 1986 repealed the exception for complete liquidations in §1363(e)(1) as part of its general repeal of §§336 and 337 nonrecognition while preserving the exception in §1363(e) for tax-free reorganization distributions of stock or securities. Moreover, the 1986 Act expanded §1374, tax-

---

for nonrecognition treatment as to sales of the transferee's stock that it had received in the reorganization exchange. Presumably, the court did not intend to hold that the transferor-corporation must recognize gain when it distributes the transferee's stock to its shareholders in complete liquidation pursuant to plan (1954 Code §336 clearly seemed to protect the distributing corporation here, as it also would in the case of a §355 distribution). As to the mutual exclusivity of the liquidation and reorganization provisions generally, one can argue that the pre-1986 law statutory scheme certainly did not, on its face, purport to effect this result. The coexistence of 1954 Code §336 with acquisitive reorganization liquidations was clear; see also 1954 Code §311(d), which did not apply to reorganization liquidations according to the regulations (supra ¶ 9.34), presumably since §311(a) or §336 did so apply. Also, application of §331 (or §302) principles at the distributee level in the §356 boot context was relatively well settled. Finally, the parity approach for 1954 Code §§336 and 337 (supra ¶¶ 11.07 and 11.61) added a further argument against court's holding in the FEC opinion.

Contra to FEC is *General Housewares Corp. v. US*, 615 F2d 1056 (5th Cir. 1980), for the reasons described above—that is, there is no essential incompatibility between the liquidation nonrecognition rules of 1954 Code §337 and the reorganization provision where the liquidating corporation sold part of the stock of the acquiring corporation, received in a prior Type C reorganization exchange, to third persons in order to raise cash for the payment of its debts; 1954 code §337 applied to the sale, and no gain was recognized thereon.

But for other decisions that the reorganization provisions preempt the liquidation rules of 1954 Code §337, see American Mfg. Co., supra note 70; James Armour Inc., supra note 120; Ralph C. Wilson, supra note 121; Abegg v. CIR, 429 F2d 1209 (2d Cir. 1970), cert. denied, 400 US 1008 (1971); Retail Properties, Inc., ¶ 64,245 P-H Memo. TC (1964); infra ¶ 14.54.

See generally Austin, The Applicability of Section 337 to Sales to Third Parties in a "C" Reorganization: The *FEC Liquidating* and *General Housewares* Decisions, 66 Calif. L. Rev. 623 (1978); Ordower, Separating Statutory Frameworks: Incompatibility of the Complete Liquidation and Reorganization Provisions of the Internal Revenue Code, 25 St. Louis U.L.J. 9 (1981). For resolution of this problem by the Tax Reform Act of 1986, see infra para. 2; see also Technical Corrections Act of 1987, H.R. 2636, §118(d)(4) (essentially reinstating the pre-1986 version of §361, infra note 335).

ing built-in gains on dispositions of property within 10 years after electing S corporation status.

The Tax Reform Act of 1984 also amended the Type C reorganization definition to require complete liquidation of the transferor corporation pursuant to the reorganization (unless waived by Service) in order to qualify as a Type C reorganization, thus eliminating the possibility that any boot could be retained and thereby become taxable at the corporate level.

Preliminary proposals by the staff of the Senate Finance Committee submitted in 1983 would have modified these rules as follows: (1) No gain or loss would be recognized to the corporate transferor in a qualified carry-over basis asset acquisition if all assets were transferred and no boot was received; (2) if boot was received on the transfer (including, for this purpose, debt securities) or if appreciated assets were retained, the corporate transferor would be required to distribute all of its assets to its shareholders or creditors pursuant to a plan of complete liquidation within 12 months in order to avoid recognition of gain; and (3) if the transferor failed to so liquidate, *net* gain (i.e., the excess of the consideration received over the aggregate basis of the transferred assets) would be recognized to the extent of the boot received and the potential gain in retained assets and taxed to the corporate transferor as long-term capital gain, per se, regardless of underlying character.

> *To illustrate:* (1) T transferred all of its assets, which had a basis of $20 and a value of $100, for $100 of P stock in a carry-over basis acquisition, no gain would be recognized, whether or not T liquidated; (2) if P paid $50 cash and $50 of stock for all of T's assets, T had to completely liquidate, or be taxed on $50 of long-term capital gain; and (3) if T retained $10 of assets (with a basis of $2), and transferred the rest of its assets for $90 of stock, T had to also completely liquidate or be taxed on $8 of capital gain on the retained assets.

Under the final 1985 version of the staff report, however, the above system was dropped in favor of a mandatory liquidation requirement (within 12 months of the acquisition) for *all* qualified asset acquisitions. Since liquidation would be required in order to constitute a qualified asset acquisition, the type of consideration received by target would be irrelevant; either it would liquidate and thereby avoid recognition,[334] or, if it failed to liquidate, the acquisition would result in full recognition of gain or loss; what the acquiring corporation pays for the properties is irrelevant to these results. Thus, in the prior example, T would have to liquidate (within 12 months) to

---

[334] Except to the extent that it distributed retained assets; receipt of boot would cause recognition to the shareholder-distributees, however. Note that the Tax Reform Act of 1984 required liquidation of the transferor pursuant to the plan, §368(a)(2)(G); supra note 114.

obtain nonrecognition treatment on its $80 potential gain under (1), while it would be taxable in full on the $80 gain under (2) if it failed to liquidate. Finally, under (3), *T* would be taxable on the $8 potential gain on its retained assets even though it did liquidate, while it alternatively would be taxed on the full $72 of gain from the transfer to *P* if it failed to liquidate (although not the gain on the retained assets).

The Tax Reform Act of 1986 generally repealed §§336 and 337 (see Chapter 11), but an exception was retained in §336(c) for reorganization distributions of stock or securities that are tax-free to the distributee-recipients; the transferor, however, will be taxable on a distribution of appreciated boot. Another provision in the 1986 Act revised §361 to provide generally in §361(a) that the transferor corporation will not recognize gain or loss on an exchange of its property pursuant to a plan of reorganization (regardless of the consideration received) and in §361(b)(1) that §§336 and 337 will not apply to any liquidation pursuant to a plan of reorganization, but that no gain or loss will be recognized on *any* disposition of stock or securities received from the acquiring corporate party to such reorganization, §361(b)(3). However, the Technical Corrections Act of 1987 proposes to undo the 1986 revision of §361 and return, in effect, to the 1954 Code version of that provision.

2. Nonrecognition: Revised 1986 §361 rules. The Tax Reform Act of 1986, as part of the technical corrections title, revised §361 in several significant substantive respects. Thus, §361(a) provides flatly that no gain or loss will be recognized to the corporate transferor party to a reorganization on *any* exchange of property pursuant to the plan of reorganization (regardless of the type of consideration received in the transaction). Section 361(b)(1) then goes on to oust §§336 and 337 from application to a reorganization liquidation, despite the general repeal of nonrecognition treatment under those sections in the 1986 Act (thus codifying at least the reasoning of the *FEC Liquidating Corp.* decision), but also provides, in §361(b)(3), that no gain or loss will be recognized on *any* disposition (pursuant to the reorganization plan) of stock or securities of a party to the reorganization that were received pursuant to the reorganization plan (thus apparently codifying the result in the *General Housewares* decision). The 1986 Act revision also overruled *Minnesota Tea* in §§361(b) and 368(a)(2)(G)(i) and now specifically permits liquidating distributions of stock or securities to creditors of the transferor under the reorganization plan. Finally, distributions of appreciated property consisting of untransferred retained assets (i.e., taxable boot) in the required reorganization liquidation transaction are subjected to full gain recognition under a provision similar to the rules of §311 (see Chapters 7 and 9) by §361(c)—that is, gain (but *not* loss) will be recognized on the distribution of such properties, (other than stock or securities entitled to be distributed tax-free to the recipients in the reorganization).[335] Moreover, §1363(e) was amended to eliminate the exception for complete liquidation distributions by S corporations, but the exception for tax-free reorganization distributions of stock or securities was retained, reminiscent of the rules of §361.

As a result of these amendments, transferor corporations (both C and S corporations) should never recognize gain or loss under §361 (except to the extent that untransferred appreciated assets are distributed in the required liquidation), even though boot is received in the transaction, and even though distributions are made to creditors as well as to shareholders of the liquidating transferor corporation.

Congress's proposal to revise §361 in the Technical Corrections Act of 1987 would, as mentioned earlier, return to the pre-1986 version of that provision, but with specific provisions in new §361(c) that protect the transferor from recognition of gain on the distribution of "qualified property" (i.e., stock or securities of the corporate parties to the reorganization, including options) pursuant to the plan of reorganization (including distributions to creditors). Thus, §§361(a) and 361(b) will return to the pre-1986 version, while §361(c) essentially provides for parity treatment with §311 on distributions of boot (i.e., recognition of gain, but not loss).

3. Assumption of liabilities. For purposes of §361, §357(a) provides generally that the assumption of the transferor's liabilities or the taking of property subject to liabilities (if consistent with the existence of a reorganization) will not constitute boot under §361(a). However, if tax avoidance motives apply to the assumption of any liability or if no business purpose can be proved therefor, §357(b) provides that *all* such liabilities must be treated as boot (although §357(b) will *not* disturb qualification as a Type C reorganization). In view of this penal aspect of §357(b), seemingly concerned with assumptions of liabilities that constitute a disguised payment of boot to the transferor, courts have tended to apply it with a merciful hand. If the liabilities assumed or to which the properties are subject exceed their basis, gain

---

[335] Note, however, that securities cannot be received tax-free by shareholders under §354 (infra ¶ 14.34), nor can they be so received by security holders to the extent that their principal amount exceeds that of the securities surrendered in the exchange. Does §361(c) override §361(b)(3) and thereby cause taxable gain to the liquidating corporation on the distribution? It would seem that it should not, but the statutory language is inartfully drafted at best on this point.

See Peaslee, Current and Quotable: Peaslee Sees 'Zero Basis' Problems Arising Under Amended Section 361, 34 Tax Notes 725 (1987); Eustice, Comment, 35 Tax Notes 283 (1987).

But the Technical Corrections Act of 1987 in §118(d)(4) successfully repairs §361 by essentially reverting to the pre-1986 version of that provision.

must be recognized by the transferor under §357(c) if the transfer occurs in a Type D reorganization,[336] but not otherwise.

A transferor corporation that received property constituting boot under §361 if retained could avoid this result by distributing the property under §361(b)(1), a result that was mandated after 1984 by §368(a)(2)(G) for Type C reorganizations; but this escape hatch was not available if the boot was created by §357. Although considered as money by virtue of §357, an assumption of the transferor's liabilities could not be distributed to its shareholders in any meaningful way.[337]

Under the Finance Committee staff's final report on reform of Subchapter C, the tax avoidance motive test of §357(b) would be replaced with an objective test that would limit non-boot assumptions to "qualified indebtedness," defined by proposed §357(b) as purchase money debt either of the transferor or that has a nexus to the transferee's use of the acquired property of its business. Like the 1986 amendments to §361, however, receipt of boot at the corporate level would be essentially a meaningless event under the staff proposal, since no gain would be recognized by the transferor in a carry-over basis acquisition regardless of the type of consideration received.

4. Basis. The applicable basis provision for the corporate transferor of property is §358, which provides that nonrecognition property (i.e., stock or

---

[336] Rev. Rul. 75-161, 1975-1 CB 114 (§357(c) applied to Type D reorganization even though also qualified as a Type A; ruling noted that §357(c) could have been avoided by having merger in reverse order, so liabilities not assumed by surviving corporation); Rev. Rul. 76-188, 1976-1 CB 99 (§357(c) applies to parent's transfer of substantially all its assets to new subsidiary because transaction was §351 exchange, even though it also constituted a Type C reorganization; fact that §351 and Type C reorganization can overlap does not oust §357(c) of jurisdiction).

Compare Rev. Rul. 78-330, 1978-2 CB 147 (parent cancellation of subsidiary debt prior to subsidiary merger into affiliated subsidiary in order to avoid §357(c) gain did not constitute §357(b) tax avoidance). See also Rev. Rul. 79-289, 1979-2 CB 145 (§357(c) not applicable to a Type F reorganization even though transaction also a Type D; Rev. Rul. 75-161 and Rev. Rul. 76-188 distinguished).

See generally Cooper, Negative Basis, 75 Harv. L. Rev. 1352 (1962), to the effect that §357(c) should have been made applicable to Type C rather than (or in addition to) D reorganizations; Steiner, Liabilities in Excess of Basis in Corporate Reorganizations—When Should Gain Be Recognized, 6 J. Corp. Tax'n 39 (1979).

[337] See Minnesota Tea Co. v. Helvering, supra note 327; Rev. Rul. 75-450, 1975-2 CB 328. But see §368(a)(2)(G)(i), as amended by the Tax Reform Act of 1986, which allows distribution to creditors as well; §361(a), as amended in 1986, supra para. 2. But see Joint Comm. Staff Explanation of Technical Corrections to the Tax Reform Act of 1986, JSC-11-87, at 26, n.7 (May 13, 1987) (not intended to change §357 rules).

See also Joint Comm. Staff Description of the Technical Corrections Act of 1987, JCS-15-87, at 283, n.1 (June 15, 1987) (same).

securities) received by the transferor in exchange for its property takes a substituted basis: its basis for the transferred property, increased by any gain (and decreased by any loss) recognized to the transferor on the exchange, and decreased by any boot received. In addition, §358(d) provides that basis must be reduced by any liabilities assumed (or taken subject to) by the transferee on the exchange.[338] These rules are generally unimportant to the transferor corporation in a reorganization if it liquidated as a part of the reorganization plan. In a Type C reorganization, however, liquidation of the transferor formerly was not necessary, so that the basis of stock or securities received in exchange for its property could have been important in this situation; but after the Tax Reform Act of 1984, the transferor is required to liquidate pursuant to the plan, unless waived by Service, so these rules should no longer be important for the Type C reorganization either.

The Finance Committee staff's final report on the reform of Subchapter C proposed a somewhat different approach, although with comparable results. Under this proposal, the consideration received in a qualified asset acquisition would take a fair market value fresh-start basis (whether the transferor elects nonrecognition treatment or not), thus purging any potential gain or loss in that property and avoiding recognition of gain or loss on the mandatory liquidation required to obtain tax-free treatment on a carryover basis asset acquisition.[339] The Tax Reform Act of 1986 did not accept this cost-basis approach in §361(b)(2); that provision merely states that boot takes the same basis as it had in the hands of the acquiring corporation, increased by gain recognized to that party on the *payment* of the boot (i.e., fair market value). If this is all that §361(b)(2) accomplishes (establishing a fair market value basis rule for boot received by the transferor), it seems to have added little, if anything, to the comparable basis rule of §358(a)(2), which also provides for a fair market value boot basis rule. The Technical

---

[338] As to the possibility of a negative basis for stock or securities where assumed liabilities exceed the transferor's basis for its property, see Easson v. CIR, 294 F2d 653 (9th Cir.) 1961; Cooper, supra note 336.

[339] Since the transferor only was required to liquidate within 12 months of the acquisition, however, interim fluctuations in value could trigger taxable gain or loss on the liquidation distribution; §368(a)(2)(G) of current law requires distribution pursuant to the plan, and the possibility for such interim value changes is considerably less likely. See supra ¶ 14.32, para. 2. The fresh-start basis rule for all consideration received in reorganization was contained in §361(b)(2) of the 1986 Senate bill, but the final Conference version of the Tax Reform Act of 1986 did not contain this fresh-start basis proposal. Instead, §361(b)(2) provides that the basis of boot received be the same as its basis in the hands of the paying corporation (adjusted for recognized gain or loss in the payment transaction), a provision that seems to add little, if anything, to the results obtained under current law §358(a)(2) (basis of boot is fair market value), except the possible creation of a potential zero-basis problem if the transferee gives its own boot note; infra note 340.

But see the Technical Corrections Act of 1987, which adds new §358(f) and gives §358 priority once again by repealing the basis rule of 1986 law §361(b)(2).

Corrections Act of 1987 recognizes this anomaly by repealing the 1986 law §361 basis provision.

A technical problem was created, however, by this 1986 revision of §361(b)(2), providing a basis for boot received by the transferor derived from its basis in the hands of the payor corporation, adjusted for recognized gain or loss. Ordinarily, this figure is the same as under the boot basis rule of §358(a)(2) (which also continues to apply here), likewise providing that the basis for boot value is its value; but suppose the acquiring corporation gives its own note (and that note is not a security)? A taxpayer ordinarily has a zero basis in its own note,[340] so that the transferor would inherit that zero basis under §361(b)(2)–although not under §358(a)(2)–and would then recognize gain on the required liquidation distribution under §361(c). It seems unlikely that Congress intended to create this problem, but it apparently succeeded in doing so inadvertently. The Technical Corrections Act of 1987 addresses this problem by repealing §361(b)(2) and returning to the §358 basis priority regime of pre-1986 law, adding new §358(f).

An even more curious result stemming from the continued jurisdiction of the §358 basis rules over §361 exchanges is the fact that §358(a)(1) would seem to apply to *all* the property received by the transferor in the reorganization exchange (both boot and nonrecognition stock or securities), since §361(a) confers nonrecognition status per se on the exchange transaction. It seems even more unlikely that Congress intended *this* result; but there is a square, and unresolved, conflict between §§358(a)(1) and 361(b)(2). This unfortunate tinkering with well-settled statutory rules succeeds in creating uncertainty at best, and potentially bizarre results, in what should otherwise be a garden variety tax-free reorganization acquisition (although the Technical Corrections Act of 1987 resolves such confusion by returning to the pre-1986 law basis rules).

5. Examples. Consider the following examples, in which *T* holds two business assets, *X* (with a basis of $20 and a value of $120) and *Y* (with a basis of $80 and a value of $30), and also has outstanding debts of $30 (held by *C*). *T* is wholly owned by individual shareholder *A*, whose basis for his *T* stock is $40 (and its value $120). Acquiring corporation *P* will acquire *T*'s assets in what is assumed to be a qualified §368 reorganization.

Example 1. *T* merges into *P* for $120 of *P* stock, with *P* assuming *T*'s debt to *C*. *T* has no gain on the *T-P* exchange under §361(a), and *T* also

---

[340] See Peaslee, supra note 335; and Eustice, supra note 335. As to the zero basis rule, see Velma Alderman, 55 TC 662 (1971); supra ¶ 3.06, note 69; see also Rev. Rul. 74-503, 1974-2 CB 117. But see the Technical Corrections Act of 1987, which repeals the special boot basis rule of 1986 law §361(b)(2).

has no gain under §361(b)(3) on the distribution of the *P* stock to *A*, even though *T*'s basis for the *P* stock was $70 under §358(a)(1) and §358(d)(1) ($100 less $30 debt assumption). *A* has no gain under §354(a)(1) and takes a $40 basis in the *P* stock under §358(a)(1). *P* takes a carry-over basis for *T*'s *X* and *Y* assets under §362(b) (and also inherits *T*'s tax attributes under §381).

Example 2. *T* merges into *P* for $60 of *P* stock, $60 cash, and assumption of *T*'s debt (a valid Type A reorganization under Rev. Proc. 77-37). *T* has no gain on the *T-P* exchange under §361(a), *T*'s basis in the *P* stock is $10 under §358 ($100 less $60 cash less $30 debt assumption); but *T* has no gain on the liquidating distribution to *A* under §361(b)(3). *A* has $60 of recognized boot gain under §356(a)(1) and takes a $20 basis in the *P* stock (which has a remaining built-in potential gain of $20). *P*'s results are the same as Example 1.

Example 3. Assume the same facts as in Example 2 except *P* gives $60 of bonds (securities) instead of cash. Again, *T* has no gain under §361(a), and takes a $70 basis in the *P* stock and bonds, allocated $35 to each under §358(b)(1). On the liquidating distribution to *A*, *T* has no gain on the *P* stock but may have $25 of gain on the distribution of the *P* bonds (because the bonds are taxable boot to *A*) if §361(c) overrides §361(b)(3) (a result worse than the receipt of cash!) *A*'s results are the same as Example 2, as are *P*'s (who gets no basis stepup for *T*'s gain under §362(b) because that gain was not recognized on the *T-P* exchange). The Technical Corrections Act of 1987, however, takes care of this problem by providing for nonrecognition treatment to *T* on its distribution of the bonds in proposed §361(c)(2).

Example 4. Assume the same facts as in Example 2 except that *P* gives its own short-term note of $60. Again, *T* has no gain on the *T-P* exchange under §361(a), and *A*'s tax results are the same as in Example 2. *T*, however, has the following possibilities as to the *P* boot note: *T* could take a $60 fair market value basis for the note under §358(a)(2) (and a $10 basis for the *P* stock), in which event no gain would result to *T* on the liquidating distribution to *A*; alternatively, *T* could take a zero basis in the *P* note under §362(b)(2) (*P*'s basis in its own obligation being zero[341]), and thereby recognize $60 of gain on the distribution to *A* under §361(c); finally, §358(a)(1) may apply (since receipt of the note by *T* was tax-free under §361(a)), in which event the note would take an allocated $35 basis and *T* would recognize $25 of gain on its distri-

---

[341] See supra note 340.

bution to *A* under §361(c). However, the Technical Corrections Act returns to pre-1986 law so that *T* takes a $60 basis for the boot and thus has no further gain on its distribution.

Example 5. *T* transfers all its assets to *P* for $150 of *P* voting stock in a C reorganization (*P* does not assume *T*'s debt to *C*). *T* transfers $30 of the *P* stock to *C* and $120 of the *P* stock to *A*. *T* has no gain on the distribution to creditor *C* under §361(b)(3) and the flush language in §361(b) (thus, one of the holdings in Rev. Rul. 70-271 is overruled[342]); *P* also does not recognize gain on the distribution of the *P* stock because of §361(b)(3). *A* has no gain under §354(a)(1) and takes a $40 basis in the *P* stock under §358(a)(1). *C* has no gain or loss if his debt is a security (§354(a)(1)) but has taxable gain or loss if it isn't. *P* has the same results as Example 1.

Example 6. Assume the same facts as in Example 5, except that *T* sells $30 of *P* stock and pays off *C* with the proceeds (the *General Housewares* pattern). The flush language of §361(b) literally does not protect *T* here (it only covers *distribution* of the stock or securities to the creditor), so that *T* might have $10 of gain on this sale ($30 less $20, the allocable §358(a)(1) basis for the portion of the *P* stock sold). *A*'s result would be the same as Example 5, as would *P*'s (*P* would get no basis stepup for *T*'s gain recognized on the sale of the *P* stock). The Technical Corrections Act of 1987, in proposed §361(b)(3), clearly rejects *General Housewares* and will tax *T* on $10 of gain here.

Example 7. *T* transfers the *X* business to *P* for $120 of *P* voting stock (*P* does not assume *T*'s debt to *C*) in a C reorganization (the substantially all requirement is satisfied under Rev. Proc. 77-37, since the *X* business is 80 percent of gross and 100 percent of net assets). *T* sells $30 of *P* stock and pays off *C* with the proceeds; *T* then liquidates, distributing the $90 of *P* stock and the *Y* business (worth $30) to *A*.

T has no gain on the *T-P* exchange and takes a $20 basis in the *P* stock under §358(a)(1). *T* arguably has a $25 gain on the *P* stock sale, if §361(b)(3) does not apply (allocable basis for the stock sold was $5). On the liquidation, *T* has no gain on the *P* stock (basis $15, value $90)

---

[342] Rev. Rul. 70-271, 1970-1 CB 166, (distribution in kind of the *P* stock to creditors triggered taxable gain to *T*). But the Conference Report, H.R. Rep. No. 841, 99th Cong., 2d Sess. 844, n.1 (1986) warns that *T* might have debt discharge gain if the value of the *P* stock is less than the face of *C*'s debt claim; infra ¶ 14.58.

Under proposed §361(c)(3) in the Technical Corrections Act of 1987, no gain or loss results on the distribution to creditors of "qualified property" (stock or securities of the corporate parties).

under §361(b)(3) and also apparently has no loss on the distribution of the Y business to A under §361(c) (a §311 parity result). A has $30 of boot gain under §356(a)(1) and takes a $40 substituted basis in the P stock (and a $30 stepped down basis in the Y business boot). P takes a $20 carry-over basis for the X business (and inherits *all* of T's tax history under §381). The Technical Corrections Act of 1987 confirms these results to T (i.e., gain of $25 on the P stock sale and no loss on the distribution of the Y business).

Example 8. Assume the same facts as in Example 7, except that instead of selling the P stock, T sells the Y business and pays off C with the proceeds. T now has a $50 loss on the sale of Y (§336 does not apply because of §361(b)(1) and no other provision would deny T's loss, including §361(c), which only covers distributions, not sales). On the liquidation, T has no gain on the distribution of the $120 of P stock (basis $20) under §361(b)(3). A also has no gain under §354(a)(1) and takes a $40 basis in the P stock. P's results are the same as in Example 7. (The Technical Corrections Act of 1987 apparently does not change these results.)

Example 9. Assume the same facts as in Example 7, except that P assumes T's debt to C (and consequently pays only $90 of voting stock). The acquisition is still a good Type C reorganization under Rev. Proc. 77-37 because T transferred 80 percent of its gross and 100 percent of its net assets to P. T has no gain on the T-P exchange, and takes a ($10) basis in the P stock ($20 less $30 debt assumption). On the liquidation distribution of P stock (potential gain of $100), T has no gain on that distribution under §361(b)(3) and also has no loss on the distribution of the Y business. A's results are the same as Example 7, as are P's.

Example 10. If the Y business has a $5 basis (i.e., a built-in gain instead of loss), T would have a recognized gain of $25 on the distribution of the Y business to A in Example 7 and Example 9 and also would have a recognized gain of $25 on the sale of this business in Example 8.

Example 11. Instead of the X and Y businesses being held directly, assume that both of those businesses are in wholly owned, five-year aged subsidiaries, XS and YS, and that T's basis for its XS and YS stock is $20 and $80 respectively—that is, T is a pure holding company with two active business subsidiaries whose inside asset bases are $20 and $80 respectively, and the liabilities are owed by T.

(a) If XS merges into P for $120 of P stock, XS has no gain on the XS-P exchange under §361(a), takes a $20 basis for the P stock under §358(a)(1), and has no gain under §361(b)(3) when it distributes the *P* stock in liquidation to *T* (although §337, as amended in 1986, also might apply to *XS* here, §361(b)(1) preempts that provision in view of the *XS-P* reorganization, and the Technical Corrections Act of 1987 preserves this result in new §361(c)(4)). *T* has two possible nonrecognition rules to rely on here: §332 (liquidation of its subsidiary *XS*) and §354(a)(1) (exchange of stock in a reorganization). If §332 applies, *T* takes a $20 carry-over basis from *XS* for the *P* stock under §334(b); if §354 applies, *T* takes a §358 substituted basis for the *P* stock (which on these facts happens to be the same number, $20, a result that would rarely occur in practice). The *P* stock would be "trapped" in *T*, however, since *T* is not a party to the *XS-P* reorganization. *P* takes a $20 carry-over basis from *XS* under §362(b) and inherits *XS*'s tax attributes under §381.

(b) If *YS* merges into *P* for $30 of *P* stock, *YS*'s built-in loss of $50 gets shifted into the basis of *P* stock, and *T* would hold the *P* stock after *YS*'s liquidation with a basis of $80 (either a carry-over from *YS* under §334(b) or substituted from *T*'s *YS* stock under §358(a)(1), also $80). *P* takes *YS*'s $80 carry-over basis but would be subject to the built-in loss limitations of §382(h) (see Chapter 16).

(c) If *T* exchanges its *XS* stock with *P* for *P* stock in a B reorganization, *T*'s basis rule for the *P* stock clearly is §358(a)(1) in this case, and *T*'s nonrecognition rule is exclusively §354(a)(1). *P* takes a $20 carry-over basis for the *XS* stock under §362(b) and *XS*'s tax history and inside asset basis continue unchanged.

(d) A Type B reorganization exchange of *YS* stock for *P* stock likewise results in nonrecognition of *T*'s loss on the *T-P* exchange, but *P* would be subject to the built-in loss rules of §382(h) on its acquisition of *YS* (see Chapter 16).

(e) *T* spins off its *XS* stock to *A* in a §355 distribution. *T* has no gain under §311(a) on the distribution of the *XS* stock, and *A* allocates its $40 *T* stock basis ratably between the *XS* and *T* stock under §358(b) in proportion to their relative values. (On these facts, since the *XS* stock is worth $120, it would draw off all of *A*'s *T* stock basis, since the *T* stock would be worth $0 after the distribution (see Chapter 13), the assets being offset by liabilities).

(f) A spin-off of *YS* stock to *A* would result in no loss to *T* under §311(a), and *A* would allocate one fourth, or $10, of his *T* stock basis to the *YS* stock under §358(b) (relative values are $30 and $90).

    (g) If *T* liquidates in a split-up, *T*'s only available nonrecognition rule is §311(a). (Section 361(b)(3) only applies to a reorganization, and this distribution, while tax-free to *A* under §355, is not a Type D reorganization because *T* was an existing holding company structure (see Chapters 7 and 13)). However, the Technical Corrections Act of 1987 proposes to add new §355(c), which specifically protects *T* in this case.

    6. Current reform proposals: Corporate acquisitions and basis election. The staff of the Senate Finance Committee, in its preliminary report on the reform and simplification of Subchapter C of 1983, proposed a fundamental restructuring of the rules governing corporate acquisitions and liquidations; the final version of these proposals (including draft statutory language) was released in 1985. Both reports recommended that §§336 and 337 be repealed (advice that was accepted in the Tax Reform Act of 1986 (see Chapter 11)) and that corporate transferors recognize gain or loss on any transfer of assets that results in a cost basis for the property to the transferee. The treatment of corporate acquisitions would be placed on a specific electivity system—that is, cost-basis or carry-over basis treatment would be expressly elected by the parties rather than, as under present law, being elected transactionally.

    The key to the proposed corporate acquisition regime is basis. In a qualified stock or asset acquisition, if cost-basis is elected, then gain or loss is to be recognized at the corporate level (as discussed in Part B), while if basis is preserved through a carry-over basis election, no gain or loss will result to the corporate transferor. Thus, a cost-basis election acquisition will trigger full corporate level recognition of both gain and loss with, however, an exception for "unallocated acquisition premium" (i.e., excess consideration paid for goodwill and the like), for which the parties could separately elect carry-over basis and nonrecognition treatment.

    Treatment of the transferor corporation in a qualified asset acquisition where carry-over basis treatment is elected by the corporate parties is a relatively straightforward matter under the Senate Finance Committee staff's final report. Under this system, the transferor never recognizes gain or loss on a carry-over basis qualified asset transfer under proposed §361(a), regardless of the consideration received; basis for all consideration received also takes a fresh start fair market value basis. Gain or loss may result under proposed §311(a) on the mandatory complete liquidation within 12 months, however, to the extent that the distribution consists of retained assets (or if the value of the consideration received has changed between the acquisition and the liquidation dates). Liquidating distributions to creditors also are permitted, thus reversing the law that existed until 1986, when amendments were made that now permit such distributions. Failure to liquidate within 12 months, however, will trigger full recognition to the transferor. The target's tax attributes pass over to the acquiring corporation along with asset basis, but the acquiring corporation in a stock acquisition is required to determine its basis for that stock under the basis conformity rule of proposed §1020 (discussed in the next section) by reference to the target's net inside asset basis.

Special complex rules are provided where the transferor is a controlled subsidiary and boot is paid in the acquisition. The general thrust of these provisions apparently allows purging of corporate level gain if all corporations in the direct chain completely liquidate within 12 months (treatment similar to the chain liquidation rules of former 1954 Code §337(c)(3), before its repeal by the Tax Reform Act of 1986). Proposed §§356(e) and 358(c) set forth the operating rules applicable to parent subsidiary chains (which are some of the more challenging features of the staff proposals). The 1986 law rules governing subsidiary liquidations (new §337) are discussed in Chapter 11.

Election of cost-basis treatment for the acquisition would result in full recognition of gain or loss at the corporate level under proposed §361(b), regardless of the type of consideration paid by the acquiring corporation. A special exception is provided for acquisition premium (e.g., goodwill), for which the parties can separately elect nonrecognition and carry-over basis treatment. The election covers all assets of the acquired corporation, but separate elections can be made for separate entities owned by the acquired corporation. The rules of §338, discussed in Chapter 11, would be conformed to reflect the above proposals (i.e., full corporate level recognition and basis adjustment of all assets to fair market value).

Thus, qualified stock acquisitions in a cost-basis election transaction would trigger corporate level recognition of gain or loss and inside asset-basis adjustments (to fair market value) for the acquired corporation, regardless of how the transferor's shareholders are taxed—that is, the shareholders could receive tax-free treatment to the extent that they receive qualified consideration (i.e., stock of the acquiring corporation) independently of corporate level recognition or nonrecognition.

The election between cost-basis and carry-over basis treatment would be made corporation-by-corporation (not asset-by-asset) under proposed §365(c). Thus, selectivity as to entities would be permitted (unlike under §338 of present law), but asset selectivity would be prohibited. As to the latter, a two-year consistency period (which could increase to three years in the case of stock acquisitions) would be provided to prevent avoidance of the asset selectivity prohibition. The election as to the acquired corporation would govern any assets held by such corporation within one year of the acquisition and ultimately acquired during the consistency period.

However, inconsistent treatment of nonamortizable intangibles (e.g., goodwill) would be permitted under proposed §365(b)(2), although mandatory carry-over basis treatment is prescribed by proposed §365(d) for related party (under §304 principles) acquisitions, and mandatory cost-basis treatment is required by proposed §365(f) if the acquiring party is a nontaxpaying entity.

The following examples illustrate the corporate level operation of these proposals. (Assume T has operating business, X, and also owns all of the stock of operating subsidiary S.)

Example 1a: P acquires all of S's assets for P stock and elects carry-over basis. S has no gain under proposed §361(a) on the transfer to P and takes a new basis for the P stock under proposed §362(b)(2) (and thus has no gain on its required liquidation into T). T has no gain or loss under either §332 or 354(a) on the liquidation of S, but T's basis in the P stock is governed by proposed §358(c)(1). (T takes the *lower* of its basis in S stock or the value of the P stock as the basis of the P stock; thus, T's potential gain in the S stock is preserved, but loss is purged.) Note that the P stock is trapped at the T level: Since T is not a party, it cannot distribute that stock to its shareholders tax-free under proposed §354; moreover, T will be taxable on the distribution of that stock under proposed §311. P takes over S's asset basis and tax history.

Example 1b: If P elects cost-basis, S will have full recognition under proposed §361(b)(2), a new basis in the P stock under proposed §362(b)(2), and no further gain or loss on the liquidation into T. T has the same results as in Example 1a (i.e., no gain or loss under §354 and a special substituted, or stepped-down, basis for the P stock under proposed §358(c)(1)). P does not get S's tax attributes here; rather they pass to T on S's liquidation.

Example 2a: P acquires the S assets for a mixture of cash and stock and elects carry-over basis. S's results are the same as in Example 1a, but T now has taxable boot gain under proposed §356. If T liquidates, however (although it need not), T's boot gain is purged by the special rule of proposed §356(e)(1)(C)(ii), and it also gets a new basis in the P stock under proposed §358(c)(2). T will be taxable under proposed §311 on the distribution of the X assets (although not on the P stock). T's shareholders have a fully taxable liquidation result, since T is not a party to the acquisition.

Example 2b: If P elects cost-basis, S's results are the same as in Example 1b. T's results depend upon whether or not it liquidates (although it need not). If T does not liquidate, it is excused from tax on its boot gain by proposed §356(e)(1)(C)(i) (the special surrogate tax rule, which excuses T because S was fully taxable); T also obtains a new basis for the T stock under proposed §358(c)(2). If T does liquidate, its results (and that of its shareholders) are the same as in Example 2a.

Example 3a: P acquires all the S stock for P stock and elects carry-over basis. T's and S's results are the same as in Example 1a.

Example 3b: Alternatively, if T was a pure holding company for the S stock, §354(c) would allow T's shareholders to obtain tax-free treatment for the P stock (by treating the transaction as an asset acquisition and thereby making T's stock party stock). However, T apparently is still stuck with the proposed §358(c)(1) substituted (or stepped-down) basis for the P stock, and hence under proposed §311, would recognize gain (although not loss) on the distribution.

Example 3c: P elects cost-basis. The results to S are the same as in Example 1b and presumably are also for T (and even in Example 3b where T was a pure holding company).

Example 4a: P acquires the S stock for a mixture of cash and stock and elects carry-over basis. S's results are the same as in Example 1a, while T's results are the same as in Example 2a, as are those of its shareholders.

Example 4b: P elects cost-basis. The results to S are the same as in Example 1b, and those of T and its shareholders are the same as in Example 2b.

Example 5a: P acquires all of T's X assets (worth half of T). The transaction is not a qualified asset acquisition, since P failed to acquire enough assets of T (i.e., 70 percent of gross and 90 percent of net). Hence, T has merely sold X.

Example 5b: T could tailor itself by spinning off S under §355 (nontaxable to T as well under proposed §311(c)) and then having P acquire the X assets in a good qualified asset acquisition. Alternatively, T could drop the X assets into new subsidiary S-2, and have P do a stock acquisition of S-2; here, the incorporation of S would be protected from decontrol arguments by proposed §351(e)(1)(B), and the tax consequences would be the same as in Example 3a.

Example 6a: P acquires *all* of T's assets (including the S stock) for P stock and elects carry-over basis for both T and S (although different elections are possible). A special bifurcation rule in §364(e)(1) treats the acquisition of the X assets as an asset acquisition and of the S stock as a stock acquisition. Thus, T has no gain or loss on the X asset transfer under proposed §361(a), and the P stock received therefor takes a new basis under proposed §362(b)(2). T has no gain or loss under §354(a) on the S stock transfer, but takes the special basis (substituted or stepped-down) for the P stock received under proposed §358(c)(1). On T's required liquidation, it will have taxable gain (but no loss) under proposed §311 for the P stock with the substituted basis. Unlike the case in Example 3a, however, T's shareholders obtain full nonrecognition on their T stock by virtue of §354(c), as in Example 3b.

Example 6b: P elects cost-basis (for both T and S, although it need not). S has full gain or loss under proposed §361(b), as in Example 3b. T has full gain or loss on the X transfer and a new basis in the P stock, but not in the S stock to which §354 still applies (although so does the special basis rule of proposed §358(c)(1), so that gain, but not loss, will be recognized on T's liquidation distribution of this P stock). T's shareholders have the same result as in Example 6a (§354(a) and proposed §358 treatment on the exchange of their T stock for P stock).

Example 6c: Note that cost or carry-over elections can be made alternatively for the S and X acquisitions; entity inconsistency is permitted here.

Example 7a: P acquires all the T stock for P stock and elects carry-over basis for both T and S (although it need not). T and S have no gain or loss, and T's shareholders have §354 nonrecognition and a §358 basis for their P stock (i.e., the same results as a Type B reorganization under current law).

Example 7b: If P paid boot to some (or all) of T's shareholders, they would have gain but no loss with respect to the boot. Unlike present law, however, the receipt of the P stock would still be tax-free.

Example 7c: If P elects cost-basis for both T and S, S has full recognition of gain or loss under proposed §361(b)(1); T similarly has full gain or loss recognition under proposed §361(b)(2) (including gain or loss on the S stock).

Example 7d: P can elect inconsistently here as to T and S (cost-basis for T and carry-over for S, or vice versa).

Example 8: P acquires all the assets of T, including the stock of S, for cash, and a cost-basis election is made as to T only. T recognizes gain or loss on all of its X assets (including the S stock), and P obtains a fair market value basis for T's directly owned X assets (but not the S stock, the basis for which would be determined by reference to S's inside net asset basis under the basis conformity rule of proposed §1020). If cost-basis treatment was elected only as to S, S would recognize gain or loss, and P would obtain a fair market value basis for the S stock (and S would obtain a fair market value basis for its assets). In either case, T must liquidate within 12 months.

Example 9: P acquires all of the stock of T for cash and elects cost-basis treatment for T and S; T and S recognize gain or loss on all of their assets (but T will not recognize gain or loss on the S stock here), and the basis of the T and S assets (including the S stock), is adjusted to their fair market values.

Example 10: If both T and P were 50 percent owned subsidiaries of H, cost-basis treatment could not be elected—that is, carry-over basis treatment would be mandatory for both stock and asset acquisitions from such related persons.

Example 11: If P were a foreign corporation (or other tax exempt type of entity), cost-basis treatment would be mandatory for any of the above acquisitions under §365(f).

¶ 14.33 TREATMENT OF CORPORATE TRANSFEREE: Sections 362 AND 1032

1. Nonrecognition. A corporation that acquires property in exchange for its stock is protected from recognition of gain or loss thereon by §1032 (see Chapter 3); this is true whether or not the transaction constitutes a reorganization under §368. Section 1032 also protects the acquiring corporation from recognition of gain or loss if the stock given in the exchange is treasury stock rather than newly issued stock; this provision, enacted in 1954, changed prior law, under which gain or loss could be recognized by a corporation if it dealt with its treasury stock as it would with the shares of another corporation.[343]

---

[343] Rev. Rul. 71-364, 1971-2 CB 182 (excess cash retained by transferor to pay liquidation expenses but not fully expended; not taxable when paid over to transferee pursuant to reorganization). But see Rev. Rul. 72-327, 1972-2 CB 197 (payment of boot in kind a taxable exchange to the acquiring corporation); Rev. Rul. 72-464, 1972-2 CB 214 (acquiring corporation recognizes gain to extent debt claims against acquired corporations are satisfied in the acquisition and the amounts received therefor exceed the basis of the debts); see also §361(b)(2), supra ¶ 14.32, para. 4, which is slated for repeal.

Where the transferee corporation issues securities in addition to stock as part of the consideration for the acquired property, the authority for nonrecognition is less clear; presumably the acquisition is a purchase of property by the transferee to this extent and, as such, does not involve recognition of gain or loss. Although this result is not prescribed by an express statutory provision, it is so well established and widely assumed that, no doubt, none was thought necessary by Congress.

Where property is acquired by a controlled subsidiary corporation in exchange for its parent's stock (in a *Groman*[344] triangular acquisition), however, nonrecognition treatment to the transferee corporation may not be afforded by §1032. For example, suppose that the parent corporation contributes its own stock to the subsidiary, which then uses this stock as the consideration for the stock or properties acquired from another corporation. Section 1032 applies only to a corporation whose *own* stock is given in exchange for property and hence would not seem to protect the subsidiary from recognition of gain in such a case of an exchange of its parent's stock for property. In Rev. Rul. 57-278, however, the Service ruled (without discussion) that no gain or loss was recognized by the subsidiary in such a case,[345] apparently on the assumption that the transaction was no different, in substance, from a direct acquisition by the parent followed by a dropdown of the acquired assets into the subsidiary, in which case §1032 would apply to protect the subsidiary from recognition of gain or loss.[346] If the

---

[344] Groman v. CIR, supra note 28.

[345] Rev. Rul. 57-278, 1957-1 CB 124 (passage of stock through subsidiary transitory conduit).

[346] Statutory support for nonrecognition treatment of the acquiring subsidiary seems questionable. In the case of an asset-for-stock acquisition (i.e., a Type C reorganization), §361 would be the only possibility, but that provision has ordinarily been thought to be concerned with the treatment of the property transferor rather than the acquiring party. Moreover, the subsidiary would not retain any continuity of interest with respect to the consideration that it gives in the exchange (its parent's stock), so that a fundamental requisite for nonrecognition treatment would be lacking as far as the subsidiary is concerned. In the case of a stock-for-stock acquisition (a Type B reorganization), the literal language of §354(a) seems more hospitable to nonrecognition treatment for the acquiring corporation, but even here the transaction may be vulnerable under continuity principles. While the continuity of interest doctrine (supra ¶ 14.11) ordinarily functions as a condition to reorganization status, its scope and radiations may be sufficiently broad to cause the infusion of continuity principles into the nonrecognition provisions of §§354 and 361 and hence to require the acquiring corporation to recognize gain in this situation. On the other hand, it may be argued that §§354 and 361 confer nonrecognition treatment on a transactional basis (i.e., if the transaction fits these sections, both sides obtain protection thereunder).

But Prop. Regs. §1.1032-2 (1980) provides nonrecognition for the subsidiary on the exchange of its parent's stock in forward subsidiary mergers, and triangular

acquisition fails to qualify as a reorganization (Type A, B, or C), however, recognition of gain or loss to the subsidiary may be more difficult to avoid, although the distinction between taxable and tax-free acquisitions seems irrelevant to this issue.[347]

2. Basis of acquired property. Under §362(b), property acquired by a corporation in connection with a reorganization[348] ordinarily takes a carry-over basis equal to the transferor's basis, increased by any gain recognized to the transferor on such transfer.[349] Since recognition of gain by the transferor is affected by whether it completely liquidates pursuant to the plan under §368(a)(2)(G), the transferee corporation has a lively interest in the transferor's continued existence. If the transferor fails to liquidate pursuant to the reorganization, the transaction becomes a taxable purchase acquisition by the transferee, entitling it to claim a §1012 cost basis for the acquired

---

Types B and C reorganizations. The general theory of Rev. Rul. 57-278 thus seems to be accepted by the proposed regulations (although apparently without a conduit limitation present in the ruling). Even so, the subsidiary can recognize gain or loss if it pays property boot, see Prop. Regs. §1.1032-2(c), Example (1). See "Comment" on these proposed regulations, supra ¶ 14.15, note 151, by N.Y. State Bar Association, Tax Section.

Proposals by the staff of the Senate Finance Committee for the reform of Subchapter C would amend §1032 to include parent, grandparent, great-grandparent, and so forth, stock within the ambit of §1032, without regard to whether the acquisition was taxable or tax-free.

[347] See also Rev. Rul 70-305, 1970-1 CB 169 (§1032 not applicable to subsidiary sales of its parent's stock); see generally Committee on Corporate Taxation, Sale or Exchange by a Subsidiary Corporation of Its Parent Corporation's Stock, 47 Taxes 146 (1969); infra note 355 and ¶ 14.53, para. 5. Prop. Regs. §1.1032-2 is silent on the subsidiary's treatment in a taxable purchase acquisition; but the Finance Committee staff's proposal would extend §1032 protection here as well; supra note 346.

See also Rev. Rul 73-427, 1973-2 CB 301 (subsidiary mere conduit for parent's stock); Rev. Rul. 74-503, 1974-2 CB 117 (corporation always has zero basis in its own stock). Rev. Rul. 80-189, 1980-2 CB 106 (subsidiary gets cost basis for parent's stock in §304(a)(2) acquisition).

[348] The scope of the phrase "in connection with a reorganization" is unclear. It seems somewhat looser than the usual requirement of an exchange "in pursuance of a plan of reorganization," for which see supra ¶ 14.11, para. 10.

[349] See supra ¶ 3.11; see also Truck Terminals, Inc. v. CIR, 314 F2d 449 (9th Cir. 1963) (basis not stepped up by gain erroneously reported by transferor on exchange); American Credit Corp., ¶ 73,033 P-H Memo. TC (1973) (general application of §362(b) carry-over basis rules); Arkansas Best Corp., 83 TC 640 (1984), rev'd on other issues, 800 F2d 215 (8th Cir. 1986), cert. granted, 107 S. Ct. 1564 (1987) (transferee equitably estopped to deny carry-over basis where acquisition occurred 15 years earlier and was treated as a reorganization by both parties; duty of consistency, or quasi-estoppel, doctrine applied here). See also Prop. Regs. §1.453-1(f)(3)(ii) (basis step-up delayed if transferor reports boot gain under §453).

properties and a clean slate for its tax history, since §381 (see Chapter 16) would not apply in that case. On the other hand, even if the transferor liquidates pursuant to the plan (as it must in order for the acquisition to constitute a reorganization), the transferee corporation does not obtain a stepped-up basis for any gain recognized to the transferor's *shareholders* because of its boot distributions.[350]

If the acquisition transaction fails to qualify as a reorganization, the transferee corporation is entitled to a cost basis for the acquired properties under §1012, presumably equal to the fair market value of the consideration paid by it.[351] Moreover, the transferee's right to a cost basis in this situation is not affected by the fact that no gain or loss was recognized to it on the exchange under §1032.

Under the Finance Committee staff's proposed reform of Subchapter C, the transferee's basis for assets acquired in an elective carry-over basis qualified acquisition would be the same as under §362(b) of current law (i.e., carry-over from the transferor *without* any step-up for gain recognized by the transferor).[352] This new regime would be elective at the corporate level, however, and the type of consideration paid would be irrelevant to the basis results.

---

[350] See Schweitzer & Conrad, Inc., supra note 36 (refer also to id. at 547–548); Levin, The Case for a Stepped-Up Basis to the Transferee in Certain Reorganizations, 17 Tax L. Rev. 511 (1962); Rev. Rul. 72-327, 1972-2 CB 1978 (no step-up for gain to *acquiring* corporation).

[351] See Moore-McCormack Lines, Inc., 44 TC 745 (1965) (acq.); Nassau Lens Co. v. CIR, 308 F2d 39 (2d Cir. 1962). But see Arkansas Best Corp., supra note 349 (transferee estopped to deny carry-over basis under duty of consistency doctrine); Simmonds Precision Prods., Inc., 75 TC 103 (1980) (open basis where consideration not susceptible to valuation).

For the possibility of OID on the acquisition of property for debt securities, see §§1273(b)(3) and 1274, and supra ¶ 4.42 (generally, the issue of debt for property can create OID and even debt issued in a reorganization can create issue discount), supra ¶¶ 4.40 and 14.17.

See generally Porter, The Cost Basis of Property Acquired by Issuing Stock, 27 Tax Lawyer 279 (1974); Amerada-Hess Corp. v. CIR, 517 F2d 75 (3d Cir. 1975), cert. denied, 423 US 1037 (1975) (traded market value of stock controlled over parties' barter-equation method; parties not bound by barter equivalent price in agreement); supra ¶ 11.11.

[352] The transferor in a carry-over basis acquisition would never recognize gain under the proposed new system (as is also the case under current law after the 1984 and 1986 amendments), since it would be required to liquidate in order to meet the definition of a qualified asset acquisition; supra ¶¶ 14.21 and 14.32, para. 6.

If cost-basis treatment is elected by the corporate parties, the acquiring corporation's basis for the acquired assets would be its cost under §1012, supra ¶ 14.32, para. 6.

3. Basis of acquired stock. Although §362(b) prescribes a carry-over basis for property received by the transferee corporation in a reorganization, it does not apply if such property consists of stock or securities in a corporation that is a party to the reorganization unless they were acquired by the exchange of the transferee's stock or securities (or stock or securities of its parent) as consideration.[353] The general purpose and effect of these provisions is to confine determination of the transferee's basis for its acquired property to the carry-over basis rules of §362(b). These provisions were amended in 1968 to read as above; prior to 1968, §§362(b) and 358(e) provided for carry-over basis treatment only where the property was acquired by the "issuance of stock or securities of *the* transferee," and in *Firestone Tire & Rubber Co.*, the Tax Court interpreted the "issuance" language of those sections to mean original issuance, so that the taxpayer transferee in a Type B reorganization was held entitled to use the substituted basis of its treasury stock (under §358) in determining the basis of the stock acquired in the exchange.[354] The court reached this conclusion in large part by reliance on the pre-1954 rule that a corporation could recognize gain or loss on the disposition of its treasury stock; this aspect of the opinion was undermined by the enactment of §1032 in 1954, and the decision was finally overruled in 1968 by the amendment of §362(b) (and §358(e)) to read "exchange" rather than "issuance."[355]

---

[353] See also §358(e), which similarly provides that the substituted basis rules of §358 do not apply to property acquired by the exchange of the transferee's (or its parent's) stock or securities as consideration for the transfer; Rev. Proc. 81-70, 1981-2 CB 729 (guidelines for estimating basis of stock acquired in a Type B reorganization where shareholders do not respond to requests for information, and providing for the use of statistical sampling techniques to estimate basis in lieu of surveying each shareholder of acquired corporation); Rev. Proc. 87-3, 1987-1 IRB 27 (no ruling on sampling procedures); see also proposed §358(f) (in the Technical Corrections Act).

[354] Firestone Tire & Rubber Co., 2 TC 827 (1943) (acq.).

[355] TIR 1160 (1972) holds that Firestone was overruled by the 1954 Code and the Service will apply the principles of the 1968 legislation retroactively to all 1954 Code years (the April 1968 proposed carry-over basis regulations, §§1.358-4 and 1.362-1, were reproposed and adopted by TD 7422 in June 1976). See also Rev. Rul. 72-327, 1972-2 CB 197 (no step-up in basis for gain recognized on payment of boot in kind). In Rev. Rul. 74-503, 1974-2 CB 117, the Service ruled that *Firestone* was overruled by the 1954 Code and that a corporation always has a zero basis in its own stock, even where that stock had been purchased for cash on the open market. See Banoff, How IRS' New Zero-Basis Approach Will Affect Corporate Tax Planning, 42 J. Tax'n 96 (1975); Comment, The Zero Basis Dilemma, 41 Chi. L. Rev. 93 (1973); supra note 347. But see Rev. Rul. 80-189, 1980-2 CB 106 (subsidiary has cost basis for parent's stock acquired in §304(a)(2) transaction).

See also Prop. Regs. §§1.358-6 and 1.1032-2, proposed on December 29, 1980 (dealing with zero basis problems in triangular reorganizations); infra para. 4, this section, supra note 346; ITT & Cos., 77 TC 60 (1981), aff'd per curiam, 704 F2d 252 (2d Cir. 1983) (parent gets cost basis equal to value of its stock on conversion of

In 1964, the definition of a Type B reorganization was expanded to include acquisitions of stock in exchange for stock of the parent of the acquiring corporation, but Congress inadvertently neglected to make a corresponding change in the basis rules of §362(b) so that a technical argument could have been made that the carry-over basis rules of §362(b) did not apply to the transferee because stock of *the* transferee was not used as consideration for the transfer. Since Regs. §1.358-4 provided (before 1968) that §358 did not apply where stock of the transferee's parent was issued as consideration for the transfer, there appeared to be a hiatus between §§358 and 362(b). If both were inapplicable, the transferee's basis for the stock presumably was its cost under §1012 (i.e., the fair market value of the parent's stock). This possibility suggested that the transferee might be able to liquidate the acquired corporation in a later unrelated transaction and thereby obtain a stepped-up basis for its assets under former §334(b)(2) or to elect to step up basis under §338, the successor to former §334(b)(2) (see Chapter 11). As a matter of policy, however, such a stepped-up basis for the assets was hard to reconcile with the fact that the stock was acquired in a tax-free transaction; and the Service's position on this issue was at first unclear.[356]

Regulations were adopted in 1976 to cure this technical gap by providing that transactions involving stock or securities of a corporation in control of the transferee (i.e., its parent) were subject to the §362(b) basis rules, not those of §358. The 1968 legislation, discussed previously, sanitized these proposals by amending §§358(e) and 362(b) to make it plain that the carry-over basis rules of §362(b) applied to the stock acquired in such a triangular Type B reorganization.[357]

4. Parent's outside basis for subsidiary stock in triangular acquisition reorganizations. On December 29, 1980, Prop. Regs. §§1.358-6(a), 1.358-

---

subsidiary's debt into parent's stock); National Can Corp. v. US, 687 F2d 1107 (7th Cir. 1982) (contra; parent has zero basis for subsidiary's debt).

[356] See XIX ABA Tax Section Bull., No. 2, at 128 (Jan. 1966). For a pre-1954 transaction involving this problem, see Georgia-Pacific Corp. v. US, 264 F2d 161 (5th Cir. 1959) (stepped-up basis allowed for assets acquired in merger under *Kimbell-Diamond* principle); see also South Bay Corp. v. CIR, supra note 102; Long Island Water Corp., supra note 70. See also materials cited supra notes 347 and 355; American Potash & Chem. Corp. v. US, supra note 56; supra ¶ 14.13.

[357] Regs. §§1.358-4 and 1.362-1; see TIR 1160, supra note 355.

For the parent's basis in a subsidiary acquired through a reverse merger under §368(a)(2)(E), see Prop. Regs. §1.358-6(c)(2) (1980), which keys outside stock basis to the subsidiary's inside net *asset* basis (whether or not a phantom subsidiary is involved). However, a transition rule in Prop. Regs. §1.358-6(c)(5) gives the parent an election to claim the Type B carry-over stock basis if higher in Rev. Rul. 67-448 type acquisitions (infra para. 4, this section).

6(b), and 1.358-6(c) were proposed, which would allow the parent to adjust the basis of its subsidiary's stock in the case of triangular Type A, B, and C reorganizations as if the parent had directly acquired the target company's assets or stock in a two-party reorganization and then dropped that property into its subsidiary.[358] Thus, in a triangular asset acquisition (Types A or C), the parent can step up the basis in its subsidiary's stock by the inside net basis (basis less liabilities assumed) of the target company's assets; in a triangular Type B, the parent can step up the basis for its subsidiary's stock by the amount of the shareholders' bases in the target company; for a reverse merger under §368(a)(2)(E), the proposed regulations in §1.358-6(c) state that basis is determined under the triangular *asset* acquisition rules (as if the parent first acquired net assets and then dropped them back into the acquired subsidiary via a reincorporation.[359]

But the proposed regulations, in §§1.358-6(a)(3), 1.358-6(b)(3), and 1.358-6(c)(3), require a downward adjustment for the value of any consideration not furnished by the parent *in* the reorganization. Read literally, this provision could result in a negative basis to the parent for its subsidiary's stock where the subsidiary effects the acquisition with old and cold parent stock. For example, if the target's net asset basis is $700, the parent's basis for its subsidiary's stock is $100, and the subsidiary gets all of the target's assets using old and cold parent stock worth $1,000, the proposed regulations' adjustment mechanics would leave the parent with a minus-$200 basis in its subsidiary's stock (i.e., upward adjustment of $700, the target's asset basis, and downward adjustment of $1,000, the value of consideration not furnished by parent). The arguably correct answer here is that the parent simply has no basis adjustment for its subsidiary's stock as a result of the acquisition (presumably, the final version of the regulations will reach this result).

5. Current reform proposals for controlled subsidiary's outside stock basis. The staff of the Senate Finance Committee, in its 1983 preliminary report on the reform and simplification on Subchapter C, proposed a uniform outside basis rule for a controlled subsidiary's stock in the hands of its parent that would be derived, in *all* cases, by reference to the inside net basis of the subsidiary's assets. Adjustments to outside stock basis would be made

---

[358] Comment, N.Y. State Bar Association, Tax Section, Report on Reverse Triangular Mergers and Basis-Nonrecognition Rules in Triangular Reorganizations, 36 Tax L. Rev. 395 (1981).

[359] The proposed regulations, §1.358-6(c)(5), provide a transition rule, however, giving the parent an election to claim the Type B carry-over stock basis, if higher, in Rev. Rul. 67-448 "phantom" subsidiary acquisitions.

when and to the extent that changes occurred in inside net asset basis (i.e., basis less liabilities). Adjustments would be required to reflect minority interests; for example, if *P* owned only 80 percent of *S*, *P*'s basis for *S*'s stock would only reflect 80 percent of *S*'s net asset basis.

This proposal would replace the rules of present law, which give the parent a substituted stock basis if the subsidiary is incorporated, a carry-over basis if the stock is acquired in a reorganization, and a cost basis if the stock is purchased. Moreover, the investment basis adjustment rules of the consolidated return regulations would be repealed under the proposal (see Chapter 15).

The staff's final 1985 report refined and codified the basis conformity concept first described in general terms in its preliminary report and contains proposed §1020 dealing with the basis conformity rules. One added feature in the final report is the creation of premium and discount accounts, special short-lived accounts that disappear three years after the acquisition year and are designed to give the buyer corporation a special basis adjustment (up or down) where outside stock acquisition cost differs from inside asset basis (a situation that can only arise when cost basis treatment is *not* elected). A premium account arises when the price paid for the subsidiary's stock exceeds inside asset basis; a discount account arises when the cost of the stock is less than inside asset basis. Moreover, these accounts can fluctuate during their three-year life to reflect corporate level realized gains and losses attributable to preacquisition built-in appreciation or depreciation in value.[360]

The major influence of proposed §1020 would arise when the parent seeks to dispose of its subsidiary in a taxable acquisition: Subsidiary liquidations result in a carry-over asset basis to the parent, and its basis in the subsidiary's stock disappears. The effect of proposed §1020 in the case of a sale of the subsidiary's stock generally would be the same as if the parent liquidated its subsidiary, reincorporated it, and then sold its stock. Thus, the parent's gain or loss on the sale would be the same whether the subsidiary sold its assets or the parent sold the subsidiary stock.

For example, if subsidiary *S* holds assets with a value of $100 and a basis of $40, *P*'s sale of *S* will give rise to the same $60 of gain whether *S* sells its assets and liquidates into *P* or whether *P* sells the stock of *S*, since *P*'s basis for the *S* stock will conform to *S*'s basis for its assets under proposed §1020.

---

[360] Realized built-in gains decrease the premium account and increase the discount account; realized built-in losses increase the premium account and decrease the discount account. This entire system disappears, however, after three years following the acquisition year.

6. Carry-over of the transferor's tax attributes to the transferee. In addition to inheriting the tax basis of property acquired from the transferor in a reorganization, the transferee corporation steps into the shoes of the transferor with respect to such tax attributes as its earnings and profits, accounting methods, and carry-overs for net operating and capital losses. This area is governed by the detailed rules of §381, enacted in 1954 (see Chapter 16).

¶ 14.34   TREATMENT OF STOCKHOLDERS AND SECURITY HOLDERS: SECTIONS 354, 356, AND 358

1. Nonrecognition and boot in general. Recognition of gain or loss to exchanging shareholders and security holders in a reorganization is governed generally by the rules of §354(a)(1), which provides that "no gain or loss shall be recognized if stock or securities in a corporation a party to a reorganization are, in pursuance of the plan of reorganization, exchanged solely for stock or securities in such corporation or in another corporation a party to the reorganization."[361] If the transaction constitutes a reorganization, if the exchanges are pursuant to a plan of reorganization, and if the stock or securities are those of a party to a reorganization, §354(a)(1) takes hold and provides for nonrecognition of gain or loss on the respective exchanges of stock or securities.[362]

---

[361] For the terms used in §354(a)(1), see supra ¶¶ 14.31 (stock or securities), 14.11 (plan of reorganization), and 14.30 (party to reorganization).

See also §356(f), referring to §§61(a)(1) and 2501 for special rules if a §354 exchange results in a gift or has the effect of compensation. The warning hardly seems necessary; moreover, to the extent that the exchange has these adventitious effects, it should not be regarded as "a transaction described in section 354."

See Rev. Rul. 73-233, 1973-1 CB 179 (non-pro rata exchange held partially taxable; capital contribution of stock by majority shareholder to induce minority shareholders to vote for merger by increasing their share of consideration resulted in a taxable exchange by the contributing shareholder with respect to his contributed stock (and an increase in the basis of his new stock acquired in the reorganization) and §61 ordinary income to the minority shareholders who received additional stock in the merger as consideration for their votes); see also Rev. Rul. 74-269, 1974-1 CB 87.

An exchange in a Type D reorganization is subject to §354(a)(1) only if it meets the additional conditions of §354(b); otherwise, as discussed supra ¶ 14.16, it is subject to §355 (supra ch. 13).

[362] Rev. Rul. 70-271, 1970-1 CB 166, holds that stock received by a shareholder-creditor in his creditor capacity is taxable to both the distributing corporation and the creditor (if his basis for the debt differs from the value received in satisfaction of his claim). Compare Rev. Rul. 75-94, 1975-1 CB 111, which held that additional shares received to bring exchange price up to originally contemplated level, as represented by acquiring corporation, were tax-free under §354(a)(1) as a receipt pursuant

The nonrecognition rule of §354(a)(1) is applicable only if the exchange is solely for stock or securities of a corporation that is a party to a reorganization. Moreover, §354(a)(2)(A) (enacted in 1954) provides that the general nonrecognition rule of §354(a)(1) does not apply if (1) the principal amount of securities received exceeds the principal amount of securities surrendered or (2) securities are received and no securities are surrendered. (For this purpose, the term "securities" presumably means only debt securities.) By virtue of these restrictions, a shareholder whose proprietary interest is upgraded in a reorganization to that of a creditor (or a security holder whose creditor status is enhanced through receipt of obligations in a greater principal amount) will have to recognize his gain pro tanto, as though he had received money in the exchange. Accordingly, the taxpayer's realized gain will go wholly tax-free under §354(a)(1) only if (1) stock and/or securities are surrendered solely for stock, (2) securities are surrendered solely for securities in an equal or lesser principal amount, or (3) securities are surrendered for stock and securities in an equal or lesser principal amount.[363]

The purpose of these restrictions is to apply the continuity of interest test (taxpayer-by-taxpayer) to the exchanges in a reorganization. Another purpose of these provisions is to block the security bailout device, whereby

---

to the plan of reorganization (acquiring corporation had represented certain values and shares were paid in satisfaction of shareholders' claims for material misrepresentation by acquiring corporation).

See also Rev. Rul. 73-552, 1973-2 CB 116 (partial exchange of stock received in Type C reorganization protected by §354(a) as well; but complete liquidation of target required after 1984 amendment).

[363] See Jack L. LeVant, supra note 320 (compensatory stock option not securities); William H. Husted, supra note 320; Rev. Rul. 68-473, 1968-2 CB 191; §83(g), added by the Tax Reform Act of 1969; Rev. Rul. 79-155, 1979-1 CB 153 (terms of security modified to such an extent in reorganization assumption that transaction deemed to constitute an exchange, but tax-free per §354(a)(1)).

But the Bankruptcy Tax Act of 1980 amended §354(a)(2) to make property received that is attributable to accrued interest (including any accrued OID) taxable to the exchanging creditor (to the extent such interest accrued during his holding period). See supra ¶ 14.20 and infra ¶ 14.58.

The Tax Reform Act of 1984 extended the OID rules to all exchanges of property for debt, whether or not traded and whether or not in a reorganization. Moreover, this legislation (in §1276) also characterized accrued *market* discount as the equivalent of interest to the holder and taxes such income at the time the bond is disposed of; however, if the bond is exchanged for another bond of equivalent face amount, the discount taint would carry-over into the new bond under §§1276(c)(2) and 1276(d)(1)(B). See generally supra ¶¶ 4.40, 4.42, and 4.44; supra ¶ 14.17, paras. 2, 3, and 4.

Under the Finance Committee staff's final 1985 report on the reform of Subchapter C, securities received in excess of the basis of securities surrendered would be taxable to the exchanging security holder—that is, securities would be boot per se for gain recognition purposes.

debt obligations could be issued pro rata to shareholders with a view to their subsequent retirement at capital gain rates, thus effecting a distribution of corporate earnings and profits without dividend consequences. The effect of §354(a)(2) is similar to the result in *Bazley*,[364] except that gain is recognized under §354(a)(2) only if gain is realized by the taxpayer on the exchange, whereas *Bazley* treated the securities as a dividend, generating ordinary income to the extent of the corporation's earnings and profits.[365] Thus, if a shareholder exchanged stock with a basis of $100 for stock with a value of $50 and bonds with a value of $75, *Bazley* would require recognition of income to the extent of $75, the fair market value of the bonds. If, however, the transaction qualifies as a reorganization, §§354(a)(2) and 356(a)(1) would limit recognition of the shareholder's gain to $25 (the amount of his realized gain). (Under the Finance Committee staff's final report on the reform of Subchapter C, however, securities would be boot per se for gain recognition purposes, even when received in exchange for other securities of an equal or lesser principal amount.[366])

On its face, §354(a) seems to leave no leeway for the receipt of money or other property in the exchange. However, the cross-reference of §354(a)(3) takes us to §356, governing the receipt of boot in an exchange that would otherwise qualify under §354. Thus, if the exchange involves the receipt of other property or money in addition to property that can be received tax-free, reference must be made to the boot rules of §356.

Section 356 relaxes the stern injunction in §354(a)(1) that the exchange must be solely for stock or securities. If the taxpayer receives boot as well as nonrecognition property, his gain, if any, is to be recognized, but in an amount not in excess of the boot.[367] The receipt of boot does not, however, permit the taxpayer to recognize any loss he may have sustained on the

---

[364] Bazley v. CIR, supra note 5.

[365] Supra ¶ 14.17, para. 4; see also Regs. §1.301-1(*l*).

[366] If securities received do not exceed the basis of securities surrendered, however, loss would continue to be unrecognized under the staff proposal.

[367] If securities are the *sole* consideration received in an exchange where no securities are surrendered—that is, a shareholder exchanges his stock solely for bonds—the transaction seems to be entirely outside the rules of §§354 and 356. See Regs. §1.354-1(d), Example (3). In this situation, the exchange resembles a redemption of stock (supra ch. 9), as suggested by the cross-reference to §302 in the regulations. If the distribution of bonds is disproportionate rather than pro rata, the result under §302 may be the recognition of capital gain or loss, rather than dividend income; see also supra ¶ 14.17, para. 4, for the relation of *Bazley* to disproportionate exchanges.

See Rev. Rul. 69-6, 1969-1 CB 103 (all-cash merger; held a §331 liquidation to shareholders of absorbed corporation); Rev. Rul. 77-19, 1977-1 CB 84 (held a §302 redemption); Rev. Rul. 77-415, 1977-2 CB 311.

See also Rev. Rul. 74-515, 1974-2 CB 118 (shareholders of acquired corporation who *only* receive cash (or, presumably, only debt securities) in merger for their stock

exchange (see §356(c)). These principles may be illustrated by the following example:

(1)	Received by taxpayer:	
	(a) Stock (fair market value)	$10,000
	(b) Securities (fair market value)	5,000
	(c) Money	2,500
		$17,500
(2)	Less: basis of stock surrendered	5,000
(3)	Gain realized on exchange	$12,500
(4)	Gain recognized under §356(a)(1) (line (3), or (1)(b) plus (1)(c), whichever is lesser)	$ 7,500

If the shareholder's basis for the stock surrendered had been $15,000, he would have realized a gain of only $2,500 on the exchange, and only this amount would have been recognized under §356(a). If his basis had been $20,000, he would have realized a loss of $2,500 on the exchange, but it would have gone unrecognized by virtue of §356(c).[368] (The final report of the Finance Committee staff on the reform of Subchapter C would, however, allow recognition of loss to a shareholder who receives only boot (i.e., unqualified consideration such as cash, debt, or property other than stock of a party to the acquisition[369]) or to a security holder who receives no stock or securities of a party to the acquisition. Loss would still be unrecognized if the security holder receives securities of a party.)

---

are not in the §354 or §356 computation mechanism; as to them, transaction merely a redemption tested under §302 (presumably with §318) for dividend equivalency).

As to the possibility of creating OID on the exchange, see supra note 363 and ¶ 14.17, paras. 3 and 4.

[368] Rev. Rul. 68-23, 1968-1 CB 144 (the taxpayer must compute gain or loss separately on different blocks of exchanged stock that had different bases; no netting of gain and loss); see also Rev. Rul. 74-515, 1974-2 CB 103 (shareholders of acquired corporation who owned both common and preferred stock and who exchanged their common stock for common stock of the acquiring corporation and their preferred stock for cash must compute the tax consequences separately for each class of stock exchanged; thus, the common-for-common exchange was wholly tax-free under §354(a)(1) while the preferred-for-cash exchange was held not to be essentially equivalent to a dividend on the facts and hence was taxable as capital gain to the extent that cash exceeded the basis of the preferred, while no loss was recognized if basis exceeded the cash by virtue of §356(c)); Estate of Charles A. Smith, supra note 317.

If the taxpayer *pays* as well as receives boot in the reorganization exchange, such payments presumably can be set off against the boot received in computing his recognized gain on the transaction; see Regs. §§1.1031(b)-1(c) and 1.1031(d)-2, Example (2).

[369] Supra ¶ 14.30, para. 3.

Gain required to be recognized under §356(a)(1) because debt boot was received can, as a result of revisions to §453 in 1980, be reported on the installment method if the exchange otherwise qualifies for this provision (e.g., the debt boot received and the securities exchanged are not publicly traded).[370]

The treatment of securities as other property is determined by §356(d), which states generally that securities will be treated as boot except in cases where securities are permitted to be received without recognition of gain under §354 or §355. If the securities do not qualify as nonrecognition property, the amount of boot is either the fair market value of the excess of principal amount received over principal amount surrendered or, if no securities are surrendered, the fair market value of the principal amount received. In applying these principles, the regulations treat a portion of the fair market value of *each security received* as boot, based on the ratio that the total excess principal amount bears to the total principal amount of all such securities received. For example, if two securities with a total principal amount of $100 are surrendered for two securities with total principal amount of $150 (one of which has a value of $75 and the other $60), one third of the fair market value of each security received constitutes boot, or $25 and $20 respectively.[371]

---

[370] For the possibility of reporting installment obligation boot under the pre-1980 version of §453, see Rev. Rul. 65-155, supra ¶ 3.05. The Installment Sales Revision Act of 1980 added §453(f)(6), providing for §453 treatment in the context of reorganization nonrecognition exchanges (but unlike Rev. Rul. 65-155, §453(f)(6) disregards nonrecognition property in computing the payments and total contract price elements of a §453 fraction). See Prop. Regs. §1.453-1(f)(2) (1984) for application of §453 to §356(a) boot gain. See generally, N.Y. State Bar Association, Tax Section, A Report on Proposed Regulations Under Section 453(f)(6)–Installment Obligations Received in Certain Nonrecognition Exchanges, 24 Tax Notes 297 (1984); Friedman, An Analysis of Nonrecognition Exchanges and Installment Rules Under the Recent Proposed Regulations, 61 J. Tax'n 158 (1984).

But the Tax Reform Act of 1986, in §453(k)(2)(A), denied the use of §453 for disposition of traded stock or securities.

[371] See Regs. §1.356-3, which is based on the Committee Reports.

The imputed interest rules of §483, and the OID rules of §1272, to the extent that they convert principal to interest, will affect the computation of principal amount under §356. See supra ¶¶ 4.40–4.42 and note 363.

The gain required to be recognized under §§356(a)(1) and 356(d) on exchanges of securities is apparently treated as capital gain, by virtue of §356(a)(2), to the extent not attributable to accrued interest, and hence taxed separately under §354(a)(2)(B), notwithstanding how such gain would have fared under §1271. For the OID possibilities on the new debt, see §1273(b)(3) (if traded), and §1274 (if not traded), and the limitations of §1275(a)(4).

See generally Rev. Rul. 71-427, 1971-2 CB 183 (recognized boot gain to taxpayer who exchanged debt securities for new common stock and cash taxed as capital gain because cash was received in his creditor capacity). But under the Tax Reform Act of

The foregoing discussion has been based on the assumption that there was a reorganization as defined by §368(a)(1) and that the boot received by the taxpayer, although requiring the partial or complete recognition of his gain, was not inconsistent with the existence of a reorganization. An example is a statutory merger in which the consideration is partly stock of the surviving corporation and partly money or other property; another is a Type C reorganization in which some money is used, in addition to voting stock, pursuant to the authorization in §368(a)(2)(B). In these cases, there is a reorganization so far as the definition in §368(a)(1) is concerned, and the receipt of boot simply requires any taxpayer who realized gain on the exchange to recognize his gain pro tanto.

For many years, it had been assumed by tax lawyers that the use of any consideration that is not tolerated by the *definitional* subparagraphs of §368(a)(1) (e.g., the use of money in a stock-for-stock transaction in violation of the solely for voting stock rule of §368(a)(1)(B) or the use of money beyond the amount permitted by §368(a)(2)(B) in an asset acquisition) would destroy the possibility of a reorganization, making such provisions as §§354, 361 and 381(a)(2) totally inapplicable for want of a reorganization. This basic idea was undermined in 1956 by *Howard v. CIR*, which held that certain shareholders, who exchanged their stock solely for stock of the acquiring corporation, could take advantage of the nonrecognition rules of §354, even though the acquiring corporation paid cash to other transferor shareholders.[372] The court reached this conclusion by reliance on the "but for" language of §356(a)(1); since the transaction would have qualified as an exchange of stock *solely* for voting stock of the acquired corporation if the cash boot was disregarded, the court held that §354 applied and that no gain was to be recognized by those shareholders who received no cash or other boot. But this approach ultimately was rejected by the Supreme Court in *Turnbow v. CIR*, which held that a transaction must constitute a reorganization under the definitional rules of the 1939 Code predecessor of §368 before taxpayers can resort to the nonrecognition rules of §§354 and 356.[373] The staff of the Senate Finance Committee proposals for the reform of Subchapter C would, however, determine shareholder treatment in a qualified corporate acquisition[374] independently of corporate level recognition or nonrecognition, in effect adopting the severability approach of the *Howard* case.

1984 (supra note 363), any taxable gain attributable to accrued market discount is taxed as ordinary interest income to the holder under §§1276(a)(1) and 1276(a)(3), supra ¶ 4.44; see also §354(a)(2)(B), supra note 363.

For possible application of §453 to recognized gain, see supra note 370.

[372] Howard v. CIR, supra note 88.

[373] Turnbow v. CIR, supra note 76. See Vernava, supra note 76; supra ¶ 14.13.

[374] See supra ¶ 14.21.

Thus, shareholders would be permitted to receive qualified stock tax-free in an acquisition without regard to the tax treatment of the transaction at the corporate level or the terms of the exchange with other shareholders.[375]

2. Character of recognized gain. The amount of gain to be recognized having been determined under §356(a)(1), the provisions of §356(a)(2) then determine whether it will be taxed as a dividend or as capital gain. Section 356(a)(2) provides that if the exchange has the "effect of the distribution of a dividend," the taxpayer's recognized gain must be so treated to the extent of his ratable share of post-1913 earnings and profits; the remainder of the recognized gain, if any, is treated as gain from the exchange of property (i.e., as capital gain, unless the taxpayer is a dealer in securities). The dividend within gain approach of §356(a)(2), under which the shareholder reports dividend income only if and to the extent that he realizes gain on the exchange, may be illustrated as follows: If the taxpayer realized a gain of $100 on the exchange, $50 of which was recognized because of the receipt of boot, the maximum amount of dividend income that could arise under §356(a)(2) would be $50; if the realized gain had been only $20, dividend income would be limited to $20; and if the realized gain had been zero (because the amount realized was equal to the adjusted basis of the stock given up), there would be no dividend income.[376] The Tax Reform Act of 1986, however, repealed the capital gain rate benefits (for both corporations and individuals), thus rendering the boot dividend question much less important for individuals after 1986 (although *not* for corporations).[377]

Several other features of the boot dividend rules of §356(a)(2) should also be noted:

(1) This provision refers only to accumulated earnings and profits, unlike the ordinary dividend rules of §316(a), which support divi-

---

[375] For discussion of these proposals, see infra para. 5, this section, and supra ¶ 14.32, para. 6.

[376] But proposals by the staff of the Senate Finance Committee would abolish the dividend within gain limitation of present §356(a)(2) and tax boot dividends under §§301 and 316 principles, without regard to realized gain or loss. See infra para. 5, this section.

As to the impact of capital gain repeal by the Tax Reform Act of 1986, see infra note 377.

[377] Boot dividend consequences for noncorporate shareholders will have no rate disadvantages after the 1986 amendments, since they will be taxable in the same way as capital gain (shareholders with capital losses, however, will still prefer capital gain classification). Corporate shareholders will almost always prefer boot dividend treatment (in view of the §243 deduction), but this was the case under prior law as well. Boot dividends also will have important earnings and profits consequences, even under the 1986 law.

dend treatment if either current or accumulated earnings are present[378];

(2) The taxpayer's dividend income is limited to his ratable share of earnings under §356(a)(2), a restriction that may not apply under §316 (see Chapter 7);

(3) In testing for existence of the requisite earnings and profits, and for "dividend equivalence," §356(a)(2) looks to the effect of a direct distribution by the transferor corporation;[379] and

(4) As to corporate distributees, Regs. §1.356-1(d) does not apply the lower of value or basis rule of §301(b)(1)(B). As a result, the boot dividend rules of §356(a)(2) seem to constitute an independent dividend test, apart from the ordinary dividend rules of §§301 and 316.[380] For this reason, the Service at one time regarded §356 dividends as not qualifying for the intercorporate dividends-received deduction of §243 or the former dividends-received exclusion of §116, although recent decisions have allowed the §243 deduction for such dividends, and the Service now agrees.[381] (The Finance Committee staff's proposals for the reform of Subchapter C would revise the boot rules of §356 in the following manner: (1) Dividend effect would be tested by assuming a hypothetical redemption from the acquiring corporation; (2) if dividend consequences result, tax-

---

[378] But see Vesper Co. v. CIR, 131 F2d 200 (8th Cir. 1942); supra ¶¶ 7.01, 7.02, and 9.01.

[379] In the case of mergers and similar acquisitions between commonly controlled corporations, however, the Service and at least one circuit use earnings of both the transferor and transferee corporations to measure the boot dividend: Rev. Rul. 70-240, 1970-1 CB 81; Davant v. CIR, 366 F2d 874 (5th Cir. 1966), cert. denied, 386 US 1022 (1967) (boot treated as either a *Bazley*-§301 dividend or a boot dividend measured by earnings of both the acquired and acquiring corporation); see also Reef Corp. v. CIR, supra note 32 (redemption severable from contemporaneous reorganization transaction). Contra American Mfg. Co., supra note 70 (only earnings of transferor); Estate of John L. Bell, ¶ 71,285 P-H Memo. TC (1971); Atlas Tool Co., 70 TC 86 (1978), aff'd, 614 F2d 860 (3d Cir. 1980) (boot dividend limited to transferor's earnings account).

[380] CIR v. Estate of Bedford, 325 US 283 (1945), however, implies that the definition of §316 is infused into §356(a)(2).

[381] For discussion of the Service's position that a reorganization boot dividend did not constitute a true dividend, see Kanter, The Changing Complexion of the B Reorganization, 45 A.B.A. J. 1317, 1319 (1959); US v. E.I. du Pont de Nemours Corp., 177 F. Supp. 1, 9 (N.D. Ill. 1959). But the §243 deduction was allowed for a boot dividend in King Enters., Inc. v. US, supra note 67; American Mfg. Co., supra note 70.
See generally Rev. Rul. 72-327, 1972-2 CB 197, for treatment of a boot dividend in kind paid to a corporate shareholder (fair market value, rather than basis, measures the amount and basis of the property to the distributee; dividend limited to ratable share of earnings; and dividend qualifies for §243 deduction).

ability would be determined under §§301 and 316 principles (i.e., the dividend within gain limitation would be repealed); and (3) earnings of the acquired corporation and any party to the acquisition whose stock or securities were received would be combined to measure the amount of the dividend.[382])

As a result of some imprecise statements in *CIR v. Bedford's Estate*, it was assumed for many years that §356(a)(2) automatically converted any recognized gain into dividend income, to the extent of the distributing corporation's earnings and profits, where the taxpayer continued as a shareholder after the exchange.[383] It is a long step, however, from the facts of the *Bedford* case (which involved cash distributed in a recapitalization to discharge arrearages in preferred dividends) to the automatic dividend conclusion; later cases properly retreated from this view,[384] which in turn prompted the Service to finally abandon its mechanical approach to §356(a)(2).[385] Rather than an automatic dividend approach (which Congress

---

[382] See infra this section, para. 5. Repeal of capital gain rates by the Tax Reform Act of 1986, supra note 377, would have a greater impact under the staff's Subchapter C proposal in view of this intention to eliminate the gain limitation and to combine earnings of the two corporations.

[383] See CIR v. Estate of Bedford, supra note 380; Regs. §1.356-1(c), Example (1).

[384] For earlier decisions, see Idaho Power Co. v. US, 161 F. Supp. 807 (Ct. Cl. 1958), cert. denied, 358 US 832 (1958); Hawkinson v. CIR, 235 F2d 747 (2d Cir. 1956); William H. Bateman, supra note 317; Ross v. US, 173 F. Supp. 793 (Ct. Cl.), cert. denied, 361 US 875 (1959).

For later developments, see Wright v. US, 482 F2d 600 (8th Cir. 1973) (boot distributed non-pro rata in consolidation of affiliated corporations not a dividend; taxpayer's interest in former corporations was 85 percent before and only 62 percent after). The appellate court in *Wright* specifically rejected the automatic dividend rule. See also Shimberg v. US, 577 F2d 283 (5th Cir. 1978), cert. denied, 439 US 115 (1979) (*Wright* distinguished and Rev. Rul. 75-83, 1975-1 CB 112, applied); James H. Johnson, 78 TC 564 (1982) (receipt of boot in recapitalization to compensate for passed dividends held equivalent to dividend); Donald E. Clark, 86 TC 138 (1986) (agreed to follow *Wright* and reject *Shimberg*; but facts and circumstances caveat).

Proposals by the staff of the Senate Finance Committee would adopt the view of the *Wright* and *Clark* cases and reject *Shimberg* in testing for dividend equivalence under §356(a)(2); infra para. 5, this section.

[385] The Service formally abandoned the automatic dividend approach in Rev. Rul. 74-515, 1974-2 CB 118, and Rev. Rul. 74-516, 1974-2 CB 121, adopting instead §302(b)(1) "dividend equivalence" analysis; see also Rev. Rul. 75-83, 1975-1 CB 112.

Rev. Rul. 74-515 held that cash boot paid in a merger to holders of both common and preferred stock of the acquired corporation (who received common in exchange for their common and cash for their preferred) was not the equivalent of a dividend on the facts, but apparently without consideration of §318; both corporations were widely held. In Rev. Rul. 74-516, cash boot distributed in a non-pro rata split-off was found to be taxable as capital gain because of the substantially disproportionate effect of the transaction; the disproportionate effect was tested by com-

had explicitly adopted in §§356(b) and 356(e), thus implying a more flexible approach elsewhere),[386] the phrase "has the effect of a distribution of a dividend" as used in §356(a)(2) suggests an analysis of the facts similar to that employed under §§302(b)(1), 302(e)(1), and 306(c)(1)(B)(ii).[387] Although there is no explicit statutory coordination between the stock redemption rules of §§302 and 346 and the boot distribution rule of §356(a)(2)[388], the courts and the Service now agree that the principles developed in interpreting §302 are applicable as well to cases under §356(a)(2).[389]

---

paring the taxpayer's interest in the distributing corporation with the interest he would have retained had he not received the distributed stock). See also Rev. Rul. 84-114, 1984-2 CB 90 (in a recapitalization, test for boot dividend equivalence under §302 principles, including *Zenz* step doctrine; here, boot did not have dividend effect under *Davis* because holder's interest dropped from 28 to 23 percent of vote and also effected a meaningful reduction in dividend and liquidation rights).

Legislation enacted in 1982 extended the attribution rules of §318 to §356(a)(2) in testing for dividend equivalence under the reorganization boot rules (effective for distributions after August 31, 1982).

[386] For earlier articles on the scope of *Bedford*, see Darrell, The Scope of CIR v. *Bedford's Estate*, 24 Taxes 266 (1949); Wittenstein, Boot Distributions and §112(c)(2): A Re-Examination, 8 Tax L. Rev. 63 (1952); Moore, Taxation of Distributions Made in Connection With a Corporate Reorganization, 17 Tax L. Rev. 129 (1961); Shoulson, Boot Taxation: The Blunt Toe of the Automatic Rule, 20 Tax L. Rev. 573 (1965).

More currently, see Gerson, Boot Dividends and the Automatic Rule: *Bedford*. Revisited, 11 Wm. & Mary L. Rev. 841 (1970); Levin, Adess & McGaffey, Boot Distributions in Corporate Reorganizations–Determination of Dividend Equivalency, 30 Tax Lawyer 287 (1977); Ronds, Section 356(a)(2): A Study of Uncertainty in Corporate Taxation 38, U. Miami L. Rev. 75 (1983); Gately & Pratt, Dividend Equivalency–Are the Tests Changing? 7 J. Corp. Tax'n 53 (1980); Peterson, Comment, Determining Dividend Equivalence of "Boot" Received in a Corporate Reorganization–*Shimberg v. United States*, 32 Tax Lawyer 834 (1978); Golub, "Boot" in Reorganizations–The Dividend Equivalency Test of Section 356(a)(2), 58 Taxes 904 (1980); Fleming, Reforming the Tax Treatment of Reorganization Boot, 10 J. Corp. Tax'n 99 (1983); Kayser, The Long and Winding Road: Characterization of Boot Under Section 356(a)(2), 39 Tax L. Rev. 297 (1984); Hankin & Lerer, Wright v. Wrong: The Final Solution to the Dividend Equivalence Problem, 23 Santa Clara L. Rev. 1 (1983).

[387] See supra ¶¶ 9.06 and 9.08; infra ¶ 14.35.

[388] For proposals to achieve coordination in this area, see XVIII ABA Tax Section Bull., No. 4, at 42–45 (July 1965).

[389] See cases and rulings supra notes 384 and 385, and articles supra note 387, see also Viereck v. US, 1983-2 USTC ¶ 9664 (Cl. Ct. 1983) (boot distribution not a partial liquidation because no contraction of business enterprise; total business continuity so distribution equivalent to a dividend); Rev. Rul. 66-365, 1966-2 CB 116, where the Service ruled that cash received in lieu of fractional shares in a Type A, B, C, or D reorganization is treated under §302 as a redemption of such fractional interests if not separately bargained for consideration (this principle also was applied in a recapitalization exchange, Rev. Rul. 69-34, 1969-1 CB 105, and in a Type F reorgani-

But even if, as now seems to be the case, a §302(b)-type analysis applies to §356(a)(2), the cases and the Service still are in conflict as to the precise formula for its application to fusion reorganizations.[390] If boot is received in exchange for "section 306 stock," a special rule is applicable by virtue of §356(e); whether the shareholder realizes gain or loss on the exchange, the fair market value of the boot is treated as an ordinary distribution under §301, which means that it will be taxed as a dividend to the extent the distribution is covered by the distributing corporation's current and post-1913 earnings and profits.[391]

3. Basis. Exchanging shareholders and security holders determine their basis for property acquired in a §354 exchange under §358(a), which provides that the basis of stock or securities received (nonrecognition property) must be the same as the basis of the property transferred, decreased by the fair market value of any boot received and increased by the amount of any gain (and by the amount of any dividend income) recognized on the exchange.[392] Under §358(a)(2), any boot received in the exchange takes a fair

---

zation by Rev. Rul. 74-36, 1974-1 CB 85); Rev. Rul. 81-81, 1981-1 CB 122 (forced cash received in a recapitalization exchange by minority shareholders in lieu of fractional shares of "section 306 stock" not dividend either; Rev. Rul. 66-365 amplified and amnesty of §306(b)(4)(A) applied).

[390] In Rev. Rul. 75-83, 1975-1 CB 112, the Service held that in applying §302(b)(2) principles to §356(a)(2), the transaction is to be treated as a hypothetical redemption of the *acquired* corporation's stock, not the acquiring corporation's stock, for the boot; Wright v. US, supra note 384, which adopted the latter method, will not be followed on this point. Accord with Rev. Rul. 75-83 is Shimberg v. US, supra note 384; accord with *Wright* is Donald E. Clark, supra note 384.

Current proposals would abolish the dividend within gain limitation and would accept the view of the *Wright* case that dividend equivalence should be tested by reference to a hypothetical redemption of the *acquiring* corporation's stock; see infra para. 5, this section.

[391] For priority rules where both "section 306 stock" and other stock are exchanged by the taxpayer, see Regs. §1.356-4. For treatment of recapitalization exchanges of common stock and "section 306 stock" for new common stock and boot, see Rev. Rul. 76-14, 1976-1 CB 97 (exchange by controlling shareholder; "agreement" allocated cash to common stock; held cash allocated to "section 306 stock" first, not arm's-length transaction because taxpayer controlling shareholder); Rev. Rul. 76-15, 1976-1 CB 98 (similar exchange by shareholders of public corporation, where cash allocated by agreement to common, respected because arm's-length transaction and §306 taint preserved because shareholder also received new "section 306 stock" in exchange for old "section 306 stock"). See also Rev. Rul. 81-81, 1981-1 CB 122.

[392] Rev. Proc. 77-37, 1977-2 CB 568, assumes a maximum issue of shares in a contingent stock acquisition for purposes of computing an interim basis on the shares actually issued.

market value basis. Rev. Rul. 70-271[393] also holds that shareholders who assume liabilities of the corporation make a capital contribution thereby and can step up their §358 stock basis accordingly.[394]

If several classes of stock or securities are received in the exchange as nonrecognition property, §358(b)(1) requires an allocation of the basis of the property surrendered between the various classes of stock and securities received in the exchange, and Regs. §1.358-2(b)(2) requires the allocation to be made in proportion to their respective market values, presumably determined at the time of the exchange.[395] For this purpose, stock or securities in different corporations are treated as separate classes of stock or securities, and stock or securities in the same corporation will be so treated if they have differing rights or preferences.

> *To illustrate:* If the basis of the property surrendered was $8,000 and the taxpayer received in exchange common stock worth $3,000 and preferred stock worth $9,000, the basis of the common stock would be $2,000 and that of the preferred $6,000. Assuming no later fluctuations in value, the taxpayer will realize $1,000 of gain on a subsequent sale of his common stock and $3,000 of gain on a sale of his preferred stock; his total gain of $4,000, it will be noted, is equal to the gain realized but unrecognized on the initial §354 exchange.
>
> If, in addition to the above consideration, the taxpayer received other property with a value of $3,000 on the exchange, gain would be recognized to that extent and the basis of the boot would be its fair market value ($3,000). The basis of the common and preferred stock received in the exchange would be $8,000 (the basis of property given up, $8,000, less boot of $3,000, plus recognized gain of $3,000), to be allocated between the common and preferred stock in proportion to their relative fair market values (one fourth and three fourths, respectively).

---

[393] Rev. Rul. 70-271, 1970-1 CB 166.

[394] An interesting conflict of basis rules could arise if a wholly owned subsidiary transfers all of its assets for stock in a Type C reorganization and then liquidates into its parent under §332: Is the parent's basis for the stock of the acquiring corporation determined under §334(b)(1) by reference to the subsidiary's asset basis therefor (i.e., §358), or is it determined under §358 by reference to the parent's basis for its stock of the subsidiary? See Kansas Sand & Concrete Co., 462 F2d 805 (10th Cir. 1972) (indicating the liquidation basis rules preempt the reorganization basis rules where a §332 liquidation is involved). But cf. American Mfg. Co., supra note 70 (indicating that the reorganization rules can preempt even a §332 liquidation situation). If the subsidiary's asset basis is significantly higher than the parent's stock basis, arguing for §332 exclusive status would give the parent a better basis result under the basis rules of §334(b)(1). After 1984, however, liquidation pursuant to the reorganization is required (supra ¶ 14.14), so that §332 may well be inapplicable here.

[395] See Regs. §1.368-3(b)(2).

If a shareholder or security holder owning more than one class of stock or securities receives, with respect thereto, other stock or securities in a non-recognition transaction under §354, Regs. §1.358-2(a)(4) requires a separate basis computation for each class.

To illustrate: If a taxpayer owning stock with a basis of $4,000 and securities with a basis of $6,000 receives in exchange for his stock two classes of stock with respective values of $2,000 and $6,000 and receives with respect to his securities two classes of securities with respective values of $3,000 and $6,000, the basis allocation would be as follows: The $4,000 basis of the stock surrendered would be allocated between the two classes of stock received in proportion to their relative values (i.e., $1,000 and $3,000 respectively); the basis of the securities surrendered likewise would be allocated among the securities received in exchange therefor in proportion to the relative fair market values of the securities received (i.e., $2,000 and $4,000).

If a single class of stock or securities is surrendered in a nontaxable §354 reorganization exchange consisting of securities acquired by the taxpayer at different dates or for different prices, determination of the substituted basis for the stock or securities received in exchange therefor is ordinarily determined by reference to an average cost basis for the stock or securities surrendered, at least if specific shares or securities received cannot be identified with specific items surrendered.[396] The average cost rule is an exception to the general rule of Regs. §1.1012-1(c) that if securities are sold by a taxpayer who purchased or acquired such properties at different dates or at different prices and the lot from which such securities are sold cannot be adequately identified, gain or loss on the sale thereof must be calculated on the first-in-first-out method.[397] The theory of the average cost exception is that the securities surrendered in a reorganization exchange lose their identity in the securities received because the latter are acquired at one time in a single transaction. The average cost rule is limited, however, to acquisi-

---

[396] See Rev. Rul. 55-355, 1955-1 CB 418. On the extent to which the average-cost rule is merely a principle of administrative convenience, inapplicable if precise identification is feasible, see Bloch v. CIR, 148 F2d 452 (9th Cir. 1945), discussing earlier cases; Leonard Osrow, 49 TC 333 (1968) (acq.).

See also TAM 7946005, 1979 Fed. Taxes (P-H) ¶ 55,756 (where shares specifically identified, tracing allowed; not required to use average cost approach); compare Rev. Rul. 85-164, 1985-2 CB 117 (aggregate basis of assets in §351 exchange must be allocated to stock and securities received in proportion to relative values of latter; no tracing allowed).

[397] See Rev. Rul. 61-97, 1961-1 CB 394; Curtis v. US, 336 F2d 714 (6th Cir. 1964).

tions of stock or securities in a nontaxable reorganization exchange; in addition, it has been held that the rule does not apply where the exchange involves stock or securities of a single corporation received in a recapitalization or Type F reorganization.[398]

While the average cost basis has been sanctioned as a proper method for determining the §358 substituted basis of stock or securities *acquired* in certain nontaxable reorganization exchanges, it should be noted that the exchanging shareholders and security holders must determine their gain or loss separately with respect to each identifiable block of stock or securities *transferred* by them in the exchange. Hence, both gains and losses can be realized by a taxpayer in the same transaction where different blocks of stock or securities are transferred in the exchange. Also, it seems relatively well established that the taxpayer cannot net the gains against the losses in this situation, since the transfer of each identifiable block of stock or securities constitutes a separate transaction for gain or loss computation purposes.[399]

4. Stock dividend aspects. Since the amendments to §305 by the Tax Reform Act of 1969, transactions that otherwise would be tax-free under §354(a) must still clear the hurdles of §305(b) to obtain complete nonrecognition treatment. The basic rules of §305 are considered in detail in Chapter 7 and certain special §305(b) problems of recapitalization exchanges were considered earlier in this chapter. It should be noted, however, that §305(b) problems can also arise in acquisitive reorganizations and divisive reorganizations, especially where preferred stock is issued in the transaction.[400]

---

[398] See Kraus v. CIR, 88 F2d 616 (2d Cir. 1937); Leonard Osrow, supra note 396; Rev. Rul. 85-164, 1985-2 CB 117 (rule does apply to §351 exchange as well).

[399] See Rev. Rul. 68-23, 1968-1 CB 144; Curtis v. US, supra note 397; US Holding Co., 44 TC 323 (1965) (acq.), and cases cited therein. For other discussions of §358, see supra ¶¶ 3.10 and 14.32, para. 4.

[400] Thus, Rev. Rul. 75-179, 1975-1 CB 103, involved preferred stock issued in a merger having a call premium beyond the 10 percent safe haven of the regulations under §1.305-5(b)(1); but the Service ruled that the premium was reasonable on the facts, so no future tax liability arose under §305(b)(4) from the issuance of the stock. Similarily, Rev. Rul. 75-468, 1975-2 CB 115, involved preferred stock issued in an acquisitive merger reorganization where the call premium was only 5 percent at the time the exchange ratio was fixed, but because of declines in the market value of the target company's stock before closing, the premium exceeded the 10 percent safe haven line; again the Service granted amnesty from §305(b)(4). Both these rulings, however, are clear warnings that §305(b) can overlap and override the nonrecognition provisions of §354(a). See also Rev. Rul. 81-190, 1981-2 CB 84 (same in tender offer deal); and Regs. §1.305-5(d), Example (6); see Rev. Rul. 77-19, 1977-1 CB 84 (20 isolated redemptions during prior three-year period, two of which were dividends, followed by going-private merger for cash, treated as a redemption; held not a

5. Current reform proposals. The staff of the Senate Finance Committee, in its report on the reform and simplification of Subchapter C, proposed to amend the boot rules of §356 in the following manner:

(1) Shareholder nonrecognition treatment would be determined independently of corporate level recognition or nonrecognition (in effect accepting the view of the *Howard* case);

(2) The dividend within gain limitation of present law would be repealed (and earnings of *both* the target and the acquiring corporation would be used to measure that dividend); and

(3) Boot dividend equivalence would be tested by assuming a hypothetical redemption of the *acquiring* corporation's stock (the *Wright* case approach) rather than of the *acquired* corporation's stock (the *Shimberg* case approach).[401]

Thus, shareholders who receive only qualified stock in a qualified corporate acquisition would be entitled to nonrecognition treatment in full on their exchange, even though other shareholders receive cash, and even though cost-basis and recognition treatment is elected at the corporate level. If a shareholder receives both qualified stock and boot, dividend equivalence is tested by assuming a full issuance of stock followed by a hypothetical redemption of such stock for the boot by the acquiring corporation. If dividend equivalence results, it will be taxed in full as such, regardless of the shareholder's realized gain or loss on the exchange and measured by the combined earnings of the target and acquiring corporations.[402]

¶ 14.35   "SECTION 306 STOCK" RECEIVED IN CORPORATE REORGANIZATIONS

Chapter 10 discussed the use of preferred stock as a method of bailing out corporate earnings and profits at the capital gain rate, along with §306,

---

periodic redemption plan under §305(c) so as to trigger taxable stock dividend consequences to the continuing shareholders under §305(b)(2) despite increase in their equity interests).

[401] Supra notes 372, 375, 376, 385, and 390. See generally Milner, Boot Under the Senate Finance Committee's Reorganization Proposal: A Step in the *Wright* Direction, 62 Taxes 507 (1984).

[402] Repeal of capital gain rate benefits for both corporations and individuals by the Tax Reform Act of 1986 will sharply downgrade the boot dividend issue for individuals after 1986 (unless they have high basis stock exchanges in the transaction or other capital losses); corporate shareholders, however, will now even more strongly prefer dividend treatment (to get the §243 deduction rate benefit), supra note 377.

the statutory remedy enacted in 1954. Since a distribution of preferred stock to the common shareholders in a corporate recapitalization is an obvious alternative to the declaration of a dividend of preferred stock, it was essential for the statutory remedy to reach recapitalizations as well as stock dividends.[403] Moreover, reorganizations of other types (e.g., a merger of a corporation into a second corporation owned by the same shareholders under which they receive preferred stock in exchange for their common stock in the absorbed corporation) could also be used to lay the foundation for a bailout. The drafters of §306, therefore, provided that stock received by a shareholder in pursuance of a plan of reorganization must be "section 306 stock" in his hands if:

(1) It is not "common stock;"[404]

(2) With respect to its receipt, the shareholder's gain or loss went unrecognized to any extent by reason of Part III of Subchapter C (i.e., §§354 and 356); and

(3) The effect of the transaction was substantially the same as the receipt of a stock dividend, or it was received in exchange for "section 306 stock."

If preferred stock is received pro rata by the common shareholders in a Type E reorganization (recapitalization), it will ordinarily have substantially the same effect as the distribution of a stock dividend;[405] the same would

---

[403] Even before the enactment of §306 in 1954, the Service was cautious about the bailout potential of preferred stock received in a tax-free recapitalization. See Rev. Rul. 54-13, 1954-1 CB 109, last sentence; Estate of Rosenberg, 36 TC 716 (1961). For 1954 Code years, see Rev. Rul. 66-332, 1966-2 CB 108; Rev. Rul. 81-91, 1981-1 CB 123 (stock not "section 306 stock," even though preferred as to dividend and liquidation rights, because participated in earnings and equity growth as well).

However, repeal of capital gain rate benefits by the Tax Reform Act of 1986 should materially reduce the significance of §306, supra note 377.

[404] Compare Rev. Rul. 75-222, 1975-1 CB 105 (stock issued in recapitalization was common stock, not "section 306 stock," even though it had right to receive cash dividends where other class of common received less, or no, dividends and other class was convertible into the stock, but not vice versa; in all other respects, the two classes were identical), with Rev. Rul. 75-236, 1975-1 CB 106 (stock distributed in recapitalization was "section 306 stock" because limited and preferred as to dividend and liquidation rights under principles of Regs. §1.305-5(a), even though such stock was the only class of stock outstanding with vote). See supra ¶ 10.03.

[405] See Rev. Rul. 59-84, 1959-1 CB 71. But see Rev. Rul. 79-287, 1979-2 CB 130 (preferred stock received in Type F reorganization in exchange for same number of old preferred with identical terms not "section 306 stock;" transaction not substantially the same as receipt of a stock dividend); Rev. Rul. 82-118, 1982-1 CB 56 (same for new preferred received in triangular forward merger where substantially the same as old "section 306 stock" exchanged therefor); Rev. Rul. 82-191, 1982-2 CB 78 (pre-

usually be true of preferred stock received in a Type A (merger) or Type C (property for voting stock) reorganization of brother-sister corporations. The cash substitution test of Regs. §1.306-3(d), (see Chapter 13), however, is more sweeping, since it is not limited to recapitalizations or reorganizations involving affiliated corporations; Example (1) thereof states flatly that preferred stock issued in a statutory merger is "section 306 stock" without specifying any facts other than the surrender of common stock for a combination of common and preferred of the acquiring corporation. If the transaction is pro rata, the cash substitution test would lead to this result; but if a distribution of cash in lieu of the preferred would not be a dividend under §356(a)(2) because not paid pro rata, "section 306 stock" status is harder to justify.[406]

In the past, the Service ordinarily ruled that preferred stock issued in a merger of two publicly held corporations was "section 306 stock," but simultaneously granted absolution under §306(b)(4) on the ground that the transaction was not in pursuance of a tax avoidance plan. Subsequently, however,

---

ferred stock, voting and limited, issued in recapitalization exchange for all of shareholder's voting common held "section 306 stock" where shareholder purchased all of a new issue of nonvoting common as part of the same plan; thus, transaction as a whole had bailout potential).

[406] The reach of the cash substitution test obviously depends upon the scope of the *Bedford* case (CIR v. Estate of Bedford, supra note 380); if it is limited as suggested by the discussion supra ¶ 14.34, notes 384 and 385, a significantly disproportionate distribution of preferred stock would not lead to "section 306 stock" status. See Alexander & Landis, Bail-Outs and the Internal Revenue Code of 1954, 65 Yale L.J. 909, 923–937 (1956); Rev. Rul. 81-186, 1981-2 CB 85 (preferred stock received by sole shareholder on recapitalization exchange not "section 306 stock" where taxpayer concurrently gave away all of his common pursuant to a unitary plan; cash dividend would have been §302(b)(3) under *Zenz* principles).

See also US v. Davis, 397 US 301 (1970), discussed supra ¶ 9.06, finding dividend equivalence automatically in the case of pro rata redemptions by a closely held corporation. Rev. Rul. 70-199, 1970-1 CB 68 ("section 306 stock" in recapitalization), applied the *Davis* dividend equivalence principle to a pro rata exchange for preferred stock.

See also Rev. Rul. 79-274, 1979-2 CB 131 (receipt of voting preferred pro rata in §351 exchange that also constituted a Type B reorganization; held, preferred "section 306 stock" if transferee corporation has earnings in its first year; transaction essentially equivalent to a stock dividend even though also qualified as §351 exchange). For analysis of this ruling, see Corry, Preferred Stock Issued in Tax-Free Exchanges: Does Section 306 Apply? 35 Tax L. Rev. 113 (1979).

Section 306(c)(3), added by Tax Equity and Fiscal Responsibility Act in 1982, now specifically covers preferred stock issued in a §351 exchange if cash issued in lieu of such stock would have resulted in a dividend under §304(b)(2)(A) principles, supra ¶ 10.03, para. 3.

See Rev. Proc. 77-37, 1977-2 CB 568, for ruling guidelines on when convertible preferred stock will not be considered "section 306 stock."

it has frequently taken the more direct step of ruling that the stock is not "section 306 stock." [407]

The impact of the cash substitution test on a shareholder who has no gain on the exchange—and who therefore would not have realized any dividend income under §356 if cash had been distributed to him—is not clear. The rulings mentioned earlier [408] do not specify that the shareholders realized gain, but see Rev. Rul. 56-586, [409] under which the stock received is apparently classified as "section 306 stock" only to the extent that the shareholder realized a gain on the exchange.

The statutory scheme of §306(c)(1)(B) seems to leave several gaps in coverage. If a transaction is similar to a reorganization but fails to qualify (e.g., for want of a business purpose), preferred stock received cannot be "section 306 stock" under §306(c)(1)(B), even though it has bailout potential. [410] If the transaction is not only a reorganization but also qualifies as an exchange under §1036, it might be argued that §306(c)(1)(B) is inapplicable on the ground that the shareholder's gain or loss went unrecognized because of §1036, rather than by reason of Part III of Subchapter C. Moreover, the cash substitution test presents certain difficulties as applied to stock received in a reorganization in that the transaction might not have been a reorganization if cash had been used in lieu of stock; hence the hypothetical cash might not have been taxed as a dividend. [411]

---

[407] See Rev. Rul. 56-116, 1956-1 CB 164; Rev. Rul. 57-212, 1957-1 CB 114 (§306(b)(4) applicable even though stock was to be redeemed under a sinking fund arrangement); Rev. Rul. 56-223, 1956-1 CB 162; Rev. Rul. 57-103, 1957-1 CB 113. For current practice, see Rev. Proc. 77-37, 1977-2 CB 568.

See also Rev. Rul. 60-1, 1960-1 CB 143 (preferred stock issued in merger to preferred shareholders of surviving corporation, some of whom also owned a small percentage of its common stock, did not constitute "section 306 stock").

See generally Trimble, The Treatment of Preferred Stock Distributions in Reorganizations Under Section 306 of the Internal Revenue Code of 1954, 19 Tax L. Rev. 345 (1964); Note, Exclusion From §306 Treatment in Unifying Reorganizations, 76 Harv. L. Rev. 1627 (1963); Kanter, Voting Preferred Stock Given in "B" Reorganization May Be Section 306 Stock, 39 Taxes 88 (1961); Metzer, The Impact of Section 306 Upon Convertible Preferred Stock Issued in a Corporate Reorganization, 116 U. Pa. L. Rev. 755 (1968); Corry, supra note 406.

[408] Id.

[409] Rev. Rul. 56-586, 1956-2 CB 214.

[410] It should be noted that excluding the transaction from §368(a) does not necessarily mean that the shareholder will be taxed on the exchange; his basis for the stock surrendered may be equal to or greater than the value of the stock received. It is possible that preferred stock received in such a transaction could be classified, in some circumstances, as "section 306 stock" under §306(c)(1)(A) (preferred stock dividend).

[411] See also, on this point, §306(c)(2), which might be used as a shield by the taxpayer.

Repeal of capital gain rate benefits by the Tax Reform Act of 1986 will confine §306 to a relatively modest role in the case of individual shareholders, since the consequences of "section 306 stock" status will no longer impose the differential rate burdens of prior law, although "section 306 stock" status is still not a desirable result even after the 1986 amendment.

¶ 14.36   REORGANIZATIONS OF FOREIGN CORPORATIONS: SECTION 367

Section 367 formerly provided that in determining the extent to which *gain* (but not loss) would be recognized in the case of exchanges described in §354, §355, §356, or §361, a foreign corporation would not be considered as a corporation unless, *before* such an exchange, it was established to the satisfaction of the Service that the exchange was "not in pursuance of a plan having as one of its principal purposes the avoidance of Federal income taxes." The Tax Reform Act of 1976 significantly modified §367 by abolishing the *advance* ruling requirement for certain transactions described in §367(a) (although retaining the requirement of a ruling therefor), and by dropping the ruling requirement altogether for transactions described in §367(b). The Tax Reform Act of 1984 amended §367 once again by dropping the ruling requirement as well for §367(a), and instead imposing a system of toll charges on outbound transfers of certain tainted assets.

Since corporate status is essential to a tax-free reorganization (by reason of the use of the term "corporation" in §§368(a)(1), 354, and 361), a failure to satisfy §367 could result in the recognition of any gain realized by any participant to the reorganization; some of the gain thus recognized may have to be reported as ordinary income by virtue of such provisions as §1245, §1248, §1249, or §1250. Section 367 is considered in detail in Chapter 17.

PART D.   SPECIAL PROBLEMS IN REORGANIZATIONS

¶ 14.50   INTRODUCTORY

We have now considered the basic provisions relating to the definition of a reorganization and the treatment of the parties thereto. The material that follows deals with special problems and aspects of reorganizations warranting further comment.

The Tax Equity and Fiscal Responsibility Act legislation in 1982 extended §318 attribution principles to the definitional testing of "section 306 stock" status in §306(c)(4).

The judicial doctrines of business purpose, step transaction and continuity of business enterprise are of special, if not unique, importance in the reorganization area. Also discussed in this section are reorganizations involving less than all, or substantially all, of the acquired corporation's properties that have given rise to numerous technical and practical problems, and the prereorganization strip-off techniques that have evolved in this area. Acquisitions by, and of, affiliated corporations likewise have spawned an extensive body of law. The liquidation-reincorporation problem has been referred to in Chapters 3, 9, and 11, but the primary discussion of this subject is in this section. Assumption of liability problems and matters relating to contingent, or conditional reorganizations, likewise have created a substantial body of law and lore, as discussed subsequently. Finally, the consequences of nonreorganization status, or quasi-reorganization transactions, are considered in this chapter, as are special problems of insolvency reorganizations.

¶ 14.51 JUDICIAL DOCTRINES AND LIMITATIONS: BUSINESS PURPOSE, CONTINUITY OF BUSINESS ENTERPRISE, AND STEP TRANSACTIONS

1. Business purpose in general. The regulations under §368 take seriously the business purpose requirement, referring at no less than three points to language culled from the fountainhead of learning on this subject, the *Gregory* case.[412] Thus, Regs. §1.368-1(b) states that the reorganization provisions are concerned with "readjustments of corporate structures ... required by business exigencies;" and Regs. §1.368-1(c) elaborates on this theme by providing that a

> "scheme, which involves an abrupt departure from normal reorganization procedure in connection with a transaction on which the imposition of a tax is imminent, such as a mere device that puts on the form of a corporate reorganization as a disguise for concealing its real character, and the object and accomplishment of which is the consummation of a preconceived plan having no business or corporate purpose,"

is not a plan of reorganization. For the unconvinced, this message is repeated in Regs. §1.368-2(g), which states that the transactions must be "undertaken for reasons germane to the continuance of the business of a corporation," and that the statute "contemplates genuine corporate reorga-

---

[412] Gregory v. Helvering, 293 US 465 (1935). See supra ¶ 13.02.

nizations which are designed to effect a readjustment of continuing interests under modified corporate forms.[413]

Although *Gregory* may mean all things to all people, its essence is an instinctive judicial attitude that a transaction should not be given effect for tax purposes unless it serves a purpose other than tax avoidance. Thus, a transaction heavily laden with tax avoidance motives may be disregarded as a sham, or its form may be recast so as to reflect its economic substance, or interdependent steps in a single transaction may be collapsed in order to prevent overreaching taxpayers from doing indirectly what they cannot do directly. As elsewhere in the law of taxation, the lawyer's passion for technical analysis of the statutory language should always be diluted by distrust of a result that is too good to be true. On the other hand, cases like *Cumberland Public Service Co.*[414] bear constant witness to the fact that the deliberate choice of a tax-free (or low-tax) route is as often as not given full effect.[415]

Granting that *Gregory* lays down a general principle of tax law that in order to fit within a particular provision of the statute a transaction must comply not only with the letter of the section, but must have a business purpose (other than a desire to avoid taxes) that falls within its spirit as well, the question then arises as to *whose* business purpose—the corporation's, its shareholders', or both—is controlling. The regulations[416] seem to focus primarily on corporate business purpose as the critical test. But in *Lewis v.*

---

[413] See Wortham Mach. Co. v. US, supra note 119; compare American Bronze Corp., 64 TC 1111 (1975) (merger of affiliated corporations engaged in same business had valid business purpose and requisite continuity; acquired corporation still in business at time of merger even though it had sold off assets of another business shortly before merger); Atlas Tool Co., supra note 379; George R. Laure, 70 TC 1087 (1978) (fusion of dormant loss brother corporation into sister corporation failed to qualify as Type A because of lack of business purpose), rev'd, 653 F2d 253 (6th Cir. 1981) (merger had valid business purpose).

[414] Cumberland Pub. Serv. Co., 338 US 451 (1950), discussed at ¶ 11.07.

[415] See also ¶ 9.07 (bootstrap acquisitions). See generally Eustice & Lyon, Federal Income Taxation, 36 NYU L. Rev. 642–643 (1961). On the business purpose requirement as it relates to corporate reorganizations, see Spear, "Corporate Business Purpose" in Reorganization, 3 Tax L. Rev. 225 (1948); Michaelson, "Business Purpose" and Tax Free Reorganization, 61 Yale L.J. 14 (1952); Bittker, What Is "Business Purpose" in Reorganizations? 8 NYU Inst. on Fed. Tax'n 134 (1950); Note, State of Mind Analysis in Corporate Taxation, 69 Colum. L. Rev. 1224 (1969); Chirelstein, Learned Hand's Contribution to the Law of Tax Avoidance, 77 Yale L.J. 440 (1968); Lipnick, Business Purpose and Income Taxes: From *Gregory* to *Goldstein*, 46 Taxes 698 (1968); supra ¶ 1.05.

More currently, see Willens, The Role of Form in Subchapter C, 57 Taxes 717 (1979); Isenberg, Musings on Form and Substance in Taxation, 49 U. Chi. L. Rev. 859 (1982); Willens, The Significance of Form: Some Subchapter C Manifestations, 12 J. Corp. Tax'n 72 (1985).

[416] Regs. §§1.368-1(b) and 1.368-1(c).

CIR, the court refused to distinguish between corporate purpose and share-holder purpose in the case of a closely held corporation, rejecting the tax-payer's contention that a transaction did not constitute a reorganization because it lacked a corporate business purpose.[417] Similarly, in *Parshelsky's Estate v. CIR*, the business purpose doctrine was interpreted as requiring an evaluation of all the non-tax avoidance motives for the transaction, those of the corporation, and of its shareholders as well; the court went on to hold that reorganization treatment could not be denied merely because the only purpose therefor was a shareholder, rather than a corporate, purpose.[418] The court did emphasize, however, that the shareholder purpose must be a reason other than avoidance of taxes.[419]

2. Continuity of business enterprise. In addition to denouncing shams and disguises, the regulations provide that reorganization requires "a continuity of the business enterprise under modified corporate forms."[420] In several cases where an alleged reorganization was only a step in the winding up of business activity, courts have treated it as part of a taxable liquidation transaction rather than a tax-free reorganization exchange. Thus, in *Standard Realization Co.*, the Tax Court held that a transfer of all of a corporation's assets to a second corporation controlled by the shareholders of the transferor was not a reorganization, although it complied with the literal requirements of a Type D reorganization, because the transferee was to sell the assets under a preconceived plan rather than to continue in a business.[421] Similarly, in *Pridemark, Inc. v. CIR*, reorganization treatment was denied where a corporation's business assets were sold to an unrelated purchaser and its business activity was suspended for over a year.[422] The court there stated that the old business had been liquidated, and that the creation of a new corporation to engage in a similar line of business did not constitute a continuation or reactivation of the old business enterprise.[423] Accordingly,

---

[417] Lewis v. CIR, 176 F2d 646 (1st Cir. 1949).

[418] Estate of Parshelsky v. CIR, 303 F2d 14 (2d Cir. 1962).

[419] See Rafferty v. CIR, 452 F2d 767 (1st Cir. 1971), cert. denied, 408 US 922 (1972), for analysis, refinement, and, in some ways, disagreement with the business purpose test of the *Lewis* and *Parshelsky* cases.

[420] Regs. §1.368-1(b).

[421] Standard Realization Co., 10 TC 708 (1948) (acq.).

[422] Pridemark, Inc. v. CIR, 345 F2d 35 (4th Cir. 1965).

[423] See also George Graham, 37 BTA 623 (1938); on the meaning of complete liquidation, see supra ¶ 11.02.

In US v. Adkins-Phelps, Inc., supra note 25, it was held that the business continuity test was satisfied where suspension of business activity was merely temporary; *Pridemark* was distinguished.

where there is a complete termination of corporate business activity or such an interruption of the business activity that its continuity is broken, the liquidation provisions take precedence over the reorganization provisions.

It should be noted, however, that liquidation of one of the corporate parties to a reorganization transaction (as distinguished from a termination of *business* activities) is not inconsistent with the concept of reorganization. In fact, many reorganization plans contemplate, or even require, the liquidation of at least one of the corporations. Thus, in the *Lewis* case,[424] it was held that reorganization treatment applied where the corporation sold two of its three lines of business; and, because of a temporary inability to sell the third, placed it in a new corporation pending a sale, and liquidated. The termination of business cases did not apply, said the court, merely because the corporation contemplated a sale of its assets at some time in the future if the business was in fact carried on at the corporate level in the interim.

In addition, the continuity of business enterprise requirement does not demand that the new corporation engage in the same or a similar business as its predecessor; all that is required is that there be continuity of business activity. For example, in *Becher v. CIR*, it was held that a transfer of assets to a corporation controlled by the transferor's shareholders was a reorganization, even though the transferor's business was terminated, some of its assets were distributed in partial liquidation, and the transferred assets were invested by the transferee in an entirely different business.[425] After flirting with a contrary view for a period of years, the Service at first agreed with *Becher* that continuity of *a* business enterprise, whether it was carried on before the reorganization by a party thereto or not, was sufficient.[426] How-

---

[424] Lewis v. CIR, supra note 417.

[425] Becher v. CIR, 221 F2d 252 (2d Cir. 1955).

[426] See Rev. Rul. 63-29, 1963-1 CB 77, revoking Rev. Rul. 56-330, 1956-2 CB 204, after its approach was rejected in Bentsen v. Phinney, 199 F. Supp. 363 (S.D. Tex. 1961); see also Morley Cypress Trust, 3 TC 84 (1944) (acq.); Pebble Springs Distilling Co. v. CIR, 231 F2d 288 (7th Cir.), cert. denied, 352 US 836 (1956); see also supra ¶ 14.19.

Rev. Rul. 63-29 was suspended by Rev. Rul. 79-433, 1979-2 CB 155, pending its revision to reflect the proposed regulations issued Dec. 28, 1979 on business continuity, infra note 427. But holding of Rev. Rul. 63-29 was republished by Rev. Rul. 81-25, 1981-1 CB 132 (no business continuity required for *transferee*; Rev. Rul. 79-433 superseded); Rev. Rul. 85-197, 1985-2 CB 120; and Rev. Rul. 85-198, 1985-2 CB 120 (test on group-wide basis in case of affiliated corporations).

See generally Tarleau, "Continuity of Business Enterprise" in Corporate Reorganizations and Other Corporate Readjustments, 60 Colum. L. Rev. 792 (1960); Freeman, Leveraged Buy-Outs: Cash Company and Investment Company Reorganizations, 6 J. Corp. Tax'n 239 (1979).

For recent continuity of business enterprise cases, see Wortham Mach. Co. v. US, supra note 118; American Bronze Corp., supra note 413; Atlas Tool Co., supra note 379 (not necessary for transferee to continue business of transferor); see also

ever, new regulations on continuity of business enterprise were proposed in December 1979[427] and became final in December 1980[428] as Regs. §1.368-1(d), which require that the transferee corporations either (1) continue the transferor's historic business or (2) continue to use a significant portion of the transferor's historic business assets in a business. The regulations note that the fact that the transferee is in the same line of business as the transferor tends to establish the requisite business continuity, but is not alone sufficient; moreover, if the transferor has more than one business, continuity requires that the transferee need only continue a significant line of the transferor's business. Finally, the transferor's historic business is that that it most recently conducted; however, a business entered into as part of an overall plan to achieve a tax-free reorganization will not qualify. A corporation's historic business assets will include various intangibles, such as goodwill, patents, and the like, whether or not they have a tax basis, and determination of the significance at the line of business or the assets transferred is a question of fact.

The proposed regulations applied only to asset transfers (raising the curious and inexplicable implication that stock-for-stock Type B reorganizations will not be subject to these limitations), but the final regulations remedied this oversight.[429] The regulations might also have some unintended side

---

George R. Laure, supra note 413 (business continuity existed, even under new regulations' test because transferee retained significant portion of transferor's historic business assets; 27 percent, by book value, significant); Rose v. US, 640 F2d 1030 (9th Cir. 1981) (generally similar to *Atlas Tool* in finding reincorporation transaction to be a Type D, but court expressly refused to apply a business continuity requirement for reorganization status here).

[427] Concurrently with these proposals, the Service issued Rev. Proc. 79-68, 1979-2 CB 600, suspending issuance of rulings on business continuity pending adoption of the regulations, while Rev. Rul. 79-433, 1979-2 CB 155, suspended Rev. Rul. 63-29, 1963-1 CB 77, pending its revision to reflect the new proposals (although Rev. Rul. 63-29 was reinstated by Rev. Rul. 81-25, 1981-1 CB 132). Finally, Rev. Rul. 79-434, 1979-2 CB 155, ruled that a corporation that sold its assets and was acquired by an investment company did not satisfy the business continuity requirement (the substance of the transaction was deemed merely to constitute a purchase of stock by the transferor). Compare Ltr. Rul. 8027017, [1980] 9 Fed. Taxes (P-H) ¶ 55,246 (asset sale for cash, followed by transfer of cash to regulated investment company for stock, followed by liquidation; held, §337 applied to first step because second step not a tax-free reorganization under continuity of business enterprise principles; hence, no conflict between §§337 and 368).

[428] The regulations are effective for acquisitions occuring 30 days after Dec. 29, 1980; of special significance is the Treasury's preamble to the regulations, which constitutes an extensive brief supporting their validity (see 1981 (CCH) Fed. Tax Rep. ¶ 6343, Vol. 10).

[429] See also Rev. Rul. 81-92, 1981-1 CB 133 (business continuity requirement did apply to Type B reorganization). But see Rev. Rul. 81-247, 1981-2 CB 87 (post acqui-

effects in the liquidation-reincorporation area, where taxpayers are seeking methods to avoid application of the reorganization rules.[430] Moreover, the business continuity requirement could restrict the Type G insolvency reorganization rules where, as is frequently the case, the reorganizing debtor corporation drastically scales down its historic business activities or assets as a consequence of its reorganization in the bankruptcy proceeding.

The regulations set out five examples in §1.368-1(d)(5) illustrating the business continuity doctrine. Example (1) illustrates that the transferee need only continue one of the transferor's lines of business (two of its three equal lines were sold prior to the reorganization, but continuation of one of those businesses was adequate since it was a significant line).[431] Example (2) illustrates acceptable asset continuity, while Examples (3), (4), and (5) illustrate situations where the requisite business continuity is lacking. In Example (3), the transferee sold its operating assets and became an investment company three and one-half years prior to the purported reorganization; in Example (4) the transferee acquired the transferor after the latter had sold its operating assets for cash and notes; in Example (5) the transferee sold off the transferor's assets after the acquisition and discontinued that line of business (all steps being effected pursuant to the plan of reorganization in these examples).[432]

Continuity of the prereorganization historic business may also be important in other contexts (e.g., in §355 transactions (see Chapter 13), in the limitations on carry-over of tax attributes under §382 (see Chapter 16), and in the reincorporation area (discussed later in this chapter).

---

sition dropdowns won't affect continuity); Rev. Rul. 82-34, 1982-1 CB 59 (does not apply to recapitalization); Rev. Rul. 85-197, 1985-2 CB 120, and Rev. Rul. 85-198, 1985-2 CB 120 (affiliated group lookthrough rule).

[430] See Atlas Tool Co., supra note 426; George R. Laure, id; Rose v. US, id; infra ¶ 14.54.

[431] Rev. Rul. 85-197, 1985-2 CB 120, and Rev. Rul. 85-198, 1985-2 CB 120 (affiliated group lookthrough rule for continuity test—that is, business of subsidiary is business of holding company parent; continuity satisfied if end up with a significant subsidiary of target, even though conducted through a second-tier subsidiary of acquiring group); see also supra notes 427 and 429.

[432] See generally Beller & Brown, IRS Mounts Double-Barreled Attack on "Cash Reorganizations" With Mutual Funds, 53 J. Tax'n 76 (1980); Aidinoff & Lopata, The Continuity of Business Enterprise Requirement and Investment Company Reorganizations, 58 Taxes 914 (1980); Faber, Continuity of Interest and Business Enterprise: Is It Time to Bury Some Sacred Cows? 34 Tax Lawyer 239 (1981); Bloom, The Resurrection of a Dormant Doctrine: Continuity of Business Enterprise, 7 J. Corp. Tax'n 315 (1981); Libin, Continuity of Business Enterprise: The New Regulations, 39 NYU Inst. on Fed. Tax'n ch. 4 (1981); Westin, Investment Company Reorganization With "Cash Companies" and the Continuity of Business Enterprise Doctrine: One Current View, 16 New Eng. L. Rev. 413 (1981); Faber, supra note 53; supra ¶ 14.11, para. 10.

3. Step transactions. Like the business purpose doctrine, the judicial requirement that all integrated steps in a single transaction must be amalgamated in determining the true nature of a transaction is applied in every nook and cranny of the tax law, not merely in the field of corporate reorganizations; examples are sprinkled freely throughout this book.[433] Whether the first in a series of steps is old and cold or is instead part of a unitary plan has considerable importance in the reorganization area, however, and the step doctrine has been applied both to create and to deny reorganization status for various types of single transactions.

A business transaction, like the rest of life, often has no sharp beginning or clearly defined end, but it is often necessary in practice to cut it, usually chronologically, into constituent elements for tax purposes. If the segments are sliced too thin, however, the tax results may be unfair to the government, the taxpayer, or to both. As a consequence, a series of formally separate steps may be amalgamated and treated as a single transaction if they are in substance integrated, interdependent, and focused toward a particular end result. In viewing an organic whole, the courts often state that an integrated transaction must not be broken into its constituent steps or, conversely, that the separate steps must be fused in determining the overall tax consequences of the transaction. Although the step-transaction principle is not limited to government counsel, in practice it seems most often to be applied at the request of the Treasury, rather than over its opposition.[434]

---

[433] E.g., whether a transferor has control "immediately after the exchange" under §351 (supra ¶ 3.09); whether a purchase of stock coupled with a liquidation is equivalent to a purchase of assets (supra ¶ 11.44); whether assets of a partially owned corporation can be acquired in a tax-free reorganization (infra ¶ 14.53); and whether a liquidation, followed or preceded by a reincorporation of all or part of the assets of the liquidating corporation, constitutes a liquidation or a reorganization (supra ¶ 11.05; infra ¶ 14.54). For other illustrations, see the works cited supra ¶ 1.05. See generally West Coast Marketing Corp., supra note 106; Regs. §§1.351-1(c)(2), 1.351-1(c)(5) ("plan in existence" and subsequent steps "however delayed"). See also supra ¶ 14.11, para. 10 (plan of reorganization), infra ¶ 14.52.

Further recent step transaction decisions of significance are Blake v. CIR, 697 F2d 473 (2d Cir. 1982); Security Indus. Ins. Co. v. US, 702 F2d 1234 (5th Cir. 1982); and Superior Coach of Fla., 80 TC 895 (1983) (cash purchase of stock, followed by asset fusion transactions linked to destroy continuity of interest).

[434] See generally Rev. Rul. 79-250, 1979-2 CB 156 (substance of each of a series of steps will be recognized and step transaction doctrine not applied if step has independent economic significance, is not a sham, and was undertaken for a valid business purpose). But compare Rev. Rul. 83-142, 1983-2 CB 68 (disregard transitory interim steps that would disqualify an otherwise qualified reorganization where steps taken to comply with local law).

See also McDonald's of Zion, Inc., 76 TC 972 (1981) (postfusion stock sales didn't break continuity, even though previously planned and intended because sales and reorganization not mutually interdependent; end result test of *King Enterprises* rejected), but reversed, 688 F2d 520 (7th Cir. 1982) (continuity broken by planned sales under

There seems to be no universally accepted test, however, as to when (and for that matter how) the step-transaction doctrine will be applied in a given case, and it may be that the concept has different meanings for different contexts. Thus, some courts speak of the test in terms of interdependence of the steps (i.e., whether one or more of the steps would have been fruitless without completion of the series), while others describe it as involving intended or expected end results. On the other hand, where there are two or more straight paths to the same end result, the taxpayer is not required to take the most expensive route.[435]

Some courts on occasion have limited the step-transaction approach to cases where the taxpayer is under a binding commitment to take the later steps (rather than a mere expectation that they will occur),[436] but this standard may be reserved for situations where the taxpayer, rather than the government, is seeking to invoke the doctrine.[437]

For illustrations of the multifaceted aspects of this principle, see generally *American Potash & Chemical Co. v. US*[438] and *King Enterprises Inc. v. US*.[439] Whatever the standard, the vagueness of its scope may be a virtue in restraining overly ambitious taxpayers and their advisers.

4. Effect of current reform proposals. Current proposals by the staff of the Senate Finance Committee would sharply downgrade in importance (and, in the case of the business purpose, continuity of proprietary interest, and continuity of business enterprise limitations, would repeal) the doctrines discussed here in the case of qualified corporate acquisitions. The staff's proposed corporate acquisition system would replace considerations of business purpose, continuity of business enterprise, and continuity of proprietary interest, with a specific election system for recognition or nonrecognition treatment at the corporate level. While the step transaction doctrine would

---

step transaction principles). Compare Robert A. Penrod, 88 TC No. 79 (1987); James H. Johnson, 78 TC 564 (1982) (subsequent sale of stock received in recapitalization not part of recapitalization transaction); ITT & Cos., 77 TC 60 (1981), aff'd per curiam, 704 F2d 252 (2d Cir. 1983) (conversion transaction not part of prior reorganization transaction in which convertible securities were issued); Chirelstein & Lopata, Recent Developments in the Step-Transaction Doctrine, 60 Taxes 970 (1982).

The classic articles on the step-transaction question are Paul & Zimet, Studies in Federal Taxation 200 (West, 2d Ser., 1938); Mintz & Plumb, Step Transactions in Corporate Reorganizations, 12 NYU Inst. on Fed. Tax'n 247 (1954).

[435] See supra ¶ 9.07; see, e.g., Glacier State Elec. Supply Co., 80 TC 1047 (1983).

[436] CIR v. Gordon, supra note 56.

[437] See Jacobs, Supreme Court Further Restricts the Step Transaction Doctrine, 29 J. Tax'n 2 (1968).

[438] American Potash & Chem. Co. v. US, supra note 56.

[439] King Enters., Inc. v. US, supra note 67.

continue to have some vitality even under the new elective nonrecognition rules, its role would be a relatively marginal one at most.

¶ 14.52   DISPOSITION OF UNWANTED ASSETS IN CONNECTION WITH A REORGANIZATION

This section is concerned with a special aspect of the step-transaction problem (i.e., when the acquiring corporation is interested in obtaining only part of the assets of the transferor corporation, what tax consequences arise if the unwanted assets are stripped off in anticipation of the impending transfer of the wanted assets. The disposition of unwanted assets in this context can be effected by (1) a sale of these properties to third parties, (2) a distribution in kind to shareholders of the transferor corporation, or (3) a tax-free distribution under §355 (see Chapter 13). The discussion that follows will focus on the way these modes of ridding the transferor corporation of the unwanted assets affect the reorganization status of the simultaneous or subsequent transfer of the wanted assets; but attention must also be given to other statutory provisions that may govern the treatment of the transferor corporation or its shareholders.[440]

To make the discussion more concrete, it will be assumed that *T* Corporation owns and operates two separate five-year-old businesses; that the assets of both businesses have appreciated in value substantially, and are about equal in value; that *T* has a large earnings and profits account; that *P* Corporation wishes to acquire one business for voting stock in a tax-free reorganization but does not want to acquire the other; and that *T* and its shareholders will receive less than 80 percent of *P*'s stock and hence will not be in control of *P* after the exchange within the meaning of §368(c).

---

[440] If the unwanted assets are not substantial (so that the fusion can qualify as a Type C reorganization), it was formerly possible to have a later independent tax-free liquidation under §333 with respect to the retained properties (earnings and profits having been drawn off to the transferee by §381). For analysis of this possibility, see Note, Combining a Section 333 Liquidation with a "C" Reorganization, 56 Cornell L.Q. 665 (1971).

But legislation enacted in 1984 now requires complete liquidation of the transferor corporation pursuant to the plan of reorganization in order to qualify as a Type C reorganization (unless such liquidation requirement is waived by regulations), the Tax Reform Act of 1984, adding §368(a)(2)(G). Moreover, legislation in 1986 repealed §337 (supra ¶ 11.06), and §333 as well (supra ¶ 11.62).

For general discussion, see Bucholz, Disposing of Unwanted Assets in Corporate Mergers and Acquisitions, 38 Tax Lawyer 161 (1984); Walter, Unwanted Assets in Taxable and Tax-Free Corporate Acquisition: Old Wine in New Bottles, 63 Taxes 897 (1985).

1. Taxable strip off of unwanted assets. If T sells the unwanted assets to an unrelated purchaser for cash, transfers the wanted assets to P for its voting stock, and liquidates, the T-P exchange may not constitute a Type C reorganization because it is not a transfer of substantially all of T's properties under §368(a)(1)(C). As a result,[441] T would have to recognize its gain on both this transfer and on the sale of the other business for cash unless it met the requirements of former §337 (before its repeal by the Tax Reform Act of 1986, as discussed in Chapter 11). If the formalities were observed, and if the shareholders of T acquired only a nominal stock interest in P (e.g., if the transfer was to a large, publicly held corporation), this ordinarily was not difficult, and T's shareholders would then realize capital gain or loss on its liquidation. If they obtained a larger interest in P, however, the Service may have contested the applicability of former §337, but its objections may not be acceptable to the courts.[442]

If instead of selling the unwanted business, T distributed it to its shareholders in exchange for stock, the transaction would constitute a taxable event to both T (as a result of the repeal of §§311 and 336 nonrecognition treatment by the Tax Reform Act of 1986) and to T's shareholders (either as a dividend under §301 or more likely as capital gain or loss under §302). A subsequent merger of T into P (or a transfer of all of T's remaining assets for voting stock of P in a §368(a)(1)(C) practical merger) may qualify as a reorganization if T is completely liquidated, as would automatically be the case in a true merger (and as is, after 1984, required for the Type C reorganization as well). Since the unwanted assets have passed out of T Corporation in a *taxable* transaction, reorganization treatment with respect to the subsequent transfer by T to P of the wanted assets may be permissible under §§368(a)(1)(A) and 368(a)(1)(C).

---

[441] See supra ¶ 14.14; Helvering v. Elkhorn Coal Co., supra note 122; see also West Coast Marketing Corp., supra note 106; Rev. Rul. 70-140, 1970-1 CB 80; supra ¶ 3.15.

[442] Compare CIR v. Berghash, supra note 32 (no reorganization where only 50 percent continuity of control by shareholders of the selling corporation); James Armour, Inc., supra note 119 (held a Type D reorganization where 100 percent continuity of control, even though only 51 percent of selling corporation's assets were transferred, which amount was held to be substantially all because all essential operating assets were transferred). See infra ¶ 14.54; Rev. Rul. 79-273, 1979-2 CB 125 (distribution of stock of unwanted subsidiary in connection with taxable stock purchase via cash reverse merger held a *Zenz* §302(b)(3) complete termination transaction).

Legislation enacted in 1984 lowered the statutory control threshold for nondivisive Type D reorganizations to 50 percent (with §318 attribution) by adopting the control test of §304(c) (i.e., at least 50 percent of vote *or* value, supra ¶ 9.12), thus making it easier to find a reorganization in the above-described transaction; the Tax Reform Act of 1984, adding new §368(c)(2), moved to §368(a)(2)(H) in 1986.

There does not seem to be any substantially all requirement for statutory mergers and Type B reorganizations, and the shareholders of T presumably retain the necessary continuity of interest in the transferred properties through their receipt of the P Corporation's stock.[443] However, Type C reorganization treatment may be more difficult to sustain in this case if the distributed assets must be considered for purposes of the substantially all test under the *Elkhorn Coal* case.[444] It can be argued that this distribution should not be considered, however, since, unlike *Elkhorn*, the unwanted assets passed out of corporate solution in a taxable transaction; hence, the transaction was essentially nondivisive in character, even when considered in its entirety.[445] In fact, the Service may argue for a reorganization on these facts so as to assert boot dividend treatment to the shareholders of T with respect to their prior receipt of its unwanted assets, [446] and taxability of T on that transaction as well.

On the other hand, if the retained unwanted assets are substantial in relation to the transferred wanted assets, as here, the transaction may lack sufficient resemblance to a merger under general reorganization theory (which ordinarily contemplates a fusion of the properties of one corporate enterprise with another). In this situation, the shareholders' continuity of proprietary interest (and possibly corporate continuity of business enterprise as well) may be so lacking as to deny reorganization treatment. Finally, as a result of amendments to §§311 and 336 by the Tax Reform Act of 1986, the distributing corporation will be taxable under §311 or §336(a) (see Chapter 9) if it distributes the unwanted assets in exchange for its stock or as a dividend (or partial liquidation) distribution.[447]

---

[443] See supra ¶ 14.11.

[444] Helvering v. Elkhorn Coal, supra note 122.

[445] See supra ¶ 14.14; Rev. Rul. 58-68, 1958-1 CB 183 (prior taxable spin-off did not affect later statutory merger) (but Rev. Rul. 58-68 was revoked by Rev. Rul. 83-114, 1983-2 CB 66 (not taxable spin-off because of planned merger, or threshold business motivated capital contribution)); Curtis v. US, supra note 397; Rev. Rul. 57-114, 1957-1 CB 122 (merger not affected by subsequent taxable split-off exchange between acquiring corporation and a shareholder of both the acquired and acquiring corporation); Ralph C. Wilson, supra note 121.

See also Rev. Rul. 70-172, 1970-1 CB 77 (dividend of unwanted assets in anticipation of Type B reorganization did not violate "solely" requirement); supra ¶ 14.13.

But see Rev. Proc. 77-37, 1977-2 CB 568, requiring consideration of threshold distributions to pay off dissenters, for stock redemptions, or for the payment of extraordinary dividends in applying the substantially all test if such distributions are part of the plan of reorganization.

[446] See supra ¶ 14.34.

[447] The Tax Reform Act of 1986 repealed all of the exceptions to corporate-level nonrecognition on the distribution of appreciated assets, whether the distribution is a dividend, a partial, or a complete liquidation, supra ¶¶ 7.21, 9.34, and 11.06.

2. Tax-free spin-off followed by reorganization. In the *Elkhorn Coal* case, the transferor, *T* Corporation, spun off its unwanted assets by transferring these properties to a newly created corporation and distributing its stock in a transaction that qualified for nonrecognition treatment under the provisions of §§355 and 368(a)(1)(D). This step was part of a plan in pursuance of which *T* then transferred the rest of its assets to *P* Corporation in what purported to be a Type C reorganization. If these two steps had been unrelated events, this result would clearly have been appropriate, since the wanted assets constituted all of *T* Corporation's properties after the spin-off. But the court in *Elkhorn* held that the two steps were part of a single integrated transaction and that the unwanted assets, which were spun off in the earlier step, had to be considered in determining whether *T* Corporation had transferred substantially all of its properties under §368(a)(1)(C); since substantially all the assets did not pass to the acquiring corporation under this approach, Type C reorganization treatment was denied.

It should be noted that if the taxpayer had prevailed in *Elkhorn*, the substantially all requirement would have been virtually nullified, at least for the well informed. Also, it was significant in *Elkhorn* that the unwanted assets remained in corporate solution, having been separated from the assets to be transferred in a nontaxable transaction, and they were substantial in amount as compared to the transferred properties; hence, *T* Corporation was attempting to continue operation of the retained business in the newly created corporate vehicle and at the same time to obtain nonrecognition treatment with respect to that part of its assets transferred to the acquiring corporation. This divisive feature of the *Elkhorn* transaction perhaps explains the Court's reluctance to treat the two steps as unrelated, since the substantially all requirement was then, as it is today, aimed precisely at discouraging this result.

The tax-free character of the preliminary spin-off transaction in the *Elkhorn* situation is determined by reference to §§355 and 368(a)(1)(D) (or §351), which matters are considered in detail in Chapter 13.[448] For purposes of this discussion, however, two important aspects of §355 should be noted: (1) The device clause of §355(a)(1)(B) denies nonrecognition treatment where the transaction is used principally as a device for the distribution of earnings and profits and (2) the active trade or business rules of §355(b) require that both the distributing corporation and the spun-off corporation be engaged in an active business immediately after the distribution and that

---

But a tax-free reorganization and §355 distributions continue to be nontaxable at the corporate level as well.

[448] See also supra ¶ 14.16. Qualification of the distribution under §355 is also important to the distributing corporation, since taxability will result to it unless the distribution constitutes a valid §355 transaction.

such business must have been conducted for five years prior to the distribution. Moreover, the distributing corporation will be taxable under §311(b)(1) or §336, after their amendment by the Tax Reform Act of 1986, unless the distribution qualifies for §355.

The device clause of §355(a)(1)(B) seems concerned primarily with a possible bailout of corporate earnings at capital gain rates (i.e., the type of transaction involved in the *Gregory* case).[449] As such, this provision may not be violated where shareholders of the distributing corporation subsequently exchange their stock in a tax-free transaction. In the case of a *taxable* transfer, however, the shareholders may have converted potential dividend income into capital gain if the prior spin-off distribution qualifies for nonrecognition treatment under §355, and this is the result that §355(a)(1)(B) is designed to discourage. Also, continuity of interest principles are inherent in the device clause, and any taxable shareholder stock sales could fail to pass muster on this score as well.[450]

Two important decisions involved the tax consequences of a spin-off transaction coupled with a statutory merger unifying reorganization. In *Curtis v. US*, unwanted assets were spun off to shareholders of the transferor corporation, which then transferred the rest of its assets to the acquiring corporation in a statutory merger, with the latter emerging as the surviving corporation.[451] The court held that the spin-off distribution constituted a taxable dividend because the transaction failed to satisfy the requirement of §355(b)(1)(A) that *the* distributing corporation be engaged in business immediately after the distribution; the distributing corporation no longer existed, said the court, since it was absorbed by the acquiring corporation in the later statutory merger (which was part of the same transaction). *CIR v. Morris Trust* involved virtually identical facts except that the transferor corporation's existence continued under the particular consolidation statute there involved; the court held that the spin-off qualified for nonrecognition treatment under §355 and that there was no incompatibility between combined divisive and acquisitive reorganizations.[452]

In neither case did the Service attack the reorganization status of the subsequent statutory mergers,[453] although, as noted above, if the Type C

---

[449] Gregory v. Helvering, supra note 412. Repeal of capital gain rate benefits by the Tax Reform Act of 1986 may downgrade the role of the device clause of §355(a)(1)(B), however.

[450] See, e.g., Rev. Rul. 55-103, 1955-1 CB 310; supra ¶ 13.07.

[451] Curtis v. US, supra note 397.

[452] CIR v. Morris Trust, 367 F2d 794 (4th Cir. 1966).

[453] See also Rev. Rul. 57-114, 1957-1 CB 122; Rev. Rul. 58-68, 1958-1 CB 183; Rev. Rul. 70-172, 1970-1 CB 77; Rev. Rul. 70-434, 1970-2 CB 83. But see infra note 455.

reorganization route had been used, it could have been vulnerable under *Elkhorn* and the substantially all requirement (if sufficiently large amounts of assets had been held back from the transfer). *Curtis* would presumably have gone the other way had the transferor corporation been the surviving corporation in the merger; if so, it turns on a highly technical reading of §355 and on the parties' choice of form. The *Morris* case, on the other hand, seems to reach the proper result, and the Service agreed to follow it.[454]

One final point: Assuming the tax-free character of the preliminary spin-off transaction, does it make any difference whether the wanted assets are the properties that are separated in the initial §355 transaction, or must §355 be used only to carve out the properties that are to be left behind in the subsequent acquisition? It would seem that both these patterns should be treated alike, but published rulings by the Service suggest that a planned integrated acquisition of the spun-off corporation is not permissible (at least when that corporation is newly created as part of the overall transaction).[455]

---

[454] In Rev. Rul. 68-603, 1968-2 CB 148, the Service agreed to follow the *Morris Trust* case (CIR v. Morris Trust, supra note 452) to the extent it holds that (1) the active business requirement will be satisfied even though the distributing corporation subsequently merges; (2) the control requirement of §368(a)(1)(D) will not be violated by a merger of the transferor after the distribution; and (3) there was a valid business purpose for that transaction.

Prop. Regs. §1.355-2(c)(2) (1977) generally accepts the *Morris Trust* principle that tax-free reorganization exchanges do not trigger a violation of §355; see also Rev. Rul. 78-251, 1978-1 CB 89.

See generally Massey, Disposal of Unwanted Assets in Connection With a Reorganization, 22 Tax L. Rev. 439 (1967); Cohen, Tax-Free Acquisition of Part of a Corporation's Assets by Combining a Spin-Off With a Unifying Reorganization, 26 NYU Inst. on Fed. Tax'n 849 (1968); N.Y. State Bar Association, Tax Section, Report on the Ancillary Tax Effects of Different Forms of Reorganizations, 34 Tax L. Rev. 477, 527 (1979); Handler, Variations on a Theme: The Disposition of Unwanted assets, 35 Tax L. Rev. 389 (1980); Bucholz, supra note 440; Walter, id.

[455] See Rev. Rul. 70-225, 1970-1 CB 80 (transfer of wanted assets to new subsidiary and spin-off of its stock to sole shareholder who exchanged it for stock of acquiring corporation; held gain recognized to distributing corporation (not under §351 because control lost); dividend to distributee shareholder (not under §355 because not valid Type D reorganization at the corporate level); entire transaction treated as a taxable exchange of property for stock at the corporate level, followed by a distribution of acquired stock as a dividend).

Compare Rev. Rul. 70-434, 1970-2 CB 83 (spin-off of unwanted assets, 23 percent, followed by acquisition of distributing corporation in Type B reorganization; held a valid Type B reorganization). In short, form still counts here.

See also King v. CIR, 458 F2d 245 (6th Cir. 1972) (stock of existing five-year subsidiary spun off and transferred, per plan, to another corporation in tax-free exchange; no assertion by Service that this step affected prior spin-off because postdistribution control not essential here); Rev. Rul. 72-530, 1972-2 CB 212 (acquiring corporation's premerger pruning of unrelated subsidiary via spin-off distribution for business reasons was valid §355 distribution); Rev. Rul. 75-406, 1975-2 CB 125

If the spun-off company stays behind, however, the Service generally permits acquisition of the stock or assets of the distributing corporation on a tax-free basis.[456] (It may be that the Service is seeking to prevent acquisition of the wanted business with a clean slate of tax attributes, since the transaction involved in Rev. Rul. 70-225,[457] had it qualified as a reorganization, would not have constituted a §381 transaction (see Chapter 16)).

With these observations in mind, the following examples will deal with certain variations on the *Elkhorn* pattern, based on the facts assumed earlier.

Example 1: T spins off the wanted assets by transferring them to S Corporation (a newly created controlled corporation) and distributed the S stock to its shareholders. S then transfers all of its assets to P solely in exchange for the latter's voting stock (in a Type C or Type A reorganization), after which S liquidates. This transaction is clearly vulnerable under *Gregory*, since S is a mere conduit for the transfer of T's wanted assets to P.[458] As such, its corporate existence should be ignored, and the transaction should be treated as a taxable exchange between T and P (of the wanted assets for P stock), followed by a dividend (or partial liquidation) distribution of the P stock to T's shareholders.

Example 2: If S was not liquidated in Example 1, its separate corporate existence could not be ignored under *Gregory*. However, the spin-off transaction still would be vulnerable under §355(b)(1)(A), since S would be a mere holding company after it transfers all of its assets for P stock.[459] In addition, *Elkhorn* may deprive the transfer of assets of Type C reorganization status, since, if the steps are collapsed, substantially all of the assets have not passed to S. Moreover, S's failure to liquidate would vitiate the Type C reorganization under §368(a)(2)(G) after 1984 amendments requiring this step.

Example 3: If P acquired all the stock of S (rather than its assets) in a stock-for-stock exchange, results could be different. The spin-off trans-

---

(spin-off of eight-year existing subsidiary, followed by merger of spun-off subisidiary into acquiring corporation, held valid §355 transaction and merger).

[456] Rev. Rul. 70-434, 1970-2 CB 83.

[457] Rev. Rul. 70-225, 1970-1 CB 80.

[458] Gregory v. Helvering, supra note 412; see also West Coast Marketing Corp., supra note 106.

[459] See also Rev. Rul. 58-68, 1958-1 CB 183 (but Rev. Rul. 58-68 was revoked by Rev. Rul. 83-114, 1983-2 CB 66); Rev. Rul. 70-140, 1970-1 CB 73.

S would have to liquidate in order to have a good Type C reorganization by virtue of §368(a)(2)(G) (added by the Tax Reform Act of 1984).

action would not be subject to the *Curtis* attack, since both *T* and *S* continue in existence after the distribution (assuming that *P* did not, by prearrangement, liquidate *S* to obtain its assets, in which case the result would be equivalent to an asset acquisition). As to the device clause of §355, however, the spin-off is vulnerable unless the exchange between *T*'s shareholders and *P* can be treated as a Type B reorganization; if it is so treated, they have disposed of their *S* stock in a nontaxable exchange, and as indicated earlier, this seems compatible with the device provision. Literally, their exchange seems to qualify under §368(a)(1)(B), but there are rulings to the contrary asserting that the transaction constitutes in substance a transfer of the wanted assets for the stock of the acquiring corporation.[460] So viewed, it would be denied reorganization status as involving less than substantially all of *T*'s assets. It is by no means clear that this approach would be accepted if the matter were litigated, however, at least if *S* is kept alive rather than liquidated by *P*.

Example 4: If *T* spins off its *unwanted* assets (by transferring them to *S* and distributing the *S* stock to its shareholders), and *T*'s shareholders then exchange their *T* stock for *P*'s voting stock, the plan has the same economic effect as the plan described in Example 3; but it is possible that its claim to Type B treatment would be stronger. To apply Rev. Rul. 54-96,[461] it would be necessary to view the acquisition by *P* of the stock of an *existing* corporation (*T*) as the equivalent of an acquisition of assets; by contrast, the ruling itself emphasized that the acquired corporation was newly created. Unless the courts respond with a new judicial doctrine—possibly similar to the "substantially all of the enterprise" notion of *Elkhorn*, only dealing with stock acquisitions rather

---

[460] See Rev. Rul. 54-96, 1954-1 CB 111. Unless the transaction is regarded as a transfer of assets, however, it seems to meet the requirement of §368(a)(1)(B). See West Coast Marketing Corp., supra note 106; Rev. Rul. 70-140, 1970-1 CB 73.

Rev. Rul. 54-96 also held that the initial transfer of assets by *T* to *S* did not qualify under §351, since control was disposed of by prearrangement; on this issue, see supra ¶ 3.09; Rev. Rul. 70-225, 1970-1 CB 80. Compare Rev. Rul. 75-406, 1975-2 CB 125, and Rev. Rul. 78-251, 1978-1 CB 89.

An attack based on the theory of Rev. Rul. 54-96 might be avoided if *T* exchanged the *S* stock directly with *P*, rather than distributing such stock to its shareholders and having them make the exchange; but in this event, the *P* stock could not be distributed tax-free by *T* to its shareholders, since *T* is not a party to a reorganization (supra ¶ 14.30). Moreover, this transaction would suffer the further disadvantage of being taxable to *T* on its distribution of the *P* stock under §311(b)(1) (no exception would apply to protect *P* here), supra ¶ 7.21, as a result of amendments to §311 by the Tax Reform Acts of 1984 and 1986.

[461] Rev. Rul. 54-96, 1954-1 CB 111.

than asset acquisitions–Type B reorganization status should prevail on these facts.[462]

The Service may attack the tax-free status of the previous spin-off transaction under the device clause of §355(a)(1)(B), however, and a warning to this effect was contained in Rev. Rul. 58-68.[463] It should be noted that the continuity of interest principle is satisfied in this example, since the shareholders of *T* have an interest in both the unwanted assets (through their ownership of *S*) and the wanted assets (through the *P* stock received in exchange for their *T* stock); hence, one of the basic ingredients for reorganization treatment is present, and perhaps this fact should prevail in determining its status. This is also true in the plan described in Example 3.

3. Current reform proposals. The staff of the Senate Finance Committee, in its final report for the reform of Subchapter C (released on May 20, 1985), proposed to completely overhaul the corporate acquisition rules. These proposals would specifically permit preacquisition tailoring transactions of the type described in this section without violating the substantially all requirement of those proposals (in effect, the *Elkhorn Coal* doctrine would be repealed under the proposed new acquisition regime).[464]

¶ 14.53 AFFILIATED CORPORATIONS: SPECIAL ACQUISITION PROBLEMS AND TECHNIQUES

Reorganization transactions involving affiliated corporations raise certain special problems, the following of which are considered herein: (1) the treatment of upstream and downstream mergers ((i.e., the fusion of a subsidiary into its parent or of a parent into its subsidiary); (2) corporate fissions whereby a parent-subsidiary structure is created; (3) acquisitions of stock or assets of one corporation by another corporation under common control; (4)

---

[462] See Rev. Rul. 70-434, 1970-2 CB 83, approving this type of transaction; see also Rev. Rul. 78-251, 1978-1 CB 89.

[463] But see Rev. Rul. 83-114, 1983-2 CB 66, revoking Rev. Rul. 58-68. Regs. §1.355-2(b)(1) speaks of a "sale or exchange" in connection with a §355 distribution; if this language is interpreted to mean taxable exchanges, the instant transaction would not be vulnerable under the device clause. See Rev. Rul. 55-103, 1955-1 CB 31, applying the device clause to taxable stock sales and relying on the continuity of interest principle to reach this result. But see Rev. Rul. 78-251, 1978-1 CB 89 (acquired parent corporation paid cash to dissenting shareholders in Type B reorganization following spin-off of unwanted subsidiary; held not a device). See Prop. Regs. §1.355-2(c)(2) (1977); see also Rev. Rul. 70-434, 1970-2 CB 83.

[464] See Staff Technical Explanation, 99th Cong., 1st Sess. 224 (1985).

acquisitions of stock or assets where the acquiring corporation already owns part (but not control) of the stock of the acquired corporation (the *Bausch & Lomb* problem[465]); and (5) acquisitions of stock or assets by a subsidiary corporation in exchange for stock of its parent (the *Groman-Bashford* problem[466]).

1. Parent-subsidiary fusions. A statutory merger of an 80-percent owned subsidiary into its parent corporation is controlled by the nonrecognition provisions of §332 (see Chapter 11), which override the reorganization rules to the extent that the two may conflict.[467] This may occur, for example, where the parent has purchased control of the subsidiary in order to obtain its assets and then immediately liquidates (by statutory merger) the newly purchased subsidiary for this purpose. The parent's basis for the assets received from the subsidiary was previously determined under former §334(b)(2), before it was replaced by a §338 in 1982, rather than under the reorganization basis rules of §362(b).[468] Replacement of §334(b)(2) with §338,[469] however, resolved any basis overlap issue here by assuring the par-

---

[465] Bausch & Lomb Optical Co. v. CIR, supra note 135.

[466] Groman v. CIR, supra note 28; Helvering v. Bashford, supra note 29.

[467] See Regs. §1.332-2(d).

[468] This result was reached even before the *Kimbell-Diamond* rule was codified by former §334(b)(2), supra ¶ 11.45. See South Bay Corp. v. CIR, supra note 102. The carry-over rules of §§381 and 382 (infra ch. 16, Parts B and C) are applied differently in certain respects, depending upon whether a transaction is a §332 liquidation under §381(a)(1) or a reorganization under §381(a)(2). But see American Mfg. Co., supra note 70.

Compare American Potash & Chem. Corp. v. US, supra note 56 (buyer could argue for *Kimbell-Diamond* basis even though former §334(b)(2) not applicable and consideration consisted solely of buyers' stock). See supra ¶¶ 14.13 and 11.45; infra note 471.

See also Kansas Sand & Concrete Co., supra note 394 (former §334(b)(2) basis rules preempt §362(b) reorganization basis rules on merger of purchased subsidiary into parent); Madison Square Garden Corp., 58 TC 619 (1972) (former §334(b)(2) basis for assets received for its stock interest; but §362(b) basis for rest of assets received in merger of less than 100 percent owned subsidiary), reversed on the basis question, 500 F2d 611 (2d Cir. 1974) (held that the taxpayer was entitled to a full stepped-up basis for all of the assets); Yoc Heating Corp., supra note 25 (parent's purchase of 85 percent of stock of old subsidiary; old subsidiary transferred assets to new subsidiary; held not a Type F or D reorganization because continuity broken); May B. Kass. supra note 25; Security Indus. Ins. Co. v. US, 702 F2d 1234 (5th Cir. 1983) (cash purchase of stock, liquidation, reincorporation transfer to sister subsidiary not a reorganization; cash purchase killed continuity of interest); Superior Coach of Fla., 80 TC 895 (1983) (same).

[469] Legislation enacted in 1982 (described supra ¶ 11.46) replaced §334(b)(2) with an elective provision, §338, under which the parent could elect to have its

ent a §334(b)(1) carry-over basis on the liquidation of its purchased subsidiary (either stepped up, if §338 is elected, or historic, if it is not). Similarly, the carry-over of the subsidiary's net operating loss would be governed by §381(a)(1), while §382, which is applicable to statutory mergers, would be inapplicable to the liquidation distribution but would, as a result of the Tax Reform Act of 1986 amendments, now apply to the first-step stock purchase transaction (see Chapter 16).[470] Cash purchases of 50 percent (or less) of the stock, followed by an integrated merger of the acquired corporation into the acquiring corporation, however, could also qualify as a Type A reorganization under the Service's continuity of interest guidelines.[471]

The treatment of minority shareholders of the liquidating subsidiary corporation who acquire stock of the parent is less clear.[472] Regs. §1.332-2(d)

---

purchased subsidiary treated as if it had sold its assets and then repurchased those assets (without an actual liquidation occurring).

[470] Moreover, if the liquidation was governed by former §334(b)(2), then §381(a)(1) did not apply, in which event the liquidated subsidiary's tax history disappeared.

However, under legislation enacted in 1982, supra note 469, all actual liquidations under §332 give rise to §334(b)(1) carry-over basis and §381 carry-over of tax history treatment to the extent any tax history of the subsidiary remains (i.e., where §338 is not elected by the purchasing parent).

Before the 1986 Tax Reform Act amendments, §382 was inapplicable to §§332–334(b)(1) liquidations, and applied to the stock purchase transaction only if the subsidiary's business was discontinued; after 1986, however, the mere fact of a more than 50 percent chance of ownership will be enough to trigger application of the §382 limitations; infra ¶ 16.24.

[471] See King Enters., Inc. v. US, supra note 67 (purchase of stock in exchange for cash (49 percent) and stock (51 percent), followed by planned merger into new parent corporation held a Type A reorganization, with boot dividend, to selling shareholders). Where more than 50 but less than 80 percent of the stock is acquired by purchase, continuity of interest requirements are harder to satisfy and reorganization treatment would be unlikely if too large a portion of the consideration consisted of nonequity interests; see cases supra note 468; see also Cannonsburg Skiing Corp., ¶ 86,150 P-H Memo. TC (1986).

See generally Pugh, Combining Acquired and Acquiring Corporations and Their Subsidiaries: Some Anomalies of Form and Substance, 35 Tax L. Rev. 359 (1980); Levin & Bowen, supra note 67; Mopsick, *Yoc Heating Corp.* and Two-Step Asset Acquisitions, 1 J. Corp. Tax'n 235 (1974); Bruce, Liquidations and Reorganizations: *Madison Square Garden* and *Kass*, 30 Tax L. Rev. 303 (1975); Henderson, supra note 67; supra ¶¶ 11.45, 14.11–14.13, and 14.15.

Proposals by the staff of the Senate Finance Committee (supra ¶ 14.21) would treat the acquisition transaction as a stock acquisition if 80 percent stock control was acquired as the first step, regardless of subsequent events.

[472] May B. Kass, supra note 25 (purchase of 80 percent of stock, followed by merger of subsidiary into parent, resulted in taxable liquidation to minority shareholders due to lack of continuity of interest). The court in *Kass* also noted in dictum that old and cold stock held by the parent corporation counts for continuity of inter-

can be interpreted to permit reorganization nonrecognition treatment for them, in tandem with liquidation nonrecognition treatment for the parent under §332. In view of the general preeminence of §332 in the statutory scheme, however, the minority shareholders may have to recognize gain or loss on the liquidation of their stock interests in the subsidiary.[473]

If the merger is downstream however, reorganization treatment is the order of the day. Thus, in *Edwards Motor Transit Co.*, a holding company whose only asset was stock of its 100 percent subsidiary was merged into the subsidiary in a transaction that qualified as a reorganization under §368(a)(1)(A).[474] In several earlier decisions, the Service had unsuccessfully argued that the merger of a parent holding company into its operating subsidiary was the equivalent of a liquidation of the parent, but the courts disagreed.[475] It is understood that the Service rules favorably on a statutory merger of an operating parent into its operating subsidiary. At one time,

---

est purposes; for a contrary Service ruling position, treating such stock as neutral, see Krane, Current Problems in Acquisitive Reorganizations, 51 Taxes 737 (1973); see also supra notes 468 and 471. But the Service now agrees that old and cold stock counts for continuity testing; see Gen. Couns. Mem. 39,404 (Sept. 14, 1985), summarized by Bloom, Private Letter Rulings, 13 J. Corp. Tax'n 73 (1986); see also Baline, New Opportunities, 65 J. Tax'n 138 (1986).

[473] See generally Seplow, Acquisition of Assets of a Subsidiary: Liquidation or Reorganization, 73 Harv. L. Rev. 484, 511 (1960); MacLean, "Creeping Acquisitions," 21 Tax L. Rev. 345, 357 (1966) (contra).

But see Performance Sys., Inc. v. US, supra note 272 (upstream merger of 100 percent subsidiary into parent held valid Type F reorganization; parent's stock old and cold; §332 and reorganization rules can be applied in tandem); accord Movielab, Inc. v. US, supra note 272; Eastern Color Printing Co., supra note 271; Rev. Rul. 75-561, 1975-2 CB 129 (agrees with cases that parent-subsidiary fusions via merger also a Type F reorganization). Compare Cannonsburg Skiing Corp., supra note 471 (no Type F if integrated cash purchase of subsidiary stock); and 1982 amendments limiting Type F to single operating company, supra ¶ 14.18, note 257.

See also Casco Prods. Corp., supra note 261; American Mfg. Co., supra note 70; compare Aetna Cas. & Surety Co. v. US, supra note 47.

In Rev. Rul. 69-617, 1969-2 CB 57, the merger of a less than 100 percent (but more than 80 percent) subsidiary into its parent, followed by a transfer of the old subsidiary's assets to a new 100 percent owned subsidiary, was held to constitute a tax-free Type A reorganization to *all* parties (including the minority shareholders). Apparently, the planned reincorporation of the assets in the new subsidiary prevented liquidation treatment to the minority shareholders.

[474] Edwards Motor Transit Co., ¶ 64,317 P-H Memo. TC (1964).

[475] See H. Grady Manning Trust, 15 TC 930 (1950) (nonacq.); CIR v. Estate of Gilmore, 130 F2d 791 (3d Cir. 1942); CIR v. Estate of Webster, 131 F2d 426 (5th Cir. 1942); see also Isidor Kahn, 36 BTA 954 (1937), aff'd per curiam sub nom. Helvering v. Einhorn, 100 F2d 418 (2d Cir. 1938); CIR v. Kann, 130 F2d 797 (3d Cir. 1942).

See generally Stuetzer & Bergen, Upstairs and Downstairs Mergers, 10 NYU Inst. on Fed. Tax'n 1267 (1952); Cohn, Downstairs Mergers, 7 NYU Inst. on Fed.

however, the Service would not rule in a case where the parent owned less than 80 percent of the subsidiary's stock, which was its only asset, presumably on the theory that the effect of the merger was a mere liquidation of the parent, but recently the Service has indicated in Rev. Rul. 78-47[476] that even here a true reorganization can occur.[477] Moreover, in Rev. Rul. 57-465, the Service approved nondivisive Type D reorganization treatment for the merger of a parent holding company into its wholly owned subsidiary where the subsidiary's stock constituted over one-half of the parent's assets.[478]

This judicial willingness to see the reorganization provisions take precedence over the liquidation rules in the case of downstream mergers operates as an appropriate inducement to the simplification of corporate structures, a policy similar to that that inspired the enactment of §332. As to upstream mergers, §332 itself provides tax-free treatment to an 80 percent parent corporation. Thus, the elimination of an unnecessary tier of corporations can be accomplished on a tax-free basis whether it is the parent or the subsidiary that is marked for extinction.

2. Parent-subsidiary fission. Creation of a parent-subsidiary structure can most easily be effected by transferring assets to a new controlled corporation pursuant to §351 (see Chapter 3), subject to the restrictions on creation of multiple corporations discussed in Chapter 15. On occasion, however, the parties' ancestral needs are more intricate. For example, a

---

Tax'n 1202 (1949); Piper, Combining Parent and Subsidiary Corporations, 16 NYU Inst. on Fed. Tax'n 375 (1958).

[476] Rev. Rul. 78-47, 1978-1 CB 113.

[477] See Rev. Rul. 78-47, 1978-1 CB 113 (fusion of holding company into 5 percent owned subsidiary was valid Type C reorganization even though subsidiary's stock constituted 71 percent of parent's properties; substantially all test satisfied by assets other than subsidiary's stock).

[478] See Rev. Rul. 57-465, 1957-2 CB 250, citing Helvering v. Leary, 93 F2d 826 (4th Cir. 1938), and Schoellkopf v. Helvering, 100 F2d 415 (2d Cir. 1938), which similarly applied the Type D reorganization provisions to downstream merger patterns; see also New York Fruit Auction Corp., 79 TC 564 (1982) (no basis step-up for subsidiary assets on downstream merger of parent into subsidiary after purchase of subsidiary stock; but §338, supra ¶ 11.46, solves this blunder after 1982).

In approving reorganization treatment, Rev. Rul. 57-465 emphasized the nondivisive character of the transaction, although it appeared to be troubled by the substantially all requirement of §354(b)(1)(A) in view of the fact that the parent's principal asset was the subsidiary's stock, which was acquired by the latter for cancellation rather than as an asset. See also Rev. Rul. 78-47, 1978-1 CB 113; Rev. Rul. 70-223, 1970-1 CB 79 (downstream merger of parent into subsidiary was a reorganization even though form was adopted to avoid recapture of income to subsidiary had it been liquidated into parent in a former §334(b)(2) liquidation, supra ¶ 11.45); Rev. Rul. 78-287, 1978-2 CB 146 (downstream merger as Type F reorganization).

corporation may seek to create an intervening parent holding company between itself and its shareholders in order to facilitate acquisition or diversification programs, to preserve its legal existence so as to retain franchise and contract rights, to escape regulation problems, and so forth. This modern corporate version of subinfeudation, by the creation of instant ancestry, can be effected by either of the following alternative routes (among others): [479]

(1) *T* Corporation creates a subsidiary, *P*, which in turn creates a second-tier subsidiary, *S*. *T* then merges into *S* in exchange for stock of *P* in a triangular merger, with the result that *S* now holds *T*'s operating assets, *P* holds all the stock of *S*—that is, *P* is *S*'s parent—and *T*'s former shareholders hold stock of *P* instead of *T*, *T* having dissolved. [480]

(2) *T* causes the creation of new corporation *P*, which then acquires all the stock of *T* from *T*'s shareholders in exchange for *P* stock either in a Type B reorganization or in a §351 transaction (or both), with the result that *T* is now a wholly owned subsidiary of *P*, and *T*'s former shareholders own stock of *P* in lieu of their *T* stock. [481]

3. Brother-sister acquisitions. If both the acquired corporation and the acquiring corporation are owned by the same shareholders in the same proportions, it is difficult to *avoid* reorganization treatment where assets or stock of one such corporation are acquired by the other. It is possible, however, that the transaction could be classified as a redemption of stock of a related corporation under §304 (e.g., if stock is acquired for stock and bonds of the acquiring corporation) (see Chapter 9), or that the net effect of the transaction would be substantially the same as the distribution of a dividend under *Bazley*[482] (e.g., if assets of one related corporation are acquired for stock and

---

[479] The illustrations of the parent-subsidiary fission technique described in the text were not intended to indicate that those two methods were the exclusive routes to such end; for example, the reverse merger technique of §368(a)(2)(E) can also be used for this purpose; supra ¶ 14.15.

[480] See Rev. Rul. 77-428, 1977-2 CB 118, approving such a transaction; see also Rev. Rul. 78-397, 1978-2 CB 150 (circular cash flow in §368(a)(2)(D) merger disregarded as transitory step).

[481] See generally Levin, The New Subsidiary-Merger Statute and Other Current Tax Problems in Acquisitions, 47 Taxes 779 (1969). See also Rev. Rul. 70-433, 1970-1 CB 82; Rev. Rul. 72-274, 1972-1 CB 97 (creation of new parent holding company did not change the affiliated group for purposes of the §243 100 percent dividends-received deduction); Rev. Rul. 77-428, 1977-2 CB 118.

For an example of parent-subsidiary fission via the §351 route, see Rev. Rul. 74-502, 1974-2 CB 116.

[482] Bazley v. CIR, supra note 5.

bonds of the other related corporation). (These matters are closely related to the liquidation-reincorporation area, discussed in the next section.)

A corporation can acquire its sibling in a variety of tax-free transactions. For example, if it is merged into its affiliate pursuant to a state merger law, the transaction constitutes a Type A reorganization. The Tax Court, in *Norman Scott, Inc.*, held that such a transaction constituted a tax-free Type A reorganization even where the acquired brother corporation was insolvent and where shareholders of the absorbed corporation was also creditors of that corporation (so that stock received by them in the exchange was obtained in their capacity as creditors, rather than as stockholders).[483]

Where the transfer took the form of a Type C reorganization, classification under §368(a)(1)(C) depended upon what the transferor corporation did with the transferee's stock received in the exchange. If the transferor liquidated and distributed this stock to its shareholders in a transaction covered by §354(b) (as it must after 1984 by virtue of §368(a)(2)(G)), then the transaction is classified as a Type D reorganization under the preemption rules of §368(a)(2)(A)—that is, where a reorganization is described in both subsections (C) and (D) of §368(a)(1), the Type D reorganization rules take precedence. If, on the other hand, the transferor does not distribute the transferee's stock under §354, the transaction will not qualify as a Type C reorganization after 1984; nor does it constitute a Type D reorganization (since there has been no distribution of stock as is required by §354(b)(1)(B)).[484] (As discussed in the next section, however, the liquidation-reincorporation doctrine can apply to such a transaction.)

The acquisition of stock of a brother corporation by a sister corporation solely in exchange for voting stock of the latter could constitute a Type B reorganization if, immediately after the exchange, the sister corporation is in control of its former sibling (in effect, this transaction would change the family relationship from brother-sister to parent-subsidiary). Accordingly, the exchanging shareholders would not recognize gain or loss on their

---

[483] Norman Scott, Inc., supra note 33. But compare Superior Coach of Fla., Inc., supra note 468 (stock purchase by shareholder of acquiring corporation, followed by merger of target into aquiring corporation not a reorganization; continuity killed by stock purchase step). See supra ¶ 14.12.

[484] In Rev. Rul. 69-413, 1969-2 CB 55, a transfer of assets by a 99 percent subsidiary to a new 100 percent subsidiary solely for voting stock of the parent could not constitute a triangular Type F reorganization (even though it was a valid triangular Type C) because the parent was not a party to a Type F reorganization under §368(b); see also Rev. Rul. 74-545 and Rev. Rul. 76-188, 1976-1 CB 99 (overlap of Type C and Type D); Rev. Rul. 75-383, 1975-2 CB 127; Rev. Rul. 78-130, 1978-1 CB 114.

But see Aetna Cas. & Surety Co. v. US, supra note 47; Bogaard, Corporate Reorganizations, 4 J. Corp. Tax'n 251 (1977), which seems to undercut Rev. Rul. 69-413.

respective exchanges by virtue of §354(a), and the acquiring corporation would obtain an inherited basis for the stock of its new subsidiary under §362(b). Moreover, in the event of a later (unrelated) liquidation of this subsidiary, §332 would apply to prevent recognition of gain or loss to the parent, and the carry-over basis rules of §334(b)(1) would apply, since the stock was not acquired by purchase within the meaning of §338(h)(3). This technique could be useful in shifting loss carry-overs or other favorable tax attributes of the brother corporation to the acquiring sister corporation without running the gauntlet of §§269 and 382 (even after its amendment by the Tax Reform Act of 1986), whether or not the two steps—acquisition of the stock and the subsequent liquidation—are treated as separate. Even if the steps are collapsed, as the Service has indicated they would be if effected pursuant to a unitary plan, so that the transaction would be treated as an asset acquisition, neither §382 nor §269 would apply because of the common control exception to these provisions.[485]

If the sister corporation has less than 80 percent control of its affiliate after the exchange of stock, §368(a)(1)(B) will not apply and the transaction will be fully taxable to the exchanging stockholders (although §1032 will still protect the acquiring corporation from recognition of gain). Even more important, however, §304 would not apply to such gain or loss because that provision requires a distribution of property by the acquiring corporation, and §317(a) states that a corporation's own stock does not constitute property for this purpose. Thus, the antibailout defenses of §304 can be circumvented by using stock of the less-than-controlling sister corporation as the consideration for the exchange rather than cash or debt. Most attractive for this purpose would be nonvoting preferred stock, which, because issued in a fully taxable transaction, would not constitute "section 306 stock" and hence could be readily sold to outsiders without further gain or loss or dilution of the insiders' control. This constitutes a variation on the classic stock dividend bailout device (now largely interdicted by §306), the major difference arising from the fact that the stockholders take their capital gain at the first stage of the transaction rather than later when the distributed stock is sold to outsiders.[486]

The absorption of one commonly controlled corporation by its affiliate may also resemble a Type F reorganization (i.e., a mere change in identity, form, or place of incorporation). As noted earlier, the Service has taken this position and courts have agreed.[487] (However, proposals by the staff of the

---

[485] See supra ¶ 14.13; infra ¶¶ 16.21, 16.23, 16.24, and 16.25.

[486] See supra ¶ 9.12.

[487] Home Constr. Corp. v. US, supra note 272 (merger of 123 affiliated corporations was Type F reorganization where identity of shareholder ownership and business continuity existed); accord, Rev. Rul. 75-561, 1975-2 CB 129 (revoking Rev.

Senate Finance Committee would treat all brother-sister fusion acquisitions as mandatory carry-over basis transactions, regardless of the form of the consideration or the structure of the acquisition.)

4. Acquisition of assets of a partially controlled subsidiary: The *Bausch & Lomb* case. In *Bausch & Lomb Optical Co. v. CIR*, the taxpayer owned 79 percent of the stock of a subsidiary corporation.[488] In order to acquire its assets, the taxpayer issued its stock in exchange for all the assets; the subsidiary then liquidated, distributing the parent's stock pro rata to all of its shareholders. The outside shareholders of the subsidiary thus became minority shareholders of the parent. The various steps were held to constitute a single plan having the effect of a taxable liquidation (to the extent of the assets received in exchange for the parent's 79 percent stock interest), rather than a tax-free Type C reorganization, on the theory that the assets were acquired by the taxpayer in consideration for its stock of the subsidiary rather than in exchange for its own voting stock, as required by §368(a)(1)(C).[489] (With the repeal of §§336 and 337 nonrecognition by the Tax Reform Act of 1986, *Bausch & Lomb* will also affect the liquidating

---

Rul. 69-185, 1969-1 CB 108); see also TFI Cos. v. US, supra note 272. But the Tax Equity and Fiscal Responsibility Act amendments to the Type F definition go back to the Rev. Rul. 69-185 rule and overrule Rev. Rul. 75-561, supra ¶ 14.18 (where at least two operating affiliates are involved).

[488] Bausch & Lomb Optical Co. v. CIR, supra note 135.

[489] For a similar result under the 1954 Code, see Grede Foundries, Inc. v. US, supra note 135; see also supra notes 471 and 473.

See generally discussions by Seplow and MacLean, supra note 473. See also articles by Henderson, Levin & Bowen, Bruce, and Mopsick, supra note 67.

Although the various opinions in the *Bausch & Lomb* case are unclear, it would seem that the parent corporation would have been entitled to nonrecognition treatment under §1032 with respect to that portion of the subsidiary's assets acquired in exchange for the parent's own stock (i.e., the 21 percent minority interest portion). Moreover, the transferor subsidiary presumably would have been entitled to nonrecognition treatment under former §336 with respect to that portion of its assets distributed to the parent in liquidation. On the other hand, that portion of the subsidiary's assets transferred to the parent for the latter's voting stock might be treated as a taxable transaction, since no nonrecognition rule applies to this portion of the transfer, unless it could be claimed that former §337 (supra ¶ 11.61), before its repeal by the Tax Reform Act of 1986, applied to such gain. However, this aspect of the transaction may merely be viewed as a non-pro rata liquidation distribution by the subsidiary, in which event it would be protected from recognition of gain or loss by the former general rule of 1954 Code §336 (supra ¶ 11.06), before its repeal by the Tax Reform Act of 1986.

Although the nonrecognition rules of §§336 and 337 were generally repealed by the Tax Reform Act of 1986, supra ¶ 11.06, nonrecognition treatment for the liquidating subsidiary corporation continues to apply under newly relabeled §337 for distributions to its controlling parent pursuant to liquidations under §§332 and 334(b),

subsidiary, triggering taxable gain to that corporation as well, unless §§332 and 337 apply, as discussed in Chapter 11.)

The opinion, which is brief and cryptic, may have been based on the continuity of interest principle, in that the parent's former stock investment in its subsidiary was extinguished by these transactions. On the other hand, it is difficult to envision how the taxpayer's interest in its subsidiary's assets could have risen to a much higher level: It now owned directly that that it formerly owned indirectly through its stock interest in the subsidiary, although, to be sure, this is also the consequence of a complete liquidation. In any event, the *Bausch & Lomb* decision restricts use of a Type C reorganization where the acquiring corporation already owns part of the stock of the corporation whose assets are to be acquired.

There are, however, several possible variations on the *Bausch & Lomb* pattern that should be noted:

(1) If the transferor corporation had remained alive for business reasons, the acquisition of its assets would have been solely in exchange for voting stock of the acquiring corporation, as required by §368(a)(1)(C).[490] Hence, the transferor and the transferee would have obtained nonrecognition treatment on the exchange by virtue of §§361 and 1032, respectively.[491] This escape, however, is no longer available after 1984 amendments in §368(a)(2)(G) requiring the transferor to liquidate.

(2) If the parent in *Bausch & Lomb* had at least 80 percent control of the subsidiary, its acquisition of all the latter's assets in exchange for its own stock would have been tax-free under §§332 (as to the assets acquired in liquidation) and 1032 (as to the assets acquired for its own stock). As to the subsidiary, it might be viewed as having sold 20 percent of its assets to the parent for the latter's stock in a taxable transaction (unless the pre-1986 version of §337, before

---

supra ¶ 11.49. But distributions to minority shareholders are taxable under new §337, while losses on such distributions are not deductible under §336(d)(3), supra ¶ 11.49.

[490] But see §368(a)(2)(G) added by the Tax Reform Act of 1984, supra note 114 (transferor must completely liquidate in a Type C, unless waived by Service).

[491] For the former use of 1954 Code §311(a) and former §311(d)(2)(A) (before their amendments in 1982, 1984, and 1986) to effect tax-free exchanges of their respective stock interests, see Rev. Rul. 79-314, 1979-2 CB 132; see also Rev. Rul. 80-101, 1980-1 CB 70 (applying principle of Rev. Rul. 79-314 to situation where one of exchanging corporations was completely liquidated; *X* owned 70 percent of *Y* and *Y* owned 25 percent of *X*; on complete liquidation of *Y*, held that §§311(a)(2) and 311(d)(2)(A) applied to portion of *X* stock received back by *X* on *Y*'s liquidation). But see supra ¶ 9.34 for amendments to §311 by the Tax Equity and Fiscal Responsibility Act of 1982, which overrule these rulings. Moreover, the Tax Reform Act of 1984 further contracted §311(d), and the Tax Reform Act of 1986 eliminated it completely.

its repeal, applied[492]) and as having distributed the rest of its assets (to the parent) and the parent's stock (to the outside shareholders) in a distribution that generated neither gain nor loss under §336 (under new §337, such a distribution continues to be tax-free, even after the 1986 amendments) for subsidiary distributions to its controlling parent under §332. Alternately, the subsidiary may claim full protection under §336 (now relabeled as §337 by the Tax Reform Act of 1986) on a non-pro rata liquidation theory.[493] The minority shareholders would presumably have to recognize their gain or loss on exchanging their stock in the subsidiary for stock in the parent unless they are protected by Regs. §1.332-2(d),[494] and the subsidiary now will recognize gain (but not loss) on distributions to the minority shareholders under revised §§337(a) and 336(d)(3).

(3) If the acquiring corporation owned 20 percent or less of the acquired corporation's stock, the boot relaxation rules of §368(a)(2)(B) would come to the rescue and permit the transaction to qualify as a Type C reorganization, provided the 20 percent limit on the use of boot in such transaction was not exceeded by virtue of an assumption of liabilities. All the parties would then obtain nonrecognition treatment on their exchanges, except that the acquiring corporation would recognize gain or loss under §§331 and 1001(c) on its exchange of its stock in the acquired corporation for the assets attributable thereto.[495]

---

[492] Supra note 489. But see former 1954 Code §337(c)(2)(A), and supra ¶ 11.61. However, §337 was repealed by the Tax Reform Act of 1986, supra ¶ 11.61.

[493] Under the 1986 amendments repealing §336, however, the subsidiary has recognized gain (but no loss) on actual distributions to the minority shareholders. But newly revised §337 provides for nonrecognition to the subsidiary to the extent it distributes property to its parent in a §§332–334(b) liquidation. see supra ¶¶ 11.06 and 11.49.

[494] See discussion at notes 472 and 473. But see Rev. Rul. 69-617, 1969-2 CB 57. While liquidation of an 80 percent subsidiary did not afford §337 protection to the subsidiary if §332 applied, minority shareholders could get the credit provided by former §337(d); moreover, §337 was repealed by the Tax Reform Act of 1986; supra ¶ 11.61.

See also former §337(c)(3), as amended in 1976 and 1978, allowing subsidiary's use of §337 if parent is also liquidated within the 12-month period of the subsidiary's plan; supra ¶ 11.61.

However, under the Tax Reform Act of 1986 rules, the subsidiary would be protected from recognition on distribution to its parent, but not to its minority shareholders.

[495] The parent's basis for the acquired assets is a §362(b) carry-over basis without any increase for gain recognized to it on the transaction under Rev. Rul. 72-327, 1972-2 CB 197; the subsidiary's nonrecognition rule presumably would be the boot distribution provision of former §361(b)(1)(A), although possibly 1954 Code §337

(4) It is understood that the Service will permit the acquiring corporation in a *Bausch & Lomb* situation to sterilize its stock in the subsidiary (if such interest is a relatively minor one),[496] by transferring it to another subsidiary, in which event the acquiring corporation will obtain all of the acquired corporation's assets in exchange for its voting stock; on the acquired corporation's liquidation, the parent's stock will go partly to its other subsidiary and partly to the outside shareholders of the acquired corporation.

Granting that the *Bausch & Lomb* decision largely interdicts use of the Type C reorganization to effect a "creeping acquisition" of stock *and* assets of the acquired corporation, it is relatively clear that the stock alone could be acquired in a creeping Type B reorganization.[497] Thus, a stock-for-stock exchange between the acquiring corporation and the other shareholders of the acquired corporation could qualify as a Type B reorganization, even though the acquiring corporation already owned part of the stock of the corporation to be acquired.[498] A prompt liquidation of the acquired corporation, however, would render the transaction vulnerable under the *Bausch &*

(before its repeal by the Tax Reform Act of 1986) might apply to the 20 percent segment. But cf. FEC Liquidating Corp. v. US, supra note 333; General Housewares Corp. v. US, supra note 333.

Although amendments to §361 by the Tax Reform Act of 1986 (supra ¶ 14.32, para. 2) provide generally for no gain recognition under §361(a) and also preempt §§336 and 337 in §361(b)(1), if the distribution to the 20 percent parent is deemed to be a liquidating distribution under *Bausch & Lomb*, new §361(c) could tax the subsidiary on gain (but not loss) with respect to that part of the transaction.

[496] See Rev. Rul. 68-526, 1968-2 CB 156 (valid Type C reorganization where unrelated operating corporation acquired all assets of parent and its 60 percent subsidiary corporation in a single exchange, after which the transferor corporations were liquidated; *Bausch & Lomb* not applicable because acquiring corporation owned no stock of acquired corporations prior to transaction).

[497] See discussion supra ¶ 14.13.

[498] But see Rev. Rul. 69-294, 1969-1 CB 110 (plan whereby parent acquired all of the stock of a second-tier subsidiary, 80 percent of whose stock was owned by its 100 percent owned first-tier subsidiary, by liquidating the first-tier subsidiary under §332 and then exchanging its own stock for the stock held by the 20 percent minority shareholders did not constitute a Type B reorganization because parent acquired the 80 percent stock interest of second-tier subsidiary in a liquidation exchange rather than in exchange for its own stock).

In Rev. Rul. 69-585, 1969-2 CB 56, however, the Service found a valid Type B reorganization where 75 percent of the stock was acquired solely for voting stock and the other 25 percent was acquired as a dividend in kind from the acquiring corporation's 100 percent subsidiary.

Compare Rev. Rul. 73-28, 1973-1 CB 187 (parent's acquisition of all the stock of a second-tier subsidiary from first-tier subsidiary in exchange for parent's stock held a valid Type B reorganization; parent's basis §362(b); subsidiary's basis §358(a)); and Rev. Rul. 74-35, 1974-1 CB 85 (stock for stock acquisition, followed by dividend

Lomb case. Accordingly, if the Type B reorganization technique is adopted, the newly acquired subsidiary must be kept alive for a decent interval to avoid step-transaction arguments.

The Service has also approved statutory merger acquisitions in the *Bausch & Lomb* situation,[499] a result implied in the Second Circuit opinion in the *Bausch & Lomb* case.[500] In addition, the Service has ruled that *Bausch & Lomb* does not apply if the acquired assets end up in a controlled subsidiary of the acquiring corporation. In this ruling, the acquiring corporation first transferred its own stock to a newly created subsidiary, which then acquired the assets in exchange for such stock; the acquired corporation was then liquidated. The theory of the ruling was that the same result could have been accomplished by use of a Type B reorganization and that no difference in tax should occur where the method adopted had, in substance, the same effect.[501] Thus, the *Bausch & Lomb* case has been limited to those situations where the ultimate transferee of the acquired assets obtains some of them through a liquidation rather than in exchange for its own stock. So limited and distinguished, the case now is mainly a trap for the uninformed; for the well-advised taxpayer, the exceptions have nearly supplanted the general rule,[502] a result that will confer tax-free treatment to both sides of the transaction, even after 1986 amendments.

Assuming that assets of a corporation cannot be acquired tax-free in exchange for stock of the transferor already held by the acquiring corporation (unless §332 applies), one would instinctively assume that if the acquir-

---

distribution of unneeded investment assets (30 percent of total) still essentially a stock acquisition because 70 percent of properties remained in corporate solution).

[499] Rev. Rul. 58-93, 1958-1 CB 188; see also Rev. Rul. 85-107, 1985-2 CB 107 (Type D reorganization not subject to *Bausch & Lomb*).

[500] See Point to Remember No. 10, 25 Tax Lawyer 571 (1972) (in merger of more than 50 percent, but less than 80 percent, owned subsidiary into parent. Service requires, for a favorable ruling, that minority shareholder group acquire stock of the parent equal to 50 percent of their former minority interest; if they fail to obtain this amount, the Service will decline to rule). But see supra notes 471, 472, and 473; Rev. Rul. 78-47, 1978-1 CB 113.

[501] See Rev. Rul. 57-278, 1957-1 CB 124. As to the status of Type A , B, and C triangular acquisitions, see supra ¶¶ 14.13–14.15. The technique approved in the ruling has a result similar to that achieved by Example (4) in the text. But see Rev. Rul. 69-48, supra note 136 (Rev. Rul. 57-278 does not apply where initial stock purchase transaction is merely a step in unitary reorganization plan because it would not have qualified as a Type B reorganization); Rev. Rul. 85-138, 1985-2 CB 122 (extending theory of Rev. Rul. 69-48 to payments by sister subsidiary on behalf of acquiring brother corporation); Rev. Rul. 72-354, 1972-2 CB 216 (parent can purge itself of tainted stock by unconditional sale to an unrelated buyer prior to the shareholder vote on the plan of reorganization); C.E. Graham Reeves, supra note 46.

[502] See also Rev. Rul. 85-107, 1985-2 CB 107 (*Bausch & Lomb* not applicable to Type D definition because no reference to solely for voting stock).

ing corporation obtains part of the transferor's assets in its capacity as a *creditor* of the transferor, similar taxable results would follow. Yet in this situation, two decisions of the Tax Court[503] have held that the liability assumption rules of §§357 (a) and 368(a)(1)(C) prevent recognition of gain to the transferor corporation (and presumably to the transferee as well), notwithstanding the fact that the assumed liabilities were owed to the acquiring corporation and were, in effect, canceled in the acquisition transaction. If *Bausch & Lomb* is based on continuity of interest principles, we are left with the unusual result that a receipt of property in exchange for the assumption and cancellation of debt obligations (i.e., a quasi-cash consideration) gives a superior nonrecognition result to that involving a receipt in exchange for voting stock, just the converse of what ordinarily passes for the continuity of interest requirement.[504]

5. *Groman-Bashford* **triangular acquisitions: Special problems.** As noted earlier, the *Groman* and *Bashford* decisions[505] (which held that stock of the acquiring corporation's parent company did not carry the requisite continuity of interest "genes") have been gradually modified by Congress over the course of the years.[506] The continuing problem with split consideration

---

[503] See Arthur L. Kniffen, 39 TC 553 (1962) (acq.); Edwards Motor Transit Co., supra note 474. But see Rev. Rul. 70-271, 1970-1 CB 166; Rev. Rul. 72-464, 1972-2 CB 214 (gain recognized to creditor).

[504] See supra ¶ 14.11 and infra ¶ 14.55. But see Rev. Rul. 72-464, 1972-2 CB 214. The Service apparently views *Bausch & Lomb* as a boot problem; see Rev. Rul. 85-107, 1985-2 CB 107.

But the Senate Finance Committee staff's final report on the reform of Subchapter C apparently perpetuates the *Bausch & Lomb* concept in proposed §364(c)(3) (defining qualified asset acquisitions by excluding assets acquired in a distribution).

[505] Groman v. CIR, supra note 28; Helvering v. Bashford, supra note 29.

[506] See Rev. Rul. 69-413, 1969-2 CB 55; see also Rev. Rul. 69-265, 1969-1 CB 109; supra ¶ 14.31, para. 3; Rev. Rul. 72-576, 1972-2 CB 217 (§368(a)(2)(D) triangular merger into subsidiary for stock of parent not spoiled by planned drop down into second-tier subsidiary because §368(a)(2)(C) protects second phase of transaction). But see Aetna Cas. & Surety Co. v. US, supra note 47; Bogaard, supra note 484.

See also Rev. Rul. 77-449, 1977-2 CB 110 (successive §351 dropdowns per single plan held separate tax-free §351 transactions despite plan to pass assets to second-tier subsidiary); Rev. Rul. 83-34, 1983-1 CB 79 (same where first- and second-tier subsidiaries only 80 percent owned); Rev. Rul. 84-30, 1984-1 CB 114 (continuity not violated when stock of acquiring corporation passed upstream to target's grandparent).

See generally N.Y. State Bar Association, Tax Section, Report on the Ancillary Tax Effects of Different Forms of Reorganizations, 34 Tax L. Rev. 477, 519 (1979); Murray, How to Avoid Loss of Continuity of Interest Through Stock Remoteness in a Reorganization, 59 J. Tax'n 8 (1983); Murray, IRS Revocation of "Stock Remoteness" Posture May Have Positive Effect on Reorganizations, 60 J. Tax'n 352 (1984).

acquisitions (i.e., where stock of *both* the parent *and* the subsidiary is used) has already been pointed out, however, and attention must also be given to the effect of these cases on the status of acquisitions in which the stock of more remote corporations in a chain are used.

For example, the parent's stock may be used as consideration for a transfer of the assets of the acquired corporation to a sub-subsidiary of the parent or the assets may be acquired by a subsidiary and then transferred to a sub-subsidiary. Such acquisitions of the assets by a second-tier subsidiary presumably were approved as valid Type C reorganizations by the Service in Rev. Rul. 64-73, where both subsidiaries were 100 percent controlled by their respective parents.[507] The ruling stated that its conclusion was influenced by Congress' desire to remove the *Groman* and *Bashford* continuity of interest problem from the Type C reorganization area.

Whether this ruling would apply to a triangular Type B reorganization under the similar anti-*Groman* amendment in 1964 (in which event there would be four tiers of corporations) remains to be seen;[508] judgment must also be reserved on such acquisitions where the parent owns less than 100 percent of the subsidiary and/or the latter owns less than 100 percent of the sub-subsidiary. There seems little reason to object on continuity of interest grounds to acquisitions by remote subsidiaries if there is 100 percent affiliation with the parent; but if the stock ownership at each level is less than complete, there will be a gradual thinning of interest as additional tiers are added. Perhaps the 80 percent benchmark that is so widely used as a standard in the corporate nonrecognition provisions will prove useful in applying the anti-*Groman* rules to these situations.

Another problem in this area was the possible overlap between the Types A and C reorganization provisions. Many states permit a subsidiary to consummate a statutory merger with another corporation through use of its parent's stock. If this transaction constitutes a reorganization under §368(a)(1)(A), there is greater leeway in the type of consideration that can be paid by the acquiring corporation than in a Type C transaction.

The Service initially ruled that *Groman-Bashford* principles prevented effective use of the Type A provisions in this situation,[509] but Congress amended the statute in 1968[510] to provide for a special category of subsidi-

---

[507] Rev. Rul. 64-73, 1964-1 CB 142.

[508] See Rev. Rul. 74-564, 1974-2 CB 124; Rev. Rul. 74-565, 1974-2 CB 125; see also Rev. Rul. 77-449, 1977-2 CB 110; Rev. Rul. 83-34, 1983-1 CB 79; and Rev. Rul. 84-30, 1984-1 CB 114.

[509] See Rev. Rul 67-326, 1967-2 CB 143 (acquisition of assets for stock of parent by state law merger held not a Type A reorganization, so no nonrecognition per §361 or §354 because parent not a party; but will be acceptable if qualified as a Type C reorganization).

[510] Section 368(a)(2)(D).

ary-merger that generally permitted Type A reorganization treatment for a merger into a controlled subsidiary of the parent if no stock of the subsidiary is used. Reverse mergers (where a subsidiary is created by a contribution to capital of stock of the parent and then merged into the corporation to be acquired) had to satisfy the solely for voting stock requirements of §368(a)(1)(B), however,[511] since this form of acquisition, according to the Service, constituted a constructive Type B reorganization; but the statute again was modified (in 1971) by §368(a)(2)(E), which created yet another special category of subsidiary merger and conferred Type A treatment on such transactions if the special conditions of that provision are satisfied.[512]

As noted in Part C, 1968 amendments to §§358(e) and 362(b) clarified a technical gap in the statute relating to the basis of property acquired in a *Groman* triangular Type B reorganization (i.e., basis carries over from the transferors); it was also noted there that the acquiring corporation in a *Groman* reorganization does not recognize gain or loss when it pays for property with its parent's stock, despite the technical nonapplication of §1032. The Service apparently views these transactions either as if the parent paid the consideration on behalf of its subsidiary (thereby making a tax-free capital contribution to it), or as if the parent had acquired the property directly and then dropped the assets into the controlled subsidiary, which also is nontaxable.

If the transaction does not qualify as a reorganization, however, matters are less clear on these points.[513] For example, if the transaction was a taxable triangular asset acquisition, could the selling corporation obtain protection under former §337, before its repeal in 1986, even though the amount of parent stock received in exchange for the assets constituted 50 percent of its outstanding stock (but less than 80 percent, so that §368(c) control was not present)? The Service might assert reorganization treatment in this case because of the high continuity of interest maintained by the sellers in the buyer corporation[514] even though a technical reorganization is lacking.

---

[511] Rev. Rul. 67-448, 1967-2 CB 144.

[512] These matters are considered supra ¶ 14.15. See Rev. Rul. 74-564, 1974-2 CB 124; Rev. Rul. 74-565, 1974-2 CB 125.

[513] See Committee on Corporate Taxation, supra note 347; Comment, The Zero Basis Dilemma in Nonqualifying Triangular Acquisitions, 41 U. Chi. L. Rev. 92 (1973); Rev. Rul. 74-503, 1974-2 CB 117.

But see Prop. Regs. §1.358-6 (parent's basis in subsidiary's stock after triangular asset or stock reorganization; generally treat as if a direct acquisition by parent followed by drop down), and Prop. Regs. §1.1032-2 (extension of §1032 nonrecognition to subsidiary in triangular reorganizations). See supra ¶ 14.33, paras. 1 and 4.

[514] See the "reincorporation" discussion, infra ¶ 14.54. But repeal of §337 by the Tax Reform Act of 1986 would make such an assertion unlikely in view of full taxability to the transferor on the transaction; supra ¶ 11.61.

On the buyer-subsidiary's side, the transaction could result in taxable gain or loss to it (unless §1032 applies, which would not technically be true if stock of the *parent* is used as the consideration), in which event the subsidiary's basis for its parent's stock becomes crucial. If the parent's stock is contributed by it to the subsidiary, §362(a) apparently would provide for a carry-over basis from the parent; if the subsidiary purchases the parent's stock on the open market, using its own funds, the basis would be its cost under §1012.[515] Is the parent entitled to nonrecognition under §351 (see Chapter 3) when it transfers its own stock (either newly issued or treasury stock) to the subsidiary in exchange for stock of the subsidiary or as a capital contribution? Apparently so, although the property status of unissued stock may be questioned.

If stock, rather than assets, is acquired in a taxable triangular transaction, can the acquiring corporation use §338 to step up the basis of the assets of the acquired corporation (see Chapter 11), or does the acquisition fail to satisfy the purchase requirements of §338(h)(3), in which event basis would carry over to the transferee under §334(b)(1) on a liquidation of its newly acquired subsidiary? It would seem that §338 could be used by the buyer corporation here (whether or not it recognizes gain or loss on the acquisition of the stock), since no carry-over basis rule would apply because the transaction would not constitute a reorganization and §338(h)(3)(A) thus would not be violated.[516]

Much of the above remains to be fully clarified, however, and few published rulings or cases have focused precisely on these issues.[517]

----

[515] See Rev. Rul. 80-189, 1980-2 CB 106 (subsidiary gets cost basis on purchase of parent's stock from parent's shareholders in §304(a)(2) transaction).

Compare ITT & Cos., 77 TC 60 (1981), aff'd per curiam, 704 F2d 252 (2d Cir. 1983) (parent gets cost basis equal to value of its stock upon conversion of subsidiary debt into parent stock) with National Can Corp. v. US, 520 F. Supp. 567 (N.D. Illl. 1981) (parent has no basis for subsidiary's debt on conversion into its stock), aff'd, 687 F2d 1107 (7th Cir. 1982).

[516] See Rev. Rul. 73-427, 1973-2 CB 301 (treat as taxable stock purchase); see also Rev. Rul. 79-273, 1979-2 CB 125 (taxable stock purchase via all-cash reverse merger coupled with distribution of stock of unwanted subsidiary treated as §302(b)(3) *Zenz* sale-redemption transaction); see also Prop. Regs. §§1.358-6 and 1.1032-2 (1980). Repeal of §337 by the Tax Reform Act of 1986 (supra ¶ 11.61) largely moots §338, however, since an election will trigger full recognition at the corporate level in the target.

[517] For related matters, see supra ¶¶ 3.02, 3.12, 3.13, 9.32, 11.05, 11.44, 11.45, and infra ¶ 14.54. But see Rev. Rul. 74-503, 1974-2 CB 117 (corporation's basis for its own stock always zero); Prop. Regs. §1.1032-2 (1980) (nonrecognition to subsidiary on triangular reorganization acquisition using parent's stock); Prop. Regs. §1.358-6 (1980) (parent's basis for subsidiary's stock after triangular asset or stock reorganization; as if parent acquired assets or stock directly and dropped them into subsidiary). See supra ¶ 14.33. (These provisions do not apply to taxable acquisitions, however.)

6. Reform proposals. Preliminary proposals by the staff of the Senate Finance Committee issued in 1983 proposed to drastically overhaul and simplify the corporate acquisition rules of present law. Under these proposals, the following significant changes would be made: (1) All triangular acquisitions would be classified as stock acquisitions under the new system; (2) remote parent stock would constitute qualified consideration so long as the acquiring corporation (or corporations) was in a direct chain with the corporation whose stock was utilized in the acquisition; (3) §1032 would be expanded to include nonrecognition on the use of parent (or grandparent) stock, whether or not the acquisition was tax-free; and (4) a parent's basis for stock in a controlled subsidiary would be determined by reference to the subsidiary's inside net asset basis (i.e., adjusted basis, less liabilities) in all cases. The staff's final report, released in 1985, contained most of these proposals (except that only reverse mergers would be classified as stock acquisitions, rather than *all* triangulars, as was suggested in the preliminary report).

¶ 14.54   REINCORPORATIONS: LIQUIDATION VS. REORGANIZATION

1. General patterns and stakes. The liquidation of one corporation coupled with a transfer of all or a part of its assets to a related corporation owned by substantially the same shareholders was a device that, if taken at face value, could serve a variety of tax-avoidance purposes. Most notable in this respect was the bail-out of accumulated earnings and other unneeded liquid assets of the liquidating corporation at capital gains rates (before repeal of §1202 by the Tax Reform Act of 1986[518]), while, at the same time, operation of the business continued in corporate form. Other reincorporation advantages, which could be equally attractive in a given case, include a step-up in the tax basis for various assets of the business;[519] elimination of the earnings and profits account (and the concomitant exposure to the §531 penalty tax); injection of preferred stock into the corporation's capitalization without the §306 taint; issuance of debt securities without dividend consequences; and recognition of a deductible capital loss with respect to the shareholders' stock in the liquidating corporation.

---

[518] Loss of capital gain benefits as a result of the 1986 amendments removed one of the primary motivations for the reincorporation gambit.

[519] Repeal of the corporate-level nonrecognition rules of §§336 and 337 (supra ¶¶ 11.06 and 11.61) eliminated another prime incentive for liquidating. As a result of these two reforms (i.e., eliminating capital gain benefits and taxing the liquidating corporation on its property distributions), reincorporation transactions, even if they succeed in avoiding classification as a reorganization, will rarely, if ever, be worth the effort.

These various goals could be achieved by a number of routes, which, however complex, usually fell into one of two patterns: (1) the complete liquidation of the original corporation, followed by a prearranged transfer of all or a part of its essential operating assets to a second, and usually newly organized, controlled corporation or (2) a transfer by the original corporation of all or a part of its operating assets to a second corporation controlled by its shareholders (which may, but need not, be newly organized by them), followed by a complete liquidation of the transferor corporation. In both of these patterns, it was essential to the taxpayers' plans that the liquidation rules, rather than the reorganization provisions, applied to the transaction in question; otherwise, most of the hoped-for goals could not be accomplished.[520]

In general, the concept of complete liquidation envisions a final termination of the *corporate* enterprise (either through a sale of its assets to outsiders followed by a distribution of the sale proceeds to its shareholders or by a distribution in kind of the assets to its shareholders, so that they may either sell these properties or continue to operate the business in noncorporate form). The applicable statutory pattern for liquidations, found in §§331–338, provided generally (before the Tax Reform Act of 1986 amendments) for nonrecognition at the corporate level, capital gain or loss for the shareholders, and a new fair market value basis for the liquidating corporation's assets (see Chapter 11);[521] this regime was drastically changed in 1986, however, to full recognition at the corporate level and repeal of capital gain rate benefits.

Reorganization, on the other hand, as noted by Regs. §1.368-1(b), involves continuity of business operation under modified corporate forms, coupled with a continuity of shareholder investment in that enterprise. In keeping with this premise, the statute provides not only for nonrecognition of gain or loss by the various parties to the reorganization exchanges, but for continuation of the tax basis for the properties involved therein and for inheritance of the acquired corporation's other tax attributes as well. Also important, however, was the possibility of dividend income by virtue of the boot dividend provisions of §356(a)(2), a risk not present in the case of a true liquidation (although repeal of capital gain benefits in 1986 largely neutralized this particular issue).

It is apparent that the reincorporation device sought the best of both of these worlds (i.e., liquidation *tax* treatment, but the economic benefits of a

---

[520] For other references to the liquidation-reincorporation problem, see supra ¶¶ 3.20 (reincorporations and §351), 11.05 (reincorporations and §331), 13.15 (reincorporations and split-ups); and 9.12 (reincorporations and §304).

For extensive coverage of this area, before its virtual repeal by the legislation noted above, see the Fourth Edition of this work at ¶ 14.54).

[521] But see supra notes 518 and 519.

reorganization), and it was here that the problems began. As an initial matter, it should be noted that the step-transaction doctrine, discussed earlier in Part D, was a major factor in this area; taxpayer hopes for success turned largely on their ability to divorce the liquidation transaction from the eventual transfer of the assets of the disappearing corporation to its affiliated transferee. If these steps were collapsed, however, and treated as a single transaction, resemblance to a tax-free reorganization became more pronounced. When this resemblance became overpowering, the transaction was classified as a reorganization, and the liquidation rules were supplanted by the provisions applicable to reorganizations. In a sense, the reincorporation doctrine could be viewed as an extension of the *Court Holding Co.* decision[522]—that is, distributions to shareholders followed by their prearranged transfer of the property to another controlled corporation could be treated instead as if the distributing corporation had effected the transfer, with the shareholders being treated as merely a conduit to convey the property to its ultimate destination in the successor corporation.

Alternatively, it could be argued that the liquidation and reincorporation transactions should be disregarded as a sham, and that the net distribution of assets to the various shareholders should be treated as an ordinary dividend under the general provisions of §301. The Service's efforts to provide such a nonreorganization framework for its attack on the reincorporation problem reached a zenith in Rev. Rul. 61-156,[523] where the judicial attitudes of *Bazley* and *Gregory*[524] (which are, in turn, largely codified by Regs. §§1.301-1(l) and 1.331-1(c), stating that a liquidation or other corporate readjustment may have the effect of a dividend distribution under §301), were blended with the step-transaction doctrine and the Types E and F reorganization provisions of §368(a)(1). This approach was largely accepted by the Fifth Circuit,[525] but other courts generally were restrained in their technical analysis of such transactions, and were content to rely on the more

---

[522] CIR v. Court Holding Co., 324 US 331 (1945); supra ¶ 11.07 and note 412.

[523] Rev. Rul. 61-156, 1961-2 CB 62.

[524] Bazley v. CIR, supra note 5; Gregory v. Helvering, supra note 412.

[525] See Davant v. CIR, supra note 379; Reef Corp. v. CIR, supra note 32; Hjorth, Liquidations and Reincorporations—Before and After *Davant*, 42 Wash. L. Rev. 737 (1967). But see Security Indus. Ins. Co. v. US, supra note 468.

The Service nonliquidation approach was also adopted in Telephone Answering Serv. Co., 63 TC 423 (1974), aff'd, 546 F2d 423 (4th Cir. 1976), cert. denied, 431 US 914 (1977), where a nonqualifying split-up was held not to constitute a complete liquidation (so that the corporation's sale of the stock of one of its subsidiaries did not qualify for §337).

See also Rev. Rul. 76-429, 1976-2 CB 97 (liquidation of subsidiary into parent, followed by reincorporation of part of old subsidiary's business, held merely a partial liquidation).

traditional concepts of reorganization and liquidation in reaching their con-clusions.[526] On the other hand, if there was no significant change in propor-tionate shareholder interests and substantially the same business was contin-ued in the transferee corporation, the Service's *Bazley*-section 301 approach (i.e., that the net effect of the transaction was merely a dividend distribution of corporate earnings ratably among the continuing shareholders) persisted as an alternative judicial solution in this area.[527]

2. Legislative evolution (and solution). Reincorporation was a problem before the 1954 Code. In *Bard-Parker Co. v. CIR*, the court insisted on amal-gamating a dissolution and reincorporation, "since those two transfers were but procedural steps used to complete what, in substance, constituted a sin-gle transfer."[528] A different spirit animated *US v. Arcade Co.*, which refused to consolidate the steps because the shareholders, on receiving the old cor-poration's assets in liquidation, "were under no contractual obligations to form a new corporation or to transfer their assets to a new corporation in return for stock therein";[529] although never specifically overruled, the case did not inspire confidence. Even when the liquidation and reincorporation were regarded as successive steps in the consummation of a single plan, how-ever, the pre-1954 cases had to meet the argument of taxpayers that the transaction could not be a reorganization because it lacked a business pur-pose or because it was not undertaken, in the words of Regs. §1.368-2(g), "for reasons germane to the continuance of the business" of the corpora-tion.[530]

In these cases under the 1939 Code, the government had at its disposal the argument (which was successful in several instances, although not uni-

---

[526] For extensive analysis of these decisions, which relied primarily on an expan-sive interpretation of the Type D reorganization provisions (supra ¶ 14.16), see the Fourth Edition of this work at ¶ 14.54.

[527] See also §346(b), added by the Tax Equity and Fiscal Responsibility Act of 1982, granting broad regulatory authority to the Service to deal with various transac-tions that have the effect of a partial liquidation; see supra ¶ 9.08.

[528] Bard-Parker Co. v. CIR, 218 F2d 52 (2d Cir. 1954), cert. denied, 349 US 906 (1955).

[529] US v. Arcade Co., 203 F2d 230 (6th Cir.), cert. denied, 346 US 828 (1953).

[530] For cases rejecting the *Arcade Co.* approach and treating such transactions as reorganizations under the 1939 Code coupled with the distribution of taxable boot, see Survaunt v. CIR, 162 F2d 753 (8th Cir. 1947); Lewis v. CIR, 176 F2d 646 (1st Cir. 1949). See also Liddon v. CIR, 230 F2d 304 (6th Cir.), cert. denied, 352 US 824 (1956) ("the Tax Court was correct in analyzing what was done in this case from the point of view of its overall net effect, rather than to permit one isolated transaction in a series to determine the tax consequences"); Walter S. Heller, 2 TC 371 (1943) (nonacq.), aff'd, 147 F2d 376 (9th Cir. 1945), cert. denied, 325 US 868 (1945).

formly) that the transaction was a reorganization under §112(g)(1)(D) of the 1939 Code. This provision was the predecessor of §368(a)(1)(D) of the 1954 Code, providing for Type D reorganizations, but the 1954 changes in the definition of a Type D reorganization precluded application of this provision to many of the transactions described above,[531] although the courts evidenced a remarkably flexible attitude in applying the Type D reorganization to reincorporation transactions.[532] Moreover, the 1954 contraction of the Type D reorganization did not mean that the liquidation-reincorporation route to tax avoidance was wide open, since it was also possible to bring these transactions under the aegis of §368(a)(1)(E) or §368(a)(1)(F), with

---

[531] The major thrust of these changes was twofold: First, all divisive Type D reorganization transactions must pass through the statutory strainer of §355, a provision of considerable technicality and complexity; second, all other Type D reorganizations must satisfy the requirements of §354(b)(1), which provides, in brief, that substantially all the assets of the transferor must pass to the acquiring corporation, and that the transferor corporation, in effect, must liquidate. Both these changes made it considerably more difficult for many reincorporation transactions to be classified as Type D reorganizations, although some courts, it may be noted, have risen to the challenge; supra ¶ 14.16.

But see Rev. Rul. 77-191, 1977-1 CB 94, for an example of a divisive reincorporation transaction (pro rata distribution of one of two separate businesses, followed by reincorporation of distributed business, held tax-free §355 split-off, not a partial liquidation).

[532] E.g., James Armour, supra note 120, involving a sale of all the operating assets of one corporation to a commonly owned sister corporation and finding a Type D reorganization under §§368(a)(1)(D) and 354(b) with a boot dividend under §356 (a)(2); the court held that (1) an actual exchange of stock was unnecessary here, since the same shareholders already owned 100 percent of both corporations (so that issuance of additional shares would be a meaningless gesture), and (2) substantially all the assets were transferred under §354(b)(1)(A), even though their value was only 51 percent of total assets (the court here tested substantially all by reference to the corporation's *operating* assets only); see also David T. Grubbs, supra note 177, where failure to liquidate was held not to violate §354(b)(1)(B) on the facts (sole continuing shareholder kept transferor alive as his own personal investment company; court in effect found a constructive distribution on the special facts present in the case).

As to the requirement of an actual exchange of stock, see CIR v. Morgan, 288 F2d 676 (3d Cir.), cert. denied, 368 US 836 (1961); Davant v. CIR, supra note 379; Reef Corp. v. CIR, supra note 32; American Mfg. Co. v. CIR, supra note 70; and Atlas Tool Co. v. CIR, supra note 379. But compare Warsaw Photographic Assocs., 84 TC 21 (1985) (lack of actual stock exchange not ignored when shareholdings not identical).

On interpreting "substantially all" to mean *operating* assets (rather than total assets), see Moffatt v. CIR, supra note 121 (service business; technical staff was principal asset); Smothers Co. v. US, 1983-2 USTC ¶ 9664 (Cl. Ct. 1983) (transfer of beneficial use sufficient); Rose v. US, supra note 426; Rev. Rul. 78-47, 1978-1 CB 114. But cf. Regs. §1.368-1(d) (1980), supra ¶ 14.51, para. 2 (historic business continuity requirement).

respect to the exchange of stock in the old corporation for stock in the new corporation, coupled with a distribution of bonds or other property.[533]

The House version of the 1954 Code contained special provisions dealing with the reincorporation device, but this section was dropped in conference with the statement, "It is the belief . . . that, at the present time, the possibility of tax avoidance in this area is not sufficiently serious to require a special statutory provision," and that these questions "can appropriately be disposed of by judicial decision or by regulation within the framework . . . of the bill."[534] Regs. §§1.331-1(c) and 1.301-1(1) attempted to provide a framework for attack on the reincorporation problem by stating that a liquidation or other corporate readjustment may have the effect of a dividend distribution under §301. The influence of *Bazley* is manifest in these regulations, which were applied in Rev. Rul. 61-156, in the fashion described above.[535] The efficacy of this line of attack, and of other approaches under the 1954 Code met with mixed results at best,[536] and the search for a legislative solu-

---

[533] The *Survaunt* and *Lewis* cases (Survaunt v. CIR, supra note 530; Lewis v. CIR, supra note 530) relied on the boot provisions to find a dividend, so that the dividend within gain restriction (supra ¶ 14.34) was applicable. If the distribution of the bonds or other properties is treated as an independent distribution that coincides in time with the reorganization, however, it would be taxable as a dividend under §301. See Bazley v. CIR, supra note 5, discussed supra ¶ 14.17; see also Telephone Answering Serv. Co., supra note 525, and generally cases and rulings, supra notes 523 and 525.

[534] H.R. Rep. No. 2543, 83d Cong., 2d Sess. 41 (1954).

[535] Rev. Rul. 61-156, 1961-2 CB 62. For comprehensive discussions of this problem, see Lane, The Reincorporation Game: Have the Ground Rules Really Changed? 77 Harv. L. Rev. 1218 (1964); Pugh, supra note 471; Hewitt, Liquidations v. Reincorporations and Reorganizations: The Current Battle, 15 Tul. Tax. Inst. 187 (1965); Nicholson, Liquidation-Reincorporation, Tax Mgmt. Portfolio (BNA) No. 335-2 (1984).

For analysis of the pre-1954 decisions and of various proposals for change, see MacLean, Problems of Reincorporation and Related Proposals of the Subchapter C Advisory Group, 13 Tax L. Rev. 407 (1958).

[536] See generally supra note 532 for examples of some of the Service's more notable successes here. See also Rev. Rul. 70-240, 1970-1 CB 81.

But where shareholders of the original corporation ended up with less than 80 percent of the stock of the acquiring corporation, courts uniformly refused to find a reorganization; see, e.g., Joseph C. Gallagher, 39 TC 144 (1962); Berghash v. CIR, supra note 32; Breech v. US, 439 F2d 409 (9th Cir. 1971); Stephens, Inc. v. US, 464 F2d 53 (8th Cir. 1972), cert. denied, 409 US 1118 (1973). These decisions also held that §318 attribution did not apply for the 80 percent control test. But see Ringwalt v. US, 549 F2d 89 (8th Cir.), cert. denied, 432 US 906 (1977) (stock deemed to be owned through grantor trust, held to be beneficially owned); Stanton v. US, 512 F2d 13 (3d Cir. 1975) (effective control over who got stock of transferee sufficient to find control for reorganization status). See also, on the control and continuity requirements generally, Security Indus. Ins. Co. v. US, 702 F2d 1234 (5th Cir. 1983); Superior Coach of Fla., Inc., supra note 25.

tion continued unabated from shortly after passage of the 1954 Code[537] until it eventually bore fruit, most notably in the Tax Reform Acts of 1984 and 1986.[538]

Beginning in 1958, various proposals were advanced to combat the reincorporation device. One of the earlier proposals was to cut back the effect of the 1954 changes in the Type D reorganization by reducing the control requirement for nondivisive transactions from 80 to 50 percent,[539] including some indirect asset transfers in the Type D definition and amending §356 (relating to boot) to include situations in which the shareholders do not receive any stock or securities.[540] Another approach was to repeal §354(b) and provide a special boot rule to deal with the nondivisive bailout pattern in reincorporation cases; one version of this proposal left the 80 percent control rule unchanged, but a revised proposal accepted a reduction to 50 percent. Elimination of the substantially all requirement of §354(b)(1)(A) would strike more deeply at the heart of the reincorporation problem; despite the flexible construction of this phrase in *Armour* and other cases,[541] it remained a principal stumbling block for the government in attacking reincorporation transactions. Finally, application of the constructive ownership rules of §318 to this area seemed imperative if various indirect control devices were to be effectively blocked.[542] Nothing much came of these sug-

---

Moreover, sufficient interruption of the original corporation's business activity was held in several cases to prevent a finding of reorganization; see, e.g., Pridemark, Inc. v. CIR, supra note 422; William C. Kind, 54 TC 600 (1970) (acq.); Lester J. Workman, ¶ 77,378 P-H Memo. TC (1977); see also Regs. §1.368-1(d)(1980) (historic business continuity requirement for reorganization status); Note, The Role of the Continuity of Business Enterprise Requirement in Liquidation-Reincorporations, 35 Tax Lawyer 737 (1982); and Mandelkern, "Continuity of Business Enterprise" and the Liquidation-Reincorporation Battle: Is Treas. Reg. §1.368-1(d) a Trojan Horse? 34 U. Fla. L. Rev. 822 (1982).

[537] See MacLean, supra note 535; XVIII ABA Tax Section Bull., No. 4, at 40 (July 1965). See also Comment, The Liquidation-Reincorporation Device—Analysis and Proposed Solution, 14 Vill. L. Rev. 423 (1969); Wood, A Proposed Treatment of Reincorporation Transactions, 25 Tax L. Rev. 282 (1970).

[538] The 1984 Act modified the Type D reorganization definition in §368(c)(2) (moved to §368(a)(2)(H) in 1986) to conform to the control line of §304(c), supra ¶ 14.16, notes 169 and 178; the 1986 Act repealed §§336, 337, and the capital gain rate benefits of §§1201(a) and 1202, supra notes 518 and 519. See also §346(b), added by the Tax Equity and Fiscal Responsibility Act of 1982, supra note 527.

[539] This proposal was finally accepted in the Tax Reform Act of 1984, supra note 538.

[540] Supra note 537.

[541] Supra note 532.

[542] Supra note 536. The Tax Reform Act of 1984, in §368(c)(2) (moved to §368(a)(2)(H) in 1986), supra note 538, finally imposed a modified §318 regime on

gestions, however, until 1982, when the Tax Equity and Fiscal Responsibility Act legislation modified §346(b)[543] to grant regulatory authority to define when a particular transaction had the effect of a partial (rather than a complete) liquidation.

In 1983, the preliminary report by the staff of the Senate Finance Committee on the reform of Subchapter C proposed to materially expand the scope of the Type D reorganization and otherwise combat the liquidation-reincorporation problem by the following amendments: (1) The control line for the nondivisive Type D reorganization would be lowered from 80 percent to 50 percent (with §318 attribution as well); (2) asset acquisitions from related transferors (i.e., 50 percent common ownership, with §318), would be denied a cost basis election (i.e., corporate level nonrecognition treatment, carry-over basis, and carry-over of tax history would be mandatory); (3) the boot dividend-within-gain limitation would be repealed; and (4) the earnings and profits limitation for dividend distributions would be repealed; and (5) §§336 and 337 would be repealed. The staff's final 1985 report contained the first four of these proposals but dropped the recommended repeal of earnings and profits; instead, earnings of both the acquired and acquiring corporation would be combined for purposes of measuring the dividend amount. The general intent of these proposals was to achieve greater parity between §304 (see Chapter 9) and the related party asset acquisition rules.

The Tax Reform Act of 1984 adopted only the first of these proposals, lowering the control definition line for nondivisive Type D reorganizations to 50 percent of vote *or* value (with §318 attribution, but only to and from 5 percent shareholders), in conformity with the control definition in §304(c).[544] The Finance Commitee staff's final report of May 20, 1985 likewise adopted the §304(c) common control definition line. While the staff's final report abolished the technical Type D reorganization as unnecessary

---

the control definition for nondivisive Type D reorganizations (based on the control definition of §304(c), supra ¶ 9.12).

[543] Supra note 527. Section 346(b) essentially codified the decision in Telephone Answering Serv. Co., supra note 525 (corporation engaged in business directly and through two 100 percent owned subsidiaries desired to sell the stock of one of its subsidiaries tax-free under §337; it adopted plan of complete liquidation, sold the subsidiary's stock for cash, transferred its directly owned operating assets (about 15 percent of total assets) to a newly organized subsidiary, and dissolved, distributing the sales proceeds and the stock of its remaining two subsidiaries pro rata to its shareholders; held §337 did not apply because taxpayer was not completely liquidated, even though transaction did not constitute a D reorganization under §355 or §354(b)(1)(A); case was first victory for Service on nonliquidation theory). But see Lester J. Workman, supra note 536 (fact that proceeds from sale of operating assets by liquidating corporation were reincorporated in a new entity by shareholder following their distribution did not deprive old corporation of §337 benefits on that sale).

[544] Supra note 538.

(since related party asset acquisitions would be subject to mandatory carry-over basis treatment under the new acquisition system), the practical effect would be the same as under the 1984 Act amendments to the Type D rules.

The Tax Reform Act of 1986,[545] however, repealed §§336 and 337 and thereby attacked the reincorporation device from a different perspective. This general elimination of corporate level nonrecognition treatment on the sale or distribution of its appreciated assets has effectively eliminated one of the principal tax incentives for attempting the reincorporation gambit. Moreover, the 1986 Act's repeal of the capital gain rate benefits in §§1201(a) and 1202 removed the other prime motivation for a liquidation-reincorporation transaction. After 1986, it will be a rare case indeed where attempting a reincorporation gambit would be financially advisable, even if one could be assured of avoiding classification as a reorganization (which became considerably more difficult as a result of the 1982 and 1984 amendments).[546]

3. Examples. The present status of this area can be illustrated by the following examples, in which *T* Corporation has appreciated operating assets with a value of $500 (basis $200) and liquid nonoperating assets (e.g., cash) of $500. *T* is owned 100 percent by *A*, whose basis for his *T* stock is $100:

Example 1: A liquidates *T* and shortly thereafter transfers all of the operating assets to a new corporation, *P*, in exchange for its stock. If the separate steps are respected, and liquidation and reincorporation treatment prevails, *T* now (as a result of the Tax Reform Act of 1986) has full recognition of gain on the distribution. *A* has $900 of gain under §331,[547] *P* takes over the operating assets with a $500 basis under §§334(a) and 362(a), and *A*'s basis for his *P* stock is $500 under §358. If reorganization treatment prevails (e.g., Type D or possibly Type F), *T* has no gain under §361, *A* probably has a §356(a)(2) boot dividend of $500 (to the extent covered by *T*'s earnings), *P* takes a $200 §362(b) basis for the assets (and inherits *T*'s tax attributes under §381), and *A*'s basis for his *P* stock is $100 under §358. Nonreorganization, or *Bazley*-§301 dividend treatment, would give the same result on these facts.[548]

---

[545] Supra notes 518, 519, and 538.

[546] Supra notes 527 and 538.

[547] The Tax Reform Act of 1986 repealed the special capital gain deduction of §1202, supra note 518 (hence, both *A*'s and *T*'s gains are taxable at the same rates as ordinary income); the 1986 Act also repealed the corporate-level nonrecognition rules of §§336 and 337, supra note 519.

[548] *A*'s boot dividend under §365(a)(2) would be taxable at the same rate as capital gain, however, after the Tax Reform Act of 1986 amendments, supra note 518.

Example 2: If, instead, *A* had first organized *P* with $500 cash, and *T* had then sold its operating assets to *P* for $500 and liquidated, liquidation treatment would give the same results as in Example 1. Reorganization treatment similarly would give the same result as in Example 1.[549]

Example 3: If *A*'s stock basis in *T* was $1,200 instead of $100, liquidation treatment could result in a deductible capital loss of $200 under §331; reorganization treatment, however, would give no loss (or dividend) to *A*, and his basis in the *P* stock would be $700 under §358 ($1,200 less $500 boot). *Bazley*-§301 dividend treatment, on the other hand, would result in a dividend to *A* to the extent of *T*'s earnings (even though *A* has a realized loss).

Example 4: If *P* is an existing corporation owned 100 percent by *B* (the son of *A*), the sale by *A* of all of his *T* stock to *P*, followed by *P*'s liquidation of *T*, would be a §304 transaction for *A* (see Chapter 9), with the likelihood of dividend treatment (because *A*'s ownership of *T* would continue under §318, so the distribution would be pro rata and hence a dividend under §302(b)(1)). Moreover, *P* would not obtain a §338 basis for the *T* assets because of §338(h)(3)(A) and §338(h)(3)(C) (purchase from a related seller), discussed in Chapter 11.

Example 5: If *X* instead had sold its *assets* to *P* and then liquidated, *Berghash* held that there could not be a reorganization on continuity

---

Bazley and §301 treatment may give different results from the rules of §356(a)(2) where boot is greater than realized gain, where accumulated earnings are less than the boot, or where the distribution is non-pro rata. See supra ¶¶ 14.17 and 14.34. While this approach was approved in Davant v. CIR, supra note 379, as an alternative ground for its decision, no difference in result from the court's views of §356(a)(2) occurred on the facts; this approach was rejected, however, in American Mfg. Co., supra note 70.

The Tax Reform Act of 1986 repeal of §336 (supra note 519) taxes *T* in full on its $300 of gain with respect to the distributed operating assets (at the regular ordinary rates as well); the Senate Finance Committee staff proposal on the reform of Subchapter C also would tax *T* without exception (query, would *P* also take the mandatory carry-over basis under proposed §365(d) related party acquisition rules?).

[549] But *T* might have been denied §337 treatment under Telephone Answering Serv. Co., supra note 543, and §346(b) (added by the Tax Equity and Fiscal Responsibility Act amendments, supra note 527) on the ground that *T* did not completely liquidate—i.e., the transaction, at best, had only a *partial* liquidation effect. This approach would result in full recognition to *T* (but *P* would still get a cost basis for the assets, and *A* would get capital gain).

Under the Tax Reform Act of 1986 repeal of §337, however (supra note 519), even if complete liquidation treatment prevailed, *T* would be fully taxable on its gain from the sale of the operating assets.

grounds because §318 did not apply to reorganization transactions. Thus, *A* obtained capital gain on the liquidation of *T* and *P* took a cost basis for the *X* assets.[550] As a result of the Tax Reform Acts of 1984 and 1986, however, §318 applies to determine control (the control definition here being 50 percent of vote or value); thus, the transaction would probably be a Type D reorganization after the 1984 Act, with the same results as Example 2. Even if liquidation treatment prevailed, *T*'s gain would be fully recognized under the 1986 Act and taxed at ordinary rates, as would *A*'s gain.

¶ 14.55 ASSUMPTION OF LIABILITIES: EFFECT ON REORGANIZATION STATUS

1. In general. In *US v. Hendler*, the Supreme Court held that assumption and payment of the transferor corporation's bonded indebtedness by the acquiring corporation constituted boot to the transferor.[551] In view of the 1934 Revenue Act's restrictive changes in the definition of reorganization (limiting the consideration that could be paid in what is now the Type C reorganization to voting stock of the acquiring corporation), the *Hendler* decision was viewed as a practical embargo upon the Type C reorganization under the 1934 provisions, since the assumption of liabilities was essential in the reorganization of most going concerns. In addition, confusion was rampant in the lower courts as to the precise scope of *Hendler*, guaranteeing an abundance of litigation and a long period of uncertainty.

Moreover, taxpayers who had relied on the Service's pre-*Hendler* position that liability assumptions did not create boot in a reorganization faced the prospect of deficiency assessments if the statute of limitations had not run on the year of the exchange. The Service, meanwhile, was threatened with refund claims for open years in which taxpayers had sold their stock without increasing their basis to reflect the taxable character (under *Hendler*) of the prior exchange, as well as claims by transferee corporations for an increased basis on assets received in pre-*Hendler* reorganizations. For these reasons, Congress retroactively overturned the *Hendler* decision in

---

[550] But the Tax Reform Act of 1984 (supra note 538) now will apply §318 to the Type D control definition (and also will lower the control threshold to 50 percent), so that reorganization and boot dividend treatment can apply to *T* and *A*, and *P* will take a carry-over basis for the acquired assets. Thus, *Berghash* (supra note 536) has been overruled. However, even if complete liquidation treatment prevailed here, the Tax Reform Act of 1986 repeal of §337 (supra note 519) would tax *T* in full on its sale of assets to *P* (at ordinary gain rates as well), although *P* would get a cost basis for the *T* assets here.

[551] US v. Hendler, supra note 22.

1939 as to all prior years during which the issue was still open. In brief, the anti-*Hendler* legislation provided that:

(1) The assumption of, or taking subject to, liabilities should be disregarded in determining whether an acquisition was solely for voting stock in a Type C reorganization;

(2) The assumption of liabilities would not, as a general rule, constitute boot to the transferor unless there was no business purpose for the assumption or it was merely a device to avoid taxes (§357); and

(3) The transferor's basis for nonrecognition property received in the exchange (i.e., stock or securities) was required to be reduced by the amount of the assumed liability,[552] but the acquiring corporation's basis for its acquired properties was not affected by its assumption or payment of the transferor's liabilities (unless gain was recognized to the transferor, in which case basis could be increased to that extent).[553]

In 1954, these rules were amplified in two respects: (1) In applying the boot relaxation rules of §368(a)(2)(B), liabilities are treated as cash; and (2) gain must be recognized to the transferor of property in a Type D reorganization if the liability exceeds its basis.[554]

Despite the 1939 intent on the part of Congress to reverse the effects of the *Hendler* case, numerous problems still remain in this area, the most important of which are dealt with in the discussion that follows.[555]

2. Definition of "liability." It may be that the term "liability," for purposes of the above provision, is limited to passive obligations for the payment of money and does not include such active contractual obligations as the duty to perform services, supply or repair goods, lease or license prop-

---

[552] Section 358(d); see supra ¶ 14.32.

[553] H.R. Rep. No. 855, 75th Cong., 1st Sess. 20 (1939).

[554] For application of §357(c) to a Type D reorganization that also constituted a Type A reorganization, see Rev. Rul. 75-161, 1975-1 CB 114; Rev. Rul. 76-188, 1976-1 CB 99 (§357(c) applied to §351 exchange that also constituted a Type C reorganization; overlap does not oust §357(c) of jurisdiction).

Compare Rev. Rul. 78-330, 1978-2 CB 147 (parent's cancellation of subsidiary's debt to avoid §357(c) gain on merger of subsidiary into another affiliate respected; not §357(b) tax avoidance). See also Rev. Rul. 79-289, 1979-2 CB 145 (§357(c) not applicable to a Type F reorganization even though transaction also a Type D).

[555] See N.Y. State Bar Association, Tax Section, Report on the Ancillary Tax Effects of Different Forms of Reorganizations, 34 Tax. L. Rev. 477, 478 (1979); Levitan, Dealing With Liabilities in a Reorganization, 39 NYU Inst. on Fed. Tax'n ch. 8 (1981).

erty, refrain from competition, and so forth. On the other hand, it does not seem to be necessary that the obligation be fixed or determinable; thus, contingent liabilities should be counted unless remote or speculative.[556]

As a general matter, the liability assumption rules are not limited to long-term capital obligations; current expense obligations (for interest, taxes, compensation, rent, royalties, and the like) should also be treated as liabilities for this purpose, at least if they accrued at or prior to the date of assumption.[557] Unaccrued liabilities for such expense items, on the other hand, may stand on a different footing. It is doubtful, for example, whether a tenant's obligation to pay rent for the balance of the lease term should be treated as a liability for this purpose (although there is accounting authority for recognizing such obligations in the liability section of the balance sheet, rather than in a footnote thereto); so also in the case of unaccrued interest on indebtedness or future liabilities with respect to pension or profit-sharing plans.[558] Section 381(c)(16) (Chapter 16) seems to provide an alternative treatment in certain reorganizations with respect to *unaccrued* liabilities of the transferor that are not reflected in the consideration paid by the acquiring corporation for the transferred properties; in this situation, the acquiring corporation steps into the transferor's shoes with respect to the liabilities and is entitled to a deduction when the obligation matures or is paid, a result not normally obtainable in a case where accrued liabilities are assumed.[559]

---

[556] Rev. Rul. 68-637, 1968-2 CB 158, held that assumption of an acquired corporation's unexercised warrants and stock options qualified as a valid liability assumption under §368(a)(1)(C) and did not constitute boot. See also Rev. Rul. 70-269, 1970-1 CB 82 (substitution of stock options severable from concurrent Type B reorganization; no recognized gain or loss); Rev. Rul. 73-301, 1973-2 CB 215 (definition of liability in partnership context under §752; contractual obligation to perform services not a §752 liability); George F. Smith, 84 TC 889 (1985); Tiller, Contributing Partnership Interests to a Corporation: "Liabilities" After Smith, 2 J. Part. Tax'n 316 (1986).

[557] See e.g., Stockton Harbor Indus. Co. v. CIR, 216 F2d 638 (9th Cir. 1954), cert. denied, 349 US 904 (1955); New Jersey Mortgage & Title Co., 3 TC 1277 (1944) (acq.); Roosevelt Hotel Co., supra note 118; Alcazar Hotel Co., 1 TC 872 (1943); Peabody Hotel Co., 7 TC 600 (1946) (acq.); see Regs. §1.279-5(e)(1), defining indebtedness for purposes of §279 as being determined under generally accepted accounting principles (e.g., short-term debt, nonrecourse debt, and contingent liabilities if the contingency is likely to become a reality); see also §1275(a)(1) (definition of "debt" for OID rules, supra ¶ 4.40); Prop. Regs. §1.1275-1(b)(1).

But see §357(c)(3), added by the Revenue Act of 1978 (expense liabilities not counted under §357(c) if deductible by cash-basis transferor; supra ¶ 3.06).

[558] If a portion of an assumed liability would constitute imputed interest under §483 or §1274, there is a possibility that it could be excluded in computing the amount of liabilities assumed.

[559] See, e.g., Magruder v. Supplee, 316 US 394 (1942) (assumed liability treated as part of the acquiring party's cost for the property); see also Schuh Trading Co. v. CIR, supra note 113; VCA Corp., 566 F2d 1192 (Ct. Cl. 1977).

The treatment of reorganization expenses bears special mention. In the *Southwest Consolidated Corp.* case, the Supreme Court held that the acquiring corporation could not assume any liability "whose nature and amount were determined and fixed in the reorganization," on the theory that such a liability, although having its origin in a prereorganization liability of the transferor, was not a "liability of the other [corporation]" within the meaning of §368(a)(1)(C).[560] This seems to bar the assumption of a liability that is adjusted *in* the reorganization process, and thus severely restricts the use of §368(a)(1)(C) in bankruptcy cases. But courts have held that *Southwest Consolidated* does not forbid the acquiring corporation from assuming and paying expenses of the reorganization proceeding itself, a result that seems sensible in view of the fact that assets may be retained by the transferor to discharge its liabilities without violating the substantially all requirement of §368(a)(1)(C).[561] Despite this, the Service at one time would not issue favorable rulings on the assumption of liabilities for the reorganization expenses of a solvent transferor,[562] but more recently it was announced that favorable rulings could be obtained here as well.[563]

---

[560] Helvering v. Southwest Consol. Corp., supra note 33. The case involved a judicial insolvency reorganization in which creditors were entitled to the equity interest in the debtor's properties; the debtor borrowed cash to pay off dissenting creditors, and the assumption of this liability by the acquiring corporation was viewed by the Supreme Court as an indirect payment of cash in violation of the solely for voting stock requirement.

See also Rev. Rul. 73-102, 1973-1 CB 186 (assumption of acquired corporation's liability to pay dissenters held boot per *Southwest Consolidated* because liability created in the reorganization). Compare Rev. Rul. 76-365, 1976-2 CB 110.

[561] See Roosevelt Hotel Co., supra note 118, and other cases cited supra note 557; Southland Ice Co., supra note 118; Westfir Lumber Co., supra note 118; Rev. Rul. 56-345, 1956-2 CB 206; discussion supra ¶ 14.14.

See also Rev. Rul. 76-365, 1976-2 CB 110 (assumption of target company's expenses for evaluating other unsuccessful offers held valid liability assumption in Type C reorganization).

[562] See Rubenfeld, supra note 90.

The treatment of liabilities created pursuant to express terms of the reorganization agreement (e.g., from warranties, indemnities, and the like, given by the buyer to the seller) presumably ought to be handled separately from the reorganization, since these obligations do not seem to constitute additional consideration for the acquisition (i.e., boot); rather, they merely go to the protection of the quality of the consideration given by the buyer. If the parties provide for discharge in voting stock of the buyer in the event payment is required, the arrangement should clearly qualify; see supra ¶ 5.06, para. 4.

See generally infra ¶ 14.56.

[563] Rev. Rul. 73-54, 1973-1 CB 187, held that assumption and payment of the acquired corporation's reorganization expenses did not result in the payment of boot by the acquiring corporation; expenses that can be assumed and paid by the acquiring corporation are those solely and directly related to the reorganization (e.g., legal,

If a particular liability fails to qualify for treatment as an assumed liability under §357(a) or §368(a)(1)(C), the amount thereof will be treated as the receipt of boot by the transferor that could (unless the boot relaxation rule of §368(a)(2)(B) applies[564]) disqualify the transaction as a Type C reorganization. In the case of a Type B reorganization, receipt of *any* boot by the transferor apparently will infect the entire reorganization; statutory mergers, on the other hand, are tested under general continuity of interest standards, which allow more leeway for nonproprietary consideration.

The ubiquitous stock vs. debt issue (see Chapter 4) can arise in the reorganization area: If an alleged debt owed to shareholders is found to be an additional stock investment on their part, a purported assumption thereof by the acquiring corporation, evidenced by its own debt securities, would constitute additional consideration. As boot, this might generate gain to the shareholder, prevent the exchange from qualifying as a Type B or Type C reorganization, and/or impair the transaction's ability to satisfy the continuity of interest requirement. Conversely, a transaction that is allegedly a taxable purchase might, if the buyer's deferred payment obligations are held to constitute stock under the thin capitalization principle, constitute a reorganization, although this possibility, so far as Type B and Type C reorganizations are concerned, is made remote by the fact that the consideration must be *voting* stock.[565]

3. Definition of "assumption." In a statutory merger, the surviving corporation assumes the liabilities of the absorbed corporation by operation of law; but in a Type C reorganization, the acquiring corporation will often issue its own debt instruments to replace those of the transferor corporation. In *Helvering v. Taylor*, it was held that such an exchange constituted an assumption even though the parties failed to use the word "assume."[566] If the terms and conditions of the liability are substantially changed, however, the transaction may go beyond a mere assumption and constitute the creation of a new liability, as in *Stoddard v. CIR*, where the issuance of mortgage

---

accounting, appraisal, and administrative costs of the reorganization); other expenses cannot be assumed as liabilities by the acquiring corporation.

See also Rev. Rul. 76-365, 1976-2 CB 110 (expenses of evaluating acquiring corporation's offer treated as qualified reorganization expense).

[564] See, e.g., Rev. Rul. 73-102, 1973-1 CB 186.

[565] For a case rejecting this argument, see W.H. Truschel, supra note 48. But see Reef Corp., ¶ 65,072 P-H Memo. TC (1965), aff'd and rev'd on other grounds, supra note 32.

See Rev. Rul. 72-343, 1972-2 CB 213 (interim financing tied into contemplated merger not a true loan; instead, advances treated as part of consideration for assets and thus taxable boot to transferor corporation).

[566] Helvering v. Taylor, 128 F2d 885 (2d Cir. 1942).

bonds to replace claims of unsecured creditors of the transferor corporation was held to be more than a mere assumption of liabilities.[567] (Since the fair market value of the bonds received was less than the taxpayer's basis for the claims surrendered, he was allowed to deduct his loss under §165.) In general, however, courts have been quite liberal in allowing modifications of the terms of an assumed liability, especially if the change merely extends the maturity date or reduces the interest rate.[568]

It is often a close question, however, whether the acquiring corporation has (1) assumed (or taken subject to) liabilities and paid them off, which is permissible or (2) paid cash as part of the consideration, which is not permissible (except possibly in a Type A reorganization or, within the limits set by §368(a)(2)(B), in a Type C reorganization).[569]

Where the liability is owed by the transferor corporation *to* the acquiring corporation, and the latter cancels the debt as part consideration for acquisition of the properties, matters become more difficult. Does the discharge and *satisfaction* of such an indebtedness constitute an assumption? In *Arthur L. Kniffen*, it was held that it did in the context of a §351 exchange, so that the transferor debtor was protected from boot treatment by

---

[567] Stoddard v. CIR, 141 F2d 76 (2d Cir. 1944).

[568] See New Jersey Mortgage & Title Co., supra note 557 (test was whether new bonds were substituted for old, not the extent of modification of interest and maturity terms); Southland Ice Co., supra note 118 (issuance of new income mortgage bonds to replace 50 percent of the principal of old mortgage bonds held an assumption); Rev. Rul. 79-155, 1979-1 CB 153 (merger of *T* into *P*'s controlled subsidiary, *S*; *P* and *S* jointly assumed *T*'s debts and also substantially modified terms thereof; held, §357(a) assumption nonrecognition for *T*, and §354(a)(1) exchange nonrecognition for security holders); Regs. §1.368-2(j)(5) (in reverse merger, liability assumption treated as a capital contribution to target and as a §354 exchange by security holder). But see supra note 85.

See also §279(h)(2) (added by the Tax Reform Act of 1969, supra ¶ 4.26), providing that assumption of tainted "corporate acquisition indebtedness" causes the assuming corporation to step into the shoes of the acquired corporation with respect to such liabilities.

[569] See generally Stockton Harbor Indus. Co. v. CIR, supra note 557, and cases cited therein, holding that prompt payment of assumed liabilities by the acquiring corporation did not affect qualification of the prior transaction as an assumption. If the transferor incurred the liability in contemplation of the reorganization, however, prompt payment by the assuming party may be viewed more hostilely; for a possible line of attack, see the provisions of §357(b) and the discussion supra ¶ 3.06. The test to be applied in such cases is whether the assumption transaction was merely a disguised method for the payment of cash boot, a standard that is easier to state than to apply.

See also Rev. Rul. 80-240, 1980-2 CB 116 (mere transitory accommodation borrowing in agency capacity not true liability assumption transaction; taxpayer not acting for own benefit here; merely assisting in meeting nontax requirements).

§357(a).[570] The theory of the *Kniffen* case was followed in *Edwards Motor Transit Co.*, where the debtor merged into its wholly owned creditor-subsidiary in a §368(a)(1)(A) statutory merger.[571] In both cases, the Tax Court held that the identity of the creditor was irrelevant under §357(a) and that the net result was the same as if the assumed debt had been owed to a third party and had been discharged by the acquiring corporation immediately after its assumption. This approach is difficult to reconcile with the treatment of intercorporate debt on the liquidation of a debtor-subsidiary by its creditor-parent where the latter recognizes gain or loss in its capacity as creditor, although the subsidiary is protected from recognition treatment by virtue of §332(c).[572]

4. Continuity of interest problems. As noted earlier, Regs. §1.368-2(d)(1) warns that an assumption may "so alter the character of the transaction as to place the transaction outside the purposes and assumptions of the reorganization provisions." This statement seems to be concerned primarily with the continuity of interest principle. Hence, if the acquisition is made primarily for assumption of the transferor's liabilities with only a trivial amount of voting stock to sweeten the bargain, the transaction more nearly resembles a foreclosure proceeding than a reorganization. Thus, reorganization treatment may be denied where the former holders of the proprietary interest in the property are

---

[570] Arthur L. Kniffen, supra note 503.

[571] Edwards Motor Transit Co., supra note 503.

[572] Supra ¶ 11.42. Bausch & Lomb Optical Co. v. CIR, supra note 135, discussed supra ¶ 14.53, holds that acquisition of a part of the transferor's assets in exchange for its stock, already held by the acquiring corporation, did not satisfy the solely for voting stock requirement of §368(a)(1)(C). But apparently the acquiring corporation will be permitted to receive at least part of the transferor's assets in its capacity as a creditor because of the special liability assumption rules of §§357 and 368(a)(1)(C), although this superior treatment seems difficult to justify. But see Rev. Rul. 72-464, 1972-2 CB 214 (gain to creditor can occur here).

Interim financing of the acquired corporation by the acquiring corporation pending final closing of the acquisition may give rise to boot problems if such loans are considered to be part of the price paid by the acquiring company; but the spirit of Arthur L. Kniffen, supra note 503, and Edwards Motor Transit Co., supra note 503, seems essentially to the contrary. See Rev. Rul. 72-343, 1972-2 CB 213; see also Rev. Rul. 70-271, 1970-1 CB 166 (discharge, or disposition, of unassumed liabilities in a Type C reorganization; satisfaction in kind to unrelated creditors a taxable event to debtor corporation; same for property payments to shareholder-creditors in their creditor capacity; but shareholder assumption of liquidating corporation's liabilities not taxable to corporate debtor because a capital contribution by them to corporation); Rev. Rul. 75-450, 1975-2 CB 328. But see revised (in 1986) §361, supra ¶ 14.32, para. 2.

virtually eliminated in the transaction.[573] An illustration in Regs. §1.368-2(d)(3) approves an assumption of liabilities equal to 50 percent of the value of the transferred properties; anything over this figure could be vulnerable under general continuity of interest principles.

Although voting stock of the acquiring corporation's parent has been permissible as the proprietary consideration in a Type C reorganization since 1954, apparently the acquiring corporation is the only one that may *assume* the transferor's liabilities (although taking *subject* to liabilities seems to be more flexible). Thus, in a *Groman*[574] triangular acquisition, it may not be permissible for the acquired assets to pass directly to a subsidiary where the parent assumes the transferor's liabilities, since the subsidiary would be viewed as the acquiring corporation for this purpose; and the same objection might be made even if the assets go first to the parent and then to the subsidiary. Where the subsidiary assumes the transferor's liabilities, it may be possible for the parent to guarantee its obligaton, however; this would not appear to constitute an assumption by the parent, since it is only secondarily liable on the debt. It is understood that several favorable rulings have been issued by the Service on such an arrangement, and a liberal approach to this question seems in order.[575]

5. Current reform proposals. The Finance Committee staff's final 1985 report on the reform of Subchapter C proposed to replace the tax avoidance test of §357(b) (and the draconian infection of all liabilities if one bad assumption exists) with an objective rule that would limit §357(a) treatment

---

[573] See, e.g., Civic Center Fin. Co. v. Kuhl, supra note 119, where the sole consideration was the assumption of liabilities; supra ¶ 14.11.

[574] Groman v. CIR, supra note 28.

[575] See Rev. Rul. 64-73, 1964-1 CB 142, for a relaxed view of triangular transactions. But see Rev. Rul. 70-107, 1970-1 CB 78 (parent's assumption of liabilities caused taxable boot where the subsidiary was the acquiring corporation); Rev. Rul. 70-224, 1970-1 CB 79 (parent's assumption of liabilities was permitted even though assets were transferred directly to its controlled subsidiary rather than acquired by parent and retransferred to the subsidiary; the parent had control over the assets and hence was treated as if there had been a direct acquisition followed by a dropdown of the assets into the subsidiary). The distinction between these two rulings, aside from form, is not instantly apparent.

See also Rev. Rul. 73-257, 1973-1 CB 189 (subsidiary and parent may assume various liabilities of acquired corporation in §368(a)(2)(D) triangular merger; reorganization status unaffected, and §357(a) protects assumptions from boot status).

Regs. §1.368-2(b)(2) provides that a parent is a party to the exchange for purposes of §357(a) in a §368(a)(2)(D) subsidiary merger; Regs. §1.368-2(j)(5) provides that liability assumptions in a reverse merger under §368(a)(2)(E) do not affect qualification as such (assumption treated as a capital contribution; if securities are exchanged, §§354 and 356 apply). But see rulings supra note 85.

to assumptions of qualifying indebtedness. Qualifying indebtedness, for this purpose, is defined as debt incurred by the transferor in acquiring the transferred property or debt that has a sufficient nexus to the transferee's use of the acquired property in its business. Whether this proposal represents an improvement over current law is dubious, since the inevitable wait for interpretative regulations and court decisions could take decades to arrive at the point where we are now under §357(b)—that is, the scope of §357(b) seems to be relatively well settled and well understood, and the lack of any recent case law under this provision may well indicate that the section is working just fine as is.[576]

¶ 14.56 CONTINGENT CONSIDERATION ACQUISITIONS AND RELATED PROBLEMS

1. General. In view of the uncertainties that typically surround the conclusion of a business bargain, the parties understandably may want to review their estimates of value after a period of time in the light of intervening changes in circumstances and expectations.[577] The contractual mechanisms for adjusting the terms of the initial transaction to take account of subsequent events include the following: (1) contingent consideration acquisitions or price holdback clauses (i.e., open, or adjustable, price terms); (2) escrows, pledges, or other stakeholder-type security arrangements, including rights in the acquiring corporation to take back part of the stock it paid as consideration on specified contingencies; (3) rights to withdraw or

---

[576] Amendments to §361 in 1986 (supra ¶ 14.32, para. 2) effectively eliminate the possibility of taxable boot at the corporate level (thus, the only consequence of §357(b) boot would be for §368 definitional purposes). But see the Technical Corrections Act of 1987 proposals, supra note 337.

[577] See Houston, How Warranties Can Be Used to Control Tax Consequences in Corporate Acquisitions, 28 J. Tax'n 22 (1968); Sugarman, Drafting Clauses of Escape in Agreements With Uncertain Tax Consequences, 12 S. Cal. Tax Inst. 131 (1960); Barker, Planning Business Transactions in View of Uncertainties in Tax Law, 16 S. Cal. Tax Inst. 79 (1964); see also Ziegler, Extricating a Corporation From a Change in Circumstances: Reversing or Modifying a Reorganization or a Liquidation, 29 NYU Inst. on Fed. Tax'n 313 (1971); Bartolini, Avoiding or Adjusting to a Change in Status of Acquisition; Taxable to Non-Taxable, or Vice Versa; Obtaining a Ruling; When Not to Apply, id. at 433; Alfred, How to "Undo" an Acquisition With Minimum Fuss and Tax Cost, 35 J. Tax'n 272 (1971); Dubin, Unscrambling an Acquisition, 49 Taxes 849 (1971); Odell, Terminating Corporate Marriages: Divorce or Annulment, 30 NYU Inst. on Fed. Tax'n 961 (1972); Littenberg & Reinstein, Deconglomeration—Tax and Business Problems Associated With the Divestiture of a Recently Acquired Business, 1972 S. Cal. Tax Inst. 101; Davis, Tax Problems of Modification of Previously Entered-Into Tax-Free Reorganizations on Account of Breach of Warranty, 32 NYU Inst. on Fed. Tax'n 593 (1974); Banoff, Unwinding or Rescinding a Transaction: Good Tax Planning or Tax Fraud, 62 Taxes 942 (1983).

back out from the transaction if certain contingencies occur (i.e., put-back or rescission, rights in either the sellers or the buyers); (4) warranty, indemnity, or guaranty clauses (adjustment rights); and (5) conditional or executory agreements that are not to be consummated until certain conditions occur (e.g., creeping acquisitions). Alternatively, the parties may simply negotiate a new deal to reflect the changed circumstances. It should be noted that advance stripping of the target company to rid it of unwanted assets is also part of this general scene.[578]

The tax consequences of these adjustment mechanisms are considered in the discussion that follows. Common problems in all of these devices, however, have been discussed previously: the continuity of interest doctrine, the definition of stock or securities, and the definition of voting stock. Another problem is how final a transaction must be before it is considered a closed transaction, and, once closed, what happens upon later adjustments (including a complete rescission of the initial transaction).[579]

2. Contingent consideration transactions.[580] As noted previously, the *Carlberg* and *Hamrick* cases held that contingent rights to acquire additional stock did not constitute boot when issued in connection with a reorganization, since the taxpayer's rights could give rise to nothing but stock under the agreement, and hence did not violate the continuity of interest principle.[581] The Service agreed to follow *Hamrick* (where the contingent rights were not readily marketable), but refused to follow *Carlberg* (because the certificates of contingent interest there involved were negotiable).[582]

Subsequently, the Service issued guidelines as to when favorable rulings would be issued in contingent stock transactions[583] (i.e., if (1) there is a busi-

---

[578] See supra ¶ 14.52; see also the mirror subsidiary alternative, infra ¶ 15.23, para. 5.

[579] For the common law background to these problems, see Burnet v. Logan, 283 US 404 (1931); Arrowsmith v. CIR, 344 US 6 (1952); Brown v. CIR, 380 US 563 (1965); US v. Davis, 370 US 65 (1962).

[580] See Tillinghast, Contingent Stock Pay-Outs in Tax-Free Reorganizations, 22 Tax Lawyer 467 (1969); Murphy, Contingent Share Reorganizations, 1969 S. Cal. Tax Inst. 255; Jacobs, Corporate Reorganizations—Deferred Stock Distributions Tax Mgmt. Portfolio (BNA) No. 166-2d (1971); Reum & Steele, Contingent Payouts Cut Acquisition Risks, 48 Harv. Bus. Rev. No. 2, at 83 (1970).

[581] See Carlberg v. US, supra note 304; James Hamrick, supra note 168; see also Rev. Rul. 66-112, 1966-1 CB 68 (agreeing with *Hamrick* but not *Carlberg*); Rev. Rul. 67-90, 1967-1 CB 79 (issue of additional stock contingent on value of acquiring corporation's stock allowed); Rev. Rul. 73-205, 1973-1 CB 188 (contingent stock payout based on adjustment in conversion ratio of convertible preferred did not result in boot).

[582] Rev. Rul. 66-112, 1966-1 CB 68.

[583] Rev. Proc. 77-37, 1977-2 CB 568; Rev. Proc. 84-42, 1984-1 CB 521, added an additional guideline for contingent stock and escrowed stock rulings: The issue of

ness purpose for the delayed issue of stock (such as indeterminacy of values); (2) the delayed stock is payable within five years; (3) there is a ceiling on the number of shares that can be issued; (4) at least 50 percent of the maximum number of shares of each class of stock is issued in the initial distribution; (5) either the agreement is not assignable or the rights to additional shares are not readily marketable; (6) the rights can give rise only to the receipt of additional stock; and (7) the rights are given in exchange for stock or assets of the acquired corporation (not as disguised compensation, royalties, and the like). While adherence to these guidelines is usually advisable as a matter of prudence, it should be noted that the cases are considerably more liberal, and a guideline footfault does not necessarily render the transaction taxable.

Several aspects of the guideline requirements bear noting, however, as well as certain special problems created by these transactions:

(1) The business purpose condition seems relatively easy to satisfy, especially since the Service agrees that inability to agree on the value of even listed securities will justify a holdback arrangement. [584]

(2) The five-year limitation seems concerned with the requirement that stock be issued pursuant to a plan of reorganization; perpetual rights tend to resemble royalty or profit-sharing arrangements rather than closed exchanges for present value. On the other hand, the rights in *Hamrick* provided for a seven-year payout term, and those in *Carlberg* had no time limit. [585]

(3) The ceiling requirement likewise seems concerned with excessively speculative deals that more nearly resemble licenses than exchanges, but it also seems related to problems in the computation of basis. In computing gain or loss on sales in the interim, the Service assumes that all contingent shares will be earned, thus maximizing gains and minimizing losses on such interim transactions. [586]

---

contingent stock or release of escrowed stock must not be triggered by events within the control of the shareholders, or by a Service audit, and the trigger mechanism must be an objective and readily ascertainable event; superseded (in part) by Rev. Proc. 87-3, 1987-1 IRB 27.

[584] Rev. Rul. 67-90, 1967-1 CB 79.

[585] See also Burnet v. Logan, supra note 579; Brown v. CIR, supra note 579. On the plan requirement generally, supra ¶ 14.11, para. 10.

[586] Rev. Proc. 77-37, 1977-2 CB 568, assumes full earnout of contingent shares, exclusive of those attributable to interest, for purposes of computing interim basis of stock actually issued.

If the full amount of contingent shares is not earned, a shareholder's unassigned basis attributable to his contingent rights to receive these shares presumably should

(4) The 50 percent down payment requirement is more obscure, but this limitation may be viewed as a buttress to the five-year term and ceiling rules against overly speculative (i.e., license-type) transactions.

(5) The limitation requiring that the rights give rise solely to the receipt of additional stock is obviously based on the continuity of interest principle, but a distinction should be drawn here between Type A and Types B or C reorganizations. In the latter, only *voting* stock is allowed, so the possibility of receiving accrued dividends on the withheld stock in the form of cash could, if treated as part of the acquisition price, destroy the tax-free character of the reorganization, although payment of accrued dividends in additional voting stock seems allowable. In a statutory merger, by contrast, consideration other than voting stock is allowable, so that accrued dividends on the contingent shares paid in cash would merely be taxable to the recipient as ordinary income without affecting the validity of the reorganization (even if deemed to be connected to the initial selling price).

(6) Nonmarketability of the contingent stock issue rights seems to be required by the Service because of the possibility that accrued cash dividends on the contingent shares might be converted into capital gain by a sale of the underlying claim.[587]

(7) Contingent stock issue payments can give rise to imputed interest income under §483,[588] although Regs. §1.483-2(a)(2) (which was

---

be allocated to the stock still held by him at such time; if all shares have been sold, however, a capital loss deduction would seem appropriate. See Arrowsmith v. CIR, supra note 579; Rees Blow Pipe Mfg. Co., 41 TC 598 (1964) (nonacq.), aff'd per curiam, 342 F2d 990 (9th Cir. 1965); Rev. Rul. 55-119, 1955-1 CB 352; supra ¶ 9.32.

[587] As to whether a particular item is readily marketable, see §453(f)(5). Compare Brundage v. CIR, 275 F2d 424 (7th Cir.), cert. denied, 364 US 831 (1960) (ordinary income on sale of stock with accrued dividend rights), with Oscar L. Mathis, 47 TC 248 (1966) (acq.) (sale of stock with accrued dividend arrears, capital gain); see supra ¶ 7.07.

[588] For application of §483 to contingent stock issue transactions, see Rev. Rul. 70-300, 1970-1 CB 125 (determination of §483 interest factor under various earnout formulas; also methods for avoiding §483). See cases cited supra note 307; Jerrold L. Kingsley, 72 TC 1095 (1979), aff'd, 662 F2d 539 (9th Cir. 1981) (and cases cited). But see infra note 591.

On the potential dangers of paying minimum interest in cash, rather than stock, see Tillinghast, supra note 580, at 473. Payment of interest (real or imputed) seems to be severable from the main consideration, however, and ought not to affect its tax-free status; see Prop. Regs. §1.483-5(b)(1); infra note 589 (OID rules apply in lieu of §483 here).

If minimum interest is payable in specifically designated shares, these, of course, will be taxable as ordinary income when received, but these shares will then obtain a

applicable to §483 before its revision in 1984) stated that such interest income would not constitute boot that destroys reorganization status (i.e., it is severable from the principal payments that must be solely voting stock).[589] If the parties provide for interest at the specified minimum rate or higher (payable either in stock or, more dangerously, in cash), however, §483 can be avoided.

However, legislation enacted in 1984[590] largely supplanted §483 with expanded coverage of the original issue discount rules in §§1272 and 1273; these provisions apply, however, only if the obligation to issue contingent stock is treated as a "debt instrument" under §1275(a)(1), which defines such term as "any obligation." In any event, the imputed interest characterization rule of §483 now will be computed in the same general manner as under the original issue discount rules, although the *timing* would differ under these two provisions: OID interest is taxed currently on a compound economic accrual basis, while §483 interest is taxable under the normal accounting rules.[591]

(8) If the acquiring corporation is in turn absorbed by another corporation, which proceeds to substitute its stock for that of the acquiring corporation to satisfy the latter's contingent stock obligation, the reorganization status for the first acquisition could be imperiled (or, at the least, the second corporation's stock would be taxable) because the second corporation is not a party to the first reorganization. An acceleration clause (or a provision to issue a compro-

---

cost basis and hence can be identified and sold without additional gain or loss. See Rev. Rul. 70-300, supra.

[589] See also Rev. Rul. 73-298, 1973-2 CB 173 (§483 applies to contingent stock issued to compensate sellers for decline in value of buyer's stock; not a mere guaranty to selling shareholders against decline in value; instead, additional stock was part of price and hence §483 applied); supra note 307, and cases there cited. For continued severability under the 1984 OID and imputed interest rules, see Prop. Regs. §§1.1274-4(e)(1) and 1.483-5(b)(1).

[590] The Tax Reform Act of 1984, adding §§1274 and 1275 and amending §483; see generally ¶¶ 4.41 and 4.42.

[591] The amount of imputed interest under the two provisions would be the same, however, since §483 imputed interest would be under the same formula as §1274 issue discount.

Contingent stock transactions should probably be handled under the contingent payment rules of §483(f), although §1275(d) similarly envisions application of the OID rules to contingent payment obligations. Moreover, the OID rules specifically take priority over §483 under §483(d)(1). Prop. Regs. §1.1275-1(b)(1) says that the deferred payments in stock are debt instruments for purposes of the OID rules, however, thus ousting §483. See Lokken, The Time Value of Money Rules, 42 Tax L. Rev. 1 (1986).

For proposed regulations dealing with contingent payment transactions, see Prop. Regs. §§1.483-5 and 1.1275-4 (1986); see generally Walter & Strasen, Innovative Transactions, 64 Taxes 488 (1986); Walter & Strasen, Contingent and Adjustable Stock in a Public Context, 65 Taxes 439 (1987).

mised number of shares) in the contingent acquisition agreement could avoid this problem; another method would be to deposit the unearned contingent shares in escrow, providing for the distribution of earned shares of the issuer (or a successor) pursuant to the earn-out schedule, and for the return of any unearned shares to the issuer or its successor.[592]

(9) The effect of contingent stock issue terms on net operating loss carry-over computations under §382 is noted in Chapter 16; the stock dividend aspects under amended §305(b) are considered in Chapter 7.

3. Escrow arrangements. Instead of merely promising to issue additional shares if earnings meet specified levels, if disputed liabilities are satisfactorily settled, and so forth, the acquiring corporation may place the shares in escrow under an arrangement by which the escrow agent will transfer them to the shareholders of the acquired corporation if the conditions are satisfied by a designated date, but otherwise will return them to the acquiring corporation.[593] Because escrowed stock may be viewed as having been actually issued and transferred (despite the possibility of its return to the acquiring corporation), there may be a greater willingness to treat the transaction as closed for reorganization purposes, especially if the transferor is entitled to the dividends or to vote the stock in the interim. For a possible analogy, see Rev. Rul. 70-120, holding that §483 does not apply to shares deposited in escrow where the beneficial interests were not transferable and where the holders of the beneficial interests reported dividends currently and were entitled to vote the escrowed stock;[594] in other words, the escrowed shares were considered to be issued and outstanding rather than a deferred payment.

Whether the escrow device can be used to circumvent the guideline requirements of Rev. Proc. 77-37 however, was initially unclear. For example, if substantially all the consideration was tied up in escrow for an unreason-

---

[592] See Rev. Rul. 75-237, 1975-1 CB 116 (contingent stock issued under acceleration clause in original agreement or under subsequently negotiated agreement held tax-free under §354(a)(1) because acquired pursuant to plan of reorganization under Regs. §1.368-2(g) and Rev. Rul. 75-94, 1975-1 CB 111.

But see Rev. Rul. 75-456, 1975-2 CB 128 (mere reincorporation via a Type F reorganization during pay-out term will not result in payment of new stock).

[593] See Rev. Proc. 77-37, 1977-2 CB 568, and Rev. Proc. 87-3, 1987-1 IRB 27, with guidelines for escrows.

See also Jacobs, Escrows and Their Tax Consequences, 39 NYU Inst. on Fed. Tax'n ch. 5 (1981); Fleming, Rethinking Contingent Price Reorganizations, 9 J. Corp. Tax'n 3 (1982).

[594] Rev. Rul. 70-120, 1970-1 CB 124. But see Feifer v. US, 500 F. Supp. 102 (N.D. Ga. 1980) (§483 not applicable to release of escrowed stock even though tax-payer's voting rights restricted).

ably long period of time, the arrangement might be so tentative that it could fail to qualify as a present tax-free reorganization. On the other hand, it seems reasonably clear that the full rigors of Rev. Proc. 77-37 should not apply to escrow agreements in view of the fundamental differences between escrows and contingent share arrangements. While the Service now applies most, although not all, of the limits of Rev. Proc. 77-37 to escrows,[595] it seems that the latter are somewhat more flexible than contingent share plans.

If some of the escrowed shares are returned to the issuing corporation because of an event that triggers forfeiture of those shares, it is unclear whether the beneficial holders of the escrowed shares are deemed to have made a taxable exchange of those shares.[596] If the recaptured stock is transferred in satisfaction of an obligation (liquidated or unliquidated) of the shareholder to the acquiring corporation (e.g., in satisfaction of a liability for breach of a warranty or representation in the contract), the *Davis* case indicates that taxable gain or loss may result to the transferor.[597] The result seems likely if the repossessed shares are taken at current values and if the transferor has the right to substitute other property for the escrowed stock in the event of a repossession.

On the other hand, *Rees Blow Pipe Manufacturing Co.* and *McGlothlin v. CIR* offer support for the contrary view (i.e., that the transfer is merely a nontaxable adjustment to the terms of the original reorganization exchange),[598] and this view seems to be inspired by the *Arrowsmith* principle, which holds that the character of subsequent aspects in a single transaction is controlled by the prior related elements of that transaction.[599] This approach seems more appropriate if the identical stock is snapped back pursuant to a condition subsequent string thereon in the original agreement (especially if the shares are repossessed on the basis of their initial negotiated value).[600]

---

[595] Supra note 593. See also Rev. Proc. 84-42 1984-1 CB 521, and Rev. Proc. 87-3 1987-1 IRB 27, for additional guidelines applicable to contingent stock and escrowed stock rulings.

[596] See supra note 580.

[597] US v. Davis, supra note 579; Rev. Rul. 78-376, 1978-2 CB 149 (in addition to recognition of gain or loss on the forfeiture, basis of remaining shares stepped up by value of shares forfeited).

[598] Rees Blow Pipe Mfg. Co., supra note 586; McGlothlin v. CIR, 370 F2d 729 (5th Cir. 1967).

[599] Arrowsmith v. CIR, supra note 579; see also Rev. Rul. 83-73, 1983-1 CB 84.

[600] See Rev. Rul. 76-42, 1976-1 CB 102 (repossession of escrowed stock on failure to meet earnings levels did not result in taxable gain or loss; mere adjustment of original price per plan of reorganization; shares repossessed at initial negotiated value and taxpayer had no right to substitute other property; basis of repossessed stock added to basis of stock still held); Rev. Rul. 76-334, 1976-2 CB 108 (no gain or

The acquiring corporation, in any event, would not seem to be in receipt of income from repossession of its stock; rather, it has merely received a downward adjustment to its purchase price for the acquired properties. However, the reacquired shares could be considered as damages to the recipient, in which event they might be taxable as ordinary income if the underlying claim was for lost profits; otherwise, the receipts would seem to constitute a nontaxable return of capital or reduction of purchase price.

If the escrowed shares are forfeited because of failure to attain designated earnings levels, it seems relatively clear that no gain or loss should result to either party, since the repossession of shares ordinarily would not be in satisfaction of a liability, and thus the *Davis* debt discharge analogy would not be applicable.[601]

4. Back-out rights, put-back rights, and other rescission situations. If either the transferors or the acquiring corporation retain the right (or are compelled in certain events) to rescind their initial bargain, uncertainty as to the tax consequences rapidly escalates. For example, will an option to put back the acquiring corporation's stock be considered boot to the transferors, thereby destroying Type B or Type C reorganization status? Will call or redemption rights in the acquiring corporation affect continuity of interest? Will the right in the acquiring corporation to rescind all or part of the acquisition affect the substantially all requirement of a Type C reorganization? Will taxable gain or loss result to the parties on a partial or complete rescission? Finally, do the acquired corporation's tax attributes (e.g., loss carryovers, earnings and profits, and so forth) go back to it or remain with the acquiring corporation on a rescission?

Rev. Rul. 69-265 held that put-type rights entitling the shareholder to exchange stock of the acquiring corporation for stock of the acquiring cor-

---

loss on forfeiture of escrowed shares per terms of escrow, using initial negotiated values, because of breach of representations and warranties by acquired corporation; mere adjustment of price, and basis of retained stock adjusted to reflect forfeiture; but cash received in settlement of dispute over amount of forfeiture taxable under §302). Compare Rev. Rul. 78-376, 1978-2 CB 149 (taxable exchange at current values).

[601] See generally Eustice, supra note 213. If the cancellation of indebtedness-mortgage foreclosure analogy is applied to forfeited share situations (i.e., by treating them as pledged property security devices), gain or loss will result to both the debtor (unless one of the exceptions to debt cancellation income applies) and the creditor in this situation, a result that seems unfortunate in view of what the parties are trying to accomplish here, i.e., protect against the possibility that the terms of the initial bargain may have to be adjusted to take account of subsequent changes of circumstances. Unfortunately, this is also one of the prime reasons for the use of mortgage or pledge-security arrangements.

See Rev. Rul. 76-42 1976-1 CB 102 (no income to forfeiting shareholders).

poration's parent did not constitute boot (at least if not exercisable for five years) so as to destroy Type C reorganization status.[602] In effect, this ruling seems to sanction an exchange-put arrangement and maybe even a cash-put term if the price is not fixed at grant. Moreover, continuity of interest is not interrupted, according to Rev. Rul. 66-23, even though the transferors are required to divest themselves of the transferee's stock within seven years so long as at least five years of unrestricted ownership existed.[603] Finally, Rev. Rul. 68-22 held that a discretionary right by the acquiring corporation to redeem 10 percent of its shares annually did not adversely affect reorganization status,[604] while Rev. Rul. 78-142 held that conditional rescission rights inherent in the stock did not constitute severable boot.[605] From this it would seem that rescission rights in either the transferor or the transferee should not ordinarily constitute boot to the transferors (or affect continuity of interest of the reorganization) if the proprietary interest of the acquired corporation's shareholders in the acquiring corporation lasts, or could be expected to last, for a reasonable duration (five years seems to be the Service's rule of thumb here).

The transferee's right to return part of the acquired assets to the transferor (or its shareholders), on the other hand, could cause trouble under the substantially all requirement under §§368(a)(1)(C), 368(a)(2)(D), and 368(a)(2)(E),[606] in view of the fact that it has not irrevocably taken over the requisite quantum of the transferor's properties. Although the transferee ordinarily is always free to dispose of part or, for that matter, all of the acquired corporation's assets in a subsequently agreed sale to third parties without adversely affecting the reorganization,[607] the acquiring corporation's option to return significant portions of the acquired properties to the former owners seems to stand on a different footing in view of the transferee's lack of an irrevocable commitment to take substantially all the assets. Absent any decided cases or published rulings on this point, extreme caution should be exercised in drafting this type of agreement if §368(a)(1)(C) or triangular merger classification is desired.[608]

---

[602] Rev. Rul. 69-265, 1969-1 CB 109.

[603] Rev. Rul 66-23, 1966-1 CB 67.

[604] Rev. Rul. 68-22, 1968-1 CB 142.

[605] Rev. Rul. 78-142, 1978-1 CB 111. See generally ¶¶ 14.11 and 14.13.

[606] Supra ¶¶ 14.14 and 14.15.

[607] But see Regs. §1.368-1(d), supra ¶ 14.51, para. 2 (continuity of business requirement).

[608] For comparable problems, see supra ¶ 14.52, where the transferor strips off potentially unwanted assets on the threshold of the acquisition. See also Regs. §1.368-1(d), supra ¶ 14.51, para. 2 (continuity of business requirement); and infra ¶ 15.23, para. 5 (post-transaction tailoring with mirror subsidiaries).

If the transferee returns all or part of the stock of the acquired corporation (after a previously tax-free Type B acquisition), §311(b) (see Chapter 11) ordinarily will cause recognition of gain to the distributing corporation unless the reexchange of stocks qualifies as a tax-free split-off under §355 (see Chapter 13), in which event §311(b) would not apply.

If all or part of the acquired properties are put back to the transferors for cash, the unwinding transaction is, of course, a taxable event to the selling party. If, however, the entire transaction is rescinded and the original consideration is returned in kind, it could at least be argued that no gain or loss should be recognized to either party in this situation on the ground that matters merely revert to their preacquisition status (perhaps the annulment or possibility of reverter analogy is appropriate here—that is, the original corporate marriage is dissolved nunc pro tunc). The *Rees Blow Pipe* and *Arrowsmith* decisions lend support to this treatment, but its successful use probably requires the continued existence of the acquired corporation after the first transaction,[609] and probably a relatively short interval between the initial acquisition and later rescission; if boot had been paid, or if a loss carry-over was consumed, the complexities may be too great to support use of the *Arrowsmith* nonrecognition theory.

If the rescission transfers instead are treated as a "divorce" (i.e., an independent transaction from the original acquisition), however, *Davis*[610] and the mortgage foreclosure analogy[611] would require recognition of gain or loss to the exchanging parties.[612] Classification of the rescission transaction as a taxable or a tax-free event also would control the ultimate location of the tax attributes inherited by the acquiring corporation under §381 (see Chapter 16) in the original transaction. If the rescission is tax-free, the unconsumed attributes apparently could return to the orig-

---

[609] The transferor corporation's existence could be preserved after a Type C asset reorganization if it does not liquidate (which it is not required to do); the same would be true in a Type B stock acquisition. Type A statutory merger acquisition ordinarily results in the dissolution of the acquired corporation, however, and it would require considerably more effort to resurrect the transferor. A §368(a)(2)(D) triangular merger seems to be functionally equivalent to a Type B reorganization (at least if a new subsidiary is used as the acquiring vehicle), and it should at least be technically feasible to effect a rescission of this type of transaction. A §368(a)(2)(E) reverse merger results in the continued existence of the acquired corporation, and in this respect is much like the Type B reorganization in its rescindability.

See Rev. Rul. 80-58, 1980-1 CB 181, for the Service's treatment of rescissions generally (no gain or loss if return to status quo in same taxable year; otherwise, unwinding transaction a taxable event).

[610] US v. Davis, supra note 579.

[611] Supra note 601.

[612] See Rev. Rul. 78-119, 1978-1 CB 277 (Type B reorganization unwound in same year by §355 split-off not true rescission because parties not returned to identical original positions—they each kept interim dividends).

inal transferor (if it is still in existence) as if the original transaction had never occurred.[613] If the rescission is a taxable event, however, the transferor's inherited tax attributes should remain with the acquiring corporation.

As an alternative to the theories described above, §355 may be available to effect a tax-free non-pro rata split-off of the acquired corporation back to its original owners (assuming the five-year active business requirements can be satisfied).[614] This would have the additional benefit of protecting the distributing corporation from the gain recognition rules of §311(b).[615] The possibility of using §355 to unwind the prior acquisition on a tax-free basis is technically easier to envision if the prior transaction was a Type B stock acquisition (or a reverse merger, which seems to be a functional equivalent), although it could theoretically be used to unscramble an asset deal as well.

5. Damages for breach of original agreement. If the acquiring corporation violates a representation, warranty, or guaranty term in its agreement with the acquired corporation, payment of cash damages to the transferors to satisfy this liability would not be treated as boot (which thereby could adversely affect the prior reorganization) if the subsequent transaction is severable from the original acquisition. If the later transaction is independent, the damage proceeds ordinarily would be taxable to the recipients, possibly as capital gain if the requisite sale or exchange can be found; but perhaps they could be characterized under *Arrowsmith, McGlothlin,* and *Rees Blow Pipe* as a nontaxable capital adjustment to the original consideration received in the acquisition (i.e., the acquiring corporation stock), in which event they might be applied to reduce the basis for such property.

Tax-free recovery of basis treatment for these receipts might also be obtained by analyzing the character of the underlying claim for which the damages are received: If the claim relates to a capital item (i.e., the property received in the initial acquisition), the damage proceeds should be classified as capital recoveries; if the claim relates to loss of income, however, taxability as ordinary income would result. On the other hand, connecting the damage payments to the initial acquisition might retroactively destroy reorgani-

---

[613] For an analogy, see Regs. §1.453-6(b), dealing with repossession of property sold on a deferred payment basis where title is retained by the seller.

[614] For an illustration of the use of a non-pro rata tax-free split-off under §355 to unwind a prior Type B reorganization, see Rev. Rul. 71-383 1971-2 CB 180; Rev. Rul. 78-119, 1978-1 CB 277.

[615] Supra ¶ 9.34. For the conditions of §355, see generally supra ¶¶ 13.01–13.15.

zation status (at least if paid in cash), in which event the entire transaction would be treated as a taxable event retroactively.[616]

The payor corporation ordinarily would be required to add such amounts to its basis for the assets acquired in the original acquisition unless they could be characterized as ordinary business expenses, deductible under §162, which seems unlikely in view of the origin of the claim test of the *Woodward* and *Hilton Hotel* cases.[617]

If the acquiring corporation discharges its obligation by paying additional stock to the transferors, no gain or loss would result to the payor by virtue of §1032; the value of such payment, however, apparently would increase its basis for the acquired properties in the same manner as a cash payment of damages for breach of the acquisition agreement. These results assume severability from the original acquisition transaction, however. If the payment of additional stock is characterized under the *Arrowsmith* principle by reference to the tax-free nature of the initial reorganization transaction, no step-up in basis would occur. By the same token, taxability to the recipients of these additional shares also would depend upon whether the subsequent payment is separate or connected to the initial acquisition transaction; severability would result in taxable income to the recipients, while connection treatment would allow receipt of the shares without recognition of gain. As a practical matter, it would seem advisable to require any additional payments by the acquiring corporation for its breach of the acquisition agreement to be made in voting stock of that corporation if the tax-free character of the original reorganization is to be assured; this would also give the transferors the chance to obtain nonrecognition on the receipt of these shares by analogy to the contingent stock issue authorities.[618]

Where the *transferors* are the defaulting parties under the agreement, cash payments on their part to the acquiring corporation presumably should be treated as capital expenditures by the payors and as tax-free adjustments

---

[616] See Victor E. Gidwitz Family Trust, 61 TC 664 (1974) (payments by majority shareholder of acquired corporation to minority shareholder as consideration for refraining from blocking merger held taxable as capital gain; cash was additional consideration for their stock; but compare Rev. Rul. 76-334, 1976-2 CB 108 (cash paid to settle dispute over amount of escrowed stock to be forfeited held not part of initial reorganization so solely requirement not violated; gain on stock forfeited for cash taxed as separate §302 redemption). But see Tribune Pub. Co. v. US, 57 AFTR2d 1267 (D.C. Wash. 1986) (pro rata damages were dividends).

[617] See Woodward v. CIR. 397 US 572 (1970); US v. Hilton Hotels Corp., 397 US 580 (1970). See generally supra ¶ 5.04.

[618] Supra para. 2. See Rev. Rul. 75-94, 1975-1 CB 111 (payment of additional stock by acquiring corporation to satisfy claims by acquired corporation's shareholders under federal and state securities laws for material misrepresentation by acquiring corporation as to value of its stock held tax-free under §354(a)(1) as receipt "in pursuance of the plan of reorganization").

to the purchase price by the payee corporation.[619] If part of the acquiring corporation's shares are repossessed to satisfy this obligation (e.g., where shares had been placed in escrow for a certain period), recognition of gain or loss to the parties depends upon whether the *Arrowsmith* relation back approach is adopted or whether the subsequent transaction is treated as an independently taxable event on the order of a mortgage foreclosure.[620]

As noted earlier in this section, these questions are not as yet fully resolved, but it would seem preferable not to require recognition of gain or loss to the parties in this situation on the ground that they are merely pulling a condition subsequent string and adjusting the terms of the initial transaction to reflect the original expectations of the parties to the agreement. In a sense, the contractual promises of the transferor can be viewed as an asset (or at least a potential asset) of the acquired corporation that subsequently ripens into a present right to adjust the purchase price (i.e., reclaim part of the original consideration) in the event of a breach by the transferor. This type of adjustment would not seem to be an appropriate time to impose a tax (or allow a deduction) in view of the parties' intent to continue with the original deal on reformed or modified terms. Perhaps the statement in Regs. §1.1001-1(a) (that a taxable exchange only occurs on the receipt of property "differing materially in kind or extent") could provide support for the conclusion that what has happened here in substance is a mere adjustment or modification of the *same* continuing property interest, rather than an exchange of one property for another.[621]

6. Other adjustment or tentative acquisition devices. If the parties are unsure of their willingness to lock up the deal until resolution of various contingencies, other more tentative arrangements than those discussed previously may be in order. For example, the acquiring corporation may obtain merely an option to acquire the stock or assets of the target company. If cash is paid for the option, however, it seems unlikely that the acquisition could be completed on a wholly tax-free basis in view of the fact that the consideration paid for the option would undoubtedly be connected to the amounts

---

[619] See Freedom Newspapers, Inc., ¶ 77,429 P-H Memo. TC (1977) (so held, even where adjustment of price paid by third person, citing *Arrowsmith*); see also Rev. Rul. 83-73, 1983-1 CB 84, which likewise so holds (purchase price adjustment per indemnity agreement).

[620] Supra notes 600 and 601; Rev. Rul. 76-334, 1976-2 CB 108 (no gain or loss on forfeiture of escrowed shares because of seller default; also, cash paid by buyer to settle dispute over size of forfeiture not part of initial reorganization; taxable instead as separate redemption transaction under §302).

[621] See supra notes 2 and 4.

paid upon the subsequent exercise of the optionee's rights.[622] If the potential acquirer allows its option rights to lapse, §1234 would govern the character of its loss (by reference to the nature of the property subject to the option). The optionor's premium for granting the option generally would be taxed as ordinary income to the optionor upon lapse of the option.[623] Conversely, if the option is exercised, the premiums would be treated as part of the consideration for the properties subject to the option (i.e., boot), which would render the acquisition partially or fully taxable, depending upon whether the transaction was an attempted Type A, B, or C reorganization. If the option premium is paid in voting stock of the acquiring corporation-optionee, however, boot treatment should not apply, and the entire transaction (assuming the option is exercised) could be effected on a tax-free basis; lapse of the option would give rise to ordinary income for the optionor (measured by the value of the optionee's stock, presumably at the time of lapse), while the optionee apparently would be entitled to a deduction under §1234, ordinarily as a capital loss, measured by the value of its stock as of such date.[624]

Instead of a mere option to acquire stock or assets, the parties may make an executory contract providing for closing at such time as the various conditions precedent to execution of the transaction are satisfied. This type of arrangement is nothing more than an agreement *to* reorganize (as opposed to a present reorganization), and its subsequent execution (or termination) should not give rise to any special tax problems other than those discussed in preceding portions of this chapter, which seem ample enough under the circumstances.

¶ 14.57   QUASI-REORGANIZATIONS: NONQUALIFYING, OR TAXABLE, REORGANIZATIONS

If the purported reorganization fails to qualify as such under the definitional rules of §368, (discussed in Part B), its tax treatment is controlled by

---

[622] Compare Richard M. Mills, 39 TC 393 (1962) (concurring opinion); Rev. Rul. 72-198, 1972-1 CB 223; §1032 (as amended in 1984).

[623] But see §1234(b) (short-term capital gain or loss to grantor of option on stocks and securities on lapse of option), added by the Tax Reform Act of 1976.

See also Rev. Rul. 72-198, 1972-1 CB 223 (premium ordinary income to grantor on lapse of option to acquire grantor's own stock); Rev. Rul. 80-134, 1980-1 CB 187 (unilateral extension of exercise date by grantor as lapse of old warrant). But the Tax Reform Act of 1984 extended §1032 protection to the corporate grantor on the cancellation or lapse of options to acquire its stock.

[624] If the grantor receives its option premium in kind (i.e., in the optionee's voting stock) and resells that stock before the acquisition takes place, taxability of the sales proceeds presumably could be suspended until such time as the option is exercised or lapses; see Rev. Rul. 72-198, 1972-1 CB 223; and supra ¶ 7.44.

other Code provisions dealing with sales, liquidations, redemptions, and dividends. Thus a taxable asset acquisition (even though effected in whole or in part with stock of the acquiring corporation) would nevertheless be treated under the liquidation rules discussed in Chapter 11, while taxable recapitalizations and the like would be handled under principles discussed in Chapter 7 (dividends) and Chapter 9 (redemptions). In other words, the fact that the transaction functionally resembles a reorganization in the colloquial sense is irrelevant in determining the tax treatment afforded to the respective parties.[625] It should be noted, however, that reorganization status may be conferred on a transaction that the parties intended, or hoped, would be taxable as a liquidation, as discussed earlier in this chapter.

¶ 14.58 INSOLVENCY REORGANIZATIONS: COLLATERAL ASPECTS

1. General. The Bankruptcy Tax Act of 1980 significantly revised the tax treatment of insolvency reorganizations in Section 4 of the Act, as discussed previously. The other principal section of the Act, Section 2, overhauled the debt cancellation rules of prior law in §§108 and 1017.[626] While

---

[625] See, e.g., Rev. Rul. 69-6, 1969-1 CB 104 (all-cash merger held a sale of assets by absorbed corporation, to which §337 could apply, and a liquidation to the shareholders under §331); see also Rev. Rul. 77-19, 1977-1 CB 84; West-Shore Fuel Inc. v. US, 453 F. Supp. 956 (W.D.N.Y. 1978), aff'd, 598 F2d 1236 (2d Cir. 1979) (no §453 for shareholders; merger transaction a corporate-level asset sale, not a shareholder-level stock sale); but see §453(h) (1980 amendment).

Compare Home Sav. & Loan Ass'n v. US, supra note 27 (all-cash acquisition because of lack of continuity of interest regarding acquiring corporation's consideration, held taxable stock purchase followed by §334(b)(2) liquidation).

See generally Rachofsky, The Reorganization That Fails: Tax Consequences of an Involuntarily Taxable Reorganization, 32 NYU Inst. on Fed. Tax'n 639 (1974); Bruce, Liquidations and Reorganizations: Madison Sqaure Garden and Kass, 30 Tax L. Rev. 303 (1975); Tufts, The Taxable Merger, 7 J. Corp. Tax'n 342 (1981).

See also supra ¶ 14.19 (investment company fusion as taxable exchanges); infra ¶ 16.24 (under §382(g)(3)(B), a taxable reorganization can, to the extent regulations provide, trigger an ownership change under §382).

[626] For description of prior law, see Krantz, Loss Carryovers in Chapter X Reorganizations, 16 Tax L. Rev. 359 (1961); Eustice, Cancellation of Indebtedness and the Federal Income Tax: A Problem of Creeping Confusion, 14 Tax L. Rev. 225, 267–270, 277–279 (1959): Tillinghast & Gardner, Acquisitive Reorganizations and Chapters X and XI of the Bankruptcy Act, 26 Tax L. Rev. 663 (1971); see also Berger, Acquisitions of Financially Troubled Businesses, 50 Taxes 809 (1972). See generally Report of the Commission on Bankruptcy Laws (July 30, 1973), for proposed revisions in the tax rules for insolvency reorganizations. For an extensive analysis of this report, see Plumb, The Tax Recommendations of the Commission on the Bankruptcy Laws—Reorganizations, Carryovers, and the Effect of Debt Reduction, 29 Tax L. Rev. 227 (1974); Plumb, Bankruptcy and

these latter provisions were not technically part of the tax-free reorganization provisions of Subchapter C, they frequently arise in the context of an insolvency reorganization proceeding (especially recapitalizations), are an integral aspect of that proceeding, and, in many cases, may be even more significant in their tax impact to the respective parties than the Subchapter C rules. It is for this reason that they are considered at this point.

The initial version of Section 2(a) of the Bankruptcy Tax Act (proposed by the House in November of 1979) substantially revised §108(a) by strictly limiting the exclusion for gains attributable to the discharge of indebtedness solely to insolvency situations (i.e., where either (a) the discharge occurred in a title 11 proceeding (the debt was discharged in a Bankruptcy Act proceeding pursuant to a court approval plan) or (b) the debtor taxpayer was insolvent (liabilities exceeded the value of the debtor's assets). In the latter case, the exclusion was limited by §108(a)(3) to the extent that the debtor was insolvent immediately prior to the discharge. In 1980, however, these proposals were revised by the House to continue the elective exclusion—basis reduction treatment for gains derived by solvent debtors from the discharge of qualified business indebtedness, §§108(a)(1)(C), 108(c), and 108(d)(4) (in which case the basis of *depreciable* property only would be reduced to the extent thereof if basis reduction treatment was affirmatively elected by the debtor in the manner prescribed by §108(d)(4)), and this version prevailed in the final act. Six years later, however, in the Tax Reform Act of 1986, solvent corporations were totally excluded from the regime of §§1017 and 108.[627]

The key provision of amended §108, however, is §108(b), which requires various tax attributes of the debtor to be reduced in a prescribed order (i.e., first, net operating losses of the year of discharge and carry-overs *to* such year, then investment tax credit carry-overs to or from such year and then capital losses of such year and carry-overs to such year) to the extent the debt cancellation gain was excluded from gross income under §108(a). If any remaining exclusion exists after the above reductions, then basis of the debtor's property is to be reduced under §1017. Finally, foreign tax credit carry-overs are to be reduced by any remaining excluded amounts. Such reductions are made dollar for dollar (except for credits, where the reduction

---

Insolvency: Effects of Debt Reduction on Loss Carryovers and Basis, 2 J. Corp. Tax'n 173 (1975). For analyses of these provisions, see articles supra note 285. See also Afosky, Discharge of Indebtness Income in Bankruptcy After the Bankruptcy Tax Act of 1980, 27 St. Louis U.L.J. 583 (1983); Peaslee, Discharge of Indebtness Through its Acquisition by a Person Related to the Debtor—An Analysis of Section 108(e)(4), 37 Tax L. Rev. 193 (1982).

[627] The Tax Reform Act of 1986 reverted to the original 1979 House bill proposal and repealed the elective exclusion provisions of §§108(a)(1)(C), 108(c), and 108(d)(4) for qualified indebtness of solvent debtor corporation.

See generally supra ¶ 4.25.

is 50 cents for each dollar of exclusion). These reductions are made after the tax is determined for the year of discharge, current year's losses are reduced before carry-overs, and carry-overs are reduced on a first in, first out basis.

The final version of §108 also provides an election in §108(b)(5) for the debtor to reduce the basis of its depreciable property before any reduction in tax attributes. (For this purpose, §1017(b)(3) provides that dealer real estate can be treated as depreciable property and that parent corporations filing consolidated returns can apply the depreciable basis reduction to stock of their subsidiaries if the latter agree to a corresponding basis reduction in their depreciable property.) The stated purpose of this amendment was to give the debtor flexibility in determining whether it wanted to preserve either its net operating loss carry-overs, or its depreciation deductions following the debt discharge transaction. To the extent that a debtor elects to reduce its basis for depreciable property, §1017(d) subjects such reductions to recapture rules similar to §§1245 and 1250, as the case may be, on an early disposition of such property.

The final version of §108(e)(1) also provides that the involvency exceptions of §108(a) are exclusive. However, §§108(e)(2) and 108(e)(5) contain two additional exceptions apart from the general exclusion rules of §108(a): First, reduction of purchase money debt of a solvent purchaser will be treated as a purchase price adjustment, and second, income will not be recognized from the discharge of undeducted expense liabilities. Presumably, this latter exception from gross income will not trigger the tax attribute reduction rules of §108(b). Finally, §108(e)(4) provides that debt acquired by related persons will be deemed to have been acquired directly by the debtor.[628]

The 1980 version of §108 treated debt cancellation gains of solvent debtors in substantially the same manner as those of insolvent debtors, affording to both the election either to reduce the basis of depreciable assets (subject to later recapture of such reductions under §§1245 and 1250) or, by not so electing, to cause its various tax attributes (e.g., loss carry-overs) to be reduced in the prescribed statutory order of §108(b)(2) (in the case of insolvent debtors) or be currently taxed (in the case of solvent debtors). However, the Tax Reform Act of 1986 abandoned the approach of the original legislation and removed solvent debtors from the regime of §§108 and 1017 in toto.

Another major substantive change proposed by the House version of the Act was in §108(f), which removed the protection of §§118 and 1032 for corporate debtors that discharged their debts by issuing additional stock or by means of a capital contribution of the debt. Debt cancelled by the issuance of stock was to be treated as if it had been cancelled for cash equal to the value of the stock; debt cancelled in a capital contribution was treated as

---

[628] See Peaslee, supra note 626.

if it had been paid in cash equal to the creditor's *basis* for the cancelled debt. The first of these rules was inapplicable, however, if the debt was a security within the meaning of §165(g)(2) (so no partial worthlessness deduction could be claimed therefor by the creditor under §166), and the debt constituted a security for purposes of §354 (so that gain or loss would not be recognized to the creditor on the exchange transaction). For purposes of this provision, stock of a parent of the debtor is treated as stock of the debtor, and the "debtor" includes a successor corporation. To the extent gain was deemed to be realized under this provision (whether by a solvent or an insolvent debtor), it was subject to the elective basis reduction or the tax attribute reduction rules of §108(b)(5) or §108(c) noted above.

> *To illustrate:* If *D* Corporation bought in its nonsecurity debt of $100 by issuing stock worth $60, *D* would be deemed to receive $40 of income as a result of the transaction. If the value of the stock was $100, no income would result. If the debt was contributed to *D*'s capital (without the issuance of additional stock by *D*), income to *D* would result to the extent the face of the debt exceeded the creditor's basis therefor. If the cancelled debt constituted a security under §165(g)(2) and if the debt for stock exchange qualified for nonrecognition treatment under §354, no debt cancellation income would result from a debt for stock exchange transaction. To the extent income was realized as a result of proposed §108(f), however, it was subject to the treatment prescribed by §§108(a), 108(b), and 108(c).

The Senate version, however, dropped the stock-for-debt rules proposed by the House bill (although not the capital contribution rule), and retained the general rule of §1032, which protected the debtor corporation from debt cancellation gain in such cases; this version prevailed in the final 1980 legislation. Instead, §108(e)(7) provided for a special recapture rule that tainted stock received by a creditor to the extent that he claimed an ordinary loss on the debt. However, subsequent legislation enacted in 1984 removed solvent corporations from the equity-for-debt exception, and legislation enacted in 1986 required partial loss of tax carry-overs on equity-for-debt exchanges even by insolvent corporations.[629]

To the extent income is excluded under §108(a) and a basis reduction is required under §108(b)(2)(D), §108(b)(5), or §108(c), §1017 takes hold (although no longer on an elective basis) and requires the basis of the debtor's

---

[629] The Tax Reform Act of 1984, supra note 216, enacting §108(e)(10), and The Tax Reform Act of 1986, supra note 216, enacting §382(*l*)(5)(C). (The 1986 Act also completely removed solvent corporations from the jurisdiction of §§108 and 1017; supra note 627.)

As to the effect of §382(*l*)(5)(C), see infra ¶ 16.25, para. 6.

property to be reduced pursuant to regulations prescribed under this provision (as was the case under pre-1980 law if §1017 were elected). Basis reduction is limited to the excess of the aggregate basis of properties held by the taxpayer after the discharge over unpaid liabilities (i.e., basis cannot be reduced below zero, nor below the amount of the debtor's remaining liabilities). If excluded debt exceeds available property basis, no income will result to the debtor if it is insolvent (although the Service took a contrary position under prior law, as discussed in Chapter 11). Finally, §1017(c)(2) provides that a basis reduction under §1017 does not trigger recapture of investment credits under §47 (thus overruling a contrary position taken by the Service).[630] To the extent that the basis of any property is required to be reduced, §1017(d) provides that recapture rules similar to §§1245 and 1250 will apply on the disposition of such basis-reduced properties.[631]

2. Examples. In the following examples, *D* Corporation is involved in a title 11 proceeding, it has substantial net operating loss carry-overs, and its liabilities exceed the value of its assets (i.e., it is insolvent) unless otherwise stated.

Example 1: *D* satisfies its outstanding debts at less than face by paying cash. *D* has no income on the cancellation under §108(a)(1)(A), but must reduce its tax attributes in the manner prescribed in §108(b) (first its loss carry-overs, then credit carry-overs, then property basis, and so on)[632] unless it elects instead under §108(b)(5) to first reduce the basis of "depreciable property" (which term also includes a special look-through rule under §1017(d)(3)(D) to reduce the basis of stock in *D*'s affiliated subsidiaries if the subsidiaries correspondingly agree to reduce the basis of their depreciable property).

Example 2: If *D* instead satisfied its debts by issuing additional stock (and/or warrants to buy its stock), no §108 cancellation of debt amounts resulted in *D* under the original §108 provisions enacted in

---

[630] But see Panhandle Eastern Pipeline Co. v. US, 654 F2d 35 (Ct. Cl. 1981) (no investment tax credit recapture on §1017 basis reduction); accord, Carolina, Clinchfield & O. Ry., 82 TC 888 (1984); Rev. Rul. 84-134, 1984-2 CB 6 (revoking earlier rulings to the contrary).

[631] The Bankruptcy Tax Act amendments were effective generally for transactions occuring in 1981 (but taxpayers could elect to apply the amended rules to insolvency proceedings commenced after October 1, 1979, and a special transition rule delayed the effect of the tax attribute reduction rules of §108(b) until 1982 for insolvent debtors).

[632] If tax attribute reductions are less than the debt cancellation gain, however, no income results to *D* under §108(a)(1)(A).

1980; amendments by the Tax Reform Act of 1986, however, require *D* to reduce the amount of its tax attribute carry-over (losses, credits, and so on) by an amount equal to one-half of the debt cancellation profit on the issuance of its stock.[633]

Example 3: If *D* was not involved in a title 11 proceeding, but was insolvent, the results in Example 2 would be the same (unless *D* became solvent as a result of the debt discharge, in which event it would realize taxable income to that extent).

Example 4: If *D* is a solvent corporation and is not involved in a title 11 proceeding, any gain realized on the satisfaction of its debts (either with cash, new debt, or *D* stock) will result in currently taxable income to *D* as a result of amendments by the Tax Reform Act of 1986.

Example 5: If *D* is wholly owned by solvent *P* Corporation, *P*'s purchase of *D*'s debts at less than their face will result in current §108 gain to *D* under the related party rules of §108(e)(4)(A), thereby triggering tax attribute reductions under §108(b). If *P* subsequently contributes that debt to *D* as a capital contribution, *D* could again realize §108 gain as a result of the capital contribution rule in §108(e)(6) (to the extent that *P*'s basis in the debt is less than its face), but regulations are supposed to be issued under §108(e)(4)(A) to prevent double counting of the gain in such cases (although they have not been as yet). If *D* instead subsequently paid its debt to *P* in full, to the extent that the payment is in excess of the debt's then value, that excess presumably will be a dividend by *D* to *P*.

Example 6: If *D*'s wholly owned subsidiary, *S*, buys in *D*'s debt at less than its face, *D* will realize immediate §108 gain under the related party rules of §108(e)(4)(A) (triggering the tax attribute reductions of §108(b)). Subsequent payments by *D* to *S* could result in a capital contribution by *D* to *S* if the amount paid is greater than the value of the debt. Conversely, a distribution of the debt by *S* to *D* would be a dividend to the extent of the value of the debt (since *S* would recognize gain under §311(b)(1) to the extent the value of the debt exceeded *S*'s basis, and, if the value was less than *S*'s basis, the dividend amount would be measured by value), but no additional debt cancellation gain should result to *D* from the distribution.

---

[633] New §382(*l*)(5)(C), supra note 629. Any creditor that claimed an ordinary deduction on the debt cancellation transaction would have the stock received therein tainted with an ordinary income potential to that extent by §108(e)(7).

CHAPTER 15

Affiliated Corporations

PART A.   MULTIPLE CORPORATIONS

¶ 15.01   INTRODUCTORY

Section 11(a) of the Code imposes a tax "on the taxable income of *every* corporation" (emphasis added), which language seems to imply that every corporation is a separate taxable entity whether it is affiliated with other corporations or not. This separate-entity assumption is a good starting point for analysis. It must, however, be qualified—as is also true of the Code's references to individuals—by a variety of statutory provisions and judge-made principles that sometimes treat affiliated taxpayers differently from taxpayers that are unencumbered by family relationships.

These limitations on the separate-entity approach to corporations reflect two quite different policy concerns: (1) recognition that a single enterprise might be artificially divided between two or more related corporations in order to exploit statutory tax allowances and other provisions such as progressive rates and tax allowances subject to dollar limits; and (2) recognition that transactions between affiliated corporations do not usually have the same economic effect as transactions between the group as a whole and the outside world. The first concern accounts for the limitations examined in Part A of this chapter, including the requirement that the members of a controlled group of corporations must share a single accumulated earnings credit.[1] The second concern accounts for a smaller but nevertheless important number of provisions, such as (1) the privilege accorded to an affiliated group of corporations to file a consolidated return that, roughly speaking, disregards intercompany income and expenses in order to tax the members of the group solely on income generated by the group's transactions with outsiders and (2) the 100 percent dividends-received deduction granted by §243(a)(3) for dividends paid by one member of an affiliated group of corporations to another.[2]

Aside from whatever business or other nontax reasons may stimulate taxpayers to use two or more corporations rather than a single one to carry on their business activities, the following tax advantages may be sought or achieved:

(1) Avoidance of dollar ceilings on tax allowances, such as the amount of taxable income qualifying for the lowest corporate rate prescribed by §11(b) and the aggregate amount of corporate capital specified by §1244, relating to corporations whose stock qualifies for special treatment when it is sold at a loss or becomes worthless.

(2) Separate elections for such matters as accounting methods, taxable years, depreciation methods, bad debt reserves vs. specific write-offs of bad debts, inventory valuation methods, and the foreign tax credit.

(3) Opportunity to shift some activities to a corporation where they will be subject to a more favorable tax regime than the rest of the taxpayer's activities (e.g., segregating foreign source, insurance, or banking income in a separate corporation subject to special rules).

---

[1] Section 1561(a)(2), discussed infra ¶ 15.02.

[2] See infra ¶ 15.20 (consolidated returns) and supra ¶ 5.05 (dividends-received deduction).

(4) Avoidance of personal holding company status by segregating activities that qualify for exemption by themselves but that taint other activities if combined with them in a single taxable entity.

(5) Qualification of a segment of a work force for a tax-favored employee benefit plan (subject to §§414(b) and 52(a)).

(6) Segregation of deductions and losses from particular activities in an S corporation if this status is not wanted for other segments of the business.

(7) Favorable treatment for anticipated or potential sales, mergers, liquidations, intrafamily gifts or bequests, and other adjustments that can be effected on a tax-free basis for some operations but not for others or that will trigger the recognition of only a limited amount of income if confined to assets segregated in a separate corporation.

In seeking to achieve these and other favorable tax results, the taxpayer must take into account a wide variety of weapons in the Service's arsenal that diverge in many respects. Among the specific features of these weapons are the following:

1. Potential targets. Some of the Service's weapons against multiple corporations can be aimed at only a narrowly circumscribed target (e.g., §179, limiting the component members of a controlled group of corporations to a single dollar-limited amount of additional first-year depreciation). Others can be fired almost at random against any perceived taxpayer abuse (e.g., §482 empowering the Service to "distribute, apportion, or allocate gross income, deductions, credits, or allowances" between or among two or more organizations, trades, or businesses owned or controlled by the same interests). Some restrictions are concerned only with corporations (e.g., §1561), others apply as between both corporations and individuals or partners (e.g., §482), and still another (§269A) is limited to corporations and their employee-owners.

2. Definition of "control." Some provisions define "control" by reference to objective circumstances, such as percentages of stock ownership (e.g., §1563), while others employ vaguer concepts (e.g., §482, which refers to organizations that are "owned or controlled directly or indirectly by the same interests"). Some prescribe attribution rules for determining stock ownership (e.g., §1563); others do not (e.g., §269(a)).

3. Type of business. Some restrictions apply only to particular types of business activities (e.g., §269A, applying to personal service corporations), and others apply only to foreign corporations (e.g., §§951–954). Still others are unlimited in their reach (e.g., §482).

4. Taxpayer purpose. Some restrictions on multiple corporations apply only if the Service establishes, or the taxpayer fails to disprove, the existence of a tax-avoidance purpose (e.g., §1551), while others apply without regard to the taxpayer's purpose (e.g., §1561). If the taxpayer's business purpose is a defense, the restriction might be viewed by students of mediaeval philosophy as an application of Occam's razor: "Entia non sunt multiplicanda praeter necessitatem" (entities ought not to be multiplied beyond what is necessary).

5. Intragroup transactions. Some provisions apply only to transactions between two or more related persons (e.g., §267(a)(1), relating to losses); others are not dependent on intrafamily transactions (e.g., §1561). Some apply to both transactions within the group and those with outsiders (e.g., the consolidated return regulations).

6. Source of restrictions. Some restrictions are prescribed by Congress in the form of statutory provisions (e.g., §1561), some are judge-made (e.g., the business purpose doctrine and assignment of income principles), and others rest primarily on regulations (e.g., the consolidated return rules and the treatment of investments in a subsidiary in applying the accumulated earnings tax).

7. Further congressional erosions of the corporate entity principle. Numerous other Code provisions enacted by recent legislation provide for the aggregation of controlled corporations in applying their various rules, either by treating such related corporate groups as a single person or by denying the particular tax benefit sought from an affiliate's separate corporate status. The following are examples of the former treatment.

(1) Section 864(e) requires allocation of interest and expenses of affiliated groups (determined under §1504) as if the group were a single corporation (see Chapter 17).

(2) Exemptions for small corporations from the mandatory accrual method of §448, the cost-capitalization rules of §263A, and the modified completed-contract method rules of §460, all added in 1986, are determined on a related group aggregation basis (using a modified affiliation definition derived from §1563(a), substituting more than 50 percent for 80 percent), as discussed in the following section;

(3) Stock purchases by affiliated members (determined under §1504) of the acquiring group are aggregated for purposes of §338 by §338(h)(8) (see Chapter 11); and

(4) The §453C proportionate payment rules of current law treat an affiliated group as one taxpayer (aggregation here being determined under §52).

The following are examples of the latter treatment of affiliated groups.

(1) Section 265 cannot be avoided by using related persons under §7701(f), as discussed later in this chapter;

(2) Under §§1239 and 453(g), depreciable property sales between §267 related parties are denied capital gain and installment sale deferral benefits;

(3) Bargain debt purchases by §267 affiliates of the debtor corporation trigger immediate discharge gain under §108(e)(4);

(4) Resales by §318 related buyers end §453 deferral for the first related seller;

(5) Members of a §1504 affiliated group cannot elect subchapter S by virtue of §1361(b)(2)(A) (see Chapter 6); and

(6) The benefits of the Accelerated Cost Recovery System cannot be obtained for pre-effective date property through churning transactions within an affiliated group (relationship here is determined under §267(b), substituting 10 percent for 50 percent) under §168(f)(5)(A).

This is only a partial listing of situations where Congress, the courts, or the Service has expanded on the basic multiple corporation statutory package of §§243(b), 482, 1501, and 1561 to frustrate taxpayer attempts to obtain particular tax benefits through the use of multiple corporate entities.

¶ 15.02   LIMITATIONS ON MULTIPLE TAX BENEFITS FOR MEMBERS OF CONTROLLED GROUPS OF CORPORATIONS

1. Introductory. If corporate income is taxed at two or more rates, it is possible to obtain a tax advantage—analogous to that obtained through income-splitting between parents and children—by dividing a business enterprise between two or more corporations (in the absence, of course, of an applicable statutory or judge-made restriction). Assuming, for example, a corporate rate structure under which the first $100,000 of taxable income is taxed at 20 percent and amounts above $100,000 are taxed at 30 percent, the tax liability for an enterprise conducted through a single corporation that generates $600,000 of taxable income per year will be $170,000 ($100,000 at 20 percent plus $500,000 at 30 percent). If, however, the enterprise can be conducted through six corporations, each generating $100,000 of taxable income, the aggregate tax liability will be only $120,000 (6 × 20 percent of $100,000). A similar phenomenon can occur whenever a tax allowance is subject to a dollar ceiling, such as the $250,000 accumulated earnings tax credit.

The multiplication of corporate entities in order to transcend dollar limits on tax allowances became especially widespread during the 1950s, when real estate subdividers perfected the technique of creating separate corporations for groups of adjacent lots or houses, designating their otherwise identical entities by arbitrary letters when they ran out of children's names and fanciful labels. Some manufacturers followed suit by creating a separate sales corporation for each region or state in which their products were sold. In the early 1960s, when the problem of such so-called alphabet corporations was perceived as acute, the only weapons available to the Service were cumbersome ones, requiring a case-by-case analysis of the taxpayer's purpose (e.g., §§269 and 1551) or of all the relevant facts and circumstances (e.g., the assignment of income and business purpose doctrines).[3]

2. Limit on multiple tax benefits imposed by §1561. Responding in 1964 to this deficiency in prior law, Congress enacted §1561, which prescribes "mechanical, objective tests" in order to "curb the abuse of multiple incorporation."[4] Under the current version of §1561, the component members of a controlled group of corporations (as defined) must divide four tax benefits among themselves as though the entire group were only one corporate entity. This division must take place without regard to whether there are

---

[3] For §§269 and 1551, see infra ¶ 16.21 and this section, ¶ 15.02, para. 6, respectively; for the assignment of income and business purpose doctrines, see supra ¶ 1.05 and infra ¶ 14.51. For leading early cases illustrating the Service's tactics in dealing with alphabet corporations, see Aldon Homes, Inc., 33 TC 582 (1959) (successful attack under §22(a) of 1939 Code, predecessor of §61(a)), and cases there cited; Shaw Const. Co. v. CIR, 323 F2d 316 (1963) (income of 88 real estate corporations allocated to one affiliated construction corporation).

For a detailed examination of the multiple corporation problem and its historical background, see the Fourth Edition of this treatise at ¶¶ 15.01–15.05.

[4] US v. Vogel Fertilizer Co., 455 US 16, 26 (1982).

For §1561, see generally Dooher, Multiple Corporations, Tax Mgmt. Portfolio (BNA) No. 55-5th (1984).

valid business reasons for conducting the enterprise through two or more corporations and even if each member of the group is engaged in a different line of business and they engage in no transactions with each other. These four tax benefits are as follows:

(1) The amounts in each taxable income bracket.[5] For example, if the first $25,000 of corporate income is taxed at 20 percent, the next $50,000 at 25 percent, and amounts above $75,000 at 30 percent, each member of the group is taxed at 20 percent on its ratable share of the first bracket amount, at 25 percent on its share of the second bracket amount, and so forth.

(2) The $250,000 allowance in computing the accumulated earnings credit.[6]

(3) The $40,000 alternative minimum tax exemption, including its phaseout as alternative minimum taxable income rises above $150,000.[7]

(4) The $2 million exemption amount for purposes of computing the superfund tax of §59A.

These benefits must be divided equally among the corporations that are component members of the controlled group on December 31 of their respective taxable years unless they elect an alternative apportionment plan pursuant to regulations.[8] If a corporation cannot use its allocable share of the benefit in question (because, for example, it suffers a loss for a particular year), the amount is not reallocated to other members of the group.

3. Other restrictions on multiple tax benefits. Section 1561's one-group/one-allowance barrier to the multiplication of tax benefits by the use of multiple corporations was subsequently incorporated, with minor variations, in various other provisions of the Code, with the result that the component

---

[5] Section 1561(a)(1). This rule also includes the phaseout of the lower bracket progressive rate benefits in §11(b) (which starts at $100,000 and ends at $335,000 of taxable income), supra ¶ 5.01 (i.e., the phaseout operates on a group basis).

[6] Section 1561(a)(2). The amount is reduced to $150,000 if any member of the group is subject to §535(c)(2)(B), relating to certain personal service corporations. For the accumulated earnings credit, see generally supra ¶ 8.09.

[7] Section 1561(a)(3). For the AMT, see supra ¶ 5.08.

[8] For alternative apportionment plans, see Regs. §1.1561-3. If all members of the group are in the top bracket (34 percent for 1988, starting at $75,000) and the group's income exceeds the §11(b) phaseout line of $335,000, the group is taxable at a flat 34 percent, regardless of how its members apportion.

members of a controlled group are also treated as a single corporation for the following purposes:

(1) The dollar limits on the dollar-for-dollar reduction of tax liability by the general business credit and on the amount of used property taken into account for investment credit purposes.[9]

(2) The $10,000 limit on the first-year depreciation allowance granted by §179.[10]

(3) Various provisions relating to qualified pension and other employee benefit plans, such as the qualification, participation, and vesting rules.[11]

In addition, dividends received by one member of an "affiliated group of corporations" from another member of the group (defined by §243(b)(5) substantially the same as for purposes of §1501, relating to consolidated returns) qualify for the 100 percent dividends-received deduction allowed by §243(a)(3) only if the common parent so elects under §§243(b)(2) and 243(b)(3) (and only if dividends come from earnings during the period of affiliation); in such event, the members of the group are treated as one corporation in electing the foreign tax credit under §901(a) and in computing the minimum accumulated earnings credit.[12] Since such an affiliated group ordinarily also constitutes a controlled group for purposes of §1561(a), restrictions relating to the minimum accumulated earnings credit usually apply in any event. A §243(a)(3) consent, therefore, seldom imposes an additional burden on corporations that have no foreign operations, particularly since an election can be terminated under §243(b)(4) if such operations are undertaken at a later time.

---

[9] Sections 38(c)(1), 38(c)(2), and 38(c)(4)(B); §§48(c)(2)(A), 48(c)(2)(C), and §48(c)(3)(C), incorporating §1563(a)'s definition of "controlled group," but with a 50 percent inclusionary benchmark (rather than 80 percent). However, this credit was repealed in 1986.

[10] Section 179(d)(6); evidently the group is also treated as a single corporation in applying the §179(b)(2) phaseout. For the meaning of "controlled group," see §179(d)(7), incorporating §1563(a)'s definition, but with a 50 percent inclusionary benchmark.

[11] Section 414(b), which requires that such principles be applied as if all members of a controlled group of corporations constituted a single employer. See generally Bittker, Federal Taxation of Income, Estates and Gifts (Warren, Gorham & Lamont, Inc., 1981), ¶ 61.3.2. See also supra ¶ 15.01.

[12] Section 243(b)(3) attaches other consequences to the election (relating to §1562, surtax exemptions, and estimated taxes) that have become obsolete because of intervening statutory changes. See generally Rev. Rul. 85-144, 1985-2 CB 86; Rev. Rul. 84-154, 1984-2 CB 61 (qualification of newly organized holding company for the deduction).

4. Controlled group of corporations. The crucial term "controlled group of corporations" is defined by §1563(a) to include three categories of affiliation:

(1) **Parent-subsidiary controlled group** (i.e., one or more chains of corporations connected with a common parent corporation through stock ownership, determined by voting power or value, of 80 percent or more). Under §269B(a)(2), so-called stapled interests (i.e., restrictions permitting the stock of one corporation to be transferred only if stock of another corporation is also transferred) can create a parent-subsidiary relationship.[13]

(2) **Brother-sister controlled group** (i.e., two or more corporations where five or fewer persons who are individuals, estates, or trusts own 80 percent (by voting power or value) of each corporation and also own more than 50 percent (by voting power or value) of each corporation, taking each person's ownership into account for the latter computation only to the extent of their smallest holding in any of the brother-sister corporations). The over 50 percent requirement is not satisfied if, for example, *A* and *B* (who are unrelated individuals) own two corporations in the proportions 75 to 25 and 25 to 75, respectively (since together they are regarded as owning only 50 percent of each corporation); but it would be satisfied if the proportions were 74 to 26 and 26 to 74. Moreover, in applying the five or fewer persons requirement, stock is taken into account only if the shareholder owns stock in each corporation.[14] Thus, if *C* and *D* own two corporations in the proportions 75 to 25 and 100 to 0, the 80 percent requirement is not satisfied because *D*'s stock ownership must be disregarded. The 80 percent requirement (as well as the 50 percent requirement) would be satisfied, however, if *C* and *D* owned the corporations in the proportions 75 to 25 and 99 to 1.

---

[13] See Eustice, The Tax Reform Act of 1984, ¶ 4.05[5] (Warren, Gorham & Lamont, Inc., 1984), and authorities cited; see also Note, Stapled Stock and I.R.C. Section 269B: Ill-Conceived Changes in the Rules of International Tax Jurisdiction, 71 Cornell L. Rev. 1066 (1986).

[14] See US v. Vogel Fertilizer Co., supra note 4 (holding invalid regulations that applied five or fewer person requirement on single or in combination basis); Prop. Regs. §1.1563-1 (revising regulations to conform to *Vogel Fertilizer* case by providing that each person whose stock ownership is taken into account for purposes of the 80 percent requirement must be a person whose ownership is counted in applying the over 50 percent requirement); see also Complete Fin. Corp. v. CIR, 766 F2d 436 (9th Cir. 1985) (person owning stock only by attribution properly counted under *Vogel Fertilizer* case; in applying over 50 percent requirement, attributed stock does not dilute ownership of persons from whom it is attributed).

See generally Smith & Peacock, Brother-Sister Multiple Corporations: The *Vogel Fertilizer Co.* Decision Resolves The *Fairfax* Issue, 9 J. Corp. Tax'n 346 (1983).

(3) **Combined group** (i.e., three or more corporations, each of which is a member of a parent-subsidiary group or a brother-sister group, and one of which is a common parent corporation).

In determining whether a corporation fits into one of these categories, some types of stock are excluded from consideration, and qualifying stock can be attributed from one person to another under elaborate constructive ownership rules. Nonvoting preferred stock and treasury stock are ordinarily excluded; excludability of other types of stock depends on whether a parent-subsidiary or a brother-sister group is involved. As to parent-subsidiary groups, if the parent owns directly or constructively 50 percent or more (by voting power or value) of a subsidiary's stock, stock of the subsidiary is excluded if it is held by certain deferred compensation trusts, by officers or 5 percent or more shareholders of the parent, or by employees of the subsidiary if the stock is held under certain restricted rights of disposition. In the case of brother-sister groups, stock held by certain employee trusts, by employees subject to restrictions in disposing of the stock, or by certain controlled charitable organizations is excluded if the five or fewer individuals, trusts, or estates that must satisfy the 50 and 80 percent requirements own directly or constructively 50 percent or more (by voting power or value) of the stock. The effect of these exclusions is to concentrate stock ownership, thus increasing the likelihood that two or more corporations constitute a controlled group, in order to frustrate avoidance of these provisions through tactics that reduce dominion over the stock in form but not in substance.[15]

Moreover, constructive ownership rules provide for the attribution of stock depending upon whether a parent-subsidiary or a brother-sister group is involved. For parent-subsidiary groups, constructive ownership is limited by §1563(d)(1)(B) to stock that is subject to an option. For brother-sister groups, attribution is more extensive, since §1563(d)(2)(B) incorporates the constructive ownership rules of §1563(e). In brief, these rules attribute stock in the following situations: (1) when stock subject to an option is attributed to the holder thereof; (2) when stock held by a partnership, is attributed to 5 percent (or more) partners in proportion to their interests; (3) when stock held by a trust or estate is attributed to 5 percent (or more) beneficiaries in proportion to their maximum actuarial interests; (4) when stock held by a

---

[15] See Mid-America Indus. v. US, 477 F2d 1029 (8th Cir. 1973); Crow-Burlingame Co., 65 TC 785, aff'd without opinion, 547 F2d 1173 (8th Cir. 1976) (parent-subsidiary group found because stock held by employees of subsidiaries was excluded in view of repurchase options running to investment company organized and dominated by parent); Tribune Publishing Co., 731 F2d 1401 (9th Cir. 1984) (parent had right of first refusal on subsidiary's stock; stock therefore excluded, and parent-subsidiary controlled group existed). But see Superior Beverage Co. of Marysville, Inc. v. CIR, 525 F2d 186 (9th Cir. 1975) (reciprocal restrictions precluded requisite control).

corporation is attributed to its 5 percent (or more) shareholders (computed by value) in proportion to their interests; and (5) when stock held by specified family members is attributed to related members, subject to certain conditions and limitations.

Finally, §§1563(f)(2) and 1563(f)(3) provide that

(1) Double or chain attribution of stock will be possible (except between family members);

(2) The option attribution rule will take precedence over all others;

(3) Ownership will be attributed, in the event of alternatives, in such manner as to create a controlled group; and

(4) Constructive ownership will take precedence over the stock exclusion rules if this will create a controlled group.[16]

5. Component members of controlled group. The restrictions of §1561(a) apply only to the "component members" of a controlled group of corporations, a term that is defined by §1563(b) to mean a corporation that is either (1) a member of a controlled group on the December 31 falling within its taxable year unless it is excluded by virtue of §1563(b)(2), or (2) "an additional member" of the group under §1563(b)(3), which embraces certain corporations that were members of the group for one-half or more of the taxable year preceding December 31, even though they were not members on that date. Section 1563(b)(2) excludes from the group certain special status corporations: (1) corporations exempt from tax under §501; (2) nonresident foreign corporations; (3) "franchised corporations" as defined by §1563(f)(4); and (4) corporations that have been members of the group for less than one-half the number of days in their taxable year that precede the December 31 membership determination date.[17]

Finally, if a corporation is a member of more than one group, §1563(b)(4) provides that it may belong to only one; and, in determining the group to which it is to be assigned, the regulations will control.[18]

---

[16] See, e.g., Regs. §1.1563-3; see also Northwestern Steel & Supply Co., 60 TC 356 (1973) (constructive ownership rules constitute one-way street into controlled group status; someone else's constructive ownership does not reduce taxpayer's actual ownership); Yaffe Iron & Metal Corp. v. US, 593 F2d 832 (8th Cir.), cert. denied, 444 US 843 (1979) (attribution rules applied to brother-sister controlled group); Complete Fin. Corp. v. CIR, supra note 14 (same).

[17] See also Regs. §1.1563-1(b)(2)(ii)(c) (excluding nontaxable S corporations).

[18] See Regs. §1.1563-1(c), which assigns such a corporation to the group of which it is a member by virtue of its owning 80 percent in value of another corporation's stock. But see Regs. §1563-1(c)(2) (allowing corporation to elect which brother-sister group to be a member of).

6. Disallowance of rate differentials and accumulated earnings credit under §1551: co-existence with §1561. Section 1551, which was originally enacted in 1951, anticipated §1561 by more than a decade in attacking the use of multiple corporations to shift income to low corporate tax brackets and to get more than one accumulated earnings credit. It applies, however, only if the following conditions are met:

(1) Property (other than money) is transferred, either by a corporation or by five or fewer individuals who control a corporation, to a second corporation;

(2) The transferor or transferors control the transferee corporation for part of the latter's taxable years;

(3) The transferee was either created for the purpose of acquiring the transferred property or was not actively engaged in business at the time of the acquisition; and

(4) The transferee fails to establish by the clear preponderance of the evidence that obtaining the benefit of a low income tax bracket or the accumulated earnings credit was not a major purpose of the transfer.

Since "control" is defined by §1551(b) in substantially the same way as by §1563,[19] a corporation that is vulnerable to attack under §1551 will usually be a component member of a controlled group of corporations for §1561 purposes; if so, it can be attacked by the Service more easily under §1561, which applies without regard to the taxpayer's purpose and whether or not property is transferred from one member of the group to another. Thus, although the enactment of §1561 was not intended to supersede §1551,[20] it has fallen into desuetude in recent years; indeed, there has been only one reported case since 1975 in which the Service asserted a deficiency under §1551, and in that case the taxpayer prevailed.[21]

---

[19] See H.R. Rep. No. 413, 91st Cong., 1st Sess. 76 (1969), reprinted in 1969-3 CB 384. But see US v. Vogel Fertilizer Corp. supra note 4, at 33, n.13 (definitions not identical).

[20] See H.R. Rep. No. 749, 89th Cong., 1st Sess. (1964), reprinted in 1964-1 CB 242 (Part 2); the continued validity of §1551 was assumed by the Tax Reform Act of 1986, which made a technical conforming change in §1551(c).

[21] Massey's Auto Body Shop, Inc., ¶ 78,414 P-H Memo. TC (1978) (§1551 inapplicable; taxpayer established business purpose for transfer).

For important cases interpreting §1551, see V. H. Monette & Co., 45 TC 15 (1965), aff'd, 374 F2d 116 (4th Cir. 1967); Hiawatha Home Builders, Inc., 36 TC 491 (1961); Bush Hog Mfg. Co., 42 TC 713 (1964) (acq.); Challenger, Inc., ¶ 64,338 P-H Memo. TC (1964); Coastal Oil Storage Co. v. CIR, 242 F2d 396 (4th Cir. 1957); James Realty Co. v. US, 280 F2d 394 (8th Cir. 1960); Perfection Foods, Inc.,

Section 1551, however, can reach a few taxpayers that are beyond the jurisdiction of §1561, such as (1) members of a controlled group that are not component members because of the entity exclusions of §1563(b)(2); (2) corporations that meet the control requirement of §1551 (which is satisfied if control exists "during any part of the taxable year of [the] transferee corporation") but that do not belong to a controlled group on December 31 or for the period specified by §1563(b)(3); and (3) corporations that are controlled for purposes of §1551 but not under §1563 because the latter provision disregards nonvoting preferred stock. Moreover, in unusual circumstances, the Service might choose to proceed under §1551 rather than under §1561 because §1551 denies the rate differential or accumulated earnings credit to the transferee corporation in toto, while §1561 apportions these amounts among the component members of the controlled group. Finally, although there is evidently no precedent for this action, it is possible that the Service could employ §1561 to apportion a tax benefit between transferor and transferee corporations, thus reducing the amount available to the transferor, and then successfully invoke §1551 to prevent the transferee from using the residue.

7. Section 269: Acquisitions of controlled corporations for tax-avoidance purpose. If any person or persons acquire, directly or indirectly, control of a corporation for the principal purpose of avoiding federal income taxes by obtaining a deduction, credit, or other allowance that would not otherwise be available, the Service can disallow the allowance under §269. "Control" is defined as the ownership of at least 50 percent (by voting power or value) of the acquired corporation's stock.

This provision, which is examined in detail later in this treatise,[22] was enacted in 1943, more than 20 years before the enactment of §1561. The two continue to exist side by side, although the Service naturally prefers to invoke §1561, which avoids an inquiry into the taxpayer's purpose, in cases of overlapping jurisdiction.

If the requisite purpose can be established, however, §269's coverage is broader than §1561 in two respects. First, control exists under §269 if a 50 percent stock ownership benchmark is satisfied; §1563 is satisfied only if its 80 percent and over-50 percent conditions are both met. Second, any deduction, credit, or other tax allowance can be disallowed when §269 applies; §1561 affects only the income tax brackets of §11(b), the accumulated earn-

---

¶ 65,015 P-H Memo. TC (1965) (leasing of assets constituted a §1551 transfer), and others noted at ¶ 15.02 in the Third and Fourth Editions of this treatise. See generally Eustice, Federal Income Tax Problems Arising From Transactions Between Affiliated or Controlled Corporations, 23 Tax L. Rev. 451 (1968).

[22] See infra ¶ 16.21. But see Dorba Homes, Inc. v. CIR, 403 F2d 502 (2d Cir. 1968) (§269 cannot be invoked where only one corporation was acquired).

ings credit, and the AMT exemption, and these must be apportioned among the component members of the controlled group rather than disallowed in their entirety.

¶ 15.03 ALLOCATION OF INCOME AND DEDUCTIONS AMONG RELATED CORPORATIONS

1. In general. Section 482 constitutes one of the Service's principal weapons for policing the fairness of transactions between related enterprises, including affiliated corporations, that cannot or do not file consolidated returns. The section provides, in brief, that gross income, deductions, credits, and other allowances of related taxpayers may be reallocated by the Service in order to prevent the evasion of taxes or clearly reflect the income of the related organizations.[23] The major function of §482 is the prevention of artificial shifting, milking, or distorting of the true taxable incomes of commonly controlled enterprises, but its concern is with economic reality rather than the taxpayer's motivation or purpose; thus, the objective of §482 "is to place a controlled taxpayer on a tax parity with an uncontrolled taxpayer."[24]

In treating related corporations as separate entities dealing with each other at arm's length, the §482 regulations contrast sharply with the consolidated return regulations. The latter in general treat the affiliated group as a

---

[23] For the history and constitutionality of §482, see Richard D. Foster, 80 TC 34, 140–142 (1983), aff'd without discussion of this issue, 756 F2d 1430 (9th Cir. 1985), cert. denied, 106 S. Ct. 793 (1986).

See generally McCawley, Section 482: The Statute and the Regulations, Tax Mgmt. Portfolio (BNA) No. 115-3d (1982); McCawley, Section 482: Special Problems, Tax Mgmt. Portfolio (BNA) No. 116 (1983); Higinbotham, Asper, Stoffregen, & Wexler, Effective Application of the Section 482 Transfer Pricing Regulations, 42 Tax L. Rev. 293 (1987). Fuller, Section 482 Revisited, 31 Tax L. Rev. 475 (1976), which cites some of the numerous earlier articles on this subject; Eustice, Affiliated Corporations Revisited: Recent Developments Under Sections 482 and 367, 24 Tax L. Rev. 101 (1968).

For the weight of the taxpayer's burden when the Service invokes §482 and the time when it must give notice of its intention to do so, see Richard D. Foster, supra, at 142–144, and cases there cited; Dolese v. CIR, 811 F2d 543 (10th Cir. 1987); Abatti v. CIR, 644 F2d 1385 (9th Cir. 1981); Silvano Achiro, 77 TC 881 (1981).

[24] See Your Host, Inc. v. CIR, 58 TC 10, 24 (1972), aff'd, 489 F2d 957 (2d Cir. 1973), cert. denied, 419 US 829 (1974) ("section 482 does not deal with motivation and purpose . . . but with economic reality"); Regs. §1.482-1(b)(1) (purpose of §482 "is to place a controlled taxpayer on a tax parity with an uncontrolled taxpayer"), quoted with approval by the Supreme Court in First Sec. Bank of Utah, 405 US 394, 400 (1972).

The final sentence of §482, added in 1986, in effect imposes a profit-sharing approach (to replace the normal separate entity concept) in the case of income attributable to intangibles (e.g., patents and industrial know-how) transferred from one related party to another. See infra text at notes 60–62.

single economic and taxable entity by washing out intrafamily transactions (such as the use of one corporation's property, funds, or employees by another member of the affiliated group) and by computing income or loss on the basis of the consolidated group's transactions with the outside world.[25] Under the quite different separate-entity approach of §482, income or loss can be—in fact, must be—recognized even when parent-subsidiary and brother-sister corporations deal solely with each other.

In determining the true taxable income[26] of each controlled entity, §482 seems to amalgamate several pervasive themes and policies of the tax law: tax-avoidance principles, the assignment of income doctrine, general deduction theories, and clear reflection of income under the parties' accounting methods. It is often difficult, however, to determine which of these various principles is being applied, either singly or together, in a given situation; and many of the decisions in this area do not readily yield to precise and consistent analysis. Even the regulations are guilty of this failure to distinguish among the various facets and functions of the section.

Given this goulash of imprecise concepts, it may be surprising to find §482 described as a more precise device for dealing with tax avoidance than these other doctrines and provisions.[27] As a *diagnostic* tool, §482 leaves much—indeed, almost everything—to be desired, since it lays down no principles to determine *when* taxes are being evaded or income is not clearly reflected. Thus, it is clearly subordinate to §61(a) and the assignment of income doctrine, which, although vague, are substantive rules determining what is taxable and to whom. Section 482 does not purport to discharge this function; it has the quite different, although important, function of prescribing what the Service can do if amounts that should be reported or deducted are not, in fact, reported or deducted by the proper party, and it accordingly comes into play only if and when the income reported by related parties does not conform to the threshold substantive rules.[28]

---

[25] For consolidated returns, see generally infra ¶ 15.20. For the possibility of a quasi-consolidation of income under §482, see infra text at note 45.

[26] Regs. §1.482-1(b)(1).

[27] Foglesong v. CIR, 621 F2d 865, 872 (7th Cir. 1980); for a later installment in this litigation, see infra note 29.

[28] For the complex relationship between §482 and the statutory nonrecognition provisions, see Eli Lilly & Co., 84 TC 996, 1114–1130 (1985), and G. D. Searle & Co., 88 TC 252 (1987) (extensive analysis, concluding that §482 allocations are justified, despite a transaction's seeming qualification for nonrecognition, in two narrowly defined situations: (1) tax-motivated transfers preparing the way for a disposition of the transferred property on favorable tax terms not available to the transferor and (2) nonrecognition transfers that artificially separate income from related expenses). *Eli Lilly & Co.* and *G.D. Searle & Co.* review the earlier cases in detail; see also Ruddick Corp. v. US, 643 F2d 747 (Ct. Cl. 1981) (divided court), on remand, 1983-2 USTC ¶ 9480 (Cl. Ct. 1983), aff'd without opinion, 732 F2d 168 (1st Cir. 1984) (§482 inapplicable to gain on recipient's disposition of tax-free dividend in kind unless distribu-

On the other hand, as a *remedial* tool, §482—especially as augmented by the regulations—can properly be described as more precise than the underlying substantive rules, because it permits all aspects of the distortion to be corrected, including the returns of related parties who have reported too *much* income because the taxpayer under examination has reported too *little*.[29]

Section 482 allocation problems arise from a wide variety of dealings between related enterprises. The principal transactional patterns giving rise to §482 questions are the sharing of facilities, properties, and services among the members of a controlled group without proper allocation of costs; the transfer of income-producing assets or activities to a related entity; and loans, leases, licenses, sales, or service transactions between related enterprises not conforming to an arm's-length standard, whether the price is inadequate or excessive.[30]

To put §482 allocations in proper perspective, it is useful to recall that the Treasury has traditionally relied on §482 to correct artificial intragroup pricing policies employed by taxpayers to achieve two principal goals: (1) in the domestic area, to shift income from the top income bracket of one corporation to the bottom (or zero) brackets of related corporations; and (2) in the foreign area, to shift income from a domestic corporation taxable on its world-wide income to affiliated foreign corporations that are not generally subject to U.S. tax on their foreign source income.[31] Since the enactment of §1561, however, the first objective—multiplication of low tax brackets— has been virtually impossible, as explained earlier in this chapter.[32] The second objective has become increasingly less attractive as foreign countries have

---

tion was motivated by tax-avoidance rather than business purpose, but lack of business purpose, and thus tax-avoidance purpose, found on remand); General Elec. Co. v. US, 3 Cl. Ct. 289 (Cl. Ct. 1983) (§482 applied to loss from parent's sale of assets obtained in §332 tax-free liquidation of subsidiary); Dolese v. CIR, supra note 23 (§482 applied in context of partnership nonrecognition rule for distributions). See generally Note, Section 482 and the Nonrecognition Provisions: Resolving the Conflict, 77 Nw. U. L. Rev. 670 (1982).

[29] Foglesong v. CIR, supra note 27; for a later installment in this litigation, see Foglesong v. CIR, 691 F2d 848 (7th Cir. 1982) (§482 allocation not proper because shareholder who worked exclusively for his personal service corporation was not engaged in a separate trade or business to which income received by corporation could be allocated). Contra, Stanley W. Haag, 88 TC No. 32 (1987). For more on the latter issue, see infra text at notes 35–36 and supra ¶ 2.07.

[30] For the application of §482 to midstream incorporations and liquidations resulting in the separation of future income from previously deducted expenses, see supra ¶¶ 3.17 and 11.07 respectively.

[31] See generally Surrey, Treasury's Need to Curb Tax Avoidance in Foreign Business Through Use of §482, 28 J. Tax'n 75 (1968).

[32] Supra ¶ 15.02. But the avoidance potential still exists where one of the affiliates is a loss company able to shelter the diverted income with its carry-overs.

imposed higher rates on the affiliated foreign corporation, and it is now an appealing goal primarily if income can be shifted to a foreign affiliate that is subject only to the nominal taxes of a tax-haven country. With this decline in the big game population, the Service has gone hunting with §482 less frequently in recent years, although trophies may still occasionally be bagged on both domestic and foreign safaris.

2. **"Two or more organizations, trades, or businesses" requirement.** Section 482 applies only "[i]n the case of any two or more organizations, trades, or businesses." This phrase is defined quite broadly by the regulations to cover practically any type of taxable entity or enterprise having independent significance for tax purposes, including corporations, associations, partnerships, proprietorships, trusts, and estates, whether they are domestic or foreign, taxable or tax exempt, and regardless of whether they are parties to a consolidated return.[33] Moreover, §482 has been applied to a holding company on the theory that it conducted a "business" within the meaning of §482 through its subsidiaries; the same result might have been reached by holding that it was an organization, whether it conducted a business or not.[34]

It is quite clear that §482 applies to transactions between a corporation and a sole proprietorship operated by the corporation's controlling shareholder, or between a corporation and a partnership of its shareholders, since the proprietorship or partnership business is different from the corporation's. If, however, a corporation deals with its controlling shareholder solely in his or her capacity as an investor, the individual's activities do not constitute an organization, trade or business and hence do not bring §482 into play.[35] A troublesome intermediate problem arises if the transactions are between the coporation and a controlling individual whose only trade or business is the performance of services for the corporation. An important Court of Appeals decision holds that §482 does not sanction an allocation of personal service income from a corporation to its controlling shareholder-employee in this situation; but the court was divided, and there is weighty

---

[33] See Regs. §§1.482-1(a)(1) and 1.482-1(b)(2).

[34] Asiatic Petroleum Co. v. CIR, 79 F2d 234 (2d Cir.), cert. denied, 296 US 645, reh'g denied, 296 US 664 (1935); see also Sunshine Dep't Stores, ¶ 81,586 P-H Memo. TC (1981) (estate constituted an organization, and, assuming arguendo that conduct of a business is also necessary for §482 allocation, it participated in a business by virtue of its controlling interests in other business entities).

[35] See Whipple v. CIR, 373 US 193, 202 (1963) ("investing is not a trade or business and the return to the taxpayer, though substantially the product of his services, legally arises not from his own trade or business but from that of the corporation").

authority upholding such allocations in similar, although not identical, circumstances.[36]

3. Common ownership or control. Section 482 applies only if the organizations, trades, or businesses are "owned or controlled directly or indirectly by the same interests." The disjunctive (common ownership *or* common control) indicates that either circumstance by itself should be sufficient, and the term "indirectly" suggests the relevance of attribution. Although the full panoply of constructive ownership principles, such as those found in §318, has not been imported into §482, the courts have not hesitated to apply attribution principles in determining whether ownership or control existed in a particular situation.[37]

---

[36] Foglesong v. CIR, supra note 29 (case remanded to determine whether dividends paid to taxpayer's children were taxable to him on assignment of income grounds); for cases upholding §482 allocations in situations that were arguably analogous to *Fogelsong*, see Borge v. CIR, 405 F2d 673 (2d Cir. 1968) (entertainment services performed by controlling shareholder for corporation that subcontracted services to third parties, producing profits, offset by losses from other activities); Ach v. Cir, 358 F2d 342 (6th Cir.), cert. denied, 385 US 899 (1966) (successful proprietorship transferred to corporation controlled by owner's son; portion of business profits allocated to transferor, who continued to manage enterprise); Rubin v. CIR, 460 F2d 1216 (2d Cir. 1972) (management services furnished to controlled corporation, which contracted services to third party for higher amount); Stanley W. Haag, supra note 29. See also Dolese v. CIR, supra note 23 (separate businesses found).

For §269A, enacted in 1982 to sidestep the "separate business" issue in the case of certain personal service corporations performing services primarily for one other entity, see supra ¶ 2.07.

See generally Wood, the *Keller, Foglesong,* and *Pacella* Cases: Section 482 Allocations, Assignments of Income and New §269A, 10 J. Corp. Tax'n 65 (1983); Manning, The Service Corporation—Who Is Taxable on Its Income?: Reconciling Assignment of Income Principles, Section 482 and Section 351, 37 U. Miami L. Rev. 653 (1983).

For earlier discussions of the first *Foglesong* decision, see Burdett, *Foglesong's* Section 482 Approach May Threaten Closely-Held Personal Service Corporations, 53 J. Tax'n 330 (1980); McFadden, Section 482 and the Professional Corporation: The *Foglesong* Case, 8 J. Corp. Tax'n 35 (1981); Feuer, Section 482, Assignment of Income Principles and Personal Service Corporations, 59 Taxes 564 (1981).

[37] See Hall v. CIR, 294 F2d 82 (5th Cir. 1961); Charles Town, Inc. v. CIR, 372 F2d 415 (4th Cir.), cert. denied, 389 US 841 (1967); Ach v. CIR, supra note 36; Grenada Indus., Inc., 17 TC 231 (1951), aff'd, 202 F2d 873 (5th Cir.) cert. denied, 346 US 819 (1953); South Tex. Rice Warehouse Co. v. CIR, 366 F2d 890 (5th Cir. 1966), cert. denied, 386 US 1016 (1967) (family attribution); Sunshine Dept. Stores, Inc., supra note 34 (indirect control by same interests found; actual control existed regardless of record ownership; either common ownership or common control, direct or indirect, sufficient). But see Van Dale Corp., 59 TC 390 (1972) (no common control where 60 percent shareholder of one corporation owned only 25 percent of other corporation); Robert M. Brittingham, 66 TC 373 (1976) (no common control where

A parenthetical phrase in §482, stating that it applies to two or more organizations whether or not affiliated, seems at first blush to contradict the statutory requirement that the organizations be owned or controlled by the same interests. This reference, however, is evidently intended to make it clear that §482 applies to related corporations whether or not affiliated in the technical sense of qualification to file consolidated returns.[38]

The regulations adopt a broad interpretation of the relationship issue, stating that "the term 'controlled' includes any kind of control, direct or indirect, whether legally enforceable, and however exercisable or exercised," and adding that "it is the reality of the control which is decisive, not its form or the mode of its exercise."[39] Moreover, the same provision of the regulations states that a presumption of control arises "if income or deductions have been arbitrarily shifted." Also, it does not appear to be necessary that the persons with control expect to gain a direct economic benefit from exercising their power; it is enough that control is exercised in a non-arm's-length manner to distort the taxable income of the controlled enterprises.

Another point to be noted is that ownership or control of the requisite two or more organizations or businesses must be held, directly or indirectly, by the same interests. As a rule, the requisite mutuality of interest between the persons who own or control the particular entities involved is not difficult to determine. On occasion, however, competing corporations may organize a jointly owned subsidiary whose function is to supply its owners with raw materials or to perform services on behalf of the parents at a price equal to or even below the subsidiary's cost therefor. In an important decision by the Court of Appeals for the Second Circuit, §482 was held applicable to this situation on the ground that the parent corporations together were engaged in a business (as de facto partners or joint venturers) in creating the subsidiary, that this business was separate from the subsidiary's business, and that both businesses were under common control, even though the parents had no shareholders, directors, or officers in common.[40]

4. Scope of Service's authority. The language authorizing the Service to "distribute, apportion, or allocate gross income, deductions, credits or

---

one corporation owned by two brothers and their families and other corporation owned solely by one of the brothers), aff'd, 598 F2d 1375 (5th Cir. 1979) (mere friendliness not enough; different economic interests existed); see also a companion case, Dallas Ceramic Tile v. US 598 F2d 1382 (5th Cir. 1978).

[38] See infra ¶ 15.21.

[39] Regs. §1.482-1(a)(3).

[40] CIR v. B. Forman Co., 453 F2d 1144 (2d Cir.), cert. denied, 407 US 934, reh'g denied, 409 US 899 (1972); see Nauheim, B. Forman & Co., Inc.—A Crucial Test of the Future of Section 482, 26 Tax Lawyer 107 (1973).

allowances" has generated a number of interpretative questions that were once hotly debated but now seem settled. First, the authority to allocate gross income has been construed to encompass an allocation of taxable or net income, on the ground that this is merely a direct route to a destination that could be reached indirectly by allocating the gross income and deductions of the related entities.[41]

Second, the reference to "gross income" empowers the Service to require related corporations to recognize income on dealings with each other (e.g., sales and loans), even though the transaction has not yet generated any income from outside the group.[42] This practice has been castigated as illegitimate on the ground that §482 authorizes the Service only to allocate income that has already been realized, not to create income,[43] but it would obviously be administratively cumbersome and sometimes impossible to trace the economic effect of intragroup transactions over time until they ultimately play out in dealings with outsiders;[44] the "separate entity" concept employed by the regulations necessarily implies that income can be generated by transactions within the controlled group itself.

Third, although the regulations state that §482 is not intended to produce a result "equivalent to a computation of consolidated taxable income," it may, in unusual circumstances, have substantially this effect (e.g., if a business enterprise is artifically split between two corporations, one of which is found to be a sham).[45] Unlike a consolidated return, however, such a determination does not require the group's income to be aggregated year after year; the facts and circumstances prevailing in each taxable year must instead be examined to determine whether the related corporations are viable separate entities or not.

Fourth, §482 is concerned with the shifting of income and tax allowances, not with the taxpayer's exercise of elections granted by the

---

[41] For cases upholding this logical shortcut, see Hospital Corp. of Am., 81 TC 520, 592–593 (1983), and cases there cited.

[42] See Latham Park Manor, Inc., 69 TC 199 (1977), aff'd mem. 618 F2d 100 (4th Cir. 1980) (extensive analysis), and cases there cited.

[43] See, e.g., Smith-Bridgman & Co., 16 TC 287 (1951) (acq.), and cases there cited. But see Central Bank of S. v. US, 58 AFTR 2d 86-5319 (N.D. Ala. 1986) (creation of income doctrine relied on to defeat §482). See generally King & Dinur, Tax Court Gives In on Creation-of-Income Issue Under 482: What Decision Means, 48 J. Tax'n 66 (1978).

[44] For cases attempting to trace the sources and uses of allocated income, see Aladdin Indus., Inc., ¶ 81,245 P-H Memo. TC (1981).

[45] Regs. §1.482-1(b)(3); Hamburgers York Road, Inc., 41 TC 821 (1964) (acq.). The separate entity approach of Regs. §1.482-2, which routinely requires income to be reported on intragroup transactions, ordinarily produces the antithesis of a consolidated return; see supra text at note 25.

Code. Thus, if a taxpayer chooses to conduct a business in corporate form rather than as a proprietorship or to conduct foreign activities through a foreign corporation, §482 does not authorize the Service to allocate the resulting income back to the taxpayer—provided, of course, that the chosen instrument is a viable entity rather than a sham and that it carries on the activities generating the income.[46] It must be acknowledged, however, that it is not always easy to draw this line between a permissible choice of the vehicle through which income will be generated, and a vulnerable assignment of income.[47]

A final notable aspect of the allocation authority created by §482 is that it is entrusted to the discretion of the Service.[48] Thus, it cannot be invoked by the taxpayer to correct an artificial pricing policy for intragroup transactions that boomerangs and increases the group's aggregate tax liability above what would have been due if the members of the group had dealt at arm's length with each other. Moreover, a timely notice of action under §482 saddles the taxpayer with a heavier than normal burden of proving that the determination is unreasonable, arbitrary, or capricious.[49]

5. Correlative adjustments, set-offs, and reimbursements. The regulations under §482 provide that an adjustment to the income of one member of a controlled group (a so-called primary adjustment) must be accompanied

---

[46] See CIR v. First Sec. Bank of Utah, supra note 24 (divided court) (subsidiary's income from insurance business could not be allocated under §482 to parent that was not permitted by federal law to engage in insurance business): Sayersville Nat'l Bank v. US, 613 F2d 650 (6th Cir. 1980) (*First Security Bank* principle applied to bank that chose not to apply for insurance license under state law; exercise of power to refer business to a related entity does not trigger application of §482). But see Rev. Rul. 82-45, 1982-1 CB 89 (*First Security Bank* principle not applicable to foreign law restrictions); see also Hospital Corp. of Am., supra note 41, at 595–602 (taxpayer entitled to divert business opportunity to related corporation; hence no justification for allocating all income to taxpayer; but §482 allocation upheld to extent of income attributable to related corporation's uncompensated use of taxpayer's facilities, services, and expertise). For the effect of nonrecognition provisions, see supra note 28.

[47] The Supreme Court itself was divided on this point in the *First Security Bank* case, supra note 24. See generally supra ¶¶ 1.05 and 2.07.

[48] Regs. §1.482-1(b)(3); see also Richard H. Foster, supra note 23, at 191–195 (§482 a sword for Service, not a shield for taxpayer).

[49] For taxpayer's burden in a §482 case, see Roger M. Dolese, 82 TC 830, 838–839 (1984), aff'd, 811 F2d 543 (10th Cir. 1987), and cases there cited. For decisions that §482 is a sword available only to the Service, see Richard Foster, supra note 23; OTM Corp. v. US, infra note 51. For the taxpayer's right to have the issue of abuse of discretion determined by a jury, see Wilson v. US, 530 F2d 772, 776 (8th Cir. 1976) (question of fact for jury; error to grant directed verdict). For the Service's obligation to give timely notice of its intention to rely on §482, see Silvano Achiro, supra note 23.

by appropriate correlative adjustments to other members of the group involved in the allocation.[50]

> *To illustrate:* X Corporation sells property with a basis of $75 and fair market value of $100 to Y Corporation, owned by the shareholders of X, for $80. Y later sells the property to an uncontrolled third party for $105 (its then fair market value), and X and Y report income of $5 and $25 respectively. When the Service increases X's income from the sale to $25 (fair market value of $100 less X's basis of $75), this primary adjustment triggers a correlative adjustment to Y's income (i.e., a reduction of the amount reported by Y from $25 to $5, the gain Y would have realized and reported had it purchased the property from X for $100, the price that would have prevailed between uncontrolled taxpayers).

Recognizing that artificial prices may be employed as a general practice when related taxpayers deal with each other and that benefits may flow in both directions, the regulations require the district director, on making an adjustment, to "consider the effect of any other non-arm's length transaction between [the related taxpayers] in the taxable year which, if taken into account, would result in a set-off against any allocation which would otherwise be made."[51] Thus, to extend the preceding example, if Y rendered to X uncompensated services worth $8, this amount would be taken into account as a set-off, so that the net primary and correlative adjustments would increase X's income to $17 (from the $5 amount reported), reflecting the $8 set-off against the primary adjustment, and reduce Y's income to $13 (from the $25 amount reported), reflecting the $8 set-off against the correlative adjustment.

The regulations also state that "the district director shall consider the effect upon such members of an arrangement between them for reimburse-

---

[50] Regs. §1.482-1(d)(2). For deemed correlative adjustments if the related party's U.S. income tax liability will not be currently affected for any pending current year (e.g., because the adjustment increases the basis of a factory that has not yet been placed in service and hence has not generated any current depreciation deductions), see id., Examples (1) – (3).

[51] Regs. §1.482-1(d)(3); for the procedures governing set-off claims, see Rev. Proc. 70-8, 1970-1 CB 434. See also OTM Corp. v. US, 572 F2d 1046 (5th Cir.), cert. denied, 439 US 1002 (1978); (taxpayer cannot force Service to invoke §482 and make correlative adjustments instead of disallowing excessive deductions under §162); Continental Equities, Inc. v. CIR, 551 F2d 74 (5th Cir. 1977) (correlative adjustment not available as set-off or equitable recoupment to taxpayer subject to primary adjustment; Tax Court has no equitable power to impose recoupment). Query whether the taxpayer can compel the Service to comply with the set-off regulations once it invokes its authority under §482, even though it cannot be compelled to take the first step; see supra note 23.

ment . . . if the taxpayer can establish that such an arrangement in fact existed during the taxable year under consideration."[52] This cryptic announcement, which does not seem to have elicited any discussion in the litigated cases or published rulings, presumably would encompass arrangements such as an agreement between a domestic parent and a foreign subsidiary for the construction of a foreign plant to be owned jointly. Under this agreement, the subsidiary would take the initiative and defray the expenses as they were incurred, subject to reimbursement with interest when the project was completed.

Because of the permissible scope and heavy evidential weight of a §482 allocation, taxpayers rarely greet them with enthusiasm.[53] Even so, action by the Service under §482 occasionally may be a boon to the taxpayer, or at least the lesser of two evils. For example, if X Corporation and Y Corporation are under common control, and X charges Y excessive amounts for services rendered to it, the Service can disallow Y's excess deductions under §162 without making any change in X's return. If X seeks a refund for the tax it paid on the amount disallowed as a deduction by Y, the refund might well be denied on the ground that X received the full amount under a claim of right and with no obligation to refund any part of it. By contrast, a primary adjustment of Y's return under §482 would ordinarily be coupled with a correlative adjustment to X's return.

6. Specific situations. Detailed guidelines for the application of §482 to a variety of intragroup transactions are provided by the regulations,[54] and these are summarized briefly below:

---

[52] Regs. §1.482-1(d)(3); see also Rev. Proc. 70-8, 1970-1 CB 434. Note also the regulations' statement that set-off adjustments are to be made at arm's-length market values (without regard to any safe harbor rules in Regs. §1.482-2).

[53] But see Surrey, supra note 31, at 75 (§482 worry is symbol of status, since it usually means taxpayer qualifies for a tax preference).

[54] Regs. §1.482-2, originally promulgated in 1968, covers the most common intragroup transactions, but not all-inclusively, and it does not explicitly prescribe rules for transactions between members of the group and third parties, although a member's dealings with outsiders can give rise to a §482 allocation. See, e.g., Richard H. Foster, supra note 23, at 156 (§482 applied to income from sale to outsiders of property previously received by seller from related party in tax-free §351 transfer); Northwestern Nat'l Bank of Minneapolis v. US, 556 F2d 889 (8th Cir. 1977) (§482 applied to parent corporation's deduction for charitable contribution of property previously received by it as dividend from subsidiary); Dolese v. CIR, supra note 23 (§482 applied to charitable contribution by partners following disproportionate distribution of property by partnership controlled by taxpayer who also controlled other partner, a corporation).

(a) Loans and advances. In the case of bona fide indebtedness between related parties (excluding, for example, contributions to capital and distributions with respect to stock), §482 can be employed by the Service to allocate an arm's-length rate of interest if the actual arrangement either bears no interest or carries a rate that is not equal to an arm's-length charge.[55] For this purpose, a rate is deemed to be at arm's length if it falls between specified safe harbor boundaries, ordinarily not less than 100 percent and not more than 130 percent of the applicable federal rate, as prescribed by regulations. Loans payable in foreign currency do not qualify for the safe harbor rules, nor do loans by professional lenders.

Before reaching §482, however, a number of other provisions dealing explicitly with imputed interest must be taken into account, including §483 (imputed interest on deferred payments attributable to the sale or exchange of property), §467 (certain rental agreements), §1274 (original issue discount on certain debt instruments issued for property), and §7872 (certain loans with no interest or below-market interest). In many situations, these priority remedies will restore the patient to tax health, leaving no need for a §482 pill.

(b) Services. Performance of services for, or on behalf of, another member of the group for less than an arm's-length consideration will result in an allocation that reflects the relative benefits intended from those services.[56] This benefits adjustment is generally based on the cost of the services rather than their value (although full, rather than marginal, cost accounting is required here). If, however, the services are an integral part of the business, a value allocation reflecting a profit factor will be required.[57] If the benefits of the services are remote or indirect, however, allocation is not required, and if

---

[55] The description in the text is based on Prop. Regs. §1.482-2(a) (1986), since Regs. §1.482-2(a), as currently in force, does not take account of legislation enacted (in 1984) after it was promulgated. For the power of the Service to impute interest under §482, see Latham Park Manor, Inc., supra note 42 (correlative adjustment procedures, supra note 50, rebut creation-of-income argument, supra note 43); Sunshine Dep't Stores, Inc., supra note 34.

[56] Regs. §1.482–2(b).

[57] For a services allocation case where the taxpayer successfully avoided a §482 allocation of supervisory domestic home office costs to its foreign subsidiaries, see Young & Rubicam, Inc. v. US, 410 F2d 1233 (Ct. Cl. 1969). See also Nat Harrison Assoc., Inc., 42 TC 601 (1964) (acq.); Columbian Rope Co., 42 TC 800 (1964) (acq.); Johnson Bronze Co., ¶ 65,281 P-H Memo. TC (1965); Edwin D. Davis, 64 TC 1034 (1975); Elvin V. Jones, 64 TC 1066 (1975); United States Steel Corp. v. CIR, 617 F2d 942 (2d Cir. 1980) (in determining arm's-length price by considering comparable transactions between unrelated parties, "comparable" does not mean identical); Hospital Corp. of Am., supra note 41 (§482 allocation upheld to reflect subsidiary's non-arm's-length use of parent's intangibles and parent's substantial services for benefit of subsidiary).

the group allocates costs pursuant to sound accounting practices, the results will not be disturbed.

(c) Use of tangible property. Intragroup lessees must pay an arm's-length rent for their use of an affiliate's property, or an allocation will be made under §482.[58] If neither the owner nor the user was engaged in the leasing business, the rent could have been determined previously under a formula prescribed in the regulations, but this formula was withdrawn in 1986.[59]

(d) Transfer or use of intangibles. If intangible property rights are made available to affiliates for other than an arm's-length consideration, the regulations require an adjustment to reflect an arm's-length charge for the use of such property, generally based on the value of the benefits conferred.[60] If the intangible is developed by one of the affiliates, however, the §482 adjust-

---

For other recent service allocation cases where the Service succeeded in obtaining adjustments under §482 to reflect the failure to properly charge for services rendered on behalf of affiliates, see Eli Lilly & Co., supra note 28; G.D. Searle & Co., supra note 28; Ciba-Geigy Corp., 85 TC 172 (1985); Stanley W. Haag, supra note 29.

[58] Regs. §1.482-2(c); see Revel D. Cooper, 64 TC 576 (1975) (corporate use of shareholder assets rent-free permitted Service to allocate fair rental income charge from corporation to shareholder under §482); Robert A. Boyer, 58 TC 316 (1972) (§482 allocation where related lessee delayed payment of rent and used proceeds to improve the property); Diefenthal v. US, 367 F. Supp. 506 (E.D. La. 1973) (intercompany charter of ships made at arm's-length rates, so §482 assertion rejected); accord, Preston W. Carroll, ¶ 87,057 P-H Memo. TC (rent charged to shareholders at proper rate).

See also Thomas B. Fegan, 71 TC 791 (1979) (bargain lease; imputation of arm's-length rent per §482 upheld); White Tool & Mach. Co., ¶ 80,443 P-H Memo. TC (1980), aff'd, 677 F2d 528 (6th Cir.) cert. denied, 459 US 907 (1982) (excess rents between brother-sister corporations properly reallocated under §482); Peck v. CIR, 752 F2d 469 (9th Cir. 1985) (shareholder contribution of property to corporation and leaseback at excessive rent; §482 applied to deny excess rent deduction by shareholder); Powers v. CIR, 724 F2d 64 (7th Cir. 1983) (lease at excessive rent and sublease at bargain rent triggered §482 allocation).

[59] Prop. Regs. §1.482-2(c)(2)(ii) deleted the prior safe-harbor formula for leases (but not for subleases).

[60] Regs. §1.482-2(d); G.D. Searle & Co., supra note 28 (imputation of arm's-length royalty to clearly reflect parent's income following transfer of intangibles in a §351 exchange); R.T. French Co., 60 TC 836 (1973) (patent license between affiliates had arm's-length terms, and hence taxpayer's royalty payments to foreign affiliate properly deductible); Ciba-Geigy Corp., supra note 57 (taxpayer's royalty rate for license of intangibles held reasonable on facts; rate was arm's-length, and Service abused discretion in arguing for lower rate).

See Comment, The Application of Section 482 to the Transfer or Use of Intangible Property, 17 UCLA L. Rev. 202 (1969); see also Jenks, Section 482 and the Nonrecognition Provisions: The Transfer of Intangible Assets, 32 Tax Lawyer 775 (1979); Adess, The Role of Section 482 in Nonrecognition Transactions—The Outer

ment is delayed until completion of the property and its transfer at a non-arm's-length price to other members of the group.

The definition of intangible property for §482 purposes is extremely broad, limited only by the requirement that the property have substantial value independent of the services of individuals.[61] If the parties have entered into a bona fide cost-sharing arrangement, however, the allocation, if any, will be based on the relative costs incurred by the members in the development of the property. Such an arrangement is defined as one where the participants have attempted in good faith to bear their respective shares of the costs and risks of development on an arm's-length basis comparable to the terms unrelated parties would have adopted.

In the case of intangibles transferred by one related party to another after 1986, however, these principles yield to the final sentence of §482 (added in 1986), which in effect imposes a profit-sharing approach for income attributable to intangibles (which will fluctuate throughout the use of those intangibles). Although the effect of this restriction on (or, perhaps, abandonment of) the normal separate entity arm's-length standard of the regulations remains to be worked out, the legislative objective was to insure "that the division of income between related parties reasonably reflect[s] the relative economic activity undertaken by each"; this may imply that the transferor must report (and that the transferee can deduct) a higher amount (a so-called super-royalty) than the license fee that would result from arm's-length bargaining between unrelated parties.[62]

(e) Intercompany sales. If tangible property is sold to affiliates at other than an arm's-length price, the regulations require an adjustment to reflect a proper arm's-length price, determined first by reference to comparable

---

Edges, 57 Taxes 946 (1979); and Note, Section 482 and the Nonrecognition Provisions: Resolving the Conflict, supra note 28.

[61] For examples of other attempts to define the property status of various intangible rights, see Rev. Rul. 64-56, 1964-1 CB (Part 1) 133 (know-how); Rev. Proc. 69-19, 1969-2 CB 301 (same); Rev. Rul. 65-261, 1965-2 CB 281 (right of publicity); Rev. Rul. 64-235, 1964-2 CB 18 (goodwill of a service business).

See Hospital Corp. of Am., supra note 41 (§482 allocation triggered by subsidiary's uncompensated use of parent's name, reputation, experience, guaranty of performance, and management system); Eli Lilly & Co., supra note 28 (transfer of intangibles to subsidiary could not be disregarded under §482 where no flip-resale by transferee and no midstream mismatch of income and deductions). But see G.D. Searle & Co., supra note 28 (arm's-length royalty could be imputed under §482 to clearly reflect parent's income despite valid §351 transfer of the intangibles to subsidiary); infra note 62.

[62] H.R. Conf. Rep. No. 841, 99th Cong., 2d Sess. II–937 (1986). See generally Granwell & Hirsh, The Super Royalty: A New International Concept, 33 Tax Notes 1037 (1986); G.D. Searle & Co., supra note 28, anticipated this provision in many respects.

uncontrolled sales, if there are any.[63] In the absence of such sales, the adjustment is to be determined next by the resale price method, which reduces the related buyer's outside selling price for the goods by an appropriate markup, or finally by use of the cost-plus method,[64] which applies an appropriate markup to the related seller's cost of production. If none of these methods is suitable, the regulations permit the use of any other appropriate method.[65]

This approach is obviously more an art than a science, and it requires a detailed factual and economic analysis. The courts, however, have tended to paint with a broader brush than the regulations in this contentious area have done, recognizing the wraithlike quality of intercompany pricing problems, but nevertheless approving the Service's §482 allocations in cases of seriously distorted dealings between affiliates.[66]

7. Collateral effects of §482 adjustments. Like a rock thrown into a placid pool, a §482 adjustment can create waves that have unexpected results. For example, an allocation of interest under §482 may be—to shift

---

[63] Regs. §1.482-2(e); Eli Lilly & Co. v. US, 372 F2d 990 (Ct. Cl. 1967), discussed by O'Connor, Can Intercorporate Pricing Arrangements Avoid Being Upset by Section 482?, 26 J. Tax'n 262 (1967). See also Eli Lilly & Co., supra note 28, for a more (although not totally) successful experience by the same company in the Tax Court; Rafferty, The Profit-Split Method of Income Allocation in Intercompany Pricing Disputes: The *Eli Lilly* case 64 Taxes 662 (1986); infra note 65.

[64] Ross Glove Co., 60 TC 569 (1973) (cost-plus method used for §482 allocation from intercompany sales); Robert M. Brittingham, supra note 37 (Service's use of customs value to determine arm's-length price an error where taxpayer established other value by evidence); Edward K. Edwards, 67 TC 224 (1976) (manufacturer's list price not controlling; no one in the trade charged list); E.I. duPont de Nemours & Co. v. US, 608 F2d 445 (Ct. Cl. 1979), cert. denied, 445 US 962 (1980) (use of resale price method rejected because no comparable resellers; Service arm's-length price determination accepted). Fuller, Problems in Applying the 482 Intercompany Pricing Regulations Accentuated by *duPont* Case, 52 J. Tax'n 10 (1980); and Webb, *duPont* and *United States Steel* Exacerbate Section 482 Intercompany Pricing Regulations, 10 J. Corp. Tax'n 152 (1983).

Legislation enacted in 1986 adopted §1059A, which limits §482 import prices to claimed customs values.

[65] The *duPont* case, supra note 64, upheld the Service's use of the fourth method as reasonable where taxpayer failed to prove it was entitled to any of the first three pricing methods (which will typically be the case in this area); see also Eli Lilly & Co., supra note 28 (use of fourth method, a reasonable profit split, based on functional analysis of relative values of members' contributions to income production process, where other methods not available on facts). See Fuller, supra note 64; Rafferty, supra note 63.

[66] See generally Schindler & Henderson, Intercorporate Transfer Pricing—1985 Survey of Section 482 Audits, 29 Tax Notes 1171 (1985). See also Higinbotham, Asper, Stoffregen, & Wexler, Effective Application of the Section 482 Transfer Pricing Regulations, 42 Tax L. Rev. 293 (1987).

metaphors—the final straw that converts an ordinary business corporation into a PHC, generating a tax burden in addition to that generated by the §482 adjustment. Section 482 allocations can also negate Subchapter S elections, render corporations vulnerable to the accumulated earnings tax imposed by §531, or destroy their eligibility for the special tax status accorded to real estate investment companies under §857. Conversely, a §482 allocation may occasionally turn out to be beneficial to a corporation (e.g., by qualifying it for a special tax status through a reduction of the proportion of tainted items in its income stream). Such windfalls are likely to be rare, however, since only the Service can invoke §482, and it is not likely to do so if the allocation's peripheral consequences will be counterproductive.

Section 482 allocations have ramifications of another type, reflecting the fact that an adjustment neither changes the financial terms on which the underlying transaction occurred nor creates a debt or account receivable in favor of the corporation that was overcharged. Hence, no deduction can be taken to reflect the related party's failure to obtain or inability to compel repayment of the excess.[67]

> *To illustrate:* If *X* Corporation sells property worth $150 to *Y*, a related corporation, for $100, a §482 allocation can impute $50 of additional gross income to *X* (and a correlative $150 basis to *Y*); but it does not alter the fact that *Y* paid only $100 for property worth $150, and may later sell the property for this amount. Thus, to the extent of the $50 disparity, *X* is poorer and *Y* is richer than they were before the transaction; this economic fact of life continues to exist despite the §482 allocation. If, instead, *X* sold property worth $100 to *Y* for $150, the §482 allocation tax burden should flow in the opposite direction (i.e., from *X* to *Y*) in order to correct the fact that *Y* overpaid for the property by $50 (*X*'s correlative adjustment presumably being a reduction in its sales price to $100).

Under Rev. Proc. 65-17, however, the parties can make tax-free transfers of funds to conform their accounts to reflect the allocation (e.g., by arranging for *Y* to remit to *X* the $50 below-market amount in the first case or for *X* to refund to *Y* the excessive $50 charge in the second case), provided the Service concludes, on examining all the facts and circumstances, that the original transaction did not have tax avoidance as one of its purposes.[68]

---

[67] See Cappuccilli v. CIR, 668 F2d 138 (2d Cir.), cert. denied, 459 US 822 (1982); A.J. Eisenberg, 78 TC 336 (1982).

[68] Rev. Proc. 65-17, 1965-1 CB 833; see also Rev. Rul. 82-80, 1982-1 CB 89 (original price treated as adjusted §482 price for purposes of later events and transactions).

If permission to make such a corrective transfer of funds is not requested or is denied, then the bargain element (or the excessive sales price portion) of a transaction between brother-sister corporations may, under principles examined earlier in this work, be taxed as a constructive distribution by the transferor to their common parent, coupled with a contribution by the parent to the transferee's capital.[69]

If the preceding example is varied by assuming that Y is X's wholly owned subsidiary (and also that there was no corrective payment under Rev. Proc. 65-17), then the $50 bargain benefit accruing to Y in the first case evidently would be treated by the Service as a contribution by X to Y's capital.[70] If, on the other hand, Y were the parent in the bargain sale case, the transaction would be treated as a taxable constructive distribution from X to Y which would be eligible for the §243 dividends-received deduction.[71] Similarly, if X, the parent, overcharged Y, its subsidiary, for the property, a constructive dividend of the excessive $50 paid from Y to X could result; and if Y were the parent in the overcharge case, a capital contribution from Y to X could result from Y's overpayment to its subsidiary X.[72]

---

[69] In the overpayment case, the party overpaying for the property would be the source of the constructive dividend, and the payee would be the recipient of the capital contribution. See supra ¶ 7.05 text at notes 118–121; see also William H. Bell, III, ¶ 82,660 P-H Memo. TC (1982) (corporation owned by individuals paid excessive fees to related corporation in order to benefit family shareholders of payee; held §482 allocation warranted; allocated amounts properly taxed as constructive dividends to shareholders of payor corporation). But see White Tool & Mach. Co., supra note 58 (excessive rentals corrected by §482 allocation; constructive dividend treatment not warranted because economic benefit to individual shareholders was derivative and corrected by §482 allocation). To the extent that *White Tool* treats the excessive payments as fully neutralized by §482, it is inconsistent with the *Bell* case, and it seems erroneous, since the §482 allocation does not alter the fact that the payee corporation received and retained an unwarranted amount of cash.

See generally, Jenks, Constructive Dividends Resulting From Section 482 Adjustments, 28 Tax Lawyer 83 (1970); Cliff & Cohen, Collateral Fictions and Section 482, 36 Tax Lawyer 37 (1982).

[70] The §482 adjusted sales price to X and Y would be $150, and X would be treated as contributing $50 of that amount to Y. The deemed transfer would be tax-free to the subsidiary under §118 and would increase the parent's basis for its stock in the subsidiary under §1016, supra ¶ 3.13. But see Huber Homes, Inc., 55 TC 598 (1971) (no §482 income to parent on bargain sale to its subsidiary). Compare Sol Lessinger, 85 TC 824 (1985) (theory of Rev. Rul. 64-155, 1964-1 CB 138, that bargain sale a constructive §351 exchange with boot, supra ¶ 3.05).

[71] Such eligibility results because $50 of X's §482 adjusted sales price ended up in the hands of Y. See Regs. §1.301-1(j), and supra ¶ 7.05. For §243, see supra ¶ 5.06.

[72] As to constructive dividend treatment, see supra ¶ 7.05; for capital contributions, see supra ¶ 3.13. See also articles supra note 69.

8. International double taxation. Section 482 adjustments can have particularly troublesome ramifications where the foreign subsidiary of a domestic parent pays foreign income taxes on income that is allocated under §482 to its parent (e.g., because the Service finds that the prices charged by the parent for goods sold to the subsidiary were too low). Unless the foreign taxing authorities agree to a similar adjustment, the subsidiary will use the artifically low purchase price in computing its profit on selling the property to its foreign customers; and it will, therefore, have to pay foreign taxes on income that is also taxed to its parent in computing the latter's U.S. tax liability.

This so-called economic double taxation may be prevented or mitigated by (1) an agreement between U.S. and foreign tax authorities under the competent authorities procedures of a bilateral tax treaty, or (2) operation of the U.S. foreign tax credit, since the foreign income tax will be taken into account in computing the so-called indirect foreign tax credit when the subsidiary's profits are paid to the parent.[73] The treaty remedy for avoiding economic double taxation, however, is cumbersome at best, and it is not available for all foreign countries.[74] The foreign tax credit does not depend on the cooperation of a foreign government, but has its own limitations: A distribution by the subsidiary may not be currently feasible, and, even when it occurs, the complex statutory limits of §904 may reduce the credit below the foreign taxes actually paid.[75] Another remedy for this problem is the tax-free transfer procedure of Rev. Proc. 65-17, summarized previously.[76]

¶ 15.04　GENERAL INCOME AND DEDUCTION PRINCIPLES IN THE MULTIPLE CORPORATION CONTEXT

In addition to possible application of the statutory provisions and principles considered in preceding sections, transactions between affiliated corporations may fail to accomplish their tax expectations because of numerous other income, deduction, timing, and characterization rules (under §§61,

---

[73] See generally McCawley, supra note 23, 116 Tax Mgmt. at A-39.

[74] See Rev. Proc. 70-18, 1970-2 CB 493 (competent authorities procedures); Rev. Rul. 76-508, 1976-2 CB 225 (income of foreign subsidiary allocated to U.S. parent under §482; if foreign subsidiary does not ask for foreign tax adjustment and U.S. parent does not invoke competent authorities' procedures of Rev. Proc. 70-18, extra foreign taxes of subsidiary not creditable under §902); amplified by Rev. Rul. 80-231, 1980-2 CB 219.

[75] See infra ¶ 17.11; Bittker, Federal Taxation of Income, Estates and Gifts (Warren, Gorham & Lamont, Inc., 1981), ¶ 69.2.

[76] Supra text at note 68. See Schering Corp., 69 TC 579 (1978) (foreign tax imposed on repatriation distribution qualifies for §901 credit).

162, 163, 165, 267, 446, 451, 453(g), 461, 1239, 7701(f), and 7872) that are considered in the following text. In addition, the form of the particular corporate structures involved in a given situation (i.e., parent-subsidiary or brother-sister corporations) will materially affect the tax problems created by transactions between members of the group.

Considered in this section are various transactions involving affiliated corporations in which §482 is not (or cannot be) invoked by the Service but in which income nevertheless is created, accelerated, or recharacterized, deductions are disallowed or deferred, or the transactions themselves are disregarded under other Code provisions or judge-made principles.[77] Although many of these principles are not limited to affiliated corporations, the existence of affiliated status is frequently central to their application.

1. Sham transactions. It has long been the rule that transactions lacking in economic substance or reality will be disregarded for tax purposes. The fouintainhead of this approach is, of course, the renowned case of *Gregory v. Helvering*,[78] but other equally well-known applications can be found in the *Higgins, Griffiths*, and *Knetsch* decisions.[79] These general principles and attitudes, sounding in tax avoidance, business purpose, and form versus substance, have been applied in a number of cases involving sales of property between related corporations at a loss.[80] One of the more striking illustrations of the sham transaction approach is *National Lead Co. v. CIR*, where the court held that a loss sale of stock by a parent corporation to its wholly owned subsidiary in 1937 lacked economic reality because of the parent's continuing control over the property for 15 years following the alleged

---

[77] For discussion of the corporate entity doctrine and when the corporation will be respected as such, see supra ¶¶ 1.05 and 2.10.

For assignment of income issues in the context of personal service corporations, see supra ¶ 2.07. See generally Stanley W. Haag, 88 TC No. 32 (1987), and cases cited.

[78] Gregory v. Helvering, 293 US 465 (1935), supra ¶¶ 1.05 and 13.02.

[79] Higgins v. Smith, 308 US 473 (1940) (loss sale to wholly owned corporation disregarded as sham); Griffiths v. CIR, 308 US 355 (1939) (purported installment sale through a wholly owned corporate conduit disregarded as sham); Knetsch v. US, 364 US 361 (1961) (borrowing transaction disregarded as a sham); see also Goldstein v. CIR, 364 F2d 734 (2d Cir. 1966), cert. denied, 385 US 1005 (1967) (no economic profit potential apart from tax savings).

[80] See Crown Cork Int'l Corp., 4 TC 19 (1944), aff'd per curiam, 149 F2d 968 (3d Cir. 1945); Bank of Am. Nat'l Trust & Sav. Ass'n, 15 TC 544 (1950), aff'd per curiam, 193 F2d 178 (9th Cir. 1951); Investors Diversified Servs., Inc. v. CIR, 325 F2d 341 (8th Cir. 1963); White-Delafield-Morris Corp., ¶ 63,325 P-H Memo. TC (1963); Northern Pac. Ry. v. US, 378 F2d 686 (Ct. Cl. 1967) (loss on sale by parent to subsidiary disallowed). But see infra notes 104 and 106.

sale.[81] Accordingly, the parent corporation was taxable on dividends and profits from the resale of such property by the subsidiary in the intervening years. Although it was too late to attack the initial loss deduction on the prior sale under *Higgins*, the parties assumed that the loss should not have been allowed. However, the court held that the parent corporation was still the owner of the property for tax purposes because the sham character of the original sale continued. The separate corporate existence of the subsidiary was not totally disregarded by the court, however; rather, it merely held that the intercorporate sale had no reality for tax purposes and hence must be disregarded. This result is less drastic than that in those cases that completely disregarded the separate corporate identity.

2. Income creation outside of §482. With the passage of §7872 in 1984, loans between parent-subsidiary corporations on interest terms below a prescribed statutory rate are covered primarily by this provision rather than by §482.[82] When applicable to a case involving below market rate loans, §7872 provides for imputation of an appropriate market interest rate in such transactions (for both the lender and the borrower). In addition, collateral tax consequences to the parties will result if the bargain interest element has the effect of a capital contribution, a dividend, compensation, or other taxable benefit, as the case may be. If the below market interest rate loan is a demand loan, the imputation computations (and the attendant collateral tax consequences) are made ratably on an annual basis; if the loan has a fixed term, however, interest is imputed under the OID rules, while the bifurcated collateral tax consequences attributable to the bargain interest spread (i.e., the dividend, compensation, and so forth) occur *immediately* at the time of the loan.[83]

Sales of property at a bargain price between parent-subsidiary corporations also can generate imputed gain without the Service needing to resort to

---

[81] National Lead Co. v. CIR, 336 F2d 134 (2d Cir. 1964); see also Goldstein v. CIR, supra note 79.

[82] See Prop. Regs. §§1.482-2(a)(3)(ii) and 1.482-2(a)(4), Example (2). For the constructive dividend aspects of a §7872 below-market loan by the corporation, see supra ¶ 7.05, para. 4. For the order of priority if §§482 and 7872 overlap, see Prop. Regs. §1.7872-2(a)(2)(iii).

For the prior case law overturned by §7872, see Hardee v. US, 707 F2d 661 (Fed. Cir. 1983), and cases cited.

As to §7872 generally, see Eustice, The Tax Reform Act of 1984, ¶¶ 2.02[3] and 3.04[2][d] (Warren, Gorham & Lamont, Inc., 1984), and supra ¶ 4.40; Lokken, The Time Value of Money Rules, 42 Tax L. Rev. 1, 200–251 (1986); Pearle, Interest-Free and Below Market Gift Loans, 26 Tax Mgmt. Memo. (BNA) No. 1, at 3 (1985). Regulations under §7872 were proposed on August 15, 1985.

For interest imputation under the OID rules of §§483 and 1274, see supra ¶¶ 4.40–4.42.

[83] Thus, §7872 codifies the Service's argument that was rejected in Greenspun v. CIR, 670 F2d 123 (9th Cir. 1982).

the mechanism of §482 adjustments. Thus, if a parent corporation sells appreciated property to its controlled subsidiary at a discount price (i.e., one that is less than the property's true value), the spread between market value and selling price is ordinarily treated as a nontaxable capital contribution by the parent to its subsidiary, but this transaction could also be converted into a constructive §351 exchange with boot.[84] Conversely, if a subsidiary sells appreciated property to its parent at a bargain price, Regs. §1.301-1(j) states that the discount element (i.e., the spread between purchase price and value) constitutes a distribution of property under §301 and hence is taxable as a dividend to the extent covered by earnings and profits of the subsidiary,[85] while the subsidiary will be taxed under §311(b)(1) as if the property had been sold to the parent at its market value.[86]

Other instances of bargain dealings between parent-subsidiary corporations (e.g., leases, licenses, and undercompensated services) are primarily patrolled by §482, but, in the absence of §482, the possibility of constructive dividend treatment can also arise, at least in cases where the §243 deduction would not apply.[87]

Bargain purchases and sales of property between brother-sister corporations create a different set of problems, most notably the possibility that constructive dividend treatment may occur to the *shareholders* of the commonly controlled corporations from such transactions.[88] Moreover, treatment of the corporate parties to such sales is complicated by the remoteness of their relationship (i.e., there is not a direct stock ownership connection here as compared with the parent-subsidiary situation). As a general matter,

---

[84] See, e.g., Simon v. CIR, 285 F2d 422 (3d Cir. 1960). See also Regs. §§1.1001-1(e) and 1.1015-4, dealing with the computation of gain or loss to the transferor and basis to the transferee where property is disposed of in a part-gift, part-sale transaction; Huber Homes, Inc., supra note 70 (no §482 income to parent on bargain sale to subsidiary).

But the Service could invoke Rev. Rul. 64-155, 1964-1 CB 138, which held that a capital contribution to a wholly owned foreign subsidiary constituted a constructive §351 exchange with boot for purposes of §367. If such a transaction is treated as a constructive §351 exchange with boot, taxable gain could be generated to the extent of the boot; if, on the other hand, the normal bargain sale rules apply, the seller realizes taxable gain only to the extent that the selling price exceeds its basis for the property (conversely no loss is recognized in such a transfer). The possibility of treatment as a constructive §351 exchange was endorsed by the Tax Court in Sol Lessinger, 85 TC 824 (1985) (which rejected the requirement in Abegg v. CIR, 429 F2d 1209 (2d Cir. 1970), that stock had to be received in order to have a §351 exchange). Supra ¶ 3.13.

[85] For the constructive dividend possibility, see supra ¶ 7.05; see also supra ¶ 7.23.

[86] For §311 imputed sale treatment, see supra ¶¶ 7.21 and 7.22.

[87] Supra ¶¶ 5.05 and 7.05 (these situations typically arise where either the subsidiary or the parent is a foreign corporation).

[88] Supra ¶ 7.05, para. 8.

it would seem that bargain sales between brother-sister corporations may be less vulnerable to constructive dividend arguments than sales at an excessive price. In the latter situation, courts seem more willing to treat the excessive portion of the sales price as a constructive distribution to shareholders of the affiliated corporations, at least where control is concentrated in a small number of stockholders.

In the case of a bargain purchase, the typical remedy is an imputation under §482 of a fair price for the property (generating additional income for the selling corporation and a higher basis for the purchaser).[89] A recasting of the transaction as (1) a sale of an appropriate portion of the property for the amount actually paid, (2) a simultaneous constructive distribution of the remaining portion of the property to the shareholders,[90] and (3) a contribution by them of this part of the property to the purchasing corporation's capital is also a possibility here. Finally, a hypothetical bargain purchase of the property by the shareholders of the first corporation (generating dividend income equal to the discount[91]), followed by a hypothetical bargain resale of the property by them to the second corporation could also result.

The treatment of the corporate parties to a non-arm's-length sale, absent application of §482 by the Service, is even less clear. Presumably the general rules relating to bargain purchases and sales could apply,[92] subject, of course, to an alternative reallocation of income or deductions under §482. One of the few decisions to face this problem squarely is *Challenger, Inc.,* involving the treatment of excessive rental receipts in the hands of the affiliated lessor corporation.[93] The court there found that the excessive rentals did not constitute taxable income to the recipient, although the precise grounds for this conclusion were unclear. The opinion noted that the amounts in question could be characterized either as a nullity, a capital contribution by the lessee to the lessor, or a constructive dividend to the common shareholder followed by capital contributions to the lessor corporation, all of which would result in tax-free treatment to the payee.[94] As noted in the

---

[89] Supra ¶ 15.03, para. 7

[90] With a taxable gain to the distributing corporation on that distribution under §311(b)(1), see supra ¶ 7.21.

[91] Also with a taxable gain to the first corporation on the distribution under §311(b)(1), see supra ¶ 7.21.

[92] Supra notes 84–86; see generally Wurzel, The Tax Basis for Assorted Bargain Purchases: The Inordinate Cost of "Ersatz" Legislation, 20 Tax L. Rev. 165 (1964).

[93] Challenger, Inc., ¶ 64,338 P-H Memo. TC (1964).

[94] But cf. Sterno Sales Corp. v. US, 345 F2d 552 (Ct. Cl. 1965), in which disallowed excessive compensation payments by a brother corporation were nevertheless held taxable as compensation income to the payee sister corporation; the taxpayer attempted to characterize these receipts as capital contributions from its shareholder,

preceding section, however, a §482 reallocation of income or deductions is preferable to the mere disallowance of excessive payments, since the former approach gives a corresponding adjustment to the income of the taxpayer *from* whom such items are allocated.

Where property is sold at a *premium* price (i.e., one in excess of its market value) between parent and subsidiary corporations, the tax problems are primarily those of the seller. For example, if a parent corporation sells property to its subsidiary at an excessive price, the premium element of the selling price will most likely be treated as a dividend distribution to the parent. In this situation, the issue is characterization of the type of income realized by the seller (i.e., whether the premium portion of the selling price will be treated as some other type of income, such as a dividend, rather than as proceeds from the sale of property).[95]

Where a subsidiary sells property to its parent at a premium, on the other hand, the excessive charge should most likely be treated as a capital contribution by the parent to the subsidiary (and subsequent refunds by the subsidiary would ordinarily result in dividend treatment to the parent). These conclusions, however, assume that the Service does not invoke the reallocation rules of §482 in order to reflect an arm's-length fair market value price for such related party dealings, in which event the tax results would be controlled by the provisions of that section and the regulations thereunder. (The consequences of a §482 allocation are considered in the preceding section.)[96]

3. Income recharacterization and acceleration. Sales of depreciable property between related[97] corporations result both in a recharacterization of gain (as ordinary rather than capital) to the selling affiliate under §1239

---

but the court held the parties to the form of their transaction (i.e., compensation), notwithstanding the excessive character thereof.

[95] See supra ¶ 7.05. Subsequent refunds of these overcharges by the parent may, in turn, be deductible under §162 and possibly subject to the special claim of right rules of §1341. More likely, however, would be classification of these repayments as additional capital contributions (supra ¶ 3.13) by the parent that would be nontaxable to the subsidiary under §118 and nondeductible to the parent under §263.

[96] See Rev. Rul. 82-80, 1982-1 CB 89 (use true §482 price in original transaction if qualifying for tax-free repatriation treatment of Rev. Proc. 65-17; one level of adjustment only—§482 adjustments not endless chain of constructive transactions).

[97] The Tax Reform Act of 1986 conformed the relationship line of §§1239 and 453(g) to §267 (i.e., more than 50 percent of vote or value); moreover, the Act amended §453(g)(1)(B)(ii), dealing with contingent payment sales between related parties that are reportable under the open transaction method, by providing that the seller must use ratable basis recovery and the buyer must delay its basis step-up until gain is reported by the related seller.

and the denial of deferral for such gain under §453(g)(1) unless the taxpayer is able to prove to the Service's satisfaction that the sale did not have as one of its principal purposes the avoidance of federal income tax under §453(g)(2).[98] Moreover, if inadequate interest is charged on deferred payment debt obligations, the OID rules of §1274 (and §483) may be invoked.[99]

4. General deduction principles: Disallowance or deferral. Intercompany loans, leases, licenses, services, or sales effected between members of an affiliated group of corporations frequently raise threshold questions of deductibility under the general deduction provisions of §§162, 163, 165, 167, or 267. As an initial matter, the close relationship between the parties does not of itself prevent current deductibility with respect to a particular item, although this fact does inspire judicial scrutiny into the bona fides of the arrangement. On the other hand, it should be noted that an expense must qualify as an ordinary and necessary business outlay to come within the purview of §162, interest must be paid or incurred on a valid indebtedness to be deductible under §163, and losses must be sustained in a genuine closed or completed transaction to be deductible under §165.[100] The fact that the parties are related, although not fatal, nevertheless imposes upon them a practical duty that they "turn square corners" in their dealings with each other, lest the transaction fail to satisfy these basic statutory requirements and presuppositions of deductibility.

For example, with respect to business expenses, not only must the item in question satisfy the ordinary and necessary standard of §162, but it must be proximately connected to the business activities of the taxpayer claiming deduction therefor as well.[101] The problem of expenses for the benefit of

---

[98] But cf. LDS, Inc., ¶ 86,293 P-H Memo. TC (1986) (installment sale between affiliates held equity capital contribution, even though parties initially treated transaction as a sale; issue was §453B disposition, and parties later changed position that transaction was not a true sale and won).

Establishment of no tax avoidance may be an easier task after 1986 in view of the repeal of capital gain rate benefits generally for corporations and individuals.

[99] Supra ¶ 4.42.

[100] Note that denial of a deduction is a more drastic result than reallocation of that item under §482, supra ¶ 15.03. See also §7701(f), enacted in 1984, which authorizes regulations to apply §265 on a related person basis (as defined). See Eustice, supra note 82, ¶ 3.04[2][c].

[101] Expenses for the benefit of another taxpayer cannot be deducted under §162. See, e.g., Interstate Transit Lines v. CIR, 319 US 590 (1943); Deputy v. du Pont, 308 US 488 (1940).

The rule that expenses for the benefit of another taxpayer are not deductible under §162 is illustrated by decisions involving the right of a joint venture corporation to deduct the excess expenses of furnishing services to its parents when it charges them less than its expenses because it realizes profits on business with outsid-

another taxpayer frequently arises in the context of related company transactions: Typical is the case where certain properties, facilities, or services of the enterprise are shared by various members of an affiliated group without proportionate contribution on their part of the costs thereof. In this situation, the Service may seek to disallow that part of a particular taxpayer's expenses that represents a disproportionate share of these costs[102] or, as is more frequently the case, attempt to reallocate such deductions among members of the group under the authority of §482. Whichever approach is adopted, the fundamental question remains the same—that is, who in substance actually incurred the deductions in question and obtained the benefits therefrom?

Another hurdle to be faced by related corporate taxpayers engaging in transactions with one another (in addition to the arm's-length requirement of §482) is the matter of the fairness of their arrangement: Because of the parties' close affiliation, courts will carefully scrutinize various intragroup transactions for evidence of lack of arm's-length dealing, and, if the terms of the bargain are found to be unconscionable, deductibility of a particular expenditure may be impaired in whole or in part, an approach that is more drastic than the reallocation mechanism of §482. Thus, deductions have been denied for excessive payments of compensation, rent, royalties, and the like, where the price adopted by the parties was deemed to be unreasonable.[103] On the other hand, it is clear that related corporations can deal with

---

ers. See Chicago & W. Ind. R.R. v. CIR, 303 F2d 796 (7th Cir. 1962) (deductions denied), a decision that was later vacated because of the enactment of §281 (see 310 F2d 380 (7th Cir. 1962)); Anaheim Union Water Co. v. CIR, 321 F2d 253 (9th Cir. 1963) (contra); see also Baltimore Aircoil Co. v. US, 333 F. Supp. 705 (D. Md. 1971) (subsidiary held to be a mere branch, or division, of parent, and hence parent could deduct expenses paid on its behalf); CIR v. B. Forman Co., supra note 40 (expenses for benefit of another entity disallowed under §162 principles).

[102] See Columbian Rope Co., supra note 57; Campbell County State Bank, Inc. v. CIR, 311 F2d 374 (8th Cir. 1963); Northern Natural Gas Co. v. CIR, 362 F2d 781 (8th Cir. 1966); Local Fin. Corp. v. CIR, 407 F2d 629 (7th Cir. 1969). But see First Security Bank of Utah v. CIR, supra note 24.

See also the various captive insurance subsidiary cases, where separate entities are respected, but deduction is denied for purported premiums because arrangement is not insurance (no risk shifting or distribution, but only the economic equivalent of a self-insurance reserve) (e.g., Beech Aircraft Corp. v. US, 797 F2d 920 (10th Cir. 1986); Humana Inc. & Subsidiaries, 88 TC 197 (1987); Clougherty Packing Co. v. CIR, 811 F2d 1297 (9th Cir. 1987), and cases there cited).

[103] See, e.g., Challenger, Inc., supra note 93; E-Z Sew Enters., Inc. v. US, 260 F. Supp. 100 (E.D. Mich. 1966); Potter Elec. Signal & Mfg. Co. v. CIR, 286 F2d 200 (8th Cir. 1961); Southeastern Canteen Co. v. CIR, ¶ 67,183 P-H Memo. TC (sale-leaseback deal; excessive rent disallowed); Sparks Nugget, Inc. v. CIR, 458 F2d 631 (9th Cir. 1972), cert. denied, 410 US 928 (1973); OTM Corp. v. US, supra note 51; Peck v. CIR, supra note 58 (corporate leaseback of contributed property to share-

each other on a tax-deductible basis so long as the transactions in question have economic reality and are conducted with a reasonable degree of fairness. [104]

Loss sales between related corporations formerly were not subject to automatic disallowance under §267 (disallowing losses and certain other deductions arising from transactions between certain related taxpayers) unless one of the corporations was a foreign or domestic PHC. [105] Despite— or perhaps because of–this omission, these transactions regularly invoked a hostile attitude on the part of the Service. Although it might be argued that the implied requirement of §165(a) that a loss must be evidenced by a closed transaction was not satisfied when property was sold by one member of an economic family to another member of the same family, in point of fact,

---

holder at excessive rent resulted in denial of excess deduction for shareholder under §482).

[104] See, e.g., Ransom W. Chase, ¶ 65,202 P-H Memo. TC (1965); Doornbosch Bros., 46 TC 199 (1966) (acq.). But see Crosby Valve & Gage Co. v. CIR, 380 F2d 146 (1st Cir.), cert. denied, 389 US 976 (1967) (no charitable deduction for contribution by subsidiary to its tax-exempt parent), noted in 36 U. Cinc. L. Rev. 331 (1967); C.F. Mueller Co., 55 TC 275 (1970) (same, unfortunately, for N.Y.U.).

See also Mackinac Island Carriage Tours, Inc. v. CIR, 455 F2d 98 (6th Cir. 1972) (rent deduction allowed, even though not an arm's-length transaction, because terms reasonable); Tampa & G.C.R.R. v. CIR, 56 TC 1393 (1971), aff'd per curiam, 469 F2d 263 (5th Cir. 1972) (intercompany debt held equity; court noted subsidiary's accrual of interest deduction and parent's failure to accrue interest income as evidence of equity status); R.T. French Co., supra note 60; Rev. Rul. 76-88, 1976-1 CB 52 (losses sustained from arm's-length exchanges between wholly owned brother-sister subsidiaries held deductible; §§267 and 482 not applicable; losses not denied per se because of common control); Pechiney Ugine Kuhlmann Corp., ¶ 86,244 P-H Memo. TC (loss sale at fair price with business purpose).

In the case of intercompany loans, the major difficulty encountered by the parties is classification of the transaction as a true loan, supra ch. 4, Part A. If that hurdle is overcome, the tax consequences of a lending transaction follow as a matter of course and are relatively well settled. Thus, interest paid or incurred thereon is deductible under §163, collections on the debt must be treated as such, and losses from the inability to collect the claim are deductible as bad debts under §166. But legislation enacted in 1984, §7701(f), applies the rules of §265(2) on a related person basis (as defined by regulations); see Eustice, supra note 82.

[105] However, legislation enacted in 1984 significantly expanded the related corporate group definition in §267(b)(3) by incorporating the controlled group definition of §1563(a) (supra ¶ 15.02), but substituting "more than 50 percent" for "at least 80 percent" (§§267(b)(3) and 267(f)(1)); thus, the scope of the former §267 loss disallowance rules was materially expanded. On the other hand, under §267(f)(2), losses between controlled corporations are no longer disallowed; rather, they are deferred until certain triggering events under principles similar to the consolidated return regulations' deferred intercompany transaction rules (infra ¶ 15.23, para. 3). See Eustice, supra note 82, ¶¶ 2.03[5] and 3.04[2][b]; and supra ¶ 5.04, para. 1.

such transactions were honored for tax purposes if bona fide and if the price was reasonable under all the circumstances.[106]

Amendments to §267(f) by the Tax Reform Act of 1984 extended the coverage of §267 to related corporate taxpayers (i.e., where there is more than 50 percent common control) and changed the loss disallowance rule to a loss deferral provision under principles similar to the consolidated return regulations.[107] Temporary regulations[108] were issued under this provision in November of 1984, and, while they generally conform to the consolidated return deferred intercompany transaction regulations, the loss-triggering events are fewer, and the timing of such losses is stretched out over a longer period.[109] In effect, these regulations impose an independent set of deferred intercompany transaction rules for losses between related corporations that do not file consolidated returns, and these rules are more rigorous than those applicable in the consolidated return system.[110]

Assuming that a particular transaction does not give rise to a proper deduction (under §§162, 163, 165, and so forth) for one related corporate party (and the Service does not invoke the reallocation rules of §482), the problem remains as to the treatment of the other related party to the transaction. For example, if a deduction for compensation, rent, or royalty payments is disallowed to the payor as being excessive, how should the payee corporation treat such amounts? This problem is primarily one of determining the proper classification for the item in question. Thus, such amounts may be treated either as disguised dividends (if received by a parent corpo-

---

[106] See General Indus. Corp., 35 BTA 615 (1937) (acq.); Apex Corp., 42 TC 1122 (1964) (acq.); Brost Motors, Inc., ¶ 48,226 P-H Memo. TC (1948); CIR v. Offutt, 336 F2d 483 (4th Cir. 1964). But see Northern Pac. Ry. v. US, supra note 80.

The difficult questions, of course, are whether the transaction is fair and whether it has economic reality, both of which factors must be satisfied before the loss deduction will be permitted; it is here that the close relationship between the buyer and seller corporation invites special judicial scrutiny as to the bona fides of the parties' agreement.

See also Pechiney Ugine Kuhlmann Corp., and Rev. Rul. 76-88, 1976-1 LB 52 (losses on exchanges between wholly owned brother-sister subsidiaries held deductible). But see §267(f), supra note 105.

[107] Supra note 105.

[108] TD 7991, 1985-1 CB 71, issuing Temp. Regs. §1.267(a)-2T (dealing with the deduction matching rules of §267(a)(2)), §§1.267(f)-1T (loss deferral rules where consolidated returns not filed), and 1.267(f)-2T (loss deferral rules where consolidated returns are filed).

[109] E.g., losses are not triggered merely because the seller ceases to be an affiliated member of the group (the loss shifts to the buying member), and the loss trigger through the buyer's depreciation deduction is slower and lower (being keyed to depreciation that would have been claimed by the seller-member had the sale not occurred).

[110] See Temp. Regs. §1.267(f)-2T, infra ¶ 15.23, para. 3.

ration from its subsidiary), as nontaxable capital contributions (if received by a subsidiary from its parent), as additional compensation (if received as such, notwithstanding the excessive character thereof), or they may simply be ignored as a nullity if the entire transaction is treated as a sham.[111] However, if §482 is invoked by the Service to *reallocate* deductions or income among related corporations, the results could differ from the situation in which a deduction is merely disallowed to one related corporate taxpayer.

5. Timing problems. If an accrual-method corporation claims a deduction for an item of expense arising in a transaction with another related corporation on the cash-receipts method, will this fact either require that the cash-basis member include a correlative income item in its return for the year in question, or, alternatively, that the accrual-method member delay taking its deduction until the connected income item is reportable? As a general rule, the answer is no, assuming that the transaction passes muster under business purpose and economic reality standards.[112] In this connection, it is interesting to consider the treatment prescribed by the consolidated return regulations in a comparable situation.[113] With respect to various nondeferred intercompany transactions that would result in the reporting of correlative income and deduction items in different taxable years, these regulations provide, in general, that both the income and the corresponding deduction items must be delayed until the later of these two years and be accounted for together at that time.

However, legislation enacted in 1984 expanded the coverage of §267 to related corporate taxpayers and changed the deduction disallowance rule for delayed payment of accrued expenses and interest to a matching concept (i.e., mandatory cash-basis method for the payor's deduction if the related payee is also on the cash-basis method of accounting).[114] The principal purpose of these amendments was to conform the timing of income, deductions,

---

[111] See Challenger, Inc., supra note 93 (excessive rentals paid by a brother corporation are not taxable to the payee sister corporation). But see Sterno Sales Corp. v. US, supra note 94. See generally supra ¶ 7.05; supra text at notes 84–92.

[112] See CIR v. Fender Sales, Inc., 338 F2d 924 (9th Cir. 1964).

[113] See Regs. §1.1502-13(b)(2); see also Regs. §1.707-1(c) (treatment of guaranteed payments to partners); infra ¶ 15.23, para. 3.

[114] The Tax Reform Act of 1984, amending §267(b)(3) and adding new §267(f) to cover controlled *corporate* groups as defined in §1563(a) but using a more than 50 percent common control test (supra note 105). For temporary regulations under this provision, see supra note 108. See generally Eustice, supra note 105; supra ¶ 5.04, para. 1; infra ¶ 15.23. The deduction matching rules of §267(a)(2) do not apply to the OID rules of §1274 or the imputed interest rules of §7872, but do apply to the interest character rules of §483 according to these regulations, supra ¶ 4.42.

The Tax Reform Act of 1986 added §267(a)(3), authorizing application of the §267(a)(2) matching rules by regulation to payments to any foreign persons.

and losses within members of an affiliated group of corporations (as newly defined, more than 50 percent common control) to deny acceleration of otherwise allowable deductions until such time as the related payee-member includes such item in income or, in the case of intragroup loss sales, until the related purchaser disposes of the property to someone outside the related corporate group.

The Service may also invoke constructive receipt principles in this situation, however, and require earlier inclusion of an item of income in the cash-basis member's return on the grounds that it was unqualifiedly subject to its command. This argument may be persuasive if the potential payor is a wholly owned subsidiary of the payee, although even here courts seem reluctant to apply this approach merely on a showing that the amount in question was owed.[115] Matters may eventually turn, however, on a question of degree in this situation. If a court determines that a cash-basis taxpayer is excessively delaying the inclusion of income generated by dealings with related parties, it may be more willing to invoke constructive receipt theory to remedy what it feels is an abuse of the cash-basis accounting privilege. Conversely, the Service may seek to prevent the current accrual of a deduction by the potential payor corporation on the ground that the taxpayer had no genuine intention (or ability) to pay the item in question. As a general matter, this approach has met with less favor in the courts, at least where the accrual-method corporate taxpayer is under no *legal* contingencies with respect to its obligation,[116] but §267(a)(2), if applicable, will now accomplish this result automatically.

If it determines that a taxpayer's method of accounting does not clearly reflect income, the Service has the power, under §446(b), to require a change to an accounting method that, under the circumstances, does clearly reflect income.[117] Moreover, the allocation rules of §482 are a formidable statutory obstacle to related taxpayer efforts to distort their incomes by improper accounting practices.

---

[115] See generally Hyland v. CIR, 175 F2d 422 (2d Cir. 1949); R.E. Hughes, Jr., 42 TC 1005 (1964); Sheraton Plaza Co., 39 TC 697 (1963).

[116] See Zimmerman Steel Co. v. CIR, 130 F2d 1101 (8th Cir. 1942). But cf. Burlington-Rock Island R.R., 321 F2d 817 (5th Cir. 1963); and see Tampa & G.C.R.R. v. CIR, supra note 104 (where court emphasized lack of consistency in subsidiary's accrual of interest deduction while parent failed to accrue interest income; debt held to be equity, and interest deductions denied to subsidiary).

Note also §453(g) (no §453 deferral on installment sale of depreciable property to §267 related buyer unless showing of no tax avoidance), supra notes 97 and 98.

[117] See, e.g., Susan Carter, 9 TC 364 (1947) (acq.), aff'd, 170 F2d 911 (2d Cir. 1948); Williamson v. US, 292 F2d 524 (Ct. Cl. 1961); Jud Plumbing & Heating, Inc. v. CIR, 153 F2d 681 (5th Cir. 1946); Standard Paving Co. v. CIR, 190 F2d 330 (10th Cir. 1951). But cf. Sol C. Siegel Prods., Inc., 46 TC 15 (1966).

6. Relation of §267 to §482. The related party rules of §267 were materially overhauled by the Tax Reform Act of 1984, which converted the former disallowance rule of that section to a deduction matching rule in the case of various expense items owed by accrual-basis taxpayers to related cash-basis payees. It also provided that losses on sales between related *corporate* taxpayers are to be deferred under principles similar to those applicable under the consolidated return regulations.[118] Section 267 is triggered by the mere objective fact of relationship[119] (and the related party categories were considerably expanded by the 1984 Act), regardless of whether the transactions were effected at arm's length (as is necessary for the invocation of §482); but proposed temporary regulations[120] under §267 provide that §482 is to be applied initially before the application of §267, although the latter provision is viewed as a backstop to §482 in cases where that section is difficult to apply. In any event, the loss deferral rules of §267(f) are closely related to §482 and should materially strengthen the Service's hand in dealing with various related party transactions.

PART B.   CONSOLIDATED RETURNS

¶ 15.20   INTRODUCTORY

Section 1501 provides that an affiliated group of corporations may elect to file a consolidated return in lieu of separate returns. The basic principle of the consolidated return is that the group is taxed upon its consolidated taxable income, representing principally the results of its dealings with the outside world after the elimination of intercompany profit and loss. The tax is computed at the usual rates, except that only one graduated bracket benefit is allowed regardless of the number of includable corporations.[121] With certain exceptions, an affiliated group that elects to file a consolidated

---

[118] See supra note 105, and ¶ 5.04, and infra ¶ 15.23.

[119] The deduction matching rules of §267(a)(2) also involve a mismatch of accounting methods (i.e., accrual-basis payor and cash-basis payee); the loss deferral rules of §267(f)(2) apply only to affiliated corporate groups (more than 50 percent common control). The Tax Reform Act of 1986, in §267(a)(3), extended the deduction matching rule to expense and interest accruals payable to foreign persons, even though unrelated, as provided by regulations.

[120] TD 7991 (1984), proposing Temp. Regs. §§1.267(a)-2T, 1.267(f)-1T, and 1.267(f)-2T, supra note 108.

[121] Upon the filing of a consolidated return election, the accumulated earnings tax of §531 and the PHC tax of §541 (supra ch. 8, Parts A and B, respectively) are also computed on a consolidated basis. See Regs. §1.1502-43 (1984) (§531); infra

return must continue to do so in later years unless conditions change so as to make the filing of such returns substantially less advantageous. The statutory provisions governing consolidated returns (§§1501–1504) are quite brief, mainly because §1502 provides that the Secretary of the Treasury

> shall prescribe such regulations as he may deem necessary in order that the tax liability of any affiliated group of corporations making a consolidated return and of each corporation in the group, both during and after the period of affiliation, may be returned, determined, computed, assessed, collected, and adjusted, in such manner as clearly to reflect the income tax liability and the various factors necessary for the determination of such liability, and in order to prevent avoidance of such tax liability.

Pursuant to this authority, the Treasury has promulgated a lengthy and intricate set of regulations that for practical purposes constitute the law of consolidated returns.[122]

Consolidated returns date from the excess profits tax of 1917, when the Treasury required their use by affiliated corporations in order to prevent the arbitrary shifting of income within the group. With the repeal of the World War I excess profits tax and the enactment of the antecedent of §482 (permitting a reallocation of income among two or more businesses under common control in order to reflect income more accurately (discussed earlier in this chapter), Congress made the filing of consolidated returns optional, and they remained so for the period 1921–1933. For the period 1934–1941, the privilege of filing consolidated returns was abolished except for railroad cor-

---

¶ 15.23, para. 9. No regulations under §1502 dealing with the PHC tax rules of §541 have been proposed as yet.

[122] See Regs. §§1.1501–1.1504. A comprehensive revision of the regulations was promulgated, in proposed form, in 1965; most of the proposed regulations were finally adopted on September 7, 1966 in substantially the same form as proposed. See articles cited in Selected Tax Reading, 24 Tax L. Rev. 303 (1969); Caps, What Every Business Lawyer and Accountant Must Know About the Law Regarding Consolidated Returns, 1969 S. Cal. Tax Inst. 191; Peel, The Consolidated Return Election—The Sword of Damocles, 28 NYU Inst. on Fed. Tax'n 619 (1970); see also Crestol, Hennessey & Rua, The Consolidated Tax Return, (Warren, Gorham & Lamont, Inc., 1980) for extensive treatment of this area; Eisenberg, Consolidated Returns: Family Ties for Financial Gain, 64 Taxes 907 (1986).

As to the inviolability of the §1502 regulations, see American Standard, Inc. v. US, 602 F2d 256 (Ct. Cl. 1979) (part of regulations held invalid; change of treatment arbitrary and unreasonable; also promulgation violated notice requirements of Administrative Procedures Act).

The 1966 final regulations apply to years beginning after 1965; the old regulations continue applicable to prior years and are designated by the addition of the letter "A" (e.g., Regs. §1.1502-1 became Regs. §1.1502-1A).

porations and a few others. With the adoption of the World War II excess profits tax, however, the consolidated return election was reinstated, subject to an additional tax of 2 percent of consolidated taxable income. The principal statutory changes since then were the reduction, in 1954, of the intercorporate stock ownership requirement from 95 percent to 80 percent, and the repeal, in 1964, of the additional 2 percent tax.[123] But legislation restricting the benefits of multiple corporations in 1964 and 1969[124] has significantly encouraged the filing of consolidated returns.

¶ 15.21   ELIGIBILITY TO FILE CONSOLIDATED RETURNS

A consolidated return may be filed by an affiliated group of corporations, a term that is defined by §1504 to mean certain includable corporations connected in a specified way through stock ownership.

An "includable corporation" is any corporation except:

(1) Corporations exempt from taxation under §501,[125] unless includable by §1504(e).

(2) Insurance companies subject to taxation under §801, unless made eligible by §1504(c).

(3) Foreign corporations, unless within the limited exception of §1504(d) (100 percent subsidiary formed to comply with foreign law).[126]

(4) Corporations electing the benefits of §936 (possessions corporations).[127]

---

[123] A detailed examination of the formidable corpus of rules embodied in the consolidated returns regulations (supra note 122) is beyond the scope of this treatise. The standard work is Peel, Consolidated Tax Returns (Callaghan & Co., 1984). The various Tax Management Portfolios by Kronovet and others on consolidated returns are also useful.

[124] Supra ¶ 15.02.

[125] Supra ¶ 1.06.

[126] See also Rev. Rul. 71-523, 1971-2 CB 326 (§1504(d) not applicable, and hence Canadian subsidiary not an includable corporation, where foreign subsidiary used merely to qualify for a privilege or benefit of a foreign law program limited to domestic corporations by that law); contra, United States Padding Corp., 88 TC 177 (1987) (subsidiary formed to comply with foreign government policy or practice qualified); infra ¶ 17.04.

[127] Burke Concrete Accessories, Inc., 56 TC 588 (1971), rejected the holding of Rev. Rul. 65-293, 1965-2 CB 323, and held that a loss corporation could waive §931 possession status and be included in a consolidated return; the corporation was not entitled to the benefits of §931, said the court, where no benefits arose from that

(5) Regulated investment companies and other specialized pass-through entities subject to tax under Subchapter M.

(6) Small business corporations electing to be taxed under Subchapter S (discussed in Chapter 6).

(7) Domestic international sales corporations (or former DISCs) and foreign sales corporations (discussed in Chapter 17).

The stock ownership rule of §1504(a) requires that the affiliated group consist of one or more chains of includable corporations connected through stock ownership with a common parent corporation (which must also be an includable corporation) in the following manner:

(1) Stock with at least 80 percent of the total voting power and at least 80 percent of the total value of each of the includable corporations (other than the common parent) must be owned directly by one or more of the other includable corporations.

(2) The common parent must own directly stock with at least 80 percent of the total voting power and 80 percent of the total value of at least one of the other includable corporations.[128]

(3) Stock ownership can be aggregated in certain cases under Regs. §1.1504-34.[129]

The prescribed amount of stock must, under §1504(a), be owned directly by members of the affiliated group, so that two corporations whose stock is owned by an individual or group of individuals[130] or by a nonincludable corporation do not constitute an affiliated group of corporations.[131]

---

section. The Service agreed with *Burke* in Rev. Rul. 73-498, 1973-2 CB 316, and the Tax Reform Act of 1976 codified this view. See infra ¶ 17.13.

[128] The affiliated group definition was amended in 1984 to require 80 percent ownership of total vote and value; prior to that amendment, ownership of 80 percent of voting power and 80 percent of each class of nonvoting stock was required; see infra note 136.

[129] For controversy over these aggregation rules in the context of mirror subsidiary acquisitions, see infra notes 168 and 175.

[130] The suggestion of Libson Shops, Inc. v. Koehler, 353 US 382 (1957), that the corporations there involved, owned by the same individuals in the same proportion, could have filed a consolidated return is erroneous.

Compare Gunlock Corp., Inc., ¶ 82,105 P-H Memo. TC (contribution of sister stock to brother corporation allowed filing of consolidated return).

[131] See West Boylston Mfg. Co. v. CIR, 120 F2d 622 (5th Cir. 1941); Regs. §1.1502-2A(b)(1) (for pre-1966 years); current regulations, however, are silent on this point. But ownership of record is not required; beneficial ownership will suffice. See Rev. Rul. 55-458, 1955-2 CB 579 (stock in escrow qualifies); Rev. Rul. 70-469,

The 80 percent stock ownership requirement of §1504 was a relaxation, enacted in 1954, of pre-1954 law, which set the test of affiliation at 95 percent. Private law problems can be created by an election to file a consolidated return, which may be beneficial to the group as a whole at the expense of the minority shareholders of one of the included corporations.[132] In this connection, it should be noted that every includable corporation must participate in the consolidated return[133]; it is not possible to exclude a particular corporation because of possible objections by its minority shareholders.

Under §1504(a), it is necessary to determine whether at least 80 percent of the total voting power of all classes of stock of each includable corporation (other than the parent) is owned by another member of the group. The term has come to mean the power to elect the directors and to exclude the power to vote on such extraordinary events as merger, sale of assets, and so forth.[134]

1970-2 CB 179 (stock held by nominee); Rev. Rul. 68-623, 1968-2 CB 404 (leased stock not owned for this purpose); Miami Nat'l Bank, 67 TC 793 (1977) (bailed, or pledged, stock still sufficiently owned so that its assignment to parent corporation enabled it to file consolidated return with acquired subsidiary); see also Rev. Rul. 69-591, 1969-2 CB 171 (can have de facto §351 transaction even though no formal issue of shares; filing of consolidated return with subsidiary allowed); Gunlock Corp., supra note 130 (held that sufficient transfer of sister corporation stock to brother corporation occurred); Rev. Rul. 84-79, 1984-1 CB 190 (grantor and sole beneficiary of revocable voting trust is the direct owner of the stock for §1504 purposes).

[132] Until now, minority shareholders seem to have been relatively ignorant or complacent unless they have been lying in ambush. But see Western Pac. R.R. v. Western Pac. R.R., 345 US 247 (1953), 206 F2d 495 (9th Cir. 1953), 216 F2d 513 (9th Cir. 1954); Johnson, Minority Stockholders in Affiliated and Related Corporations, 23 NYU Inst. on Fed. Tax'n 321 (1965).

See generally Singleton v. CIR, 569 F2d 863 (5th Cir. 1978) (subsidiary's distribution to parent and minority shareholders held dividend despite argument that subsidiary only reimbursing parent for use of its losses on consolidated return).

For collection of authorities on minority shareholders' rights in this area, see Brudney & Chirelstein, Fair Shares in Corporate Mergers and Takeovers, 88 Harv. L. Rev. 297, at ns.53, 54 (1974).

[133] Regs. §§1.1502-75(a), 1.1502-75(b), and 1.1502-75(e); see also Regs. §§1.1502-76(a), 1.1502-76(b), and 1.1502-76(c). As to time for includability, see Rev. Rul. 80-169, 1980-1 CB 188 (include in consolidated return on day after acquisition date). For the possibility of short-term membership, see Priv. Ltr. Rul. 81-18-011, 1981 Fed. Taxes (P-H) ¶ 55,261 (liquidation one day after entry into group; still includable).

[134] See IT 3896, 1948-1 CB 72 (discussing method of computing total voting power where one class of stock could elect one director and another class the remaining six directors) (but IT 3896 was declared obsolete in Rev. Rul. 68-100, 1968-1 CB 572); Anderson-Clayton Secs. Corp., 35 BTA 795 (1937) (prior law); Rev. Rul. 69-126, 1969-1 CB 281 (determination of voting power).

In applying the stock ownership rules of §1504(a), the term "stock" has never included nonvoting stock that is limited and preferred as to dividends. Such stock may be owned by persons outside the affiliated group, and for this reason is sometimes used by one or more members of the affiliated group to raise equity capital.[135]

Because of the relative ease with which the stock affiliation rules of §1504(a) could be manipulated (to fall in, or out of, affiliation status virtually at will), reforms were enacted in 1984[136] to require that the requisite 80 percent stock ownership exist with respect to *both* total voting power stock *and* total value of stock (both voting and nonvoting), but to exclude stock that is nonvoting, nonconvertible, and limited and preferred as to both dividends and in liquidation.[137] Affiliation will terminate under new §1504(a)(2)

If a class of stock can vote on routine matters that are ordinarily entrusted to the directors, it might be regarded as having voting power even though it could not elect directors. Query also the effect of stockholders' voting agreements on the computation of total voting power (if the agreement decreases a member's power below the 80 percent benchmark, loss of affiliation status could result; see §1504(a)(5), establishing authority to deal with various manipulative practices by regulation).

See Rev. Rul. 78-119, 1978-1 CB 156 (parent's right to vote temporarily suspended during litigation, held not fatal), cited with approval in 1984 Conference Report, infra note 138.

[135] As to the meaning of "nonvoting stock," see Erie Lighting Co. v. CIR, 93 F2d 883 (1st Cir. 1937) (stock that cannot vote for directors is nonvoting stock despite power to vote on increase of capital stock or indebtedness, number of directors, time of stockholders' meetings, and so forth); Vermont Hydro-Electric Corp., 29 BTA 1006 (1934) (acq.) (preferred stock with right to vote for directors only on default in dividends is nonvoting stock until contingency occurs); Rudolph Wurlitzer Co. v. CIR, 81 F2d 971 (6th Cir.), cert. denied, 298 US 676 (1936) (stock with power to vote for directors under Illinois law is not nonvoting stock despite attempt to eliminate such power in articles of incorporation); IT 3896, supra note 134; Tannebaum, Nonvoting Stock for the Consolidated Return, 29 Taxes 679 (1951). As to the meaning of "limited and preferred as to dividends," see Pioneer Parachute Co. v. CIR, 162 F2d 249 (2d Cir. 1947) (participating preferred is not limited as to dividends, even in a year in which nothing is paid beyond the preference); Erie Lighting Co. v. CIR, supra (contra). See also Rev. Rul. 69-126, 1969-1 CB 281.

In addition, Rev. Rul. 71-83, 1971-1 CB 268 (cumulative, nonvoting convertible preferred stock not counted in determining the 80 percent voting power test of §1504(a)); Rev. Rul. 79-21, 1979-1 CB 290 (participating preferred is stock).

For a related definition of "preferred stock" in the stock dividend area, see Regs. §§1.305-5(a) and 1.305-5(d), Examples (8) and (9); supra ¶ 7.43.

[136] The Tax Reform Act of 1984, revising §1504(a) (generally effective for years beginning after 1984). See Eustice, supra note 82, ¶ 3.04[1]; N.Y. State Bar Association, Tax Section, Report on Tax Reform Act of 1984 Amendments to Section 1504(a), The Definition of Affiliated Group, 28 Tax Notes 895 (1985).

[137] See §1504(a)(4). The Tax Reform Act of 1986 amended §1504(a)(4)(C) to provide for redemption rights not in excess of original issue price (allowing a reasonable redemption or liquidation premium). The definition of excluded stock under

if the requisite ownership of vote or value drops below either of the dual 80 percent lines, and, if affiliated status of a member terminates under this provision, §1504(a)(3) requires that five years must elapse before that member can reaffiliate (unless waived). Moreover, §1504(a)(5) broadly authorizes antiavoidance regulations to deal with attempts to finesse these limitations by the issuance of warrants, options, convertible securities, and so forth, and that also permit the waiver of inadvertent terminations due to valuation footfaults. [138] Thus, it is harder to affiliate under §1504 after the 1984 amendments, but, conversely, it is easier to disaffiliate, although the statute now imposes a five-year waiting period before consolidation returns can again be filed.

If a corporation is acquired by another corporation solely in order to make use of its tax attributes on a consolidated return, the requisite affiliation may be found lacking on business purpose grounds, despite compliance with the literal terms of the statute. [139] Denying the parent the right to use an acquired subsidiary's pre-affiliation and post-affiliation losses on a consolidation return to offset its postaffiliation profits can also result under §269. [140] For some purposes, it would be immaterial whether the acquisition was found to violate §269 or the requisite affiliation was found to be lacking; but for other purposes, the latter ground is more drastic, since it would require separate returns, perhaps for all time, whereas §269 might disallow only the use on the consolidated return of the deduction, credit, or other tax benefit that motivated the acquisition. [141] As will be seen, the consolidated return

---

§1504(a) is virtually identical to §382(c) of the 1976 Act's proposed amendment to §382, infra ¶ 16.22, para. 2.

[138] See §1504(a)(5). Under §60(b) of the Tax Reform Act of 1984, special effective date rules are provided for corporations affiliated on June 2, 1984. See Conf. Rep. No. 861, 98th Cong., 2d Sess. 833, 834 (1984).

[139] Elko Realty Co. v. CIR, 29 TC 1012, aff'd per curiam, 260 F2d 949 (3d Cir. 1958); see also American Pipe & Steel Corp. v. CIR, 243 F2d 125 (9th Cir.), cert. denied, 355 US 906 (1957) (consolidation denied under §269); J.D. & A.B. Spreckels Co., 41 BTA 370 (1940) (consolidation denied under *Gregory*); Book Prod. Indus., Inc., ¶ 65,065 P-H Memo. TC (1965).

[140] Infra ¶ 16.21.

[141] But see Zanesville Inv. Co. v. CIR, 335 F2d 507 (6th Cir. 1964), cases discussed therein (allowing use of post-affiliation losses, and discussion infra ¶ 15.24. See also Hawaiian Trust Co. v. US, 291 F2d 761 (9th Cir. 1961) (consolidation privilege and losses both allowed, despite attack under §269 and *Spreckles* theories). But see R.P. Collins & Co. v. US, 303 F2d 142 (1st Cir. 1962) (Service successfully invoked §269 to deny post-affiliation loss deductions on the consolidated return); Hall Paving Co. v. US, 471 F2d 261 (5th Cir. 1973) (§269 can apply to post-acquisition losses via eligibility to file a consolidated return (following *Collins* and rejecting *Zanesville*); remanded for further proceedings on the merits of whether the acquisition was for the prohibited purpose); see discussion of these cases infra ¶ 16.21.

regulations themselves impose certain automatic restrictions (regardless of purpose) on the use of the preaffiliation net operating losses and some post-affiliation losses as well when membership in the affiliated group changes, as do similar limitations in §382; [142] but they do not go so far as to deny that the new member is part of the affiliated group. The approach of *Elko Realty Co.,* which appears to deny affiliation for all purposes, is more far-reaching.

¶ 15.22   THE ELECTION TO FILE A CONSOLIDATED RETURN

A consolidated return may be made only if all corporations that at any time during the taxable year have been members of the affiliated group consent to the consolidated return regulations prescribed under §1502. [143] Under Regs. §1.1502-75(a)(2), the affiliated group must continue to file on a consolidated basis in subsequent taxable years unless the following occurs (Regs. §1.1502-75(c)):

(1) The Service, for good cause, grants permission to discontinue filing consolidated returns; [144] and

(2) The Service, in its discretion, grants blanket permission to all groups or to a particular class of groups, if any provision of the Code or regulations is amended so as to have a substantial adverse effect on the filing of consolidated returns vis-à-vis separate returns. [145]

---

[142] The limitations of §382, as reformed in 1986 (infra ¶¶ 16.23–16.25) will probably overshadow all of the restrictions noted above.

[143] The taxpayer's consent to the regulations does not preclude an attack on the Treasury's authority to issue a particular provision. See Corner Broadway-Maiden Lane, Inc. v. CIR, 76 F2d 106 (2d Cir. 1935). See generally Peel, supra note 123.

For a decision upholding the binding election feature of the regulations, see Regal, Inc., 53 TC 261 (1969). But see American Standard, Inc. v. US, supra note 122 (change in regulations held invalid, arbitrary, and unreasonable, and violated notice requirements of Administrative Procedures Act); compare J.A. Tobin Constr. Co., 85 TC 1005 (1985) (failure to elect due to mistaken interpretation of regulations not curable).

[144] For illustration of procedures to be followed in requesting a good cause permission, see Rev. Proc. 70-4, 1970-1 CB 417 (no blanket permission because of the Tax Reform Act of 1969).

[145] Under the pre-1966 regulations, Regs. §1.1502-11A, groups had an automatic right to shift back to separate returns upon the acquisition of a new member or upon a substantially adverse amendment of the Code or of the §1502 regulations (the Service ordinarily announced whether, in its opinion, such an amendment had occurred; see, e.g., Rev. Rul. 58-471, 1958-2 CB 429 (three-year carry-back of net operating

The regulations make each member of the affiliated group severally liable for the entire tax (including any deficiency), with a qualification for subsidiaries that are sold before the tax is assessed (Regs. §1.1502-6). This liability cannot be reduced by intercompany agreements, but presumably an agreement will be effective as between the parties. Under §1552, a method is provided for allocating the tax liability in computing each corporation's earnings and profits.[146]

The parent corporation, by Regs. §1.1502-77, is made the agent of all includable corporations to receive deficiency notices, to file refund claims, to execute waivers of the statute of limitations, and so forth.[147]

¶ 15.23 COMPUTATION OF CONSOLIDATED TAXABLE INCOME AND TAX LIABILITY: IN GENERAL

1. In general. The tax liability of an affiliated group filing a consolidated return is computed on its consolidated taxable income. The starting point is the separate taxable income of each includable corporation, computed in accordance with the rules applicable to separate corporations, but with the elimination of profits and losses from transactions between members of the affiliated group and of dividend distributions within the group and the segregation of the group's capital gains and losses, charitable contributions, transactions under §1231, net operating losses and certain other items. After these adjustments, the separate taxable incomes are combined, and capital gains and losses, charitable contributions, §1231 transactions, net operating losses, and so forth, are computed on a consolidated basis and taken into account. There are many vexing accounting adjustments in this process of converting the taxable incomes of the separate corporations into

---

losses, in lieu of former two-year carry-back, warrants new election); Rev. Rul. 56-681, 1956-2 CB 597 (extension of 30 percent normal tax rate on corporations does not permit new election). But the 1966 amendments shifted completely to a locked-in permission of the Service approach. See Rev. Proc. 70-4, 1970-1 CB 417.

[146] See Rev. Rul. 73-605, 1973-2 CB 109, for illustration of a §1552 tax allocation agreement; see also Marvin E. Singleton, Jr., 64 TC 320 (1975) (subsidiary's distribution to parent not a dividend where facts showed payment to compensate parent for subsidiary's tax savings attributable to being included in consolidated return), rev'd, 569 F2d 863 (5th Cir. 1978).

[147] The regulations also state that the parent is the agent of the other members of the group for conducting proceedings in the Tax Court, Regs. §1.1502-77. But see Community Water Serv. Co., 32 BTA 164 (1935), stating that the court's rules of procedure take precedence. See generally Craigie, Inc., 84 TC 477 (1985) (authority of parent to settle tax issues of former subsidiary upheld).

the affiliated group's consolidated taxable income, but they are beyond the scope of this treatise.[148]

Whether an affiliated group should elect to file a consolidated return depends upon a variety of complex and competing factors. Among the principal advantages of consolidation are the following: (1) Operating losses of an affiliate can be offset against profits of other members of the group; (2) certain intercorporate distributions can be received tax-free from other members of the group (Regs. §1.1502-14); and (3) gain or loss on certain intercompany transactions is deferred, under elaborate rules found in Regs. §1.1502-13, until realized outside the group or by virtue of certain other triggering events. These opportunities became relatively more attractive in 1964, when the additional 2 percent tax on consolidated taxable income was eliminated and the advantages of filing separate returns (e.g., the multiplication of surtax exemptions) were restricted vis-à-vis affiliated groups,[149] and became even more attractive by 1975 when multiple surtax exemptions finally expired.[150] On the other hand, filing a consolidated return carries with it certain disadvantages, including:

(1) The requirement of consistent elections and accounting periods within the group (but Regs. §1.1502-17(a) permits separate accounting *methods* for each member under the general rules of §446);

(2) The rule that, to the extent losses of one affiliate are used to reduce consolidated taxable income, the basis of stock or obligations of the loss corporation must be correspondingly reduced (Regs.

---

[148] See Peel, supra note 123; Seidler & Carmichael, Accountants' Handbook §23 (Wiley, 6th ed., 1981), and articles supra notes 122 and 123.

While the general theory of consolidated returns is similar to the joint return treatment of spouses, it has been unclear whether this analogy can be carried to its ultimate extreme; for example, if one member of the group is guilty of fraud (e.g., intentionally claiming an improper deduction), is the penalty of §6653 imposed on tax deficiencies of the entire consolidated group or merely on the separate deficiency of the offending member? (Under such circumstances, the election to file consolidated returns could prove expensive indeed because an errant affiliate can expose the entire group to the consequences of its actions). Note that there is no rule comparable to the innocent spouse provisions of §6013(e) for consolidating corporations; however, the Tax Reform Act of 1986, §6653(b)(1)(A), now generally limits the penalty to that portion of the deficiency attributable to the fraud.

See Note, Application of the Civil Fraud Penalty to Consolidated Returns, 34 Tax Lawyer 801 (1981) (for pre-1986 law).

[149] Supra ¶ 15.02.

[150] Id. For possibility that consolidated groups may offer an escape from the passive activity loss restrictions of the 1986 Tax Reform Act, see Snyder & Gonick, Affiliated Corporate Groups for Real Estate Investments: The Syndication Vehicle of the Future?, 14 J. Corp. Tax'n (1987).

§1.1502-19 allows recapture of certain excess losses attributable to a subsidiary);

(3) The general limitation that the members of a consolidated group must share a single graduated rate bracket amount, accumulated earnings tax credit, and any other special exemption or credit (a result that §1561 would compel, however, even without consolidation;

(4) The regulatory requirement that certain intercompany transactions must be taken into account currently (Regs. §1.1502-13);

(5) The fact that the consolidated return regulations are so complicated, and in many instances, inordinately so; and, finally,

(6) The fact that the election is a binding one (absent the above-mentioned rare instances where a new election may, with Service consent, be permitted).

The balancing of these considerations can itself be one of the tax adviser's more difficult assignments: The practical response to a consolidated return issue is often to request an extension of time for more thorough deliberation.

2. Outline of consolidated return regulations structure. The current consolidated return regulations, applicable to taxable years beginning after 1965, completely revised both the substance and format of the prior regulations. In general, the regulations consist of four major subject headings: (1) computation of the group's net consolidated tax liability, which consists of its regular tax liability less applicable credits (Regs. §§1.1502-2–1.1502-6); (2) computation of consolidated taxable income (which, in turn, is divided into three principal subheadings: computation of separate taxable incomes of the various affiliates (Regs. §§1.1502-12–1.1502-19), computations of various consolidated items (Regs. §§1.1502-21–1.1502-27); and special rules pertaining to basis, stock ownership, and earnings and profits (Regs. §§1.1502-31–1.1502-34)); (3) provisions dealing with special taxes and taxpayers (e.g., alternative capital gains tax (now repealed), accumulated earnings tax, mutual savings banks, insurance companies, and so forth.) (Regs. §§1.1502-41–1.1502-47); and (4) administrative and procedural rules (Regs. §§1.1502-75–1.1502-80).

The computation of an electing group's consolidated tax liability involves the following steps: (1) The separate taxable income (or loss) of each member of the affiliated group is determined as if a separate return had been filed (subject to certain special rules and adjustments for such items as intercompany transactions, intercompany distributions, accounting methods, inventories, and so forth) (Regs. §1.1502-12); (2) these separate taxable incomes are then combined to arrive at consolidated taxable income; (3) various other separately computed consolidated items (e.g., consolidated net operating loss deduction, capital gain, §1231 gain or loss, charitable contributions, and so forth) are then taken into account (Regs. §1.1502-11); (4) gross consolidated tax liability is then computed by adding up the various taxes imposed by §§11, 55, 531, 541, and 1201, among others on the consolidated taxable income of the group as determined above; and (5) from this figure, the consolidated investment credit and the consolidated foreign tax credit are subtracted (Regs. §1.1502-2).[151]

The basic concept underlying these provisions is that the consolidated group constitutes, in substance, a unitary economic enterprise, despite the existence of technically distinct legal entities; as such, its tax liability ought to be based on its dealings with outsiders rather than on intragroup transactions. This unitary enterprise concept lies at the heart of the treatment, both past and present, of intercompany transactions, which, in general, are eliminated in computing the group's consolidated taxable income. In effect, the results resemble in many respects the joint return treatment of a husband and wife.[152]

The most important features of this computation procedure are its treatment of intercompany transactions, distributions, acquisitions, accounting methods, inventories, net operating loss deductions, investment basis adjustments, and accumulated earnings. These matters will be considered in the paragraphs that follow.

3. Intercompany transactions. Among the most significant features of the 1966 regulations were changes in the treatment of intercompany transactions. For this purpose, a distinction is made between two types of intercompany transactions[153]: (1) so-called deferred intercompany transactions, which are subject to the deferred accounting rules and which consist of sales

---

[151] The investment credit was repealed, however, in 1986. The consolidated return regulations have yet to reflect even the initial 1969 version of the minimum tax; for discussion of the current 1986 law AMT provisions, see supra ¶ 5.08.

Several technical and substantive changes in the consolidated return regulations were proposed in 1971 and became final in 1972. In large part, these provisions constituted a reproposal of previous regulations amendments that were not adopted in the 1966 overhaul of the consolidated return regulations; in some instances, the earlier proposals were modified to reflect taxpayer comments and other considerations, while in others, new proposals were added. A technical explanation and summary of these proposed amendments was issued by the Treasury in a Treasury Department News Release on August 24, 1971, published in 1971 P-H Taxes, ¶ 55, 458.

[152] In 1984, enactment of §1042 eliminated gain on interspousal property transfers (providing instead for a carry-over basis); this rule is similar to the pre-1966 regulations' treatment of intercompany transactions. Moreover, income and deductions of both spouses are generally combined on a joint return, as is the case with a consolidated return.

[153] Intercompany transactions do not include distributions with respect to a member's stock (e.g., dividends, redemptions, or liquidations), however, or a contri-

or exchanges of property, the performance of services where the expense thereof is capitalized, and any other capitalized expenditures between members of the group and (2) all other intercompany dealings such as the payment of currently deductible interest, rent, royalties, or compensation by one member of the group to another that are not subject to the deferred accounting treatment. With respect to these latter items, the approach of the regulations is to require the payor and the payee to deduct and to include such amounts *currently*, depending on their respective accounting methods; however, the item of income and the correlative deduction therefor ordinarily must be reflected in the same taxable year. The net effect of this treatment is, of course, a wash so far as the group's consolidated taxable income is concerned. [154]

The treatment of deferred intercompany transactions, on the other hand, is more complicated and represented a major change from pre-1966 law. For these items, the regulations adopt a deferral or suspense account approach, whereunder intercompany profits and losses are deferred by recording them in a suspense account until the subsequent occurrence of certain specified events; these events will then trigger the reporting of both the amount and character of such items by the member of the group that originally earned the profit or sustained the loss. In general, this treatment follows the traditional accounting practice of attributing gain or loss from an intercompany transaction to the member that actually earned or incurred

---

bution to capital on which no gain is realized. See generally Rev. Rul. 85-133, 1985-2 CB 192 (definition requires actual, not hypothetical, transaction).

However, distributions in kind (other than in complete liquidation) that result in recognition of gain or loss to the distributing corporation under the §311 (as amended in 1984 and 1986 to require all nonliquidation distributions to result in full recognition of gain) are to be treated under the deferred intercompany transactions rules. Regs. §1.1502-14(c)(1). For the §311 gain recognition rules, see supra ¶¶ 7.21 (1986 amendments) and 7.22 (prior law).

[154] See Regs. §1.1502-13(b). Compare the results under §482 and other Code provisions on a separate return basis, supra ¶¶ 15.03 and 15.04. See also Rev. Rul. 74-589, 1974-2 CB 286 (cash-method parent prepaid rent to its wholly owned accrual-basis subsidiary, both filing consolidated returns; held, transaction a deferred intercompany transaction, and hence, parent deduction and subsidiary inclusion must be made ratably over term to which prepayment relates).

See also 1984 legislation, supra ¶ 15.04, notes 105 and 114, amending §267 to impose mandatory matching rules for affiliated corporate groups. Both the House and Senate Committee Reports state that these amendments were not intended to affect corporations filing consolidated returns; H.R. Rep. No. 432, Part 2, 98th Cong., 2d Sess. 1580 (1984); S. Rep. No. 169, 98th Cong., 2d Sess. 496 (1984); see also H.R. Rep. No. 861, 98th Cong., 2d Sess. 1033 (1984). Since the consolidated return regulations impose their own matching regime for nondeferred intercompany transaction items, application of §267(a)(2) would add nothing to the treatment of these items. But see infra note 156 for intercompany loss rules, which override the §1502 regulations.

it. Under the earlier regulations, however, such profits or losses were, in effect, shifted to another member of the group: This occurred as a result of certain rules, which provided for elimination of such gains or losses from the selling member's return with a corresponding carry-over of the basis of such property to the purchasing member, when then reported gain or loss thereon when the property was sold to an outsider.[155] The amended regulations, on the other hand, while similarly deferring the gain or loss from such transactions until the property is sold to an outsider (or until certain other specified events occur), assign the ultimate profit or loss from such transactions to the particular member that produced it.

> *To illustrate:* Suppose that *P* sold property, having a basis of $80 and a value of $100, to its wholly owned subsidiary, *S*, during a period when *P* and *S* were filing consolidated returns; in a later year, *S* resold the property to *A*, an outsider for $110. Under the pre-1966 regulations, the intercompany profit of $20 was eliminated from the computation of consolidated taxable income, and *S* carried over *P*'s $80 basis for the property. On reselling the property to *A* for $110, *S* reported the entire $30 of gain, even though $20 thereof reflected appreciation in value during *P*'s ownership of the property.
>
> The amended regulations, however, tax $20 of the profit to *P*—but only in the taxable year of the resale to *A*—and give *S* a cost basis of $100 (rather than a carry-over basis of $80) for the property, so that the remaining $10 is taxed to it. Thus, each member of the group is taxed on the portion of the gain that it earned. Moreover, the *character* of *P*'s gain (capital or ordinary) is the same as it would have been had *P* made the sale directly, rather than by means of an intercompany transaction through *S*.[156]

---

[155] See Regs. §1.1502-31A(b)(1)(i).

[156] See generally Regs. §§1.1502-13(b)–1.1502-13(h), and 1.1502-31(a).

As to characterization of deferred intercompany gain, see, e.g., Regs. §1.1502-13(h), Example (1) (parent had §1231 capital gain status on its sale to dealer subsidiary, even though subsidiary's resales were ordinary gain under §1221(1) dealer rules).

But see the 1984 amendments to the §267 loss disallowance rules, supra ¶ 15.04, note 105, which imposed rules similar to the deferred intercompany transactions regulations, §267(f). However, both the House and Senate Committee Reports state that this legislation is not intended to apply to corporations filing consolidated returns, supra note 154. For temporary regulations under this provision, see TD 7991, supra note 108; infra text at note 162. These regulations override the consolidated return regulation rules in the case of loss sales and, in general, impose a more restrictive regime on the timing and amount of such losses, despite indications in the Committee Reports, supra, that §1.267(f) would not apply in the consolidated return context. For §267 generally, see supra ¶ 5.04, para. 1.

The purpose of this change in the treatment of intercompany sales was to prevent the result sanctioned in several litigated cases, which permitted consolidated groups to avoid completely the tax on intercompany sales (e.g., where *P* sold the *stock* of *S* after transferring property to it and the new buyer liquidated *S* under a prior rule that enabled *P* to obtain a stepped-up basis for *S*'s assets.[157] This ploy is not possible under the revised regulations, since *P*'s deferred intercompany profit must be recognized if either the buying member or the selling member leaves the affiliated group before the property has been sold to an outsider.[158]

Other events that will trigger recognition of deferred gain or loss include:

(1) Depreciation or amortization deductions on the property by the purchasing member trigger a partial restoration of the deferred gain or loss, the amount thereof being reported at the same rate at which the asset is depreciated.[159]

---

[157] Before 1982, §334(b)(2) allowed *P* to obtain the basis stepup; this provision was replaced in 1982 by §338, which gives comparable basis results by treating the transaction as a deemed asset purchase, supra ¶ 11.45 (old rule), ¶ 11.46 (1982 rule).

See Henry Beck Builders, Inc., 41 TC 616 (1964) (intercompany profit of parent that was properly eliminated from consolidated taxable income held not taxable when parent sold its subsidiary's stock); accord, CIR v. United Contractors, Inc., ¶ 64,068 P-H Memo. TC (1964), aff'd per curiam, 344 F2d 123 (4th Cir. 1965). The Service agreed to follow the *Beck* case for tax years ending before 1965, TIR 764 (Sept. 28, 1965); this acquiescence apparently is embodied in Regs. §1.1502-13(h), Example (17) (although the facts therein differ from the *Beck* transaction). See also Rev. Rul. 67-412, 1967-2 CB 317.

For the earnings and profits effects of intercompany profits under the pre-1966 regulations, see Henry C. Beck Co., 52 TC 1 (1969), supra ¶ 7.03.

[158] Regs. §1.1502-13(f)(1)(iii). Regs. §1.1502-13(c)(3) allows the group to elect (with the consent of the Service) to report intercompany gains and losses currently, however. See generally Rev. Proc. 82-36, 1982-1 CB 490 (information checklist and guidelines for consent not to defer gain or loss on intercompany transactions). If §267 applies, however, infra note 162, temporary regulations issued under that provision deny the nondeferral election; Temp. Regs. §1.267(f)-2T(c).

See Rev. Rul. 72-321, 1972-1 CB 285 (where subsidiary with deferred intercompany inventory gain is sold to a new parent and included in its consolidated return, such gain is included only in the income of the old consolidated group when it leaves that group). But see Rev. Rul. 81-84, 1981-1 CB 451 (deferred intercompany transaction rules, applicable to intragroup sales, control over ELA trigger rules of Regs. §1.1502-19).

[159] See Regs. §1.1502-13(d), providing that the amount of recapture is that percentage of the deferred gain or loss that the amount of the annual depreciation deduction bears to the asset's depreciable basis (i.e., cost less salvage value). For example, if the asset in the text example was depreciable, was held by *S* for use (rather than sold to *A*), and had a useful life of 10 years and a salvage value of $20, and if *S* used straight-line depreciation, *P* would report 10 percent of its $20, or $2,

(2) The filing of separate returns by members of the group triggers a restoration of all deferred inventory profits or losses and, if consolidated returns were filed for less than three consecutive years preceding the filing of separate returns, all other deferred gains or losses.

(3) The worthlessness, collection, or redemption of debt obligations or stock that were the subject of a deferred intercompany transaction will trigger recognition of such deferred gain or loss.

(4) If the acquired property is resold by the purchasing member on the installment method (under §453), deferred gain is reported ratably by the selling member as collections are made by the affiliated purchasing member of the group.

The revised treatment of intercompany transactions was criticized as violating the single corporate taxpayer concept of the consolidated returns provisions;[160] but, in view of the broad delegation of regulatory authority effected by §1502, no attempts have been mounted to contest the regulations on this point. Although profits and losses from some types of intercompany transactions are currently taxable (and deductible) under these rules while others are handled under the deferred accounting treatment discussed above, the major thrust of the provisions is concerned with the *identification of the proper taxpayer* to report such items rather than with the question of recognition or nonrecognition of profits. Moreover, although the consolidated return is based on the theory that intercompany transactions should in general be disregarded, it also assumes that the group's gains from transactions with outsiders will be fully recognized at the proper time; seen in this light, the changes were justified, and the cases that allowed some gains to escape taxation[161] rested on defects in the old regulations rather than on any concept inherent in the consolidated return itself.

Section 267(f), enacted by the Tax Reform Act of 1984, generally imposes a further parallel deduction deferral system for losses on sales

---

of deferred profit annually (i.e., $8 of annual depreciation over $80 depreciable basis, or annual depreciation rate (10 percent), times the deferred profit of $20). Moreover, the profit must be reported as ordinary income by P in this situation, regardless of the character of the asset in its hands when sold to S. In effect, these provisions treat the depreciation of the asset by S as a gradual sale or consumption thereof by S.

But see Regs. §1.1502-3(f)(2) (no ITC recapture where property is transferred within the group unless transfer occurs pursuant to §334(b)(2) liquidation (and, presumably, also in a §338 election, the 1982 replacement of that provision)); compare Rev. Rul. 82-20, 1982-1 CB 6 (exception to recapture of Regs. §1.1502-3(f)(2) not applicable where transferee of property leaves the group pursuant to a single plan, here by split-off distribution of its stock).

[160] See Dale, Consolidated Return Regs. Introduce New Concepts for Taxing Inter-Company Profits, 24 J. Tax'n 6 (1966).

[161] Supra note 157.

between "related corporations" (i.e., those with more than 50 percent common control). Thus, §267(f)(2) provides "such loss shall be deferred until the property is transferred outside the controlled group and there would be recognition of loss under consolidated return principles or at such other times as may be prescribed in regulations." Temporary regulations[162] issued under this provision state that the rules of Regs. §1.1502-13 generally are to govern such losses, but then go on to set out various exceptions to this general rule that result in fewer triggering events and a more gradual restoration of the deferred losses (i.e., the recognition triggers are lower in amount and slower in their rates than the §1502 deferred intercompany transaction regulations). In effect, these regulations establish a separate deferral regime for intercompany losses that overrides the consolidated return rules and creates a more restrictive recognition system than the latter provisions.

The temporary §267 regulations provide that losses are *not* triggered by: (1) the seller or buyer leaving the consolidated group (so long as they remain members of the §267(b) controlled group); (2) filing of separate returns; and (3) dispositions to other persons who are still related to the seller or buyer under §267(b). In addition, §267(f)(2) will override an election not to defer under the consolidated return regulations. Moreover, special rules apply in the case of depreciable property and receivables for determining the amount and timing of the restoration.[163]

The differing results that can occur under the temporary §267 regulations and the deferred intercompany transaction regulations of Regs. §1.1502-13 are illustrated by the following examples in which *P* has two wholly owned subsidiaries, *X* and *Y*, and a third subsidiary, *Z*, which is owned 55 percent by *P*.

> *Example 1.* *X* sells real estate used in its business to *Y* and realizes a $100 loss; both the temporary §267 regulations and the §1502 regulations defer this loss until such time as *Y* disposes of the property. If *Y* resells the property to *Z* (an unconsolidated, but still related affiliate), the deferred loss would be triggered to *X* under the §1502 regulations, but not under the temporary §267 regulations.

> *Example 2.* In Example 1, if separate returns are subsequently filed (and the property constitutes inventory in the hands of buyer *Y*), the deferred loss is triggered to *X* under the §1502 regulations but not under the temporary §267 regulations.

> *Example 3.* In Example 1, if stock of either *X* or *Y* is transferred to *Z* (and *X* or *Y* thus ceases to be a member of the group), *X*'s loss is trig-

---

[162] TD 7991, issuing Temp. Regs. §§1.267(a)-2T, 1.267(f)-1T, and 1.267(f)-2T.
[163] Temp. Regs. §§1.267(f)-2T(g), 1.267(f)-2T(h), and 1.267(f)-2T(j).

gered under the §1502 regulations but not the temporary §267 regulations.

Example 4. If *P* liquidates *Y* under §332, neither the §1502 regulations nor the temporary §267 regulations trigger *X*'s deferred loss (and the same result is true if *P* liquidates *X* instead of *Y*). The same result would obtain if *X* merged into *Y* or *Y* merged into *X* (although, if *X* and *Y* merged into *Z* and *P* does not acquire enough stock to require includability of *Z* in the consolidation, a §1502 trigger would occur, but not a §267 trigger, since *X* (or *Y*), while ceasing to be a member of the *P* group, would still be related under §267).

4. Intercompany distributions. Dividend distributions between members of a consolidated group are eliminated from the computation of consolidated taxable income by Regs. §1.1502-14(a)(1).[164] This treatment is consistent with the theory that the group is, in effect, a single taxable enterprise and that such earnings have already been reflected in the consolidated return and taxed once to the group. Note, however, that the investment basis adjustment rules of Regs. §1.1502-32 generally require that the parent's basis for its common stock in the subsidiary (and, to a limited extent, the preferred stock, but not obligations) must be reduced on account of such distributions whether made from current earnings, from earnings accumulated in prior consolidated return years (after 1965), or from pre-affiliation accumulated earnings.[165] However, distributions from earnings of affiliation years in which no consolidated return was filed or from consolidated return years before 1966 do not reduce stock basis.

The theory of these basis rules is that such earnings have already been capitalized or reflected in an upward adjustment in the parent's basis for its stock in the subsidiary and that a tax-free distribution of the earnings should

---

[164] Rev. Rul. 72-230, 1972-1 CB 209 (in determining gross income for §861(a)(2)(A) special source rules, dividends received by parent from other members of an affiliated group count as gross income, even though such dividends are eliminated in determining consolidated taxable income (i.e., "eliminated" means deducted, not excluded, for this purpose)).

In computing the book income preference for AMT purposes under §56(f), supra ¶ 5.08, excluded dividends presumably also would be excluded here; see §56(f)(2)(C)(i); S. Rep. No. 313, 99th Cong., 2d Sess. 532 (1986). But in the case of the ACE preference of §56(g), excluded dividends apparently *are* counted in the base; see §§56(g)(4)(B) and 56(g)(4)(C)(ii), H.R. Rep. No. 841, 99th Cong., 2d Sess. 275 (1986). But see H.R. Rep., id, at 278 (compute preference on consolidated basis if consolidated returns filed).

[165] See Garvey, Inc. v. US, 726 F2d 1569 (Fed. Cir. 1984) (regulation requiring reduction in stock basis for distribution from preaffiliation earnings valid even though subsidiary acquired in a basis carry-over Type B reorganization).

result in a corresponding reduction of basis. Such a reduction will increase the parent's gain (or decrease its loss) on a later sale of its stock in the subsidiary. The exception for distributions out of earnings accumulated in post-affiliation pre-consolidation years, or in pre-1966 consolidated return years, recognizes that those accumulations are not reflected in the parent's basis for the distributing corporation's stock and hence do not constitute a return of capital. [166]

Nondividend distributions (i.e., return of capital distributions under §§301(c)(2) and 301(c)(3) that are not covered by earnings) likewise are tax-free to the distributee under the regulations. However, the distributee must reduce its stock basis in the distributing corporation by the amount of such distribution; distributions in kind are taken into account only by reference to the distributing corporation's *basis* for the property, regardless of value, plus any gain recognized to the distributing corporation because of the distribution (which, after amendments to §311, will always result).

The distributee's basis for property so distributed likewise is its basis in the hands of the distributing subsidiary (increased by gain recognized to it on the distribution). [167] If the nondividend distribution exceeds the parent's stock basis for its investment in the subsidiary, the excess becomes part of an excess loss account (in effect a negative basis item), with results considered later in this section.

Distributions in cancellation or redemption of stock (i.e., liquidations, partial or complete, and §302 stock redemptions) produce the following results:

(1) If §332 applies to the liquidation, as would ordinarily be the case, the normal nonrecognition and basis rules of §§332 and 334 apply. [168]

---

[166] See Rev. Rul. 72-498, 1972-2 CB 516 (treatment of §356(a)(2) boot dividend in consolidated return context; relationship to intercompany dividend and intercompany transaction rules; boot distribution out of pre-1966 earnings excludable as intercompany dividend; but distribution out of post-1965 earnings not excludable dividend because earnings reflected in parent's positive basis adjustment to subsidiary's stock; thus, latter distribution taxable capital gain to parent and not deferred intercompany transaction because merger of subsidiary broke consolidated return status with parent).

For more on this aspect, see the investment basis adjustment, infra para. 8.

[167] Regs. §1.1502-31(b)(1). Note that as a result of amendments to §311, supra ¶ 7.21, appreciated property will always take a basis equal to its value in view of the full gain recognition required by §311(b)(1). Loss property, by contrast, will take a carry-over basis, resulting in a shift of the potential loss to the distributee.

[168] For §332, see supra ¶ 11.40. See also Regs. §1.1502-34 (stock owned by group members aggregated in applying §332); Rev. Rul. 74-441, 1974-1 CB 105 (a qualified §334(b)(2) liquidation even though stock of liquidating subsidiary owned by various

(2) The rare case of a taxable *complete* liquidation will result in current recognition of gain to the parent only to the extent that the amount of cash distributed by the liquidating subsidiary exceeds the parent's stock basis (after any basis adjustments under Regs. §1.1502-32) plus liabilities of the subsidiary assumed, or taken subject to, by the parent. Current losses will be allowed only if the distribution consists solely of cash.

(3) Other liquidation distributions and stock redemptions to which §302 applies (such cases will be rare in view of the high stock ownership level of the parent) do not result in current recognition of gain or loss to the parent-shareholder, even where cash distributed exceeds stock basis (except in cases of complete liquidation); rather, any gain or loss of the shareholder is deferred until occurrence of one of the events that would trigger an excess loss account (e.g., filing separate returns, sale or worthlessness of the remaining stock of the subsidiary, the distributee or distributor ceasing to be a member of the group, and so forth). Property distributed in such a transaction takes a *substituted* basis, determined by reference to the parent's adjusted basis of the stock exchanged therefor (reduced by distributed cash), under principles similar to the basis rules of former §§334(c) and 334(b)(2) (Regs. §1.1502-31). [169]

---

members of the group, none of whom had owned 80 percent, but all of whom as a group owned 100 percent; aggregation rules of Regs. §1.1502-34 applied so that stock ownership test satisfied). For additional rulings on the stock aggregation rules of Regs. §1.1502-34, see Rev. Rul. 70-141, 1970-1 CB 76; Rev. Rul. 74-598, 1974-2 CB 425; Rev. Rul. 75-383, 1975-2 CB 127.

But see legislation enacted in 1982 (infra note 169), which replaced former §334(b)(2) with new §338, under which the purchaser of a controlling stock interest can elect to treat the acquisition as an asset purchase rather than a stock purchase, supra ¶ 11.46. All actual §332 liquidations now result in a §334(b)(1)/§381 carry-over of basis and tax attributes.

For a special acquisition technique relying on the aggregation rules of Regs. §1.1502-34 (i.e., the mirror subsidiary device), see Sheppard, Mirror Moves: Life Without the *General Utilities* Rule, 32 Tax Notes 847 (1986); see also Faber, 32 Tax Notes 1022 (1986); Faber, 32 Tax Notes 1205 (1986); Sheppard, 33 Tax Notes 281 (1986); Hiegel & Schler, 33 Tax Notes 961 (1986); Baker, 33 Tax Notes 1073 (1986); Sheppard, 33 Tax Notes 988 (1986), and 34 Tax Notes 538 (1987).

For discussion of this technique, see infra para. 5; for a variation relying on the IBA regulations, see infra para. 8 at note 186.

[169] Partial liquidation distributions in the context of the consolidated return regulations at one time offered an extremely attractive method of acquiring a stepped-up basis for certain selected assets of a newly purchased subsidiary without recognition of gain to the parent and with no immediate recapture income to the subsidiary (and *no* investment tax credit recapture at all, supra note 159). Concern over what were perceived to be unwarranted tax benefits from such transactions resulted in corrective legislation, the Tax Equity and Fiscal Responsibility Act of 1982, which repealed partial liquidation treatment for all corporate shareholders, supra ¶ 9.08.

If the *distributing* corporation is required to recognize gain on a distribution in kind (other than in complete liquidation) because of the application of §311(b)(1), the gain is to be treated under the deferred intercompany transaction rules of Regs. §1.1502-13.[170] As noted in Chapter 7, gain recognition will occur in *all* such cases under §311(b)(1) as a result of legislation enacted in 1984 and 1986, while losses are not recognized under §311(a)(2) (and no exceptions exist for this latter rule). Distributions in complete liquidation, on the other hand, are treated under the regular liquidation rules (discussed in Chapter 11)—that is, gain or loss is recognized to the distributing corporation to the same extent and in the same manner as if separate returns had been filed.[171] Because of legislation enacted in 1986, complete liquidation sales and distributions generally result in full recognition of gain and (with certain special exceptions) loss under §336; but liquidating distributions to an 80 percent parent in a qualified §332 liquidation continue to receive nonrecognition treatment under 1986 Code §337 (which replaced a much broader 1954 Code provision that provided generally for nonrecognition treatment on liquidating sales of property).[172]

Under this legislation, such distributions now are treated as ordinary dividends and hence take a carry-over basis from the distributing corporation (increased by any recognized gain). Recognized gain under §311(b)(1) (supra ¶ 7.21) continues to be treated as a deferred intercompany transaction, however.

Legislation enacted in 1984 provided for full recognition of *gain* to the distributing corporation for nonliquidating distributions to corporate shareholders (a rule that was extended to *all* nonliquidating distributions in 1986 and to most liquidating distributions as well, infra notes 170–172).

[170] Section 311 was tightened in 1982 to require full corporate level recognition of gain (but not loss) on stock redemption and partial liquidation distributions of property to corporate shareholders; in 1984, §311 was amended again to tax gain, but not loss, on any nonliquidating property distribution to corporate shareholders. See supra ¶ 7.22.

In 1986, §311 was tightened yet again to require full recognition of gain on any nonliquidating distribution of property to any shareholder, supra ¶ 7.21, the only exception being for §355 distributions.

[171] Regs. §1.1502-14(c)(2). Moreover, ITC recapture would occur in a former §334(b)(2) liquidation under Regs. §1.1502-3(f)(2)(iii). See the 1982 legislation, supra ¶ 11.46, which replaced §334(b)(2) with §338 (an elective rule allowing the buyer corporation to elect to treat stock purchase as asset purchase), so that all §332 liquidations are basis carry-over transactions under §334(b). But ITC recapture presumably occurs in the target's final separate return if §338 is elected; supra ¶ 11.47.

For repeal of the corporate level nonrecognition rules of 1954 Code §§336 and 337 by the Tax Reform Act of 1986, see infra note 172.

[172] Under 1986 Code §336, all liquidating sales result in full recognition of gain and, in most cases, loss. As to the latter, exceptions are provided in §336(d) for (1) distributions to §267 related persons that are either non-pro rata or consist of any property acquired in a tax-free transaction from a corporation's shareholders within five years and (2) certain distributions of property that had a built-in loss when acquired from its shareholders.

Gains and losses on intercompany obligations are, in general, handled similarly to the deferred intercompany transactions discussed above—that is, they are generally deferred until such later events as a disposition to an outsider or retirement of the obligation,[173] in keeping with the theory that the consolidated group is a single taxable enterprise and that only its dealings with outsiders have genuine significance. At such time they generally are taken into income ratably over the remaining term of the obligation. Gain or loss from retirement or cancellation of the obligation, however, is taken into account currently at that time. Losses from worthlessness of an obligation likewise are deferred over the remaining term of the obligation, until they are canceled, or until certain other designated triggering events occur that end deferral.

5. Mirror subsidiary acquisitions. A specialized form of acquisition transaction developed in the 1980s involves the use of so-called mirror subsidiaries, which are separately created entities pretailored to receive particular assets of subsidiary members of the target group. Under this technique, the acquiring corporation funds newly organized subsidiaries with cash; these subsidiaries then jointly purchase all the stock of the target corporation. Relying on the stock aggregation rules of Regs. §1.1502-34,[174] the subsidiaries then liquidate the target under §332, with the target's assets passing upstream to the various mirror subsidiaries in a tax-free §332 liquidation. By selling the stock of the mirror subsidiaries, the acquiring corporation can then sell off unwanted portions of the target group with no further gain or

---

But qualified §332 liquidations are still not taxable to the distributing subsidiary under 1986 Code §337, except to the extent distributions to minority shareholders occur, in which case gain, but not loss, is recognized under §§337(a) and 336(d)(3).

If the subsidiary distributes property to an outstanding minority interest, it will be taxable on gain, but not loss to the extent property is distributed to such minority shareholders, but not otherwise. This represents a change from the house bill, which would have taxed the subsidiary proportionally to the extent of the minority interest outstanding on the plan date unless such interest was purchased or redeemed for cash; see H.R. Conf. Rep. No. 841, 99th Cong., 2d Sess. 202 (1986).

For discussion of the 1986 legislation repealing the *General Utilities* doctrine, see supra ¶¶ 7.20, and 11.06; for the subsidiary's treatment, see supra ¶ 11.49.

[173] Regs. §1.1502-14(d). But see Velvet O'Donnell Corp., 1983-1 USTC ¶ 9225 (Cl. Ct. 1983) (no deferral of worthless bad debt loss if debt becomes worthless before affiliation, even though loss claimed in parent's consolidated return with acquired debtor-subsidiary); First Nat'l Bank of Little Rock, 83 TC 202 (1984) (bad debt reserve additions for intercompany loans deferred).

[174] Supra note 168. See also §338(h)(8) for similar affiliate aggregation rules in determining whether a qualified acquisition has occurred under that provision, supra ¶ 11.47. For a variation, see infra note 186.

For another variation, using §304 (supra ¶ 9.12), see Vanderwolk, Restructuring an Affiliated Corporation Using Section 304, 65 Taxes 241 (1987).

loss, since the parent's basis for the stock of the subsidiaries holding those assets would equal their value.

Whether the 1986 Code's §337, providing for nonrecognition at the subsidiary level in a §332 liquidation, also applies here is not entirely clear,[175] although the consolidated return regulations currently in force plainly indicate that it should. Since inside asset basis is not stepped up as a result of these transactions (assuming no §338 election is made), the policy underlying the 1986 repeal of the *General Utilities* principle would not appear to have been abused by such transactions, even though corporate-level tax has been escaped (or, more accurately, deferred) as a result of this technique.

> *To illustrate:* T has operating division X and also wholly owns two subsidiaries, T-1 and T-2. P creates three mirror subsidiaries, P-1, P-2, and P-3, which jointly acquire all the T stock with cash contributed by P; T is then liquidated into P's three subsidiaries, with the T-1 and T-2 stock passing to P-1 and P-2 and T's operating assets in X passing to P-3. P can then sell P-1, P-2, or P-3 with no further gain or loss,[176] since its basis for the P-1, P-2, and P-3 stock will be comparable to the value of that stock.

6. Accounting methods and inventory. Another significant modification of the regulations in 1966 permits each member of the consolidated group to determine its method of accounting under §446 as if it were filing a separate return.[177] Under the pre-1966 regulations, the members were required to adopt consistent accounting methods unless the Service consented to the use of different methods. The adoption of consistent accounting *periods* by the affiliates is still necessary, however, such period being determined by reference to that of the common parent.[178] Moreover, where the requisite affilia-

---

[175] See articles and comments supra note 168. See also Kliegman, Do Mirror Transactions Survive the 1986 Act?, 66 J. Tax'n 206 (1987); Sheppard, Mirror Transactions Go Forward, 35 Tax Notes 1057 (1987). For a variation on the mirror transaction (which relied on the IBA regulations, infra para. 8), see discussion infra note 186; for Service response to this alternative, see Notice 87-14, 1987-4 IRB 21.

For addition of mirror transactions to the no ruling list, see Rev. Proc. 87-23, 1987-21 IRB 18 (under study).

[176] See generally supra ¶ 11.49 and ¶ 14.15. For similar target tailoring techniques (which, however, antedate acquisition rather than follow it as here), see supra ¶ 14.52.

[177] Regs. §1.1502-17. See generally Rev. Rul. 85-133, 1985-2 CB 192 (parent not entitled to use §453 because it did not sell on the installment method, even though subsidiary extended credit to buyers; Service would not recharacterize arrangement as installment sale by parent and deferred sale of receivables to subsidiary).

[178] Regs. §1.1502-76.

tion is established during the common parent's taxable year, all of its income for the year must be included in the consolidated return; income of the other affiliates, however, is included in the consolidated return for only that part of the parent's taxable period during which they were members of the affiliated group.[179]

> *To illustrate.* If *P* acquired all the stock of *S* on June 30 and elected to file a consolidated return for that year, all of *P*'s income would be included in such return, while *S*'s income would be included for the period July 1–December 31. *S* would file a separate return with respect to its pre-consolidation income. (Members of the group for 30 days or less during the year can elect not to be part of the group for that year.)

The treatment of intercompany inventory transactions is governed by the provisions of Regs. §1.1502-18, which, in general, adopts the deferral technique described above; the thrust of these rules is to tax the profit from intercompany sales of inventory items to the member of the group that earned it, but only when the property is sold to an outsider. Moreover, special adjustments to inventories are required when an affiliated group filing separate returns switches to a consolidated return. These adjustments are necessary in order to normalize the group's income for the year of change to consolidated reporting as well as to prevent the tax windfall or distortions that might occur if inventories were not adjusted to take account of preconsolidation intercompany inventory transactions.

7. Treatment of net operating losses. One of the most commonly cited advantages of filing a consolidated return is the rule that current operating losses of one affiliate can be offset against profits of another affiliate in computing consolidated income (or loss) of the group. If losses of some members of the group exceed profits of other members of the group, a consolidated net operating loss results, and the rules relating to the computation of the consolidated net operating loss deduction are found in Regs. §1.1502-21.[180]

---

[179] See Rev. Rul. 67-189, 1967-1 CB 255, holding that the newly acquired subsidiary does not have to annualize its income for the preaffiliation part-year separate return; Rev. Rul. 70-378, 1970-2 CB 178 (same); see also Petroleum Heat & Power Co. v. US, 405 F2d 1300 (Ct. Cl. 1969) (income deferred from short separate return year taxed in consolidated return year); Regs. §1.1502-76(b).

[180] But see Regs. §1.1502-32, requiring the basis of the loss affiliate's stock held by other members of the group to be reduced to the extent that its losses are availed of by the group (either currently or as carry-back or carry-over deductions) in computing consolidated taxable income. These matters (together with the effect of losses in excess of stock basis, the so-called excess loss account) are considered infra para.

8. Investment basis adjustments and excess loss accounts. In order to put into force the principles discussed previously relating to intercompany distributions and net operating losses, the regulations prescribe a system of special annual investment basis adjustments in Regs. §1.1502-32. These provisions generally require the parent to make annual, year-end adjustments to the basis of its common and preferred stock in each of its subsidiaries to reflect the economic results of that subsidiary's operations for the year (i.e., its earnings, losses, and distributions). They thus create a floating, or fluctuating, basis. In brief, the basis of all stock (common and preferred) is increased for undistributed current earnings and profits of the subsidiary, and the basis of common stock only is increased for such subsidiary's share of any consolidated net operating, or net capital, losses that are not carried back and absorbed in a prior year (i.e., unused losses of the subsidiary). Basis of common stock only is reduced for utilized losses of a subsidiary (i.e., current deficits for the year and the subsidiary's allocable share of any net operating, or net capital, losses from prior years that are carried over into, and absorbed during, the current year); basis of common and preferred is reduced for §301(c)(2) nondividend return of capital distributions and for dividend distributions out of earnings accumulated during consolidated return years (after 1965) or from earnings accumulated in preaffiliation years of the subsidiary. These adjustments are in addition to any other basis adjustments to the stock that may be required by §1016 (e.g., capital contributions or return of capital dividends).[181]

---

8. See also infra ¶ 15.24 for various limitations on the use of losses in the consolidated return area; and §382, infra ¶¶ 16.23–16.25.

See also TD 7685, 1980-1 CB 192, promulgating temporary regulations under amendments to the §465 at-risk rules by the Revenue Act of 1978 for corporations filing consolidated returns; Regs. §5.1502-45. These regulations provide that if a parent corporation meets the stock ownership test of §465(a)(1)(C), a subsidiary's loss from an activity to which §465 applies (i.e., an activity other than the holding of real estate and equipment leasing) will be allowed in a consolidated return only to the extent that the parent is at risk in the activity of the subsidiary as of the close of the subsidiary's taxable year. See Blanchard, Application of the "At Risk" Rules to Consolidated Groups, 36 Tax Lawyer 661 (1983). The Tax Reform Act of 1986 extended §465 to real estate; see Snyder & Gonick, supra note 150.

In Prop. Regs. §1.1502-21(b)(4) (July 31, 1984), it is provided that §381 transfers between members generally only will consume one year of the carry-over (unless subject to the separate return limitation year rules, in which case two years are absorbed); see also Prop. Regs. §1.1502-21(g), which provides rules for waiving consolidated net operating loss carry-backs.

[181] Regulations under §§1.1502-11 were amended on December 29, 1972 by adding new paragraph (b) in order to resolve a circular basis adjustment problem that could arise under the IBA rules of Regs. §1.1502-32 when stock of a subsidiary was disposed of (because of interdependent variables in the computation mechanics of these provisions). The solution adopted by the regulations is first to compute the IBA

The purpose of the IBA rules is to avoid duplication of tax on the parent's investment gain attributable to accumulated earnings of its subsidiary that have already been taxed to the group in the consolidated return or a double deduction for losses that have already been utilized by the group in computing consolidated tax liability. Note that the primary upward and downward basis adjustments are based on current *earnings* and *profits* or *deficits* rather than taxable income.[182] The IBA for the parent's common and preferred stock in a particular subsidiary is to be made separately and presumably on a share-by-share basis (rather than on an aggregate, or average, basis), for each class of stock. These adjustments resemble the fluctuating basis rules for shareholders of Subchapter S corporations who likewise

---

for the stock disposed of on the basis of tentative consolidated taxable income or loss (*without* regard to gain or loss on the stock disposition); then, the amount of any loss carry-overs attributable to the subsidiary that may be carried into the taxable year of disposition are limited to such tentative consolidated taxable income (thus preventing endless absorption of those carry-overs by any disposition gain, without tax benefit); finally, if there is gain on the disposition of the subsidiary's stock, the portion of a consolidated net operating loss attributable to the disposed subsidiary is removed from the computation of consolidated taxable income (thus avoiding a circular absorption of that loss against the disposition gain). This removed loss is treated as a loss that is sustained in the year of disposition and may be carried either to a CRY of the group or to a SRY of the subsidiary in the same manner as such losses ordinarily are carried.

See also example infra text at note 185.

[182] For computation of the earnings, or deficit, components of the IBA, see Regs. §1.1502-33. See generally Axelrod, The Basis for Using E&P in Consolidated Return Basis Adjustments, 12 J. Corp. Tax'n 227 (1985); Bean, Consolidated Returns: The Complexities Involved in an Earnings and Profits Study, 13 J. Corp. Tax'n 54 (1986).

See Priv. Ltr. Rul. 79-46-008, 1979 Fed. Taxes (P-H) ¶ 54,696, dealing with the interaction of the §312(k) earnings and profits limitations with the IBA rules; that is, §312(k) limitations reduce the IBA negative adjustment for the parent's stock in the subsidiary, resulting in a basis gap to the extent, accelerated depreciation exceeds §312(k) straight-line depreciation. In effect, the parent has a higher outside stock basis than would otherwise occur absent §312(k). This effect was magnified by the new ACRS depreciation system and the safe-harbor leasing rules of §168(f)(8) under the Economic Recovery Tax Act of 1981; §312(n), added in 1984, requires earnings and profits computations to be made on the basis of economic income notions. See supra ¶ 7.03, which further inflates earnings and magnifies the outside basis gap effect. Accord, Woods Inv. Co., 85 TC 274 (1985); see Zimmerman, Tax Court Allows Double Tax Benefit for Consolidated Return Filers, 64 Taxes 216 (1986). The Service will not appeal *Woods*, Ann. 86-32, 1986-12 IRB 26, but instead will change the regulations.

Preliminary proposals by the staff of the Senate Finance Committee on September 22, 1983 proposed abolishing the IBA system of the consolidated return regulations and establishing a uniform outside basis rule for stock of a controlled subsidiary determined by reference to the subsidiary's inside net asset basis; the final report, released on May 20, 1985, also proposed to scrap the IBA rules in favor of proposed §1020, supra ¶ 14.33, para. 5.

increase the basis of their stock for undistributed earnings and reduce basis for losses and distributions.[183] While simple in basic concept, the IBA rules are intricate and confusing in detail;[184] a few simple examples will illustrate the general scope of their operation.

Assume that P has two newly created and wholly owned subsidiaries, X and Y, with which it files a consolidated return for the first year of existence, year one. P's initial basis for its stock of X is $50 and $100 for its stock of Y. P has $100 of earnings for year one (and for any other year unless stated).

Example 1. If X has current earnings of $10 in year one and Y has losses (current deficit) of $20, P's basis for its stock of X will be increased by X's $10 of undistributed earnings to $60, and its basis for Y's stock will be reduced to $80 by the $20 of Y's losses which were used to reduce consolidated taxable income during year one.

Example 2. If X distributed $8 of its year one earnings to P in the above example (a tax-free distribution to P, as discussed earlier in this section), P's positive basis adjustment would only be $2 (i.e., the undistributed amount of X's current earnings). If X instead distributed $15 to P in year one ($X$ having no accumulated earnings from prior years), P's basis for its X stock would be reduced by $5 (the §301(c)(2) return of capital amount) to $45. If P reinvested $10 of this distribution by a capital contribution to X, P's basis for the X stock would be stepped up to $55 to reflect this amount. (An elective deemed dividend-capital contribution procedure is provided in Regs. §1.1502-32(f)(2), which accomplishes the same net result without an actual transfer of funds.)

---

[183] Supra ch. 6, especially ¶¶ 6.01 and 6.06. See also the comparable treatment of partnerships, where the basis of the partners for their interests in the partnership is adjusted to reflect current earnings, losses, and distributions of the partnership under §705 and the special basis adjustment rules under the former §334(b)(2) regulations, supra ¶ 11.45.

[184] For discussion of these provisions, see Dring, Handling Investment Adjustments and Excess Losses Under the New Consolidated Return Regulations, 27 J. Tax'n 166 (1967); Kern & Rendell, The New "Excess Loss" Concept in the New Consolidated Return Regulations: An Analysis, 27 J. Tax'n 206 (1967); Dring, How the Consolidated Regulation Amendments Clarify the Investment Basis Adjustment Rules, 39 J. Tax'n 266 (1973); Dring, The Investment Adjustment Rules of the Consolidated Return Regulations: How They Work, 39 J. Tax'n 330 (1973); Axelrod, supra note 182; Bean, supra note 182; Rubin, Consolidated Returns: Basis Adjustment for Distributions Out of Pre-Acquisition Earnings and Profits, 34 Tax L. Rev. 649 (1979); see also Garvey, Inc. v. US, supra note 165.

But see current proposals, supra note 182 to scrap the IBA rules and determine outside stock basis by reference to inside net asset basis. See supra ¶ 14.33, para. 5.

Example 3. If (returning to the facts of Example 1) *X* lost $5 and *Y* earned $15 in year two, *P*'s basis for its stock in *X* at the end of year two, would be reduced by the $5 of *X*'s loss to $55, and its basis for the *Y* stock would be increased by *Y*'s $15 of earnings to $95.

Example 4. If, during year 3, *X* sells property and sustains a capital loss of $30 and has ordinary income of $10, while *Y* has a current operating deficit of $15, *P*'s IBA to the basis of its *X* stock is a net increase of $10 (i.e., a negative current deficit adjustment of $20 and a positive adjustment of $30 for the capital loss that could not be used currently or as a carry-back in computing consolidated taxable income (assuming the group had no capital gain in years 1, 2, and 3)); its IBA for the *Y* stock is a reduction of $15, the amount of *Y*'s current loss used in computing consolidated taxable income of the group. If the group had incurred a $30 capital gain in year 1 against which *X*'s capital loss of $30 could have been carried back and absorbed, however, *P*'s IBA to its *X* stock would be a decrease of $20, the current deficit of *X*, there being no positive adjustment for unused capital losses attributable to *X*.

Example 5. If, for year 1, *P* has current earnings of $10 (rather than $100), *X* breaks even and *Y* has a current operating deficit of $15, *P*'s sale of the *Y* stock for $110 on December 31 will result in a gain to *P* of $20 under Regs. §1.1502-11(b), as amended in 1972. Sale of the *Y* stock for $80, on the other hand, will result in a $10 capital loss to *P* under those regulations. These results occur because, in the first instance, *P*'s gain from the sale of its *Y* stock is *not* considered in determining the amounts available to absorb *Y*'s current deficit on the consolidated return for year 1, so that the net negative IBA to the *Y* stock is only $10 (i.e., a decrease of $15 for the deficit of *Y*, and an increase of $5 for the unused consolidated net operating loss attributable to *Y*), resulting in a gain of $20 to *P* on the sale of its *Y* stock ($110 less adjusted basis of $90).[185] In the second situation, where the *Y* stock was sold for $80, the *Y* stock basis is likewise determined by subtracting *Y*'s $15 deficit and adding the $5 of positive IBA for the unused consolidated net operating loss attributable to *Y*, giving *P* a $90 basis for its *Y* stock and a $10 capital loss.

---

[185] See supra note 181 for description of the 1972 amendments dealing with this situation. Prior to these amendments, *P* realized a $25 gain on the sale of *Y* stock because *P*'s gain on the *Y* stock sale created income to absorb *Y*'s loss on the consolidated return with a consequent net negative IBA to the *Y* stock of $15, resulting in a gain of $25.

Example 6. *P* buys all the stock of *Z* for $100 in January of year 1, and *Z* sells property at a gain of $10 in the same year, resulting in a step-up in *P*'s basis for the *Z* stock to $110. If *P* then sells the *Z* stock for $100, its $10 loss can be set off against the gain recognized by *Z* on its asset sale in the consolidated return (either currently, if both occur in the same year, or by way of carry-back).[186]

Perhaps the most important feature of the IBA rules is the fact that the negative adjustments to stock basis prescribed therein (for example, §§301(c)(2) and 301(c)(3) nondividend distributions and utilized operating or capital losses) do not stop at zero, and thus can create a negative basis for the parent's stock in the subsidiary. This account, defined by Regs. §1.1502-32(e)(1) as an excess loss account, represents a potential income item in the hands of the parent, recognition of which will occur on the happening of certain designated disposition events provided for in Regs. §1.1502-19(b).[187] If a disposition event occurs that triggers recognition of income from an ELA, the income ordinarily will be deemed to be capital gain rather than ordinary income if the subsidiary is solvent at the time of recognition; if it is

---

[186] For the Service response to this tactic, see Notice 87-14, 1987-4 IRB 21. See also Sheppard, The Prodigal Son of Mirror, 34 Tax Notes 444 (1987). The Service has proposed to amend the regulations (effective Jan. 6, 1987), denying *P* a basis step-up for the $10 of built-in gain when it acquired *Z*. For use of §304 as a planning vehicle, see Vanderwolk, supra note 174.

[187] A disposition under Regs. §1.1502-19(b), for this purpose, includes not only a sale or other transfer of the subsidiary's stock, but also the worthlessness of such stock, the discharge of an indebtedness of the loss affiliate under certain circumstances, the discontinuance of filing consolidated returns, and certain other constructive stock dispositions of a highly technical character. The result of these disposition rules is to make the ELA a volatile potential income item. But see Rev. Rul. 81-84, 1981-1 CB 451 (sale of stock with ELA taint to another member of consolidated group not a trigger of ELA; sale a deferred intercompany transaction per Regs. §1.1502-13(c)(1), and these provisions control over ELA trigger rules).

Where the subsidiary's stock is canceled or redeemed in a partial liquidation (or in a §302(a) redemption), however, ELA gain is deferred by Regs. §1.1502-19(a)(3) until one of the other constructive disposition events provided for in Regs. §1.1502-19(b)(2) occurs. But see 1982 legislation (supra note 169), which abolished partial liquidation treatment for corporate shareholders.

Regs. §1.1502-19(a)(3) deferral treatment is not applicable, however, to taxable complete liquidations; if liquidation is a tax-free §§332/334(b)(1) liquidation, the ELA account is purged by virtue of §1.1502-19(e).

Finally, various tax-free transfers of stock or assets of an ELA subsidiary do not trigger recognition of the ELA by virtue of Regs. §§1.1502-19(d) and 1.1502-19(e).

See also Rev. Rul. 73-73, 1973-1 CB 371 (ELA recapture rules override §1071 nonrecognition rules dealing with sales to effectuate Federal Communications Commission policies. But see Rev. Rul. 81-84, supra.

insolvent (as specially defined), however, ordinary income will generally result.[188]

The pre-1966 regulations, by contrast, did not reduce the parent's basis for its interest in the subsidiary below zero, regardless of the amount of the subsidiary's losses availed of by the group in the consolidated return. This fact created a distortion in the net economic consequences from the overall transaction if a subsidiary's deductible tax losses exceeded the parent's net investment in the stock of the subsidiary.

> *To illustrate:* P and its wholly owned subsidiary have been filing consolidated returns, P's basis for its investment in S is $100, and S suffers net operating losses of $100 in year 1 and $50 in year 2. These losses are fully absorbed as current offsets, carry-overs, or carry-back deductions in the determination of the group's consolidated taxable income. In year 3, P sells all of S's stock for $70. Under the pre-1966 regulations, P's $100 basis for its stock in S would be adjusted down to (but not below) zero by the year 1 and year 2 losses, which were availed of in the consolidated return. As a result, P would recognize $70 of capital gain on selling its S stock, although the consolidated return would have reflected $150 of deductions in respect of a net investment outlay of only $30 (i.e., $100 paid by P for S stock, less $70 received on its sale). In contrast, P is currently required to report a capital gain of $120 on selling the stock of S, this amount being the excess loss account of $50 ($150 of deductions taken in excess of P's $100 stock basis in S) plus the $70 proceeds of sale. Thus, the tax returns, reporting $150 of deductions and $120 of gain, correspond to the economic results to P of its investment in S ($100 paid for stock, less $70 received on sale).

The excess loss account rules of Regs. §1.1502-19 were revised in 1972 to allow a parent that disposes of part or all of its common stock of a subsidiary with respect to which there is an excess loss account to elect to apply such account to the reduction of basis of its other stock (common or preferred) and debt investment in the subsidiary that is not disposed of in the transaction; in effect, no excess loss account income need be reported by the

---

[188] The proposed regulations had provided for recapture in full as ordinary income upon a designated disposition event; the final regulations pulled back considerably from this approach, reserving ordinary income treatment primarily for certain specifically defined insolvency situations.

See Covil Insulation Co., 65 TC 364 (1975) (regulations requiring recapture of ELA account valid; negative basis rules of Regs. §1.1502-32(e) and inclusion triggers of Regs. §1.1502-19 held valid exercise of regulatory authority under §1502; also, treatment of ELA recapture income as ordinary income where subsidiary insolvent held valid).

parent until there has been a complete recovery by the parent of its entire investment (both equity and debt) in the subsidiary through distributions, utilization of losses, sales, and so forth.[189]

An ELA status with respect to stock in a particular subsidiary can be purged in any one of the following ways:

(1) Additional capital contributions will reduce or eliminate the ELA, with any excess contribution causing a step-up in stock basis; capital contributions in the form of property presumably are considered by reference to the contributed property's basis, although the proposed regulation's specific statement to that effect was dropped in the final version.

(2) Earnings of the subsidiary will likewise reduce the parent's ELA by increasing basis under Regs. §1.1502-32.[190]

(3) Under Regs. §1.1502-19(e), an ELA will be eliminated if the subsidiary is liquidated into the parent under §332 and the carry-over basis rules of §334(b)(1) apply; if the subsidiary is merged into another affiliated member of the group, however, the ELA with respect to stock of the disappearing member is transferred to the parent's basis for its stock of the acquiring member, which may create an ELA with respect to that stock.

(4) The regulations were revised in 1972 to allow an excess loss account to be purged by a downstream merger of the parent into its subsidiary (in addition to the prior rules, which allowed purging of the account by an upstream merger or liquidation of the subsidiary into its parent).

(5) Under Regs. §1.1502-33(d), a group can elect to apportion the consolidated tax liability among the various affiliates in such a manner as to reduce ELAs of particular members (e.g., reimbursement by profit members to loss affiliates for the tax benefits received on the

---

[189] For prior law, see Georgia Pac. Corp., 63 TC 790 (1975) (ELA regulations valid; ELA capital gain triggered where parent disposed of loss subsidiary stock in reorganization transfer of all parent's assets (Type C reorganization); no reduction of ELA for parent loans to subsidiary as required by pre-1971 regulations; post-1971 regulations now allow such loans to offset ELA recapture, but old rules still valid despite this change, and taxpayer bound by them).

[190] For the election (applicable only to pre-1976 years) to include current earnings of a subsidiary in the current earnings of its parent (as if such earnings had been distributed currently up the chain), see Regs. §1.1502-33(c)(4)(iii); for the requirement (after 1975) that current earnings be so included, see Regs. §1.1502-33(c)(4)(ii).

For the special deemed dividend election to treat accumulated earnings of a subsidiary as if they had been distributed as a dividend to its immediate parent on the first day of the year, see Regs. §1.1502-32(f)(2); for an illustration of this computation, see Rev. Rul. 75-212, 1975-1 CB 107.

consolidated return may be treated as a capital contribution which reduces ELA).[191]

9. Accumulated earnings tax. Regulations were finalized in 1984 relating to the accumulated earnings tax aspects of an affiliated group of corporations filing consolidated returns.[192] These regulations state generally that an affiliated group is treated as a single corporation in determining whether its earnings have been allowed to accumulate in excess of its reasonable business needs. In testing whether the group is subject to liability for the §531 tax, earnings and profits of the group are determined under the rules of Regs. §1.1502-33, except that earnings adjustments attributable to IBA computations are not considered.

The regulations also make plain that earnings of one member can be accumulated for the needs of another member. If the group is deemed to have accumulated its earnings unreasonably, the tax is imposed on the group's consolidated accumulated taxable income (after the consolidated adjustments described in §535(b);[193]), reduced by the consolidated dividends-paid deduction and by the consolidated accumulated earnings credit. In computing the consolidated dividends-paid deduction, however, distributions to other members generally are excluded; hence, it is only dividends paid to nonmember shareholders of the group that qualify for the §561 deduction as it relates to §531 tax computations.

10. Credits. Regs. §1.1502-3 sets forth the rules for determining the consolidated investment credit of the group, while Regs. §1.1502-4 deals with the consolidated foreign tax credit.[194] While the ITC was repealed in 1986, certain provisions continue in force under grandfathering rules. Among the principal features of these provisions are the following:

---

[191] See Rev. Rul. 73-605, 1973-2 CB 109 (effect of tax allocation agreement under §1552 and of payments between members pursuant to that agreement). See generally Sacks, Intercompany Federal Income Tax Allocation Agreements, 13 J. Corp. Tax'n 40 (1986).

But note Regs. §1.1502-6(c) (member agreements have no effect on the several liability of group members for the tax).

[192] Prop. Regs. §1.1502-43, adopted by TD 7937, 1984-1 CB 187. See also Gottesman & Co., 77 TC 1149 (1981) (compute §531 tax separately in absence of final regulations; existing regulations did not require consolidation for this tax). These regulations were initially proposed in 1968 but were withdrawn without explanation in 1971.

[193] Supra ¶ 8.09.

[194] The foreign tax credit regulations are woefully out of date (see infra ¶ 17.11). See Prop. Regs. §1.1502-9 (foreign loss recapture rules). Numerous other credits have yet to be reflected in final regulations under §1502.

(1) The consolidated ITC of the group is determined by aggregating the credits earned by each member of the group for the year; however, for this purpose, the qualified investment of a member that acquires such property in an intercompany transaction does not include gain or loss realized by the transferor member (whether or not deferred) under Regs. §1.1502-3(a)(2).

(2) The amount of the credit is limited by the consolidated tax liability of the group for the year (after the foreign tax credit and without consideration of additional taxes generated by §56, §47 (ITC recapture), §531, or §541).

(3) Credits that cannot be used currently become part of the group's consolidated carry-back and carry-over accounts under Regs. §1.1502-3(b), subject to the limitations described in Regs. §§1.1502-3(c), 1.1502-3(d) and 1.1502-3(e), as discussed in the following section.

(4) Under §1.1502-3(f), early dispositions of ITC property *outside* the group will result in recapture of the credit under §47; however, intragroup transfers do not trigger recapture (unless the disposition transaction constitutes a §334(b)(2) liquidation) under Regs. §1.1502-3(f).[195]

¶ 15.24 LIMITATIONS ON APPLICATION OF CONSOLIDATED RETURN PRINCIPLES

1. Regulation limitations on separate to consolidated return inbound transactions. The consolidated return regulations contain their own automatic protective measures against the acquisition of a loss corporation in order to apply its net operating loss deductions (or other favorable tax attributes) against the income of the more prosperous members of the group. In general, pre-affiliation losses can be used in computing post-affiliation consolidated taxable income only to the extent that the new member of the group contributes to the consolidated income. Similar limitations are imposed with respect to such other tax attributes as capital loss, investment credit, and foreign tax credit carry-overs.[196] This limitation, defined as a separate return limitation year by Regs. §1.1502-1(f), is reminiscent of the con-

---

[195] See §1.1502-3(f)(3), Examples, especially Example 5. Compare Rev. Rul. 82-20, 1982-1 CB 6 (recapture triggered by planned disposition of transferee corporation's stock outside the group). See also Prop. Regs. §1.1502-3 (1984) (conforming the regulations to various changes in the ITC provisions after 1966). But the Tax Reform Act of 1986 repealed the ITC, effective in 1986.

[196] See Regs. §1.1502-21(c) (net operating losses); Regs. §1.1502-3(c) (investment credit carry-overs); Regs. §1.1502-4(f) (foreign tax credit carry-overs); Regs. §1.1502-

tinuity of business enterprise doctrine of the *Libson Shops* case, which denied the use of pre-merger losses against post-merger profits produced by business units different from those that incurred the losses.[197] It should be noted that corporate tax attribute carry-overs in the consolidated return context are treated less favorably in this respect than carry-overs based on the direct acquisition of assets, which are subject to the rules of §§381 and 382 (see Chapter 16). While numerous limitations apply to tax-free asset acquisitions, it is relatively clear that the continuity of business enterprise approach of *Libson Shops* is not one of them. This lack of parallelism between stock acquisitions (followed by the filing of consolidated returns) on the one hand and asset acquisitions on the other is difficult to justify as a policy matter, other than for the technical reason that the subsidiary is still a separate entity rather than a mere division.[198]

The consolidated return regulations permit net operating losses (or other tax attributes) attributable to a SRLY to be carried forward to a CRY, without regard to the loss corporation's income in the later year, however, provided that the loss corporation either is the common parent of the group or was a member of the affiliated group on each day of the loss year.[199] This

---

22(c) (capital loss carry-overs). See generally J.A. Tobin Constr. Co., 85 TC 1005 (1985).

See also Woolford Realty Co. v. Rose, 286 US 319 (1932), in which the Supreme Court similarly disallowed a carry-over for pre-affiliation losses against post-affiliation consolidated taxable income before the regulations contained an explicit limitation; Salem, How to Use Net Operating Losses Effectively Under the New Consolidated Return Regulations, 26 J. Tax'n 270 (1967).

[197] Libson Shops, Inc. v. Koehler, supra note 130, discussed infra ¶ 16.26.

[198] But the Tax Reform Act of 1986 materially revised §382 and provided for essentially parallel treatment of stock and asset acquisitions, infra ¶ 16.23. See also Prop. Regs. §§1.1502-21(c)(3) and 1.1502-21(c)(4) (July 31, 1984) (application of SRLY rules where intragroup §381(a) transactions).

[199] Regs. §§1.1502-1(f) and 1.1502-21(c). Legislation enacted in 1982 (Tax Equity and Fiscal Responsibility Act of 1982), however, restricted the ability of a loss group to apply its own loss carry-overs against income generated upon the purchase of a subsidiary and its liquidation under former §334(b)(2). Section 338 replaced §334(b)(2) with an elective rule under which the purchasing corporation could elect, within eight and one-half months after buying control of the subsidiary, whether to treat the stock purchase as if it were an asset purchase. If §338 is elected, the acquired subsidiary is deemed to have sold its assets and immediately repurchased them, both such events occurring *outside* of the buyer's consolidated return. Thus, the buyer acquires its subsidiary with a clean slate (and the subsidiary reports its gain in its final separate return (or in its former consolidated group's return). See generally supra ¶ 11.47.

If §338 is not elected (or if no election is made and the acquired subsidiary is liquidated under §332), the subsidiary retains its tax history and asset basis (or its tax history and basis carry over to the distributee-parent, since all §332 liquidations will be §334(b)(1) §381 transactions).

provision substantially incorporated a 1965 amendment to the pre-1966 consolidated return regulations,[200] which permitted similar benefits for engaged but unmarried corporations with respect to consolidated returns filed in 1964 and thereafter.[201]

It should be noted that, although the consolidated return regulations (and various other limitation provisions, such as §269[202]) generally discourage profitable affiliated groups from acquiring loss corporations to take advantage of their loss carry-over deductions, the converse of this rule does not necessarily hold true. A loss group is presumably free to acquire a profitable subsidiary where there has been no material change in stock ownership of the acquiring group's common parent corporation (i.e., where there has not been a reverse acquisition), as discussed later in this section, and apply its own unused net operating loss carry-over deductions against income generated by the newly acquired corporation. In this latter respect, however, the regulations added a new refinement, the consolidated return change of ownership. This term is defined by Regs. §1.1502-1(g) as a more than 50 percentage point change of ownership in the common parent corporation that occurs during a two-year period, resulting from a purchase, a redemption, or a combination thereof as defined in §382(a)(4) of the 1954 Code (before its amendment in 1986, as discussed in Chapter 16). If such a change of ownership occurs, the group's consolidated operating losses sustained before the change in ownership can be carried over to consolidated return years ending after the change only to the extent that those corporations that were members of the group before the change generate income in these later years.[203] This limitation is aimed at the acquisition of a loss group by the owners of a profitable corporation, who then seek to apply the former's loss carry-overs

---

[200] TD 6813, 1965-1 CB 436.

[201] For an illustration of the interaction of §381(c)(1) and the SRLY rules of §1.1502-21(c), see Rev. Rul. 75-378, 1975-2 CB 355 (group had filed separate returns and elected multiple benefits, so SRLY rules applied, then filed consolidated returns, and loss subsidiary subsequently liquidated into parent).

See generally Wolter Constr. Co., 68 TC 39 (1977) (losses sustained by sister corporation not available in consolidated return when group turned into parent-subsidiary structure; SRLY restrictions apply since amnesty available only where a common parent present during years losses sustained; regulations valid in view of their legislative character and fact that losses would have been allowed under §§269, 381, and 382 irrelevant in view of regulations' denial therefor); aff'd, 634 F2d 1029 (6th Cir. 1980) (common parent exception to SRLY definition not applicable to commonly controlled brother-sister corporations).

[202] Infra ¶ 16.21.

[203] See Regs. §1.1502-21(d). For an analogy to this approach, see 1954 Code §382(a) (prior to its amendment in 1986), infra ¶ 16.22.

Moreover, similar limitations apply to other favorable tax attributes of the group as well (e.g., investment credits, foreign tax credits, and capital losses).

against the latter's income on a consolidated return. This rule, in effect, merely extends to an acquired group the general principle that the losses of an acquired subsidiary are locked into that member and can be carried over only against its own income.[204]

Regs. §1.1502-21(e) also incorporates the limitations of 1954 Code §382 (before its amendment in 1986, as discussed in Chapter 16) as an additional limitation on the use of net operating loss carry-overs by the group. If that provision applied to the transaction, however, the consequences were more drastic than the limitations provided by the consolidated return regulations. The net operating loss carry-overs were disallowed in full under 1954 Code §382(a) if there was a change of business (by *any* member of the group) and a change of ownership (with respect to stock of the parent or of a member). The carry-overs were abated under 1954 Code §382(b) if continuity of interest on the part of former shareholders of the loss corporation dropped below 20 percent. Legislation enacted in 1986, however, materially revised the limitation rules of §382, but these amendments have not yet been reflected in the consolidated return regulations presently in force. (The 1986 legislation did, however, specifically retain the consolidated return SRLY and CRCO limitations.)[205]

Another concept adopted by the regulations to prevent trafficking in loss corporations by consolidated groups is the "reverse acquisition" definition of Regs. §1.1502-75(d)(3) (i.e., an acquisition of stock or assets, whether or not constituting a reorganization, where shareholders of the acquired member end up owning more than 50 percent by value of stock of the acquiring corporation). Although the transaction formally resembles a minnow swallowing a whale, the regulations reverse the substance of the acquisition for tax purposes: The group of which the acquiring corporation is the common parent is treated as ceasing to exist, the technical acquiring member is treated as becoming the common parent of a new group, and the tax attributes of the members of the old group are deemed to have arisen in SRLYs (i.e., these attributes are frozen into the old members and can only be used against future profits of the old members on the consolidated return).[206] Thus, acquisitions *by* loss groups, which are putatively permitted

---

[204] See Rev. Rul. 84-33, 1984-1 CB 186 (two newly formed subsidiaries of parent during year of CRCO treated as old members, even though not technically such because not in existence for year prior to CRCO, because their assets and businesses were derived solely from old member parent).

[205] See infra ¶¶ 16.23–16.25 for a detailed discussion of §382 and the 1986 amendments; see specifically ¶ 16.25, para. 7.

[206] The provisions of Regs. §1.1502-75(d) were amended in 1972 to clarify the effects of reverse acquisitions and downstream mergers on the taxable years of the participants; Regs. §1.1502-76(b) also was revised to specify which corporation is to be regarded as the common parent in the case of reverse acquisitions and down-

without limitation under the regulations, first must be scrutinized under the relative size test of the reverse acquisition rules to see which party to the acquisition is to be subject to the SRLY strictures of Regs. §1.1502-1(f) and the CRCO rules of Regs. §1.1502-1(g). [207]

The consolidated return regulations also inhibit the acquisition of a corporation with built-in losses or other deductions (such as depreciated stock in trade, plant, equipment, or capital assets and debts that are about to become worthless) for the purpose of using these losses or other deductions generated thereby to offset post-affiliation consolidated taxable income attributable to other members of the group. [208] In general, built-in deductions are defined by the regulations as those that are economically accrued by the subsidiary in a SRLY prior to its acquisition but that are technically realized (by sale, write-off, worthlessness, abandonment, and so forth) after such acquisition in a consolidated return year as well as depreciation deductions attributable to the built-in loss element of an asset.

The term does not, however, include operating deductions or losses that are incurred economically *and* for tax recognition purposes *after* affiliation (including, for this purpose, those incurred in rehabilitating the acquired corporation). [209] These deductions are not entirely disallowed by the regula-

---

stream mergers for purposes of the rule that the group must include the income of the common parent for its entire taxable year and the income of each subsidiary for that portion of the year during which it is a member of the group.

See Rev. Rul. 82-152, 1982-2 CB 205 (merger of second-tier subsidiary into common parent of affiliated group did not cause termination of the group; Regs. §1.1502-75(d)(2)(ii) downstream merger principle applied here, even though not literally covered).

See also Prop. Regs. §1.1502-75(d)(4) (July 31, 1984) (clarification of reverse acquisition rules in the case of §368(a)(2)(E) reverse-merger transactions).

[207] See generally Rev. Rul. 72-322, 1972-1 CB 287, for an example of application of the reverse acquisition rules (may apply even though one of the corporations in a reorganization was not a member of an affiliated group prior to its acquisition); Rev. Rul. 72-30, 1972-1 CB 286; see also Rev. Rul. 73-303, 1973-2 CB 315; Rev. Rul. 76-164, 1976-1 CB 270 (in computing 50 percent ownership test, ignore old and cold stock acquired in prior unrelated transaction).

[208] Regs. §1.1502-15; see Rev. Rul. 79-279, 1979-2 CB 316 (normal operating expenses of cash-method subsidiary that were accrued in its pre-acquisition short period and paid in the consolidated return year held subject to built-in deduction limitations).

For similar limitations on built-in losses under 1986 Code §382(h), see infra ¶ 16.25, para. 4.

[209] See Mississippi Steel Corp., ¶ 71,018 P-H Memo. TC (1971) (loss allowed; postacquisition events caused the loss).

Compare Canaveral Int'l Corp., 61 TC 520 (1974) (use of built-in loss on consolidated return denied by §269 for years prior to regulation amendments). Note also that §269 can be applied to deny post-acquisition losses that would not otherwise be

tions; rather, they are treated as if sustained by the acquired corporation prior to its acquisition (in a SRLY). Hence, such deductions are subject to the limitations on the carry-over of pre-acquisition losses discussed above (i.e., they can be deducted only from the post-affiliation income generated by the new member). Thus, the acquired corporation's assets that reflect such built-in deductions must be segregated so that the subsequently realized losses therefrom will be taken only against the income of that corporation. This sanction does not apply if the corporation was acquired more than 10 years before the taxable year in question or if the aggregate basis of its assets (other than cash or goodwill) did not exceed the value of those assets by more than 15 percent.[210] Moreover, the limitations apparently do not apply to the acquiring group's *own* built-in deductions, although it is possible (but not certain) that a CRCO of the common parent's stock would bring the limitations of Regs. §1.1502-21(d)[211] into play so as to restrict such deductions to income of the old members of the group.

The built-in deduction rules of Regs. §1.1502-15 were revised and tightened in 1972 to prevent utilization of such potential losses through the device of having an older member of the group act as the ultimate acquisition receptacle for the assets (e.g., by transferring the built-in loss assets to an older member in a §351 exchange or by arranging the acquisition so that an older member of the group is the acquiring corporation, such as in a triangular merger); instead of focusing on the *member* of the group that has the built-in deduction and the date of its acquisition, the revised regulations apply the built-in deduction limitations to the *assets* acquired by the group in a tax-free, basis carry-over acquisition.

Legislation enacted in 1982 added a further restriction on acquisitions of subsidiaries by an affiliated group.[212] Under pre-1982 law, a loss group could purchase the stock of a profit subsidiary, liquidate it under former §334(b)(2), and offset any triggered income (or ITC recapture tax) against its loss carry-overs (and ITC carry-overs) in the consolidated return. To curb this practice, §338 replaced former §334(b)(2) with a short fuse (eight and one-half months) election, under which a corporation purchasing control of the stock of another corporation can treat the transaction as a deemed asset purchase. The effect of an election under §338 is to trigger any gain or ITC recapture tax liability outside of the purchaser's consolidated return (the

---

inhibited by the consolidated return regulation limitations; see Hall Paving Corp. v. US, supra note 141.

[210] See Rev. Rul. 83-14, 1983-1 CB 199 (for this purpose, parent's ELA in subsidiary's stock is subtracted from aggregate asset basis in determining whether built-in loss limitation applies).

[211] Supra note 203.

[212] Supra note 199; supra ¶ 15.23, notes 168, 169, and 171.

result that would have occurred if assets, rather than stock, had been acquired). If §338 is not elected (or if no election is made and the subsidiary is liquidated under §332), its asset basis and tax history will be preserved (or carried over), and no recapture will result.

Finally, legislation enacted in 1986[213] repealed the corporate level non-recognition rules of former §§336 and 337 (except for qualified §332 liquidations). The 1986 legislation also dealt with so-called dual resident corporations in §1503(d), by imposing an SRLY-type limitation on such entities (under which losses of the U.S. corporation cannot be used—currently or by carry-over—to offset U.S. taxable income of any other member of the affiliated group[214] if such losses also served to reduce foreign tax liability of any foreign corporation).[215]

These principles may be illustrated by the following examples in which P and its wholly owned subsidiary, S file consolidated returns.

Example 1. If P and S have profits, and if P acquires all the stock of loss company, T (either by purchase, or in a tax-free reorganization), P and S cannot make use of T's loss carry-overs on the consolidated return because of the SRLY rules.

Example 2. If, instead, P and S had the loss carry-overs and T was a profitable corporation, P's acquisition of T and use of its profits to absorb consolidated loss carry-over deductions is not prohibited by the regulation so long as the acquisition of T by P does not constitute a reverse acquisition (i.e., T's shareholders do not end up owning more than 50 percent of the value of P's stock) and so long as there is no CRCO of P.

Example 3. If the acquisition of T in Example 2 constitutes a reverse acquisition by P, however, P and S's loss carry-overs are treated as having arisen in SRLYs (i.e., they can only be used against future profits of P and S (the old members) on the consolidated return).

Example 4. If a CRCO occurs with respect to P in Example 2 above, P and S (the old members) will be limited in the use of their loss

---

[213] Tax Reform Act of 1986, supra note 172. For the mirror subsidiary problem, see supra text at notes 174–176.

[214] See H.R. Rep. No. 841, 99th Cong., 2d, Sess. 656–658 (the intent of this amendment is to prevent the double use of the loss against both U.S. and foreign taxable income).

[215] The "double-dip" utilization of losses is what is restricted by this provision; that is, if no foreign taxes of any member of the group are reduced by the loss, this limitation is inapplicable.

carry-overs to their own future profits (the income of the new member, *T*, cannot be utilized to absorb the carry-overs in the consolidated return).

Example 5. If both a CRCO and a reverse acquisition occur with respect to *P* and *T* in Example 2, *P* and *S* continue to be treated as the old members and their loss carry-overs can only be used against their future profits.

Example 6. If *P* and *S* have operating loss carry-overs (and ITC carry-overs) and *P* (or *S*) purchases all of *T*'s stock (*T* being a profitable corporation), and *T* is then promptly liquidated under §332, *P* (or *S*) under pre-1982 law would have obtained a stepped-up basis for *T*'s assets, and *T*'s recapture gain could be set off by the *P-S* group's loss carry-over. Under the 1982 amendments, however, *P* is put to a choice: Liquidate *T* under §332 and have *T*'s basis and tax history carry over, or make the §338 election, under which *P* (or *S*) would be treated as if *T*'s assets had been purchased, and *T*'s gain must be reported in *T*'s separate return rather than in the *P* group's consolidated return.

Example 7. If *S* has a loss that also is used to reduce foreign tax liability of *P*'s foreign subsidiary, under §1503(d) this "double-dip" loss is restricted to any future taxable income generated by *S*.

2. Rules applicable for consolidated to separate return outbound transactions. The rules governing the carry-over or carry-back of consolidated net operating losses *from* a consolidated return year *to* a separate return year of the members of the group are found in Regs. §1.1502-79(a). In brief, these provide that:

(1) That portion of an unabsorbed consolidated net operating loss that is attributable to an affiliate who was a member of the group during the year the loss was sustained may be carried back or carried forward to a separate return year of such member; the portion of the loss attributable to each member of the group is determined on the basis of the relative amounts of separate net operating losses of each member of the group which sustained losses during the year.[216]

---

[216] Note, however, that Regs. §1.1502-79(a)(1)(ii) requires the consolidated net operating loss carry-over attributable to the departing member *first* to be absorbed by any available consolidated income of the group for the CRY in which such member leaves the group; only the unabsorbed amount of such carry-over stays with the

(2) That portion of a consolidated net operating loss that is attributable to a member of the group not in existence in a potential carry-back year will be carried back to prior consolidated return years of the group (or to the equivalent separate return year of the common parent), provided such member became a member of the group immediately after its organization.[217] (The offspring rule of Regs. §1.1502-79(a)(2), described previously, would be clarified and significantly restricted, however, by pending regulations proposed on July 31, 1984).

(3) Under the proposed regulation, losses attributable to a member whose stock becomes worthless during or subsequent to the consolidated net operating loss year were attributed solely to such member. These losses ordinarily would be wasted, since they could not be carried forward to later consolidated return years of the continuing members of the group.[218] This provision was omitted from the final regulations, however, which are silent on the question.[219]

---

departing member when it leaves the group. As Regs. §1.1502-79(a)(4), Example (2) indicates, loss carry-overs attributable to the departing member can be drained off from such member by the existence of consolidated taxable income of the group for the entire year of the departure.

[217] Rev. Rul. 74-610, 1974-2 CB 288 (consolidated net operating loss attributable to new second-tier subsidiary can be carried back to SRY of first-tier subsidiary but not to SRY of parent); Rev. Rul. 80-79, 1980-1 CB 191 (consolidated net operating loss carry-back generated by newly organized parent corporation cannot be carried back to SRY of member subsidiaries; theory of Rev. Rul. 74-610 elaborated); Rev. Rul. 75-54, 1975-1 CB 293 (consolidated unused investment credits of two sister subsidiaries can be carried back to separate return year of common parent). To the same effect under prior law, see Rev. Rul. 64-93, 1964-1 CB 329; see also Rev. Rul. 69-263, 1969-2 CB 171. But see J.A. Tobin Constr. Co., supra note 196 (dictum contra to Rev. Rul. 80-79).

See also Electronic Sensing Prods., Inc., 69 TC 276 (1977) (carry-back attributable to losses of subsidiary cannot be taken to parent's SRY because subsidiary in existence during that year and filed separate return; hence, carry-back could only go to SRY of subsidiary); J.A. Tobin Constr. Co., supra (carry-back generated by parent not allowed in SRY of subsidiary because parent, although inactive, mistakenly filed separate return; also, carry-back generated by sister subsidiary had to be carried to its immediate parent, not its sibling, under Rev. Rul. 74-610).

[218] But see US v. Northern R.R., 334 F2d 936 (1st Cir. 1964), reaching a contrary result; there, the court permitted carry-over of a consolidated net operating loss generated by the sale of assets of two subsidiaries (which thereafter became dormant) to later SRYs of the parent. To the same effect is Joseph Weidenhoff, Inc., 32 TC 1222 (1959) (acq.); Hawaiian Trust Co. v. US, supra note 141; see also F.C. Donovan, Inc. v. US, 261 F2d 470 (1st Cir. 1958); J.A. Tobin Constr. Co., supra note 196.

[219] Worthlessness of the member's stock, however, is an event that will trigger recognition of the parent's ELA with respect to such member under Regs. §1.1502-

These principles set out in (1) and (2) above can be illustrated by the following example:

> *To illustrate:* Assume that *P* was organized on January 1 of year 1 and filed a separate return for that calendar year. *P* formed *S*, a subsidiary, on June 30 of year 2, and *P* and *S* thereafter filed a consolidated return for year 2. On January 1 of year 3, *P* purchased all the stock of *T*, which had been filing separate returns for prior years. *P*, *S*, and *T* join in filing a consolidated return for year 3, during which period the group sustains a consolidated net operating loss of $100, $10 of which is attributable to *P*, $30 to *S*, and $60 to *T*. Only $40 of the consolidated net operating loss (that portion attributable to *P* and *S*), can be carried back to *P*'s year 1 separate return year; any unconsumed portion of this amount is then carried to *P* and *S*'s year 2 consolidated return year to the extent of their income for such period. The portion of the year 3 consolidated loss attributable to *T* ($60) is carried back to *T*'s separate return years; the unconsumed portion, if any, is carried forward as part of the group's consolidated net operating loss carry-over deduction to post-year 3 years if *P*, *S*, and *T* continue to file consolidated returns.

3. Other limitations on survival of corporate tax attributes applicable to affiliated groups. The consolidated return regulations specifically warn that the Code, or other general principles of law, continues to apply to affiliated groups to the extent not excluded thereby; of special note in this respect is the express reference in these regulations to §§269 and 482.[220] Hence, intercompany (or extragroup) transactions may result in a reallocation of the group's income and/or deductions under §482 in order to clearly reflect its income (as discussed earlier),[221] or in a limitation of net operating loss carry-overs of a newly acquired affiliate under §382(a), or a disallowance of benefits for tax-motivated acquisitions under §269 (see Chapter 16).[222]

19(b)(2), so that the loss carry-over could then be absorbed by income generated from this event.

[220] Regs. §1.1502-80.

[221] For example, if one member of the group is subject to SRLY restrictions, other members may be tempted to inflate the restricted member's earnings by dealing with it on non-arm's length terms.

[222] See R.P. Collins & Co. v. US, supra note 141, and Hall Paving Co. v. US, supra note 141, in which §269 was invoked to deny not only built-in losses of a newly acquired affiliate, but also post-affiliation operating losses generated thereby, which the court held to be "tarred with the same brush." Regs. §1.1502-15 may be contrary to the *Collins* and *Hall Paving* decisions on the latter point. Compare Zanesville Inv. Co. v. CIR, supra note 141, where the court refused to apply §269 to disallow deduc-

As to the relationship of the *Libson Shops* doctrine[223] to the consolidated returns area, see *F.C. Donovan, Inc. v. US.*[224] Note also that the consolidated return regulations themselves incorporate limitation principles similar to *Libson's* continuity of business enterprise approach where pre-affiliation tax attributes are sought to be carried into a consolidated return. On the other hand, where affiliated corporations file consolidated returns during the period when a particular member's tax attributes are generated, it is generally assumed that *Libson* would not apply to restrict the transfer of these attributes to other members of the affiliated group, since the fact of filing consolidated returns causes the group to be treated as a single business enterprise.

---

tions for post-affiliation losses incurred by a recently acquired corporation that filed a consolidated return with the profitable affiliate. See discussion infra ¶ 16.21; Adlman, Recent Cases Increasingly Extend Section 269 to Disallow Post-Acquisition Operating Losses, 17 J. Tax'n 282 (1962).

See also discussion of the *Spreckels* and *Elko Realty* decisions, supra note 139, where the provisions of §269 (or general business purpose principles) were invoked to deny inclusion of the acquired corporation as a member of the affiliated group, a more drastic approach than disallowing the use of its tax attributes in the group's consolidated return.

For an argument that the consolidated return regulations' limitations are sufficient here, see Dunn, The New Consolidated Return Regulations May Preempt the Field in Determining the Allowance of Operating Losses, 23 Tax L. Rev. 185 (1968); see generally Goldman, Joining or Leaving an Affiliated Group Which Files a Consolidated Return: A Checklist, 36 Tax L. Rev. 197 (1981); see also Snyder & Gonick, supra note 150.

[223] Infra ¶ 16.26.

[224] F.C. Donovan, Inc. v. US, supra note 218.

CHAPTER 16

Corporate Tax Attributes: Survival and Transfer

PART A.　BACKGROUND AND INTRODUCTION

¶ 16.01　CORPORATE TAX ATTRIBUTES IN GENERAL

In general, a corporation is treated as an independent taxable entity, unaffected by either the identity of its shareholders or changes in their composition, as discussed in Chapter 1. Moreover, changes in the character of its business activity ordinarily do not affect its tax position. The same can also be said of changes in its financial structure, such as refinancing operations, recapitalizations, and the like. However, the combination of a change in business, a change in financial structure, and a change in stock ownership may have unfavorable tax consequences to the corporation despite its continuity as a legal entity. In addition, if the corporation participates in a merger or consolidation or if all or a part of its assets are acquired by another corporation, a myriad of difficult tax questions arises. Does the transferor corporation's taxable year end? Does the basis of the transferred properties carry over to the acquiring corporation? Does the acquiring corporation inherit the predecessor corporation's earnings and profits (or deficit) and net operating loss and capital loss carry-overs? Must or may new elections be made by the acquiring corporation as to the accounting methods, inventory valuation, depreciation practices, and installment sales of the transferor corporation?

Before the enactment of the 1954 Code, there were statutory rules providing for the carry-over of basis for property transferred in tax-free reorganization exchanges (see Chapter 14), but the transfer of other corporate tax attributes was not spelled out in the statutes; and some courts relied heavily on form in determining whether the "new" corporation was or was not a continuation of the old corporation. In 1954, Congress set forth specific rules in §381 to provide for the carry-over of some corporate tax attributes in certain tax-free acquisitions. But the list of items that carry over to the transferee was not exhaustive, and not all tax-free transfers were included in the statutory scheme. Thus, the confusion of prior law was perpetuated as to these uncodified matters.

Moreover, numerous other statutory provisions and judicial doctrines must be considered in determining the survival quotient of various corporate tax attributes. Thus, §382 limits the use of a corporation's net operating loss carry-overs; §269 prohibits certain acquisitions whose principal purpose is the avoidance of taxes; §446(b) empowers the Service to adjust certain tax accounting practices in order to clearly reflect income; §482 permits allocation of income and deductions among related taxpayers to prevent avoidance of taxes or to clearly reflect income; §61 is interpreted to require that "income must be taxed to the one who earns it"; §1551 (before its virtual demise in 1975) denied surtax exemptions and minimum accumulated earnings tax credits to corporations created for the major purpose of tax avoidance; §1561 (the de facto replacement of §1551) automatically does the same if a controlled group exists; and finally, the judicial principles and attitudes inspired by *Gregory v. Helvering* and applying to tax avoidance, sham, business purpose, form versus substance, and economic reality are a brooding omnipresence in this area.[1]

This combination of a technical and complicated statute, interspersed with vague and uncertainly applied judicial doctrines, makes the task of the tax adviser a formidable one indeed. Moreover, the careful attorney must be able to sense, perhaps instinctively, the outer limits of judicial tolerance with respect to a particular transaction in order adequately to advise at what point a court is liable to invent a new judicial doctrine (or revitalize an old one) to strike down what is a case of abuse. Although this approach does not yield ready answers, it is nevertheless essential to understanding the realities of the tax law in this area.

As an initial matter, the following factors have at one time or another been emphasized by the courts and Congress in determining whether a corporation's tax attributes will survive business, legal, and financial readjustments of its corporate enterprise: (1) the form of the readjustment (i.e., whether the transaction affects the corporation's "continuity of legal entity"); (2) continuity of the corporation's business activities; (3) continuity of its shareholder ownership; and (4) the element of tax windfall or tax avoidance with respect to the transaction (i.e., whether tax motives, as opposed to business or nontax motives, animated the arrangement). Negotiability of a corporation's tax attributes seems to depend, in the final analysis, on the taxpayer's showing of a favorable balance of these factors.

The difficult matter, however, is to determine which of these factors is to be considered as controlling in a given case and how much weight is to be given to a particular factor in making this determination. The subject has been in a state of flux for decades, and Congress's attempts at legislative specificity, culminating in the overhaul of §382 by the Tax Reform Act of 1986, have still not resolved many of the conflicts that can develop between taxpayers and the government in this area. It seems safe to say, however, that the judicial climate is hostile to taxpayer efforts to secure corporate tax benefits by merger or other forms of acquisition; some judges and commentators apparently feel that traffic in corporate tax benefits (most notably net operating loss carry-overs) is akin to original sin, although not all authorities are so disposed.[2] In any event, the taxpayer must thread his way through a

---

[1] Gregory v. Helvering, 293 US 465 (1935), discussed supra ¶¶ 13.02 and 14.51.

[2] See Tarleau, The Place of Tax Loss Positions in Corporate Acquisitions, cited in Joint Committee on the Economic Report, Federal Tax Policy for Economic Growth and Stability, 84th Cong., 1st Sess. 513, 610 (1955). Compare Staff Report of the FTC, Economic Report on Corporate Mergers, Part A, Hearings Before the Sub-

formidable array of statutory provisions and court decisions, most of which are designed to separate bona fide business transactions from those freighted with tax-avoidance motives.

Before turning to an analysis of these matters, several observations should be made. Most of the litigation and statutory complexities in this area relate to net operating loss carry-over and carry-back deductions, and hence this tax attribute will receive the major emphasis in the materials that follow. However, numerous other corporate tax attributes may be important in a given case: for example, earnings and profits or deficits; graduated rate brackets and minimum accumulated earnings tax credits; tax credits; accounting methods and elections; and potential loss situations (i.e., high-basis corporate assets with low current values). In general, the principles applicable to the survival of net operating loss carry-overs apply with equal force to these other corporate tax attributes and will be so treated in the ensuing discussion, but there are some exceptions, as will be noted hereafter.

On the special role of tax motive in this area, it should be noted that several statutory provisions specifically turn on the presence or absence of tax-avoidance motives or purposes with respect to a particular transaction; many of these sections have been noted at other points in this work. On the other hand, the statute also contains many rule of thumb provisions designed to block certain tax advantages by establishing mechanical tests rather than attempting to plumb the taxpayer's state of mind. Moreover, the Code also sanctions certain elections and other choices, even though tax motivation is obviously the determining factor.[3] Finally, if a particular

---

comm. on Antitrust and Monopoly of the Senate Judiciary Comm., 91st Cong., 1st Sess. (1969), for a more hostile view of tax loss carry-overs.

More currently, see Joint Committee on Taxation, Special Limitations on the Use of Net Operating Loss Carryovers and Other Tax Attributes of Corporations (JCS-16-85), May 21, 1985, a Staff pamphlet describing various proposals to limit the use of loss carry-overs prepared for hearings of the Ways and Means Subcommittee on Select Revenue Measures, held on May 22, 1985 (reprinted in DTR (BNA) No. 94, May 22, 1985).

[3] State of mind controlling: §269; §1551; the device clause of §355(a)(1)(B) (supra ¶ 13.07); §367 (infra ¶ 17.40); §357(b) (supra ¶ 3.06); §531 (supra ch. 8, Part A); §341 (supra ¶ 12.01).

Rules of thumb: §267 (losses on sales between related taxpayers); §541 (personal holding company penalty tax, supra ch. 8, Part B); §§355(b) and 302(e)(2) (five-year active business rules for corporate divisions and partial liquidations, supra ¶¶ 13.06 and 9.08–9.12); §382 (limitations on corporate net operating loss carry-overs); §1561 (controlled group benefits, supra ¶ 15.02).

Elections: §333, before its repeal in 1986 (tax-free liquidations, supra ¶ 11.62); §338 (stepped-up basis acquisitions, supra ¶ 11.46); §337, before its repeal in 1986 (tax-free liquidation sales, supra ¶ 11.61); §1361 (Subchapter S elections, supra ch. 6); §1501 (consolidated return election, supra ¶ 15.20).

transaction is too heavily laden with tax-avoidance motives or if it appears to lack economic reality, courts may ignore it as a sham or collapse the interdependent steps into what is essentially a single transaction; here one invariably sees a citation to *Gregory v. Helvering.* [4] Thus, some tax motivated transactions are acceptable, others are not, and in still other situations, tax motivation is merely a neutral factor. Determining in which of the above categories a particular transaction belongs is, of course, the difficult question, and, as one would expect, courts are not unanimous in their treatment. At the very least, however, the presence of tax motives with respect to a transaction tends to poison the atmosphere, so that courts will scrutinize the facts with special care to see whether the transaction is in substance what it purports to be in form.

¶ 16.02   ACQUISITION OF TAX BENEFITS: A CHRONOLOGY OF MAJOR DEVELOPMENTS

1. Legislative chronology in general. Before attempting an analysis of the cases and statutory provisions relating to the survival of corporate tax attributes, a brief review of the historical developments in this area may prove helpful. Congress, with an assist from the courts, has constructed a formidable defense against taxpayer efforts to traffic in net operating losses and other corporate tax benefits. As early as the Revenue Act of 1924, when the predecessor of §482 was enacted, the statute empowered the Service to reallocate income and deductions among related taxpayers in order to prevent avoidance of taxes and to clearly reflect income. Moreover, the net operating loss provisions of the 1939 Code restricted the use of net operating losses to "the taxpayer" who sustained the loss (1939 Code, §122).[5] In 1943, the predecessor of §269 was enacted (1939 Code, §129), the terms of which disallowed any deduction, credit, or other allowance in the case of certain acquisitions of stock or property where the principal purpose of the acquisition was income tax avoidance. The Revenue Act of 1951 added a more limited provision (the predecessor of §1551), disallowing multiple surtax exemptions where tax avoidance was the major purpose for creation of the corporation, and the 1954 Code

---

See generally Cohen, Taxing the State of Mind, 12 Tax Executive 200 (1960); Note, State of Mind Analysis in Corporate Taxation, 69 Colum. L. Rev. 1224 (1969).

[4] Gregory v. Helvering, supra note 1, discussed supra ¶¶ 13.02 and 14.51.

[5] As will be seen (infra ¶ 16.26), the reference to "the taxpayer," which became very important under the 1939 Code, was omitted from the corresponding provision (§172) of the 1954 Code.

broadened this provision to include multiple accumulated earnings tax credits as well (see Chapter 15).

In 1954, Congress legislated generally in the corporate carry-over area, providing first in §381 that certain items of a corporation's tax history would survive certain types of corporate adjustments, but going on in §382 to limit the survival of net operating loss carry-overs where prescribed continuity of business and continuity of ownership standards were not satisfied. In 1971, the provisions of §382 were broadened to cover a wider list of carry-over items by the enactment of §383; subsequently, Congress drastically overhauled §382 in the Tax Reform Act of 1976, materially tightening its application and effect (but this provision never became effective); and finally, the Tax Reform Act of 1986 succeeded in revising the limitations of §382.[6]

In a related legislative development, the Revenue Act of 1964 launched a major assault on the multiple corporation problem by a combination of the carrot and the stick—that is, affiliated groups willing to renounce multiple surtax exemptions could either file a consolidated return or get complete tax immunity for their intragroup dividends under §§243(a)(2) and 243(b); but members of an affiliated group that did not travel one of these routes had to give up their right to multiple exemptions (§1561) or pay an additional tax of 6 percent on a certain portion of their income for the privilege of retaining multiple exemptions. The Tax Reform Act of 1969 followed up this attack on the tax shelters of affiliated groups by providing in §1564 for the automatic abolition of their benefits in stages over a six-year period commencing in 1970.[7] These provisions have largely supplanted the tax-avoidance rules of §1551.

2. Major judicial developments. On the judicial scene, things began badly for taxpayers with the case of *Woolford Realty Co. v. Rose,* where the Supreme Court held that preaffiliation net operating losses of an acquired corporation could not be deducted in computing the postaffiliation consolidated return income of the affiliated group, stating that "the reaction of an impartial mind is little short of instinctive that the deduction is unreasonable and cannot have been intended by the framers of the statute."[8] Several years later, in *New Colonial Ice Co. v. Helvering,* net operating loss carry-overs again were denied.[9] There, assets of the loss corporation were

---

[6] For §381, see infra Part B. The history of §382 is discussed infra ¶¶ 16.22 and 16.23.

[7] See generally supra ¶ 15.02.

[8] Woolford Realty Co. v. Rose, 286 US 319 (1932).

[9] New Colonial Ice Co. v. Helvering, 292 US 435 (1934).

absorbed by a newly created corporation organized for the purpose of taking over the business of the loss corporation, which sought to offset these losses against its current income. The reorganization transaction in *New Colonial* probably constituted a Type F reorganization under present law, but did not qualify as a Type A (statutory merger) reorganization. The Court held that the resulting corporation was not the same taxpayer as the corporation that sustained the losses (despite the fact that the creditors, capital structure, and businesses of both corporations were substantially identical); accordingly, it was not entitled to carry over the losses of its predecessor as a deduction against current income.

In effect, the Court adopted an entity theory with regard to the survival of net operating loss carry-overs and thereby restricted the deduction for such losses to the same legal entity that incurred the loss. The *New Colonial* doctrine dominated the reorganization scene for two decades, and well-advised taxpayers tried to arrange to have the loss corporation emerge as the surviving corporation in a reorganization transaction so that its loss carry-overs (or other beneficial tax attributes) would be preserved; this in turn led to some unwieldy amalgamations, and instances of "minnows swallowing whales" were fairly common during this period.

In *Helvering v. Metropolitan Edison Co.*, however, tax attributes were held to carry over to a successor corporation where the reorganization took the form of a statutory merger; the issue was the successor corporation's right to deduct unamortized bond discount on its predecessor's obligations assumed by operation of law in the merger, and the Court noted that in a statutory merger, "the corporate personality of the transferor is drowned in that of the transferee." [10] Moreover, courts fairly consistently held that an acquired corporation's accumulated earnings and profits account carried over to the acquiring corporation in a nondivisive corporate fusion transaction. The leading case on this point is *CIR v. Sansome.* [11] The *Sansome* doctrine was said to be grounded not on a theory of continuity of corporate enterprise, but rather on the need to prevent avoidance of tax on the absorbed corporation's accumulated earnings; [12] with this as its rationale, the

---

[10] Helvering v. Metropolitan Edison Co., 306 US 522 (1939).

[11] CIR v. Sansome, 60 F2d 931 (2d Cir.), cert. denied, 287 US 667 (1932).

[12] Compare CIR v. Phipps, 336 US 410 (1949) (deficit of subsidiary liquidated tax-free into its parent did not absorb the parent's accumulated earnings and profits), with *Sansome;* see also CIR v. Munter, 331 US 210 (1947); US v. Snider, 224 F2d 165 (1st Cir. 1955).

For discussion of the pre-1954 treatment of earnings and profits and deficits in a reorganization, see Rice, Transfers of Earnings and Deficits in Tax-Free Reorganizations: The Sansome-Phipps Rule, 5 Tax L. Rev. 523 (1950); Note, Corporate Reorganizations and Continuity of Earning History: Some Tax Aspects, 65 Harv. L. Rev. 648 (1952).

Sansome principle played a limited role in determining the extent to which other corporate tax attributes survive a tax-free acquisition.

The *New Colonial* and *Metropolitan Edison* cases occupied center stage in the carry-over area until enactment of the 1954 Code. During this period, carry-overs generally could be preserved if taxpayers were careful to continue the existence of the loss corporation's legal entity. An extreme example of this approach was *Alprosa Watch Corp.,* where the Tax Court allowed various loss deductions despite radical changes in the taxpayer corporation's stock ownership and business activities.[13] All of the taxpayer's stock had been sold to new owners, who then proceeded to discontinue the loss business and embark on a new line of activity—in effect, all that continued was the corporate shell.[14]

Thus, as of the date of the enactment of the 1954 Code, the survival of corporate tax attributes was determined primarily by reference to the form of the particular acquisition transaction. The entity theory of *New Colonial* was the dominant theme, permitting favorable corporate tax characteristics to be preserved by having the corporation whose tax attributes were most desirable emerge as the surviving corporation. Alternatively, for those with

---

For the 1954 Code rules, see Halperin, Carryovers of Earnings and Profits, 18 Tax L. Rev. 289 (1963); Nesson, Earnings and Profits Discontinuities Under the 1954 Code, 77 Harv. L. Rev. 450 (1964); Testa, "Earnings and Profits" After Bankruptcy Reorganization, 18 Tax L. Rev. 573 (1963).

[13] Alprosa Watch Corp., 11 TC 240 (1948).

[14] Similarly, carry-overs and carry-backs generally were allowed across the line of corporate fusion where the reorganization transaction took the form of a statutory merger. In Stanton Brewery, Inc. v. CIR, 176 F2d 573 (2d Cir. 1949), for example, operating losses of a wholly owned subsidiary that merged into its parent holding company were allowed as a carry-over to the parent. Similarly, Newmarket Mfg. Co. v. US, 233 F2d 493 (1st Cir. 1956), cert. denied, 353 US 983 (1957), allowed a carry-back of post-acquisition losses after a profitable corporation had reincorporated in another state through a statutory merger into its wholly owned subsidiary. If the acquisition did not follow the statutory merger route but took the form of a §332 liquidation or a Type C practical merger, however, carry-over of the transferor corporation's tax attributes ordinarily was denied under the principle of *New Colonial Ice.*

See also Koppers Co. v. US, 134 F. Supp. 290 (Ct. Cl. 1955), cert. denied, 353 US 983 (1957) (carry-back of post-merger excess profits tax credits to pre-merger taxable years of affiliated group that had been filing consolidated returns allowed); E. & J. Gallo Winery v. CIR, 227 F2d 699 (9th Cir. 1955) (surviving corporation in statutory merger allowed to carry over operating loss deductions of absorbed corporation); Patten Fine Papers, Inc. v. CIR, 249 F2d 776 (7th Cir. 1957) (no carry-over on §332 liquidation): Dumont Airplane & Marine Instruments, Inc., 28 TC 1308 (1957) (same for Type C reorganization); compare F.C. Donovan, Inc. v. US, 261 F2d 470 (1st Cir. 1958) (liquidation of subsidiary under §332; post-liquidation losses arising from the former subsidiary's business allowed as carry-backs to pre-liquidation years of the subsidiary).

stronger nerves, the *Metropolitan Edison* statutory merger route offered a reasonable chance of success if, under local law, it could be shown that the absorbed corporation's legal identity was submerged by operation of law into that of the acquiring corporation. While subject to the criticisms that formal legal doctrines inevitably inspire, matters were reasonably predictable in this area, at least for the well advised.

However, in *Libson Shops v. Koehler,* the Supreme Court overturned (or ignored) several well-settled assumptions in this area, propounded a new doctrinal limitation on the carry-over of corporate tax attributes, and stirred up a hornet's nest of confusion, the outer limits of which may still be unresolved.[15] *Libson* involved a statutory merger of 16 brother-sister corporations (all owned by the same shareholders in the same proportions, and each of which operated a separate retail store) into another similarly controlled corporation, which then sought to apply the pre-merger net operating losses of three of those corporations against its post-merger income. The loss stores continued to lose money after the merger. The carry-over was denied on the ground that the income against which the deduction was claimed was not produced by "substantially the same business which incurred the losses"; the net operating loss deduction was intended to average out the income from a single business, said the Court, not to permit the pre-merger losses of one business to be offset against the post-merger income of another business. *Newmarket* and *Koppers*[16] were distinguished as involving essentially a single business enterprise.

Libson Shops's loss tracing test thus injected a new requirement into the carry-over area and enabled the Court to avoid deciding whether to follow the strict entity theory of *New Colonial* or instead to adopt the "merger of identity by operation of law" approach of *Metropolitan Edison.* Moreover, the *Libson* opinion seemed concerned with the possibility of a tax windfall if the carry-overs had been allowed as deductions. Absent the merger, operating losses of the three loss corporations could not have been offset against profits of the other corporations, since consolidated returns had not and could not have been filed prior to the merger.[17]

The current status of the *Libson* decision, which has generated an inordinate amount of judicial, administrative, and academic turmoil, is considered fully later in this chapter.

---

[15] Libson Shops v. Koehler, 353 US 382 (1957).

[16] Koppers Co. v. US, supra note 14; Newmarket Mfg. Co. v. US, supra note 14.

[17] A consolidated return could not have been filed by the 16 corporations unless there had been a reshuffling of stock ownership to give them a common parent; see supra ¶ 15.21. For the continued presence of *Libson*-type limitations in the consolidated return regulations provisions, see supra ¶ 15.24.

3. Revision of the 1954 Code statutory regime. After 22 years of traffic control under the 1954 Code rules of §§381 and 382, Congress returned to the carry-over scene in the Tax Reform Act of 1976, which extensively amended §382 to substantially broaden the scope and impact of that provision. This provision had a delayed effective date, however, which was repeatedly extended until 1986, when Congress finally repealed the 1976 provisions retroactively.[18]

Interest in §382 reform revived in the ensuing decade, and preliminary proposals by the staff of the Senate Finance Committee, released on September 22, 1983, sought to replace the present acquisitive reorganization rules of §368 with an elective carry-over basis (and tax history) system for all qualified corporate acquisitions. These proposals also would have replaced §§269 and 382 (and the 1976 Act pending amendments thereto) with a new set of objective limitations under which the acquiring corporation would be denied any greater benefit than would have been available before the acquisition.[19] The staff's final report was released on May 20, 1985, and the loss carry-over limitation proposal was materially revised in the final version. The dual limitation approach in the preliminary proposal was replaced with a single limitation, based on the acquisition value of the loss corporation, the key feature of which was adoption of the neutrality principle.[20]

The Tax Reform Act of 1986, in its extensive revision of §382, generally adopted an approach similar to the Senate Finance Committee staff's May 1985 final report by providing for a single limitation based on acquisition value and a prescribed absorption rate, which is triggered by a significant

---

[18] See discussion infra ¶ 16.22 for a description of the 1976 proposals.

Moreover, §269A, added by the Tax Equity and Fiscal Responsibility Act of 1982, provided for broadened §482-type allocation powers to deal with personal-service corporations. See supra ¶¶ 2.07 and 15.03.

Also, the Tax Equity and Fiscal Responsibility Act of 1982 repealed §334(b)(2) and replaced these provisions with §338, under which the purchasing corporation can elect to treat a controlling stock purchase as a deemed asset acquisition (supra ¶ 11.46). Since August 31, 1982, all §332 liquidations result in basis carry-over under §334(b)(1) and tax history carry-over under §381(a)(1) (if a §338 election has *not* been made).

[19] These preliminary proposals were greatly influenced by the American Law Institute Federal Income Tax Project, Subchapter C: Proposals of the American Law Institute on Corporate Acquisitions and Dispositions (1982); see also Bacon & Tomasulo, Net Operating Losses and Credit Carryovers: The Search for Corporate Identity, 20 Tax Notes 835 (1983); Nichols, Net Operating Loss Carryovers and Section 382, 21 Tax Notes 609 (1984); supra ¶ 14.21.

[20] See also Joint Comm. on Taxation, Special Limitations on the Use of Net Operating Loss Carryovers and Other Tax Attributes of Corporations (JCS-16-85), May 21, 1985, supra note 2; Camp, Carryovers of Net Operating Losses Following Changes in Corporate Ownership, 43 NYU Inst. Fed. Tax'n ch. 3 (1985), and articles supra note 19.

(i.e., more than 50 percent) shift in the ownership of the loss corporation. This provision is considered in detail later in this chapter.

¶ 16.03 STATUTORY AND TRANSACTIONAL PATTERNS IN GENERAL

1. General. Statutory provisions relating to the survival of corporate tax attributes can be grouped into three categories, depending upon the particular function that the provision is intended to perform: (1) the basic carry-over rules of §381, which provide, with limitations, that certain enumerated tax attributes will pass from one corporation to another when the transaction constitutes a certain type of tax-free reorganization or liquidation; (2) various restrictions or limitations on the enjoyment of corporate tax attributes (such as §§269 and 382), designed to discourage acquisitions of corporations primarily because of their favorable tax characteristics; and (3) an elaborate network of provisions dealing with the multiple corporation problem, intended to reduce or eliminate undue tax advantages by operating through multiple corporate entities (e.g., §§243(b), 482, 1551, and 1561 (which has effectively supplanted §1551)), considered in Chapter 15. Alternatively, these provisions can be classified on the basis of the various transactional patterns that may invoke their operation: (1) provisions applicable to acquisitive transactions whereby one corporation absorbs the stock or assets of another (e.g., §§269, 381, and 382); (2) those that apply to divisive transactions whereby one corporation splits itself into two or more separate entities (e.g., §§243(b), 1551, 1561); and (3) those that deal with the effect of various transactions between related members of an affiated group (e.g., §§61, 446(b), and 482). Moreover, the special problems of affiliated corporations that elect to file consolidated returns are part of the statutory tapestry in this area, especially in view of the 1964 Revenue Act's announced policy of encouraging the filing of such returns. Also important to an overall view of this general area are those judicial tax avoidance doctrines concerned with matters of sham, form versus substance, business purpose, and economic reality, principles that may be invoked to safeguard the statutory provisions from the erosive effects of transactions excessively laden with tax avoidance motives. Finally, the Treasury regulations, with respect to these various statutory provisions, are of more than usual importance, especially in the consolidated returns area, where they are for all practical purposes the substantive law.

2. Acquisitions: Transactional patterns and potential limitations. Before turning to an analysis of these provisions, a brief summary of the possible transactional patterns that can occur, and of the sections potentially applicable thereto may prove helpful. In the case of acquisitive transactions, the transaction may be either taxable or tax-free and may consist of the transfer of either stock or assets of the acquired corporation. Moreover, the corporation whose favorable tax attributes are sought to be preserved may, depending upon the form of the acquisition, end up as the surviving corporation or, alternatively, may be absorbed by the other corporation.

For example, assume that *L* Corporation has a history of operating losses and *G* Corporation a history of profits and that they are owned by unrelated shareholders. If *L* buys *G's* profitable business assets for cash, it seems clear that *L's* loss carry-over deductions will not be affected by this transaction; neither §269 nor §382 (in its old or new version) would apply, and the Service has ruled that a corporation's tax attributes will not be affected (and the principles of the *Libson Shops* case will not be applied) where the corporation merely changes the character of its business.[21] As a policy matter, a loss corporation should be able to overcome its losses by acquiring profitable businesses so long as there is no substantial change in the ownership of the loss corporation. Similarly, if *L* buys *G's stock* and either liquidates *G* under §332 or keeps it alive and files consolidated returns, the Service has indicated that it will not apply *Libson Shops* or §269 (even though that provision is technicially applicable in this situation) to disallow *L's* own loss carry-over deductions.[22]

If *G* purchases *L*'s assets for cash, however, *L*'s tax attributes will not carry over to *G*, since the transaction does not constitute one of the specified types of tax-free acquisitions covered by §381(a). Hence, *L*'s tax attributes remain with it and can only be availed of against future income earned in any new ventures that *L* might undertake. If *G* buys *L*'s stock and promptly liquidates *L* under §332, the carry-over of *L*'s loss history was denied under pre-1982 law, since the liquidation of *L* was subject to the stepped-up basis rule of former §334(b)(2) and thus did not constitute a §381 transaction.[23] Alternatively, *G* may attempt to avail itself of *L*'s operating losses by filing consolidated returns with *L* (or by merging

---

[21] See Rev. Rul. 63-40, 1963-1 CB 46; Joseph Weidenhoff, Inc., 32 TC 1222 (1959); US v. Jackson Oldsmobile, Inc., 371 F2d 808 (5th Cir. 1967); Anbaco-Emig Corp., 49 TC 100 (1967) (acq.) (no de facto dissolution where corporation sold operating assets and remained inactive for two years before starting a new business; net operating losses of old business allowed as carry-overs.)

[22] See Rev. Rul. 63-40, 1963-1 CB 46; Regs. §§1.1502-21(c)(3), Example (2), and 1.1502-1(f)(2).

[23] As a result of amendments made by the Tax Equity and Fiscal Responsibility Act of 1982, however, §334(b)(2) was repealed and replaced by an elective deemed asset sale rule, §338, supra ¶ 11.46. Thus, if §338 is elected, *L*'s tax history will be purged; but if §338 is not elected, it will be preserved and carry over to *G* under §381(a)(1) on the liquidation (subject, however, to possible denial by §269(b)).

downstream into *L*), but here the provisions of §269 are a major hurdle. Also, amendments to §382 by the Tax Reform Act of 1986 will result in a limitation on the use of *L*'s losses if the change of ownership exceeds 50 percent (the change of business rule of the 1954 Code version of §382(a) was dropped). Moreover, as will be noted subsequently, courts also applied *Libson Shops* to deny *L*'s net operating loss deductions against the post-acquisition profits from *G*'s business; it was not clear, however, whether *Libson Shops*, which arose under the 1939 Code, would be applied to a taxable year governed by the 1954 Code,[24] although the 1986 amendments to §382 finally seem to have resolved this question.

If the assets of *G* are absorbed by *L* in a tax-free reorganization (e.g., by way of a Type A or Type C reorganization), §381 by its terms does not apply with respect to the corporate tax attributes of *L*; rather, that provision deals only with the tax attributes of the acquired *transferor* corporation, in this case *G*. Hence, the loss tracing principle of *Libson Shops* may prevent *L*'s loss carry-overs from being used to offset subsequent profits of the acquired business. Moreover, §382 will serve to limit the use of *L*'s loss carry-overs if the shareholders of *L* do not retain at least a 50 percent (raised from 20 percent by the Tax Reform Act of 1986) continuity of interest in the combined corporate enterprise. Finally, §269(a)(2) could apply if the principal purpose of the acquisition was to secure the benefits of a deduction that *L* would not otherwise enjoy.

If *L* instead acquires the *stock* of *G* (in a Type B reorganization), the 1954 Code version of §382(b) does not, by its terms, apply (unless *L* promptly liquidated *G* under §332, in which case the steps may be collapsed and treated, in substance, as an asset acquisition subject to old §382). But the Tax Reform Act of 1986 amendments to §382 extended the reach of that provision to stock acquisitions (and to triangular reorganizations as well) so that the step-transaction approach should ordinarily no longer be needed by the Service in this type of acquisition. Moreover, §269(a)(1) would also be applicable, so that if tax avoidance motives inspired the acquisition, this fact could defeat *L*'s attempts to use its loss carry-overs against profits of the acquired corporation (e.g., by filing consolidated returns with *G*). However, if the tax avoidance standard of §269 is satisfied, the consolidated return regulations apparently permit the loss corporation (*L*) to file a consolidated return with its newly acquired subsidiary *G* and to use its remaining loss carry-overs against the income of the profitable subsidiary (*G*) in a consoli-

---

[24] Compare Maxwell Hardware Co. v. CIR, 343 F2d 713 (9th Cir. 1965) (*Libson* superseded by 1954 Code); Clarksdale Rubber Co., 45 TC 234 (1965) (*Libson* partially displaced by 1954 Code); with J.G. Dudley Co. v. CIR, 298 F2d 750 (4th Cir. 1962) (*Libson* survives 1954 Code); and US v. Jackson Oldsmobile, Inc., supra note 21 (*Libson* applies, but taxpayer satisfied its tests). See infra ¶ 16.26.

dated return (see Chapter 15), assuming the transaction was not a reverse acquisition.

If *G* instead acquires the assets of *L* in a tax-free Type A or Type C reorganization, §381 clearly applies to the carry-over of *L*'s tax attributes to G. Moreover, the Service ruled, in Rev. Rul. 58-603, that *Libson* would not be applied to transactions of this sort, since they are specifically covered by §381(a).[25] However, §§269(a)(2) and 382 (in both its old and new versions) clearly apply in this situation, and the limitations of these provisions must be satisfied before *L*'s loss carry-over can be used by *G*.

The principles described in the preceding examples can be summarized by the following table:

Transactions	*Applicable rules*
(1) *G* acquires *L* assets in Type A or Type C reorganization	§§269(a)(2), 381, 382
(2) *G* acquires *L* stock in Type B reorganization and:	New §382 (1986 Act)
(a) files consolidated returns	§269(a)(1) and SRLY
(b) liquidates *L* (§332)	§§269(a)(2) (if step), §381, old 382(b) (if step)
(c) merges downstream into *L*	§§269(a)(2), old 382(b), and maybe *Libson*
(3) *L* acquires *G* assets in Type A or Type C reorganization	§§269(a)(2), 382, and maybe *Libson*
(4) *L* acquires *G* stock in Type B reorganization and:	New §382 (1986 Act)
(a) files consolidated returns	§269(a)(1), and SRLY
(b) liquidates *G* (§332)	§§269(a)(2), old 382(b) (if step), and maybe *Libson*
(c) merges downstream into *G*	§§269(a)(2) 381, old 382(b)
(5) *G* purchases *L* assets	None (no §381)
(6) *G* purchases *L* stock and:	New §382 (1986 Act)
(a) files consolidated returns	§§269(a)(1), old 382(a), and SRLY
(b) liquidates *L* (§332) and:	
(i) §334(b)(2) applies (§338 election)	None (no §381); (tax history purged like line (5))
(ii) §334(b)(1) applies (no §338 election)	§§269(b), 381, old 382(b) (no §338)
(c) merges downstream into *L*	269(a)(2), old §§382(b), and maybe *Libson*
(7) *L* purchases *G* assets	None
(8) *L* purchases *G* assets, but substantial change of *L* stock ownership	§269(a)(1), new §382 (1986 Act)

---

[25] Rev. Rul. 58-603, 1958-2 CB 147.

(9) *L* purchases *G* stock and:

    (a) files consolidated returns   §269(a)(1)

    (b) liquidates *G* (§332)   §381(a)(1)

    (c) merges downstream into *G*   §§381(a)(2)

3. Separations. Corporate separations (or the initial creation of multiple corporate entities) are not covered by the carry-over rules of §381 (although new §382 now can apply); even so, the Service possesses a formidable array of defenses against taxpayer abuses of the multiple corporation device. In addition to the previously noted rules of §269, which have been held applicable to corporate split-ups as well as to amalgamation transactions,[26] consideration also must be given to the interrelated provisions of §§243(b), 482, 1551, and 1561 (as well as to those general judicial principles involving assignment of income, recognition of the corporate entity, form versus substance, sham transactions, and lack of business purpose). Moreover, if an affiliated group of corporations files consolidated returns, the detailed provisions of the regulations under §1502 must also be consulted, a task of no small proportions at best. These matters are considered in detail in Chapter 15.

PART B.   CARRY-OVERS AND §381

¶ 16.10   IN GENERAL

Section 381 was enacted in 1954 to provide a comprehensive set of rules for the preservation of tax attributes, to be "based upon economic realities rather than upon such artificialities as the legal form of the reorganization."[27] The drafters hoped to protect taxpayers against the loss of favorable

---

[26] See, e.g., James Realty Co. v. US, 280 F2d 394 (8th Cir. 1960); Coastal Oil Storage Co. v. CIR, 242 F2d 396 (4th Cir. 1957); infra ¶ 16.21; supra ¶ 15.02.

The Tax Reform Act of 1986 version of §382 can apply to non-pro rata divisions that effect a substantial ownership change, infra ¶ 16.24.

[27] S. Rep. No. 1622, 83d Cong., 2d Sess. 52 (1954).

See Worthy, Carryover of Deductions, Credits and Other Tax Attributes in Corporate Adjustments and Reorganizations, 44 Taxes 919 (1966); Kaufman, Application of a Loss Carryover of One Business Against Profits From Another Business; Libson Shops, and Sections 381, 382 and 269, 24 NYU Inst. on Fed. Tax. 1199 (1966); Asimow, Detriment and Benefit of Net Operating Losses: A Unifying Theory, 24 Tax L. Rev. 1 (1968); Comment, Net Operating Loss Carryovers and Corporate Adjustments: Retaining an Advantageous Tax History Under Libson Shops and

tax attributes as well as to prevent the avoidance of unfavorable ones by paper reorganizations. The statutory rules are applicable if assets of a corporation are acquired by another corporation under the following circumstances:

(1) In a liquidation of a subsidiary under §332 unless a §338 election is made;[28]

(2) In a reorganization under §§368(a)(1)(A) (statutory merger or consolidation); 368(a)(1)(C) (acquisition of substantially all of the properties of one corporation for voting stock of another); 368(a)(1)(D) and 368(a)(1)(G) (transfer of assets to a controlled corporation or pursuant to an insolvency proceeding, but only if §§354(b)(1)(A) and 354(b)(1)(B) apply); or 368(a)(1)(F) (change in identity, form, or place of organization only).[29]

If the assets are acquired in a transaction fitting within one of the above categories, the acquiring corporation "shall succeed to and take into account" the items specified in §381(c) (i.e., net operating loss carryovers, earnings and profits, capital loss carry-overs, accounting methods, and a number of others). These items are inherited by the acquiring corporation subject to the operating rules of §381(b) and to certain limitations imposed by §381(c).[30] Because §381(c) enumerates the items to be carried forward instead of flatly providing that the acquiring corporation must step into the shoes of the transferor for all purposes, it might be inferred that unmentioned items do not go over. But the Senate Report on the 1954 Code states that §381 "is not intended to affect the carry-over

---

Sections 269, 381, and 382, 69 Yale L.J. 1201 (1960). These articles cite the most important of the very extensive earlier discussions of this area.

See also McGaffey, Utilization of Net Operating Losses, 51 Taxes 613 (1973); Milefsky, Utilization of Acquired Corporate Loss Carryovers, 3 J. Corp. Tax'n 28 (1976); N.Y. State Bar Association, Tax Section, Report on the Ancillary Tax Effects of Different Forms of Reorganizations, 34 Tax L. Rev. 477, 495 (1979).

[28] Supra ¶¶ 11.40–11.48. If §338 is elected, the subsidiary's tax history is purged; if §338 is not elected, the subsidiary's tax history carries over to the parent, subject to §269(b) (infra note 37); see supra ¶ 11.46.

[29] Supra ¶¶ 14.12, 14.14–14.16, 14.18, and 14.20.

[30] For a possible restriction on the ostensible scope of §381, see Rev. Rul. 58-603, 1958-2 CB 147, hinting that if a loss corporation is acquired in order to carry over its tax attributes to another corporation through the medium of a reorganization within the meaning of §381(a)(2), the absence of a business purpose may mean that there is no reorganization (see Regs. §1.368-1(b)), and hence that §381(a)(2) will not come into play to preserve the tax attributes for the successor corporation.

Note also the restrictions on the carry-over of net operating losses imposed by §382, infra ¶¶ 16.22–16.25.

treatment of an item or tax attribute not specified in the section."[31] It may be, therefore, that other items (e.g., amortizable research and experimental expenditures under §174, organizational expenditures under §248, soil and water conservation expenditures under §175, and foreign tax credit carry-overs under §904(d)), which are hardly distinguishable from a policy standpoint from some of those specified in §381(c), may also be carried forward; but the pre-1954 case law may be relevant to these unenumerated tax attributes.

The Senate Report also states that §381 is not intended to affect the carry-over treatment of items or tax attributes in corporate transactions not described in §381(a). Among the unlisted transactions, in which some items or attributes might be carried over, are transfers of property from one corporation to another in corporate divisions under §355 (see Chapter 13), insolvency reorganizations under former §371 (before its repeal in 1980), and some transfers of property to subsidiary corporations under §351.[32] Like the items mentioned in the previous paragraph, these transactions may be governed by the pre-1954 case law, including the loss tracing theory of *Libson Shops* and perhaps the continuity of entity theory of *New Colonial.*[33]

It should be noted that the acquiring corporation is not dependent upon §381 for the preservation of its *own* tax attributes (since §381 deals only with the tax characteristics of the transferor or distributor corporation); hence, these items will continue unimpaired even though not specified in §381(c), unless some other statutory provisions or case law principles apply.[34]

---

[31] S. Rep. No. 1622, supra note 27, at 277.

[32] As to earnings and profits in such transactions, see §312(h) and Regs. §§1.312-10 and 1.312-11.

[33] See infra ¶ 16.14 and note 77. See generally Tillinghast & Gardner, Acquisitive Reorganizations and Chapters X and XI of the Bankruptcy Act, 26 Tax L. Rev. 663 (1971); Plumb, The Tax Recommendations of the Commission on the Bankruptcy Laws—Reorganizations, Carryovers, and the Effect of Debt Reduction, 29 Tax L. Rev. 227 (1974); Glancy, Carrying Losses Through Chapter X and Chapter XI Reorganizations, 28 Tax Lawyer 27 (1974); Plumb, Bankruptcy and Insolvency: Effects of Debt Reduction on Loss Carryovers and Basis, 2 J. Corp. Tax'n 173 (1975).

The Bankruptcy Tax Act of 1980 (supra ¶ 14.20), however, created a new insolvency reorganization, the Type G, which also became a §381(a)(2) transaction if nondivisive in character.

[34] But see Stanton Brewery, Inc. v. CIR, supra note 14, for the difficulty of determining which, if any, corporation survives in a statutory merger or consolidation. See also the discussion infra Part C of the statutory and judicial limitations which may prevent a corporation's use of its own or acquired tax attributes (e.g., §§269 and 382 and the loss tracing doctrine of *Libson Shops*).

¶ 16.11　SECTION 381(a) TRANSACTIONS

The carry-over rules of §381 apply to two categories of tax-free asset acquisitions: liquidations of controlled subsidiaries under §332 if the adjusted basis of the transferred assets carries over to the parent on the liquidation and various acquisitive and nondivisive reorganization asset transfers. If the transaction fails to qualify as a tax-free liquidation or reorganization under the definitional provisions applicable thereto, the transferor's tax attributes will not carry over to the transferee. Thus, initial satisfaction of the definitional rules of §332 (see Chapter 11) or §368(a) (Chapter 14) is necessary before consideration can be given to the effects of §381.

1. Liquidation of controlled subsidiary: Section 381(a)(1). Under pre-1954 law, the *New Colonial* continuity of entity doctrine was ordinarily thought to bar a transfer of a subsidiary's tax attributes to its parent on a §332 liquidation.[35] If the liquidation took the form of a statutory merger, however, the Second Circuit held that tax attributes of the transferor corporation carried over to the transferee "by operation of law."[36] The 1954 Code altered the reliance on form in this area by permitting the carry-over of a subsidiary's tax attributes in a §332 liquidation if the tax basis of the subsidiary's assets carries over to the parent under §334(b)(1).[37]

If the subsidiary is insolvent, however, §332 does not apply to the liquidation, and hence the carry-over rules of §381 do not come into play. In this

---

[35] See, e.g., Patten Fine Papers, Inc. v. CIR, supra note 14; contra, F.C. Donovan, Inc. v. US, supra note 14. See generally supra ¶ 16.02.

[36] Stanton Brewery, Inc. v. CIR, supra note 14.

[37] Prior to 1982, §381(a)(1) did not apply to a §332 liquidation if the basis of the transferred assets was determined by reference to the cost of the subsidiary's stock under §334(b)(2) (supra ¶ 11.45); but legislation enacted in 1982 replaced §334(b)(2) with an election mechanism in §338 to treat stock purchase acquisitions as deemed asset purchases, supra ¶ 11.46. If the §338 election is not made, or if an actual liquidation under §332 occurs, tax history (and asset basis) carries over under §§334(b)(1) and 381(a)(1) (subject to the limitations of §§382 and 269). The abolition of §334(b)(2) by the Tax Equity and Fiscal Responsibility Act of 1982 thus means that all §332 liquidations result in §381(a)(1) tax history carry-over transactions (assuming that the purchased subsidiary's tax history has not been purged by a §338 election). For possible application of §269(b) (tax motivated nonelection of §338), see infra ¶ 16.21.

If the liquidation qualifies both under §332 and as a reorganization, it is probably to be treated as a liquidation by virtue of Regs. §1.332-2(d); this may be important in applying §382, which covers §381(a)(2) transactions but not, presumably, §381(a)(1) transactions; infra ¶ 16.24.

See Pacific Transp. Co., ¶ 70,041 P-H Memo. TC (1970) (§334(b)(2) liquidation via statutory merger not a reorganization for §381 carry-over purposes), rev'd on other grounds, 483 F2d 209 (9th Cir. 1973).

situation, the parent is entitled to deduct the loss on its stock or debt investments in the subsidiary and to carry any such losses to other years under §172 (net operating losses) or §1212(a) (capital losses); but the subsidiary's own tax attributes are extinguished by its liquidation.[38]

2. Reorganizations: Section 381(a)(2). The strict continuity of legal entity approach with respect to the survival of corporate tax attributes, inspired by *New Colonial* (and modified to some extent by the statutory merger exception of *Metropolitan Edison*), was rejected by the drafters of the 1954 Code. Thus §381(a)(2) lists five categories of corporate fusions (Types A, C, and F reorganizations and certain nondivisive Types D and G[39] reorganizations) where tax attributes of the transferor will carry over to the transferee. In each of these situations, the transferor corporation is in effect absorbed by the transferee; but it is no longer necessary, as was the case under pre-1954 law, for taxpayers to go through the ritual of having the loss corporation emerge as the surviving legal entity in the acquisition transaction.

Section 381 does not apply, however, to corporate divisions or recapitalizations or to some transfers of property to controlled corporations under §351; these transactions remain subject to the pre-1954 rules dealing with the preservation of corporate tax attributes.[40] As a result, the *New Colonial, Libson Shops,* and *Metropolitan Edison* lines of authority retain a limited viability under both the 1954 and 1986 Codes. Moreover, since §381 deals only with the carry-over of the transferor corporation's tax attributes, the acquiring corporation must resort to other provisions of

---

[38] See Marwais Steel Co., 38 TC 633 (1962), aff'd, 354 F2d 997 (9th Cir. 1965); Rev. Rul. 68-602, 1968-2 CB 135; Swiss Colony, Inc. v. CIR, 428 F2d 49 (7th Cir. 1970). Compare Textron, Inc. v. US, 561 F2d 1023 (1st Cir. 1977) (parent allowed §165 loss deduction for worthless investment in subsidiary despite subsequent revival of subsidiary and use by it of its carry-overs from prior loss business against profits of new business). See also Natbony, Twice Burned or Twice Blessed—Double Deductions in the Affiliated Corporation Context, 6 J. Corp. Tax'n 3 (1979); supra ¶¶ 11.41 (insolvent subsidiary) and 4.22 (investor's loss deductions).

[39] The Bankruptcy Tax Act of 1980 added insolvency reorganizations that qualify under §§354(b)(1) and 368(a)(1)(G) (supra ¶ 14.20) to the types of transactions covered by §381(a)(2).

As to insolvency reorganizations before the 1980 amendments, see Tillinghast & Gardner, supra note 33; Krantz, Loss Carryovers in Chapter X Reorganizations, 16 Tax L. Rev. 359 (1961). As to the carry-over of earnings and profits in non-§381 transactions, see Regs. §§1.312-10 and 1.312-11; articles by Halperin, Nessen, and Testa, supra note 12.

[40] See Rev. Rul. 77-133, 1977-1 CB 96 (loss carry-overs stay with distributing parent corporation in §355 split-off transaction); Rev. Rul. 56-373, 1956-2 CB 217 (carry-overs disappear in a split-up).

the law to determine the preservation of its *own* advantageous tax history (most notably §§269 and 382). Consequently, §381(a)(2) offers only a limited solution to the carry-over problem in the corporate readjustment area, albeit a considerably more rational one than that which existed under pre-1954 law.

In the case of Type C reorganizations (acquisition of substantially all the assets of one corporation for voting stock of another), some uncertainty once existed as to whether the transferor corporation had to liquidate after the transfer in order for its attributes to pass over to the transferee under §381. As a general matter, such a liquidation was not until 1984 necessary in order for the transaction to qualify as a Type C reorganization, but if the transferor continued in existence (e.g., as a holding company), and its earnings and profits passed to the transferee, it would be free to distribute its accumulated earnings to its shareholders without dividend consequences. The language of §381(a)(2) seemed to support this conclusion, and the Service ruled favorably on the issue.[41] But the Tax Reform Act of 1984, in §368(a)(2)(G), required liquidation of the transferor pursuant to the reorganization in order to qualify as a Type C reorganization.

Section 381 permits inheritance of the transferor corporation's tax attributes only by *the* acquiring corporation. The regulations state that only a single corporation can constitute the acquiring corporation[42] and that it is the corporation that ultimately acquires, directly or indirectly, all the assets transferred by the transferor; if no one corporation ultimately acquires all of the transferred assets, then it is the corporation that directly acquired them, even though none are retained by it.

> *To illustrate:* If all the assets of *T* Corporation are acquired by *P* Corporation in exchange for its stock, and thereafter, pursuant to the plan of reorganization, *P* transfers one-half of these assets to its wholly owned subsidiary *A*, and the other half to a second subsidiary *B*, *P* will be treated as the acquiring corporation. If, on the other hand, all of *T*'s assets had been acquired by *A* in exchange for stock of its parent corporation *P* (or, alternatively, if the *T* assets had been directly acquired by *P* and then retransferred by it to *A*), then *A*, as the ultimate transferee of all of the assets, would be treated as the acquiring corporation and succeed to *T*'s tax attributes.

---

[41] Rev. Rul. 68-358, 1968-2 CB 156; see also Rev. Rul. 73-552, 1973-2 CB 116 (holdback of insubstantial assets in a Type C reorganization with intent to enter into new active business did not prevent carry-over of all tax attributes under §381). See also supra ¶¶ 14.14 and 14.18.

[42] Regs. §1.381(a)-1(b)(2).

The limited category of Types D and G reorganizations covered by §381(a)(2) is designed to restrict the carry-over benefits of §381 to nondivisive transactions (see Chapter 14). In effect, this type of reorganization (like that of §368(a)(1)(F), relating to mere changes in identity, form, or place of organization), involves the reincorporation of substantially all of the transferor corporation's properties in a new corporate vehicle.[43] The Service has recognized the possible overlap of Types A, C, D, and F reorganizations in this situation, and, where such a transaction satisfies the requirements of §368(a)(1)(F), it will be treated as such for purposes of §381, even if it constitutes a Type A, C, or D reorganization as well.[44]

¶ 16.12   SPECIAL OPERATING RULES: SECTION 381(b)

By virtue of §381(b)(1), the taxable year of the transferor corporation ends with the date on which it makes one of the types of transfers specified in §381(a) (except that the acquiring corporation in a Type F reorganization is treated as the transferor corporation would have been had there been no reorganization). For this purpose, Regs. §1.381(b)-1(b) provides that the date of the transfer is the day on which the transfer is finally completed, except that the date on which substantially all of the transferor's property was transferred may be used if the transferor corporation ceases all operations (other than liquidating activities) after such date. The regulations permit the retention of a reasonable amount of assets to pay liabilities or to preserve the corporate existence and go on to state that a corporation is considered to be in a state of liquidation when it ceases to be a going concern and its activities are merely for the purpose of winding up its affairs, paying its debts, and distributing its remaining properties to shareholders.[45]

A transferor corporation whose taxable year is closed by §381(b)(1) must file a return for the short taxable year period ending on such date;

---

[43] The Type G reorganization, however, can also be acquisitive in character, as are Type A and Type C reorganizations.

[44] See Rev. Rul. 57-276, 1957-1 CB 126; see also Regs. §1.381(b)-1(a)(2); Rev. Rul. 66-284, 1966-2 CB 115; Rev. Rul. 75-561, 1975-2 CB 129; Rev. Rul. 76-188, 1976-1 CB 99 (parent's tax attributes carried over to subsidiary under §381 in transaction constituting Type C reorganization as well as §351 exchange); compare Rev. Rul. 77-133, 1977-1 CB 96 (in §355 split-off; losses stay behind with parent); Rev. Rul. 56-373, 1956-2 CB 217 (same in split-up; losses thus disappear because parent liquidates).

[45] See Rev. Rul. 70-27, 1970-1 CB 83 (taxable year closed on a transfer of all operating assets except for cash retained to pay franchise tax, directors' fees, and liquidation expenses).

For the meaning of "complete liquidation," see supra ¶¶ 2.09 and 11.02.

moreover, if it remains in existence, it must file another short taxable year return for the period ending with the date on which its regular taxable year would have ended had there been no §381(a) transfer.[46] In effect, a transferor corporation that continues in existence after a §381 transaction has two short taxable year periods in lieu of its former accounting period. This closing of the transferor's taxable year also has importance in computing the net operating loss deduction that carries over to the transferee under §381(c)(1).

Under another special rule applicable to §381 transactions, §381(b)(3) states that the acquiring corporation (except in a Type F reorganization) will not be entitled to carry back a net operating loss sustained in a taxable year ending after the date of the acquisition to a prior taxable year of the transferor corporation.[47] After losing several decisions on the question of whether two or more affiliated operating companies could combine in a Type F reorganization,[48] the Service generally conceded that parent-subsidiary and brother-sister fusions would so qualify if there was complete identity of

---

[46] However, in view of the requirement in §368(a)(2)(G) that the transferor corporation in a Type C reorganization must liquidate pursuant to the reorganization plan (supra ¶ 16.11, text at note 41), continued existence of the transferor for any appreciable period would be rare; in addition, the transferor in a Type A reorganization always liquidates by operation of law, while the Types D and G reorganizations covered by §381(a)(2) likewise effectively require liquidation of the transferor.

[47] This provision overrules the result in F.C. Donovan, Inc. v. US, supra note 14. But see Bercy Indus., Inc. v. CIR, 640 F2d 1058 (9th Cir. 1981) (forward triangular merger into new shell subsidiary not subject to §381(b)(3) limitation, even though transaction not a Type B or Type F reorganization; no tracing problems here, so post-fusion losses can be carried back to pre-fusion year of acquired corporation; court seemed to view transaction as functional equivalent of a Type B).

[48] See Estate of Stauffer v. CIR, 403 F2d 611 (9th Cir. 1968) (merger of two active affiliated corporations was a Type F reorganization for this purpose); see also Home Constr. Corp. v. US, 439 F2d 1165 (5th Cir. 1971) (merger of 123 commonly controlled corporations a Type F reorganization; post-reorganization losses carried back to pre-fusion years); Performance Sys. Inc. v. US, 382 F. Supp. 525 (M.D. Tenn. 1973), aff'd per curiam, 501 F2d 1338 (6th Cir. 1974) (same for upstream merger of a wholly owned subsidiary into parent); accord, Movie Lab Inc. v. US, 494 F2d 693 (Ct. Cl. 1974); Eastern Color Printing Co., 63 TC 27 (1974) (acq.) (liquidation of operating subsidiary by merger into holding company parent whose only asset was stock of the subsidiary, also a Type F reorganization; Tax Court did not abandon its position that merger of two operating companies does not constitute an F reorganization); Aetna Casualty & Sur. Co. v. US, 568 F2d 811 (2d Cir. 1976) (merger of 61 percent subsidiary into 100 percent newly organized subsidiary a Type F reorganization, at least for §381(b)(3) carry-backs, supra ¶ 14.53, para. 1). See also Bercy Indus., Inc. v. CIR, supra note 47 (forward triangular merger into shell subsidiary not limited by §381(b)(3); decision goes even further than Aetna). See generally McManus, Judicial Law Making: The Liquidation of a Corporation Treated as an F Reorganization, 2 J. Corp. Tax'n 273 (1975).

shareholder interests, the same (or an integrated) business was carried on by the corporation before and after the transactions, and uninterrupted business continuity exists;[49] but the Tax Equity and Fiscal Responsibility Act of 1982 amended the Type F definition and limited that provision to the reorganization of a single operating company.[50]

However, a post-acquisition net operating loss can be carried back by the acquiring corporation to its *own* preacquisition taxable years under the general rules of §172.[51]

¶ 16.13 CARRY-OVER ITEMS AND COMPUTATION MECHANICS: SECTION 381(c)

Section 381(c) enumerates 26 tax attributes of the transferor corporation that carry over to the transferee.[52] The most important of these attributes, and the principles governing their application to the transferee, are the following:

---

[49] Rev. Rul. 75-561 1975-2 CB 129 (loss carry-backs, however, will be subject to *Libson*-type tracing limitations; infra ¶ 16.26); see also Rev. Rul. 78-287, 1978-2 CB 146 (principles of Rev. Rul. 75-561 apply to downstream mergers if tests satisfied); National Tea Co., 83 TC 8 (1984), aff'd, 793 F2d 864 (7th Cir. 1986) (no carry-back because of failure to trace).

But see Berger Mach. Prods., Inc., 68 TC 358 (1977) (merger of four active brother-sister corporations not a Type F reorganization because no identity of relative shareholder interests); Romy Hammes, Inc., 68 TC 900 (1977) (merger of active brother-sister corporations not a Type F because of substantial shifts of shareholder interests, change of business and inability to trace losses) (compare with Romy Hammes, however, TFI Cos. v. US, 40 AFTR2d 5688 (C.D. Cal. 1977) (held a Type F under Rev. Rul. 75-561)); Security Indus. Ins. Co. v. US, 702 F2d 1234 (5th Cir. 1983) (stock purchase, liquidation, and retransfer of operating assets to sister subsidiary not a Type F; continuity broken by stock purchase); Superior Coach of Fla., Inc., 80 TC 895 (1983) (stock purchase by shareholder of acquiring corporation followed by merger into acquiring corporation not a §381 carry-over transaction); Cannonsburg Skiing Corp., ¶ 86,150 P-H Memo. TC (1986) (continuity broken by stock purchase step).

See generally supra ¶ 14.18, para. 3.

[50] This amendment was effective for transactions after August 31, 1982. But see Bercy Indus. Inc. v. CIR, supra note 47 (not literally covered by the 1982 amendment); moreover, Eastern Color Printing Co., supra note 48, probably would reach the same result under the 1982 amendment.

[51] See Regs. ¶ 1.381(c)(1)-1(b); for more on the net operating loss carry-over, see infra ¶ 16.13.

[52] On the possibility that other tax attributes may carry over, see the discussions supra ¶ 16.10 and infra ¶ 16.14, note 77.

1. Net operating loss carry-overs. The rules and limitations respecting inheritance of the transferor corporation's net operating loss carry-overs are found in §381(c)(1). These provisions are at points extraordinarily complex, and the regulations are even more so. Moreover, as will be subsequently noted, the form of the acquisition can still have a considerable effect in this area despite the 1954 Code's avowed aim of eliminating such distinctions.

The principal computational rules with respect to the carry-over of net operating losses from the transferor corporation to the acquiring corporation are as follows:

(1) The acquiring corporation obtains all of the transferor's unused net operating loss carry-overs, even though it acquires less than 100 percent of the acquired corporation's assets under Regs. §1.381(c)(1)-1(c)(2).

(2) If the transferor corporation continued in existence after the transfer, any post-transfer losses sustained could be carried back to its *own* pre-transfer taxable years, but could not be used by the acquiring corporation as carry-backs or carry-overs under Regs. §1.381(c)(1)-1(b) (however, the continued existence of the transferor for any appreciable period is no longer possible under §368(a)(2)(G)).

(3) The transferor corporation's taxable year closes on the effective date of the §381 transfer,[53] and this short taxable year period counts as a full year in computing the carry-back and carry-over time periods of §172(b)(1) with respect to its net operating losses under Regs. §1.381(c)(1)-1(e)(3).

(4) Under §381(c)(1)(A), the first period to which unused loss carry-overs of the transferor are to be carried is the taxable year of the acquiring corporation ending after the effective date of the §381 transfer, which period also counts as a full year in applying §172(b)(1).[54]

(5) Under §381(c)(1)(B), only part of the acquiring corporation's taxable income (computed on a daily basis) for the year during which the two corporations are combined can be offset by a net operating loss *deduction* attributable to loss carry-overs of the transferor under Regs. §1.381(c)(1)-1(d).

---

[53] Sections 381(b)(1) and 381(b)(2), supra ¶ 16.12.

[54] Because of this rule, acquisition of the loss company on the last day of that corporation's taxable year is necessary to avoid consumption of an extra loss carry-over year.

(6) Post-acquisition losses of the *acquiring* corporation cannot be carried back to pre-acquisition taxable years of the *transferor* corporation, but such losses can be carried back to prior taxable years of the *acquiring* corporation under the carry-back rules of §172 under Regs. §1.381(c)(1)-1(b).

(7) Section 381(c)(1)(C) contains elaborate rules for tracing the extent to which, and the sequence in which, the net operating loss carry-overs of both the transferor and the acquiring corporations are absorbed under §172(b)(2), Regs. §§1.381(c)(1)-1(e) and 1.381(c)(1)-1(f).

To illustrate: In the following examples, both the transferor corporation (*T*) and the acquiring corporation (*P*) use a calendar year accounting period. In addition, the acquisition transactions are effected on July 1, the midpoint of the acquiring corporation's taxable year.

Example 1: *P* Corporation owns 80 percent of *T*, which has unused loss carry-overs. *P* liquidates *T* under §332 and thereby obtains 80 percent of its assets. *P* is entitled to all of *P*'s loss carry-overs.

Example 2: *T* merges into *P*, and *P* is the surviving corporate entity; thereafter, *P* sustains a net operating loss. *P* is not entitled to carry back this loss to pre-acquisition taxable years of *T* because of §381(b)(3); however, *P* can carry back this loss to its own pre-acquisition taxable years under Regs. §1.381(c)(1)-1(b).[55]

Example 3: *T* transfers substantially all of its assets to *P* in a Type C reorganization; *T* continues in existence after the transfer and subsequently sustains net operating losses. Those losses could be carried back by *T* to its own prior taxable years, but could not be used in any way by *P*. (After 1984, however, because *T* would be required to liquidate, this situation would only rarely occur (e.g., if *T* retained "insubstantial loss assets" and sold them before liquidating).)

Example 4: At the start of year 1 (the acquisition year) *T* has an unused loss carry-over from three years earlier in the amount of $100. *T* earns

---

[55] If the acquisition had taken the form of a statutory consolidation of *T* and *P* into *Z* however, *Z*'s post-consolidation losses could not be carried back to pre-consolidation years of either *T* or *P*. Regs. §1.381(c)(1)-1(b), Example (2). Thus, if one of the combining corporations is a potential loss candidate and if a carry-back of the loss is preferable to a carry-forward, the parties should seek to preserve its legal entity.

$20 during the 183-day short period (January 1–July 1 of year 1) preceding the transfer of its assets to *P*. The $100 loss carry-over is first applied against *T*'s $20 of income for its short fiscal year ending July 1 of year 1; the unused portion ($80) is then carried to *P*'s year 1 taxable year under §381(c)(1)(A). However, *P*'s net operating loss deduction with respect to such loss is limited to 50 percent of its year 1 taxable income by virtue of §381(c)(1)(B). Thus, if *P* earned $60 of income for its year 1 taxable year, it would be entitled to claim only $30 of the $80 loss carry-over from *T* as a deduction in its year 1 return. The unused portion of *T*'s loss carry-over ($50) would then be carried to *P*'s year 2 taxable year. This would be the last available year of such loss, however; although its normal life would continue through year 3 (i.e., the fifth year after the loss arose, which was three years previous to year 1),[56] the loss aged by two years in year 1, by reason of the two short taxable years into which that year was broken.[57]

Example 5: If *P* in Example 4 also had a net operating loss carry-over of $40 from three years previous, matters become more intricate. Section 381(c)(1)(C) provides generally (first sentence) that where loss years of the transferor and the acquiring corporations overlap, priority of consumption is given to losses of the transferor. The second sentence of §381(c)(1)(C) goes on to provide, however, that in applying the loss carry-over tracing rules of §172(b)(2), *P*'s year 1 taxable year must be split into two separate periods, the pre-acquisition part year and the post-acquisition part year (since the transfer from *T* occurred within *P*'s year 1 taxable year) and that loss carry-overs from *T* will only be absorbed by the post-acquisition part year taxable income of *P* for year 1 (prorated on a daily basis). Consequently, *P*'s year-3 loss carry-over would first be applied against *P*'s year 1 pre-acquisition part year taxable income of $30; the unused $10 portion would then be carried to the post-acquisition part year, but, since the $80 loss carry-over from *T* is entitled to priority by

---

[56] The Tax Reform Act of 1976 added two years to the life of a carry-over (effective for losses incurred in years ending after 1975). The 1976 Act amendments to §172 also permit taxpayers to waive loss carry-backs. The Economic Recovery Tax Act of 1981 added eight years to carry-over lives (extending the carry-over term from 7 to 15 years, effective for losses in years after 1975). Before these amendments, the carry-over period was five years.

[57] If *P* (the profit company) had merged into *T* (the loss company) in the previous example, the result would differ in that *T*, as the surviving company, would not lose an extra year in the life of its year 3 loss carry-over. *P*'s taxable year would close on the date of the transfer, but not *T*'s.

virtue of the first sentence of §381(c)(1)(C), this $10 of *P*'s unused loss would carry over to *P*'s year 2 taxable year.[58] Because of these rules, the party with the larger and older carry-overs should, where possible, generally be cast as the acquiring corporation.

2. Earnings and profits. Another major corporate tax attribute that carries over to the acquiring corporation under §381 is the earnings and profits (or deficit) account of the transferor, §381(c)(2). The applicable rules codify much of the pre-1954 case law on this subject. Thus, the *Sansome* rule (earnings and profits of transferor carry over to the corporation that acquires its assets in a tax-free reorganization), and the *Phipps* restriction (deficit in transferor's earnings and profits cannot be applied against transferee's accumulated earnings and profits) are codified by §§381(c)(2)(A) and 381(c)(2)(B), as is the hovering deficit rule of the *Snider* case (deficit inherited from transferor can be applied against transferee's post-acquisition earnings and profits).[59]

The regulations elaborate on these general principles by providing that (1) earnings inherited from the transferor become a part of the acquiring corporation's *accumulated* earnings account (and thus have no effect on computation of its current earnings for the year of acquisition);[60] (2) current dividend distributions by the acquiring corporation during the year of acquisition come out of its current earnings account before consideration can be given to any deficits inherited from the transferor; (3) in determining the dividend status of current distributions by the acquiring corporation, deficits inherited from the transferor corporation have no effect on the acquiring corporation's accumulated earnings account; if, on the other hand, there are inherited earnings, they are reduced for this purpose by only a ratable por-

---

[58] While *P*'s taxable year is split into two parts for purposes of applying the tracing and consumption rules of §172(b)(2), it counts as one taxable year in applying the carry-back and carry-over time limits of §172(b)(1) to losses of the acquiring corporation (i.e., in the example, year 1 counts as only one year for *P*'s year-3 loss carry-over). See Regs. §1.381(c)(1)-1(f)(2).

[59] Supra note 12. See also Monroe v. US, 304 F. Supp. 1080 (E.D. La. 1969) (pre-1954 Code reorganization; where only 20 percent of book value of assets passed to transferee in merger, only 20 percent of transferor's deficit in earnings and profits carried over per *Sansome* rule; other 80 percent of assets distributed in partial liquidation). See generally supra ¶ 16.02.

[60] If the acquiring corporation has an accumulated deficit, the inherited earnings are not offset by it; see Regs. §1.381(c)(2)-1(a)(5). This provision is contrary to a dictum in CIR v. Phipps, supra note 12, stating that pre-acquisition deficits of the acquiring corporation offset accumulated earnings inherited from the transferor; but it is supported by §381 itself. See Sid Luckman, 56 TC 1216 (1971) (parent's accumulated deficit not offset by earnings and profits inherited from liquidated subsidiary).

tion of the acquiring corporation's current deficit (computed on a daily basis); and (4) in determining the amount of the transferor's earnings and profits inherited by the acquiring corporation, distributions by the transferor to its shareholders (other than the acquiring corporation) pursuant to the plan of reorganization or liquidation reduce such earnings, whether the distribution occurs before or after the effective date of the §381 transfer.[61]

3. Accounting methods. Section 381(c)(4) provides generally that the acquiring corporation must continue to use the accounting method used by the transferor on the date of the §381 transfer if both corporations have been using the same method prior thereto; otherwise, the method to be used is to be determined under regulations adopted by the Service (which, in effect, will be entitled to the force of law in view of the express statutory delegation of authority). As to what constitutes a method of accounting, §446 and the regulations thereunder provide, in brief, that this term includes not only a taxpayer's overall accounting method (i.e., the general method used in computing its taxable income such as the cash or accrual method), but the accounting treatment of any material item of income or deduction (e.g., bad debts; research and experimental expenses; long-term contracts; intangible drilling expense elections; and so forth).

Thus, the accounting method rules of §381(c)(4) are one of the broader categories of carry-over items covered by §381, possibly reaching many items not originally thought subject to carry-over.[62] It should also be noted

---

[61] Such distributions could include boot distributions by the transferor to its shareholders pursuant to the reorganization plan and distributions to minority shareholders on the liquidation of a subsidiary owned less than 100 percent by its parent. Regs. §1.381(c)(2)-1(c). For illustrations of these principles, see Regs. §1.381(c)(2)-1(a)(7), Examples (1)–(7); see also Halperin and Nesson, supra note 12; see also Rev. Rul. 71-364, 1971-2 CB 182 (distribution of retained cash a boot dividend, citing Regs. §1.381(c)(2)-1(c)(1), even though distribution made one year after reorganization transfer of other assets).

[62] See, e.g., Rev. Rul. 70-241, 1970-1 CB 84 (unamortized §248 expenses carry over as a method of accounting item); Rev. Rul. 70-83, 1970-1 CB 85 (completed contract method carries over to transferee). But see Rev. Rul. 68-350, 1968-2 CB 159 (foreign tax credits not a method of accounting for §381(c)(4) purposes).

See also VCA Corp. v. US, 40 AFTR2d 5429 (Ct. Cl. Tr. Div.), aff'd per curiam, 40 AFTR2d 6047 (Ct. Cl. 1977) (relationship of §381(c)(4) to §381(c)(16); deduction of assumed contingent liability denied under §381(c)(16) because shareholder of acquired corporation agreed to indemnify acquiring corporation for this item, and hence it was reflected in price paid; but deduction allowed under §381(c)(4) and regulations thereto, reimbursement a capital contribution to acquiring corporation); accord with *VCA Corp.,* is Rev. Rul. 83-73, 1983-1 CB 84 (deduction under §381(c)(4) by acquiring corporation; reimbursement by shareholder of acquired corporation not income; mere purchase price adjustment and capital contribution with step-up of stock basis); see supra ¶ 14.56.

that §381(c) deals specifically with various other item accounting methods of the transferor (e.g., inventories, §381(c)(5); depreciation methods, §381(c)(6); installment sales, §381(c)(7); and assumed expense liabilities, §381(c)(16)). These specific provisions apply in lieu of the general accounting method rules of §381(c)(4).

If a change of accounting method (either in an overall or an item method) is required because of the §381 transaction, the adjustment rules of §481, designed to prevent doubling up of income or deductions when accounting methods are changed, must be considered; moreover, Regs. §1.381(c)(4)-1(a)(2) warns that §§269 and 482 may be applicable, notwithstanding the fact that §381(c)(4) ordinarily assures carry-over treatment. Accordingly, integration of a transferor's accounting methods with those of the acquiring corporation can create problems of no small dimension, the major aspects of which are considered in the following discussion. [63]

(a) Continuance of transferor's accounting methods. If the transferor corporation and the acquiring corporation have the same accounting methods, then the acquiring corporation will step into the shoes of the transferor with respect to various elections and items of income or deduction of the transferor that, because of its method of accounting, have not been included or deducted in computing its taxable income prior to the date of the §381 transfer. Such items will retain their character in the hands of the acquiring corporation.

To illustrate: If *T* Corporation and *P* Corporation are both on the cash-basis method of accounting (or, alternatively, if both are on the accrual method), *P* must continue to use *T*'s overall accounting method after it acquires the assets of *T* in a transaction covered by §381(a). This is true whether *P* integrates *T*'s business into its own operations or instead preserves the *T* business as a separate division. Hence, if *T*, as of the date of the transfer, has currently unreportable ordinary income items in the amount of $100 and $20 of currently nondeductible ordinary

---

[63] See generally Eames, Accounting Method Considerations in Corporate Reorganizations With Special Attention to Section 381 Transactions, 23 NYU Inst. on Fed. Tax'n 853 (1965).

For rulings on the §481 aspects of §381, see Rev. Rul. 67-103, 1967-1 CB 117 (transferor's unused §481 adjustments carry over to transferee); Rev. Rul. 68-527, 1968-2 CB 162 (transferee inherits transferor's §481 transitional adjustment items); Rev. Rul. 70-128, 1970-1 CB 124 (transferee whose method was changed after acquisition of transferor can use latter's pre-1954 §481 adjustments arising from such change); superseded (and corrected) by Rev. Rul. 72-578, 1972-2 CB 244 (acquired corporation's unfavorable pre-1954 adjustments should not be taken into account in determining §481 additional tax adjustment triggered by Service change of inventory valuation of acquiring corporation; acquiring corporation steps into shoes of acquired corporation re §481 adjustments).

expense obligations, *P* must continue *T*'s treatment with respect to these items and include or deduct them when received, paid, or accrued (as the case may be), depending on its accounting method.

If the transferor and acquiring corporations use different methods of accounting, the regulations provide that the acquiring corporation must continue to use the transferor's accounting methods if the acquired business is continued as a separate and distinct enterprise, so that if *T* operated a service business and used the cash method of accounting and *P* operated a manufacturing business and used the accrual method, *P* would have to continue using the cash method of accounting with respect to the acquired service business if it was operated as a separate division after the acquisition.[64] If the acquiring corporation wishes to adopt a different accounting method from the one required by these principles, it may do so only with the consent of the Service, which may be granted subject to such terms, conditions, and adjustments as are necessary to clearly reflect income.[65]

(b) Change of accounting method required. If the transferor corporation and the acquiring corporation use different methods of accounting in their businesses, and the transferred business is not continued as a separate and distinct enterprise by the acquiring corporation, a change of accounting method is required by the regulations subject to any adjustments that may be necessary under §446(b) or §481 in order to give proper effect to the change. Which corporation's overall accounting method is to be used depends upon the principal accounting method test—that is, if the acquiring corporation's accounting method is the principal method, then the transferor's accounting method must be converted to this system; if, on the other hand, the transferor's method is the principal method, the acquiring corporation's accounting method must be changed.

The principal accounting method is determined by comparing the adjusted asset bases and gross receipts of the component businesses. If one business predominates on both of these counts, its method is to be employed; otherwise, the Service will determine the method, or combination of methods, to be used. In either event, as stated above, appropriate adjustments may be required to avoid duplicating or omitting items of income and deduction. Moreover, if the Service determines that the principal accounting method will not clearly reflect income, he may provide for the use of a method that will clearly reflect the income of the acquiring corporation.[66]

---

[64] See Regs. §§1.381(c)(4)-1(b)(2) and 1.381(c)(4)-1(b)(3); on the meaning of "separate business," see Regs. §1.446-1(d). But see §448, added by the Tax Reform Act of 1986, limiting the use of the cash method (supra ¶ 5.07).

[65] Regs. §1.381(c)(4)-1(d).

[66] See generally Regs. §§1.381(c)(4)-1(c) and 1.381(c)(4)-1(d).

4. Assumption of liabilities. If, in a transaction to which §381(a) applies, the acquiring corporation assumes (by agreement or operation of law) a liability (not yet taken into account by the transferor) that would, but for the transfer, have been deductible by the transferor when paid or accrued by it, §381(c)(16) permits the acquiring corporation to deduct the liability when, under *its* method of accounting, it is able to claim a deduction therefor (i.e., when paid if the acquiring corporation is on the cash method, or when accrued, if it is on the accrual method). However, if the transfer is by way of a transaction specified in §381(a)(2) (i.e., certain acquisitive reorganizations), §381(c)(16) does not apply to assumed obligations that are reflected in the price paid by the acquiring corporation for the transferred assets.[67] In determining whether a liability was reflected in the acquiring corporation's purchase price for the transferred assets, the regulations provide for a presumption in favor of nonreflection, in the absence of facts showing that (1) the parties were aware of a specific liability and (2) they reduced the consideration paid for the transferred assets by a specific amount to take account of it.[68]

If §381(c)(16) does not apply to a particular liability assumption, either because the transferor was entitled to take it into account at or before the date of the transfer under its regular accounting method or because the liability was reflected in the price paid by the acquiring corporation for the transferred assets, the regulations provide that its treatment will be governed by the method of accounting rules of §381(c)(4).[69]

5. Other §381(c) items. Section 381(c) lists numerous other tax attributes of the transferor that qualify for carry-over treatment under §381(a):

(1) *Capital loss carry-over, §381(c)(3).* The limitations on the carry-over of this item are similar to those discussed in connection with net operating loss carry-overs.

(2) *Inventory methods, §381(c)(5).* These provisions are similar to the carry-over rules relating to accounting methods.

---

[67] This restriction does not apply to §332 liquidations of subsidiary corporations, although the carry-over rules of §381 ordinarily apply to such transactions by virtue of §381(a)(1).

[68] See Regs. §1.381(c)(16)-1(c), Examples. Note also that §381(c)(16) applies only to liability assumptions; merely taking subject to the liability will not suffice. For other aspects of the assumption of liabilities in a reorganization, see supra ¶ 14.55. But see VCA Corp. v. US, supra note 62; Rev. Rul. 83-73, 1983-1 CB 84.

[69] See VCA Corp. v. US, supra note 62; Rev. Rul. 83-73, 1983-1CB 84.

See also Rev. Rul. 71-496, 1971-2 CB 315 (§1341 computation by acquiring corporation with respect to §381(c)(16) assumed liability deduction item goes back into year of acquired corporation to which it relates).

(3) *Depreciation methods, §381(c)(6).* The acquiring corporation steps into the shoes of the transferor with respect to its accelerated depreciation methods for the transferred assets (but only to the extent that the basis of the acquired depreciable assets is not in excess of their basis in the hands of the transferor).[70]

(4) *Installment method, §381(c)(8).* The acquiring corporation steps into the shoes of the transferor with respect to §453 obligations acquired therefrom.

(5) *Amortization of bond discount and premium, §381(c)(9).* An acquiring corporation that assumes bonded indebtedness of the transferor must continue to treat issue discount or premium thereon (and, according to the regulations, bond issue expenses as well) in the same manner as did the transferor.[71]

(6) *Excess contributions to qualified deferred compensation plans, §381(c)(11).* The acquiring corporation succeeds to any unused deductions or excess contributions carry-overs that would have been available to the transferor under §404.[72]

(7) *Recovery of prior deductions of the transferor, §381(c)(12).* The acquiring corporation is subject to the tax benefit rules of §111 with respect to any postacquisition recoveries of items previously deducted by the transferor, such recoveries being taxable to it in the same manner as would have occurred had the transferor obtained the recovery.

---

[70] Thus, if the acquiring corporation obtains a stepped up basis in whole or in part for the acquired depreciable assets (because it paid boot to the transferor which was taxable to it under §361(b)(1)(B)), the acquiring corporation is not entitled to use accelerated depreciation methods on this excess portion of the assets' adjusted basis. See Regs. §§1.381(c)(6)-1(b) and 1.381(c)(6)-1(g); Rev. Rul. 66-345, 1966-2 CB 67.

By virtue of new §381(c)(24), added by the Economic Recovery Tax Act of 1981, cost recovery treatment for the acquired corporation's recovery properties passes over to the acquiring corporation if the basis of such property is a carry-over basis.

[71] As to what constitutes an assumption for this purpose, see Regs. §1.381(c)(9)-1(d), which provides generally that an exchange or substitution of the acquiring corporation's bonds for those of the transferor in a §381 transaction will be so treated. Note, however, that this provision does not apply if the transferee merely takes subject to the liability. For similar problems under §357, see discussion supra ¶ 14.55.

Section 381(c)(9) partially codifies the holding of Helvering v. Metropolitan Edison Co., supra note 10, which permitted carry-over of bond issue discount deductions.

[72] See Musto, Carryover Problems of Compensation Plans in Corporate Reorganizations, 25 J. Tax'n 270 (1966); Metzer, The Qualified Deferred Compensation Plan of an Acquired Corporation: Basic Considerations in a Corporate Acquisition, 118 U. Pa. L. Rev. 688 (1970).

(8) *Involuntary conversions under §§381(c)(13) and 1033.* The acquiring corporation is treated in the same manner as the transferor in applying the nonrecognition rules of §1033.

(9) *General business credit, §381(c)(25).* The acquiring corporation presumably steps into the shoes of the transferor with respect to its unused general business credits under §47(b)(2) and Regs. §1.47-3(e), at least where the acquired assets are continued in use by the acquiring corporation as investment tax credit or investment credit property.[73]

¶ 16.14   NON-§381(a) TRANSACTIONS AND NON-§381(c) ITEMS

As noted earlier, §381 does not cover all the possible corporate tax attributes or all the possible forms of tax-free reorganization that can raise a carry-over problem. With respect to these unenumerated items and transactions, three interpretations are possible: (1) No carry-over occurs because §381 is the exclusive provision for carry-over treatment; (2) carry-overs of unspecified tax attributes can occur under some residual policy of §381 where the acquisition transaction is similar to a §381(a) transfer (a theory that is specifically rejected by the regulations); (3) carry-overs of unspecified items and transactions are controlled by the pre-1954 rules, including the *New Colonial* continuity of entity theory and the loss tracing requirement of *Libson Shops*; and (4) foreign tax credit carry-overs may stand on their own special footing here, since, while unmentioned in §381(c), they are specifically mentioned in the limitations provisions of §383[74] (added in 1971).

In *Denver & Rio Grande Western Railroad v. CIR,* the Tax Court took a long step toward adoption of the first approach, holding that tax attributes of a transferor could carry over to an acquiring corporation *only* if the transaction is mentioned in §381(a).[75] This position seems erroneous in view of the express statements in the Committee Reports that §381 "is not intended to affect the carry-over treatment of an item or tax attribute not specified in

---

[73] But see Shop Talk, Interplay of Investment Credit Recapture and Subchapter S, 53 J. Tax'n 127 (1980) (discussing investment tax credit recapture problems when ITC property of a Subchapter S corporation is acquired in a tax-free reorganization).

The Economic Recovery Tax Act of 1981 extended the ITC carry-over term of §39 from 7 to 15 years (effective for credit years after 1973); but the Tax Reform Act of 1986 repealed the general business credit in 1986.

[74] See Rev. Rul. 80-144, 1980-1 CB 80. Regs. §1.383-3(b)(1), dealing with limitations on foreign tax credit carry-overs under §382(b) analogizes such items to the carry-over rules of §381(c)(23) (now §381(c)(25)) for investment credits.

[75] Denver & R.G.W.R.R. v. CIR, 38 TC 557 (1962) (acq.).

the section or the carryover treatment of items or tax attributes in corporate transactions not described in §381(a)," and that "no inference is to be drawn from the enactment of this section whether any item or tax attribute may be utilized by a successor or a predecessor corporation under existing law."[76] These statements appear to support approach (3) in the preceding text, and may be the foundation for Regs. §1.312-11, providing for a carry-over of earnings and profits in certain circumstances that are not covered by §381.[77]

PART C.   LIMITATIONS ON ENJOYMENT OF CORPORATE TAX ATTRIBUTES

¶ 16.20   INTRODUCTORY

The carry-over of tax attributes from one corporation to another (either under the pre-1954 case law or under the 1954 Code rules of §381) can lead to the acquisition of corporations primarily because of their favorable attributes. Although on occasion any of the items that are preserved for the acquiring corporation may be a valuable prize, the most commonly sought attribute is a net operating loss carry-over; for many years advertisements for defunct corporations with such carry-overs have appeared in the financial pages of the metropolitan and financial press. As will be seen in the discussion that follows, however, the Service is armed with numerous statutory and judicial weapons to combat such tax motivated transactions:

---

[76] See S. Rep. No. 1622, supra note 27, at 277.

[77] See Rev. Rul. 68-350, 1968-2 CB 159 (carry-over of foreign tax credit under §904(d), a non-§381(c) item, and adopting the third approach); CIR v. Joseph F. Seagram & Sons, 394 F2d 738 (2d Cir. 1968) (last in, first out inventory layers carried over on capital contribution, a non-§381 transaction); see also Rev. Rul. 72-452, 1972-2 CB 438 (§904(d) foreign tax credit carry-overs allowed after a Type C reorganizaton; Rev. Rul. 68-350 modified to allow carry-overs, subject to *Libson*-type limits, in a Type C reorganization as well as a Type A; thus Service has abandoned *New Colonial* continuity of entity theory regarding non-§381(c) items); Rev. Rul. 72-453, 1972-2 CB 439 (same for §§332–334(b)(1) liquidation of subsidiary with §904(d) carry-overs if parent carries on subsidiary's business; but ruling unclear whether §904 limitations apply only to post-fusion taxable income of subsidiary's business). But see Philadelphia & Reading Corp. v. US, 602 F2d 338 (Ct. Cl. 1979) (transferee in §351 transaction could make an election generated by transferor; §381 not exclusive section for tax attribute carry-over); Rev. Rul. 80-144, 1980-1 CB 80 (Rev. Rul. 68-350 and Rev. Rul. 72-452 held obsolete in view of §383 amendments; §383 preempts carry-over treatment of items mentioned therein and *Libson* limits not applicable).

(1) Section 269, which disallows any deduction, credit, or other allowance involved in certain acquisitions of stock or property with the principal purpose of income tax avoidance.

(2) Section 382, which limits the use of net operating loss carry-overs where a substantial change in the corporation's stock ownership is effected in any manner, whether by purchase, new issue, redemption, reorganization, or a combination thereof.[78]

(3) The *Libson Shops* doctrine, which may prohibit the carry-over in a reorganization of losses against profits of a different business.

(4) Various other general principles sounding in sham, tax avoidance, business purpose, form versus substance, clear reflection of income, step transactions, and assignment of income, and derived in large part from *Gregory v. Helvering*.

Some of these provisions and general principles depend for their applicability on the taxpayer's motives or state of mind (e.g., §269); others adopt mechanical rules of thumb to eliminate probing into tax motivation as such (e.g., §382); others depend on the economic consequences of the transaction (e.g., *Libson Shops*); some are concerned with whether the form of a particular transaction has independent substance, apart from its tax benefits (e.g., *Gregory*). Litigation has been extensive on all of these points, and, as one would expect, matters unfortunately are not entirely clear. The materials that follow consist of only a sample (and a highly selective one at that) of the many decisions in this area in the hope that the major trends and points of conflict may be illuminated without bogging down in detail. Moreover, the principal focus will be on the survival of net operating loss deductions, although other tax attributes can, and often do, raise similar problems.

Of the various limitations, §382 is by far the most important, especially since 1986.[79] While §269 continues to apply after the 1986 amendments, its role will be greatly diminished, and the *Libson Shops* doctrine has been almost completely superseded by the 1986 legislation. Section 269, however,

---

[78] An attempt to revise §382 in 1976 never became effective; infra ¶ 16.22. Section 382 finally underwent extensive revision in 1986, infra ¶ 16.23.

The 1954 version of §382 had a bifurcated regime, one set of rules (§382(a)) being applicable to stock purchase ownership change transactions (coupled with substantial business change), and the other set of rules (§382(b)) being applicable to the asset reorganizations specified in §381(a)(2) (where the shareholders of the loss corporation failed to retain a minimum ownership interest (i.e., 20 percent) in the loss corporation).

[79] For discussion of §382 under the 1954 Code rules, see the Fourth Edition of this treatise at ¶¶ 16.22 and 16.23. For the attempt to revise §382 in 1976, see id. at ¶ 16.24.

will be considered first, primarily because it was the first legislative effort at restricting the acquisition of corporate tax benefits.

¶ 16.21 ACQUISITIONS TO AVOID INCOME TAX: SECTION 269

1. Introductory. Section 269 provides for the disallowance of deductions and other tax benefits when tax avoidance is the principal purpose for the acquisition of control of a corporation or for certain transfers of property from one corporation to another. This statutory restriction was originally enacted in 1943, principally to curb a growing market for defunct corporate shells.[80] These hollow entities were in demand because the World War II excess profits tax exempted a corporation's normal profits, based on its historic earnings or invested capital; some owners of booming war businesses hoped to shield themselves against taxable excess profits by carrying on their activities through a corporation with a history of high normal earnings or a high level of invested capital. The repeal of the excess profits tax at the end of World War II eliminated this particular stimulus to so-called trafficking in corporate shells; but the practice continued as a method of acquiring other advantageous tax attributes, such as operating and capital loss carry-forwards and built-in losses (i.e., assets with a high adjusted basis but low current value).

Although the Treasury was not wholly devoid of weapons against acquisitions motivated solely by the hope of avoiding taxes,[81] §269 was enacted in 1943 on the Treasury's recommendation to provide a more specific statutory foundation for an attack on these devices. Section 269 is applicable if:

(1) Any person or persons (including, by virtue of §7701(a)(1), a corporation) acquire control of a corporation, directly or indirectly; or

(2) Any corporation acquires, directly or indirectly, property of another corporation if the latter corporation was not controlled, directly or indirectly, immediately before the acquisition by the

---

[80] Thus, a seller advertised in the New York Times in 1943: "For sale. Stock of corporation having 1943 tax loss deduction $120,000. Sole assets are $80,000 in cash and equivalent." A buyer advertised in the Wall Street Journal that he wanted "to acquire all the outstanding stock of a corporation with original invested capital of several hundred thousand dollars with present assets at nominal values." See Rudick, Acquisitions to Avoid Income or Excess Profits Tax: Section 129 of the Internal Revenue Code, 58 Harv. L. Rev. 196 (1944).

[81] See Rudick, supra note 80, at 216–222. For continued vitality of these nonstatutory remedies, see Regs. §1.269-2(b).

acquiring corporation or its shareholders and if the acquiring corporation's basis for the property is determined by reference to the transferor corporation's basis; and

(3) The principal purpose of the acquisition is evasion or avoidance of federal income tax by securing the benefit of a deduction, credit, or other allowance that such person or corporation would not otherwise enjoy. [82]

"Control" is defined by §269(a) to mean the ownership of stock possessing at least 50 percent of the total combined voting power of all classes of stock entitled to vote or at least 50 percent of the total value of all classes of stock. The statutory reference to a tax allowance is construed broadly by the regulations to encompass "anything in the internal revenue laws which has the effect of diminishing tax liability." [83]

Because discussions of §269 frequently focus on the purchase of loss corporations to serve as shells for the conduct of a successful business whose profits are to be offset by a carry-over of the losses of prior years, it is important to note that §269 is not confined to such transactions, and that it may embrace devices in which the acquired corporation is not even kept alive or is newly created for a tax avoidance purpose. The potential range of §269 is illustrated by the regulations, which refer to (1) the acquisition of a corporation with current, past, or prospective credits, deductions, net operating losses, and so forth in order to bring these allowances into conjunction with the income of a profitable enterprise; (2) the acquisition by a corporation of property having a basis materially in excess of fair market value in order to generate tax reducing losses, presumably by selling the property or taking depreciation deductions with respect to it; and (3) the transfer of business assets producing a high level of profits to a subsidiary with large net operating losses if the parent could not arrange to inherit the loss carry-overs by liquidating the subsidiary and using the losses to offset its own income. [84]

---

[82] The transfer must have occurred on or after October 8, 1940, the date when the Excess Profits Tax of 1940 was enacted.

For §269(b), relating to certain tax motivated liquidations following so-called qualified stock purchases, see supra ¶ 11.46 and note 37.

Under former §269(c), enacted in 1954 but repealed in 1976, the payment of a purchase price that was disproportionate to the tax basis of the acquired corporation or property and the tax benefits resulting from the acquisition were prima facie evidence of the principal purpose of evasion or avoidance of federal income tax. For discussion of this presumption, see the Third Edition of this treatise at ¶ 16.21.

For general discussions of §269, see Watts, Acquisitions Made to Avoid Taxes: Section 269, 34 Tax L. Rev. 539 (1979); Bowen & Sheffield, Section 269 Revisited, 61 Taxes 881 (1983).

[83] Regs. §1.269-1(a).

[84] See Regs. §1.269-3(c)(2).

2. Scope and operation. When §269 is applicable, the taxpayer's purpose of securing the benefit of a deduction, credit, or other allowance that he would not otherwise enjoy is frustrated by the simple device of denying "such deduction, credit, or other allowance."[85] When §269 was in its infancy, the Tax Court enunciated the theory that §269 could not be used to deprive the *acquired* corporation of tax allowances;[86] but this interpretation, which would have sapped §269's vitality for taxpayers with the foresight to keep the acquired corporation alive, has long since been rejected. Thus, *CIR v. British Motor Car Distributors, Ltd.,* the Court of Appeals for the Ninth Circuit stated:

> We should be closing our eyes to the realities of the situation were we to refuse to recognize that the persons who have acquired the corporation did so to secure *for themselves* a very real tax benefit to be realized by them *through* the acquired corporation and which they could not otherwise have realized.[87]

Although §269 has most frequently been applied to deny the carry-over of net operating losses to a period following a change in control of a corporation or the acquisition of loss-generating assets in a tax-free transaction, its reach is considerably broader than these two tax benefits. Thus, in *Army Times Sales Co.,* §269 was applied to disallow corporate deductions for interest paid on the corporation's bonds and to convert a sole shareholder's claim for capital gain treatment on the redemption thereof into ordinary income.[88] Other examples of deductions, credits, or allowances that may be denied under §269 include foreign tax credit carry-overs; investment credit carry-overs; depreciation deductions; rental deductions; capital, ordinary, or §1231 losses; earnings and profits deficits; minimum accumulated earnings tax credits under §535(c)(2); the privilege of filing consolidated returns; and losses from the sale of assets acquired with a built-in loss at the date of the acquisition.[89]

---

[85] By virtue of §269(c), deductions and other allowances need not be disallowed in toto when the statutory conditions are satisfied but can instead be disallowed in part, apportioned between the relevant corporations, and so forth; but this mitigating authority has evidently not been exercised in any public rulings or decisions.

[86] Alprosa Watch Corp., 11 TC 240 (1948).

[87] CIR v. British Motor Car Distribs., Ltd., 278 F2d 392 (9th Cir. 1960); see also Vulcan Materials Co. v. US, 446 F2d 690 (5th Cir.), cert. denied, 404 US 942 (1971) (§269 applied on merger of profit into loss corporation even though latter's shareholders maintained control after merger).

[88] Army Times Sales Co., 35 TC 688 (1961).

[89] See J.T. Slocomb Co. v. CIR, 334 F2d 269 (2d Cir. 1964); Luke v. CIR, 351 F2d 568 (7th Cir. 1965) (built-in loss disallowed and capital gain treatment denied);

On the other hand, some tax benefits are immune to disallowance (or virtually so) under §269, even though they are allowances within the meaning of the statutory language, because Congress intended to grant the benefit provided specified statutory conditions were met regardless of the taxpayer's desire to reduce its tax burden. Thus, in an early ruling, the Service held that the creation of a Western Hemisphere Trade corporation (which was entitled to a reduced tax rate under pre-1976 law), was not tax avoidance within the meaning of §269, even though the corporation was created for the principal purpose of qualifying for the rates applicable to such corporations:

> It appears from the structure [of the provisions governing Western Hemisphere Trade corporations], and the apparent purpose thereof, that Congress sought to make this relief available to any domestic corporation, provided only that it could satisfy the gross income and other specific requirements of [the relevant] sections of the Code.[90]

The same rationale protects S corporations and life insurance companies from losing their tax benefits, even if they are organized for the principal purpose of securing these tax allowances;[91] it also applies to a miscellany of other situations, such as the incorporation of an existing sole proprietorship or partnership to take advantage of the fact that the bottom corporate tax rate is lower than the top personal rate.

3. Section 269 transactions. As noted previously, §269 embraces two principal types of transactions: (1) acquisitions of control (i.e., stock of a corporation (§269(a)(1))); and (2) tax-free acquisitions of one corporation's assets by a previously unrelated corporation (§269(a)(2)). If either transaction is effected for the prohibited tax avoidance purpose, the hoped-for tax benefits can be denied.

Acquisition of control within the meaning of §269(a)(1) includes not only a direct purchase of stock sufficient to bring the acquiring party's own-

---

Borge v. CIR, 405 F2d 673 (2d Cir. 1968) (post-acquisition corporate losses in excess of former §270 limit on individuals disallowed); Canaveral Int'l Corp., 61 TC 520 (1974) (acq.) (built-in loss for high-basis, low-value asset denied in stock purchase transaction).

[90] IT 3757, 1945 CB 200; Rev. Rul. 70-238, 1970-1 CB 61 (same).

[91] See Modern Home Fire & Cas. Ins. Co., 54 TC 839, 851–854 (1970) (acq.), and cases there cited. For other tax allowances shielded by the same principle, see Sam Siegel, 45 TC 566 (1966) (acq.) (§269 cannot be used to disregard corporate entity and tax income directly to shareholders); Supreme Inv. Corp. v. US, 468 F2d 370 (5th Cir. 1972) (§269 inapplicable to old §334(b)(2) stepped up basis rules, which preempted §269 subjective intent analysis); Rocco, Inc., 72 TC 140 (1979) (creation of subsidiary to change accounting method); cases cited infra notes 115–117.

ership up to the requisite 50 percent level, but also tax-free acquisitions and indirect methods of acquiring control of a corporation (e.g., the redemption of the stock of other shareholders, the use of chains of controlled corporations, and possibly even the use of convertible debentures or options to acquire additional stock, although matters are less clear in these latter situations).[92] Although §269(a)(1) is not explicit on this point, presumably all persons whose acquisitions of stock were motivated by the forbidden tax avoidance purpose are to be aggregated in computing control; but it would seem reasonable for a shareholder's tax avoidance purpose to infect not only the stock owned by him directly and indirectly (e.g., through a dummy, trust, or other entity), but also, in some circumstances, stock owned by his spouse, minor children, and possibly other intimates.[93]

The regulations give three nonexclusive examples of transactions that may constitute a control acquisition under §269(a)(1): (1) the acquisition of a corporation having current, past, or prospective tax benefits intended to bring these items into conjunction with the income of a profitable enterprise; (2) the creation of two or more corporations instead of a single corporation in order to obtain multiple corporation benefits;[94] and (3) the separation of profitable assets from assets producing net operating losses by transferring the income producing assets to a controlled corporation and thereafter using losses generated by the retained assets to produce loss carry-back refunds.[95] Another likely candidate for application of §269(a)(1) is a transaction of the type involved in *Diamond A Cattle Co. v. CIR*, where an individual acquired control of a corporation engaged in a cyclical business and liquidated the enterprise in midstream (i.e., after incurring expenses but before realization of the related income therefrom).[96] The result was to generate large net operating loss carry-back refunds.[97]

---

[92] See Swiss Colony, Inc. v. CIR, supra note 38 (control acquired through combination of repossession of previously sold stock and purchases from third parties).

[93] Section 269 does not adopt the constructive ownership rules of §318, as does §382, however, so such attribution ought to be selective rather than automatic. See Dorba Homes, Inc. v. CIR, 403 F2d 502 (2d Cir. 1968) (spouses' stock not attributed to husbands; must be actual, or beneficial, control); Rev. Rul. 80-46, 1980-1 CB 62 (§318 not applicable to give acquiring corporation 50 percent control through attribution from sole stockholder; held, transaction a §269(a)(1) control acquisition); Emory, "Control" Under Section 269 Is a Labyrinth of Complexity, 53 J. Tax'n 181 (1980).

[94] See infra note 99 and the discussion supra ¶¶ 15.02 and 15.03.

[95] Regs. §1.269-3(b).

[96] Diamond A Cattle Co. v. CIR, 233 F2d 739 (10th Cir. 1956).

[97] The deduction was allowed in the *Diamond A* case under the general net operating loss provisions of §172; but the Service did not specifically assert §269, an oversight that is not likely to be repeated.

For discussion of the midstream liquidation problem, see supra ¶ 11.07.

The second category of transactions covered by §269 is the acquisition of the *assets* of one corporation by another corporation if (1) the basis for the assets carries over to the transferee and (2) the corporations were not under common control immediately prior to the acquisition. The major focus of this provision is on tax-free reorganizations, since these transactions generally activate the carry-over rules of §381;[98] but the regulations state, and the decisions generally agree, that §269(a)(2) has a considerably broader reach. Thus, in the *Coastal Oil Storage Co.* case, §269(a)(2) was applied to disallow a newly created subsidiary corporation's surtax exemption on the ground that the subsidiary could not have enjoyed the benefit of the surtax exemption without acquiring the property producing the income from or against which the exemption was claimed.[99]

There are, however, many types of asset acquisitions that are not covered by §269(a)(2): (1) acquisitions from noncorporate transferors (but §269(a)(1) could apply to this situation if the transferors obtain 50 percent control of the transferee); (3) purchases or other taxable transactions where the transferee obtains a cost basis for the acquired properties under §1012;[100] (3) like-kind exchanges under §1031, which result in an exchanged rather than transferred basis to the transferee; (4) acquisitions of cash, which does not have a tax basis; and (5) acquisitions from a corporation that is controlled (under the 50 percent test of §269) by the acquiring corporation or its shareholders.[101]

---

[98] Supra ¶ 16.11.

[99] Coastal Oil Storage Co. v. CIR, supra note 26. For the use of §269(a)(1) to disallow surtax exemptions of multiple corporations created by individual shareholder transferors, see James Realty Co. v. US, supra note 26; Joe Dillier, 41 TC 762 (1964), aff'd per curiam sub nom. Made Rite Inv. Co. v. CIR, 357 F2d 647 (9th Cir. 1966); Bobsee Corp. v. US, 411 F2d 231 (5th Cir. 1969); supra ¶ 15.02.

But contrary to the principle of *Coastal Oil*, the Second Circuit has held that §269 could not be invoked to deny a surtax exemption in a case where the acquisition was of control by an individual of only one corporation. See Dorba Homes, Inc. v. CIR, supra note 93.

For an alternative statutory remedy for the multiplication of the tax allowance involved in *Coastal Oil,* see §1561, supra ¶ 15.02.

[100] See O'Mealia Research & Dev., Inc., 64 TC 491 (1975) (integrated transaction where subsidiary acquired assets purchased by parent, held not a §269(a)(2) transaction, since subsidiary in effect obtained a cost basis therefor; parent a mere conduit for passage of property to subsidiary, and hence not a transferor within meaning of §269(a)(2); followed principle of Yoc Heating Co., 61 TC 168 (1973)).

[101] This common control exception to the applicability of §269(a)(2) relates to transfers between brother-sister corporations and to transfers pursuant to the liquidation of a controlled subsidiary under §332. However, *Coastal Oil* ignored this exception where the assets were transferred by the parent corporation *to* a newly created subsidiary in a §351 transaction (a result that may also be reached in downstream mergers of the parent into its subsidiary and in contributions to the subsidi-

While §269(a)(2) does not apply to asset transfers between commonly controlled corporations, there is no such common control exception for §269(a)(1); [102] but the existence of such control may prove helpful to taxpayers on the primary issue of tax avoidance, at least in situations where the facts are unclear as to the principal purpose for the transaction or are susceptible of varying interpretations. Moreover, in situations where true common control exists, §269(a)(1) ought to be applied with restraint in view of the fact that the transaction can in most instances be just as easily arranged as an asset acquisition of the §269(a)(2) variety, in which case it would be beyond the reach of §269. On the other hand, courts faced with this argument have so far refused to show much leniency, despite the admittedly harsh results accruing because of the particular form that the taxpayer elected to follow. [103]

4. The forbidden tax-avoidance purpose. The crux of §269 is the forbidden state of mind that motivates the particular transaction (i.e., the principal purpose of evasion or avoidance of federal income tax). [104] As with most statutory provisions turning on the taxpayer's motive or intent, considerable difficulty in application is to be expected, and §269 has proved to be no

---

ary's capital by its parent, since the transferee does not control the transferor here either). See Regs. §§1.269-3(c)(2) and 1.269-6, Example (3). Moreover, transitory common control immediately prior to the relevant asset acquisition presumably would be ignored in applying this exception, as has been the case with similar provisions. For possible analogies, see discussion supra ¶ 3.09; Regs. §§1.382(a)-1(e)(2) and 1.382(b)-1(a)(6); Rev. Rul. 67-274, 1967-2 CB 141; see also Rev. Rul. 67-202, 1967-1 CB 73 (contribution of stock of brother corporation to sister corporation, followed by immediate liquidation; held in substance an asset acquisition under §269(a)(2) protected by the common control exception).

[102] See Brick Milling Co., ¶ 63,305 P-H Memo. TC (1963). But see Southland Corp. v. Campbell, 358 F2d 333 (5th Cir. 1966), where the court in effect applied a common control exception to §269(a)(1) as well. See also WOFAC Corp. v. US, 269 F., Supp. 654 (D.N.J. 1967).

[103] But see Southland Corp. v. Campbell, supra note 102.

[104] As passed by the House in 1943, §269 was applicable if tax avoidance was one of the principal purposes of the acquisition. The language was changed by the Senate on the recommendation of the Senate Finance Committee that "the section should be operative only if the evasion or avoidance purpose outranks, or exceeds in importance, any other one purpose." See S. Rep. No. 627, 78th Cong., 1st Sess. 59 (1943), reprinted in 1944 CB 973, 1017; Stange Co., ¶ 77,007 P-H Memo. TC (1977) (business purpose for acquisition, even though tax aspects of carry-over considered; tax avoidance, but not the principal purpose); VGS Corp., 68 TC 563 (1977) (same); see also Malat v. Riddell, 383 US 569 (1966) (construing primarily as used in §1221).

See generally Blum, Motive, Intent and Purpose in Federal Income Taxation, 34 U. Chi. L. Rev. 485 (1967); Note, State of Mind Analysis in Corporate Taxation, 69 Colum. L. Rev. 1224 (1969).

exception to this rule. The question is, of course, one of fact, and, despite the presumption of correctness attaching to the assertion of a deficiency, the early litigation under §269 produced surprisingly few government victories.[105]

Subsequently, however, the judicial climate changed, possibly because cases were selected by the Service with greater care. The *Coastal Oil* case is a striking illustration of this skeptical attitude on the part of courts as to why the taxpayer chose one tax route over all others or why it selected a particular loss corporation for acquisition.[106] While this critical judicial attitude does not go as far as to compel the taxpayer to adopt the least favorable tax route out of several possible alternatives, it does seem to require a showing that the choice of the most favorable tax route was motivated by substantial business reasons in addition to the opportunity to obtain the particular tax benefits inherent in the method selected.[107]

---

[105] Thus, in a number of cases involving the transfer of property by a corporation to newly created subsidiaries, it was found as a fact that the creation of additional corporate entities served various business purposes (e.g., limiting liability, avoiding exclusive franchises and loan restrictions, and creating the reputation of local control) and was not for the principal purpose of tax avoidance. See Berlands, Inc., 16 TC 182 (1951) (acq.); Alcorn Wholesale Co., 16 TC 75 (1951) (acq.); see also WAGE, Inc., 19 TC 249 (1952) (acq. and nonacq.); Commodores Point Terminal Corp., 11 TC 411 (1948) (acq.) (finding that other transactions, alleged by the government to violate §269, served business purposes).

[106] Coastal Oil Storage Co. v. CIR, supra note 26; see also, e.g., James Realty Co. v. US, supra note 26 (multiple real estate development corporations); Elko Realty Co. v. CIR, 29 TC 1012, aff'd per curiam, 260 F2d 949 (3d Cir. 1958) (§269 applied to deny right to file consolidated return with subsidiary whose stock was purchased presumably in anticipation of using future excess of depreciation allowances over income as an offset to consolidated income); Industrial Suppliers, Inc., 50 TC 635 (1968) (§269 applied to disallow net operating loss carry-over); PEPI, Inc., 448 F2d 141 (2d Cir. 1971).

[107] For an extended statement of §269's tax-avoidance trigger, see Regs. §1.269-2(b). For cases finding the requisite tax-avoidance purpose, see Canaveral Int'l Corp., supra note 89 (purchase of stock of corporation with high-basis, low-value asset; held §269 applies to deny use of high basis in consolidated return for depreciation and loss on latter sale; while valid business purpose for acquiring asset, no business purpose for form of acquisition adopted such as purchase of stock); Inductotherm Indus., ¶ 84,281 P-H Memo. TC (1984) (§269 applied because stock acquisition route followed only to get loss carry-overs). For taxpayer successes in rebutting the application of §269, see Princeton Aviation Corp., ¶ 83,735 P-H Memo. TC (1983) (business purpose for acquisition; taxpayer wanted to expand space and seller would only sell stock); D'Arcy-MacManus & Masius, Inc., 63 TC 440 (1975) (business purpose for acquisition; expansion and diversification not tax avoidance, so no §269; taxpayer's awareness of net operating loss not fatal, nor was existence of tax planning to allow use of loss carry-overs; transaction switched from stock acquisition (Type B reorganization) to asset acquisition (Type C reorganization) for this

Some of the criteria that have been considered in determining whether an acquisition satisfies the business purpose standard of §269 are:

(1) whether the acquiring parties were aware of the challenged tax benefits at the time of the acquisition, and, if so, whether they took them into consideration,[108]

(2) whether the acquired corporation has a going business that will continue to be operated on a substantial scale after the acquisition (the acquisition of a corporation that is virtually a shell, or whose assets are suitable only for liquidation, is not likely to survive an attack under §269);

(3) whether the acquisition of control or assets is necessary or useful to the acquiring person's business or investment activities (i.e., whether the acquiring party was expanding or diversifying its business activities via the acquisition route rather than by internal growth or made the acquisition to protect its competitive position);[109]

(4) the relative value of the acquired tax benefit as compared to the economic profit inherent in the enterprise;[110]

(5) whether the challenged benefit could have been used by the taxpayer absent the particular acquisition transaction (i.e., whether

---

purpose but such planning did not trigger §269); VGS Corp., supra note 104 (tax-avoidance purpose, but not the principal purpose; business reasons predominated).

[108] See Hawaiian Trust Co. v. US, 291 F2d 761 (9th Cir. 1961) (postacquisition tax motives did not retroactively infect the transaction under §269); Power-Line Sales, Inc., ¶ 77,043 P-H Memo. TC (1977) (knowledge of tax losses not fatal; parties did not know they could use losses against profits of other corporations); Supreme Inv. Corp. v. US, 320 F. Supp. 1328 (W.D. La. 1970) (expertise of tax advice triggered tax avoidance motive for §269), reversed on other grounds, supra note 91 (not a §269 transaction).

Suppose that the acquiring person's advisers offer no hope for survival of the acquired corporation's tax benefits because of §269; will evidence of this advice be relevant (or persuasive) on the issue of tax avoidance if the transaction is consummated in any event? It would seem so, subject of course to reasonable limits of credibility. In this regard, see Arwood Corp., ¶ 71,002 P-H Memo. TC (1971).

[109] This factor seems related to the "reasonable needs of the business" test of §533(a), applied with respect to the accumulated earnings tax. See generally John B. Stetson, ¶ 64,146 P-H Memo. TC (1964) (distribution outlet); Glen Raven Mills, Inc., 59 TC 1 (1972) (acq.) (taxpayer needed source of supply; purchase of stock okay because shareholder would not sell assets); D'Arcy-MacManus & Masius, Inc., supra note 107 (expansion and diversification valid business purpose for acquisition, even though tax planning regarding net operating losses).

[110] See R.P. Collins & Co. v. US, 303 F2d 142 (1st Cir. 1962) (dissent).

enjoyment of the tax benefit flows directly or proximately from the acquisition transaction);

(6) if the acquisition is by a purchase of stock rather than assets, whether this route was the more feasible method of acquiring the business or assets of the acquired corporation;[111] and

(7) if assets are acquired in a nontaxable reorganization, whether such method was more feasible than a cash purchase thereof.[112]

Two final points relating to §269's tax avoidance purpose requirement deserve attention. First, if the principal purpose of a transaction was the capture of a particular tax benefit, the Service seems authorized to disallow any other tax allowances stemming from the tainted acquisition, even if by themselves they might not have stimulated the transaction.[113] Second, the relevant date in determining whether tax avoidance was the principal purpose for an acquisition is presumably the date when the acquisition was planned or occurred. Thus, a tax-infected transaction following an innocent acquisition should not retroactively bring §269 into force, assuming, of course, that the two were not integral parts of a single transaction.[114]

---

[111] In Baton Rouge Supply Co., 36 TC 1 (1961) (acq.), taxpayers were able to purchase various properties they desired only if they agreed, in addition, to buy the stock of the loss company (of whose tax benefits they were unaware at the time of purchase). This factor seems tangentially related to the principles of the *Kimbell-Diamond* case, supra ¶ 11.44, which held that an acquisition of stock in order to acquire assets will be treated, in substance, as a direct asset acquisition. See also Canaveral Int'l Corp., supra note 89.

[112] D'Arcy-MacManus & Masius, Inc., supra note 107 (switch from stock acquisition to asset acquisition to allow acquiring corporation to use net operating losses not fatal under §269 where good business purpose for acquisition, expansion, and diversification).

[113] Zanesville Inv. Co., 38 TC 406 (1962), rev'd on other grounds, 335 F2d 507 (6th Cir. 1964). It is not clear whether this principle extends to the treatment of losses sustained *after* the date of the §269 acquisition, however. Compare R.P. Collins & Co. v. US, supra note 110 (deduction for post-acquisition operating losses denied under §269 as tainted by taxpayer's unrelated pre-acquisition tax-avoidance purpose), with Zanesville Inv. Co. v. CIR, supra (deductions for post-acquisition losses allowed; purpose of §269 was to prevent distortion of income through the use of *someone else's loss* or a built-in loss). See also US v. Hall Paving Co., 471 F2d 261 (5th Cir. 1973) (following *Collins*); Herculite Protective Fabrics Corp. v. CIR, 387 F2d 475 (3d Cir. 1968) (following *Zanesville*): Inductotherm Indus., supra note 107 (computations).

[114] See Hawaiian Trust Co. v. US, supra note 108; Capri, Inc., 65 TC 162 (1975) (*Hawaiian Trust* rule followed; acquisition of 56 percent stock interest in one transaction, without tax avoidance, followed by later separate acquisition of 80 percent control so it could file consolidated returns and use losses, held not hit by §269 because separate acquisition steps and no retroactive infection of first purchase); compare Jupiter Corp. v. US, 2 Cl. Ct. 58 (Cl. Ct. 1983) (creeping acquisition; intent at time control

5. Tax allowance that taxpayer "would not otherwise enjoy." A feature of §269 that is easily overlooked because it is ordinarily satisfied is that it applies only to tax allowances that the acquiring taxpayer "would not . . . enjoy" but for the acquisition. In one of the few cases to construe this requirement, the taxpayer was a corporation formed by investors to effect a bootstrap acquisition, pursuant to which it borrowed a substantial portion of the purchase price to be paid for the stock of the acquired corporation, purchased the stock with these funds plus additional sums contributed by its shareholders, filed a consolidated return with its newly acquired subsidiary, and then had the subsidiary distribute a dividend that the taxpayer used to discharge its purchase money indebtedness.[115] The Service attacked this transaction under §269, alleging that the taxpayer was not entitled to file a consolidated return with the subsidiary (or, if it was, that it was not entitled to eliminate the intercompany dividend, as is normal on consolidated returns) and that if a consolidated return was not proper, the dividend did not qualify for the dividends-received deduction of §243.

The Tax Court rejected all of these assertions, stating that, regardless of the taxpayer's purpose in effecting the transaction in this manner, it did not thereby obtain a tax benefit that it would not otherwise have enjoyed. The court noted that other methods could have been used in making the acquisition, all of which would have produced the same net effect for tax purposes as the method chosen by the parties (i.e., the acquisition of another corporation with a limited equity investment). The purpose of §269, said the court, is to prevent a distortion of the taxpayer's net income, as "where a taxpayer is attempting to secure the benefit of built-in tax advantages, typically a net operating loss carry-over, by combining two corporations via an acquisition."[116] Here, the purchasers merely obtained, through their use of an intervening holding company to effect the acquisition, control of the desired enterprise with a limited out of pocket investment, a result that did not contravene the limitations of §269. In a later Tax Court case of similar import, the court distinguished between a tax motivated *acquisition* and a tax motivated *method* used to effect a business motivated acquisition, and it refused to apply §269 to a transaction of the latter type.[117]

---

was acquired the crucial date and tax avoidance here); R.P. Collins & Co. v. US, supra note 110; J. T. Slocomb Co. v. CIR, supra note 89; Temple Square Mfg. Co., 36 TC 88 (1961); cases cited supra note 108. See generally supra ¶ 14.51, para. 3.

[115] Cromwell Corp., 43 TC 313 (1964). For bootstrap acquisitions, see supra ¶ 9.07.

[116] Id. at 320. See also Rev. Rul. 63-40, 1963-1 CB 46 (mere change of business not enough to invoke §269): Zanesville Inv. Co. v. CIR, supra note 113.

[117] Arwood Corp. supra note 108; see also Cherry v. US, 264 F. Supp. 969 (C.D. Cal. 1967); Daniel F. Keller, 77 TC 1014 (1981), aff'd, 723 F2d 58 (10th Cir. 1983). But see §269A, supra ¶ 2.07. See supra notes 90 and 91.

¶ 16.22   SECTION 382: THE PRE-1987 STATUTORY REGIME

1. 1954 Code provisions. On the ground that §269 had proved to be ineffectual as a weapon against the traffic in loss corporations because it required proof that tax avoidance was the primary purpose of the transaction, Congress in 1954 enacted two new restrictions on the net operating loss carry-over.[118] The first was §382(a), applicable to changes of ownership through the purchase of stock, which provided for the complete disallowance of the carry-over if, roughly speaking, 50 percent of the corporation's stock changed hands in a two-year period and if the corporation's old trade or business was abandoned. The second restriction was §382(b), applicable only to changes of ownership through a tax-free reorganization under which the carry-over was reduced proportionately if the old owners received less than 20 percent of the stock of the reorganized corporation and was eliminated if they received none. Neither restriction was dependent upon a showing of a tax-avoidance purpose; the function of both was to reduce or eliminate the carry-over in appropriate cases even though they could not be brought within §269.[119]

(a) Section 382(a). As enacted in 1954, §382(a), one of the few statutory provisions under which a change in stock ownership impinges on the corporation's tax attributes, provided that a net operating loss deduction[120] could not be carried forward if (1) at the end of the corporation's taxable year, its 10 principal shareholders owned a percentage of the corporation's outstanding stock (taken at total fair market value) that was 50 percentage points or more greater than they owned at the beginning of the prior taxable year;[121] (2) the increase resulted from a purchase of stock from an unrelated person

---

[118] For §269, see supra ¶ 16.21. For the 1954 legislation, see S. Rep. No. 1622, 83d Cong., 2d Sess. 53 (1954).

[119] For the resulting reduced significance of §269 so far as net operating losses are concerned, see S. Rep. No. 1622, 83rd Cong., 2d Sess. 284 (1954); S. Rep. No. 938, 94th Cong., 2d Sess. 206 (1976); 1986 Conf. Rep., H.R. Rep. No. 841, 99th Cong., 2d Sess. II-194 (1986); infra notes 130, 139, 148, and 156.

See generally infra ¶ 16.25, para. 7(a).

[120] The 1954 Code version of §382(a) only disallowed net operating loss deductions arising from net operating losses of prior years that were carried over to the year of change of ownership and change of business and to subsequent years; current operating losses incurred in such year apparently were unaffected by §382(a) for that year (but even these would be disallowed as carry-overs to subsequent years). Regs. §1.382(a)-1(h)(2).

[121] An increase in percentage points was not identical with an increase in percentage. Thus, if *A* owns 80 percent of the stock and *B* 20 percent, and *B* purchases 10 percent from *A* so that the stock is held 70 percent by *A* and 30 percent by *B*, *B*'s interest has increased by 50 percent but by only 10 percentage points. His ownership would have to rise to 70 percent before §382(a) could become applicable.

or from a decrease in the amount of stock outstanding; and (3) the corporation did not continue to carry on a trade or business substantially the same as that conducted before any change in stock ownership. These conditions were refined by the 1954 legislation and regulations in considerable detail. Thus, ownership of stock was determined by reference to the constructive ownership rules of §318 (see Chapter 9); related persons were treated as a single person in determining the 10 principal stockholders; the purchase of stock in a holding company or of an interest in a trust or partnership could be treated as a purchase of stock in the loss corporation itself; and "stock" meant all shares except nonvoting stock that was limited and preferred as to dividends.

Conditions (1) and (2) in the preceding paragraph were of course satisfied in the blatant case of an outright purchase of all of the stock of a loss corporation by outside interests; but they could also be satisfied by less drastic changes in ownership, such as the purchase by outside interests of one third of the stock coupled with a redemption (except under §303) of another one third from the original shareholders. Moreover, nothing in §382(a) required a showing that the purchase and redemption were part of a single plan to shift ownership, and such a requirement would have conflicted with the desire of the 1954 drafters to lay down relatively mechanical rules to avoid the probing into purpose required by §269. Thus, §382(a) could be invoked even if the redemption occurred a year after the acquisition of stock as a result of an unanticipated disagreement among the shareholders; similarly, the independent acquisition of stock by 10 unrelated investors also could bring §382(a) into play.[122]

While §382(a) clearly applied to a control-shifting disproportionate stock redemption for cash or other property, the same economic effect could be accomplished on a tax-free basis via a recapitalization exchange or by a non-pro rata split-off or split-up distribution. Application of §382(a) to these situations was less certain, although the Service ruled that §382(a) would not be triggered by a nontaxable §355 distribution.[123]

---

[122] See generally Regs. §§1.382(a)-1(c), 1.382(a)-1(d), 1.382(a)-1(f), and 1.382(a)-1(g). But see Maxwell Hardware Co. v. CIR, supra note 24 (for a well-tailored acquisition that avoided §382(a)).

The regulations as of 1987 still do not reflect the 1964 changes in the sidewise attribution rules, discussed supra ¶ 9.03. See Regs. §§1.382(a)-1(c), Example; 1.382(a)-1(d)(3), Example (2).

[123] Note that a tax-free recapitalization exchange of common stock for new non-voting preferred stock could cause a prohibited change of ownership under §382(a) because the preferred would not constitute stock under §382(c), and thus the transaction could be treated as a redemption under old §382(a)(1)(B)(ii) (even though the exchange was tax-free to the shareholder under §§354(a)(1) and 368(a)(1)(E)). See supra ¶ 14.17.

Section 382(a) was applicable only if the requisite change in ownership was accompanied by purchase (or by a decrease in the outstanding stock) and hence did not reach changes that resulted from gifts, bequests, or exchanges that were tax-free in whole or in part.[124] Moreover, since the term "purchase" was defined by §382(a)(4) to exclude a transaction between related persons, as defined by §382(a)(3), §382(a) did not destroy the carry-over if the corporation was transferred within the same economic group.

Although the rules with respect to changes in stock ownership were quite precise and ordinarily caused little difficulty, the same could not be said of the change of business limitations of §382(a)(1)(C), which required that the corporation continue (until the close of the two-year period) to carry on a business substantially the same as that conducted before the first increase in stock ownership.[125] Of course, a blatant discontinuance of the old

---

A non-pro rata split-off under §355 also literally could result in a prohibited change of ownership to the continuing shareholder under the "decrease" rules of §382(a)(1)(B)(ii) (as could a non-pro rata partial liquidation distribution); but Rev. Rul. 77-133, 1977-1 CB 96, ruled that §382(a) did not apply to tax-free §355 split-off transactions, citing Committee Reports to the 1954 Code to the effect that §382(a) was not intended to apply to reoganizations; moreover, the ruling stated that the same conclusion will apply under amended 1976 §382(a). See supra ¶¶ 13.01–13.15.

[124] Query: Would stock acquisitions from the loss corporation constitute a purchase under §382(a)(4)? It would seem that they could, at least if the buyers took a cost basis for such stock under §1012, but the regulations were unclear on this point. See Regs. §1.382(a)-1(e); Rev. Rul. 75-248, 1975-1 CB 125 (acquisition of additional stock in a tax-free §351 exchange is not a purchase under old §382(a)(4), but such an acquisition in a taxable exchange would constitute a purchase); see also Rev. Rul. 77-81, 1977-1 CB 97 (creditors' acquisition of 85 percent of debtor's stock in exchange for their claims not a purchase because transaction a §351 exchange).

Moreover, §351(d)(2), added by the Bankruptcy Tax Act of 1980, denied §351 property status for non-security debts of the transferee, thus overruling Rev. Rul. 77-81 and expanding the category of transactions that could constitute a taxable purchase of stock under §382(a).

[125] Because of interpretative difficulties and uncertainties of this provision, the Tax Reform Act of 1976 and the Tax Reform Act of 1986 both abolished the change of business test under §382(a); under the new version of this provision, a prohibited shift of ownership is the sole touchstone for application of its limitations.

Section 382(a)(1)(C), relating to the continuation of the old business, did not contain a time limit. In conjunction with §§382(a)(1)(A) and 382(a)(1)(B), however, it seemed to mean that if all the stock of a calendar year corporation changed hands on January 1, the carry-over would be entirely lost if the old business were abandoned during year 1, that it would be lost for year 2 and later years if the business were abandoned during year 2, and that it would not be affected (at least not by §382(a)) if the business were continued until year 3. See Regs. §1.382(a)-1(h)(1), stating that the critical time period for change of business starts with the first increase in owner-ship, which is counted for the 50 percent test. But a change in business made in contemplation of a change in stock ownership will be pushed forward to such date. See Regs. §1.382(a)-1(h)(3); see also supra note 120.

business, coupled with an entry into a totally unrelated activity, would clearly fall within §382(a)(1)(C), but such radical change would often be sufficient proof that tax avoidance motivated the acquisition of the corporation's stock, making §269 applicable to the transaction and §382(a) unnecessary. [126]

Confusion rapidly accelerated, however, when the new owners were sufficiently astute (and the tax stakes sufficiently alluring) to continue the old business to some extent. What was "the same business enterprise" for purposes of §382(a)(1)(C)'s continuity rule? Did the old business have to be continued on the same scale or could it be contracted and, if so, to what extent? Could a new line of business be added or the old business expanded; if so, were there any limits to such growth? What was the effect of a suspension or cessation of business activities, either temporary or total and either voluntary or involuntary? Was it sufficient that one out of several separate businesses previously conducted by the corporation be continued; if so, could manufacturing activities be continued and sales activities dropped (or vice versa), or were both of these functions merely part of a single integrated business? What was a business, as opposed to mere investment activity, for purposes of these rules? What relationship, if any, did §382(a)(1)(C) bear to the "same business" or loss tracing doctrine of the *Libson Shops* case? Finally, what if the old shareholders of the corporation abandoned the loss business, shifted to a different business, and *then* sold their stock to new owners who intended to continue the new business? These and other questions were dealt with at length in Regs. §1.382(a)-1(h) and in the decisions interpreting §382(a)(1)(C), [127] and—of more importance as far as current law

---

[126] For §269, see supra ¶ 16.21.

Query whether the abolition of §334(b)(2) by the Tax Equity and Fiscal Responsibility Act of 1982, supra ¶ 11.46, would raise business continuity problems if *no* §338 election were made and the purchased loss subsidiary were liquidated in a §332–§381(a)(1) transaction by the acquiring corporation? Literally, *such* corporation, having been liquidated into its parent, was no longer carrying on the required business activities; however, §381 may well supply the missing continuity link in this situation, especially in view of the fact that §382(a) was not designed, or intended, to cover §381 transactions. But see §269(b) (tax-avoidance liquidation plan within two years after §338 stock purchase where no §338 election), enacted by the Tax Reform Act of 1984.

Conversely, if a §338 election were made (so that the target-subsidiary was deemed to have sold its assets and immediately repurchased them), §382(a) should not be applied to deny the target corporation's use of its *own* loss carry-overs against any taxable income generated on the deemed sale, since those carry-overs would be so available in the case of a true liquidation; see Temp. Regs. §§1.338-4T(k)(3) and 1.338(h)(10)-1T(e)(3), which so hold.

[127] For cases and rulings applying the change of business rule of the 1954 version of §382, see the Fourth Edition of this treatise; ¶ 16.22. For other provisions embod-

is concerned—difficulties in applying the 1954 business continuity concept led Congress, in 1986, to enact a substantially less demanding alternative.[128]

(b) Section 382(b). In addition to totally disallowing the net operating loss carry-over where (roughly speaking) 50 percent of the corporation's stock changed hands and the old business was abandoned, the drafters of the 1954 Code imposed a limitation, embodied in §382(b), on the carry-over where the corporation went through one of the tax-free reorganizations listed in §381(a)(2).[129] The limitation came into play if the shareholders of the loss corporation received, in exchange for their stock and as a result of the reorganization, less than 20 percent of the stock (taken at fair market value) of the acquiring corporation.[130] The limitation operated in mathematical stages—that is, if the original shareholders received only 15 percent of the reorganized corporation, 25 percent of the carryover was disallowed; if they received 10 percent, 50 percent was disallowed; if they received 5 percent, 75 percent was disallowed—it applied, unlike §382(a), even though the original business was continued. An example of the operation of §382(b) was the merger of a loss corporation into a profitable corporation: If the shareholders of the loss corporation received less than 20 percent of the stock of the merged corporation,[131] the net operating loss carry-over would be reduced as provided by §382(b)(2).

---

ying a business continuity concept, see §355(b), discussed supra ¶ 13.06; see also Libson Shops v. Koehler, supra note 15; infra ¶ 16.26; supra ¶ 14.51, para. 2.

[128] See §382(c)(1), discussed infra ¶ 16.25; see also supra ¶ 14.51, para. 2.

[129] For more extensive discussion of §382(b), see the Fourth Edition of this treatise at ¶ 16.23; see also supra ¶ 16.11.

[130] Although §382(b) was inapplicable if the shareholders of the loss corporation received 20 percent or more of the reorganized corporation's stock, the carry-over could be disallowed under §269. See S. Rep. No. 1622, supra note 119, at 84 ("the fact that a limitation under [§382] does not apply shall have no effect upon whether section 269 applies"), in the light of which the statement in the same report that "if the shareholders of the old corporation have 20 percent of the stock of the new corporation the loss carryover is available to the new corporation without diminution" must be regarded as loose language: The carry-over in such an instance would be available without diminution by §382(b), but it nevertheless ran the gauntlet of §269. See Regs. §1.269-6. Moreover, the statement just quoted must also be modified in another respect: The test under §382(b) was not whether the loss corporation's shareholders *had* the requisite percentage of the reorganized corporation's stock, but whether they *received* that much stock in exchange for their old stock. Stock in the reorganized corporation that was acquired by them in other ways did not count except to the limited extent provided by former §382(b)(3). See Kerns Bakery of Va., Inc., 68 TC 517 (1977); Commonwealth Container Corp. v. CIR, 393 F2d 269 (3d Cir. 1968).

[131] Like §382(a), §382(b) measured ownership of stock in terms of fair market value (excluding nonvoting stock that was limited and preferred as to dividends).

The percentage limitation was not applicable to the carry-over, however, if both corporations were owned by substantially the same persons in the same proportion; thus, the carry-over was not reduced by §382(b) even though less than 20 percent of the reorganized corporation's stock was issued in exchange for the stock of the loss corporation if, in effect, there was merely a merger of two corporations owned in the same proportion by the same interests.[132]

If a small loss corporation was acquired tax-free by a large profit corporation in a triangular Type A or Type C reorganization—that is, a subsidiary of the acquiring corporation was used to receive the assets of the loss company in exchange for stock of the parent—the 20 percent test of §382(b)(2) was applied by looking through the parent corporation and determining the shareholders' continuity as if they owned stock (of equivalent value) of the subsidiary rather than of the parent.[133] Although this method of computing the denominator (i.e., the subsidiary's stock value) in making the 20 percent continuity computation protected the carry-over against invasion, it should be noted that the carry-over is vested in the subsidiary, not in the parent. This is because the subsidiary is the acquiring corporation under §381(a)(2), and this meant that the carry-over could be used only against the subsidiary's income. (Moreover, the consolidated return regulations impose a similar limitation on the use of the acquired corporation's tax attributes in the consolidated return). In effect, then, the triangular asset reorganization was treated essentially the same as a Type B stock-for-stock reorganization; §382(b)(6) merely served to prevent immediate dilution of the loss carry-

---

The 1976 version of §382(b) applied a dual continuity test, looking both to participating stock and stock, whichever was lower. See infra this section, para. 2.

See Kerns Bakery of Va., Inc., supra note 130 (§382(b) applied where less than 20 percent of surviving corporation's stock received in merger; continuity test applied by persons, not §318 "groups"); see also Consolidated Blenders, Inc. v. US, 600 F. Supp 999 (D.C. Neb. 1984) (multiple loss corporation mergers into a single corporation; held, could aggregate loss companies' shareholders to meet 20 percent threshhold; Regs. §1.382(b)-1(a)(5), requiring separate computations, invalid); but rev'd, 785 F2d 259 (8th Cir. 1986) (regulations valid; no aggregation allowed); Kliegman, Multiple Acquisitions and the Carry-Over Rules, 65 J. Tax'n 94 (1986).

[132] See Commonwealth Container Corp. v. CIR, supra note 130 (common control exception not applicable to merger of loss corporation into profitable corporation where shareholders who owned 100 percent of former and 75 percent of latter before merger ended up with 78 percent of latter; carry-over reduced by 35 percent because loss company shareholders only received 13 percent of profit company's stock in merger); see also Kerns Bakery of Va., Inc., supra note 130; Regs. §1.382(b)-1(d)(2), Examples (1)–(4).

[133] See §382(b)(6); Regs. §1.382(b)-1(g)(1), Example; see also Rev. Rul. 86-52, 1986-1 CB 204 (§382(b)(1) applies to §368(a)(2)(E) reverse merger using a transitory subsidiary, but so does §382(b)(6) look-through rule, so loss carry-overs not reduced). For triangular reorganizations, see supra ¶ 14.15.

overs at the time of the acquisition. One further point: prompt liquidation of the subsidiary would open the transaction to characterization as an acquisition of assets by the parent, with the result that the transferor shareholders' interest (and hence the size of the carry-over) would be determined by reference to their percentage of ownership of the parent's stock rather than the subsidiary's.[134]

Suppose the stock ownership (of either the acquired or acquiring corporation) was adjusted on the eve of the acquisition by a recapitalization that converted outstanding debt (or nonvoting preferred stock, which, by virtue of §382(c), was ignored for purposes of §382) into common stock. If the threshold recapitalization was severable from the acquisition, the new shareholders would enter into the §382(b) continuity computation when they exchanged their stock for stock of the acquiring corporation. If the two steps were treated as part of a single transaction, however, the new shareholders could be treated as acquiring their stock in the recapitalization exchange rather than in the acquisitive reorganization transaction. The Service indicated a lenient attitude in allowing recapitalization exchanges in advance of a contemplated acquisition to stand as independent transactions for purposes of §382(b); a ruling that permitted a recapitalization to set the stage for a tax-free spin-off distribution under §355[135] evidences considerable flexibility on the part of the Service in this respect.[136]

---

[134] See Rev. Rul. 67-274, 1967-2 CB 141; Regs. §1.382(b)-1(a)(6). For a decision applying the principles of Rev. Rul. 67-274, see Resorts Int'l, Inc., 60 TC 778 (1973), aff'd on this issue, 511 F2d 107 (5th Cir. 1975), where a stock for stock acquisition followed by a planned §332 liquidation was treated as a unitary asset acquisition for purposes of applying the limitations of §382(b). Both the Tax Reform Act of 1976 and the Tax Reform Act of 1986 amendments to §382(b) obviate this problem by testing continuity at the parent level.

When §334(b)(2) was repealed (for liquidations after August 31, 1982) by the Tax Equity and Fiscal Responsibility Act of 1982, all §332 liquidations became §334(b)(1)–§381(a)(1) transactions. Moreover, both the Senate Finance Committee Report and the Conference Committee Report specifically state that the new statutory rules preempt the *Kimbell-Diamond* principle; S. Rep. No. 494, 97th Cong., 2d Sess. 192 (1982), H.R. Rep. No. 760, 97th Cong., 2d Sess. 536 (1982). Thus, attempts to convert stock acquisitions into asset acquisitions under step transaction principles may be more difficult under the 1982 regime (although this approach may have continued vitality in cases where the stock acquisition was tax-free, and hence was not governed by §338 because it did not constitute a qualified purchase). See also §269(b), added by the Tax Reform Act of 1984, which applies to tax motivated §332 liquidations within two years of a §338 stock purchase; supra ¶ 16.21.

[135] Rev. Rul. 69-407, 1969-2 CB 50.

[136] See also Rev. Rul. 77-227, 1977-2 CB 120 (issuance of nonvoting preferred stock dividend to shareholders of acquiring corporation prior to acquisition of loss corporation for purpose of enabling latter's shareholders to receive 20 percent of former's stock and thereby meet §382(b) line held to be acceptable planning device;

Although the constructive ownership rules of §318 were made applicable to §382(a) transactions by §382(a)(3), §318 did not apply to §382(b). Thus, options, warrants, and convertible debentures presumably were not to be considered outstanding stock for purposes of §382(b); moreover, continuity percentages were computed by reference to the shareholders' actual, rather than constructive, ownership. [137]

2. 1976 Senate Finance Committee proposals. In 1976, the Senate Committee on Finance announced that the time had come to impose more effective restrictions on trafficking in net operating loss carry-overs by (1) coordinating the rules applicable to taxable and tax-free acquisitions involving loss companies; (2) curing weaknesses in the rule-of-thumb aspects of prior law; and (3) ending uncertainties caused by the change-of-business rule in §382(a) and the subjective state of mind test of §269. [138]

The Senate Finance Committee therefore proposed that §382(a) be tightened and clarified in the following manner:

(1) The business continuity test of §382(a)(1)(C) would be dropped; thus, mere change of ownership would be enough to trigger §382(a);

(2) The triggering change of ownership by purchase would be raised from 50 to 60 percentage points;

(3) The all-or-nothing disallowance rule would be replaced by a proportional reduction approach—that is, for each point of change

---

stock dividend had independent significance here; same principle will apply to amended §382(b) rules). But see Regs. §1.382(b)-1(c).

[137] Regs. §1.382(c)-1. But see World Serv. Life Ins. Co. v. US, 471 F2d 247 (8th Cir. 1973) (§382(b) continuity satisfied by transferor loss corporation's ownership of acquiring corporation's stock; distribution to shareholders not necessary and regulation's implications to contrary invalid); compare Kerns Bakery of Va., Inc., supra note 130 (no §318 in §382(b)). However, see also Consolidated Blenders, Inc. v. US, supra note 131 (cannot aggregate shareholders for 20 percent test where mergers of multiple loss companies into one corporation; regulation so holding is valid).

See Rev. Rul. 76-36, 1976-1 CB 105 (Service will not follow *World Service* decision; on downstream merger of parent into loss subsidiary, §382(b) applied and §382(b)(3) common control exception not applicable; but special rule of §382(b)(5) did apply and cut down the loss of carry-overs because stock of subsidiary was worth 10 percent of combined value of the group; in effect, if subsidiary worth 20 percent of group, downstream merger will not cause loss of carry-overs; ruling also noted that §332 liquidation not covered by §382(b)). For comment on *World Service* and Rev. Rul. 76-36, see Friedrich, The Sad Case of Section 382(b)(5): Indirect Stock Ownership May Not Be Taken Into Account for Purposes of Net Operating Loss Carryovers, 2 J. Corp. Tax'n 465 (1976).

[138] S. Rep. No. 938, 94th Cong., 2d Sess. 206 (1984).

above 60 percent, a specified proportion of the carryover would be denied (thus coordinating the purchase rules of §382(a) with the treatment of mergers under §382(b));

(4) The change of ownership time span would be increased from two to three years, and the shareholder test group increased in size from 10 to 15;

(5) Losses incurred in the acquisition year would be covered by the revised limitations (prior law did not directly hit these losses, since it dealt only with loss carry-over deductions);

(6) A change of ownership would be tested by the greater of the increase in voting power or value;

(7) Section 351 exchanges were added to §382(a) transactions;

(8) Any combination of stock purchases, redemptions, or §351 exchanges would trigger application of §382(a);

(9) A special single-taint rule would be provided to cover the case where no change of ownership occurred after the first year; and

(10) The Service was authorized to provide regulations governing hybrid potential equity interests, which were to be treated as the equivalent of the underlying stock (e.g., convertibles).[139]

The Senate Finance Committee also proposed to significantly tighten the provisions of §382(b) in the following manner:

(1) The minimum continuity of interest line for shareholders of the loss corporation would be doubled from 20 percent to 40 percent;

(2) The limitations of §382(b) would be made applicable to Type B reorganizations;

(3) Coincidentally with the foregoing, triangular reorganizations also would be subject to §382(b) by testing shareholder continuity with respect to their actual interest in the *parent's* stock; and

(4) Shareholder stock ownership would be measured solely by reference to participating voting stock of the acquiring corporation, defined by proposed §382(c)(2) as voting stock which was not limited and preferred as to earnings or assets.

The language and basic structure of §382(b), except for the above proposed changes, was virtually identical. Thus, the common ownership exception of §382(b)(3) was unchanged, the consumption mechanism of

---

[139] Id. The Senate Report also envisioned a modest role for §269 under this regime.

§382(b)(4) (by which phantom income, to the extent of the disallowed carry-over, is generated for purposes of absorbing the carry-overs) was continued unchanged, and the special attribution rule of §382(b)(5) was continued in virtually the same form in the proposed legislation. While proposed §382(b), as amended, would have been significantly more restrictive than existing law, the basic language and organization of that provision would have continued to be readily recognizable.

3. The 1976 amendments. The Senate Finance Committee's proposals, after substantial technical changes by the Conference Committee,[140] were enacted into law in 1976, subject, however, to a postponed effective date. This date was repeatedly postponed by Congress until 1986, when the 1976 rules were retroactively repealed and a substantially revised version of §382 was enacted to govern post-1986 transactions.[141]

4. Extension of §382 limits to carry-overs of certain tax credits and capital losses. Under §383, originally enacted in 1971, the limitations applied by §382 to net operating loss carry-overs were extended to the carry-over of certain unused tax credits and capital losses.[142] As amended in 1986, §383 limits the carry-over of excess general business credits, minimum tax credits, foreign tax credits, and net capital losses in a manner consistent with §382's limits on the carry-over of net operating losses, provided there is an ownership change as defined by §382(g).[143]

5. Ownership aspects: Section 382(c). The shareholder continuity rules under the 1976 version of §§382(a) and 382(b) determined ownership of the requisite amount of stock by reference to the value of either participating stock or stock, whichever produced the more onerous tax result. This version of §382(c) contained special definitions of the terms "stock" and "participating stock" that applied throughout §§382(a) and 382(b) and that had the effect of classifying a corporation's equity capital structure into three categories for purposes of this provision: nonstock, participating stock, and stock.

---

[140] See Eustice, The Tax Reform Act of 1976: Loss Carryovers and Other Corporate Changes, 32 Tax L. Rev. 113 (1977).

[141] For the sources of discontent with the 1976 rules and an analysis of the 1986 version of §382, see generally infra this section, para. 7, and ¶ 16.23. For a detailed examination of the defunct 1976 rules, see the Fourth Edition of this treatise and 1987 Cumulative Supplement No. 2, ¶ 16.24.

[142] See S. Rep. No. 437, 92nd Cong., 1st Sess. 63 (1971), reprinted in 1972-1 CB 559, 594.

[143] For §382(g), see infra ¶ 16.24.

The latter consisted of all equity interests not specifically exempted by §382(c)(1). Examples of stock included voting preferred and convertible preferred as well as common stock.

Nonstock was defined in the negative by §382(c)(1) as stock that met all of the following tests:

(1) It was not entitled to vote (presumably this meant a present vote).[144]

(2) It was fixed and preferred as to dividends and did not participate in corporate growth to any significant extent.

(3) Its redemption and liquidation rights did not exceed par or paid in capital with respect to such stock (except that a reasonable redemption premium, although *not* a liquidation premium, was allowed.)

(4) It was not convertible.

In short, this type of stock interest was the classic prototype preferred stock interest.[145] Economically, it more nearly resembled debt than equity in view of its extremely limited interest in the corporate enterprise and hence would not be treated as carrying continuity genes for purposes of §382.

Participating stock was defined by §382(c)(2) as stock (whether voting or nonvoting) that represented an interest in earnings *and* (note, *not* "or") assets that were not limited in amount or percentage. This type of stock was essentially common stock, since it represented an unlimited equity interest in the residual growth of the enterprise.[146] It should be noted that participat-

---

[144] See, e.g., Rev. Rul. 71-83, 1971-1 CB 268; Rev. Rul. 72-72, 1972-1 CB 104 (holding, respectively, that stock was not voting stock even though convertible into voting stock and that stock subject to a five-year voting trust restriction was not voting stock). Compare Rev. Rul. 73-28, 1973-1 CB 187 (stock voting stock even though not votable because held by subsidiary).

[145] See Regs. §1.305-5(a) (an analogous definition of preferred stock); see also §1504(a)(4), added by the Tax Reform Act of 1984, supra ¶ 15.21, which contains virtually identical language for defining excluded preferred stock; infra note 159.

[146] Regs. §1.305-5(a) (similar distinctions between common and preferred stock based upon whether the stock has a significant participation in corporate growth or instead has a cap on its interest in the enterprise).

There are rulings under §306(c)(1)(A) that take a similar approach in defining common stock: Rev. Rul. 75-222, 1975-1 CB 105 (common even though preferred as to dividends); Rev. Rul. 75-236, 1975-1 CB 106 (not common because of cap on interest in corporate growth, even though only stock with voting rights); Rev. Rul. 76-386, 1976-2 CB 95 (common even though subject to right of first refusal at book value); Rev. Rul. 76-387, 1976-2 CB 96 (common even though no voting rights).

But for purposes of §382(c)(2), the only stock that clearly would qualify as participating stock was that described in Rev. Rul. 76-387; the other interests were lim-

ing stock would also constitute stock, although the converse was not true, while nonstock was totally excluded from the computations of §382. Finally, the Treasury was authorized by §382(c)(3) to determine, by regulations, whether various hybrid equity interests (including convertible debt) were to be included or excluded from classification as stock or participating stock by reason of special conversion and call rights, interests in earnings and assets, priorities and preferences as to distributions of earnings or assets, and the like.[147]

6. Other indirect changes in carry-over rules. The Senate Committee report indirectly effected a major downgrading of §269 when it stated that, while §269 would be retained for transactions not expressly covered by new §382 (i.e., "to deal with 'built-in loss' transactions and other exchanges or transfers which are apparent devices to exploit continuing gaps in the technical rules for tax avoidance purposes"), "the committee believes, however, that §269 should not be applied to disallow net operating loss carryovers in situations where part or *all* of a loss carryover is permitted under the specific rules of §382, unless a device or scheme to circumvent the purpose of the carryover restrictions appears to be present."[148] This language is reminiscent of similar statements of the Senate Committee in 1954 when it enacted §382 but that were ignored by the Service in drafting the regulations under §269.[149]

Similar comments as to the vitality of the *Libson Shops* doctrine noted the considerable uncertainty associated with this decision and stated that "in view of the changes made in present law in the amendment, the committee believes that the so-called *Libson Shops* approach should have no application to determining net operating loss carry-overs after stock purchases or reorganizations in tax years *for which the amendment is effective.*"[150] Did this

---

ited in some respect. Query: Would common stock subject to a typical buy-sell agreement formula price restriction qualify as participating stock? If based on book, it may well not, but, if based on values, it should.

[147] Presumably warrants would continue to be treated as not stock or securities. But cf. §305(d)(1). The treatment of contingent issue stock rights as present stock for purposes of §382 continued to be unclear even under the 1976 rules. Section 382(c)(3) seemed broad enough to permit the Treasury to deal with these problems, as well as those doubtful label interests specifically enumerated in §382(c)(3). While the rest of §382 had a delayed effective date, §382(c) well may have become effective at once, on October 4, 1976.

[148] S. Rep. No. 938, supra note 138.

[149] Supra note 130.

[150] S. Rep. No. 938, supra note 138, at 206 (emphasis added).

But this language was clarified in the conference report by a statement that "the conferees intend that no inference should be drawn from [the Senate] discussion con-

mean that *Libson Shops* had vitality *until* such date: the period from 1954 until 1976? Arguably, the Senate Committee report had breathed new life into what many had viewed as a dead issue.

7. Subsequent reform developments. General disenchantment with the 1954 Code §382 regime and equal distaste for the 1976 proposed reforms stimulated Congress to return to the carry-over scene in the 1980's. The opening salvo occurred in 1983, when the staff of the Senate Finance Committee, in a preliminary report submitted September 22, 1983, proposed to replace the 1976 Act provisions of §382 (and §269 as well) with a new set of objective tax history carry-over limitations, under which an acquiring corporation would be denied any greater benefit after an acquisition than would be available before an acquisition. The staff's final report was released two years later, on May 20, 1985, and contained specific statutory draft language as well as general and technical explanations. The final report version of the §382 loss carry-over limitations dropped the dual limitation approach of the preliminary report, however, and instead adopted a single limitation based on the acquisition value of the target corporation. The staff's proposals for the reform of §382 ultimately found their way into the 1986 tax reform legislation (in recognizable form, although differing considerably in numerous technical details).

The reformers of §382 found the 1954 Code version of §382 both too rigorous when it applied (for example, §382(a) completely eliminated carry-overs) and too lax in its application (for example, §382(a) could be avoided relatively easily in continuing the loss corporation's business for a decent interval, while §382(b) could be finessed in a variety of ways, principally through the device of acquiring stock in a Type B reorganization or triangular merger). Moreover, the differing limitations in §§382(a) and 382(b) were irrational, as were the myriad technical uncertainties surrounding the change of business rules of §382(a)(1)(C). The 1976 reform attempt was found deficient for similar reasons—that is, it punished those who triggered its application too harshly, while leaving open numerous avenues of escape from the activation of the limitation. Moreover, the 1976 version of §382 was felt to be overly complex (a condition that was *not*, however, materially improved in the 1986 version).

The reform developments leading up to the Tax Reform Act of 1986 are discussed in detail in the following section.

---

cerning the applicability or nonapplicability of the *Libson Shops* case, either generally or as to specific types of transactions, in determining net operating loss carry-overs to tax years governed by present law." S. Conf. Rep. No. 1236, 94th Cong., 2d Sess. 450 (1976).

¶ 16.23 SECTION 382: THE TAX REFORM ACT OF 1986 AMENDMENTS—BACKGROUND, EVOLUTION, AND OVERVIEW

1. General. The staff of the Senate Finance Committee submitted a preliminary report on the reform and simplification of Subchapter C on September 22, 1983. One of the major elements of this report was a proposal to replace the existing limitations on corporate net operating loss (and certain other) carry-overs with a new system of limitations, which were intended to permit a loss corporation to use its tax carry-overs following a change of ownership only to the extent that it could have used them had there been no such change of ownership. The report alleged that the then-current rules were both too lax and too restrictive in attempting to confine the carry-over provisions to their primary function of income averaging.

The stated goals of the 1983 proposals were threefold: (1) to provide for tax neutrality on the disposition of corporations that possess favorable tax carry-over characteristics (i.e., to eliminate both incentives and disincentives for the acquisition); (2) to limit the use of corporate tax benefits generated under one set of owners to the income attributable to the pool of capital that generated such benefits; and (3) to provide objective rules that could be applied and administered with greater certainty.[151]

The preliminary staff proposals did not contain specific statutory language, but the staff's final report, released on May 20, 1985, did contain a draft bill reflecting the proposed amendments, as well as general and technical explanations to these provisions. Hearings were held before the Ways & Means Subcommittee on Select Revenue Measures on these and other proposals to amend the loss carry-over limitations on May 22, 1985,[152] and similar hearings were held before a Senate Finance Subcommittee on September 30, 1985.[153] The final version of §382, as ultimately enacted by the Tax Reform Act of 1986 on October 22, 1986, bears a noticeable resemblance both in basic structure and technical detail to these proposals.

A bifurcated approach was first proposed in the preliminary report. This approach consisted of the purchase rule (which consisted generally of

---

[151] These preliminary proposals were greatly influenced by the American Law Institute Federal Income Tax Project, Subchapter C: Proposals of the American Law Institute on Corporate Acquisitions and Dispositions (1982); see also Bacon & Tomasulo, supra note 19; Campisano & Romano, On the Benefits of Loss Recoupment: A Response, XXI Tax Notes, No. 3, at 209 (1983); Nichols, Net Operating Loss Carryovers and Section 382, supra note 19.

[152] See Joint Committee staff pamphlet prepared for use at these hearings, supra note 2.

[153] The Treasury testimony at these hearings (which generally supported the Finance Committee staff proposal for revision of §382), is reprinted in 190 DTR (BNA) J-10 (1985).

acquisitions of stock control or assets in a carry-over basis transaction for consideration *other* than stock) and the merger rule (i.e., carry-over basis acquisitions for stock). Ownership shifts by means of a stock redemption were governed by the purchase rule, and ownership shifts through the issuance of new stock by the loss corporation were treated under the merger rule. Each provision would have had its own set of specific (and different) rules. But the staff's final report abandoned the dual limitation approach of the preliminary proposals and switched to a single limitation based on acquisition value of the loss corporation immediately prior to the limitation triggering event and further limited to an annual utilization rate based on the applicable long-term federal interest rate of §1274(d). Moreover, the pool of capital concept of the preliminary proposals was abandoned by the final version in favor of an acquisition price-based limitation.

The underlying theory of the final proposal was the so-called neutrality principle (i.e., abolition of both incentives and disincentives for an acquisition of the loss corporation). By removing the potential for a tax profit from the acquisition, it was felt that only economically motivated transactions would result. The impetus for the staff's final report approach to loss carryover limitations stemmed from a proposal by the ABA Tax Section,[154] which was basically similar to (although considerably more liberal than) the final staff report regime.

The remainder of this section traces the evolution of the final Tax Reform Act of 1986 version of §382 from the initial proposals of the Finance Committee staff in 1985 to its eventual passage in the 1986 Act. Readers for whom such background is not relevant can find more pertinent technical explanations of current §382 in the two following sections.

2. The final staff proposals (May 1985). The staff's final proposal to revise §382 proposed to limit the use of corporate loss carry-overs and the like after a specified triggering event, which generally would be defined in new §382A as a substantial (more than 50 percent) change in control of the loss corporation. These rules operated to limit the amount of taxable income after a change in control that could be offset by losses arising prior to the change; the limitation each year following such a change would be determined initially (and permanently) by the value of the loss corporation at the time of the change multiplied by the applicable federal long-term rate under §1274(d). These rules were designed to replace both the 1954 and 1976 ver-

---

[154] See Jacobs, Tax Treatment of Net Operating Losses and Other Tax Attribute Carryovers, 5 Va. Tax Rev. 701 (1986); see also Joint Committee staff pamphlet prepared for Ways and Means hearings on May 22, 1985, supra note 2; Bacon & Tomasulo, supra note 19 (whose purchase price amendment antedated the ABA proposal); Camp, supra note 20.

sions of §§382 and 383 and also to supplant §269 and any lingering *Libson Shops* limitations.

> *To illustrate:* If *L* corporation had $100 of loss carry-overs and *P* acquired all of *L*'s stock for $50 (the value of *L*) at a time when the AFR was 10 percent, the amount of *L*'s post-change taxable income that could be offset by the pre-hange carry-overs would be limited to a $5 annual ceiling (in effect, *L* could never consume all of its carry-overs on these facts, since the maximum §172 life of a carry-over is only 15 years, and it would take *L* 20 years to earn out the losses under these facts). If, on the other hand, *P* acquired all of *L*'s stock for $200, the annual loss utilization limitation ceiling would be $20, and *L* could earn out its loss carry-overs in five years, assuming it generated enough taxable income during these years. Thus, the higher the price that *P* paid for *L*, the more rapid the absorption of *L*'s carry-overs.

The two basic ownership change transactional patterns that would trigger application of this proposed §382 limitation were: (1) a "more than 50 percent owner shift" (which was generally a stock acquisition transaction) and (2) a more than 50 percent equity structure change (which would arise in the case of a qualified asset acquisition transaction). Thus, the owner shift transaction was essentially comparable to §382(a) of the 1954 Code (and would encompass stock ownership changes effected by redemptions, recapitalizations, conversions, and new stock issues), while the equity structure change transaction would be comparable to the 1954 Code §382(b). The testing period for determining whether the applicable change has occurred was the three-year period preceding the date of change (1954 law required only a two-year lookback). Changes by less-than-5-percent shareholders would be disregarded in determining whether a stock ownership change occurred, while acquisitions of stock by death, gift, or divorce would not count. In testing whether a control shift had occurred, pure preferred stock, described in §1502(a)(4), would be disregarded (although such stock *would* be counted in determining the annual loss limitation amount value of the loss corporation).

These proposals also contained a series of intricate special rules dealing with the following issues: (1) midyear ownership changes (where daily proration rules were provided); (2) substantial (i.e., 25 percent) built-in gains and losses of noncash assets recognized within five years after the triggering ownership change (i.e., in situations where the loss corporation had substantially depreciated or appreciated assets at the date of the ownership change, recognized built-in losses would be subjected to the general §382 loss limitation rules in the year they were recognized, while recognized built-in gains would increase the amount of the annual loss limitation); (3) successive ownership changes of the loss corporation; (4) capital contributions within two years of the ownership change (the so-called anti-stuffing rule, which was designed to inhibit attempts to inflate the value of the loss company and the consequent annual loss limitation figure); (5) investment companies (which would be denied any carry-over if at least two-thirds of the value of their total assets consisted of "assets held for investment," which term, however, was not statutorily defined); and (6) ownership changes effected in title 11 insolvency proceedings (here *no* owner shift trigger event would result if shareholders *and* creditors of the loss corporation maintained at least a 50 percent stock ownership interest in the reorganized corporation, but three years of interest deductions on debt converted into equity in the title 11 proceeding would be denied in computing the loss carry-over deduction, and, moreover, if another change occurred within two years, the carry-overs would be totally eliminated). The Technical Explanation section of the staff's final report contained 19 examples illustrating the application of the proposed new loss carry-over limitation proposals that were recommended for careful study in understanding how these limitations would operate.

3. The House Bill Tax Reform Act (December 1985). The loss limitation rules proposed by the House Tax Reform Bill version of §382 were basically the same as those contained in the Senate Finance Committee staff proposal. Thus, the specified triggering events that activated the limitation provisions were keyed to substantial (more than 50 percent) shifts in the ownership or equity structure of the old loss corporation, and carry-overs would be limited by the net value of the loss corporation immediately before those events multiplied by a specified recovery rate (although in this instance the rate would be the long-term *tax exempt* rate). However, unlike the staff proposal, the rules did *not* replace §269 (or the consolidated return regulations limitation), although they did replace the 1954 and 1976 versions of §382 and preempt the *Libson Shops* doctrine.

While the similarities between the Senate staff and the House bill proposals in term of basic approach and technical implementation provisions were greater than their differences, there nevertheless were several significant technical variations between the two. The following are the principal ones:

(1) The House bill imposed a continuity of business enterprise limitation on any limitation triggering transaction that had to be satisfied for two years after the triggering event (a limitation that was based on the §368 regulations principles in Regs. §1.368-1(d));

(2) The House bill excluded pure preferred stock, as defined in §1504(a)(4), from the determination of the acquisition value limitation (unlike the staff proposal); while acquisition value of the loss corporation ordinarily was determined *before* the triggering event, in the case of redemptions and certain insolvency transactions, the House bill provided that value was to be determined *after* the trig-

gering event (which generally would result in a lower limiting amount);

(3) The House bill provided *no* exceptions from the owner-shift trigger event definition, except that less-than-5-percent shareholders were disregarded (although all non-5-percent shareholders were required to be aggregated and treated as one shareholder for this purpose);

(4) The House bill excluded divisive Types D and G reorganizations from the equity structure change trigger event definition;

(5) The House bill provided no special exception for insolvency transactions (i.e., Type G reorganizations and equity for debt exchanges in title 11 and other proceedings), save for testing acquisition value *after* the triggering event, rather than before, as was the general rule (and which would thus deny *any* carry-over by an insolvent corporation);

(6) The House bill rules on built-in losses were more stringent (the built-in gain or loss limitation period was 10 years rather than five, and the de minimis line was only 15 percent rather than 25 percent);

(7) The House bill's anti-stuffing rule for capital contributions looked back three years rather than two in eliminating pre-trigger capital contributions from the acquisition value amount; and

(8) The House bill dealt with the passive asset problem by providing a scale-back rule (if passive assets were one third or more of total assets) in lieu of the total disallowance cliff approach proposed in the staff bill. [155]

4. Senate Bill Tax Reform Act (June 1986). The Finance Committee's tax reform proposal of March 18, 1986, included the staff's 1985 §382 proposal, although in slightly altered form. Thus, the utilization rate was changed from long-term to mid-term AFR, the insolvency exception was tightened to require that exchanging creditors in an insolvency proceeding must have held their debt for at least one year before *filing* the insolvency proceeding (or the debt must have arisen in the ordinary course of business), the built-in loss limitation would not apply to depreciation deductions, and §269 would be retained. The Senate proposal was effective in 1987 (the 1976 Act provisions being retroactively repealed to January 1, 1986), and this legislation passed the Senate on June 24, 1986.

---

[155] For analysis of the House Bill, see N.Y. State Bar Association, Tax Section, Report on the Net Operating Loss Provisions of the House-Passed Version of H.R. 3838, 31 Tax Notes 1217 (1986): Stone & Jacobs, An Analysis of the Net Operating Loss and Excess Credit Carryforwards Under H.R. 3838, 31 Tax Notes 725 (1986); Jacobs, supra note 154.

A comparison of the three principal §382 proposals (i.e., the ABA proposal, the Senate Finance Committee staff proposal (which was virtually identical to the Senate Bill), and the House bill) is contained in the following table.

TABLE 16-1

Comparison of §382 Proposals

Features	ABA Proposals on Corporate Acquisition	Senate Finance Committee Staff Proposals	House Tax Reform Bill
1. Limitation			
(a) Gross cap amount	120% of value	Equity value	Equity value
(b) Annual utilization rate	24% over 5 years	§1274(d) (taxable)	§1274(d) (tax exempt)
(c) Continuity of historic business	None	None	Yes (§368 test only)
(d) Measure	Include capitalized old debt	Net equity (all)	Exclude preferred stock
(e) Time of measure	Before trigger	Before trigger	Before trigger (except for redemptions and insolvencies)
(f) Items covered	NOLs, carry-over losses, credits	NOLs, carry-over losses, credits	NOLs, carry-over losses, credits
2. Owner shift trigger			
(a) Size	More than 50%	More than 50%	More than 50%
(b) Exceptions	Yes	Some, but fewer	None
(c) Test period	Integrated plan	3 years	3 years
(d) Shares covered	Participating stock only; ignore less than 5% shareholders	Ignore preferred stock; ignore less than 5% shareholders	Ignore preferred stock; aggregate all small shareholders and treat as one shareholder
(e) Market value fluctuations	Silent	Ignore	Ignore
3. Equity structure shift trigger			
(a) Definition	No separate rule	Any qualified asset acquisition	Any reorganization except divisive
(b) Size (continuity of old shareholder)	Less than 50%; ignore 5%	Less than 50%	Less than 50%

Features	ABA Proposals on Corporate Acquisition	Senate Finance Committee Staff Proposals	House Tax Reform Bill
4. Antistuffing rule			
(a) Period	2 years	2 years (or longer if a plan)	3 years
(b) Exceptions	Yes-business needs	None	De minimis
5. Passive assets	No limit	No carry-over if ⅔ of value	Scale-back if ⅓ of value
6. Built-ins			
(a) Term	5 years	5 years	10 years
(b) Exceptions	None	25% de minimis	15% de minimis
7. Insolvency proceedings	Exception for creditor exchanges for stock	Generally not a trigger event (but only one bite and lose interest)	No special rules
8. Other limitations	Preempt §269 and *Libson*	Preempt §269 and *Libson*	Maintain all except *Libson*

5. Final Conference version—The Tax Reform Act of 1986. The final version of §382, as drafted by the Conference Committee, blended and refined both the House and Senate bill proposals (although the House bill seems to have been dominant in this process), but also introduced some new technical provisions of its own. The basic structure of §382 of the 1986 Code, however, is still clearly recognizable from the 1985 Finance Committee staff proposals. Thus, the specified events that activate the limitation provisions are keyed to substantial (more than 50 percentage points) shifts in the ownership or equity structure of the old loss corporation, and that corporation's tax attribute carry-overs generally are limited by its net equity value immediately before those events, multiplied by a specified recovery rate (here the House bill long-term *tax exempt* rate was adopted in §382(f)). Moreover, §269 and the consolidated return regulation limitations are preserved, but the 1954 and 1976 versions of §382 are replaced, and the *Libson Shops* doctrine is finally interred.[156]

The principal features of new §382 are the following:

(1) Section 382(a) generally limits the amount of loss carry-overs and the like that can be set off annually against the taxable income of the loss corporation (similar to the SRLY limitations of the consolidated return regulations) to its "section 382 limitation," which is defined in §382(b) as the loss corporation's value before the

---

[156] See H.R. Rep. No. 841, 99th Cong., 2d Sess. 194 (1986).

triggering event multiplied by the applicable long-term tax exempt bond rate of §382(f).

In determining the value of the loss corporation, §382(e)(1) measures the net equity value of *all* the loss company's stock (including pure preferred), but §382(e)(2) determines value in the case of redemption ownership shifts immediately *after* the redemption (as did the House bill).

(2) The House bill's continuity of business enterprise limitation was adopted in §382(c)(1) (under which *no* carry-overs will be allowed unless business enterprise continuity exists for two years after the limitation triggering event); but §382(c)(2) allows the carry-over against any built-in gains of the loss company, and any §338 election gains, when they are recognized.

(3) Stock acquired by death, gift, or divorce gets to tack the holding period of the transferor under §382(*l*)(3)(B) (while §382(*l*)(3)(C) disregards stock acquired by certain employee stock ownership plans); this represents a compromise between the House bill (which provided for *no* exceptions from the owner shift triggers), and the Senate bill (which totally excluded such transactions).

(4) The House bill provision that aggregated all less than 5-percent shareholders and treated them as one shareholder was adopted in §382(g)(4)(A).

(5) Transactions excluded from the equity structure (i.e., reorganization) change triggered by §382(g)(3)(A) are divisive Types D and G reorganizations (the House bill proposal) and also Type Fs (new in the final version); but §382(g)(3)(B) also *includes* taxable reorganization-type transactions, public offerings, and the like, as provided—prospectively only—by regulations (a new provision).

(6) The final legislation in §382(h) generally adopted the more lenient Senate bill rules for built-in gains and losses (i.e., where the loss corporation has substantial noncash asset appreciation or depreciation in value before the limitation triggering event); thus, the de minimis threshold is 25 percent and the applicable post-trigger recognition period is five years.

(7) Moreover, the Conference bill adopted the Senate proposal for anti-stuffing limitations in §382(*l*)(1) (which ignores pre-change capital contributions intended to inflate the value of the loss company).

(8) However, the House bill passive asset rule was accepted in §382(*l*)(4)(A)—that is, if more than one third of the loss company's assets are investment assets, the value of the loss corporation will be reduced by the amount of such assets, net of allocable debt, (but investment companies, such as regulated investment

companies and real estate investment trusts, are exempted from this rule by §382(*l*)(4)(B)(ii), a new addition).

(9) The rules for insolvency transactions in §382(*l*)(5), though based on the Senate bill proposal, were significantly contracted in the final legislation. Thus, while no limitation generally will be triggered if stockholders and qualified creditors (i.e., those who have either held their claims for 18 months before the *filing* of the insolvency proceeding or whose claims arose in the ordinary course of business) retain ownership of at least 50 percent (of vote and value) of the loss corporation, loss carry-overs will be reduced by three years of interest deductions on debt converted to stock and also by one-half of any gain realized by the debtor in paying off its debt claims with stock.

   Moreover, §382(*l*)(5)(D) allows only one insolvency shift every two years, while §382(*l*)(6) tests the loss corporation's value after the insolvency transaction if §382(*l*)(5) does not apply (this provision was contained in the House bill).

(10) Finally, a megadelegation to regulations is made by §382(m) (for that matter, there are 22 such delegations throughout the extensive provisions of §382), that should ensure a high degree of uncertainty until those regulations are forthcoming and, when they eventually do appear, a regulation corpus that will inevitably be monumental in size and complexity (as much, perhaps, as the §338 morass).

The Conference Committee report also contains 25 useful (and essential) examples illustrating the operation of the new §382 rules.

In summary, the new §382 rules, as a practical matter, seem destined to virtually eliminate any significant loss carry-over transfer possibilities, except in those cases where the acquired company's losses are relatively incidental to its business enterprise. Why Congress felt it still needed §269 (or, for that matter, the consolidated return regulation SRLY rules) is difficult to perceive, since §382, as effective in 1987, has effectively barred the assignability of significant corporate loss carry-over and tax credit carry-over attributes.[157]

---

[157] However, §269 covers a broader range of corporate tax attributes than §§382 and 383; thus, a diminished role for §269 should result only in those situations where these sections overlap; infra ¶ 16.25, text at note 230.

   For analyses of the final version of §382, see Eustice, Kuntz, Lewis, & Deering, The Tax Reform Act of 1986 (Warren, Gorham & Lamont, Inc., 1987) ¶ 2.04; Peaslee & Cohen, Section 382 as Amended by the Tax Reform Act of 1986, 33 Tax Notes 849 (1986); Wooton, Section 382 After the Tax Reform Act of 1986, 64 Taxes 874 (1986);

The following table contains a tabular summary of the principal features of §382. A more detailed analysis of the events that activate application of the §382 limitations and of the operation of those limitations is found in the two subsequent sections.

TABLE 16-2

Final §382 Rules

Feature	Rule
1. Limitation	
(a) Gross cap amount	Taxable income, to extent of net equity value times rate
(b) Annual utilization rate	Long term tax exempt bond rate
(c) Continuity of historic business	Required for two years
(d) Measure	All stock (including preferred)
(e) Time of measure	Before trigger (except for redemption triggers and certain insolvencies)
(f) Items covered	NOLs, carry-over losses, and credit carry-overs
2. Owner Shift trigger	
(a) Size	Increase of more than 50 points
(b) Exceptions	Gift, death, divorce, ESOPs
(c) Test period	3 years
(d) Shares covered	Ignore pure preferred stock, but aggregate all small shareholders and treat as one
(e) Market value fluctuations	Ignore
3. Equity structure trigger	
(a) Definition	Decline of more than 50 points in any reorganization (except divisive or Type F) including taxable "reorganization type" transactions and public offerings (prospectively by regulations)
(b) Overlap	Has priority generally (if worse result); can be cumulative
(c) Size (continuity of old shareholders)	Less than 50%
4. Antistuffing rule	
(a) Period	2 years (or longer if a plan)
(b) Exceptions	By regulation
5. Passive assets	Scale-back if exceed ⅓ of value (net of debt)

Silverman & Keyes, New Limitations on NOL Carryovers Following the Tax Reform Act: Part I, 66 J. Tax'n 194 (1987), Part II, 66 J. Tax'n 258 (1987); infra note 158.

Feature	Rule
6. Built-ins	
(a) Term	5 years after trigger
(b) Exceptions	25% de minimis (and no depreciation deductions)
7. Insolvency proceedings	Generally exempt (if an 18-month creditor holding period); but one bite only every 2 years, and scale-back NOLs by ½ of cancellation of debt amount on discharge with stock and by 3 years of interest deductions on converted debt
8. Other limitations	Maintain all except *Libson*

¶ 16.24   SECTION 382: CHANGE OF OWNERSHIP TRIGGER

1. General. The key to the operation of §382, as amended in 1986, is the statutory ownership change definition of §382(g)(1), which, if activated, brings into play the "section 382 limitation" of §382(b).[158] Under this limitation, pre-change "net operating loss carry-overs (and also built-in losses) of the old loss corporation can only be used against post-change taxable income of the new loss corporation to the extent of an annual cap based on the equity value of the loss corporation at the time of the ownership change event multiplied by a designated annual rate of return (the long-term Federal tax exempt interest rate of §1274(d)). (As explained below, the terms "old loss corporation" and "new loss corporations" are defined terms of art; if the change triggering the application of §382 involves only a shift in the stock ownership of a single corporation, rather than its reorganization, the same corporation is an "old loss corporation" before the ownership shift and a "new loss corporation" thereafter.) Note that, unlike under 1954 Code law, carry-overs are not reduced (or eliminated) here; rather, utilization of the carry-overs is subjected to an annual limitation based on a statutory rate of return on the loss company's value and on its post-change income.

An ownership change under amended §382 consists generally of any change in ownership of the loss corporation's stock aggregating more than 50 percentage points (by value) over a three-year period, whether occurring

---

[158] The sole criteron for application of the 1986 §382 limitations is a change of ownership; continuity of business is generally irrelevant (with the exception of the special §382(c) business continuity requirement; infra ¶ 16.25).

See Rizzi, Section 382 and the Trigger Rules: Is Congress Beating a Dead Horse?, 14 J. Corp. Tax'n 99 (1987); articles supra note 157.

as a result of taxable (or nontaxable) stock acquisitions, new issues, conversions, redemptions, recapitalizations, reorganizations, or any combination thereof.

Two basic types of ownership change are prescribed by §382(g). The first is an owner shift involving a 5-percent shareholder under §382(g)(2), and the second an equity structure shift under §382(g)(3). The owner shift transaction typically involves a stock acquisition of some sort, whether taxable or tax-free and whether from the loss corporation directly or from its shareholders; an equity structure shift generally involves any reorganization under §368 (except divisives and Type Fs), including (although prospectively only by regulations) even taxable reorganizations. In many situations, these two types of ownership change overlap (e.g., a recapitalization can be both an owner shift and an equity structure shift transaction). No substantive differences seem to exist between the two types of transaction (except possibly as to effective dates), and, in view of the fact that combinations of the two trigger events can affect a statutory change, there seems to be little practical significance in the statute's dual definition approach.

In any event, it is clear that the 1986 version of §382 envisions a considerably wider range of owner-shifting transactions than its 1954 Code predecessor. Moreover, the expansion of §382 in 1986 was accompanied by a revision of §383, which limits the carry-over of specified credits and capital losses to bring its ownership shift trigger into harmony with revised §382.

2. Definitions and special rules. Amended §382 contains several new and specialized terms of art that must be considered before turning to the general operation of that provision. Thus, §382(k)(6)(A) provides that the term "stock" generally includes all types of equity interests except so-called pure preferred stock that is excluded under the consolidated return rules of §1504(a)(4) (i.e., nonvoting, nonconvertible, nonparticipating preferred stock that is not callable at an excessive premium and was not issued at an excessive discount).[159] Regulatory authority is granted by §382(k)(6)(B), however, to either expand or contract the definition of the term "stock."[160]

---

[159] Supra ¶ 15.21; see also a similar provision in §382(c) of the 1976 version of §382, supra notes 144 and 145.

[160] See H.R. Rep. No. 841, supra note 156, at II-173, suggesting when regulations should disregard stock, (e.g., in cases where its equity interest is disproportionately small (or large) vis-à-vis total stock value and where what would otherwise be pure preferred stock has a vote). Mentioned by name as a candidate for disregarding stock status is Maxwell Hardware Co. v. CIR, supra note 24; also to be disregarded is preferred stock that becomes voting merely because dividends are passed; see also Rev. Rul. 82-150, 1982-2 CB 110 (high-cost option treated as ownership equivalent because exercise economically certain).

Finally, §382(k)(6)(C) provides that all determinations of the percentage of stock held by any shareholder are to be made on the basis of the value, rather than the number of shares.[161]

A "5-percent shareholder" is defined by §382(k)(7) as any person owning 5 percent or more of the loss corporation's stock at any time during the three-year testing period. Status as a 5-percent shareholder is important for purposes of the owner shift definition, since only such shareholders are considered in making that determination. Moreover, under a special aggregation rule in §382(g)(4)(A), all less than 5-percent shareholders are aggregated and treated as one 5-percent shareholder.

The term "loss corporation" is defined by §382(k)(1) as any corporation entitled to use a net operating loss carry-over or having potential built-in loss deductions; the old loss corporation is the loss corporation that generated the loss before the relevant ownership change event, while the new loss corporation is the loss corporation that can use the loss after the change event (subject to the §382 limitation) under §§382(k)(2) and 382(k)(3). Moreover, the new loss corporation and the old loss corporation may be the *same* corporation or they may be different corporations (a phenomenon similar to that under §338 (discussed in Chapter 11), where two corporations may exist for tax purposes while only one exists for state law purposes). "Pre-change loss" is defined by §382(d)(1) as losses and carry-overs ending with the date of the ownership change, and a "post-change year" under §382(d)(2) means any year ending after the change. Finally, §382(j) defines the "change date" as the day on which the final component resulting in the ownership change occurs.

Special constructive stock ownership rules are prescribed in §382(*l*)(3)(A), which provides that §318 attribution rules generally apply in determining stock ownership but with the following modifications: (1)All §318(a)(1) family members are aggregated and treated as one owner under §382(*l*)(3)(A)(i) (thus, sales between family members will be disregarded); (2) stock owned *by* various entities (corporations, partnerships, trusts, or estates) is attributed out *in full* to the beneficial owners in proportion to their interests, regardless of the extent of that interest, and also is treated as *not* being owned by the entity under §382(*l*)(3)(A)(ii) (i.e., there is a full lookthrough attribution rule, regardless of any threshold ownership inter-

---

[161] Using value rather than number of shares to determine changes of ownership practically ensures disputes about control premiums, blockage discounts, and minority interest discounts, especially in close cases.

However, §382(*l*)(3)(D) provides that changes in proportionate ownership attributable solely to changes in the values of different classes of stock will not be considered; the statutory focus, in other words, is on stock transfers, not fluctuations in stock values.

est); [162] (3) no stock is attributed *into* entities unless regulations provide otherwise under §382(*l*)(3)(A)(iii); and (4) stock subject to options (including, for this purpose, various option-type rights [163]) is presumed to be owned by the holder of the option if an ownership change results from that presumption under §382(*l*)(3)(A)(iv).

3. Owner shift involving a 5-percent shareholder: Section 382(g)(2). Almost any change of proportionate stock ownership involving a 5-percent shareholder is covered by this rule, including changes effected by a stock purchase, a new issue, a redemption, a conversion (of common stock, preferred stock, or debt), a corporate division, or a corporate reorganization. However, by virtue of §382(*l*)(3)(B), stock transferred by reason of gift, death, divorce, or separation is effectively ignored—that is, the transferee tacks the ownership of the transferor. Moreover, §382(*l*)(3)(C) ignores employer security stock acquired by an ESOP or by a participant in such a plan if the ESOP has, or acquires, at least 50 percent of the value of the employer securities.

Since ownership changes are based on the value [164] rather than the number of shares owned, uncertainty will exist at the fringes of the statutory lines due to the possibility of minority discounts, control premiums, and the like. Thus, a shareholder owning 6 of 100 shares may not be a 5-percent shareholder if a minority discount factor applies (as it most likely would if the minority interest were also nonvoting); on the other hand, a shareholder owning 50 of 100 shares may own more than 50 percent by value, especially if ownership of the other 50 shares is dispersed (thereby giving the 50 percent shareholder de facto control).

Note also that owner shift transactions can be affected by the special rules of §382(k)(6)(A), ignoring preferred stock, and in cases where regulatory authority under §382(k)(6)(B) is exercised to treat certain options and other corporate elements as stock or, conversely, to treat stock as nonstock. [165] Moreover, the attribution rules of §382(*l*)(3)(A) [166] can affect not only the existence of a 5-percent shareholder, but also whether an owner shift involving such a shareholder has occurred. These rules can either help

---

[162] This provision is one of the more significant modifications of the stock ownership rules; as a result of this rule, ownership continuity is tested exclusively at the beneficiary level.

[163] The statute refers to "any contingent purchase, warrant, convertible debt, put, stock subject to a risk of forfeiture, contract to acquire stock, or similar interests." See H.R. Rep. No. 841, supra note 156, at II-183.

[164] See §382(k)(6)(C).

[165] Supra note 160.

[166] Supra text at notes 162 and 163.

(e.g., intrafamily stock sales are effectively ignored), or hurt (e.g., attribution can concentrate stock ownership), but the lack of attribution into entities (unless regulations provide otherwise) prevents stock ownership from concentrating into entity hands as a result of ownership by their respective beneficiaries.

By virtue of the special aggregation rule in §382(g)(4)(A), every corporation has at least one 5-percent shareholder, since all less than 5-percent shareholders are aggregated and treated as one 5-percent shareholder. As a result of this rule, a publicly owned loss company that has no 5-percent shareholders will not be subjected to §382, regardless of the extent of the trading volume in its shares, so long as no person acquires a 5-percent interest during the three-year test period.[167]

4. Equity structure change: Section 382(g)(3). An equity structure shift includes most corporate reorganizations under §368 and is not concerned with the existence of 5-percent shareholders; this is a transactional test rather than a specific shareholder test. Under §382(g)(3)(A), any §368 reorganization is an equity structure shift except divisive Types D and G reorganizations, and Type F reorganizations. Thus, Types A, B, C, E, and nondivisive D and G reorganizations (as well as their triangular variants) all will constitute equity structure shifts. Moreover, §382(g)(3)(B) grants *prospective* only regulatory authority to treat taxable reorganizations, public offerings, and similar transactions as equity structure shifts.[168] This authority will make no difference if the transaction also effects an owner shift involving a 5-percent shareholder but could make a difference if the corporation has no 5-percent shareholders under the special aggregation, segregation, and tracing rules of §382(g)(4).

5. Ownership increase of more than 50 percentage points within the three-year testing period. The statute in §382(g)(1) requires not only the existence of an ownership change event, but also a change of significant magnitude (i.e., more than 50 percent) before it is activated. Moreover, this change must occur within a limited period, generally the three-year period prescribed under §382(i). The three-year period is a moving

---

[167] H.R. Rep. No. 841, supra note 156, at II-174, Example 1.

[168] H.R. Rep. No. 841, supra note 156, at II-178; see also §382(m)(5) (to be redesignated as §382(m)(4) by the 1987 Technical Corrections Act) (prospective regulatory authority to subject public offerings, recapitalizations, and possibly Type F reorganizations to the special §382(g)(4) aggregation, segregation, and tracing rules, infra paragraph 6 of this section).

Another candidate for similar transaction treatment under §382(g)(3)(B) may be a §332 liquidation.

timeframe that looks back from the date of any ownership change; thus, a series of unrelated purchases adding up to more than 50 percentage points within the three-year statutory period can trigger application of §382. The three-year period is shortened, however, in two, generally helpful, instances: First, if an ownership change occurs, a new testing period cannot begin until the day after such change (thus avoiding double counting in overlapping periods); second, the period does not start before the first day of the first year in which the carry-overs arose (although this exception will not apply to corporations with a net built-in loss unless that loss arose in such year).

It should be noted that the change required is more than 50 percentage *points* of ownership, not a 50 percent change. For example, if a shareholder owning 10 percent of loss corporation L increases his ownership in L to 30 percent, no statutory change has occurred, since his increase has only been 20 percentage points (even though his ownership percentage increased 300 percent). Moreover, the percentage change is measured by value, not number of shares, so that if 5-percent shareholder A buys an additional 50 percent of loss company L's stock, his percentage point number increase is only 50 percentage points (not enough); in view of A's outright control of L, however, a value premium probably exists and hence could result in a trigger of §382.

6. Special aggregation, segregation, tracing, and attribution rules: Section 382(g)(4). As noted previously, §382(g)(4)(A) aggregates all less than 5-percent shareholders and treats this group as a single 5-percent shareholder. This rule can either help or hurt, depending on the transaction involved. Thus, stock trading among small shareholders will not in itself cause an ownership change for a loss corporation that never has any persons who are 5-percent shareholders.[169] On the other hand, ownership concentrating purchases by a person who is, or becomes, a 5-percent shareholder can trigger an ownership change (for example, if A buys 26 percent of loss company L's stock from the public, and, within three years, B also acquires 25 percent from the public, an owner shift transaction has occurred).[170] Conversely, dispersal by less than 5-percent shareholders of stock ownership from closely held 5-percent shareholder hands into widely held public ownership also can effect a change of ownership (for example, if loss corporation L is wholly

---

[169] Supra note 167.

[170] If A and B purchase only 6 percent each of L's stock, however, there has been no ownership change (since the increase by 5-percent shareholders A and B is only 12 percentage points).

See H.R. Rep. No. 841, supra note 156, at II-174, Example 2, and II-175, Example 6.

owned by *A* and issues 51 percent of its stock to the public, an owner shift will occur).[171]

Under §§382(g)(4)(B)(i) and 382(g)(4)(C), less than 5-percent shareholders can be segregated into two or more groups, each of which will be treated as a separate 5-percent shareholder in determining whether an equity structure shift or an owner shift transaction constitutes a statutory change of ownership.[172] The group segregation rule typically applies in the case of acquisitive reorganizations involving two or more publicly owned corporations. Thus, if public loss corporation *L* merges into public profit corporation *P*, the post-merger shareholder group is segregated into two separate 5-percent shareholders, the *L* group and the *P* group; depending upon which group dominates in the new loss corporation, an ownership change will, or will not, occur.[173]

However, the statute in §382(m)(5) grants prospective regulatory authority to apply the aggregation and segregation rules of §382(g)(4) to a single corporation (e.g., a recapitalization or public issue of stock). For example, a public offering of stock by a widely held loss corporation having no 5-percent shareholders would not constitute an owner shift change transaction because the corporation has only a single 5-percent shareholder both before and after the stock issue under §382(g)(4)(A).[174] However, if and when regulations are issued under §382(m)(5), an owner shift can occur if those regulations segregate the shareholders of the loss company into pre- and postpublic offering groups (effective, however, only as of the date such regulations are issued).

Since multiple transactions that occur within the testing period are combined in determining whether an ownership change has taken place,[175] a special tracing convention is prescribed in §§382(g)(4)(B)(ii) and

---

[171] See H.R. Rep. No. 841, supra note 156, at II-175, Examples 4 and 5.

If *L* also had another shareholder, *B*, who owned 4 percent of *L* (and *A* owned 96 percent), a public offering of 49 percent presumably would not trigger a §382 ownership change if *B* is included with the public 5-percent shareholder group (an increase from 4 to 53 percent is only a 49 point change); exclusion of *B* at the start and inclusion at the end of the offering, however, would trigger §382.

[172] Section 382(g)(4)(B)(i) is the equity structure shift group segregation rule; §382(g)(4)(C) is the comparable group segregation rule for ownershift transactions.

[173] See H.R. Rep. No. 841, supra note 156, at II-177, Example 8. If *P*'s shareholders end up with more than 50 percent of the surviving corporation's stock, an ownership change will occur; if *L*'s shareholders maintain at least 50 percent ownership, it will not.

[174] See H.R. Rep. No. 841, supra note 156, at II-178, Example 10. But the Conference Report, at footnote 7, citing Rev. Rul. 78-294, 1978-2 CB 141, states that a firm commitment underwriter would become a 5-percent shareholder, despite its intention to remarket the stock as soon as possible; query this conclusion?

[175] See H.R. Rep. No. 841, supra note 156, at II-175, Example 3.

382(g)(4)(C) that provides a statutory presumption (rebuttable by proof) that acquisitions of stock in subsequent transactions after an equity structure shift or an owner shift event has occurred are deemed to have been made proportionately from all persons who owned stock just before that particular event.[176] The arbitrary proportional purchase presumption was inserted as a practical response to the difficulties of tracing actual stock ownership changes in the case of publicly held corporations, where the corporation frequently is unable to track the sellers of its shares. However, if the loss corporation can prove who actually sold the stock, the presumption can be overcome.[177]

Finally, the special stock attribution rules of §382(*l*)(3)(A) round out the statutory regime for computing ownership changes under §382(g), most notable of which are the entity look-through rules of §382(*l*)(3)(A)(ii) and the broad application of the attribution rules relating to option attribution in §382(*l*)(3)(A)(iv);[178] The latter rule applies, however, only if the effect is to trigger an ownership change.

7. Examples. In the following examples, *L* is a loss corporation, wholly owned by *A* (which may be a single individual, a single corporation, or a public group of less than 5-percent shareholders). *P* is a profit corporation that is wholly owned by *B* (either an individual, a corporation, or the public).

Example 1. L merges into *P* (or vice versa), after which *A* owns 40 percent of the surviving corporation. Both an equity structure shift and an owner shift has occurred here, whether or not *L* and *P* were publicly owned corporations.[179] However, if *A* obtains at least 50 percent of the surviving corporation stock, no change would result (because the change must be more than 50 percentage points).[180]

---

[176] See H.R. Rep. No. 841, supra note 156, at II-179–II-182, Examples 11–18.

[177] Id., Example 18.

[178] Supra notes 162–163. See also H.R. Rep. No. 841, supra note 156, at II-183, Example 19 (contingent right to receive additional shares in the loss company triggered an ownership change). Note that the contingent issue stock option rule can only *create* a statutory change of ownership; it will never prevent it (i.e., the option rule is a one way street running in favor of triggering §382).

[179] If *L* and *P* were publicly held, the *A* and *B* groups would each be separate 5-percent shareholders under the aggregation rule of §382(g)(4)(A) and the group segregation rule of §382(g)(4)(B)(i); supra notes 169–173.

[180] If *A* was a single shareholder and *P* was publicly held, however, *A*'s 50 percent interest could be worth more than 50 percent if a control premium attaches to *A*'s stock. The converse case, where *L* is publicly held, would likewise result in *P*'s 50 percent interest being worth more by virtue of his control premium.

Example 2. B buys 10 percent of *L* stock from *A*; subsequently, *L* merges into *P* and the *L* shareholders obtain 55 percent of *P* stock, 5.5 percent to *B* and 49.5 percent to *A*.

An equity structure ownership change occurs here as a result of the merger transactions, since *P*'s shareholder, *B*, has increased his ownership with respect to *L* by 50.5 percent (5.5 percent received in the merger for the stock of *L* that *B* previously purchased and 45 percent as a result of *B*'s ownership of *P* prior to the merger.

If *P* had merged into *L* for 45 percent of *L* stock, the same result would occur, since *B* would increase his ownership in *L* by the same 50.5 percentage points (45 percent in the merger and 5.5 percent by virtue of his prior ownership of *L*).[181]

Example 3. *L* and *P* merge, with *A* receiving 50 percent of *P* stock (no ownership change occurs at this point). Subsequently, *C* buys 5 percent of surviving *P* stock. An ownership change will result under the proportional purchase presumption rule of §382(g)(4)(B)(ii) unless it can be proved that *C* purchased the stock from *B* rather than ratably from *A* and *B*.[182]

Example 4. *L* acquires all of *B*'s *P* stock for *L* voting stock in a Type B reorganization, after which *B* owns 51 percent of *L*. Both an owner shift and an equity structure shift change of ownership occurs (unless *A* and *B* were related family members).

The same would be true if *P* acquired *L* stock in a Type B reorganization and *A* did not receive at least 50 percent of *P*'s stock value in the transaction.[183]

Example 5. *L* merges into *P*'s wholly owned subsidiary, *S*, for stock of *P* equal to 49 percent of *P*'s value. This is both an owner shift and an

---

[181] H.R. Rep. No. 841, supra note 156, at II-179, Example 11.

[182] Supra notes 175–177; H.R. Rep. No. 841, supra note 156, at II-179, Example 13, and II-182, Example 18.

[183] If *P* subsequently liquidates *L* under §332 (with *L*'s carry-overs passing upstream to *P* under §381(a)(1), supra ¶ 16.11), *L*'s carry-overs apparently should continue to be limited under §382, since *L* can be viewed as the old loss corporation and *P* would become the new loss corporation here under §382(k)(3). (If not, the limitations of §382 could be finessed by the simple device of acquiring stock and then liquidating under §332); supra note 168. The statutory language of §382(k)(3) seems defective on this point, however, since *P* is technically not a new loss corporation, but rather is a *successor* to the new loss corporation *L*.

But see Joint Comm. Staff General Explanation of the Tax Reform Act of 1986, JCS-10-87, at 314 (May 4, 1987) ("Blue Book") (adds "successor" language to §382(k)(3)); see also the Technical Corrections Act of 1987, H.R. 2636, §106(d)(10), adding new §382(*l*)(8) (successor same entity). See infra notes 234, 236, and 250.

equity structure shift change of ownership, since the S stock (which represents new loss corporation S) is attributed out to P's shareholders under the lookthrough attribution rule of §382(l)(3)(A)(ii), and the B shareholder group has increased its ownership in old loss corporation L by more than 50 percent.[184] The same would be true if the transaction had been structured as a reverse merger under §368(a)(2)(E) rather than a forward merger under §368(a)(2)(D).

Example 6. Assume L is publicly owned by A; L issues stock to the public equal to 51 percent of L's value. Until regulations are issued under §382(m)(5), no change of ownership results here because L has only one 5-percent shareholder, the public, before and after the stock issue under §382(g)(4)(A).[185] If L were closely held by A, however, the public issue transaction would trigger a §382 owner shift change without regulations.[186]

However, once regulations are issued under §382(m)(5) (and effective as of such time), an ownership change can result under the group segregation rules of §382(g)(4)(B)(i) (the pre-issue and post-issue groups would each be separate 5-percent shareholders).[187]

Example 7. B purchases 40 percent of L stock from A; subsequently L redeems the rest of A's shares for cash. An owner shift occurs through the combination of these two steps, whether A is a public group or the sole shareholder of L.

Moreover, even if B's ownership in L was old-and-cold (i.e., of 3 years' duration), L's redemption of A's stock in itself would operate to effect an owner shift change, since B's ownership of L has increased by more than 50 percentage points as a result of the redemption of A.[188]

If A and B were a single public group, regulations to be issued under §382(m)(5) may segregate the L shareholders into two separate 5-percent groups under §382(g)(4)(B)(i), thereby resulting in an owner shift under §382(g)(2).[189]

If the redemption of A's stock is effected by issuing pure preferred stock to A, the transaction is also an equity structure shift recapitalization change of ownership under §382(g)(3) (since the preferred is not treated as stock for purposes of the ownership change rules under

---

[184] H.R. Rep. No. 841, supra note 156, at II-184, Example 21.

[185] Supra note 174.

[186] Supra note 171.

[187] Supra note 174.

[188] H.R. Rep. No. 841, supra note 156, at II-177, Example 9.

[189] Id. Until such regulations are issued, however, no ownership change would result in this case.

§382(k)(6)(A)). If A subsequently reexchanges his preferred stock for 60 percent of L's common stock (or if the preferred is exchanged for, or becomes, participating or voting preferred, and hence is treated as stock), another owner shift change will result from this event as well.

Example 8. Assume that L is owned 60 percent by A and 40 percent by B. If L splits off an aged subsidiary, S, to A in exchange for all of A's stock in L, the transaction constitutes an owner shift change for L, although not an equity structure shift, and also not an owner shift change for S. If, instead, the split-off flowed to B in exchange for B's L stock, the owner shift change would occur as to S, although not L.[190]

A pro rata spin-off to A and B, however, would not cause a change of ownership of either L or S, since L's shareholders already are deemed to own S under the entity attribution rules of §382(*l*)(3)(A)(ii).[191] A pro rata split-up liquidation of L would terminate L's tax history, but would not affect S's.[192]

Example 9. A and B transfer all of their stock of L and P to newly organized holding company H, with A getting 40 percent of H and B getting 60 percent. An owner shift change results here for L because B's interest in L (by attribution from H under §382(*l*)(3)(A)(ii)) has increased from 0 to 60 percent; but if A and B each took back 50 percent of H stock, no ownership change would result.[193]

Example 10. P buys all of L's assets for cash. This transaction has no effect on L under §382, and L merely augments its loss carry-overs by any loss realized on the sale of its assets. If P buys L's stock and elects §338, L's carry-overs are usable by L against any gain recognized as a result of the §338 election, but L's tax history otherwise is purged (and the basis of its assets stepped down to fair market value).

Example 11. L buys all of P's assets for cash. This also is not a §382 trigger event. If L buys P's stock and elects §338, no §382 consequences result; but L cannot set off its carry-overs against the gain required to be recognized by P on the §338 election.[194]

---

[190] Id. at II-176, Example 7.

[191] Id. at II-181, Example 17.

[192] See Rev. Rul. 56-373, 1956-2 CB 217 (parent's tax history disappears in split-up); see also Rev. Rul. 77-133, 1977-1 CB 96 (loss carry-overs stay with distributing parent corporation in a split-off, since not a §381 transaction); supra ¶ 13.12, para. 6.

[193] See H.R. Rep. No. 841, supra note 156, at II-184, Example 20.

[194] The gains recognized on a §338 election occur outside of the L-P consolidated return on the day before P enters the L-P group, supra ¶¶ 11.46 and 11.47.

Example 12. *L* has 100 equal 1 percent shareholders. As a result of a self-tender redemption transaction, 75 percent of *L*'s stock is redeemed, leaving *L* with 25 equal 4 percent shareholders. No owner shift occurs here because of the aggregation rule of §382(g)(4)(A) (there is still only one 5-percent shareholder) unless and until regulations under §382(m)(5) segregate the pre- and post-redemption shareholders into two separate 5-percent shareholder groups. The same result would occur if the 25 shareholders purchased the stock from the other shareholders.

Example 13. *L* and *P* each contribute assets to new partnership *L-P*. Any attempt to allocate the use or benefit of *L*'s loss carry-overs to *P* via the partnership allocation rules will be vulnerable to the Treasury's broad antiabuse regulations under §382(m)(3). [195]

¶ 16.25   SECTION 382: OPERATION OF THE LIMITATION

1. General. Once §382 is activated by a prescribed change of ownership event, the limitation of §382(a) takes hold and restricts the amount of taxable income that can be offset by the taxpayer's net operating loss carry-overs in taxable years (or part-years) after the change of ownership; parallel restrictions are imposed by §383 on the carry-over of capital losses and certain credits. Note that, unlike the 1954 Code version of §382 (which restricted the *losses* that could be carried forward), the 1986 Code rule of §382 limits the amount of *income* that can be offset by the carry-overs to the "section 382 limitation." The "section 382 limitation" is defined by §382(b)(1) as an amount equal to the value of the old loss corporation multiplied by the long-term tax exempt rate of §382(f) (which is to be determined monthly by reference to §1274(d) principles). If the amount of the limitation exceeds taxable income for any year, such excess is carried forward and added to the limitation in the succeeding taxable year under §382(b)(2).

Thus, if *P* acquires all the stock of loss company *L*, which has a value of $100, in a month when the applicable rate was 5 percent, the annual limitation on the amount of taxable income that can be offset by carry-overs would be $5 (which limitation is permanent for the life of the carry-overs). If

---

If *L* liquidates *P* under §332, however, *L* can sell the *P* assets and use its loss carry-overs to shelter the gains recognized on those sales. See generally Rev. Rul. 63-40, 1963-1 CB 46.

[195] See H.R. Rep. No. 841, supra note 156, at II-194–II-195. These regulations also are expected to be retroactive to date of enactment, October 22, 1986, which should serve to restrain the taking of aggressive positions here.

both L and P are loss corporations and they combine with a third corporation, Q, in a transaction that constitutes an ownership change for both L and P, the section 382 limitations are computed separately for L and P, based on their respective values prior to the change.[196]

The annual section 382 limitation is intended to approximate the amount of income that the loss company could have produced as a return on equity, absent the acquisition, had it invested its capital in tax exempt securities. The limitation incorporates an implicit tax avoidance restriction in that the limitation applies more stringently to cases where the amount of the carry-overs is high in comparison with the corporation's value; conversely, the lower the carry-over in relation to value, the less significant will be the limitation on the ability to use those carry-overs.

The value of the loss corporation generally is determined under §382(e)(1) immediately before the change in ownership event; however, §382(e)(2) determines value immediately after the event in any case where a redemption occurs *in connection with* an ownership change.[197] For this purpose, pure preferred stock *is* included in the value determination.[198] The price paid for the stock ordinarily will determine its value, but the Conference Report warns that price is not conclusive on the value issue, such as in cases where a control premium is paid for part of the stock.[199] Because of the rule in §382(e)(2) that redemptions effected in connection with the ownership change reduce the value cap of §382(e), acquiring corporations would be well advised to avoid bootstrap acquisition techniques in acquiring a loss company. Thus, if P buys 51 percent of L's stock for $110 when the total value of L is $200, and then causes L to redeem the balance of its stock for $90 in a related transaction, the section 382 limitation will be $110.[200]

---

[196] H.R. Rep. No. 841, supra note 156, at II-186, Example 22; see also Consolidated Blenders Inc. v. US, supra note 131 (limitation also computed separately for each corporation under 1954 Code §382 rules).

[197] Moreover, §382(m)(4) authorizes regulations to provide for similar treatment in the case of corporate contractions and §382(l)(6) likewise determines value after the event in the case of certain insolvency transactions not covered by the special insolvency rules of §382(l)(5), infra this section, para. 6.

[198] See also H.R. Rep. No. 841, supra note 156, at II-187 (regulations to be issued under §382(k)(6)(B) also will include various equity flavored interests such as options, warrants, convertible debt, contracts to acquire stock, and other similar interests in determining stock value).

[199] Id. But the Conference Report also notes that if a control block is acquired within a 12-month period, regulations will permit a gross-up of the price paid for all of the target's stock.

[200] Id., Example 23. By contrast, if the redemption was not connected to the ownership change event, or if P buys the rest of L's stock from L's shareholders for $90, the limitation would be $200, the full preredemption value of L.

2. Mid-year change rules. Unless the ownership change occurs on the last day of the loss corporation's taxable year, which is atypical, special rules are needed to deal with cases where the change date[201] occurs at some point during the loss corporation's year. Different rules apply here, depending upon whether the loss company's change year is a profit year or a loss year. If the change year is a profit year, §382(b)(3)(A) allows carry-overs to be set off against profits earned prior to the change date without limitation; for purposes of the mid-year rules, taxable income is prorated on a daily basis (except for recognized built-in gains and losses, which §382(h)(5) requires to be specifically traced because they are readily identifiable). Income earned after the change date is limited by a pro rata portion of the "section 382 limitation" under §382(b)(3)(B).

If the change date occurs during a loss year of the corporation, §382(d)(1)(B) subjects only the pre-change portion of the change year loss to the "section 382 limitation," such amount again being determined on a prorated daily basis (except for identifiable recognized built-in gains and losses, which fall into that part of the year in which they occur). Losses arising after the change date (other than built-in losses) are not subject to limitation under §382.[202]

3. Special modifications of the "section 382 limitation." Several special rules modify the computation of the "section 382 limitation," either by reducing it or increasing it, depending upon the particular rule involved.

(a) Reduction for capital contributions (the anti-stuffing rule). Under §382(l)(1), attempts to inflate the value of the loss corporation by pre-change capital contributions will be disregarded if they are made as "part of a plan a principal purpose of which is to avoid or increase any limitation under this section." Contributions within two years of the ownership change date, however, are deemed to be part of such a plan unless regulations provide otherwise. Without such a rule, the value cap of §382(e) could be increased dollar for dollar by capital contributions made in anticipation of a planned sale of the loss company.

The Conference Report instructs, however, that regulations are to exempt the following contributions: (1) those made on formation of the corporation (other than assets with a net built-in loss); (2) contributions before the first loss year; and (3) contributions to meet operating costs.[203] The

---

[201] The change date is defined by §382(j) as the date on which the last component of the ownership change occurs.

[202] For an example of the operation of the mid-year change rules, see H.R. Rep. No. 841, supra note 156, at II-188, Example 24.

[203] H.R. Rep. No. 841, supra note 156, at II-189.

report also suggests that the regulations can permit offsets for subsequent distributions and for assets that would reduce the limitation under the passive asset rule of §382(*l*)(4), infra.[204]

If the loss company consists of an affiliated group of corporations, the "section 382 limitations" apply separately to each loss member of the group.[205] While downstream capital contributions to loss affiliates would be covered, and disregarded, by the anti-stuffing rule of §382(*l*)(1), upstream (or lateral) transfers of assets from other members of the group by distribution, liquidation, or reorganization are not subject to this limitation and thus could augment the value limitation of the transferee member.[206]

(b) Reduction for passive assets. If the loss corporation has an excessive amount of passive assets (i.e., nonbusiness, or investment, assets that exceed one third of gross assets), the value of the loss corporation is reduced by the amount of such assets (less an allocable portion of any debt).[207] In determining the amount of investment assets, a look-through rule in the case of 50 percent owned subsidiaries (by vote and value) is provided by §382(*l*)(4)(E), under which the parent is deemed to own a ratable portion of its subsidiaries' assets rather than their stock. Pass-through entities to which subchapter M applies (RICs, REITs, and so forth) are not subject to this limitation, presumably because their business consists of holding investment assets.

The statute merely defines nonbusiness assets as assets held for investment, and the Conference Report is not much more helpful, noting only that assets held as an integral part of the conduct of a business (such as funded reserves of banks and insurance companies) are not investment assets.[208] Cash and marketable securities, however, ordinarily would be investment assets unless cash is the business of the corporation (e.g., a bank, a check cashing business, a consumer loan business). Ambiguous status assets would be real estate, which can range in character from an active business under §355(b) (see Chapter 13) to a purely passive investment activity (e.g., §1375,

---

[204] For the definition of "capital contributions" (which typically are, but need not be, pro rata by the shareholders), see supra ¶ 3.13. Purchases of stock from the corporation by a new shareholder ordinarily should not be covered by this rule, since he would not likely be acting to avoid §382 (but such purchases, if greater than 50 percent of the loss company's stock, could trigger the application of §382 in their own right).

[205] Supra note 196.

[206] E.g., if a profitable parent liquidates its loss subsidiary, the subsidiary's carry-overs flow up to the parent under §381(a)(1) (supra ¶ 16.11), and the parent's assets could then be taken into account in determining the value limitation applicable to these inherited carry-overs.

[207] Under §382(*l*)(4)(D), debt is allocated proportionately by formula (relative gross values) and not traced to any particular asset.

[208] H.R. Rep. 841, supra note 156, at II-190.

discussed in Chapter 6). Thus, ownership and operation of a hotel, a commercial office building, or an apartment building, where significant services are required to be rendered to tenants, should constitute business assets, while holding a warehouse under a long-term net lease to other users would constitute investment property.[209]

(c) Increase for recognized built-in gain. At the time of the ownership change, the loss company may have substantially appreciated assets despite the existence of its loss carry-overs. If the corporation's net built-in gain on the change date[210] is substantial (i.e., more than 25 percent of the gross value of its non-cash assets),[211] it can increase the amount of its "section 382 limitation" (and not merely the value of the loss company) under §382(h)(1)(A), if such gain is recognized in any post-change taxable year during the five-year recognition period.[212] However, if built-in gains do not exceed the 25 percent threshold or are recognized outside of the five-year recognition period, no adjustment will be made.

Built-in gains for this purpose include only gains existing at the time of the ownership change; post-change appreciation does not count under §382(h)(2)(A). However, §382(h)(1)(C) provides that the built-in gain rules also include gains recognized as a result of an election under §338 (to the extent not previously taken into account).[213] Note also that while the built-in gain rules apply asset by asset, §382(h)(1)(A) and §382(h)(3)(A) also pre-

---

[209] For analogous areas, see supra chs. 6, 8, and 13. The assets only have to be business assets, however, not *active* business assets, to escape this limitation.

[210] For another built-in gain provision (involving conversion of a C corporation to Subchapter S status), see §1374 (supra ¶ 6.07). The built-in gain rule requires a determination of all asset values at the date of the ownership change in order to arrive at the potential built-in gain of each particular asset and also to determine the aggregate net gain amount. The burden of proof is on the taxpayer to establish the existence, the amount, and the timing of each such gain. Presumably appraisals will be essential to establish such values at the date of the ownership change, which is the critical point under these provisions.

[211] Section 382(h)(3)(B)(ii) excludes cash and cash-type items. As to the latter, the Conference Report at II-191 refers to §368(a)(2)(F)(iv), supra ¶ 14.19, and marketable securities having a stable value (e.g., CDs and T-bills).

[212] The recognition period of §382(h)(1) is the five *calendar years* following the change date; for example, if the change date is July 1, 1987, gains recognized in December 1992 are still timely.

Note that the recognition period for built-in gains subject to tax in the hands of an electing S corporation under §1374 is 10 years from the effective date of the election; supra ¶ 6.07.

[213] This rule allows the loss company to use its own loss carry-overs against any gain triggered by a §338 election, supra ¶ 11.46. For an expansive definition of "built-in gains" under §1374 (supra ¶ 6.07), see Announcement 86-128, 1986-52 IRB 22.

scribe an overall limitation of aggregate net built-in gain on all assets at the time of the ownership change (e.g., if the corporation has a built-in gain of $100 for one asset and a built-in loss of $50 for another, its maximum built-in gain adjustment would be $50).[214] Valuation of assets generally is determined immediately before the change date, except that, if a redemption occurs in connection with the ownership change, values must be adjusted downward to reflect the redemption. Finally, assets subject to the anti-stuffing rules of §382(*l*)(1) are disregarded for purposes of the built-in gain adjustment as well.

As previously noted,[215] built-in gains are not subject to the daily proration rules of §382(b)(3) in the case of midyear ownership changes, since these transactions are identifiable as to the time of their recognition under §382(h)(5).

4. Limitation on built-in losses. Section 382(h) also deals with built-in losses on the date of the ownership change, but subjects these losses to limitation under §382 if they are recognized during the five-calendar-year post-change recognition period.[216] As in the case of built-in gains, losses must be (1) accrued at the time of the ownership changes (post-change declines, if proved, are not limited), (2) substantial in amount (i.e., greater than the 25 percent de minimis threshold), and (3) recognized within a limited period (five years). Regulatory authority is granted by §382(h)(6) to treat deductions that accrue on or before the change date as built-in losses; the Conference Report mentions deductions deferred by §267 or §465, but specifically excludes depreciation.[217]

In valuing assets for purposes of determining whether a net built-in loss exists at the date of an ownership change, §382(h)(8) provides a special limitation on inside asset values where 80 percent or more of the loss company's stock is acquired within a 12-month period. Under this rule, asset values cannot *exceed* (but can be *less* than) the grossed up amount paid for the

---

[214] Moreover, if the gain asset declines in value by 60 percent after the change date, the built-in gain adjustment would be reduced to $40 (i.e. postchange declines in value affect only the particular asset, not the initial overall limitation).

[215] Supra this section, para. 2.

[216] If current deduction for the loss is denied, §382(h)(4) converts the disallowed loss to a carry-over, subject to continuing limitation under §382; presumably, the carry-over's mortality period will run from that year.

For comparable limitations under the consolidated return regulations, see Regs. §1.1502-15, supra ¶ 15.24.

[217] H.R. Rep. No. 841, supra note 156, at II-191; but §621(d)(1) of the 1986 Act directs the Treasury to study whether depreciation deductions should be subject to this rule and report back to Congress before 1989.

stock, adjusted for liabilities of the corporation and other relevant items.[218] Thus, if loss company stock is acquired at a discount, the effect will be either to reduce net built-in gain or to increase net built-in loss.

5. Continuity of business enterprise limitation. While the general operation of §382 merely limits the utilization of loss carry-overs, §382(c)(1) totally eliminates them (retroactively to the date of change) if the loss company fails to continue the business enterprise of the loss corporation for two years after the change of ownership event.[219] This limitation is not the same business continuity test of former 1954 Code §382(a), however; instead, according to the Conference Report,[220] it is the business continuity test applicable to §368 reorganizations under Regs. §1.368-1(d),[221] which is less stringent than the 1954 Code version of §382. The §382(c) business continuity test thus requires the loss corporation to continue its historic business or continue to use a significant portion of its historic business assets for the requisite two-year period. This limitation can be viewed as a backstop to the passive asset rules of §382(l)(4), discussed previously, which focus on the character of the loss corporation's pre-change business activities, while §382(c) requires continuance of significant business activity or assets for two years after the ownership change event.

Changes in business locations, key employees, or even the elimination of substantial lines of business should not violate §382(c)(1), so long as a significant historic line of business, or historic business activity, continues within the meaning of the §368 regulations and any authorities developed thereunder.[222] Moreover, if the regulations exempt a particular transaction, such an exemption should apply under §382(c) as well.[223] Even if §382(c)(1) is violated, §382(c)(2) still allows the loss company to use its own carry-overs to the extent of recognized built-in gains and any gains

---

[218] For a similar rule in the case of §338 elections, see Temp. Regs. §1.338(b)-1T, supra ¶ 11.47.

[219] The section 382 limitation becomes zero as of the change date; thus, if the business continuity test is failed in the second year of the two-year period, no carry-overs are allowed for the first post-change year as well (and amended returns will have to be filed to reflect this retroactive denial of any deduction taken in that year).

[220] H.R. Rep. No. 841, supra note 156, at II-189.

[221] Supra ¶ 14.51, para. 2.

[222] See also Rev. Rul. 85-197, 1985-2 CB 120 (business of subsidiary is imputed to parent); Rev. Rul. 85-198, 1985-2 CB 120 (continuity test is on a group-wide basis in the case of affiliates); Rev. Rul. 81-25, 1981-1 CB 132 (test not applicable to acquiring corporation); Rev. Rul. 81-247, 1981-2 CB 87 (post-acquisition drop-downs do not affect continuity); Rev. Rul. 82-34, 1982-1 CB 59 (no business continuity requirement for a recapitalization).

[223] E.g., Rev. Rul. 81-25, 1981-1 CB 132, and Rev. Rul. 82-34, 1982-1 CB 59.

triggered by a §338 election. In effect, the §382(c)(1) requirement has imposed the same business continuity standard that is necessary to effect a tax-free reorganization on any change of ownership transaction that triggers the application of §382.

6. Insolvency rules.   Special rules in §382(*l*)(5) apply to a loss corporation that is under the jurisdiction of a court in a title 11 or similar case (see Chapter 14), the general effect of which is to treat certain creditors of the debtor loss corporation as if they were equity shareholders. Thus, in a title 11 reorganization proceeding that results in continued 50 percent (or greater) ownership (tested by vote *and* value) on the part of the corporation's shareholders and historic creditors (i.e., creditors that either have held their claims for the 18-month period preceding the *filing* of the title 11 proceeding or are historic ordinary business trade creditors[224]), §382(*l*)(5)(A) provides that no limitation under §382 will be triggered.

However, §382(*l*)(5)(B) requires that loss carry-over deductions must be reduced dollar for dollar by the amount of any interest deductions taken (on debt that was converted into stock in the title 11 proceeding) during the pre-change part-year period and for the preceding three years. The theory here is that the converted debt was in substance equity for the three-year disallowance period.[225] Moreover, §382(*l*)(5)(C) further reduces the carry-overs by one-half of any debt cancellation gain that was excluded from §108 income treatment under the insolvency exception for equity-debt swaps in §108(e)(10)(B). If part of the excluded debt cancellation gain consists of previously deducted interest (three years of which also reduces carry-overs under §382(l)(5)(B)), a duplicative reduction is nevertheless required by §382(l)(5)(C). Finally, §382(l)(5)(D) completely eliminates carry-overs running from the period before the first ownership change that qualified for the bankruptcy exception if a second ownership change of any kind occurs within two years of the first change—that is, only one bite at the loss company is allowed every two years.[226]

The debtor corporation can elect under §382(*l*)(5)(H) not to have the special insolvency exception apply (subject to regulation terms and condi-

---

[224] Section 382(*l*)(5)(E). In order to qualify, the ordinary course of business creditor must have been the continuous beneficial owner of that claim (i.e., he must be the historic trade creditor.)

[225] Presumably, interest is disallowed under this rule, whether or not the former creditor counts for purposes of the 50 percent continuity rule. If this interest is also cancelled in the proceeding by issuing stock with a value less than the cancelled debt, one-half of this excluded gain also reduces carry-overs under §382(*l*)(5)(E).

[226] The Conference Report, supra note 156, at II-192, indicates that loss carry-overs generated between the two ownership changes would not be eliminated but would merely be subject to limitation under §382 on the second acquisition.

tions) and instead be subject to the normal §382 limitations. In view of the carry-over reduction rules for pre-change interest and debt cancellation gains, election out of §382(*l*)(5) may well be preferable. If such an election is made, or if §382(*l*)(5) does not otherwise apply, §382(*l*)(6) determines the value limitation of §382(e) immediately after the ownership change event, thereby taking into account stock acquired by creditors in the reorganization.

The special bankruptcy rule does not apply to informal workouts that occur outside the formal jurisdiction of a bankruptcy court, but the Treasury is directed to study informal workouts and report back to Congress before 1988.[227]

7. Other limitations. Despite the stringent new limitations provided by the 1986 version of §382, Congress was unwilling to abandon various other statutory and regulatory limitations on the negotiability of corporate tax attributes, although it apparently did put to death *most* of any lingering application of the *Libson Shops* doctrine.[228] However, the significance of these other limitations is bound to be greatly diminished in view of the pervasive effects of the §382 limitations.

(a) Relation of §382 to §269. While §269 technically continues to apply with unabated force, it is difficult to envision many cases where taxpayers could harbor the requisite tax avoidance principal purpose contained in that provision in view of the tightly restricted use of carry-overs imposed by the mechanical rules of §382 in cases where this provision also applies to the sought-after tax benefits. Thus, an economically motivated taxpayer who acquires a loss company that is subject to a 5 percent earnout limitation under §382 would most likely have given little if any thought to making effective use of its tax loss history. Almost any transaction to which §269 could apply also seems to be equally subject to §382; in fact, the transactional coverage under the 1986 version of §382 is even broader than §269 in several instances (e.g., §382 can apply to a public stock offering, while §269(a)(1) probably would not; owncr shifts involving pure preferred stock

---

[227] Tax Reform Act of 1986, §621(d)(2). Special favorable temporary rules (applicable only until 1989) also are provided in §382(*l*)(5)(F) for reorganizations of insolvent thrift institutions. Generally, §382 will not be triggered by such a reorganizing thrift institution if shareholders, creditors, and depositors maintain at least a 20 percent stock interest in the thrift (counting deposits as stock for this purpose). The carry-over cutback rules for interest and debt cancellation gains and the disallowance rule for second ownership changes do not apply to these transactions.

[228] H.R. Rep. No. 841, supra note 156, at II-194; this holds true only if the transaction is subject to §382.

now are caught by §382, but could be tailored to escape §269;[229] §318 attribution applies generally to §382, while it does not apply as such to §269).

On the other hand, §382 requires an ownership change of *more* than 50 percentage points of stock value in order to constitute a triggering event. Section 269(a)(1), by contrast, only requires a 50 percent change of control measured by vote *or* value. Thus, 50-50 joint ventures are not caught by §382 but could result in a §269(a)(1) control acquisition. Moreover, control shifts among less than 5-percent shareholders do not generally activate §382, while §269(a)(1) could apply to such acquisitions (e.g., a loss company with no 5-percent shareholders can, until contrary regulations are issued, be acquired by a group of 21 equal unrelated persons without triggering a §382 change of ownership). In addition, §382 does not apply if the more than 50 percent control shift occurs outside of the three-year test period of §382(i); §269 has no such mechanical time frame. Finally, while §§382 and 383 cover those favorable tax attributes that have the greatest potential significance, they do not exhaust all the possibilities to which §269 could apply (e.g., earnings deficits, various rapid amortization writeoffs, favorable tax elections, and so forth).[230] Regardless of these continuing differences, §269, although technically unaffected by the 1986 legislation, seems destined to play at most an interstitial and relatively minor supporting role under the amended statutory regime. Section 382, while not yet a one-person show, has definitely been recast as the star performer, at least as far as the loss carry-over drama is concerned.

(b) Relation to §338. If stock control of a loss company is acquired in a §338 qualified purchase transaction, election of §338 generally purges the acquired corporation of its tax history, including loss carry-overs and built-in losses, since a taxable liquidation is deemed to occur on the acquisition date.[231] But the acquired corporation can fully use its own loss carry-overs against any built-in gain required to be recognized on the §338 election (even if the business continuity requirement of §382(c) is violated).[232]

On the other hand, if §338 is not elected (as would ordinarily be the case where the target corporation has favorable tax benefits that would be

---

[229] See e.g., Maxwell Hardware, Inc. v. CIR, supra note 24.

[230] Loss carry-overs and built in losses are covered by §382; §383 extends §382 treatment to capital loss carry-overs, excess business credits, minimum tax credits, and foreign tax credits.

For some of the potential tax benefits to which §269 could apply, see the list of corporate carry-over items in §381(c), supra ¶ 16.13. See also Prop. Regs. §1.269 A-1(a)(6).

[231] Supra ¶ 11.46. Note also that the acquired corporation's taxable gains or losses occur outside of the purchasing corporation's consolidated group, id.

[232] Supra note 213; see also supra this section, para. 5. See generally Temp. Regs. §1.338-4T(k)(3); Temp. Regs. §1.338(h)(10)-1T(e)(3).

purged by electing §338), use of the target's carry-overs will be limited by §382(a) as discussed at the beginning of this section. If the parent subsequently liquidates its acquired loss subsidiary under §332, however, no gain or loss results to either the liquidating subsidiary (under §337) or to its parent (under §332), and the subsidiary's tax history carries over to the parent under §381(a)(1); this liquidation transaction would not effect a second change of ownership, since it would constitute neither an owner shift nor an equity structure shift transaction.[233] Moreover, the distributee-parent does not fit comfortably within the statutory definition of "new loss corporation" in §382(k)(3) (the corporation to which the §382 limitation applies); rather, it is the subsidiary that clearly is the new loss corporation for purposes of §382(a),[234] and that corporation disappears in the liquidation.

It seems highly unlikely, however, that the limitation of §382 can be avoided by the simple expedient of liquidating a newly acquired loss subsidiary. Unfortunately, the statutory language of §382 does not respond clearly to this sort of transaction unless and until (if ever) the antiabuse regulations of §382(m)(3) are so drafted (which they easily could be under the broad delegation contained therein). Perhaps §381 will cause the limitations of §382 to carry over as an inherited tax attribute or possibly §381 will cause new loss company status to carry over, in either case subjecting the parent corporation to the §382 limitations. Moreover, §269(b), enacted in 1984, can apply to tax motivated liquidation plans adopted within two years of a §338 stock purchase and nonelection of §338;[235] tax avoidance would seem to be a high probability here if the parent were attempting to finesse §382 with this maneuver.[236]

---

[233] Supra ¶ 16.24. Under the constructive ownership look-through rule of §382(*l*)(3)(A)(ii), the subsidiary's stock is deemed to be owned by the parent's shareholders (and *not* by the parent); thus, no ownership change occurs on the liquidation, assuming no underlying change in the parent's stock ownership.

Moreover, a §382(g)(3)(A) equity structure change requires a §368 reorganization, which a §332 liquidation is not (unless effected by merger); query whether the regulatory authority in §382(g)(3)(B) to include similar transactions as equity structure changes will cover a §332 liquidation, supra note 168. For §381(a)(1), see supra ¶ 16.11.

[234] On the other hand, §382(k)(3) may be broad enough to encompass a second new loss corporation (or, more exactly, a *successor* new loss corporation that obtained such status as a result of §381); see supra note 183 (but see proposed §382(*l*)(8) in the pending Technical Corrections Act of 1987).

[235] Supra ¶ 16.21 and note 82; supra note 134.

[236] Note, however, that plans adopted more than two years after the acquisition date avoid §269(b) as well: §269(b)(1)(C); this period does not appear to be extendable, as is the consistency period of §338(h)(4)(B), supra ¶ 11.47.

But the Technical Corrections Act of 1987, supra note 183, fixes this gap in proposed new §382(*l*)(8); so also does the Blue Book, supra note 183.

(c) Relation to consolidated return rules. As previously noted, the consolidated return regulations have their own set of limitations that restrict the ability of affiliated groups to acquire other corporations having favorable tax attributes with a view to the use of those attributes in the consolidated return (e.g., the SRLY and consolidated return change of ownership limitation rules, and the built-in loss limitation rules). The Conference Report states that these limitations will continue to apply.[237]

In many respects, the §382 limitation rules resemble the consolidated return SRLY rules, since SRLY losses, like losses limited under §382, can only offset taxable income generated by that particular member of the group. Moreover, the built-in deduction rules of the consolidated return regulations also subject these deductions to the SRLY limitations in a manner similar to the treatment of those losses under §382.[238] However, the consolidated return regulations specifically incorporate §382 into their limitations, and also give priority to §382.[239] As a result, it seems likely that the 1986 version of §382 will also come to overshadow the consolidated return regulation limitations where the two overlap, which will be the case in most instances.

(d) Libson Shops doctrine. The Conference Report specifically notes that the *Libson Shops* doctrine (a 1939 Code decision that limited the use of loss carry-overs to the income of the business unit that produced the loss), is not to apply in cases where §382 also applies.[240] Since the breadth of §382 is probably sufficient to absorb virtually all of those instances in which *Libson Shops* might also apply (even if that decision had continuing vitality under the 1954 Code, an issue on which the courts were in conflict), we have probably seen the last of that decision.[241]

(e) Anti-abuse regulations. The statute, in §382(m)(3), contains a broad delegation of regulatory authority for the Treasury to draft such regulations

---

[237] Supra ¶ 15.24; see H.R. Rep. No. 841, supra note 156, at II-194, stating that these limitations (SRLY and CRCO) continue to apply notwithstanding enactment of amended §382.

Note, however, that the definition of a CRCO in Regs. §§1.1502-1(g) and 1.1502-21(d) is based on the stock ownership change provisions of former 1954 Code §382(a).

[238] However, the built-in deduction rules in Regs. §1.1502-15 apply more broadly than the built-in loss rules of §382; the former has a de minimis line of only 15 percent and applies to depreciation deductions, while the latter has a 25 percent de minimis line and does *not* cover depreciation, supra notes 216 and 217.

[239] Regs. §1.1502-21(e). Note however, that these regulations refer to the 1954 Code version of §382.

[240] Supra note 228; infra ¶ 16.26.

[241] For extensive analysis of *Libson Shops*, see infra ¶ 16.26.

(retroactively) "as is necessary to prevent the avoidance of the purposes of this section . . . including the avoidance . . . through the use of related persons, pass[through] entities or other intermediaries." The Conference Report[242] points out that the primary concern here is the use of partnerships in which taxable income is allocated to a loss partner without a concurrent allocation of economic benefit to that partner. The Conference Report also authorizes the Treasury to deal with this issue under §382 (in lieu of the partnership allocation rules of the §704(b) regulations[243]) by restricting the use of losses to offset distributable partnership income and by taxing such income at the highest marginal rate or reallocating such income to other partners.

8. Examples. Operation of the "section 382 limitation" can be illustrated by the following examples in which it is assumed (unless otherwise stated) that the applicable statutory change of ownership has occurred.[244] *L* is the loss company, wholly owned by *A*; *P* is a profit company, wholly owned by *B*.

Example 1. *A* sells all his *L* stock to *P* for $100 at a time when the long-term tax exempt rate is 5 percent. *L*'s carry-overs can only be offset against its post-change taxable income to the extent of $5 per year (pro-rated in the change year).

If *L* has built-in losses, those losses become subject to the §382 limitation if recognized within five years after the change; if, instead, *L* has built-in gains on the change date, carry-overs can be absorbed to the extent of those gains if recognized within five years of the change.

Example 2. Assume the same facts as in Example 1, except that *A* sells half of his *L* stock to *P* for $50 and *L* redeems the rest for $50. The annual §382 limitation here is $2.50 (reflecting the reduction of *L*'s stock value caused by the redemption).

---

[242] Supra note 195.

[243] As to the §704(b) regulations, see Lokken, Partnership Allocations, 41 Tax L. Rev. 545 (1986); see also Gunn, The Character of a Partner's Distributive Share Under the "Substantial Economic Effect" Regulations, 40 Tax Lawyer 121 (1986); Bailis & Hartung-Wendel, Meeting the Economic Effect Test Under Section 704(b) Regulations, 3 J. Part. Tax'n 311 (1987): Shapleigh & Hoskins, How to Satisfy the Substantiality Requirement Under Section 704(b) Regulations, 3 J. Part. Tax'n 291 (1987); Close & Kusnetz, The Final Section 704(b) Regulations, 40 Tax Lawyer 307 (1987).

[244] See also H.R. Rep. No. 841, supra note 156, at II-186, Example 22, and at II-188, Example 24.

Example 3. L buys all of P's stock from B, after which L sells its business assets and invests the proceeds in its new subsidiary P; §382 has no application here; neither, absent special facts, does §269.[245]

Example 4. L sells all its operating assets for cash and invests the proceeds in marketable securities; L is then acquired by P (either by merger or an acquisition of L stock). Under the passive asset rules of §382(*l*)(4), the value of L is reduced by its passive assets (presumably 100 percent here), so no use could be made by P here of L's carry-overs.

Example 5. P acquires all of L's stock, and, within two years, L sells all of its operating assets. L flunks the business continuity test of §382(c)(1), and its §382 limitation is reduced to zero retroactively, back to the date of its acquisition by P.[246]

Example 6. L was incorporated in year one and merged into P in year two. The anti-stuffing rule of §382(*l*)(1) applies in full here and none of L's carry-overs (including built-in losses) could be available to P (although the Conference Report indicates that incorporation transactions should be exempted by regulation from this rule).[247]

Example 7. L has two classes of stock, common (worth $100) and pure preferred (worth $900), and A sells all of his common stock to P for $100. An ownership change occurs here (the preferred is ignored), but the amount of the §382 value limitation is $1,000 (§382(e)(1) includes the preferred in valuing L's stock).

If, instead of preferred stock, A held $900 of debt, the §382 limitation if $100, the equity value of L. Moreover, if A contributes the debt to L within two years of the acquisition by P, the $900 capital contribution would be disregarded under the anti-stuffing rule of §382(*l*)(1).

Example 8. L is involved in a title 11 proceeding. Under the court approved plan, L's creditor, C, acquires 100 percent of L's stock; depending upon whether C qualifies as a historic (18-month) creditor or a historic ordinary course of business creditor, this event may or may not constitute an ownership change under §382.[248]

---

[245] See Rev. Rul. 63-40, 1963-1 CB 46.

[246] Under §382(c)(2), however, L could use its carry-overs against any recognized built-in gain (or if P elects §338, L's gains recognized as a result of that election could be offset by L's carry-overs).

[247] Supra note 203.

[248] Supra notes 224–227.

If C is not a qualified creditor, §382 is triggered, but the limitation would be measured after the change under §382(l)(6). If enough creditors are qualified to meet the 50 percent continuity line of §382(l)(5), the §382 limitation does not apply, but L must reduce its carry-overs by three years of interest deductions and half of any excluded debt cancellation gains (even though part of that debt gain was attributable to disallowed interest). Moreover, if another ownership change occurs within two years, L's carry-overs would be terminated under the one-bite rule of §382(l)(5)(D).

Example 9. P acquires all of L's stock in year 1 (a change of ownership activating §382). In year 2, P liquidates L under §332. Assuming that §269(b) does not apply to totally disallow L's carry-overs,[249] P would succeed to L's unused carry-overs under §381(a)(1); but it is unclear whether P would also take these carry-overs impressed with the §382 limitation applicable to L, since the liquidation of L does not constitute a second ownership change under §382.[250] On the other hand, the carry-over principles of §381 may be flexible enough to cause L's §382 limitation to be treated as a carry-over attribute in the hands of P.

¶ 16.26　THE *LIBSON SHOPS* LOSS TRACING TEST AND ITS RAMIFICATIONS

In the long-famous case of *Libson Shops, Inc. v. Koehler*, the Supreme Court announced a controversial limitation on the survival of net operating loss carry-overs after a statutory merger, based on a loss tracing or continuity of business enterprise theory.[251] The taxpayer was a corporation into which 16 other corporations (each operating a separate retail store), all owned by the same shareholders in the same proportion, were merged; the surviving corporation sought to apply the pre-merger net operating losses of three of these absorbed corporations to the aggregate post-merger income of the combined group. The stores formerly operated by the loss corporations continued to produce losses. The Court disallowed the carry-overs, "since the income against which the offset is claimed was not produced by substantially the same businesses which incurred the losses"; and, in examining the legislative history of the net operating loss rules, the Court found that they

---

[249] Supra notes 235 and 236.

[250] Supra notes 183, 233, and 234. See also supra ¶ 16.13, and proposed amendment by the Technical Corrections Act of 1987, note 183.

[251] Libson Shops v. Koehler, supra note 15. For extensive analysis of *Libson*, see the Fourth Edition of this treatise at ¶ 16.26.

were designed to permit "a taxpayer to set off its lean years against its lush years" but not "to permit the averaging of the pre-merger losses of one business with the post-merger income of some other business which had been operated and taxed separately before the merger"; instead, the Court ruled that Congress was concerned "with the fluctuating income of a single business."[252]

Although *Libson Shops* was decided in 1957, it arose under pre-1954 law; important changes in the governing statutory rules since then have dramatically limited *Libson Shops'* jurisdiction in some areas and have rendered it irrelevant in others, as explained in the following paragraphs.

1. The effects of §§381 and 382. For the taxable years before the Court in *Libson Shops* (1948–1949), there were no statutory provisions explicitly providing for the inheritance of a corporation's operating loss carry-overs by a successor corporation or for the disallowance of inherited carry-overs in the event of a change of ownership or business. The enactment in 1954 of §§381 and 382, however, arguably preempted both of these issues, leaving no room for a judge-made restriction on a successor corporation's right to use carry-overs inherited from its predecessor. Although this theory has some support,[253] the less sweeping principle (i.e., that "*Libson Shops* has no application to cases decided under the 1954 Code *where the provisions of sections 381 and 382 apply*"[254]) is more widely accepted. Thus, if a change in owner-

---

[252] Id. at 387. In so ruling, the Supreme Court gave no attention to another possible reading of legislative objective in allowing unused losses to be carried to other taxable years: measurement of the taxpayer's ability to pay taxes *over the long haul* rather than year by year. This rationale suggests that losses and income should be amalgamated without regard to the sources from which they are derived. The legislative history's reference to "a business" on which the Court relied for its contrary theory of legislative purpose was only an example and creaks under the weight placed on it by the Court.

For problems in determining whether a post-change business is the same business that produced the loss carryovers, see the Fourth Edition of this treatise at ¶ 16.26.

[253] Maxwell Hardware Co. v. CIR, supra note 24 (1954 Code "destroyed the precedential value" of *Libson Shops*). The committee reports on the Tax Reform Act of 1976 state that *Libson Shops* should not be applied to taxable years affected by the 1976 amendments to §382; but query the effect of this opinion, given the retroactive repeal in 1986 of the 1976 rules. See S. Rep. No. 938, 94th Cong., 2d Sess. 206 (1976), reprinted in 1976-3 CB 57, 244 (*Libson Shops* not applicable to future years); H.R. Conf. Rep. No. 1236, 94th Cong., 2d Sess. 450 (1976), reprinted in 1976-3 CB 807, 854 (no inferences intended regarding application of *Libson Shops* to taxable years governed by present law). For the repeal of the 1976 amendments, see supra notes 141 and 157.

[254] Daytona Beach Kennel Club, Inc., 69 TC 1015, 1033 (1978), citing other cases (emphasis added). Substantially the same point—preemption for transactions

ship or a corporate reorganization brings §§381 and 382 into play, the net operating loss carry-over can be used if and to the extent prescribed by §382, even if it does not satisfy the loss tracing principle of *Libson Shops.* On the other hand, if a transaction is not described by §382 (e.g., an ownership change not meeting the standards of §382(g)), the italicized language quoted above implies that loss carry-overs can be used only if they satisfy the *Libson Shops* test.

Although such a residual role for *Libson Shops* may be defensible in some non-§382 situations, there are others in which the application of *Libson Shops* would produce a bizarre result. Assume, for example, that two taxpayers claiming the benefit of net operating carry-overs are identical in all respects, except that the first underwent an ownership change within the meaning of §382(g)(1) because it has one 5-percent shareholder, while the second was not subjected to §382 because no shareholder owned 5-percent or more of its stock. On these facts, the first corporation might be entitled to use its carry-overs in full because they were below the §382 limit; but the second corporation's carry-overs—arising from identical pre-change facts and applied against identical post-change income sources—could be disallowed in full because *Libson Shops* is more restrictive than §382. It strains credulity to believe that this disparity is consistent with the legislative purpose in enacting §382.

2. Net operating loss carry-backs. Section 172 provides for both carry-backs and carry-overs of operating losses, but §§381–382 limit themselves to carry-overs. *Libson Shops* was also concerned solely with carry-overs, but its loss tracing rationale is equally applicable to carry-backs. Unless the enactment of §382 is construed as implicitly endorsing the unrestricted allowance of carry-backs, it can be persuasively argued—and the Court of Appeals for the Seventh Circuit has held—that the loss tracing principle of *Libson Shops* remains valid for net operating loss carry-backs.[255]

3. Other carry-overs. The loss tracing principle enunciated in *Libson Shops* emerged from the Supreme Court's review of the legislative history of the statutory predecessor of §172, and there is no a priori reason to believe that the legislative history of any, let alone all, of the other tax carry-overs allowed by the Code embodied an analogous tracing principle. For example,

---

covered by §382 (as amended in 1986)—is to be found in the Conference Committee's report on the Tax Reform Act of 1986; this permits the application of *Libson Shops* to other transactions if indeed it does not enforce that outcome by negative implication. See H.R. Rep. No. 841, supra note 156, at II-194.

[255] National Tea Co. v. CIR, 793 F2d 864 (7th Cir. 1986), and cases cited.

it is arguable that the ITC's function of encouraging capital expenditures would be better served by allowing taxpayers to apply their ITC carry-overs to taxes generated by income from any business activities, rather than applying the same business restriction enunciated by *Libson Shops* for net operating loss carry-overs. Not surprisingly, however, there is a tendency to extend *Libson Shops* to other carry-overs, at least in the absence of a distinctive legislative history evidencing a contrary congressional intention. Thus, in 1968, the Service in effect applied the *Libson Shops* rationale to the foreign tax credit without referring to its legislative history or even citing *Libson Shops* itself. [256]

Before this seemingly mechanical extension of *Libson Shops* had been tested by litigation, however, Congress enacted §383, applying §382 principles to the foreign tax credit; the Service thereafter withdrew its 1968 ruling, stating that §383 had "preempted prior law" regarding the carry-over of foreign tax credits in transactions subject to §383. [257] It seems likely that the Service will adopt the same position for the other credit carry-overs governed by §383. [258]

¶ 16.27 OTHER LIMITATIONS ON SURVIVAL OF CORPORATE TAX ATTRIBUTES

While the foregoing limitations on survival of corporate tax attributes constitute a formidable array of statutory and judicial defenses, the Service has yet another series of more general weapons at its disposal that may be invoked in egregious cases of tax manipulation and abuse. These have been noted at other points in this work; what follows is a checklist rather than a full discussion:

1. Business purpose and economic reality. If a transaction fails to qualify as a reorganization because it lacks a business purpose, §381(a) will not come into play to preserve the tax attributes of the transferor corporation for the successor corporation. [259]

---

[256] Rev. Rul. 68-350, 1968-2 CB 159.

[257] Rev. Rul. 80-144, 1980-1 CB 80.

[258] For the scope of §383, see supra text at notes 142–143 and supra note 230.

[259] See American Bronze Corp., 64 TC 1111 (1975) (reorganization upheld and carry-over allowed where taxpayer proved business purpose and continuity of business enterprise); compare Wortham Mach. Co. v. US 521 F2d 160 (10th Cir. 1975) (no business purpose for merger; acquired corporation inert and insolvent; so carry-overs denied for lack of reorganization status).

2. Recognition of the corporate entity. If the corporate enterprise is of such an evanescent or dormant character as to lack economic reality, its status as a separate entity may be disregarded. Because the courts seem reluctant to ignore the separate entity status of a corporation,[260] this line of attack has been reserved for extreme cases.

3. Assignment of income principles. In a sense, the *Libson Shops* doctrine and its subsequent judicial extensions can be viewed as an offshoot of the general principle that income must be taxed to the one who earns it or to the owner of the property that produces it.[261] Where there is a change of ownership, allowing the post-change income to be offset by losses or other items whose economic cost fell on the old shareholders is the same as allowing the new owners to avoid the tax burden of their income. Even if ownership does not change, a transfer of tax benefits from one taxable entity to another raises assignment of income problems. On the other hand, the carry-over rules of §381 (and the limitations of §§269 and 382) probably restrict assignment of income principles to a limited role in this area, and this conclusion seems borne out by the paucity of decided cases resorting to this approach.[262]

4. Reallocation of income or deductions under §482. The Service has broad discretionary power under §482 to reallocate income, deductions, credits, or other allowances between or among related taxpayers to clearly reflect income.[263]

See also Regs. §1.368-1(d), imposing continuity of business enterprise limitations similar to those in 1954 Code §382(a) and 1986 Code §382(c). For §382(c), see supra ¶ 16.25, para. 5.

[260] See, e.g., Raymond Greenberg, 62 TC 311 (1974), aff'd per curiam, 36 AFTR2d 5479 (6th Cir.), cert. denied, 423 US 1052 (1976); Arthur T. Beckett, 41 TC 386 (1963), aff'd sub nom. Maxwell Hardware Co. v. CIR, supra note 24; Ach v. CIR, 385 F2d 342 (6th Cir.), cert. denied, 385 US 899 (1966); see also Sam Siegel, supra note 91 (entity upheld despite tax motives for creation of foreign corporation); supra ¶ 2.07.

[261] See generally Lyon & Eustice, Assignment of Income: Fruit and Tree as Irrigated by the P.G. Lake Case, 17 Tax L. Rev. 293 (1962); supra ¶¶ 1.05 and 2.07.

[262] See Rubin v. CIR, 429 F2d 650 (2d Cir. 1970), reversing Tax Court holding that payment by one corporation to another was taxable to dominant individual shareholder of both corporations on the ground that the rules of §482 should be applied rather than the blunt tool of assignment of income theory; Stanley W. Haag, 88 TC No. 32 (1987).

[263] See Borge v. CIR, supra note 89; Rubin v. CIR, supra note 262; Stanley W. Haag, supra note 262.

For an invitation to the Service to use §482 where the parties successfully avoid the clutches of §§269 and 382, see *Maxwell Hardware Co. v. CIR*.[264] It should be noted, however, that §482 authorizes only the reallocation of income or deductions; it does not permit disallowance of deductions, and hence cannot be used in the same manner as §§269 and 382, which provide for total disallowance (or severe limitation) of various beneficial tax allowances.

5. De facto dissolution. A corporation in the process of liquidation may eventually reach such a point of dormancy that its corporate existence will be held to have terminated; consequently, operating losses or other tax benefits generated after this event cannot be carried back to prior years of viability.[265] On the whole, however, courts have been reluctant to apply the de facto dissolution theory to disallow net operating loss carry-backs generated during the process of liquidation.[266]

Before leaving this area, a word of caution seems in order. The preceding materials may have created the impression that corporate tax attributes will survive adjustments and changes in a corporation's stock ownership, financial structure, legal entity, or business enterprise only in rare and unusual cases. In point of fact, however, the scope of corporate carry-overs is a

---

[264] Maxwell Hardware Co. v. CIR, supra note 24.

[265] See generally in this respect Rev. Rul. 61-191, 1961-2 CB 251, where the Service ruled that post-liquidation net operating losses and excess profits tax credits could not be carried back to pre-liquidation years of a corporation that had been dissolved de facto. See also Willingham v. US. 289 F2d 283 (5th Cir.), cert. denied, 368 US 828 (1961), for an application of this approach, although with overtones of *Libson Shops*, to a corporation that had passed through a major insolvency reorganization. But see Jacqueline, Inc., ¶ 77,340 P-H Memo. TC (1977).

[266] See, e.g., US v. Jackson Oldsmobile, Inc., supra note 21; Joseph Weidenhoff, Inc., supra note 21; Anbaco-Emig Corp., supra note 21. For problems raised by corporations that liquidate in midstream, see supra ¶ 11.07; see also supra ¶ 2.09 for the tax treatment of corporations in the process of winding up; Tillinghast & Gardner, supra note 33; see also Jacqueline, Inc., supra note 265; Daytona Beach Kennel Club Inc., supra note 254 (Willingham not applicable to 1954 Code).

More currently, see Rev. Rul. 74-462, 1974-2 CB 82 (Rev. Rul. 61-191, 1961-2 CB 251, distinguished, and no de facto liquidation of a corporation in process of complete liquidation even though operating business terminated, where it retained assets as a reserve for contingent liabilities from pending lawsuits and where it continued to defend against those suits and to prosecute actions brought by it).

But see Textron, Inc. v. US, supra note 38 (parent allowed §165(g)(3) loss deduction for investment in subsidiary despite its later revival with new business and use of loss carry-overs against profits of new business; no argument that subsidiary had de facto liquidated when parent claimed §165 deduction, although such would have appeared to be the government's strongest position here). See Natbony, supra note 38.

broad one (especially since the 1954 Code), and denial of these benefits may well be the exception rather than the rule. Although the Service's position in litigated cases may suggest implacable opposition to any and all transfers of tax attributes, many, if not most, corporate reorganizations and other adjustments pass smoothly through the audit or tax ruling process with their carry-overs intact. The reader, therefore, should not focus so exclusively on the barriers to a transfer of attributes as to overlook the likelihood of their preservation.

In short, the hole is an important part of the doughnut (although the doughnut has shrunk in size and soured in taste considerably as a result of the 1986 reforms under §382).

CHAPTER 17

Foreign Corporations and Foreign-Source Income

PART A. TAXATION OF FOREIGN CORPORATIONS IN GENERAL

¶ 17.01 INTRODUCTORY

The taxation of foreign corporations and the treatment of foreign-source income is a vast and highly intricate subject, well beyond the intended coverage of this treatise; and the purpose of this chapter is to provide merely an introduction to the basic principles.[1]

---

[1] See generally Postlewaite, International Corporate Taxation, Tax and Estate Planning Series (Shepard's/McGraw-Hill, 1980); Ross, U.S. Taxation of Aliens and Foreign Corporations: The Foreign Investors' Tax Act of 1966, 22 Tax L. Rev. 277

As a general rule, U.S. domestic corporations are taxed on their worldwide income regardless of its source. Exceptions to this rule exist only to prevent taxation of foreign income by multiple national sovereigns (such "double taxation" is mitigated by the foreign tax credit system) and, to a more limited extent, to promote U.S. policy interests abroad (e.g., foreign sales corporations, possessions corporations, and domestic international sales corporations). Foreign corporations pay U.S. tax at regular corporate rates only on net income that is effectively connected to a U.S. trade or business, while their gross U.S.-source investment income is taxed separately at a flat 30 percent rate (with no deductions); however, capital gains and other nonrecurring U.S.-connected income is usually not subject to tax, nor is interest from U.S. investments that qualifies for special treatment under §881. Special rules also govern foreign investments in U.S. real estate.

Before turning to these questions, however, it is important to examine the general rules that define the source of income and deductions,[2] the income's "effective connection" to a U.S. trade or business,[3] and the nature (trade or business vs. investment) and location (within or without the United States) of a taxpayer's economic activity.[4] These definitions determine which of the tax rules discussed below must be applied in order to calculate the U.S. tax liability of foreign corporations and domestic recipients of foreign-source income. Moreover, various bilateral tax treaties frequently will alter the results under the basic statutory regime and constitute an important aspect of this area.[5]

For many years, the taxation of foreign persons and foreign-source income suffered from congressional neglect. The Revenue Act of 1962, however, effected an overhaul of the taxation of foreign corporations owned by U.S. taxpayers; and before its changes were fully digested, Congress enacted the Foreign Investors' Tax Act of 1966, materially revising the taxation of nonresident aliens and foreign corporations. Administrative changes during

---

(1967); Tillinghast, The Foreign Investors' Tax Act of 1966, 20 ABA Tax Section Bull. 87 (Jan. 1967); Tax Mgmt. (BNA) Portfolio Series on foreign income problems.

See also generally Kingson, The Coherence of International Taxation, 81 Colum. L. Rev. 1151 (1981); Ross, A Perspective on International Tax Policy, 26 Tax Notes 701 (1985).

[2] See Dailey, The Concept of the Source of Income, 15 Tax L. Rev. 415 (1960); Krahmer, Federal Income Tax Treatment of International Sales of Goods: A Reevaluation of the Title-Passage Test, 17 Tax L. Rev. 235 (1962); Rosch, Travel and Entertainment Expense Deductions for Nonresident Aliens: An Analysis and Critique, 21 Tax L. Rev. 103 (1965).

[3] See Garelik, What Constitutes Doing Business Within the United States by a Nonresident Alien Individual or a Foreign Corporation?, 18 Tax L. Rev. 423 (1963).

[4] See Ross, supra note 1.

[5] Infra ¶ 17.02, para. 4.

this period were no less extensive, including the 1968 regulations under §482 (the major impact of which related to the foreign area) and the issuance, also in 1968, of guidelines under §367 rulings relating to tax-free exchanges involving foreign corporations. Tax treaties between the United States and foreign countries also play a major role in this area, often changing materially the tax results that would otherwise obtain under domestic statutory law.

Congress renewed its interest in the foreign area in the early 1980s and, in the Tax Reform Act of 1984, effected major changes in the §367 rules, exempted portfolio interest income from tax, replaced the DISC rules with a new deferral system, the Foreign Sales Corporation, and made numerous other complex technical changes.[6] The Tax Reform Act of 1986 ranged even more broadly across the foreign tax landscape, exacting significant amendments to the source rules, the foreign tax credit rules, the taxation of foreign corporations doing business in the United States, and the controlled foreign corporation rules. It also set out a new set of statutory rules dealing with foreign currency transactions.[7]

The 1986 Act also materially affected the foreign area by dramatically lowering both individual and corporate rates, as discussed in Chapter 5.

¶ 17.02　BASIC DEFINITIONS AND CONCEPTS

1. Source of income and deductions. Sections 861 and 862 provide a set of source rules for some, but not all, types of income, while §863 deals with the treatment of items not specified in §861 or §862. Sections 861(a) and 862(a) provide the following general source rules for income:

(a) Interest. The source of interest income is generally determined by reference to the residence of the debtor: Interest paid by residents of the United States constitutes domestic-source income, while interest paid by foreign residents is foreign-source income (§§861(a)(1) and 862(a)(1)).[8]

---

[6] See Eustice, The Tax Reform Act of 1984: A Selective Analysis, ch. 4 (Warren, Gorham & Lamont, Inc., 1984).

[7] Infra ¶ 17.02, para. 5. See also Eustice, Kuntz, Lewis & Deering, The Tax Reform Act of 1986, ch. 4 (Warren, Gorham & Lamont, Inc., 1987).

[8] Two principal exceptions to these principles are found in §§861(a)(1)(A) and 861(a)(1)(B). First, §861(a)(1)(A) treats interest as foreign-source if the debtor satisfies the requirements of §861(c)—that is, 80 percent of its gross income for a three-year period is attributable to an active business in a foreign country (or U.S. possession); second, §861(a)(1)(B) treats interest on deposits in foreign branches of U.S. banks as foreign-source.

For the taxability of interest paid by foreign debtors, see infra ¶ 17.04, para. 2.

(b) Dividends. The source of dividend income generally depends upon the nationality of the corporate payor—that is, distributions by U.S. corporations constitute domestic-source income, while dividends of foreign corporations are foreign-source income (§§861(a)(2) and 862(a)(2)).[9]

(c) Compensation for personal services. The source of income from the performance of personal services depends upon the place of performance of the services (§§861(a)(3) and 862(a)(3)).[10]

(d) Rents and royalties. Rent or royalty income has its source at the location, or place of use, of the leased or licensed property (§§861(a)(4) and 862(a)(4)).[11]

(e) Sale of real property. Gain from the sale of real estate has its source at the place where the property is situated (§§861(a)(5) and 862(a)(5)).

(f) Sale of personal property. Gain from the sale of personal property has its source at the "place of sale," which is generally held to be the place where title to the goods passes (§§861(a)(6) and 862(a)(6)).[12] However, the

---

[9] The principal exceptions to this rule are the following:

(1) Dividends paid by a domestic corporation that has a §936 election in effect (infra ¶ 17.13) are foreign-source.

(2) Dividends paid by a foreign corporation are foreign-source income under §861(a)(2)(B) if less than 25 percent of its gross income for the applicable three-year period was effectively connected to a U.S. business; otherwise, a ratable portion of its dividend payments will be considered U.S.-source income.

(3) In computing the foreign tax credits of the shareholders of a foreign corporation, dividends paid by a foreign corporation are foreign-source income to the extent that they exceed 100/85 of the deduction allowed thereon by §245 (supra ¶ 5.05; infra ¶ 17.04).

For the treatment of dividends paid by *domestic* corporations that derive the bulk of their income (80 percent) from an active foreign situs business, see §881(d), infra ¶ 17.03; for the treatment of dividends paid by a *foreign* corporation engaged in a U.S. business that is subject to the branch profits surrogate tax rules of §884, see infra ¶ 17.04, para. 2.

[10] A commercial traveler exception applies to a nonresidential alien present in the United States for 90 days or less if his gross income does not exceed $3,000 and if he is working, in effect, for a foreign employer. Similar, although more liberal, exceptions are common in the tax treaties.

[11] See Rev. Rul. 68-443, 1968-2 CB 304 (royalties for use of foreign trademark were foreign-source income even though initial sale of trademarked goods occurred in United States); Wodehouse v. CIR, 178 F2d 987 (4th Cir. 1949) (allocation of proceeds from the sale of U.S. and Canadian serial rights); Rev. Rul. 86-156, 1986-52 IRB 18 (equipment rentals are business profits, not royalties).

[12] See Rev. Rul. 55-677, 1955-2 CB 289, applying the place of sale test without reference to how the property was acquired, thus suggesting that acquisitions by exchange, gift, or inheritance will be covered by the personal property general source rule.

Tax Reform Act of 1986 materially revised and restricted the passage of title source rule in §865 to provide that the source of gain from the sale of personal property generally is determined by the seller's residence; the title passage rule was retained for gain from sales of inventory personal property, but additional exceptions are provided for income that is effectively connected to a U.S. business and for recapture income (both sourced to the dominant economic residence of the seller).[13]

There are some difficult definitional aspects to the application of the source rules to various types of income: Do the interest-source rules apply to imputed interest under §483 (as indicated by Regs. §1.861-2(a)(4)), to original issue discount income under §1272,[14] or to market discount ordinary income under §1276?[15] How is one to treat "collapsed interest" income from the sale of the right to such income (Regs. §1.1441-4(h) exempts accrued interest on bonds between interest dates from withholding requirements, notwithstanding the domestic source and general taxability of such interest income to the seller)? Is the source of interest paid by the guarantor of an obligation the residence of the primary debtor or that of the guarantor?[16]

With respect to the "dividend" source rules, what constitutes a "dividend" for this purpose; that is, is the term limited to "ordinary" dividend distributions under §§301 and 316 (see Chapter 7), or does it include such extraordinary corporate distributions as ordinary gain from the sale of "section 306 stock" (as indicated by §306(f)), taxable stock dividends under §305(b), redemption distributions that fail to qualify for §302(a) sale treatment (see Chapter 9), distributions in partial or complete liquidation taxable as capital gain under §331 (or as ordinary gain if the distributing corpora-

---

Employee bargain purchases that result in compensation income (compare §83) should be handled under the compensation source rules of §861(a)(3), and shareholder bargain purchases that create dividend income to the purchaser should be governed by the dividend source rules of §861(a)(2).

[13] H.R. 3838, §1211(a) enacting §865, infra text at notes 24–30.

[14] Sections 871(a)(1)(C), 881(a)(3), and 1441(c)(8), enacted in 1971, provide that OID is taxed currently (to the extent that there is stated interest) if the obligation was issued after March 31, 1972 and has a term of more than six months. See also Rev. Rul. 68-333, 1968-1 CB 390, holding that the interest source rules should be applied here (this conclusion is derived from a statement in Staff of Senate Comm. on Finance, 89th Cong., 2d Sess. 24 (1966), Report on Foreign Investors' Tax Act of 1966, at 24, that issue discount income follows the interest source rules). See generally supra ¶ 4.40. For the Service's definition of "interest" (as opposed to "compensation" for services), see Rev. Rul. 70-540, 1970-2 CB 101, amplified by Rev. Rul. 74-607, 1974-2 CB 149. See also infra note 96.

[15] Section 1276(a)(4) states that market discount is interest except to a foreign taxpayer; supra ¶ 4.44.

[16] See Rev. Rul. 70-377, 1970-2 CB 175 (residence of principal debtor controls source of interest paid by guarantor).

tion is a collapsible corporation as defined in §341 (see Chapter 12), and boot dividends under §356(a)(2) distributed in the context of a corporate reorganization (see Chapter 14)?[17] Regs. §1.861-3(a)(1) states that "dividends" for this purpose means distributions defined in §316, thus indicating that some corporate distributions, even if treated as ordinary income under various Code provisions, do not constitute dividends for this purpose. Conversely, the mere fact that the distribution is "extraordinary" (e.g., a taxable stock dividend, a constructive dividend (see Chapter 7), or a dividend equivalent redemption) will not affect its treatment as a dividend under §861(a)(2) if it constitutes a distribution out of earnings and profits for purposes of §316.

With respect to compensation income, earnings derived from the performance of personal services are not always instantly identifiable, but instead may constitute royalty income from a license of property or the proceeds of a sale of property. These classification difficulties, which are especially troublesome in the area of "know-how" transfers,[18] are illustrated by *Karrer v. US.*[19] Another issue: What is the source of payments for negative services (e.g., noncompetition agreement proceeds), and how are proceeds from the sale of the taxpayer's contractual rights to earn compensation-type income (which are taxable as ordinary gain under assignment of income principles) to be treated here?[20] Purported licensing transfers of real or per-

---

[17] For a decision that §356(a)(2) boot dividends qualified for the §243 dividends-received deduction, see King Enterprises, Inc. v. US, 418 F2d 511 (Ct. Cl. 1969); see also Rev. Rul. 69-235, 1969-1 CB 190 (capital gain dividends of a regulated investment company follow dividend source rules); De Nobili Cigar Co. v. CIR, 143 F2d 436 (2d Cir. 1944) (dividend rules for source and taxability purposes, but capital gain redemption not taxable to foreign shareholder); Hay v. CIR, 145 F2d 1001 (4th Cir. 1944), cert. denied, 324 US 863 (1945) (liquidation gain determined under dividend source rules).

But see Rev. Rul. 72-87, 1972-1 CB 274 (§301(c)(3) capital gain dividend subject to withholding even though not taxable to foreign recipient).

[18] See Rev. Rul. 64-56, 1964-1 CB 133; Rev. Proc. 69-19, 1969-2 CB 301, amplified by Rev. Rul. 71-564, 1971-2 CB 179, and Rev. Proc. 74-36, 1974-2 CB 465.

[19] Karrer v. US, 152 F. Supp. 66 (Ct. Cl. 1957); see Lokken, The Sources of Income From International Uses and Dispositions of Intellectual Property, 36 Tax L. Rev. 233 (1981).

[20] See Korfund Co., 1 TC 1180 (1943) (source of payments for noncompetition covenant is the area where payee agreed not to compete); Rev. Rul. 74-108, 1974-1 CB 248 (same); Realty Loan Corp., 478 F2d 1049 (9th Cir. 1973) (gain on sale of right to earn future income ordinary, rather than capital, gain, but seller could report gain on installment method of §453 as a sale of property). See generally Eustice, Contract Rights, Capital Gain, and Assignment of Income—The Ferrer Case, 20 Tax L. Rev. 1 (1964).

See generally Ken Linesman, 82 TC 514 (1984); Stemkowski v. CIR, 690 F2d 40 (2d Cir. 1982); Rev. Rul. 87-38, 1987-20 IRB 7.

sonal property raise similar classification problems in that the transaction instead may constitute a sale rather than a license of the property, or, conversely, the consideration may be attributable to the performance of services rather than to the transfer of property.[21]

Until 1986, gains from the sale of personal property ordinarily had their source at the place of sale (i.e., the place where beneficial title to the property (as opposed to a security title) passed from the seller to the buyer and where the latter succeeded to the burdens and benefits of ownership). While the passage of title test usually determined source of income from the sale of goods, Regs. §1.861-7(c) warned that "when the transaction is arranged in a particular manner for the primary purpose of tax avoidance, the foregoing rules will not be applied," and that "in such cases, all factors of the transaction, such as negotiations, the execution of the agreement, the location of the property, and the place of payment will be considered, and the sale will be treated as having been consummated at the place where the *substance of the sale* occurred." Although courts agreed that the passage of title test might be inapplicable on certain facts, the cases uniformly applied it.[22] The regulation's caveat seemed limited to those unusual situations where the transaction was so lacking in economic reality that its form should have been disregarded for tax purposes; but the fact that the parties arranged the passage of title to reduce taxes was not fatal if the form adopted had commercial reality. The passage of title test was criticized because of its manipulative possibilities, but other approaches (e.g., origin of the goods, destination of the goods, place of execution of the contract, "all the facts and circumstances," "balancing of contacts" tests) similarly were found wanting, and for many years Congress showed no clear disposition to substitute any of these alternatives.[23]

---

[21] See §1253 (added by the Tax Reform Act of 1969), requiring license treatment for transfers of franchises, trademarks, and trade names where the transferor retains a continuing economic interest in the property (including a right to payments contingent on productivity, use, or disposition). Compare §1235(a), where a sale of patent rights is not affected by the form of the selling price (i.e., payments can be made periodically over the term of the transferee's use and can be measured by the economic productivity of the property without destroying sale treatment). See Regs. §1.871-11(c) (ignore §1253 in determining sale status for §§871(a)(1)(D) and 881(a)(4) rules).

See generally Lokken, supra note 19; see also Pierre Boulez, 83 TC 584 (1984) (royalties vs. compensation; held compensation).

[22] See, e.g., US v. Balanovski, 236 F2d 298 (2d Cir. 1956), cert. denied, 352 US 968 (1957); A.P. Green Export Co. v. US, 284 F2d 383 (Ct. Cl. 1960).

[23] See Krahmer, supra note 2, for extended analysis of the title-passage test. There were, however, two statutory inroads on the title-passage test: The foreign-base company sales income rules of §954(d) override the passage-of-title test (see infra Part D); moreover, in §864(c)(4)(B)(iii), Congress in effect adopted a destina-

The Tax Reform Act of 1986, however, substantially revised the source rules applicable to personal property dispositions in new §865 and generally adopted residence[24] of the seller as the touchstone for sourcing gains (and losses[25]) from the sale or exchange of such property, whether tangible or intangible. The passage of title test was retained for inventory property in §865(b) (although the Treasury was directed to study this rule and report back to Congress in 1987).[26] Other exceptions to the seller-residence source rule are:

(1) Depreciable (or amortizable) property recapture gain is sourced under §865(c)(1) to the place where depreciation-type deductions are claimed[27] to the extent of such recapture gain (any excess gain is sourced by §865(c)(2) under the *inventory* property rules);

(2) Contingent payments for the sale of intangible property are sourced by §865(d) under the royalty rules of §861(a)(4) (i.e., place of use), while fixed payments are sourced under the general sale source rules;[28]

---

tion test (although under a different label) for determining income effectively connected to a U.S. business.

See also Rev. Rul. 70-304, 1970-1 CB 163, where the Service applied an origin of the goods test for gain realized from insurance proceeds received on goods lost or destroyed in transit; Rev. Rul. 75-263, 1975-2 CB 287 (gain to U.S. corporation from exchange of stock of subsidiary pursuant to conversion of debt is sourced at place of exchange, foreign or U.S., as the case may be; no tax avoidance for place of exchange because taxpayer had no control over location of conversions).

[24] Residence is specially defined in §865(g)(1) for individuals to mean "tax home" (i.e., the test for deductibility of away-from-home travel expenses under §162), and U.S. corporations are residents per se (while foreign corporations are nonresidents per se). But §865(g)(2) provides that a U.S. resident cannot be treated as a resident of another country with respect to a sale of personal property unless a meaningful foreign income tax is paid on that sale (at an effective rate of at least 10 percent).

See Eustice, Kuntz, Lewis, & Deering, supra note 7, ¶ 4.04[2]; General Explanation of the Tax Reform Act of 1986, prepared by the staff of the Joint Comm. on Taxation, JCS-10-87, at 916–923 (May 4, 1987).

[25] The rules for sourcing losses are to be provided in regulations, §865(h)(1), which are generally expected to follow the gain-source rules (subject to anti-abuse rules).

[26] H.R. 3838, Act §1211(d). This study is directed to take into account the 1986 Act's lower tax rates and congressional trade concerns.

[27] But §865(c)(3)(B) sources recapture gain to the place where the property is *predominantly* (presumably more than 50 percent) used on an all or nothing basis, except for property described in §48(a)(2)(B).

[28] Payments for goodwill, however, are sourced to the country in which such goodwill was generated under §865(d)(3).

(3) Inventory gains attributable to an "office or other fixed place of business"[29] are sourced by §865(e) to the situs of that business under rules similar to the effectively connected provisions of §§864(c)(4) and 864(c)(5);[30] and

(4) Stock in a foreign affiliate (as defined in §1504(a)) is sourced outside the United States by §865(f) if the subsidiary has an active foreign business and the sale of its stock is made in the foreign country where it derived more than 50 percent of its gross income for three years.

The fixed place of business source rules of §865(e)(2), which provide for sourcing of a foreign taxpayer's income to a U.S. fixed business situs if the income is attributable to that U.S. business, essentially preempt the effectively connected foreign-source income rules of §864(c)(4).

The geographical source of items not specified in §§861 and 862 is to be determined under §863, which commences in §863(a) with a grant of authority to the Treasury to issue regulations on this subject. This authority has been exercised only in the case of natural resources; Regs. §1.863-1(b) provides that the situs of a farm, mine, oil or gas well, other deposits, or timber ordinarily determines the source of the income therefrom. Section 863(b) deals with items of income whose source is partly within and partly without the United States (i.e., income from transportation services rendered partly within and partly without the United States); income from the sale of inventory property "produced" (defined by §864(a) to include created, fabricated, manufactured, extracted, preserved, cured, or aged) without and sold within the United States or vice versa; and income from the purchase of inventory within a possession and its sale within the United States. Regs. §§1.863-3–1.863-5, provide allocation methods and formulas (reminiscent of the §482 allocation principles (see Chapter 15)) for these situations. The regulations relating to §863(b)(2) (production without and sale within the United States and vice versa) attempt to separate the manufacturing profits of an integrated business from its selling profits, an obviously difficult task.

The Tax Reform Act of 1986 revised the rules of §863 as follows:

---

[29] Two aspects of §865(e) apply here: First, §865(e)(2) provides that foreign taxpayers with a U.S. business situs must source gains that are effectively connected to that business in the United States; second, §865(e)(1) provides that U.S. taxpayers can source gains abroad if there was material foreign participation in the transaction by a foreign situs business (and the transaction was subject to significant foreign taxes).

[30] Section 865(e)(3). In effect, the §865(e) rules have subsumed the provisions of §§864(c)(4) and 864(c)(5) and converted those rules into a source-based regime. See infra para. 3.

(1) Special rules governing the source of transportation income are contained in §863(c), which assigns all income from transportation that both begins and ends in the United States to the United States and assigns half of transportation income to the United States if the transportation either begins *or* ends in the United States (a new 4 percent tax on gross U.S. source transportation income is provided in §887, and the reciprocal exemption rules of §883(a) are materially restricted by new §883(c));

(2) Section 863(d) provides special source rules for income from outer space and offshore ocean activities (which income would be assigned to the country of residence); and

(3) Section 863(e) provides special source rules for international communications income (which is sourced to U.S. persons to the extent of 50 percent and to foreign persons to the extent of 50 percent except to the extent attributable to a fixed U.S. business situs).

The source rules for deductions are less specific than those for gross income; Sections 861(b), 862(b), and 863(a), and 863(b) merely provide that taxable income from domestic or foreign sources is to be determined (1) by properly apportioning or allocating expenses, losses, and other deductions to the items of gross income to which they relate and (2) if an allocation to particular items or classes of gross income is not feasible, a ratable portion of the deductions must be allocated or apportioned between the domestic and foreign-source income of the taxpayer. In short, expenses that are directly attributable to a particular item or classes of income are allocable to that income; general or indirect expenses that cannot be definitely traced to particular items or classes of income are to be divided among all items of income on the basis of an appropriate allocation formula.[31]

Before 1977, Regs. §1.861-8(a) allocated indirect deductions under a relative gross income formula, but amendments were proposed in 1966 that provided that deductions that cannot be definitely allocated to a particular item or class of income (but that are related to the production of income, as opposed to such personal deductions as alimony, medical expenses, and the like) must be apportioned on the basis of all the facts and circumstances, considering such factors as relative amounts of gross income, gross sales or

---

[31] See generally Missouri Pac. R.R. v. US, 411 F2d 327 (8th Cir. 1969); International Standard Elec. Corp. v. CIR, 144 F2d 487 (2d Cir. 1944), cert. denied, 323 US 803 (1945); Grunebaum v. CIR, 420 F2d 332 (2d Cir.), cert. denied, 397 US 1075 (1970), for apportionment of direct and indirect expenses between foreign-source and domestic-source income. See also F.W. Woolworth Co., 54 TC 1233 (1970) (nonacq.) (state taxes, interest, home office, and travel expenses allocated exclusively to domestic operations); Rosch, Travel and Entertainment Expense Deductions for Nonresident Aliens: An Analysis and Critique, 21 Tax L. Rev. 103 (1965); Owens, The Foreign Tax Credit 249–254 (Harvard University, 1961).

receipts, expenses incurred, assets used, salaries paid, space utilized, and time spent, unless the taxpayer has adopted a reasonably consistent procedure under its own accounting system.[32] The 1966 proposals were revised on several occasions,[33] a process that culminated in 1977 with the promulgation of an elaborate set of regulations inspired by the earlier rules dealing with specific types of deductions (interest, research and development expenses, stewardship expenses) and also laying down general principles for other items. The 1977 rules, which constitute a bible for the cost accountant, are too lengthy and complex to be usefully summarized, but they are copiously illustrated with examples.[34]

The Tax Reform Act of 1986 requires corporate members of an affiliated group to allocate all income and expenses between U.S. and foreign income on a consolidated group basis in new §864(e), although corporations that are not eligible to join in a consolidated return can continue to allocate expenses on a separate company basis.[35] Allocation of interest expense can only be made on the basis of assets; the gross income allocation method is eliminated. In allocating expenses, tax-exempt income and tax-exempt assets are not to be taken into account.[36]

---

[32] Prop. Regs. §1.861-8(a)(4)(i) (1966); see also §482, supra ¶ 15.03 (to which these proposals were closely related).

[33] For discussions of these various proposals, see Cole, Highlights of the Proposed Regulations on Allocation and Apportionment of Deductions, 39 J. Tax'n 272 (1973); Committee on Deductions From Foreign Source Income, N.Y. State Bar Association, Tax Section, Proposals for Improvement of Rules for Allocation of Deductions Between Foreign and US Source Income, 29 Tax L. Rev. 597 (1974); Fuller & Granwell, The Allocation and Apportionment of Deductions, 31 Tax Lawyer 125 (1977); Plaia, Use of Holding Company by Corporation Can Cut Impact of Allocation Regulations, 48 J. Tax'n 122 (1978); Bischel, Optimizing Benefits From R&D Expenses Under Allocation and Apportionment Regs, 48 J. Tax'n 332 (1978); Levey, Allocating Foreign Source Income, 12 J. Corp. Tax'n 174 (1985).

[34] See Regs. §1.861-8(g) for examples. For analogous principles and approaches, see §482, supra ¶ 15.03.

[35] H.R. 3838, §1215(a), adding §864(e). However, §1216 of the 1986 Act provided temporarily (for one year) that half of U.S.-performed research and development expenses are allocable to the U.S.-source income, with the remaining portion being allocable on the basis of gross sales or gross income; thereafter the suspended R&D allocation in Regs. §1.861-8(e)(3) will take effect. See Joint Comm. Staff General Explanation of the Tax Reform Act of 1986, supra note 24, at 956–961.

For background of the R&D allocation question, see Joint Comm. on Taxation, Description of Proposals Relating to Research and Development Act of 1987 (S.58) and Allocation of R&D Expenses to U.S. and Foreign Income (S.716) JCS-6-87 (Apr. 2, 1987).

[36] See H.R. Conf. Rep. No. 841, 99th Cong., 2d Sess. 604–606 (1986); Joint Comm. Staff General Explanation of the Tax Reform Act of 1986, supra note 24, at 941–956.

2. Trade or business: Existence and location. Of central importance to the U.S. taxation of foreign persons is whether they are engaged in a trade or business, and, if so, whether it is located within the United States.[37] Before 1966, the former issue ordinarily was controlled by §162(a)'s concept of trade or business,[38] so that such factors as the presence or absence of a profit motive, the continuity, regularity, and substantiality of the taxpayer's activities, and the nature of the activities (investment vs. business) were considered in determining the existence of a trade or business. Although the ordinary manufacturing, mining, mercantile, or service enterprise caused little difficulty, it was often difficult to determine whether the ownership of rental real estate and dealings in stocks, securities, and commodities were merely investment activities or instead constituted the conduct of a trade or business.[39] These difficulties were increased by the facts that business activities can be conducted by agents on the taxpayer's behalf and that a corporation is not engaged in business merely because of its corporate status.[40]

---

[37] See generally Garelik, What Constitutes Doing Business Within the United States by a Nonresident Alien Individual or a Foreign Corporation, 18 Tax L. Rev. 423 (1963). See also Isenberg, The "Trade or Business" of Foreign Taxpayers in the United States, 61 Taxes 972 (1983).

[38] Before its amendment in 1966, §871(c) provided that the term "trade or business" included a nonresident alien's performance of personal services within the United States at any time during the year (with a minor exception for some commercial travelers), but not transactions in stocks, securities, or commodities through a resident broker or similar agent. See CIR v. Nubar, 185 F2d 584 (4th Cir. 1950), cert. denied, 341 US 925 (1951); Fernand Adda, 10 TC 273 (acq.), aff'd per curiam, 171 F2d 457 (4th Cir. 1948).

See generally Georges Simenon, 44 TC 820 (1965) (on the business "at any time" point); Regs. §1.864-3(b), Example (3).

[39] For real estate, see Pinchot v. CIR, 113 F2d 718 (2d Cir. 1940); Elizabeth Herbert, 30 TC 26 (1958) (acq.); Jan C. Lewenhaupt, 20 TC 151 (1953), aff'd per curiam, 221 F2d 227 (9th Cir. 1955); Inez de Amodio, 34 TC 894 (1960), aff'd, 299 F2d 623 (3d Cir. 1962) (passive ownership of real property not a business, but active management of the property personally or through agents was a business); see also §§856(c) and 856(d) for similar problems in defining business vs. investment in the real estate area; Rev. Rul. 75-23, 1975-1 CB 290 (foreign corporation investing as limited partner in U.S. real estate projects through U.S. limited partnership held engaged in business in United States and taxable under §882).

In the securities trading area, see Fernand Adda, supra note 38 (extensive trading through discretionary agent held a business); CIR v. Nubar, supra note 38 (extensive trading by alien physically present in the United States held a business); Edward de Vegvar, 28 TC 1055 (1957) (acq.) (investment, not business).

[40] For cases where activities of an agent on behalf of the alien caused a finding of U.S. business, see the *Adda, Lewenhaupt,* and *Amodio* cases, supra notes 38 and 39. See also Rev. Rul. 55-282, 1955-1 CB 634.

For decisions that a corporation can be a mere investor, see Continental Trading, Inc. v. CIR, 265 F2d 40 (9th Cir.), cert. denied, 361 US 827 (1959) (mere holding

These rules were modified by the Foreign Investors' Tax Act of 1966, which provided that trading in stocks, securities, or commodities, regardless of the frequency, size, or extent of the transactions, will not ordinarily constitute the conduct of a trade or business for alien individuals or foreign corporations.[41] Thus, §§864(b)(2)(A)(i) and 864(b)(2)(B)(i) provide that such trading through a resident broker, commission agent, custodian, or other independent agent does not constitute a U.S. business if the taxpayer does not have an office or other fixed place of business through which such transactions are effected, under §864(b)(2)(C). Section 864(b)(2)(A)(ii) also protects trading in securities for the taxpayer's own account from business status, even if conducted by the taxpayer personally or through discretionary agents or employees (thus overruling the *Nubar* and *Adda* cases[42]); this exception does not apply to securities dealers, however, or to corporations whose principal business is trading for their own account if their principal office is located in the United States.[43]

A similar exception in §864(b)(2)(B)(ii) applies to commodities[44] (except that a corporate trader is not disqualified from the benefits of this provision even if its principal office is located in this country). Thus, dealers (whether corporate or individual) can avoid business status only if they effect their transactions through brokers and maintain no U.S. trading office; a corporate trader (other than a personal holding company or the like) can avoid U.S. business status only if its principal office is located abroad; individual and personal holding company traders, however, can speculate with abandon, even through a U.S. office.

---

company); Abegg v. CIR, 429 F2d 1209 (2d Cir. 1970) cert. denied, 400 US 1008 (1971) (investment rather than business).

[41] See Roberts, US Taxation of Foreign Taxpayers' Stock or Security Transactions: An Analysis, 33 J. Tax'n 66 (1970); Regs. §§1.864-2(c) and 1.864-2(d).

[42] CIR v. Nubar, supra note 38; Fernand Adda, supra note 38.

[43] However, a corporation that is, or but for §542(c)(7) or §543(b)(1)(C) would be a personal holding company (supra Ch. 8) can trade for its own account, even though its principal office is located in this country; §864(b)(2)(A)(ii). The theory of this provision is apparently that such companies are, in effect, individual enterprises, and should be so treated. Regs. §1.864-2(c)(2)(iii) states that a corporation can have only one principal office and lists the functions relevant to this determination. (Foreign mutual funds are thus provided with a roadmap for avoiding U.S. business status). See Roberts, Taxation of Stock or Securities Transactions of Foreign Corporations and Partnerships, 33 J. Tax'n 146 (1970).

[44] Commodities are defined by §864(b)(2)(B)(iii) to mean the kind of property customarily dealt with on an organized commodity exchange, and the transaction must be one customarily transacted at such place; Regs. §1.864-2(d)(3) adds that the term does not include "goods or merchandise in the ordinary channels of commerce."

In the case of real estate holdings, foreign corporate and individual investors are permitted to elect to treat their real property income as business income by §§871(d) and 882(d). The election is revocable only with consent of the Service and applies to all real estate holdings, which, but for the election, would not be considered a trade or business. The utility of such election is limited, however, by §897(a)(1) (the Foreign Investment in Real Property Tax Act of 1980), which treats gain or loss from the sale of a U.S. real property interest as effectively connected to a U.S. trade or business. A U.S. real property interest, for this purpose, is defined by §897(c) to include not only direct ownership of U.S. real estate, but also an interest in a U.S. real property holding company (defined by §897(c)(2) as a domestic corporation more than 50 percent of whose assets, specially defined, consist of U.S. real property interests).[45] Presumably, §897 merely establishes the manner in which such gain or loss is to be taxed; that is, the foreign owner should not be deemed to be in a U.S. business for other purposes.[46]

Whether the taxpayer is considered to be engaged in a trade or business within the United States depends upon the nature and extent of its economic contacts with this country.[47] It is clear that the entire business operation need not be centered in the United States. The difficult question is how much of the business functions must be located here to create a U.S. business situs. Relevant factors in determining the extent of economic penetration in the United States for this purpose are location of (1) production activities; (2) management (i.e., direction and control of the enterprise); (3)

---

[45] See Feder & Parker, The Foreign Investment in Real Property Tax Act of 1980, 34 Tax Lawyer 545 (1981); Feingold & Alpert, Observations on the Foreign Investment in Real Property Tax Act of 1980, 1 Va. Tax Rev. 105 (1981); and Kessler, Adjusting to FIRPTA, 61 Taxes 960 (1983); see also §831 of the Economic Recovery Tax Act of 1981, for various technical amendments to the Foreign Investment in Real Property Tax Act provisions. See TD 7999, 1985-1 CB 189 (1984), for final regulations under §897.

[46] For legislation establishing a withholding system for taxable Foreign Investment in Real Property Tax Act of 1980 transactions, see the Deficit Reduction Act of 1984, adding §1445, providing for a 10 percent withholding tax on the purchase of a U.S. real property interest from a foreign person, subject to numerous exceptions and conditions set out in §§1445(b)–1445(e). Temporary regulations under §1445 were issued on Dec. 26, 1984, in TD 8000, 1985-1 CB 296. See Eustice, supra note 6, ¶ 4.03[4]; Knight & Noyes, The New FIRPTA Withholding and Investment Disclosure Rules, 13 Tax Mgmt. Int'l 312 (1984); Hudson, Karp, Langer, & Warner, An Analysis of the New FIRPTA Withholding Requirements, 24 Tax Notes 573 (1984).

[47] See generally US v. Balanovski, supra note 22 (U.S. business); CIR v. Spermacet Whaling & Shipping Co., 281 F2d 646 (6th Cir. 1960) (no U.S. business); CIR v. Consolidated Premium Iron Ores, Ltd., 265 F2d 320 (6th Cir. 1959) (no U.S. business); Rev. Rul. 55-182, 1955-1 CB 77; Rev. Rul. 62-31, 1962-1 CB 367; Rev. Rul. 63-113, 1963-1 CB 410; Rev. Rul. 65-263, 1965-2 CB 561; Rev. Rul. 75-23, 1975-1 CB 290.

distribution activities (e.g., storage of goods, solicitation of orders, advertising and promotion, clerical functions, showroom and samples, credit functions); and (4) such other business functions as purchasing, financial activities, research, servicing of products, transportation, and the like. Moreover, the type of business (extractive, manufacturing, trading, service) is a factor, since some ventures, such as mining or manufacturing, are inherently local in character. Finally, the taxpayer's formal structure (parent-subsidiary corporations, brother-sister corporations, or separate branches or divisions of a single corporation) has an important bearing on this question.

A fully integrated enterprise that manufactures and sells its total output in the United States, and that is managed and controlled here, is clearly a U.S. trade or business. At the other end of the spectrum is the wholly foreign enterprise that merely ships products to customers in this country but has no other economic contacts with the United States. Between these two extremes, however, the presence of a U.S. business situs has to be determined on a case by case basis, and identification of the point at which mere business *with* the United States crosses the line and becomes business *within* the United States is a function of the above-noted factors. As a general rule, the more deeply a foreign corporation becomes enmeshed in the economic and commercial structure of this country, the more likely it will be found to have established a business nexus here.

Section 864 does not contain a general definition of business location for purposes of the taxation of foreign persons, but specific business situs rules (or their functional equivalents) are prescribed for some fields. Thus, §864(b)(1) states that performance of personal services at any time within the United States constitutes a business within this country; and §864(b)(2)(A)(ii) and Regs. §1.864-2(c)(2)(iii) (relating to determination of the location of the taxpayer's "principal office") contain numerous illustrations. Section 864(c)(5)(A) ("office or other fixed place of business" in the United States) offers guidance on the business situs question, stating that the business of an independent agent will not be attributed to its foreign principal, while a local "dependent" agent (i.e., one subject to the taxpayer's direction and control), acting on behalf of his foreign principal, will constitute a U.S. business of the foreign principal if the agent has either (1) discretionary authority to bind his foreign principal (and regularly exercises it) or (2) a local stock of merchandise from which he regularly fills orders on behalf of the foreign principal. A nondiscretionary agent, on the other hand, will not cause his foreign principal to have a U.S. office if no stock of goods is maintained in this country. (Regs. §1.864-7(d) elaborate on these rules.) The regulations also state that a person who buys and resells goods for his *own* account (a distributor) is not an agent for this purpose.

These same regulations deal with other aspects of the U.S. office or fixed place of business concept, and provide that (1) "fixed facilities" (such as a factory, store, or other sales outlet, workshop, or mine) in this country will constitute a "fixed place of business" under §864(c)(5)(A); (2) general supervisory management activity in this country by a corporation that controls the foreign taxpayer will not create a U.S. office (if confined to policy matters and if the foreign affiliate has its own manager who conducts its daily affairs); (3) employee activity on behalf of a foreign employer, carried on through an office located in this country, will constitute a domestic office of the employer;[48] and (d) offices of related persons will not, without more, be attributed to the foreign affiliate. These provisions are similar to the principles for determining whether a permanent establishment exists in this country under our tax treaties.[49] If the foreign taxpayer is found to have an office or other fixed place of business in the United States under §864(c)(5)(A) or a U.S. permanent establishment under a tax treaty, this would a fortiori constitute a U.S. business situs, since the requirements of the latter are less rigorous. On the other hand, it has been held that a U.S. business does not necessarily constitute a U.S. permanent establishment.[50]

3. Income effectively connected with a U.S. business. One of the key concepts adopted by the Foreign Investors' Tax Act of 1966 was the "effectively connected" principle,[51] whereby income effectively connected with a U.S. business would be taxable at the normal rates (on a net basis after allowance of appropriate deductions), while U.S.-source investment income would be taxed on a gross basis at the special 30 percent rate applicable to foreign nonresident persons (or lower treaty rate, where applicable), without allowance for any deductions.

Prior to this amendment, nonresident foreign taxpayers with a U.S. trade or business were taxable on all income from U.S. sources, whether or not such income was attributable to the business, under the force of attraction principle. Under the 1966 amendments, by contrast, a foreign taxpayer distinguishes between its business income and its investment income under §864(c), segregating them and computing the tax on each under the various

---

[48] Regs. §1.864-7(e) clarified the employee activity rule by tying in generally to the agent rules (but also emphasized that employee activity at a fixed facility can constitute a U.S. office, and a new example was added that seems based on the facts and holding of Rev. Rul. 62-31, 1962-1 CB 367).

[49] For which, see generally Williams, Permanent Establishments in the United States, 29 Tax Lawyer 277 (1976).

[50] See Inez de Amodio, supra note 39 (so holding).

[51] See generally Ross, supra note 1; Lokken, supra note 19; Sitrick, The Effectively Connected Concept in the Foreign Investors' Tax Act of 1966, 45 Taxes 2 (1967); Roberts, Force of Attraction: Impact of the FITA of 1966 on the Code, 28 J. Tax'n 232 (1968); Dale, Effectively Connected Income, 42 Tax L. Rev. (1987).

provisions applicable thereto. As a result of the abolition of the force of attraction principle[52] (with a minor exception noted subsequently), foreign taxpayers now occupy a dual tax status with respect to their activities in this country (i.e., that of an investor (taxable on such income under §871(a) or §881) and that of a trade or business enterprise (taxable on such income under §871(b) or §882)). Before the effectively connected rules of §864(c) become applicable, however, there must be a finding of a U.S.-centered trade or business under the principles discussed previously.[53]

The principal provision dealing with the definition of effectively connected business income, §864(c)(2), states that in determining whether U.S.-source income of the type described in §§871(a) and 881(a) (i.e., dividends, interest, rents, other "fixed or determinable annual or periodic income," and capital gains) is effectively connected with a U.S. business, two factors must be considered: the "asset use" test (i.e., whether the income is derived from assets used, or held for use, in the business); and the "business activities" test (i.e., whether the activities of the business were a material factor in the production of the income).[54] If the periodical income described in §864(c)(2) has a sufficiently proximate economic nexus with the U.S. business under these tests, it is treated as business income for purposes of §§871(b) and 882; otherwise it is taxed as investment income under §§871(a) and 881(a). A substantially direct economic relationship between the income and the business is required before such income will be treated as effectively connected to the business. The regulations and examples, however, embody a noticeable bias against effectively connected treatment for income derived from the ownership or sale of securities. This may be explained by the fact that portfolio investments typically would fall outside the scope of the taxpayer's normal business activities. In the case of stock investments, this tendency against business connection classification may be inspired by Treasury reluctance to permit use of the §243 deduction by foreign corporate shareholders.

Assistance in applying the effectively connected periodical income tests of §864(c)(2) may be found in other areas of the law. Thus, securities that are deemed integrally connected to ordinary business functions under the *Corn*

---

[52] Force of attraction was also eliminated from those treaties where it still applied by virtue of §894(b), if such elimination helps the taxpayer. See §110 of the 1966 Act (uncodified), which allows treaty-covered foreign taxpayers to choose either effectively connected or force of attraction treatment. See generally Roberts, Force of Attraction: How the FITA of 1966 Affects Treaties, 28 J. Tax'n 274 (1968); Ross, supra note 1; Dale, supra note 51.

[53] See Regs. §§1.864-6 and 1.864-7.

[54] See Regs. §1.864-4(c) for elaboration of these provisions and for illustrations, derived in large part from the House Ways and Means Committee Report on the 1966 Act, H.R. Rep. No. 1450, 89th Cong., 2d Sess. (1966); Rev. Rul. 86-154, 1986-52 IRB 14.

Products doctrine[55] similarly should be effectively connected under §864(c)(2); moreover, if a particular loan or investment could avoid non-business classification under the *Whipple* tests,[56] it would probably also be effectively connected to a business under §864(c)(2).[57] On a less direct level, if an investment in stocks or securities would cause unreasonable accumulation tax troubles under §531 (see Chapter 8), as an unrelated investment, it ought not to be treated as an effectively connected investment under §864(c)(2) (or vice versa). Finally, the definition of unrelated business income for purposes of §511 (in the tax-exempt organization area) may have some tangential relevance under §864(c)(2) as well.

By virtue of §864(c)(3), a limited force of attraction principle still exists with respect to U.S.-source ordinary income that is not described in §871(a) or §881(a).[58] This type of income is deemed effectively connected with a U.S. business, regardless of an actual relationship under the usual tests. This "basket clause" is important, however, only if the foreign taxpayer has a trade or business in the United States at some time during the year in which such income becomes taxable; if so, all nonperiodical ordinary income from U.S. sources for that year is attracted to that business and taxed as business income under §882.[59]

Finally, §864(c)(4) provides that foreign-source income is to be treated as effectively connected with the conduct of a U.S. business if it meets certain conditions, which look both to the type of income involved and to its

---

[55] Corn Prods. Ref. Co. v. CIR, 350 US 46 (1955), discussed supra ¶ 4.20.

[56] Whipple v. CIR, 373 US 293 (1963), discussed supra ¶ 4.22.

[57] See Regs. §1.864-4(c)(6)(i) for such an illustration.

[58] For example, gain from the sale of property described in §§1221(1)–1222(4) (dealer property, depreciable business property, artistic property, and business receivables); gain under §1221(2) from the sale of long-term or short-term §1231 property; ordinary gain resulting from the "netting" process of §1231; gain resulting from the depreciation recapture rules of §§1245, 1250, 1251, and similar provisions; and ordinary gain from a disposition that does not qualify as a sale or exchange under §1222 (e.g., collection of a claim not covered by §1271, cancellation of a contract not covered by §1241, involuntary conversions not covered by §1231, or nonperiodic gain under §1253). But see §897(a) (U.S. real estate per se trade or business income or loss under Foreign Investment in Real Property Tax Act). See Feder & Parker, supra note 45.

Applicability of the §864(c)(3) basket clause to quasi-capital gains, while not clear in the regulations, seems to have been specifically covered by a statement in the House Committee Report to FITA, H.R. Rep. No. 1450, 89th Cong., 2d Sess. 61 (1966), which stated that gains from the sale of capital assets are not included in this provision. Thus, §341 gain would be excluded, even though such gain is ordinary, because the stock is still a capital asset, while §1231 gain on business property would be included, even though treated as capital gain, because such property is not a capital asset by virtue of §1221(2).

[59] See generally Regs. §§1.864-3 and 1.864-4(b).

relationship to the taxpayer's U.S. activity. The purpose of §864(c)(4), in conjunction with §882, is to prevent foreign corporations from using the United States as a tax haven for income that has its economic genesis here but can be manipulated into a foreign-source mold. In this respect, the effectively connected foreign-source income rules play a different role from their major function of separating business income from investment income. Section 482 principles (see Chapter 15) are clearly recognizable in these provisions, in that §864(c)(4) attempts to assign taxability of the income in question to the economic enterprise that in fact "earned" it, regardless of technical source rules.[60]

The conditions for application of §864(c)(4) are:

(1) A U.S. office or other fixed place of business, defined by §864(c)(5)(A) and the regulations in a manner quite similar to the permanent establishment definitions of tax treaties, must be present (Regs. §1.864-7);

(2) The income in question must be "attributable" to such office, as defined in §§864(c)(5)(B) and 864(c)(5)(C) (i.e., the office must be a material factor in the production of the income and must regularly carry on activities of the type giving rise to the income, and the income must be properly allocable[61] to the office) (Regs. §1.864-6); and

(3) The income must consist of rents or royalties for the use of intangible personal property or gains from the sale of such property derived by a taxpayer engaged in the active conduct of a licensing or rental business;[62] dividends, interest, and capital gains of a financial or securities trading business (unless the taxpayer can avoid trade or business status under the liberalized definition provisions of §864(b)(2) with respect to its securities trading activities); or gains from the sale of tangible or intangible personal property described in §1211(1) (i.e., dealer property) through such office

---

[60] See Regs. §1.864-5.

[61] The purpose of this rule seems to be to incorporate the general source rule principles of §863 (and possibly the notions of §482 as well) into the determination of the amount of such income attributable to the U.S. office; in this respect, §864(c)(5)(C) specifically limits income from the sale of tangible personal property to the amount that would have constituted U.S.-source income under §863(b)(2) if the sale had been within, rather than outside, the United States.

[62] But final Regs. §1.864-6 added a new Example (2) in §1.864-6(b)(2)(i), dealing with a motion picture film and television program-distribution business (query the effect of Walt Disney Prod. v. US, 480 F2d 66 (9th Cir. 1973), cert. denied, 415 US 934 (1974), holding that films are *tangible* personal property for purposes of the investment credit).

for ultimate consumption in the United States (i.e., "import" or U.S. destination sales).[63]

It should be noted that §864(c)(4)(B) is limited generally to items of controllable source income and thus does not cover all the possible types of foreign-source income. For example, income from sales or leases of real property is not included, nor is rental income from leasing tangible personal property, nor is compensation for services.[64] Moreover, §864(c)(4)(D) excludes two additional categories of income from the coverage of §864(c)(4)(B): (1) dividends, interest, or royalties paid by a more than 50 percent owned foreign subsidiary; and (2) Subpart F income (whether or not taxed to the domestic shareholders under the rules of §951 (discussed later in this chapter). Thus, a domestic parent corporation with controlled foreign subsidiaries must steer a perilous course between the new effectively connected foreign-source income rules of §864(c)(4)(B) (application of which will result in taxability of the foreign subsidiary under §882 on such income) and the controlled foreign corporation rules of §951 (application of which will result in taxability of the parent on the subsidiary's Subpart F income).

The Tax Reform Act of 1986, however, has largely subsumed the effectively connected income foreign-source rules of §864(c)(4) by the new source rule provisions of §865(e)(2), since income that formerly was subject to §864(c)(4) treatment now will be characterized as U.S.-source income under §865(e)(2).[65] The Tax Reform Act of 1986 provided for a lookback rule in new §864(c)(6) to deal with the case of deferred income items; this provision requires that such income be treated as effectively connected in the year it becomes taxable if it was effectively connected in the year the income was generated, thus overruling regulations to the contrary.[66] The 1986 Act also adopted §864(c)(7), which treats income as being effectively connected to a

---

[63] Export sales through the U.S. office are excepted from these provisions, however, if a non-U.S. office (not necessarily one in the country of destination) participated materially in the sale. Regs. §1.864-6(b)(3)(i) defines "material participation" as including solicitation of orders, negotiating contracts, or other significant incidental services necessary for the sale, but not including mere final approval of the sale, warehousing or storage functions, serving as the title-passage situs, or clerical functions.

[64] See also Rev. Rul. 73-227, 1973-1 CB 338 (interest income of a foreign finance subsidiary not §864(c)(4)(B) income; hence, only taxed if U.S.-source, but foreign finance subsidiary had active business in United States, so U.S.-source income taxed per §864(c)(2), while foreign-source income exempt); see also Regs. §1.864-4(c)(5)(i), holding that a foreign finance subsidiary is not engaged in a banking or financial business; Rev. Rul. 75-253, 1975-1 CB 203.

[65] Supra text at notes 24–30.

[66] Regs. §§1.864-3(b), Example (1), and 1.871-8(c)(2), Example (2).

U.S. business where assets used in that business are sold within 10 years after ceasing to be used in the U.S. business.[67]

4. Tax treaties. The role of bilateral tax treaties in the taxation of foreign persons on their U.S.-source income is frequently of even greater importance than the basic statutory regime applicable to those transactions. Thus, treaties can operate to (1) reduce (or even eliminate) the rate of U.S. tax on certain types of U.S. income derived by foreign taxpayers situated in the treaty-partner country, (2) override various statutory source rules, (3) exempt certain types of income or activities from taxation, by one or both treaty-partner countries, or (4) extend credit for taxes levied by one country to situations where the domestic law would not so provide.

Although the principal thrust of our bilateral tax treaties is to mitigate the potential for double taxation arising from overlapping tax jurisdictions (e.g., income source arising in one country while the taxpayer is resident in the other country), other general purposes for tax treaties include the prevention of tax avoidance and evasion, resolution of technical disputes between the treaty partners over administration of various treaty provisions, and avoidance of excessive taxation by one jurisdiction (where foreign rates exceed the U.S. rate). Other policies, grounded in economic and foreign policy considerations, may also animate a particular treaty provision, although by and large these latter purposes occupy a relatively minor role in the U.S. treaty system.[68]

Tax treaties generally cover a more limited economic universe than that encompassed by a particular country's domestic tax laws, being concerned as they are with the typical types of economic intercourse between the treaty partners. Thus, coverage is limited to residents of the contracting party states and generally only applies to nationwide taxes levied by a party country. Moreover, the tax base included in a particular treaty is selective, rather than universal, consisting of the sum of the particular treaty articles granting rights to tax (or exempting from tax) various categories of income arising from within one of the party states (unmentioned items continue to be governed by domestic tax rules). When applicable, however, a treaty generally will override a conflicting statutory provision (at least if the treaty is of more recent vintage (e.g., §§894(a) and 7851(d)), although on occasion the United States has specifically provided that a newly enacted provision will override

---

[67] H.R. 3838, §1242, adding new §§864(c)(6) and 864(c)(7) (effective in 1987); see Eustice, Kuntz, Lewis, & Deering, supra note 7, ¶ 4.05[2]. For a similar 10-year tainting provision, see §1374, supra ¶ 6.07.

[68] See generally Rosenbloom, Current Developments in Regard to Tax Treaties, 40 NYU Inst. on Fed. Tax'n ch. 31 (1982); Bissell, The Treasury's Model Income Tax Treaty: An Analysis and Appraisal, 3 Int'l Tax J. 9 (1976).

a conflicting treaty rule.[69] Finally, the general intent of a treaty is to confer tax benefits (at least as to substantive tax law provisions), so that a resident of a treaty state is always free to apply domestic U.S. tax law rules if a better tax result arises under the latter.

The treaty process involves several unique features that tend to set it apart from the method of enactment of domestic tax legislation. A tax treaty is essentially a country to country bilateral contract (negotiated by the executive branches of each country) that attempts to harmonize, albeit imperfectly, two different overlapping tax regimes. As such, political compromise is inevitable in this area, and the resulting document is usually a far less detailed codification of general principles than is the case with domestic tax law legislation. Moreover, the usual legislative participants in the domestic tax law process are absent in the treaty negotiation system (the House has no direct input at all on treaties, except via the legislative override route, and the Senate Finance Committee is likewise excluded from the treaty process; the Senate at large votes the treaty up or down, or occasionally reserves as to a particular provision). Thus, the State Department (in consultation with Treasury) initially negotiates the treaty, and the Senate Foreign Relations Committee holds hearings on the resulting product of those negotiations.

Our tax treaties fall generally into three broad categories: (1) old style treaties with various developed countries (e.g., Switzerland, Italy, the Netherlands, and Sweden) that were negotiated years ago, before the numerous changes in the U.S. tax law that have been effected since the 1954 Code; (2) new style treaties, based largely on the Organization for Economic Cooperation and Development model tax treaty, again primarily with developed countries (e.g., Germany, France, the United Kingdom, and Japan); and (3) treaties with various developing countries (based loosely on a United Nations model draft treaty) that reflect the fact that the parties thereto are not of equal rank in their economic prowess (these treaties are still relatively rare, and those that exist are generally not as extensive in scope as those with the developed countries).

Several common definitional concepts permeate our various tax treaties (both old and new style) with developed countries. Thus, the taxpayer is required to be a resident in one of the party states before the treaty can apply to such person, and most of the newer treaties attempt to define that term.[70] Moreover, investment income is treated differently from business

---

[69] E.g., the Subpart F rules of 1962 (infra ¶ 17.31) so provided, as does §269B(d) enacted by the Tax Reform Act of 1984 (see Eustice, supra note 6, ¶ 4.05[5]). Many of the provisions in the recent 1986 tax reform legislation provide for treaty overrides in whole or in part; see Forry & Karlin, 1986 Act: Overrides, Conflicts, and Interactions With U.S. Income Tax Treaties, 35 Tax Notes 793 (1987).

[70] See also §7701(b) (definition of "U.S. resident"), enacted by the Tax Reform Act of 1984; Eustice, supra note 6; ¶ 4.04.

income under the treaties; the former (e.g., dividends, interest, rents, royalties, and the like)[71] is usually either tax-exempt or subject to a reduced rate of tax by the source country, while business profits are taxable only if the taxpayer has a permanent establishment in the source country.[72] Income from personal services is generally taxed more leniently than under U.S. tax law rules—that is, longer periods of presence are allowed, and higher dollar limits are permitted—and certain special categories of service income may be completely exempted from tax (e.g., government employees, teachers, students, athletes, and entertainers). Finally, many of the treaties deal specifically with income from shipping and air transport, natural resources, pensions, and government service, either assigning such income to a specific source or exempting it from tax in whole or part.

The U.S. tax liability of U.S. taxpayers is not directly affected by the tax treaty system (apart from certain collateral effects, through the U.S. foreign tax credit, where the treaty operates to reduce, or eliminate, a particular foreign tax liability). Thus, the principal focus of tax treaties as it relates to U.S. tax liability is with respect to foreign taxpayers investing (or doing business) in the United States. But it should be noted that the U.S. tax law on occasion may operate unilaterally, apart from the treaties, to eliminate the potential for double taxation—for example, the recent elimination of tax on U.S.-source portfolio interest income derived by certain foreign persons in the Tax Reform Act of 1984 obviates the need for treaty relief for such income;[73] moreover, the foreign tax credit provisions (discussed later in this chapter) constitute the principal mechanism by which U.S. taxpayers are shielded from overlapping tax burdens on their foreign-source income. Consequently, tax treaties occupy a minor role in those situations where U.S. domestic tax law operates of its own force to deal with potential double taxation.

Recently, a major thrust of U.S. treaty policy (and current legislative policy as well) has been centered on three goals:

(1) To sharply limit the so-called "treaty shopping," or third party use, problem where a foreign taxpayer artificially claims residence in a treaty country in order to obtain the benefits of a treaty exemption or rate reduction provision;

---

[71] See Dale, Withholding Tax on Payments to Foreign Persons, 36 Tax L. Rev. 49 (1980).

[72] See discussion supra paras. 2 and 3 for similar concepts under U.S. tax law rules defining a U.S. trade or business and income effectively connected thereto; Williams, Permanent Establishments in the United States, 29 Tax Lawyer 277 (1976).

[73] See Eustice, supra note 6, ¶ 4.30[2]; but this same legislation extended U.S. withholding rules (in §1445) to U.S. real property gains; id., ¶ 4.03[4].

(2) To expand the flow of information exchange between the two treaty partners; and

(3) To expand efforts at mutual assistance for compliance in order to prevent tax-avoidance (mainly by U.S. taxpayers operating offshore through various tax-haven jurisdictions).

All new treaties contain a specific antiabuse provision attempting to curb third country use of the treaty by taxpayers who are not economically present in the treaty country, and Treasury has been actively attempting to insert such provisions in older treaties through renegotiation efforts as well.[74] On the compliance front, expansive information exchange clauses are being actively pushed (with the focus on obtaining admissible evidence, and not merely general information, at the core of these efforts).[75] Finally, the U.S. withholding tax rules were recently tightened by regulation as a result of legislation enacted in 1982,[76] and administrative efforts to materially tighten compliance in the foreign tax arena have been a high priority goal in recent years.[77]

Many of these efforts to spur compliance in the foreign tax area have stemmed from congressional perceptions that significant tax avoidance by U.S. taxpayers has been present and that major efforts are necessary to insure that purportedly offshore activities will no longer be tolerated as a means to avoid or evade U.S. taxation; the U.S. tax treaty system has become a significant component in this area.

5. Foreign currency. The tax rules relating to foreign currency have general application to the matters considered in this chapter. Thus, questions of timing, source, and character of foreign currency gain or loss trans-

---

[74] A model clause is contained in Article 16 of the Treasury's Model Tax Treaty draft; for recent ruling attacks on this practice, see Rev. Rul. 84-153, 1984-2 CB 383; see also Rev. Rul. 84-152, 1984-2 CB 381.

[75] See generally Symposium, Compelling Discovery in Transnational Litigation, 16 J. of Int'l Law & Pol. No. 5 (Summer 1984); see also Aland, Expanding IRS Access to Foreign-Based Documentation and Information in U.S. Tax Audits and Litigation, 64 Taxes 890 (1986).

[76] See Prop. Regs. §1.1441-6 (1984) (replacing the self-certification system of former law with new official certification requirements that must be satisfied before a purported foreign person will be entitled to claim treaty tax benefits); these regulations were mandated by §342 of the Tax Equity and Fiscal Responsibility Act of 1982.

[77] See also Rev. Rul. 84-152, 1984-2 CB 381, §6038A (added by the Tax Equity and Fiscal Responsibility Act of 1982), requiring reporting for foreign-owned U.S. corporations; §982 (added by the Tax Equity and Fiscal Responsibility Act of 1982), forbidding use of records in tax litigation where the taxpayer failed to previously produce those *records* for Service examination; Symposium, supra note 75, and supra notes 70 and 71.

actions, the extent to which income (or loss) is recognized due to fluctuations in foreign currency (and the character of that income or loss), the effect of currency translation timing on the foreign tax credit rules (both the direct and indirect foreign tax credits), and the general rules applicable to the proper measure of net income or loss derived by a foreign business venture conducted in non-U.S. currency, generate considerable uncertainty and complexity.[78] In 1980, the Treasury released a discussion draft[79] on foreign currency, in which it proposed a comprehensive system of rules dealing with the treatment of foreign currency in a business context. The Treasury's 1985 reform proposals[80] picked up on this theme, and the Tax Reform Act of 1986 generally accepted them.[81]

In brief, these provisions generally require that:

(1) The taxpayer use its functional currency for all U.S. tax computation purposes under §985 (functional currency is that currency which is used by a separate business unit in keeping its books and in which a significant part of its business activities are conducted unless use of the dollar is elected or the dollar is used primarily in the conduct of its activities).

(2) In computing the tax of any shareholder on distributions from a foreign corporation, earnings and profits of the foreign corporation must be computed in its functional currency, and in the case of actual or deemed distributions to any domestic 10 percent corporate shareholders, such earnings must be translated into dollars during the years earned under §986 (any gain or loss on that translation is ordinary);

(3) Foreign taxes must be translated into dollars when paid under §986(b) (additional deficiencies are to be translated into dollars when the adjustment is made, but tax refunds are to be translated at the rate when initial payment was made);

---

[78] See generally for prior law: Miller, Foreign Currency Translations: A Review of Some Recent Developments, 33 Tax Lawyer 820 (1980); Samuels, Federal Income Tax Consequences of Back-to-Back Loans and Currency Exchanges, 33 Tax Lawyer 847 (1980); and H.R. Rep. No. 426, 99th Cong., 1st Sess. 449–471 (1985).

[79] Printed in the Federal Register on Dec. 11, 1980 (also reproduced in 1981 Fed. Tax Rep. (CCH) Vol. 81 (10), ¶ 6267). This proposal is analyzed by Newman, Tax Consequences of Foreign Currency Transactions: A Look at Current Law and Analysis of the Treasury Department Discussion Draft, 36 Tax Lawyer 223 (1983), and by the ABA, Tax Section, Report on the U.S. Treasury Department Discussion Draft on Taxing Foreign Exchange Gains and Losses, 36 Tax L. Rev. 425 (1981).

[80] See Horst, Foreign Exchange Gains and Losses: What Are the Issues? 28 Tax Notes 1393 (1985).

[81] H.R. 3838, §1261, adding §§985–989; see O'Neill & Lee, Federal Income Tax Treatment of Foreign Currency Transactions After the Tax Reform Act of 1986, 33 Tax Notes 185 (1986).

(4) Taxable income of a foreign branch that is conducted in a functional currency other than dollars must be translated using the profit and loss translation method only under §987 (the net worth method is no longer permitted); and

(5) Exchange gain or loss arising from various financial assets or liabilities that are denominated in one or more nonfunctional currencies (e.g., debt instruments, trade receivables or payables, and various financial futures instruments) are treated generally under §988 as an increase or decrease in ordinary income or loss—that is, they are characterized as interest income or expense to the extent provided in regulations under §988(a)(2), but are sourced under §988(a)(3) either at the residence of the taxpayer or the principal place of business of the qualified business unit of the taxpayer to which the particular item relates).[82]

These provisions should provide a framework to establish a coherent set of rules for the tax treatment of foreign currency questions; although not all questions are resolved, and although the resolution of those questions that were dealt with may itself create problems, it is clear that this area of the law has been improved by these provisions.[83]

¶ 17.03   FOREIGN CORPORATIONS NOT ENGAGED IN UNITED STATES BUSINESS: SECTION 881

Section 881 imposes a flat 30 percent tax (without allowance for any deductions or credits) on designated categories of income from U.S. sources (defined generally as fixed or determinable annual or periodic investment-type income, such as dividends, interest, rents, and royalties) that are not effectively connected with the conduct of a U.S. trade or business.[84] This may be reduced (or eliminated) by treaty provisions, however, and §894(b) incorporates the effectively connected principle into those treaties that do not specifically so provide, thus preserving the favorable treaty rate for the

---

[82] For the treatment of cross-border interest rate "swap" transactions, see Rev. Rul. 87-5, 1987-3 IRB 6; and IRS Advance Notice 87-4, 1987-3 IRB 7.

[83] See generally Joint Comm. Staff General Explanation of the Tax Reform Act of 1986, supra note 24, at 1068–1114.

[84] Newman & Co. v. US, 423 F2d 49 (2d Cir. 1970), held that a dividend in kind to a foreign corporate shareholder is to be valued under the lower of basis or value rule of §301(b)(1)(B), but was overruled by the Revenue Act of 1971, which added §§301(b)(1)(D) and 301(d)(3) to the Code, providing that the measure of a dividend in kind (and its tax basis) to the distributee is fair market value if such dividend is not effectively connected to a U.S. business of the distributee.

investment income of a foreign taxpayer even though it has a permanent establishment in the United States.[85]

However, the Tax Reform Act of 1984[86] repealed the tax (and withholding) on portfolio interest income (including OID) derived by foreign corporations if such income is not effectively connected to a U.S. trade or business. The tax exemption of §881(c)(1) is not available to foreign banks (except with respect to U.S. government debts), foreign corporations that are 10 percent shareholders of the U.S. debtor, or to interest received by a controlled foreign corporation from a related person under §881(c)(3). Other portfolio interest received by a CFC is exempt from tax (and withholding), but flows through currently to its shareholders as U.S.-source income under §881(c)(4). Portfolio interest is defined in §881(c)(2) as interest on (1) bearer debt that is exempt from the registration requirements of §163(f)(2)(B) (because its ownership by U.S. persons is effectively blocked) or (2) registered debt where the withholding agent has received an acceptable certification that the holder is not a U.S. person.[87]

The Tax Reform Act of 1986 established the following intricate taxability regime for payments of dividends and interest by domestic "80–20 companies" (i.e., those whose income and activities are essentially from foreign sources under §861(c)):[88]

(1) Interest paid to unrelated creditors (defined in §954(d)(3)) retains its character as foreign-source in full, and hence is not taxable under §881(a)(1);

(2) Interest paid to related creditors retains its foreign-source status only in proportion to the payor's foreign-source gross income under the look-through rules of §861(c)(2);[89]

---

[85] See supra note 52. But see Rev. Rul. 74-63, 1974-1 CB 374 (U.S.-source dividends not effectively connected to U.S. business taxed at treaty rate of 15 percent; foreign-source income exempted by treaty even though that income was effectively connected to U.S. business and hence would have been taxable under §864(c)(4)(B) rules).

[86] Pub. L. No. 98-369, §127(b), 98 Stat. 678, adding §881(c). See Eustice, supra note 6, ¶ 4.03[2]; Feingold & Fishman, The DRA's Elimination of the "Withholding" Tax on Portfolio Interest, 62 J. Tax'n 170 (1985); Wales, Repeal of 30 Percent Withholding: A Case Study in Complexity, 12 J. Corp. Tax'n 352 (1985).

[87] These provisions were explained in Temporary and Proposed Regulations issued on August 22, 1984, by TD 7965, 1984-2 CB 38, and TD 7967, 1984-2 CB 329. See generally Granwell, Repeal of the 30 Percent Withholding Tax on Interest Paid to Foreigners, 13 Tax Mgmt. Int'l 306 (1984); Feingold & Fishman, supra note 86; Wales, supra note 86.

[88] Supra note 8 (i.e., 80 percent of its gross income for the three-year period preceeding the year of payment of the dividends or interest is derived from an active business *in* a foreign country).

[89] The foreign-source portion of such interest thus is not taxed under §881(a).

(3) Dividends paid, although fully sourced as U.S. income,[90] nevertheless are excused from U.S. tax and withholding by §§881(d) and 1441(c)(10) to the extent of the payor-corporation's §861(c)(2) proportional foreign-source gross income percentage.[91]

The principal definitional problems under §881 are whether a particular item of income constitutes "fixed or determinable annual or periodic income" within the meaning of §881(a)(1).[92] Regs. §1.1441-2(a)(1) states that this term "is merely descriptive of the character or class of income," whether or not paid in a lump sum, a statement inspired largely by the decision in *CIR v. Wodehouse*,[93] which held a foreign author taxable on his receipt of lump-sum proceeds for the transfer of magazine serial rights to a U.S. publisher. Conversely, Regs. §1.1441-2(a)(3) states that income derived from the sale of real or personal property is not annual or periodic income. Since rents or royalties constitute annual or periodic income, while proceeds from the sale or exchange of property do not (even when payable in installments), the sale vs. license distinction has special importance to foreign taxpayers: If the transaction constitutes a sale or exchange, gain will not be taxable under §881 provided it is not effectively connected with a U.S. business.[94] Thus, foreign corporations can derive substantial amounts of nonbusiness capital or ordinary gain from sales to U.S. purchasers without fear of U.S. tax on such income, regardless of its source. Conversely, corporations forfeit the

---

[90] Supra note 9, §861(a)(2)(A).

[91] H.R. 3838, §1214, amending §§861(a)(1) and 861(a)(2) (source rules), adding new §§861(c), 881(d), and 1441(c)(10); see H.R. Conf. Rep. No. 841, 99th Cong., 2d Sess. 601–603 (1986); Joint Committee Staff General Explanation of the Tax Reform Act of 1986, supra note 24, 936–941.

[92] See generally Rev. Rul. 58-479, 1958-2 CB 60 (lump-sum commissions paid by marine suppliers to personnel of foreign ships constitute periodic income, as do prizes, awards, and wagering winnings); Rev. Rul. 64-51, 1964-1 CB 322 (proceeds of redemption of life insurance or endowment policy are periodic income); Rev. Rul. 74-555, 1974-2 CB 202, modified by Rev. Rul. 76-283, 1976-2 CB 222 (royalties periodic income); Lokken, supra note 19.

But see Rev. Rul. 69-244, 1969-1 CB 215 (capital gain dividends of regulated investment company not periodic income); IT 3781, 1946-1 CB 119 (reorganization boot dividend not periodic income).

[93] CIR v. Wodehouse, 337 US 369 (1949).

[94] Capital gains of foreign corporations are thus either wholly exempt from tax under §881, if not effectively connected to a U.S. business or (after 1986) subject to the regular §11(b) rates under §882 if connected to a U.S. business; the stakes for ordinary gains of a foreign corporation likewise are no tax vs. the regular §11 corporate tax rates on such income. But ordinary gain from U.S. sources will be attracted to a U.S. business under §864(c)(3) and hence will be taxable under §882 (infra ¶ 17.04).

right to nonbusiness deductions or credits if they compute their tax under §881.

Two other categories of U.S.-source income are contained in the list of items subject to the 30 percent rate of §881(a) (if not effectively connected to a U.S. business):

(1) Gain attributable to accrued, but untaxed, OID on the sale or exchange of an OID obligation[95] (§881(a)(3)(A)) and payments of interest (or principal) attributable to accrued but untaxed OID (net of any withholding tax on such payments) (§881(a)(3)(B)); [96]

(2) Gains from the sale of intangible personal property (patents, copyrights, trademarks, etc. to the extent contingent on future productivity of the property (§§881(a)(4) and 865(d)(1)(B)). The source of contingent payment gains is determined under the royalty source rules of §861(a)(4); the source of fixed payment gains is determined under the personal property sale rules of §865, and such gains are not subject to tax under §881. [97]

¶ 17.04　FOREIGN CORPORATIONS ENGAGED IN UNITED STATES BUSINESS: SECTIONS 882 AND 884

1. Section 882 in general. In addition to the 30 percent tax of §881 on the gross investment income of a foreign corporation from U.S. sources,

---

[95] For the treatment of OID generally, see supra ¶¶ 4.40–4.43.

[96] As to market discount (supra ¶ 4.44), §1276(a)(4) states that market discount gain is to be treated as interest *except* for purposes of §§881 and 1441.

See generally Eustice, supra note 6, ¶ 4.03[3]; Feingold & Cappuccio, U.S. Taxation of OID Income to Foreign Persons After the 1984 Tax Reform Act, 24 Tax Notes 1007 (1984).

For evolution of the treatment of OID under §881, commencing with the Foreign Investors' Tax Act of 1966, followed by the Tax Reform Act of 1969, the Revenue Act of 1971, the Tax Reform Act of 1982, and the Tax Reform Act of 1984, see the fourth edition of this work at ¶ 17.03, note 56.

[97] Supra text at note 28. For example, if *F* Company sold a zero-basis patent to a U.S. buyer for fixed annual payments of $100 per year plus annual contingent payments measured by 10 percent of the buyer's earnings therefrom, *F*'s collection of $300 in year 1 under the contract would result in $200 (the contingent portion), being treated as a taxable contingent payment under §881(a)(4); if *F* collects $200 in year 2, only the $100 contingent portion would be taxable; if *F* collects only $100 in year 3, nothing would be taxable under §881, since there are no contingent proceeds. See Regs. §1.871-11 for computation mechanics under these provisions. Before amendment in 1986, §871(e) treated *all* gain as contingent for any year in which contingent payments constituted more than half of the gain (e.g., in the first year of the example), but this provision was repealed in 1986.

See generally Lokken, supra note 19.

§882(a) imposes the regular §11 tax (both on ordinary income and, after 1986, on business capital gains) on any taxable income (net of applicable deductions) effectively connected with the conduct of a trade or business within the United States. In this respect, a foreign corporation engaged in U.S. business is treated essentially the same as a domestic corporation, with the following exceptions:

(1) By virtue of §§882(c)(3), 901(b)(1), and 901(b)(4), a foreign corporation is not entitled to claim the foreign tax credit (except to the limited extent provided in §906).

(2) It cannot file, or be included in, a consolidated return because of §1504(b)(3) (except for the special case of certain Mexican and Canadian title-holding subsidiaries, which are treated under §1504(d) as domestic corporations for purposes of the consolidated return rules).[98]

(3) By virtue of §542(c)(7), it will not be subject to the 28 percent personal holding company tax of §541 if *all* its stock is owned by nonresident alien individuals during the last half of its taxable year. (The penalty tax of §541 is not needed in this situation because nonresident alien individuals are only taxed at a 30 percent rate on their investment income from U.S. sources; but if the corporation has U.S. shareholders, §541 can apply even though the corporation is only taxable under §881.)

(4) Foreign corporations cannot qualify for the special benefits of former §921 or §991, but *only* a foreign corporation can qualify for the benefits of current §921.

(5) Certain exchanges involving foreign corporations are subject to the special requirements of §367.

(6) By virtue of §882(c)(1), foreign corporations are allowed deductions only to the extent such items are connected with income that is effectively connected with the U.S. business. Section 882(c)(2) provides further that the corporation must file a "true and accurate return" in order to be entitled to its deductions or credits.[99]

---

[98] For illustrations of §1504(d), see Rev. Rul. 69-182, 1969-1 CB 218; Rev. Rul. 70-379, 1970-2 CB 179; Rev. Rul. 71-253, 1971-2 CB 326 (§1504(d) not applicable where foreign corporation used only to get the benefit of a foreign law program restricted to corporations organized under laws of that country). But see U.S. Padding Corp., 88 TC No. 11 (1987) (contra to Rev. Rul. 71-523).

[99] Applied literally, this provision could deny all deductions to a corporation that guesses wrong on the treatment of a single item on its return; but the Service has evidently reserved application of this penalty for no return, pro forma return, or unjustifiably late return cases.

Since a foreign corporation may be taxed on certain foreign-source income as well as domestic-source income, if it is connected to a U.S. business, the "connection" requirement of §882(c)(1) performs a different function from the taxable income source provisions of §861(b), which latter section requires deductions to be properly apportioned or allocable to U.S.-source income in computing the U.S.-source taxable income component of the corporation's §882 tax base. A final point: Whether taxable under §881 or §882, foreign corporations can also be subject to the penalty tax of §531 if they unreasonably accumulate U.S.-source earnings for the purpose of avoiding tax with respect to their shareholders. This risk arises, however, only if distributions by the corporation to its shareholders would have been subject to U.S. tax.

A foreign corporation investing in U.S. real estate can elect to be taxed on a net basis with respect to income from rentals, royalties, or sales thereof as if it were engaged in real estate business in this country under §882(d). The election is revocable only with the consent of the Service (unlike the similar election under many treaties, which can be made on a year-by-year basis), and it applies to all the corporation's real estate interests. (It does not trigger application of the basket clause of §864(c)(3), however, for the taxpayer's other U.S.-source income.) The §882(d) election seems of modest utility, since a corporate investor in real estate will ordinarily be considered engaged in a true business with respect to its real estate activities if it does anything more than merely own real property under long-term net leases. For a really passive investor, however, a §882(d) election will ensure the benefit of the deductions attributable to its real estate operations, but it should be noted that the election will include any capital gain on a sale of the property as well as rental income. [100]

For no-return cases, see Taylor Secs., Inc., 40 BTA 696 (1939) (return not filed until after Tax Court petition; deductions denied); Blenheim Co. v. CIR, 125 F2d 906 (4th Cir. 1942) (acq.) (same).

For loss of deductions where the return contained inadequate information, see Gladstone Co., 35 BTA 764 (1937) (acq.); Blenheim Co. v. CIR, supra (taxpayer filed PHC schedule but not Form 1120).

See also Robert M. Brittingham, 66 TC 373 (1976) (taxpayer lost deductions for failure to file true and accurate return because of substantial omissions of income; mere filing of return not enough, return must be reasonably accurate, which was not here).

Deductions were allowed, even though the return was delinquent, in Anglo-American Direct Tea Trading Co., 38 BTA 711 (1939) (nonacq.); Ardbern Co. v. CIR, 120 F2d 424 (4th Cir. 1941).

[100] Of course, if the taxpayer incorporates the real estate and later sells it in an independent transaction, the sale will generate capital gain (or loss) because the stock will be a capital asset. This assumes that the two steps are not treated as a single integrated transaction amounting to an indirect sale of the real estate itself.

The effectively connected rules of the Foreign Investors' Tax Act of 1966 abolished several tax shelters formerly available to foreign corporations by the force of attraction principle. Thus, a foreign corporation could engage in a U.S. real estate business that yielded a high gross income but a low net income or even a loss, and thereby obtain the §243 deduction with respect to dividend income from its U.S. portfolio investments. Moreover, losses from the real estate business could be applied against its investment income, thereby reducing or eliminating its §882 tax. These devices are no longer available, since the foreign corporation's investment income is taxed on a gross basis under §881, while its business earnings are subject exclusively to §882. [101]

If a foreign corporation is engaged in trade or business within the United States, its shareholders and creditors are subject to these important collateral tax consequences:

(1) If 25 percent or more of the foreign corporation's gross income for the applicable three-year period was effectively connected with the U.S. business, a ratable share of its dividends (based on the ratio of effectively connected gross income to the aggregate gross income) constitutes U.S.-source income under §861(a)(2)(B). [102]

See Rev. Rul. 75-23, 1975-1 CB 290 (foreign corporate limited partnership in U.S. business); Rev. Rul. 73-522, 1973-2 CB 226 ("net-net" lease not U.S. business; lessor taxed on gross rents without deductions).

But under §897(a)(1)(B) of the Foreign Investment in Real Property Tax Act, a foreign corporation is taxable on sales of U.S. real estate (directly or indirectly owned) under §882 as per se U.S. business income; supra note 45. Moreover, by virtue of §897(d)(1), most foreign corporations (and, after 1986 amendments, domestic corporations as well, supra ¶ 7.21) are required to recognize gain on the distribution or sale of a U.S. real property interest notwithstanding §331, §336, or §337 (unless the distribution is a carry-over basis transaction). See Feder & Parker, supra note 45. For legislation that imposed a withholding system on taxable Foreign Investment in Real Property Tax Act gains, see §129 of the Tax Reform Act of 1984, adding new §1445; supra note 46.

[101] It is not clear whether a foreign corporation must take its §881 investment income into account in computing a net operating loss under §172(c) on its other business operations (or the extent to which such loss is absorbed in carry-back or carry-over years).

But H.R. Rep. No. 1450, 89th Cong., 2d Sess. 78-79 (1966), states that only §882 business income counts in computing a §172(c) net operating loss, and only business income is utilized in absorbing a net operating loss deduction under §172(b) rules.

[102] A similar second-level source rule also applied to interest in former §§861(a)(1)(C) and 861(a)(1)(D), but these provisions were repealed by the Tax Reform Act of 1986 and replaced with the branch profits tax rules of §884, infra para. 2 of this section. The 1986 Act also lowered the §861(a)(2)(B) second-level dividend source rule threshold from 50 to 25 percent. See supra notes 8 and 9.

(2) Under §245, the foreign corporation's corporate shareholders may be entitled to the 80 percent dividends-received deduction (in limited situations, 100 percent) for a similarly computed ratable share of dividends received from the corporation.[103]

2. Branch profits tax: Section 884. The Tax Reform Act of 1986 generally replaced the second-level source rules for dividends and interest paid by foreign corporations engaged in business within the United States[104] with a new special surrogate tax levied on the foreign corporation itself.[105] This provision, called the "branch profits tax," is contained in §884 and would tax the foreign corporation on its "effectively connected earnings and profits" attributable to the U.S. branch as defined by §884(d). The general approach here is to treat the U.S. branch business as if it had been a U.S. subsidiary. Thus, the foreign corporation is taxable at a flat 30 percent rate (or lower applicable treaty rate) on its "dividend equivalent amount," defined in §884(b) as U.S. effectively connected earnings and profits (increased by net "disinvestment" in the branch for the year, defined as a decrease in "net U.S. equity," and decreased by net positive investment, or an increase in "net U.S. equity," in the branch). Section 884(e)(1) overrides treaties unless the foreign corporation is a "qualified resident" (defined in §884(e)(4)(A)(i) as one organized in the treaty country and having at least 50 percent of its stock owned by residents of that country (i.e., an anti-"treaty shopping" rule)).[106] Another special anti-abuse rule in §884(e)(4)(A)(ii) is designed to prevent erosion of the taxable base through payment of substantial amounts of interest (at least half its income) to nonresidents.

---

[103] Section 245(d) provides that dividends in kind are to be valued by the lower of basis or value rule of §301(b)(1)(B); ordinarily, such dividends are measured by value (§301(b)(1)(C)).

For amendments to §245 by the Tax Reform Act of 1986, see H.R. 3838, §1226, amending §245(a); H.R. Conf. Rep. No. 841, 99th Cong., 2d Sess. 628–630 (1986); supra ¶ 5.05, para. 4.

[104] Supra note 102.

[105] H.R. 3838, §1241(a), enacting new §884; see H.R. Conf. Rep. No. 841, 99th Cong., 2d Sess. 646–650 (1986); Joint Comm. Staff General Explanation, supra note 24, at 1035–1047.

See Blessing, The Branch Tax, 40 Tax Lawyer (1987); Feingold & Rosen, New Regime of Branch Level Taxation Now Imposed on Certain Foreign Corporations, 66 J. Tax'n 2 (1987); Delta, Branch Profits Tax Under the TRA 1986, Tax Mgmt. Int'l 39 (1987); N.Y. State Bar Association, Tax Section, The Branch Profits Tax: Issues to Be Addressed in the Regulations, 34 Tax Notes 607 (1987).

[106] Vettel, Branch-Level Tax and Treaty Overrides, 35 Tax Notes 632 (1987); Forry & Karlin, supra note 69.

According to IRS Advance Notice 86-17,[107] however, the branch profits tax of §884 will not be triggered for the year that the foreign corporation completely terminates *all* of its U.S. business activities (and such activities stay terminated); nor will §884 tax liability be increased by asset transfers of the foreign corporation to another foreign corporation in a §332 liquidation or a tax-free §368 acquisitive reorganization. Finally, the §884 tax will not be imposed if the branch is actually incorporated as a U.S. subsidiary in a §351 transaction.

The treatment of interest payments by the U.S. branch is dealt with in §884(f)(1), which provides that such interest has a U.S. source to the extent of the greater of the branch's interest payments or interest deductions (in the latter case, the excess of interest deducted over interest paid is taxable under §881(a) as if there had been a deemed loan by the foreign corporation to its U.S. branch; the applicable treaty rules of §884(e)(3)(B) apply to interest payments under §884(f)(1) as well).

The second-tier source rule for interest was repealed by the Tax Reform Act of 1986, but the second-tier source rule for dividends was retained, although the threshold was changed to 25 percent. However, even if dividends become U.S. source under this rule, §884(e)(3)(A) exempts such dividends from tax if a treaty does not prevent the application of the §884(a) branch profits tax.

Note that a foreign corporation engaged in a U.S. trade or business through a branch faces the unappetizing prospect of not only being taxed under §882 at the §11 top rate of 34 percent, but also faces paying a tax of 30 percent on the branch's net U.S. earnings and profits (and further being subject to the new §55 alternative minimum tax regime on its book profits preference, until 1990, and thereafter on its earnings and profits preference as well).

¶ 17.05   SPECIAL-PURPOSE FOREIGN CORPORATIONS

1. Foreign shipping companies. Under §883(a)(1), earnings of a foreign corporation derived from the operation of foreign flag ships are exempt from tax, regardless of source or business situs, if the "flag" country grants a reciprocal exemption for U.S. taxpayers.[108] However, the Tax Reform Act of

---

[107] Released on Nov. 24, 1986, published in 1986-2 IRB 19 (1986).

[108] Time or voyage charter fees presumably are counted as operating earnings for this purpose, but bareboat charter hire apparently is not. See also Rev. Rul. 70-263, 1970-1 CB 158 (interest on funds arising from shipping business, and temporarily deposited with U.S. banks, qualifies as exempt shipping income under §883); Rev. Rul. 74-170, 1974-1 CB 175 (lessor earnings from time and voyage charters qualify for §883 exemption; but rent from bareboat charter (à la net lease) does not because mere passive rental income (unless engaged in shipping business and such

1986 effected a substantial revision of the rules applicable to shipping (and other transportation) income, the general effect of which was to significantly tighten the taxation of such activities.[109]

2. Offshore investment funds. Because of the liberal 1966 amendments to the trade or business definitional rules in §864(b)(2), foreign investment funds, formed for the purpose of trading in U.S. securities or commodities, gained in popularity.[110] The key to successful operation of these investment funds, generally owned primarily or solely by non-U.S. shareholders, is the accumulation of trading profits free of the U.S. capital gain tax. This could be accomplished by taking care to have the principal office of the fund located abroad (Regs. §1.864-2(c)(2)(iii)). Moreover, U.S. taxation of the fund's dividends and interest income could be reduced or eliminated by incorporation of the fund in a favorable treaty rate jurisdiction.

The all-foreign-owned investment fund is relatively simple from a tax standpoint, once the trade or business problem is resolved; but complications arise if domestic shareholders participate in the fund. The PHC and FPHC provisions of §§541 and 551 must be faced, as well as the tainted stock provisions of §§1246, 1247, and 1291–1297, and the controlled foreign corporation rules of §§951 and 1248, discussed in later sections of this chapter.

3. International finance subsidiaries. Domestic tight money conditions abroad gave birth to the curious financing vehicle known as the "international finance subsidiary."[111] In brief, here is how one variant of the IFS

---

lease merely incidental activity); lessee earnings qualify, whether his charter is a time, voyage, or bareboat charter hire); Rev. Rul. 73-350, 1973-2 CB 251 (ship or aircraft must be registered in same country where corporations organized to qualify for §883(a) exemption); Rev. Rul. 73-350 was revoked by Rev. Rul. 75-459, 1975-2 CB 289 (not necessary that ship or aircraft be documented in same country as where corporation organized to qualify for §883 exemption).

For allocation of transportation income, see §863(b)(1), Regs. §1.863–4. For new source rules, see supra ¶ 17.02; infra note 109.

[109] H.R. 3838, §1212, providing for new source rules in §863(c)(2), for a new 4 percent tax on gross U.S.-source transportation income (§887), and amending §883(c) to restrict the reciprocal exemption of §883(a).

[110] See Comment, The Off-Shore Hedge Fund, 8 Colum. J. Transnat'l L. 79 (1969); Note, United States Taxation and Regulation of Offshore Mutual Funds, 83 Harv. L. Rev. 404 (1969); Sitrick, U.S. Taxation of Stock and Securities Trading Income of Foreign Investors, 30 J. Tax'n 98 (1969); Roberts, U.S. Taxation of Foreign Taxpayers' Stock or Security Transactions: An Analysis, 33 J. Tax'n 66 (1970); Roberts, Taxation of Stock or Securities Transactions of Foreign Corporations and Partnerships, 33 J. Tax'n 146 (1970).

[111] See Boffa, International Finance Subsidiaries, Tax Mgmt. Portfolio (BNA) No. 215-2d (1972); Report on International Finance Subsidiaries, 28 Tax L. Rev. 439

worked: The domestic parent set up its controlled IFS in the Netherlands Antilles, and the IFS then issued its bonds or other debt instruments to foreign lenders. (The obligations were guaranteed by the U.S. parent and were often, but not always, convertible into stock of the parent.) The IFS then loaned the proceeds of the debt issue to the U.S. parent on terms that more or less tracked the provisions of the IFS's obligations. (A nominal tax toll had to be paid to the Netherlands Antilles as the host country, which enabled the interest paid by the parent to its IFS to qualify for the tax treaty exemption under the United States-Netherlands tax treaty.) Interest payments by the IFS to its bondholders were not subject to U.S. tax or withholding because of the special source rules of §861(a)(1)(C). When the dust settled, the U.S. parent had borrowed funds abroad (through its IFS conduit) without subjecting the interest thereon to the §1441 withholding tax. [112]

However, repeal of the tax and withholding on portfolio interest income for foreign lenders by the Tax Reform Act of 1984[113] should largely obviate the need to use the IFS structure, which was a major reason for enactment of the 1984 amendments.

PART B.   DOMESTIC CORPORATIONS WITH FOREIGN-SOURCE INCOME

¶ 17.10   INTRODUCTORY

U.S. corporations ordinarily are taxable under §11 on their entire net income "from whatever source derived" without allowance for the foreign situs of the income. While taxability on worldwide income is the basic statutory pattern in the Code, there are several significant exceptions, grounded on the belief that foreign-source earnings may have a special character. [114]

(1973); Lederman, The Offshore Finance Subsidiary: An Analysis of the Current Benefits and Problems, 51 J. Tax'n 86 (1979).

See generally Rev. Rul. 74-464, 1974-2 CB 46; and Rev. Rul. 78-230, 1978-1 CB 274.

[112] But see Rev. Rul. 84-153, 1984-2 CB 383 (IFS held to be mere conduit and U.S. affiliate was the true borrower). See also Rev. Rul. 84-152, 1984-2 CB 381 (foreign parent loan to Antillies subsidiary, which reloaned funds to U.S. affiliate, held mere conduit and transaction treated as direct loan by foreign parent to its U.S. subsidiary). See supra ¶ 17.02, para. 4.

[113] Supra note 86. See also Rev. Rul. 84-153, 1984-2 CB 383, and Rev. Rul. 84-152, 1984-2 CB 381.

[114] See generally Norr, Jurisdiction to Tax and International Income, 17 Tax L. Rev. 431 (1962); Surrey, Current Issues in the Taxation of Corporate Foreign Invest-

Thus, the foreign tax credit provisions reflect a long-standing congressional policy to alleviate multiple taxation of the same items of income, while the Western Hemisphere trade corporation deduction of §922 (which was repealed in 1976) and the former exclusion (now a credit) for certain income from possessions of the United States by §936 are designed to confer economic incentives on corporations that conduct their affairs in a manner responsive to this country's special interests in these areas.

Although Congress has gone part way toward a system of special taxation for the foreign-source income of domestic corporations, it has so far resisted appeals for complete tax exemption and for broad-based deferral of tax for such income, even though many foreign tax jurisdictions have adopted such a territorial approach to the taxation of foreign-source income of their resident taxpayers. Thus, the U.S. treatment of foreign-source earnings of domestic taxpayers is a compromise between contending tax philosophies: We have adopted the theory that foreign-source income should not be subject to double taxation, and hence allow a credit for foreign taxes levied thereon, but not the general principle that such income is entitled to complete exemption from or deferral of U.S. tax.[115]

Although it is ordinarily advantageous to a taxpayer whose business activities give rise to foreign-source income to have such business classified as a foreign person (and hence not subject to current U.S. tax on such income), this is not invariably true. Thus, a domestic corporation may prefer the U.S. tax treatment afforded to particular items of income or deduction, and conduct its foreign business activities through an unincorporated foreign branch or a domestic subsidiary in order to obtain these benefits. For example, losses of one division can be offset against profits of other divisions in computing the taxpayer's aggregate taxable income (or consolidated returns can be filed by a domestic corporate group with the same net result). Other U.S. tax benefits that may be controlling in a given situation include the percentage depletion deduction and the lower rate applicable to capital gains (the latter of which, however, was repealed in 1986).

The Tax Reform Act of 1976 revised the calculus for conducting foreign business operations in several important respects, repealing the Western Hemisphere trade corporation §922 deduction (with a four-year phase-out period), changing the former §931 possessions corporation exclusion to a credit (in §936), tightening the deemed-paid credit rules of §902 (that is,

---

ment, 56 Colum. L. Rev. 815 (1956); Surrey, The United States Taxation of Foreign Income, 1 J. Law & Econ. 72 (1958).

[115] But deferral of U.S. tax on the export earnings of certain specially defined domestic international sales corporations was proposed in 1970, and passed, in modified form, by the Revenue Act of 1971, Pub. L. No. 91-178; they are considered infra ¶ 17.14; these provisions in turn were replaced by the foreign sales corporation legislation (§§921–927) in 1984; infra ¶ 17.14.

gross-up now will apply across the board), restricting the tax credit limitations in §904, modifying the controlled foreign corporation provisions in several important respects, and completely revising the §367 provisions (which, in turn, were revised again in 1984).

Moreover, the Tax Reform Act of 1986 materially revised and significantly restricted the rules dealing with the taxation of foreign-source income.[116] Thus, the 1986 legislation (1) sharply restricted the foreign tax credit provisions of §§901–904, (2) contracted the potential for tax deferral with respect to foreign income by tightening the controlled foreign corporation provisions and the foreign investment company rules, (3) established a new statutory regime for foreign currency transactions, (4) modified the source rules in several important respects, and (5) cut back or tightened numerous other provisions dealing with the taxation of foreign income and activities. On a more basic level, the dramatic rate reductions effected by the 1986 Act will have a major impact on planning both the structure and economic feasibility of foreign business operations and investment.

The tax factors and stakes involved in choosing the form through which a foreign business venture is to be conducted are summarized in the following table (in which it is assumed that the earnings are from foreign sources and are not effectively connected to a U.S. business):

	Foreign Branch	Domestic Subsidiary	Foreign Subsidiary
§367 apply?	No	No	Yes
Operation			
Current §11 tax on foreign earnings?	Yes	Yes	No (unless §951)
Current loss offset?	Yes	Yes (if §1501)	No
Special U.S. tax benefits?	Yes	Yes (e.g., §936)	No
§531 tax exposure?	N.A.*	Yes	No (generally)
Direct §901 credit?	Yes	Yes	No
Indirect §902 credit when dividends paid?	N.A.*	No	Yes
Gross-up?	N.A.*	No	Yes
Dividends received deduction?	N.A.*	Yes	No (unless §245)
§482 exposure?	Yes	Yes	Yes
Subpart F exposure?	N.A.*	No	Yes
Sale, Liquidation, Reorganization			
Taxable?	N.A.*	§331 capital gain	§1248 dividend
Tax-free?	N.A.*	No §367	§367 applies

* Since a foreign branch is not a separately taxed entity, N.A. denotes "not applicable;" but cf. §884.

---

[116] See Eustice, Kuntz, Lewis, & Deering, supra note 7.

¶ 17.11 FOREIGN TAX CREDIT

1. In general. The most important provisions of the Code relating to the taxation of foreign-source income of domestic taxpayers are §§901–908, which prescribe the foreign tax credit mechanism. A detailed description of this subject is beyond the scope of this treatise,[117] but its more salient features will be described briefly.

The purpose of the foreign tax credit is to eliminate double taxation of foreign-souce income. In effect, the foreign tax is treated as a down payment on the domestic taxpayer's U.S. tax liability with respect to that income. In general, §901 provides the following rules with respect to the foreign tax credit:

(1) Only foreign "income taxes" (or, under §903, taxes paid in lieu of an income tax) can be credited,[118] property taxes, excise taxes, value added taxes, sales taxes, succession or transfer taxes, payroll taxes, user fees or license fees, customs levies, and the like do not qualify;[119]

(2) Only the foreign tax itself is creditable, not interest or penalties thereon;

(3) The taxpayer must bear the legal liability for the tax, not merely its economic burden;[120]

(4) The credit is limited to normal tax and surtax, excluding the penalty taxes of §531 or §541, but is allowed in restricted amounts against AMT liability;[121]

(5) The credit is elective (but if the credit is elected, the taxpayer thereby waives deductibility for such taxes under §275(a)(4));

---

[117] See generally Owens, The Foreign Tax Credit (Harvard University Press, 1961); Owens & Ball, The Indirect Credit (Harvard University Press, 1975); Schoenfeld, Some Definitional Problems in the Deemed Paid Foreign Tax Credit of Section 902: "Dividends" and "Accumulated Profits," 18 Tax L. Rev. 401 (1963). For 1976 amendments to the foreign tax credit, see Dale, The Reformed Foreign Tax Credit: A Path Through the Maze, 33 Tax L. Rev. 175 (1978) (dealing with 1976 amendments).

[118] See discussion infra text at notes 123–127. Income taxes also include war profits and excess profits taxes under §901(b).

[119] Section 901(f), enacted in 1975, denies tax status for certain payments to foreign countries for oil and gas if the taxpayer has no economic interest in the oil and gas to which §611(a) applies or if the price thereof differs from fair market value.

[120] See Biddle v. CIR, 302 US 573 (1938); Rev. Rul. 87-14, 1987-6 IRB 14; Rev. Rul. 63-51, 1963-1 CB 407, modified by Rev. Rul. 74-525, 1974-2 CB 411; Rev. Rul. 68-128, 1968-1 CB 381. But constructive payment of the tax will suffice. Rev. Rul. 57-106, 1957-1 CB 242.

[121] Supra ¶ 5.08; §59(a).

(6) An election can be revoked within the applicable statute of limitations for refunds, and the right to elect arises anew each year;

(7) The election to credit foreign taxes must be made for all creditable taxes and cannot be claimed on a partial basis; and

(8) Finally, cash-method taxpayers can elect to claim credit for foreign taxes on the accrual method by virtue of §905.[122]

The requirements that must be met by foreign income taxes in order to be creditable under the foreign tax credit provisions of §901 have undergone substantial change in recent years. Several sets of proposed regulations were issued,[123] culminating in final regulations issued as such on October 6, 1983.[124]

The touchstone of creditability under these regulations is the comparability of the foreign tax to an "income tax" in the U.S. sense.[125] The regulations require that the foreign tax must be compulsory and not a payment for

---

[122] The Service has ruled that the §901 credit is not subject to the *Dixie Pine* contested liability doctrine (Dixie Pine Prods. Co. v. CIR, 320 US 516 (1944)) but relates back to the year in which it was incurred after liability is finally determined. Rev. Rul. 58-55, 1958-1 CB 266; Rev. Rul. 70-290, 1970-1 CB 161.

For the possibility of bunching credits in the year of an election to accrue foreign taxes under §905, see Jose Ferrer, 35 TC 617 (1961) (acq.).

[123] Proposed Regulations issued June 20, 1979; Temporary and Proposed Regulations issued November 12, 1980; and Proposed Regulations issued April 5, 1983. For an analysis of these proposals, see Hannes & Levey, *Inland Steel* in the Court of Claims: What Will Its Impact Be On The Foreign Tax Credit Area?, 57 J. Tax'n 74 (1982); Hannes & Levey, How Regulatory and Judicial Analysis of the Foreign Tax Credit Differ: Regs. v. *Inland Steel,* 57 J. Tax'n 162 (1982); Ad Hoc Committee on Foreign Tax Credit, ABA, Tax Section, Comments Regarding Proposed Foreign Tax Credit Regulations, 33 Tax Lawyer 35 (1979).

[124] Promulgated by TD 7918 (1983), 1983-2 CB 113.

For analysis of the final regulations, see Lieberman, Whether and to What Extent a Foreign Tax Is Creditable Under Final Regulations, 60 J. Tax'n 98 (1984); Isenberg, The Foreign Tax Credit: Royalties, Subsidies, and Creditable Taxes, 39 Tax L. Rev. 227 (1984); and Bouma, The Final Foreign Tax Credit Regulations: Through the Looking Glass, 62 Taxes 554 (1984).

[125] The regulations require predominant comparability to an income tax in the U.S. sense; they also require that the levy must first constitute a "tax" (i.e., be compulsory and not be a payment for a specific economic benefit). But the all or nothing approach of the earlier proposals on this latter point was replaced by a splitting concept where the particular payment contains elements of both a tax and a payment for an economic benefit. Income tax comparability is determined under a three-part test derived from Inland Steel Co. v. US, 677 F2d 72 (Ct. Cl. 1982), which decision is analyzed in the articles cited supra note 123.

See also Schering Corp., 69 TC 579 (1978) (foreign taxes imposed on tax-free §482 repatriation held creditable under §901); Maynard Waxenberg, 62 TC 594 (1974) (nondeductible excise vs. deductible property tax); ABA, Tax Section Report,

a specific economic benefit, and they set down a three-part test of comparability: the realization test, the gross receipts test, and the net income test, all of which must be met to attain creditability. The Service explained that this test is derived from the *Inland Steel* case,[126] and the mechanics of the test are set out with extensive examples in Regs. §§1.901-2(b)(1)–1.901-2(b)(4). A more comprehensive treatment of the new regulations, however, is best left to more specialized literature.[127]

2. The derivative (or deemed paid) foreign tax credit of §902. A domestic corporation that owns at least 10 percent of the voting stock of a foreign corporation[128] is entitled by §902 to claim a credit for the foreign income taxes paid by the foreign corporation on its accumulated profits in the year in which the domestic corporation receives a dividend from the foreign corporation. This derivative (or "deemed paid") credit roughly parallels the dividends-received deduction of §243. That is, §243 alleviates double domestic taxation of a domestic corporation's earnings at the corporate level, while §902 eliminates double international taxation of earnings at the corporate level where a *foreign* corporation is involved. (Dividends paid by a foreign corporation do not ordinarily qualify for the §243 deduction, and a foreign corporation cannot be included in a consolidated return.) If the foreign corporation in turn owns at least 10 percent of the voting stock of another foreign corporation, the domestic corporation can obtain a credit under §902(b) for foreign income taxes paid by the second-tier foreign corporation.

Prior to 1971, the derivative tax credit was not allowed for tax payments by third-tier subsidiaries, and taxes paid by a second-tier foreign corporation did not qualify unless it was owned to the extent of 50 percent or more by the first-tier foreign corporation. Section 902 was amended in 1971, however, to (1) reduce the percentage applicable to second-tier foreign corporations from 50 percent to 10 percent and (2) permit third-tier foreign

---

The Creditability of Foreign Income Taxes: A Critical Analysis of Revenue Rulings 78-61, 78-62 and 78-63, 32 Tax Lawyer 33 (1978).

[126] Supra note 125.

[127] Articles supra notes 123, 124, and 125; see also supra note 117.

[128] If the 10 percent test is satisfied, the U.S. corporate shareholder can claim the §902 credit for dividends paid on all its stock in the foreign corporation, whether or not such stock is voting stock. Morever, the crucial time for determining the requisite ownership apparently is the time when the dividend is received, in view of the fact that only the person who receives the dividend is entitled to use §902. See Steel Improvement & Forge Co., 36 TC 265 (1961), rev'd on other grounds, 314 F2d 96 (6th Cir. 1963); see also, Rev. Rul. 84-6, 1984-1 CB 178 (the 10 percent voting stock requirement means 10 percent of voting power (i.e., electable directors, not value or number of shares); Leher, Minimizing Foreign Currency Transactions in Computing the Indirect Foreign Tax Credit, 17 J. Corp. Tax'n 165 (1984).

corporations to qualify if owned to the extent of 10 percent or more by the second-tier corporation, subject to conditions set out in §902(b)(3) to prevent qualification if the domestic parent's interest in its progeny is too diluted—that is, the U.S. parent must have at least a 5 percent indirect investment in its second-tier and third-tier affiliates. More remote subsidiaries, however, do not qualify under the 1971 amendments, even if there is 100 percent ownership from top to bottom.

When the second-tier corporation receives dividends from the third-tier corporation, the former is deemed to have paid its pro rata share of the foreign income taxes actually paid by the latter; next, on receiving dividends from the second tier, the first-tier corporation is deemed to have paid *its* pro rata share of the foreign income taxes actually paid, or deemed to have been paid, by the second-tier corporation; finally, dividends received by the domestic parent similarly convey upward a credit for income taxes paid, or deemed to have been paid, by the first-tier corporation.

The §902 credit is generally determined by multiplying the foreign income taxes of the foreign corporation by a fraction (which can never exceed 100 percent) consisting of dividends received over accumulated profits of the foreign corporation. The three principal definitional concepts under §902 are "dividends," "accumulated profits,"[129] and "foreign taxes paid on or with respect to such accumulated profits," none of which are defined with gemlike clarity. Regs. §1.902-1(a)(6) states that the term "dividends" for this purpose (the numerator of the §902 fraction) is limited to distributions taxable as "ordinary dividends" under §316 (see Chapter 7). Courts have generally agreed that capital gain distributions (e.g., distributions in partial or complete liquidation, or distributions in redemption of stock that qualify for sale treatment under §302(a)) do not qualify for §902.[130] If the courts had decided otherwise on this question, the foreign tax credit computations could have been distorted because the distribution gain would have been taxable at the capital gain rate, while the foreign taxes of

---

[129] See Schoenfeld, supra note 117; see also Rev. Rul. 71-65, 1971-1 CB 212 (treatment of dividends in kind for purposes of the §902 credit computations); Rev. Rul. 77-483, 1977-2 CB 244 (amount of distribution is value, but charge to earnings is adjusted basis); Rev. Rul. 87-14, 1987-6 IRB 14 (not limited to profits allocable to U.S. shareholders on whom tax was actually imposed).

[130] See US v. Associated Tel. & Tel. Co., 306 F2d 824 (2d Cir. 1962), cert. denied, 371 US 950 (1963) (complete liquidation); Fowler Hosiery Co. v. CIR, 301 F2d 394 (7th Cir. 1962) (partial liquidation).

The treatment of §356(a)(2) reorganization boot dividends at one time was not entirely clear. The court of claims held that such dividends qualify for the §243 deduction in a decision that ought to apply to §902 with equal force. See King Enterprises, Inc. v. US, supra note 17; American Mfg. Co., 55 TC 204 (1970) (same); Rev. Rul. 74-387, 1974-2 CB 207 (same).

the subsidiary could have been credited in full, producing a credit in excess of the U.S. capital gain rate on the underlying gain.

Because of the §902 credit, dividend treatment for a particular distribution may be preferable to capital gain treatment; this reversal of roles may cause a corporate shareholder to attempt a dividend strip-out of the subsidiary's earnings before a contemplated sale of the subsidiary's stock or a complete liquidation, in the hope that a §902 credit can be obtained for the threshold dividends. If these steps are collapsed, however, the purported dividend may instead be treated as part of the selling price for the stock (or as an advance liquidation distribution), not qualified for the §902 credit.[131]

Accumulated profits of the foreign corporation (the denominator) are, in general, equated with earnings and profits of the foreign corporation and are determined in accordance with domestic law principles.[132] Adoption of these principles has the virtue of correlating the denominator of the §902 computation with the definition of dividends (the numerator), thus avoiding the possible distortions that could arise if different definitional approaches were used for the numerator and the denominator of the §902 fraction. It must be acknowledged, however, that earnings and profits is a concept of no small confusion in its own right (as has been noted previously), and that practical difficulties often arise in getting the relevant information from a foreign corporation which the U.S. stockholder may not control. The fundamental definitional problem with respect to the term "accumulated profits" may be that §902 requires the meshing of two concepts which do not readily fit (i.e., the dividends numerator of the §902 fraction, which must clearly be determined under U.S. tax law principles, and the creditable foreign taxes of a foreign corporation, which must of necessity be controlled by foreign tax rules); the accumulated profits denominator of the §902 fraction is thus

---

[131] See, e.g., Steel Improvement & Forge Co. v. CIR, supra note 128; Waterman S.S. Corp. v. CIR, 430 F2d 1185 (5th Cir. 1970), cert. denied, 401 US 939 (1971). Casner v. CIR, 450 F2d 379 (5th Cir. 1971), extended the principles of the *Waterman* case and treated a threshold sale dividend as part of the sale price (and as taxable dividend income to the buyer) even though the buyer did not supply the funds for payment of this dividend, as in *Waterman*.

But see Rev. Rul. 75-493, 1975-2 CB 108 (Service will not follow *Casner*, but will continue to follow *Waterman*).

[132] If the domestic shareholder elects to be governed by the special earnings and profits rules and regulations of §964(a), the determination is to be made under rules substantially similar to those applicable to domestic corporations. Rev. Rul. 63-6, 1963-1 CB 126; Regs. §§1.902-1(e)–1.902-1(g), and 1.964-1, and 1.964-2. See generally Schoenfeld, supra note 117; Owens, supra note 117; see also Rev. Proc. 68-23, 1968-1 CB 821; infra ¶ 17.43.

See generally, Champion Int'l Corp., 81 TC 424 (1983) (tracing and timing rules). But the Tax Reform Act of 1986 in §1202(a) changed the annual peel-back rule, and instead now computes accumulated earnings on a multi-year aggregate basis; infra note 141.

assigned the thankless task of attempting to reconcile that that is, by definition, probably irreconcilable—that is, it is the base on which the foreign taxes are presumably paid, and it is also the fund from which the dividends are determined. Thus, it is small wonder that considerable confusion has long enveloped its precise definition.[133]

Since the §902 credit for taxes paid or incurred by a foreign corporation is tied to its dividends, it is not available until the earnings of the foreign corporation are repatriated, in whole or in part, to the domestic parent.[134] Because of this functional relation of the §902 credit to the foreign corporation's dividends, the Court held, in the landmark *American Chicle* case,[135] that only foreign taxes attributable to the foreign corporation's net earnings available for the distribution of dividends to its shareholders could be claimed as a credit under §902; taxes attributable to earnings used to pay the foreign taxes themselves could not be credited under §902 because these earnings were not available for distribution as dividends and hence were not subjected to the double taxation which Congress sought to avoid by §902.

Thus, if foreign corporation *F* earned $100 of profits subject to $40 foreign taxes and distributed the remaining $60 as a dividend to its domestic corporate shareholder *P*, only $24 of *F*'s taxes would be creditable under §902 and the *American Chicle* limitation; the other $16 of foreign taxes were attributable to the $40 of earnings that *F* used to pay the taxes themselves. It

---

[133] See H.H. Robertson Co., 59 TC 53 (1972) (relation of dividend in kind rules to foreign tax credit computations; followed principle of Rev. Rul. 71-65, 1971-1 CB 212; good general discussion of accumulated profits and earnings and profits concepts and how §902 computation works in multiple-year tracing stituations; also reaffirms annual peel-back principle for computation of §902 credit, first decided in General Foods, 4 TC 209 (1944) (acq.); but see amendments by the Tax Reform Act of 1986, infra note 141.

See also Rev. Rul. 74-550, 1974-2 CB 209 (deficits absorb accumulated profits in reverse chronological order and if deficit wipes out accumulated profits for a year, foreign taxes for that year become permanently locked into that year and cannot be drawn out by subsequent years' dividends; but also held that post-dividend deficits will not retroactively deny §902 credit for dividends paid in that year); Champion Int'l Corp., supra note 132 (foreign loss carry-backs reduce *both* the numerator and the denominator of the §902 fraction); infra note 141.

[134] See IR 1703 (1976), issuing Rev. Rul. 76-508, 1976-2 CB 225 (where income of foreign subsidiary *F* is allocated to U.S. parent *P* under §482, and *F* does not seek foreign tax refund and *P* does not invoke competent authorities treaty procedures of Rev. Proc. 70-18, 1970-2 CB 493, extra foreign taxes of *F* not creditable to *P* under §902); amplified by Rev. Rul. 80-231, 1980-2 CB 219 (overpaid foreign taxes are presumed refundable, and hence increase earnings and profits as of original year due; if taxes are refunded, no further effect; if taxes not refunded, presumption rebutted and earnings reduced for original year of accrual. If taxpayers fail to pursue refund diligently, foreign overpayment treated as voluntary and no reduction of earnings for earlier year; instead, earnings reduced for year refund rights lapse).

[135] American Chicle Co. v. US, 316 US 450 (1942).

should be noted, however, that *P* was taxed only on *F*'s *after-tax* profits, since *F*'s taxes were deductible in determining the amount of its earnings available for distribution as a dividend to *P* under §§301(c)(1) and 316. Thus, *F*'s foreign taxes served the dual function of reducing the amount of dividends taxable to its shareholder, *P*, and of constituting a credit against *P*'s U.S. taxes on that dividend. Because of this combination of a deduction and a credit for *F*'s foreign taxes, the overall foreign and domestic tax burden on the $100 of foreign-source earnings would only be $44.80 where the foreign business was conducted through a separate foreign subsidiary ($40 on *F*, and $4.80, after the §902 credit, on *P*'s $60 of taxable dividends from *F*). On the other hand, if the foreign business had been conducted by a branch, rather than through a separate foreign subsidiary, the total tax burden would have been $48 ($40 of foreign taxes and $8 of U.S. taxes ($48 less a credit of $40 under §901)).[136]

The Revenue Act of 1962 attacked this preference for the use of foreign subsidiaries by amending the computation rules of §902 and adding §78, requiring the domestic corporate shareholder to gross up the foreign taxes that are creditable under §902 (i.e., to treat them as a constructive dividend for purposes of computing its tax under §61 on the dividend income received from the foreign corporation). Under this gross-up approach, the domestic corporate shareholder first computes its deemed-paid foreign tax credit under §902(a)(1) without the *American Chicle* limitation and then includes this amount in its gross income as a dividend under §78.[137] This equalizes the treatment of foreign subsidiaries and unincorporated branches with respect to the foreign tax credit for the *distributed* earnings of the subsidiary (although a disparity between the two structures remains with respect to undistributed earnings[138]).

---

[136] These calculations assume a U.S. rate of 48 percent (which, however, has been lowered to 34 percent by the Tax Reform Act of 1986). See S. Rep. No. 1881, 87th Cong., 2d Sess. 67 (1962), for tables demonstrating this result. The maximum tax rate differential advantage in this situation occurred when the foreign tax rate was exactly half the U.S. tax rate, with the rate differential declining ratably as the foreign rate approached either the U.S. rate or zero.

[137] The gross-up dividend of §78 applies only at the domestic corporate level, however; dividends by second-tier foreign subsidiaries are not grossed up at the first-tier foreign subsidiary level.

It should be noted that §78 dividends constitute gross income for all purposes, not merely the computation of the shareholder's foreign tax credits; thus, unfavorable collateral effects under §§531, 541, 1361, and similar provisions can be created by the gross-up rules of §78.

[138] Unless the Subpart F rules of §951 apply (infra Part D), domestic taxation of a foreign subsidiary's income is deferred until repatriation of the income to the domestic corporation, resulting in potential tax advantage.

Using the facts in the above example, *P*'s foreign credit under §902(a)(1) would be $40, rather than $24—that is, all the foreign taxes of *F* are creditable under §902, including the amount attributable to the $40 of its earnings used to pay the taxes—but *P*'s dividend income is $100, rather than $60 (i.e., $60 of actual dividends plus $40 of gross-up constructive dividends under §78), thus raising the total tax burden on the $100 of foreign earnings to $48 ($40 of foreign taxes paid by *F* and $8, net of credits, paid by *P*). This is the same result that would have obtained if *F* had been operated as a branch rather than as a separately incorporated foreign subsidiary.[139] If *F* had instead distributed only $30 of its earnings as a dividend to *P*, accumulating the remaining $30 of its after-tax profits, *P*'s §902 credit would be $20 (i.e., foreign taxes of $40 times the $30 dividend over *F*'s after-tax profits of $60) and *P*'s dividend income would be $50 ($30 actual plus $20 of §78 gross-up income), upon which it would pay a net tax, after credits, of $4. *P* would not be taxable on *F*'s undistributed earnings (unless the Subpart F rules of §951 apply), however, whereas if *F* were only a branch of *P*, *P* would be taxable currently on the full $100 of *F*'s earnings (and would claim the full $40 of credit for *F*'s foreign taxes). Thus, full equality between branches and subsidiaries is approached by the 1962 legislation, but a disparity remains with respect to the accumulated foreign earnings of the business.[140]

The Tax Reform Act of 1986 converted the computation of the deemed paid foreign tax credit under §902 to a system utilizing a multiyear pool of accumulated earnings and profits on a prospective basis (after 1986); moreover, earnings and profits are to be determined under the CFC rules of §964. Thus, the annual "peel-back" computation method of prior law[141] was replaced with an earnings "pooling" approach. Consequently, foreign tax credits will not be lost due to the occurrence of intervening deficit years, nor, conversely, could taxpayers derive artificially higher deemed paid credits by

---

[139] But note that the gross-up computation can produce a more favorable tax result for the taxpayer than the pre-1962 approach in cases where the effective foreign tax rate exceeds the effective U.S. tax rate (a result more likely to occur after the U.S. rate reductions effected by the Tax Reform Act of 1986). This occurs because of the abolition of the *American Chicle* limitation by §902(a)(1). For example, if *F*'s foreign taxes were $60 and it paid a $40 dividend to *P*, gross-up gives *P* creditable taxes of $60 on the $100 dividend ($40 plus $60), while the pre-1962 rules would allow only $24 of §902 credit for the $40 of dividends. While U.S. taxes on the dividends in both cases would be zero because of the §902 credit, *P* would have a larger carry-over with gross-up.

[140] An exemption from the gross-up rules for dividends paid by less developed country corporations was repealed in 1976. See Dale, supra note 117.

[141] Supra notes 132 and 133.

carefully timing a subsidiary's distributions to occur in high tax years (i.e., the "rhythm method" of dividend distributions). [142]

3. Limitations on foreign tax credits: Section 904. Foreign taxes are not always allowed in full as credits against domestic tax liabilities; §904(a) instead limits the credit to the amount of U.S. taxes attributable, roughly speaking, to the taxpayer's foreign-source income, including dividends from its foreign subsidiary. [143] The basic §904(a) limitation is expressed as a fraction: U.S. taxes (before credits), times foreign-source taxable income over total taxable income. The effect of this limitation is that foreign-source income is taxed at the higher of the U.S. or foreign effective rate; in effect, the United States will give way to a foreign jurisdiction, but only up to the level of the effective U.S. tax rate on that income. If the foreign rate is greater, no relief is granted for the excess.

Other features of the §904 limitation worthy of special note are:

(1) Section 904(c) allows a two-year carry-back and a five-year carry-forward of foreign tax credits that are currently unused because of the limitations of §904(a). [144] This allows the taxpayer to average his foreign tax credits from year to year, where the effective foreign tax rate on foreign-source earnings fluctuates; but carry-backs and carry-overs between per-country and overall limitation years are not allowed by virtue of §904(e). Section 904(c) is of no help, however, if the effective foreign tax rate chronically exceeds the effective U.S. rate. The mechanics of §904(c) are similar to the net operating loss carry-over rules of §172 and the capital loss carry-over rules of §1212. [145]

---

[142] H.R. 3838, §1202(a), amending §902. See IRS Advance Notice 87-6, 1987-3 IRB 8 (regulations to be issued on transition rules); see Eustice, Kuntz, Lewis, & Deering, supra note 7, ¶ 4.02[5].

[143] See generally Kaplan, The Limitless Limits of the Foreign Tax Credit, 45 Wash. L. Rev. 347 (1970). For amendments to §904 by the Tax Reform Act of 1976, see Dale, supra note 71; Lokken, The Effects of Capital Gains and Losses on the Credit for Foreign Income Taxes, 30 Fla. L. Rev. 40 (1977).

[144] See Regs. §1.904-2 (carry-back and carry-forward of credits). For procedural aspects of the foreign tax credit carry-back rules of §904(c), see Rev. Rul. 71-533, 1971-2 CB 413 (10-year statute of limitation applies for foreign tax credit carry-back triggered by net operating loss carry-back from later year); Rev. Rul. 71-534, 1971-2 CB 414 (interest on refund attributable to foreign tax credit carry-back triggered by net operating loss carry-back starts to run from close of loss year that created the net operating loss carry-back).

[145] Foreign tax credit carry-overs are not listed as inheritable tax attributes in §381(c); supra ¶ 16.13; see generally Rev. Rul. 68-350, 1968-2 CB 159, modified by Rev. Rul. 72-452, 1972-2 CB 438, allowing the carry-over of §904(c) credits in a stat-

(2) Section 904(d) is designed to eliminate the practice of averaging down the effective foreign tax rate on foreign-source income (and thus avoiding the limitation of §904(a)) by generating additional foreign-source income taxable at a low foreign rate. The limitation of §904(d) attacks such devices by the simple expedient of requiring a separate §904(a) computation for the taxpayer's various categories of "separate-basket" income, thus preventing this type of income from being averaged with other forms of foreign income in the §904(a) limitation.

The Tax Reform Act of 1986 greatly expanded the separate-basket limitation regime of §904(d) to cover what are now eight specified categories of foreign-source income.[146] A special look-through rule is provided by §904(d)(3) in the case of dividends, interest, rents, and royalties received from controlled foreign corporation payors; under this rule, these receipts are subject to separate limitation computations only to the extent the payor's own income would be subject to such limitations.[147]

(3) Sections 904(b)(2) and 904(b)(3) limit the use of foreign-source capital gains in the §904 numerator in the following manner: (1) A foreign corporation could only include five eighths of foreign-source capital gains in the numerator and five eighths of all capital gains in the denominator (thus neutralizing the rate averaging effects of capital gains in the §904 limitation); (2) certain "portable," or controllable source, capital gains could only be included in the numerator if subjected to foreign taxes of at least 10 percent; and (3) U.S.-source capital losses will reduce foreign-source capital

---

utory merger reorganization if the *Libson Shops* limitations of Rev. Rul. 59-395, 1959-2 CB 475, supra ¶ 16.26, are satisfied.

The Revenue Act of 1971 added §383 to the Code, which subjects foreign tax credit carry-overs to the limitations of §382 (but still does not list such item as a §381(c) carry-over).

For amendments to the carry-over limitation rules of §§382 and 383 by the Tax Reform Act of 1986, see supra ¶¶ 16.23–16.25.

[146] These (five of which are new in the 1986 Act) are listed in §§904(d)(1) and 904(d)(2) as follows: (1) passive income (defined in §904(d)(2)(A) generally by reference to §954(c), the FPHC income definition, infra ¶ 17.32); (2) high withholding tax interest income (defined in §904(d)(2)(B) as a gross-basis tax of at least 5 percent); (3) financial services income; (4) shipping income; (5) dividends from uncontrolled subsidiaries that qualify for the §902 credit; and (6) three categories of income attributable to FSCs and DISCs (infra ¶ 17.14). Extensive definitional refinements of the various separate-basket categories are contained in §904(d)(2).

[147] For descriptions of this fearsomely intricate regime, see Joint Comm. Staff General Explanation of the Tax Reform Act of 1986, supra note 24, at 852–906; Eustice, Kuntz, Lewis, & Deering, supra note 7, ¶ 4.02; see also IRS Advance Notice 87-6, supra note 142.

gains, thus reversing the contrary holding of Rev. Rul. 73-572.[148]
Section 904(b)(4) also provides that income that is taken into
account in computing the new possessions credit of §936 is
excluded from both the numerator and the denominator of the
§904 limiting fraction.

(4) A special loss recapture rule is included in §904(f), the general purpose of which is to reduce the §904(a) numerator (foreign-source
taxable income) by the amount of previous foreign-source losses
that had been utilized by the taxpayer in reducing his overall U.S.
taxes (in effect, §904(f) "re-sources" subsequent foreign profits to
the U.S. to compensate for the fact that prior foreign losses were
deductible against U.S.-source income).[149]

(5) The alternative per-country limitation was abolished in 1976 for
years after 1975; thus, the only general limitation on the credit
under §904(a) is the "overall" limitation (that is, foreign-source
taxable income over worldwide taxable income).

(6) Further adjustments to the provisions of §904 were made by the
Tax Reform Act of 1984; the new provisions, §§904(d)(3) (a special
recharacterization rule) and 904(g) (a special resourcing rule) were
imposed in an effort to reduce further manipulation of the credit
limitations imposed by §904.[150]

(7) Special limitations are contained in §907 restricting the tax benefits
of foreign oil and gas operations in the following manner: Section
907(a) limits the amount of foreign taxes on "foreign oil and gas
extraction income" that could be claimed as a credit under §901,
and §907(b) applies a §904(d)-type limitation to the allowable
credit—that is, the limitations of §904 apply separately to foreign
oil-related income.

(8) Sections 908 and 999 further restrict foreign tax credits by providing that credits will be denied for foreign taxes paid on income
generated by virtue of cooperation with an international boycott
(although such taxes can be deducted).

---

[148] Rev. Rul. 73-572, 1973-2 CB 289; see also Dale, supra note 117, at 196–202.

[149] For detailed analysis of this complex provision, see Dale, supra note 117, at
209–221.

For the impact of this provision on §367(a), see Hershey Foods Corp., 76 TC
312 (1981). For a clarification amendment, see the Tax Reform Act of 1986,
§1203(a), adding §904(f)(5); see also Eustice, Kuntz, Lewis, & Deering, supra note 7,
¶ 4.02[4]; Joint Comm. Staff General Explanation, supra note 147, at 909–914.

[150] Pub. L. No. 98-369, §122, 98 Stat. 678, (adding new §§904(d)(3)) and §121
(adding new §904(g)); see Eustice, supra note 6, ¶ 4.05[2]. The first of these amendments, §904(d)(3), was repealed by the Tax Reform Act of 1986 as part of the amendments to §904(d); supra note 147.

The rigors of the above limitation regime, when coupled with the major rate reductions in §11(b) effected by the Tax Reform Act of 1986, seem destined to result in significant amounts of unusable foreign tax credits, at least where domestic corporations are doing business in countries that impose meaningful income-type tax burdens.

¶ 17.12   WESTERN HEMISPHERE TRADE CORPORATIONS

Prior to 1976, a special deduction was allowed by former §922 to a corporation that met the definition of a western hemisphere trade corporation in §921. Although a WHTC had to be engaged in foreign operations to satisfy the definition rules of §921, it was a domestic taxpayer for other U.S. tax purposes. Thus, a WHTC could organize, reorganize, or liquidate tax-free without a §367 ruling; its foreign-source earnings were currently taxable under §11, and domestic losses could be currently offset against its foreign profits; it could join in a consolidated return; dividends paid by a WHTC to corporate shareholders qualified for the §243 deduction (or for elimination in a consolidated return if the affiliated group to which the WHTC belonged elected to be taxed under §1501). Conversely, the §902 credit did not apply to dividends received from a WHTC, and the "effectively connected" rules of §864(c) and the Subpart F rules of §951 had no application to a WHTC.

The Tax Reform Act of 1976 repealed the WHTC provisions, subject to a transition period ending in 1980.[151]

¶ 17.13   POSSESSIONS CORPORATIONS: SECTION 936

In 1976, Congress enacted §936, relating to so-called possessions corporations, to replace former §931, under which these entities had operated for many years.[152] Although the 1976 rules differ materially from pre-1976 law, they continue the basic principle that earnings from U.S. possessions will

---

[151] For discussion of the western hemisphere trade corporation device, see the third edition of this work at ¶ 17.12; and Tillinghast, The Western Hemisphere Trade Corporation: Comparision With Locally Incorporated Entities; Its Utility: Its Future, 28 NYU Inst. on Fed. Tax'n 437 (1970).

[152] For former §931, see the third edition of this work at ¶ 17.13; and see generally Dale, Operating a Business in Puerto Rico Under the Industrial Incentive Act of 1963, 28 NYU Inst. on Fed. Tax'n 359 (1970); Sorlien, Tax Effects of Various Ways in Which United States Companies Can Do Business in Puerto Rico, 28 NYU Inst. on Fed. Tax'n 387 (1970); Goldberg, Tax Effects Upon Getting Out of Puerto Rico: Timing; Techniques; Sale or Liquidation of Business, 28 NYU Inst. on Fed. Tax'n 413 (1970).

not be subject to U.S. taxation.[153] Under prior law, foreign-source income of qualified §931 corporations was exempt from U.S. tax (in essence, a §931 corporation was treated like a foreign corporation in that its foreign-source income was not subject to U.S. tax, it was not entitled to claim most of its deductions or any of its foreign tax credits, its dividend distributions to corporate shareholders qualified for the §902 derivative tax credit, although not for the intercorporate dividends-received deduction of §243, and it was generally immune from exposure to the §531 tax).[154]

Section 936 replaced this pattern with a credit approach, which provision allows qualified electing §936 corporations a credit for their ordinary U.S. taxes[155] attributable to (1) foreign-source taxable income derived from active business within a possession and (2) income from qualified possession-source investment income (defined in §936(d)(2) as earnings from investments in a possession, the funds for which were derived from a possession business and reinvested in a possession). The credit rules of §936 must be affirmatively elected by the qualified corporation (§936(e)), and such election is binding for 10 years unless the Service consents to an earlier revocation. The basic test for qualification under §936(a)(2) contains a two-pronged 80 percent-75 percent rule—that is, 80 percent of its gross income must be derived from possessions sources for the applicable three-year period and 75 percent of its gross income also must be derived from the conduct of an active business during such period within a possession.[156] Also, under §936(h), income from intangibles (e.g., patents, know-how, trademarks, and contracts) is excluded from the calculation and is allocated to the U.S. affiliates of the §936 corporation.[157]

---

[153] See generally Griggs, Operating in Puerto Rico in the Section 936 Era, 32 Tax L. Rev. 239 (1977); Woods & Arbutyn, How the TRA Changes Tax Climate for Using Possessions and WHTC Corporations, 46 J. Tax'n 92 (1977).

[154] The foreign corporation analogy was not complete, however, since §367 rulings were not necessary for transactions involving such corporations, nor were they subjected to the controlled foreign corporation provisions of Subpart F.

[155] The credit is not allowed against the taxes imposed by §59A, §531 or §541 by virtue of §936(a)(3).

[156] Section 936(b) continued the rule of old §931(b) that amounts received within the United States do not qualify for the special credit benefits of this provision. See Rev. Rul. 58-486, 1958-2 CB 392. But the Tax Reform Act of 1986 eased this rule by allowing U.S. receipts of active business income from unrelated payors.

[157] The Tax Reform Act of 1986 modified the intangibles rules of §936(h) in an important respect, requiring an arm's-length royalty charge based on income attributable to the intangibles, H.R. 3838, §1231; see H.R. Conf. Rep. No. 841, 99th Cong., 2d Sess. 631–634 (1986); see also Granwell & Hirsh, The Super Royalty: A New International Tax Concept, 33 Tax Notes 1037 (1986); Griggs, Recent Changes in the Taxation of Section 936 Corporations, 33 Tax Notes 1053 (1986); Joint

The domestic corporation theme is further refined by allowing a §936 corporation to claim a §901 credit for foreign taxes imposed on its nonpossession-source foreign income (by virtue of §936(c)); however, no foreign tax credit or deduction will be allowed for income that is taken into account in computing the credit under §936(a), and such income is taken out of both the numerator and denominator of the §904 limitation by virtue of §904(b)(4).[158] Dividends paid by a §936 corporation to corporate shareholders now will qualify for the intercorporate dividends-received deductions of §243, but a §936 corporation still will not be eligible to file a consolidated return by virtue of §1504(b)(4). Finally, §936(g)(1) exempts income that qualifies for the §936(a) credit from the accumulated taxable income base of §535, while §936(g)(2) includes assets that produce income eligible for the §936 credit as reasonable business needs under §537.

> *To illustrate:* If U.S. parent P has a wholly owned subsidiary S, which derives at least 80 percent of its gross income from sources within a possession and 50 percent of its income from an active business therein, S can elect the benefits of §936; if all of S's taxable income qualifies for the §936(a) credit, S will pay no U.S. tax, since the §936(a) credit will completely eliminate its U.S. tax liability on such income. Any foreign taxes paid on such earnings are not allowable either as a §901 credit or as a §164 deduction to S by virtue of §936(c); dividends paid by S to P qualify for the §243 deduction[159] (but not the §902 credit), and any foreign taxes imposed thereon do not qualify for credit or deduction in the hands of P by virtue of §901(g). P is not entitled to file a consolidated return with S so long as the latter's election is in effect. If S derives some nonpossession-source foreign income (within the 20 percent tolerance permitted by §936(a)(2)), any foreign taxes imposed thereon will qualify for the §901 credit, but §904(b)(4) excludes all of S's §936(a) income from the limitation fraction of §904(a). If P liquidates S under §332, no §367 ruling is necessary (and P is not entitled to any credit or deduction for foreign taxes imposed thereon).

The possessions corporation provisions of §936 effectively serve their avowed purpose of restricting the tax benefits available from such operations to those earnings generated from activities within the possession (or

---

Comm. Staff General Explanation of the Tax Reform Act of 1986, supra note 24, at 999–1006.

[158] Also, §901(g) denies a foreign tax credit or deduction (to shareholders) for any foreign taxes attributable to distributions by §936 corporations.

[159] Either the general 80 percent deduction of §243(a)(1) or the special 100 percent deduction of §243(a)(3). See §243(b)(1)(C).

possessions), thus eliminating what was considered to be one of the principal defects of prior law.

¶ 17.14 FOREIGN SALES CORPORATIONS AND THEIR ANTECEDENTS

1. Introductory. In an effort to spur U.S. export sales, Congress since 1972 has provided tax preferences for special U.S. corporations set up to export U.S. goods abroad. This preference began with the creation of special tax treatment for domestic international sales corporations in 1972 and now continues with similar treatment for foreign sales corporations, which were created to replace DISCs for tax year 1985 and beyond. Although the DISC form was in large part abandoned by the U.S. in 1984 in response to complaints by European nations that the DISC program constituted an illegal export subsidy in violation of the GATT,[160] the provisions and benefits of the new FSC program contained in §§921–927 are strikingly similar to those of the DISC program in §§991–997. An abbreviated treatment of each program is presented below.

2. Domestic international sales corporations: Sections 991–997. In general, DISCs were domestic corporations whose income, for tax years beginning after 1971 and continuing through 1984, was derived primarily from export sales, lease transactions, and certain other export-related activities and investments and whose assets consisted predominantly of qualified export-related assets. The principal function of a DISC was to handle the export sales and leasing activities of a domestic enterprise. Such a corporation was not subject to federal income tax if it elected to be treated as a DISC; instead, approximately one-half of the DISC's earnings was taxed currently to its shareholders as constructive dividends even though not distributed, and the rest of its earnings were not taxable to the shareholders until actually distributed or until a shareholder disposed of his DISC stock in a taxable transaction or the corporation ceased to qualify as a DISC, at which time they were includable, at the shareholder level, as a dividend. In effect, taxation was deferred for approximately one-half of the export earnings of the DISC, the other half being subject to current taxation, as constructive dividends, at the shareholder level. After 1976, however, the tax

---

[160] See Deficit Reduction Act of 1984, S. Rep. No. 169, 98th Cong., 2d Sess. 634–635 (1984) (providing an excellent discussion of the controversy over the status of DISCs under the GATT).

deferral benefits were limited to qualified export receipts in excess of 67 percent of average gross receipts of the DISC for a four-year base period.[161]

Tax deferral treatment of a DISC was an all or nothing proposition. Tax preference was granted only to those corporations for which at least 95 percent of its gross receipts consisted of qualified export receipts (generally those arising from export sales or lease transactions and other export-related activities), and at least 95 percent of its assets (using adjusted basis) at the close of the taxable year consisted of qualified export assets (generally those assets that were export-related, such as property held for sale or lease abroad, and the nonmanufacturing operating assets associated with such export activities). These qualification requirements were much more restrictive than the new FSC rules, which grant tax preference to the foreign income of a FSC regardless of its percentage of the corporation's gross receipts.

3. Foreign Sales Corporations: Sections 921–927. Title V of the Tax Reform Act of 1984 replaced, in large part, the DISC formulation of prior law with a new, equally complex export incentive device, the FSC, which is designed to meet European objections under the GATT to the former DISC taxation framework.

Although the statutory provisions of the FSC legislation defy concise explanation, the core of the FSC framework is apparent from the following definitions:

(a) A foreign sales corporation is defined by §922(a) as a foreign corporation organized under the law of any qualified foreign country (1) that has an adequate tax information exchange agreement in place with the United States[162] or in a possession; (2) that has no more than 25 shareholders; (3) that does not have outstanding preferred stock; (4) that has an office located in a qualified foreign host country and maintains a set of permanent tax records at that office (and in the United States as well); (5) whose board of directors includes at least one nonresident alien individual; (6) that is not a

---

[161] For a general discussion of DISCs, see Gourevitch, DISC's Ability to Defer Tax on Income Restricted by TRA of 1976, 46 J. Tax'n 9 (1977); Rothkoph, DISC: Qualifying Under the New Export Income Laws: Advantages and Hazards, 36 J. Tax'n 130 (1972); DISC: A Handbook for Exporters (published by the Treasury); see also the fourth edition of this work for a more detailed analysis of the DISC rules.

[162] Section 927(e)(3) defines the information exchange requirement to include bilateral or multilateral agreements for the exchange of information appropriate to the enforcement of civil and criminal tax laws and tax treaties certified by Treasury as meeting the above purpose.

See generally Symposium on Compelling Discovery and Disclosure in Transnational Litigation, 16 NYU J. of Int'l L. & Pol. 957 (1984).

member of a controlled group with a DISC member; and (7) whose taxable year (under §441(h)) conforms to the taxable year of its majority stockholder.

(b) "Big FSC-small FSC" status is determined primarily by the size of gross receipts (namely, gross receipts of no more than $5 million) and the filing of an election to be treated as such under §922(b).

(c) Export property gives rise to the tax-favored income for a FSC under §927(a). It consists generally of property of U.S. origin destined for use or consumption outside the United States, namely, property manufactured, produced, grown, or extracted in the United States (including depletable products except for oil and gas) by a person other than a FSC, which is then transferred to or through the FSC for use, ultimate consumption, or disposition outside the United States (i.e., is exported through the FSC).[163] Certain property is excluded from export property status by §927(a)(2): intangibles, property leased by an FSC to affiliates, oil and gas property, subsidized property, and property in short supply.

(d) Foreign trading gross receipts is a specially defined category of tax-favored income in §924(a) that consists of proceeds from the sale or lease of export property, from ancillary services related to such sale or lease of export property, from construction or architectural service fees with respect to non-U.S. projects, and from certain limited types of managerial services.[164] To qualify as foreign trade gross receipts, however, two foreign presence tests in §§924(c) and 924(d) must be satisfied (*except* in the case of small FSCs):[165] (1) the foreign management test[166] (which is relatively easy to satisfy), and (2) the foreign economic processes test[167]

---

[163] No more than 50 percent of the value of such property can be attributable to imported articles, however.

[164] Managerial services rendered to an unrelated FSC in furtherance of the production of other qualified export receipts can qualify, but only if the FSC has at least 50 percent of its gross receipts from such other export activities as well under §924(a)(5).

[165] Small FSCs are excused from these tests by §924(b)(2).

[166] The foreign management test of §924(c) will be met if all director and shareholder meetings are outside of the United States, its principle bank account is foreign, and all dividends, professional fees, and salaries are disbursed from that foreign bank account.

[167] Section 924(d) provides that the FSC must participate (outside the United States) in the solicitation, the negotiation, or the making of the contract giving rise to the foreign gross receipts transaction and that at least 50 percent of that transaction's cost must be incurred by the FSC (or at least 85 percent of the costs of each of two of the five listed activities for determining the alternative cost requirement in §924(e), which are (1) advertising and sales promotion, (2) processing of orders and arranging for delivery, (3) transportation, (4) billing and collection, and (5) assumption of credit risk).

(which focuses on transactional participation by the FSC). Both of these tests are designed to ensure that the FSC, unlike a DISC, is actually located abroad and conducts a real business enterprise outside the United States.

(e) Exempt foreign trade income is, under §923, the tax benefit amount that is granted with respect to the FSC's qualified income (i.e., gross income attributable to FTGR); this exemption depends upon whether or not the FSC's income is determined under the special administrative transfer pricing rules of §925.[168] If those rules are used, then the exempt amount is 16/23 of foreign-trade income; if not, then the exempt amount is 32 percent. Section 921(b) requires that a proportionate amount of deductions must be allocated to the exempt foreign trading income, and §921(c) denies any credits (other than foreign tax credits) to a FSC.

In its simplest form, use of the FSC structure would involve a U.S. manufacturing parent organizing a foreign sales subsidiary in a qualified host country (i.e., one with an acceptable tax information-exchange agreement) and selling its products to the FSC, which would then resell such products abroad. (Alternatively, the FSC could operate as a commission agent with respect to such export sales.) Depending upon whether the special administrative profit-split rules of §925 are involved or whether actual prices (subject to §482) are used, the FSC would be entitled to exclude either 16/23 or 32 percent of its income (less allocable deductions) and would be taxable on the rest.[169] Distributions out of exempt income earnings qualify for a 100 percent deduction to a domestic corporate shareholder under §245(c).

If a qualified FSC derives qualified foreign export receipts under the preceding rules, the applicable amount (in §923) is excluded from gross income and allocable deductions are disallowed by §§921(a) and 921(b). (Credits, other than the foreign tax credit, are denied by §921(c).) The rest of the FSC's net income is taxable under §921(d) as effectively connected U.S.-source income unless the special §921(d)(1)(B) provides that the FSC will be taxed like a regular foreign corporation on such foreign-trade income. Interest income, dividends, royalties, other investment income, and carrying charges on credit sales will be taxable as effectively connected U.S.-source income.

Distributions by a FSC (while not required) are deemed to come first from the FSC's qualified foreign-trade income earnings under §926(a). Distributions to foreign shareholders of the FSC from its foreign trade earnings

---

[168] There are two special related party transfer pricing systems under §925(a) of the Code. The first allows the FSC to make a taxable income profit equal to 1.83 percent of foreign trading gross receipts; the second would split combined taxable income of the related party and the FSC in a 77-to-23 ratio. These rules can be used only if the FSC performs all of the activities listed in §924(e); supra note 167.

[169] For examples see Deficit Reduction Act of 1984, S. Rep. No. 169, 98th Cong., 2d Sess. 648–651, 655–656.

are treated as U.S.-source business income under §926(b), while distribution of such earnings to U.S. corporate shareholders generally are exempt (i.e., they qualify for the 100 percent dividends received deduction of §245(c)).[170]

4. The transition from DISC to FSC. While the FSC rules generally replace the DISC provisions, "small" DISCs (i.e., those with $10,000,000 or less of qualified export receipts) can continue to defer taxability under the DISC rules. Section 995(f) imposes a special interest charge on the shareholders of these "old" DISCs, however, based on the deferred tax liability attributable to the income retained by the DISC. The FSC rules generally became effective in 1985, but special transition rules were provided to deal with conversion from the DISC to the FSC system.[171] The new FSC legislation also makes the conversion from DISC to FSC considerably less painful by granting tax-deferred income accumulated in an existing DISC at the time of the changeover a permanent exemption from U.S. taxation.[172]

¶ 17.15   INTERNATIONAL BOYCOTTS: SECTION 999

The Tax Reform Act of 1976 denied various tax benefits attributable to foreign earnings that were generated by participation in, or cooperation with, an international boycott; thus, §908 denies credit (although not a deduction) for foreign taxes on boycott-related income. Sections 995(b)(1)(F)(ii) and 927(c)(2) deny DISC and FSC benefits for such income, and §952(a)(3) denies tax deferral for such earnings produced by a controlled foreign corporation. The basic statutory provisions dealing with boycotts are in §999.[173]

---

[170] Section 245(c)(2) permits the 100 percent deduction only for dividends from *exempted* foreign trade earnings in cases where the special pricing rules of §925 are not used. If those special rules are used, all dividends from foreign trade earnings qualify.

[171] See the Tax Reform Act of 1984, H.R. Rep. No. 861, 98th Cong., 2d Sess. 659–661.

[172] The Tax Reform Act of 1984, §805(b)(2). This amnesty is not total; it merely converts the tax-deferred DISC income to previously taxed income, which then can be withdrawn without further tax.

See generally Eustice, supra note 6, ¶ 4.05[1]; Sharp, Steele, & Jacobson, Foreign Sales Corporations: Export Analysis and Planning, 63 Taxes 163 (1985); Granwell & Rosensweig, An Analysis of the Foreign Sales Corporation Provisions and Rules, 28 Tax Notes 1266 (1985); for Temporary Regulations, see TD 7993, 1985-1 CB 248, and TD 7994, 1985-1 CB 258, issued Dec. 12, 1984.

[173] See generally Flynn, International Boycotts, 29 So. Calif. Tax Inst. 139 (1977); Rubenfeld, Legal and Tax Implications of Participation in International Boy-

---

PART C. FOREIGN PERSONAL HOLDING COMPANIES AND FOREIGN INVESTMENT COMPANIES

¶ 17.20 INTRODUCTORY

The foreign personal holding company provisions (§§551–558) were enacted in 1937 after a congressional investigation brought to light the formation of a number of "incorporated pocketbooks" in the Bahama Islands, Panama, and Canada by citizens of the United States. Dividends, interest, and other types of investment income were thus realized by U.S.-owned corporations domiciled in countries with low or no income taxes; and the corporations might also be employed to avoid U.S. taxes on the sale of the income-producing property, to create deductions to their affiliates or shareholders, and for more esoteric manipulations.

For jurisdictional and administrative reasons, Congress decided to close this set of tax loopholes by taxing the U.S. shareholders of foreign personal holding companies on their proportionate shares of the corporation's undistributed income, rather than by imposing a penalty tax on the corporation itself. The constitutionality of this procedure was assumed in *Eder v. CIR*.[174]

Somewhat similar in form and function to the closely held foreign investment company was the foreign-based mutual fund, which, although widely held (and hence not subject to the foreign personal holding company provisions), was owned primarily by domestic shareholders. It was designed

---

cotts, 32 Tax L. Rev. 613 (1977); Kaplan, Income Taxes and the Arab Boycott, 32 Tax Lawyer 313 (1979).

For boycott determination ruling procedures, see Rev. Proc. 77-9, 1977-1 CB 542. See also Temp. Regs. §7.999-1 for computing the boycott factor, adopted by TD 7467, 1977-1 CB 243 (Feb. 2, 1977). Boycott Form 5713, with instructions and schedules, was issued in mid-1977; new guidelines, which superseded the earlier guidelines, were published in 1978-1 CB 521.

174 Eder v. CIR, 138 F2d 27 (2d Cir. 1943); see also Helvering v. National Grocery Co., 304 US 282 (1938), as to the power of Congress to tax undistributed corporate income to the shareholder; Alvord v. CIR, 277 F2d 713 (4th Cir. 1960), holding that the FPHC tax could not be imposed on the majority shareholder of a FPHC for years in which the United States, as the result of a tax assessment, prevented the distribution of its income.

See Alexander, Foreign Personal Holding Companies and Foreign Corporations That Are Personal Holding Companies, 67 Yale L.J. 1173 (1958); Lerner & Kirschbaum, Foreign Personal Holding Companies, Tax Mgmt. Portfolio (BNA) No. 103-2d (1986); Lowe, Curacao Investment Companies: Some Shoals in a Tax Haven, 16 Tax L. Rev. 177 (1961).

For the early history of these provisions, see Rudick, §102 and Personal Holding Company Provisions of the Internal Revenue Code, 49 Yale L.J. 171 (1939); Paul, The Background of the Revenue Act of 1937, 5 U. Chi. L. Rev. 41 (1937).

to serve as an investment vehicle for the tax-free accumulation of income that was not taxed (or taxed very lightly) by the country of incorporation and that was simultaneously exempt from U.S. taxation because it was derived from foreign sources. Congress responded to this problem in the Revenue Act of 1962 by providing, in general, for ordinary income treatment when the shareholder sold or exchanged his stock.

Legislation enacted in 1984 revised and tightened the foreign personal holding company and foreign investment company provisions.[175] The Tax Reform Act of 1986 enacted an entirely new regime for the taxation of U.S. shareholders of passive foreign investment companies (such shareholders generally will be charged interest for the deferral privilege or, alternatively, will be taxed currently on the corporation's undistributed income if the PFIC elects such treatment).[176]

¶ 17.21 FOREIGN PERSONAL HOLDING COMPANIES: DEFINITION

"Foreign personal holding company" is defined by §552 to mean any foreign corporation (except tax-exempt corporations and certain foreign banking corporations) that meets the following two conditions:

(1) At least 60 percent (50 percent in some instances) of its gross income for the taxable year is "foreign personal holding company income." This term (whose scope is similar to "personal holding company income" under pre-1964 law (see Chapter 8)) is defined by §553 to include the following categories of income: (a) dividends, interest, and royalties; (b) the excess of gains over losses from sales of stocks, securities, and commodity futures contracts;[177] (c) income from an estate or trust or from the sale of an interest therein; (d) income from certain personal service contracts; (e) compensation for the use of corporate property by a 25 percent shareholder; and (f) rents, if they constitute less than 50 percent of gross income.

In keeping with the purpose of the FPHC provisions,"gross income" is defined by §555(a) for this purpose to include foreign-source income as well as income from domestic sources.

[175] The Tax Reform Act of 1984, §§132 and 134 (enacted July 18, 1984); see Eustice, supra note 6, ¶ 4.05[3].

[176] H.R. 3838, §1235, enacting new §§1291–1297; see H.R. Conf. Rep. No. 841, 99th Cong., 2d Sess. 640–645 (1986); infra ¶ 17.25.

[177] Mariani Frozen Foods, Inc., 81 TC 448 (1983), aff'd sub nom. Gee Trust v. CIR, 761 F2d 1410 (9th Cir. 1985) (stock gain includes profit attributable to foreign currency fluctuation; currency gain not a separate commodity profit here).

(2) At any time during the taxable year, more than 50 percent in vote or value of the corporation's outstanding stock is owned, directly or indirectly, by not more than five individuals who are citizens or residents of the United States. Section 554 applies constructive ownership rules that are virtually identical to those for domestic PHCs.[178]

By virtue of §542(c)(5), the FPHC provisions take precedence over the PHC provisions, but a foreign corporation that is not a FPHC may be caught up in the meshes of the PHC provisions (unless immunized by §542(c)(7)), or it may be subject to the accumulated earnings tax of §531.

¶ 17.22   TAXATION OF FOREIGN PERSONAL HOLDING COMPANY INCOME TO SHAREHOLDERS: SECTION 551

Once it is determined that a corporation is an FPHC, each U.S. shareholder is required by §551(b) to include in gross income the amount he would have received as a dividend if his share of the corporation's undistributed FPHC income had been distributed to him. "Undistributed foreign personal holding company income" is defined by §556 as taxable income, with certain adjustments, less the dividends-paid deduction of §561.[179] Because the U.S. shareholder is taxed on undistributed income, he is permitted to increase the basis of his stock as though the constructive dividend had been reinvested in the corporation as a contribution to capital.[180] However, FPHCs are also subject to §1014(b)(5)—that is, basis of stock is not stepped up on a stockholder's death.

---

[178] Supra ¶ 8.23; but see Estate of Nettie Miller, 43 TC 760 (1965) (nonacq.), holding that (1) stock owned by foreigners was not attributable to their brother, a U.S. citizen, so as to make the corporation a FPHC, when the brother was not himself a sharcholder; and (2) certain bearer warrants (with voting and dividend rights) were stock. But the Tax Reform Act of 1984 amended the constructive ownership rules of §544 in new §544(c) to essentially codify the result in *Nettie Miller* (i.e., stock of nonresident individual not attributed to U.S. citizen or resident under family rules, except for spouse).

The Tax Reform Act of 1986 (H.R. 3838, §1222(b)) tightened the stock ownership requirement of §552(a)(2) by testing such ownership in terms of vote *or* value; prior to this amendment, only value was used.

[179] Supra ¶ 8.24; under §562(b) liquidating distributions by an FPHC do not qualify for this deduction. See also John D. Gray, 71 TC 719 (1979) (timing of FPHC constructive dividend income where corporation on fiscal year, U.S. shareholders on calendar year, and FPHC status terminated by U.S. shareholders' sale of their stock).

[180] Mariani Frozen Foods, Inc., supra note 177 (stock basis step-up for deemed capital contribution occurs at end of FPHC's taxable year).

Several features of these rules bear special comment. The constructive dividend of §551 is assigned to all U.S. shareholders (individual or corporate) who were shareholders on the last day on which the U.S. group (i.e., the five or fewer individual U.S. shareholders owning more than 50 percent) existed; thus the guilty infect the innocent, once FPHC status is found to exist.[181] Owners of FPHCs cannot hide behind a foreign corporation to avoid liability in view of §551(f), which provides that income will flow through foreign entities interposed between U.S. taxpayers and the FPHC to the ultimate beneficiaries.[182] The constructive dividend mechanism of §551 is similar to the Subchapter S rules of §1361 (see Chapter 6), with the important exception that the latter are elective, rather than mandatory; §551 also resembles the controlled foreign corporation rules of §951 (discussed later in this chapter) and, where the two overlap, §951 controls by virtue of §951(d).[183] The constructive dividend base of §556 includes capital gains as well as ordinary investment income from dividends and interest, unlike the §§531 and 541 corporate penalty taxes, which exclude capital gains from the corporate penalty tax. Moreover, there is no deficiency dividend procedure for FPHCs as there is for domestic PHCs.

¶ 17.23 FOREIGN PERSONAL HOLDING COMPANY VS. UNITED STATES PERSONAL HOLDING COMPANY

The relationship between the PHC provisions of §541 and the FPHC rules of §551 can become quite intricate, although the possibility of overlap was materially reduced by changes in the PHC definition rules effected by the Foreign Investors' Tax Act of 1966.[184] The major 1966 Act change in the

---

[181] But see Silvio Gutierrez, 53 TC 394 (1969), aff'd per curiam, 29 AFTR2d 358 (D.C. Cir. 1971) (alien shareholder only taxed under §551 on portion of FPHC income attributable to that part of the year he was a resident of the United States).

[182] The Tax Reform Act of 1984, §132(b), added §551(f), which imposes an income imputation tracing rule through tiers of various foreign entities, thus eliminating the use of foreign entity circuit breakers to stop the flow of FPHC income.

[183] This result came about when the Tax Reform Act of 1984 amended §951(d) to resolve a conflict in the cases in favor of priority for §951. For the background of this amendment, see Woo, *Estate of Lovett*: The Continuing Conflict Between the Code Provisions Governing Controlled Foreign Corporations and the Foreign Personal Holding Company Regulations, 10 J. Corp. Tax'n 242 (1983).

[184] See generally Hochberg, The Foreign Investors' Tax Act: Its Impact on Personal Holding Companies, 27 J. Tax'n 118 (1967).

Section 542(c)(5) provides that §551 prevails over §541 if the two overlap. See also Mariani Frozen Foods, Inc., supra note 177 (concurrent application of FPHC and PHC rules to affiliated chain; constructive dividend from FPHC subsidiary turned parent into a PHC).

PHC definition area was the amendment of §542(c)(7), which generally excludes foreign corporations (other than ones that have §543(a)(7) loaned-out services income) from the definition of PHCs if *all* of their outstanding stock during the last half of the year is owned by nonresident aliens. Moreover, §545(a) was amended to provide that if a foreign corporation is owned 90 percent or more by foreign shareholders during the last half of its taxable year, the §545(a) tax base only includes that portion of the undistributed PHC income equal to the highest percentage of stock owned by U.S. persons during such period.[185] The general purpose of these amendments was to eliminate the all foreign owned investment company from the ambit of §541 in view of the fact that nonresident alien individuals became taxable on their gross U.S.-source investment income under the new rules at only the flat 30 percent rate of §871(a); hence, §541 was no longer necessary to prevent the use of foreign corporations to shelter investment income of such persons from the progressive individual tax rates.[186]

The salient differences between the provisions of §§541 and 551 are summarized generally by the following table:

Definition	§541 PHC	§551 FPHC
Type of income	§543 (rents tougher,[187] but no capital gain)	§553 (rents easier,[188] but includes capital gain)
Percentage of tainted income	60 percent of adjusted ordinary gross	60 percent of gross
Stock ownership	Five or fewer individuals own more than 50 percent during last half of year	Five or fewer individuals own more than 50 percent at any time
Overlap	Yields to §551	Controls over §541

(continues)

---

[185] Note that this provision technically eliminates all taxable §545 income if the foreign corporation is 100 percent foreign-owned during the last half of its taxable year.

But compare §545(d), which provides that taxable income for purposes of §545(a) includes only §543(a)(3) (loaned-out services) income, less allocable deductions, in the case of a 100 percent foreign owned foreign corporation. How this provision relates to §545(a) (which only includes income in proportion to U.S. stock ownership) remains to be seen.

[186] Note that as a result of the Tax Reform Act of 1986 rate amendments, the top rate of §§11 and 541 is 28 percent, two points lower than the rates in §§871 and 881.

[187] The provisions defining rents as PHC income were materially tightened by the Revenue Act of 1964; supra ¶ 8.22.

[188] Section 553 continued the pre-1964 exemption for rents as FPHC income if they constitute 50 percent or more of gross income.

Mechanics and Operation	§541 PHC	§551 FPHC
Who taxed	The corporation	All U.S. shareholders [189]
Method	28 percent penalty tax	Constructive dividend and step-up of stock basis
Foreign tax credits?	Yes, but only against §11 tax	No pass-through to shareholders
Tax base	Capital gain eliminated	Capital gain included
Escape batch?	§547 deficiency dividend	None
Effect on shareholders	None	No stepped-up basis at death

¶ 17.24   FOREIGN INVESTMENT COMPANIES: SECTIONS 1246 AND 1247

A popular accumulation device prior to 1962 was the foreign investment company, typically based in Canada, Bermuda, or Curacao.[190] Like the FPHC device, foreign investment companies offered an attractive method for a large group of U.S. shareholders to convert ordinary dividend and interest income into capital gain. Such a company would be lightly taxed (or not taxed at all) in the country of its organization and similarly would pay no U.S. tax, since it invested in foreign securities and had no taxable U.S.-source income. Thus, the current earnings of the company could be accumulated virtually tax-free: The U.S. shareholders would not be taxed currently on these accumulations; and the enhanced value of the shareholders' stock due to this accumulation feature would ultimately be taxed as capital gain on the sale or redemption of the stock.[191]

The Revenue Act of 1962 attacked this device in one of two ways, depending upon the election that the foreign investment company made. Under the first alternative, the U.S. shareholder will realize ordinary income on the sale or redemption of his stock in a foreign investment company[192] to

---

[189] The 1984 legislation imposed an income imputation rule through tiers of foreign entities as well; supra note 182.

[190] See Lowe, supra note 174.

[191] Rev. Rul. 60-192, 1960-1 CB 142, allowed capital gain on redemption of stock in a Canadian mutual fund, despite the stated policy of the fund to accumulate all current earnings.

[192] Defined in §1246(b) as a foreign corporation that is either registered under the Investment Company Act of 1940 or is engaged in a similar business and at least 50 percent of its stock (by vote or value) is owned by U.S. persons. The stock ownership threshold was lowered by the Tax Reform Act of 1984 (formerly the line had been more than 50 percent of value).

the extent of his ratable share of the earnings accumulated by such company (after 1962) during the period he held his stock under §1246. The burden of establishing his ratable share is on the shareholder, and if he fails to prove this figure, the entire gain will be ordinary income under §1246(a)(3). Similarly, the ordinary income potential of such tainted stock will survive a gift of the stock, a tax-free exchange of the stock, and the death of the holder of such stock.[193]

As an alternative to the above treatment, §1247 allowed a foreign investment company registered under the Investment Company Act of 1940 to elect to have the U.S. shareholders taxed substantially like shareholders in domestic regulated investment companies under §§851–855. The election had to be made before 1963 and was binding for all future years. This meant that the U.S. shareholder would be taxed currently on the ordinary income of such an investment company, since 90 percent of this income had to be distributed annually; capital gains were passed through and taxed at the shareholder level, whether distributed or not.[194] If, as expected, most foreign investment companies took the latter treatment, the tax advantages of predominantly U.S.-owned foreign mutual funds were effectively neutralized after 1962. It is hard to quarrel with this result, since the growth of these funds was largely due to the tax advantage they offered to U.S. investors.

The type of foreign investment company covered by the provisions of §§1246 and 1247 should be compared with the offshore investment funds (described earlier in this chapter). In the former situation, the statute generally requires at least 50 percent ownership (of vote or value) by U.S. persons for the provisions of §§1246 and 1247 to apply; moreover, the typical investment pattern of such corporations was investing or trading in the stock or securities of other foreign corporations. By contrast, the offshore fund is predominantly foreign-owned and is formed for the purpose of investing in stock or securities of U.S. corporations. Since these funds ordinarily are structured so as not to be engaged in business within the U.S., they are taxable only on dividends, interest, and rents from domestic sources under §881; capital gains are exempt, since they do not constitute fixed or determinable annual or periodic income.

It was possible, although perilous, to push a foreign investment company into the cracks between §§551, 951, 1246 and 1247, however, if care

---

The Tax Reform Act of 1984 also expanded the definition of §1246(b) to include trading in commodities, futures contracts, forward contracts, and options.

[193] For example, on a transfer to a controlled corporation under §351, §1246(c) provides that both the corporate transferee and the shareholder would have tainted stock. For the death rules, see §1246(e).

[194] But the shareholder could increase his basis to reflect the undistributed capital gain that he was required to include in income; §1247(e)(2).

was taken to divide ownership of the corporation in a complex fashion. Thus, if stock ownership was spread equally among 11 or more unrelated individuals, neither §541 nor §551 could apply (since five or fewer persons must own more than 50 percent of the stock under those sections); this tactic also avoids classification as a controlled foreign corporation under §§957 and 1248, which are applicable only if more than 50 percent of the corporation is owned by U.S. persons, but in making this determination take account of 10 percent shareholders only. However, foreign ownership of more than 50 percent is required to avoid §1246 status, regardless of how widely the stock is held. This can be achieved if the foreign corporation is owned five-elevenths by five equal, unrelated U.S. shareholders, and six-elevenths by six equal, unrelated foreign shareholders. Needless to say, a creature of so complex a parentage is not likely to be encountered frequently or to survive for long without a fatal family quarrel. In any event, the PFIC rules established by the Tax Reform Act of 1986 will ensnare *any* U.S. investor in a PFIC, regardless of the level or dispersion of that ownership. Thus, the PFIC rules should largely swallow the more modestly targeted rules of §1246.

¶ 17.25 PASSIVE FOREIGN INVESTMENT COMPANIES: SECTIONS 1291–1297

The Tax Reform Act of 1986 created an entirely new system for the taxation of U.S. shareholders who invest in a passive foreign investment company. A PFIC is defined by §1296(a) as any foreign corporation that has either (1) 75 percent of its gross income as passive income (defined in §1296(b)(1) by reference to the passive income definition under the §904(d) separate basket rules, but with an exception for real banks and insurance companies in §1296(b)(2)) or (2) 50 percent (by value) of its assets as passive assets (i.e., assets producing, or held for the production of, passive income). No U.S. ownership size limitation is provided here; the definition instead focuses entirely on the corporate-level income and asset characteristics and, as a result, is much broader in scope than the provisions discussed in the preceding section.

The U.S. shareholder of PFIC is hit with an interest charge on the value of the deferral privilege by §1291 when he disposes of his PFIC stock (or receives substantial distributions thereon); alternatively, if the PFIC elects "qualified election fund" status under §1295, the shareholder is taxed currently under §1293 on the undistributed earnings of the PFIC (and the §1295 election is permanent). The shareholder, however, can defer payment of the tax on undistributed income imposed under §1293 by electing an extension of time to pay such tax under §1294, although failure of the fund to elect under §1295 will deny stepped-up basis at death for the investors under §1291(e), in a similar manner as the rules of §1246(e). The net effect of these provisions is to remove the economic benefit attributable to tax deferral for those who choose to invest in passive foreign investment vehicles.[195]

Qualification as a PFIC has the following additional collateral consequences:

(1) The accumulated earnings tax does not apply under §532(b)(4);

(2) The PHC rules of §541 do not apply under §542(c)(10);

(3) If the FPHC rules of §551 also apply to a PFIC that elected current taxability status as a QEF, §551 takes priority under §551(g);

(4) A similar rule also gives §951 priority if it overlaps a QEF/PFIC under §951(f); and

(5) The PFIC rules preempt §1246 for post-1986 earnings and profits under §1297(b)(7).

¶ 17.26   ACCUMULATED EARNINGS TAX ASPECTS

The regulations have long provided that §531 is applicable to a foreign corporation, whether resident or nonresident, with respect to its U.S.-source income if any of its shareholders would be subject to U.S. tax on distributions of the foreign corporation.[196] Thus, a U.S.-owned foreign corporation doing business in the United States, or deriving income from U.S. sources, could be subject to the §531 tax if it unreasonably accumulates its income (see Chapter 8). Conversely, if none of the foreign corporation's income would be taxable on distribution from the foreign corporation or if all of the foreign corporation's income is foreign source the §531 tax would not apply, either because the shareholder tax-avoidance purpose would be lacking in the first instance or because the §535 tax base (which is derived from taxable income) would be zero in the second.

Attempts to insulate U.S.-owned foreign corporations from exposure to the §531 tax by creating tiers of foreign corporations (e.g., a foreign parent holding company, incorporated in a taxhaven country, with a controlled foreign subsidiary deriving income from the United States, that distributes all of its current earnings to the foreign parent) inspired enactment of §535(d)

---

[195] See H.R. Conf. Rep. No. 841, 99th Cong., 2d Sess. 640–645 (1986); Joint Comm. Staff General Explanation of the Tax Reform Act of 1986, supra note 24, at 1021–1034 (1987). See also Rubenfeld, Passive Foreign Investment Companies: The Pentapus Becomes the Sextapus: Or Does It?, 36 Tax Notes 199 (1987).

[196] Regs. §1.532-1(c).

in 1984,[197] preserving U.S.-source treatment for the initially U.S.-source income as it flows up the chain of foreign corporations and hence subjects the corporation ultimately accumulating such income to the §531 tax.

PART D.　CONTROLLED FOREIGN CORPORATIONS

¶ 17.30　INTRODUCTORY

Under §§881 and 882, foreign corporations generally are taxed on their income from U.S. sources only, and a foreign corporation not engaged in trade or business here is taxed on such income only to the extent that it is derived from dividends, interest, and other "fixed or determinable annual or periodical" sources.[198] Because the foreign-source income of a foreign corporation is not generally subject to U.S. taxation (while domestic corporations are taxed on their worldwide income), American corporations and individuals frequently find it advantageous to segregate their foreign business activities in a foreign corporation, especially if the country in which the operations are conducted taxes business income at a lower rate than the United States. In this way, no U.S. tax need be paid until the foreign corporation's earnings are repatriated in the form of dividends or a liquidating distribution to its U.S. shareholders or until they sell their stock. At that time, the shareholders report their receipts or profit as dividend income or capital gain, as the case may be.[199] If dividends are received by a domestic corporation owning at least 10 percent of the voting stock of the foreign corporation, it is entitled to a foreign tax credit for its share of the subsidiary's foreign income taxes as deemed-paid or derivative credit under §902(a).[200]

When the foreign corporation and its U.S. parent (or its U.S. shareholders, if it is not a wholly owned subsidiary) are engaged in several aspects of a single enterprise—for example, if the foreign corporation is a sales subsidiary of a U.S. manufacturer—their intercompany transactions take on a special

---

[197] The Tax Reform Act of 1984, H.R. 4170, §125, adding §535(d). See Eustice, supra note 6, ¶ 3.05[2][b].

[198] The source rules are prescribed by §§861–864, which make no special reference to foreign corporations. See Dailey, supra note 2; supra ¶¶ 17.02–17.04.

[199] The shareholder's gain on a sale or liquidation of a corporation may be taxable as ordinary income, under rules enacted in 1962, if it is a foreign investment company (supra ¶ 17.24), a PFIC (supra ¶ 17.25), or a controlled foreign corporation; infra ¶ 17.34.

[200] Under §902(b), the deemed paid credit also extends to second- and third-tier foreign corporations in the circumstances described supra ¶ 17.11. See generally supra Parts A and B of this chapter.

importance because the foreign corporation's share of the enterprise's world-wide income is not taxed by the United States until repatriation. In recent years, the Service manifested a much greater interest in these arrangements than previously, recognizing that the deferral of U.S. tax on earnings that are segregated in the foreign corporation may continue for many years, perhaps permanently. In demanding that the foreign corporation and its domestic parent adopt an arm's-length pattern for their intercompany transactions, the Service relies primarily on §482 (reallocation of income, deductions, etc., among related taxpayers), but it also can call upon assignment of income principles, form vs. substance, the step transaction doctrine, and §446(b) (accounting method must clearly reflect income) as sources of authority.[201]

In 1961, the Treasury asked Congress to provide detailed rules for the allocation of income and expenses arising in foreign operations, and the House version of the Revenue Act of 1962 amended §482 accordingly; this change was eliminated in conference, however, with a statement that the Treasury "should explore the possibility of developing and promulgating regulations under [§482, as it exists] which would provide additional guide-lines and formulas for the allocation of income and deductions in cases involving foreign income."[202] In 1966, the first installment of proposed regulations pursuant to this legislative direction were issued, and final regulations were adopted in 1968. These administrative procedures recognized that the reallocation of income or deductions after the close of a taxable year had unusually complex ramifications in the domestic-foreign arena, since the foreign corporation's foreign income taxes were computed in accord with the original arrangements between the parties and would not necessarily be refunded merely because the United States determined that the foreign subsidiary had received too large a share of the enterprise's worldwide income. Moreover, §482 allocations may alter the character of amounts received by

---

[201] See Asiatic Petroleum Co. v. CIR, 79 F2d 234 (2d Cir. 1935), cert. denied, 296 US 645 (1935); Hay v. CIR, supra note 17; see also supra ¶ 1.05. The source rules (supra ¶ 17.02) contain their own allocation principles; see Regs. §§1.863-1 and 1.861-8 (1977).

See generally Plumb & Kapp, Reallocation of Income and Deductions Under Section 482, 41 Taxes 809 (1963); general discussion supra ¶ 15.03.

See also Treasury Department News Release, Study of Administration of §482 to International Business Transactions Between US Corporations and Their Foreign Subsidiaries (Jan. 8, 1973), reported in 1973 Fed. Taxes (P-H) ¶ 54,956; Bischel, Tax Allocations Concerning Inter-Company Pricing Transactions in Foreign Operations: A Reappraisal, 13 Va. J. Int'l L. 490 (1973); Note, Multinational Corporations and Income Allocation Under Section 482 of the Internal Revenue Code, 89 Harv. L. Rev. 1202 (1976).

[202] See 4 Hearings on President's 1961 Tax Recommendations, House Committee on Ways and Means, 87th Cong., 1st Sess. 3534–3551 (1961); H.R. Rep. No. 2508, 87th Cong., 2d Sess. (1962), reprinted in 1962-3 CB 1129 and 1146.

the foreign corporation's shareholders and their right to the foreign tax credit.[203]

Before 1962, the statutory pattern of exempting foreign corporations from U.S. tax on their foreign-source income and taxing these earnings to their U.S. shareholders only on repatriation—the deferral privilege—was subject to an exception for FPHCs. As already explained, the tax-avoidance potential of such corporations is nullified by requiring their U.S. shareholders to report the corporate income as earned, even if it is not distributed to them. In 1962, a similar, yet more far reaching, requirement was enacted for "controlled foreign corporations," under which their U.S. shareholders must currently report their pro rata share of certain categories of foreign income, even though it is not distributed to them. Because the 1962 rules embrace foreign corporations engaged in ordinary business operations, however, they are far more important than the FPHC provisions. In addition to taxing the U.S. shareholders of a controlled foreign corporation on its undistributed foreign income, §1248 provides that the shareholder's gain on a sale, exchange, or redemption of the stock of such a corporation or on a liquidating distribution is taxable as ordinary dividend income, rather than as capital gain, in circumstances described later in this section.

¶ 17.31   THE "CONTROLLED FOREIGN CORPORATION"

In examining the 1962 rules applicable to "controlled foreign corporations,"[204] it should be borne in mind that no change was made in the traditional tax pattern for foreign corporations, under which foreign-source income ordinarily is not taxed to the corporation itself. Whether or not foreign corporations with U.S. shareholders could be subjected to the full force of U.S. taxation on their foreign income without violating international law, there are obvious difficulties in imposing such a tax if the corporation has some foreign shareholders; and Subpart F, like the FPHC provisions, sidesteps the problem by selecting the corporation's U.S. shareholders as its target. In an effort to cover every contingency, the rules of Subpart F share the complexity that typifies virtually all Code provisions dealing with foreign corporations and transactions, yet in the end it turns many tasks over to the Treasury to discharge by regulations.[205] The description of Subpart F that

---

[203] For detailed discussion of §482, see supra ¶ 15.03.

[204] Subpart F (§§951–964) of Part Il, Subchapter N of the 1954 Code.

[205] See generally McDonald, Controlled Foreign Corporations, 5 Inst. on Priv. Inv. & Inv. Abroad 5 (Southwestern Legal Foundation 1963); O'Connor, United States Taxation of Earnings of American-Controlled Foreign Corporations, 42 Taxes 588 (1964); Harris, Foreign Base Companies Under the 1962 Act; Relief Provisions and Areas for Tax Planning, 1964 So. Calif. Tax Inst. 287; Tillinghast, Problems of

follows has been kept within manageable limits only by ruthlessly suppressing many details. In particular, the special rules applicable to income from insuring U.S. risks and to corporations organized in Puerto Rico are not set out. Moreover, the discussion assumes that the income of the foreign corporation in question is attributable entirely to foreign sources, so that no U.S. tax was payable.

1. Corporations subject to Subpart F. The heart of Subpart F is the "controlled foreign corporation," defined by §957(a) as a foreign corporation more than 50 percent of whose total combined voting power or value is owned by U.S. shareholders on any day of the taxable year in question.[206] A "United States shareholder" is a "United States person" (defined by §7701(a)(30) to mean a citizen or resident of the United States, a domestic partnership or corporation, or a nonforeign trust or estate) who owns 10 percent or more of the corporation's total combined voting power. For these purposes, and for others, stock owned indirectly and constructively as well as directly is taken into account by §958.[207]

---

the Small or Closely Held Corporation Under the Revenue Act of 1962, 22 NYU Inst. on Fed. Tax'n 697 (1964); Friedman & Silbert, Final Regulations on Controlled Foreign Corporations and Less Developed Country Corporations, 22 NYU Inst. on Fed. Tax'n 811 (1964); Ross, United States Jurisdiction to Tax Foreign Income, XL1Xb Studies on International Fiscal Law (Int'l Fiscal Ass'n, Hamburg 1964); Olsen & Choate, Foreign Operations—Base Companies, Tax Mgmt. Portfolio (BNA) No. 23-4th (1976).

The enactment of Subpart F, under which the income, earnings and profits, and other financial data for foreign corporations are more important than under pre-1962 law, brought to the fore a number of difficulties in the computation of such amounts for enterprises whose books and records are often inconsistent with U.S. standards, and that have not had to make the elections (e.g., accounting and depreciation methods) that are usually a prerequisite to the determination of earnings and profits. See articles by Weiss, Hutchison, Stock, & Wilcox, 23 NYU Inst. on Fed. Tax'n 981, 1017, and 1059 (1965); Weiss, Earnings and Profits and the Determination of the Foreign Tax Credit, 43 Taxes 849 (1965).

[206] The Tax Reform Act of 1986 amended the definition in §957(a) (from a vote-only test of ownership to one of vote or value); see H.R. Conf. Rep. No. 841, 99th Cong., 2d Sess. 626. See generally Eustice, Kuntz, Lewis, & Deering, supra note 7, ¶ 4.03[2].

[207] See Alexander, Controlled Foreign Corporations and Constructive Ownership, 18 Tax L. Rev. 531 (1963); on the constructive ownership rules of §318, see supra ¶ 9.03

For attempts to use "paired" or "stapled" stock arrangements to avoid CFC status, see Cliff, Pairing: A Technique for Avoiding Controlled Foreign Corporation Status and Other Burdens of U.S. Taxation, 57 Taxes 530 (1979); Corry, Stapled Stock—Time for a New Look, 36 Tax L. Rev. 167 (1981).

But the Tax Reform Act of 1984 addition of §269B dealt with the stapled stock problem in the foreign area (and other contexts) by providing that a foreign entity

The most important foreign corporations, in size if not in number, classified as CFCs are wholly owned subsidiaries of domestic corporations, as to which the elaborate rules of indirect and constructive ownership will either be unnecessary (because all the stock is owned directly by the domestic parent) or readily applied (e.g., to reach a foreign corporation whose stock is held by a foreign subsidiary of the domestic corporation). For other foreign corporations, however, there are difficult issues of statutory construction in working out the web of imputed ownership as well as problems in ascertaining the facts.[208] These determinations, moreover, must be made not only at year's end, but from day to day, since if a CFC enjoys (if that is the proper word) that status for only part of the year, the amount taxable to its shareholders is appropriately reduced by §951; and if the period is less than 30 consecutive days, none of its income is attributable to them.

It will be noted that a foreign corporation can be wholly owned by U.S. citizens without becoming a CFC (e.g., if the voting stock is equally divided among 11 or more unrelated individuals); the ownership rules require not only that *more* than 50 percent of the voting power or value be U.S.-owned but also that it be concentrated in a limited number of hands.

2. Attribution of income to "United States shareholders" of CFC. Every "United States shareholder" of a CFC (i.e., a "United States person" who

---

whose stock is stapled to that of a domestic entity is taxed as a domestic corporation. See Eustice, supra note 6, ¶ 4.05[5]; infra ¶ 17.35.

[208] See Garlock, Inc. v. CIR, 489 F2d 197 (2d Cir. 1973), cert. denied, 417 US 911 (1974), for an attempted decontrol device—an issue of voting preferred equal to 50 percent of the vote—that failed because the reality of control remained with the former parent-shareholder corporation; Kraus v. CIR, 490 F2d 898 (2d Cir. 1974) (decontrol device failed because no real shift of 50 percent voting power to new investors who purchased preferred stock carrying 50 percent of vote); Estate of Edwin C. Weiskopf, 64 TC 78 (1975), aff'd per curiam (2d Cir. 1976) (corporation held a CFC, even though technically a 50-50 deadlock vote situation, because U.S. shareholders retained control over economic life of corporation through control of its sole source of business and other matters); Koehring Co. v. US, 583 F2d 313 (7th Cir. 1978) (informal control existed, even though 55 percent of voting stock owned by U.K. corporation; implied agreement that foreign stockholder would vote as directed by the U.S. shareholder); but compare CCA, Inc., 64 TC 137 (1975) (nonacq.) (foreign shareholders had 50 percent vote, actively participated in affairs of the corporation, and had real opportunity to alter course of its affairs; limited dividend and equity rights did not destroy voting power).

The above-cited cases also would likely be caught by the CFC definition of the Tax Reform Act of 1986, supra note 206 (i.e., more than 50 percent of vote or value). The final Conference Report, H.R. Conf. Rep. No. 841, 99th Cong., 2d Sess. 627 (1986), however, specifically endorses Regs. §1.957-1(b) to deal with cases of "real" U.S. effective control.

owns directly, indirectly, or constructively 10 percent or more of the corporation's combined voting power) is required by §951 to report his pro rata share of its "attributable income" (a nonstatutory phrase, used here for convenience only). Although stock owned constructively is taken into account in determining whether the shareholder owns the requisite 10 percent, his pro rata share of the CFC's attributable income is computed by reference to the stock owned by him directly or through other foreign corporations or entities in which he is beneficially interested.

Since the purpose of Subpart F is to require the shareholder to report his share of the CFC's *undistributed* income, the amount imputed to him by §951 is so computed as to exclude amounts actually distributed by the corporation. To the extent that undistributed income is taxed to the shareholder, his basis for his stock is increased by §961 (as though the imputed distribution had been reinvested by him); subsequent distributions of these previously taxed amounts are receivable tax-free under §959 (having already paid their way), and the basis of the stock is then reduced. These changes in the basis of the stock are similar to the adjustments prescribed by the Code for FPHCs and Subchapter S corporations.[209]

If the shareholder to whom income is imputed is a domestic corporation, §960 provides that the attributed income is to be treated as a dividend in computing the deemed-paid foreign tax credit of §902. A similar provision is applicable to individual shareholders who elect to be taxed at the corporate rates under §962.

¶ 17.32　INCOME ATTRIBUTED TO SHAREHOLDERS OF CONTROLLED FOREIGN CORPORATIONS

The income that is attributable to the CFC's U.S. shareholders under §951(a)(1) consists of two components: Subpart F income and increase in earnings invested in U.S. property. In more detail, these components are as follows:

1. Subpart F income. The CFC's Subpart F income (defined by §952) consists of its "foreign base company income," determined under §954, plus certain "insurance income," as provided in §953.[210]

---

[209] The Subpart F provisions were held constitutional in Garlock, Inc. v. CIR, supra note 208 and Albert L. Dougherty, 60 TC 917 (1973), supplemented, 61 TC 719 (1974) (same despite partially retroactive effect). See supra ¶ 17.22, and ch. 6.

[210] The Tax Reform Act of 1976 added two new categories of Subpart F income to §952; §952(a)(3), boycott-generated income as determined under §§999 and

The term "foreign base company income" is defined in detail by §954, but the label itself implies an effort to restrict the common practice of using a foreign base company in international business operations to shelter foreign-source income from *foreign* taxes as well as U.S. taxes. The device takes many forms, but the shelter at which §954 strikes most directly is the sale of goods manufactured in the United States to a subsidiary incorporated in one foreign country (the base country), with the subsidiary in turn selling the goods to an affiliated corporation organized in the country where the goods are to be resold to the ultimate consumer (or to unrelated wholesalers). By adroitly fixing the prices at which the goods are sold by the parent to the base company and by the base company to the affiliate or sub-subsidiary in the country of destination, the lion's share of the spread between the cost of the goods sold and the price paid by the unrelated buyers can be segregated in the base company; and if it is organized in a country that imposes no income tax or treats the base company's profit as exempt foreign-source income, the taxes paid by the parent to the United States and by the sub-subsidiary to the country of destination are minimized. (The same result may be achieved without a sub-subsidiary if the tax law of the country of destination exempts the foreign base company from local tax (e.g., because it has no local "permanent establishment" or because of a treaty with the base company's country of incorporation.)) The device, to be sure, must run the gauntlet of §482, but in practice this statutory weapon is used primarily to insure that an appropriate fraction of the gross profits is reported by the parent, not to allocate income from the foreign base company to the foreign sub-subsidiary in order to prevent the latter from avoiding taxes in its country of incorporation.

Why, however, should the United States be concerned with an avoidance of taxes in the country of destination? The stated purpose of the 1962 provisions was the elimination of artificial stimulation to foreign investment, but the legislation strikes primarily, as stated, at tax inducements offered by base countries; if the country in which the goods are to be sold or the services performed wishes to reduce its rates, the U.S. investor may take advantage of *this* stimulus by operating through a corporation organized in the country of destination.

952(a)(4), illegal bribes or other payments within the meaning of §162(c) paid by or on behalf of the CFC directly or indirectly to a government official; §952(a)(5) (income from countries supporting terrorism) was added to the list in 1986.

The Tax Reform Act of 1986 broadened the scope of Subpart F income from passive investments, banking, and insurance, and narrowed the exceptions from Subpart F income treatment. See H.R. Conf. Rep. No. 841, 99th Cong., 2d Sess. 609–628 (1986); Eustice, Kuntz, Lewis, & Deering, supra note 7, ¶ 4.03; Joint Comm. Staff General Explanation of the Tax Reform Act of 1986, supra note 24, at 962–987.

Returning to the statutory details, FBCI is defined by §954 to consist of the items described in (a), (b), (c), and (d) below, adjusted as described in (e).

(a) Foreign personal holding company income: Section 954(c). This concept is patterned on the definition of FPHC income found in §553 and consists of dividends, interest, royalties, and similar categories of passive income; but the definition is relaxed in some respects (primarily to exempt certain amounts derived from the active conduct of a trade or business or received from a related person having a legitimate connection with the country in which the CFC is incorporated) and tightened in others (i.e., rents are included without limitation). The Tax Reform Act of 1985 broadened the scope of the FPHC income category in §954 by including all gains from the sale of property giving rise to passive income, gains from commodity (and commodity futures) transactions, foreign currency gains, and income equivalent to interest (rents and royalties developed in, or used in, the country of incorporation of the CFC are generally excepted, but the exception for FPHC income received by banking or insurance companies was repealed).[211]

(b) Foreign base company sales income: Section 954(d). This category consists, roughly speaking, of income derived by the CFC from selling personal property that it purchased from a related person (e.g., a domestic parent engaged in manufacturing) or from buying personal property (e.g., raw materials) for sale to a related person if the property is both produced and sold for use outside the country in which the CFC is incorporated.[212]

If the CFC is engaged in manufacturing in one foreign country and sells its products in another foreign country, the sales in the second country may generate "foreign base company sales income" under the complex "branch"

---

[211] H.R. 3838, §1221, amending §954(c), expanding the Subpart F status of insurance income and repealing §954(b). See generally Eustice, Kuntz, Lewis, & Deering, supra note 7, ¶ 4.03[7].

[212] A "related person" for computing FBCI is defined by §954(d)(3); in general, ownership of more than 50 percent of the vote or value of the CFC's stock is controlling. The Tax Reform Act of 1986 tightened the related person definition of §954(d)(3) by adding "value" (as an *alternative*) to the more than 50 percent stock ownership test and adding controlled partnerships, trusts, and estates to the related group.

"Foreign-base company sales income" and "foreign-base company services income" are defined by reference to the place where property is manufactured, goods are to be used or consumed, services are performed, etc., and these geographical references create many troublesome questions. See Fimberg, The Foreign Base Company Engaged in Selling Activities: A Reappraisal of the Conduct of Foreign Business, 1965 So. Cal. Tax Inst. 237 and 254–259; see also Dave Fischbein Mfg. Co., 59 TC 338 (1972) (acq.) (no FBC sales income because subsidiary's activities constituted manufacturing, or at least major assembly, within meaning of §954 regulations).

rule of §954(d)(2). This provision requires the CFC's branch to be treated as a wholly owned subsidiary in certain circumstances, with the result that the sales component of the CFC's income will constitute foreign base company sales income even though there is no formally organized related party.

(c) Foreign base company services income: Section 954(e). This category consists, again roughly speaking, of income from the performance of technical, managerial, engineering, commercial, and similar services, which are performed outside the country of the CFC's incorporation for a related person.[213]

> *To illustrate these components of FBCI:* If *P*, a U.S. corporation, owns all the stock of *S*, a Swiss corporation, FBCI will arise if (1) *S* buys goods from *P* and resells them outside Switzerland; (2) *S* buys goods outside Switzerland and resells them to *P*; (3) *S* performs services for, or on behalf of, *P* outside Switzerland; or (4) *S* is a holding company receiving dividends, interest, rents, or royalties from a payor which is not a related Swiss business corporation (i.e., a related subsidiary organized and doing business in Switzerland). In category (1), if the goods had been sold in Switzerland (the country of incorporation), no tainted income would result; similarly, in category (2), if the goods had been purchased in Switzerland, there would be no FBCI. In category (3), tainted income could be avoided either by performing the services in the country of incorporation or by avoiding performance of services for, or on behalf of, a related party. Similarly, in categories (1) and (2), no tainted income would result from the purchase and sale of goods by *S* if it did not deal with its parent, *P*.

(d) Other components of FBCI. Two other categories of FBCI, foreign base country shipping income, §954(f), and foreign base country oil related income, §954(g), were added to the list in 1976 and 1982 respectively.

(e) Adjustments to FBCI: Section 954(b). In computing these components of FBCI, §954(b)(4) excludes income that is subject to an effective foreign tax greater than 90 percent of the top §11 rate (34 percent), since taxes are not significantly reduced by the base country device in this case.[214]

---

[213] See Holleman, United States Taxation of the Overseas Construction Industry, 23 Tax L. Rev. 155 (1968).

[214] The Tax Reform Act of 1986 replaced the subjective tax-avoidance safe-harbor rule of prior §954(b)(4) with an objective test based on effective foreign tax rates essentially comparable to the U.S. rate. See generally Eustice, Kuntz, Lewis, & Deering, supra note 7, ¶ 4.03[4]. This exclusion safe harbor will play a more important role in view of the expansion of the scope of the CFC rules in 1986.

If, after applying these rules, the FBCI is less than the *lesser* of 5 percent of gross income or $1 million, none of its income is treated as FBCI; if the percentage is between 5 and 70, the actual amount is treated as FBCI under §954(b)(3).[215]

At this point, each of the components of FBCI is reduced by the expenses and other deductions properly attributable to it, so as to convert gross income into net income.[216]

2. "Increase in earnings invested in United States property." The CFC's "increase in earnings invested in United States property"—the second component of attributable income—consists of the amount (if any) by which its earnings invested in U.S. property at year-end exceed the earnings so invested at the beginning of the year.[217] "United States property" means any property (if acquired after December 31, 1962) that is tangible property located in the United States, stock of a domestic corporation, an obligation of a U.S. person, or a right to use a patent, copyright, invention, secret formula, or similar property in the United States if it was acquired or developed by the CFC for such use; but U.S. bonds, bank deposits, certain debts arising in the ordinary course of business from the sale or processing of property, certain property used in transporting persons or property in foreign commerce, and an amount equal to *certain* (but *not all*) pre-1963 earnings and profits[218] are excluded from the term "United States property."[219]

---

[215] For taxable years before 1976, the corresponding percentages were 30 and 70; for taxable years before 1986, the percentages were 10 and 70.

The Tax Reform Act of 1986 adopted the de minimis threshold of §954(b)(3) as the lesser of 5 percent of gross income or $1 million. See Eustice, Kuntz, Lewis, & Deering, supra note 7, ¶ 4.03[3].

[216] The Tax Reform Act of 1986, H.R. 3838, §1221(f), also repealed the chain deficit rules of §952(d); see H.R. Conf. Rep. No. 841, 99th Cong., 2d Sess. 621–626 (1986); Eustice, Kuntz, Lewis, & Deering, supra note 7, ¶ 4.03[6].

[217] See Stone, US Taxation of Profits Withdrawn From Foreign Corporations Under the Revenue Act of 1962, 5 Inst. on Priv. Inv. & Inv. Abroad 85 (Southwestern Legal Foundation 1963); Jenks, Controlled Foreign Corporation's Investment in United States Property: A New Dividend Concept, 21 Tax L. Rev. 323 (1966); Bissell, Controlled Foreign Corporations—§956, Tax Mgmt. Portfolio (BNA) No. 232-3d (1986).

[218] Albert L. Dougherty, supra note 209 (dividend generated under §956 includes earnings accumulated prior to effective date of Subpart F enactment).

[219] Sections 956(b)(2)(F) and 956(b)(2)(G) exempt investments in stock or obligations of U.S. corporations (other than a shareholder of the CFC) in which the CFC's U.S. shareholders own less than 25 percent of the voting stock, and investments in movable property (except ships and planes) used on the continental shelf for mineral exploration and development; other special exemptions are found in §§956(b)(2)(H) and 956(b)(2)(I).

Shareholders of a CFC thus are taxed on their pro rata share of an increase in their investment in U.S. property without regard to the *source* of the earnings that made the increase possible. This component of attributable income thus differs from Subpart F income, which is imputed to the share-holder because of the source from which it is derived; the increase in U.S. investments instead is imputed to the shareholder on the very different theory that the CFC's earnings have been repatriated pro tanto, even though not distributed by a formal dividend.[220] This constructive repatriation provision will reach such methods of indirectly placing the CFC's foreign earnings at the disposal of its parent as making a long-term loan to it and purchasing U.S. property (e.g., an industrial plant or office building) for lease to it.[221] In appropriate circumstances, some arrangements of this character might have been treated as constructive distributions to the parent corporation even under pre-1962 law, but §956 provides the government with a more certain remedy.

Because Subpart F income is defined by reference to the source of earnings, while the CFC's "increase in earnings invested in United States property" is not, the same earnings (if invested in U.S. property) could be counted twice, were it not for §959(a). By virtue of this provision, earnings that enter into the corporation's Subpart F income are excluded in computing its increase in earnings invested in U.S. property.[222]

The CFC provisions may be put into perspective if we note that by and large they will not affect a foreign corporation if its ownership is widely dispersed, its income is derived from manufacturing,[223] it is incorporated in

---

[220] For operation of §956 generally, see Clayton E. Greenfield, 60 TC 425 (1973), aff'd, 506 F2d 972 (5th Cir. 1975) (various loans and advances by foreign sister corporation to domestic affiliate held taxable under §956 as increase in investment of earnings in U.S. property on facts; no part of such loans were constructive dividends, however); Gulf Oil Corp., 87 TC 548 (1986) (payables balance was a single obligation, even though reflected results of many intercompany transactions).

For the relationship between §§551 and 951 with respect to §956 investments in U.S. property, see §951(d), supra note 183 (§951 priority).

[221] Rev. Rul. 74-436, 1974-2 CB 214 (computation of §956 dividend illustrated); Rev. Rul. 76-125, 1976-1 CB 204 (pledge of CFC stock by shareholder to secure personal bank loan held equivalent to a guaranty of the loan by the CFC and a §956 investment in U.S. property thereby); D.K. Ludwig, 68 TC 979 (1977) (nonacq.) (Rev. Rul. 76-125 rejected); Rev. Rul. 76-192, 1976-1 CB 205 (indirect loan transaction held §956 investment in U.S. property). But see §1297(b)(6) (pledge of PFIC stock, supra §17.25, a deemed disposition).

[222] See Rev. Rul. 76-538, 1976-2 CB 230 (Subpart F income taxed to U.S. share-holders and reinvested in U.S. property also covered by §956, but double tax avoided by §959(a)(2) rules).

[223] For a CFC operating in two countries, however, see the branch rule of §954(d)(2).

the country in which its business activities are performed, or its business is not related to a U.S. enterprise controlled by its shareholders. The CFC rules are applicable primarily to sales and service affiliates of U.S. enterprises (and then only if the country of incorporation is different from the country in which the goods have their origin or destination or the services are perfomed) and to foreign holding companies. Even when applicable, the CFC rules are of limited importance if the foreign subsidiary is subject to high foreign income taxes, since the U.S. tax on the parent resulting from the attribution of Subpart F income to it may be largely or wholly offset by its deemed-paid foreign tax credit arising from the subsidiary's foreign tax payments. In such circumstances, of course, the pre-1962 deferral privilege enjoyed by the parent was of little value, so it may not be missed.

¶ 17.33   SUBPART F RELIEF PROVISIONS

Several provisions that mitigate the full force of Subpart F have already been mentioned: the disregard of FBCI if it amounts to less than the lower of 5 percent of the CFC's gross income or $1 million of the CFC's gross income; the exclusion from FBCI of certain amounts if tax avoidance is not present; and the 30-consecutive-day rule for determining whether anything is to be attributed to the CFC's shareholders. Under another relief provision, §962, an individual shareholder of a CFC may elect to be taxed at corporate rates on the income imputed to him by §951(a), in which event he is entitled to employ the derivative foreign tax credit as though he were a domestic corporation. If the election is made, however, later actual distributions are includable in gross income to the extent that they exceed the tax previously paid. The election approximates the result that would have been reached if the foreign income had been earned and fully distributed (after corporate tax) by a domestic corporation; it would then have been taxed at the U.S. corporate rate (subject to the foreign tax credit) in the year when the income was earned, and the corporation would have been able to distribute only the balance (i.e., the earnings less taxes) to its shareholders.[224]

¶ 17.34   SALE OR LIQUIDATION OF CONTROLLED FOREIGN CORPORATIONS: SECTION 1248

Under pre-1962 law, the shareholder's gain on a sale of stock in a foreign corporation, on some redemptions of stock, and on a partial or com-

---

[224] See generally Albert L. Dougherty, supra note 209 (timing of election and binding effect).

plete liquidation of the corporation constituted, with minor exceptions, captial gain. Rather than repatriate its foreign earnings in the form of dividends taxable as ordinary income, therefore, the shareholders of a foreign corporation might allow the earnings to accumulate and then sell their stock or liquidate the corporation, reporting their profit as long-term capital gain.

To discourage such transactions, §1248 was enacted in 1962 to require the gain realized by certain U.S. persons on the sale, exchange, or redemption of stock, or on the liquidation of a foreign corporation, to be treated as a dividend to the extent of the earnings and profits that were accumulated after 1962 and during the period the shareholder held his stock.[225] These rules apply only if at some time during the five-year period preceding the transaction,[226] the corporation was a CFC and the shareholder owned (directly, indirectly, and constructively) 10 percent or more of its voting power. Although the shareholder's 10 percent ownership must have coincided with the corporation's status as a CFC, §1248 applies even though neither of these conditions is satisfied when the gain is realized. In determining the amount of earnings and profits under §1248, amounts that were previously included in the shareholder's gross income under §951 (constructive distributions) are excluded; and there are several other qualifications and limitations on the strict application of §1248.[227] If the shareholder is a corporation, the amount treated as a dividend by §1248 may qualify for the deemed-paid credit of §902. If the shareholder is an individual, §1248(b) provides a limit on the tax payable (so as to moderate the effect of throwing the accumulated earnings into the shareholder's ordinary income in a single year), which looks to the tax burden that would have been imposed if the controlled foreign corporation had been a domestic corporation.[228]

A significant amendment to the CFC rules was effected by the Tax Reform Act of 1976, which expanded the transactional coverage of §1248. Prior to its amendment, §1248 did not reach various nonrecognition transfers covered by former §311, §336, or §337 (before their repeal in 1986), with

---

[225] See generally Irell & Stone, Understanding Section 1248—The New Tax Law Regarding Sales or Liquidations of Foreign Corporations, 1964 So. Calif. Tax Inst. 321; Foster, Controlled Foreign Corporations—Section 1248, Tax Mgmt. Portfolio (BNA) No. 240-3d (1986); supra note 205.

[226] For successful escape from the §1248 taint through use of a foreign trust and a delayed sale of the stock (after five years), see David E. Hart, ¶ 83,364 P-H Memo. TC (1983).

[227] Brigham v. US, 539 F2d 1312 (3d Cir. 1976), and Pielemeier v. US, 543 F2d 81 (9th Cir. 1976), hold that §1245 recapture gain is included in earnings for §1248 dividend computations.

[228] Hoover v. US, 348 F. Supp. 502 (C.D. Cal. 1972) (individual entitled to use §§921 and 922 in computing §1248(b) limitations on tax for §1248 dividend; Regs. §1.1248-4(e)(1)(i) to contrary invalid).

the result that the potential dividend taint inherent in CFC stock could be purged by distributing such shares as a dividend in kind, or in liquidation, which transactions resulted in a stepped-up basis for the shares. But §1248(f)(1) specifically triggers application of §1248 dividend recapture upon distributions in kind and most liquidation sales of the shares under §337.[229]

The 1976 amendments were further strengthened by legislation enacted in 1984 [230] in response to attempts to purge §1248 status by having the CFC acquire all (or a majority) of the stock of its widely held U.S. parent in exchange for stock and cash of equivalent value issued by the CFC; if these expatriating exchanges of stock were successful, shareholders of the former U.S. parent corporation would become shareholders of the CFC and, because of the wide dispersion of stock ownership, such stock would no longer be subject to §1248 treatment in the hands of those shareholders (and the former publicly held parent would become a controlled subsidiary of its former subsidiary).[231] However, §1248(i) recharacterizes this transction as a deemed distribution of the CFC stock by the U.S. corporation to its shareholders in redemption of its stock (in an amount equal to the difference between the value of the constructively distributed CFC stock[232] and the deemed distributing corporation's basis for that stock). Thus, §1248 dividend income is triggered to the deemed distributing corporation under §1248(f).

Section 1248 is best viewed as a backstop to Subpart F. Taken together, and disregarding a variety of minor exceptions, these provisions require the principal U.S. shareholders of a CFC to report their pro rata share of its accumulated earnings as a dividend either under (1) §951, when the earnings

---

[229] Gain is not triggered, however, if the shares are distributed in a carry-over basis dividend in kind or §332 liquidation transaction (§1248(f)(2)), since the potential dividend taint inherent in the distributed shares will be preserved in the hands of the distributee; §1248(f)(3) also provides a limited exception for certain §337 sales. See also Rev. Rul. 74-106, 1974-1 CB 237 (§1248 applics only to sales, etc., by U.S. shareholders of a CFC).

See generally Klein, Scope of Section 1248—Disposition of Stock in a Controlled Foreign Corporation—As Expanded by the Tax Reform Act of 1976, 4 J. Corp. Tax'n 336 (1978).

[230] The Tax Reform Act of 1984, H.R. 4170, §133, adding §1248(i).

[231] An example illustrating the abusive transaction addressed by this legislation is found in the Committee Report to both the House and Senate versions; H.R. Rep. No. 432, Pt. 2, 98th Cong., 2d Sess. 1327 (1984); S. Rep. No. 169, 98th Cong., 2d Sess. 372 (1984).

[232] The value of the constructively distributed CFC stock would be equal to the spread between the value of the hypothetically redeemed parent stock and the value of such stock excluding the value attributable to the CFC (i.e., the value of the CFC stock held by the U.S. parent before the transaction).

are realized by the corporation or (2) §1248, when they sell or exchange their stock or the corporation is liquidated.[233] However, repeal of the capital gain rate benefits by the Tax Reform Act of 1986, and reduction of the individual top rate to 28 percent (in 1988), reduces the significance of the capital gain vs. ordinary income distinction and hence the importance of the §1248 recharacterization rule.

¶ 17.35　THE SCOPE OF THE CONTROLLED FOREIGN CORPORATION PROVISIONS

The limited nature of the CFC provisions is readily apparent in the preceding discussion of these provisions. CFC treatment will not encompass a foreign corporation if its ownership is widely dispersed, its income is derived from manufacturing, it is incorporated in the country in which its business activities are performed, or its business is not related to a U.S. enterprise controlled by its shareholders. The CFC rules are applicable primarily to sales and service affiliates of U.S. enterprises (and then only if the country of incorporation is different from the country in which the goods have their origin or destination or the services are performed) and to FPHCs. Even when applicable, the CFC rules are of limited importance if the foreign subsidiary is subject to high foreign income taxes, since the U.S. tax on the parent resulting from the attribution of Subpart F income to it may be largely or wholly offset by its deemed-paid foreign tax credit arising from the subsidiary's foreign tax payments.

Futhermore, several provisions of the Code act to mitigate the full force of Subpart F: Those already mentioned include §954(b)(3), which disregards FBCI if it amounts to less than the lower of 5 percent of the CFC's gross income or $1 million; §954(b)(4), which excludes from FBCI certain amounts if tax avoidance is not present by virtue of high foreign tax rates; and the 30-consecutive-day rule for determining whether anything is to be attributed to the CFC's shareholders under §951(a)(1). Under another relief provision, §962, an individual shareholder of a CFC may elect to be taxed at corporate rates on the income imputed to him by §951(a), in which event he is entitled to employ the derivative foreign tax credit as though he were a domestic corporation.

Despite these weaknesses of the CFC provisions, the interaction of §§951–964 and 1248 seemingly combine to produce a significant check on

---

[233] Rev. Rul. 75-143, 1975-1 CB 275 (if property transferred in §351 exchange is §1248 stock, any boot gain will be recognized as dividend under §1248); Estate of Edwin C. Weiskopf, supra note 208 (purported bootstrap stock sale (i.e., sale of stock, liquidation, and use of cash by buyer to pay sellers the purchase price) held in substance a liquidation of the corporation by the selling shareholders).

tax deferral and conversion of income from ordinary to capital gain status. Evidence of this can be found in the ongoing struggle by tax practitioners to evade the CFC provisions. For example, prior to 1984, repeated attempts were made by taxpayers to purge §1248 status by having the CFC acquire all (or a majority) of the stock of its widely held U.S. parent in exchange for stock and cash of equivalent value issued by the CFC. If these expatriating exchanges of stock were successful, shareholders of the former U.S. parent corporation would become shareholders of the CFC and, because of the wide dispersion of stock ownership, such stock would no longer be subject to §1248 treatment in the hands of those shareholders (and the former publicly held parent would become a controlled subsidiary of its former subsidiary).[234] However, §1248(i), passed in 1984, recharacterizes this transaction as a deemed distribution of the CFC stock by the U.S. corporation to its shareholders in redemption of its stock (in an amount equal to the difference between the value of the constructively distributed CFC stock[235] and the deemed distributing corporation's basis for that stock), thus triggering §1248 dividend income to the deemed distributing corporation under §1248(f).

Another device for avoiding classification as a CFC, used prior to 1984, involved the pairing, or "stapling," of the stock of two or more entities so that a stockholder could not trade the stock of one entity separately from the other. If stock ownership of the paired entities were sufficiently dispersed, this device of turning a former parent-subsidiary structure into a linked, or paired, brother-sister structure resulted in the avoidance of CFC tax provisions.[236] In order to combat this practice, Congress passed §269B of the Code as part of the Tax Reform Act of 1984, which provides at §269B(a)(1) that if a domestic and foreign entity are stapled entities, the foreign entity will be domesticated, and therefore taxable as a U.S. taxpayer. Section 269B(c) defines a "stapled entity" as any business organization (i.e., corporation, partnership, trust, association, or estate), "stapled entities" as a group of two or more entities if more than 50 percent of beneficial ownership in each entity consists of stapled interests, and "stapled interests" as those for which, by reason of form of ownership, restrictions on transfers, or other terms or conditions, the transfer of one interest cannot be effected without transfer of the other. Broad regulation authority is granted by §269B to prescribe any regulations necessary to prevent tax avoidance through stapling, including, but not limited to, providing for the extent to which one of the entities is to be treated as owning the other.

Thus, if attempts at creative evasion can be deemed a measure of the effectiveness of a Tax Code provision, the treatment of CFCs under the

---

[234] Supra note 231.

[235] Supra note 232.

[236] Supra note 207.

Code seems to prevent far more tax avoidance and deferral than a first glance at its provisions might suggest. Repeal of capital gains and reduction of individual and corporate tax rates by the Tax Reform Act of 1986 may well operate to lessen pressures on the CFC regime.

PART E.　ORGANIZATION, LIQUIDATION, AND REORGANIZATION OF FOREIGN CORPORATIONS: SECTION 367

¶ 17.40　INTRODUCTORY: BACKGROUND, EVOLUTION, AND SCOPE OF §367

1. In general. Perhaps the central conflict of jurisprudence is between the desire for consistency and uniformity of law versus the desire to do justice, which often requires ad hoc decisionmaking tailored to the merits of each particular case or transaction. Throughout the Code, Congress has sought a balance between these frequently conflicting goals of uniformity and flexibility through a combination of strict rules governing given sets of transactions, combined with broad authority delegated to the Service to issue regulations that may profoundly alter the scope and implementation of those rules.

Section 367 of the Code is one of several tax provisions that give the Service greater discretion and flexibility in the application of other Code provisions in order to prevent the use of the latter provisions for tax avoidance.[237] Since §367 has undergone substantial change over the past 20 years, the following material initially presents a short history of §367's development before moving to a description of its current provisions.

2. Initial provisions. In its original incarnation, §367 provided that in determining the extent to which gain (but not loss) would be recognized in the case of exchanges described in §332, §351, §354, §355, §356, or §361, a foreign corporation would "not be considered as a corporation" unless, *before* such an exchange, it was established to the satisfaction of the Service that the exchange was "not in pursuance of a plan having as one of its principal purposes the avoidance of Federal income taxes."[238] Since corporate status is

---

[237] Other examples include §§482 (supra ¶ 15.03), 1502 (supra ¶ 15.20), 382 (supra ¶ 16.23), and 269 (supra ¶ 16.21).

[238] For the pre-1976 Act version of §367, see generally McDonald, Section 367—A Modern Day Janus, 64 Colum. L. Rev. 1012 (1964); Ross, The Impact of the Revenue Act of 1962 on Reorganizations and Other Rearrangements Involving For-

essential to a tax-free organization, liquidation, or reorganization (by reason of the use of the term "corporation" in §§332, 351, 368(a)(1), 354, and 361), a failure to satisfy §367 resulted in recognition of any gain realized by the participants to a transaction governed by that section. Section 367 could, moreover, be brought into play by a transaction found to be a reorganization even though cast in another form.[239] On the other hand, since §367 applied only to the recognition of gain, a failure to obtain advance clearance from the Treasury did not exempt any realized loss from nonrecognition; and if the transferor realized both gains and losses on the transfer, failure to obtain a favorable ruling under §367 required gains to be recognized under §367 while losses went unrecognized.[240]

It was usually assumed that the requirement under the former version of §367 that clearance by the Service *before* the exchange occurred could not be excused at the taxpayer's behest, no matter how persuasive an excuse was offered for failure to apply for a ruling. This may have been too dogmatic a conclusion, but it was a good working hypothesis; and it argued for wariness in transactions with foreign corporations, lest what was thought to be outside the ambit of §367 proved, after the fact, to be within its scope, and taxable because the requisite advance ruling was not obtained.

In 1971, §367 was amended by §367(b) to allow obtaining the ruling *after* the exchange in a highly limited category of transactions (i.e., Type F reorganizations of foreign corporations). In 1976, §367 again was amended, this time more broadly, to allow post-transaction rulings in certain instances and to abolish the ruling requirement altogether in others.[241] If the taxpayer

---

eign Corporations, 22 NYU Inst. on Fed. Tax'n 761 (1964); Landis & Currier, The Future of Section 367, 25 Tax Lawyer 253 (1972).

On the special reporting rules applicable to transactions with foreign corporations, see §§964(c), 6038, and 6046; for discussion, see Kanter, Congress Expands Information Reporting Requirements for Foreign Corporate Operations, 42 Taxes 84 (1964).

[239] See, e.g., Retail Properties, Inc., ¶ 64,245 P-H Memo. TC (1964) (involving a taxpayer that sold assets to its controlled foreign subsidiary in reliance on §337; on holding that the transaction constituted a Type D reorganization under reincorporation principles (supra ¶ 14.54), the court required the transferor to recognize its realized gain because no §367 ruling had been obtained); see also cases infra note 265, and infra note 326.

[240] See Rev. Rul. 67-192, 1967-2 CB 140; Rev. Rul. 71-433, 1971-2 CB 325 (no netting of unrealized gains and losses for §1491 tax computations either); Rev. Rul. 76-333, 1976-2 CB 104 (failure to include proper description of transferred property vitiated entire ruling; omitted property tainted entire transaction).

[241] For the 1976 Act version, see Gosain, Foreign Corporations: Recognition of Gain Under §367–Half a Century of Metamorphosis, 9 J. Corp. Tax'n 203 (1982); Dolan & Horowitz, Reorganizations of Foreign Corporations Under §367(b): Issues and Recommendations, 38 Tax L. Rev. 321 (1983); Pugh & Samuels, Tax-Free International Corporate Combinations Under New Sections 367 and 1491, 30 Tax Lawyer

deliberately refrained from requesting a ruling in order to achieve a taxable transaction with a concomitant step-up in basis, however, the Service ruled that §367 was a one-way street on the ground that the section was enacted solely to close a tax loophole.[242] It should also be noted that there were no cases on the taxpayer's right to judicial review of an unfavorable ruling. Although some remedy might have been theoretically available in an aggravated case of arbitrary action, business opportunities were not likely to wait while a new cause of action was being judicially established.[243]

By its terms, §367 was concerned only with "determining the extent to which gain would be recognized" under the statutory provisions listed therein; but the transactions to which §367 applied, including reorganiza-

---

263 (1977); Alpert & Feingold, Tax Reform Act Toughens Foreign Transfer Provisions of 1491 and Liberalizes 367, 46 J. Tax'n 2 (1977).

The Tax Reform Act of 1984, however, finally dropped the ruling requirement altogether.

[242] See Rev. Rul. 64-177, 1964-1 CB 141; Hay v. CIR, supra note 17, supplies some support for this view, but on an extreme set of facts; see also Rev. Rul. 76-90, 1976-1 CB 101 (Rev. Rul. 64-177 followed where U.S. subsidiary sold assets, claiming §337, and liquidated into foreign parent under §332 without a §367 ruling); former Temp. Regs. §7.367(a)-1(g) (1977) (same); Prop. Regs. §1.367(a)-1(e)(4) (1982), (same); and final Regs. §1.367(a)-1(e)(4) (same), TD 7954, 1984-1 CB 107 (1984).

But for abolition of the ruling requirement in 1984, see infra note 258.

[243] For administrative review procedures under these provisions, see Rev. Proc. 73-5, 1973-1 CB 751. The Tax Reform Act of 1976 established a declaratory judgment for review by the Tax Court of §367 determinations in new §7477; for procedures for obtaining rulings under §367, as amended by the 1976 Act (and administrative remedies), see Rev. Proc. 77-5, 1977-1 CB 536. In addition, see generally Dittler Bros., 72 TC 896 (1979) (declaratory judgment for taxpayer granted under §7477; no tax avoidance; review standard is whether Service determination supported by "substantial evidence;" seven dissenters thought proper standard was abuse of discretion). But see Gerli & Co., 73 TC 1019 (1980) (taxpayer's failure to include toll charge income imposed by §367 ruling subjected it to 5 percent penalty of §6653(a)), reversed, 668 F2d 691 (2d Cir. 1982) (imposition of automatic toll charge not proper; Service did not discharge its responsibility to determine whether liquidation of subsidiary involved tax avoidance, and facts showed no tax-avoidance effects; taxpayers not bound by previous acceptance of toll charge as condition for favorable §367 ruling).

For other more recent taxpayer victories under the declaratory judgment procedures of §7477, see Hershey Foods Corp., 76 TC 312 (1981) (no tax avoidance proved); Kaiser Aluminum & Chem. Corp., 76 TC 325 (1981) (acq.) (same); Robert Pitcher, 84 TC 85 (1985).

See Weiss, Reversing the Advance Ruling Under Section 367 of the Code, 8 J. Corp. Tax'n 235 (1981); and Lowry, Review of the Tax Court's Decision in *Hershey Foods Corp.*, 60 Taxes 224 (1982); Weiss & Levenson, The Impact of *Gerli* on Judicial Review of Section 367 Rulings: An Analysis of the CA-2 Opinion, 56 J. Tax'n 330 (1982).

Legislation in 1984 (infra note 258), however, dropped the declaratory judgment proceedings of §7477 and switched to a notice requirement; the Tax Reform Act of 1984, §§131(d) and 131(e), repealing §7477 and adding §6038B.

tions, have many collateral consequences. If a §367 ruling was not obtained, so that gain had to be recognized by the participants in a reorganization under §§354 and 361, did the other effects of a reorganization (e.g., a carry-over or substituted basis for the transferred property or a transfer of earnings and profits and other corporate tax attributes) nevertheless apply? A literal reading suggested that the failure to satisfy §367, and hence failure to qualify the exchanges under §§354 and 361, also prevented the collateral attributes of reorganization treatment from applying. The basis rules of §358, for example, apply only to "an exchange to which section 351, 354, 355, 356, 361, or 371(b) applies"; §362(b) contemplates the nonrecognition of gain to the transferor; and §381 applies only if the transfer is one to which §361 applies. The guidelines of Rev. Proc. 68-23 seemed to adopt this "transactional" approach—that is, if gain must be recognized, the entire transaction would be treated consistently, so that the transferee's basis was its cost, the transferor's tax attributes do not carry over, and so forth,[244] and the Tax Reform Act of 1976 amendments to §367, especially those in §367(b)(2), echoed this transactional theme. If, on the other hand, nonrecognition treatment applied with respect to the various exchanges (whether because of a favorable §367 ruling or because such a ruling was not necessary), the Service took the position that the carry-over rules of §381 and the rules of §§358 and 362(b) applied, even though the transaction involved only foreign corporations and created no immediate U.S. tax consequences to the parties.[245]

3. The 1968 Guidelines. In 1968, after nearly a decade of administrative consideration, the Service issued a detailed guideline in Rev. Proc. 68-23 as to when favorable rulings ordinarily would be issued under the former version of §367, thus finally ending the conspiracy of silence that had enveloped this area since the passage of §367 in 1932.[246] These guidelines provided tax-

---

[244] Rev. Proc. 68-23, 1968-1 CB 821.

[245] To the same general effect are Prop. Regs. §1.367(a)-1(e)(2) (1982) (taxable gain and basis results affected, but §381 tax-attribute carry-overs and losses are not affected by failure to comply). Final regulations were promulgated by TD 7954, 1984-1 CB 107 (1984), Regs. §1.367(a)-1(e)(2) (same). But these regulations were replaced by a new set of temporary regulations in 1986 to reflect amendments to §367(a) by the Tax Reform Act of 1984, infra notes 258 and 260.

[246] Rev. Proc. 68-23, 1968-1 CB 821; for discussion of the 1968 Guidelines, which were amplified by Rev. Proc. 75-29, 1975-1 CB 755; Rev. Proc. 76-20, 1976-2 CB 560, modified by Rev. Proc. 77-17, 1977-1 CB 577; Rev. Proc. 76-4, 1976-1 CB 453, modified by Rev. Proc. 76-44, 1976-2 CB 668, and Rev. Proc. 76-24, 1976-1 CB 563; see Eustice, Affiliated Corporations Revisited: Recent Developments Under Sections 482 and 367, 24 Tax L. Rev. 101 (1968); Beimfohr, Tax-Free Exchanges With a Foreign Corporation: Section 367; The Guidelines Analyzed, 28 NYU Inst. on Fed. Tax'n 455 (1970); Sitrick, Section 367 and Tax Avoidance: An Analysis of the Section 367 Guidelines Will Be Applied to Asset Acquisition Situations, 29 J.

payers and their counsel with significant insights into the Service's policies and practices. They were issued contemporaneously with revised regulations under §482 (see Chapter 15) and were closely related to those provisions. The guidelines were intended to assist taxpayers by setting out certain ground rules for the issuance of favorable rulings under the pre-1976 version of §367 in typical transactions arising under that provision and to provide for various "toll charges" as a condition for issuance of the ruling depending on the type of transaction involved. [247]

The 1968 guidelines covered a wide range of corporate adjustments, and the standards required for obtaining a favorable §367 ruling became more readily ascertainable in many situations that heretofore had to be gleaned from direct contact with the appropriate ruling office or by hearsay from other practitioners. The preliminary sections (Guidelines §§1 and 2) set forth the purpose and background for these provisions, while the major operative portion of the guidelines (§3) set forth the particular transactions (corporate organizations, reorganizations, and liquidations) covered by §367 and the rules for issuance or nonissuance of a §367 ruling thereunder. Finally, the last two sections (§§4 and 5) dealt with special problems in the §367 area (earnings and profits, collateral effects, etc.). There were numerous changes and refinements in the details of these provisions, some of which varied significantly from the earlier proposals. Many, if not most, of the changes, however, were primarily technical in nature and were fairly limited in scope.

4. The Tax Reform Act of 1976. In 1976, Congress enacted a major revision of §367 and its related provisions. [248] Among the reasons given for

---

Tax'n 362 (1968); Kurlander, Jurisdictional Questions Under §367, 46 Taxes 730 (1968); Herskovitz, New Section 367 Guidelines Encourage Stock Acquisitions of Corporations, 30 J. Tax'n 154 (1969); Comments on Guidelines for Rulings Under Section 367 (Report of Special Committee on Section 367 Policies of the Tax Section of the N.Y. State Bar Association), 23 Tax L. Rev. 151 (1969); see also Robert Pitcher, supra note 243 (legal effect of guidelines; failure to meet tests not fatal).

[247] For example, outbound §351 transfers to foreign corporations were conditioned upon payment of tax on the gain inherent in transferred inventory and receivables; and conversely, repatriating §332 liquidations of foreign subsidiaries were conditioned upon payment of tax as a dividend by the U.S. parent on the subsidiary's accumulated foreign earnings.

Though supplanted by specific statutory amendments in 1976 and 1984 (infra notes 248 and 258), the guidelines' general principles and policies are readily recognizable in many of the statutory and regulations provisions.

[248] For detailed analyses of the 1976 changes, see articles supra note 241; see also Staff of the Joint Comm. on Taxation, 94th Cong., 2d Sess., General Explanation of the Tax Refom Act of 1976, at 258 (CIR Print 1976), reprinted at 1976-3 Vol. 2 CB 270 (hereinafter cited as the General Explanation).

amending §367 were: (1) undue delay often encountered by taxpayers, resulting from the necessity of securing an advance ruling regardless of the business exigencies supporting the transaction; (2) transactions where the particular corporate adjustment involved only foreign corporations, which, although technically covered by the §367 advance ruling requirement, nevertheless were consummated without obtaining the necessary ruling and without advance knowledge of the transaction on the part of U.S. shareholders, thus resulting in inadvertent taxability to such shareholders, even though the ruling clearly would have been issued had it been requested; (3) unfair application of the dividend or gain recognition toll charges in certain transactions; and (4) inability of taxpayers effectively to challenge Service decisions under §367 through litigation. Congress also felt that it was generally desirable to replace the present ad hoc case-by-case ruling approach with more public regulations governing the tax consequences of certain transactions subject to this provision.

The 1976 Act dealt with these problems by providing separate rules for two functionally different groups of transactions: (1) expatriating, or outbound, transfers of property (other than stock or securities of a foreign corporation) from the U.S. to a foreign person and (2) all other transfers, i.e., repatriating, or inbound, transfers of property into the United States and those that are exclusively foreign in effect.

As to the first group, the favorable ruling requirement was retained, but application therefore could be made as late as 183 days after the beginning of such transfer under §367(a)(1);[249] moreover, such rulings, or the nonissuance of a ruling, were subject to judicial review;[250] finally, §367(a)(2) author-

---

[249] The General Explanation, supra note 248, at 261, stated that an intentional failure to obtain a required ruling will not automatically result in taxability because "the Secretary may require non-recognition treatment of the transfer in those situations he decrees appropriate even in the absence of a ruling." This statement did not appear in the official Committee Reports of the House Ways and Means Committee, Senate Finance Committee, or Conference Committee; it codified the Service's published view that it can waive §367 if it chooses. Rev. Rul. 64-177, 1964-1 CB 141; Rev. Rul. 76-90, 1976-1 CB 101; see also former Temp. Regs. §7.367(a)-1(g) to the same effect; Regs. §1.367(a)-1(e)(4) (1982) (same as to Service power to waive intentional failure to comply); Regs. §§1.367(a)-1(c) (time and manner of ruling), 1.367(a)-1(d) (persons who must file), 1.367(a)-1(e) (failure to comply), and 1.367(a)-1(f) (protests and appeals).

As noted infra note 258, legislation in 1984 repealed the ruling requirement of former §367(a) and established a new set of limitations and toll charges for outbound transfer based on objective factors.

[250] Section 7477 established a declaratory judgment review procedure in the Tax Court of the Service's actions either in refusing to rule, or in ruling adversely, or on unacceptable terms, with respect to the transaction. See Rev. Proc. 77-5, 1977-1 CB 536, for ruling procedures and administrative remedies under §367 as amended in 1976.

ized the Service to designate by regulations those transactions where no ruling would be required, either because tax avoidance possibilities clearly do
not exist or the amount of the §367 toll charge can be readily ascertained.[251]

As to the second group of transactions, the ruling requirement was
completely eliminated; instead, §367(b) directed the Treasury to promulgate
regulations as to when a foreign corporation is to be considered a "corporation"[252] and dealing specifically with the various tax effects of such transactions, including questions of gain recognition, current dividend treatment,
deferral, basis, and earnings and profits adjustments. In effect, §367(b) went
public as to the transactions governed thereby, spelling out the applicable
ground rules in regulations rather than by private ruling.[253]

The function of the first category of provisions was to prevent expatria-
tion of appreciated movable property away from the taxing jurisdiction of
the United States; the purpose underlying the second category was to protect the integrity of the CFC rules of §§951 and 1248 by ensuring that U.S.
dividend taxation would be imposed upon the repatriation of untaxed earnings of a foreign corporation, and that such tax would be imposed at the
appropriate time (either currently or at some later triggering event) on the
potential §1248 dividend income inherent in the stock of controlled foreign
corporations to the extent of the post-1962 accumulated earnings attributable to such stock.

Examples of outbound transfers subject to the 1976 law ruling requirements of §367(a)(1) were §351 transfers by U.S. persons to a foreign corpo-

---

See generally Dittler Bros., supra note 243 (taxpayer won under §7477 because
Service was unable to support its determination of tax avoidance by substantial evidence). Accord: Hershey Foods Corp., supra note 243; Kaiser Aluminum & Chem.
Corp., supra note 243; Gerli & Co. v. CIR, supra note 243 (automatic toll charge
improper where no showing of tax-avoidance effect). But see current law to the contrary, infra note 258.

[251] See former Temp Regs. §7.367(a)-1(b)(5) for the extremely limited exercise of
this authority (in effect, the excepted transaction category of the temporary regulations is similar to the late ruling provisions of former §367(b), enacted in 1971 to
permit after the fact rulings for certain reincorporation-type transactions).

[252] Taxpayers also were entitled to judicial review of these regulations, although
the chances of successfully prevailing on the issue of whether the regulation, as
applied to the taxpayer's case, "are not necessary or appropriate to prevent avoidance of Federal income taxes" was remote.

[253] These regulations strongly resembled the ruling guidelines of Rev. Proc. 68-
23, 1968-1 CB 821; see Pugh & Samuels, supra note 241; Temp. Regs. §§7.367(a)-1–
7.367(c)-2; for analyses of these regulations, see Clark, New Temporary Section 367
Regulations, 56 Taxes 405 (1978); N.Y. State Bar Association, Tax Section, Report
on the Proposed Regulations Under Section 367 (1978), reprinted in 34 Tax. L. Rev.
79 (1978); see also Kingson, The Theory and Practice of Section 367, 37 NYU Inst.
on Fed. Tax'n ch. 22 (1979). New temporary regulations under §367(b) governing
stock transfers were proposed on December 23, 1982.

ration, §332 liquidations of U.S. subsidiaries into their foreign parent, and acquisitions of the stock or assets of U.S. corporations by foreign corporations in a Type B, Type C, or Type D reorganization.[254] Exchanges where the only transfer of property out of the United States is stock of a foreign corporation which is a party to the exchange were (and are) treated as transfers *into* the United States and thus subject to §367(b), since the concern here is avoidance of dividend tax on the accumulated earnings of the foreign corporation.[255]

Examples of other transfers that are governed by the regulations promulgated under §367(b) are (1) inbound, or repatriating, transfers, such as a §332 liquidation of a foreign subsidiary of a U.S. parent, and acquisitions of the stock or assets of foreign corporations in Type B, Type C, or Type D reorganizations and (2) exclusively foreign exchanges, such as an acquisition of the stock of a CFC by another foreign corporation, and acquisition of the stock of a CFC by another CFC controlled by the same shareholders, acquisition of the assets of a CFC by another foreign corporation, recapitalization of a foreign corporation, or the transfer of property by one CFC to its foreign subsidiary.[256] Liquidation of a second-tier foreign subsidiary into a first-tier foreign subsidiary and various other combinations of exchanges involving stock of foreign corporations also are governed by the regulations under §367(b)(2), which provide for the timing and character of gain recognition or nonrecognition, as the case may be, and for various adjustments to earnings and profits and bases arising from such transactions.[257]

---

[254] Also treated as an outbound transfer is a Type C reorganization between two unrelated domestic corporations where the acquiring corporation is controlled by foreigners; see General Explanation, supra note 248, at 260 n.1. Other types of indirect outbound transfers include triangular reorganization between two domestic corporations where stock of a foreign parent is used as the consideration, termination of a §1504(d) election, and reclassification of a foreign enterprise as a corporation; see Temp. Regs. §1.367(a)-1T(c) (1986).

[255] See IR 85-62, issuing Ann. 85-95. 1985-27 IRB 18; Terr, Announcement 85-95—Outbound Stock Transfers, 12 J. Corp. Tax'n 393 (1985); see also Temp. Regs. §§1.367(a)-3T(b)(1) (1986) and 1.367(a)-3T(d)(1) (1986), to the same effect under the 1984 version of §367(a), infra note 258.

[256] The General Explanation, supra note 248, stated (at note 264) that it expected the regulations to provide for no immediate tax on these exclusively foreign transfers. See Temp. Regs. §§7.367(b)-1–7.367(b)-12 (1977), which generally follow this approach so long as the potential §1248 taint is preserved as a result of the transaction.

[257] Amended §367 was effective generally for transfers after 1978; until then, the old rules continued to apply, but with the new 183-day ruling procedure substituted for the old advance ruling requirement for transfers after October 9, 1975. For Temporary Regulations under these provisions, see Temp. Regs. §§7.367(b)-1–367(b)-12 (1977). These regulations strongly reflect the 1968 §367 guidelines in Rev. Proc. 68-

5. The Tax Reform Act of 1984 amendments to §367(a). In 1984, §367 was revised once again to strengthen the outbound transfer provisions of §367(a), which the Congress felt had been weakened by court decisions.[258] The tax-avoidance principal purpose test (and the mandatory ruling requirement) were replaced with an objective effects test, based largely on the 1968 guidelines approach, which generally permits outbound transfers of property for use in an active foreign business, but also imposes a toll charge on the transfer of certain designated categories of tainted assets (where the tax-avoidance potential is deemed to be unacceptably high).

The principal reasons asserted for amending §367(a) were the following:

(1) Application of the subjective tax-avoidance principal purpose test had been weakened by a series of Tax Court cases[259] and generally was causing administrative difficulty for the IRS;

(2) The mandatory ruling requirement procedure was becoming burdensome for both taxpayers and the Service, and the declaratory judgment procedure of §7477 gave taxpayers an unintended advantage through their full control over the nature of the factual evidence on which both the ruling and declaratory judgment determinations were based;

(3) Outbound transfers of U.S. developed intangibles were resulting in a mismatching of tax benefits and burdens with respect to the deductions and subsequent income from such property (development costs could be deducted against U.S. income, while subsequent earnings on the intangibles would not be subject to any significant U.S. or foreign taxes);

(4) Replacement of the subjective tax-avoidance principal purpose test with an objective active foreign business asset use test (subject to designated categories of tainted assets, which would be subject to current exit toll charges) was thought to be a more effective mechanism for policing the potential for tax avoidance on such transactions; and

---

23, 1968-1 CB 821, although some modifications were made to reflect Congress's express intentions to liberalize these provisions. See Rev. Proc. §3.03, 1977-1 CB 536.

[258] The Tax Reform Act of 1984, §131, abolished the mandatory ruling requirement altogether and switched to an objective effects test (with a notice procedure) in new §367(a). See generally Eustice, supra note 7, ¶ 4.02. See also H.R. Rep. No. 432, Pt. 2, 98th Cong., 2d Sess. 1315 (1984); S. Rep. No. 169, 98th Cong., 2d Sess. 360 (1984). The Ways and Means Report specifically disapproved of the *Dittler Bros.* and *Hershey Foods* decisions.

[259] E.g., Dittler Bros., supra note 243 (Service not able to meet substantial evidence standard; taxpayer wins under §7477).

(5) Incorporation of a foreign loss branch, whose prior foreign losses had reduced U.S. tax on foreign income (a situation not covered by the recapture rules of §904(f)), was thought to be an appropriate time to recapture the tax benefits derived from those prior losses.

Consequently, the 1984 legislation revised the outbound transfer rules of §367(a) and essentially adopted the objective approach of the 1968 guidelines, with certain modifications, abandoning the mandatory ruling requirement and the subjective tax-avoidance principal purpose standard of prior law. Tainted assets subject to a current toll charge were specifically listed in the statute and conformed closely, although not identically, to the categories listed in the 1968 guidelines. Special rules were provided for transfers of intangibles (which were treated as if they had been sold for a contingent price). Moreover, incorporation of a foreign loss branch triggered a special recapture rule (thus complementing the §904(f) recapture rules). Finally, the Act established a notification requirement for §367 transfers and a set of penalties for intentional failure to comply with that requirement (and also extended the statute of limitations if the requisite notice is not given).[260]

5. Transactions governed by §367: In general. As noted above, §367 (both the old and new versions) applies only to exchanges falling under §§332, 351, 354, 355,[261] and 361 where corporate status is essential to operation of their nonrecognition rules. Thus, a transfer to a controlled foreign corporation under §351 falls under §367, as does the liquidation under §332 of a foreign subsidiary by a domestic parent or of a domestic subsidiary by a foreign parent, as well as, for the same reason, a reorganization involving the participation of a foreign corporation, either as transferor or transferee.

Nonrecognition sections not listed in §367 (e.g., §§337, 1032, and 1036), however, do not require §367 clearance for their application,[262] nor do non-

---

[260] Temporary regulations were issued under the 1984 Act version of §367 on May 15, 1986, Regs. §§1.367(a)-1T–1.367(a)-7T, and 1.367(d)-1T. See Terr, The Tax Treatment of Outbound Transfers, 17 J. Corp. Tax'n 79 (1987).

[261] The Tax Reform Act of 1986 moved §355 from §367(a) to §367(e)(1) and revised §367(e) to include outbound §355 distributions and §332 liquidations (under this provision, §355 distributions by a U.S. corporation to a foreign person, and §332 liquidations of a U.S. subsidiary into a foreign parent, will not qualify for nonrecognition treatment at the distributing corporation level). But see H.R. Conf. Rep. No. 841, 99th Cong., 2d Sess. 202 (1986) (but may get nonrecognition on a §332 liquidation if appreciated assets remain in the United States). See IRS Advance Notice 87-5, 1987-3 IRB 7 (foreign-to-foreign liquidations under §367(e)(2), infra ¶ 17.43).

[262] See, e.g., Rev. Rul. 64-156, 1964-1 CB 139 (recapitalization that also qualified as a §1036 exchange did not need §367 ruling); Temp. Regs. §7.367(b)-4(c) (1977); Rev. Rul. 66-171, 1966-1 CB 181 (same for Type F reorganization that also fell under §1036); Temp. Regs. §7.367(b)-4(d); Rev. Rul. 72-420, 1972-2 CB 473. But these

recognition sections that are not dependent on the corporate status of the foreign corporation (e.g., a transfer by a foreign corporation to a controlled domestic corporation under §351). Thus, the fact that the transferred property consists of stock of a foreign corporation does not necessarily make §367 applicable if the foreign corporation's corporate status is not essential to nonrecognition treatment (e.g., a transfer of stock of a foreign corporation under §351 to a controlled domestic corporation).[263] As noted above, §367 applies only to exchange transactions where potential gain exists for one of the exchanging parties; exchanges resulting in the realization of loss do not fall within its provisions. The same principle applies if the exchange results in neither gain nor loss.[264] Finally, many other types of property transfers which do not purport to qualify as tax-free exchanges under the sections listed in §367 (e.g., taxable liquidations, sales, leases, licenses, loans, or the like) do not require §367 rulings even though one of the participants is a foreign corporation.[265]

At one time it was thought that §367 rulings were necessary only in cases where immediate U.S. tax consequences would arise from the transaction (i.e., currently recognized gain). This view had to be refined, however, to take account of the wide range of collateral tax effects flowing from a given transaction, some of which could have at least an indirect current impact on U.S. taxpayers (e.g., earnings and profits determinations, foreign tax credits), or even a direct current impact on U.S. taxpayers under Subpart F.[266]

---

rulings were declared obsolete by Rev. Rul. 78-381, 1978-2 CB 347, in view of the 1976 Act amendments to §367(b). See also the status of capital contributions (which were made subject to §367 in 1971 by §367(c)(2), overruling prior decisions, infra note 265); Rev. Rul. 79-150, 1979-1 CB 149 (a Type F reorganization to which §1036 applied need not comply with §367 notice requirement). Also §356 was added to the §367(a) outbound transfer regime by The Tax Reform Act of 1984, supra notes 241 and 260.

[263] See Rev. Rul. 55-45, 1955-1 CB 34; Rev. Rul. 70-433, 1970-2 CB 82 (§351 transfer of stock of foreign corporation to a domestic corporation allowed even though also a Type B reorganization).

[264] See Rev. Rul. 68-43, 1968-1 CB 146.

[265] But see Retail Properties, Inc., supra note 239; American Mfg. Co., supra note 130; Abegg v. CIR, supra note 40, involving purportedly taxable liquidations that were recast as reorganizations for §367 purposes. See supra ¶ 14.54. As to capital contributions, see 1971 amendments, supra note 262. See also infra note 326.

But see Hospital Corp. of Am., 81 TC 520 (1983) (diversion of business opportunity to foreign subsidiary not a property transfer for purposes of §367); LeBeau & Dostart, Offshore Tax Planning May Be Favorably Affected by Recent *Hospital Corp.* Decision, 60 J. Tax'n 294 (1984).

[266] See Rev. Rul. 64-157, 1964-1 CB 139 (§367 ruling required because recognition of gain would generate currently taxable Subpart F income to U.S. parent corporation), but superseded by Temp. Regs. §7.367(b)-5(e); Construction Aggregates Corp. v. US, 350 F. Supp. 726 (N.D. Ill. 1972) (failure to obtain §367 ruling on

Moreover, the Service encouraged taxpayers to seek §367 rulings, even where no immediate U.S. tax consequences were present, if the parties desired certainty as to the future U.S. tax consequences of the deal. On the other hand, if U.S. tax rules were completely unimportant to all parties to the transaction (e.g., a reorganization of two foreign corporations, both of wholly foreign ownership), §367 was clearly inapplicable. [267]

It was in the area of reorganization exchanges that §367 had its broadest and most intricate impact, since §§354, 355, and 361 all require corporate status of a participating foreign corporation for their application. Thus, both the transferor and the transferee must be corporations in Types A, C, and D reorganizations in order for the nonrecognition provisions of §361 to apply. If one or both of such corporations were foreign corporations, gain would be recognized to the transferor on the exchange of its property for stock of the transferee. Also, the provisions of §§354 and 355 require exchanges thereunder to involve corporate stock or securities; hence, a failure to satisfy §367 would render the entire transaction taxable if one of the corporations whose stock was either transferred or received was a foreign corporation. Since §1032 is not among the nonrecognition sections to which §367 applies, however, a corporation acquiring property in exchange for its stock is protected from recognition of gain by §1032 even if other parties to the transaction had to recognize gain because of a failure to obtain a ruling under §367.

7. Tax avoidance under §367. The tax-avoidance standard contemplated by §367 must be viewed in the larger context of the rules dealing with the taxation of foreign income. The special gloss of these provisions on the tax-avoidance doctrine under §367 is of particular importance in determining whether the transaction will pass muster with the Service. One of the principal efforts of the Service in applying §367 to the reorganization area is to prevent the tax-free repatriation of previously untaxed foreign earnings; but if the earnings remain in foreign corporate solution after the reorganization, favorable treatment under §367 can be expected. Other tainted transactions that prevent favorable §367 treatment include attempts to isolate and expatriate assets for sale so as to reduce potential U.S. taxes thereon and

---

liquidation of second-tier subsidiary into first-tier subsidiary created FPHC income to latter corporation which was currently taxable to U.S. parent under §551; §367 ruling necessary per Rev. Rul. 64-157 even though transaction occurred before 1962 rules of §951; §551 FPHC rules had same general theory).

[267] The ruling requirement was dropped in 1976 for all non-outbound transactions covered by §367(b) and was dropped totally for outbound transfers under §367(a) by the Tax Reform Act of 1984, supra note 258.

efforts to divert income from possible U.S. taxation.[268] The business purpose requirement for a valid reorganization (see Chapter 14) is independent of the tax-avoidance standard that must be satisfied under §367; although similar in some respects, it seems clear that the Service viewed the §367 showing of no tax avoidance as requiring more than mere proof of a business purpose for the reorganization, although the latter is certainly a minimum prerequisite here. Even the 1968 guidlines did not prescribe precise criteria for determining whether the transaction had as one of its principal purposes the avoidance of federal income taxes. For example, whether transfers resulting in a *deferral* of taxes can be distinguished from those resulting in a permanent reduction is still a murky question.[269] However, legislation enacted in 1984 dropped the tax-avoidance principal purpose test for outbound transfers and switched to an objective effects test, based on the 1968 guidelines with toll charges for designated categories of tainted assets.[270]

---

[268] Thus, an obvious theme in the §367 guidelines was prevention of taxpayer efforts to reorganize out of the §1248 taint with respect to stock of a foreign corporation and to block transactions that resulted in elimination of CFC status, unless the shareholders consented to a §1248 toll charge on their stock. Also prevalent in §367 is the notion that U.S. taxpayers should not be allowed to expatriate domestically generated income.

Note that §367 is concerned with the avoidance of U.S., not foreign, taxes. For possible analogies, see other "state of mind" provisions such as §§269, 357(b), 482, 531, and 1551. See generally Note, State of Mind Analysis in Corporate Taxation, 69 Colum. L. Rev. 1224 (1969).

For illustration of Service tax-avoidance analysis in a §367(a) outbound transfer, see Priv. Ltr. Rul. 8,305,036, 1983 Fed. Taxes (P-H) ¶ 54,820.

[269] See, e.g., Rev. Rul. 78-201, 1978-1 CB 91 (deferral of U.S. taxes on future foreign earnings of incorporated branch resulted in tax avoidance on facts, and previously deducted losses of branch had to be recaptured as ordinary foreign-source income upon incorporation of the branch).

But the recapture theory of Rev. Rul. 78-201 was rejected by Hershey Foods Corp., supra note 243, and Kaiser Aluminum & Chem. Corp., supra note 243 (deferral of future U.S. taxes not avoidance under §367). See Lowry, supra note 243; see also Robert Pitcher, supra note 243 (no tax avoidance; valid business reasons for transaction; failure of Service to enter into closing agreement an important factor in court's decision); Mars, Inc., 88 TC No. 19 (1987) (ruling rejected despite 1984 Act history).

But see Rev. Rul. 81-4, 1981-1 CB 126 (foreign currency per se taxable if exported in outbound transfer; like marketable liquid assets and cannot leave U.S. without toll charge).

Recent legislation (supra note 258) disagreed with, and overruled, *Dittler Bros.,* replacing the tax-avoidance principal purpose test with an objective exit toll charge system for outbound transfers of tainted assets similar to the approach of the 1968 guidelines.

[270] Supra note 258; for regulations under the 1984 version of §367, see supra note 260.

¶ 17.41　SECTION 367: CURRENT LAW AND REGULATIONS

1. Outbound transfers: Section 367(a). As amended by the Tax Reform Act of 1984, §367(a)(1) provides generally that transfers of appreciated property by a U.S. person to a foreign corporation in connection with any exchange described in §§332, 351, 354, 355, or 361 will be currently taxable to the transferor. Moreover, §367(e) applies similar principles to outbound liquidation distributions under §§336 and 355 (thus, full recognition on the distribution of tainted assets now will be required here, not merely on recapture gains).[271] This sweeping general rule is then modified by new §367(a)(3)(A), however, which reconfers nonrecognition treatment for assets used in the active conduct of a trade or business outside the U.S. (subject to expansion or contraction by regulations).[272] Assets that are ineligible for the active foreign business exception (i.e., tainted assets) are listed in new §367(a)(3)(B): (1) inventory and copyrights (not subject to the special rules of §367(d)); (2) installment obligations and receivables; (3) foreign currency or property denominated in foreign currency; (4) intangibles not subject to the special treatment under §367(d); and (5) property that is presently leased (other than to the transferee). Categories (1), (2), and (5) are carried over from the 1968 guidelines; catagory (3) is new.[273]

Stock or securities of a foreign or domestic corporation, property likely to be leased by the transferee, and transfers of limited partnership interests are not automatically tainted; rather they are to be tested under the general active foreign business asset use standard of §367(a)(3)(A).[274] But a transfer of stock of a U.S. corporation to a foreign corporation in a Type B reorganization apparently now will be covered by §367(a)(1), since none of the exceptions in §367(a)(2) or §367(a)(3)(A) can apply.[275] Outbound transfers of intangibles to a foreign corporation in any exchange under §351 or §361

---

[271] The Tax Reform Act of 1986 repealed the nonrecognition rule of §336 (supra ¶ 11.06), but retained it for §332 liquidations at the subsidiary level in revised §337 (supra ¶ 11.49); the 1986 Act also moved §355 to §367(e)(1) and provided for general taxability of expatriating §332 liquidations in §367(e)(2); supra note 261; infra ¶ 17.43.

For temporary regulations under §367 as amended in 1984, see supra note 260.

[272] For application of these rules, see Temp. Regs. §1.367(a)-2T (1986); Terr, supra note 260, at 80–81.

[273] But see Rev. Rul. 81-4, supra note 269. See generally Temp. Regs. §§1.367(a)-5T (1986) and 1.367(a)-4T (1986).

[274] See Temp. Regs. §§1.367(a)-3T(e) and 1.367(a)-4T (1986).

[275] See 1986 Temp. Regs. §1.367(a)-1(c)(2)(ii), 1.367(a)-3(c)(1). But see Temp. Regs. §§1.367(a)-3(b)(1) and 1.367(a)-3(d)(1), supra note 255 (Type B reorganization involving *two* foreign corporations is subject to §367(b), not §367(a)); see also Terr, supra note 255, at 83–86 for limited exceptions provided in the §367(a) regulations; see generally infra ¶ 17.44.

are treated, under §367(d), as a deemed sale of such property for a contingent price payable over the useful life of the property (and the periodic income therefrom is characterized as U.S.-source ordinary income).[276]

Incorporation of a foreign loss branch will trigger current recognition of gain to the extent of the previously deducted foreign losses under new §367(a)(3)(C), less any amounts recaptured under §904(f)(3). Thus, the general principle of Rev. Rul. 78-201 is codified by the new law, but income is recognized only to the extent of the lesser of appreciation on the transferred assets or the amount of the previously deducted losses.[277] Recognized gain under this provision is characterized as foreign-source ordinary income.

To illustrate: T incorporates a foreign branch that has deducted $100 of prior losses (none of which are recapturable under §904(f)(3)); T transfers tainted assets with $30 of potential gain and untainted assets with $90 of potential gain. T recognizes $120 on the transfer ($30 under §367(a)(3)(B) and $90 under §367(a)(3)(C); if potential gain on the untainted assets was only $60, then $90 would be recognized on the transfer; if potential gain on untainted assets was $110, then $130 would be recognized.

2. Other transfers: Section 367(b). As amended by the Tax Reform Act of 1976, §367(b) applies to all other transfers (i.e., inbound (or repatriating) transfers of property into the United States and those that are exclusively foreign in effect).

As to the second group of transactions governed by §367(b), the ruling requirement was completely eliminated in 1976; instead, §367(b) directed the Treasury to promulgate regulations as to when a foreign corporation is to be considered a corporation and dealing specifically with the various tax effects of such transactions, including questions of gain recognition, current dividend treatment, deferral, basis, and earnings and profits adjustments. Thus, §367(b) went public as to the transactions governed thereby, spelling out the applicable ground rules in regulations rather than by private ruling.[278]

Examples of other transfers that are governed by the regulations promulgated under §367(b) are (1) inbound (or repatriating) transfers, such as a §332 liquidation of a foreign subsidiary of a U.S. parent, and acquisitions of the stock or assets of foreign corporations in Type B, Type C, or

---

[276] See Temp. Regs. §1.367(d)-1T (1986); for the 1986 Tax Reform Act super royalty amendment, see Granwell & Hirsh, The Super Royalty, supra note 157.

[277] Supra notes 245 and 269; see generally Temp. Regs. §1.367(a)-6T (1986); Terr, supra note 260.

[278] Supra note 253.

Type D reorganizations and (2) exclusively foreign exchanges, such as an acquisition of the stock of a CFC by another foreign corporation, and acquisition of the stock of a CFC by another CFC controlled by the same shareholders, acquisition of the assets of a CFC by another foreign corporation, recapitalization of a foreign corporation, or the transfer of property by one CFC to its foreign subsidiary.[279] Liquidation of a second-tier foreign subsidiary into a first-tier foreign subsidiary and various other combinations of exchanges involving stock of foreign corporations also are governed by the regulations under §367(b)(2), which provide for the timing and character of gain recognition or nonrecognition, as the case may be, and for various adjustments to earnings and profits and bases arising from such transactions.[280]

3. Regulations under §367. The statutory regime of §367 has been extensively explicated by a series of elaborate regulations, in temporary form, commencing in 1977,[281] and culminating with the issuance of temporary regulations under the 1984 outbound rules of §367(a) in 1986.[282] Although the length and intricacy of these regulations defies a concise summary of their provisions, the salient points will be noted here and in the material that follows.

Pursuant to the congressional mandate of the 1976 Act, regulations were issued under §367, although in temporary form, on December 30, 1977. The outbound transfers governed by §367(a)(1) were dealt with in Temp. Regs. §7.367(a)-1, which continued the requirement that a no-tax-avoidance ruling be obtained in order to recognize the corporate status of a foreign corporation (although such ruling could now be filed after the fact if the filing occurs within 183 days of the beginning of the transfer). The guideline principles of Rev. Proc. 68-23 continued to be applicable to these transactions (although the regulations were silent on this point).[283]

The only exchange excepted from coverage under §367(a) was a classic Type F reorganization (Temp. Regs. §7.367(a)-1(b)(5)). Also of special note was Temp. Regs. §7.367(a)-1(g), which reiterated the Service's view that §367 is a one-way street and a ruling could be forced on a taxpayer who attempted to use the absence of a required ruling to its advantage.[284]

---

[279] Supra note 256, infra para. 3.

[280] Supra note 257, infra para. 3.

[281] Supra notes 253, 256, and 257, dealing with §367(b).

[282] Regs. §§1.367(a)-1T–1.367(a)-7T, and 1.367(d)-1T (1986), supra note 260, dealing with the 1984 Act amendments to §§367(a) and 367(d).

[283] Rev. Proc. 68-23, 1968-1 CB 821; Rev. Proc. 77-5, 1977-1 CB 536 at §3.03.

[284] Supra notes 242, 249, and 251.

The 1977 proposed regulations were replaced with a new set of proposed regulations in 1982, which became final in 1984,[285] but these regulations were replaced in turn by new temporary regulations in 1986 to reflect the amendments to §367 by the Tax Reform Act of 1984 (including abolition of the ruling requirement and the subjective tax-avoidance test of former §367(a)).[286]

At the core of the 1977 Temporary Regulations under §367, however, were those provisions dealing with §367(b)'s other transfers. These rules, found in Temp. Regs. §§7.367(b)-1–7.367(b)-12, constitued a defense mechanism to §1248. To the extent that the Service feels that the transaction is likely to result in an escape from the provisions of §1248, an immediate dividend toll charge will be imposed; by contrast, if the §1248 taint is preserved following the transaction, no immediate toll charge will be imposed. This theme of blocking attempts to effect a tax-free repatriation of foreign generated earnings and profits is the key to most of the intricacies of the temporary regulations.

Temp. Regs. §7.367(b)-1 sets out the general purpose of these provisions and requires, in §7.367(b)-1(c), that any person in receipt of potential income as a result of a §367(b) transaction must notify the district director with which his normal return would be filed of this fact. Section 7.367(b)-2 provides general definitions, the key ones being the "section 1248 amount" in §§7.367(b)-2(d) and 7.367(b)-2(e). Temp. Regs. §7.367(b)-3 provides special rules with respect to various computations under §1248, earnings and profits, and foreign tax credits. Section 7.367(b)-4 sets forth various transactional preference rules in the case of overlapping provisions (namely, that §351 or §361 initially took precedence over §368(a)(1)(B) if both applied to the same transaction, a priority that was reversed, however, by subsequent regulations,[287] that §1036 takes precedence over §354, and that the Type F reorganization for purposes of §367(b) only involves a single corporate entity, not the more expansive version sanctioned formerly by courts and the Service.[288]

The rules of Temp. Regs. §7.367(b)-4(b) were revised by temporary regulations, issued on December 23, 1982, dealing with the treatment of transfers of stock of foreign corporations that constitute both a §351 (or §361) exchange and a §354-Type B reorganization. These regulations subjected such

---

[285] TD 7954, 1984-1 CB 107, effective June 7, 1984.

[286] Supra note 260 and para. 1 of this section.

[287] Temp. Regs. §7.367(b)-4(b) (1982); Temp Regs. §§1.367(a)-3T(b)(1) and 1.367(a)-3T(d)(1) (1986); supra note 255.

[288] Rev. Rul. 79-150, 1979-1 CB 149 (example of §1036 priority over §354); changes in the Type F reorganization definition by the Tax Equity and Fiscal Responsibility Act of 1982 now limit this type of reorganization to single operating companies as well; supra ¶ 14.18, para. 3.

transactions to §367(b) (rather than §367(a) as under the former version), with the result that the §1248 toll charges would apply (unless the §1248 taint was preserved in the new stock). Moreover, realized gain in excess of the §1248 taint on the transferred stock would be recognized (unless the transferor was a U.S. person and obtained a §367(a)(1) ruling or the transferor was a U.S. shareholder of both the transferred corporation and the transferee, so that the §1248 taint was preserved in the transferee's stock).

Section 7.367(b)-5 deals with complete liquidations of foreign subsidiaries; if the liquidation is into a domestic parent corporation, the parent in effect is given the option of paying a dividend toll charge based on the full earnings and profits account of the foreign subsidiary or of treating the transaction as if the subsidiary's stock had been sold in a fully taxable §1248 transaction (in either case, however, the subsidiary's asset basis carries over to the parent as if §334(b)(1) applied). Liquidation of a remote tiered foreign subsidiary into another foreign subsidiary does not trigger any immediate toll charge under these proposals, however, because foreign earnings remain in foreign corporate solution.

Sections 7.367(b)-7–7.367(b)-12 spell out the treatment of various stock and asset reorganizations under §367(b), and the two key sections in this pattern are §§7.367(b)-7 and 7.367(b)-9. The theme of these provisions is preservation of the §1248 taint; if the §1248 dividend taint would be lost as a result of the transaction, then an immediate dividend toll charge is imposed by Temp. Regs. §7.367(b)-7(c), but if the §1248 taint is preserved, the earnings and profits tracing rules and basis adjustment rules of §7.367-9 take hold. Of special importance in this latter respect are the earnings and profits adjustment provisions in §§7.367(b)-9(c) and 7.367(b)-9(d) and the basis adjustment rules in §§7.367(b)-9(e) and 7.367(b)-9(f).

Section 7.367(b)-10 deals with §355 divisive distributions that fall within the scope of §367(b) and echo the toll charge theme of the above regulations sections based upon the extent to which §1248 dividend potential is preserved, or lost, as a result of the transaction. Section 7.367(b)-11 deals with post-transaction deficits, and §7.367(b)-12 relates to various post-transaction triggering events (distributions and dispositions of stock), where the initial transaction did not result in an immediate §367 toll charge with respect to that stock. The 17 examples of Temp. Regs. §7.367(b)-13, issued on October 4, 1979, illustrate the operation of the §367(b) regulations' principles outlined above.[289]

---

[289] For analysis of these regulations by their principal draftsman, see Kingson, supra note 253, N.Y. State Bar Association, Tax Section, Report on the Examples Under Section 367(b), 35 Tax L. Rev. 317 (1980). Example (14) of Temp. Regs. §7.367(b)-13 was amended by TD 7863, 1983-1 CB 80 (1982) to reflect the change in the treatment of §§351–354 overlap transactions involving stock of a foreign corporation by Temp. Regs. §7.367(b)-4(b); supra note 287.

4. Collateral amendments by Tax Reform Acts of 1976 and 1984. While life became more bearable for taxpayers under §367, the rules of a comparable provision, §1491 (the excise tax on transfers of appreciated property by U.S. persons to foreign trusts, corporations, and partnerships) were considerably broadened to include all transfers (taxable or tax-free) of any type of property (not just stock or securities) to foreign trusts, corporations and partnerships, and to raise the excise tax rate from 27.5 to 35 percent. The tax applies to taxable transactions as well as nontaxable transfers (except that transfers to foreign corporations only cover capital contributions under this provision), but if gain is recognized to the transferor *at the time* of the transfer, such gain will reduce the amount subject to the §1491 excise tax. In lieu of being subject to the 35 percent excise tax of §1491, §§1057 and 1492(3) allow taxpayers to elect to treat the transfer as a presently taxable sale subject to normal tax rates, thus affording taxpayers who wish to accelerate income (e.g., to absorb expiring net operating losses) with a ready mechanism to effect their goals.

Transfers to tax-exempt organizations are not subject to the §1491 tax, however, and §§1492(2) and 1494(b) exempt transfers that are either "described in §367," or for which the taxpayer elects (before the transfer) application of the "principles of §367" even though the transfer is not so described.[290]

With the repeal of the mandatory ruling requirement in 1984 (and also the declaratory judgment procedure of §7477), Congress was unwilling to rely solely on the audit process to police outbound transfers subject to §367(a). Consequently, the new law established a notification requirement and a set of penalties for failure to comply with that requirement in new §6038B, so that the Service will continue to be aware of transfers subject to §367(a). The penalty for noncompliance with the notice requirement is 25 percent of the gain realized on the exchange (unless it is shown that such failure is due to reasonable cause and not to willful neglect). In addition, the statute of limitations is tolled during the period which the required notice has not been given (§6501(c)(8)).

¶ 17.42 TRANSFERS TO AND BY FOREIGN CORPORATIONS UNDER §351

1. Background: The pre-1984 rules. In the case of expatriating outbound transfers under §351 (i.e., transfers of property to a controlled foreign

---

[290] But see Rev. Rul. 82-112, 1982-1 CB 59 (§1491 tax not applicable to capital contribution by U.S. parent to 100 percent owned foreign subsidiary consisting of stock of the subsidiary; transfer described in §367(b)(1), so §1491 not applicable).

corporation), the 1968 guidelines in §3.02(1) provided that transfers ordinarily would receive a favorable §367 ruling if the transferred property was devoted to the active conduct of a trade or business *in* a foreign country or countries and such business either required a substantial investment in fixed assets of the business or constituted a wholly foreign trading enterprise.[291] The apparent requirement of an all-foreign trading enterprise may well have precluded establishment of a foreign sales subsidiary (with appreciated property) if it intended to purchase goods from a domestic affiliate, although this provision may have been limited to transactions that constituted a device for increasing income diverted to the subsidiary above a normal wholesaler's profit.[292]

The categories of tainted assets that, under the guidelines, could not be transferred in such an exchange consisted of two basic classifications: those assets that could not be transferred at all and those that could not generally be transferred. The first category of absolutely tainted assets included all inventory-type assets, untaxed receivables, artistic property, stock or securi-

---

[291] As amended in 1984, however, §367(a)(3)(A) merely requires the conduct of an active business *outside* of the United States and use of the transferred assets in that business; see Temp. Regs. §1.367(a)-2T(b)(4) (1986) (test satisfied if primary managerial and operational activities conducted outside United States and substantially all of assets are located outside United States, infra para. 2).

[292] See Rev. Rul. 78-201, 1978-1 CB 91 (incorporation of foreign branch that had incurred prior deductible losses; held, ruling conditioned on transferor's recognition of ordinary foreign source income equal to prior deducted losses—in effect a tax benefit recapture toll charge).

For further amplifications of Rev. Rul. 78-201 principles, see Rev. Rul. 80-163, 1980-1 CB 78 (recapture rule of Rev. Rul. 78-201 applies to full extent of prior losses even though this amount is greater than transferor's realized gains on §351 property transfer); Rev. Rul. 80-246 1980-2 CB 125 (amount of §367 gain toll per Rev. Rul. 78-201 reduced by §904(f)(3)(A) loss recapture income); Rev. Rul. 80-247, 1980-2 CB 127 (losses that must be recaptured under Rev. Rul. 78-201 include expenses related to branch property abandoned as worthless); Rev. Rul. 80-293, 1980-2 CB 128 (loss recapture on incorporation of foreign partnership limited to losses incurred by partnership after U.S. partners acquired their interests in the partnership); Rev. Rul. 81-82, 1981-1 CB 127 (no netting of gains and losses of separate divisions; also, must recapture all losses of loss divisions even though not all assets transferred); Rev. Rul. 81-89, 1981-1 CB 129 (integrated foreign branches of affiliated corporations filing consolidated returns can combine profits and losses).

The courts uniformly rejected Rev. Rul. 78-201, however; see Mars, Inc., 88 TC 428 (1987) (and cases cited).

Amendments to §367(a) in 1984 adopt the principle of Rev. Rul. 78-201 and reject the decision in *Hershey Foods* but limit the amount of recapturable income on the incorporation of a foreign loss branch to the potential gain on the transferred assets under new §367(a)(3)(C); infra para. 2. See generally Temp. Regs. §1.367(a)-6T (1986).

ties (with two exceptions[293]), and property that was expected to be sold or disposed of by the transferee.[294] The second, or semi-aromatic, category included leased or licensed property (unless leased or licensed to the transferee), property expected to be leased or licensed by the transferee, and patents, trademarks, or similar intangibles (domestic or foreign) that were expected to be used in connection with a domestic business (i.e., an attempted farmout of domestically generated income from such intangibles).[295]

---

[293] (1) Stock or securities of a less developed country corporation to a controlled less developed country corporation holding company, as defined in §902(d)(2) and (2) stock or securities of a foreign corporation if the transferee controlled such corporation after the exchange, within the meaning of §368(c) and if the foreign corporation whose stock or securities were transferred met the tests of §954(c)(4)(A) (i.e., was a holding company for an active subsidiary and both corporations were in the same country). In order for both of these exceptions to apply, however, the above requirements had to be expected to continue for the reasonably foreseeable future. See Guidelines §§3.02(1)(a)(iii)(A) and 3.02(1)(a)(iii)(B).

See also Rev. Rul. 81-4, 1981-1 CB 126 (export of appreciated foreign currency subject to per se toll charge; similar to marketable securities). But see Kaiser Aluminum & Chem. Corp., supra note 243 (rejects mechanical per se toll charge rules; taxpayer showed no tax avoidance, so entitled to §367 ruling notwithstanding guidelines automatic tax); Gerli & Co. v. CIR, supra note 243 (per se toll charge on §332 liquidation rejected in absence of showing of tax avoidance, even though taxpayer had accepted toll charge as condition of favorable §367 ruling); Robert Pitcher, supra note 243 (formation of foreign holding company held tax-free; valid business reasons for transaction, not tax avoidance; failure to meet guidelines not fatal).

[294] For similar tainted asset approach under 1984 Act §367(a)(3)(B), see Temp. Regs. §1.367(a)-5T (1986), infra para. 2.

[295] See Guidelines §§3.02(1)(b)(iii), 3.02(1)(b)(iv), and 3.02(1)(c) (Examples). In the case of domestic intangibles, the prohibited use was in connection with a domestic business or with the manufacture of goods (either foreign or domestic) for consumption in the United States. In the case of foreign intangibles, the prohibited use was in connection with the sale of domestically manufactured goods.

See also Rev. Rul. 79-288, 1979-2 CB 139 (corporate name and associated goodwill held property where protectable under law of country of transfer and hence §367 ruling necessary; but not property where name not protectable and no goodwill transferred so no §367 ruling needed regarding this aspect of transfer; ruling is silent, however, on taxable status of second transaction); Hospital Corp. of Am., supra note 265 (diversion of business opportunity to foreign subsidiary not a transfer of property under §367(a) or §351): LeBeau & Dostart, Offshore Tax Planning May Be Favorably Affected by Recent *Hospital Corp.* Decision, 60 J. Tax'n 294 (1984); Priv. Ltr. Rul. 8305036, 1983 Fed. Taxes (P-H) ¶ 54,820 (net leased farm properties; no ruling because tax-avoidance taint found on facts).

For the property status of know-how transfers under §351, see Rev. Rul. 64-56, 1964-1 CB 133; for guidelines on the status of know-how under §§351 and 367, see Rev. Proc. 69-19, 1969-2 CB 301.

For the more stringent 1984 rules applicable to outbound transfers of intangibles, see §367(d), Temp. Regs. §1.367(d)-1T (1986); infra para. 2.

The 1968 guidelines were clear that the transfer of tainted assets did not infect the transfer of nontainted assets for §367 purposes. Moreover, if a gain with respect to any tainted assets was required to be recognized before a §367 ruling was issued, the transfer of such property would be treated as a taxable exchange for all collateral purposes such as basis and holding period determination and the character of such gain. In this latter respect, the guidelines adopted the transactional approach for situations where gain was required to be recognized by virtue of §367. Under this view, if the exchange was taxable, various other tax attributes flowing from that transaction, such as basis and holding period, were determined as if the nonrecognition rules did not apply.

2. The 1984 rules. Amendments to the outbound transfer rules of §367(a) in 1984[296] dropped the tax-avoidance principal purpose test, repealed the mandatory ruling requirement (and the declaratory judgment procedure of §7477), and adopted an objective active foreign business asset use test,[297] with designated categories of tainted assets, based largely on the 1968 guidelines (although with certain modifications). The statutory list of tainted assets in §367(a)(3)(B) generally follows the 1968 guideline categories (i.e., inventory, artistic property, untaxed receivables, leased property), adds one new category (foreign currency and property denominated in foreign currency), but removes the treatment of stocks and securities of foreign corporations, property expected to be leased, and property expected to be sold from the per se tainted category, and instead subjects such assets to testing under the general active foreign business use standard.[298] Outbound transfers of intangibles under §§351 and 361 are treated as deemed sales for a contingent price to the foreign corporate transferee (and gain is recognized ratably as U.S.-source ordinary income) under §367(d)[299] (other outbound

---

[296] Supra ¶ 17.41, note 258. Temporary regulations, reflecting these amendments, were proposed on May 16, 1986, supra note 260.

[297] Both Committee Reports state that *Dittler Bros.*, supra note 243, would not satisfy this standard of active foreign business; H.R. Rep. No. 432, Pt. 2, 98th Cong., 2d Sess. 1320; S. Rep. No. 169, 98th Cong., 2d Sess. 365; see generally Temp. Regs. §1.367(a)-2T (1986); Terr, supra note 260, at 80.

[298] The Committee Reports, supra note 297, both state that transfers of stock such as that in the *Kaiser Aluminum* case, supra note 243, would qualify under §367(a)(3)(A) for nonrecognition treatment; see Temp. Regs. §1.367(a)-3T(e).

For per se tainted assets, see Temp. Regs. §1.367(a)-5T(1986); for special treatment of particular assets, see Temp. Regs. §1.367(a)-4T (i.e., partial taint for tax benefit attributable to U.S. depreciation recapture; property to be leased tainted unless an active foreign leasing business (see Rev. Proc. 80-14, 1980-1 CB 617); property likely to be sold tainted). See generally Terr, supra note 260.

[299] The Tax Reform Act of 1986 amended §367(d)(2)(A) to require that the imputed royalty must be "commensurate with the income attributable to the intangi-

transfers of intangibles are treated as tainted assets). Finally, the foreign loss branch recapture principles of Rev. Rul. 78-201 are generally codified by new §367(a)(3)(C).[300]

3. Nonoutbound transfers. Where the property transferred in a putative §351 transaction flows from one foreign corporation to another foreign corporation, the transaction, with one exception (where part of the property was stock of a foreign corporation subject to §1248), ordinarily qualifies for automatic tax-free treatment, since it is governed by the other transfer regulations under §367(b).[301] Transfers *by* a foreign corporation to a U.S. controlled corporation under §351 are not subject to §351, however, since corporate status of the transferor is not necessary here.[302]

¶ 17.43 LIQUIDATION OF CONTROLLED SUBSIDIARY UNDER §332

1. Inbound repatriating liquidations. Where a foreign subsidiary is liquidated into its domestic parent corporation, the 1968 Guidelines §3.01(1) required as a condition to the §367 ruling that the domestic parent corporation include as a dividend its share of the earnings and profits of the foreign subsidiary attributable to the domestic parent's stock. Determination of the amount of this dividend was set forth in §4 of the Guidelines, which required that the parent corporation include its share of the subsidiary's earnings for pre-1963 years under the principles of Rev. Rul. 63-6[303] and for post-1962 years under the rules of §§1248(c) and 1248(d). Some, but not all, of the exceptions of §1248(d) applied to this computation, and special computation mechanics were spelled out for determination of the earnings of less developed country corporations, foreign investment companies, and corporations organized in U.S. possessions.[304]

---

ble;" see Granwell & Hirsh, The Super Royalty, supra note 157. As to §367 generally, see Temp. Regs. §1.367(d)-1T (1986), and Terr, supra note 260, at 89–93.

[300] Supra note 292; see Temp. Regs. §1.367(a)-6T (1986), and Terr, supra note 260, at 87–88.

[301] See Temp. Regs. §7.367(b)-8 (1977) for the treatment under §367(b).

[302] Supra note 263.

[303] Rev. Rul. 63-6, 1963-1 CB 126.

[304] See Guidelines §§4.01 and 4.02. If the foreign corporation was a foreign investment company within the meaning of §1246(b), earnings attributable to post-1963 years would be taxed as a dividend. Earnings of a foreign corporation that had already been subjected to U.S. taxation, under either §951 or §11, were excluded under the guidelines.

This aspect of the 1968 guidelines was superseded by the 1976 amendment to §367(b) and, more specifically, by Temp. Regs. §7.367(b)-5, which likewise provided that the dividend toll charge on liquidation of a foreign subsidiary by its U.S. parent is either the entire earnings and profits of the subsidiary attributable to the parent's stock (including pre-1963 earnings), or, alternatively, the entire potential gain with respect to such stock, as if there had been a fully taxable sale thereof (although the carry-over basis rules of §334(b)(1) and the carry-over of tax attributes rules of §381 still would apply to this latter transaction).

2. Outbound expatriating liquidations. Where a foreign parent corporation liquidates its domestic subsidiary, the outbound expatriating transfer analogy of §351 was applied by the 1968 Guidelines, which rules in turn were largely codified in the 1984 amendments to §367.[305] Thus, the same types of assets that are forbidden for §351 exchange transfers similarly can not be transferred to the foreign parent via a liquidation transaction.[306] Note that if the *parent* is not engaged in a trade or business in the United States or, if so engaged, where the liquidation gain is not effectively connected with the conduct of that business, the parent will not be taxable on its gain under §881 or §882, even though the gain did not qualify for nonrecognition treatment by virtue of §367; thus, the parent corporation does not ordinarily need §332 for protection of *its* liquidation gain, in which event application of §367 is of no special consequence to it. However, failure to satisfy §367(a) principles (i.e., the outbound transfer rules) precludes corporate status for the foreign parent under §367(a)(1), which in turn eliminates nonrecognition protection for a domestic subsidiary under current law §337(a),[307] which requires application of §332 to the liquidation for its operative rules. Moreover, a controlled subsidiary's nonrecognition treatment under §337 is sub-

---

But see Gerli & Co. v. CIR, supra note 243 (automatic toll charge improper in absence of showing of tax-avoidance effect; no tax avoidance on facts here, even though taxpayer had accepted toll as condition to favorable §367 ruling; Service has duty to determine whether or not tax avoidance existed on liquidation of foreign subsidiary).

[305] Supra note 258; §§367(a) and 367(d); Temp. Regs. §§1.367(a)-1T–1.367(a)-7T, and 1.367(d)-1T (1986), supra note 260.

[306] Guidelines §3.01(2); 1984 law §367(a)(30)(B); Temp. Regs. §§1.367(a)-3T(d), 1.367(a)-4T, and 1.367(a)-5T (1986); Terr, supra note 260.

[307] The Tax Reform Act of 1986 repealed the nonrecognition rules of pre-1986 law §§336 and 337 (supra ¶ 11.03), but retained nonrecognition for distributions by a subsidiary that liquidates into its parent under §332 (supra ¶ 11.49).

For problems under the pre-1986 law rules involving the interaction of §§332, 337, and 367, see Rev. Rul. 76-90, 1976-1 CB 101, and ¶ 17.43 of the Fourth Edition of this treatise.

ject to §367 by virtue of §367(e)(2), which provides that §337(a) will not apply to a §337 liquidation into a foreign parent except to the extent provided by regulations.[308]

3. Foreign-to-foreign liquidations. Where a foreign subsidiary corporation is liquidated into a parent corporation that is also a foreign organization, the 1968 Guidelines stated flatly that a favorable §367 ruling would automatically be issued.[309] Thus, second-tier foreign subsidiaries can be liquidated into first-tier foreign subsidiaries without proving any special nontax avoidance factors under §367, and this same result occurs under new §367(b)—that is, no ruling is necessary and no current toll charge will be imposed on such a transfer.

¶ 17.44 REORGANIZATION OF FOREIGN CORPORATIONS

1. Type B reorganizations. The general approach of the §367 regime applicable to stock-for-stock Type B reorganization exchanges has been to correlate these rules with the provisions relating to outbound exchanges under §367(a) and, in addition, to the special statutory dividend provisions of §1248 applicable to §367(b) transactions. However, there was no corresponding attempt in the initial 1968 Guidelines to relate the Type B reorganization acquisition rules with the Guideline provisions relating to §332 liquidations. Thus, in the case of an acquisition of stock of a foreign corporation by a domestic corporation in a Type B reorganization transaction, the 1968

---

[308] But H.R. Conf. Rep. No. 841, 99th Cong., 2d Sess. 202 (1986), states that regulations may permit nonrecognition here if the assets remain in the United States.

In IRS Advance Notice 87-5, 1987-3 IRB 7, the Service announced that regulations will be promulgated to address foreign-to-foreign liquidations in the context of the repeal of the *General Utilities* rule. These regulations (which will be effective retroactively to years beginning in 1987) will provide generally for recognition of gain or loss on the liquidation of a subsidiary into its foreign parent, but the regulations will provide an exception to this general rule of recognition where the subsidiary is also foreign (except in cases where the subsidiary has a U.S. real property interest subject to §897 or has domestically based assets used in a U.S. business). The regulations will also exempt liquidations of domestic subsidiaries in cases protected by treaty (until such time as the Treasury is not successful in renegotiating such treaties to obtain appropriate anti-treaty shopping protection).

[309] See Guidelines §3.01(3); Temp Regs. §7.367(b)-5(c) (1977) likewise imposes no toll charge on the liquidation of one foreign subsidiary into its foreign parent; see also IRS Advance Notice 87-5, supra note 308 (future Treasury regulations under §367(e)(2), added by the Tax Reform Act of 1986, will continue this general amnesty in the case of foreign-to-foreign liquidations, except in cases where §897 applies or the subsidiary has U.S. business assets).

Guidelines stated flatly that a favorable §367 ruling automatically would be issued, even though shareholders of the acquired foreign corporation could purge their transferred stock of its §1248 taint as a result of the exchange (a defect that was remedied, however, by regulations issued under §367(b), as amended in 1976).[310] Where a foreign corporation acquired stock of a domestic corporation in a Type B reorganization exchange, the guidelines contained a specific cross-reference to the §351 rules if the shareholders whose stock was acquired ended up with 80 percent control of the acquiring corporation (i.e., if there was a reverse acquisition).[311] If the domestic corporation's shareholders did not control more than 50 percent of the acquiring foreign corporation, on the other hand, a favorable ruling ordinarily was issued (unless the domestic corporation's assets consisted principally of stock or securities). The guidelines also permitted so-called triangular Type B reorganization acquisitions (i.e., an acquisition for stock of the acquiring corporation's parent company).

Under the 1976 and 1984 amendments to §367, acquisition of a U.S. corporation by a foreign corporation in a Type B reorganization has an expatriating effect with respect to the exchanging U.S. shareholders and hence is governed by the outbound transfer rules of amended §367(a).[312]

---

[310] See Guidelines §3.03(1)(e). But see §5.02, warning that dividend income might have to be recognized by shareholders of a foreign corporation in a stock-for-stock exchange in order to prevent permanent avoidance of §1248 income with respect to their stock. Under the 1976 law rules of §367(b) and Temp. Regs. §7.367(b)-7(c)(1) (1977), however, a toll charge is now imposed on the exchanging U.S. shareholders of a CFC in this case.

[311] See Guidelines §3.03(1)(d). For similar treatment under the 1976 version of §367(a), see Temp. Regs. §7.367(b)-4(b). In the absence of a §351 effect, however, §367(b), rather than §367(a) applied; consequently no ruling was necessary in this case and the temporary regulations imposed no toll charge on that transaction. For the 1984 law rules, see Temp. Regs. §1.367(a)-3T(c), infra note 312.

[312] The 1984 amendments to §367(a), supra ¶ 17.41, dropped the mandatory ruling requirement for §367(a) (and generally codified the toll charge rules for tainted asset transfers of the 1968 Guidelines). But such transactions are literally taxable under §367(a)(1) (even though stock of the U.S. corporation is not a listed tainted asset), since the exception of §367(a)(3)(A) does not apply and no other provision of §367(a) confers nonrecognition to the exchanging shareholders. See Temp. Regs. §1.367(a)-3T(c).

These regulations, however, provide for four exceptions to this general rule of taxability in Temp. Regs. §1.367(a)-3T(c)(2)-(5): (1) where the transferred stock qualifies for the active business exception (based on the *Kaiser Aluminum* fact pattern, supra note 243); (2) where U.S. transferors obtain only a limited interest in the foreign corporate transferee (i.e., less than 20 percent of vote and value, with §958 attribution, or more than 20 but less than 50 percent as a group with the particular U.S. transferor owning less than 5 percent of vote and value); (3) where all U.S. transferors own less than 50 percent of the transferee and the transferor files a closing agreement under Temp. Regs. §1.367(a)-3T(g) (agreeing to recognize gain upon the

Conversely, Type B reorganization acquisitions of *foreign* corporations by U.S. corporations are governed by the rules of §367(b), which impose a toll charge (to the extent of any potential §1248 dividend income) on the exchanging U.S. shareholders of the foreign corporation.[313]

In the case of stock-for-stock acquisitions by one foreign corporation of the stock of another foreign corporation, the rules of both the 1968 Guidelines and of §367(b), as amended in 1976, were considerably more elaborate, focusing primarily on the degree of shareholder control over the respective foreign corporations in a given situation. Thus, the 1968 Guidelines[314] provided that where the controlling shareholders of the acquired corporation (which was a CFC) ended up with more than 50 percent control of the acquiring corporation (as defined in §954(d)(3) as voting control or value) and where the acquired corporation met the requirements of §954(c)(4)(A)— that is, the acquired corporation was organized under the laws of the same country as the acquiring corporation, and a substantial part of the former's assets was used in the conduct of business within such country–a favorable ruling would be issued. However, if the acquiring corporation was not a CFC within the meaning of §957(a), shareholders of the acquired corporation had to recognize any potential dividend income on their transferred stock to the extent provided in §1248. In short, a Type B reorganization involving two foreign corporations that constituted, in effect, a reverse acquisition was entitled to a §367 ruling only if CFC status (and the concomitant §1248 dividend potential) was preserved in the transaction, and then only if the newly acquired subsidiary was organized and engaged in business in the same country as that of the acquiring corporation.

If shareholders of the acquired foreign corporation did not obtain more than 50 percent control of the acquiring foreign corporation, a §367 ruling generally would be issued unless the *acquiring* corporation was not a CFC (in which event the §1248 dividend toll had to be paid by the transferor shareholders). However, if shareholders of the acquired corporation obtained 80 percent control of the acquiring corporation after the exchange transaction, then the guideline rules relating to §351 transfers applied.

The general thrust of these rules was to prevent escape from the tainted stock provisions of §1248 through tax-free exchanges designed to purge the transferor shareholders of their potential dividend income risks. If the stock acquired by the transferors constituted stock in a CFC, the §1248 taint con-

---

occurence of certain triggering events within five years after the transaction); and (4) on certain transfers of stock as compensation for services. See generally Terr, supra note 260, at 83–86.

[313] The rules of §367(b), rather than §367(a), apply here; supra note 287, infra note 315.

[314] Guidelines §§3.03(f) and 3.03(g).

tinued and the issuance of a favorable §367 ruling ordinarily would follow. Where the transaction constituted a §351 exchange as well as a Type B reorganization, the 1968 Guidelines treated it as a §351 transaction[315] and the 1977 Temp. Regs. §7.367(b)-4(b) continued that treatment.

The 1976 amendments of §367(b) abolished the ruling requirement for foreign-to-foreign Type B reorganizations but provided, in §367(b) and Temp. Regs. §7.367(b)-7, that a toll charge will be imposed on any exchanging U.S. shareholders of an acquired CFC unless the potential §1248 dividend inherent in their stock was preserved following the transaction. Moreover, Temp. Regs. §§7.367(b)-4(b) and 7.367(b)-13, Example (14), (1982), subject transfers of foreign corporate stock to a foreign corporation in a §368(a)(1)(B) reorganization to the rules of §367(b) (even though the transaction also constituted a §351 exchange).[316] Thus, the §1248 toll charge regime of Temp. Regs. §7.367(b)-7 applies (unless the §1248 taint is preserved in the transferee's stock under Temp. Regs. §7.367(b)-9). Moreover, even realized gain in excess of the §1248 amount also must be recognized here unless the §1248 taint is preserved in the transferee's stock held by the transferor after the exchange.

These principles can be illustrated by the following examples in which it is assumed, unless otherwise stated, that D is a domestic corporation with all U.S. shareholders and F is a foreign corporation with all foreign shareholders.

Example 1. If D acquired all the stock of F solely in exchange for its voting stock in a Type B reorganization, the 1968 Guidelines stated that favorable §367 treatment would apply regardless of relative shareholder control of the two corporations; the same result occurs under new §367(b) as amended in 1976 (and no charge will be imposed). However, if F's shareholders were U.S. persons and F were a controlled corporation, §367(b) and Temp. Regs. §7.367(b)-7(c)(1), impose a current §1248 toll charge on the exchanging F shareholders.

Example 2. If F instead acquired all the stock of D, the transaction would be treated as an expatriating transfer under §367(a)[317] and generally would be taxable to D's shareholders.

---

[315] See also Rev. Rul. 70-433, 1970-2 CB 82. But Temp. Regs. §7.367(b)-4(b) (1982) reverse the priority rule of the former 1977 regulations and treat the transaction as a B reorganization governed by §367(b); see Terr, Announcement 85-95—Outbound Stock Transfers, 12 J. Corp. Tax'n 393 (1985); Temp. Regs. §§1.367(a)-3T(b)(1) and 1.367(a)-3T(d)(1) (1986) (same), supra note 287.

[316] See Temp. Regs., id.

[317] See Temp. Regs. §1.367(a)-1T(c)(2)(ii) (1986) (an outbound transfer even in the case of a transfer of stock to a domestic subsidiary for stock of its foreign par-

Example 3. If *D* were also a foreign corporation (and were classified as a controlled foreign corporation because of its U.S. shareholders), *D*'s acquisition of *F* stock in a Type B reorganization would not trigger a taxable toll charge under §367(b) if *F*'s shareholders did not have more than 50 percent control of *D* after the exchange; under §367(b), no toll charge is applied to *F*'s shareholders because no §1248 taint was present in their *F* stock.

Example 4. If *F* instead acquired *D*'s stock in Example 3 (and *D*'s shareholders did not have more than 50 percent control of *F* after the exchange), §367 and Temp. Regs. §7.367(b)-7(c)(1) imposes the §1248 toll charge on *D*'s shareholders because *F* was not a CFC.

Example 5. If *D*'s shareholders did obtain more than 50 percent control of *F* in the transaction in Example 4, *D*'s shareholders would have to include a §1248 dividend in this situation if *F* was not a CFC; but if *F* was also a CFC, *D*'s shareholders would not have to pay a current §1248 toll, since their §1248 taint would be preserved in their stock.[318]

Example 6. If *D*'s shareholders acquired 80 percent control of *F* in the exchange (so §351 could also apply), Temp. Regs. §7.367(b)-4(b) (1982) apply §367(b) principles to the transaction (and the §1248 toll charge of Temp. Regs. §7.367(b)-7, unless the taint is preserved in *F*'s stock by Temp. Regs. §7.367(b)-9). Moreover, even gain in excess of the §1248 amount (if any) must also be recognized by *D*'s shareholders unless the transaction results in a §1248 taint shift to *F*'s stock under Temp. Regs. §7.367(b)-9.[319]

2. Asset acquisitions: Type C reorganizations. Asset acquisitions by a foreign corporation from a domestic corporation are treated in the same manner as an expatriating §351 transfer under §367(a).[320] Where the acquisi-

---

ent); §367(a)(1), as added by the Tax Reform Act of 1984, will tax the exchanging U.S. shareholders in this transaction, since no express exception applies (except to the extent a regulation amnesty is granted under §367(a)(5)); see supra note 312 for exceptions to taxability in Temp. Regs. §1.367(a)-3T(c) (1986).

[318] See Temp. Regs. §§7.367(b)-7(b) and 7.367(b)-9.

[319] See Temp. Regs. §7.367(b)-13, Example (14), for illustration of these provisions; supra notes 315 and 316.

[320] Note that a Type C reorganization is the only "asset route" available where a foreign corporation is involved, since it is not possible to have a "statutory merger" involving a foreign corporation according to the Service. See Regs. §1.368-2(b). But see Rev. Rul. 74-297, 1974-1 CB 84, holding that a merger of a domestic corporation into a domestic subsidiary of a foreign parent for stock of the parent qualified as a

tion is made by a domestic corporation from a foreign corporation, on the other hand, the analogy is to the rules under §367(b) dealing with §332 liquidations. Here, any U.S. shareholders of the acquired foreign corporation must include the appropriate amount of §1248 dividend income with respect to their stock in the foreign corporation (or the appropriate amount of §1246 ordinary gain if the acquired corporation happened to be a foreign investment company).[321] Moreover, if a domestic corporation owned 20 percent or more of the foreign corporation's stock, the domestic corporate shareholder must include an appropriate amount of either §1246 gain or of regular dividend income with respect to that stock (since after the reorganization it would be a corporate shareholder of a domestic corporation and thus entitled to the dividends-received deduction of §243). Thus, Temp. Regs. §7.367(b)-7(c)(2) adopts the §332 repatriation analogy and requires inclusion by an exchanging U.S. *corporate* shareholder of the foreign transferor of an amount equal to the lesser of (1) all the earnings and profits attributable to the transferred stock or (2) all the gain attributable to such stock (as if it had been sold). Noncorporate shareholders of the foreign transferor need only include the potential §1248 dividend income attributable to their stock.[322]

Where the acquisition is effected between two foreign corporations, the 1968 Guidelines required payment of a §1248 dividend toll by shareholders of the acquired foreign corporation if the latter was a CFC at the time of the stock exchange (or at any time within five years prior thereto), whether or not the acquiring corporation also was classified as a CFC.[323] While the par-

---

good triangular merger under §368(a)(2)(D) (although a §367 ruling was necessary here). The same result would occur under new §367(a), although the ruling could be issued after, rather than before, the transaction. For results under the 1976 amendments of §367(a), see supra ¶ 17.40 at note 254, and Temp. Regs. §7.367(a)-1(b)(3)(ii).

For results under the 1984 amendments to §367(a), which dropped the mandatory ruling requirement and switched to a tainted asset toll charge system based largely on the 1968 Guidelines, see supra ¶¶ 17.41 and 17.42.

[321] A Type F reorganization of two foreign corporations may have qualified for the late ruling provisions of former §367(b), however, which was added in 1971. But this provision was replaced in 1976 by new §367(a)(2), which gave the Service the power to designate certain transactions as excepted exchanges. For the limited exercise of this power, see Temp. Regs. §7.367(a)-1(b)(5) (which resembles the former late ruling definition of old §367(b)).

But see Temp. Regs. §7.367(b)-4(d) (1977), and supra notes 262 and 288.

[322] Temp. Regs. §7.367(b)-7(c)(1).

[323] See Guidelines §3.03(1)(c). In TIR 1354 (1975), the Service announced an alternative mechanism (via closing agreement) to satisfy the §1248 toll charge in the future; the former closing agreement procedure locked in pre-reorganization earnings until certain triggering events (e.g., acquiring corporation ceased to be a CFC, shareholders ceased to be U.S. persons, shareholders ceased to own 10 percent, acquiring corporation ceased to be in business or its stock became worthless, or shareholder

allelism of the asset acquisition rules to the stock acquisition rules was evident in this situation, differences did exist. In the case of asset acquisitions, no distinction was made for situations where the acquiring corporation was also a CFC, unlike the result in a stock for stock Type B reorganization. Also, the reverse acquisition situation was not covered by the asset reorganization rules (i.e., where a "minnow swallowed a whale," the economic consequences of the transaction may be such that the acquired and acquiring parties should be reversed to reflect the substance of the deal). But the Service's concern with reorganizing out of CFC status was a common theme in both types of acquisition, although the roadblocks erected in the asset acquisition situation appeared to be somewhat more formidable than those for stock acquisitions.

However, under the 1976 amendments to §367(b), stock acquisitions and asset acquisitions are treated with greater consistency; thus, §367(b)(2) authorized the Service to provide regulations dealing with the tax consequences of exchanges of stock in foreign corporations by U.S. persons, and Temp. Regs. §§7.367(b)-7 and 7.367(b)-9 provide generally that no current toll charge will be imposed on the transaction so long as it has no repatriating effect and so long as any potential §1248 dividend income attributable to transferred stock is preserved after the transaction.[324]

3. Reincorporations and divisions: Type D reorganizations. The 1968 Guidelines dealing with asset acquisition reorganizations applied with equal force to Type D reorganization transactions whether the reorganization took the form of a nondivisive reincorporation transaction or instead constituted a divisive reorganization.[325] Thus, the expatriating reincorporation (i.e.,

---

disposed of all or part of his tainted stock). Under the revised closing agreement procedure, tainted earnings could be reduced by dividends and post-reorganization deficits, and includable dividends on triggering events were limited to potential gain on the tainted stock at the time of a trigger event. For guidelines on these agreements, see Rev. Proc. 75-29, 1975-1 CB 754, modified by Rev. Proc. 76-4, 1976-1 CB 543, and Rev. Proc. 76-44, 1976-2 CB 668, amplified by Rev. Proc. 76-24, 1976-1 CB 563.

The Tax Reform Act of 1976, in §367(b), gave the Service power to deal with this situation by regulations; for the regulatory treatment, see Temp. Regs. §§7.367(b)-7 and 7.367(b)-9; supra ¶ 17.41; see also Rev. Proc. 76-20, 1976-1 CB 560 (Type F reorganizations of multiple corporations that satisfy the conditions of Rev. Rul. 75-561, 1975-2 CB 129, discussed supra ¶ 14.18, are still subject to guideline rules dealing with Type C asset reorganizations); Temp. Regs. §§7.367(b)-4(d) and 7.367(b)-7(a) (same).

[324] See supra ¶ 17.41.

[325] See Guidelines §3.03(1)(a), 3.03(1)(b), and 3.03(1)(c). For similar results under the 1976 amendments, see Temp. Regs. §§7.367(a)-1(b)(3), 7.367(b)-7(a), and 7.367(b)-4(d).

reincorporation of a domestic corporation in a foreign country) was covered by the guideline rules dealing with §351 transfers.[326] On the other hand, domesticating reincorporations fell within the principles of §3.03(1)(b) of the guidelines, which in turn adopted the analogy of §332 liquidations.[327] Likewise, transactions involving the reincorporation of one foreign corporation into another foreign corporation were covered by the principles of §3.03(1)(c), dealing with asset acquisitions by one foreign corporation from another foreign corporation.[328] It seemed, however, that an all-foreign nondivisive Type D reorganization was less vulnerable to attack under §367, since the assets and earnings continued in foreign corporate solution. More-

---

[326] For an example of the consequences of failure to obtain a §367 ruling where an alleged liquidation transaction was held instead to constitute a nondivisive Type D reorganization, see Abegg v. CIR, supra note 40 (gain recognized to domestic transferor corporation); Retail Properties, Inc., supra note 239 (attempted §337 transaction with foreign subsidiary converted to a Type D reorganization; gain recognized because of failure to obtain §367 ruling); American Mfg. Co., supra note 130 (attempted sale of assets by domestic subsidiary to foreign sister subsidiary, where losses exceeded gains, resulted in taxation of gains because a Type D reorganization and no §367 ruling).

The 1984 legislative amendments to §367(a) (supra note 258) dropped the mandatory ruling requirement and switched to a tainted asset toll charge system for outbound asset transfers, based largely on the 1968 Guidelines. For regulations under the outbound transfer rules of §367(a), see supra note 260.

But see Rev. Rul. 87-27, 1987-15 IRB 5 (change from U.S. to foreign corporate status a Type F reorganization and no adverse §367(a) consequences will result here).

[327] Rev. Rul. 75-383, 1975-2 CB 127 (foreign subsidiary's transfer of all assets to U.S. subsidiary without issue of additional stock held a Type D reorganization and §367 ruling necessary); see Temp. Regs. §7.367(b)-7(c)(2) for similar treatment of these transactions under new §367(b)(2) as amended by the 1976 Act (although no ruling is required here, a current toll charge analogous to repatriating §332 liquidations is imposed; supra ¶ 17.43).

[328] But cf. Rev. Rul. 66-171, supra note 262, holding that exchanges by shareholders of a single foreign corporate entity that merely changed its name did not require a §367 ruling since the transaction was governed by §1036 as well as §354. See also Rev. Rul. 72-420, 1972-2 CB 473, holding that no §367 ruling is necessary on conversion of a Naamloze Vennootschap corporation to a Besloten Vennootschap corporation, even though the transaction constituted a Type F reorganization, because §1036 also governed the stock exchange (corporation was still the same corporation here; so §1036 applied). But these rulings were declared obsolete by Rev. Rul. 78-381, 1978-2 CB 347. However, see Rev. Rul. 87-27, supra note 326.

See also Point to Remember No. 1, 25 Tax Lawyer 565 (1972) (change of country of incorporation—Service will not impose §1248 toll charge on a Type F reorganization where place of incorporation of first-tier subsidiary changed from one country to another); Point to Remember No. 5, 25 Tax Lawyer 566 (1972) (need a §367 ruling on a §1504(d) election, which is treated as a reorganization involving foreign corporations; also need §367 on termination of §1504(d) status and the §351 guideline tools will be imposed); Temp. Regs. §7.367(a)-1(b)(3)(iv) (1984) (same); Temp. Regs. §1.367(a)-1T(c)(5) (1986) (same).

over, there was no possibility of evading the taint of §1248 in this situation. The 1976 amendments in §367(b) adopted the view that no current dividend toll charge will be imposed where the §1248 taint is preserved in the stock of the successor corporation.[329]

Where the transaction takes the form of a divisive reorganization (i.e., one where the distribution of stock by the transferor corporation is governed by the provisions of §355, rather than those of §354(b)(1)), analysis of the §367 consequences must proceed on two separate levels. First, the §367 consequences of the preliminary transfer of assets (if any) to the controlled subsidiary corporation must be considered, and, second, the §367 consequences of a distribution of the stock of such controlled subsidiary corporation pursuant to §355 must be determined. The initial asset transfer, in addition to constituting a reorganization under §368(a)(1)(D), also qualifies as a transfer to a controlled corporation under §351; as such, the rules applicable to §351 exchanges apparently apply to this stage of the reorganization transaction. Thus, if assets of a domestic corporation are transferred to a foreign subsidiary, the tainted-assets approach of the outbound transfer rules of §367(a) presumably apply to this step. If assets are transferred by a foreign corporation to a foreign subsidiary, the 1976 Act amendments to §367(b) apply, and no toll charge will be imposed at this stage of the transaction. If the transfer is from a foreign corporation to a domestic subsidiary, §367 is inapplicable, since corporate status of the transferor is unnecessary for nonrecognition treatment under §351.

When stock of the transferee subsidiary is distributed by the transferor corporation under §355 as the second stage of a divisive reorganization transaction, the 1968 Guidelines referred to some (but not all) of these distributions. Thus, if the spin-off distribution of stock resulted from a domesticating transfer of assets by the foreign corporation to the spun-off domestic subsidiary, §3.03(1)(b) of the Guidelines required inclusion of a §1248 dividend by U.S. shareholders of the distributing foreign corporation with respect to their stock deemed exchanged in the distribution transaction; §367(b) (as amended in 1976) and Temp. Regs. §7.367(b)-10(i) likewise impose the §1248 toll charge at this point on *non*corporate U.S. shareholders of the foreign distributing corporation. However, if the shareholder is a U.S. corporation, the repatriation §332 liquidation approach is adopted by Temp. Regs. §7.367(b)-10(j). On the other hand, the 1968 Guidelines were silent where the spin-off flowed in the opposite direction—where assets were transferred by a domestic corporation to a foreign subsidiary, whose stock then was distributed under §355 to U.S. stockholders of the transferor corporation. Presumably, no special difficulties arose in this situation, since the initial asset transfer had to pass muster under the outbound transfer rules of

---

[329] See Temp. Regs. §§7.367(b)-7(b) and 7.367(b)-9, supra ¶ 17.41.

§367(a) dealing with §351 exchanges, and §367 would apply to this phase of the transaction.[330]

When both the distributing corporation and the spun-off subsidiary corporation were foreign entities, §3.03(1)(c) of the 1968 Guidelines required inclusion of a §1248 dividend by the U.S. shareholders of the distributing corporation if the distributing corporation was a CFC (to be determined with respect to the shareholders' stock of the distributing corporation deemed exchanged in the distribution). Payment of a §1248 dividend tax in this latter situation seemed inappropriate where stock of the spun-off subsidiary also constituted §1248 stock of a CFC,[331] and the 1976 Act amendments of §367(b) (and Temp. Regs. §7.367(b)-10)) now provide that a current §1248 toll charge is no longer required in cases where the §1248 taint is preserved in the hands of the U.S. distributee shareholders.[332]

One final point: By virtue of amendments to §1248(f) by the Tax Reform Act of 1976, distributions by *domestic* parent corporations of stock of their CFCs will result in current recognition of §1248 dividend income to the distributing parent corporation with respect to that stock by virtue of the distribution transaction.[333]

---

[330] But the 1986 temporary regulations under §367(a), supra note 260, reserve §355 questions. The Tax Reform Act of 1986, §631(d), provides in §367(e)(1) that, on a §355 distribution by a U.S. corporation to a foreign person, gain will be recognized as provided by regulations.

[331] But see Rev. Rul. 76–13, 1976–1 CB 96 (foreign subsidiary's transfer of movable assets (about to be seized by foreign country of location) to a new foreign subsidiary and distribution of its stock to U.S. parent, held valid §355 distribution if §367 ruling obtained); amplified and superseded by Rev. Rul. 78–383, 1978–2 CB 142. But see Rev. Rul. 83–23, 1983–1 CB 82 (§1248 toll charge applied if distributed subsidiary's stock not CFC stock; was not here because domestic corporate shareholder had to decontrol to comply with foreign decree requiring local ownership of 60 percent).

[332] But see §367(e)(1), added by the Tax Reform Act of 1986 (§355 distribution by U.S. corporation taxable to the extent provided in regulations); supra notes 330 and 331.

[333] See Temp. Regs. §7.367(b)-10(b), which notes this result.

Table of Cases

[References are to paragraphs (¶) and to notes (n.).]

[References are to paragraphs (¶) and to notes (n.).]

[References are to paragraphs (¶) and to notes (n.).]

[References are to paragraphs (¶) and to notes (n.).]

[References are to paragraphs (¶) and to notes (n.).]

[References are to paragraphs (¶) and to notes (n.).]

[References are to paragraphs (¶) and to notes (n.).]

[References are to paragraphs (¶) and to notes (n.).]

[References are to paragraphs (¶) and to notes (n.).]

[References are to paragraphs (¶) and to notes (n.).]

[References are to paragraphs (¶) and to notes (n.).]

Table of IRC Sections

[References are to paragraphs (¶) and to notes (n.).]

[References are to paragraphs (¶) and to notes (n.).]

[References are to paragraphs (¶) and to notes (n.).]

[References are to paragraphs (¶) and to notes (n.).]

[References are to paragraphs (¶) and to notes (n.).]

[References are to paragraphs (¶) and to notes (n.).]

[References are to paragraphs (¶) and to notes (n.).]

[References are to paragraphs (¶) and to notes (n.).]

[References are to paragraphs (¶) and to notes (n.).]

[References are to paragraphs (¶) and to notes (n.).]

IRC §

356(a)(2) .... 3.19 & n.203; 13.07;
13.11 & n.112;
13.15 n.151; 14.17 & n.241;
14.34 & ns. 371, 376, 380, 384,
385, 390; 14.35; 14.54 & ns. 532,
548; 15.23 n.166; 17.02 & n.17;
17.11 n.130
356(b) 13.11; 13.13; 14.34
356(c) 13.06 n.56; 13.11; 14.13
n.77; 14.34 & n.368
356(d) ... 14.11; 14.17; 14.31; 14.34 &
n.371
356(d)(2) 14.31
356(d)(2)(B) 13.11 n.107; 14.17
356(d)(2)(C) 13.11 n.107
356(e) 10.05 n.40; 13.11; 14.32;
14.34
356(e)(1)(C)(i) 14.32
356(e)(1)(C)(ii) 14.32
356(f) 14.34 n.361
357.... 3.06 & n.70; 3.11; 14.02; 14.13
n.92; 14.30; 14.32; 14.55 &
n.572; 16.13 n.71
357(a) .... 3.06 & n.62; 3.10; 14.15
n.158; 14.32; 14.53; 14.55 & ns.
568, 575
357(b) ...... 3.06 & ns. 62, 63, 65–67,
76; 3.10; 3.11 n.118; 11.42
n.142; 14.14; 14.32 & n.336;
14.55 & ns. 554, 569, 576; 16.01
n.3; 17.40 n.268
357(b)(1) 3.06
357(c) ..... 3.06 & ns. 67, 69, 76; 3.10
& n.114; 3.11 n.118; 3.19 &
n.210; 5.06; 10.04 n.29; 11.42
n.142; 13.06 n.55; 13.11 n.111;
14.16 n.181; 14.18 n.266; 14.32
& n.336; 14.55 ns. 554, 557
357(c)(1) 3.19
357(c)(3) ..... 3.06 & n.72; 3.10 n.114;
3.11 n.118; 14.55 n.557
357(c)(3)(A)(i) 3.06 n.70
357(d)(2) 3.11 n.118
358.......... 3.01 & n.6; 3.06; 3.10 &
n.110; 3.13 n.147; 3.17; 4.24;
5.06; 13.12 & n.116; 14.02;
14.15; 14.30; 14.32; 14.33 &

IRC §

n.353; 14.34 & ns. 394, 399;
14.54; 17.40
358(a) 14.34; 14.53 n.498
358(a)(1) 3.10; 14.32
358(a)(1)(B)(i) 3.10 n.110
358(a)(1)(B)(ii) 3.10; 4.62 n.261
358(a)(2) .... 3.10; 13.12; 14.32 &
n.339; 14.34
358(b) 14.32
358(b)(1) 3.10; 14.32; 14.34
358(b)(2) 13.12 n.116
358(c) 13.12 n.116; 14.32
358(c)(1) 14.32
358(c)(2) 14.32
358(d) ..... 3.06 & ns. 70, 71; 3.10 &
n.114; 14.32; 14.55 n.552
358(d)(1) 14.32
358(d)(2) 3.10 n.114
358(e) ....14.33 & n.353; 14.53
361......... 3.19; 7.03; 11.06 & n.54;
11.47; 11.49; 12.02; 12.07;
13.06; 13.12 & n.132; 13.15
n.158; 14.02; 14.11; 14.14 n.125;
14.15 & n.166; 14.20; 14.30;
14.31; 14.32; 14.33 n.346; 14.34;
14.36; 14.53 & ns. 495, 509;
14.54; 14.55 ns. 572, 576; 17.40;
17.41; 17.42
361(a) ...3.01; 3.03; 4.60 n.232; 13.03;
13.06 n.56; 13.15 n.147; 14.11;
14.31 & n.318; 14.32 & ns. 324,
337; 14.53 n.495
361(b) 14.32
361(b)(1) 13.12; 14.32; 14.53 n.495
361(b)(1)(A) 14.53 n.495
361(b)(1)(B) 14.32; 16.13 n.70
361(b)(2) .. 14.32 & n.339; 14.33 n.343
361(b)(3) 13.03 n.10; 13.12; 13.15;
14.32 & ns. 327, 335
361(c) ..... 11.06 & n.54; 11.49; 13.03
n.10; 13.12 & ns. 131, 132;
14.20; 14.32 & n.335; 14.53
n.495
362....... 3.01; 3.11; 3.12; 3.17; 7.03;
11.47 n.201
362(a) .. 3.10 n.110; 3.11; 14.53; 14.54
362(a)(1) 3.06; 3.11 n.118; 3.13
362(a)(2) 3.13 n.144; 9.12 n.177

[References are to paragraphs (¶) and to notes (n.).]

[References are to paragraphs (¶) and to notes (n.).]

[References are to paragraphs (¶) and to notes (n.).]

[References are to paragraphs (¶) and to notes (n.).]

[References are to paragraphs (¶) and to notes (n.).]

[References are to paragraphs (¶) and to notes (n.).]

[References are to paragraphs (¶) and to notes (n.).]

[References are to paragraphs (¶) and to notes (n.).]

[References are to paragraphs (¶) and to notes (n.).]

[References are to paragraphs (¶) and to notes (n.).]

Table of Treasury Regulations

[References are to paragraphs (¶) and to notes (n.).]

[References are to paragraphs (¶) and to notes (n.).]

[References are to paragraphs (¶) and to notes (n.).]

[References are to paragraphs (¶) and to notes (n.).]

[References are to paragraphs (¶) and to notes (n.).]

PROPOSED REGULATIONS

[References are to paragraphs (¶) and to notes (n.).]

[References are to paragraphs (¶) and to notes (n.).]

Table of Revenue Rulings, Revenue Procedures, and Other IRS Releases

[References are to paragraphs (¶) and to notes (n.).]

REVENUE RULINGS

[References are to paragraphs (¶) and to notes (n.).]

[References are to paragraphs (¶) and to notes (n.).]

[References are to paragraphs (¶) and to notes (n.).]

[References are to paragraphs (¶) and to notes (n.).]

[References are to paragraphs (¶) and to notes (n.).]

[References are to paragraphs (¶) and to notes (n.).]

[References are to paragraphs (¶) and to notes (n.).]

[References are to paragraphs (¶) and to notes (n.).]

Index

[References are to paragraphs (¶).]

[References are to paragraphs (¶).]

[References are to paragraphs (¶).]

[References are to paragraphs (¶).]

[References are to paragraphs (¶).]

[References are to paragraphs (¶).]

[References are to paragraphs (¶).]

[References are to paragraphs (¶).]

Reverse mergers, 14.15, 14.33, 14.53

Rights, stock purchase, 4.62, 7.41, 7.44, 13.03, 13.11

Royalties, 1.03, 8.22

S

S corporations
  See also Closely held corporations
  basis of stock, 6.01, 6.05–6.08
  corporate status, 6.01
  deductions, 5.03, 6.05–6.07
  disqualification, election termination by, 6.04
  distributions of previously taxed income, 6.08
  earnings and profits, 6.08
  election, 6.01–6.04
  election after termination, 6.05
  eligibility, 6.01, 6.02
  inadvertent terminations, 6.04
  multiple corporations, 15.01
  partnerships vs., 3.18, 6.01
  passive investment income, 6.04, 6.07
  pass-throughs to shareholders, 6.06
  revocation, election termination by, 6.04
  shareholders, generally, 6.01, 6.02
  stock limitations, 6.01, 6.02
  and Subchapter C corporations, 6.09
  successor corporations, 6.04
  taxable income, 6.01
  tax benefits, 1.03, 5.01, 5.09, 16.21
  tax preference items, 5.01, 503, 6.06
  tax shelters, 5.03, 6.05–6.07
  termination of election, 6.01, 6.04

Safe harbor distributions, 9.10

Salaries, 1.02, 1.03, 7.05

Sales
  See also Exchanges
  of assets, 16.21
  between affiliated corporations, 15.04
  bootstrap, 7.07, 9.07, 10.06
  capital gain or loss treatment, 4.20
  collapsible corporations, 12.03
  complete liquidations, 11.01–11.11
  dividends vs., 9.01–9.12
  foreign corporations, 17.02, 17.14, 17.34

  losses on, 4.22
  property, and §351 transactions, 3.14
  related party, 3.05, 3.11, 3.14
  reorganizations, 14.01, 14.11
  Section 306 stock, 10.04
  of stock, 1.07, 4.21, 10.04

Section 269 acquisitions, 16.21

Section 306 stock, 10.03
  bailouts, 10.02, 10.07
  corporate divisions, 13.03, 13.11, 13.13
  dispositions, 10.04
  exceptions, 10.05
  reorganizations, 14.17, 14.35
  uses, 10.06

Section 338 stock, 11.47, 11.48

Section 341 assets, 12.05–12.07

Section 351 transactions, 3.01
  assumption of liabilities, 3.06
  basis, 3.10, 3.11
  boot, 3.05
  capital contributions, 3.13
  classification, 3.03
  collateral problems, 3.18
  continuity of interest doctrine, 3.04
  control, 3.07–3.09
  dividends vs., 3.16
  gain or loss on issue/sale of, 3.01, 3.12
  midstream transfers, 3.17
  property transfers, 3.02
  reincorporations, 3.20
  reorganizations, 3.19
  sale vs., 3.14
  for Section 306 stock, 10.03
  solely in exchange, 3.05
  transfers to foreign corporations, 3.21
  transfers to investment companies, 3.15

Section 355 transactions, 13.07, 13.11, 13.14

Section 382 acquisitions, 16.22-16.25

Section 1244 stock, 4.24

Securities
  See also Bonds; Debt securities; Stock
  accrued interest in exchange for, 3.02
  assumption of liabilities, 3.06

[References are to paragraphs (¶).]

[References are to paragraphs (¶).]

[References are to paragraphs (¶).]